HANDBOOK OF COUNSELING PSYCHOLOGY

THIRD EDITION

Edited by

Steven D. Brown
Robert W. Lent

John Wiley & Sons, Inc.
New York • Chichester • Weinheim • Brisbane • Singapore • Toronto

We dedicate this edition to:

My parents (Irvin and Elma Brown), wife (Linda Heath),
and children (Zachary and Kathryn Brown)
for their love and unwavering support.

SDB

My mother (Gladys Lent), brother (Steve Lent),
life partner (Ellen Lent), and son (Jeremy Lent)
for their enduring love and innumerable kindnesses.

RWL

This publication is designed to provide accurate and authoritative information in regard to
the subject matter covered. It is sold with the understanding that the publisher is not engaged
in rendering professional services. If legal, accounting, medical, psychological or any
other expert assistance is required, the services of a competent professional person
should be sought.

Library of Congress Cataloging-in-Publication Data:

Handbook of counseling psychology / edited by Steven D. Brown and
Robert W. Lent. — 3rd ed.
p.   cm.
Includes bibliographical references and index.
ISBN 0-471-25458-4 (alk. paper)
1. Counseling. 2. Psychology, Applied. I. Brown, Steven D.
(Steven Douglas), 1947– . II. Lent, Robert W. (Robert William),
1953–
BF637.C6H315   2000
158′.3—dc21   99-16054

Printed in the United States of America.

10 9 8 7 6 5 4

Contributors

D. Craig Anderson, PhD
University Counseling Services
Virginia Commonwealth University
Richmond, Virginia

Sharon K. Anderson, PhD
School of Education
Colorado State University
Ft. Collins, Colorado

Consuelo Arbona, PhD
College of Education
University of Houston
Houston, Texas

David L. Blustein, PhD
Department of Counseling, Educational, and
    Developmental Psychology
Boston College
Boston, Massachusetts

Daniel M. Bolt, PhD
Department of Educational Psychology
University of Wisconsin—Madison
Madison, Wisconsin

Michael T. Brown, PhD
Graduate School of Education
University of California—Santa Barbara
Santa Barbara, California

Steven D. Brown, PhD
Department of Leadership, Foundations, and
    Counseling Psychology
Loyola University Chicago
Wilmette, Illinois

Jean Carter, PhD
Independent Practice
Washington, D.C.

J. Manual Casas, PhD
Graduate School of Education
University of California—Santa Barbara
Santa Barbara, California

Eric C. Chen, PhD
Division of Psychological and Educational
    Services
Fordham University at Lincoln Center
New York, New York

Madelyn N. Coleman, MA
Department of Educational and Counseling
    Psychology
University of Missouri—Columbia
Columbia, Missouri

Jeanine M. Driscoll, PhD
Department of Medicine
Duke University Medical Center
Durham, North Carolina

Carolyn Zerbe Enns, PhD
Cornell College
Mt. Vernon, Indiana

Ruth E. Fassinger, PhD
Department of Counseling and Personnel
    Services
University of Maryland
College Park, Maryland

Nadya A. Fouad, PhD
Department of Educational Psychology
University of Wisconsin—Milwaukee
Milwaukee, Wisconsin

Myrna L. Friedlander, PhD
Department of Educational and Counseling
    Psychology
University at Albany, State University of
    New York
Albany, New York

Jairo N. Fuertes, PhD
Division of Psychological and Educational
    Services
Fordham University at Lincoln Center
New York, New York

Charles J. Gelso, PhD
Department of Psychology
University of Maryland
College Park, Maryland

Rodney K. Goodyear, PhD
Division of Counseling Psychology
University of Southern California
Los Angeles, California

Paul A. Gore, Jr., PhD
Department of Psychology
Southern Illinois University
Carbondale, Illinois

Leslie S. Greenberg, PhD
Department of Psychology
York University
Toronto, Ontario
Canada

Christine R. Guzzardo, MS
Division of Counseling Psychology
University of Southern California
Los Angeles, California

P. Paul Heppner, PhD
Department of Educational and Counseling
Psychology
University of Missouri—Columbia
Columbia, Missouri

Beryl Hesketh, PhD
Faculty of Science
The University of Sydney
Sydney, Australia

Clara E. Hill, PhD
Department of Psychology
University of Maryland
College Park, Maryland

Robert D. Hill, PhD
Department of Educational Psychology
University of Utah
Salt Lake City, Utah

Mary Ann Hoffman, PhD
Department of Counseling and Personnel
    Services
University of Maryland
College Park, Maryland

Cindy L. Juntunen, PhD
Department of Counseling
University of North Dakota
Grand Forks, North Dakota

Karen Strohm Kitchener, PhD
College of Education
University of Denver
Denver, Colorado

Dennis M. Kivlighan, Jr., PhD
Department of Educational and Counseling
    Psychology
University of Missouri—Columbia
Columbia, Missouri

Wendy L. Kliewer, PhD
Department of Psychology
Virginia Commonwealth University
Richmond, Virginia

Nancy E. Ryan Krane, PhD
The Ball Foundation
Glenn Ellyn, Illinois

Robert W. Lent, PhD
Department of Counseling and Personnel
    Services
University of Maryland
College Park, Maryland

Susan L. Morrow, PhD
Department of Educational Psychology
University of Utah
Salt Lake City, Utah

Ted Packard, PhD
Department of Educational Psychology
University of Utah
Salt Lake City, Utah

Joseph G. Ponterotto, PhD
Division of Psychological and Educational
    Services
Fordham University at Lincoln Center
New York, New York

Le'Roy E. Reese, PhD
Centers for Disease Control and Prevention
Division of Violence Prevention
Atlanta, Georgia

Steven B. Robbins, PhD
Department of Psychology
Virginia Commonwealth University
Richmond, Virginia

James Rounds, PhD
Department of Educational Psychology
University of Illinois at Urbana-Champaign
Champaign, Illinois

Mary Lee Smith, PhD
Educational Policy Studies
Arizona State University
Tempe, Arizona

Gerald L. Stone, PhD
University Counseling Service
The University of Iowa
Iowa City, Iowa

Jane L. Swanson, PhD
Department of Psychology
Southern Illinois University
Carbondale, Illinois

Brian L. Thorn, PhD
Department of Educational Psychology
University of Utah
Salt Lake City, Utah

Terence J.G. Tracey, PhD
Division of Psychology in Education
Arizona State University
Tempe, Arizona

Ma. Teresa Tuason, PhD
Department of Educational and Counseling
   Psychology
University at Albany, State University of
   New York
Albany, New York

Elizabeth M. Vera, PhD
Department of Leadership, Foundations, and
   Counseling Psychology
Loyola University Chicago
Wilmette, Illinois

Bruce E. Wampold, PhD
Department of Counseling Psychology
University of Wisconsin—Madison
Madison, Wisconsin

Serine Warwar, MA
Department of Psychology
York University
Toronto, Ontario
Canada

Elizabeth Nutt Williams, PhD
Department of Psychology
St. Mary's College of Maryland
St. Mary's, Maryland

Roger L. Worthington, PhD
Department of Educational and Counseling
   Psychology
University of Missouri—Columbia
Columbia, Missouri

Preface

This edition, like its two predecessors, has three primary objectives: (1) to provide a scholarly, critical review of important areas of counseling psychology activity; (2) to elaborate future directions for research, highlighting suggestions that may advance knowledge and stimulate further inquiry; and (3) to present specific suggestions for counseling practice that derive from the literature in counseling psychology and related disciplines. As in the first two editions, we asked authors to take a crossdisciplinary, integrative, critical, and direction-pointing approach to their chapters—and to do all this within strict page limits! We were once again fortunate to work with an outstanding and dedicated group of scholars, and we are grateful for the contributions that their chapters make to the scientist-practitioner knowledge base of counseling psychology.

Although all three editions of the *Handbook* share the same essential objectives, this volume departs from the earlier editions in its content, organization, and approach to knowledge accumulation. To ensure that this edition would adequately represent the field's current breadth and vigor, we surveyed a large group of leading scholars and practitioners in counseling psychology, and we also conducted a content analysis of all issues of the *Journal of Counseling Psychology* published between 1990 and 1998. Survey questions asked respondents (1) whether the major sections of the first and second editions still accurately represented the field, (2) which topics and chapters should be retained and which should be dropped, and (3) what new topics and chapters should be added. The survey and content analysis results led us to revise this edition in several important ways.

First, there appears to be growing sentiment in the field that the career/educational and personal counseling dichotomy, which has historically characterized counseling psychology (and the first two editions of the *Handbook*), is artificial. Thus, in this edition we eliminated the separate section on Career and Educational Counseling that appeared in the first two editions, and, instead, distributed chapters on career and educational topics throughout the *Handbook*. Following an opening section on professional and scientific issues (a *Handbook* mainstay), this edition contains sections on human development across the life span (Part II), preventive and developmental interventions (Part III), and counseling interventions (Part IV). These sections capture the developmental, preventive, and remedial themes that have historically been prominent in counseling psychology, and that continue to mark the field's distinctiveness. In each of these sections, career and educational topics are included, along with topics that do not focus as specifically on, but nonetheless are often intertwined with, career and educational concerns.

Second, inquiry on issues of human diversity in counseling psychology has grown at a remarkable pace in recent years. Accordingly, this edition attempts to convey state-of-the-art thinking and research on the developmental and counseling implications of gender, race, ethnicity, sexual orientation, social class, and culture. Expanding on coverage of diversity themes in previous *Handbook* editions, there are now chapters devoted to the role of gender and sexual orientation (Chapter 11) and race/ethnicity and social class (Chapter 12) in human development, and gender and sexual orientation (Chapter 19) and culture (Chapter 20) within the context of counseling. In addition to this focused coverage, we asked authors to incorporate attention to diversity issues into all *Handbook* chapters.

Third, several chapters have been added to this edition because they reflect relatively new, reinvigorated, or substantially expanded areas of involvement by counseling psychologists. Such topics include qualitative research methods (Chapter 7), preventive interventions with school-age youth (Chapter 13), promoting school-to-work transitions (Chapter 14), the process and outcome of group counseling (Chapter 24), and the process and outcome of couples and family counseling (Chapter 25). Fourth, several chapters reprise topics that were covered only in the first edition and that warrant coverage again because they represent areas in which there has been vigorous professional or scientific activity over the ensuing years. These include chapters on recent history of organized counseling psychology (Chapter 1), scientific training (Chapter 4), and the process (Chapter 21) and outcome (Chapter 22) of individual counseling.

Several other chapters in this edition provide different perspectives on previously covered *Handbook* topics. For example, the retirement and leisure counseling chapter of the second edition has been replaced with a more broadly focused chapter on preventive interventions with older adults (Chapter 16), and the previous coverage of adult career concerns has been updated with a chapter on promoting career development in the workplace and preventing workplace adjustment difficulties in contemporary society (Chapter 15). Prior chapters on life-transition coping have been replaced by a focus on subjective well-being and positive development (Chapter 10).

Similarly, prior attention to the academic adjustment of college students has been augmented by a new chapter on the development of academic aspirations and achievements of school-age youth (Chapter 9). The latter two topics (well-being, academic development), despite their centrality to the developmental and normative emphases of counseling psychology, have surprisingly received only limited or inconsistent attention from researchers in our field. We hope the inclusion of these topics in this edition of the *Handbook* will stimulate renewed interest in them by established and new scholars in counseling psychology.

In summary, the third edition of the *Handbook of Counseling Psychology* has a revised section arrangement that more satisfactorily reflects current thinking about our field and its subject matter. It also contains five chapters on new topics that were not included in the earlier editions, four chapters that reprise topics that were covered in the first edition only, four chapters that provide a substantially refocused coverage of second edition topics, and expanded coverage of diversity themes. The remaining chapters on ethical issues (Chapter 2), counselor supervision and training (Chapter 3), psychometrics (Chapter 5), quantitative data analyses (Chapter 6), vocational theory (Chapter 8), health promotion (Chapter 17), theories of change (Chapter 18), and career intervention (Chapter 23) are retained from previous editions as representing areas of continued inquiry or interest. These chapters will, therefore, reflect the latest trends and findings in their respective literatures; each will also present a somewhat unique perspective relative to coverage in prior *Handbook* editions because these reoccurring chapters were written by different authors this time around.

One other new feature of this edition deserves mention. In summarizing findings across studies, we asked authors to take into account current thinking about how knowledge is cumulated and applied in the social sciences. In particular, considering the shortcomings of null hypothesis significance testing strategies, we asked authors to avoid drawing conclusions based on the relative number of significant and nonsignificant findings in the literatures they were reviewing. Instead, whenever possible, they were asked to report effect sizes and to discuss the consistency of effect sizes across studies as a way to judge both the cumulativeness and practical importance of research findings. We also asked authors to use commonly accepted guidelines in interpreting effect sizes and to consider context in judging the practical importance of an effect (e.g., even small effect sizes may have practical significance in certain contexts).

Not coincidentally, this edition includes a chapter that addresses a number of relevant issues regarding the cumulativeness and application of quantitative findings in counseling psychology and related fields (Chapter 6). This chapter is complemented by coverage of developments in psychometrics (Chapter 5) and qualitative research methodology (Chapter 7). Together, we hope this triad of chapters will become required reading in research methods courses in counseling psychology.

ACKNOWLEDGMENTS

We have many people to thank for their critical help throughout this project. First, we thank those colleagues who took time out of their busy schedules to respond to our content survey: Don Atkinson, Betsy Altmaier, Nancy Betz, David Blustein, Steve Danish, Ruth Fassinger, Nadya Fouad, Kathy Gainor, Charlie Gelso, Lucia Gilbert, Rod Goodyear, Jo-Ida Hansen, Marty Heesacker, Punky Heppner, Beryl Hesketh, Clara Hill, John Horan, Brent Mallinckrodt, Don Pope-Davis, John Romano, Jim Rounds, Mark Savickas, Cal Stoltenberg, Jerry Stone, Linda Subich, Tony Tinsley, Terry Tracey, Bruce Wampold, and Roger Worthington. This edition of the *Handbook* owes much to their thoughtful and insightful comments. We also thank Jennifer Simon, our editor at Wiley, and the colleagues and students at our respective universities for their support and patience throughout this project. Finally, editing a book of this type requires incredible forebearance from one's family. We are, therefore, deeply grateful for the support, inspiration, and understanding provided to us by our families.

STEVE D. BROWN
ROBERT W. LENT

Contents

PART I
Professional and Scientific Issues

CHAPTER 1

The Maturation of Counseling Psychology: Multifaceted Perspectives, 1978–1998

P. PAUL HEPPNER
J. MANUAL CASAS
JEAN CARTER
GERALD L. STONE

The history of counseling psychology has been previously documented through a number of different venues, reflecting particular events, such as the founding of the Division of Counseling Psychology of the American Psychological Association (APA) (e.g., Scott, 1980); the founding of the *Journal of Counseling Psychology* (e.g., Wrenn, 1966); definitions of counseling psychology at particular points (e.g., Jordaan, Myers, Layton, & Morgan, 1968); or historical developments within a particular time period (e.g., Robinson, 1964). Larger historical analyses of the Division (e.g., Meara & Myers, 1999), and oral histories with senior members of the counseling profession (see P.P. Heppner, 1990, 1997) have also been conducted. In addition, the history of the field is reflected in the major counseling journals and books, as well as various reviews that have analyzed patterns in the literature (e.g., Borgen, 1984; Brayfield, 1963). Perhaps most notably, two books also appeared in the early 1980s, *The History of Counseling Psychology* (Whiteley, 1980) and *Counseling Psychology: A Historical Perspective* (Whiteley, 1984b) which documented the roots of counseling psychology; its early organizational initiatives, major publications, addresses, and committee reports; as well as significant social forces and environmental influences affecting the field.

Whiteley (1984a, 1984b) divided the history of counseling psychology into seven historical periods, spanning the years from 1908 to 1984. During the 1970s, counseling psychology had engaged in considerable consolidation and consensus on professional identity; training and practice were closely linked, centering primarily on skills used in college and university counseling centers, and on developmental needs, as well as adjustment and vocational/career concerns. The training programs largely prepared faculty and other counseling psychologists who took positions in higher education, including counseling and student personnel work; often they were housed in departments or colleges of education, reflecting the strong bond with education. The identity of counseling psychology was strongly connected with the roles and activities of counseling itself. Faculty in counseling psychology programs had considerable control over the content and format of the training they provided, and practicing counseling psychologists reflected that training directly. Both the education of counseling psychologists and the practice of counseling psychology seemed to be mostly internally driven by the specialty itself at this time.

Whiteley's (1984a, 1984b) analyses were the last historical documentation of the counseling psychology profession as a whole. Many events have transpired within and outside of counseling psychology since the early 1980s, and the profession has changed in many ways, in some cases profoundly. For example, multicultural or diversity issues were not mentioned in the previous historical reviews (save Meara & Myers, 1999); since the early 1980s, significant strides have been made to integrate diversity issues into the counseling profession, and numerous books on this topic have

3

appeared (e.g., Atkinson, Morten, & Sue, 1979; Ivey, Ivey, & Simek-Morgan, 1980; Pedersen, 1988; Ponterotto, Casas, Suzuki, & Alexander, 1995; Sue & Sue, 1981; Suzuki, Meller, & Ponterotto, 1996). Likewise, the health care industry has had a major impact, for example, in creating market opportunities for applied professions including counseling psychology (Cummings, 1995).

This chapter documents major developments within the field of counseling psychology since the late 1970s. The counseling psychology profession has not progressed in a vacuum: rather, it has been influenced by social, cultural, economic, and governmental forces as well as by numerous professional issues, nationally and globally. These forces have led to changes within universities, affecting demands on faculty as well as the education and training of future counseling psychologists. Although cause-and-effect relationships among major historical events are difficult if not impossible to isolate, the first section of this chapter will identify some of the broader issues and governmental policies that provide a context for understanding the continuing evolution of the counseling psychology profession in the last 20 years. It is important to note that while cultural forces provide the challenges and opportunities, individuals make the decisions; thus we will mention many of these individuals and their perspectives.

The second section of this chapter discusses developments within professional organizations that have influenced counseling psychology over the last 20 years. Specifically, this section focuses on developments within the (1) Division 17 (Counseling Psychology) of the APA, (2) Council of Counseling Psychology Training Programs, (3) Association of Counseling Center Training Agencies, and (4) American Counseling Association. It also includes multicultural and diversity developments within the American Psychological Association and Division 17, and documents major changes in practice and training in counseling psychology.

An important aspect of a discipline's history is the accumulated research of that discipline. Analyses of research trends provide important information about the discipline's ability to extend relevant knowledge bases which is, in essence, the lifeblood of the discipline. The third section of this chapter briefly sketches developments in the theoretical and empirical research literature over the last 20 years. Trends in six areas are discussed: (1) methodological diversity; (2) counseling interventions, process, and outcomes; (3) career counseling; (4) multicultural counseling; (5) issues of gender and sexual preference; and (6) supervision. Although there are many other important areas, these areas clearly depict significant developments in the knowledge bases of counseling psychology as well as increased methodological sophistication of the investigations. The fourth and final section discusses several major challenges that confront the counseling psychology profession as the new millennium begins.

A few initial caveats are in order. Analyzing the history of a professional discipline is a difficult and often subjective task. To provide a broad and multifaceted analysis, the first author selected co-authors who would provide expertise on quite different topics as well as provide alternative perspectives. Nonetheless, because of the time span of 20 years, space limitations, and our own biases, there will necessarily be omissions of events, people, and developments. Writing the chapter was further complicated by anticipating potential multiple uses and audiences, from beginning graduate students in counseling psychology with little knowledge of the history to retired professionals who helped shape the field. Because understanding the history of the profession is often an important part in the training of the next generation of counseling psychologists, we placed the greatest emphasis on the educative function of our analysis.

EXTERNAL FORCES AND THE CULTURAL CONTEXT

It is commonly noted that social, cultural, economic, and governmental forces affect the development of disciplines (e.g., Potter, 1967). The discipline of counseling psychology is no exception (e.g., McGowan, 1965; Meara & Myers, 1999; Scott, 1980; Whiteley, 1984a, 1984b). In this section, we sketch some of the major external forces that provided the context for the development of counseling psychology during the last two decades. Sometimes the context for a particular issue has evolved over a broader time frame (e.g., the increasingly diverse society), and thus a wider historical lens is needed to understand these professional developments.

Cultural Issues and Legislation

A major change in the U.S. culture in the past 20 years reflects a growing awareness of the tremendous diversity that exists among the people who inhabit this country. Such awareness was greatly facilitated by individuals from the following groups that were becoming more visible and vocal relative to their social and political rights and needs: racial/ethnic minorities, women, gays and lesbians, individuals with disabilities, and the elderly. Given space limitations, selective attention is given to some of the major forces, events, and issues relative to the rights and needs of these groups. Since federal legislation has been a major external force that has shaped the professions of counseling and psychology starting in 1917 (e.g., Smith-Hughes Act), special attention is given to legislation that has had a direct bearing on these groups. As society became more sensitive to various social movements and changes, so did the counseling profession (Sue & Sue, 1998); rather profound changes were to follow, although slowly.

Racial/Ethnic Minorities

Awareness of and interest in racial/ethnic minority populations began to increase slowly during the mid-1950s and took on stronger momentum in the 1960s as reflected by such events as the 1954 Supreme Court decision of *Brown vs. the Kansas Board of Education,* the Civil Rights movement of the 1960s, the passage of the Civil Rights Act in 1964, and dramatic demographic changes. In essence, the struggle that began in Montgomery, Alabama, with the bus boycott in 1955 "ultimately transformed race relations in thousands of American communities" (Faragher, Buhle, Czitrom, & Armitage, 1997). *Brown vs. the Kansas Board of Education* forced Americans to begin acknowledging the inequities of "separate but equal" policies. The Civil Rights movement and the Black Power movement, in particular, served as a catalyst for raising the consciousness of many people to the needs of various powerless, disenfranchised groups, including persons of color, women, gays and lesbians, elderly, and physically challenged persons. Moreover, as a result of increased immigration and a high birth rate, a period of significant growth for racial/ethnic minority groups began in the late 1960s and continues to this day. For instance, the 1980s and 1990s witnessed an increasing immigrant and racial/ethnic population in the United States, especially on the East and West Coasts. The 1990 census revealed that half of the population of greater Los Angeles was Hispanic, African American, or Asian, and 27% were foreign-born residents (Faragher et al., 1997). The U.S. population was becoming increasingly diverse in terms of racial and cultural backgrounds, which created specific needs for the delivery of mental health services.

Women

Many of the forces that affected the status of women reflect larger changes in American Society as a whole, such as the Civil Rights movement. As with racial/ethnic minorities, a strong belief in government's role in addressing social ills resulted in a number of legal actions and legislation aimed at addressing the status of women in education and in the work force (American Psychological Association [APA], 1995). Most of the legislation was aimed at dismantling barriers in the workforce that had limited women's freedom to make choices (see the Report of the Task Force on the Changing Gender Composition of Psychology, APA, 1995). In 1966, the National Organization for Women (NOW), sparked in part by Betty Friedan's *The Feminine Mystique* (1963), pledged to bring women's participation into the mainstream of American society (Faragher et al., 1997). The women's liberation movement stimulated a wide range of activities such as the implementation of affirmative action programs, state equal opportunity laws, and the development of women's studies programs and research centers. The strong impetus for positive change for women in the 1960s and 1970s was slowed down somewhat in the more conservative era that started in the late 1970s and continued with the Reagan and Bush Administrations (APA, 1975). Reflecting a change in the last decade, Betz and Fitzgerald (1993) concluded that the psychology of gender and its implications for counseling may well be the fastest-growing area within counseling psychology in the 1990s.

Gays, Lesbians, and Bisexuals

As reported in Atkinson and Hackett (1998), the Kinsey reports (Kinsey, Pomeroy, & Martin, 1948; Kinsey, Pomeroy, Martin, & Gebhard, 1953) and subsequent research (e.g., Kingdon, 1979) demonstrated that, conservatively, about 10% of the population is predominantly homosexual. By most recent census figures, this population would be well over 20 million individuals. This group has been subject to many of the same kinds of discrimination and harassment experienced by other oppressed minority groups (Atkinson & Hackett, 1998; Fassinger, 1991), namely, intolerance, oppression, lack of legal protection, harassment, loss of jobs, violence, religious prejudice, medical and psychological malpractice (e.g., pathologizing homosexuality), and political persecution. Although many writers contend that the fight for gay and lesbian rights came to life with the Stonewall Riots in 1969, others note that gay liberation, like the women's movement, was made possible by the Civil Rights movement and other social and cultural forces prevalent at this time (Kaiser, 1997). Several organizations promoting gay and lesbian rights began demonstrating for social rights in the latter part of the 1960s (e.g., Gay Liberation Front, Gay Activist Alliance), and by the mid-1970s, Gay Pride marches around the United States were drawing nearly 500,000 participants (Faragher et al., 1997). Relative to psychology, in 1975, the APA adopted an official policy stating that "homosexuality per se implies no impairment in judgement, stability, reliability, or general social or vocational capabilities" (Conger, 1975, p. 63). However, it was not until the publication of the *DSM-III-R* in 1987 that psychiatry removed homosexuality from its taxonomy of pathological conditions (American Psychiatric Association, 1987). Some writers, like Kaiser (1997), addressing such visibility and accomplishments, contend that in America "no other group has ever transformed its status more rapidly or more dramatically than lesbians and gay men" (p. vii). Others like Fassinger (1991) and Melton (1989), underscored the continued prevalence of disapproval and stigmatization of gays and lesbians in American society, and suggest that the AIDS epidemic has played a major part in the maintenance, exacerbation, or justification of such attitudes.

Persons with Disabilities

From a historical perspective, state and federal governments did not significantly address the needs of persons with disabilities until the twentieth century (Hohenshil & Humes, 1979). According to some writers (Rubin & Roessler, 1978), the negative by-products of industrialization, the tragedies of World War I, and a growing humanitarian philosophy served as the impetus for the increased attention. Relative to counseling, the profession's involvement with persons with disabilities was tied to the vocational rehabilitation movement that emerged in the 1920s. The National Civilian Rehabilitation Conference was first convened in 1924 and was renamed the National Rehabilitation Association (NRA) in 1927. Over the next three decades, vocational rehabilitation shifted from an educational emphasis, to a social work approach, and then to a vocational guidance approach. In the mid-1950s, research psychologists began to develop an interest in varied aspects of disabilities. This interest helped to spur the formation of rehabilitation psychology as a specialization.

According to Atkinson and Hackett (1998), until the 1960s, the formation of a cohesive social or political group representing persons with disabilities was not possible because of the diverse experiences and communication differences that existed among such persons. However, the social and political movements of the 1960s brought the realization to persons with disabilities that, like racial/ethnic minorities, they too shared the common experiences of oppressed individuals. Such a realization resulted in the formation of a Persons-with-Disabilities Civil Rights movement. The activity of the movement between 1965 and 1975 was such that Abeson (1976) referred to this time as the "era in which the battle cry for public policy advances changed from charitable solicitations to declarations of rights" (p. 5). As with racial/ethnic minorities, the movement resulted in federal legislative actions and rulings designed to protect and advance the rights of persons with disabilities, such as the Rehabilitation Act of 1973 and later the Americans with Disabilities Act of 1990, which supported vocational rehabilitation and counseling for people with disabilities (for an overview of such legislation, see Atkinson & Hackett, 1998).

The increased advocacy on the part of persons with disabilities and the concomitant legislation could not help but impact the realm of psychology. This impact can only increase further given the fact that as the number and percentage of elderly in the U.S. population increases, so does the number and percentage of people with disabilities. At present, there is still not a clear consensus on what constitutes a disability, even among governmental agencies; consequently, clear-cut estimates of the number of persons with disabilities in the United States are not available. However, according to a recent estimate, there were approximately 43 million Americans with disabilities in 1990 (National Council on Disability, 1995).

The Elderly

Unlike the previous groups addressed in this section who are often defined by existing criteria or who have established criteria by which to define themselves, the determination of who is elderly and who is not is arbitrary at best (Atkinson & Hackett, 1998). A major reason for this is the U.S. culture's fascination with "eternal youth." With such a commitment, many individuals hesitate to label or define themselves as elderly until well over 65. The Social Security Act of 1935 "had a major impact on our perceptions of who is an elder and who is not when it identified 65 as the magic age for determining who will receive full Social Security benefits" (p. 12). Given that people are living longer, and that there is a financially driven effort to increase the age of qualification for full Social Security benefits, 65 may no longer be the defining point for the elderly. The number of elderly people living in the United States has been increasing steadily since 1830. As they increased in numbers, they also developed an awareness of their political power, especially at the voting booth. With such awareness, they established themselves politically through such organizations as the American Association of Retired Persons (AARP), which was founded in 1958. In addition, in most cities' senior centers, programs, and advocacy groups have been established to serve the needs of the elderly. Federal legislation, such as the Older Persons Comprehensive Counseling Assistance Act of 1983, has provided for counseling of the elderly. Although the elderly have become more visible in the social, economic, and political realm, applied psychologists have often generally ignored this group (e.g., training programs seldom provide course work on aging; see Atkinson & Hackett, 1998; Hill, Thorn, & Packard, this volume).

Children and Adolescents

In addition to legislation previously mentioned, a series of legislative acts were passed in the 1970s and 1980s that had direct bearing on counseling as it relates to children—the most powerless group in the United States. Such acts included: (1) the Educational Amendments of 1976, which included major support for counseling and vocational guidance in the schools; (2) the Comprehensive Employment and Training Act of 1973, which included counseling for potential school dropouts, economically disadvantaged, and unemployed adults; (3) the Education for All Handicapped Children Act of 1977, which involved mainstreaming of special education students; and (4) Title IX resolutions, which included educational interventions to reduce sex bias in the schools, particularly with regard to athletics. More recently, the School-to-Work Opportunities Act of 1994 established a framework for the development of work opportunities systems in all states (see Blustein, Juntenen, & Worthington, this volume). More money has been appropriated for this act than the National Defense Education Act of 1958, which had an enormous impact on the counseling profession (see Bourne, 1988). In essence, federal legislation has been a major external force that has shaped American society, including the psychological and counseling professions (Herr, 1985). These legislative acts and others reflect some of the nation's priorities regarding children, unemployment, underemployment, people with disabilities, women's rights, civil rights, and educational and occupational opportunities—all of which have provided professional opportunities for a wide range of professionals, including counseling psychologists.

Economic and Social Issues

Economic issues have played a major role in American society, and subsequently counseling psychology, in the last 30 years. In the early 1960s, the United States was enjoying an economic boom. "An expanding economy, cheap energy, government subsidies, and a dominant position in the marketplace had made the hallmarks of 'the good life' available to more Americans than ever" (Faragher et al., 1997, p. 894). It was an era of expansion and "new frontiers." The mid-1960s also brought President Johnson's Great Society program and the War on Poverty, which ushered in a range of programs such as Job Corps, Neighborhood Youth Corps, Community Action Programs, Medicare, and Aid to Families with Dependent Children. As Meara and Myers (1999) noted, the unprecedented legislation during this time created many opportunities for psychologists. The early 1980s brought an economic downturn and increasing dependence on foreign oil, and by the end of that decade, the nation faced tougher economic competition from countries around the world (Faragher et al., 1997); this economic downturn would affect a wide range of institutions, including universities.

Beginning in the late 1960s, and well into the 1980s, psychology experienced a tremendous boom, with many undergraduate students claiming it as a major, and record numbers entering graduate school in psychology. Moreover, mental health care was increasingly recognized in the late 1970s as an important part of overall health care, and the need for mental health practitioners was increasing dramatically. Psychologists from various practice specialties were entering the health care system in larger numbers, pursuing jobs in community mental health centers, hospitals, clinics, and independent practice.

There were dramatic shifts in external forces that shaped psychology in the late 1970s. Organized psychology engaged in several major advocacy initiatives to support psychologists' right to independent participation in the health care market, such as pursuit of licensure, freedom of choice legislation, and inclusion in health care programs. Licensure defined those who were qualified as "psychologists," while freedom of choice legislation (which precludes discrimination based on degree of provider), and inclusion in health care reimbursement gave psychologists equal footing with other participants in the market. These initiatives had a major impact on counseling psychology. As professional psychology became more active in the health care market, the job market for the practice of psychology increased dramatically, particularly in independent practice. As the delivery of mental health services changed from institutions to individual practitioners, credentialing of mental health service providers became "more intense, and indeed, more political" (Herr, 1985, p. 398). These demands affected the structure and focus of professional organizations in education and psychology. The tighter American economy and health care reform of the early 1990s brought escalating competition among independent practitioners as well as various mental health professional groups. Later in the 1990s, demands for accountability and standardization of valid treatments would add further restrictions and pressures on the health care market.

Due partially to economic difficulties within the general economy and in higher education in the 1980s and 1990s, more attention was given to obtaining externally funded grants for research. This put more pressure on academic faculty to conduct more research, and more importantly to compete against each other to obtain external funding. Toward the close of the 1990s, between 75% to 80% of the APA accredited programs in counseling psychology were in colleges of education. Counseling and clinical psychologists housed in psychology departments often found considerable overlap in their training activities, which created tension when resources were scarce. Within colleges of education, counseling psychologists often reported an uneasy fit with narrowly defined K–12 college missions (e.g., Brooks, Elman, Fouad, Spokane, & Stoltenberg, 1989; Lent, Lopez, & Forrest, 1988). As Meara and Myers (1999) noted, a few counseling psychology programs lost support and were terminated.

During the mid-1990s, the U.S. economy began an unprecedented "bull" market of growth, but toward the close of the decade, economic downturns in Asia affected other regions of the world, including the United States. An increasing focus on regional and international solutions to problems confronting the world gave rise to the term "global economy." Communication advances began linking people within the United States and across the globe, and electronic mail and the Internet promoted more and faster communications. The implications of globalization and rapid electronic communication in general are just beginning to be recognized.

DEVELOPMENTS IN PROFESSIONAL ORGANIZATIONS: IMPLICATIONS FOR PRACTICE AND TRAINING

This section discusses a number of major developments within national professional organizations that have played a role in the changing roles in practice and training in counseling psychology. The most central organization is the Division of Counseling Psychology of the APA (Division 17). Division 17 celebrated its fiftieth anniversary in 1996, and it continues to be a vital core of the counseling psychology profession. We begin by documenting significant and broad ranging changes in the Division in the last 20 years. Next we discuss the emergence and growth of the Council of Counseling Psychology Training Programs (CCPTP), which consists primarily of training directors of counseling psychology programs. CCPTP began in the mid-1970s and has become a nationally recognized entity within the counseling psychology profession, and psychology generally. The third organization we discuss is the Association of Counseling Center Training Agencies (ACCTA), which started in 1978 and consists primarily of counseling center training directors. Like CCPTP, ACCTA has grown substantially in the last 20 years and today plays a critical role within counseling psychology and organized psychology, particularly with regard to pre-doctoral internships. Next we briefly discuss developments in the American Counseling Association (ACA). The ACA has a long history, with a series of different names over the years. Whereas historically this organization was intertwined with counseling psychology, increasingly ACA has focused on counselors at the masters and doctoral level. The final focus of this section is on organizational efforts and accomplishments related to diversity issues within the APA in general and Division 17 in particular. Our treatment of these issues begins well before 1980, because some of these events have not been widely documented within the literature, and they provide a context for understanding the more recent evolution of diversity issues in counseling psychology.

The Division of Counseling Psychology

Counseling psychology was a charter division (Division 17) of the APA in 1946, initially identified as the Division of Personnel and Guidance Psychologists; in 1955 its name was changed to the Division of Counseling Psychology (see Scott, 1980, for a review of earlier years). The Division has a long and distinguished history spanning over 50 years; for an excellent historical overview of the Division from 1946–1996, see Meara and Myers (1999). As of this writing, Division 17 had over 3,300 members, making it one of the most popular APA divisions. The purpose of the Division, as reflected in its bylaws, has been to extend and promote the practice of a broad range of counseling and guidance activities, encourage and support research on counseling activities, develop professional standards and ethical codes, and promote the professional education and training of members of the profession (Scott, 1980).

To record observations about the most important historical events within the Division from the late 1970s to the present, 19 of the last 20 presidents of the Division (one was deceased) were asked to comment on some of the most important events during their presidency. Past presidents of the Division during this time period were: Samuel Osipow (1978), Carl Thoreson (1979), Allen Ivy (1980), Donald Blocher (1981), Henry Borow (1982), Ursula Delworth (1983), Donald Zytowski (1984), Lyle Schmidt (1985), George Gazda (1986), Lawrence Brammer (1987), James Hurst (1988), Naomi Meara (1989), Leo Goldman (1990), Michael Patton (1991), Bruce Fretz (1992), Janice Birk (1993), Jo-Ida Hansen (1994), Kathleen Davis (1995), Dorothy Nevill (1996), and Gerald Stone (1997). Since this project began, Bruce Walsh (1998) and Rosie Bingham (1999) have since served as president as well. Thirteen of the 19 past presidents responded; their observations will be used to document various aspects of the Division's history in the last 20 years. For more details, readers are referred to the minutes of the Division meetings held during annual APA conventions and mid-year meetings, all of which are published in *The Counseling Psychologist* each year.

Reorganization, Transitions, and Accreditation Issues

As reflected in a number of writings (e.g., Meara & Myers, 1999; Whiteley, 1984a, 1984b), counseling psychology and Division 17 in the 1960s and 1970s established a definitional core around developmental issues, focusing on client strengths and psychoeducational interventions. Standards for training were in place, and the Division established a viable, recognized organization representing counseling psychology. The late 1970s brought considerable "rethinking" of professional identity and roles in the profession (Whiteley, 1984a, 1984b). Donald Blocher (president in 1981) reflected on this period:

> In my view, the 15 years between the 1964 Greyston conference and the beginning of the 1980s was a kind of coming of age for the Division, and for the field, itself. The governance of the Division was in the hands of a relatively small group of very dedicated and committed people, most of who had been students or colleagues of the people who had helped to found the Division and who launched the field of counseling psychology . . . The governance of the Division was very informal and often decisions were made . . . on the basis of an informal consensus of like-minded friends and colleagues. This mode of operation was an effective and appropriate way to operate for most of the fifteen year period . . . In the late 70s it began to be apparent that the old way of doing business was no longer adequate. In one sense the governing group was relatively closed. The organization and its governance system was not attracting the newer and younger people. Important new constituencies such as private practice, government and community agency psychologists were not well represented. As a group the leadership, myself included, tended to obsess about the status of the field within APA and to feel powerless and excluded from many of the sweeping developments that were taking place in professional psychology such as licensing and credentialing requirements, third party payments and Psy D. programs. (personal communication, December 24, 1997)

Subsequently, Blocher began several initiatives, such as appointing a special committee (Lyle Schmidt, Naomi Meara, Tom Magoon) to "put the Division on a more formal and business-like footing" (D. Blocher, personal communication, December 29, 1997).

During the late 1970s and early 1980s, however, counseling psychology was being pushed in a new direction, in part due to the systematic effort to define all of professional psychology as a health care profession. Although the APA Committee on Accreditation had been in existence since 1950, the National Register developed criteria for the designation of doctoral programs in professional psychology to assist state licensing boards in the review of credentialing of psychologists who had not graduated from APA accredited programs. Some of the major criteria included a clear designation as a psychology program with an identifiable psychology faculty, and a psychologist responsible for the program. These criteria became the basis for licensing and other credentialing of psychologists. It also provided the basis for determining who was eligible for listing in the National Register of Health Service Providers in Psychology. Although there was a "grandparenting" period for previous graduates, that period was limited, and future graduates needed to have come from a clearly defined psychology program.

The consequences for counseling psychology and for Division 17 were significant and lasting. First and foremost, counseling psychology as a specialty was forced to choose whether to align most closely with counseling and its roots in personnel and guidance, or most closely with psychology. The differences would be dramatic. If counseling psychology chose to remain more closely aligned with the activity of counseling, the field would forego the benefits of the psychology designation (e.g., the increased job market, income, prestige), but would be among the most educated of the counseling professions, and thus have greater prestige and income relative to that group. Alignment with psychology would mean moving toward psychology's training requirements and ensuring that psychologists (as opposed to counselor educators or student personnel experts) would be responsible for the training, as well as for the professional practice of psychology. With Norm Kagan (president in 1977) strongly promoting licensure for psychologists, and Sam Osipow (president in 1978) serving on the Board of Directors of the National Register of Health Service Providers in Psychology, counseling psychology moved toward a much stronger primary identification as a psychological specialty, albeit with continued ambivalence.

Given that APA accreditation required designation as a "psychology program" (meaning that training would be psychological in nature, and thus the program would be housed in a department which included the word psychology in the name of the department), counseling psychology training programs moved quickly to achieve accreditation by shifting program requirements to incorporate psychology-based core content. The number of accredited counseling psychology programs increased at a fast pace. For example, in both 1970 and 1975, only 22 programs in counseling psychology were accredited. By 1980, two more programs had been accredited. In the five years between 1980 and 1985, however, the number jumped to 44, and by 1990, 59 were accredited. In 1995, there were 68 accredited training programs, reflecting a growth rate from 1980 to 1995 of over 180%, which "significantly increased Division 17's numbers and its voice in APA governance, especially as related to accredited specialties within the APA" (G. Gazda, personal communication, December 29, 1997):

> Within this context, the Division again engaged in self-reflection, goal setting, and change. Inasmuch as so many radical changes were being proposed by the APA in 1986–1987 that would significantly affect Division 17, I proposed a Third National Conference for Counseling Psychology—Planning the Future—as my Presidential Project. It was organized during my year as president and implemented during my year as immediate past-president in the spring of 1988.

Lawrence Brammer (president in 1987) described the conference:

> About three hundred participants heard eleven position papers. Working groups discussed thirteen basic issues that were identified by the planning group under George Gazda the year before. Twenty recommendations covered a range of issues including relationship to APA, management problems in Division 17, under representation of various ethnic, gender, disabled, and interest groups in Division 17 governance, encouragement of ethnic and cultural diversity, need for strategic planning, need for regional conferences, need for more contacts with related professional groups, and unresolved licensing matters. (personal communication, December 30, 1997)

A major theme throughout all of the Conference's invited work groups was the importance of counseling psychology's traditional awareness of "viewing people and their behavior . . . (within) a sociocultural context influenced by variables of culture, ethnicity, gender, sexual orientation, age, and sociohistorical perspective" (Rude, Weissberg, & Gazda, 1988, p. 426). The recommendations from this conference set in motion a wide range of activities related to education and training, science, practice, and professional issues that would affect the members and leadership of the Division for many years. (For more details on this conference, see Brammer et al., 1988; Gelso et al., 1988; Kagan et al., 1988; Meara et al., 1988; Rude et al., 1988; Zytowski, Casas, Gilbert, Lent, & Simon, 1988).

Thus, the early 1980s was a time of many beginnings, endings, and transitions, sometimes with very small steps. Many changes were occurring in the APA, and subsequently within counseling psychology. In addition to a number of organizational changes made within the Division, important beginnings were also made to recognize outstanding accomplishments of individual members. For example, in 1987 Brammer increased "the professional awards from one (The Leona Tyler Award) to five, including recognition of young professionals, research achievements, outstanding practice, and outstanding dissertations" (L. Brammer, personal communication, December 30, 1997). Also at this time, the Student Affiliate Group (SAG) was begun at the initiative of Carl Davis, Patrick Sherry, and others at the University of Iowa (Meara & Myers, 1999). At present, SAG has over 300 members, publishes a newsletter, and holds meetings and often presents a symposium at the annual APA conference.

Membership Concerns: Expanding the Traditional Base of Counseling Psychology

Several membership-related concerns from the late 1970s persisted and even increased into the 1980s and early 1990s. Leo Goldman (president in 1990), summarized some aspects of this concern:

> One of my major concerns during my term as president of Division 17 was the limited pool from which were drawn our committee members and chairs, nominated and elected officers, and editorial board members. The under-represented included members of minority groups, full-time practitioners, newer members, and people living on the East and West Coasts. During my year as president-elect (1988–1989), therefore, I made an effort to draw large numbers from all those groups into active involvement in these leadership and governance roles. But I think that this must be a continuing effort, in part because these groups tend not to feel fully identified with what has been largely a white, middle-of-the-country, academic organization. (personal communication, December 18, 1997)

The concerns of Goldman were shared by others who purported that "insiders" in the Division, primarily from four universities (Minnesota, Ohio State, Missouri, and Maryland, the so-called "MOMM cartel"), received a disproportionate number of awards, and appointments to editorial boards and committees (e.g., Horan & Erickson, 1991).

Consequently, several efforts were made to address the needs of a range of members in the Division. Largely through the efforts of a very strong Committee on Women over a period of years, the absence of women in various roles had been well redressed as the 1990s began (see the diversity section later in this chapter for a summary of efforts made to respond to the interests and needs of women, racial/ethnic minorities, gay, lesbian, and bisexuals). We will briefly summarize here several efforts to respond to the needs and interests of independent practitioners.

From the late 1970s through the 1990s, increasing numbers of new graduates were moving outside of higher education, and into the private sector in a variety of positions, particularly in the health care marketplace. Early health care economics were based on a fee-for-service where the providers of health care set the fee for treatment and were reimbursed directly, primarily by government programs, insurance plans, or consumers. Rising medical costs later made such a system prohibitive in the 1990s for many individuals and health insurance companies. Subsequently, the health care industry would undergo a major change in the 1990s; rather than reimbursing services directly, government and employers increasingly contracted these services to private managed care organizations (MCOs), which served as an intermediary to reduce health care costs and to enhance accountability of health care.

Presidents of Division 17 throughout the 1980s expressed considerable concern that the Division was not responding sufficiently to the needs of the practitioners who were in these nontraditional settings. The hard-won consensus on professional identity within counseling psychology in the 1970s was breaking down, and both faculty and students were unprepared for the implications of these new career paths. Overall, the reaction to MCOs by the psychology practice community in the mid- to late-1990s was primarily negative, from strong condemnation—"Managed care is an immoral system" (Shore, 1996, p. 324)—to voicing professional concerns (see Phelps, Eisman, & Kohout, 1998), with a few less negative exceptions (e.g., Belar, 1995; Cummins, 1995). As counseling psychology increasingly participated in APA-driven practice initiatives, organized counseling psychology was forced to respond to numerous legal, legislative, and financial matters related to independent practice. The increased need to attend to matters outside the traditional purview of either academic psychology or practice within higher education settings created both opportunity and conflict. The business and political aspects of participation in the health care system created conflict for many counseling psychologists (see Patton, 1992). Because a growing number of counseling psychologists were financially dependent on the health care market, organized counseling psychology began to attend to the needs of those practitioners.

Although concerns were expressed about the practitioners of the specialty, the Executive Boards of the Division had typically been composed of academic counseling psychologists who had limited experience with the issues of full-time practice and, in particular, full-time independent practice. Counseling psychology practitioners had frequently joined other APA divisions and thus been unavailable for service to the Division. Faith Tanney was a notable early exception, serving on the Executive Board from 1983–1987.

A small cadre of practitioners in various nontraditional settings (e.g., Norma Simon in independent psychotherapy practice, Sandy Shullman in organizational development, Cheryl Carmin in health and hospital practice) maintained a strong identification with counseling psychology and continued to assume active roles on committees. In an early effort in the Division (1988), the Board responded with enthusiasm to a proposed Ad Hoc Committee on Independent Practice. Over the next several years, the Ad Hoc Committee became a standing committee (1991), and then a Section in 1996. In 1990 and 1991, respectively, independent practitioners Christine Courtois and Jean Carter were elected to the Board; in addition, Helen Roehlke and Jim Spivack, both of whom were housed in counseling centers, were elected to the Executive Board in 1991 and 1992, respectively. Melba Vasquez, also in independent practice, was elected as a Division Council Representative in 1994. At the end of the 1990s, Carter, was elected president of the Division. Thus, a practitioner focus became more prominent on the Executive Board of the Division in the 1990s.

Reorganization of Division Structure to Meet the Needs of the 1990s

In the late 1980s and early 1990s, there was more frequent discussion within the Executive Board about the viability of the Division's organizational structure. The governance of the Division had become sprawling and unwieldy, and the ability of the Division to be both responsive to the needs of members and to APA initiatives was severely hampered. Presidents of the Division were burdened by the organizational structure and the demand to attend to a tremendous range of issues.

Presidents Meara (1988), Patton (1991), and Fretz (1992), concerned about the organizational structure and member involvement, all encouraged dialogue on improving the organizational structure of the Division. Patton (personal communication, December 31, 1997) recalled two main goals of some of the early discussions: (1) to help the Division relate more effectively to its parent organization, the APA; and (2) to make the Division more accessible and responsive to new and younger members. Fretz promoted a planning retreat for the Executive Board in May of 1992;

Puncky Heppner and Jean Carter organized and facilitated the retreat, which produced a new organizational structure for the Division. The Division maintained its governance by an Executive Board composed of officers elected for three years by the membership: past-president; president; president-elect; secretary; treasurer; and vice presidents for diversity and public interest, education and training, practice, and science; and three representatives to the APA Council of Representatives. The four new vice-president positions were created to parallel the structure of the larger APA, to serve the diverse interests of the Division's membership, and to create opportunities for active, external involvement and advocacy of issues related to the APA Directorates.

Other new additions included member groups consisting of Sections (which comprise groups of 50 or more voting members of the Division with an active and unitary interest), Special Interest Groups (SIGs; 10 or more voting members of the Division with a particular interest), and Special Task Groups (STGs; appointed by the president for no longer than two years to complete specific tasks). The Division also maintained a host of Committees, the Student Affiliate Group (SAG), Editors (of the Division's *Newsletter* and *The Counseling Psychologist*), Historian, Liaisons and Monitors, as well as International Liaisons and Contacts. Committees, much like the committee structure of the APA, carry out important functions such as awards (Awards and Recognition Committee, Fellowship Committee), continuing education (Continuing Education and Regional Conferences Committee), membership (Membership Committee), and convention programming (Program Committee). The various Divisional liaisons represent the Division to relevant APA Committees, task forces, and other psychological organizations, including international organizations. They help to ensure that the Division remains active in relevant policy and diplomatic efforts. As of 1999, four formal liaisons to Division 17 exist, representing other psychological organizations concerned with training and/or counseling centers: Association of Counseling Center Training Agents (ACCTA), Association of Psychology Postdoctoral and Internship Centers (APPIC), Association of University and College Counseling Center Directors (AUCCCD), and the Council of Counseling Psychology Training Programs (CCPTP).

The implementation phase of the reorganization spanned the presidencies of Birk (1993), Hansen (1994), and Davis (1995):

> This change in structure provided the exciting opportunity for the Executive Board to be more proactive on behalf of the membership. However, we quickly discovered that the Division's financial state was not sufficiently robust to allow us to actually move ahead with very many of our ambitious plans . . . a budget increase was approved at the business meeting during my term . . . (which) allowed the Division to have a large presence within APA and psychology . . . The convergence of the reorganization of the Executive Board, the establishment of Sections, and the dues increase has in my opinion fostered tremendous vitality within Division 17. As a result counseling psychology has greater visibility in, impact on, and effectiveness within APA and the profession. (J. Hansen, personal communication, March 16, 1998)

The reorganization of the Division has been very successful in increasing member involvement, facilitating closer ties to the four APA Directorates (e.g., Education), and promoting proactive planning of initiatives and collaborative ties to other professional organizations. For example, in terms of increasing member involvement, six sections have been created since the reorganization of the Division (four will be discussed in the Diversity section). The Society for Vocational Psychology: A Section of the Division of Counseling Psychology reflects both the long history of vocational and career psychology within counseling psychology and the large number of members committed to this central component of the specialty. This section (previously the Vocational Behavior and Career Intervention Special Interest Group) was established in 1996 to encourage, promote, and facilitate contributions to research, teaching, practice, and public interest in vocational psychology by Division members. It is a very large section with many members who have a great deal of energy and enthusiasm. Its vitality is reflected in a wide array of activities such as convention programming, books, and sponsoring a national conference series as well as international meetings. Conferences have included "Convergence in Theories of Career Choice and Development" (1992); "Toward Convergence in Career Theory and Practice" (1994); "Vocational Interests: Meaning, Measurement, and Use in Counseling" (1996); and "The Role of Contextual Factors in Vocational Development" (1999). In addition, a working conference on "School to Work Transition: Defining the role of Vocational Psychology" was held in 1996. Counseling psychologists' increasing movement into the health care system and into a significant role in mind-body linkages is reflected in the Counseling Health Psychology Section. This section also sponsored a successful conference in 1998, "Groups, Health, and Disease: Psychosocial Models for Prevention."

All the Division's vice presidents have begun to attend meetings of relevant APA groups, providing valuable advocacy for counseling psychologists. One significant test of the value of these intergroup connections came when the Health Care Finance Administration (HCFA), which administers federal health care programs, released a new regulatory definition of the term *clinical psychologist*. The term was used in legislative language and had the potential to create significant difficulties for counseling psychologists. Although the Practice Directorate of the APA had been advocating for a definition that would not be discriminatory to counseling psychologists, this new definition concerned counseling psychologists. Through the relationships already built with other groups, and working with the Practice Directorate, Division 17 led an effective and organized objection to the new definition, which was subsequently returned to HCFA for further work; in 1998, an acceptable nondiscriminatory definition was released that included counseling psychologists. As another example, in 1995, Sandy Shullman was appointed as the Division's Federal Advocacy Coordinator, marking the Division's first official involvement in federal legislative matters. In sum, the reorganization was a:

> quantum leap in establishing the vitality of the profession of counseling psychology . . . The creation of sections and SIGs has led to a significant increase in the number of counseling psychology research conferences, convention programs, newsletters and special sections in our journals, almost all involving substantial numbers of younger psychologists. (B. Fretz, personal communication, November 30, 1997)

The 1990s also witnessed three other major initiatives within Division 17: (1) integration of science and practice, (2) generic accreditation and specialty designation, and (3) further expansion of the membership base. (The latter development will be discussed in the Diversity section later in the chapter).

Promoting the Integration of Science and Practice

The integration of science and practice has a long history in psychology and counseling psychology. Briefly, the early APA was primarily identified as a learned scientific society devoted to the advancement of the discipline through research. In 1946, the APA reorganized by bringing together the earlier learned society of science with the separate, more applied organization, the American Association of Applied Psychology. Although there have been many benefits to this merger, it has also created a challenge for integrating science and practice, and was the source of conflict and change in the 1980s and 1990s. In the 1980s, there was growing dissatisfaction within some groups in the APA who felt that the APA had moved too far away from a scientific society to become a professional guild. After a major attempt to reorganize the APA in 1987, a number of psychologists left the APA, some of who formed the American Psychological Society.

A few years later as concerns were echoed about integrating science and practice within counseling psychology, Patton (personal communication, December 31, 1997) chose as his presidential theme, "Science into Practice and Practice into Science," to counter the lack of integration of science and practice in doctoral and internship training programs. A task force chaired by Puncky Heppner, then Secretary of the Division, was charged with formulating a set of recommendations to present to the membership for achieving: (1) integration of science and practice throughout the doctoral training curriculum, (2) improved training for students in both qualitative and quantitative research methods, and (3) the development of more critical thinking and writing by students. The task force report (P.P. Heppner, Carter, et al., 1992) has assisted curriculum reform in some training programs (e.g., P.P. Heppner et al., 1999) and influenced the "model training program" project, authored by a joint CCPTP/Division 17 task force (see Murdock, Alcorn, Heesacker, & Stoltenberg, 1998).

Generic Accreditation and Specialty Designation

As professional practice and training became more homogeneous across practice specialties in the late 1980s and 1990s (as it must if it is to meet standardized licensing requirements and generic "psychologist" descriptions), concerns were raised about the uniqueness of both new and established specialties in professional psychology. Moreover, there were some efforts to create a generic predoctoral training sequence (Fox, Kovacs, & Graham, 1985), which caused some to fear that predoctoral training specialties like counseling and clinical psychology would be eliminated. The Joint Council on Professional Education in Psychology (JCPEP) was formed in 1988 from the leadership of practice divisions of the APA to consider a coherent and consistent policy for predoctoral education and training in professional psychology. In 1990, JCPEP recommended establishing a formal process for specialty and proficiency recognition, which would apply both to new and existing specialties (clinical, counseling, school, and industrial/organizational). In 1995, the APA Council of Representatives (the elected representatives that form the governing body of the APA) created the Commission for the Recognition of Specialties and Proficiencies in Professional Psychology (CRSPPP) to fulfill the 1990 recommendation of JCPEP.

With the creation of CRSPPP came the requirement that existing specialties apply for redesignation as a specialty, to be evaluated for distinctiveness in their scope and focus. Division 17 quickly began preparing its petition for redesignation, as did Division 12 (clinical psychology) and Division 16 (school psychology). At the same time, CCPTP, in conjunction with Division 17, began developing a model training program in counseling psychology, specifying the ideals inherent in such training:

> It was important that the Division work with CCPTP and ACCTA to develop two official documents that were to shape how counseling psychology would be defined in the future. Although the Model Training Proposal would officially be presented by CCPTP and the Division would officially present the Specialty Definition, the profession needed input from all affiliated groups. (K. Davis, personal communication, January 17, 1998)

As the specialty redesignation petitions were submitted, problems began surfacing. First, the petitions for clinical psychology and counseling psychology revealed a high degree of overlap between the two areas, particularly in the practice arena (subsequently both the counseling and clinical petitions were returned to the petitioners for revision). Second, counseling psychologists were concerned about the term *clinical* being used as a modifier for several new specialties and proficiencies (e.g., clinical health psychology). Although the term was being used to imply *applied* or *professional* specialties, there was potential for it to be misinterpreted by the public and in legislation and regulation, to the detriment of counseling psychologists.

Counseling psychology representatives raised these concerns with CRSPPP and on the floor of the APA Council. Responding to counseling psychology's concerns in 1997, APA president Norm Abeles appointed a task force to address use of the term *clinical*. Rosie Bingham (then president-elect of Division 17) and Jean Carter served on this task force, which proposed that no future specialties or proficiencies would use the term *clinical* as a modifier. The task force also endorsed a plan, developed by the Board of Professional Affairs (chaired by Melba Vasquez) and the Practice Directorate, that would promote use of the new term, *health service psychologist,* in a way that was inclusive of counseling psychologists. Counseling, clinical, and school psychology representatives also developed a proposal to create archival definitions of their respective specialties that recognized and retained their historical place as specialties in the field (see APA, 1999, for the archival description of counseling psychology). These consensus positions were accepted by the Council of Representatives in 1998, marking an era of cooperation that promises to help unify the field without eliminating any of the foundational specialties.

Leadership within the APA

At the same time organized counseling psychology was extending considerable effort to achieve a stronger and clearer voice within organized psychology, individual counseling psychologists were assuming numerous leadership roles within the larger APA. For example, in 1998, 7 of the 14 current or designated APA Board of Directors members were trained as counseling psychologists. In addition, in that same year, 81 counseling psychologists served on other important APA governance bodies, such as the Committee on Accreditation.

Summary

In sum, Division 17 has undergone tremendous change during the last 20 years. In the early 1980s, the Division made a concerted move to identify more exclusively with organized psychology. In addition, the Division began to broaden its membership base and develop more formal operating procedures to conduct Division activities. A decade later, the organizational structure of the Division expanded but in the process had become unwieldy. Moreover, the market economy created more opportunities for counseling psychologists in the private sector, and the needs of the membership as well as pressing issues in organized psychology created new issues in practice and training that demanded attention within the profession. Thus, in the early 1990s, the Division leadership began a major reorganization of the administrative structure of the Division. This was intended to further expand the membership, improve the administrative structure, and facilitate closer ties to the APA directorates. As the 1990s came to a close, greater attention was being given to the diverse needs of a broader range of individuals (e.g., independent practitioners, people of color) within the Division. Simultaneously, the Division has become increasingly involved in central decision making processes within organized psychology. In essence, the Division has developed a structure to respond internally to a diverse membership base as well as externally to the larger APA, and in a way promote unity in diversity. The unity/diversity theme is analogous to states within the United States, or divisions within the APA. Much like the early APA's use of divisions, it is hoped that the four vice-presidential offices and functions, Sections, and SIGs will be building blocks and tension release mechanisms necessary for Division 17 to increase its vitality and growth while maintaining unity.

Council of Counseling Psychology Training Programs

In the mid-1970s, the Council of Counseling Psychology Training Programs (CCPTP) was officially established. This group, consisting primarily of training directors of counseling psychology programs, has served as an important conduit for information about training in counseling psychology. To help document the CCPTP's history, the current and all past presidents of CCPTP were asked to provide their recollection of the most important events during their involvement with CCPTP; 10 of the 18 responded.

Although Barbara Kirk provided the initial impetus for this organization, Bruce Fretz was most instrumental in establishing CCPTP, serving as the first chair from 1975 to 1979:

> Barbara Kirk had become aware that there was a Council of University Directors of Clinical Programs (CUDCP) that was meeting at APA with some modest support from APA. She suggested that counseling psychology programs should become part of that group . . . I was asked by the Division to talk with them about having the counseling program directors meet with them. In my meeting with CUDCP, they were reasonably cordial, but . . . [not particularly welcoming]. (B. Fretz, personal communication, December, 1997)

It became clear to Fretz and several other counseling psychology representatives that the creation of a separate training directors' organization would be in the best interests of counseling psychology. "We established ourselves as a formal organization, setting up a board, elections, etc. Dick Weigel did a yeomen's job on getting the bylaws written" (B. Fretz, personal communication, December, 1997).

The chairs of CCPTP, along with the dates of their appointments are as follows: Bruce Fretz (1975–1979); Lyle Schmidt (1979–1980); Naomi Meara (1980–1981); David Dixon (1981–1982); Janice Birk (1982–1983); Jim Lichtenberg (1983–1984; 1985–1986); Gerald Stone (1984–1985); Kathleen Davis (1986–1987); Sharon Robinson (1987–1988); Franz Epting (1988–1989); Thomas Dowd (1989–1990); Susan Phillips (1990–1992); Andy Horne (1992–1993); Elizabeth Holloway (1993–1994); Michele Boyer (1994–1995); Greg Neimeyer (1995–1996); Robert Lent (1996–1997); Nancy Murdock (1997–1998); and Robert McPherson (1998–1999). Since its inception, one-third of CCPTP chairs have been women, and all but one have been White.

During the early years, the focus of CCPTP was mainly on providing information about setting up a training program, and providing a forum to discuss issues that were important to training directors. For example, CCPTP organized and developed a Training Manual for Program Directors in the mid-1980s. Almost from its inception, CCPTP conducted annual surveys of counseling psychology programs, and documented various aspects of the training programs, such as: (1) faculty rank, size, and demographics; (2) student body size, demographics, internship placement, job placement; and (3) occasional special topics such as information about impaired students. Especially as accreditation standards changed in the late 1970s, CCPTP played a major role in helping programs to interpret the criteria and move toward accreditation.

In the early to mid-1980s CCPTP also focused on internship standards, developing training experiences to enhance the competitiveness of counseling psychology intern applicants. Another issue that surfaced in the mid-1980s and continues at the time of this writing, was the unique needs of counseling psychology training programs housed in colleges of education. In essence, concerns were raised about the match between mission statements within some colleges of education and the training goals of counseling psychology programs (e.g., Brooks et al., 1989; Lent et al., 1988).

Although CCPTP would become more active within the national domain of professional psychology in the 1990s, the organization also increased its role in providing information and support to the training directors of counseling psychology programs. In this regard, annual midwinter conferences were established in the early 1990s, with meetings organized around themes such as the new APA accreditation guidelines, and training issues such as internship supply and demand. Andy Horne (personal communication, January 3, 1998) described the first national conference:

> The conference was informal and quite unstructured, intentionally, so that training directors could identify issues of concern and the group could work collaboratively to address concerns, issues, and directions. We had approximately 70 people attend and it was a very active conference with heated discussions, calls for action, and walks in the woods . . . the conference was so stimulating and professionally involving that those in attendance recommended having a conference each year.

An Outstanding Graduate Student Award was introduced at the 1995 midwinter meeting "to recognize the instantiation of the training values of CCPTP within the context of graduate student excellence" (G. Neimeyer, personal communication, December 26, 1997).

The midwinter conferences have continued with great success by responding to important training issues; in essence, CCPTP, and the midwinter meeting in particular, provides the best vehicle to address the day-to-day as well as large-scale educational and training concerns of program directors in counseling psychology. For example, CCPTP has organized discussions around the burgeoning interest regarding prescription privileges in the 1990s. As part of the agenda to expand the practice of psychology in the public interest, the APA's official position has been to support prescription privileges for appropriately trained professional psychologists (see Cullen & Newman, 1997; Gutierrez & Silk, 1998). As part of the prescription privileges movement, the APA has developed model state legislation for prescriptive authority, postdoctoral training curriculum, and a psychopharmacology examination. Progress on this issue may be modest due to the political realities of medicine's dominance in the health care industry, as well as considerable ambivalence within professional psychology. Organized counseling psychology has not taken a stand for or against prescription privileges for counseling psychology. CCPTP and other counseling organizations will likely be involved with this training issue in the future.

In the mid-1980s and early 1990s, a major shift occurred within the focus of the organization; CCPTP increased its involvement in the national professional psychology scene. Susan Phillips (chair, 1991–1992) recalled:

> In 1982, Betsy Altmaier—a member of the Committee on Accreditation at that time—was just leaving her term on the CCPTP Board, and provided valuable wisdom about the accreditation storm that was brewing. At issue was, first, who would be in a position to make accreditation policy, and second, what that policy would be. Also on the horizon were the efforts of JCPEP (Joint Council on Professional Education in Psychology) and specialty designation. Suddenly, the very existence of counseling psychology was threatened, and together, CCPTP and the Division 17 Representatives to Council (Jo-Ida Hansen and Jim Hurst) were galvanized into political action. There was considerable skirmishing and collaborating with other relevant groups—I recall spending a lot of time with folks from [other training organizations], reinforcing our presence and educating about what counseling psychology was all about. Finally, at the APA Convention in 1991, the Division 17 Representatives to Council were able to secure two seats for CCPTP on the new Committee on Accreditation, reflecting parity with the Clinical and School Psychology constituent groups. CCPTP nominated Betsy Altmaier and Mike Patton for those two seats on the first new Committee on Accreditation (CoA). (personal communication, January 13, 1998)

Betsy Altmaier chaired the Committee on Accreditation (CoA) as the new accreditation guidelines were adopted and the scope was expanded to include postdoctoral programs (see APA, 1997). She provided strong leadership in revising the guidelines with a goal of encouraging both creativity and accountability; she later received the APA Award for Distinguished Contribution to Education and Training for her service. Michael Patton subsequently chaired the CoA in 1998 during the difficult process of clarifying the necessary separation of program accreditation from APA governance.

CCPTP has also remained active in other national issues in professional psychology. For example, after the accreditation criteria were revised, CCPTP recognized a need to "develop some coherent core organizing features common to doctoral training in counseling psychology" (G. Neimeyer, Personal communication, December 26, 1997). CCPTP and Division 17 formed a joint writing project to draft a model training program for doctoral training in counseling psychology. This document has been forwarded to the CoA to assist site visitors and CoA members in understanding and defining the core features of counseling psychology; the document has subsequently been published in *The Counseling Psychologist* (see Murdock et al., 1998).

Likewise CCPTP cooperated with Division 17 in 1996–1997 in preparing and supporting the petition to recognize counseling psychology as a psychological practice specialty. In addition, other efforts resulted in representing counseling psychology's training interests during APA's

Board of Education Affairs meetings as well as the annual meetings of The Council of Chairs of Training Councils, a superordinate group including the chairs of the various training councils (e.g., clinical psychology, school psychology):

> I think these advocacy and liaison activities were among the most important of CCPTP's activities. We worked hard to increase and strengthen CCPTP's advocacy efforts and liaison relationships with other key players in the training of professional psychologists. An important strategy was to have a few CCPTP representatives become well-versed in the national scene (i.e., the key issues and personalities in professional psychology training at the national level), and to serve in this advocacy role for at least 2 to 3 years. By building such continuity and sophistication with the issues, we hoped to better collaborate with other organizations that influenced graduate education and training policies within psychology. (R. Lent, personal communication, January 12, 1998)

Summary

In sum, during the last 20 years, CCPTP has witnessed tremendous growth in numbers, coupled with concomitant strength within professional psychology. Although the organization's central mission of responding to the education and training needs of counseling psychology training directors and programs across the United States remains center stage, the visionary leadership of CCPTP has also established itself as a strong voice for training in counseling psychology, and psychology in general. Lent nicely articulated the utility of this focus:

> Although not particularly glamorous or public, I think such advocacy at the grass roots and higher echelon levels is absolutely essential to the health and well being of counseling psychology's training mission. Given that we are a David in relation to the Goliath status of clinical psychology and its rapidly growing PsyD/professional school juggernaut, it is essential that we become (and remain) as organized and proactive as possible, forging alliances, drafting initiatives, and anticipating threats to our autonomy. It is only by remaining alert and clever, and by using our political skills wisely, that we can maintain agency in helping to shape the future of professional psychology training—rather than becoming hapless bystanders (or victims) in the highly competitive and rapidly changing atmosphere of professional psychology and the larger health care marketplace. (personal communication, January 12, 1998)

Association of Counseling Center Training Agencies

The conceptualization of doctoral training models for counseling psychologists have evolved steadily since 1949, and a number of national conferences have focused on this issue (Ann Arbor Conference of 1949, Northwestern Conference of 1951, Greystone Conference of 1964, Georgia Conference of 1988). Holloway and Roehlke (1987) noted that it was not until the 1970s that the internship came to be viewed as a substantive part of graduate education, in part due to a growing concern within the profession for quality control in graduate training. In 1979, accreditation standards, along with specific criteria, were developed by the APA (see APA, 1979) that required the predoctoral internship as a necessary component of the doctoral degree in professional psychology. The coordinating body for doctoral internships is now APPIC (Association of Psychology Post-Doctoral and Internship Centers). This group establishes policies and procedures for selecting interns.

The Association of Counseling Center Training Agencies (ACCTA) was started in 1978 and remains intact today "to bring people who are doing training in counseling centers together to talk about common problems that we are facing" (L. Douce, personal communication, January 30, 1998). Early in 1978, informal talks were held among a handful of internship program directors at several large counseling centers about problems related to intern selection; after several discussions and meetings, ACCTA was officially founded at the American Personnel and Guidance Association convention in Detroit in March, 1978, by a group of about eight training directors. Helen

Roehlke was a central figure in the early development of ACCTA, serving as president for its first seven years, and has remained involved throughout ACCTA's existence.

Thirteen training directors attended the first ACCTA Conference in 1978. According to Roehlke (personal communication, April, 1998), the group endorsed three goals for the organization:

1. To represent the interests of counseling center training agencies at a national and state level in matters pertaining to the education and credentialing of counseling psychologists, specifically in the areas of internship and practicum training.
2. To provide liaisons between other groups involved in the training and credentialing of counseling psychologists, including the Council of Counseling Psychology Training Program Directors, Association of University and College Counseling Center Directors, Association of Psychological Internship Centers (now APPIC), and the APA Accreditation Committee.
3. To provide a forum for discussion of issues related to the procedures and process of training interns and practicum students.

Some of the issues initially discussed were (1) requesting endorsement and recognition by the Counseling Center Directors; (2) intern recruitment, selection, and negotiation, including possibilities for adopting a uniform application form and computer matching procedure for intern selection; and (3) establishing formal relationships with what is now the APPIC, CCPTP, and the APA Accreditation Office. The group also participated in exchanging information regarding intern evaluation criteria and procedures, standards of training for supervisors, program administration, monetary support for internships, and content/components of internship training.

ACCTA was highly influential in facilitating and enhancing the development of intern training in counseling centers during the late 1970s and throughout the 1980s. Presidents of the organization have included: Helen Roehlke (1979–1985), Louise Douce (1986–1988), Jim Spivack (1989–1990), Kathy Boggs (1991–1992), Martha Christiansen (1993–1994), Lynda Birckhead (1995–1996), and Emil Rodolfa (1997–1998). Five of the seven presidents have been women, all of them White.

ACCTA also created several activities that became traditions, and these speak to the interactive climate that was created within this group in the 1980s and 1990s. Typically, the first night of their conferences involved program sharing and innovation (e.g., sharing evaluation forms of interns, evaluation forms of supervisors, competency lists). ACCTA was a process-oriented group, and offered a great deal of social support and intimacy for its members:

> That's where you went to share your problems with someone who did the job like you did . . . it was sitting down and talking about your lives and who you were, what you were doing. We were not only good therapists but a number of us were just plain intimacy addicts where we established pretty close relationships. A lot of people would articulate that leaving ACCTA was harder then leaving their jobs. (L. Douce, personal communication, January 30, 1998)

Reflective of the growing awareness of the role of cultural factors in American society in the 1980s, attention was directed to cultural issues within the group. For example,

> One [of these activities] is cultural sharing which happens the last night where people chose to share something from their culture; it can be music, a dialogue, a structured kind of thing, anything. Sometimes they are light and humorous, and other times they are deep and very powerful. I remember one discussion of some new people who were in biracial marriages; they discussed some of the pressures and issues they face. Another time there was a diverse racial group who talked about their experiences as interns and students, and some of the racial incidents that happened to them. (L. Douce, personal communication, January 30, 1998)

Another tradition is singing; meetings are often started or ended with singing. Sometimes song books are used; other times songs are written by the group that speak to counseling centers, or ACCTA, with melodies of popular songs that most people know. "They write songs that reflect the misery of the times; when there were budget crises, there were songs about no money" (E. Rodolfa, personal communication, January 31, 1998). Most importantly, as Douce noted, "it's really spiritual in many ways . . . not religious based, but really speaking to what affirms people's spirit and traditions, and that's really wonderful" (L. Douce, personal communication, January 30, 1998):

> Important topics of discussion [at annual meetings] that evolved into ACCTA policies and procedures were intern supervision processes, which developed into recommended standards; APA accreditation and reaccreditation workshops, which became yearly presentations; multicultural diversity discussions and workshops, which evolved into ACCTA's diversity scholars program; and intern impairment, which developed into model due process procedures . . . The current ACCTA Clearinghouse, which matches unplaced intern candidates and Counseling Center sites with unfilled slots, was first mentioned in 1982 and then established in 1986. Although initially the Clearinghouse was utilized only by a small number of candidates/sites, in 1998, 25 sites and 40 intern applicants used this service.
>
> Increases in the membership, the number of attendees at the annual conferences, and the number of APA accredited internship programs have also been important accomplishments for ACCTA. For example, in 1978–79, there were about 20 members; 13 people attended the 1978 meeting . . . At the most recent 1997 meeting, there were 71 Training Directors present; and ACCTA's current membership numbers over 120. In 1978, there were only four APA accredited programs; in 1998 there are over 40. (H. Roehlke, personal communication, April, 1998)

In the mid-1980s, a major shift occurred within the organization; ACCTA began to enter the political arena of the APA. "We had a critical mass of people who wanted to have a voice in what happened. Part of my role as president of ACCTA was bringing that organization into the political arena of the larger APA" (L. Douce, personal communication, January 30, 1998). One of the first instances was formulating responses to the initial draft of accreditation criteria. A second was an early version of using a computer to match potential interns with sites, which APPIC was promoting:

> More recently, ACCTA members have been involved in developing postdoctoral residency standards, designing a uniform application form for intern candidates, the APPIC/APA Supply and Demand Conference, and the recent proposal for computer matching for intern selection. These many activities have resulted in ACCTA . . . becoming a major player in the political arenas related to intern education and training. (H. Roehlke, personal communication, April, 1998)

The supply-and-demand dilemma is currently a major training problem; in essence, there are considerably more trainees seeking internships than there are available internship positions. This dilemma has received a lot of publicity and concern that resulted in a joint APA-APPIC conference in 1997. Recent data (e.g., Oehlert & Lopez, 1998) confirmed the speculations about an internship imbalance; the number of students seeking APA-accredited internships for 1996–1997, 1997–1998, and 1998–1999 exceeded the number of APA-accredited internship slots by between 300 and 500 students per year. The consequences for trainees and the profession is unclear at this time. With a potential bottleneck effect, training could take longer and be even more expensive. It may also affect decisions made by undergraduate students, given these hurdles and the changing health care environment, to seek another profession or to obtain a degree requiring less training, resulting in fewer psychologists and less access to doctoral-level mental health services for consumers. ACCTA and other counseling psychology organizations will likely be involved in this issue in the future.

Summary

In the last 20 years, ACCTA has evolved from a small group of 20 members to over 120 at the time of this writing. Its central focus remains bringing training directors together to talk about common education and training issues in university counseling centers. At the 1998 conference in Colorado, "there were approximately 30 new program directors, either new programs with new directors, or old programs with new directors, all interested in learning how to do this job" (E. Rodolfa, personal communication, January 31, 1998). Moreover, in the last decade the leadership in ACCTA has become a strong force within organized psychology, particularly with regard to pre and post doctoral internship training. Through innovative leadership, ACCTA has not only responded to the immediate personal and professional needs of its members, but also the more encompassing training issues within organized psychology.

American Counseling Association

The American Counseling Association is a confederation of relatively autonomous counseling organizations reflecting a wide range of professional interests. The umbrella organization dates back to 1952, with several name changes that depict changing professional foci over the decades. The American Personnel and Guidance Association (APGA) was established in 1952 as a unified structure for four national organizations: the National Vocational Guidance Association (NVGA); American College Personnel Association (ACPA); National Association of Guidance and Counselor Training (NAGCT; now the Association for Counselor Education and Supervision, ACES); and the Student Personnel Association for Teacher Education (now the Association for Humanistic Education and Development, AHEAD). These groups "sought common cause within the larger association umbrella, but did so with an intent to retain the capability to advance the special interests of their divisions" (Herr, 1985, p. 396). The APGA changed its name to the American Association of Counseling and Development (AACD) in 1983, and in 1992 to the American Counseling Association (ACA).

The membership of APGA primarily had an educational orientation within schools and universities and had considerable overlap with membership in Division 17 of the APA. As Pepinsky noted (in Claiborn, 1985) "pioneers in counseling and counseling psychology were people who had credit ratings in both psychology and education" (p. 11), and thus often belonged to and attended both the annual meetings of the APGA and APA. In fact, Frank Robinson, as treasurer of the emerging APGA organization, recalled how the APGA headquarters were initially established "in the old carriage house that was in the back of the APA Building . . . at a very reasonable rent" (Meara, 1988, p. 213). However, over the ensuing decades, an ever-increasing split has separated what is now the ACA and APA.

Norm Gysbers (personal communication, September, 1998) noted that a major shift occurred between the two organizations as third-party payments became more prevalent in the early 1980s, which placed increasing emphasis on accreditation and licensure as entrance into the psychology profession. In essence, the APA began to focus on credentialing *psychologists,* while the ACA then concentrated on credentialing *counselors.* Accreditation of doctoral programs in counseling psychology was housed in the APA in the late 1970s, and licensure was tied to accredited programs in various states. Partly as a means of protecting its membership, in the early 1980s the APGA created an independent Council for Accreditation of Counseling and Related Educational Programs (CACREP). CACREP was designed to promote quality preparation of counselors, particularly at the masters level but also the doctoral level. Another means of protecting its membership has been through credentialing (N. Gysbers, personal communication, September, 1998). As the delivery of mental health services has changed from institutions, particularly schools and universities, to insurance plans and community settings, accountability in the form of credentialing of mental health service providers has become increasingly important. In 1983, the APGA developed the National Board for Certified Counselors (NBCC) to review counselor credentials and administer examinations to certify counselors (Herr, 1985). NBCC and CACREP have been instrumental in promoting licensure of professional counselors at the masters and doctoral level.

Summary

In the last 20 years, the umbrella organization of what is now called the ACA has undergone two name changes to reflect new initiatives in new eras (see Herr, 1985). The ACA has become an active player in the national and international lives of professional counselors. Increasingly, the organization has moved from "a learned society to become more of a trade association" (N. Gysbers, personal communication, September, 1998), and has become very active in accreditation and credentialing of professional counselors at both the masters and doctoral level. Whereas it was once very common for counselors and counseling psychologists to hold membership in both organizations, and although to some extent that is still true, it seems that there has been less membership overlap and collaboration between the ACA and Division 17 of APA over time.

Diversity Issues in the APA and Division 17

This section *selectively* and, more or less chronologically across three time periods, identifies accomplishments on the part of the larger profession, in particular the APA and, more specifically, Division 17, to: (1) improve the status and treatment of oppressed individuals from diverse groups (for space reasons, primarily racial/ethnic minorities, but also women, gays and lesbians, persons with disabilities, and the elderly) within the general social-cultural context; (2) address diversity in its organizational structures and ethical principles and standards; (3) increase the representation of persons from diverse groups within the professional ranks; and (4) identify and develop the process by which the needs of persons from under-represented and oppressed groups could be more adequately addressed through the development of multicultural/diversity curricula and educational/training experiences required of all counseling psychologists. To this end, it attends, not only to policy and organizational changes, but to major conferences and events sponsored by the APA and Division 17 that helped to further the development of diversity issues, and served to remind the profession of the continuing needs of persons from oppressed and under-represented groups. In order to understand the accomplishments relative to diversity in the last two decades, it is necessary to provide a longer historical framework that helps to put such accomplishments into perspective. This general and more extensive historical coverage is intended to provide a larger organizational context from which to understand Division 17's multicultural/diversity efforts and accomplishments.

Pre 1980: Early Beginnings

Early sporadic efforts relative to diversity focused on the elderly and persons with disabilities. For instance, the Division on Maturity and Old Age of the APA was organized in 1945. The first National Conference on the Psychological Aspects of Aging was convened in 1953. In 1958, rehabilitation psychology was formally recognized as a division, the National Council on Psychological Aspects of Disability (Division 22). Although emphasis was given to the study of persons with disabilities, the APA did not provide leadership in the area of disability rights (Atkinson & Hackett, 1998). This changed in the 1970s when psychologists with disabilities began to lobby the APA for greater access to conventions. Such lobbying resulted in the establishment of the Task Force on Psychology and the Handicapped by the APA Board of Social and Ethical Responsibility for Psychology in 1979.

One of the early efforts by the APA to address racial/ethnic minority concerns was the establishment in 1963 of the Ad Hoc Committee on Equality of Opportunity in Psychology (CEOP). In

1967, CEOP was made a standing committee and more formally given the task of formulating policy related to the education, training, employment, and status of minority groups in psychology. This Committee helped to spur the APA into more direct and decisive actions relative to racial/ethnic minorities through the publication in 1969 of its national survey of 398 Black psychologists. It reported that between 1920 and 1966, the 10 top-rated departments of psychology had produced 24% of all doctorates in psychology, but only 0.5% of the Black doctorates in psychology. In addition, 48% of the respondents believed that race had limited their professional opportunities (APA, 1997). Over the years, the responsibilities of this Committee increased significantly in relation to the four major racial/ethnic groups (i.e., Asian Americans, African Americans, Hispanics, and Native Americans).

Wanting to increase the APA's efforts to address the needs of people of color, representatives from the major racial/ethnic minority groups eventually established their own respective associations within the APA: the Association of Black Psychologists (1968), the Association of Psychologists Por La Raza (1970), the Asian American Psychological Association (1972), and the Society of Indian Psychologists (1975). In essence, these associations continued to highlight three major issues: (1) the extremely limited number of racial/ethnic minority psychologists as well as graduate and undergraduate students in psychology; (2) the APA's failure to address social problems, such as poverty and racism; and (3) the inadequate representation of minorities in the APA governance structure.

The Board of Social and Ethical Responsibility in Psychology (BSERP) was created in 1971 to oversee three committees—the Committee on Academic Freedom and Conditions of Employment, what was later to be called the Committee on Women, and the Committee on Equality of Opportunity in Psychology—as well as a myriad of task forces dealing with social and ethical issues. The Vail Conference, held in 1973, gave strong impetus to the APA's efforts to address professional training for racial/ethnic minorities, something that previous training conferences had ignored. In fact, a Task Group on Professional Training and Minority Groups was included in the conference (Korman, 1974). As a result of this conference, the implementation of affirmative action programs and the identification, recruitment, admission, and graduation of minority students was designated as a basic ethical obligation. In addition, the participants underscored their belief that all students be prepared to function professionally in a pluralistic society. The conference participants also proposed changes that were more structural in nature, including the creation of APA minority boards and committees.

As a result of issues raised by the Association for Women in Psychology, in 1970 the Council of Representatives of the APA established a Task Force on the Status of Women to collect information and develop guidelines and recommendations for both academic and nonacademic settings. This task force became an ad hoc Committee on Women in 1972, and a continuing Committee on Women in Psychology in 1973. (For details relative to the mission of this committee, see APA, 1996.) A major focus of this committee was to address the under-representation of women in the APA. To take on broader issues and play a larger part in the governance of the APA, in 1973 Division 35 (Psychology of Women) was also established. In 1975, the APA Task Force on Sex Bias and Sex Role Stereotyping report laid the foundation for researchers to examine the existence of four kinds of therapist bias that could impact women: fostering traditional sex roles, biased expectations of and devaluation of women, sexist use of psychoanalytic concepts, and treatment of women as sex objects, including seduction of female clients (APA, 1975).

A major boost to the representation of racial/ethnic minority students in psychology was the establishment of the APA Minority Fellowship Program (funded by NIMH) in 1974. This program sought to increase the representation of ethnic minorities in psychology by providing stipends to students and by helping psychology departments improve their capabilities to address cultural diversity. Melba Vasquez, reflecting on this program and its impact on the inclusion of ethnic minority persons in the APA, shared the following thoughts:

My involvement [in the APA] was a result of two things: I was in the first cohort of recipients of an APA Minority Fellowship in 1975. The program initially socialized Fellows into the profession in various ways, including supporting attendance at the APA Conventions. Also, my mentors . . . were active in Division 17. They got me connected to other active folks in their network . . . (personal communication, May 14, 1998)

To accommodate a growing number of diverse groups that were airing their needs and concerns to the APA, the responsibilities delegated to the Committee on Equality of Opportunity in Psychology and the Board of Social and Ethical Responsibility in Psychology were broadened from specific issues of race (especially involving Blacks) to include all minorities, as well as a myriad of other issues of social importance but not directly concerned with minority affairs. Subsequently, racial/ethnic minority professionals expressed concern that broadening the focus of these bodies could very likely impede the expected progress of racial/ethnic minorities within the APA. This concern eventually served as a major impetus for the Dulles Conference of 1978, which examined the means of expanding the roles of culturally diverse people in psychology. In fact,

the seminal event in the last 20 years of the history of ethnic minority affairs at the American Psychological Association was the so-called 'Dulles Conference' . . . The Conference was jointly funded by the APA and NIMH, and brought together several dozen psychologists representing the major recognized ethnic minority groups: American Indian/Alaska Natives, Asian/Pacific Americans, Blacks and Hispanics. The major focus of the Conference was to recommend to the APA steps that the Association could take to increase the participation of these groups in the governance and activities of the APA. The meetings were intense, full of energy and optimism, and permeated with a sense that the time for APA to act was at hand. (E. Olmedo, personal communication, April 27, 1998)

Conferees expressed the need for a clearer focus on minority affairs in the APA, including establishment of a Board of Minority Affairs, a Minority Affairs Office, and eventually a racial/ethnic minority division. The APA Board of Directors and, subsequently, the Council of Representatives, took action establishing (1) the Office of Ethnic Minority Affairs in 1979 (Esteban Olmedo served as its first director); and (2) an Ad Hoc Committee on Minority Affairs.

In reference to Division 17, an Ad Hoc Committee on Women was established by Janice Harrison and Jean Parson in 1970, focusing on the needs of women clients, students, and professionals (Meara & Myers, 1999). One early example of the Committee's activities was the development of the Principles Concerning the Counseling and Therapy of Women (1979), which were principles designed to assist professionals is reducing sex bias. For example, several of the principles underscore the historical reliance of the discipline of psychology on men and their problems, resulting in a lack of information about women and their problems.

1980–1991: Growing Awareness and Developments

In the early 1980s, some members of the psychological community noted that little had been done in the APA to include lesbian, gay, and bisexual issues into research, training, and the curricula. Subsequently in 1980, the Committee on Lesbian and Gay Concerns (CLGC) was formed. Five years later, Division 44, the Society for the Psychological Study of Gay and Lesbian Issues was established and has played a significant part in promoting the needs of gays and lesbians in psychology.

In 1981, the Board of Ethnic Minority Affairs (BEMA) was established, which was very significant because it institutionalized within the APA governance structure a mechanism to enhance the pluralism of psychology. To insure such enhancement:

BEMA appointed liaisons and monitors to the other major boards and committees and solicited the same from them. It also sought to establish relationships with interested divisions and state associations. BEMA also made sure that when other boards and committees were considering items of import to ethnic minority constituencies, our voices would be heard. (E. Olmedo, personal communication, April 27, 1998)

Recognizing the importance of education and training issues, the first task force BEMA established was the Task Force on Minority Education and Training. The Task Force concentrated on issues relative to the training of psychologists who work with culturally-diverse populations, the under-representation of ethnic minority psychologists in the profession, and the funding of education and training opportunities for minorities in psychology. A nationwide survey was conducted to assess the specific types of culturally-relevant course material and experiences that were offered in the clinical training of graduate students. The survey results indicated very marginal inclusion of culturally-sensitive material, mostly offered at the internship level rather than at the graduate level (Wyatt & Parham, 1985). The work of this task force and the information obtained from the surveys eventually resulted in numerous recommendations for recruitment and retention of minority faculty and students as well as the integration of multicultural curricula in the graduate education and training of psychologists.

With respect to the elderly, the APA convened several conferences that focused on the need for more training relative to this group. More specifically, a conference was convened in 1981 that resulted in a number of recommendations, but fell short of putting forth action plans. This was especially true relative to curricula and service (Moses, 1992). (Another conference was convened in 1992 that also resulted in a number of recommendations for gerontological practice.)

In addition, a number of conferences were held specifically to address multicultural issues. One of these conferences that merits specific attention is the Teachers College, Columbia University, Winter Roundtable on Cross-Cultural Psychology and Education which began in 1983 under the leadership of Samuel Johnson, Jr., and has been held on an annual basis ever since. This conference, later directed by Robert Carter since 1989, has become the longest running professional education program in the United States devoted solely to cross-cultural issues. The conference centers on themes that relate to training, research, and practice. (Over the ensuing years, most major cross-cultural researchers have presented their work at this conference.)

The second BEMA task force, established in 1984, was the Task Force on Communications with Minority Constituencies, which sought to establish a network of minority psychologists in APA divisions and state associations. In 1987, the activities of this Task Force lead to the establishment of Division 45 within the APA, The Society for the Study of Ethnic Minority Issues. "Division 45 has validated and provided a conduit for ethnic minority psychological issues as well as imparting cultural diversity into mainstream psychology" (L. Comas-Diaz, personal communication, May 26, 1998).

In 1984, the Task Force on Psychology and the Handicapped recommended the establishment of a permanent Committee on Psychology and Handicaps (later renamed the Committee on Disabilities and Handicaps in 1986, and the Committee on Disability Issues in Psychology in 1991). A major responsibility of this Committee was to sensitize and educate the APA membership regarding the role that psychology can play in helping persons with disabilities to realize their potential (Atkinson & Hackett, 1998). These efforts and accomplishments served as a model for those that would be taken relative to other oppressed and diverse groups. In spite of the APA's commitment to individual needs, some writers feel it has been slow to recognize disability rights and has not been effective in promoting them (Atkinson & Hackett, 1998).

A National Conference on Graduate Education in Psychology was convened at the University of Utah in Salt Lake City in June, 1987 (see Bickman, 1987). This conference, in line with the previous Vail Conference, recognized cultural diversity as an important aspect of graduate education. Recommendations and resolutions on ways to increase the inclusion of cultural diversity within graduate education courses were offered. BEMA also developed a Task Force on the Delivery of Services to Ethnic Minority Populations. The Task Force subsequently drafted Guidelines for

Providers of Psychological Services to Ethnic, Linguistic, and Culturally Diverse Populations (Board of Ethnic Minority Affairs, 1990).

In the late 1980s, the APA reorganized itself into directorates. One consequence of this reorganization was that BEMA was eliminated and superseded by a board with a much broader purview: the Board for the Advancement of Psychology in the Public Interest (BAPPI), with Melba Vasquez as its elected chair. In Olmedo's opinion:

> that event was a significant step backward in our efforts to provide a high profile focus for ethnic minority issues within the APA. However, these efforts continue in the activities of the Committee on Ethnic Minority Affairs, which reports to BAPPI. (personal communication, April 27, 1998)

Through the efforts of the Committee on Lesbian and Gay Concerns, a task force on Lesbian and Gay Concerns (Garnets, Hancock, Cochran, Goodchilds, & Peplau, 1991) was formed. This task force investigated, defined, and categorized specific ways in which negative attitudes and misinformation may be manifested in psychological practice. The investigation resulted in a report that discussed the major types of therapist bias and misinformation regarding lesbians and gays. It also provided examples of beneficial or exemplary practice with gay/lesbian/bisexual individuals (Browning, Reynolds, & Dworkin, 1991; Fassinger, 1991; Shannon & Woods, 1991).

Within Division 17, the early 1980s witnessed a somewhat wavering commitment to the development of multicultural counseling and diversity. Allen Ivey (president in 1980) reflected:

> Clearly, the most important thing I did as president was appoint Derald Wing Sue as chair of the Professional Standards Committee. Out of this committee came the multicultural competencies (see D.W. Sue et al., 1982). The Division 17 Executive Committee voted to accept rather than endorse the competencies. I consider that the major defeat and disappointment of my time as president. I and one or two others lobbied hard, but looking seriously at multicultural issues was not for the Executive Committee at that time. I was greatly surprised and saddened by their resistance and the almost total lack of support and interest. (personal communication, November 27, 1997)

In 1982, Division 17's Education and Training Committee offered service and training recommendations regarding ethnic minorities (Myers, 1982). It was recommended that counseling psychology monitor population shifts to determine the focus of needed services and that there be renewed commitment to the recruitment and retention of minority students to help serve the needs of its population. Also at this time, a seminal position paper on cross-cultural counseling competencies (D.W. Sue et al., 1982) was published under the auspices of Division 17 in *The Counseling Psychologist*. This paper recommended that the APA adopt specific cross-cultural counseling and therapy competencies that would be used as accreditation criteria.

The Division's Committee on Women continued to evolve and attract many members and became one of the most effective committees within the Division, affecting not only the personal and professional lives of its members, but the Division, APA, and the profession of psychology as well (see Fassinger, 1996; Meara & Harmon, 1989). For example, the Principles for Counseling Women underwent extensive revision (Fitzgerald & Nutt, 1986) and were incorporated into accreditation criteria.

A stronger commitment by Division 17 to the further development of multicultural counseling was also made evident in a national conference that was held in Atlanta, Georgia, in 1987. The work groups on counseling research (Gelso et al., 1988) specifically discussed the future directions of research addressing racial/ethnic minority issues within counseling. Their recommendations focused on (1) an increased quantity of racial/ethnic minority research using accurate terminology and focusing on theory development, testing, and application; (2) a need for studies examining actual interventions in the cross-cultural area; and (3) incorporation of nontraditional or alternative research approaches (Ponterotto & Casas, 1991).

In 1988, Division 17 took the necessary steps to make its Ad Hoc Committee on Ethic and Cultural Diversity a standing committee; this committee was charged with providing input to Division 17 on service, training or research issues that impact racial/ethnic minorities. The establishment of this Committee is the result of the work and dedication of several divisional presidents, like Larry Brammer, who demonstrated a strong commitment to multicultural issues and initiatives.

1992–1999: Increased Awareness and Stronger Commitments

As the 1990s progressed, there was more evidence of increased commitment to multicultural issues, and particularly multicultural training. For example, a survey conducted in 1992 revealed that 89% of counseling psychology programs at that time were offering a multiculturally focused course in their training format (Hills & Strozier, 1992). Other surveys document the rapid growth of multicultural training in counseling curricula. For example, the "multicultural counseling" course was projected to be the fastest growing new course offered in the 1991 to 1993 period (Hollis & Wantz, 1994).

The 1992 revisions of the APA Code of Ethical Principles (APA, 1992) was notable from a diversity perspective. Fisher and Younggren (1997) saw the inclusion of the basic moral principle that centers on human diversity and nondiscrimination as one of the major changes in the focus of the current Code. Shifting from merely warning to "not cause harm," the 1992 Code takes a more proactive stance, requiring psychologists to be sensitive and respectful of diversity in the broadest sense. Furthermore, while the code directly targets the issue of *discrimination* in relationship to human diversity, it also addresses the need for professionals to be *competent* in working with distinct populations in the clinical, academic, and research environment. Although the changes have generally been well received, there have been calls to make the Code much more "enforceable" and less prone to "interpretation" (Bidell, 1998).

In 1994, the Commission on Ethnic Minority Recruitment, Retention, and Training (CEMRRAT) was established by the APA Board of Directors to (1) assess the status of, and barriers to, ethnic-minority participation in psychology and, most importantly, (2) create a five-year plan to guide APA in its efforts to address such barriers. Also, in 1995, the APA addressed the need to take into consideration individual differences and diversity as an integral part of the training program accreditation process. Specifically, the APA Council approved revised Guidelines and Principles in Professional Psychology (most notably Domain D: Cultural and individual differences and diversity), which called for programs to make:

> systematic, coherent and long-term efforts to attract and retain students and faculty from differing ethnic, racial, and personal backgrounds . . . ensure a supportive and encouraging learning environment appropriate for the training of diverse individuals," and implement "a coherent plan to provide students with relevant knowledge and experience about the role of cultural and individual diversity in psychological phenomena and professional practice . . . (APA, Office of Program Consultation and Accreditation, 1996, p. 8)

Although the APA has taken steps to address training deficiencies relative to racial/ethnic minorities, much less has been done with respect to other under-represented or oppressed groups, such as gays and lesbians. Relative to these groups, much has yet to be done in the realm of training and accreditation.

As a culmination of all the APA organization efforts documented above, in 1998 the APA president Richard Suinn underscored his and the APA's ongoing commitment to diversity: "One of the reasons I am excited about serving as APA president is my belief in the importance of mentors and role models for all students, but especially for students of racial and ethnic minorities" (R. Suinn, personal communication, June, 1998). During Suinn's presidential year, he visited numerous graduate programs in psychology to mentor and talk to graduate students.

Within the Division, the mid-to-late 1990s witnessed greater attention to diversity issues. For example, the position paper on multicultural competencies by D. Sue et al. (1982) was updated (Sue, Arredondo, & McDavis, 1992), and lead to a number of major books and instruments related to multicultural competencies (see Ponterotto, Fuertes, & Chen, this volume). These multicultural guidelines recognized that the psychological traditions informing practitioners have been associated with a limited cultural frame of reference, while clients come from a wide variety of cultural backgrounds. Given that the evolution of psychological knowledge and practice has been primarily associated with White men of European American backgrounds, these guidelines were needed to assist therapists in working with racial and ethnic minority clients in a culturally appropriate manner. The multicultural competencies were officially endorsed by the Division during the presidency of Gerald Stone (1997–1998); in addition, motions were passed to increase ethnic minority representation in the governance of Division 17 and APA Council. Allen Ivey, attending the 1998 meeting of the Executive Board at the annual meeting of the APA, remarked how much progress the Division had made on multicultural issues since his presidency in 1982 and he also noted the greater diversity among the Executive Board itself, including many more women and people of color than ever before. In fact, six women had been elected president of the Division at this point.

During the Division's reorganization, the Committee on Women was the first committee to become a section (Section on the Advancement of Women) in 1995. In 1998, it held its first conference (Advancing Together: Centralizing Feminism and Multiculturalism in Counseling Psychology), which addressed both feminism and multiculturalism in counseling psychology. An ambitious series of casebooks is planned as one outcome of the conference. Also in 1995, the Section for Lesbian, Gay, and Bisexual Awareness was officially established to (1) promote awareness of gay, lesbian, and bisexual issues that impact counseling psychology training, research, and practice; and (2) support the professional development of gay, lesbian, and bisexual psychologists and students. In 1998, a major contribution appeared in *The Counseling Psychologist* on Lesbian, Gay, and Bisexual Affirmative Training (see Croteau, Bieschke, Phillips, & Lark, 1998). In 1996, the Ethnic and Cultural Diversity Committee became the Section of Ethnic and Racial Diversity.

Rosie Bingham, the first Division 17 president who is a person of color, was elected in 1997, 51 years since the Division began. As her presidential project in 1998–1999, she and several others organized a two-day multicultural conference and summit, which was designed to (1) present state of the art issues in ethnic minority psychology; (2) facilitate difficult dialogues on race, gender, and sexual orientation; (3) forge multicultural alliances for political action and advocacy; and (4) develop strategies for multicultural organizational change:

> The idea for the proposed multicultural conference and summit arose as a result of last year's election of the first Asian American president of the American Psychological Association, Dr. Richard Suinn (only the third ethnic minority psychologist to have achieved that distinction); and the realization that three other persons of color (Lisa Porche-Burke, Derald Wing Sue, Melba Vasquez) were presidents or past presidents of Divisions 45 and 35. History was also made because our group realized that all four were counseling psychologists! Since then, we have discovered that two other Division presidents are persons of color as well (Division 44 and 36). As individuals thrust into leadership positions, we saw a three-year window of opportunity to make a meaningful difference in impacting the profession, APA and our Divisions by making them more inclusive and multicultural. All of our Divisions and/or many members have worked on issues of equal access and opportunities, racism, sexism, homophobia and other forms of prejudice and discrimination. We felt the need to spearhead change by bringing together psychologists who have worked in the areas of race relations, diversity and multiculturalism. (Sue, Vasquez, Porche-Burke, & Bingham, 1999)

Summary

Over the last 20 years, there has been increased awareness and commitment to diversity issues in the APA and Division 17. It is important to note, however, that there has often been tension and many of the changes have not come easily. Actions taken by the APA and Division 17 relative to the realm of diversity have resulted in: (1) improving the status and treatment of individuals from oppressed groups; (2) increasing the representation of persons from diverse groups in the APA organizational structure, especially at leadership levels; (3) ensuring that diversity issues and needs are addressed in the APA ethical principles and standards and taken into consideration in the accreditation process; and (4) developing a process to increase the representation of diversity issues in the curricula as well as in the educational/training experiences required of all psychologists. These results, though often slow in coming, were made possible through a variety of actions, such as the establishment of new divisions and standing committees, special APA sponsored publications and conferences, and the revision of the ethical principles and accreditation guidelines. Significant changes have been made. At this point, some additional areas for development include: (1) continuing to increase the number of racial/ethnic minority students in graduate training programs; (2) more clearly specifying and enforcing the accreditation criteria that focuses on diversity; and (3) increasing the attention given to diverse groups in both the training curricula and practicum experiences (this is especially true in relation to gays, lesbians, people with disabilities, and the elderly). Given the increased visibility of persons from diverse groups in leadership positions in both the APA and Division 17, and the growing numbers of individuals committed to diversity, it is likely that the momentum related to diversity issues will continue in the future.

MAJOR DEVELOPMENTS IN THE THEORETICAL AND EMPIRICAL RESEARCH LITERATURE

The scholarly literature of a discipline provides an important dimension within a historical analysis, reflecting knowledge and the intellectual vigor and exploration within the discipline. Although research in counseling psychology is covered extensively in other chapters in this volume, we will briefly sketch a few theoretical and empirical research trends in six significant areas of inquiry over the past 20 years: (1) changes in methodological diversity, including growing quantitative and qualitative sophistication; (2) counseling interventions, process, and outcomes; (3) career development and counseling; (4) multicultural counseling; (5) issues of gender and sexual preference; and (6) supervision.

Methodological Diversity and Sophistication

Calls for methodological diversity emphasizing alternatives to the received view of science began in the late 1970s (e.g., Gelso, 1979), and increased in the 1980s (e.g., Borgen, 1984; Gelso et al., 1988; Howard, 1984; Polkinghorne, 1984). By the early 1990s, Gelso and Fassinger (1990) noted "receptivity to alternative methodologies is now at a high pitch" (p. 373). Two years later, the first research design book in counseling was published; P.P. Heppner, Kivlighan, and Wampold (1992) concluded, "methodological diversity is essential for important advances in the field of counseling and development" (p. 11).

Despite these calls for methodological diversity, the number of articles reflecting this diversity was limited in the 1980s. For example, in 1983 Hill, Carter, and O'Farrell published one of the first intensive single-subject design studies of counseling process in the *Journal of Counseling Psychology*. Later, Hill (1989) published a book on eight cases of brief psychotherapy. Articles began appearing about training paradigms for alternative methodologies (e.g., Hoshmand, 1989; Wampold, 1986). In the 1990s, however, articles employing more diverse research methodologies became much more frequent in the journals. Moreover, researchers are also now providing methodological refinements of qualitative techniques; a recent article by Hill, Thompson, and Williams (1997) introduced a new methodology, consensual qualitative research, which employs multiple researchers to reach consensus in identifying representativeness of results across cases. This trend signals an important philosophical shift in the profession, and provides a more varied set of tools to creatively develop important and relevant knowledge bases.

During the 1980s, there were also a number of calls for the utilization of more sophisticated statistical analyses (e.g., Kerwin, Howard, Maxwell, & Borkowski, 1987). In 1987, Bruce Wampold edited a special issue in the *Journal of Counseling Psychology* which highlighted the applicability of a number of statistical techniques to counseling research, such as cluster analysis, factor analysis, discriminant analysis, multidimensional scaling, and structural equation modeling. Many of these articles were heavily cited throughout the next decade and there has been a marked increase in the quantitative sophistication of articles in counseling journals, particularly in the last 15 years.

Shifts from reliance on univariate to multivariate statistics, and from analysis of variance designs to multiple regressions, also reflect the increased sophistication in quantitative methods. In addition, more counseling researchers are examining moderating and mediating relationships among variables (e.g., Brown, Lent, Ryan, & McPartland, 1996). The testing of mediating models allows researchers to conceptualize not only direct relations among variables, but also indirect relations, which more accurately depicts many phenomena of interest to counselors. Perhaps one of the most significant statistical developments in the counseling literature has been the introduction of causal modeling (e.g., Fassinger, 1987). Structural equation modeling allows researchers to examine more complex path analyses among a large group of variables and incorporates enhanced measurement models (e.g., latent variable modeling).

As the 1990s come to a close, another special issue on advanced quantitative methods has appeared in *The Counseling Psychologist* (see Chartrand & Ellis, 1999a, 1999b), highlighting methods such as item response theory, generalizability theory, graphic analysis, and multilevel models and analysis. As a whole, methodological pluralism, enhanced sophistication of both qualitative and quantitative methods, and multi-study articles have significantly enhanced the knowledge bases within the counseling literature in the last two decades.

Counseling Interventions, Process and Outcomes

In 1984, Borgen noted three "vigorous and mainstream" (p. 581) theoretical perspectives that have tended to be the primary foci in research on counseling interventions during 1978 to 1982: cognitive-behavioral psychology, social psychological models of influence, and analytic models. Cognitive-behavioral interventions were part of the cognitive-behavioral revolution occurring at that time. For example, self-efficacy was being applied to career development (e.g., Betz & Hackett, 1981), metacognitive variables were being examined in problem solving and coping (e.g., P.P. Heppner & Peterson, 1982) and behavioral management principles were being applied to assertiveness, anxiety, and anger management training (e.g., Deffenbacher, Mathis, & Michaels, 1979). Later, Lent, Brown, and Hackett (1994) nicely expanded Bandura's work advancing a social cognitive theory of career and academic interest, choice, and performance. All of these areas greatly expanded throughout the 1980s, and into the 1990s.

The social influence literature was greatly stimulated by Strong (1968) who conceptualized counseling as an interpersonal or social influence process, and applied an attitude change model from social psychology. In the next two decades, approximately 100 empirical investigations on this topic followed (see P.P. Heppner & Claiborn, 1989; Hoyt, 1996), making it a dominant and reoccurring theme up to the mid-1980s (Wampold & White, 1985). At that point, however, serious concerns were raised about external validity, the role of client factors, and important advances in the attitude change literature from social psychology that had not been examined (see P.P. Heppner & Claiborn, 1989). Although there has been an abrupt reduction in this line of research since 1990, recently authors have articulated new extensions of social psychological research in hopes of restimulating this line of research (e.g., Forsyth & Leary, 1997; P.P. Heppner & Frazier, 1992).

A main focus within the counseling literature has been on the process and outcome of counseling of psychotherapy; in short, there has been great progress in understanding the complex processes and multidimensional outcomes of therapy. As Borgen (1984) noted, the 1970s focused on questions such as: Is Counseling Effective? Which theoretical orientation is best? These questions began to change in the 1980s to: What are the key ingredients of change? What is change, how is it measured, and from which perspective? (Highlen & Hill, 1984). The mid-1980s witnessed an important shift as investigators focused more intensively on the cognitive processes and covert behaviors of both clients and counselors inherent in the therapeutic encounter, including therapist intentions and client reactions to therapeutic events, client recall of significant therapeutic events, client intentions, and session impact. The research of the mid-1980s was characterized by increased methodological rigor and greater clarity in operationalizing constructs, and in examining the systematic linkage of process events to counseling outcomes.

Gelso and Fassinger (1990) noted that although process research in the mid-1980s flourished, research on the counseling relationship came to a standstill. Influential articles by Highlen and Hill (1984), and Gelso and Carter (1985), however, stimulated a new wave of research on the what came to be called the working alliance in the late 1980s and 1990s (e.g., Bordin, 1979; Horvath & Symonds, 1991).

The psychoanalytic perspective during the 1970s and 1980s was primarily focused on time-limited counseling (e.g., Johnson & Gelso, 1980), and measure development based on Kohut's theory of the self (Patton, Connor, & Scott, 1982). The 1990s, however, ushered in a wave of research based on analytic principles. For example, various studies have examined the interrelation of transference, working alliance, and therapist techniques (Patton, Kivlighan, & Multon, 1997), the interaction of transference and insight (Gelso, Hill, & Kivlighan, 1991), and resistance (e.g., Kivlighan, Multon, & Patton, 1996).

The 1990s witnessed an even greater focus on counseling process and outcomes, often characterized by greater methodological and statistical sophistication (e.g., Kivlighan & Shaughnessy, 1995). One of the major issues of debate in outcome research of the late 1990s pertained to identifying empirically supported treatments. Wampold, Mondin, Moody, Stich, and Benson (1997), in a meta-analysis on empirically validated treatments, concluded that it may be more fruitful to focus on the process, theory, or psychological mechanisms of change rather then trying to identify most effective treatments. Process researchers were just beginning to address race and cultural factors within the counseling process in the 1990s (e.g., Thompson, Worthington, & Atkinson, 1994). Excellent new conceptualizations integrating race and cultural factors into assessment as well as the counseling process holds a great deal of promise to guide future research (see Ponterotto et al., this volume). Likewise, process research is just beginning to be addressed in career counseling through sophisticated techniques such as hierarchical linear modeling (see M. Heppner, Multon, Gysbers, Ellis, & Zook, 1998).

Career Development and Vocational Behavior

Counseling psychology's roots in vocational psychology and career development have continued to be the strongest and most empirically mature area of research and practice within the field. In addition to the general counseling journals, four major specialty journals (the *Journal of Vocational Behavior, Career Development Quarterly,* the *Journal of Career Development* and, new in 1993, the *Journal of Career Assessment*) are prominent outlets for the theoretical and empirical work of the field. The strength of this field of research and practice can be attributed in large measure to the robust theories that have provided the groundwork for the conceptual and empirical work that followed. The "Big-Five—Bordin, Dawis/Lofquist, Holland, Krumboltz, and Super—continue to be strongly felt by means of their theoretical contributions, the effects they have had in furthering others' theory, knowledge and research, and in moving career development as a field of practice and inquiry to new heights" (Watkins, 1994, p. 324). The work of John Holland, in particular, continues to provide vigorous research and practical applications. Holland's book *Making Vocational Choices,* first published in 1973, and revised in 1997, provides a dramatic illustration of the heuristic value of his contribution to the field. In addition to the foundational theories, social cognitive theory has begun to have significant impact on the research and practice of career development (Lent et al., 1994). In the realm of theory, Savickas has outlined two important areas that the field continues to grapple with: the first is convergence of existing theories of career choice and development, the second is the "use of post-modern thought to move beyond logical positivism as the philosophy of science for theory and research about vocational behavior" (Savickas, 1995, p. 1). Also in the 1990s, the "false dichotomy" (Hackett, 1993) between career concerns and social-emotional concerns has been consistently addressed with an appeal for a more holistic approach to career development.

The role of career development in the lives of previously marginalized individuals (racial/ ethnic minorities, women, gay, lesbian, and bisexual individuals, individuals with disabilities) has been an important focus of the last two decades (e.g., Betz & Fitzgerald, 1993; Leong, 1995; Walsh & Osipow, 1994). The role of gender in the career decision-making area has been the subject of two major theoretical contributions during this time (both of which have generated a great deal of subsequent research): Gottfredson's (1981) theory of the impact of occupational gender-typing on the circumscription and compromise of career choices, and Hackett and Betz's (1981) application of Bandura's self-efficacy theory to women' career development.

Methodological advancements have also been a hallmark of this time period. For example, meta-analytic procedures, structural equation modeling, and hierarchical linear modeling have allowed for a more thorough examination of the complex relationships among career constructs. For example, Oliver and Spokane (1988) conducted an important meta-analysis across 58 vocational studies to determine the relationship between intervention characteristics and outcome. Thus, methodological diversity and sophistication have expanded during this time period to allow for greater exploration of the complex factors involved in career development.

Multicultural Counseling

A review of the counseling literature of the 1950s found very few journal articles that focused on racial/ethnic minority clients (Jackson, 1995), although the 1960s witnessed an increase in research on multicultural and cross-cultural counseling issues (Reynolds & Pope 1991). The establishment of the Association for Non-White Concerns (now called the Association for Multicultural Counseling and Development) and its journal (now named the *Journal for Multicultural Counseling and Development)* helped spur this increase. In traditional journals, articles focusing on racial/ ethnic minority groups have increased at a moderate rate. A review of 1987 to 1999 by the second author found the following representation of racial/ethnic minority-focused articles in the following three major counseling journals: *The Counseling Psychologist* (15%), the *Journal of Counseling Psychology* (11%) and the *Journal of Counseling and Development* (11%). This is marginally higher than the 10% reported by Ponterotto and Casas (1991) in their review of works in five major counseling journals between 1983 and 1985.

Some of the early articles focused on topics such as the psychology of nigrescense (Cross, 1971), acculturation (e.g., Sabogal, Marin, Ostero-Sabogal, Marin, & Perez-Stable, 1987), and counselor-client matching (e.g., Atkinson, 1983). Currently, multicultural counseling research has extended itself to all areas that fall within the realm of the counseling profession (see for example, Ponterotto et al., 1995). For example, with respect to counseling theories, a number of researchers have evaluated the efficacy of existing theories across racial and ethnic minority clients and proposed theories specifically earmarked for multicultural groups (e.g., Sue & Sue, 1990). A significant focus in the 1990s especially has been on developing theories and models of racial and ethnic identity development (e.g., black racial identity, Helms, 1984, 1990), including bi-racial identity (Kerwin & Ponterotto, 1995), intra-group variability in identity (Casas & Corral, in press), and white racial identity (see Fouad & Brown as well as Ponterotto et al., this volume).

In addition, researchers continue to examine factors related to training and practice (e.g., Berg-Cross & Chinen, 1995), such as utilization of services, accessibility of services, use of parapro-fessionals, and use of translators with non-English speaking clients. Likewise, cross-cultural perspectives are discussed within supervision (e.g., see Goodyear & Guzzard, this volume) as well as strategies for teaching multicultural counseling courses (Reynolds, 1995). A range of topics have also been addressed in the research literature related to both racial/ethnic minority groups and multicultural counseling, such as preference for counselor ethnicity, identifying counseling strategies that are effective with ethnic minority clients, culture responsive counseling, multicul-tural counseling competencies, help seeking attitudes, the psychological costs of racism, stress and coping, assessment, and counseling outcomes.

Betz and Fitzgerald (1993) concluded that the tendency to recognize the profound influence of race, culture, and ethnicity on individuals' life experiences and worldview represents a sig-nificant change in the ways that psychologists address their clients, research, and training. Their contention underscores Pedersen's (1991) perspective that multiculturalism has the potential to become the "fourth force" in psychology. Such an attainment on the part of multiculturalism is truly remarkable given the fact that in psychology, only a few years ago, "Even the Rat Was White" (Guthrie, 1976).

Issues of Gender and Sexual Orientation

The focus on gender issues has not always been the norm. Gilbert (1992) reported that in earlier periods, women were either ignored by social scientists or their experiences were interpreted and defined by men (Russett, 1989). In the late 1960s and 1970s, however, women's roles underwent rapid change, and questions were raised within psychology about bias in psychological research and misrepresentation of women (Richardson & Johnson, 1984). The upshot was (1) the develop-ment of an extensive body of literature on the psychology of women (Gilbert, 1992), and (2) the development of feminist therapy (see Enns, this volume). Counseling psychologists were involved in a broad range of activities related to gender issues in the 1970s and 1980s, but the focus was peripheral to the mainstream of the field. Gilbert aptly depicted the status of this area; the field "moved from viewing women and their issues as special to looking at how the social context of women's and men's lives influence their development, choices, and goals" (p. 383).

Perhaps the earliest lines of research that were maintained throughout the last two decades were within career development (e.g., Gottfredson, 1981; Hackett & Betz, 1981). Both of these articles have stimulated significant research throughout the subsequent years. The research on women's is-sues grew throughout the 1980s and 1990s, with increasing breadth and depth. For example, major lines of research investigated not only career choice and career development, but also mental health issues affecting women such as eating, beauty and women's self-concept, dual career fam-ily issues, sexual violence, and sexual harassment. Likewise, numerous studies examined issues af-fecting women in counseling (see Enns as well as Fassinger, this volume).

Research relevant to counseling men developed at a much slower pace. In 1978, *The Counseling Psychologist* published a special issue on counseling men; the second special issue on this topic, however, was not published until 1998, twenty years later. Undoubtedly the most instrumental line of research was spawned by O'Neil (1981) and his conceptualization of male gender role conflict. This line of research has resulted in more than fifty studies in fifteen years (see O'Neil, Good, & Holmes, 1995).

Research on counseling issues with gay, lesbian, and bisexual (GLB) individuals "is in its in-fancy" (Betz & Fitzgerald, 1993, p. 373), although three reviews in the 1990s have concluded that there is increasing activity in this area (Betz & Fitzgerald, 1993; Buhrke, Ben-Ezra, Ruprecht, & Hurley, 1992; Gelso & Fassinger, 1990). In the late 1980s and early 1990s, two major journals in counseling psychology published special issues devoted to GLB concerns in counseling psychology (Dworkin & Gutierrez, 1989; Fassinger, 1991). Recently, a third issue appeared that focused on research and theory application related to GLB-affirmative training in counseling psychology (see Croteau et al., 1998).

Supervision

In the late 1970s, the supervision literature as we now know it was just beginning. In the early 1980s, Bartlett, Goodyear, and Bradley (1983) edited a special journal issue on counseling supervision, which not only discussed theoretical models, but also summarized the research literature. A year later, Russell, Crimmings, and Lent (1984) analyzed the existing supervision literature (18 studies) in greater depth, calling for more specificity of theories, moving beyond beginning counselor trainees, and giving more attention to external validity issues.

Although the earlier theoretical models of supervision tended to be developed around the major counseling models (e.g., client-centered therapy), within the next 10 years counseling researchers proposed a number of supervision-specific models (e.g., Loganbill, Hardy, & Delworth, 1982). While earlier models pertained to "social role" models (e.g., Bernard, 1979), later models adhered to a developmental approach (e.g., Stoltenberg & Delworth, 1987). The basic assumption within the developmental models was that effective supervision must incorporate the level of counselor development, and thus differ across trainees' level of development. The 1980s and 1990s witnessed a number of empirical studies examining various aspects of the developmental models. Despite problems, the rapid growth in this research led some writers to conclude that this area has grown more than any other content area (Gelso & Fassinger, 1990).

Several major books on supervision appeared in the 1990s (e.g., Bernard & Goodyear, 1992, 1998; Holloway, 1995; Stoltenberg, McNeil, & Delworth, 1997; Watkins, 1997) which depict the development of this area of inquiry within the last 20 years. The Watkins book is an extraordinary resource with major sections devoted to theoretical approaches to supervision, training models, research, and professional issues. The text is a compendium of the most up to data knowledge in this area. Much more is known about supervision since Kell and Mueller's (1972) seminal book, and considerable progress has been made since that time.

Summary

Our examination of the research literature over the last two decades clearly reveals greater methodological diversity, and greater quantitative and qualitative sophistication. This conclusion is reflected across a number of topical areas in counseling psychology. In 1984, Borgen noted an excitement in the literature about new concepts and methods; six years later, Gelso and Fassinger noted that the searching and stirring have resulted in "exciting developments that have enriched counseling psychology" (p. 356). As the 1990s are about to end, counseling psychologists are increasingly using a broader range of methodological tools, with increasing sophistication. Although some would probably like to see faster progress (e.g., Tracey, 1999), it is an excellent sign that the methodological diversity and sophistication are increasing with each decade. The first author's father would remark, most often in reference to carpentry tasks, that "most jobs are made much easier if you have the right tools." Counseling psychology, as well as other specialty areas in psychology and education, are getting more and better research tools with each decade.

Research in counseling psychology is clearly providing important new knowledge that is furthering the development and refinement of theory. Excellent examples of theory development and refinement pertain to the working alliance (Gelso & Carter, 1985), racial identity (Helms, 1990), career self-efficacy (Lent et al., 1994), gender role conflict (O'Neil et al., 1995), and the integrated developmental model of supervision (Stoltenberg et al., 1997). One upshot of the increased knowledge bases and refined theories includes revision of counseling theories (e.g., Ivey, Ivey, & Simek-Morgan, 1993; Sue et al., 1998) and consequently counseling practice. In sum, it is abundantly clear that research in counseling psychology in the last 20 years is increasing in methodological sophistication and rigor and providing important new knowledge that is furthering the development of theories and practice relevant to counseling psychology.

CONCLUDING COMMENTS: OPPORTUNITIES AND CHALLENGES

This chapter provides a kaleidoscope of events and perceptions to document multiple dimensions of a maturing discipline within the last 20 years. In this last section, we will present our concluding comments about potential opportunities and challenges that face counseling psychology as the new millennium begins.

Challenge 1: Maintaining Unity within a Varied Discipline

Our historical analysis of the last 20 years reveals that the counseling psychology profession is strong, vibrant, politically active, and expanding. Organized counseling psychology has broadened beyond Division 17 of the APA, and now includes active, viable, assertive organizations such as CCPTP and ACCTA. In addition, there is active collaboration and overlap with other organizations such as the Association of University and College Counseling Center Directors, the Association of Psychology Postdoctoral and Internship Centers, and the American College Personnel Association. In addition, counseling psychology consists of many outstanding individuals who have provided a wealth of energy, dedication, and leadership. The combined efforts of these individuals, groups, and organizations have resulted in a strong set of voices for counseling psychology. Division 17, CCPTP, and ACCTA have not only grown in membership in the last 20 years, but have evolved administratively to respond more effectively to the needs of their members. Given the social, political, and economic changes of the last 20 years, the membership of all three organizations have changed to include more diverse membership (e.g., independent practitioners, people of color). Nonetheless, it is important to note that many counseling psychologists who are members of the APA are not members of Division 17, but rather have joined other divisions such as Divisions 14 (Industrial and Organizational Psychology), 29 (Psychotherapy), 38 (Health Psychology), 42 (Independent Practice), or 45 (Ethnic Minority Issues). Most likely these divisions are responding to important professional needs of counseling psychologists in a way that Division 17 does not. A major challenge for the future pertains to maintaining unity within organized counseling psychology while simultaneously responding to the needs of members within an extremely diverse and multifaceted discipline.

Challenge 2: Collaboration among Counseling Organizations

The combined strength of Division 17, CCPTP, ACCTA, and other organizations previously mentioned is greater than any one organization alone; although Division 17 formally represents organized counseling psychology, the profession has now evolved beyond any one organization. Collaboration among Division 17, CCPTP, ACCTA, and other groups has been and will continue to be critically important in the future. To this end, as president-elect of Division 17, Jean Carter has spearheaded the development of a Council of the Specialty of Counseling Psychology to foster additional collaboration among relevant counseling psychology organizations. Conversely, whereas in the past there had been considerable overlap between members of Division 17 and what is now called ACA and ACPA, the last 20 years have witnessed widening splits among these organizations. Although a number of external forces and internal decisions have most likely influenced this separation, functionally these splits divide the counseling profession. A challenge for the future is how the various organizations within the counseling profession will respond to both internal and external forces that may affect their future development and interrelationships.

Challenge 3: Being an Active Player by Interfacing within Organized Psychology

The evolution of Division 17, CCPTP, and ACCTA in the last 20 years has also included increasing attention to larger issues in organized psychology. It is clear that the counseling psychology profession is influenced by broad scientific, training, and practice issues within organized psychology (e.g., empirically supported treatments, prescription privileges, the supply and demand of doctoral internships) as well as larger economic and political issues (e.g., the health care revolution). The scope of such broad issues necessitates collaboration not only among counseling psychologists in various organizations (e.g., CCPTP, ACCTA), but also collaboration, negotiation, and diplomacy between counseling psychology organizations and other psychological specialty areas and mental health disciplines. A major challenge for the future of counseling psychology pertains to the profession's ability to (1) be an active player, interfacing with other specialties within organized psychology, and other disciplines outside of psychology (e.g., education, medicine), (2) respond effectively to major scientific, training, and practice issues, and as a result, (3) enhance the viability of counseling psychology.

Challenge 4: Supporting and Increasing Member Involvement

It is important that the specialty of counseling psychology not only adequately protect its domain but also bring its strengths to promoting and enhancing psychology and education in general. The recent reorganization of Division 17 has enabled it to take an active and effective role within the larger field of psychology and within the APA. The breadth of counseling psychology can also be a major asset, as it offers the skills and the flexibility for counseling psychologists to take leadership roles within organized psychology, as evidenced by the numbers of counseling psychologists who serve on the APA Board of Directors, the National Register Board of Directors, and various other boards and committees within organized psychology. Nonetheless, often the leadership within counseling psychology has to a great extent relied on a relatively small number of individuals with vision and a passion for the specialty. A challenge for counseling psychology is to identify ways to support and increase passionate involvement and representation of more members within the confines of "volunteer" organizations. Inherent in this challenge is the issue of whether the larger organizations, such as Division 17, can continue to thrive as a strictly volunteer organization, or whether some type of (paid) executive officers are needed.

Challenge 5: Maintaining an Active Research and Social Policy Agenda That Addresses Major Societal Needs

Our review of several major patterns in the empirical literature in the last 20 years revealed both increasing methodological rigor and significant advances in extending knowledge and theory development. It is clear that the discipline of counseling psychology has an active and successful research agenda, which we view as an essential and integral activity for an applied profession. Cutting edge research regularly appears in rigorous, mature, and stable journals that have "come of age." For example, the *Journal of Vocational Behavior* is almost 30 years old. The *Journal of Counseling Psychology* has been in existence for 45 years, has an excellent reputation for rigorous empirical research, and is one of the most widely circulated APA journals. *The Counseling*

Psychologist celebrated its thirtieth anniversary in 1999, and is widely cited not only within counseling psychology, but also in psychology and other disciplines, both in the United States and internationally (Flores, Rooney, Heppner, Browne, & Wei, 1999). The impact ratings of the counseling psychology journals in the Social Sciences literature are very respectable.

Nonetheless it is obviously important that the research of an applied discipline such as counseling psychology not only be useful in creating knowledge but also in helping people to resolve important problems (i.e., that is, make important contributions to society). Although it is often useful to research professional issues within the profession, it is critical that our primary research foci remain on major societal needs and improving the delivery of psychological services. A challenge for the discipline of counseling psychology is to continue to address major societal needs through its research agenda and subsequently be the basis for better practice.

A related issue pertains to the legislative process aimed at pressing societal problems. The ACA provides a useful example of contributing to the development of state and national legislation that has, in turn, provided research and training opportunities through various granting agencies for the counseling profession (see Herr, 1985). Although it can be limiting for a specialty to base its research agenda solely on granting agencies' priorities, some overlap with state and national priorities can contribute to the utility and viability of a specialty. Challenges for organized counseling psychology are, therefore, to (1) educate counseling psychologists about state and national legislative processes and opportunities, (2) promote grant writing skills as an integral part of doctoral training, (3) promote awareness of pressing social problems within the context of existing social structures and their interrelations, and (4) create research and practice opportunities for counseling psychologists via legislative advocacy efforts. Such efforts have great potential to enhance the research agenda in counseling psychology as well as to enhance the viability of the specialty.

Challenge 6: Developing Meaningful International Collaborations

Another challenge pertains to the potential internationalization of counseling psychology. Economic, cultural, technological, and social forces have created a major shift toward a "global village" zeitgeist. There are many societal needs around the globe that counseling psychologists are ideally suited to address, and the new millennium may be an optimal time to "internationalize" counseling psychology (P.P. Heppner, 1997). Moreover, the major counseling journals can play an important role in promoting cross-cultural awareness and international collaboration; the International Forum in *The Counseling Psychologist* is one example of recent developments in this area. An important challenge for organized counseling psychology involves how to develop meaningful collaborations across different cultures, which not only means effectively adapting American developments, but recognizing other countries' and other cultures' innovations and developments within mutually beneficial partnerships.

Challenge 7: Further Integrating Cultural Diversity into Counseling Psychology Research, Training, and Practice

Counseling psychology is already perceived as a leader in multicultural issues, and the discipline clearly has made significant strides in the last 20 years. At the same time, there is still a pressing need for creativity and energy in our efforts to make cultural diversity an inherent part of mainstream counseling psychology, as opposed to an area of specialization. Research that incorporates factors associated with diversity (e.g., socially constructed racial and cultural factors) into the conceptualization of counseling activities has the potential to expand significantly our research (and theoretical perspectives) on topics such as counseling process and outcomes, career counseling, supervision, and individual differences in coping and psychological adjustment (for example, see Ridley, Li, & Hill, 1998). Incorporating factors associated with diversity into our conceptualizations of counseling activities could significantly change the face of counseling psychology, and represents an important challenge for the future.

The counseling profession has come a long way in heeding to Wrenn's (1962) warnings about cultural encapsulation (for example, see Ridley, Mendoza, & Kanitz, 1994). Diversity in student admissions in counseling psychology training programs has been enhanced by affirmative action policies of the U.S. government in the last 20 years. Recent affirmative action rulings, however, in California and Texas place psychology programs in these states in a challenging position regarding some diversity goals. Although other states are not affected by these rulings and the rulings themselves may change, it is important for training programs to examine carefully their approaches to diversity recruitment and retention (for example, see Atkinson, Brown, & Casas, 1996).

The inclusion of diversity issues within training has not been without tension and frustration, and for some, the evolution has been painfully slow. Although diversity issues are now a part of every accredited counseling psychology program, a major challenge for training in counseling psychology is to integrate diversity issues throughout the training curriculum in a significant and meaningful manner. Organized counseling psychology has the potential to take major leadership roles in achieving significant advances in diversity training not only within counseling psychology, but also more broadly within psychology and education as well.

Another important training issue pertains to the emergence of recommendations/guidelines to assist the work of practitioners, such as the "Principles Concerning the Counseling and Therapy of Women" (see Fitzgerald & Nutt, 1986), "Cross-Cultural Counseling Competencies (Sue et al., 1992), and recommendations about psychotherapy practice with lesbians and gay men (Garnets et al., 1991). Such recommendations seek to enhance cultural competence and reduce biases of sexism, racism, and heterosexism. These recommendations/guidelines also begin to define what constitutes culturally appropriate practice as well as "cultural malpractice." Challenges for the future in this area will include developing criteria for cultural competence, implementation in education and training, and assessment of culturally competent practice.

Challenge 8: Further Integration of Science and Practice in Counseling Psychology Research, Practice, and Training

Counseling psychology has a long history of integrating science and practice as well as espousing the scientist-practitioner model of training (see P.P. Heppner et al., 1992). However, concerns about the viability of the scientist-practitioner model have consistently appeared in the literature (e.g., Barlow, Hayes, & Nelson, 1984), and other training models have been proposed such as the PsyD., or practitioner-scientist model. The linkage between science and practice is critical for the science, practice, and training in counseling psychology. Two major challenges for counseling psychologists are (1) to enhance the scientist-practitioner model through curriculum reform (with a major focus on critical thinking), and (2) to promote science and practice as well as their integration, in our journals and work settings (see P.P. Heppner et al., 1992). More integration of science and practice holds a great deal of potential to strength the counseling psychology profession.

Challenge 9: Closing the Gap between Training and the Needs of Practicing Psychologists, Particularly within the Health Care Arena

Training the next generation of counseling psychologists presents a number of challenges. In the 1970s, the focus of training matched the needs of practitioners within counseling psychology. Over the next two decades, the needs and interests of training and practice diverged as counseling psychology practitioners entered the independent psychotherapy market and as their practice became increasingly externally regulated and controlled. With the increase of graduates finding employment in the private sector in the 1990s, it has become increasingly apparent that the counseling psychology profession needs to train students for participation in a practice world that is not traditionally defined as counseling psychology. For example, independent practice has changed in the 1990s, moving from being largely focused on third-party payer (insurance or government) supported psychotherapy to practice that is heavily influenced by managed care and by new areas and forms of practice (e.g., business, organizational development activities, health care counseling). Within the health care arena, it is likely that future psychologists will function less in an individualistic manner and more within a collectivist context as members of an organized and integrated health care delivery system. The emphasis may be on group modalities, consultation, and interdisciplinary/collaborative models, with a majority of intervention time spent on time-limited, problem-focused assessment and intervention, psychoeducational approaches, administrative oversight, and supervision of less well-trained providers. It will be important for the future training provided by counseling psychology programs to prepare graduates adequately for various forms of practice within and outside of health care, and for the adaptability and flexibility required for successful practice in the changing market economy. Moreover, the evaluative focus within managed health care appears to offer a new opportunity for research and practice psychologists to join forces and influence the health care industry through our expertise in behavioral research. In short, a challenge for counseling psychology is to close the gap between training and the diverse needs of practicing counseling psychologists.

Challenge 10: Masters Level Training of Counseling Psychologists

A long-term professional training issue continues to be the ambivalence of psychology towards master's counseling programs and master's degree holders (Gelso & Fretz, 1992). The APA and Division 17 have consistently supported doctoral degree training and the doctoral degree as the only appropriate training and entry level. However, it has often been argued that the restrictions on the master's degree professional inhibits practice and, therefore, reduces consumer's choices as well as access to needed services, especially in rural areas with few doctoral level psychologists. Moreover, there are inconsistencies and tensions. For example, the stability of an accredited doctoral program in professional psychology, partly based on tuition money generated from large master's programs, is a reality for many contemporary doctoral programs. With the emergence of managed care in the 1990s, master's level therapists may have a wider range of practice opportunities than doctoral level psychologists because they are less expensive. Masters level training in counseling psychology remains an unaddressed issue, with accredited training and credentialing occurring within the auspices of the ACA. Masters level training provides an important challenge for both the ACA and organized counseling psychology as separate organizations, as well as an opportunity for mutually beneficial collaborative relationships between the two organizations.

The next decades will undoubtedly be a time of challenges and opportunities for organized counseling psychology. Although many economic, social, and cultural forces will surely exert an influence on counseling psychology, in the end it will be key individuals who will make the decisions in response to various challenges and opportunities that will alter the course of the field's history. Typically, the boundaries between the individual's contributions to history and the movement of greater social undercurrents are blurred (O. Flathman, personal communication, September 1, 1999). Nonetheless, it is essential to understand the interplay between individual decisions and social forces to fully comprehend the history of counseling psychology.

ACKNOWLEDGMENTS

The authors would like to express gratitude for the helpful comments on various sections of this manuscript from the following individuals: Rosie Bingham, James Croteau, Rodney Goodyear, Norm Gysbers, Mary Heppner, Helen Neville, Michael Patton, Helen Roehlke, and Bruce Wampold. Special thanks to Debbie Harms for her diligence in typing multiple drafts of this chapter, to Matt

Martens for collecting relevant data that was used in this chapter, April Schremp for cheerfully and effectively completing numerous clerical tasks, and for the numerous individuals who so graciously provided observations about the field of counseling psychology in the last 20 years.

REFERENCES

Abeson, A. (1976). Overview. In F.J. Weintraub, A. Abeson, J. Ballard, & M.L. LaVor (Eds.), *Public policy and the education of exceptional children.* Reston, VA: Council for Exceptional Children.

American Psychiatric Association. (1987). *Diagnostic and statistical manual of mental disorders* (3rd ed., rev.). Washington, DC: Author.

American Psychological Association. (1975). Report of the task force on sex bias and sex-role stereotyping in psychotherapeutic practice. *American Psychologist, 30,* 1170–1178.

American Psychological Association. (1979). *Criteria for accreditation of doctoral training programs and internships in professional psychology.* Washington, DC: American Psychological Association.

American Psychological Association. (1992). Ethical principles of psychologists and code of conduct. *American Psychologist, 47,* 1597–1611.

American Psychological Association. (1995). *Task force on the changing gender composition of psychology.* Washington, DC: Author.

American Psychological Association: Office of Program Consultation and Accreditation. (1996). *Guidelines and principles for accreditation of programs in professional psychology.* Washington, DC: Author.

American Psychological Association: Women's Program Office. (1996). *Women in the American Psychological Association: 1995.* Washington, DC: Author.

American Psychological Association: Commission on Ethnic Minority Recruitment, Retention, and Training in Psychology. (1997). *Visions and transformations: The final report.* Washington, DC: Author.

American Psychological Association. (1999). Archival description of counseling psychology. *The Counseling Psychologist, 27,* 589–592.

Atkinson, D.R. (1983). Ethnic similarity in counseling psychology: A review of research. *The Counseling Psychologist, 22,* 79–92.

Atkinson, D.R., Brown, M.T., & Casas, J.M. (1996). Achieving ethnic parity in counseling psychology. *The Counseling Psychologist, 24,* 230–258.

Atkinson, D.R., & Hackett, G. (1998). *Counseling diverse populations.* Boston: McGraw-Hill.

Atkinson, D.R., Morten, G., & Sue, D.W. (Eds.). (1979). *Counseling American minorities: A cross-cultural perspective* (1st ed.). Dubuque, IA: Brown.

Barlow, D.H., Hayes, S.C., & Nelson, R.O. (1984). *The scientist-practitioner: Research and accountability in clinical and educational settings.* New York: Pergamon Press.

Bartlett, W.E., Goodyear, R.K., & Bradley, F.O. (1983). Guest editor's introduction. *The Counseling Psychologist, 11,* 7.

Belar, C.D. (1995). Collaboration in capitated care: Challenges for psychology. *Professional Psychology: Research and Practice, 26,* 139–146.

Berg-Cross, L., & Chinen, R.T. (1995). Multicultural training models and the person-in-culture interviews. In J.G. Ponterotto, J.M. Casas, L.A. Suzuki, & C.M. Alexander (Eds.), *Handbook of multicultural counseling* (pp. 333–356). Thousand Oaks, CA: Sage.

Bernard, J.M. (1979). Supervisory training: A discrimination model. *Counselor Education and Supervision, 19,* 60–68.

Bernard, J.M., & Goodyear, R.K. (1992). *Fundamentals of clinical supervision* (1st ed.). Boston: Allyn & Bacon.

Bernard, J.M., & Goodyear, R.K. (1998). *Fundamentals of clinical supervision* (2nd ed.). Boston: Allyn & Bacon.

Betz, N.E., & Fitzgerald, L.F. (1993). Individuality and diversity: Theory and research in counseling psychology. *Annual Review of Psychology, 44,* 343–381.

Betz, N.E., & Hackett, G. (1981). The relationship of career-related self-efficacy expectations to perceived career options in college women and men. *Journal of Counseling Psychology, 28,* 399–410.

Bickman, L. (1987). Graduate education in psychology. *American Psychologist, 42,* 1041–1047.

Bidell, M. (1998). *A review of ethics and sexual orientation diversity in the American Psychological Association.* Unpublished manuscript, University of California at Santa Barbara.

Board of Ethnic Minority Affairs. (1990). *Guidelines for providers of psychological services to ethnic, linguistic, and culturally diverse populations.* Washington, DC: American Psychological Association.

Bordin, E.S. (1979). The generalizability of the psychoanalytic concept of the working alliance. *Psychotherapy: Theory, Research, and Practice, 16,* 252–260.

Borgen, F.H. (1984). Counseling psychology. *Annual Review of Psychology, 35,* 579–604.

Bourne, B. (1988). Making ideas work: Ralph Bedell and the NDEA Institutes. *Journal of Counseling and Development, 67,* 9–16.

Brammer, L., Alcorn, J., Birk, J., Gazda, G., Hurst, J., LaFromboise, T., Newman, R., Osipow, S.H., Packard, T., Romero, D., & Scott, N. (1988). Organization and political issues in counseling psychology: Recommendations for change. *The Counseling Psychologist, 16,* 407–422.

Brayfield, A.H. (1963). Counseling psychology. *Annual Review of Psychology, 14,* 319–350.

Brooks, L., Elman, N.S., Fouad, N.A., Spokane, A.R., & Stoltenberg, C.D. (1989). Counseling psychology in colleges of education: A survey of training directors. *The Counseling Psychologist, 17,* 470–476.

Brown, S.D., Lent, R.W., Ryan, N.E., & McPartland, E.B. (1996). Self-efficacy as an intervening mechanism between research training environments and scholarly productivity: A theoretical and methodological extension. *The Counseling Psychologist, 24,* 535–544.

Browning, C., Reynolds, A.L., & Dworkin, S.H. (1991). Affirmative psychotherapy for lesbian women. *The Counseling Psychologist, 19,* 177–196.

Buhrke, R.A., Ben-Ezra, L.A., Ruprecht, L.J., & Hurley, M.E. (1992). Content analysis and methodological critique of articles concerning lesbian and gay male issues in counseling journals. *Journal of Counseling Psychology, 39,* 91–99.

Casas, J.M., & Corral, C.V. (in press). Multicultural counseling. In *The Encyclopedia of Psychology.* Washington, DC: American Psychological Association.

Chartrand, J.M., & Ellis, M.V. (1999a). Introduction to advances in quantitative methods in counseling psychology I [Special issue]. *The Counseling Psychologist, 27,* 291–298.

Chartrand, J.M., & Ellis, M.V. (1999b). Introduction to advances in quantitative methods in counseling psychology II [Special issue]. *The Counseling Psychologist, 27,* 483–484.

Claiborn, C.D. (1985). Harold B. Pepinsky: A life of science and practice. *Journal of Counseling and Development, 64,* 5–13.

Conger, J. (1975). Proceedings of the American Psychological Association, for the year 1974: Minutes of the annual meeting of Council of Representatives. *American Psychologist, 30,* 620–651.

Cross, W.E., Jr. (1971). Re negro to black conversion experience: Toward a psychology of black liberation. *Black World, 20*(9), 13–27.

Cross, W.E., Jr. (1995). The psychology of nigrescence: Revising the Cross model. In J.G. Ponterotto, J.M. Casas, L.A. Suzuki, & C.M. Alexander (Eds.), *Handbook of multicultural counseling* (pp. 93–122). Thousand Oaks, CA: Sage.

Croteau, J.M., Bieschke, K.J., Phillips, J.C., & Lark, J.S. (1998). Moving beyond pioneering: Empirical and theoretical perspectives on lesbian, gay, and bisexual affirmative training. *The Counseling Psychologist, 26,* 707–711.

Cullen, E.A., & Newman, R. (1997). In pursuit of prescription privileges. *Professional Psychology: Research and Practice, 28,* 101–106.

Cummings, N.A. (1995). Impact of managed care on employment and training: A primer for survival. *Professional Psychology: Research and Practice, 26,* 10–15.

Deffenbacher, J.L., Mathis, H., & Michaels, A.C. (1979). Two self-control procedures in the reduction of targeted and non-targeted anxieties. *Journal of Counseling Psychology, 26,* 120–127.

Dworkin, S.H., & Gutierrez, F. (Eds.). (1989). Gay, lesbian, and bisexual issues in counseling [Special issue]. *Journal of Counseling and Development, 68,* 1.

Faragher, J.M., Buhle, M.J., Czitrom, D., & Armitage, S.H. (1997). *Out of many: A history of the American people.* Upper Saddle River, NJ: Prentice-Hall.

Fassinger, R.E. (1987). Use of structural equation modeling in counseling psychology research. *Journal of Counseling Psychology, 34,* 425–436.

Fassinger, R.E. (1991). The hidden minority: Issues and challenges in working with lesbian women and gay men. *The Counseling Psychologist, 19,* 157–176.

Fassinger, R.E. (Chair). (1996, August). *Division 17 section on women.* Symposium presented at the annual meeting of the American Psychological Association, Toronto, Canada.

Fisher, C.B., & Younggren, J.N. (1997). The value and utility of the 1992 ethics code. *Professional Psychology: Research and Practice, 28*(6), 582–592.

Fitzgerald, L.F., & Nutt, R. (1986). The Division 17 principles concerning the counseling/psychotherapy of women: Rationale and implementation. *The Counseling Psychologist, 14,* 180–216.

Flores, L.Y., Rooney, S.G., Heppner, P.P., Browne, L.D., & Wei, M. (1999). Trend analysis of major contributions in *The Counseling Psychologist* cited from 1986 to 1996: Impact and implications. *The Counseling Psychologist, 27,* 73–95.

Forsyth, D.R., & Leary, M.R. (1997). Achieving the goals of the scientist practitioner model: The seven interfaces of social and counseling psychology. *The Counseling Psychologist, 25,* 180–200.

Fox, R.E., Kovacs, A.L., & Graham, S.R. (1985). Proposals for a revolution in the preparation and regulation of professional psychologists. *American Psychologist, 40,* 1042–1050.

Friedan, B. (1963). *The feminine mystique.* New York: Norton.

Garnets, L., Hancock, K.A., Cochran, S.D., Goodchilds, J., & Peplau, L.A. (1991). Issues in psychotherapy with lesbians and gay men. *American Psychologist, 46,* 964–972.

Gelso, C.J. (1979). Research in counseling: Methodological and professional issues. *The Counseling Psychologist, 8,* 7–35.

Gelso, C.J., Betz, N.E., Friedlander, M.L., Helms, J.E., Hill, C.E., Patton, M.J., Super, D.E., & Wampold, B.E. (1988). Research in counseling psychology: Prospects and recommendations. *The Counseling Psychologist, 16,* 385–406.

Gelso, C.J., & Carter, J.A. (1985). The relationship in counseling and psychotherapy: Components, consequences, and theoretical antecedents. *The Counseling Psychologist, 13,* 155–243.

Gelso, C.J., & Fassinger, R.E. (1990). Counseling psychology: Theory and research of interventions. *Annual Review of Psychology, 41,* 355–386.

Gelso, C.J., & Fretz, B.R. (1992). *Counseling psychology.* Fort Worth, TX: Harcourt Brace.

Gelso, C.J., Hill, C.E., & Kivlighan, D.M., Jr. (1991). Transference, insight, and the therapist's intentions during a psychotherapeutic hour. *Journal of Counseling and Development, 69,* 428–433.

Gilbert, L.A. (1992). Gender and counseling psychology: Current knowledge and directions for research and social action. In S.D. Brown & R.D. Lent (Eds.), *Handbook of counseling psychology* (2nd ed., pp. 383–416). New York: Wiley.

Gottfredson, L.S. (1981). Circumscription and compromise: A developmental theory of career aspiration. *Journal of Counseling Psychology, 28,* 416–427.

Guthrie, R.V. (1976). *Even the rat was white: A historical view of psychology.* New York: Harper & Row.

Gutierrez, P.M., & Silk, K.R. (1998). Prescription privileges for psychologists: A review of the psychological literature. *Professional Psychology: Research and Practice, 29,* 213–222.

Hackett, G. (1993). Career counseling and psychotherapy: False dichotomies and recommended remedies. *Journal of Career Assessment, 1,* 105–117.

Hackett, G., & Betz, N.E. (1981). A self-efficacy approach to the career development of women. *Journal of Vocational Behavior, 18,* 326–339.

Helms, J.E. (1984). Toward a theoretical explanation of the effects of race on counseling: A black and white model. *The Counseling Psychologist, 12,* 153–165.

Helms, J.E. (1990). *Black and white racial identity: Theory, research, and practice.* Westport, CT: Greenwood Press.

Heppner, M.J., Multon, K.D., Gysbers, N.C., Ellis, C., & Zook, C.E. (1998). The relationship of trainee self-efficacy to the process and outcome of career counseling. *Journal of Counseling Psychology, 45,* 393–402.

Heppner, P.P. (Ed.). (1990). *Pioneers in counseling and development: Personal and professional perspectives.* Alexandria, VA: American Association for Counseling and Development.

Heppner, P.P. (1997). Building strengths as we move into the next millennium. *The Counseling Psychologist, 25,* 5–14.

Hepper, P.P., Carter, J., Claiborn, C.D. Brooks, L., Gelso, C.J., Fassinger, R.E., Holloway, G.L., Stone, G.L. Wampold, B.E., & Galassi, J.P. (1992). A proposal to intergrate science and practice in counseling psychology. *The Counseling Psychologist, 20,* 107–122.

Heppner, P.P., & Claiborn, C.D. (1989). Social influence research in counseling: A review and critique [Monograph]. *Journal of Counseling Psychology, 36,* 365–387.

Heppner, P.P., & Frazier, P.A. (1992). Social psychological processes in psychotherapy: Extrapolating basic research to counseling psychology. In S.D. Brown & R.W. Lent (Eds.), *Handbook of counseling psychology* (2nd ed., pp. 141–176). New York: Wiley.

Heppner, P.P., Kivlighan, D.M., Jr., & Wampold, B.E. (1992). *Research design in counseling* (1st ed.). Pacific Grove, CA: Brooks/Cole.

Heppner, P.P., & Petersen, C.H. (1982). The development and implications of a personal problem solving inventory. *Journal of Counseling Psychology, 29,* 66–75.

Heppner, P.P., Rooney, S.C., Flores, L.Y., Tarrant, J.M., Howard, J.K., Mulholland, A.M., Thyre, R., Turner, S.L., Hanson, K.M., & Lilly, R.L. (1999). Salient effects of practice poster sessions on counselor development: Implications for research training. *Counselor Education and Supervision, 38,* 205–217.

Herr, E.L. (1985). AACD: An association committed to unity through diversity. *Journal of Counseling and Development, 63,* 395–404.

Highlen, P.S., & Hill, C.E. (1984). Factors affecting client change in individual counseling: Current status and theoretical speculations. In S.D. Brown & R.W. Lent (Eds.), *Handbook of counseling psychology* (1st ed.). New York: Wiley.

Hill, C.E. (1989). *Therapist techniques and client outcomes: Eight cases of brief psychotherapy.* Newbury Park, CA: Sage.

Hill, C.E., Carter, J.A., & O'Farrell, M.K. (1983). A case study of the process and outcome of time-limited counseling. *Journal of Counseling Psychology, 30,* 3–18.

Hill, C.E., Thompson, B.J., & Williams, E.N. (1997). A guide to conducting consensual qualitative research. *The Counseling Psychologist, 25,* 517–572.

Hills, H.I., & Strozier, A.A. (1992). Multicultural training in APA-approved counseling psychology programs: A survey. *Professional Psychology: Research and Practice, 23,* 43–51.

Hohenshil, T.H., & Humes, C.W. (1979). Roles of counseling in ensuring the rights of the handicapped. *Personnel and Guidance Journal, 58,* 221–227.

Holland, J.L. (1979). *Making vocational choices: A theory of careers.* Englewood Cliffs, NJ: Prentice-Hall.

Holland, J.L. (1997). *Making vocational choices* (3rd ed.). Odessa, FL: Psychological Assessment Resources.

Hollis, J.W., & Wantz, R.A. (1994). *Counselor preparation 1993–1995: Vol. 2. Status, trends, and implications* (8th ed.). Muncie, IN: Accelerated Development.

Holloway, E.L. (1995). *Clinical supervision: A systems approach.* Thousand Oaks, CA: Sage.

Holloway, E.L., & Roehlke, H.J. (1987). Internship: The applied training of a counseling psychologist. *The Counseling Psychologist, 15,* 205–260.

Horan, J.J., & Erickson, C.D. (1991). Fellowship behavior in Division 17 and the MOMM cartel. *The Counseling Psychologist, 19,* 253–259.

Horvath, A.O., & Symonds, B.D. (1991). Relation between working alliance and outcome in psychotherapy: A meta-analysis. *Journal of Counseling Psychology, 38,* 139–149.

Hoshmand, L.L.S.T. (1989). Alternate research paradigms: A review and teaching proposal. *The Counseling Psychologist, 17,* 3–79.

Howard, G.S. (1984). A modest proposal for a revision of strategies in counseling research. *Journal of Counseling Psychology, 31,* 430–442.

Hoyt, W.T. (1996). Antecedents and effects of perceived therapist credibility: A meta-analysis. *Journal of Counseling Psychology, 43,* 430–447.

Ivey, A.E., Ivey, M.B., & Simek-Morgan, L. (1980). *Counseling and psychotherapy: A multicultural perspective* (1st ed.). Boston: Allyn & Bacon.

Ivey, A.E., Ivey, M.B., & Simek-Morgan, L. (1993). *Counseling and psychotherapy: A multicultural perspective* (3rd ed.). Boston: Allyn & Bacon.

Jackson, M.L. (1995). Multicultural counseling: Historical perspectives. In J.G. Ponterotto, J.M. Casas, L.A. Suzuki, & C.M. Alexander (Eds.), *Handbook of multicultural counseling* (pp. 3–16). Thousand Oaks, CA: Sage.

Johnson, D.H., & Gelso, C.J. (1980). The effectiveness of time limits in counseling and psychotherapy: A critical review. *The Counseling Psychologist, 10*(2), 4–44.

Jordaan, J.P., Myers, R.A., Layton, W.C., & Morgan, H.H. (1968). *The counseling psychologist.* Washington, DC: American Psychological Association.

Kagan, N., Armsworth, M.W., Altmaier, E.M., Dowd, E.T., Hansen, J.C., Mills, D.H., Schlossberg, N., Sprinthall, N.A., Tanney, M.F., & Vasquez, M.J.T. (1988). Professional practice of counseling psychology in various settings. *The Counseling Psychologist, 16,* 347–365.

Kaiser, C. (1997). *The gay metropolis.* New York: Harcourt Brace.

Kell, B.L., & Mueller, W.J. (1972). *Impact and change: A study of counseling relationships.* New York: Appelton-Century-Crofts.

Kerwin, C., & Ponterotto, J.G. (1995). Biracial identity development: Theory and research. In J.G. Ponterotto, J.M. Casas, L.A. Suzuki, & C.M. Alexander (Eds.), *Handbook of multicultural counseling* (pp. 199–217). Thousand Oaks, CA: Sage.

Kerwin, M.L.E., Howard, G.S., Maxwell, S.E., & Borkowski, J.G. (1987). Implications of covariance structure analysis (LISREL) versus regression models for counseling research. *The Counseling Psychologist, 15,* 287–310.

Kingdon, M.A. (1979). Lesbians. *The Counseling Psychologist, 8,* 44–45.

Kinsey, A.C., Pomeroy, W.B., & Martin, C.E. (1948). *Sexual behavior in the human male.* Philadelphia: Saunders.

Kinsey, A.C., Pomeroy, W.B., Martin, C.E., & Gebhard, P.H. (1953). *Sexual behavior in the human female.* Philadelphia: Saunders.

Kivlighan, D.M., Jr., Multon, K.M., & Patton, M.J. (1996). Development of the Missouri addressing resistance scale. *Psychotherapy Research, 6,* 291–308.

Kivlighan, D.M., Jr., & Shaughnessy, P. (1995). An analysis of the development of the working alliance using hierarchical linear modeling. *Journal of Counseling Psychology, 42,* 338–349.

Korman, M. (1974). National Conference on levels and patterns of professional training in psychology: Major themes. *American Psychologist, 29,* 301–313.

Lent, R.W., Brown, S.D., & Hackett, G. (1994). Toward a unifying social cognitive theory of career and academic interest, choice, and performance. *Journal of Vocational Behavior, 45,* 79–122.

Lent, R.W., Lopez, F.G., & Forrest, L. (1988). Counseling psychology in colleges of education: A time to leave home? *The Counseling Psychologist, 16,* 488–491.

Leong, F.T.L. (1995). *Career development and vocational behavior of racial and ethnic minorities.* Mahwah, NJ: Erlbaum.

Lerman, H. (1976). What happens in feminist therapy. In S. Cox (Ed.), *Female psychology: The emerging self.* Chicago: Science Research Associates.

Loganbill, C., Hardy, E., & Delworth, V. (1982). Supervision: A conceptual model. *The Counseling Psychologist, 10*(1), 3–42.

McGowan, J.F. (Ed.). (1965). *Counseling development in American society.* Washington, DC: U.S. Department of Labor and Department of Health, Education and Welfare.

Meara, N.M. (1988). Frank M. Fletcher: A curious career. *Journal of Counseling and Development, 66,* 210–218.

Meara, N.M., & Harmon, L.W. (1989). Accomplishments and disappointments of the Division 17 Committee on Women, 1970–1987. *The Counseling Psychologist, 17,* 314–331.

Meara, N.M., & Myers, R.A. (1999). A history of Division 17 (counseling psychology): Establishing stability amid change. In D.A. Dewsbury (Ed.), *Unification through division: Histories of divisions of the American Psychological Association* (Vol. 3, pp. 9–41). Washington, DC: American Psychological Association.

Meara, N.M., Schmidt, L.D., Carrington, C.H., Davis, K.L., Dixon, D.N., Fretz, B.R., Myers, R.A., Ridley, C.R., & Suinn, R.M. (1988). Training and accreditation in counseling psychology. *The Counseling Psychologist, 16,* 366–384.

Melton, G.B. (1989). Public policy and private prejudice: Psychology and law on gay rights. *American Psychologist, 44,* 933–940.

Moses, S. (1992). More clinicians needed to help a graying America. *Monitor, 23*(8), 34.

Murdock, N.L., Alcorn, J., Heesacker, M., & Stoltenberg, C. (1998). Model training program in counseling psychology. *The Counseling Psychologist, 26,* 658–672.

Myers, R.A. (1982). Education and training: The next decade. *The Counseling Psychologist, 10,* 39–45.

National Council on Disability. (1995). *The Americans with Disabilities Act: Ensuring equal access to the American dream.* Washington, DC: Author.

Oehlert, M.E., & Lopez, S.J. (1998). APA-accredited internships: An examination of the supply and demand issues. *Professional Psychology: Research and Practice, 29,* 189–194.

Oliver, L.W., & Spokane, A.R. (1988). Career-intervention outcome: What contributes to client gain? *Journal of Counseling Psychology, 35,* 447–462.

O'Neil, J.M. (1981). Male sex role conflicts, sexism and masculinity: Psychological implications for men, women and the counseling psychologist. *The Counseling Psychologist, 9,* 61–80.

O'Neil, J.M., Good, G.E., & Holmes, S. (1995). Fifteen years of theory and research on men's gender role conflict: New paradigms for empirical research. In R. Levant & W. Pollack (Eds.), *Foundations for a new psychology of men.* New York: Basic Books.

Patton, M.J. (1992). Counseling psychology and the organized health industry: The hazards of uniformity. *The Counseling Psychologist, 20,* 194–206.

Patton, M.J., Connor, G.E., & Scott, K.J. (1982). Kohut's psychology of the self: Theory and measures of counseling outcome. *Journal of Counseling Psychology, 29,* 268–282.

Patton, M.J., Kivlighan, D.M., Jr., & Multon, K.D. (1997). The Missouri psychoanalytic counseling research product: Relation of changes in counseling process to client outcomes. *Journal of Counseling Psychology, 44,* 189–208.

Pedersen, P.B. (1988). *A handbook for developing multicultural awareness.* Alexandria, VA: American Association for Counseling and Development.

Pedersen, P.B. (1991). Introduction to the special issue on multiculturalism as a fourth force in counseling. *Journal of Counseling and Development, 70,* 4.

Phelps, R., Eisman, E.J., & Kohout, J. (1998). Psychological practice and managed care: Results of the CAPP practitioner survey. *Professional Psychology: Research and Practice, 29,* 31–38.

Polkinghorne, D.E. (1984). Further extensions for methodological diversity for counseling psychology. *Journal of Counseling Psychology, 31,* 416–429.

Ponterotto, J.G., & Casas, J.M. (1991). *Handbook of racial/ethnic minority counseling research.* Springfield, IL: Thomas.

Ponterotto, J.G., Casas, J.M., Suzuki, L.A., & Alexander, C.M. (Eds.). (1995). *Handbook of multicultural counseling.* Thousand Oaks, CA: Sage.

Potter, R.E. (1967). *The stream of American education.* New York: Van Nostrand-Reinhold.

Principles concerning the counseling and therapy of women: Preamble. *The Counseling Psychologist, 8,* 21.

Reynolds, A.L. (1995). Challenges and strategies for teaching multicultural counseling courses. In J.G. Ponterotto, J.M. Casas, L.A. Suzuki, & C.M. Alexander (Eds.), *Handbook of multicultural counseling* (pp. 312–330). Thousand Oaks, CA: Sage.

Reynolds, A.L., & Pope, R.L. (1991). The complexities of diversity: Exploring multiple oppression. *Journal of Counseling and Development, 70*(1), 174–180.

Richardson, M.S., & Johnson, M. (1984). Counseling women. In S.D. Brown & R.W. Lent (Eds.), *Handbook of counseling psychology* (1st ed., pp. 832–877). New York: Wiley.

Ridley, C.R., Li, L.C., & Hill, C.L. (1998). Multi-cultural assessment: Re-examination, reconceptualization and practical application. *The Counseling Psychologist, 26,* 827–910.

Ridley, C.R., Mendoza, D.W., & Kanitz, B.E. (1994). Multicultural training: Reexamination, operationalization, and integration. *The Counseling Psychologist, 22,* 227–289.

Robinson, F.P. (1964). Counseling psychology since the Northwestern conference. In A.S. Thompson & D.E. Super (Eds.), *The professional preparation of counseling psychologists* (pp. 35–42). New York: Columbia University, Teachers College.

Rubin, S.E., & Roessler, R.T. (1978). *Foundations of the vocational rehabilitation process.* Baltimore: University Park Press.

Rude, S.S., Weissberg, M., & Gazda, G.M. (1988). Looking to the future: Themes from the third national conference for counseling psychology. *The Counseling Psychologist, 16,* 423–430.

Russell, R.K., Crimmings, A.M., & Lent, R.W. (1984). Counselor training and supervision: Theory and research. In S.D. Brown & R.W. Lent (Eds.), *Handbook of counseling psychology* (1st ed., pp. 625–681). New York: Wiley.

Russett, C.E. (1989). *Sexual science: The Victorian construction of womanhood.* Cambridge, MA: Harvard University Press.

Sabogal, R., Marin, G., Ostero-Sabogal, R., Marin, B.V., & Perez-Stable, E.J. (1987). Hispanic familialism and acculturation: What changes and what doesn't? *Hispanic Journal of Behavioral Sciences, 9,* 397–412.

Savickas, M.L. (1995). Current theoretical issues in vocational psychology: Convergence, divergence, and schism. In W. Bruce Walsh & S.H. Osipow (Eds.), *Handbook of vocational psychology: Theory, research and practice* (pp. 1–34). Mahwah, NJ: Erlbaum.

Scott, C.W. (1980). History of the division of counseling psychology: 1945–1963. In J.M. Whiteley (Ed.), *The history of counseling psychology* (pp. 25–40). Monterey, CA: Brooks/Cole.

Shannon, J.W., & Woods, W.J. (1991). Affirmative psychotherapy for gay men. *The Counseling Psychologist, 19,* 197–215.

Shore, K. (1996). An alternate view: Comments of Karen Shore. *Professional Psychology: Research and Practice, 27,* 324.

Stoltenberg, C.D., & Delworth, U. (1987). *Supervising counselors and therapists; A developmental approach.* San Francisco: Jossey-Bass.

Stoltenberg, C.D., McNeil, B.W., & Delworth, U. (1997). *IDM: The integrated development model of clinical supervision.* San Francisco: Jossey-Bass.

Strong, S.R. (1968). Counseling: An interpersonal influence process. *Journal of Counseling Psychology, 15,* 215–224.

Sue, D.W., Arredondo, P., & McDavis, R.J. (1992). Multicultural counseling competencies and standards: A call to the profession. *Journal of Multicultural Counseling and Development, 20,* 644–688.

Sue, D.W., Bernier, J.E., Durran, A., Feinberg, L., Pedersen, P.B., Smith, E.J., & Vasquez-Nuttall, E. (1982). Position paper: Cross-cultural counseling competencies. *The Counseling Psychologist, 10*(2), 45–52.

Sue, D.W., Carter, R.T., Casas, J.M., Fouad, N.A., Ivey, A.E., Jensen, M., LaFromboise, T., Manese, J.E., Ponterotto, J.G., & Vasquez-Nuttall, E. (1998). *Multicultural counseling competencies: Individual and organizational development.* Thousand Oaks, CA: Sage.

Sue, D.W., & Sue, D. (1981). *Counseling the culturally different: Theory and practice* (1st ed.). New York: Wiley.

Sue, D.W., & Sue, D. (1990). *Counseling the culturally different: Theory and practice* (2nd ed.). New York: Wiley.

Sue, D.W., & Sue, D. (1998). *Counseling the culturally different: Theory and practice* (3rd ed.). New York: Wiley.

Sue, D.W., Vasquez, M., Porche-Burke, L., & Bingham, R. (1999). *Multicultural conference and summit: Announcement and call for co-sponsors* [Flyer]. Authors.

Suzuki, L.A., Meller, P.J., & Ponterotto, J.G. (Eds.). (1996). *Handbook of multicultural assessment: Clinical, psychological, and educational applications.* San Francisco: Jossey-Bass.

Thompson, C.E., Worthington, R., & Atkinson, D.R. (1994). Counselor content orientation, counselor race, and black women's cultural mistrust and self-disclosures. *Journal of Counseling Psychology, 41,* 155–161.

Tracey, T.J.G. (1999). Integration of theory, research design, measurement, and analysis: Toward a reasoned argument. *The Counseling Psychologist, 27,* 299–324.

Walsh, W.B., & Osipow, S.H. (1994). *Career counseling for women.* Hillsdale, NJ: Erlbaum.

Wampold, B.E. (1986). State of the art in sequential analysis: Comment on Lichtenberg and Heck. *Journal of Counseling Psychology, 33,* 182–185.

Wampold, B.E. (Guest Ed.). (1987). Quantitative foundations of counseling psychology research [Special issue]. *Journal of Counseling Psychology, 34,* 363–479.

Wampold, B.E., Mondin, G.W., Moody, M., Stich, F., & Benson, K.H. (1997). A meta-analysis of outcome studies comparing bonafide psychotherapies: Empirically, "All must have prizes." *Psychological Bulletin, 122,* 203–215.

Wampold, B.E., & White, T.B. (1985). Research themes in counseling psychology: A cluster analysis of citations in the process and outcome section of the *Journal of Counseling Psychology. Journal of Counseling Psychology, 32,* 123–126.

Watkins, C.E., Jr. (1994). On hope, promise, and possibility in counseling psychology or some simple, but meaningful observations about our specialty. *The Counseling Psychologist, 22,* 315–334.

Watkins, C.E., Jr. (Ed.). (1997). *Handbook of psychotherapy supervision.* New York: Wiley.

Wellner, A.M. (Ed.). (1978). *Education and credentialing in psychology: Proposal for a national commission in education and credentialing in psychology.* Washington, DC: American Psychological Association.

Whiteley, J.M. (1980). *The history of counseling psychology,* Monterey, CA: Brooks/Cole.

Whiteley, J.M. (1984a). *Counseling psychology: A historical perspective.* New York: Character Research Press.

Whiteley, J.M. (1984b). A historical perspective on the development of counseling psychology as a profession. In S.D. Brown & R.W. Lent (Eds.), *Handbook of counseling psychology* (pp. 3–55). New York: Wiley.

Wrenn, C.G. (1962). The culturally encapsulated counselor. *Harvard Educational Review, 32,* 444–449.

Wrenn, C.G. (1966). Birth and early childhood of a journal. *Journal of Counseling Psychology, 13,* 485–488.

Wyatt, G.E., & Parham, W.D. (1985). The inclusion of culturally sensitive course materials in graduate school and training programs. *Psychotherapy, 22,* 461–468.

Zytowski, D.J., Casas, J.M., Gilbert, L.A., Lent, R.W., & Simon, N.P. (1988). Counseling psychology's public image. *The Counseling Psychologist, 16,* 332–346.

CHAPTER 2

Ethical Issues in Counseling Psychology: Old Themes—New Problems

KAREN STROHM KITCHENER
SHARON K. ANDERSON

The last time ethical issues in counseling psychology were reviewed comprehensively was in the 1984 *Handbook of Counseling Psychology* (Schmidt & Meara, 1984). Although Fretz and Simon (1992) briefly discussed ethics in their chapter in the 1992 edition of the *Handbook,* they dealt primarily with new developments in ethics in the late 1980s and early 1990s. As they pointed out, the literature on ethics increased substantially during that period. The interest in ethics has not abated since then; if anything, it has continued to rise. Furthermore, the increase in consumerism and the public attention focused on unethical therapist behavior in particular has led to an increase in concern about consumer welfare. Consequently, this chapter includes a more detailed discussion of the literature between 1984 and 1992, as well as subsequent work.

As counseling psychologists have moved into new work roles and settings, the populations with whom they work have changed. Moreover, the demographics of the United States continue to change rapidly. Currently, 75% of those entering the labor market for the first time are women and people of color (D.W. Sue, Arredondo, & McDavis, 1992). In addition, the population has aged. These demographic changes affect the groups with whom counseling psychologists work and influence perspectives on ethics.

Furthermore, counseling psychologists are dealing with a variety of new issues. The AIDS epidemic is one example. In 1984, most psychologists were only minimally aware of the threat of AIDS, and few had to face the difficult ethical decisions surrounding work with individuals who were infected with the HIV virus. Similarly, managed care was dimly on the horizon, and few psychologists were aware of its potential to change independent practice substantially. The result of shifting demographics, roles, and issues has increased awareness that new populations and issues bring with them new ethical challenges.

On the other hand, the literature on ethics has been uneven. Although substantial discussions of, and research on, ethical issues in psychotherapy have occurred, less attention has been paid to ethics in research or in academia. Generally, work on the ethics of research has accounted for a very small proportion of the literature in psychology (McGaha & Korn, 1995). Similarly, discussions of the ethics of teaching and academia have been almost nonexistent until recently (Kitchener, 1992b; Welfel & Kitchener, 1992).

Despite these omissions, two events have changed the nature of the dialogue on ethics since 1984: increased attention to the theoretical foundation of ethical behavior and the publication of the 1992 revision of the *Ethical Principles of Psychologists and Code of Conduct* (American Psychological Association [APA], 1992; subsequently referred to as the *Ethics Code*). Based on the work of Beauchamp and Childress (1994) in biomedical ethics, Kitchener (1984a, 1984b) argued that the profession needed to move away from a rule-bound conception of ethics to one that focused on identifying foundational ethical principles and applying those principles to difficult ethical dilemmas. She argued that the foundational principles suggested by Beauchamp and Childress were as relevant for ethical discussions in psychology as they were in medicine. These were respect for *autonomy* (i.e., respect for other's rights to make their own decisions as long as they are competent to do so), *nonmaleficence* (i.e., do no harm to consumers or research participants), *beneficence* (i.e., help others through research and practice), and *justice* (i.e., fairness). Furthermore, she suggested that the principle of *fidelity,* which includes truth telling, promise keeping, and faithfulness, should be elevated from a rule in the Beauchamp and Childress conceptualization to a principle because of its importance to the human bond that is central to relationship issues in psychology. These five principles have shaped the discussion of ethical issues and the teaching of ethics, particularly in counseling psychology (J.M. Bernard & Goodyear, 1998; Goodyear, Crego, & Johnston, 1992; Heppner, Kivlighan, & Wampold, 1992; Patton & Meara, 1992; Vasquez, 1992; Welfel, 1998), as well as other psychological specialties (Bersoff & Koeppl, 1993; Hendrix, 1991). More recently, Meara, Schmidt, and Day (1996) have argued that the rule of *veracity* or *truthfulness* ought to be similarly elevated from a rule to a principle because of its centrality to human relationships.

Although principle ethics has raised the discourse on ethics to a more critical-evaluative level, it has focused on what psychologists ought to do rather than on their ethical character. Consequently, some (Jordan & Meara, 1990; Meara et al., 1996) have argued for a focus on issues of virtue or character. Meara et al. suggested that virtue ethics, which focuses on motivation, emotion, character, ideals, and moral habits, presents a more complete account of the moral life than does a model of ethics based only on rules and principles of practice. Virtue ethics and how they might affect conceptions of moral behavior are discussed later in this chapter.

The publication of the *Ethics Code* has also shaped current discussions of ethics. The first major revision of the code since 1981, the 1992 code reflected a major departure from earlier codes in format as well as content. Although some of the changes have been criticized (Bersoff, 1994; Gabbard, 1994; Keith-Spiegel, 1994; Kitchener, 1996a; Koocher, 1994; Sieber, 1994; Sonne, 1994), the code addressed a wide variety of professional behavior that prior codes ignored. Additionally, for the first time clearly articulateded aspirational principles were stated.

The standards were written to provide clear guidelines regarding what the American Psychological Association (APA) considered to be unethical conduct. Although some have criticized the use of words like "feasible," "ordinarily," and "reasonable" for providing loopholes which place the best interests of psychologists over those of consumers (Vasquez, 1994), others have suggested that in many cases, psychologists' roles are too complex to forego the role of reasonable judgment in the application of the *Code* (Fisher & Younggren, 1997). Similarly, Payton (1994) lamented the failure of the Preamble of the 1992 *Ethics Code* to state a commitment to human welfare. However, she and others (Fisher & Younggren, 1997) noted that the code substantially strengthened psychology's stand on the importance of sensitivity to members of minority or historically oppressed groups. The *Code* also sets forth several substantially new prohibitions and requirements. Although these cannot be described in detail here, it should be noted that the *Code* includes a new section on forensics; much clearer standards regarding sexual behavior between psychologists' and their students and former clients; prohibitions about engaging in sexual harassment and entering into therapy relationships with former sexual partners; clearer statements about the rights of students, supervisees, and research participants; and stronger standards of informed consent for psychotherapy clients. Several resources offer additional explanations of many of the standards (Canter, Bennett, Jones, & Nagy, 1994; Fisher & Younggren, 1997).

The primary focus of this chapter is on applied normative ethics, which identifies the values or ethical ideals psychologists ought to hold, which values or ideals are better than others, and why they are better. Specifically the focus is on applied normative ethics as it relates to (1) the problematic nature of multiple-role relationships, (2) the use and misuse of informed consent, (3) the complex nature of confidentiality, (4) the obligation to be competent in the face of professional challenges, (5) issues of justice, and (6) virtue ethics. The first five topics were identified because they are reoccurring issues in the psychological literature on ethics that affect counseling psychologists. The discussion of virtue ethics hopefully will challenge readers to think more broadly about what it means to be an ethical psychologist. Occasionally, issues of descriptive ethics, what psychologists actually do in ethical situations, are discussed when research illuminates current ethical practice or beliefs. Additionally, at several points we include discussions of law as it interacts with professional ethics. Due to space limitations, theories of moral development or ethics training are minimally covered.

MULTIPLE ROLE RELATIONSHIPS

When psychologists are asked to describe difficult ethical issues that they face in their work, multiple role relationships are frequently identified as being the most complex (Pope & Vetter, 1992); they have also been a major source of ethics complaints against psychologists (APA, 1997a). Generally, multiple role relationships arise when an individual participates in two or more relationships with another person. The multiplicity of roles can be sequential as well as concurrent (Kitchener, 1988; Pope & Vasquez, 1991; Sonne, 1994).

Multiple role relationships are complex for several reasons. First, some multiple role relationships are unavoidable. For example, a psychologist who coaches her daughter's baseball team may play her client's daughter's team in the tournament championship. Second, the potential for harm often differs in multiple relationships between psychologists and clients, former clients, students, research participants, and supervisees. For example, the potential for harm to a student who works with her advisor on research is less than for a client who is seduced by his therapist. Third, multiple role relationships do not occur in a vacuum. A psychologist and former client may have thought ahead and established parameters for an appropriate, mutually beneficial, and ethical nonsexual, posttherapy relationship, but the public watches, judges, and builds expectations of the profession based on the professional's behavior. Fourth, the APA *Ethics Code* is silent or ambiguous about some types of multiple relationships (i.e., nonsexual posttherapy relationships).

Troublesome multiple role relationships can involve interactions that are intentional or circumstantial (Anderson & Kitchener, 1998). Unfortunately, the potential for harm does not necessarily coincide with the intentionality. Although the APA *Ethics Code* acknowledges that some multiple role relationships may be unavoidable, it warns psychologists about entering into other relationships with a consumer if the relationship might impair objectivity or interfere with the psychologist's professional effectiveness, possibly resulting in harm to the consumer.

Two studies have reported on the kinds of multiple role relationships therapists consider to be most problematic other than engaging in sexual activity with a current client (Baer & Murdock, 1995; Borys & Pope, 1989). In both, four items were rated as never ethical by psychotherapists: the sale of a product or gift to a client, the provision of therapy to a current employee, sex with a client after therapy, and the extension of an invitation to a client for a personal party or social event.

Although there is no simple formula to determine when a multiple role will be unethical or will be harmful, Kitchener (1988) used social role theory to explain such relationships inherently possess the potential for harm. It suggests that roles carry certain expectations and obligations that imply appropriate role behavior and govern role interactions. When a psychologist enters into another role with consumers, role conflict is likely to ensue because the expectations of the psychologist role may conflict with the expectations of the second role. When expectations conflict, consumers may become confused, angry, and frustrated because they are unclear about what role they are expected to play and what can be expected from the professional. Different perceptions of role expectations complicate the issue.

Role obligations may also be incompatible, resulting in divided loyalties and loss of objectivity (Kitchener, 1988). A therapist's primary obligation is to care for the welfare of the client. This obligation may conflict with obligations associated with other roles such as a supervisor. Kitchener suggested that as the incompatibility of expectations increases and role obligations diverge, the potential for harm becomes greater.

A third aspect of social role theory is role power and the power differential between two people in any relationship. Because the role of psychologist carries with it the expectations of knowledge, wisdom, and trustworthiness, it also conveys substantial amounts of power and prestige (Brown, 1994; Gottlieb, 1993). Generally, as the power differential "between the professional's and the consumer's role increases, so does the potential for exploitation" (Kitchener, 1988, p. 219) by the professional.

In summary, when role expectations conflict and the power differential is great, multiple role relationships are particularly dangerous because of the harm that can befall the consumer through exploitation, confusion, and misunderstanding. By contrast, when the power differential is small and role expectations are clear or compatible, there may be little danger of harm (Kitchener, 1988).

Sexual Relationships with Current Clients

Sexual attraction between psychologists and clients is a reality. Pope, Keith-Spiegel, and Tabachnick (1986) found that 87% of psychologists in private practice have at one time or another been attracted to their clients. Attraction, in and of itself is not unethical. On the other hand, all the major mental health professional associations have identified sexual relationships between current clients and therapists as unethical. Pope and Bouhoutsos (1986) argued that psychologists fail to make the welfare of clients a primary concern when they enter into sexual relationships with them. Based on a review of the research, Pope (1988) identified 10 client symptoms associated with sexual contact between therapists and clients, including ambivalence; feelings of guilt; a sense of emptiness and isolation; sexual confusion; impaired ability to trust; identity, boundary, and role confusion; emotional lability; suppressed rage; increased suicidal risk; and cognitive dysfunction.

In recent years, the profession has been absolutely clear that therapists should never have sex with clients nor should they ever communicate, explicitly or implicitly, that sexual intimacies are a possibility. Furthermore, it is always the therapist's responsibility to ensure that no sexual intimacies occur with clients (Pope, Sonne, & Holroyd, 1993). Even though sex with clients has been explicitly forbidden since 1981 by the American Psychological Association (APA, 1981a), studies conducted since then report that between 1% and 9% of male psychologists and .04% and 2.5% of female psychologists had been sexually involved with clients. Earlier studies reported percentages as high as 12% for male psychologists and 3% for female psychologists (Pope, 1993).

One of the more positive trends in the research on sexual contact between therapist and clients has been the apparent decrease in the reported incidence. The decrease may be real and reflect a change that has resulted from the attention that the press, the profession, and the law have paid to this issue. On the other hand, it may also reflect a reluctance to admit guilt for an illegal and unethical act, even on an anonymous questionnaire (Stake & Oliver, 1991).

Few predictors of therapists' sexual involvement with clients have been identified with the exception of gender and age (Pope, 1990). The general trend has been for older male therapists to become sexually involved with younger female patients, although male with male, female with male, and female with female cases have also occurred (Pope & Bouhoutsos, 1986). Current data suggest that this trend continues. Seventy-five percent of all cases involving sexual relationships between therapists and clients adjudicated by the APA Ethics Committee in 1996 involved male therapists with adult female clients (APA, 1997a).

The Complexity of Posttherapy Relationships

Psychology has begun to acknowledge that therapists' responsibilities to clients do not end when the formal therapy relationship is terminated. In fact, the *Ethics Code* (APA, 1992) encourages psychologists to avoid exploitive and harmful relationships during and after the professional relationship. Pope (1988) argued that it is important to avoid posttherapy relationships because some aspects of the therapeutic process continue after termination. These include (1) the residual transference of successful therapy, which Pope argues, reaches its peak during a time period of 5 to 10 years after termination; (2) the mental representation of the former therapist; and (3) the power differential. In fact, Geller, Cooley, and Hartley (1981/1982) found that after therapy individuals used the therapist's internalized image to continue the therapeutic dialogue and their personal improvement. Additionally, Buckley, Karasu, and Charles (1981) reported that participants who had been terminated from therapy for 5 to 10 years rated transference residue items and items related to returning to therapy significantly higher than participants with fewer or more years since termination.

Sexual Intimacy with Former Clients

The 1992 APA *Ethics Code* prohibited psychologists from entering into a sexual relationship with a former client for a minimum of two years after termination. After this two-year period, psychologists are responsible for proving "that there has been no exploitation" when entering into the sexual relationship (Standard 4.07). Although several states have passed legislation regarding sexual intimacy with former clients, the legislation varies from state to state (Jorgenson, 1994). Some prohibit sexual contact in perpetuity and others do not prohibit it at all.

Studies have revealed that between .6% and 4.4% of psychologists admit to starting a sexual relationship with a client after termination (Akamatsu, 1988; Borys & Pope, 1989; Pope, 1990). The belief that this behavior was ethical under some circumstances ranged from 3.9% to 11%. Lamb et al. (1994) found that when the interval between termination and the sexual activity was less than a month, most psychologists condemned the activity; however, when the interval increased, fewer respondents believed the behavior to be unethical.

There appear to be two competing arguments regarding the two-year prohibition on sexual intimacy between psychologists and former clients. Bersoff (1994), for example, stated that although the new standard upheld the principles of beneficence and nonmaleficence, it violated clients' autonomy. He argued that concern about posttermination sexual relationships was based on the belief that there would always be a power imbalance between the former therapist, who was usually a male, and the former client, who was usually a woman. This claim, he suggests, assumes that women who enter therapy will never be autonomous or able to make reasonably informed decisions about their sexual partners and disregards their moral maturity.

Others (Kitchener, 1992a; Vasquez, 1991) have suggested that the risk of harm is too great. Vasquez stated that the question is not whether a psychotherapist should have the "right to (consensual) sex with a former client" (p. 48), but rather whether psychotherapists should lay aside their personal rights for "moral and professional reasons," just as they lay aside these rights and do not enter into sexual relationships with current clients. Although the formal contract to help the client has ended, Kitchener (1992a) stressed that this does not imply that psychologists should willfully engage in activities that might undo the benefits that have accrued from their services. There, in fact, are data to suggest that harm occurs in 80% of the cases of therapist-patient sex that are initiated after therapy ends (Pope & Vetter, 1992).

POSTTHERAPY NONSEXUAL, NONROMANTIC RELATIONSHIPS

Several studies have examined psychotherapists' beliefs and behavior regarding nonsexual posttherapy relationships (Baer & Murdock, 1995; Borys & Pope, 1989; Lamb et al., 1994). The results of these studies suggest that the majority of respondents saw behaviors such as social interaction, entering into a business relationship, or developing a friendship with a former client as unethical.

Anderson and Kitchener (1996) asked psychologists to describe, from direct or indirect knowledge, nonsexual, nonromantic posttherapy relationships between psychologists and former clients. Eight types of posttherapy relationships were described: personal/friendship, social interactions, business/financial, collegial/professional, supervisory/evaluative, religious, collegial or professional plus social, and workplace. The frequency of contact with former clients varied substantially. Some involved little more than occasional social or professional contact whereas others involved such full-fledged relationships as a business partnership. Some relationships were circumstantial and often unavoidable; others were intentional. Some participants believed that posttherapy relationships of any kind were unethical and should not occur. They argued that the therapeutic relationship continues in perpetuity, the therapist should remain available to the former client for further therapy in the future, and the former client may be harmed if a posttherapy relationship occurred. Other psychologists argued that nonsexual relationships with former clients were not unethical. They indicated that termination was the end of the therapeutic relationship, compartmentalization of concurrent roles such as former therapist and business acquaintance was possible, and posttherapy relationships can naturally evolve from a therapeutic relationship. In between these two perspectives were the opinions of psychologists who suggested that at least some nonsexual posttherapy relationships can be unethical or at least "ethically awkward." Unfortunately, although the APA *Ethics Code* (1992) offers some broad general principles, it provides little specific guidance regarding these types of relationships with former clients.

Ethicists (Kitchener, 1988; Pipes, 1997; Sonne, 1994) have identified at least eight reasons for avoiding posttherapy relationships:

1. The former client may at some point wish to return to therapy with the therapist, which would be prohibited after a posttherapy relationship.
2. The power differential may continue. As a result, some clients remain vulnerable to exploitation after termination.
3. Clients develop strong feelings toward their therapists. These feelings, along with the power differential, are a powerful combination that may lead to poor objectivity by the former client which in turn can result in exploitation by the therapist.
4. The posttherapy relationship could go poorly, thus, the former client might reevaluate his or her trust in psychology.
5. When the general public views posttherapy relationships, they may believe professional boundaries are diffuse and casual.
6. Therapist objectivity for future professional service, such as testifying in court on the former client's behalf, may be compromised by the posttherapy relationship.
7. Clients may hold back information because they assume that some type of posttherapy relationship may ensue after termination.
8. In some states, posttherapy relationships may be illegal.

It is unlikely that every nonsexual posttherapy relationship will exploit, damage, or undo therapeutic gains. One guideline might be that the greater the risk of an adverse consequence, such as undermining the gains made in a psychotherapy relationship, the greater the need to avoid entering into the relationship. Anderson and Kitchener (1998) developed a four-component model that can be used to assess the potential for a nonsexual posttherapy relationship to be ethically risky. *Component 1* encourages the therapist to consider each aspect of the therapeutic contract before entering into a relationship with a former client. The psychologist might consider questions such as, How will confidentiality be handled? Were the presenting problems resolved? Did we come to clear closure, and does the client understand that returning to therapy with the psychologist will not be feasible? *Component 2* addresses the dynamics of the therapeutic bond which could include issues of transference and feelings about the former therapist that are unresolved (Pipes, 1997) and the power differential that has not changed substantially. The psychologist might ask questions such as, What was the strength of the therapeutic bond, and did the client and I process changes in it? In light of the power differential, to what extent is the former client's decision to enter into a new relationship an autonomous one? Will this posttherapy relationship undo the good that was accomplished in therapy? Did therapy encourage self-reliance and responsibility or dependence? *Component 3* uses social role theory to examine the consistency or divergence between the therapy and posttherapy role expectations and obligations. The therapist might ask questions such as, Have the former client and I clarified how our roles will change and whether our expectations are realistic? To what extent does the former client understand the ramifications of changing the relationship? How might our perceptions of each other gained in therapy influence our perceptions in our new roles? To what extent can we be equals in the new relationship? *Component 4* encourages the psychologist to self-examine the motivations for entering into the posttherapy relationship. As Anderson and Kitchener suggest, therapists can have competing values and motivations for entering into a posttherapy relationship. They suggest considering questions such as, Will the former client be exploited by the new relationship? Is the new relationship avoidable, and, if so, why do I want to enter into it? What personal benefits do I gain if I enter into this relationship?

Boundary Issues with Students and Supervisees

Psychology has begun to attend to the overlapping relationships between faculty or supervisors and students or trainees. Several studies have investigated the incidence of sexual intimacy between psychology educators and their students. Pope, Levenson, and Schover (1979) surveyed members of APA's psychotherapy division about the sexual contacts with educators that they experienced as students. Results indicated substantial gender differences. Over 16% of the females reported such contact, but only 3% of the males reported similar experiences. Subsequent studies found remarkably similar results (Glaser & Thorpe, 1986; Hammel, Olkin, & Taube, 1996; Robinson & Reid, 1985); between 13.6% and 17.9% of women psychologists report sexual contact with psychology educators. The only other study that questioned male respondents found that 2% reported such contact (Hammel et al., 1996). All these studies occurred prior to the publication of the current *Ethics Code* which prohibits sexual relationships between psychology educators and students or supervisees over whom they have evaluative or direct authority (Standard 1.19). It remains to be seen whether there has been a decrease in sexual contact with students since the publication of the code.

No studies have been completed on the incidence of sexual relationships in supervision. However, the articles that have been written suggest that it occurs frequently enough to be problematic (Bartell & Rubin, 1990; Slimp & Burian, 1994). Sexual relationships with either students or supervisees for whom the educator has an evaluative responsibility increase the risk of impairing the psychologist's judgment and the potential for exploitation.

Kitchener (1992b) argued that such relationships undermine the ethical values that faculty are trying to teach. Rather than valuing integrity, respectfulness, and truthfulness, which underlie trustful human relationships, secrecy and deceit are often modeled. As problematic are the jealousies and mistrust engendered when it is perceived that some students or supervisees are receiving favors because of special relationships.

Nonsexual forms of dual relationships between faculty and students or supervisees are not uncommon and have the potential for good or harm (Kitchener, 1992b). In actual practice, Tabachnick, Keith-Spiegel, and Pope (1991) found that 76% of faculty had asked students for small favors such as a ride home, 66% loaned money to students, 86% accepted a student's invitation to a party, and 87% accepted an inexpensive gift from a student. Additionally, 49% bartered course credit instead of salary for student research assistants.

Different role responsibilities are inherent in the multiple obligations of academic psychologists because they are accountable for enhancing the welfare of their students, as well as protecting the public from incompetent psychologists (APA, 1992). Because the role of a faculty member, like that of a therapist, carries with it unrealistic expectations about knowledge and wisdom, students may be unable to evaluate objectively inaccurate feedback or harmful recommendations if a faculty member tries to exploit them (Kitchener, 1992b). The power between faculty and students is asymmetrical. Faculty have the responsibility to make decisions about the success or failure of students who are enrolled in the program. Thus, faculty wield very real power over the outcomes of students' lives and careers. For example, Goodyear et al. (1992) offered numerous examples of research supervision of faculty who used their positions of power to exploit students by coercing them to fraudulently tamper with data, by failing to give them credit for their participation on research projects, or by plagiarizing student work directly.

On the other hand, there is opportunity for real benefit in some of the multiple roles that academics play with students. Some extra-classroom experiences can have powerful effects on the intellectual and personal growth of undergraduates (Pascarella & Terenzini, 1991). Furthermore, mentoring relationships provide opportunities for enriching learning experiences and professional development that might not otherwise be open to students.

USES AND MISUSES OF INFORMED CONSENT

Informed consent remains the bulwark of protecting the rights of consumers and research participants. Because consent requires providing information regarding the nature of psychological activities, it allows consumers the opportunity to consider whether participating in the activity would be in their best interests. It is based on the assumption that people's welfare will best be protected when they make informed decisions about events that will affect them or their loved ones.

Problematic Issues with the Meaning and Methods of Consent

Sometimes the literature on consent is difficult to interpret because it can refer to (1) legal requirements that specify what clients or research participants must be told, (2) ethical responsibilities that define how truly to help people make informed choices, or (3) an interpersonal process that elaborates how (1) and (2) are fulfilled (P.S. Appelbaum, Lidz, & Meisel, 1987). Consequently, what is understood as adequate consent depends on whether the referent is the law, the ethical responsibility, or the process. Fulfilling the spirit of consent generally can be understood to include several components, including competence, disclosure, understanding, voluntariness, and authorization (P.S. Appelbaum et al., 1987; Beauchamp & Childress, 1994). An individual must be competent to provide consent. Adequate information must be disclosed and understood. The person must have the authority to agree voluntarily and do so without being coerced, manipulated, or intimidated.

Stating the components of adequate consent may be easier than fulfilling the ethical requirements of informed consent. Many people seek treatment at a point when their competence may be compromised; as a result, participation in the consent process may be beyond their capacity (Widger & Rorer, 1984). On the other hand, this is true only if consent is conceptualized as an event that occurs at the beginning of treatment rather than a process that occurs throughout treatment. Pope and Vasquez (1991), for example, argued for a process model of consent, pointing out that as clients' symptoms lift so does their ability to understand the nature of therapy.

Research has identified several problems with written consent forms. T. Mann (1994) found that providing more information on the forms is not necessarily linked to better understanding. Participants remembered less after reading longer consent forms than after reading shorter ones, and those who signed a consent form were more likely to believe they had lost the right to sue even for negligence than those who did not sign (T. Mann, 1994). Whether they signed the consent form, the majority of participants were unable to answer several questions about important information related to the study. Because they did not understand the information, their consent was technically invalid.

Research has consistently documented that written consent forms for therapy (Handelsman, Kemper, Kesson-Craig, McLain, & Johnsrud, 1986; Handelsman et al., 1995) and research (National Commission for the Protection of Human Subjects, 1978) are written beyond the reading ability of most of the public. In fact, studies found that the reading level of written consent forms of psychologists in private practice was equivalent to an academically oriented magazine. Furthermore, the forms often contained only legally mandated information, methods of payment, or information on the limits of confidentiality (Handelsman et al.,1986, 1995). Many did not even meet minimal standards regarding the legal limits of confidentiality.

Others have raised special population questions regarding the validity of the written consent process. Pope and Vasquez (1991) point to the fact that illiteracy is a serious problem in the United States. If clients are illiterate, written consent forms are useless. As demographics shift and the number of nonnative English speakers increases, psychologists cannot assume that consumers or research participants can read consent forms written in English.

Because of the limits of written consent forms and the difficulty involved in insuring understanding, some have argued for using oral consent (T. Mann, 1994) or using a question and answer format that provides a list of questions that potential clients can ask their therapists (Handelsman & Galvin, 1988). Although no procedure is foolproof, a combination of written and oral procedures might be useful. Whichever is used, both researchers and therapists need to recognize that unless the information provided is understood, the consent is not legally or ethically valid.

Psychologists provide a variety of reasons for failing to use written consent (Handelsman et al., 1986). For example, psychologists who do not inform clients about the length of treatment report that they fail to do so because they believe it cannot be predicted (Somberg, Stone, & Claiborn, 1993). Others believe that disclosing the limits of confidentiality makes establishing a therapeutic relationship more difficult (Somberg et al., 1993; Widger & Rorer, 1984). Contrary to these worries, Sullivan, Martin, and Handelsman (1993) found that psychotherapists who used a consent procedure that included both an oral and written component were rated as more trustworthy and expert than were those who did not. Furthermore, participants who received a consent procedure were more willing to recommend the therapist to a friend and were more willing to see therapists who used one. Additionally, using a consent procedure was found to have a positive effect on judgments of therapists' experience and likeability (Handelsman, 1990).

Some consensus has developed about the information that should be disclosed to therapy clients (Bennett, Bryant, VandenBos, & Greenwood, 1990; Pope & Vasquez, 1991). In general, disclosure information should include (1) the kind of treatment or testing being provided; (2) the risks and benefits of the treatment or testing; (3) the logistics of treatment (e.g., length of appointments, length of treatment, canceling appointments, and costs); (4) information about the therapists' credentials; (5) risks and benefits of alternatives to the treatment or testing or of foregoing either; (6) the limits of confidentiality; and (7) emergency procedures. Similarly, the U.S. Department of Health and Human Services has provided explicit criteria for adequate consent in federally funded research. These criteria have set the standard for nonfunded research as well and are consistent with the requirements of the APA *Ethics Code* (1992).

With the advent of managed care, informing psychotherapy clients about the limits of confidentiality is particularly important. Clients may not know that they give up some privacy rights when they use their insurance benefits, particularly because insurance companies or HMOs do not observe the same level of confidentiality as do psychologists (Bennett et al., 1990). Similarly, clients may not understand the limits of their coverage or the risks and benefits of the short-term treatment models that are endorsed by most managed care companies. The spirit of consent requires that these issues be discussed at the beginning of treatment. The process model of consent would suggest that they be revisited periodically.

Relatively little has been written regarding informed consent issues in higher education institutions (Handelsman, 1987). Educational institutions act as if consent has been implied with students. Based on an implicit model of consent, students agree to attend given the information they have been provided regarding the institution or program they are entering. On the other hand, once they agree to participate, they are in particularly vulnerable positions, because the agreement is not between equals (Kitchener, 1992b). Consequently, the institution or faculty in charge of the program have the same responsibility required in any consent situation, namely, to provide accurate information in a language that is understandable (Handelsman, 1987). Handelsman argued that faculty should also provide students with adequate information regarding course participation and requirements. Activities that would place unusual demands on them or ones for which they may not be emotionally prepared, such as self-disclosure, participation in deceptive research, or intense group activities, would be particularly important to disclose.

Problematic Issues Using Informed Consent with School-Age Youth and Adolescents

The law has been ambivalent regarding whether adolescents are to be treated as adults or children when it comes to consent issues (Kitchener, 1999). In a 1979 Supreme Court case (*Bellotti v. Baird,* 1979), the court concluded that the constitutional rights of children cannot be equal to those of adults because (1) children have a "peculiar vulnerability"; (2) children are incapable of making "critical decisions in an informed, mature manner"; and (3) parents have an important role in child rearing. However, in *Kremens v. Bartley* (1977), the Supreme Court granted minors 14 years and older the right to voluntarily seek out or terminate therapy.

When working with minors who may be "legally incapable of giving informed consent," the APA *Ethics Code* (Standard 4.02) guides psychologists to obtain "informed permission from a legally authorized person, if such substitute consent is permitted by law." The Supreme Court cases and the *Ethics Code* suggest that psychologists should work with minors in a judicious manner, eliciting parental or guardian permission and involvement that meets ethical and legal directives.

Assent is a different issue. Children should be allowed to assent to treatment and research participation (Weithorn & Scherer, 1994). Legal issues aside, data suggest that failure to involve adolescents in the assent process can lead to negative reactions to, and a lack of cooperation in, therapy (Adelman, Lusk, Alvarez, & Acosta, 1985). Furthermore, the Department of Health and Human Services (DHHS) requires that those under the age of 18 assent to participate in research even if they cannot give legal consent (Sieber, 1992).

The ability of minors to give consent when they are able to do so legally is tied to issues of competence. Several investigators have pursued the question of minors' ability to give consent using criteria that include the ability to understand complex instructions, evidence of choice, providing rational reasons for choice, awareness of risks, and awareness of future consequences. Generally, they concluded that minors 15 years old and older have the ability to understand information related to consent and to make reasonable choices based on the information (L. Mann, Harmoni, & Power, 1989).

Even younger children between the ages of 5 and 12 exhibit some characteristics associated with the competence and understanding needed to give consent (Weithorn & Scherer, 1994). They are, at least, capable of participating in a meaningful way in mental health care and research decisions, even if their competence is not developed enough to provide true consent. However, attention needs to be paid to how information is disclosed.

On the other hand, because children have a strong tendency to acquiesce to authority (Weithorn & Scherer, 1994), counseling psychologists need to provide them the opportunity to dissent. Although this may be inconvenient for researchers because some may choose not to participate, ethically it is important because there is little justification for coercing research participation from children, particularly if it does not directly benefit them (Kitchener, 1999).

Counseling in K–12 schools offers its own unique challenges related to parental consent for counseling. Counselors in school setting have multiple constituents to please: the student, the parents of the student, administrators, teachers, and lawmakers (Quirk, 1997). Additionally, parameters around parental consent for counseling may lack clarity. A teacher may refer a student for counseling, and the student may be seen several times without parental knowledge or consent. This process violates parental rights to consent. Psychologists working in the school setting would be well advised to develop disclosure and consent procedures so that minors and their parents can be informed about the counseling process.

Whether the psychologist works in an agency or school setting, issues such as birth control and abortion are ethically and legally difficult when it comes to parental knowledge and consent. The laws governing parental involvement with issues such as these varies from state to state (Swenson, 1997). However, the Supreme Court's rulings on several cases (e.g., *Webster v. Reproductive Health Services,* 1989) provide some guidance (Hopkins & Anderson, 1990). Generally speaking, the Court has ruled that some restrictions on minors' rights to seek abortions without parental approval are legal (Swenson, 1997). According to Shields and Johnson (1992), parental consent regarding psychological services is not generally sought for court ordered treatment, cases of child abuse, drug or alcohol treatment, and when the child poses a risk to self or others. In some states, minors have the right to seek out psychological services related to birth control, drug treatment, or therapy for sexually transmitted diseases without parental notification or consent.

Problematic Consent Issues with Vulnerable Populations

There is a presumption in most of the work on informed consent that if individuals have adequate information and understand that information, they will be able to make voluntarily decisions regarding participation. Generally, however, oppression as a controlling influence that may affect the voluntariness of people's consent has not been explored (Brabeck, 1999). If people feel powerless as decision makers and are sensitive to the undue influence of those in positions of power, they may not be able to make autonomous decisions regarding participation in either research or treatment, even if they have adequate information.

Some populations are particularly vulnerable to undue influence and may easily be manipulated to participate in activities that may not be in their best interests (Sieber, 1992). These include students, women, the poor, those in dire need of psychological services, and those who are not a part of the majority culture. For example, a low-income mother may consent to treatment, desperate to get help with a child who is out of control. In the process, she signs a consent form and does so without understanding the limits of confidentiality. When she admits that she has struck her child, the psychologist files a report. For many reasons, her consent may not have been valid. In particular, her vulnerability and oppression may be controlling influences that limit her choices (Kitchener, 1999).

In research, vulnerable populations can be induced to participate by excessive inducements (Sieber, 1992) and, like therapy participants, may agree to participate when it is not in their best interests. This is especially true if they are participating in illegal activities and those activities are revealed during the research. This is a particular problem when studying behaviors such as child abuse. Although it is yet unclear whether researchers are legally obliged to report suspected child abuse (Liss, 1994), consent procedures would require informing participants ahead of time if the researcher intended to report that abuse. If researchers inform participants ahead of time that they intend to report, as Sieber (1994) points out, they may end up with skewed samples and untrustworthy responses from research participants. In this case, the advantages society might get from valid data would be sacrificed for the benefit of individual children. On the other hand, if they do not inform participants, they would be violating the participant's rights to make autonomous decisions. Additionally, although there may be ways to avoid the legal necessity to report abuse (see the section on confidentiality), there may be a moral obligation to protect a vulnerable child (Hoagwood, 1994). With vulnerable populations such as these, psychologists have a particularly strong ethical responsibility to promote understanding and nurture autonomous choice.

PROBLEMATIC ISSUES WITH MAINTAINING CONFIDENTIALITY

Although at one time professional confidentiality was considered inviolate, the last 20 years have been marked by ongoing debate regarding the importance of confidentiality and the circumstances in which it should be violated (Bok, 1983). The current APA *Ethics Code* discusses confidentiality in the aspirational principles as well as in 13 separate standards. It also provides examples of situations in which disclosures of confidential information may occur.

Responsibilities to keep and break confidentiality can be complicated by legal requirements both at the state and federal level. For example, every state requires that child abuse be reported in some cases, even without the client's consent (Kalichman, 1993). Furthermore, although all states have child abuse laws, how child abuse is defined and the requirements of reporting vary from state to state. For example, in Pennsylvania the law does not require professionals to report child abuse when they see only the perpetrator in treatment and the child being violated is not in immediate danger (Goldberg, 1997). In addition, case law, particularly that deriving from the *Tarasoff* case (*Tarasoff v. Regents of the University of California,* 1974, 1976), has been interpreted to mean that the ethical obligation to maintain confidentiality can be superseded when public safety is at risk. On the other hand, some states make maintaining client confidentiality a legal requirement, and in many states, privileged communication laws protect clients from having private information divulged in courts of law. Thus, what is most often considered to be an ethical obligation may also become a legal one.

It is no wonder that issues of confidentiality are rated as the most problematic ethical issue that practicing psychologists have to face, as well as the ones that are most frequently encountered (Haas, Malouf, & Mayerson, 1986; Pope & Vetter, 1992). These surveys and critical incident descriptions reveal that therapists are often faced with agonizing decisions about when they should keep and when they should break confidentiality.

Clients generally expect that information given to a therapist will remain confidential and are often unaware that there are many limits on confidentiality (Hillerbrand & Claiborn, 1988; Rubanowitz, 1987). In fact, in one study 69% of the respondents believed that all information provided to a mental health professional would be kept confidential, and 74% believed there should be no limits to confidentiality. Only 20% believed it should be broken when there is a danger to self or others (Miller & Thelan, 1986). The difference between clients' beliefs and the realities in which psychologists work underlines the importance of explaining the limits of confidentiality as a part of the consent process.

Problematic Confidentiality Issues in a Therapy Setting

Suicide

At some point, most practitioners will have to deal with clients who attempt, threaten, or complete suicide. In one study, 97% of the psychologists surveyed reported fearing that a client would commit suicide, and 29% had experienced at least one client suicide (Pope & Tabachnick, 1993). Both professionals and trainees find dealing with suicidal clients deeply stressful, and completed suicides often leave both professionals and trainees with feelings of grief, loss, depression, guilt, inadequacy, and self-doubt (Chemtob, Bauer, Hamada, Pelowski, & Muraoka, 1988).

Historically, breaking confidentiality to intervene with a suicidal client is based on the Christian doctrine that suicide is immoral and the assumption that suicide is not a rational decision and, thus, not an autonomous choice (Mayo, 1993). The difficulty in, and responsibility for, discriminating between rational and irrational suicide may be a further barrier to accepting that suicide sometimes may be a rational choice (Mayo, 1993). The assumption that suicide is not rational is based on the close association between it and mental problems such as depression, alcohol abuse, and other clinical symptoms. It is for reasons like these that most psychologists are taught to prevent suicide.

Because psychologists have begun to work with clients who have serious physical illnesses such as AIDS, discussions of rational suicide have begun to appear in the psychological literature with some frequency (Rogers & Britton, 1994; Werth, 1992; Werth & Liddle, 1994). The argument has been made that because death from certain diseases is particularly slow and painful, suicide might be a viable and rational alternative (Werth, 1992). If this is true, then suicide might be a rational, autonomous choice, and the ethical argument for intervening would be less salient. In fact, Werth and Liddle (1994) found that 80% of psychologists believed in rational suicide in some cases.

Many have expressed reservations about a position that supports rational suicide. Some have argued that therapists should always ally themselves with a respect for life (Boyd, 1989). In fact, the idea of rational suicide itself is controversial. Some argue that decisions to commit suicide fluctuate with the disease process and, therefore, are transitory; and if they are transitory, then they are not rational (Rogers & Britton, 1994). Additionally, cognitive impairment and depression affect rational decision making, and both are common in latter stages of some diseases (Siegel, 1986). By contrast, individuals with AIDS are more likely to report suicidal ideation and attempts early rather than later in the disease process. As the disease progresses, suicidal ideation is tied to feelings of despair, fear of dependency and physical deterioration, and observing others who have died of the same illness (Kalichman & Sikkeman, 1994). Providing clients with information about hospice care and pain management may present alternatives they have not considered (McIntosh, 1993), especially if fear of pain or being a burden on family members is a concern.

Although some may believe that requests for a hastened death from a terminal illness is common, it is important to note that physical decline does not necessarily lead to these feelings in the majority of cases (APA Public Interest Directorate, 1997). Suicidal ideation may be the effects of a treatable clinical depression. Furthermore, although some believe that patients who are in pain or terminally ill are likely to become suicidal, the writers of Directorate suggest "a person's lifelong values, temperament, and behavior are often better indicators of who is at risk for suicide thoughts when ill" (p. 2). From the perspective of the APA Public Interest Directorate in cases where individuals wish to hasten their own death, psychologists should not try to control the decision, but to help insure that the decision is free of coercion, well-reasoned, and rational.

Given the complexity of the issues involved, several authors have attempted to define the characteristics of rational suicide. These characteristics include (1) the person is competent and assessing the situation realistically; (2) mental processes are not impaired by psychological illness or distress; (3) the person is acting under his or her own free will and not being coerced by outside pressures to make the decision; (4) the decision has been considered over a period of time; (5) the person's motivation is understandable to those who can view the situation more objectively; and (6) when possible, loved ones are involved in the decision (APA Public Interest Directorate, 1997; Siegel, 1986; Werth, 1992).

The issue of rational suicide is one of the most difficult ethical issues facing psychologists. It challenges personal values and professional training. Both professionals and trainees need the opportunity to consider the issue and its ethical implications. Research is needed to evaluate whether additional social-emotional support affects suicidal ideation and how factors such as race, sex, age, and other individual differences influence risk factors (APA Public Interest Directorate, 1997). In addition, research should examine how psychologists' own beliefs and values about religion, homosexuality, drug use, and suicide affect their evaluation of rational suicide.

The Duty to Protect

One of the most well-known challenges to therapist-client confidentiality arose from the *Tarasoff* decision. Although it was initially discussed as the "duty to warn," Melton (1988) argues it is better understood as the "duty to protect" because even the decision suggested that the therapist take one of several steps to protect an intended victim against danger (*Tarasoff v. Regents of the University of California,* 1976, p. 340). The alternatives included warning the victim, notifying the police, or taking other reasonable steps. The implication of the court's decision was that confidentiality was only a prima facie or conditional obligation and that, when public safety is at risk, therapeutic confidentiality cannot be used as a shield (Daniel & Kitchener, 1999). Bok (1983) has further argued that no one should expect professionals to maintain confidentiality under such circumstances because it would make them complicitous in the acts.

In the minority opinion, Justice Clark warned that the "duty to protect" could limit the practice of therapy, deterring some from seeking treatment and negatively affecting the therapeutic alliance. In reality, research suggests that some therapists are less willing to probe for dangerousness (Wise, 1978), and revealing the limits of confidentiality may affect client's willingness to disclose extreme behaviors (Mangalmurti, 1994).

In the last 10 years, a major issue has been whether the duty to protect extends to sexual and needle partners of individuals who are infected with the HIV virus or who have AIDS. Despite the fact that the debate about this issue has been extensive (K. Appelbaum & Appelbaum, 1990; Grey & Harding, 1988; Lamb, Clark, Drumheller, Frizzell, & Surrey, 1989; Melton, 1988), authors have come to different conclusions regarding whether the criteria used in the *Tarasoff* case would apply. However, because no court has decided the issue, what exists is speculation regarding how courts might act (Stevenson & Kitchener, in press).

Most of the arguments regarding therapists' responsibilities have been couched in legal terms. Some authors have, however, argued that because contracting the HIV virus is potentially life threatening and the long-term consequences both to individuals and the public as a whole are dire, breaking confidentiality is ethically justified (K. Appelbaum & Appelbaum, 1990; Grey & Harding, 1988). It is basically argued that because AIDS is a fatal disease, the rights of the endangered person override the client's right to confidentiality. Others have pointed out that any decision to break confidentiality should be made on a case-by-case basis because the risk factors vary depending on the kind of activity in which the individuals are engaging (Kain, 1988; Lamb et al., 1989). For example, mutual masturbation carries less of a risk than does engaging in anal intercourse without the use of a condom. Furthermore, the issue is complicated by the fact that determination of risk involves a medical assessment which may be beyond the competence of psychologists to make (Kain, 1988; Lamb et al., 1989). Additionally, some have argued that a policy of breaching confidentiality may have more long-term negative consequences for society than maintaining it (Melton, 1988) because it may keep some from seeking services. In such cases, there would be less of an opportunity to intervene and change client behavior.

In cases of communicable diseases, some have argued that attempts to alter the client's behavior should precede breaching confidentiality (Kain, 1988). Alternatives might include educating the client regarding responsible behavior, addressing interpersonal issues that may impede clients from disclosing, addressing social or cultural norms that may inhibit safer sex practices or disclosure, and assisting clients to obtain condoms or sterile needles. In addition to when and whether to break confidentiality, other unresolved issues include how long psychologists ought to try clinical interventions before breaking confidentiality, and how to respond if clients generally change their behavior but have periodic lapses (Stevenson & Kitchener, in press).

Issues with Children and Adolescents

Identifying the limits of confidentiality with children and adolescents is by definition problematic because in many cases they cannot give legal consent for therapy and may not hold privileged communication rights (Daniel & Kitchener, 1999). Glenn (1980) and others have argued for "informed forced consent" meaning that the therapist would disclose information to appropriate parties (e.g., parents) after the therapist informed the child that was going to happen. Hendrix (1991) reasoned that therapists should not promise absolute confidentiality because they might not be able to keep such a promise. They should, however, disclose information only if it is in the best interests of the minor client. In addition, clients should always be told if therapists plan to disclose information and be provided the opportunity to raise objections, which respects their limited autonomy. Therapists should use clients' objections to evaluate the decision, and change it if necessary. They should attempt to minimize unforeseen problems, thus avoiding harm. He argued that such an alternative is also just because it recognizes the unique decision-making abilities of minors and treats them accordingly.

The settings in which the counseling psychologists work may differ vastly in terms of rules regarding the limits of confidentiality and, thus, may affect the ethical issues involved. Working with minors emphasizes the importance of clarifying confidentiality issues prior to beginning treatment. Gustafson and McNamara (1987) recommended meeting with both the minor client and the client's parents prior to beginning treatment to clarify the limits of confidentiality, as well as its implication for all parties.

Settings such as K–12 schools hold their own unique challenges. In some states, the law provides minimal legal parameters concerning client/student confidentiality (Fischer & Sorenson, 1996). As more schools move to a team approach to solving student problems, preserving confidentiality becomes more complicated. Teachers and administrators do not have ethical rules requiring confidentiality; therefore, it may be easier for them unthinkingly to share information about the student and student's family that is private and confidential (Quirk, 1997).

Working with minors from divorced families leads to other difficult confidentiality issues. Parents who pursue treatment for their child or who request access to their child's counseling records may not have the legal right to do so if they are not the custodial parent (Wiggins-Frame, 1995). In these cases, the psychologist should request legal documentation to verify who has the legal responsibility for the child's emotional welfare.

The Family Educational Rights and Privacy Act of 1974—FERPA (typically known as the Buckley Amendment)—can be another challenge to confidentiality. It requires disclosure of educational records to parents of children below the age of 18. However, "private notes" kept by counselors are not open to parental review (Fischer & Sorenson, 1996). Private notes are defined as notes that are not shared with anyone except a substitute. Records or notes to which two or more counselors have access are considered educational records. FERPA makes it clear that "all educational records, no matter where they are stored, in what medium they are created, or how they are labeled" shall be made available to parents upon their request (Fischer & Sorenson, 1996, p. 101). According to FERPA, custodial and noncustodial parents have equal rights to review educational records (Fischer & Sorenson, 1996).

Confidentiality and Managed Care

The face of psychotherapy has been changed dramatically by the advent of managed care. Managed care was initially a response to the escalating costs of health care and the lack of availability of services to many, particularly, the poor. Ethically, it can be viewed as a way to make the provision of health services more just or fair. Unfortunately, since its first iteration, managed care's primary strategy has been to cut costs by cutting services deemed marginal (Hersch, 1995), often by managing cases via a review process. One ethical consequence of this move is the difficulty maintaining confidentiality.

Managed care reviewers contact psychotherapist providers by phone, mail, computers, and fax machines to obtain client information with few, if any, safeguards regarding who will have access to the information once it leaves the psychologist's office (Daniel & Kitchener, 1999). The issue is made more difficult by the fact that those who review psychologists' notes may not have the same professional ethical obligations to maintain confidentiality, nor are they covered by privileged communication laws (Daniel & Kitchener, 1999). Therapists often feel compromised by the system because if they fail to divulge the information requested, the managed care company may deny the client's claim, disallow payment, or additional sessions (Murphy, DeBernardo, & Schoemaker, 1997).

Few remedies have been suggested for these problems. The APA *Ethics Code* instructs psychologists to discuss the limits of confidentiality with their clients. At minimum, clients should be informed about the potential loss of confidentiality if they use their benefits.

Although managed care companies may demand information, psychologists still have a responsibility to protect client confidentiality and, thus, should resist providing information via faxes or other communication mediums that are not secure. Additionally, they may request that information be viewed only by mental health professionals responsible for maintaining confidential records. Furthermore, if reviewers or managers are members of mental health organizations such as APA, ethics complaints can be filed against them if a client's privacy is abused (Sank, 1997).

Problematic Confidentiality Issues in Research

The fundamental issues supporting the confidentiality of research data are similar to those in psychotherapy. Some of the problems, however, are different. For example, sensitive data may be gathered and stored on large groups of people, researchers may request information on illegal activities, and confidentiality of research data does not have the same legal protection as does therapeutic information because it is not "privileged" (P.S. Appelbaum & Rosenbaum, 1989; Sieber, 1992).

Certain kinds of information gathered in research are particularly sensitive to loss of confidentiality, yet these are arguably some of the most important to study. These include studies of drug and alcohol use, violent behavior, sexual behavior including sexual orientation, AIDS/HIV status, and current criminal involvement. Sieber (1994) cautioned that even the title of a project should be chosen in a way to shield the privacy of participants who are participating in socially sensitive research if it is going to be used when recruiting participants. Furthermore, researchers should consider the kinds of measures to take to ensure that third parties, including those involved in law enforcement, cannot gain access to private information. Researchers can apply for a confidentiality certificate from the U.S. Department of Health and Human Services to help safeguard data from legal intrusions (Sieber, 1992). These certificates were authorized by Congress to encourage research on sensitive topics. Ostensibly, they allow researchers to withhold identifying information from local, state, or federal authorities.

Legally, the duty to protect has not been applied in a research setting (Daniel & Kitchener, 1999). On the other hand, even if a researcher has received a certificate of confidentiality from the U.S. Department of Health and Human Services, it remains unclear whether that researcher is exempt from mandatory state laws regarding the reporting of child abuse. Even if they are legally protected, the question of whether researchers have a moral obligation to report child abuse remains (Hoagwood, 1994). As noted earlier, the dilemma is even more complex when considering how to manage issues of consent.

Prudent counseling psychologists who are studying socially sensitive topics need to consider a variety of issues. In particular, they may want to consider ways to collect research data anonymously so that they do not have identifying information on participants. This would protect the research participants' autonomy and would remove the researcher from the position of having to make a decision that might harm the participant. If anonymous data collection is not feasible, the researcher might explore the option of getting a certificate of confidentiality. In addition, participants should be informed that if they admit to certain behaviors such as child abuse, they may be reported. Under the latter circumstances, data would need to be interpreted cautiously to inform readers about the potential bias. (See Daniel & Kitchener, 1999 for more discussion.)

THE OBLIGATION TO BE COMPETENT

Being competent is the foundation of ethical practice in all the roles played by counseling psychologists. Acting in the best interests of clients and adequately protecting consumers or research participants from inept or harmful practices are essential if counseling psychologists are going to do good and avoid harming others (Welfel, 1998). As Swenson (1997) has said, "Mental health professionals should be fully trained, keep up-to-date, and be good at what they do. Otherwise they should stop doing it" (p. 64). Yet of all the areas addressed by this chapter, competence is the hardest to define.

The APA *Ethics Code* (1992, Standard 1.04, Boundaries of Competence) defines competence in relationship to training, education, and supervision or other professional experience. In addition, it requires that psychologists remain up-to-date on current scientific and professional information (Standard 1.05, Maintaining Expertise). In other words, it hedges on the definition of competence, instead relying on methods of acquiring it. The presumption seems to be that if psychologists have participated in a formal procedure for acquiring a skill, they can perform that skill adequately. This is not necessarily the case. Competence needs to be assessed in relationship to performance of professional roles and functions (Welfel, 1998).

Kitchener (1999) suggests that competence involves having the knowledge, skills, and abilities to perform adequately professional roles and the ability to recognize when one's knowledge, skills, and abilities are inadequate or impaired. Although knowledge, skills, and abilities are closely related, they each imply a slightly different component of competence. Knowledge includes having the necessary facts or ideas, which are usually gained through study, to complete a task successfully. Although skills are based on knowledge, they involve the capacity to use the knowledge in an applied setting. Thus, one may know counseling theory, but not have the skill to use it with clients. Abilities involve the mental or physical capacity or fitness to perform a task or a role. For example, individuals may have the knowledge and skill to perform therapy, but because of mental or physical impairment, they may not be able to use them competently with clients.

One of the most difficult ethical issues facing training programs in any area of applied psychology is how competent students need to be prior to providing services to consumers. Certainly, students often feel incompetent, and if they were fully competent, they would not be in graduate programs. Ultimately, the responsibility to ensure that students are minimally competent falls on the shoulders of faculty who must evaluate students' readiness to be involved in new experiences and to provide the supervision necessary to guarantee that students will not harm consumers. This is one reason why APA accredited doctoral programs are required to evaluate all students (Forrest, Elman, & Gizara, 1997).

Impairment: A Threat to Competence

Sometimes even psychologists who are highly trained and skilled become incapacitated for periods of time. The literature on professional impairment has attempted to address this issue. In psychology, impairment has been discussed in relationship to a broad set of issues that includes personal distress, decreased professional functioning, and ethical violations (Forrest et al., 1997).

In general, impairment means a decline in functioning from prior levels of competence (Kutz, 1986, Nathan, 1986). When that definition is applied to a professional, the decline refers to a decrease in work performance as a result of personal, behavioral, or environmental factors (Nathan,

1986). The difficulty is differentiating impairment from incompetence and unethical behavior. Sometimes, but not always, impairment and incompetence lead to unethical behavior.

Bissell (1983) attempted to distinguish between incompetence, impairment, and unethical behavior with chemically dependent physicians. She defined the incompetent professional as one who was poorly trained or who failed to keep up with current professional practice or knowledge, and the unethical professional as one who was dishonest or inattentive to the welfare of others. The causes of impairment were identified as organic or mental problems or chemical dependency.

Ethically, it is difficult to decide whether impaired professionals who have committed unethical acts should be treated and allowed to return to professional practice, be punished, or both (Brown, 1997; Layman & McNamara, 1997; Orr, 1997). The question is complex because it is hard to identify whether all unethical acts are a result of impairment or incompetence. Orr argues that if impairment is a result of a psychological disorder, it ought to be diagnosable using the *DSM-IV* (American Psychiatric Association, 1994) and that if there is no diagnosable disorder it is not impairment. This, of course, leaves out physical causes of impairment.

If unethical acts occur as a result of a decline of functioning or because of a lack of knowledge or skill, there might be a possibility of remediation. In these cases, the protection of consumers would need to be balanced with the potential for saving the livelihood of the professional and the possibility that the professional, if remediated, might make a contribution to society (Orr, 1997). This assumes that the deficits are not due to an irremediable problem.

Because of the difficulty in determining the relationship of incompetence and impairment to unethical behavior, Schoener and Gonsiorek (1988) argued that when ethical violations occur an assessment of their possible causes is critical to help determine the consequences for the violator. Additionally, they suggested that some particularly severe character disorders defy remediation. In these instances, the protection of the consumer should take precedence over concern about the livelihood of the professional.

Competence in Psychotherapy

Ethical issues regarding competence in the practice of counseling and psychotherapy overlap with professional guild concerns. For example, the General Guidelines for Providers of Psychological Services (APA, 1987), the Specialty Guidelines for Counseling Psychology (APA, 1981b), and the APA *Ethics Code* (APA, 1992) attempt to identify the parameters of competent practice. To a great extent, they rely on appropriate education and supervised experience to define competence. However, as already noted, good education and credentials do not necessarily protect consumers from unethical activities or incompetent professionals.

When the profession moves beyond tying issues of competence to education and credentials, the question becomes how competence should be assessed. One alternative is to tie it to the research literature on psychotherapy outcome. For example, therapist skill and an effective working alliance have been linked to positive outcome (Lambert & Bergin, 1994). Evaluations of competence could be tied to performance of certain therapeutic skills.

It may be important to consider what characteristics, techniques, and practices lead to client deterioration and negative outcomes. Although negative outcomes have been consistently documented in controlled outcome studies (Lambert & Bergin, 1994), no particular modality seems to be responsible for these effects. Unfortunately, while the causes are still being debated it is clear that psychotherapy harms a portion of those it was designed to help. This underlines the ethical importance of outcome research that focuses on these kinds of issues and of counseling psychologists remaining knowledgeable about the psychotherapy process and outcome literature.

The recent work on empirically validated treatments (EVTs); (Chambless et al., 1996) is one attempt to bring the scientific study of psychotherapy to bear on the issue of competent practice. (See also Goodyear & Guzzardo, this volume, and Heppner et al., this volume.) This work may have both an ethical benefit and ethical downside for the consumer. On one hand, using the psychological literature to identify treatments that have been empirically validated may benefit the consumer if it helps practitioners identify more effective interventions. As Chambless et al. stated, psychologists "bear a fundamental ethical responsibility to use where possible interventions that work" (p. 10).

On the other hand, Chambless and her team members also note that just because a treatment is not on an EVT list does not mean it is ineffective, nor does a list substitute for the good judgment of practitioners about which treatment will be most effective with a particular client. In addition, some interventions and client groups have not been studied systematically. For example, no treatments specifically intended for racial and ethnic minorities meet the criteria to be called empirically validated. This does not mean that there are not good reasons to choose one treatment over another or that racial and ethnic minorities should not be treated. It remains the responsibility of the practitioner to choose the most effective treatment for a particular client at any point in time. If the work on EVTs is misused by third-party payers to prescribe treatments for clients with little consideration for the person involved, the potential for harmful consequences arises.

The ethical implications of EVTs for competent practice are just beginning to be explored. They raise the issue of identifying the most beneficial treatment for consumers and the appropriate and inappropriate use of research results. Both call attention to the need for psychologists to remain knowledgeable about the research literature in order to ensure that clients are helped and not harmed.

Competence Issues in Academia

Much more has been written regarding the issue of competence in psychotherapy than in either teaching or research. Generally, the relationship between faculty and students should be guided by the necessity to promote students' welfare (Kitchener, 1992b), which requires at minimum that faculty be competent at what they do. However, research suggests that this is not always the case. In a study of psychology educators, 4% of respondents reported teaching material they had not mastered or teaching classes without adequate preparation fairly or very often. Over 90% indicated that they did both at least on rare occasions (Tabachnick et al., 1991). The authors pointed out that the vicissitudes of daily life and the information explosion might prevent adequate preparation in some cases. The study does, however, raise the issue of what counts as minimal competence for teaching. Such questions have remained generally unaddressed in the pedagogical literature although some have argued that competence involves both content competence and pedagogical competence (Murray, Gillese, Lennon, Mercer, & Robinson, 1996). Both require a commitment to remaining current about teaching strategies and subject matter, as well as the learning needs of different student groups.

As with instruction, little attention has focused on ethical issues regarding competence in research. Rosenthal (1994) argued, however, that bad science in essence involves bad ethics because it wastes limited resources, including time and money, with little or no benefits. In addition, poor quality research can lead to inaccurate conclusions that may harm individuals, cultural groups, or society as a whole. Ultimately, incompetent research is a failure of scientific integrity because it is contrary to the core values of science, such as seeking new knowledge and accuracy of information (Kitchener, 1996b).

ISSUES OF JUSTICE IN PRACTICE AND RESEARCH

Justice, broadly conceived, means fairness (Benn, 1967). Distributive justice refers to how goods and services ought to be proportioned. In psychology, issues of justice include how the benefits and burdens associated with the profession ought to be distributed. Concern about fairly proportioning benefits would involve how psychological services ought to be distributed. Concerns about the burdens include issues such as fairly dividing the burdens of research participation.

In the past 10 years, most of the focus on justice issues in psychology has been on what it means to be fair with special populations. For example, the *Ethics Code* (APA, 1992) forbids psychologists to distribute unfairly the burdens and benefits of the profession based on "age, gender, race, ethnicity, national origin, religion, sexual orientation, disability, or socioeconomic status" (Standard 1.10). Additionally, APA has mandated that accredited psychology programs make a commitment to recruit minority students, thereby increasing the numbers of minority psychologists (APA Office of Program Consultation and Accreditation and Education Directorate, 1996). Issues such as the "duty to treat" (Melton, 1988) underserved populations and fairly distributing the burdens of psychological research have also been raised (Sieber, 1992), but these issues have received less attention. Most recently, justice issues have arisen regarding which candidates ought to receive the benefits associated with graduate education in light of the *Hopwood* decision (*Hopwood v. Texas,* 1994, 1996).

Issues of Competence, Bias, and Justice

Disparity in services to a particular group because of incompetence or bias is a fundamental violation of the principle of justice, as well as being a violation of the responsibility to benefit and not harm those whom psychologists have agreed to serve (Cayleff, 1986). Despite the rise of feminism and the increased sensitivity to women's issues in both practice and research, evidence exists that gender differences still play a negative role in the treatment of women. Take, for example, the pattern of both sexual and nonsexual multiple role relationships. Data from a variety of sources (APA, 1997a; Baer & Murdock, 1995; Borys & Pope, 1989; Pope, 1993) suggest that male therapists more often than female therapists become involved in multiple role relationships. Furthermore, male professionals, with much greater frequency than female professionals, engage in sexual intimacies with their clients who are most often females (Borys & Pope, 1989; Pope, 1990). These data suggest that gender socialization issues remain potent forces that subtly and not so subtly lead to unjust treatment for women and may also bias treatment of men.

On the other hand, over the past 10 years feminist scholarship has been on the rise in psychology (Brabeck, 1999; Lerman & Porter, 1990; Rave & Larsen, 1995). To a great extent, this work emphasizes positive ethical duties toward both women and men, including the need to address issues of oppression both with individuals and in society, to authorize individuals' experience of the world, to recognize how psychologists' power affects consumers, and to empower consumers (Brabeck, 1999; Enns, this volume; Feminist Therapy Institute, 1990; Lerman & Rigby, 1990). Although these duties go beyond simple responsibilities of justice, they emphasize that counseling psychologists may need to play a more active role in counteracting cultural assumptions and identifying ways that institutional systems devalue others. This would help ensure that both men and women receive equitable benefits from treatment and that research does not exploit them.

Similar issues have been discussed in relationship to racial and ethnic minorities. Because psychology has been so dominated by people of white European ancestry, this perspective permeates psychology and its assumptions. Yet data suggest that there are profound differences in cultural values both between and within different racial and ethnic groups (Carter, 1991). Consequently, some have questioned whether the delivery of multicultural counseling and therapy services has been morally just (Pedersen & Marsella, 1982). Certainly, perceptions of cultural insensitivity cannot help but contribute to the underutilization of mental health services by racial and ethnic minorities (S. Sue, Zane, & Young, 1994). Probably the most complete statement of ethical responsibilities for providing competent services to culturally diverse groups of people can be found in the "Guidelines for Providers of Psychological Services to Ethnic, Linguistic, and Culturally Diverse Populations" (APA, 1993).

Some have cautioned the profession about the meaning and use of foundational ethical princi-ples, such as those articulated by Kitchener (1984b) and Meara et al. (1996) with minority groups or women (Hill, Glaser, & Harden, 1995; Ibrahim, 1996). Pedersen (1995), however, argued that the principles are no less valid with racial and ethnic minorities, but that the interpretation of the principles, as well as the *Ethics Code* (APA, 1992), needs to take cultural values into considera-tion. For example, the harmfulness of certain multiple role relationships such as accepting goods for services or attending a client's special event may need to be reevaluated in different cultural contexts (LaFromboise & Foster, 1989).

Just as issues of cultural bias affect fair provision of psychological services, they can also affect assumptions that drive research. Several authors have pointed out that harmful models have been used to conceptualize research on racial and ethnic minorities (Ponterotto, 1988; D.W. Sue et al., 1992). These include models of evolutionary deficiency, genetic deficiency, and cultural defi-ciency. Generally, behavior associated with the white middle class has been presumed to be nor-mal, and behavior and beliefs associated with ethnic and racial minorities have been considered deviant. Research derived from these assumptions can hardly lead to fair or unbiased conclusions.

Issues of Justice in Graduate School Admissions

Being fair or just in the admissions process starts with the evaluation of applicants. As applica-tions are reviewed, judgments are made about who can successfully complete the program and contribute to the profession. Issues of justice are involved in defining criteria and applying the cri-teria fairly. Because the profession has taken the position that a diverse student body enriches the experience of all students and fulfills a social obligation to meet the needs of a diverse society, a critical issue has been how to meet this responsibility.

Several legal issues have begun to influence how graduate programs do so. Affirmative action demonstrated through race-preferred admission processes is one such legal issue. Amirkham, Be-tancourt, Graham, López, and Weiner (1995) suggested that affirmative action in psychology ad-missions compensated groups of people (i.e., ethnic minorities) for past injustice, corrected present inequities that exist for ethnic minorities, promoted and encouraged intellectual diversity, and fostered the presence of ethnic minority role models.

Recently, major universities have implemented policies and admission decisions that highlight the complexity and emotional intensity of affirmative action and justice issues in admissions. For example, in 1996 the University of California Board of Regents voted to eliminate race as a valid factor in admission (Inouye, 1997). The decision to eliminate affirmative action was made so that "desire for diversity" did not overshadow the "need for the best-qualified students" (Inouye, 1997).

Additionally, the *Hopwood* decision imposed legal limits on the use of affirmative action (*Hop-wood v. Texas,* 1994, 1996). This case was based on the fact that the University of Texas Law School had different admission standards, evaluation processes, and waiting lists for applicants who represented preferred minority groups. Four white students filed suit under the Equal Protec-tion Clause of the Fourteenth Amendment, alleging that they had been subjected to unconstitu-tional racial discrimination. Both the District Court and Fifth Circuit Court ruled against the Law School in favor of the plaintiffs (the white students), but for different reasons.

The District Court ruled that all categorizations based on race must meet the "strict scrutiny test" (*Regents of the University of California v. Bakke,* 1978). In other words, race could be one factor, a "plus factor," with other plus factors that would allow each applicant to be compared with other applicants on a case-by-case basis (Inouye, 1997).

Although the Fifth Circuit Court of Appeals agreed with using racial classifications to remedy "past wrongs," it stated that "diversity" is not a valid reason for race-based categorization. Thus, it took a strong stand against the use of race as a factor in admission. The Supreme Court refused to hear the case, letting the opinion stand (Kier & Davenport, 1997).

The implications of this decision may be far reaching. Although the decision only applies to Texas, it is likely other cases will be filed to generalize the decision to other states and to private as well as public institutions. In other words, training programs will need to balance the need to recruit minority students, which is mandated by the APA, with the limits on special admissions policies that allow race to be used as a special criteria in admissions.

The American Disabilities Act (ADA) may also affect how fairness is interpreted in admissions decisions. This civil rights law prohibits employers from discriminating against persons who suffer from a disability and who "with or without reasonable accommodation can perform the 'essential functions' of the employment position that such individual holds or desires" (ADA, 190, Title I, sec.101[8]). Any institution that receives federal funds must comply with the American Disabilities Act. Although the act has not been applied to educational admissions, Frame and Stevens-Smith (1995) suggest that higher education institutions could be held to the prohibitions of this law in admissions and strongly encourage training programs to identify and inform prospective students of the "essential functions" necessary for an individual in the counseling profession. Lissner (1992) suggested that there needed to be a balance between meeting "dual responsibilities of providing equal access and maintaining the mission, quality, and integrity of academic programs."

As counseling psychology programs consider the impact of the *Hopwood* decision, they may need to be more creative in providing statements about their commitment to recruit and graduate a diverse group of students as well as to provide them with a support system while they are in the program. The final report of APA's (1997b) Committee on Ethnic Minority Recruitment, Retention, and Training in Psychology provides additional suggestions. Additionally, they may need to rethink admission criteria to assure that the essential functions which psychologists must perform are identified to address the ADA.

VIRTUE ETHICS: IMPLICATIONS FOR SCIENCE, PRACTICE, AND TRAINING

In the prior sections of this chapter, a series of ethical problems were presented. In situations such as these, professional ethics codes and foundational ethical principles provide invaluable guidance. However, ethics codes and foundational ethical principles do not help psychologists understand what kind of person they ought to be, other than one who follows the code or uses ethical principles to make decisions. Similarly, they offer no explanation for why some people who know the right thing to do, fail to do it. Take, for example, psychologists who seduce clients, yet, know that the *Ethics Code* forbids such actions and that the profession will sanction them if their behavior is discovered.

Because of the limits of principle and rule-bound ethics, Meara and her colleagues (Jordan & Meara, 1990; Meara et al., 1996) argued that virtue ethics, which recognizes issues of motivation, emotion, and character, provides a more complete picture of the moral life than does an account limited to principles and rules. In fact, philosophers and psychologists have both criticized modern ethics as being too focused on doing one's duty or following rules (MacIntyre, 1981; Meara et al., 1996). Whereas principle ethics focuses on what people should do when faced with an ethical problem, virtue ethics focuses on what kind of characteristics a moral person should have.

Feminist ethicists have made similar points, arguing that current moral theory has focused too much attention on reasoning. Noddings (1984) suggested that principled ethics is ambiguous and leads to the false belief that there is more consistency in ethical decision making than is the case. Rather than arguing about universal principles, she proposed that ethics ought to concern itself with being in a caring relationship with others.

The argument is not that principle ethics is unimportant, particularly for ethical decision making. After all, even people of good character are sometimes unclear about the right choice. Rather, the argument is that ethical principles and rules are insufficient fully to understand morality. Such philosophical arguments are consistent with psychological models that differentiated between moral reasoning and having the sensitivity to recognize moral issues or the motivation to act when a moral decision has been made (Rest, 1983). Moral behavior is complex; thus, philosophically and psychologically sophisticated models are necessary to understand it.

What Is Virtue Ethics and What Ethical Issues Does It Raise?

Virtue ethics presumes that people with good character will be better able to understand and respond to ethical problems and standards than people without good character. Others may know moral rules but may cut ethical corners when they think they will not be caught. Although the idea of virtue may sound antiquated to the modern ear, it can be translated into issues involving "what a 'good' person would do in real life situations" (Pence, 1991, p. 249).

A virtue is a character trait that leads someone to do the morally right thing and to have consistent motivations and emotions. Virtue ethics suggests that the profession should be concerned with the character traits that are critical to being a "good" or ethical counseling psychologist. Although the traits might be slightly different for psychologists in practice and those doing research, there is probably a strong commonality between them (Kitchener, 1996b; Kitchener, 1999; Meara et al., 1996). It is important to consider what traits are central for ethical psychologists, and it is also important to remember that being a virtuous psychologist consists of more than particular virtues. Virtuous psychologists strive, though may not always succeed, to be ethical in their professional and personal life (Meara et al., 1996).

Meara et al. (1996) argued that several virtues—prudence or practical wisdom, integrity, respectfulness, and benevolence—are central to the practice of psychology. Kitchener (1999) suggests adding compassion (what feminists have characterized as the ethic of care) and trustworthiness because both are at the core of interpersonal relationships that are critical to practice and research on humans. Even though it is beyond the scope of this chapter, an argument could be made why each of the traits noted above are central to the ethical practice of psychology.

Psychology and the Study of Virtue

The concept of a virtue as a character trait or set of relatively stable characteristics that lead people to act in particular ways should not be foreign to psychologists. Because character traits involve an aspect of personality structure, the idea of studying character traits associated with moral behavior should be familiar ground (Drane, 1994).

Meara et al. (1996) pointed to Rest's (1983, 1994) four-component model of moral behavior as a way to organize thinking about the study of virtue. For example, Rest's first component, moral sensitivity, involves interpreting a situation as requiring moral action. It is related to the ability to discern a moral situation and be empathic with those who are affected by one's actions. These psychological processes are critical for understanding the development of compassion. Similarly, one cannot exhibit prudence (the ability to reason well about moral matters and apply that reasoning to the real world) if one does not recognize that a moral problem exists.

Studies of moral sensitivity among psychologists have not been encouraging. For example, Volker (1984) and Lindsey (1985) found that about 50% of psychology graduate students, as well as licensed psychologists, did not identify the moral content of a taped client's problem without being cued that there was an ethical dilemma in it. On the other hand, Lindsey found a positive and significant association ($r = .25$) between moral sensitivity and formal ethics coursework, suggesting that ethics education can increase sensitivity to moral issues. This is an area that needs further study (Welfel, 1992).

The second component of Rest's model involves deciding what course of action is right, fair, or just (Welfel & Kitchener, 1992). It underlies the ability to use moral reasoning to come to a conclusion about what to do or how to act when faced with an ethical problem. There is a rich psychological literature both on moral judgment (Rest, 1994) and students' reasoning about ethical issues (see Welfel, 1992 for a summary). Findings suggest that people are not equally able to make good judgments about ethical issues in their work. Because the virtue of prudence is dependent on good moral reasoning, these data are particularly relevant to understanding moral lapses and may be an important consideration in graduate admissions. Again, there is some evidence that high quality ethics education can improve ethical decision making (Bebeau, 1994; Welfel, 1992).

The third component of Rest's model, moral motivation, involves the importance given to moral values when they compete with other ones. Moral virtues such as trustworthiness would be related to the motivation to act in a moral way. Not much has been done regarding the empirical evaluation of this component (Rest, 1994).

The last component of the model involves implementing a moral action (Welfel & Kitchener, 1992). Recently, Rest (1994) has referred to it as moral character. It includes having the moral strength to follow through on what one believes to be right and good. He described it as involving ego strength, toughness, and strength of conviction, all of which are related to integrity (having a firm commitment to doing what is morally best). Again, little work has been done on this issue with psychology students. However, J.L. Bernard and Jara (1986) found that despite having an ethics course, 50% of the psychology graduate students in their sample reported that they would do less than they thought they should in a moral situation, suggesting they lacked moral integrity.

Ironically, other professions have more systematically studied the relationship between ethics education and moral behavior than has psychology. Probably Bebeau (1994) and her colleagues have done the most extensive research on the effects of professional ethics education on moral attitudes and behavior. They used Rest's four-component model as a theoretical framework for developing and evaluating an ethics curriculum for dental students. They found that ethical sensitivity, a component one process, varies greatly among both students and professionals, but that those who have a longer period of preparation for the profession showed higher levels of moral sensitivity. Lindsey's (1985) data on psychology students paralleled these findings. Bebeau (1994) also reported that ethical sensitivity could be enhanced through instruction. In terms of the second component, moral reasoning, Bebeau and her colleagues found that technically oriented dental curriculum had little impact on moral reasoning scores. In addition, prior to training many advanced dental students were unable to develop reasoned arguments for common ethical dilemmas encountered in practice. Explicit curriculum changes that gave students feedback about their moral reasoning as well as instruction about how to develop moral arguments improved moral reasoning scores.

Component three, moral motivation, was studied in relationship to professional identity. Bebeau (1994) reasoned if a professional's self-concept includes a sense of responsibility to patients and society, it provides part of a professional's motivation to be ethical. Based on her data, she concluded that students explicitly trained to consider their professional responsibility expressed a significantly greater sense of concern for others than did students who did not receive such training or practicing dentists. Bebeau's work on component four strategies is in the early stages. She is, however, investigating the personal characteristics as well as the problem solving and self-regulation skills that are essential to maintain a commitment to act in a moral way and to maintain control over the self and the situation.

In general, Bebeau's (1994) research program is a good example of theory driven research on the relationship between ethics education and moral behavior. One outcome of her systematic work to assess all four components is her observation that competence on one component does not necessarily predict competence on another either for students or practicing professionals. This suggests, for example, that students may reason well about moral problems in the abstract, but be insensitive to them in real world situations or vice versa.

Unfortunately, most studies of ethical behavior among psychology students rely on surveys of current practices and beliefs and, as Welfel (1992) has pointed out, are noticeably atheoretical. Clearly, more research is needed in this area, but research is needed that is driven by theory so that it aids in the understanding of how virtuous character and moral behavior develop and are maintained.

In summary, Rest's model provides a way to conceptualize how ethical virtues interact with ethical reasoning to produce moral behavior. There is some evidence that ethics education can increase moral sensitivity and compassion as well as prudent judgment. On the other hand, existing data are less encouraging about the development of integrity.

Implications of Virtue Ethics for Training and Admissions

Meara et al. (1996) argued that virtuous character is important for developing professionals who are sensitive to, and concerned about, ethical behavior in their professional and personal life. If this is the case, then counseling psychology needs to consider the implications of the research on moral behavior for training and admissions. Unfortunately, we have little current data to guide our decisions. As noted, evidence indicates that ethics training may improve compassion as it is related to ethical sensitivity as well as prudent judgment. The effects are, however, uneven, and it appears that many students lack firm convictions to make the right ethical choice (J.L. Bernard & Jara, 1986). For example, Fly, van Bark, Weinman, Kitchener, and Lang (1997) found that some psychology graduate students made serious and sometimes blatant ethical errors even after ethics training. These transgressions involved behavior such as discussing personal information about clients in social settings and lying to practicum supervisors. On the other hand, the data are too meager to draw firm conclusions. Bebeau's (1994) conclusions that dental students are not consistently good or poor on all of Rest's components suggest, however, that counseling psychology educators should at least consider whether the same is true of their students. In addition, her work suggests the importance of considering each of the components of Rest's model in designing ethics curriculum. The limits of the data underline the critical need for more theory-based research in this area.

What is currently known suggests that students have a difficult time recognizing ethical issues when they are embedded in complex clinical cases (Lindsey, 1985; Volker, 1984). Faculty might address this by providing students with multiple examples of complex clinical cases or research designs where ethical issues are embedded in other material. Discussions and written assignments could focus on taking the perspective of each of the players in the case and considering the consequences of different actions on each (Fly et al., 1997; Kitchener, 1986). Role-playing the effects of ethical transgressions on clients, students, or research participants or using videotaped vignette are other alternatives. Such assignments might stimulate students' moral sensitivity and, perhaps, their compassion for those whom their actions affect.

Although it is beyond the scope of this chapter to describe fully the implications of each of the components for ethics education, Rest (1983) suggested that people's capacity to make prudent moral decisions reflects basic growth in the cognitive capacity to consider and evaluate moral problems. Although age and education affect this growth, education that ignores this aspect of students' development will probably be inadequate (Fly et al., 1997; Kitchener, 1986). Failure to consider the impact of the social environment in which ethics education is occurring may also be counterproductive. This is especially true if faculty model values that contradict what is being taught about being ethical (Kitchener, 1992b). As Meara et al. (1996) suggested, ethics education cannot be relegated to a single course if it is going to have any influence on students' character.

CONCLUSION

Counseling psychology has been and continues to be confronted with ethical problems that represent old themes but address new issues. Several of those have been reviewed in this chapter. In addition, virtue ethics and its implications for science, practice, and training was addressed. It is clear that, in many cases, ethical problems do not have easy or simple answers. Often choosing between ethical alternatives in an ethical dilemma means making a decision that leaves the professional feeling uncomfortable (Kitchener, 1984b). At times, counseling psychologists may be asked to choose between alternatives that have some element of potential harm. In addition, some ethical decisions place the psychologist in a position of trying to predict the future. Even though this uncomfortable position exists, the public expects professionals to be prudent decision makers in the throes of ethical dilemmas. This being the case, it is clear that counseling psychologists need to remain current about the ethics literature and consider periodic professional training opportunities.

As already noted, large gaps in the ethics and moral behavior literature remain. Most of the theoretical literature focuses on ethical issues in practice. The research and dialogue in this area need to continue. However, the profession needs to focus more energy on ethical issues in the science of psychology and in the training of counseling psychologists. In particular, theory-driven research on ethics education is needed that helps to enhance the ethical character and behavior of psychologists.

Furthermore, the complexity of ethical issues is likely to continue and intensify as the nation's demographics change and as counseling psychologists move into new practice and research areas. If psychologists have seen ethical issues and the decision-making processes around those issues as secondary to good practice and research, those days are quickly ending. The intensified involvement of state legislatures to regulate psychology, the increased number of civil suits filed against psychologists, and the public's increased awareness and expectation that psychologists act ethically calls for the profession to see good counseling, research, and training as impossible without good or virtuous ethical behavior.

REFERENCES

Adelman, H.S., Lusk, R., Alvarez, V., & Acosta, N.K. (1985). Competence of minors to understand, evaluate, and communicate about their psychoeducational problems. *Professional Psychology: Research and Practice, 16,* 426–434.

Akamatsu, T.J. (1988). Intimate relationships with former clients: National survey of attitudes and behavior among practitioners. *Professional Psychology: Research and Practice, 19,* 454–458.

American Psychiatric Association. (1994). *Diagnostic and statistical manual of mental disorders* (4th ed.). Washington, DC: Author.

American Psychological Association. (1981a). *Ethical principles of psychologists.* Washington, DC: Author.

American Psychological Association. (1981b). *Specialty guidelines for the delivery of services.* Washington, DC: Author.

American Psychological Association. (1987). *General guidelines for providers of psychological services.* Washington, DC: Author.

American Psychological Association. (1992). Ethical principles of psychologists and code of conduct. *American Psychologist, 47,* 1597–1611.

American Psychological Association. (1993). Guidelines for providers of psychological services to ethnic, linguistic, and culturally diverse populations. *American Psychologist, 48,* 45–48.

American Psychological Association. (1997a). Report of the ethics committee, 1996. *American Psychologist, 52,* 897–905.

American Psychological Association. (1997b). *Visions and transformations, the final report: Commission on ethnic minority recruitment, retention, and training in psychology.* Washington, DC: Author.

American Psychological Association Office of Program Consultation and Accreditation and Education Directorates. (1996). *Guidelines and principles for accreditation of programs in professional psychology.* Washington, DC: Author.

American Psychological Association Public Interest Directorate. (1997). *Terminal illness and hastened death requests: The important role of the mental health professional.* Washington, DC: Author.

Amirkham, J., Betancourt, H., Graham, S., López, S.R., & Weiner, B. (1995). Reflections on affirmative action goals in psychology admissions. *American Psychological Society, 6,* 140–148.

Anderson, S.K., & Kitchener, K.S. (1996). Nonromantic nonsexual posttherapy relationships between psychologists and former clients: An exploratory study of critical incidents. *Professional Psychology: Research and Practice, 27,* 59–66.

Anderson, S.K., & Kitchener, K.S. (1998). Nonsexual posttherapy relationships: A conceptual framework to assess ethical risks. *Professional Psychology: Research and Practice, 29,* 91–99.

Appelbaum, K., & Appelbaum, P.S. (1990). The HIV antibody patient. In J.C. Beck (Ed.), *Confidentiality versus the duty to protect: Foreseeable harm in the practice of psychiatry* (pp. 121–140). Washington, DC: American Psychiatric Press.

Appelbaum, P.S., Lidz, C.W., & Meisel, A. (1987). *Informed consent: Legal theory and clinical practice.* New York: Oxford University Press.

Appelbaum, P.S., & Rosenbaum, A. (1989). *Tarasoff* and the researcher: Does the duty to protect apply in the research setting? *American Psychologist, 44,* 885–894.

Baer, B.E., & Murdock, N. (1995). Nonerotic dual relationships between therapist and clients: The effects of sex, theoretical orientation, and interpersonal boundaries. *Ethics & Behavior, 5,* 131–145.

Bartell, P.A., & Rubin, L.J. (1990). Dangerous liaisons: Sexual intimacies in supervision. *Professional Psychology: Research and Practice, 21,* 442–450.

Beauchamp, T.L., & Childress, J.F. (1994). *Principles of biomedical ethics* (4th ed.). Oxford, England: Oxford University Press.

Bebeau, M. (1994). Influencing the moral dimensions of dental practice. In J.R. Rest & D. Narvaez (Eds.), *Moral development in the professions* (pp. 121–146). Hillsdale, NJ: Erlbaum.

Bellotti v. Baird, 443 U.S. 622 (1979).

Benn, S.I. (1967). Justice. In P. Edwards (Ed.), *The encyclopedia of philosophy* (Vol. 4). New York: Macmillan.

Bennett, B.E., Bryant, B.K., VandenBos, G.R., & Greenwood, A. (1990). *Professional liability and risk management.* Washington, DC: American Psychological Association.

Bernard, J.L., & Jara, C.S. (1986). The failure of clinical psychology graduate students to apply understood ethical principles. *Professional Psychology: Research and Practice, 17,* 313–315.

Bernard, J.M., & Goodyear, R.K. (1998). *Fundamentals of clinical supervision* (2nd ed.). Needham Heights, MA: Allyn & Bacon.

Bersoff, D.N. (1994). Explicit ambiguity: The 1992 ethics code as an oxymoron. *Professional Psychology: Research and Practice, 25*(4), 382–387.

Bersoff, D.N., & Koeppl, P.M. (1993). The relation between ethical codes and moral principles. *Ethics & Behavior, 3,* 345–357.

Bissell, L. (1983). Alcoholism in physicians: Tactics to improve the salvage rate. *Postgraduate Medicine, 74,* 177–230.

Bok, S. (1983). *Secrets: The ethics of concealment and revelation.* New York: Random House.

Borys, D.S., & Pope, K.S. (1989). Dual relationships between therapist and client: A national study of psychologists, psychiatrists, and social workers. *Professional Psychology: Research and Practice, 20,* 283–293.

Boyd, K. (1989). Ethical questions. In J. Green & A. McCreaner (Eds.), *Counseling in HIV infection and AIDS* (pp. 301–313). Oxford, England: Blackwell Scientific.

Brabeck, M.M. (Ed.). (1999). *Feminist theory and ethics: Challenge and response to psychological practice.* Washington, DC: American Psychological Association.

Brown, L.S. (1994). Concrete boundaries and the problem of literal-mindedness: A response to Lazarus. *Ethics & Behavior, 4,* 275–281.

Brown, L.S. (1997). Remediation, amends, or denial? *Professional Psychology: Research and Practice, 28,* 297–299.

Buckley, P., Karasu, T.B., & Charles, E. (1981). Psychotherapists view their personal therapy. *Psychotherapy: Research & Practice, 18,* 299–305.

Canter, M.B., Bennett, B.E., Jones, S.E., & Nagy, T.F. (1994). *Ethics for psychologists: A commentary on the APA ethics code.* Washington, DC: American Psychological Association.

Carter, R.T. (1991). Cultural values: A review of empirical research and implications for counseling. *Journal of Counseling and Development, 70,* 164–173.

Cayleff, S.E. (1986). Ethical issues in counseling gender, race, and culturally distinct groups. *Journal of Counseling and Development, 64,* 345–347.

Chambless, D.L., Sanderson, W.C., Shoham, V., Bennett, S., Pope, K.S., Crits-Christoph, P., Baker, M., Johnson, B., Woody, S.R., Sue, S., Beutler, L., Williams, D.A., & McCurry, S. (1996). An update on empirically validated therapies. *The Clinical Psychologist, 49*(2), 5–18.

Chemtob, C.M., Bauer, G.B., Hamada, R.S., Pelowski, S.R., & Muraoka, M.Y. (1988). Patient suicide: Occupational hazards for psychologists and psychiatrists. *Professional Psychology: Research and Practice, 20,* 294–300.

Daniel, P.A., & Kitchener, K.S. (1999). Issues of confidentiality. In K.S. Kitchener (Ed.), *The foundations of ethical practice, research, & teaching in psychology.* Mahwah, NJ: Erlbaum.

Drane, J.G. (1994). Character and the moral life: A virtue approach to biomedical ethics. In E.R. DuBose, R.P. Hamel, & L.J. O'Connell (Eds.), *A matter of principles? Ferment in U.S. bioethics* (pp. 284–309). Valley Forge, PA: Trinity Press International.

Family Educational Rights and Privacy Act, 20 U.S.C.A. § 1232g. (1974).

Feminist Therapy Institute. (1990). Feminist therapy institute code of ethics. In H. Lerman & N. Porter (Eds.), *Feminist ethics in psychotherapy* (pp. 38–40). New York: Springer.

Fischer, L., & Sorenson, G.P. (1996). *School law for counselors, psychologists, and social workers* (3rd ed.). White Plains, NY: Longman.

Fisher, C.B., & Younggren, J.N. (1997). The value and utility of the 1992 ethics code. *Professional Psychology: Research and Practice, 28,* 582–592.

Fly, B.J., van Bark, W.P., Weinman, L., Kitchener, K.S., & Lang, P.R. (1997). Ethical transgressions of psychology graduate students: Critical incidents with implications for training. *Professional Psychology: Research and Practice, 28,* 492–495.

Forrest, L., Elman, N., & Gizara, S. (1997, August). *Professional standards for identifying, remediating and terminating impaired or incompetent trainees in psychology: A review of the literature.* Paper presented at the annual meeting of the American Psychological Association, Chicago.

Frame, M.W., & Stevens-Smith, P. (1995). Out of harm's way: Enhancing monitoring and dismissal processes in counselor education programs. *Counselor Education and Supervision, 35,* 118–129.

Fretz, B.R., & Simon, N.P. (1992). Professional issues in counseling psychology: Continuity, change, and challenge. In S.D. Brown & R.W. Lent (Eds.), *Handbook of counseling psychology* (2nd ed., pp. 3–36). New York: Wiley.

Gabbard, G.O. (1994). Reconsidering the American Psychological Association's policy on sex with former patients: Is it justifiable? *Professional Psychology: Research and Practice, 25*(4), 329–335.

Geller, J.D., Cooley, R.S., & Hartley, D. (1981/1982). Images of the psychotherapist: A theoretical and methodological perspective. *Imagination, Cognition & Personality, 1,* 123–146.

Glaser, R.D., & Thorpe, J.S. (1986). Unethical intimacy: A survey of sexual contact and advances between psychology educators and female graduate students. *American Psychologist, 41,* 43–51.

Glenn, C.M. (1980). Ethical issues in the practice of child psychotherapy. *Professional Psychology, 11,* 613–619.

Goldberg, R. (1997). Ethical dilemmas in working with children and adolescents. In D. Marsh & R. Magee (Eds.), *Ethical and legal issues in professional practice with families.* New York: Wiley.

Goodyear, R.K., Crego, C.A., & Johnston, M.W. (1992). Ethical issues in the supervision of student research: A study of critical incidents. *Professional Psychology: Research and Practice, 23,* 203–210.

Gottlieb, M.C. (1993). Avoiding exploitive dual relationships: A decision-making model. *Psychotherapy, 30,* 41–47.

Grey, L.A., & Harding, A.K. (1988). Confidentiality limits with clients who have the AIDS virus. *Journal of Counseling and Development, 66,* 219–223.

Gustafson, K.E., & McNamara, J.R. (1987). Confidentiality with minor clients: Issues and guidelines for therapists. *Professional Psychology: Research and Practice, 18,* 503–508.

Haas, L.J., Malouf, J.L., & Mayerson, N.H. (1986). Ethical dilemmas in psychological practice: Results of a national survey. *Professional Psychology: Research and Practice, 17,* 316–321.

Hammel, G.A., Olkin, R., & Taube, D.O. (1996). Student-educator sex in clinical and counseling psychology doctoral training. *Professional Psychology: Research and Practice, 27,* 93–97.

Handelsman, M.M. (1987). Informed consent of students: How much information is enough? *Teaching of Psychology, 14*(2), 107–109.

Handelsman, M.M. (1990). Do written consent forms influence clients' first impressions of therapists? *Professional Psychology: Research and Practice, 21,* 451–454.

Handelsman, M.M., & Galvin, M.D. (1988). Facilitating informed consent for outpatient psychotherapy: A suggested written format. *Professional Psychology: Research and Practice, 19,* 223–225.

Handelsman, M.M., Kemper, M.B., Kesson-Craig, P., McLain, J., & Johnsrud, C. (1986). Use, content, and readability of written informed consent forms for treatment. *Professional Psychology: Research and Practice, 17,* 514–518.

Handelsman, M.M., Martinez, A., Geisendorfer, J.L., Wagner, L., Daniel, P., & Davis, S. (1995). Does legally mandated consent to psychotherapy ensure ethical appropriateness? *Ethics & Behavior, 5,* 119–129.

Hendrix, D.H. (1991). Ethics and intrafamily confidentiality in counseling with children. *Mental Health Counseling, 13,* 323–333.

Heppner, P.P., Kivlighan, D.M., Jr., & Wampold, B.E. (1992). *Research design in counseling.* Pacific Grove, CA: Brooks/Cole.

Hersch, L. (1995). Adapting to health care reform and managed care: Three strategies for survival and growth. *Professional Psychology: Research and Practice, 26,* 16–26.

Hill, M., Glaser, K., & Harden, J. (1995). A feminist model of ethical decision making. In E.J. Rave & C.C. Larsen (Eds.), *Ethical decision making in therapy: Feminist perspectives* (pp. 18–37). New York: Guilford Press.

Hillerbrand, E.T., & Claiborn, C.D. (1988). Ethical knowledge exhibited by clients and non-clients. *Professional Psychology: Research and Practice, 19,* 527–531.

Hoagwood, K. (1994). The certificate of confidentiality at the National Institute of Mental Health: Discretionary considerations in its applicability in research on child and adolescent mental disorders. *Ethics & Behavior, 4,* 123–131.

Hopkins, B., & Anderson, B. (1990). *The counselor and the law* (3rd ed.). Alexandria, VA: American Counseling Association.

Hopwood v. State of Texas, 861 F. Supp. 551 (W.D. Tex. 1994), 78 F.3d 932, 945-448 (5th Cir. 1996).

Ibrahim, F.A. (1996). A multicultural perspective on principle and virtue ethics. *The Counseling Psychologist, 24,* 78–85.

Inouye, M. (1997). The diversity justification for affirmative action in higher education: Is *Hopwood v. Texas* right? *Notre Dame Journal of Law, Ethics & Public Policy, 11,* 385–417.

Jordan, A.E., & Meara, N.M. (1990). Ethics and the professional practice of psychologists. *Professional Psychology: Research and Practice, 21,* 107–114.

Jorgenson, L.M. (1994). *Legal liability, licensing, and malpractice insurance considerations.* Paper presented at the meeting of the American Psychological Association, Los Angeles.

Kain, C.D. (1988). To breach or not to breach: Is that the question? A response to Gray and Harding. *Journal of Counseling and Development, 66,* 224–225.

Kalichman, S.C. (1993). *Mandated reporting of suspected child abuse: Ethics, law, & policy.* Washington, DC: American Psychological Association.

Kalichman, S.C., & Sikkeman, K.J. (1994). Psychological sequelea of HIV infection and AIDS: Review of empirical findings. *Clinical Psychology Review, 14,* 611–612.

Keith-Spiegel, P. (1994). Teaching psychologists and the new APA ethics code: Do we fit in? *Professional Psychology: Research and Practice, 25*(4), 362–368.

Kier, F.J., & Davenport, D.S. (1997). Ramifications of *Hopwood v. Texas* on the process of applicant selection in APA-accredited professional psychology programs. *Professional Psychology: Research and Practice, 28,* 486–491.

Kitchener, K.S. (1984a). Ethics and counseling psychology: Distinctions and directions. *The Counseling Psychologist, 12*(3), 15–18.

Kitchener, K.S. (1984b). Intuition, critical evaluation and ethical principles: The foundation for ethical decisions in counseling psychology. *The Counseling Psychologist, 12,* 43–55.

Kitchener, K.S. (1986). Teaching applied ethics in counselor education: An integration of psychological processes and philosophical analysis. *Journal of Counseling and Development, 64,* 306–310.

Kitchener, K.S. (1988). Dual role relationships: What makes them so problematic? *Journal of Counseling and Development, 67,* 217–221.

Kitchener, K.S. (1992a). Posttherapy relationships: Ever or never? In B. Herlihy & G. Corey (Eds.), *Dual relationships in counseling.* Alexandria, VA: American Association for Counseling and Development.

Kitchener, K.S. (1992b). Psychologist as teacher and mentor: Affirming ethical values throughout the curriculum. *Professional Psychology: Research and Practice, 23,* 190–195.

Kitchener, K.S. (1996a). Professional codes of ethics and on-going moral problems in psychology. In W. O'Donahue & R.F. Kitchener (Eds.), *Psychology and philosophy.* Thousand Oaks, CA: Sage.

Kitchener, K.S. (1996b). There is more to ethics than principles. *The Counseling Psychologist, 24,* 92–97.

Kitchener, K.S. (1999). *The foundations of ethical practice, research, and teaching in psychology.* Mahwah, NJ: Erlbaum.

Koocher, G.P. (1994). The commerce of professional psychology and the new ethics code. *Professional Psychology: Research and Practice, 25*(4), 335–361.

Kremens v. Bartley, 431 U.S. 119 (1977).

Kutz, S.I. (1986). Defining "impaired psychologist." *American Psychologist, 41,* 220.

LaFromboise, T.D., & Foster, S.L. (1989). Ethics in multicultural counseling. In P. Pedersen, J. Draguns, W. Lonner, & J. Trimble (Eds.), *Counseling across cultures* (3rd ed., pp. 115–136). Honolulu: University of Hawaii Press.

Lamb, D.H., Clark, C., Drumheller, P., Frizzell, K., & Surrey, L. (1989). Applying *Tarasoff* to AIDS related psychotherapy issues. *Professional Psychology: Research and Practice, 20,* 37–43.

Lamb, D.H., Strand, K.K., Woodburn, J.R., Buchko, K.J., Lewis, J.T., & Kang, J.R. (1994). Sexual and business relationships between therapists and former clients. *Psychotherapy: Theory, Research, Practice, and Training, 31,* 270–277.

Lambert, M.J., & Bergin, A.E. (1994). The effectiveness of psychotherapy. In A.E. Bergin & S.L. Garfield (Eds.), *Psychotherapy and behavior change* (pp. 143–189). New York: Wiley.

Layman, M.J., & McNamara, J.R. (1997). Remediation for ethics violations: Focus on psychotherapists' sexual contact with clients. *Professional Psychology: Research and Practice, 28,* 281–292.

Lerman, H., & Porter, N. (1990). The contribution of feminism to ethics in psychotherapy. In H. Lerman & N. Porter (Eds.), *Feminist ethics in psychotherapy* (pp. 5–13). New York: Springer.

Lerman, H., & Rigby, D.N. (1990). Boundary violations: Misuse of the power of the therapist. In H. Lerman & N. Porter (Eds.), *Feminist ethics in psychotherapy* (pp. 51–59). New York: Springer.

Lindsey, R.T. (1985). *Moral sensitivity: The relationship between training and experience.* Paper presented at the annual meeting of the American Psychological Association, Los Angeles.

Liss, M.B. (1994). Child abuse: Is there a mandate for researchers to report? *Ethics & Behavior, 4*(2), 133–146.

Lissner, L.S. (1992). *Access to higher education for students with disabilities: What is reasonable? What is fundamental? and Who is qualified?* [On-line]. Available: http://www.rit.edu~easi/law/lissner.html

MacIntyre, A. (1981). *After virtue.* Notre Dame, IN: University of Notre Dame Press.

Mangalmurti, V.S. (1994). Psychotherapists' fear of *Tarasoff:* All in the mind? *Journal of Psychiatry and Law, 22*(3), 379–409.

Mann, L., Harmoni, R., & Power, C. (1989). Adolescent decision-making: The development of competence. *Journal of Adolescence, 12,* 265–278.

Mann, T. (1994). Informed consent for psychological research: Do subjects comprehend consent forms and understand their legal rights? *Psychological Science, 5,* 140–143.

Mayo, D. (1993, August). *The case for rational suicide.* Presented at the annual convention of the American Psychological Association, Toronto, Canada.

McGaha, A.C., & Korn, J.H. (1995). The emergence of interest in the ethics of psychological research with humans. *Ethics & Behavior, 5,* 147–160.

McIntosh, J.L. (1993, August). *Arguments against rational and assisted suicide.* Paper presented at the 101st annual convention of the American Psychological Association, Toronto, Canada.

Meara, N.M., Schmidt, L., & Day, J.D. (1996). Principles and virtues: A foundation for ethical decisions, policies and character. *The Counseling Psychologist, 24,* 4–77.

Melton, G.B. (1988). Ethical and legal issues in AIDS related practice. *American Psychologist, 43*(11), 941–947.

Miller, D.J., & Thelan, M.H. (1986). Knowledge and beliefs about confidentiality in psychotherapy. *Professional Psychology: Research and Practice, 17,* 15–19.

Morrison, C.F. (1989). AIDS: Ethical implications for psychological intervention. *Professional Psychology: Research and Practice, 30,* 166–171.

Murphy, M.J., DeBernardo, C.R., & Schoemaker, W.E. (1997). Impact of managed care on independent practice and professional ethics: A survey of independent practitioners. *Professional Psychology: Research and Practice, 29,* 43–51.

Murray, H., Gillese, E., Lennon, M., Mercer, P., & Robinson, M. (1996, December). Ethical principles for college and university teaching. *AAHE Bulletin,* 1–3.

Nathan, P.E. (1986). Unanswered questions about distressed professionals. In R.R. Kilburg, P.E. Nathan, & R.W. Thoreson (Eds.), *Professionals in distress: Issues, syndromes, and solutions in psychology* (pp. 27–36). Washington, DC: American Psychological Association.

National Commission for the Protection of Human Subjects of Biomedical and Behavioral Research. (1978). *The Belmont Report: Ethical principles and guidelines for the protection of human subjects of research* (DHEW Publication No. OS 78-0012). Washington, DC: U.S. Government Printing Office.

Noddings, N. (1984). *Caring: A feminine approach to ethics and moral education.* Berkeley: University of California Press.

Orr, P. (1997). Psychology impaired? *Professional Psychology: Research and Practice, 28,* 293–296.

Pascarella, E.T., & Terenzini, P.T. (1991). *How college affects students.* San Francisco: Jossey-Bass.

Patton, M.J., & Meara, N.M. (1992). Ethical considerations in psychoanalytic counseling. In *Psychoanalytic counseling* (pp. 288–304). New York: Wiley.

Payton, C.R. (1994). Implications of the 1992 ethics code for diverse groups. *Professional Psychology: Research and Practice, 25*(4), 317–320.

Pedersen, P.B. (1995). Culture-centered ethical guidelines for counselors. In J.G. Ponterotto, J.M. Casas, L.A. Suzuki, & C.M. Alexander (Eds.), *Handbook of multicultural counseling* (pp. 34–50). Thousand Oaks, CA: Sage.

Pedersen, P.B., & Marsalla, A.J. (1982). The ethical crisis for cross-cultural counseling and therapy. *Professional Psychology: Research and Practice, 13,* 492–500.

Pence, G.E. (1991). Virtue theory. In P. Singer (Ed.), *A companion to ethics.* Oxford, England: Basil Blackwell.

Pipes, R. (1997). Nonsexual relationships between psychotherapists and their former clients: Obligations of psychologists. *Ethics & Behavior, 7,* 27–41.

Ponterotto, J.G. (1988). Racial/ethnic minority research in the *Journal of Counseling Psychology:* A content analysis and methodological critique. *Journal of Counseling Psychology, 35,* 410–418.

Pope, K.S. (1988). How clients are harmed by sexual contact with mental health professionals: The syndrome and its prevalence. *Journal of Counseling and Development, 67,* 222–226.

Pope, K.S. (1990). Therapist-patient sexual involvement: A review of the research. *Clinical Psychology Review, 10,* 477–490.

Pope, K.S. (1993). Licensing disciplinary actions for psychologists who have been sexually involved with a client: Some information about offenders. *Professional Psychology: Research and Practice, 24,* 374–377.

Pope, K.S., & Bouhoutsos, J.C. (1986). *Sexual intimacy between therapists and patients.* New York: Praeger.

Pope, K.S., Keith-Spiegel, P., & Tabachnick, B.G. (1986). Sexual attraction to clients: The human therapist and the (sometimes) inhuman training system. *American Psychologist, 41,* 147–158.

Pope, K.S., Levenson, H., & Schover, L. (1979). Sexual intimacy in psychology training: Results and implications of a national survey. *American Psychologist, 34,* 682–689.

Pope, K.S., Sonne, J.L., & Holrody, J. (1993). *Sexual feelings in psychotherapy: Explorations for therapists and therapists-in-training.* Washington, DC: American Psychological Association.

Pope, K.S., & Tabachnick, B.G. (1993). Therapists' anger, hate, fear, and sexual feelings: National survey of therapist responses. *Professional Psychology: Research and Practice, 25,* 247–258.

Pope, K.S., & Vasquez, M.J.T. (1991). *Ethics in psychotherapy and counseling.* San Francisco: Jossey-Bass.

Pope, K.S., & Vetter, V.A. (1992). Ethical dilemmas encountered by members of the American Psychological Association: A national survey. *American Psychologist, 47,* 397–441.

Quirk, J. (1997). Professional and ethical issues in family-school mental health interventions. In D. Marsh & R. Magee (Eds.), *Ethical and legal issues in professional practice with families.* New York: Wiley.

Rave, E.J., & Larsen, C.C. (Eds.). (1995). *Ethical decision making in therapy: Feminist perspectives* (pp. 18–37). New York: Guilford Press.

Regents of the University of California v. Bakke, 438 U.S. 265, 313 (1978).

Rest, J.R. (1983). Morality. In J. Flavell & E. Markham (Eds.), *Manual of child psychology: Vol. 4. Cognitive development* (pp. 520–629). New York: Wiley.

Rest, J.R. (1994). Background: Theory and research. In J.R. Rest & D. Narvaez (Eds.), *Moral development in the professions* (pp. 1–28). Hillsdale, NJ: Erlbaum.

Robinson, W.L., & Reid, P.T. (1985). Sexual intimacies in psychology revisited. *Professional Psychology: Research and Practice, 16,* 512–520.

Rogers, J.R., & Britton, P.J. (1994). AIDS and rational suicide: A counseling psychology perspective or a slide on a slippery slope. *The Counseling Psychologist, 22,* 171–178.

Rosenthal, R. (1994). Science and ethics in conducting, analyzing, and reporting psychological research. *Psychological Science, 5,* 127–133.

Rubanowitz, D.E. (1987). Public attitudes toward psychotherapist-client confidentiality. *Professional Psychology: Research and Practice, 18,* 613–618.

Sank, L.I. (1997). Taking on managed care: One reviewer at a time. *Professional Psychology: Research and Practice, 28,* 548–554.

Schmidt, L.D., & Meara, N.M. (1984). Ethical, professional and legal issues in counseling psychology. In S.D. Brown & R.W. Lent (Eds.), *Handbook of counseling psychology.* New York: Wiley.

Schoener, G.R., & Gonsiorek, J. (1988). Assessment and development of rehabilitation plans for counselors who have sexually exploited their clients. *Journal of Counseling and Development, 67,* 227–232.

Shields, J.M., & Johnson, A. (1992). Collision between law and ethics: Consent for treatment with adolescents. *Bulletin of American Academy Psychiatry Law, 20*(3), 309–323.

Sieber, J.E. (1992). *Planning ethically responsible research: A guide for students and internal review boards* (Applied social research methods series, Vol. 31). Newbury Park, CA: Sage.

Sieber, J.E. (1994). Will the new code help researchers be more ethical? *Professional Psychology: Research and Practice, 25*(4), 369–375.

Siegel, K. (1986). Psycho-social aspects of rational suicide. *American Journal of Psychotherapy, 40,* 405–418.

Slimp, P.A.O., & Burian, B.K. (1994). Multiple role relationships during internship: Consequences and recommendations. *Professional Psychology: Research and Practice, 25,* 39–45.

Somberg, D.R., Stone, G.L., & Claiborn, C.D. (1993). Informed consent: Therapists' beliefs and practices. *Professional Psychology: Research and Practice, 24,* 153–159.

Sonne, J.L. (1994). Multiple relationships: Does the new ethics code answer the right questions? *Professional Psychology: Research and Practice, 25*(4), 336–343.

Stake, J.E., & Oliver, J. (1991). Sexual contact and touching between therapist and client: A survey of psychologists' attitudes and behavior. *Professional Psychology: Research and Practice, 22,* 297–307.

Stevenson, S., & Kitchener, K.S. (in press). Ethical issues in the practice of psychology. In J. Anderson & R. Barret (Eds.), *Ethics and AIDS: A mental health practitioners guide.* Washington, DC: American Psychological Association.

Sue, D.W., Arredondo, P., & McDavis, R.J. (1992). Multicultural counseling competencies and standards: A call to the profession. *Journal of Counseling and Development, 70,* 477–486.

Sue, S., Zane, N., & Young, K. (1994). Research on psychotherapy with culturally diverse populations. In A.E. Bergin & S.L. Garfield (Eds.), *Handbook of psychotherapy and behavior change* (pp. 783–820). New York: Wiley.

Sullivan, T., Martin, W.L., Jr., & Handelsman, M.M. (1993). Practical benefits of an informed-consent procedure: An empirical investigation. *Professional Psychology: Research and Practice, 24,* 160–163.

Swenson, L.C. (1997). *Psychology and law for the helping profession.* Pacific Grove, CA: Brooks/Cole.

Tabachnick, B.G., Keith-Spiegel, P., & Pope, K.S. (1991). Ethics of teaching: Beliefs and behaviors of psychologists as educators. *American Psychologist, 46,* 506–515.

Tarasoff v. Regents of the University of California, 529 P.2d 553 (Cal. 1974); 551 P.2d 334,331 (Cal. 1976).

Vasquez, M.J.T. (1991). Sexual intimacies with clients after termination: Should a prohibition be explicit? *Ethics & Behavior, 1*(1), 45–61.

Vasquez, M.J.T. (1992). Psychologist as clinical supervisor: Promoting ethical practice. *Professional Psychology: Research and Practice, 23,* 196–202.

Vasquez, M.J.T. (1994). Implications of the 1992 ethics code for the practice of individual psychotherapy. *Professional Psychology: Research and Practice, 25*(4), 321–328.

Volker, J.M. (1984). *Counseling experience, moral judgment, awareness of consequences, and moral sensitivity in counseling practice.* Doctoral dissertation, University of Minnesota at Minneapolis.

Webster v. Reproductive Health Services, 492 U.S. 490 (1989).

Weithorn, L.A., & Scherer, D.G. (1994). Children's involvement in research participation decisions: Psychological considerations. In M.A. Grodin & L.H. Glantz (Eds.), *Children as research subjects: Science, ethics, and law.* Oxford, England: Oxford University Press.

Welfel, E.R. (1992). Psychologists as ethics educator: Successes, failures, & unanswered questions. *Professional Psychology: Research and Practice, 23,* 182–189.

Welfel, E.R. (1998). *Ethics in counseling and psychotherapy: Standards, research and emerging issues.* Pacific Grove, CA: Brooks/Cole.

Welfel, E.R., & Kitchener, K.S. (1992). Introduction to the special section: Ethics education—An agenda for the 90s. *Professional Psychology: Research and Practice, 23,* 179–182.

Werth, J.L., Jr. (1992). Rational suicide and AIDS: Considerations for the psychotherapist. *The Counseling Psychologist, 20,* 645–659.

Werth, J.L., Jr., & Liddle, B.J. (1994). Psychotherapists' attitudes toward suicide. *Psychotherapy: Theory, Research and Practice, 31,* 440–448.

Widger, T.A., & Rorer, L.G. (1984). The responsible psychotherapist. *American Psychologist, 39,* 503–515.

Wiggins-Frame, M. (1995, Fall). Confidentiality and child consent: Guidelines for practice. *Awareness,* 25–29.

Wise, T.P. (1978). Where public peril begins: A survey of psychotherapists to determine the effects of *Tarasoff. Stanford Law Review, 31,* 165–190.

CHAPTER 3

Psychotherapy Supervision and Training

RODNEY K. GOODYEAR
CHRISTINE R. GUZZARDO

Professionals differ from members of other occupations in several important ways. Among these are the degree of autonomy with which they work, their need to make judgments under conditions of uncertainty (Sechrest et al., 1982), and their reliance on a knowledge base that is sufficiently unique and specialized that the average person would have difficulty grasping it and its implications. For these reasons, society maintains what might be understood as an implicit contract with the professions. That is, the professions are allowed to self-regulate in return for the assurance that they will place the welfare of society and of their clients above their own self-interests (see, e.g., Abbott, 1988; Cruess & Cruess, 1997; Schein, 1973; Schön, 1983).

This self-regulation includes controlling who is admitted to practice, setting standards for members' behavior, and disciplining incompetent or unethical members. Training and supervision are central to these purposes, for they are the vehicles for imparting necessary skills and for socializing novices into the profession's values and ethics while also protecting clients. As Holloway and Neufeldt (1995) note, within psychology "supervision plays a critical role in maintaining the standards of the profession" (p. 207).

It is not surprising, therefore, that the history of supervision in the mental health professions coincides with the history of those professions. Supervision as we understand it today apparently evolved primarily from two independent roots. One of those roots was in psychoanalysis. Freud reported that supervision began in 1902 with "a number of young doctors gathered around me with the express intention of learning, practicing, and spreading the knowledge of psychoanalysis" (Freud, 1986, p. 82). By the mid-1920s, psychoanalytic supervision had become a formalized process (Frayn, 1991). The second root was in social work, where supervision began with "the nineteenth century Charity Organization Societies in which paid social work agents supervised the moral treatment of the poor by friendly visitors" (D. Harkness & Poertner, 1989, p. 115). These roots have since converged into an intervention in its own right that has been informed by a number of additional influences (see, e.g., Holloway, 1992). Despite some between-discipline differences in its expression, supervision is an intervention with essential similarities across the several mental health professions (Bernard & Goodyear, 1998).

As supervision became a formalized process, it became normative for psychotherapists to assume the role of supervisor at some point during their professional development (e.g., Ronnestad, Orlinsky, Parks, & Davis, 1997; Shechter, 1990). In fact, supervision not only is one of the most common activities of counseling psychologists (Fitzgerald & Osipow, 1986; Watkins, Lopez, Campbell, & Himmell, 1986), but also of professional psychologists in general (Corrigan, Hess, & Garman, 1998; Garfield & Kurtz, 1976; Norcross, Prochaska, & Farber, 1993; Norcross, Prochaska, & Gallager, 1989). Norcross et al. (1993) found that clinical supervision edged out diagnosis and assessment as the second most frequently reported activity among members of the American Psychological Association's (APA) Division of Psychotherapy.

In contrast to supervision's importance and its relatively long history, research on its processes and outcomes began only a few decades ago. Yet during that relatively short period, research and concomitant theory-building have grown rapidly. That there now have been at least 34 reviews of supervision research (Ellis & Ladany, 1997) suggests the vitality of that work. In fact, Watkins (1995b) recently observed that "interest in, and scrutiny of, the psychotherapy supervision experience is now at an all time high" (p. 568). Evidence includes the recent special features in both the *Journal of Counseling Psychology* (see Holloway & Carroll, 1996) and the *Journal of Consulting and Clinical Psychology* (Beutler & Kendall, 1995), two recent issues in *Counselor Education and Supervision* (September and December, 1998), and the number of recent books devoted to supervision.

Research attention given to supervision, however, has been uneven across the several mental health professions, apparently in accordance with each respective profession's level of emphasis on research in general. Therefore, Tsui (1997) reported having located only 30 empirical articles concerning social work supervision that had been published over the previous 25 years. Psychologists have been the primary source of research on supervision. Moreover, this literature has been largely driven by counseling psychologists, who have made many of the more important contributions to theory and who comprise the majority of supervision researchers. Counseling psychologists' interest in supervision is reflected as well in their commitment to *preparing* supervisors, for counseling psychology programs are significantly more likely to offer a supervision course than are clinical or school psychology programs (cf. Romans, Boswell, Carlozzi, & Ferguson, 1995).

It is appropriate, therefore, that each edition of this *Handbook* has included a chapter on supervision. This convention allows readers to track the evolution of the supervision literature across time. That each supervision chapter has been written by a different author or authors enriches the coverage by broadening the perspectives reflected in the chapters.

Our primary consideration in deciding what would appear in this chapter was that the material should include empirical and conceptual literature that: (1) extended the earlier *Handbook* chapters by Russell, Crimmings, and Lent (1984) and Holloway (1992) by following up on themes and issues they had initiated and also by minimizing the redundancies between this chapter and either of theirs; (2) reflected our own interests and beliefs about what material is important; and (3) addressed some of the evolving practice issues that are affecting training and supervision.

Two other factors influenced both our choice of material and the manner in which we approached it. First, the focus of this chapter is primarily on psychotherapy supervision and training. Although there are unique contextual issues in supervising other activities such as assessment (Finkelstein & Tuckman, 1997) and career counseling (Watkins, 1993a), those are not addressed here.

Second, although we devote the greater portion of this chapter to *supervision,* we also address *training* in several sections, taking care to differentiate the two interventions. Stone (1997) made the point that the definition of supervision "occasionally suffers from cycles of inflation and deflation" (p. 265), depending on whether authors are confusing supervision with training. Although supervision and training are complementary and even overlapping functions, they are not interchangeable. The term "training," in fact, is used in two different ways in the literature. One meaning of the term concerns the teaching of discrete skills (e.g., reflecting feelings, asking open-ended questions). This typically occurs during prepracticum and similar laboratory-based skill courses. The second meaning of training is broader in connotation and refers to all of what constitutes professional preparation, including curriculum, courses, and supervised counseling experiences. Training in this sense of the word is virtually synonymous with "graduate education." For the purposes of this chapter, we consider training in the more specific, limited sense.

Space is an additional constraint on what is possible to cover in a chapter of this nature. We decided to cover topics that have been prominent in most reviews of supervision literature, including those of Russell et al. (1984) and Holloway (1992). As well, we chose to cover training and supervision related to empirically supported treatments, given the prominence of this relatively recent development. The six topics we cover are (1) supervision and training outcomes, (2) supervisory relationships, (3) the role of individual differences in supervision and training processes and goals, (4) supervisory and supervisee development, (5) evaluation in supervision, and (6) training and supervision issues concerning empirically supported treatments. We then conclude with some observations about the current status of supervision research.

OUTCOMES

No question with respect to training and supervision is more important than, Does it work? The answer, however, is complicated. In the two following subsections, we discuss the outcomes of counselor skills training, and then of supervision.

Counselor Skills Training Outcomes

One of the more important contributions to psychological education during the past several decades has been the development of protocols for training novices in basic relationship and interviewing skills. Rogers and his associates (e.g., Rogers, 1967) developed rating scales to assess the level at which therapists' demonstrated use of Rogers's (1957) relationship variables. This important step toward operationalizing those relationship attitudes or conditions was extended by two of Rogers's research associates, Robert Carkhuff and Charles Truax, who proposed procedures to teach these relationship attitudes as specific *skills* (Carkuff & Truax, 1965). Whereas some psychologists initially questioned the use of a technology to teach relationship skills (e.g., Calia, 1974), psychology educators found it useful and adopted the Carkhuff and Truax model or one of the related models that followed quickly thereafter (e.g., Danish & Hauer, 1973; Ivey, Normington, Miller, Merrill, & Haase, 1968; Kagan & Krathwohl, 1967; see Russell et al., 1984, for a more complete review of this history). It is significant that the developers of these models identified primarily as counseling psychologists and that most of the research on these models was published in counseling psychology journals. Counseling psychologists' dominance of the training literature parallels their dominance of the supervision literature.

Two decades ago, Ford (1979) concluded from his literature review that discrete counselor skills could be taught effectively, but he tempered this conclusion by noting that, "certain limitations require that these promising results be viewed as tentative rather than conclusive" (p. 119). Sufficient evidence now has accrued, however, to conclude with confidence that these systematic training models are effective in imparting the more specific relationship skills they intend to provide. For example, after reviewing studies of Ivey's Microcounseling (MC) training, Baker and Daniels (1989) concluded that the mean effect size was .83. That is, after training, these trainees scored .83 standard deviations higher than control participants on relevant measures of outcome.

Baker, Daniels, and Greeley (1990) subsequently conducted a meta-analytic review of studies of the three dominant skills training models: MC, Carkhuff's Human Resource Training (HRT), and Kagan's Interpersonal Process Recall (IPR). Although the Baker and Daniels (1989) meta-analysis had not restricted the types of samples used, the Baker et al. (1990) meta-analysis included only studies in which samples were graduate level counselor trainees. They concluded that all three models were effective, but differentially so. HRT had the greatest effect size (1.07), followed by MC (.63), and then IPR (.20). From a cost-effectiveness perspective, however, it is noteworthy that the average length of training across studies was *least* for MC ($M = 9.46$ hours), greatest for HRT ($M = 37.14$), and at an intermediate level for the IPR studies ($M = 13.83$).

Baker et al. (1990) acknowledged the smaller effect size for MC obtained in this study than in the earlier Baker and Daniels (1989) study and hypothesized that it might be a result of differences in the samples used in the studies that were reviewed. In fact, they speculated that "graduate-level counseling trainees may be more challenging to train with the MC program than are samples from other populations (e.g., undergraduates, paraprofessional, and secondary school student)" (p. 411). This explanation, however, seems counterintuitive. It may be that graduate-level counselor trainees begin skills training with a higher threshold of skills than do others and that what Baker and Daniels (1989) were observing was a ceiling effect.

Despite these generally positive conclusions about the effectiveness of the dominant training models, two particular areas concerning skills training seem to beg further attention. First, even though the evidence suggests that students trained via any of these three models can learn and demonstrate the intended skills during the training experience itself, it still is not clear how well they are able to generalize these skills to actual therapy settings. In citing studies that bring this matter into question, Lambert and Ogles (1997) hypothesized that *supervision* is an essential next step that helps trainees to make this generalization effectively. Certainly this hypothesis warrants further attention.

Second, most research concerning counselor skills training programs has focused on the acquisition of very specific counseling skills. Alberts and Edelstein (1990) are among those who have noted the absence of attention to higher order skills. It is therefore significant that one recent study documented the extent to which novice trainees in a training "laboratory" context struggled to recognize and manage personal reactions that these initial counseling experiences stimulated (E.N. Williams, Judge, Hill, & Hoffman, 1997). In qualitative analyses of open-ended material completed by seven trainees after each counseling session over the course of a semester, Williams et al. concluded that "[t]rainees also struggled with personal concerns related to conflict with their clients, reactions to specific client issues (e.g., parents, guilt, sex, abortion), and their concerns about their roles as therapists (e.g., wish to rescue or side with the client, desire to give advice or be like a friend or teacher, difficulty sticking with time limits)" (p. 397). Importantly, Williams et al. documented (via quantitative measures) that at the end of the semester these trainees were less anxious and had demonstrated greater ability to manage countertransference reactions. This study offers preliminary evidence that at least some higher order skills are being developed in prepracticum settings.

Supervision Outcomes

Holloway (1992) asserted that "the ultimate goal of supervision is counselor competence" (p. 202). Whereas a number of criteria might reasonably be used in the service of assessing supervision's success in meeting this goal (Holloway, 1984; Lambert & Ogles, 1997; Russell et al., 1984), the most stringent and arguably most important criterion is client change (Holloway & Neufeldt, 1995). As Ellis and Ladany (1997) have noted, "the impact of clinical supervision on client outcome is considered by many to be the acid test of supervision" (p. 485).

Unfortunately, evidence of supervision's effect on client outcomes remains scant. There have been few studies and those that have been conducted have not allowed definitive conclusions. For example, based on the nine such studies that they identified as having been published since 1981, Ellis and Ladany (1997) concluded that methodological and other problems made it possible to draw "few justifiable conclusions" (p. 488).

Moreover, we would add the additional limitation that these nine studies focused on session impact rather than on client symptom reduction or other treatment outcomes. As well, there have been almost no efficacy studies in supervision. In psychotherapy research, efficacy studies are conducted with a treatment manual and "consist of a brief and fixed duration of treatment, manualized treatment, a single simple disorder, and random assignment of clinic volunteers to type of treatment" (Seligman, 1998, p. 2). As will be demonstrated, these criteria present specific difficulties in terms of supervision research.

Many of the studies reviewed in the skills training literature discussed in the section above might be described as efficacy studies. They were tests of a particular model, were of fixed duration, and are based on a training protocol (i.e., the analogue of a treatment manual in psychotherapy research). Such studies are rare in supervision, however, for several reasons. One is that the extant supervision models are limited in their prescriptive possibilities for day-to-day supervisory tasks because they tend to be based on relatively general principles (e.g., developmental models positing that less structure is best for more advanced trainees; social role theories that characterize supervisor behaviors). At this point in the development of supervision models, the most salient comparisons might be between different supervisory modalities. An example is a study by Kivlighan, Angelone, and Swafford (1991) which compared live supervision with videotaped supervision.

A second reason is that supervision researchers have not generally had (or developed) manuals or protocols to ensure that a particular style of supervision is being followed with fidelity. Supervision researchers have had only the Neufeldt, Iverson, and Juntunen (1995) manual, and even it was developed for training purposes rather than to explicate a particular supervisory model (see Neufeldt, 1994). At least one prominent supervision theorist (Holloway, 1992) has expressed doubts that supervision ever will be manualized to any significant extent.

Goodyear and Bernard (1998) suggested a third reason as well: It is difficult to design a supervision efficacy study—that is, one in which a particular approach to supervision is being compared to a no-treatment, control group—that sufficiently protects clients. For psychotherapy researchers to assign clients to a control group means to withhold an active treatment from them. In most cases, this entails minimal risk to the client. But to have a no-treatment control group in supervision research might mean to allow novice counselors to work unmonitored with clients. In this case, the intervention the client receives is an *active* one, regardless of how closely the supervisee who provides the treatment is being monitored. Some researchers have argued on both ethical and practical grounds to abandon placebos in favor of comparisons with treatments of known effectiveness (e.g., Rothman & Michels, 1994). The difficulty in the case of supervision, however, is that there are no models of established effectiveness against which to calibrate the effectiveness of newer models.

In summary, most of the supervision research has addressed supervision outcomes in terms of particular trainee attitudes, skills, and behaviors (Holloway & Neufeldt, 1995), and direct links between supervision and client outcomes are yet to be established. But although it is less compelling than an empirical link, it is possible to relate supervision to client outcomes on the basis of logic and inference. For example, by knowing that (1) particular supervision processes affect trainee's working alliances with their clients (Patton & Kivlighan, 1997), and that (2) client-therapist working alliances are associated with therapeutic outcomes (Horvath & Symonds, 1991; Orlinsky, Grawe, & Parks, 1994), it is possible to infer that supervision therefore affects client outcomes.

Perhaps, then, supervision affects client outcomes indirectly, and this relationship should be conceptualized in terms of mediated, or path models. An adequate empirical test of such a model requires a much larger sample size than is usually practical in supervision research. Nevertheless, to hypothesize such a conceptual frame seems reasonable based on the available evidence.

THE SUPERVISORY RELATIONSHIP

A central theme in the supervision literature has been that the nature and quality of the supervisor-supervisee relationship affects supervision outcomes. The supervisory relationship, however, is multifaceted and can be understood from a number of perspectives. Moreover, it pervades so much of what occurs in supervision that many topics we address elsewhere in the chapter (e.g., individual differences; trainee evaluation) can be understood to bear on one or more aspects of the supervisory relationship.

This section addresses three particular relationship phenomena that have been prominent in the supervision literature. These concern parallel processes, working alliances, and social influence.

Parallel Processes

The supervisory relationship is intended to facilitate the development of the counselor-client relationship. However, in introducing the concept of what now are understood as "parallel processes," Searles (1955) made the point that the supervisor-supervisee relationship can be influenced by that of the counselor-client. Doehrman (1976) later demonstrated that parallel processes work in both directions and that supervisor-supervisee relationship phenomena can be reflected onto the counselor-client relationship as well.

Russell et al. (1984) suggested two ways that the parallel processes can be useful in supervision:

> First, as the supervisee becomes aware of the parallels in the relationships with the client and the supervisor, understanding of the client's psychological maladjustment is increased. Second, the supervisee's understanding of the therapeutic process grows in that the supervisee learns how to respond therapeutically to the client just as the supervisor has responded to the supervisee. (p. 629)

Although the concept of parallel processes has intuitive appeal to supervisors, it has been difficult to operationalize and study. Perhaps as a consequence, there have been only a few empirical examinations (McNeill & Worthen, 1989). One was a survey using a questionnaire of unknown psychometric qualities. With it, Raichelson, Herron, Primavera, and Ramirez (1997) confirmed that psychodynamic supervisors and supervisees were more likely than their nonanalytic counterparts (primarily rational emotive or cognitive behavioral) to perceive the existence and importance of parallel processes.

These few studies have used case studies based either on interviews with participants (clients, counselors, supervisors; Doehrman, 1976) or an intensive examination of within session behaviors (e.g., Alpher, 1991; Friedlander, Siegel, & Brenock, 1989) to document the existence of parallel processes. Friedlander et al., for example, observed a typical interaction pattern in counseling in which the supervisee/counselor used a leading style and the client responded with cooperation; they also observed a similar pattern to occur in supervision, where the supervisor typically used a leading style and the supervisee followed with cooperation.

These several studies have documented the presence of parallel processes. However, empirical investigations of the *usefulness* of parallel processes to which Russell et al. (1984) alluded have not been conducted except perhaps in research programs concerned with phenomena that the investigators did not themselves label as parallel processes. For example, Truax and Carkhuff (1967) had hypothesized that the level of empathy trainees demonstrate with their clients corresponds to the level of empathy their supervisors demonstrate with them; Russell et al. suggested this was a form of parallel process. With respect to this particular line of research, however, Lambert and Ogles (1997) concluded that, overall, research findings have been inconclusive. They noted that supervisory and therapeutic environments have different demands and that trainees can learn effective helping skills without the supervisor demonstrating especially high levels of empathy and other facilitative conditions.

A recent study by Patton and Kivlighan (1997) might be understood to have concerned parallel processes by the same rationale that was applied to the Carkhuff-derived studies. Significantly, they found that working alliances between supervisors and supervisees do affect those of the supervisee counselors and their clients. It is, though, but a single study and therefore should be understood as tentative.

Working Alliances

Interest in client-counselor working alliances during the past 15 years has been reflected in supervision research as well, albeit to a lesser degree. Bordin's (1983) conceptual article on working alliances in supervision has been followed by several studies. Important among these was an instrument development study describing development of a psychometrically sound instrument for assessing supervisory alliances (Efstation, Patton, & Kardash, 1990). This has given researchers an important tool that is sensitive to the uniqueness of the supervisory alliance.

Several studies have examined relationships between working alliances and particular trainee or supervisor attributes: racial identity levels of supervisor and supervisee; trainees' perceptions of role conflict and role ambiguity; and trainee experience level. Ladany, Brittan-Powell, and Pannu (1997) found that racial identity levels of supervisors and supervisees predicted strength of supervisory alliances (this study is described more fully below). Ladany and Friedlander (1995) found that the stronger some aspects of the supervisory alliance, the less role ambiguity and conflict the trainees reported.

Sumerel and Borders (1996) found that supervisees' experience level did not predict quality or strength of the supervisory alliance. Possibly experience level is not, by itself, a salient variable in predicting supervisory alliances. Alternatively, between-group differences in trainee experience levels in this study (that is, 1–$1\frac{1}{2}$ semesters of supervised experience versus 3–$3\frac{1}{2}$ semesters) may have been insufficiently large to observe such differences. Holloway (1992) has observed from her review of the literature that reliable between-group differences are most likely to be observed when comparing very beginning students with more advanced, intern level trainees.

One study has examined the impact of supervisory alliances. We already have noted that Patton and Kivlighan (1997) found strength of supervisory alliances to predict those of trainees and their clients. They found that the unbiased correlation between trainees' ratings of the supervisory alliances and clients' ratings of the counseling working alliance was .66. As well, they found that supervisory alliances were related to trainee adherence to the general psychodynamic interviewing style (unbiased correlation of .52), but not to the use of more specific techniques of the model in which trainees were being trained.

Another way to examine the working alliance is as a process that fluctuates in quality and strength as weakenings (also discussed in the literature as "tears" or "ruptures") occur, then are repaired. This perspective is virtually identical to that of Mueller and Kell (1972), who asserted that conflicts are inherent in any ongoing relationship and that the resolution of those conflicts determines whether the supervisory relationship stagnates or deepens. To examine patterns and causes of weakenings and repairs, Burke, Goodyear, and Guzzard (1998) had raters examine within-session tear-repair processes within 10 consecutive sessions of 10 supervisory dyads. Among their observations was that the more emotional, difficult to repair weakenings occurred as supervisors assumed evaluative roles. Also, that the type of weakening events varied according to experience level of the trainees (e.g., alliance weakening events with more advanced trainees were more likely to involve disagreements about theoretical or treatment planning issues). This was a descriptive study with a small number of participants. However, as the first study to examine the tear-repair process in supervisory alliances, it may stimulate further research of a more rigorous nature.

Another study concerned with weakening processes within the supervisory alliance (Nigam, Cameron, & Leverette, 1997) examined supervisory "impasses" as stalemates that lasted at least three to four weeks. As the authors acknowledge, this was a preliminary study that was limited by a relatively low response rate (23 of 44 psychiatric residents) and the use of an informal questionnaire. Nevertheless, it is interesting that 40% of the respondents reported having experienced at least one such impasse as supervisees. The usefulness of this descriptive study was in its cataloging of nine types of interpersonal problems between the supervisor and supervisee that led to impasses (e.g., boundary violations, lack of acceptance of a trainee's sexual identity, inhibition of disclosure of pertinent information).

Social Influence

The supervision literature driven by Strong's (1968; Strong & Matross, 1973) social influence model was reviewed a decade ago by Dixon and Claiborn (1987), and more recently by Stoltenberg,

McNeill, and Crethar (1995). In their review, Stoltenberg et al. noted that various studies have documented the effects that particular supervisor attributes have on ratings of their attractiveness, expertness, and trustworthiness, but that the efficacy of these cues in accomplishing actual attitudinal or behavioral change remains uninvestigated. These conclusions mirror those that have been reached about studies of social influence in counseling (see Heppner & Frazier, 1992).

There have been two recent proposals (Claiborn, Etringer, & Hillerbrand, 1995; Stoltenberg et al., 1995) to extend the social influence model in supervision to include Petty and Cacioppo's (1986) Elaboration Likelihood Model (ELM). With its more fully articulated propositions about the mechanisms of attitude change, the ELM has the potential to enrich and revitalize the social influence research. Perhaps by the next *Handbook* edition, the supervision literature will include empirical tests of ELM propositions.

INDIVIDUAL DIFFERENCES IN SUPERVISION AND TRAINING

Dawis (1992) effectively documented that individual differences have been an enduring concern of counseling psychologists. Although clients' aptitudes and traits have been given particular focus, individual differences related to such areas as gender, culture and race, and sexual orientation have been an important focus as well. For example, Ponterotto (1997) found that 89% of counseling psychology programs offer at least one multicultural counseling course, and Pope-Davis, Reynolds, Dings, and Nielson (1995) found that counseling psychology students rated themselves higher on several dimensions of multicultural competence than did clinical psychology students.

With respect to supervision and training, individual differences are of concern at two levels: that of the counselor-client relationship and that of the supervisor-supervisee. At each level, individual differences may affect the relationship between the involved parties. In the role of counselor, the trainee has particular responsibility to respond with appropriate sensitivity, knowledge, and skill to the client. The supervisor, in turn, must ensure that the trainee is fulfilling these responsibilities toward the client while *also* behaving in a parallel manner toward the trainee.

In the following subsections, we address the literature concerning five particular types of individual differences as they pertain to supervision and training: race and ethnicity, gender, sexual orientation, experience levels, and personality characteristics.

Race and Ethnicity in Training

Training in any domain requires target goals. Within the domain of multicultural counseling, the most widely employed goals are the competencies articulated by Sue et al. (1982) and later updated by Sue, Arredondoo, and McDavis (1992). Although links between these competencies and client outcomes are yet to be established empirically, they do have the force of expert judgement.

The training needs of minority students have been one focus of multicultural counselor training (cf. McNeill, Hom, & Perez, 1995). Educators, however, have also been concerned with preparing the White or Anglo counselor (e.g., Kiselica, 1998) to work with minority clients. Fowers and Richardson (1996) observed that some influential multiculturalists believe that all Whites are racist, whether they recognize it, and that the natural corollary is therefore that White trainees should undergo antiracism training (e.g., Corvin & Wiggins, 1989). This appears to be one purpose of multicultural training as it occurs in counseling psychology programs. At least two studies (Brown, Parham, & Yonker, 1996; Neville et al., 1996) now have documented that to take a multicultural counseling course increases the level of racial identity of White students.

This outcome is important because of the Helms (1990) hypothesis that higher levels of White racial identity correspond to lower levels of racism. Further support for its importance is given by

Ottavi, Pope-Davis, and Dings (1994), who found that levels of White racial identity explained variability in multicultural competencies beyond that which was accounted for by educational, demographic, and clinical variables. Ladany, Inman, Constantine, and Hofheinz (1997), on the other hand, found no significant relationship between racial identity levels (of either White or minority trainees) and trainees' consideration of multicultural issues during case conceptualization. These are not necessarily contradictory findings because of between-study differences in dependent measures: coding of written responses to a written client vignette (Ladany, Inman, et al., 1997) versus responses to a standardized measure (Ottavi et al., 1994). These tasks make different psychological demands on trainees and responses to a single written vignette may not be a satisfactory approximation of real-life behavior.

Race and Ethnicity in Supervision

Although a number of recent articles and books have addressed racial and ethnic differences within supervision at a conceptual level (e.g., Pope-Davis & Coleman, 1997), there have been surprisingly few studies. At the time of their respective reviews, Holloway (1992) was able to identify only a single study; Leong and Wagner (1994) were able to identify three. This literature is growing slowly; we were able to locate eight studies, two of which were qualitative.

Three studies have identified biases or difficulties that might exist, especially in dyads in which the supervisee is a minority group member. Vander Kolk (1974) found that, compared with their White counterparts, Black trainees anticipated that their supervisors would be less respectful, supportive, and empathic. McRoy, Freeman, Logan, and Blackmon (1986) found that a small but notable number of social work trainees (16%) and supervisors (28%) in cross-cultural supervisory relationships reported having had problems of a cross-cultural nature during supervision.

Cook and Helms's (1988) study of 225 Asian, Black, Hispanic, and Native American supervisees yielded relatively complicated findings. Although they obtained between-group differences in the extent to which trainees perceived their supervisors as being uncomfortable being with them and as providing unconditional liking of them, the lack of a White comparison group made it difficult to interpret the findings (Leong & Wagner, 1994).

Hilton, Russell, and Salmi (1995) obtained more encouraging results with respect to multiracial supervisory pairings. In their analogue study, undergraduate students counseled a coached client, receiving supervision from either a White or an African American supervisor (counseling psychology doctoral student) who offered either a high or a low level of support. In factorial ANOVAs (race of supervisor by level of support), main effects were obtained for level of support for the trainee ratings of the supervisory relationship, and for ratings of supervisor effectiveness and level of support. Importantly, there were no main effects for race on these measures; nor were there any race X support interactions.

Beutler, Brown, Crothers, Booker, and Seabrook (1996) discussed conceptual confusions that have occurred as researchers have used apparent biological identifiers such as race and sex. They argued for conceptual clarity, especially concerning the presumed psychological understructure of the particular term a researcher might be employing. It is possible that racial identity development may constitute such a psychological understructure and therefore be more salient than race in understanding cross-cultural supervision. In a study by Ladany, Brittan-Powell, et al. (1997), 105 counselor trainees completed racial identity measures for themselves and also estimated their supervisors' racial identity levels. Using a median-split, the authors then assigned trainees and supervisors to high- or low-racial identity categories and matched them into four groups: supervisor high/trainee low; supervisor low/trainee high; both high; and, both low. Racial matching was related to trainees' cross-cultural competence in that those supervised by a person of color scored higher on a competence measure than those with a White supervisor ($\eta^2 = .10$) [η^2, or eta squared, is the proportion of variance of the dependent variable that is accounted for by the independent variable]. Racial identity matching had a greater effect ($\eta^2 = .17$), however, than racial matching: Trainees supervised by someone they rated high in racial identity development (regardless of their own level of racial identity development) scored higher on a measure of cross-cultural competence. It also is noteworthy that whereas racial matching did not predict strength of working alliance, matching on level of racial identity did ($\eta^2 = .13$ for agreement on Goal/Task; .19 for Bond). Supervisors-trainee dyads in which both members were high on racial identity scored highest on these working alliance dimensions.

Finally, several studies have obtained convergent results with respect to trainees' preferences for cross-cultural supervision. Kleintjes and Swartz (1996) interviewed seven Black current and former trainees in a clinical psychology program within a historically White South African university. Respondents reported having valued two particular supervisor qualities: the ability to discuss racial issues in a matter-of-fact manner and the ability to help the trainee put concerns about race in perspective. Similarly, Fukuyama (1994) concluded her report of critical incidents and suggestions obtained from 18 racial-ethnic minority trainees with the recommendation that "supervisors initiate discussion of multicultural issues with supervisees" (p. 149). This also was the second most frequent answer given to an open-ended question that Duan, Roehlke, and Matchisky (1998) posed to 60 predoctoral interns concerning what contributed to their satisfaction with cross-cultural supervision (the most frequent response concerned feeling respected by their supervisors).

Within cross-cultural supervisory dyads, the majority of supervisors are White, whereas the majority of supervisees are racial or cultural minorities (Duan et al., 1998). This suggests that in addition to the power differential that supervisors have by virtue of their position, most of these supervisors *also* are working with supervisees who are sensitive to social power that traditionally has accrued to White people. For the supervisor to raise the issue of race or culture is the first step toward engaging one another in a constructive relationship based on mutual respect.

Gender and Supervision Processes

Worthington and Stern (1985) found male-male supervisory pairings to have the closest reported relationships, but Behling, Curtis, and Foster (1988) found just the opposite (i.e., that female-female dyads reported the closest relationships). These findings suggest that gender likely affects the quality of the supervisory relationship, although the particular patterns of these effects are not yet fully understood.

Two studies of actual supervisor-supervisee interactions indicate that gender configuration affects relational styles. Sells, Goodyear, Lichtenberg, and Polkinghorne (1997) found that conversations of female supervisor–male trainee dyads were significantly more relationship oriented (versus task oriented) than that of male supervisor–male trainee dyads. Nelson and Holloway (1990) found in sequential analyses that supervisors of both sexes were more reinforcing of male trainees' use of high power messages. They also found female trainees to be *less* likely than their male counterparts to make a high power statement following a supervisor's low power statement. Power in this study was defined as the degree of interpersonal influence a particular message would have according to Penman's (1980) system.

In summary, these few studies do suggest that supervisor and supervisee gender affects the supervisory relationship and specific processes that occur within it. With one exception, however, there has been no examination of the relationship of gender to supervision *outcomes*. Putney, Worthington, and McCullough (1992), when surveying interns in a variety of sites, found that women were perceived as more effective supervisors than were men. This provocative finding merits further exploration.

Eagly (1995) suggested that it is unlikely that the biological fact of being a woman or a man accounts for the sex differences that have been obtained in studies of social interactions. It is much more likely that these differences reflect learned social roles. Therefore, the next generation of studies might examine what specific behaviors or attitudes account for these sex differences. For example, with respect to the Putney et al. study: If those results were to be replicated, what did the women supervisors *do* differently from their male counterparts that affected the perception that they were more effective?

Gay and Lesbian Issues in Training and Supervision

Nearly 15 years ago, Carlson (1985) found that fewer than 10% of 303 surveyed department chairpersons reported that their clinical programs addressed lesbian and gay issues in their training. A few years later, Buhrke (1989) reported that almost one-third of surveyed doctoral-level graduate students reported never having received informal or formal training regarding gay or lesbian issues. A more recent study by Pilkington and Cantor (1996) suggests that gay and lesbian issues continue to receive inadequate coverage in graduate training programs.

To not cover gay or lesbian issues during training is an obvious act of omission. More problematic are the acts of commission that occur when instructors or supervisors actively exhibit gay- or lesbian-focused discrimination or bias. Pilkington and Cantor (1996) asked 64 student members of APA's Division 44 (Society for the Psychological Study of Lesbian and Gay Issues) to report up to four instances of such biases that occurred with respect to instructional materials or instructors. Students reported instances in which instructional materials and/or faculty members (1) pathologized gays and lesbians or homosexuality, (2) disparaged lesbian or gay clients or students, or (3) discussed "curing" homosexual behavior. Students also reported instances in which faculty members focused inappropriately on the sexual orientation of students or publicly disclosed a student's sexual orientation. A study of this type is important in documenting that a problem exists and the forms it may take. What it does not pinpoint, however, is either base rates or information about circumstances in which these problematic acts are likely to occur.

Gay and lesbian issues can confront supervisors at two levels: in their supervision of trainees' work with gay or lesbian clients and in their relationships with their supervisees. With respect to the former, Buhrke (1989) reported that, among a sample of doctoral-level graduate students, those who had counseled gay or lesbian clients rated supervision they had received for working with their homosexual clients to have been less helpful than that they received for their heterosexual clients. Research concerning the gay and lesbian issues as they occur within the supervisor-supervisee relationship itself, however, is still nonexistent.

Three analogue studies that focused on trainees (rather than on their faculty or supervisors) provide reassuring results. In one study, counseling and counseling psychology trainees who observed a video of a female client did not differ in their degree of liking for her whether she was introduced as lesbian or heterosexual (Liddle, 1995). In two studies of counseling and counseling psychology students, Gelso and his associates did not observe negative countertransference reactions (assessed in terms of cognitive, affective, and behavioral responses) to either actresses depicting heterosexual versus lesbian women clients (Gelso, Fassinger, Gomez, & Latts, 1995) or to actors depicting heterosexual versus gay male clients (Hayes & Gelso, 1993). In discussing their findings, Gelso et al. (1995) speculated that this might have occurred because trainees in their study scored one and half standard deviations below the mean of the normative sample on a measure of homophobia. Whereas these findings suggest some reason for optimism with respect to trainees' response to gay and lesbian clients, it is important to recognize that they were obtained with a sample at one university. In the absence of comparative data, it is not possible to know whether these findings concerning homophobia levels would generalize to trainees at other universities in other regions. Also, because the latter two studies were analogue in nature, it is difficult to know how the results concerning countertransference responses would generalize to real-life counseling and training settings.

Personality and Other Personal Style Issues

Over the past 50 years, researchers have made a number of attempts to link trainees' measured personality traits to training-related behaviors. Three particular questions have driven this research.

The first question has been whether it would be possible to identify trainee attributes or qualities that predict professional success. Attempts to use personality test data in this manner date back at least to the work of Kelly and Fiske (1951), and this remained an active area of research up until the 1970s. Scales on many instruments, including the Minnesota Multiphasic Personality Inventory (e.g., Arbuckle, 1956), the 16 Personality Factor Questionnaire (e.g., Forster & Hamburg, 1976), and the Omnibus Personality Inventory (e.g., Tinsley & Tinsley, 1977) have been examined for their predictive utility. Although individual studies have reported positive findings, the aggregated findings have not been regarded as sufficiently robust to inform admissions policies of training programs. In fact, Beutler, Machado, and Neufeldt (1994) concluded from their literature review that only a few therapist qualities have even a modest effect on therapeutic outcomes, one of those being the therapists' cognitive or conceptual level (e.g., Holloway, 1992; Holloway & Wampold, 1986).

The second question has concerned possible links between trainees' personality test data and counseling styles. An early study of this type was that of Asa (1967) who found that scores on the Dominance scale of the Edwards Personal Preference Schedule were correlated with trainees' use of "probing/projecting" interchanges. Perhaps the best-known research program of this type, however, was stimulated by the hypothesis that it is possible to differentiate two types of therapist on the basis of a 23-item scale Whitehorn and Betz (1960) developed from responses to the Strong Vocational Interest Blank. One type was hypothesized to work better with schizophrenic clients; the other, with neurotic clients. Reviewers (e.g., Carson, 1967) were optimistic about the potential usefulness of this differentiation, and at least some counseling psychologists (e.g., Stoltenberg & Dixon, 1983) employed it in their work. Eventually, however, this research program ran its course, with little evidence of its use for training programs.

The third research question has concerned the link between particular trainee attributes and their interactions with supervisors (rather than with clients). Tracey, Ellickson, and Sherry (1989), for example, examined reactance potential (the tendency to respond in an oppositional manner when a person perceives that his or her freedom has been constrained) as a moderator of supervisees' interaction styles in relationship to their supervisors. Their finding that reactance levels predicted trainees' preference for level of structure in supervision was a promising one. Only one additional study has examined this construct. Although Stoltenberg et al. (1996) found that general reactance of trainees had no relationship to predicted satisfaction with supervision, they did obtain a negative relationship between a supervision-specific reactance measure and satisfaction with supervision. Their additional finding that supervision-specific reactance correlated positively with trainee experience can be understood as supporting the developmental notion that more advanced trainees prefer less structure (e.g., Stoltenberg, McNeill, & Delworth, 1998).

Cognitive style is another trainee characteristic that has been examined as a moderator of trainees' relationship to their supervisor. The measure most often used has been the Myers-Briggs Type Indicator (MBTI); however, one study (Lochner & Melchert, 1997) employed the Keirsey Temperament Sorter as an alternative to the MBTI.

Handley (1982) found that trainee scores on the Sensing-Intuition (S-N) index (i.e., higher scores in the intuitive direction) were related to supervisors' perceptions of the quality of the supervisory relationship, satisfaction with trainee performance, and to evaluation of trainees (r^2 of .19, .22, and .22 respectively). In a partial replication, however, Carey and Williams (1986) found no significant relationship between trainees' cognitive style and supervisors' evaluations of them ($r^2 = .07$). In commenting on the between-study differences in results, Carey and Williams noted Handley's failure to correct for experimental-wise Type I error and therefore the possibility of spurious findings. Perhaps the best assessment at this point is that the relationship between S-N and trainee evaluations is inconclusive.

Several studies have examined the relationship between supervisee cognitive style and their preferences for supervisory style. Although Swanson and O'Saben (1993) found in 4 of 10 hierarchical regression analyses (among more than 235 statistical tests) that individual MBTI scales correlated with one or another perception of the supervisory environment, the block of MBTI scores was not significant in any of the analyses (and therefore precluded interpretation of significance obtained on any of the individual scales). In a canonical correlation analysis, Lochner and Melchert (1997) obtained two significant canonical functions. The canonical loadings for the first function indicated that high Sensing (low Intuition) and high Judgment (low Perception) and high Thinking (low Feeling) scores were associated with interns' preferences for task-oriented supervision (and less interpersonally sensitive supervision). Canonical correlations for the second function indicated that high Thinking (low Feeling), high Extraversion (low Introversion), and high Perception (low Judgment) scores were associated with interns' preferences for low levels of supervisor attractiveness (i.e., perceived similarity). Schacht, Howe, and Berman (1989) found that Feeling type trainees rated supervisors who they believe contributed most to their therapeutic effectiveness as significantly higher on facilitative conditions than did their Thinking type counterparts.

An important question in this line of research concerns the possibility of matching supervisor and supervisee with respect to cognitive style. Handley (1982), for example, found that cognitive style similarity between trainee and supervisor on the S-N dimension predicted higher ratings of the supervisory relationship by the supervisor.

The small but steady volume of supervision research devoted to cognitive style over the past 15 years reflects the interest that many supervision practitioners have in this topic. These several studies suggest that at least a few dimensions (especially those of Sensing-Intuition and Thinking-Feeling) are promising enough as predictors of supervisor and supervisee relationships that they merit continued exploration. Ellis and Ladany (1997) raised the important question of whether these particular cognitive styles are state or trait related within the supervisory context. All extant research has assumed traitlike dimensions.

SUPERVISEE AND SUPERVISOR DEVELOPMENT

Supervisee Development

Probably no other notion has dominated the supervision literature over the past two decades more than that trainees change with experience and training and that those changes make corresponding demands on supervisory environments. This concept was expressed in a number of models, most proposed during the late 1970s and early 1980s. Worthington (1987) was able to identify 16 such models and Watkins (1995c) later identified six more. Holloway (1987) observed a decade ago that "developmental models of supervision have become the Zeitgeist of supervision thinking and research" (p. 209).

Surprisingly, there is little new to report with respect to either models or research beyond what was reviewed by Holloway (1992) in the last edition of the *Handbook*. Perhaps the most interesting development has been the rigorous review of that literature by Ellis and Ladany (1997) who characterized it as a "disheartening experience." That is, they found that methodological problems and failures to eliminate rival hypotheses have so characterized this area of research that "data from these studies are largely uninterpretable . . . [and] little viable information about supervisee development has been gained" (p. 483). They acknowledged, however, that their conclusions differ from those of other recent reviewers (e.g., Holloway, 1992; Stoltenberg, McNeill, & Crethar, 1994).

The trainee development literature generally has not been concerned with whether trainees obtain better client outcomes as they gain more training and experience. Yet this is the assumption on which the entire training enterprise is built. Until quite recently, reviewers of the literature have concluded that level or amount of graduate education has little effect on therapeutic effectiveness (see, for example, Christensen & Jacobsen, 1994, and Dawes, 1994 for summaries of those reviews). Stein and Lambert (1995), however, were able to conclude from their meta-analysis that there was "modest but consistent" evidence for training effects for a number of client-improvement and satisfaction measures. These were the most positive conclusions to date about the effects of training. Even so, Stein and Lambert (1995) ended their article by observing that "given the enormous, national investment of physical and human resources in graduate programs, it is quite remarkable that more compelling evidence is not available that demonstrates that graduate training directly relates to enhanced therapy outcomes" (p. 194).

Supervisor Development

Research interest in trainee development may have slowed, but interest in supervisor development seems on the increase. Since Holloway's (1992) review, the several supervisor development models (Alonso, 1983; Hess, 1987; Stoltenberg et al., 1998) have been supplemented by two additional ones (Rodenhauser, 1994; Watkins, 1993c) and at least two reviews of the literature concerning supervisor development (Russell & Petrie, 1994; Watkins, 1995c). This apparent increase in interest has not, however, been matched by corresponding research. In fact, Russell and Petrie (1994) concluded from their literature review that research on supervisor development has been "virtually nonexistent" (p. 35), even though the several models do allow for specific hypotheses that might be tested.

A matter closely associated with supervisor development is the relationship between experience (both general clinical experience and specific experience as a supervisor) and supervisory competence. As Russell and Petrie's (1994) review indicated, not much research has been done on this topic since the review by Worthington (1987), who concluded that once supervisors achieve some very minimal levels of clinical experience, they function as well as highly experienced supervisors. The American Association of State Psychology Boards (1997) recently adopted the position that a psychologist should be licensed for three years before being allowed to supervise. This seems to be a clear instance in which "common sense" (that clinical experience correlates with supervisory effectiveness) has no empirical support.

EVALUATION

The fact that supervisors have evaluative responsibilities toward their trainees is a key difference between supervision and counseling (Bernard & Goodyear, 1998). This evaluative or monitoring function therefore has been central in many conceptions of supervision (e.g., Carroll, 1996; Holloway, 1992; A. Williams, 1995). Evaluation also is at the heart of our profession's implicit contract with society to control who is admitted to practice. For these reasons, it is significant that Ellis and Ladany (1997) recently concluded that "supervisee evaluation is one area of supervision that needs much attention" (p. 484).

Two particular issues are salient to evaluation in supervision. The first issue concerns the accuracy of supervisors' evaluations; the second concerns effects of evaluation on the supervision process.

Evaluation Accuracy

Ellis and Ladany (1997) suggested that one source of error in evaluating supervisees is at the level of measurement. They noted that most trainee evaluation is done in a qualitative manner, and that even supervisors who want to use a more standardized instrument would have difficulty obtaining one with suitable conceptual and psychometric qualities.

The reliance on qualitative ratings amplifies the risk of bias in assessment. A.R. Harkness and Lilienfeld (1997) proposed the term "clinical hermeneutics error" to describe the phenomenon whereby therapists so adopt their clients' perspective during treatment that they lose track of what is normative behavior and thereby underestimate the clients' level of pathology. It is easy to see how an analogous process might occur during supervision as well, perhaps even to a greater extent than in counseling.

Carey, Williams, and Wells (1988) and Dodenhoff (1981) found that supervisors' inflated their evaluations of trainees when they liked them. Borders and Fong (1991) found no significant relationships between supervisors' and external observers' ratings of supervisees at three different levels of training. This might be explained by the two groups' use of different scales to rate the supervisees or by one group having had multiple observations of the supervisee whereas the other group had a single behavior sample. Nevertheless, it seems significant that although ratings of external observers showed a linear trend whereby evaluations of trainees progressed upward according to trainee level, supervisors' ratings dipped for the middle level of trainees. Such findings suggest that supervisors' interactions with trainees during supervision sessions affects their overall ratings of the trainee.

Evaluation Effects

The fact of being an evaluator gives the supervisor a level of power that might be used to encourage trainees to engage in particular behaviors (Bernard & Goodyear, 1998). In this way, evaluation can be used for good purposes. It is the negative consequences of evaluation, however, that are of more concern. For example, Burke et al. (1998) observed instances in which the supervisor made evaluative interventions that resulted in breaches in the supervisory alliance that were not repaired during the session in which it had occurred. In Ladany, Hill, Corbett, and Nutt's (1996) study of the prevalence, content, and motivation of material that supervisees chose not to disclose to their supervisors, they observed that one motivation for nondisclosing seemed to be the supervisees' wish to manage the impressions they were making on their supervisors: The evaluative context of supervision certainly would heighten this motivation and, therefore, increase the amount of information they would withhold about thoughts, feelings, or behaviors that might give an unfavorable impression to the supervisor. Given the real and imagined consequences that evaluation has in trainees' lives, it is not surprising that Ladany, Lehrman-Waterman, Molinaro, and Wolgast (1999) found that issues with respect to monitoring and evaluating trainees were among the categories of ethical breaches that trainees reported most frequently.

TRAINING, SUPERVISION, AND EMPIRICALLY SUPPORTED TREATMENTS

The movement to identify and promulgate empirically validated (or empirically supported; EST) treatments (see Task Force, 1995) has been an important professional trend (see the chapter by Wampold, this volume). Davison (1998) has characterized the EST movement as a juggernaut that not only is affecting practice, but training as well. This is reflected, for example, in the APA's accreditation guidelines (APA, 1996) that now stipulate training in ESTs.

The attribute of ESTs most likely to affect training and supervision is that they are manual-based. More than a decade ago, Lambert and Arnold (1987) pointed out that the use of manuals has the potential to:

> (a) standardize (to a greater degree) the treatment being offered and thus allow for more concrete interventions by supervisors, (b) provide a method of training and supervising therapists to ensure that they offer a standard treatment, (c) allow for the development of rating scales to judge whether a therapy is being properly offered and thereby alert the supervisor and trainee to the need for further supervision with specific interventions. (pp. 220–221)

Counterbalancing these possible benefits are several areas that merit supervisory caution. For example, Henry, Strupp, Butler, Schacht, and Binder (1993) found that using a manual for training in time-limited dynamic psychotherapy successfully changed therapists' technical interventions, but that it had unexpected negative effects on the therapists' relationships with their clients. Specifically, the therapists became less optimistic, more authoritative and defensive, and less approving and supportive.

Fortunately, Multon, Kivlighan, and Gold (1996) subsequently obtained results that seemed to qualify the Henry et al. findings. Using the same time-limited, dynamic therapy model, Multon et al. found that trainees were able to achieve stronger working alliances with their clients even as they demonstrated increasing adherence to the manual's interviewing style. An important difference between the two studies was that whereas the trainees in the Henry et al. study were experienced therapists, those in the Multon et al. study were novices. Perhaps teaching graduate students manual-based treatments has different meaning and effects than is the case with more experienced therapists. In particular, the specific focus on skills that is required in supervising manualized treatment is consistent with the preference of beginning trainees and their supervisors.

Another area of supervisory caution stems from an otherwise positive aspect of manualized treatments. That is, the clear-cut criteria for evaluating trainee's conceptualizations and interventions can be very useful for supervisors (see, e.g., Rounsaville, O'Malley, Foley, & Weissman, 1988; Weiss & Marmar, 1993). But a reasonable concern is that supervisors of manualized treatments might rely too rigidly on measures of trainee compliance in their evaluations of trainees. In this context, it is important to note that Rounsaville et al. found that the degree to which therapists adhered to manual guidelines was not a major determinant of supervisor judgements of their skill. They found, in fact, that therapists tended to deviate from manual guidelines when working with more difficult patients and that supervisors found such deviations to be acceptable.

Holloway and Neufeldt (1995) suggested that the quality of the supervisory relationship should affect the level of trainees' adherence to a treatment manual. Patton and Kivlighan (1997) tested this hypothesis by examining the relationship between supervisor-supervisee working alliances and level of trainee compliance with a treatment manual for time-limited dynamic psychotherapy (TLDP; Strupp & Binder, 1984). They found that supervisory working alliance accounted for 27% of the variance in supervisor ratings of trainee compliance with the manualized treatment. The authors acknowledged, however, that it was not possible to determine directionality of effects and, therefore, it is possible that the quality of trainees' learning affected the working alliance.

Lambert and Ogles (1997) suggested that one unexamined area is the comparative effectiveness of supervision versus reading the treatment manual:

> Perhaps supervision is the more important aspect of training with manuals, and manuals are really not superior to any other book on psychotherapy theory. This will undoubtedly depend on the particular treatment that is under consideration as some are much more explicit than others, and some are more easily implemented than others. (p. 433)

Given the prominent role that manual-based treatments are likely to continue to have in the future, it seems imperative that more research be conducted to examine their training and supervision implications. It also seems inevitable that a parallel development would be manual-guided supervision. As was noted earlier in this chapter, the several prominent counseling skills training programs are manualized. To date, there has been only a single attempt to manualize the practice of supervision (Neufeldt et al., 1995).

CONCLUDING OBSERVATIONS

We have reviewed research concerning the more central topics in supervision research and theory. In concluding this chapter, we address a few questions regarding how that research is being conducted, with some attention to new directions.

Methodological Rigor

In the first edition of the *Handbook,* Russell et al. (1984) assessed the supervision research literature through 1981, evaluating each study in terms of 12 threats to validity (six internal; six external). Ellis, Ladany, Krengel, and Schult (1996) subsequently reviewed studies published between 1981 and 1993, hypothesizing that there would be a significant reduction in the proportion of studies that demonstrated each of these 12 validity threats. Using one-tailed z tests of proportions, they contrasted proportions obtained in the Russell et al. sample with those obtained in their more recent sample.

Ellis et al. found no between-period differences in the proportion of studies that had (1) lack of adequate controls, (2) no pretreatment assessment, and (3) confounded treatment length. Their hypotheses were confirmed for five comparisons, all concerning decreased threats to external validity. That is, in the later period, there were fewer studies with: (1) a restricted range of dependent variables, (2) nonrepresentative supervisee or supervisor population, (3) lack of follow-up assessment, (4) use of role-play or audiotaped client statements to assess supervised changes, and (5) overly brief training period.

Ellis et al. also found in 4 of the 12 comparisons that between-period differences were significant in the direction opposite to what had been hypothesized. That is, during the later period there had been an *increase* in the proportion of studies that demonstrated: (1) inadequate sample size, (2) nonrandom assignment to conditions, (3) widely discrepant cell sizes, and (4) exclusive reliance on self-report data. The first three of these concerned internal validity; the fourth, external validity.

In a subsequent study that replicated and extended that of Ellis et al. (1996), using a substantially overlapping sample, Ellis and Ladany (1997) examined a number of characteristics of the supervision research studies that had been published since 1981. Several of their key observations are summarized here.

In further analyzing,

> The 6 most pervasive threats or plausible explanations for the pattern of results across the studies reviewed here are experimentwise Type I error (76%); measures not psychometrically sound (64%); experimentwise Type II error (51%); samples neither random nor representative of the target population (39%); nonrandom assignment to treatment conditions (38%); and clear inconsistencies among the purpose, hypotheses, design-methods, and analyses (29%). (p. 459)

For the 104 supervision studies they reviewed, Ellis and Ladany (1997) reported that the median sample effect size (η^2), was .073, with an estimated median population effect size of .048 (this suggests that the independent variables accounted for 4.8% of the variance in the dependent variable across all studies). This was comparable to the estimated median population effect size of .05 for counseling psychology research in general observed in Haase, Ellis, and Ladany's (1989) review of articles published between 1970–1979 in the *Journal of Counseling Psychology.* In both the Ellis and Ladany (1997) and the Haase et al. (1989) reviews, the independent and dependent variables were those reported by the authors of the particular studies under review. Unfortunately, Ellis and Ladany (1997) also concluded that the statistical power was "meager," so that there was less than a 26% chance of detecting an effect that existed in the population, even with the medium level of population effect size (.048).

Much supervision research has relied on instruments developed for counseling research, but then adapted for supervision research (usually by reworking the items with simple word substitutions, such as "supervisor" for "counselor"). This has been problematic both because it imposes a counseling frame on supervision research and because the resulting measures have unknown psychometric properties. It is a measure of supervision research's growing maturity that there increasingly are measures developed specifically for supervision. Ellis and Ladany (1997) reviewed seven of these, finding that two were sufficiently well developed to recommend their use in both supervisory practice and research. These were the Role Conflict and Role Ambiguity Inventory (Olk & Friedlander, 1992) and a short form of the Barrett-Lennard Relationship Inventory developed specifically for clinical supervision (Schacht, Howe, & Berman, 1988).

Qualitative Research

One recent trend has been the rapid increase in the number of supervision and training studies employing qualitative methods. There were virtually none at the time of the last *Handbook,* but at least 10 studies with qualitative features have been published in recent years: Caldwell, Becvar, Bertolino, and Diamond (1997); Fukuyama (1994); Mauzey and Erdman (1997); Kleintjes and Swartz (1996); Neufeldt, Karno, and Nelson (1996); Smith, Winton, and Yoshioka (1992); Smith, Yoshioka, Winton (1993); E.N. Williams et al. (1997); Skovholt and Ronnestad (1992); and, Worthen and McNeill (1996).

The increasing volume of qualitative research concerning supervision reflects a broader trend in psychology, and in counseling psychology in particular (see Morrow & Smith, this volume). In an informal study, we searched the web site of full text articles of APA journals (going back three years), using the search words "qualitative" and "research." We found that 13 journals had published 30 such articles and that eight of these had been published in the *Journal of Counseling Psychology.* The journal with the second-highest frequency was *Professional Psychology: Research and Practice,* with four articles—two of which had been authored by counseling psychologists.

Evaluating the merit of qualitative studies is more difficult than is the case with quantitative studies. Although there are well-established conventions for evaluating quantitative studies, such conventions are much less well defined for qualitative studies. Moreover, as Hill, Thompson, and Williams (1997) have pointed out, they are grounded in a different epistemology than quantitative methods; therefore, concerns about reliability and validity are addressed in different ways. Perhaps as standards such as those suggested by Hill et al. (1997) become more widely understood and employed, a greater proportion of this research will allow trustworthy inferences to be made.

CONCLUSION

That each edition of the *Handbook* has included a chapter reviewing supervision and training literature offers "snapshots" at successive points in time. This enables a clearer appreciation of the progression of knowledge. For example, during the period between the publication of the first review (Russell et al., 1984) sufficient evidence has accrued to support educators' use of the several major counselor skills training models.

These successive snapshots also provide documentation of shifts in research emphasis across time. For example, we noted earlier in this chapter that whereas research on trainee development had been active for more than a decade, there has been little recent activity. On the other hand, it has been possible to observe increases in research activity on other topics, such as supervisory working alliances and cross-cultural supervision.

No chapter-length review could address the entire range of topics in the supervision and training literature. We were forced, therefore, to omit a number of otherwise worthy topics and developments (e.g., Larson's, 1998, new training model). As well, there were topics that were not reviewed because of a near-absence of literature. These included some established areas of supervisory practice, such as group or live supervision (two exceptions are Heppner et al., 1994; Kivlighan et al., 1991). They also included new areas that we anticipate soon *will* have a research literature. One example is between-country comparisons of supervisory traditions and practices (e.g., Holloway, 1998).

In summary, the supervision and training literature is dynamic, robust, and responsive to needs of the field (e.g., the increasing attention to cross-cultural supervision). The persistent methodological problems that have been documented (e.g., Ellis & Ladany, 1997; Russell et al., 1984) certainly merit continued attention. Nevertheless, supervision literature continues to add incrementally to our knowledge and therefore to inform practice.

REFERENCES

Abbott, A. (1988). *The system of professions.* Chicago: University of Chicago Press.

Alberts, G., & Edelstein, B. (1990). Therapist training: A critical review of skill training studies. *Clinical Psychology Review, 10,* 497–511.

Alonso, A. (1983). A developmental theory of psychodynamic supervision. *The Clinical Supervisor, 1*(3), 23–26.

Alpher, V.S. (1991). Interdependence and parallel processes: A case study of structural analysis of social behavior in supervision and short-term dynamic psychotherapy. *Psychotherapy, 28,* 218–231.

American Psychological Association. (1996). *Guidelines and principles for accreditation of programs in professional psychology.* Washington, DC: Author.

Arbuckle, D.S. (1956). Client perception of counselor personality. *Journal of Counseling Psychology, 3,* 93–96.

Asa, L. (1967). Interview behavior and counselor personality variables. *Counselor Education and Supervision, 6,* 324–330.

Baker, S.D., & Daniels, T.G. (1989). Integrating research on the microcounseling program. *Journal of Counseling Psychology, 36,* 213–222.

Baker, S.D., Daniels, T.G., & Greeley, A.T. (1990). Systematic training of graduate-level counselors: Narrative and meta-analytic reviews of three major programs. *The Counseling Psychologist, 18,* 355–420.

Behling, J., Curtis, C., & Foster, S.A. (1988). Impact of sex-role combinations on student performance in field instruction. *The Clinical Supervisor, 6*(3), 161–168.

Bernard, J.M. (1997). The discrimination model. In C.E. Watkins, Jr. (Ed.), *Handbook of psychotherapy supervision* (pp. 310–327). New York: Wiley.

Bernard, J.M., & Goodyear, R.K. (1998). *Fundamentals of clinical supervision* (2nd ed.). Boston: Allyn & Bacon.

Beutler, L.E., Brown, M.T., Crothers, L., Booker, K., & Seabrook, M.K. (1996). The dilemma of factitious demographic distinctions in psychological research. *Journal of Consulting and Clinical Psychology, 64,* 892–902.

Beutler, L.E., & Kendall, P.C. (1995). Introduction to the special section: The case for training in the provision of psychological therapy. *Journal of Consulting and Clinical Psychology, 63,* 179–181.

Beutler, L.E., Machado, P., & Neufeldt, S.A. (1994). Therapist's variables. In A. Bergin & S. Garfield (Eds.), *Handbook of psychotherapy and behavior change* (4th ed., pp. 229–269). New York: Wiley.

Borders, L.D., & Fong, M.L. (1991). Evaluations of supervisees: Brief commentary and research report. *The Clinical Supervisor, 9*(2), 43–51.

Bordin, E.S. (1983). A working alliance model of supervision. *The Counseling Psychologist, 11,* 35–42.

Brown, S.P., Parham, T.A., & Yonker, R. (1996). Influence of a cross cultural training course on racial identity attitudes of white women and men: Preliminary perspectives. *Journal of Counseling and Development, 74,* 510–516.

Buhrke, R.A. (1989). Female student perspectives on training in lesbian and gay issues. *The Counseling Psychologist, 17,* 629–636.

Burke, W.R., Goodyear, R.K., & Guzzard, C.R. (1998). Weakenings and repairs in the supervisory alliance: A multiple-case study. *American Journal of Psychotherapy, 52,* 450–462.

Caldwell, K., Becvar, D.S., Bertolino, R., & Diamond, D. (1997). A postmodern analysis of a course on clinical supervision. *Contemporary Family Therapy: An International Journal, 19,* 269–287.

Calia, V.F. (1974). Systematic human relations training: Appraisal and status. *Counselor Education and Supervision, 14,* 85–94.

Carey, J.C., & Williams, K.S. (1986). Cognitive style in counselor education: A comparison of practicum supervisors and counselors in training. *Counselor Education and Supervision, 26,* 128–136.

Carey, J.C., Williams, K.S., & Wells, M. (1988). Relationships between dimensions of supervisors' influence and counselor trainees' performance. *Counselor Education and Supervision, 28,* 130–139.

Carkhuff, R.R., & Truax, C.B. (1965). Training in counseling and psychotherapy: An evaluation of an integrated didactic and experiential approach. *Journal of Consulting Psychology, 29,* 333–336.

Carlson, H. (1985, August). *Employment issues for researchers on lesbian and gay issues.* Paper presented at the annual meeting of the American Psychological Association, Los Angeles.

Carroll, M. (1996). *Counseling supervision: Theory, skills, and practice.* London: Cassell.

Carson, R.C. (1967). A and B therapist "types": A possible critical variable in psychotherapy. *Journal of Nervous & Mental Disease, 144,* 47–54.

Christensen, A., & Jacobsen, N.S. (1994). Who (or what) can do psychotherapy: The status and challenge of nonprofessional therapies. *Psychological Science, 5,* 8–14.

Claiborn, C.D., Etringer, B.D., & Hillerbrand, E.T. (1995). Influence processes in supervision. *Counselor Education and Supervision, 35,* 43–53.

Cook, D.A., & Helms, J.E. (1988). Visible racial/ethnic group supervisees' satisfaction with cross-cultural supervision as predicted by relationship characteristics. *Journal of Counseling Psychology, 35,* 268–274.

Corrigan, P.W., Hess, L., & Garman, A.N. (1998). Results of a job analysis of psychologists working in state hospitals. *Journal of Clinical Psychology, 54,* 11–18.

Corvin, S., & Wiggins, F. (1989). An antiracism training model for white professionals. *Journal of Multicultural Counseling and Development, 17,* 105–114.

Cruess, S.R., & Cruess, R.L. (1997). Professionalism must be taught. *British Medical Journal (International), 315,* 1674–1677.

Danish, S.J., & Hauer, A. (1973). *Helping skills: A basic training program.* New York: Behavioral.

Davison, G.C. (1998). Being bolder with the Boulder model: The challenge of education and training in empirically supported treatments. *Journal of Consulting and Clinical Psychology, 66,* 153–167.

Dawes, R.M. (1994). *House of cards: Psychology and psychotherapy built on myth.* New York: Free Press.

Dawis, R.V. (1992). The individual differences tradition in counseling psychology. *Journal of Counseling Psychology, 39,* 7–19.

Dixon, D.N., & Claiborn, C.D. (1987). A social influence approach to counselor supervision. In J.E. Maddux, C.D. Stoltenberg, & R. Rosenwein (Eds.), *Social processes in clinical and counseling psychology* (pp. 83–93). New York: Springer-Verlag.

Dodenhoff, J.T. (1981). Interpersonal attraction and direct-indirect supervisor influence as predictors of counselor trainee effectiveness. *Journal of Counseling Psychology, 28,* 47–52.

Doehrman, M. (1976). Parallel processes in supervision and psychotherapy. *Bulletin of the Menninger Clinic, 40,* 3–104.

Duan, C., Roehlke, H., & Matchisky, D.J. (1998, August). *National survey of cross-cultural supervision: When the supervisor and the supervisee are different in race.* Paper presented at the annual meeting of the American Psychological Association, San Francisco.

Eagly, A.H. (1995). The science and politics of comparing women and men. *American Psychologist, 50,* 145–158.

Efstation, J.F., Patton, M.J., & Kardash, C.M. (1990). Measuring the working alliance in counselor supervision. *Journal of Counseling Psychology, 37,* 322–329.

Ellis, M.V., & Ladany, N. (1997). Inferences concerning supervisees and clients in clinical supervision: An integrative review. In C.E. Watkins, Jr. (Ed.), *Handbook of psychotherapy supervision* (pp. 447–507). New York: Wiley.

Ellis, M.V., Ladany, N., Krengel, M., & Schult, D. (1996). Clinical supervision research from 1981 to 1993: A methodological critique. *Journal of Counseling Psychology, 43,* 35–50.

Finkelstein, H., & Tuckman, A. (1997). Supervision of psychological assessment: A developmental model. *Professional Psychology: Research and Practice, 28,* 92–95.

Fitzgerald, L.E., & Osipow, S.H. (1986). An occupational analysis of counseling psychology: How special is the specialty? *American Psychologist, 41,* 535–544.

Ford, J.D. (1979). Research on training counselors and clinicians. *Review of Educational Research, 49,* 87–130.

Forster, J.R., & Hamburg, R.L. (1976). Further exploration of the 16-PF and counselor effectiveness. *Counselor Education and Supervision, 15,* 184–188.

Fowers, B.J., & Richardson, F.C. (1996). Why is multiculturalism good? *American Psychologist, 51,* 609–621.

Frayn, D.H. (1991). Supervising the supervisors: The evolution of a psychotherapy supervisors' group. *American Journal of Psychotherapy, 45,* 31–42.

Freud, S. (1986). On the history of the psychoanalytic movement. In *Historical and Expository Works on Psychoanalysis.* Harmondsworth, England: Penguin. (Original work published 1914)

Friedlander, M.L., Siegel, S.M., & Brenock, K. (1989). Parallel process in counseling and supervision: A case study. *Journal of Counseling Psychology, 36,* 149–157.

Fukuyama, M.A. (1994). Critical incidents in multicultural counseling supervision: A phenomenological approach to supervision. *Counselor Education and Supervision, 34,* 142–151.

Garfield, S.L., & Kurtz, R.M. (1976). Clinical psychologists in the 1970s. *American Psychologist, 31,* 1–9.

Gelso, C.J., Fassinger, R.E., Gomez, M.J., & Latts, M.G. (1995). Countertransference reactions to lesbian clients. *Journal of Counseling Psychology, 42,* 356–364.

Goodyear, R.K., & Bernard, J.M. (1998). Clinical supervision: Lessons from the literature. *Counselor Education and Supervision, 38,* 6–22.

Haase, R.F., Ellis, M.V., & Ladany, N. (1989). Multiple criteria for evaluating the magnitude of effects. *Journal of Counseling Psychology, 36,* 511–516.

Handley, P. (1982). Relationship between supervisors' and trainees' cognitive styles and the supervision process. *Journal of Counseling Psychology, 29,* 508–515.

Harkness, A.R., & Lilienfeld, S.O. (1997). Individual differences science for treatment planning: Personality traits. *Psychological Assessment, 9,* 349–360.

Harkness, D., & Poertner, A. (1989). Research and social work supervision: A conceptual review. *Social Work, 34,* 115–119.

Hayes, J.A., & Gelso, C.J. (1993). Male counselors' discomfort with gay and HIV-infected clients. *Journal of Counseling Psychology, 40,* 86–93.

Helms, J.E. (1990). *Black and white racial identity: Theory, research, and practice.* Westport, CT: Greenwood Press.

Henry, W.P., Strupp, H.H., Butler, S.F., Schacht, T.E., & Binder, J.L. (1993). Effects of training in time-limited dynamic psychotherapy: Changes in therapist behavior. *Journal of Consulting and Clinical Psychology, 61,* 434–440.

Heppner, P.P., & Frazier, P.A. (1992). Social psychological processes in psychotherapy: Extrapolating basic research to counseling psychology. In S.D. Brown & R.W. Lent (Eds.), *Handbook of counseling psychology* (2nd ed., pp. 141–175). New York: Wiley.

Heppner, P.P., Kivlighan, D.M., Burnett, J.W., Berry, T.R., Goedinhaus, M., Doxsee, D.J., Hendricks, F.M., Krull, L.A., Wright, G.E., Bellatin, A.M., Durham, R.J., Tharp, A., Kim, H., Brossart, D.F., Wang, L., Witty, T.E., Kinder, M.H., Hertel, J.B., & Wallace, D.L. (1994). Dimensions that characterize supervisor interventions delivered in the context of live supervision of practicum counselors. *Journal of Counseling Psychology, 41,* 227–235.

Hess, A.K. (1987). Psychotherapy supervision: Stages, Buber, and a theory of relationship. *Professional Psychology: Research and Practice, 18,* 251–259.

Hill, C.E., Thompson, B.J., & Williams, E.N. (1997). A guide to conducting consensual qualitative research. *The Counseling Psychologist, 25,* 517–572.

Hilton, D.B., Russell, R.K., & Salmi, S.W. (1995). The effects of supervisor's race and level of support on perceptions of supervision. *Journal of Counseling and Development, 73,* 559–563.

Holloway, E.L. (1984). Outcome evaluation in supervision research. *The Counseling Psychologist, 12,* 167–174.

Holloway, E.L. (1987). Developmental models of supervision: Is it supervision? *Professional Psychology: Research and Practice, 18,* 209–216.

Holloway, E.L. (1992). Supervision: A way of teaching and learning. In S.D. Brown & R.W. Lent (Eds.), *Handbook of counseling psychology* (pp. 177–214). New York: Wiley.

Holloway, E.L. (1998, July 26). *Reciprocal responsibility in supervision.* Presentation to the British Association of Supervision Practice and Research, London.

Holloway, E.L., & Carroll, M. (1996). Reaction to the special section on supervision research: Comment on Ellis et al (1996), Ladany et al. (1996), Neufeldt et al. (1996), and Worhten & McNeill (1996). *Journal of Counseling Psychology, 43,* 51–55.

Holloway, E.L., & Johnston, R. (1985). Group supervision: Widely practiced but poorly understood. *Counselor Education and Supervision, 24,* 332–340.

Holloway, E.L., & Neufeldt, S.A. (1995). Supervision: Its contributions to treatment efficacy. *Journal of Consulting and Clinical Psychology, 63,* 207–213.

Holloway, E.L., & Wampold, B.E. (1986). Relation between conceptual level and counseling-related tasks: A meta-analysis. *Journal of Counseling Psychology, 33,* 310–319.

Horvath, A.O., & Symonds, D.B. (1991). Relationship between working alliance and outcome in psychotherapy: A meta-analysis. *Journal of Counseling Psychology, 38,* 139–149.

Ivey, A.E., Normington, C.J., Miller, D.C., Merrill, W.H., & Haase, R.F. (1968). Microcounseling and attending behavior: An approach to prepracticum counselor training [Monograph]. *Journal of Counseling Psychology, 15*(Suppl.), 1–12.

Kagan, N.I., & Krathwohl, D.R. (1967). *Studies in human interaction: Interpersonal process recall stimulated by videotape.* East Lansing: Michigan State University.

Kelly, E.L., & Fiske, D.W. (1951). *The prediction of performance in clinical psychology.* Ann Arbor: University of Michigan Press.

Kiselica, M.S. (1998). Preparing anglos for the challenges and joys of multiculturalism. *The Counseling Psychologist, 26,* 5–21.

Kivlighan, D.M., Angelone, E.O., & Swafford, K.G. (1991). Live supervision in individual psychotherapy: Effects on therapist's intention use and client's evaluation of session effect and working alliance. *Professional Psychology: Research and Practice, 22,* 489–495.

Kleintjes, S., & Swartz, L. (1996). Black clinical psychology trainees at a "White" South African university: Issues for clinical supervision. *Clinical Supervisor, 14,* 87–109.

Ladany, N., Brittan-Powell, C.S., & Pannu, R.K. (1997). The influence of supervisory racial identity interaction and racial matching on the supervisory working alliance and supervisee multicultural competence. *Counselor Education and Supervision, 36,* 305–317.

Ladany, N., & Friedlander, M.L. (1995). The relationship between the supervisory working alliance and trainees' experience of role conflict and role ambiguity. *Counselor Education and Supervision, 34,* 220–231.

Ladany, N., Hill, C.E., Corbett, M.M., & Nutt, E.A. (1996). Nature, extent, and importance of what psychotherapy trainees do not disclose to their supervisors. *Journal of Counseling Psychology, 43,* 10–24.

Ladany, N., Inman, A.G., Constantine, M.G., & Hofheinz, E.W. (1997). Supervisee multicultural case conceptualization ability and self-reported multicultural competence as functions of supervisee racial identity and supervisor focus. *Journal of Counseling Psychology, 44,* 284–293.

Ladany, N., Lehrman-Waterman, D., Molinaro, M., & Wolgast, B. (1999). Psychotherapy supervisor ethical practices: Adherence to guidelines, the supervisory working alliance, and supervisee satisfaction. *The Counseling Psychologist, 27,* 443–475.

Lambert, M.J., & Arnold, R.C. (1987). Research and the supervision process. *Professional Psychology: Research and Practice, 18*(3), 217–224.

Lambert, M.J., & Ogles, B.M. (1997). The effectiveness of psychotherapy supervision. In C.E. Watkins, Jr. (Ed.), *Handbook of psychotherapy supervision* (pp. 421–446). New York: Wiley.

Larson, L.M. (1998). The social cognitive model of counselor training. *The Counseling Psychologist, 26,* 219–273.

Leong, F.T.L., & Wagner, N.S. (1994). Cross-cultural counseling supervision: What do we know? What do we need to know? *Counselor Education and Supervision, 34,* 117–131.

Liddle, B.J. (1995). Sexual orientation bias among advanced graduate students of counseling and counseling psychology. *Counselor Education and Supervision, 34,* 321–331.

Lochner, B.T., & Melchert, T.P. (1997). Relationship of cognitive style and theoretical orientation to psychology interns' preferences for supervision. *Journal of Counseling Psychology, 44,* 256–260.

Mauzey, E., & Erdman, P. (1997). Trainee perceptions of live supervision phone-ins: A phenomenological inquiry. *The Clinical Supervisor, 15,* 115–128.

McNeill, B.W., Hom, K.L., & Perez, J.A. (1995). The training and supervisory needs of racial and ethnic minority students. *Journal of Multicultural Counseling & Development, 23,* 246–258.

McNeill, B.W., & Worthen, V. (1989). The parallel process in psychotherapy supervision. *Professional Psychology: Research and Practice, 20,* 329–333.

McRoy, R.G., Freeman, E.M., Logan, S.L., & Blackmon, B. (1986). Cross-cultural field supervision: Implications for social work education. *Journal of Social Work Education, 22,* 50–56.

Mueller, W.J., & Kell, B.L. (1972). *Coping with conflict: Supervising counselors and therapists.* New York: Appleton-Century-Crofts.

Multon, K.D., Kivlighan, D.M., & Gold, P.B. (1996). Changes in counselor adherence over the course of training. *Journal of Counseling Psychology, 43,* 356–363.

Nelson, M.L., & Holloway, E.L. (1990). Relation of gender to power and involvement in supervision. *Journal of Counseling Psychology, 37,* 473–481.

Neufeldt, S.A. (1994). Use of a manual to train supervisors. *Counselor Education and Supervision, 33,* 327–336.

Neufeldt, S.A., Iverson, J.N., & Juntunen, C.L. (1995). *Supervision strategies for the first practicum.* Alexandria, VA: American Counseling Association.

Neufeldt, S.A., Karno, M.P., & Nelson, M.L. (1996). A qualitative analysis of expert's conceptualization of supervisee reflectivity. *Journal of Counseling Psychology, 43,* 3–9.

Neville, H.A., Heppner, M.J., Louie, C.E., Thompson, C.E., Brooks, L., & Baker, C.E. (1996). The impact of multicultural training on white racial identity attitudes and therapy competencies. *Professional Psychology: Research and Practice, 27,* 83–89.

Nigam, T., Cameron, P.M., & Leverette, J.S. (1997). Impasses in the supervisory process: A resident's perspective. *American Journal of Psychotherapy, 51,* 252–272.

Norcross, J.C., Prochaska, J.O., & Farber, J.A. (1993). Psychologists conducting psychotherapy: New findings and historical comparisons on the psychotherapy division membership. *Psychotherapy, 30,* 692–697.

Norcross, J.C., Prochaska, J.O., & Gallager, K.M. (1989). Clinical psychologists in the 1980's: II. Theory, research, and practice. *The Clinical Psychologist, 42,* 45–53.

Olk, M.E., & Friedlander, M.L. (1992). Trainees' experience of role conflict and role ambiguity in supervisory relationships. *Journal of Counseling Psychology, 39,* 389–397.

Orlinsky, D.E., Grawe, K., & Parks, B.K. (1994). Process and outcome in psychotherapy: Noch einmal. In A.E. Bergin & S.L. Garfield (Eds.), *Handbook of psychotherapy and behavior change* (3rd ed., pp. 270–376). New York: Wiley.

Ottavi, T.M., Pope-Davis, D.B., & Dings, J.G. (1994). Relationship between white racial identity attitudes and self-reported multicultural counseling competencies. *Journal of Counseling Psychology, 41,* 149–154.

Patton, M.J., & Kivlighan, D.M., Jr. (1997). Relevance of the supervisory alliance to the counseling alliance and to treatment adherence in counselor training. *Journal of Counseling Psychology, 44,* 108–111.

Penman, R. (1980). *Communication process and relationships.* San Diego, CA: Academic Press.

Petty, R.E., & Cacioppo, J.T. (1986). *Communication and persuasion: Central and peripheral routes to attitude change.* New York: Springer-Verlag.

Pilkington, N.W., & Cantor, J.M. (1996). Perceptions of heterosexual bias in professional psychology programs: A survey of graduate students. *Professional Psychology: Research and Practice, 27,* 604–612.

Ponterotto, J.G. (1997). Multicultural counseling training: A competency model and national survey. In D.B. Pope-Davis & H.L.K. Coleman (Eds.), *Multicultural counseling competencies: Assessment, education and training, and supervision* (pp. 111–130). Thousand Oaks, CA: Sage.

Pope-Davis, D.B., & Coleman, H.L.K. (Eds.). (1997). *Multicultural counseling competencies: Assessment, education and training, and supervision.* Thousand Oaks, CA: Sage.

Pope-Davis, D.B., Reynolds, A.L., Dings, J.G., & Nielson, D. (1995). Examining multicultural counseling competencies of graduate students in psychology. *Professional Psychology: Research and Practice, 26,* 322–329.

Putney, M.W., Worthington, E.L., & McCullough, M.E. (1992). Effects of supervisor and supervisee theoretical orientation and supervisor-supervisee matching on interns' perceptions of supervision. *Journal of Counseling Psychology, 39,* 258–265.

Raichelson, S.H., Herron, W.G., Primavera, L.H., & Ramirez, S.M. (1997). Incidence and effects of parallel process in psychotherapy supervision. *The Clinical Supervisor, 15,* 37–48.

Rodenhauser, P. (1994). Toward a multidimensional model for psychotherapy supervision based on developmental stages. *Journal of Psychotherapy Practice and Research, 3,* 1–15.

Rogers, C.R. (1957). The necessary and sufficient conditions of therapeutic personality change. *Journal of Consulting Psychology, 21,* 95–103.

Rogers, C.R. (Ed.). (1967). *The therapeutic relationship and its impact: A study of psychotherapy with schizophrenics.* Madison: University of Wisconsin Press.

Romans, J.S.C., Boswell, D.L., Carlozzi, A.F., & Ferguson, D.B. (1995). Training and supervision practices in clinical, counseling, and school psychology programs. *Professional Psychology: Research and Practice, 26,* 407–412.

Ronnestad, M.H., Orlinsky, D.E., Parks, B.K., & Davis, J.D. (1997). Supervisors of psychotherapy: Mapping experience level and supervisory confidence. *European Psychologist, 2,* 191–201.

Rothman, K.F., & Michels, K.D. (1994). The continuing unethical use of placebo controls. *New England Journal of Medicine, 331,* 394–398.

Rounsaville, B.J., O'Malley, S., Foley, S., & Weissman, M.M. (1998). Role of manual-guided training in the conduct and efficacy of interpersonal psychotherapy for depression. *Journal of Consulting and Clinical Psychology, 56,* 681–688.

Russell, R.K., Crimmings, A.M., & Lent, R.W. (1984). Counselor training and supervision: Theory and research. In S.D. Brown & R.W. Lent (Eds.), *Handbook of counseling psychology* (pp. 625–681). New York: Wiley.

Russell, R.K., & Petrie, T. (1994). Issues in training effective supervisors. *Applied and Preventive Psychology, 3,* 27–42.

Schacht, A.J., Howe, H.E., & Berman, J.J. (1988). A short form of the Barrett-Lennard Relationship Inventory for supervisor relationships. *Psychological Reports, 63,* 699–706.

Schacht, A.J., Howe, H.E., & Berman, J.J. (1989). Supervisor facilitative conditions and effectiveness as perceived by thinking- and feeling-type supervisees. *Psychotherapy, 26,* 475–483.

Schein, E. (1973). *Professional education.* New York: McGraw-Hill.

Schön, D.A. (1983). *The reflective practitioner: How professionals think in action.* New York: Basic Books.

Searles, H. (1955). The informational value of the supervisor's emotional experiences. *Psychiatry, 18,* 135–146.

Sechrest, L., Brewer, M.B., Garfield, S.L., Jackson, J.S., Kurz, R.B., Messick, S.J., Miller, N.E., Peterson, D.R., Spence, J.T., & Thompson, R.F. (1982). *Report of the task force on the evaluation of education, training, and service in psychology.* Washington, DC: American Psychological Association.

Seligman, M.E.P. (1998). The effectiveness of therapy. *American Psychological Association Monitor, 29*(5), 2.

Sells, J.N., Goodyear, R.K., Lichtenberg, J.W., & Polkinghorne, D.E. (1997). Relationship of supervisor and trainee gender and client severity to in-session verbal behavior, session impact, trainee ratings. *Journal of Counseling Psychology, 44,* 406–412.

Shechter, R.A. (1990). Becoming a supervisor: A phase in professional development. *Psychoanalysis & Psychotherapy, 8,* 23–28.

Skovholt, T.M., & Ronnestad, M.H. (1992). *The evolving professional self: Stages and themes in therapist and counselor development.* Chichester, England: Wiley.

Smith, T.E., Winton, M., & Yoshioka, M. (1992). A qualitative understanding of reflective-teams: II. Therapists' perspectives. *Contemporary Family Therapy: An International Journal, 14,* 419–432.

Smith, T.E., Yoshioka, M., & Winton, M. (1993). A qualitative understanding of reflecting teams: I. Client perspectives. *Journal of Systemic Therapies, 12,* 28–43.

Stein, D.M., & Lambert, M.J. (1995). Graduate training in psychotherapy: Are therapy outcomes enhanced? *Journal of Consulting and Clinical Psychology, 63,* 182–196.

Stoltenberg, C.D., Ashby, R.H., Leach, M., McNeill, B.W., Eichenfield, G., & Crethar, H.C. (1996, August). *Effects of supervisee reactance on the supervision relationship and satisfaction.* Paper presented at the annual meeting of the American Psychological Association, Toronto, Canada.

Stoltenberg, C.D., & Dixon, D.N. (1983). Analysis of verbal interactions of A-sub type therapists during therapy. *Psychological Reports, 53,* 115–120.

Stoltenberg, C.D., McNeill, B.W., & Crethar, H.C. (1994). Changes in supervision as counselors and therapists gain experience: A review. *Professional Psychology: Research and Practice, 25,* 416–449.

Stoltenberg, C.D., McNeill, B.W., & Crethar, H.C. (1995). Persuasion and development in counselor supervision. *The Counseling Psychologist, 23,* 633–648.

Stoltenberg, C.D., McNeill, B.W., & Delworth, U. (1998). *IDM supervision: An integrated developmental model for supervising counselors and therapists.* San Francisco: Jossey-Bass.

Stone, G.L. (1997). Multiculturalism as a context for supervision: Perspectives, limitations, and implications. In D.B. Pope-Davis, & H.L.K. Coleman (Eds.), *Multicultural counseling competencies: Assessment, education and training, and supervision.* Thousand Oaks, CA: Sage.

Strong, S.R. (1968). Counseling: An interpersonal influence process. *Journal of Counseling Psychology, 15,* 215–224.

Strong, S.R., & Matross, R.P. (1973). Change processes in counseling and psychotherapy. *Journal of Counseling Psychology, 20,* 28–37.

Strupp, H.H., & Binder, J.L. (1984). *Psychotherapy in a new key: A guide to time-limited dynamic psychotherapy.* New York: Basic Books.

Sue, D.W., Arredondo, P., & McDavis, R.J. (1992). Multicultural competencies and standards: A call to the profession. *Journal of Multicultural Counseling and Development, 20,* 64–88.

Sue, D.W., Bernier, J.E., Durran, A., Feinberg, L., Pedersen, P.B., Smith, E.J., & Vazquez-Nutall, E. (1982). Position paper: Cross-cultural counseling competencies. *The Counseling Psychologist, 10,* 45–52.

Sumerel, M.B., & Borders, L.D. (1996). Addressing personal issues in supervision: Impact of counselors' experience level on various aspects of the supervisory relationship. *Counselor Education and Supervision, 35,* 268–286.

Swanson, J.L., & O'Saben, C.L. (1993). Differences in supervisory needs and expectations by trainee experience, cognitive style, and program membership. *Journal of Counseling and Development, 71,* 457–464.

Task Force on Promotion and Dissemination of Psychological Procedures. (1995). Training in and dissemination of empirically-validated psychological treatments: Report and recommendations. *Clinical Psychologist, 48,* 3–23.

Tinsley, H.E., & Tinsley, D.J. (1977). Relationship between scores on the Omnibus Personality Inventory and counselor trainee effectiveness. *Journal of Counseling Psychology, 24,* 522–526.

Tracey, T.J., Ellickson, J.L., & Sherry, P. (1989). Reactance in relation to different supervisory environments and counselor development. *Journal of Counseling Psychology, 36,* 336–344.

Truax, C.B., & Carkhuff, R.R. (1967). *Toward effective counseling and psychotherapy: Training and practice.* Chicago: Aldine.

Tsui, M. (1997). Empirical research on social work supervision: The state of the art (1970–1995). *Journal of Social Service Research, 23*(2), 39–54.

Vander Kolk, C.J. (1974). The relationship of personality, values, and race to anticipation of the supervisory relationship. *Rehabilitation Counseling Bulletin, 18,* 41–46.

Watkins, C.E., Jr. (1993a). Career assessment supervision: Could what we don't know hurt us? *Counselling Psychology Quarterly, 6,* 151–153.

Watkins, C.E., Jr. (1993b). Development of the psychotherapy supervisor: Concepts, assumptions, and hypotheses of the supervisor complexity model. *American Journal of Psychotherapy, 47,* 58–74.

Watkins, C.E., Jr. (1995a). Pathological attachment styles in psychotherapy supervision. *Psychotherapy, 32,* 333–340.

Watkins, C.E., Jr. (1995b). Psychotherapy supervision in the 1990s: Some observations and reflections. *American Journal of Psychotherapy, 49,* 568–581.

Watkins, C.E., Jr. (1995c). Psychotherapy supervisor and supervisee: Developmental models and research nine years later. *Clinical Psychology Review, 15,* 647–680.

Watkins, C.E., Jr. (1995d). And then there is psychotherapy supervision, too [Letter to the editor]. *American Journal of Psychotherapy, 49,* 313.

Watkins, C.E., Jr., Lopez, F.G., Campbell, V.L., & Himmell, C.D. (1986). Contemporary counseling psychology: Results of a national survey. *Journal of Counseling Psychology, 33,* 301–309.

Weiss, D.S., & Marmar, C.R. (1993). Teaching time-limited dynamic psychotherapy for post-traumatic stress disorder and pathological grief. *Psychotherapy, 30,* 587–591.

Whitehorn, J., & Betz, B. (1960). Further studies of the doctor as a crucial variable in the outcome of treatment with schizophrenia patients. *American Journal of Psychiatry, 117,* 215–223.

Williams, A. (1995). *Visual and active supervision: Roles, focus, technique.* New York: Norton.

Williams, E.N., Judge, A.B., Hill, C.E., & Hoffman, M.A. (1997). Experiences of novice therapists in prepracticum: Trainees', clients', and supervisors' perceptions of therapists' personal reactions and management strategies. *Journal of Counseling Psychology, 44,* 390–399.

Worthen, V., & McNeill, B.W. (1996). A phenomenological investigation of "good" supervision events. *Journal of Counseling Psychology, 43,* 25–34.

Worthington, E.L., Jr. (1987). Changes in supervision as counselors and supervisors gain experience: A review. *Professional Psychology: Research and Practice, 18,* 189–208.

Worthington, E.L., Jr., & Stern, A. (1985). Effects of supervisor and supervisee degree level and gender on the supervisory relationship. *Journal of Counseling Psychology, 32,* 252–262.

CHAPTER 4

Scientific Training and Scholarly Productivity: The Person, the Training Environment, and Their Interaction

CHARLES J. GELSO
ROBERT W. LENT

Over the past two decades, a growing interest within our field has been evidenced in the study of factors that fuel graduate students' interest and skill in research, and more broadly in science. Theoretical constructs have been offered, and measures have been developed, to study the general topic of research training and subtopics within this general area. In contrast to the situation when Magoon and Holland (1984) addressed the topic in the first edition of the *Handbook,* a number of empirical investigations have been conducted. Magoon and Holland, for example, had little or no empirical research directly pertaining to this topic to draw on, whereas we have had the benefit of a number of studies. In general, these investigations have sought to address questions around the impact of graduate training and the training environment on outcomes such as students' attitudes toward research, sense of efficacy related to research, and research productivity. Studies have also addressed the input factor—qualities within the student that are related to these outcomes.

The aim of the present chapter is to summarize and integrate both the theoretical and empirical literature in this emergent area, an area that might be called "the making of scientists" in counseling psychology. We examine factors that contribute to this "making," and have broadly classified these factors into person, training, and the combination (additive and interactive) of person and training factors. Although the focus is on counseling psychology training, most of our review and recommendations have wider applicability, relating closely to research training in all fields within professional psychology, and perhaps to fields beyond psychology.

In addition to addressing person and training factors, we are also interested in the criterion or outcome factor. A further objective is to offer recommendations for both research and training, with the latter addressing some practical ways of enhancing scientific interest and activity among students and new professionals in the field. Our review will emphasize research on students in counseling psychology and related fields published through 1998. We also draw on relevant studies of postdoctoral professionals. Interested readers may wish to consult the literature on personal and environmental characteristics associated with scientific creativity and productivity across diverse academic fields (see, for example, Bland & Ruffin, 1992; Rushton, Murray, & Paunonen, 1987; Stumpf, 1995).

Although we cover both person and training factors, greater emphasis is given to the latter. That is because, apart from selection, we believe that programs can have their greatest impact through the training practices they implement. We should also note at the outset that it is not our intent to determine how graduate training can turn all students into scientists or, indeed, how to make all

We wish to thank Drs. Clara E. Hill and Bruce E. Wampold for their thoughtful review of an earlier draft of this chapter.

scientist-practitioners into professionals who devote half their career efforts to science and half to practice. We believe it to be neither viable nor desirable to turn all students into scientists or to strive for the idealized 50–50 split between science and practice that seems implicit in literature on the scientist-practitioner model (Gelso, 1979, 1993).

In fact, each student will find his or her place on the continuum of science and practice. The aim of this chapter is to examine what research and theory have to say about enhancing students' interest in research and science, confidence in themselves as researchers, scientific competence, and actual scientific productivity. Although some will never do science after graduate school, the chapter is based on the assumption, as discussed below, that enhancing the quality and quantity of science in counseling psychology, and increasing the number of students and professionals who are involved to some degree, are desirable goals.

In sum, then, in this chapter we address the following questions:

1. What are the desired outcomes or goals of graduate education in terms of students' scientific development?
2. What is the role of person or input factors in the development of research self-efficacy, skills, attitudes, and productivity?
3. What are the ingredients of effective research training and supervision?
4. To what extent do person and training factors combine (interactively and additively) in their effect on research attitudes, skills, efficacy, and productivity?

In the process of addressing these questions, we shall examine measures that have been developed in recent years. Finally, we offer suggestions both for the study and the practice of research training.

CONCEPTUAL AND HISTORICAL BACKDROP

Why Worry about Research Training?

Why be concerned about research training and scientific output in counseling psychology? The scientific side of counseling psychology has often been portrayed in recent times as suffering from serious ailments. Much has been written about the low productivity of graduates in this specialty (see, for example, special issues of *The Counseling Psychologist,* Vol. 3, 1979; Vol. 1, 1986; Vol. 1, 1997) and the apparent erosion of its scientific and knowledge base (Betz, 1986; Fitzgerald & Osipow, 1986; Galassi, 1989; Whiteley, 1984). The increased interest in counseling practice and the number of graduates taking practice positions has been viewed as part and parcel of this ailment (Betz, 1986; Fitzgerald & Osipow, 1986).

Although the data that we are aware of do not suggest that counseling psychology's scientific productivity is weak relative to other practice specialties in psychology (see, for example, Brems, Johnson, & Gallucci, 1996; Garfield & Kurtz, 1976; Kelly & Fiske, 1950; Price, 1963) and our observations do not support claims about the erosion of science in the specialty, we nevertheless view attention to training issues in science as essential. For one, we suggest that the production of high-quality science is not only a desirable goal for counseling psychology, but it is crucial if our field is to thrive, or perhaps even survive (Galassi, 1989; Magoon & Holland, 1984; Meara et al., 1988; Whiteley, 1984). It is hard to imagine an effective and enduring psychological helping field without the sound scientific base that itself emerges from high-quality scientific theory and research.

A second reason why attention to training issues is essential is that the graduate training situation is perhaps the most effective setting through which scientific productivity (including quality) may be influenced. Just as with training in counseling and other interventions, it is vital to establish and understand principles of how best to train students for their roles. We suggest, however, that the task of research training is more complicated than that of training in counseling. Observation (e.g., Brehms, 1994; Gelso, 1979, 1993, 1997) and research evidence (Royalty, Gelso, Mallinckrodt, & Garrett, 1986) support the idea that students typically enter graduate training with considerable ambivalence about their research ability and the role of research in their careers. Thus, if graduate training is to be effective, it must help students resolve this ambivalence in the positive direction. In this sense, training not only needs to be aimed at fostering research skill, but also research interest and motivation. We need to light a fire under our students and help them to feel efficacious, as well as teaching the research skills that undergird actual effectiveness. This situation is quite different from that for counseling training, where students tend to be highly motivated and have a more solid sense of efficacy from the outset (Gelso, 1979, 1997).

A Very Short History of Research Training

Although concerns about research training have been around for a long time, theory and research related to this topic are relatively recent. In the early 1970s, Seeman (1973) published a paper on research supervision. To our knowledge, this was the first examination of the dynamics of research supervision with the intent of offering suggestions to increase students' investment in research and ultimately their productivity. Seeman, a client-centered therapist, applied client-centered and humanistic ideas to the topic, suggesting, for example, that we need to help students search inside themselves for research ideas so that they can own those ideas, that supervisors should refrain from applying critical skills until students are able to transcend the fragile early stage of idea generation, and that when students' proposals reach some minimum level of acceptability, the supervisor should shift to a consultant role rather than what we would term an advisor-director role. Seeman's ideas were influential in the development of subsequent conceptions of research training and supervision.

In 1979, *The Counseling Psychologist* (Vol. 8, No. 3) published an issue that was partly devoted to research training (TCP, Vol. 8, No. 3). In that issue, Gelso (1979) presented a conception of the ingredients in the graduate training environment that enhances students' interest in research and ultimately their research productivity. To our knowledge, this was the first formal treatment in counseling psychology of the topic of how best to enhance and promote research interest in students. A few years later, Magoon and Holland (1984) published their *Handbook* chapter on research training and supervision. At that point, they likened research training to "an ineffective vaccine—it works for only a small proportion of students. After carrying out their theses and dissertations, only a few continue to do any research or go on to have a career in research" (p. 682). Magoon and Holland's chapter sought to identify principles and practices of training that might improve the situation.

Research on the topic of research training and supervision essentially did not exist prior to the 1980s. Of course, the topic of training scientists and researchers during graduate education has been with us for a much longer time. In fact, this topic is a fundamental part of the scientist-practitioner model of training, which has been addressed from the beginnings of counseling psychology. The research role of the counseling psychologist, for example, was attended to explicitly in the Northwestern Conference, the first national conference of counseling psychology (APA, 1952). It was also given a central place in the Georgia Conference, the third and most recent national conference in the field (see Gelso et al., 1988; Meara et al., 1988). Moreover, although the value and viability of the scientist-practitioner model of training has often been vigorously contested over the years in all fields of professional psychology, this model, with its emphasis on research and research training along with practice, has been strongly endorsed by official counseling psychology since the field's inception.

During the Georgia Conference, in the report of the research work group (Gelso et al., 1988) it was noted that research training as an area of inquiry was in its infancy. Given this fact, the group's first and foremost recommendation was for "the development of theory and the conduct of research on all aspects of research training" (p. 405). The work group also recommended that "in the graduate training situation we should focus on influencing students' sense of efficacy as scientists, their interest in doing research, and the value they place on research in their subsequent careers" (p. 405). Thus, at least some attention was given at that time to the criterion question of what it is that we hope to influence during training.

As we shall see throughout this chapter, research and theory on research training and related topics have emerged during the decades of the 1980s and 1990s. The amount is still meager, by any yardstick, but it has certainly increased, and appears to be on the rise.

THE CRITERION ISSUE, OR WHAT IS IT THAT WE HOPE TO ACCOMPLISH?

The literature on research training, and the related body of work on the scientist-practitioner model of training in counseling psychology, include much on what we are calling the "criterion issue," that is, the question of what are the desired outcomes or products of training. These literatures, however, rarely deal directly and explicitly with what the outcomes or products ought to be. In fact, as Gelso and Fretz (1992) have noted, there has never been a great deal of agreement or clarity about what the terms "scientist" and "practitioner" in the scientist-practitioner model really mean and how they ought to be actualized, either in graduate education or in the work lives of counseling psychologists (or psychologists in other specialties).

Ways of Being a Scientist

Although there are many meanings of the concept of scientist within the scientist-practitioner model, Gelso and Fretz (1992) pointed out that three primary levels of "being a scientist" have been implicit and explicit over the years. The first and perhaps minimum level refers to the "ability to review and make use of the results of research" (APA, 1952, p. 179). In essence, the counseling practitioner needs to understand empirical research and apply research findings to practice, directly or indirectly.

A second way or level of being a scientist pertains to how the practitioner goes about thinking of practice, as well as the manner in which that practice is conducted. In being scientific, the practitioner adheres to the most fundamental tenets of the scientific attitude: Think critically and be sufficiently skeptical (e.g., about theories in general and about hypotheses related to the client). During practice, the scientific practitioner also follows the scientific process of developing hypotheses based on case material, testing these hypotheses during the counseling work, and revising the hypotheses as a result of the client's response. This use of a scientific process during and as part of counseling was first elaborated many years ago by the Pepinskys (Pepinsky & Pepinsky, 1954), and has been a vital part of the scientist-practitioner model ever since.

The third and most demanding level of being a scientist involves the actual conduct of scientific inquiry (e.g., empirical research). When functioning at this level, the counseling psychologist actually does science and research. At the Northwestern Conference (APA, 1952), it was stated, "On the counseling psychologist falls the chief responsibility for conducting research upon which depends the possibility of more effective counseling. . . . We feel strongly that research must continue as a basic job of the counseling psychologist and that he [she] must be trained accordingly" (p. 176).

Gelso and Fretz (1992) noted that, while the counseling psychologist functions as a scientist at each of these levels, the field will profit most if the individual actualizes all three levels, assuming that the third level not only does include empirical research, but also embraces scholarly work that is clinical and conceptual, such as writing or presenting clinical theories and analyses. Probably most would agree that the first and second level of being a scientist can and ought to be a goal of research and scientific training in counseling psychology. Many more disagreements emerge with the third level. Should the goal be for all students to do scholarly work? To produce and publish research? Or should the goals be more attitudinally based? In the next section, we explore the goals and outcomes of research training that have been posited in the literature.

Desired Outcomes and Measures

Within the research training literature, several outcomes have been suggested and studied. The most commonly addressed outcomes of effective research training are the development of positive research attitudes and interest, research self-efficacy, skill and competence, and productivity. Each of these is discussed below, along with measures that have been developed to assess it. We have placed this section on outcomes before sections on person and training factors because an understanding of outcomes should facilitate the reader's integration of material on person and training factors.

Training outcomes or criteria may be seen as residing on a continuum. At one end of the continuum exist outcomes that are only way stations to a desired end point. We might use the term "intermediate" to describe such outcomes. On the other end are what can be called "ultimate" outcomes. These represent the end points that are sought by a given intervention (e.g., a training experience). In fact, various outcomes in the research training area (just as any area) exist at different points in this continuum. For example, research self-efficacy has been seen as one of the most central outcomes of research training (Gelso et al., 1988). At the same time, within social cognitive theory (see Brown, Lent, Ryan, & McPartland, 1996), research self-efficacy is seen as a mediating variable (what we are calling an intermediate outcome), itself influenced by other factors, such as the training environment, while also affecting outcomes that are closer to the ultimate end of the continuum (e.g., research interest, productivity). Research productivity, in fact, is implicitly seen as an ultimate criterion in much of the research training literature.

Research Attitudes and Interest

Most authors in the research training area focus on enhanced research interest and attitudes as a desired outcome of training. In the terms discussed above, most view attitudes and interest as intermediate outcomes. For example, Gelso and his collaborators (Gelso, 1979, 1993, 1997; Mallinckrodt, Gelso, & Royalty, 1990; Royalty et al., 1986) have focused on what they call research attitudes. This construct includes both interest in research and the value the student expects to place on research in a future career (subsequently referred to as interest and value). Gelso's view has been that training ought to focus on enhancing research attitudes, and that if such training succeeds, an increase in the quality and quantity of scholarly productivity (more ultimate outcomes) will naturally follow.

Bieschke and her collaborators (Bieschke, Bishop, & Herbert, 1995; Bieschke, Herbert, & Bard, 1998; Bishop & Bieschke, 1998) also focus on interest in research, which, in keeping with social cognitive career theory, is conceptualized as an intermediate outcome that prompts choice-related behaviors and, indirectly, performance. These researchers have conceptualized research interest as resulting from factors such as research self-efficacy, which, in turn, they proposed to be influenced by the research training environment.

Several measures of the research interest or attitude construct have been developed in recent years. Research attitudes as defined by Gelso and his collaborators have been assessed largely by a four-item Likert scale. The Attitude Toward Research Measure (ATRM; Royalty et al., 1986) asks respondents about their research interest and value. The ATRM has demonstrated considerable reliability and validity in each study that has employed it (Gelso, Mallinckrodt, & Judge, 1996; Kahn & Scott, 1997; Mallinckrodt et al., 1990; Royalty et al., 1986).

Bieschke and her colleagues have developed the 16-item Interest in Research Questionnaire (IRQ), and have found support both for its reliability and validity (Bieschke et al., 1995; Bishop & Bieschke, 1998). Validity was demonstrated by the finding that research self-efficacy and outcome expectations, investigative interests, and research training environment (indirectly) were predictive of IRQ responses.

A third measure within the research interest/attitude area is the Scientist-Practitioner Inventory (SPI; Leong & Zachar, 1991). The SPI taps the extent to which individuals are interested in the work activities associated with the roles of scientist and practitioner in psychology. Obviously, the Scientist scale is the one that has been used to measure research interest. The original version of the SPI contained 42 items; a shortened version (Leong & Zachar, 1993) includes 18 items. For the most part, the SPI has received support both for its reliability and validity. It has been found to correlate in theoretically expected ways with measures of personality and with scientific and practitioner work setting aspirations.

Research Self-efficacy

An intermediate outcome that has received considerable attention in recent years, the concept of research self-efficacy (RSE) draws heavily on general social-cognitive theory (Bandura, 1986; Lent, Brown, & Hackett, 1994). Betz (1986) theorized that students' research training experiences affect RSE. Positive research experiences of the sort described by Gelso (1979, 1993) should elevate RSE, whereas negative experiences should dampen it. Furthermore, Betz implied that RSE would mediate the relationship between the research training environment and research productivity. As noted earlier, the report of the research work group at the Georgia Conference (Gelso et al., 1988) also proposed RSE as a primary outcome.

There has been much interest in examining the role of RSE as it related to training experiences and to more ultimate outcomes (examined in subsequent sections). The measure used in most studies is Phillips and Russell's (1994) Self-Efficacy in Research Measure (SERM). SERM is a 33-item inventory that assesses level of confidence in performing various research tasks and the belief that the skill is possessed for the tasks. This inventory consists of four subscales (research design skills, practical research skills, quantitative and computer skills, and writing skills) and a total score. Reliability estimates are high, and validity is supported at the total score level by correlations with research training environment and productivity (Gelso et al., 1996; Kahn & Scott, 1997; Phillips & Russell, 1994), as well as by mediating the relationship of research training environment to productivity (Brown et al., 1996). Two as-of-yet unpublished measures of RSE have also appeared on the scene: The Research Self-Efficacy Scale (RSES; Greeley et al., 1989) and the Research Attitudes Measure (RAM; O'Brien, Malone, Schmidt, & Lucas, 1998). Both measures have demonstrated sound reliability estimates and beginning validity.

Research Skill and Competence

It goes without saying that training programs should seek to promote a high level of actual research skill and competence in graduate students. On the other hand, this outcome ironically has been neglected in both theory and research in the area of research training. In fact, Heppner, Kivlighan, and Wampold (1999) viewed research competence as "the missing construct" in this area. These authors pointed out that, although it is critical to enhance research attitudes and self-efficacy, it is not enough. Research training needs also to be arranged so that students develop high-level skills in a wide range of research design and methodology areas, for example, multivariate statistics, experimental and qualitative research designs, and writing. Surveys by Wampold (1986) and Royalty and Reising (1986) indicated that training was insufficient regarding several important research and statistical methods; more recently, Wampold (1998) has questioned the effectiveness of training in advanced statistical methods that have been developed in recent years. To date, however, we know of no explicit measures of, or studies that incorporate, competence as an outcome factor.

Research Productivity

Of the research training outcomes we have discussed, research productivity is most likely seen as being an ultimate outcome. At the same time, one may ask whether productivity, in fact, should be a goal of training? If by productivity we mean the quantity of production, then this outcome is quite controversial. Some advocate increased productivity (Gelso, 1993; Magoon & Holland, 1984; Whiteley, 1984), whereas others worry that attention to quantity without corresponding attention to quality might simply result in more weak research (e.g., Wampold, 1986). We suggest that although research productivity may be a useful criterion measure in some research studies, it alone cannot be an ultimate outcome of research training. Quantity and quality ought to be considered hand in hand, as a tandem of sorts. At the same time, we wonder about the value of training that focuses only on research production (cf. Altmaier & Claiborn, 1987). If training focuses on skill, self-efficacy, and attitudes, such training should ultimately affect the production of more and better scholarship.

Simple weighted (Phillips & Russell, 1994) and unweighted (Kahn & Scott, 1997; Krebs, Smither, & Hurley, 1991) systems have been used to assess productivity. Both procedures seem like reasonable ways of tapping this construct. Interestingly, quality of research has not been measured in the research training area to date, although it has been examined in studies of faculty productivity (Hanish et al., 1995; Taylor, Locke, Lee, & Gist, 1984).

Additional Outcomes

Two other outcomes have been addressed recently in the literature: research-related career goals and research outcome expectations. Kahn and Scott (1997) included research-related career goals as an ultimate outcome in their structural equation model of research training. Although this outcome was appropriate for Kahn and Scott's research, and may be quite suitable as a criterion in other studies, Heppner et al. (1999) questioned its appropriateness as a training goal. Some programs may want to use the proportion of students entering research career positions as an outcome goal, other programs may not. Heppner et al. did suggest, however, that the mission of training programs ought to include enhanced research attitudes and skills.

Research outcome expectations (expected outcomes of completing research tasks, e.g., professional advancement, contribution to knowledge) has been used as an intermediate outcome by Bishop and Bieschke (1998). This variable was found to be a highly significant intervening link between the training environment and student personality, on the one hand, and positive research interest, on the other. Such expectations appear to be a desirable intermediate outcome of research training and a fruitful criterion in research on research training.

In sum, the desired research and science-related outcomes of graduate education have been conceptualized in terms of levels of being a scientist (e.g., applying research, using scientific attitudes and processes, and actually doing research, science, and scholarly work). Outcomes can be conceptualized as existing on an intermediate-ultimate continuum, and outcomes that have been most often addressed involve research attitudes (i.e., interest and value), research self-efficacy, research skill and competence, and productivity. Measures have been developed for most of these outcomes, and beginning research efforts have been made to determine what factors affect them and what effects intermediate outcomes have on more ultimate ones. In the following sections, we examine what research and theory have to say about how person, training, and person-training interaction factors influence these outcomes.

THE ROLE OF PERSON FACTORS IN RESEARCH INTEREST AND TRAINING

The idea of person factors influencing attitudes toward research among counseling psychology students stems from the proposition that scientific work entails a set of demands that "pull for" or even require certain personal qualities if science is to be done effectively and happily by the student. Furthermore, this set of demands is seen as substantially different from the demands of practice. For example, Gelso (1979) posited that the demands of science and practice are basically contradictory, perhaps even mutually exclusive. In sum, science demands that the scientist understand the world primarily through intellect; is continually skeptical, doubting, and challenging of theories and other phenomena; is logical, controlled, deterministic; seeks to reduce ambiguities; and is able to tolerate isolation. In contrast, practice requires greater access to affective and nonintellective processes, confidence in one's theories and tactics, the ability to live in ambiguity, and satisfaction from a kind of constant intimacy.

Given such vastly different demands of science and practice, it makes sense that different kinds of people will gravitate toward these two clusters of activities. Such a notion is bolstered by the consistent findings that people with very different temperaments gravitate toward research careers and clinically oriented careers, in psychology and other fields (see Frank's, 1984, review).

Before addressing the role of person factors in the research training outcomes discussed earlier, a word should be added about what we mean by person factors. Person factors are those qualities and characteristics that the student brings into the graduate training situation. These include trait-like personality and cognitive style variables, as well as psychosocially relevant demographic characteristics such as gender, race/ethnicity, and age. We exclude from the category of person factors those personal qualities that are in themselves reactions to research and research training, are seen as modifiable by the environment, and are thus viewed as desired outcomes of research training, for example, research self-efficacy and attitudes toward research. In naming something a "person factor," there is no implication that this factor is necessarily an inherent or biologically based part of the person. Different person factors are differentially influenced by heredity, early learning, later learning, and the interaction of these determinants.

What do we know about how such person factors are associated with the science-related outcomes of graduate education? In this section, we examine the person factors that relate to research attitudes, self-efficacy, and productivity—the outcomes that have been studied most in relation to person factors. Specifically, the following clusters of questions are addressed:

1. What person factors relate to the three criteria, how, and to what extent?
2. What person factors relate to changes in these criteria during graduate education? How and to what extent?
3. How fundamental are these person factors? Where do they originate? How do they develop?

Person Factors Related to Research Attitudes, Self-Efficacy, and Productivity

Personality and Interest Patterns

The personality factor most consistently found to be associated with research attitudes, self-efficacy, and productivity is *Investigative* interest or personality, where the term investigative derives from Holland's (1985) theory of personality and vocational interests. A number of studies confirm a direct and positive relationship between scores on measures of investigative personality (e.g., as assessed by the Strong Interest Inventory) and research attitudes (Betz & Taylor, 1982; Bishop & Bieschke, 1998; Kahn & Scott, 1997; Leong & Zachar, 1993; Mallinckrodt et al., 1990; Zachar & Leong, 1992), research self-efficacy (Bieschke et al., 1995; Bishop & Bieschke, 1998), and productivity, during and after graduate school (Kahn & Scott, 1997; Krebs et al., 1991; Royalty & Magoon, 1985).

Other studies have found variables very similar to investigative personality to relate to kinds of criteria we have been addressing. For example, Goodyear and Lichtenberg (1991) found that graduate students' preference for working with ideas (in contrast to working with concrete, practical problems) was associated with attitudes toward research. Youness, Lorr, and Stefic (1985) discovered that academic psychologists (both clinical and nonclinical) differed from clinical practitioners in being more interested in working with abstract ideas, theories, and problems. Zachar and Leong (1992) found that the extent to which clinical, counseling, and experimental psychology graduate students possess objective orientations (belief in impersonal causality, behavioral content, reductionism, and quantitative analysis) was related to interest in scientific activities; alternatively, extent of subjective orientation (belief in personal will, experiential content, holism, and qualitative analysis) was negatively related to interest in science (and positively related to practitioner interests).

The only study to date that failed to support the link between Investigative personality and research attitudes/self-efficacy/productivity criteria was that of Tinsley, Tinsley, Boone, and Shim-Li (1993). However, these researchers did find that, early in graduate school, the more scientifically oriented participants scored lower on social extroversion and higher on independence than the more practice-oriented individuals.

Another related personality factor that has been supported is achievement orientation (desire to be recognized for mastering difficult tasks against high standards). Counseling students' research attitudes were found to be associated with achievement orientation (Goodyear & Lichtenberg, 1991), and academic psychologists across subfields tend to be more achievement oriented than practitioners (Youness et al., 1985).

In sum, it appears that characteristics of the investigative personality type are related to graduate students' and professionals' research attitudes, research self-efficacy, and research productivity (as well as the jobs professionals take). The investigative type tends to be achieving, independent, reserved, and planful; these characteristics, too, have been supported in studies that did not examine the investigative type per se.

Just as it is important to determine what personality factors are positively related to attitudes/self-efficacy/productivity criteria, we need to learn about those factors that are negatively related. When examining such factors as noted above, as well as additional ones (e.g., Bishop & Bieschke, 1998; Tinsley et al., 1993; Youness et al., 1985; Zachar & Leong, 1992), there also appears to be a tendency for the science-oriented counseling student to be less person oriented, and enjoy social and help-giving activities less than the practice-oriented students. These results do not imply that research-oriented students are low on such qualities. It is just that they are lower than practice-oriented persons.

Cognitive Variables

Are there cognitive factors that mediate research interest, efficacy, skill, and productivity? Experience suggests that certain cognitive styles may lend themselves more readily to the tasks and demands of scientific work, whereas other styles may be inimical to such work. For example, some (e.g., Gelso, 1997; Meehl, 1972) have speculated that students who are the better research prospects tend to prefer tight, logical, and orderly thinking (or at least have a good capacity for such thinking). By contrast, Meehl somewhat playfully referred to "muddleheadedness" (e.g., loose thinking) as not making for good science. This is not to say that there is no place for less logical, looser, "disorderly" thinking in the scientific process. Indeed, there is an important (perhaps vital) place for such thinking styles in creative science. The spirit of Gelso's and Meehl's comments, however, is that good science requires that the scientist have the capacity or thinking style that will allow him or her to make use of orderly, logical, tight thinking at the key stages of the scientific process that call for this sort of style.

The only study to our knowledge that addressed the cognitive style topic was Rardin's (1986) dissertation. Rardin found that psychotherapy researchers have more verbal/analytic cognitive styles than do practitioners, whereas practitioners possess more global/intuitive styles. This was a promising beginning, and cognitive factors need to be studied further.

Gender

Do male and female graduate students differ on the criteria that have been examined? The typical finding has been that there is no gender effect. Males and females generally do not differ in research attitudes (Bishop & Bieschke, 1998; Gelso et al., 1996; Kahn & Scott, 1997; Royalty et al., 1986), research self-efficacy (Bishop & Bieschke, 1998; Gelso et al., 1996; Phillips & Russell,

1994), or research productivity (Kahn & Scott, 1997; Phillips & Russell, 1994). Only one study to date (Kahn & Scott, 1997) supported a modest relationship of gender to research self-efficacy, with men scoring higher than women graduate students.

Indirect Effects

We have been examining the direct relationships of person factors to research attitudes/self-efficacy/productivity criteria. What about indirect effects? Statistical methods such as regression and path analysis and structural equation modeling have allowed investigators to study how person factors may relate to research training outcomes *through* some intervening variable(s).

Stemming from theoretical propositions of social cognitive theory (Lent et al., 1994), recent investigations have examined research self-efficacy (Bishop & Bieschke, 1998; Kahn & Scott, 1997) and research outcome expectations (Bishop & Bieschke, 1998) as intervening links. It has been found that Investigative personality relates to productivity both directly (as noted above) and through its effects on research self-efficacy and research outcome expectations. In other words, in these studies Investigative personality contributes to research self-efficacy and/or positive research outcome expectations, which in turn contribute to research interest (Bishop & Bieschke, 1998) and productivity (Kahn & Scott, 1997). The examination of such causal linkages represents a fruitful area of inquiry, as shall be discussed in later sections.

Person Factors in Change

We have been looking at how person factors connect to intermediate and ultimate research training outcomes. Another phenomenon that must be examined is how person factors relate to *changes* in outcome related qualities. For example, does investigative personality relate to increases in research interest or self-efficacy during the course of training? It may be that certain person factors are negatively related to research interest but that those who have high scores on that factor are positively affected by a powerful and positive research training environment. For example, although the social personality appears to enter graduate school with less positive research attitudes, might it be that this social type is readily and positively influenced by a potent research training environment?

The literature on how person factors relate to change in research relevant outcomes is strikingly sparse. Comparing students' retrospective reports of research attitudes on entrance to training versus current research attitudes, Mallinckrodt et al. (1990) discovered that, contrary to expectation, students whose attitudes toward research (interest and value) improved the most during training tended to be Social types and those with a *low* Investigative-artistic-social code, using Holland's (1985) typology. Because these types also had the least favorable research attitudes at the beginning of training, the change may have been due to statistical regression to the mean. Yet it is also possible that those with personal qualities that are not ordinarily associated with research interest and self-efficacy may change a great deal if their research training is potent. This issue will be taken up later in the chapter.

The Mallinckrodt et al. (1990) study pointed to additional findings that should be heuristically valuable. Controlling for research attitudes at entrance, current research attitudes correlated positively with investigative but negatively with enterprising type. Scores on the Investigative personality were related to research training outcome criteria on entrance to graduate school, and are related to the improvements on these same criteria during training. The more Enterprising the student, on the other hand, the less likely that student was to develop positive research attitudes during training.

How Do They Get That Way? or How Basic Are Person Factors?

In considering how basic are person factors, we come face to face with the ubiquitous nature-nurture question in psychology. To what extent are the factors that make for scientific interest and self-efficacy inherent or learned? To the extent that they are learned, how early in life does such learning occur? Just how deeply rooted are the attributes reflecting scientific interest?

In pondering these questions, Gelso (1997) was reminded of Abraham Maslow's (1954) famous statement: "A musician must make music, an artist must paint, a poet must write, if he is to be ultimately at peace with himself" (p. 91). This quote implies that the qualities making for scientific interest (and other interests) are deeply rooted in our personalities or are part of our basic nature. Such a nature argument is supported by behavior genetic studies suggesting that there is a sizable genetic contribution to basic interests (although unique environmental factors also contribute strongly to interests; see Swanson & Gore's chapter, this volume).

Despite the genetic data, it has been clear for a long time that the choice of a scientific career comes relatively late for many students. For example, in Anne Roe's (1953) seminal research on eminent male scientists, many of the psychologists did not decide on a scientific career until late in their college years. Roe offered a clue as to the factors underlying research and scientific interest: "In the stories of the social scientists and the biologists it becomes clear that it is the discovery that a boy can himself do research that is more important than any other factor in his final decision to become a scientist" (p. 80). It is noteworthy that this observation appeared to anticipate by several decades recent findings on the research self-efficacy construct.

Roe has also noted that

> [T]he discovery of the possibility of finding out things for oneself has most often come about through the experience of working on problems individually, rather than reading what others have done. Sometimes this is the result of careful preparation on the part of the teacher; sometimes it happens because the teacher is more interested in other things and leaves his students to work on their own. (p. 82)

These latter observations speak to the relative value of personal performance accomplishments, another key concept in social cognitive theory.

In sum, Gelso (1997) recently interpreted the kinds of evidence presented in this section as follows:

> [I]t appears that the psychological qualities that predispose the person toward scientific activities and a scientific career are to an important extent genetically rooted, and to an important extent learned early in life. They blend into basic personality, basic interests, and cognitive styles. Yet the ways in which these tendencies are channeled, and the specific forms in which they are enacted, and indeed the extent to which these tendencies become realized, depend on later learning events—the availability of good teachers and mentors, direct experience in doing research, and other aspects of the learning environment. Herein lies the interaction of person and environment factors. (pp. 311–312)

In subsequent sections, we examine graduate school training factors, as well as the ways in which person and training factors may combine to affect the kinds of research training outcomes that have been discussed.

THE ROLE AND INGREDIENTS OF EFFECTIVE RESEARCH TRAINING

There clearly has been an increasing interest in the topic of research training over the past two decades. At the same time, research and theory on research training sadly lags behind research and theory on its counterpart topic in the practice arena, that is, counselor training and supervision. The norm seems to now be about one or two studies a year in the general area of research training appearing in our major journals. Theoretical works are even more scant.

Our impression is that there are currently more research experiences offered to students, and research educators have greater awareness of how training experiences can affect research attitudes, certainly than when Gelso (1979) offered the first formal conception of the ingredients of effective research training. However, here, too, we believe progress to be very slow. There is little in the literature suggesting that educators are seeking to develop systematically training situations and environments that enhance students' research interest and efficacy, as well as their competence in research.

Given the state of affairs we have discussed regarding research, theory, and practice in the area of research training, what really does happen to research attitudes, self-efficacy, and skill during training? What does research have to say about changes in these criteria during one's graduate career?

Training Effects on Research Attitudes, Self-Efficacy, and Skill

Despite the difficulties noted in the above section, the data that do exist suggest that, on the whole, students develop more favorable attitudes toward research over the course of their graduate education. The degree of change tends to be small, and it is not uniform, but it appears to be consistent across the few studies that have been done on the topic.

For example, Royalty et al. (1986) surveyed 358 students in 10 counseling psychology doctoral programs. These researchers found that when students retrospectively rated their research attitudes (interest and value) on entrance to their programs, research interests were slightly below the neutral point on the scale. Their current ratings, however, were .40 higher than initial ratings on a five-point scale (SD was not reported). When asked to rate the percentage of work-time in their future careers that they would ideally devote to research, respondents' means changed from 19% at entrance (retrospective rating) to 23% currently, a statistically significant but small change.

Evidence of positive change was also found by Perl and Kahn (1983) in their survey of over 1,000 students in applied specialties in psychology. Intensive studies of single programs (Berman, 1990, 1992; Gelso, Raphael, Black, Rardin, & Skalkos, 1983) have uncovered similar results.

It must be underscored that many students do not demonstrate this pattern of increased interest, and in fact some become less favorable (Perl & Kahn, 1983). Likewise, although certain training programs appear to be especially impactful in terms of research attitudes, most have a modest positive impact, and students in some programs evidence a declining interest. Thus, a training program effect has been empirically identified (Gelso et al., 1996; Parker & Detterman, 1988; Royalty et al., 1986); and, similar to counseling research, a deterioration effect also surfaces, at both an individual and a training program level.

The literature on general effects has focused on attitudes toward research. No studies to date have examined individual or training program effects on other relevant outcome criteria (e.g., research self-efficacy or competence). Such studies are sorely needed. In addition, research is needed on the factors that underlie changes (for better and worse) in research training outcomes. Earlier we identified person factors that are related to change. We next look at training environment factors.

The Research Training Environment

The research training environment (RTE) has been offered as a major factor in accounting for changes in research attitudes, self-efficacy, and productivity. Gelso's (1979, 1993, 1997) theory of the RTE has been the only formal theoretical statement to date, and this conception has been examined in a number of empirical studies.

Gelso (1993) conceptualized the RTE as "all those forces in graduate training programs (and, more broadly, the departments and universities within which the programs are situated) that reflect attitudes toward research and science" (p. 470). These attitudes generally are seen as existing on continua, ranging from highly positive to highly negative. All constituents in an environment (faculty, students, support staff) are seen as contributing to the overall press of that environment, but since faculty have the most power to effect the environment (e.g., through selection, course offerings, control of rewards and punishments), they are seen as having the greatest responsibility.

According to Gelso (1979, 1993, 1997), students in applied specialties enter graduate training with considerable anxiety and ambivalence related to research and its role in their careers. They are not sure they can do research effectively and usually have not felt the excitement that comes from discovering things through science. The most effective research training is arranged so that the anxiety and ambivalence are resolved, and the excitement of discovery is experienced.

RTE theory was revised in 1993 and 1997 to take into account the research that had been done on its ingredients. In the most recent version (Gelso, 1997), it was proposed that research attitudes, self-efficacy, and eventually productivity will be enhanced or retarded to the extent that nine interrelated ingredients exist in the environment. The nine ingredients are described below. They are grouped under two higher order factors, interpersonal and instructional, based on a recent factor analytic study (Kahn & Gelso, 1997).

Interpersonal Factor

1. *Faculty model appropriate scientific behavior and attitudes.* It is important that faculty both do science and show that they have a passion for what they do. On the negative side, faculty who communicate that they do research just to get promoted have a deadening effect on students' attitudes.

2. *Scientific activity is positively reinforced in the environment, both formally and informally.* Encouragement, support, or other interpersonal reinforcers are probably the most influential, given the strong interpersonal orientation of counseling students.

3. *Students are involved in research early in their training and in a minimally threatening way.* Students should be involved in research from very early in graduate school. Involvement should be at a level the student can handle without significant anxiety, and, on the positive side, should allow the student to experience the exciting aspects of science.

4. *The environment emphasizes science as a partly social experience.* Given that students in applied fields are so deeply interpersonally oriented, interpersonal elements need to be present in the environment. Relationships with advisors are key; they have the potential to damage or deepen research attitudes and efficacy, depending on how supportive and stimulating they are. The existence of research teams is also important, and ideally all students would have access to such teams. This ingredient is especially important for students who are the most interpersonally oriented.

Instructional Factor

5. *It is emphasized in training that all research studies are limited and flawed in one way or another.* This takes the pressure off students by helping them understand that no research approaches perfection, and that the solution to problems in research usually create other problems. This ingredient reflects Gelso's (1979) "bubble hypothesis."

6. *Varied approaches to research are taught and valued.* Teaching a range of approaches, and that each has merits and drawbacks, enhances students' sense of efficacy and flexibility. It also allows students to choose approaches that both fit the problems being studied and are compatible with their own personalities and styles.

7. *The importance of students looking inward for research ideas and questions is emphasized when students are developmentally ready for this responsibility.* Looking inward is vital for a sense of ownership and internalization of the research ideas. But it is useful for students to first immerse themselves in research, and perhaps collaborate on others' (e.g., advisors') research so they can eventually look inward knowledgeably.

8. *Students are shown how science and practice are wedded.* Showing students how practice is a great source of research ideas, and how research bears upon practice is an important motivator, especially since even the most research-oriented students tend also to be interested in practice (Stone & Vespia, 1998).

9. *Statistics' instruction is made relevant to applied research, and emphasis is placed on the logic of design as well as statistics.* Although one need not be a statistician to be an excellent researcher, the most effective training contains statistics instruction that is sensitive to the needs of applied researchers and is sensitively taught. Insensitively taught statistics courses can traumatize students. Also, the role of the counseling researcher as a logician of science is emphasized.

Support for the theory is derived from studies that examine all nine ingredients collectively (Bishop & Bieschke, 1998; Kahn & Scott, 1997; Phillips & Russell, 1994), each of the nine ingredients separately (Gelso et al., 1996; Goodyear & Lichtenberg, 1991; Krebs et al., 1991; Mallinckrodt et al., 1990; Royalty et al., 1986), and one or another of the nine ingredients (Berman, 1990; Galassi, Brooks, Stoltz, & Trexler, 1986; Gelso et al., 1983; Royalty & Reising, 1986). As a group, these studies tend to be supportive of the theory in general, although not every ingredient or the same ingredients is confirmed from study to study, and the RTE does not correlate with every criterion used in each study. The magnitude of RTE-criterion relations varies substantially across studies, and shall be discussed next.

Some findings of RTE studies seem especially noteworthy. First, when programs are separated into those that appear to have an especially powerful impact on research attitudes as compared with other programs (Gelso et al., 1996; Royalty et al., 1986), marked differences in the RTEs of the two groups emerge, with the impactful programs having consistently more positive RTEs. In the Gelso et al. study, for example, significant RTE differences emerged between the impactful programs and the others on each of the theorized ingredients of effective RTEs. These differences were greater than half an SD on four of the nine ingredients: (1) Faculty Modeling, (2) Positive Reinforcement, (3) Early Involvement, and (4) Science as Partly Social (the four ingredients within the Interpersonal factor).

A second noteworthy finding is that the RTE appears to relate to relevant research training outcomes both directly (as noted above) and indirectly. Regarding indirect effects, recent research (e.g., Bishop & Bieschke, 1998; Kahn & Scott, 1997) suggests that the RTE influences various research training outcomes *through* its effect on variables, such as research self-efficacy, research attitudes, and outcome expectations. These indirect effects, as well as RTE by person interaction effects, will be examined in the later "person in environment" section. For now, suffice it to say that the study of indirect effects and person X environment interaction effects represent a growing edge of RTE research.

Measuring the Environment

All the studies involving Gelso's theory have used the original or revised Research Training Environment Scale (RTES). The original version (Gelso, Mallinckrodt, & Royalty, 1991; Royalty et al., 1986) contains 45 Likert items assessing 9 of the 10 RTE ingredients presented in Gelso's (1979) first theoretical statement. The revised RTES (RTES-R; Gelso et al., 1996) consists of 54 items (6 per subscale) and substantially improved on reliability at the subscale level. The validity data presented by Gelso et al. for the RTES-R also appears to be superior to the original measure, and this has been supported in subsequent research. Studies using the revised measure (Gelso et al., 1996; Kahn & Scott, 1997) have consistently reported stronger relations of RTE with outcome criteria than those employing the earlier version (e.g., Bishop & Bieschke, 1998; Mallinckrodt et al., 1990; Phillips & Russell, 1994). For example, studies using the revised measure typically report correlations in which RTE accounts for between 10% and 20% of the outcome variance, whereas the RTE accounts for less than 10% of the outcome variation in studies using the original scale. Kahn and Miller (1999) has developed an 18-item short form of the RTES-R that appears to have sound reliability and validity at the total score level (Hollingsworth, 1999; Kahn & Miller, 1999). If the total score is all the researcher desires, and if convenience is a factor, the short form appears to be a viable alternative.

Levels of Intervention

The RTE is conceptualized by Gelso in broad, overarching terms. In considering how scientific training affects students attitudes, self-efficacy, skill, and productivity, it is worth examining specifics within the overall environment. For example, Heppner, Gelso, and Dolliver (1987) discussed how research attitudes and other outcomes can be affected by events as diverse as a half-day writing workshop, a semester-long research seminar, a scholarly paper, the sequencing of research seminars, and differing research and advising models in a program. The authors also noted the importance of all faculty being of one voice in supporting the scientist-practitioner model, and in this way creating a powerful press in the environment. The propositions to be emphasized here are that (1) the training environment exerts its influence through a myriad of more specific activities and events, and (2) the effect of any given activity (e.g., a research seminar or a writing workshop) on students' research attitudes and skill is dependent on how the activity is arranged and presented to the student. A poorly or insensitively taught research seminar, for example, can do more to impede research attitudes than no seminar at all. Naturally, research is needed on how specific events and activities (including the manner in which they are presented to students) affect research relevant outcomes.

The Advisor as Mentor

Although RTE theory focuses a great deal on faculty behavior (e.g., modeling, reinforcing, stimulating), there is no particular construct or ingredient in that theory pertaining to the advisor-advisee relationship and mentoring. Likewise, there has been an absence of study within counseling psychology of advisor mentoring, its antecedents, correlates, and outcomes (Hollingsworth, 1999)—despite what appears to be general agreement on the importance of the advising relationship and mentoring (Betz, 1997; Gelso, 1979, 1993, 1997; Hill, 1997; Magoon & Holland, 1984; Mallinckrodt, 1997). The lack of theory and research is especially notable when juxtaposed with the mentoring literature that has developed in business (Burke, McKeen, & McKenna, 1993; Hunt & Michael, 1983; Kram, 1985) and in other fields within academe (Green & Bauer, 1995; Jacobi, 1991).

The data that do exist on the role of the advising and mentoring relationship underscore the major importance of this relationship. Professionals who recollect their graduate school experience comment on the centrality of the advisor-advisee relationship (Gelso et al., 1983; Royalty & Magoon, 1985) and the negative impact of lack of mentoring (Gelso et al., 1983). When graduate students respond to open-ended questions about aspects of, and experiences in, training that facilitated or impeded their research interest and self-efficacy (Gelso, 1997), many single out mentoring as a key factor—its enhancing effects when positive, and damaging effects when there exists what might be termed "negative mentoring."

Despite these valuable theoretical and empirical beginnings, there is now no formal theory of the mentoring and advising relationship during counseling psychology training (or during training in academic fields), although informal observations exist, especially in industrial/organizational psychology, that could contribute to formal theory development (e.g., Kramer & Martin, 1996; Van Dyne, 1996). There is also an absence of reliable instruments with which to study this relationship. Some promising theory-based research is currently in progress (Hollingsworth, 2000; Schlosser, 2000), but this is clearly an area of inquiry that is in its earliest stages.

Conclusions about the Effects of Research Training

To sum up the research presented in this section, it appears that research training and the training environment matter quite a bit. They have an effect, substantial at times, on students' research attitudes, self-efficacy, outcome expectations, skill, and productivity. Most of the studies to date have examined the association of the RTE to attitudes (i.e., interest and value). There has been less study of the relations of RTE and the particulars of training to the development of self-efficacy and actual competence, although the research that has looked at self-efficacy as an intermediate outcome of an effective RTE has been quite positive and promising.

There are numerous general and specific questions that await empirical scrutiny in the research training and RTE area. Research recommendations are discussed in a later section. For now, we raise the question of just how large an effect the RTE has on research relevant outcomes. Although some of the effects discovered in some of the studies are large (especially when training program rather than individual student is the unit of analysis), the magnitude of the associations is generally moderate (e.g., with RTE typically accounting for 5% to 15% of outcome variance), and supports the "accentuation effect" pointed to in the literature on the role of college on students' cognitive and emotional development (Feldman & Newcomb, 1969). Thus, "colleges accentuate what they receive, but they turn very few pussycats into tigers" (Magoon & Holland, 1984, p. 696). When applied to the research training arena, it appears that the training environment rarely transforms the student, but instead "it can take what is there and deepen it, dampen it, shape it, and alter it. . . . at times the environment can have a profound effect, actually creating a transformation of sorts" (Gelso, 1997, p. 312).

PERSON IN ENVIRONMENT

In this section, we consider two streams of inquiry. First, we review studies exploring some aspect of person by environment interaction in relation to research training or productivity outcomes. These studies have generally examined person factors, such as Holland interest types or other personality variables, in combination with aspects of the research training environment as conceptualized by Gelso (1979). Second, we review research extending social cognitive theory to research training/productivity. This research is considered within the rubric of "person in environment" because social cognitive person variables, such as self-efficacy and outcome expectations, are presumed to derive from, and change through, transactions with the environment.

Person-Environment Interaction

A few studies reviewed earlier within the sections on person or training environment factors have also examined person-environment interaction effects. Such studies are quite important, theoretically and practically, because they consider that particular environmental ingredients may well have differential effects, depending on students' training needs and other attributes. This line of research may also suggest ways in which training environments can be fine tuned to meet the needs of particular student types—rather than assuming that "one size fits all."

Royalty et al. (1986) explored the possibility that the relationship between students' perceptions of the training environment and their reported change in research attitudes would depend on students' year in graduate school. They found that five of the nine subscales of the RTES related positively to attitude changes in second-year students; six of the scales correlated with attitude change in third-year students (r's ranged from .24 to .42). However, no significant correlations were observed in first-, fourth-, or fifth-year students, and moderately negative correlations were found between five of the environment scales and attitude change in the group of sixth-year-and-beyond students.

Royalty et al. interpreted their findings as suggesting that the research environment may have most of its positive influence on research attitudes within the first few years of training. After that point, as students pursue internships and other, more individualized experiences, the program may simply have less leverage on research attitudes. Although the negative correlations among the most senior students is difficult to explain, Royalty et al. suggested that these students may represent "late finishers" for whom the positive effects of the research training environment did not "take hold."

In a somewhat related vein, Phillips and Russell (1994) explored the relationship between composite RTES perceptions and research productivity among newer (first and second year) and more advanced (fourth year and beyond) students in counseling psychology. The RTES-productivity correlation was moderate and significant only among advanced students. Viewing these findings in the context of those by Royalty et al. (1986), it may be that the training environment effects changes in research attitudes sooner than in productivity. Effects on productivity may be more gradual and only be apparent later on, assuming that they are partly a consequence of favorable attitude change and also depend on the development of research skills, as well as the accumulation of sufficient opportunities to pursue and complete scholarly projects.

Using the same sample as Royalty et al., Mallinckrodt et al. (1990) explored Holland interest theme–RTES interactions with respect to research attitude changes. Their findings indicated that two environment factors—reinforcement of student research and science as a partly social experience—related more strongly to research attitude changes among students with high- versus low-social or artistic interests. Although these few significant interactions explained only 1% to 1½% additional variance in attitude change, they nevertheless suggest ways in which the research training environment may be made more responsive to the needs of social- and artistic-type students, who comprise the majority of counseling psychology doctoral students (e.g., Krebs et al., 1991; Mallinckrodt et al., 1990). Other findings also suggest that counseling psychologists with different interest types prefer RTEs that are compatible with their type (Royalty & Magoon, 1985).

Krebs et al. (1991) examined research productivity as a function of investigative interests, RTES composite scores, and their interaction in a national survey of counseling psychologists. RTES-productivity relations were significant only among respondents with investigative theme scores in the upper two quartiles. Thus, the training environment may best promote research productivity in those with relatively strong scientific interests. A recent longitudinal study of graduate training in the physical sciences found that students' abilities and attitudes at entry predicted the amount of mentoring and research collaboration subsequently provided by their advisors (Green & Bauer, 1995). Like Krebs et al.'s findings, such results imply a sort of rich-get-richer phenomenon, pointing to the need to identify training conditions that foster the scientific development of students who enter graduate school with relatively *less* interest or skill in science.

In sum, these few studies offer preliminary evidence that certain person variables, particularly interest/personality type and developmental level, may interact with aspects of the training environment, resulting in differential outcomes. Effect sizes have generally been quite modest, and there is need to replicate these findings. However, this sort of research is crucial if the field is to address important "matching questions," such as which training ingredients work best for which students and on which outcomes?

Social Cognitive Applications

Applications of theory to research training and productivity represent a relatively new trend in the literature. To this point, studies have been derived largely from two theoretical positions: Holland's (1985) typology of interests and Gelso's (1979, 1993) theory of research training environments. However, a third theoretical framework, social cognitive theory, has also emerged as a source of hypotheses about factors that promote research outcomes in students and postdoctoral professionals. This line of research is derived from Bandura's (1986) seminal theory and, more recently, from adaptations of this theory to the study of career development processes and outcomes (Lent et al., 1994). Applications of social cognitive theory to scientist development are based on the assumption that choice of, and achievement in, scientific endeavors involve the same sorts of theoretical mechanisms that affect career development in other occupational fields.

In some ways, social cognitive career theory (SCCT; Lent et al., 1994) may be seen as complementing, rather than competing with, Holland's and Gelso's theories. For example, SCCT incorporates the influence of personality and interest on career outcomes (Holland) and also acknowledges the effects of environmental factors (Holland, Gelso). However, SCCT does differ from these other theories in some important specifics. One key difference involves the conceptualization of how the environment promotes science-related interest, choice, and performance.

Gelso's theory, for example, suggests that the training environment directly influences both research attitudes and interests (cf. Gelso et al., 1996). By contrast, social cognitive hypotheses (Betz, 1986; Lent et al., 1994) posit that the effect of the training environment operates largely indirectly by affecting certain intervening person variables which, in turn, promote interests. For instance, by providing opportunities for early, direct success with research projects, training environments help to strengthen students' research skills, along with their self-efficacy and outcome expectations (i.e., beliefs about personal research performance capabilities and about the consequences of research involvement). Increased self-efficacy and outcome beliefs would then be expected to promote interests in research pursuits, as well as subsequent science-related goals and performance behavior. As we will see, tests of such direct versus mediating hypotheses have begun to appear.

Much of the growing literature on social cognitive theory and research training or productivity outcomes can be divided into four categories: (1) linkages to interest; (2) linkages to productivity; (3) predictors and facilitators of research self-efficacy; and (4) male-female differences in research self-efficacy. Individual studies have frequently involved investigation of more than one of these topics. Perhaps the earliest sustained focus of this literature was on sex differences in self-efficacy. This focus reflected an effort to understand the basis for differential career experiences of female and male academics. Because of the centrality of this issue, we incorporate gender-related findings within the context of our review of studies of research interests, productivity, and self-efficacy correlates.

Research Interests

Several studies have examined the relation of social cognitive variables, primarily self-efficacy, to research interest. In a sample of graduate students from a wide variety of disciplines, Bieschke, Bishop, and Garcia (1996) found that research interest correlated moderately with both research self-efficacy and research involvement. Together, self-efficacy and research involvement explained 29% of interest variation. Male and female students did not differ significantly in self-efficacy ratings. O'Brien et al. (1998), studying counseling psychology students, reported that self-efficacy correlated strongly with interest in research and in the role of scientist, as well as moderately with research values.

Bieschke et al. (1995) explored the relations of self-efficacy, outcome expectations, and the research environment (as measured by Royalty et al.'s, 1986, RTES) to research interest in rehabilitation doctoral students. Although relations of self-efficacy and the RTES to interest were generally small, outcome expectations were found to correlate substantially with interest, explaining 43% of interest variation in a multiple regression. In a follow-up study with rehabilitation counseling faculty, Bieschke, Herbert, et al. (1998) found that outcome expectations once again correlated more strongly with research interests than did self-efficacy.

Two recent studies used path analysis or causal modeling designs to test hypotheses regarding the research interests of counseling psychology students. Kahn and Scott (1997) found that Holland investigative interests, RTES-composite scores, and self-efficacy jointly explained 33% of the variance in interests. The training environment affected interest both directly as well as indirectly, through self-efficacy. Although gender did not relate directly to research interest, it did correlate with self-efficacy, with men reporting higher self-efficacy.

Bishop and Bieschke (1998) found support for a model wherein research interests were jointly predicted by self-efficacy, outcome expectations, investigative interests, artistic interests (negatively), and student age. The full model accounted for 62% of interest variation. Similar to earlier findings by Bieschke and her colleagues, outcome expectations were found to be the single strongest predictor, explaining 41% of interest variation. Effects of the training environment on interest were fully mediated by self-efficacy and outcome expectations and, contrary to Kahn and Scott's (1997) findings, the relation of gender to research self-efficacy was small and nonsignificant. The big difference in the predictive efficiency of these last two studies (62% vs. 33% variance explained) may involve the addition of outcome expectations to the theoretical model. However, the two studies also used different measures of self-efficacy and research interests.

Research Productivity

Several studies have examined social cognitive variables in relation to faculty members' research productivity. In the first of these studies, Taylor et al. (1984) employed a sample of academics from diverse disciplines. They found that research self-efficacy related moderately to indices of both productivity (quantity) and quality (citation frequency). They also found support for a path model in which the effect of job involvement on productivity was mediated by self-efficacy, goals, and the tendency to work on multiple projects. The effect of self-efficacy on productivity was both direct as well as indirect via goals and multiple projects. Vasil (1992) also reported that academics' research self-efficacy correlated moderately with their research productivity. In a study of rehabilitation counseling faculty, Bieschke, Herbert, et al. (1998) found that self-efficacy, outcome expectations, and research interests each correlated moderately with research productivity, although only self-efficacy and interest accounted for significant variation in productivity after controlling for demographic, program, and rank variables. Relations of gender to self-efficacy and outcome expectations were small and nonsignificant.

Four other studies have examined social cognitive variable-research productivity relations in counseling psychology graduate student samples. Using different research self-efficacy measures, Phillips and Russell (1994) and O'Brien et al. (1998) each found that self-efficacy was substantially related to productivity. Phillips and Russell also found that self-efficacy was moderately related to training environment (composite RTES) ratings, and that advanced students reported stronger self-efficacy than beginning students. They did not find significant gender differences in self-efficacy, RTES, or productivity.

In a reanalysis of Phillips and Russell's advanced student data, Brown et al. (1996) explored the theoretical possibility that the self-efficacy mediates the effect of the training environment on productivity. Results did suggest such a mediational relationship when the data were aggregated over gender, but somewhat different patterns emerged when men and women were examined separately. In particular, for men, the training environment exerted its effect on productivity only through self-efficacy. By contrast, for women, self-efficacy only partly mediated the environment-productivity relationship. That is, training showed both a direct link to productivity as well as an indirect link via women's self-efficacy beliefs. These gender-based differences must be viewed cautiously, given the relatively small sample of advanced students on which they were based.

In their causal modeling study, Kahn and Scott (1997) examined predictors of productivity and career goals as well as research interest (the prediction of research interest was discussed earlier). Findings suggested that productivity was a function of career goals, research interests, and year in doctoral program; collectively, these variables explained 57% of the variance in productivity. Only interest yielded a direct path to career goals, accounting for 33% of the predictive variance. The effect of self-efficacy on productivity and goals was indirect, being mediated by research interests.

Predictors of Research Self-efficacy

Finally, several studies have examined factors that correlate with or facilitate research self-efficacy. Assuming that self-efficacy promotes interest and productivity, it is important to explore the types of experience that can strengthen efficacy percepts. We first consider three studies of faculty members. Schoen and Winocur (1988) found that research self-efficacy relates to research task involvement and academic rank, with more research-active and advanced faculty (who have presumably accrued more research successes) reporting stronger self-efficacy beliefs than less active and junior faculty.

Landino and Owen (1988) found that research self-efficacy was predicted by several experiential variables, such as publication experience, perceived university responsiveness, mentoring, and group participation. These authors also found gender differences in research self-efficacy, with male faculty reporting stronger self-efficacy beliefs than female faculty. However, the effect of gender on research self-efficacy was mediated by differential experiences and environmental climate variables. Vasil (1992) reported that causal attributions were related to self-efficacy, with the tendency to attribute research successes to one's personal ability being associated with stronger self-efficacy beliefs. Vasil also found that gender differences in self-efficacy (males reported higher ratings) were paralleled by differences in the frequency with which men and women performed research tasks.

Turning to research involving graduate students, studies have mostly found moderate to strong relations between indices of the training environment and self-efficacy (Bieschke et al., 1995; Bishop & Bieschke, 1998; Gelso et al, 1996; Kahn & Scott, 1997; Phillips & Russell, 1994). Self-efficacy has also been shown to be positively related to year in graduate program (Bieschke et al., 1996; Bishop & Bieschke, 1998; Kahn & Scott, 1997; Phillips & Russell, 1994) and to amount of research experience (Bieschke et al., 1996). ("Year in program" may reflect cumulative increases in research skill as a function of performance experience; cf. Heppner et al., 1999.) Finally, in a study involving masters students in rehabilitation counseling, Szymanski, Whitney-Thomas, Marshall, and Sayger (1994) found that students participating in a research course, compared with those in a quasi-control group, reported significant increases in research self-efficacy and the perceived value of research, and lowered research anxiety.

Summary of Social Cognitive Findings

Studies applying social cognitive theory to research training and productivity have yielded promising results. Self-efficacy for research tasks has typically contributed substantially to the prediction of research interest and productivity; outcome expectations have also been shown to be an important predictor of research interest; and interest was strongly predictive of research-related career goals. Although each of these conclusions is consistent with hypotheses derived from SCCT, it is important to note that there has been limited study of certain linkages (e.g., outcome expectations-interest, interest-goal) and not all findings have been theory-consonant (e.g., Kahn & Scott, 1997).

Study of self-efficacy as an intervening variable between the training environment and outcome criteria has not yielded definitive conclusions. The effect of training on interest and productivity appears to be at least partly mediated by self-efficacy (Brown et al., 1996; Kahn & Scott, 1997), and the precise nature of the mediational relationship may vary for male and female students. Outcome expectations may also add an important piece to the puzzle: Effects of training on interest were fully mediated by the combination of self-efficacy and outcome expectations in one study (Bishop & Bieschke, 1998).

On balance, at least part of the effect of the training environment on relevant outcomes may be explained by the manner in which the environment affects students' beliefs about their research competencies and the outcomes of engaging in research. However, part of the environment's effect may also be direct (or mediated by as-yet unstudied intervening variables). In addition to its theoretical interest, further study of this issue may have important practical implications. For example, subsequent findings may suggest optimal methods for modifying the training environment so as to magnify its impact on research interest and productivity. It would also be useful to study additional environmental (e.g., moderator) hypotheses derived from SCCT. For example, SCCT suggests that students' willingness to translate their interests into goals, and their goals into actions, depends partly on the supports or barriers they encounter in their environments. Thus, particular environmental supports and barriers (e.g., mentoring, job market conditions) might be examined in relation to their effects on students' research career paths.

Finally, research on predictors of, and gender differences in, research self-efficacy may offer useful suggestions for ways to promote scholarly involvement in both female and male students. It is noteworthy that male and female students and faculty do not consistently report differences in research self-efficacy, although, in a few studies (and only one in counseling psychology), males have reported stronger self-efficacy beliefs. Such differences, where they are found, may derive from experiential and environmental climate variables. Viable methods for enhancing research self-efficacy include exposure to personal success experiences with research, as well as potent vicarious and supportive experiences.

WHERE DO WE GO FROM HERE? DIRECTIONS FOR FUTURE INQUIRY

A number of recommendations for research have been offered in passing throughout the chapter. In this section, we summarize the main ones and and add further recommendations.

Progress has clearly been made in identifying important aspects of persons and environments (and, to a lesser extent, P X E interactions) that predict or promote desired research training outcomes. Much more effort is needed, however, before this domain achieves any sort of parity with advances that the field has made in studying counselor training and supervision. Given the relative newness of the research training area and the sparseness of research and theory on the topic, it is clear that empirical and theoretical work is needed on a wide range of themes.

Addressing Neglected Outcomes

Of the research outcomes that have been conceptualized and studied, the most neglected empirically are research skill/competence and research quality. It is likely that skill or competence is not unidimensional, but rather consists of a range of component skills in such domains as statistics, measurement, methodology, and writing. Of course, we would also want to develop researchers who transcend what a perceptive colleague once referred to as "having good hands" (i.e., being good research technicians). Ideally, training would also foster such skills as clarity, depth, and complexity of thinking with respect to research and science. As Betz (1986) has noted, "[W]e need to restore our focus . . . on education to think, to wonder, to learn not just content areas but the processes of learning to learn, reasoning, and problem solving" (p. 111). In sum, research is needed on person and training factors that influence these competencies, and how such competencies relate to more distal outcomes (e.g., later productivity).

Relatedly, although quantity of productivity has been used as an outcome in several studies, virtually no studies in the research training area have used quality of research as an outcome. Some studies of faculty productivity have employed a number of citations as an index of quality (e.g., Hanish et al., 1995; Taylor et al., 1984). Measures of quality need to be developed for research produced during graduate school years.

Ironically, an outcome that has been neglected thus far has been *change* in whatever criterion variable has been examined. For example, most studies focus on the relationship of certain person or environmental elements to outcomes such as research interest, self-efficacy, and productivity. In fact, such studies do not really address the bottom-line question of the training and person factors that facilitate the improvement, development, or unfolding of these criteria. The fact that a certain environmental factor is related to research interest tells us little about whether that factor facilitates strengthening of (change in) interest in research. It is the latter outcome that needs to be our primary concern.

Identifying Additional Predictors

Research has thus far identified a number of person and environment predictors of research attitudes, self-efficacy, and productivity. However, given that research behaviors—like all complex human activities—are multiply determined, it would be valuable to study additional variables and processes in relation to desired training outcomes. One promising direction includes study of the strategies that effective student researchers use to manage their time, cope with research barriers and frustrations, and set (as well as adhere to) personal developmental goals. Certain social-contextual factors, such as advising, mentoring, and peer group influences also deserve greater attention. As noted earlier, although the advisor-advisee relationship is embedded within Gelso's (1979, 1993, 1997) theory of the effective RTE, little research has directly studied this potentially crucial factor (cf. Betz, 1997; Hill, 1997). Likewise research on mentoring is clearly in its infancy in counseling, as well as other areas of psychology.

Prevailing accounts of the RTE focus almost exclusively on the role of the faculty and curriculum in shaping students' research attitudes and behavior. However, higher education research suggests that peers also play an important role in the educational socialization process (Astin, 1993). Moreover, general social learning findings indicate that similarity on such dimensions as age can strengthen modeling effects (Bandura, 1986). Thus, students likely play an important part in shaping the research culture of a training program, and they may well influence one another's research aspirations and productivity in graduate school—just as colleagues appear to do in postdoctoral job settings (cf. Bland & Ruffin, 1992). Such possibilities deserve added study.

Examining Additional Aspects of Research Training and the Research Training Environment

Most RTE studies have examined the relation between individual students' perceptions of the RTE and intermediate or ultimate outcomes. Although this focus is important, it does not get at RTE effects at the training program level. Royalty et al.'s (1986) early effort uncovered marked differences among training programs in their RTE, and two studies (Gelso et al., 1996; Royalty et al., 1986) clearly point to the effect of such differences on students' attitudes toward research. It is also clear that some programs have a powerful positive effect on their students' research attitudes and behavior, and it would be useful to study what those programs do to produce that effect. Conversely, students in other programs seem to exhibit declining research interest over the course of their graduate careers, and studies are needed to understand what accounts for this deteriorative effect.

As noted in our review, certain ingredients of effective RTEs have been identified, and there has also been an abundance of suggestions for improving research training through coursework and noncoursework experiences (e.g., research practica, workshops, research teams). Unfortunately, though, there has been little or no effort to study and compare the effects of specific training strategies on particular training outcomes. Of course, in addition to addressing more global, main effects-type questions (e.g., what works best?), it would be valuable to explore attribute (person) X treatment (specific training intervention) interactions (e.g., what works best for which students, on what criteria?). Promising student attributes to match to training strategies include Holland vocational personality types and developmental level (e.g., year in training, research experience).

Intervention research would be useful on several levels. For example, experimental and quasi-experimental studies of training components and strategies could allow for more powerful causal inferences than has been possible in the correlational research that has been done to date. Such research could also help empirically to establish "best practices" regarding research training methods. On a logistical level, experimental work would be somewhat daunting to conduct (e.g., finding sufficient numbers of students and appropriate comparison conditions within and across particular programs), calling for creative methodological and analytic solutions, such as gathering data from successive "waves" of students over several years (e.g., Tinsley et al., 1993). The yield from such research, however, could make it well worth the challenges.

Extending the Methodological, Developmental, and Cultural Range of Research

A clear and pronounced movement has occurred over the course of several years toward the use of nontraditional research approaches, especially qualitative designs, in counseling psychology (Hill, Thompson, & Williams, 1997; Morrow & Smith, this volume). Such research may be quite helpful at this point in time in the research training area. Asking students and professionals about training experiences that have been helpful and harmful, finding out faculty's perceptions of such experiences, learning about advisors' and advisees' perceptions of their working alliances, and assessing statistics professors' and students' perceptions of effective and ineffective teaching techniques are but a few examples of the many topics that can be fruitfully probed with qualitative designs in a way that supplements quantitative findings.

Accompanying the trend toward qualitative approaches has been an equally important movement toward the use of advanced statistical procedures to test theoretical propositions. In particular, structural equation modeling (Kahn & Scott, 1997), path analysis (Bishop & Bieschke, 1998), and confirmatory factor analysis (Kahn & Gelso, 1997) have recently been used to good advantage. Although such approaches offer the opportunity to study complex questions, we also believe that the more fundamental need is for good ideas, and that simple tests of such ideas are often just as elegant and useful.

A particularly useful analytic strategy has been to explore how certain variables (e.g., research self-efficacy) may mediate the relationship between a predictor (e.g., the RTE) and criterion (e.g., productivity). The assessment of indirect (mediated) effects represents a growing edge of research on research training. Likewise, the study of interaction effects, especially person X intervention interactions, remains a major need in this area (Mallinckrodt, 1997). As the research training area advances, research will move from the general "does it work?" question to the more differentiated question of what research experiences offered by which faculty within what kind of overall training environment affect graduate students in which ways at what points in their development? Naturally, this question (actually, series of questions) cannot be addressed in any single study, but it points the way to the kinds of interaction effects that need to be examined over the course of numerous investigations. The important study of how individual and cultural factors interact with training and environment factors is an important part of this thrust.

To date, most research on research training and productivity has focused on graduate students. This focus has made sense given the centrality of the training situation for the development of research attitudes and behaviors. It would be valuable, however, to extend the study of scientist development in two temporal directions—prior to and after graduate school. Graduate training is, after all, a relatively brief period in most psychologists' lives. It is preceded and followed by many formative experiences that help mold research attitudes and behaviors. Although there have been some seminal studies of the life experiences and career/life span productivity of creative researchers (e.g., Roe, 1953; Stumpf, 1995), we still know very little about experiences before and after graduate school that have helped shape scientific attitudes and behavior. We know much about which individuals and training programs in our field have been productive or impactful (e.g., Hanish et al., 1995; Howard & Curtin, 1993), but we need to know much more about the factors that promote or sustain scholarship.

Study of pregraduate school experiences and behavior should assist the field to identify practices that facilitate early development of scientific attitudes and behavior, and also aid in the prediction of such attitudes and behavior. Meanwhile, studying "working scholars" (as well as those professionals who are not involved in scholarly work) could help highlight processes central to choice of, and persistence in, scientific endeavors, particularly in the face of environmental hurdles and inevitable setbacks.

An aspect of extending the methodological and developmental range of research is the use of longitudinal designs. Such designs are extremely rare in the research training area, and are sorely needed to supplement cross-sectional and retrospective survey methods that have characterized nearly all investigations. Longitudinal approaches would be most useful to measure *change,* as discussed earlier. Cross-sectional designs simply do not allow for strong inferences about change.

It also is important to attend to cultural variables and processes in relation to research training. More needs to be known, for example, about environmental resources that support the scientific career development of students of color (Pope-Davis, Stone, & Nielson, 1997) and lesbian, gay, and bisexual researchers (Bieschke, Eberz, Bard, & Croteau, 1998). Ponterotto and Casas (in press) have recently proposed six sets of multicultural research competencies. These competencies are designed to promote a sophisticated and ethical approach to multicultural research topics, research participants, and research training.

Developing and Refining Theories and Measures

Finally, perhaps the most fundamental need for further inquiry lies in the development, application, and refinement of theories of effective research training. In fact, such theories could subsume and lend direction to all of the suggestions we have made so far. New or refined theories could serve as a source of additional constructs, measures, and interventions.

At present, three main theoretical positions have been applied to the study of research training and productivity in counseling psychology: Gelso's (1979, 1993) theory of the research training environment, Holland's (1985) theory of vocational personality and environment, and Lent et al.'s (1994) social cognitive career theory. One possible direction would involve the exploration of the ways in which these theories may complement one another. For instance, Gelso's theory focuses on the *content* of research training. Lent et al.'s social cognitive theory, on the other hand, emphasizes interest, choice, and performance *processes,* but is less specific about research training content. Empirical and theoretical work on the interface between these theories could be illuminating.

Although the application of additional career theories (e.g., Lofquist & Dawis, 1984) to the development of research attitudes and behavior could be fruitful, perhaps the field would profit most from the development of new theories. For example, whereas the three theories noted in the above paragraph encompass large domains of behavior, more specific theories (what are often referred to as minitheories) could be invaluable in many, more specific, topics within the general research training area, for example, the advising and mentoring relationship, the sequencing of training events, and ingredients of effective research or statistics courses.

Going hand in hand with the need for theory development is the need for measures to address these theories. There is perhaps nothing that warms the minds and hearts of researchers like a good measure—one that is both economical and reliable. Considerable advances have occurred in the area of measure development in research training. As new theoretical constructs emerge and as existing theories become further refined, instrument development and refinement needs to be a constant accompaniment of this progress.

SUGGESTIONS FOR THE PRACTICE OF RESEARCH TRAINING

Many implications and suggestions for the practice of research training are contained both in the previous pages of this chapter and the existing literature (e.g., Betz, 1997; Bowman, 1997; Galassi, Stoltz, Brooks, & Trexler, 1987; Gelso, 1979, 1993, 1997; Hill, 1997; Mallinckrodt, 1997; Wampold, 1986). Next we summarize the most compelling of these suggestions, and add further points based on our review. Before doing so, we look at a debate that goes to the heart of the research training enterprise.

The Student Selection Debate

A chapter such as this would be remiss if it did not examine issues and controversies regarding who and how counseling programs select for doctoral training. Led by Holland's (1986) recommendations, some have suggested that the best way to enhance research behavior and productivity is through selecting for person factors that reflect strong scientific interest and skill. Because, for example, the Investigative personality (Holland, 1985) has clearly been shown to relate to relevant research behavior, this argument suggests that if we want more and better science, we ought more systematically to select Investigative types. Instead, our training programs are too populated with Social type personalities, whose main interests revolve around counseling practice.

The flip side of this controversy is the view that our attention should focus on the training environment. Such an argument might include the notion that students enter training, on the whole, with high degrees of plasticity regarding research interest and self-efficacy. Powerful training environments will have an impact on varying personality types, not just Investigative types. Scores on Social and Investigative themes have not been found to be inversely related among counseling graduate students (Bishop & Bieschke, 1998; Kahn & Scott, 1997; Zachar & Leong, 1992); neither have Social theme scores been found to correlate negatively with research interests or attitudes. In fact, interest in and attitudes toward research among Social types may well be affected by effective research training (see Mallinckrodt et al., 1990).

In response to the first of these two positions, we would offer that selecting only Investigative types would be problematic because, in fact, most programs are not scientist-only programs, but instead are scientist-practitioner programs. Such programs need to select both for good science and good practice, and the evidence does not support the notion that Investigative types make for competent and inspired practitioners. In fact, the evidence suggests that we are indeed selecting for this joint mission. The typical counseling psychology student is not a pure Social type. The summary code (e.g., on the Strong Interest Inventory) of our students is typically Artistic-Social-Investigative (ASI; Betz & Taylor, 1982; Mallinckrodt et al., 1990). Thus, both social and investigative components are part of the mix.

The view that is proposed here is that we can have it both ways. We can select students who exhibit strong investigative elements in their application materials (e.g., documented research behavior, recommendations addressing research potential) as well as potential for excellence in practice, realizing that these two attributes likely will not be entirely balanced within a given applicant. Alternatively, we can select a mix of students—some more clearly I, S, or A types—with the intention that each will develop the primary and secondary sides of his or her personality during scientist-practitioner training. Of course, depending on a program's training philosophy and goals, faculty may wish to emphasize selection of students who report greater interest, and have demonstrated prior success, in either the scientific or practice domain. At the same time, it is important to understand that, although we can try to select and train students who have a passion for science and/or practice, when they leave our programs, each student is going to find his or her own place on the scientist-practitioner continuum.

Training and Developmental Level

Just as counseling supervision needs to take into account the developmental level of supervisees, individual research supervision, as well as the organization and sequencing of training experiences, needs to pay attention to the student's developmental level in research. As we have studied training programs over the years, our sense is that research instruction is typically not matched intentionally to students' developmental levels in most programs, except in a general way (e.g., advanced courses follow basic ones). Some programs, faculty members, and advisors, however, surely do this sort of matching. On the whole, though, training programs need to devote greater energy to thinking systematically about what sequence of training experiences will be most effective for students, and how this sequencing can be influenced by individual students' needs. For example, the first step in training is often to have students join research teams during their first semester, where the tasks given to these students depend on their level of sophistication in research. For some students, though, being on a team in the first semester may not be wise. These may be students who would do better to work individually with their advisors or who might best not be involved in research immediately. Thus, a practice recommendation is that the organization and sequencing of training events need to take into account students' developmental level and individual differences. These individual and developmental level differences have probably always been attended to carefully by great mentors (e.g., Cummings, 1996).

The Reinforcement of Research Attitudes and Behavior

Gelso (1979) considered the graduate research training situation a behavior modification task in the broadest sense. That is, students enter training with much ambivalence about research and its role in their lives, and if attitudes are to move to the positive side of the continuum, the environment must provide sufficient positive reinforcement for research behavior and attitudes. Tied to this primacy, the faculty reinforcement ingredient of Gelso's RTE theory was considered the most fundamental of his factors in the sense that it pervades all the other ingredients. In addition, of the nine ingredients in his theory, faculty reinforcement has probably received the most consistent and powerful empirical support.

It is important that research trainers think carefully about reinforcers and about the question of what programs and faculty can do to reinforce students' research behavior and attitudes. Given that counseling students are often so interpersonally oriented, we suspect that interpersonal reinforcers may be the most potent. Thus, for example, encouragement and praise from advisors, mentors, and faculty in general for research behavior should affect attitudes, self-efficacy, skill, and productivity. The excitement faculty members feel for students' ideas may be one of the most potent reinforcers of all, and students readily comment on this when asked about what in their training has affected their research interest (Gelso, 1997). So do faculty members who look back on their training and their interactions with mentors (e.g., Ashford, 1996).

There are probably also reinforcers that programs could effectively incorporate that are not as clearly and directly interpersonal. Examples of such reinforcers are giving awards for outstanding research performance, offering financial assistance for travel and research-related expenses, providing computers for research, allowing students to use undergraduate research assistants in their research, and noting outstanding achievements in department and program communiques.

We are not suggesting that students need to be constantly positively reinforced for research behavior. Nor are we ignoring the great significance of students' own internal reinforcement. We do, however, offer the view that if programs want to enhance research attitudes, self-efficacy, and productivity, faculty ought to be responsive to these phenomena through their support and encouragement in a range of ways.

Life after Graduate School: Coping with Barriers

The issue of learning to cope with research barriers also deserves some comment. Aside from internal-personal attributes, such as lack of interest in research, many practicing counseling psychologists face substantial extrinsic hurdles (e.g., heavy practice demands) to their formal involvement in scientific activities (Haynes, Lemsky, & Sexton-Radek, 1987). To boot, these hurdles often exist in the face of few extrinsic reinforcers for scientific work. These are hurdles that research trainers cannot simply dismiss. Especially within the current health care market-place, therapists' livelihoods frequently depend in part on the efficiency with which they discharge their clinical duties. Apart from marketplace considerations, however, practice settings have always presented significant barriers to scientific work. From the perspective of graduate trainers, the most discouraging part of these real-life impediments is that they diminish or wipe out the ability of many former students to pursue formal scholarship (e.g., the development of clinical theory, collaborative research projects), for which these former students may have both passion and talent.

We think it useful and important for faculty to help students during their graduate education anticipate how to cope with the barriers that are regularly manifest in practice settings, including agencies such as university counseling centers. Discussions in research seminars, professional issues courses, and special workshops could help students anticipate environmental hurdles to their scholarship. Such interventions need also to help students consider strategies for dealing with the hurdles. Although interventions will not prevent research obstacles, the availability of coping methods, and the sense of efficacy in their use, may encourage persistence toward career goals under adverse conditions. We should also note that some current students will go on to become administrators of counseling agencies. Discussions during graduate school of the ins and outs, the benefits and drawbacks, of doing research in agency settings may stimulate them to better support research-oriented staff members in their agencies.

A particularly effective vehicle through which students could learn about how to do scholarly work in the world of practice is adjunct and affiliate faculty who themselves are in practice settings. These faculty can be powerful scholarly models (Heppner et al., 1987), and they also have much wisdom to share about doing scientific work in practice settings—wisdom that full-time faculty usually cannot possess.

This discussion of scholarship in primarily practice settings requires that we underscore the need to broaden what is often seen as the ultimate goal of research training—that is, enhanced *research* productivity. Diverse forms of scholarship and theory development, as well as empirical research, need to be emphasized and legitimized as part of the scientific training mission. It may be useful to conclude with the reminder that the great therapy theories of the twentieth century were developed by individuals who were steeped in practice, who were able to find and make the time to include scholarship in their worklives. We expect that the twenty-first century will be no different. Ultimately, though, our science and practice will be enhanced by helping our students learn how scholarly work can be done in the context of practice and practice settings.

REFERENCES

Altmaier, E.M., & Claiborn, C.D. (1987). Some observations on research and science. *Journal of Counseling and Development, 66,* 51.

American Psychological Association, Division on Counseling and Guidance, Committee on Counselor Training. (1952). Recommended standards for training counseling psychologists at the doctorate level. *American Psychologist, 7,* 175–181.

Ashford, S.J. (1996). Working with doctoral students: Reflections on doctoral work past and present. In P.J. Frost & S.M. Taylor (Eds.), *Rhythms of academic life: Personal accounts of careers in academia* (pp. 153–158). Thousand Oaks, CA: Sage.

Astin, A.W. (1993). *What matters in college: Four critical years revisited.* San Francisco: Jossey-Bass.

Bandura, A. (1986). *Social foundations of thought and actions: A social cognitive theory.* Englewood Cliffs, NJ: Prentice-Hall.

Berman, P. (1990, August). *The influence of graduate training on research attitudes: A longitudinal study.* Paper presented at the annual meeting of the American Psychological Association.

Berman, P. (1992). The influence of graduate training on research attitudes, consumption, and production. In J. Grip, B. Vaughn, K. Edwards, L. Ferguson, & R. Olsen (Eds.), *Mirror, mirror on the wall: Framing new models to evaluate professional competence.* Washington, DC: American Psychological Association.

Betz, N.E. (1986). Research training in counseling psychology: Have we addressed the real issues? *The Counseling Psychologist, 14,* 107–113.

Betz, N.E. (1997). Increasing research involvement and interests among graduate students in counseling psychology. *The Counseling Psychologist, 25,* 88–93.

Betz, N.E., & Taylor, K.M. (1982). Concurrent validity of the Strong-Campbell Interest Inventory for graduate students in counseling psychology. *Journal of Counseling Psychology, 29,* 626–635.

Bieschke, K.J., Bishop, R.M., & Garcia, V.L. (1996). The utility of the Research Self-Efficacy Scale. *Journal of Career Assessment, 4,* 59–75.

Bieschke, K.J., Bishop, R.M., & Herbert, J.T. (1995). Research interest among rehabilitation doctoral students. *Rehabilitation Education, 9,* 51–66.

Bieschke, K.J., Eberz, A.B., Bard, C.C., & Croteau, J.M. (1998). Using social cognitive career theory to create affirmative lesbian, gay, and bisexual research training environments. *The Counseling Psychologist, 25,* 735–753.

Bieschke, K.J., Herbert, J.T., & Bard, C. (1998). Using a social cognitive model to explain research productivity among rehabilitation counselor education faculty. *Rehabilitation Education, 12,* 1–16.

Bishop, R.M., & Bieschke, K.J. (1998). Applying social cognitive theory to interest in research among counseling psychology graduate students: A path analysis. *Journal of Counseling Psychology, 45,* 182–188.

Bland, C.J., & Ruffin, M.T. (1992). Characteristics of a productive research environment: Literature review. *Academic Medicine, 67,* 385–397.

Bowman, S.L. (1997). Research training in counseling psychology: A former training program director's perceptions. *The Counseling Psychologist, 25,* 82–87.

Brehms, C. (1994). Taking the fear out of research: A gentle approach to teaching an appreciation of research. *Teaching of Psychology, 21,* 241–243.

Brems, C., Johnson, M.E., & Gallucci, P. (1996). Publication productivity of clinical and counseling psychologists. *Journal of Clinical Psychology, 52,* 723–725.

Brown, S.D., Lent, R.W., Ryan, N.E., & McPartland, E.B. (1996). Self-efficacy as an intervening mechanism between research training environments and scholarly productivity: A theoretical and methodological extension. *The Counseling Psychologist, 24,* 535–544.

Burke, R.J., McKeen, C.A., & McKenna, C. (1993). Correlates of mentoring in organizations: The mentor's perspective. *Psychological Reports, 72,* 883–896.

Cummings, L.L. (1996). The development of doctoral students: Substantive and emotional perspectives. In P.J. Frost & S.M. Taylor (Eds.), *Rhythms of academic life: Personal accounts of careers in academia* (pp. 147–152). Thousand Oaks, CA: Sage.

Feldman, K.A., & Newcomb, T.M. (1969). *The impact of college on students.* San Francisco: Jossey-Bass.

Fitzgerald, L.F., & Osipow, S.H. (1986). An occupational analysis of counseling psychology: How special is the specialty? *American Psychologist, 41,* 535–544.

Frank, G. (1984). The Boulder model: History, rationale, and critique. *Professional Psychology: Research and Practice, 15,* 417–435.

Galassi, J.P. (1989). Maintaining the viability of counseling psychology. *Counseling Psychology Quarterly, 2,* 465–474.

Galassi, J.P., Brooks, L., Stoltz, R.F., & Trexler, K.A. (1986). Research training environments and student productivity. *The Counseling Psychologist, 14,* 31–36.

Galassi, J.P., Stoltz, R.F., Brooks, L., & Trexler, K.A. (1987). Improving research training in doctoral counseling programs. *Journal of Counseling and Development, 66,* 40–44.

Garfield, S.L., & Kurtz, R.M. (1976). Clinical psychologists in the 1970s. *American Psychologist, 31,* 1–9.

Gelso, C.J. (1979). Research in counseling: Methodological and professional issues. *The Counseling Psychologist, 8*(3), 7–35.

Gelso, C.J. (1993). On the making of a scientist-practitioner: A theory of research training in professional psychology. *Professional Psychology: Research and Practice, 24,* 468–476.

Gelso, C.J. (1997). The making of a scientist in applied psychology: An attribute by treatment conception. *The Counseling Psychologist, 25,* 307–320.

Gelso, C.J., Betz, N.E., Friedlander, M.L., Helms, J.E., Hill, C.E., Patton, M.J., Super, D.E., & Wampold, B.E. (1988). Research in counseling psychology: Prospects and recommendations. *The Counseling Psychologist, 16,* 385–406.

Gelso, C.J., & Fretz, B.R. (1992). *Counseling psychology.* Fort Worth, TX: Harcourt Brace.

Gelso, C.J., Mallinckrodt, B., & Judge, A.B. (1996). Research training environment, attitudes toward research, and research self-efficacy: The revised Research Training Environment Scale. *The Counseling Psychologist, 24,* 304–322.

Gelso, C.J., Mallinckrodt, B., & Royalty, G.M. (1991). The Research Training Environment Scale. *Tests in Microfiche.* Princeton, NJ: Educational Testing Service.

Gelso, C.J., Raphael, R., Black, S.M., Rardin, D.K., & Skalkos, O. (1983). Research training in counseling psychology: Some preliminary data. *Journal of Counseling Psychology, 30,* 611–614.

Goodyear, R.K., & Lichtenberg, J. (1991, April). *Research interests of counseling psychology students: Person and training environment factors,.* Paper presented at the annual meeting of the American Education Research Association, Chicago.

Greeley, A.T., Johnson, E., Seem, S., Braver, M., Dias, L., Evans, K., Kincade, E., & Pricken, P. (1989). *Research Self-Efficacy Scale.* Unpublished scale, Pennsylvania State University, Erie.

Green, S.G., & Bauer, T.N. (1995). Supervisory mentoring by advisors: Relationships with doctoral student potential, productivity, and commitment. *Personnel Psychology, 48,* 537–561.

Hanish, C., Horan, J.J., Keen, B., St. Peter, C.C., Ceperich, S.D., & Beasley, J.F. (1995). The scientific stature of counseling psychology training programs: A still picture of a changing scene. *The Counseling Psychologist, 23,* 82–101.

Haynes, S.N., Lemsky, C., & Sexton-Radek, K. (1987). Why clinicians infrequently do research. *Professional Psychology: Research and Practice, 18,* 515–519.

Heppner, P.P., Gelso, C.J., & Dolliver, R.H. (1987). Three approaches to research training in counseling. *Journal of Counseling and Development, 66,* 45–49.

Heppner, P.P., Kivlighan, D.M., & Wampold, B.E. (1999). *Research in counseling* (2nd ed.). Pacific Grove, CA: Brooks/Cole.

Hill, C.E. (1997). The effects of my research training environment: Where are my students now? *The Counseling Psychologist, 25,* 74–81.

Hill, C.E., Thompson, B.J., & Williams, E.N. (1997). A guide to conducting consensual qualitative research. *The Counseling Psychologist, 25,* 517–572.

Holland, J.L. (1985). *Making vocational choices: A theory of vocational personalities and work environments.* Englewood Cliffs, NJ: Prentice-Hall.

Holland, J.L. (1986). Student selection, training, and research performance. *The Counseling Psychologist, 14,* 121–126.

Hollingsworth, M.A. (1999). *A structural model of student-faculty mentoring relationships and their role in counseling psychology research training.* Unpublished doctoral dissertation, University of Maryland, College Park.

Howard, G.S., & Curtin, T.D. (1993). Individual productivity and impact in counseling psychology. *The Counseling Psychologist, 21,* 288–302.

Hunt, D.M., & Michael, C. (1983). Mentorship: A career training and development tool. *Academy of Management Review, 8,* 475–485.

Jacobi, M. (1991). Mentoring and undergraduate academic success. *Journal of Educational Research, 61,* 505–532.

Kahn, J.H., & Gelso, C.J. (1997). Factor structure of the Research Training Environment Scale-Revised: Implications for research training in applied psychology. *The Counseling Psychologist, 25,* 22–37.

Kahn, J.H., & Miller, S.A., (1999). Measuring global perceptions of the research training environment using a short form of the RTES-R. Manuscript submitted for publication, Illinois State Uniersity.

Kahn, J.H., & Scott, N.A. (1997). Predictors of research productivity and science-related career goals among counseling psychology doctoral students: A structural equation analysis. *The Counseling Psychologist, 25,* 38–67.

Kelly, E.L., & Fiske, D.W. (1950). The prediction of success in the VA training program in clinical psychology. *American Psychologist, 5,* 395–406.

Kram, K.E. (1985). *Mentoring at work*. Glenview, IL: Scott, Foresman.

Kramer, R.M., & Martin, J. (1996). Transitions and turning points in faculty-doctoral student relationships. In P.J. Frost & M.S. Taylor (Eds.), *Rhythms of academic life: Personal accounts of careers in academic* (pp. 165–180). Thousand Oaks, CA: Sage.

Krebs, P.J., Smither, J.W., & Hurley, R.B. (1991). Relationship of vocational personality and research training environment to research productivity of counseling psychologists. *Professional Psychology: Research and Practice, 22,* 362–367.

Landino, R.A., & Owen, S.V. (1988). Self-efficacy in university faculty. *Journal of Vocational Behavior, 33,* 1–14.

Lent, R.W., Brown, S.D., & Hackett, G. (1994). Toward a unifying social cognitive theory of career and academic interest, choice, and performance [Monograph]. *Journal of Vocational Behavior, 45,* 79–122.

Leong, F.T.L., & Zachar, P. (1991). The development and validation of the Scientist-Practitioner Inventory for psychology. *Journal of Counseling Psychology, 38,* 331–341.

Leong, F.T.L., & Zachar, P. (1993). Presenting two brief versions of the Scientist-Practitioner Inventory. *Journal of Career Assessment, 1,* 162–170.

Lofquist, L.H., & Dawis, R.V. (1984). Research on work adjustment and satisfaction: Implications for career counseling. In S.D. Brown & R.W. Lent (Eds.), *Handbook of counseling psychology* (pp. 216–237). New York: Wiley.

Magoon, T.M., & Holland, J.L. (1984). Research training and supervision. In S.D. Brown & R.W. Lent (Eds.), *Handbook of counseling psychology* (pp. 682–715). New York: Wiley.

Mallinckrodt, B. (1997). Discovering research training environments that fit the students. *The Counseling Psychologist, 25,* 68–73.

Mallinckrodt, B., Gelso, C.J., & Royalty, G.M. (1990). Impact of research training environment and counseling psychology students' Holland personality types on interest in research. *Professional Psychology: Research and Practice, 21,* 26–32.

Maslow, A.H. (1954). *Motivation and personality*. New York: Harper & Row.

Meara, N.M., Schmidt, L., Carrington, S., Davis, K., Dixon, D., Fretz, B., Myers, R., Ridley, C., & Suinn, R. (1988). Training and accreditation in counseling psychology. *The Counseling Psychologist, 16,* 366–384.

Meehl, P.E. (1972). Second-order relevance. *American Psychologist, 27,* 932–940.

O'Brien, K.M., Malone, M.E., Schmidt, C.K., & Lucas, M.S. (1998). *Research self-efficacy: Improvements in instrumentation*. Poster presented at the 1998 convention of the American Psychological Association, San Francisco.

Parker, L.E., & Detterman, D.K. (1988). The balance between clinical and research interests among Boulder model graduate students. *Professional Psychology: Research and Practice, 19,* 342–344.

Pepinsky, H.B., & Pepinsky, P.N. (1954). *Counseling theory and practice*. New York: Ronald Press.

Perl, K.G., & Kahn, M.W. (1983). Psychology graduate students' attitudes toward research: A national survey. *Teaching of Psychology, 10,* 139–143.

Phillips, J.C., & Russell, R.K. (1994). Research self-efficacy, the research training environment, and research productivity among graduate students in counseling psychology. *The Counseling Psychologist, 22,* 628–641.

Ponterotto, J.G., & Casas, J.M. (in press). Individual and organizational competencies for multicultural counseling research. In J.G. Ponterotto & J.M. Casas (Eds.), *Handbook of racial-ethnic minority counseling research* (2nd ed.). Springfield, IL: Thomas.

Pope-Davis, D.B., Stone, G.L., & Nielson, D. (1997). Factors influencing the stated career goals of minority graduate students in counseling psychology programs. *The Counseling Psychologist, 25,* 683–698.

Price, D.J. (1963). *Little science, big science*. New York: Columbia University Press.

Rardin, D.K. (1986). The mesh of research and practice: The effect of cognitive style of the use of research in the practice of psychotherapy. *Dissertation Abstracts International, 46,* AAD86-25719.

Roe, A. (1953). *The making of a scientist*. New York: Dodd, Mead.

Royalty, G.M., Gelso, G.J., Mallinckrodt, B., & Garrett, K. (1986). The environment and the student in counseling psychology: Does the research training environment influence graduate students' attitudes toward research? *The Counseling Psychologist, 14,* 9–30.

Royalty, G.M., & Magoon, T.M. (1985). Correlates of scholarly productivity among counseling psychologists. *Journal of Counseling Psychology, 32,* 458–461.

Royalty, G.M., & Reising, G.N. (1986). The research training of counseling psychologists: What the professionals say. *The Counseling Psychologist, 33,* 49–60.

Rushton, J.P., Murray, H.G., & Paunonen, S.V. (1987). Personality characteristics associated with high research productivity. In D.N. Jackson & J.P. Rushton (Eds.), *Scientific excellence: Origins and assessment* (pp. 129–148). Beverly Hills, CA: Sage.

Schlosser, L. (2000). Measuring the working alliance in advisor-advisee relationships in graduate school. Unpublished masters thesis, University of Maryland, College Park.

Schoen, L.G., & Winocur, S. (1988). An investigation of the self-efficacy of male and female academics. *Journal of Vocational Behavior, 32,* 307–320.

Seeman, J. (1973). On supervising student research. *American Psychologist, 28,* 900–906.

Stone, G.L., & Vespia, K.M. (1998). *Counseling psychology students and professionals: Scientist and practitioner orientations and work environments.* Paper presented at the annual meeting of the American Psychological Association, San Francisco.

Stumpf, H. (1995). Scientific creativity: A short overview. *Educational Psychology Review, 7,* 225–241.

Szymanski, E.M., Whitney-Thomas, J., Marshall, L., & Sayger, T.V. (1994). The effect of graduate instruction in research methodology on research self-efficacy and perceived research utility. *Rehabilitation Education, 8,* 319–331.

Taylor, M.S., Locke, E.A., Lee, C., & Gist, M.E. (1984). Type A behavior and faculty research productivity: What are the mechanisms? *Organizational Behavior and Human Performance, 34,* 402–418.

Tinsley, D.J., Tinsley, H.E.A., Boone, S., & Shim-Li, C. (1993). Prediction of scientist-practitioner behavior using personality scores obtained during graduate school. *Journal of Counseling Psychology, 40,* 511–517.

Van Dyne, L. (1996). Mentoring relationships: A comparison of experiences in business and academic. In P.J. Frost & M.S. Taylor (Eds.), *Rhythms of academic life: Personal accounts of careers in academic* (pp. 159–164). Thousand Oaks, CA: Sage.

Vasil, L. (1992). Self-efficacy expectations and causal attributions for achievement among male and female university faculty. *Journal of Vocational Behavior, 41,* 259–269.

Wampold, B.E. (1986). Toward quality research in counseling psychology: Curricular recommendations for design and analysis. *The Counseling Psychologist, 14,* 37–48.

Wampold, B.E. (1998). Necessary (but not sufficient) innovation: Comment on Fox and Jones (1998), Koehly and Shivy (1998), and Russell, Kahn, Spoth, and Altmaier (1998). *Journal of Counseling Psychology, 45,* 46–49.

Whiteley, J.M. (1984). A historical perspective on the development of counseling psychology as a profession. In S.D. Brown & R.W. Lent (Eds.), *Handbook of counseling psychology* (pp. 3–55). New York: Wiley.

Youness, R., Lorr, M., & Stefic, E. (1985). Motivational patterns among three groups of psychologists. *Professional Psychology: Research and Theory, 16,* 581–584.

Zachar, P., & Leong, F.T.L. (1992). A problem of personality: Scientist and practitioner differences in psychology. *Journal of Personality, 60,* 665–677.

CHAPTER 5

Advances in Psychometric Theory and Methods

DANIEL M. BOLT
JAMES ROUNDS

The need for sound psychometric training has been recognized as imperative in the counseling profession (see AERA, APA, and NCME Standards for Educational and Psychological Testing, 1985). Counselors and counseling psychologists typically serve both as test administrators and interpreters of test results; consequently, their psychometric expertise is needed throughout the testing process. Test selection, for example, requires the ability to interpret previous psychometric research on the quality of the test, evaluate the appropriateness of the measure for the client, and justify the types of inferences intended to be drawn from test performance. Contemporary methods of assessment, such as computer-based adaptive testing, require familiarity with new aspects of test administration and their psychometric basis. Perhaps most importantly, counselors are faced with the challenge of interpreting test scores. In many settings, counselors must synthesize outcomes from multiple tests with other sources of information to help the client use test scores in identifying appropriate courses of action. Test score use in the context of decision making requires, for example, an understanding of the reality of measurement error and the utilities of test-based decisions.

This chapter addresses some recent advances in psychometric theory that are relevant to counseling psychology practice and research. One area that receives particular attention is item response theory (IRT). IRT is in large part responsible for the introduction and development of computerized adaptive testing. It has also had a very practical influence on the construction and development of paper-and-pencil tests and on how basic psychometric concepts such as test reliability are investigated. Extensions of IRT to tests measuring multiple traits and to items scored using more than two score categories make it an area of particular promise for the kinds of tests used in counseling psychology.

New and important considerations have also emerged in the context of reliability and validity assessment. We review some recent discussions of methods for estimating reliability coefficients, particularly Cronbach's alpha, as well as measures appropriate for criterion-referenced tests. Generalizability theory, which can be thought of as an extension of classical test theory, provides a framework in which multiple sources of measurement error can be investigated. Much discussion has continued to focus on the definition of test validity, particularly in light of Messick's (1989) consideration of the consequences of test use as a component of validity. The emergence of statistical methods employed in the analyses of multitrait multimethod matrices and validity generalization are also examined. Finally, the importance of ensuring that tests measure the same psychological constructs for individuals of different cultures or from different racial, ethnic, or gender groups has led to important statistical methods for assessing measurement invariance.

Recent psychometric efforts have focused on modeling test performance in ways that are consistent with insights from educational and cognitive psychology. One goal of this work is to develop

We thank Susan X Day, Melissa Holt, Lawrence Hubert, Molly McKenna, and Tom Smith for their constructive suggestions in the preparation of this manuscript.

methods that underscore the diagnostic potential of tests, a break from the usual psychometric approach that simply seeks to score individuals according to an underlying trait or ability. Cognitive psychology also has implications for the ways in which tests are designed, the types of dependent variables of interest, and the nature of tasks used to assess traits such as intelligence. In the final section of the chapter, we look at some recent approaches designed to make assessment and testing more cognitively informative.

A frequent misconception of psychometrics views the field as primarily static with well-defined rules and methods. Although many of the general questions remain the same (e.g., What is the test measuring and how accurately is it being measured?), psychometrics is also an area of considerable innovation in which new statistical tools are devised and new perspectives adopted on the measurement process in an attempt to answer these questions. Various sources provide the impetus for such developments. New methods of assessment frequently demand the development of new psychometric theory. Developments in the field of statistics, particularly statistical computation, as well as the increased speed and memory capacities of new computers, make previously insurmountable measurement problems much more tractable. Increased social sensitivities to various aspects of testing often place renewed emphasis on old psychometric questions, as has occurred, for example, in areas such as measurement invariance. We believe that a consideration of such advancements, more than contributing to appropriate test use, also permits more effective and informative testing for a broader range of applications than are available using more conventional methods.

ITEM RESPONSE THEORY

Perhaps the most influential development in psychometric theory in recent history has been the emergence of model-based measurement, or *item response theory* (IRT). IRT characterizes both test items and individuals along a common latent ability scale. As a result, IRT makes it possible to describe statistical item features such as difficulty or discrimination in ways that are not dependent on the population of individuals used for estimation. Likewise, in IRT an individual's ability level can be evaluated in a way that is not dependent on the particular test form administered. This feature allows IRT to address conveniently several important measurement issues (e.g., differential item functioning, adaptive testing, appropriateness measurement) that have traditionally been less (or not at all) approachable within the framework of classical test theory (CTT; Gulliksen, 1950). Most commonly, IRT applications have focussed on standardized ability or achievement tests using items scored dichotomously—that is, as correct or incorrect. Later in this section, we direct our attention to several more recently developed models that apply IRT to the wider variety of measures and item formats used in counseling practice and research. These include models applicable to items having multiple score categories, as occurs frequently in self-report indices (for example, using a five-point scale), and to tests that measure more than one ability. Important advances in the statistical methods and computer software used to fit item response models have improved the efficiency and accuracy of IRT modeling-based applications. We begin, however, by describing some more fundamental implications of the IRT-modeling framework for test development and evaluation. The growing popularity of IRT has had a noticeable impact on educational and psychological testing practice and has some subtle and not-so-subtle implications for how future counseling psychologists should be trained in psychometrics (see, for example, Embretson, 1996).

Foundations of Item Response Theory

On the surface, CTT and IRT differ in the level at which they model test performance. Recall that a foundational principle in CTT is the notion that a subject's observed test score (denoted X) is the sum of an unobserved true score component *(T)*, and a random error component *(E)*. Thus, the primary element of interest from a modeling standpoint in CTT is the observed test score. (For a presentation of CTT and its assumptions, see Gulliksen, 1950, or Crocker & Algina, 1986.) By contrast, IRT emphasizes the interaction of subjects and the individual test items. In IRT an item response model expresses the probability of item score as a function of a continuous latent ability, θ, corresponding to the individual, and a set of item parameters that characterize the item. For tests measuring some form of educational achievement or ability, we think of θ as representing the individual's proficiency, although it can also represent any other kind of trait measured by a psychological test. It is typically scaled so as to range between approximately −4 and 4 where, analogous to a standard normal random variable, we assume −4 represents very low levels of the trait, 0 approximately average, and 4 a very high level of the trait.

Usually in IRT we also assume that the expected score on an item should increase as the level of θ increases. For example, with dichotomously scored test items, we assume that the probability of correct response to (or, alternatively, the probability of endorsing) a test item becomes greater at progressively higher levels of θ. The specific functional relationship between this probability and θ for a given item is determined by the *item parameters* of the model and is illustrated by an *item characteristic curve* (ICC). Several examples of ICCs are displayed in Figure 5.1. We might think of an item response model as defining a particular class of such curves, with the item parameters (estimated using real test data) determining the precise shape of the curve. For example, the curves in Figure 5.1(a) are based on the one-parameter logistic item response model (1PL), more commonly known as the Rasch model (Rasch, 1960):

$$P(\theta) = \frac{\exp(\theta - b_i)}{1 + \exp(\theta - b_i)}$$

(a)

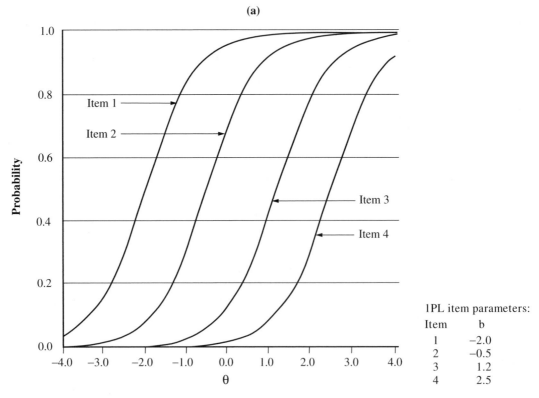

1PL item parameters:	
Item	b
1	−2.0
2	−0.5
3	1.2
4	2.5

Figure 5.1   Item Characteristic Curves for Items of 1PL, 2PL, and 3PL Models

(b)

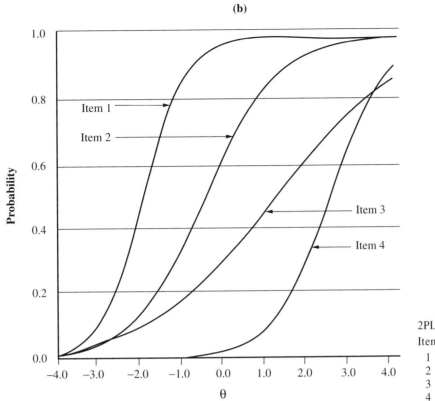

2PL item parameters:

Item	a	b
1	1.2	−2.0
2	0.7	−0.5
3	0.4	1.2
4	0.9	2.5

(c)

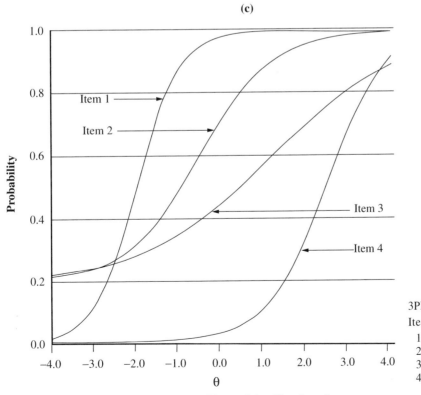

3PL item parameters:

Item	a	b	c
1	1.2	−2.0	.0
2	0.7	−0.5	.2
3	0.4	1.2	.2
4	0.9	2.5	.0

Figure 5.1   (Continued)

In a Rasch model, each item i is characterized by a single item parameter b_i representing its difficulty, and *exp* denotes the exponential function. Items having larger b values are more difficult (or less frequently endorsed) items. Mathematically, the value of b corresponds to the point on the θ-scale at which exactly 50% of examinees are expected to answer the item correctly. The items in Figure 5.1(a) are therefore increasing in order of difficulty, with item 1 being the easiest (or most frequently endorsed) item.

Extensions of this basic model have been developed to handle situations where items vary in their discriminating strength and for cases in which random guessing occurs. The items in Figure 5.1(b) are exemplars of a two-parameter logistic (2PL) model (Birnbaum, 1968). In the 2PL model, an item parameter a_i, determining the slope of the ICC, is added to the model representation used previously:

$$P(\theta) = \frac{\exp[a_i(\theta - b_i)]}{1 + \exp[a_i(\theta - b_i)]}$$

Note that the larger a is, the steeper the slope of the ICC becomes in the region of the θ-scale where the curve is maximally increasing. The reason that a is considered a discrimination parameter is that a larger a suggests the item is more effective at distinguishing between individuals having trait levels above versus below θ in that particular region of the scale. In fact, Lord and Novick (1968) demonstrated that the a parameter in the 2PL model has a direct correspondence to the item discrimination indices traditionally considered in CTT, namely the biserial and point-biserial coefficients.

Table 5.1 provides 2PL item parameter estimates for the Eysenck Personality Questionnaire (EPQ) obtained in a study by Grayson (1986). Items from the two scales "Extraversion" (E) and "Neuroticism" (N) contain a list of personal characteristics that are either endorsed or not endorsed by the test-taker as self-reflective. Data from the two scales were analyzed separately, with items from the E scale regarded as measuring a latent trait (θ) defined as extraversion and items from the N scale a latent trait defined as neuroticism. Note that the items vary both with respect to their discriminating power (a) and frequency of endorsement (b). On the N scale, for example, items such as "Nervous person" ($a = 1.933$) and "Worrier" ($a = 1.999$) are considered to be highly indicative of neuroticism, whereas items such as "Irritable person" ($a = 1.221$) and "Worry after embarrassment" ($a = 1.288$) are less indicative. In terms of frequency of endorsement, an item such as "Feelings easily hurt" ($b = -.786$) is much more frequently endorsed by individuals with lower levels of neuroticism than "Irritable person" ($b = 1.267$), which tends to be endorsed by those with higher levels of the trait. Similar comparisons can be performed for items from the E scale.

The three-parameter logistic model (3PL; Lord, 1974) is an extension of the 2PL model in which the lower tail of the ICC may be greater than zero, reflecting the potential for any individual, regardless of ability, to answer the item correctly simply by guessing the correct response. A clear example where this condition is relevant is a multiple-choice item where individuals are not penalized for guessing. The probability of guessing the correct response is determined by the parameter c, and the resulting item response function is written as:

$$P(\theta) = c_i + (1 - c_i)\frac{\exp[a_i(\theta - b_i)]}{1 + \exp[a_i(\theta - b_i)]}$$

Examples of ICCs for items that vary with respect to their guessing parameters are shown in Figure 5.1(c). Note how items 2 and 3, both having $c = .20$, have ICCs whose lower tails flatten at probabilities of .20, whereas the ICCs of items 1 and 4, both having $c = .0$, flatten at probability values of 0.

Table 5.1   2PL Parameter Estimates for Items from the Extraversion and Neuroticism Scales of the Eysenck Personality Questionnaire-Revised (Grayson, 1986)

Extraversion	a	b
1. Talkative person	1.360	−0.251
2. Rather lively	1.765	−0.742
3. Enjoy meeting people	1.864	−1.368
4. Keep in background socially	2.162	0.098
5. Take initiative making friends	1.503	−0.048
6. Get life into a dull party	2.305	0.601
7. Like mixing with people	2.434	−1.344
8. Let yourself go	1.727	−0.735
9. Like bustle and excitement	1.126	−0.322
10. Quiet when with other people	1.710	−0.179
11. People think of you as lively	1.645	−0.422
12. Get a party going	1.910	0.224

Neuroticism	a	b
1. Mood up and down	1.521	−0.195
2. Just miserable	1.318	0.290
3. Irritable person	1.221	1.267
4. Feelings easily hurt	1.396	−0.786
5. Feel "fed-up"	1.780	0.162
6. Nervous person	1.933	0.755
7. Worrier	1.999	−0.171
8. Tense or "highly strung"	1.651	1.125
9. Worry after embarrassment	1.288	−0.358
10. Suffer from "nerves"	1.710	0.680
11. Often feel lonely	1.298	0.858
12. Troubled about guilt	1.313	0.554

Nonlinearity is an important feature of logistic models that makes them appropriate for item response data. Note that although item response scores are usually bounded (e.g., 0 = incorrect, 1 = correct), the θ scale usually is not, for reasons we describe shortly. Consequently, a model in which item performance increases linearly with θ (such as in factor analysis) must restrict the steepness of the slopes of the ICCs so that the predicted item scores are not outside the bounds of the score scale. By contrast, each of the logistic models has an upper and lower asymptote so that predicted scores always remain within the score range of the item without constraining the slope of the ICC.

Although the 2PL and 3PL models are more flexible, there are unique mathematical advantages for preferring the Rasch model. In particular, the property of *specific objectivity,* possessed only by the Rasch model, means that statistically unbiased estimates of the item parameters are obtained regardless of the distribution of the latent trait in the sample of individuals used to estimate them and, likewise, statistically unbiased estimates of ability parameters are obtained regardless of the parameters of the items administered (Rasch, 1960). Later we discuss additional reasons for preferring the Rasch model in the context of item parameter estimation. Many psychometricians, however, suggest that these statistical advantages are outweighed by the superior approximation provided by the 2PL and 3PL models to real test data.

Applications of IRT models have found a place in the counseling psychology literature (Fox & Jones, 1998) and are now used successfully with a variety of different types of measures, including personality inventories (Harvey & Thomas, 1996; Steinberg & Thissen, 1996), measures of social behavior and experience (Kindlon, Wright, Raudenbush, & Earls, 1996), self-esteem (Gray-Little, Williams, & Hancock, 1997), depression (Hammond, 1995), and posttraumatic stress (King, King, Fairbank, & Schlenger, 1993), among others. As the number of IRT applications continue to grow, new models have also emerged that incorporate IRT into issues of interest in counseling psychology theory and research. Examples include models that assess developmental change over time (Meiser, 1996), incorporate external predictors along with individual ability (Zwinderman, 1991), and examine the effects of experimental treatments (Fischer, 1987) at the level of individual item responses.

Local Independence and Unidimensionality

Two key assumptions underlying IRT modeling are captured by the concepts of *local independence* (LI) and *unidimensionality*. LI states that once θ is taken into account, the item responses should be statistically independent. Equivalently, LI implies that the probability of any observable response pattern given trait level θ is equal to the product of the probabilities of the individual item scores at θ.

A related principle underlying many IRT applications is the assumption that the latent trait is unidimensional. Unidimensionality implies that the test items collectively measure only one common latent trait. Each of the IRT models considered thus far has this property, although many more recently developed IRT models permit multidimensional modeling. Generally, unidimensionality is considered a more strict requirement than that of local independence, as satisfaction of unidimensionality necessarily implies that LI also holds.

It is important when applying IRT models to consider the degree to which these conditions are satisfied by the test data. Neither assumption is likely to be satisfied perfectly, although many IRT applications allow for some relaxation of these requirements. Methods for investigating the requirements of LI (McDonald, 1981; Yen, 1981) and unidimensionality (see Hattie, 1985; Stout, 1987) have been developed. As will be considered later, this capacity to assess statistically the fit of IRT models is a very useful feature that extends to other forms of model misspecification as well.

An Item Response Theory Perspective on Testing and Measurement

Although considerable psychometric attention has been directed toward understanding the statistical underpinnings of IRT models, even more relevant for practitioners and researchers has been how the IRT modeling framework affects the ways in which fundamental psychometric concepts are represented. In many ways the IRT perspective differs from the more traditional CTT framework in which most counseling psychologists have been trained. In this section, we note some fundamental distinctions between IRT and CTT that provide a basis for many of the emerging IRT applications.

Item and Ability Parameter Invariance

A primary difference between IRT and CTT stems from the *item* and *ability parameter invariance* properties of IRT. Item parameter invariance implies that the item parameters used to characterize items in IRT can be interpreted independently of the distribution of θ for the sample of individuals that were administered the test. For example, in the case of the Rasch model where we define the difficulty of an item by the parameter b, we note that b retains the same value whether it is estimated using a group of individuals having high ability or low ability (although it may be estimated more precisely for one group compared with another). In the case of the EPQ, we therefore expect to obtain the same parameter estimates as reported in Table 5.1 regardless of whether the test is administered to a population consisting largely of extraverts or introverts. This contrasts sharply with the situation in CTT, where the classical statistics used to describe item difficulty and discrimination can only be interpreted with respect to the particular population of individuals for which they are computed. The CTT index of item difficulty, for example, is defined as the proportion of individuals who answer the item correctly, which obviously depends on the test population's level of ability. Likewise, classical item discrimination indices such as the biserial or point-biserial coefficients depend on the variance of test scores in the sample for which they are estimated.

In the same way, ability parameter invariance means that the ability parameter θ associated with each individual has the same interpretation regardless of the particular set of items the individual is administered. In IRT, an estimate of an individual's θ level is determined both by the individual's entire item response pattern and the parameters of the test items administered (the process of ability estimation is described in the next section). In CTT, characterization of ability by the number of correct answers on the test will necessarily be dependent on how easy or difficult the test items are, whereas a comparability of individuals in IRT is maintained even when different test forms of varying difficulty are administered.

These invariance properties do not, of course, overcome the need to link item or ability parameters administered in different tests to distinct individual populations. One attractive feature of the underlying θ-scale in IRT is its interval-level measurement property. Item and ability parameter estimates obtained for different test administrations will be related by a simple linear transformation. Petersen, Kolen, and Hoover (1989) provided a detailed discussion of the process of scaling IRT parameter estimates (often called "linking"), which makes IRT useful for applications such as test equating. Item and ability parameters from different administrations can be linked if there is some overlap of items or individuals across test administrations or if an assumption can be made as to the random equivalence of the test populations.

Ability Scores

A second distinction between IRT and CTT is the ability scale assumed to underlie item performance in IRT. In CTT, an individual's observed test score is an imperfect indicator of true score, which is the CTT equivalent of an individual's ability. In IRT, individual ability has a less direct association to total test score and usually must be estimated based on the entire item response pattern. Although there are various ways in which an individual's ability can be estimated, most methods are based on the *likelihood function* of the item response pattern conditional upon θ. Assuming we know (or have estimated) the item parameters for all of the items, it is possible to determine the particular θ level along the ability continuum where the observed response pattern would be most likely to occur. Suppose that having administered the 12 items from the E scale of the EPQ, a given individual produces the response pattern *111010111110*. At various levels of θ, we can compute the likelihood of this pattern using the model-based probability of each item response. The likelihood is the product of these probabilities, and is displayed in Figure 5.2. A typical estimate of ability is the point on the θ-scale at which the function is maximized. We call this the maximum-likelihood estimate of θ, and denote it as $\hat{\theta}$. Other possibilities for ability estimates based on the likelihood function are described by F.B. Baker (1992).

Relative to CTT, interpretation of the IRT ability scale is enhanced by the fact that item parameters are reported on the same scale. Given an ability estimate, one can determine an estimate of the individual's expected scores on items that may not even have been administered. Moreover, the individual's expected score for a complete test can be derived as a simple sum of the estimated probabilities of correct response across each of the items. Along these lines, attention is being directed toward an area called *proficiency scaling* (Tatsuoka, 1993), which seeks to give an interpretation to various points along the ability scale according to the specific types of items that

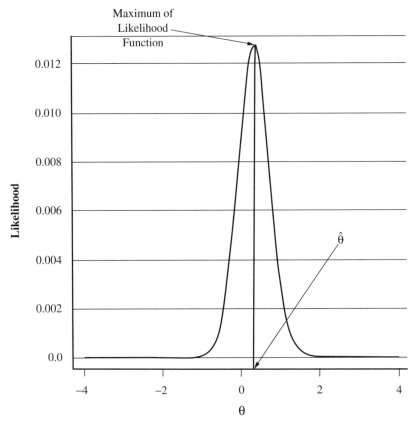

Figure 5.2   Maximum Likelihood Estimate for Response Pattern 111010111110. Based on 2PL Parameter Estimates from the EPQ-R Extraversion Scale

individuals are likely to answer correctly. Thus, while in CTT meaningful test scores are obtained only in reference to standard scores, in IRT meaningful interpretations can usually be derived from the ability and item parameter estimates themselves (Embretson, 1996).

Item and Test Information

An important concept in IRT is that of *information.* Recall that items that are highly discriminating (i.e., having large a parameters) are effective at distinguishing between individuals that lie within a particular region on the θ-scale. The specific point on the θ-scale at which the item is most discriminating (corresponding to the ability levels at which the slope of the ICC is maximally increasing) is determined by the item difficulty parameter b (along with c in the 3PL case). We say that the item provides its maximal information for individuals in this region. Intuitively, difficult items will be most informative for individuals of high ability whereas easier items will be most informative for low-ability individuals. Thus, the amount of information provided by an item varies depending on θ. We express this relationship through an *item information function,* which is determined in large part by the slope of the ICC. More specifically, the larger the slope is, the more informative the item becomes, and thus the more useful it is for ability estimation.

One attractive feature of information is that it accumulates as items are added; that is, test information conditional on θ is computed as the sum of information from each of the individual items. Figure 5.3 provides illustrations of item information functions for four items (items 3, 4, 5, and 7) from the E scale of the EPQ, as well as the resulting information function for the four items combined. Note that items 4 "Keep in background socially" ($a = 2.162$) and 7 "Like mixing with people" ($a = 2.434$) generally provide more information across the θ-scale than items 3 "Enjoy meeting people" ($a = 1.864$) and 5 "Take initiative meeting friends" ($a = 1.503$), a result that follows

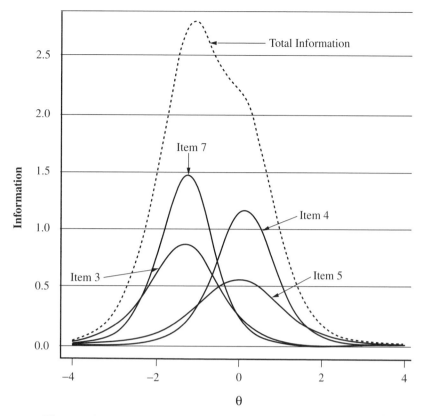

Figure 5.3 Item Information Functions and Total Information for
Items 3, 4, 5, and 7 from the EPQ-R Extraversion Scale

from the fact that items 4 and 7 are more discriminating items. An interpretation of the test information function (denoted I(θ)) follows from its relationship to the standard error of the maximum-likelihood ability estimate (denoted SE(θ)):

$$SE(\hat{\theta}) = \frac{1}{\sqrt{\sum_{i=1}^{n} I_i(\hat{\theta})}}$$

Consequently, the larger the amount of information, the smaller the standard error, implying that highly informative tests lead to accurate ability estimation. At this point, a few differences from CTT also become apparent. First, in IRT the measurement error of the test varies depending on individual ability. For the four-item subtest in Figure 5.3, maximum information is provided around $\theta = -1.4$, influenced primarily by the fact that item 7, a highly discriminating (and thus highly informative) item has difficulty parameter $b = -1.368$. By contrast, in CTT the standard error of measurement is constant for all individual ability levels. Second, whereas reliability theory in CTT emphasizes the importance of increasing the number of test items to increase test reliability (recall the Spearman-Brown formula), the concept of test information in IRT suggests the importance of selecting test items appropriate for a given individual's ability level. In IRT, short tests can also be very reliable.

Practical Implications

As mentioned earlier, one of the primary attractions of IRT has been its capacity to deal more conveniently with several aspects of test development and data analysis. In this section, we provide a few representative examples of ways the IRT properties just described have allowed IRT to enhance this process.

Test Construction and Evaluation

The concepts of test and item information are especially useful in the context of constructing and evaluating tests. Many tests need to be designed so as to provide more precise estimation of individual ability in certain regions along the θ-scale. For example, a test for assessing clinical depression seeks to distinguish those individuals at an extreme end along a "depression" scale. Alternatively, a test used for purposes of job selection that seeks to identify the top 25% of candidates should be constructed so as to be maximally informative for individuals at or near the 75th percentile. For these testing situations, the primary goal is one of determining those individuals who lie above or below a particular ability threshold, implying that the test should provide its most precise ability estimates for individuals at or near the threshold. By contrast, for a test whose primary function is to order all individuals with respect to an ability, it may be desirable to have approximately equal amounts of information at all ability levels. Lord (1977) described how the test developer can use a target information curve to represent the relative importance of accurate trait estimation at various levels along the θ-scale, and items can be selected in such a way so as to provide a total amount of information that approximates the target. Other considerations, such as item content and its match with test specifications, also need to play a role in item selection, as test information relates only to measurement error considerations.

In selecting among tests already constructed, investigators often compare the *relative efficacy* of the tests at various levels of θ. The relative efficacy of one test versus another is defined as the ratio of the first test's information at θ to that of the second test. It is therefore a function of θ, and can be interpreted as how much the second test must be lengthened to provide as much information as the first.

Adaptive Testing

A rapidly developing area in psychometrics is adaptive testing. The goal of adaptive testing is to make the assessment process more efficient by selectively administering only those items that are most useful in estimating an individual's ability level. Because the true ability level of the individual is unknown, provisional ability estimates based on individual responses to previously administered test items are used to determine the most useful item to administer next. With adaptive tests, it becomes possible to obtain estimates of an individual's ability level that are as precise as those obtained with standard paper-and-pencil tests, but by administering only a fraction of the number of items. Also, because all items are linked to a common underlying metric, the fact that different individuals are administered different items is not problematic for purposes of comparing individuals' performances. Confidence bands can be placed around ability estimates using the previously described connection between information and the standard error of the ability estimate.

The emergence of computers for purposes of testing has helped make adaptive testing a reality, as it becomes possible to program item selection algorithms that select informative items from a previously calibrated pool of potential test items. In particular, if the goal is to obtain an ability estimate for each individual within a certain criterion level of precision, items may be administered until the range of the confidence interval falls below the criterion. However, as in test construction for paper-and-pencil tests, item selection algorithms take into account more than just item information in selecting test items, including, for example, consideration of item content. One additional consideration is that of item exposure, as items that are too frequently administered may begin to compromise the security of the test. Other issues in administering a test by computer versus paper and pencil are receiving increased attention, including evaluation of dimensionality, validity, parameter estimation, scoring, and human factors issues (see Wainer et al., 1990, for an extended discussion of computer adaptive testing topics).

Appropriateness Measurement

One benefit of an item-level response model for test data is the capacity to investigate model misfit. An example of how this has been useful is in determining whether a test performs as intended for individual examinees. Test validity for an examinee is evidenced by the "typicality" of the individual's response pattern. In the process of ability estimation, it sometimes occurs that an observed item response pattern results in likelihood values that are very small across all levels of θ. For example, an examinee's item response pattern may indicate that a large number of difficult items were answered correctly although a large number of easy items were answered incorrectly. The small likelihood of observing such patterns suggests that these individuals are not behaving in accordance with the model. There could be a variety of reasons for the observation of such response patterns that suggest the test performance is not an accurate reflection of examinee ability, including careless responding, guessing, cheating, or alignment errors (i.e., when separate sheets for questions and answers are used) (Meijer, 1995).

Zickar and Drasgow (1996) developed an IRT-based methodology for identifying individuals who attempt to fake responses in a socially desirable way on personality inventories. Alternatively, such patterns may provide important information about the examinee—such as an atypical pattern of cognitive skill mastery (Tatsuoka, 1983). A variety of methods have been proposed for the purpose of identifying such response patterns, usually based in some way on the likelihood of the observed response pattern at θ (see Hulin, Drasgow, & Parsons, 1983, and the special issue of *Applied Measurement in Education,* Meijer, 1995). Figure 5.4 illustrates the likelihood functions for three item response patterns using the four items from the E scale described in Figure 5.3. Note that the pattern *0110* (response to item 3 = 0, item 4 = 1, item 5 = 1, and item 7 = 0) and, to a lesser extent, pattern *1010* provide instances of patterns we might consider atypical, recalling

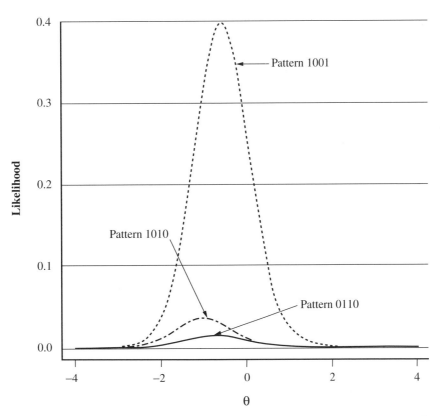

Figure 5.4 Relative Likelihood Values of Item Response Patterns 1001, 1010, and 0110 to Item Subset {3, 4, 5, 7} from the EPQ-R Extraversion Scale

that items 3 "Enjoy meeting people" and 7 "Like mixing with people" were the most frequently endorsed, whereas items 4 "Keep in the background socially" and 5 "Take initiative making friends" are relatively less frequently endorsed. Appropriateness measurement provides a good example of how IRT can be useful in investigating the validity of a test, in this case at the level of individual examinees.

Differential Item Functioning

Differential item functioning (DIF) refers to the condition in which the same item produces different item characteristic curves (ICCs) in two (or more) subpopulations of individuals. Often interest in DIF is based on determining whether one item is relatively more difficult for one subpopulation than another, in which case we would find that the ICCs modeled for the two groups separately differ with respect to their b parameters. If such is the case, we say that the item demonstrates DIF against the group for which the item has a higher b parameter. (Assuming the remainder of the test is valid, we might otherwise claim that the item displays *item bias*.) Provided the items do not also vary in their discrimination across groups, we say that the item demonstrates *uniform DIF* because it disadvantages one group versus another at all levels of θ. It is also conceivable, however, that an item may vary in terms of its discrimination across subpopulations, in which case differences in a parameters will be observed. When difficulty is the same but discrimination differs for the item among the two groups, we have the condition of *crossing DIF,* because the ICCs for the two groups will intersect. With crossing DIF, the item displays DIF against each group (and in favor of the other) over a certain range of the θ-scale.

Mackinnon et al. (1995) conducted a study contrasting the results of Grayson's (1986) study of the EPQ E and N scales with that obtained from an elderly population. Figure 5.5 provides examples of items displaying uniform and crossing DIF, respectively, in comparing item performance between Mackinnon et al.'s elderly population with the general population studied by Grayson. An example of an item displaying uniform DIF from the N scale is item 8 "Tense or highly strung." A possible explanation for its more frequent endorsement in an elderly population may be due to the somatic content of the item and the fact that the elderly are typically in poorer health. Item 10 "Suffer from nerves" displays a similar shift in the b-parameter ($b = .294$ in elderly sample, $b = .680$ in general sample). On the E-Scale, items dealing with social interaction tended to demonstrate poorer discrimination in the elderly population (Mackinnon et al., 1995). An example is item 4, "Keep in the background socially," which after being reverse scored (i.e., a response of 0 versus 1 is indicative of extraversion), produces the ICCs in Figure 5.5. An alternative explanation for the poorer discrimination in the elderly population may have to do with the fact that the item is the only one coded in reverse and the possibility that response sets are more common in an elderly population.

With DIF no reference is made to the distribution of θ for either of the two groups. In fact, the two groups may have ability distributions that differ considerably—our interest is only in the way in which the item performs in each of the two groups. As a result, we might claim that an item demonstrates DIF against a group even though, conceivably, more individuals answer the item correctly from that group.

The advantage of IRT over classical methods for assessment of DIF is discussed by Linn and Drasgow (1987). In determining whether one item is more difficult for individuals of one group than another, it is most logical from a CTT perspective to compare the proportion correct for the item within each subpopulation. Unfortunately, when the two groups also differ in terms of their distributions of ability, it becomes impossible to distinguish whether an item displaying differences in proportion correct does so because it appropriately measures the ability it should measure, or inappropriately measures something else that unfairly disadvantages one group. We return to this issue and discuss some additional methods for detecting DIF in a later section on measurement invariance.

(a) Uniform DIF

Neuroticism Item #8: "Tense or highly strung"

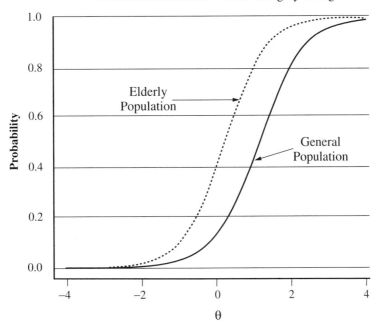

(b) Crossing DIF

Extraversion Item #4: "Keep in background socially"

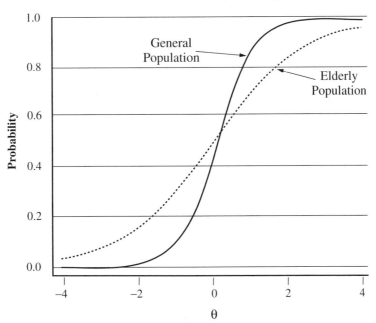

Figure 5.5 Examples of Items Displaying DIF

Model Extensions

Variations of the logistic models have been developed to handle tests with items that are scored *polytomously*—that is, using more than two score categories. Such tests are common in psychological research, especially in self-report measures, or in educational tests that permit some form of partial credit scoring. A measure of anxiety, for example, may contain items consisting of statements such as "I feel afraid" and ask the subject to respond in categories ranging from 1 = "Not at all" to 5 = "Very much." In this case, a clear ordering of the categories with respect to the underlying latent trait (anxiety) is implied, with category 1 indicating the least amount of anxiety and category 5 the most. An example of a model that could be applied in this context is Samejima's (1969) *graded response model.* In the graded response model, each score category has its own *option characteristic curve* (OCC), representing the probability that an individual scores in that category given ability or trait level θ. An example of such an item, in this case consisting of five possible score categories, is shown in Figure 5.6. Supposing that this were the item "I feel afraid," note that for all θ, there is a nonzero probability of scoring in any of the five categories, although the likelihood of scoring in the higher categories becomes larger as θ increases. For individuals very high in anxiety, the probability of endorsing category 5 becomes almost certain, as does the probability that individuals very low in anxiety endorse category 1. An example of an application of the graded response model is provided by J.G. Baker, Zevon, and Rounds (1994) who evaluated differences in the measurement features of positive and negative affect scales of Tellegen's model for mood.

Alternative models that can be used with polytomously scored items are the *partial credit* (Masters, 1982) and *nominal response models* (Bock, 1972). For a discussion on the structural differences between these models and the graded response model, see Thissen and Steinberg (1986).

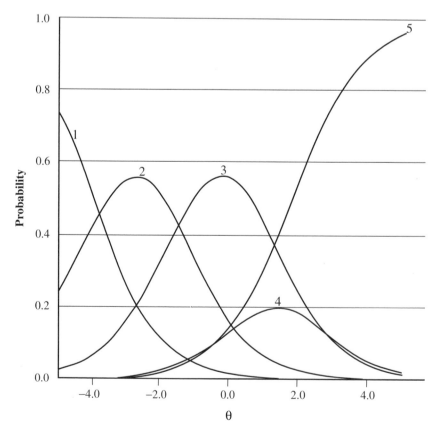

Figure 5.6 Option Characteristic Curves for Item of Graded Response Model

The partial credit model, like the graded response model, can be used when the item categories have a known ordering (e.g., higher score categories are indicative of a larger "amount" of the trait). The nominal response model does not assume a known ordering of the categories, but determines it in the process of estimating OCCs for each response category.

A current area of much research in IRT concerns the development of models to handle tests that measure more than one trait or ability. An important consideration in these models is the way in which the traits or abilities are assumed to combine or interact in determining item performance. McDonald (1967) presents nonlinear factor analysis, which assumes that abilities combine linearly, but where the item response function relating the linear combination to the probability of correct response is a nonlinear function. A similar model that is a more direct extension of the 3PL model considered earlier is the multidimensional logistic model described by Reckase (1985). Other multidimensional models (see, for example, Sympson, 1977, or Embretson, 1985) assume the abilities interact in a multiplicative way and may be applicable, for example, to items in which individuals need to execute a series of sequential steps to produce a correct answer. One result of working with a multidimensional as opposed to unidimensional model is that the probability of correct response is defined by an item response surface (i.e., we need to know more than one trait or ability value to determine the probability of correct response) rather than an ICC, as illustrated in Figure 5.7. In this case, the probability of correct response is determined by two abilities (denoted θ_1 and θ_2). Extensions of polytomous models to handle multidimensional data are also gaining increasing attention (Kelderman & Rijkes, 1994; Muraki & Carlson, 1996).

A compendium of item response models has been recently compiled by Van der Linden and Hambleton (1997). Other popular models that demonstrate the capacity of IRT to address a variety of different issues in testing include Fischer's (1973) *linear logistic model,* which expresses the difficulty parameter of the Rasch model as a function of the cognitive operations required for solving the test item; Ramsay (1991) and Mokken's (1971) *nonparametric* IRT approaches, which permit less restrictive forms for ICCs; and Hoitink (1990) and Andrich and Luo's (1993) *unfolding* models, which are appropriate for items in which scores do not strictly increase as the level of the trait becomes higher.

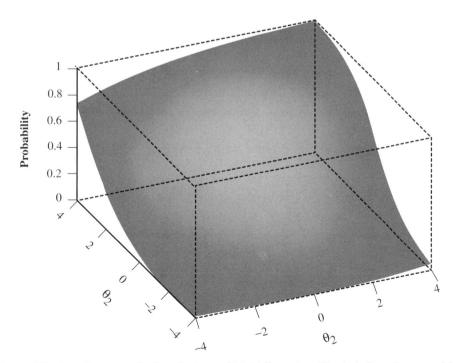

Figure 5.7   Item Response Surface for Item of Multidimensional Logistic Item Response Model

RELIABILITY AND MEASUREMENT ERROR

Two related concepts used to describe the quality of a test are its *reliability* and *validity*. Most test users are familiar with their general definitions; however, the interpretation of these terms continues to evolve, often as a consequence of new techniques developed to investigate them. We have already suggested, for example, how the emergence of IRT and test information has affected our view of measurement error and how investigations of appropriateness measurement ultimately relate to test validity. In this section, we consider some other ways in which these concepts have developed.

By reliability we mean the consistency or dependability of the measurement tool. For a standardized test, we sometimes think of reliability as corresponding to the degree to which the individual's performance would be replicated in a hypothetical readministration of the same test or an alternate form. There could be a variety of factors that contribute to inconsistencies in performance across test administrations, including conditions related to the examinee (e.g., health, amount of effort), the testing environment (e.g., distractions, the person scoring the test), or the test itself (e.g., which sample of items are selected from an item bank). Because such variables are not related to what the test is intended to measure, they are considered to be sources of *measurement error*. Traditionally, reliability has been defined in the framework of CTT. In CTT, we think of reliability as the amount of variability in observed test scores that can be attributed to variability in true scores (i.e., what the observed scores would be if there were no measurement error). The *reliability coefficient* is defined as the ratio of the variance of true scores to the variance of observed scores for examinees within the population (i.e., the amount of observed score variance explained by true score variance). Because the variance of observed scores can be expressed as the sum of the variance of true scores and the variance of error, the reliability coefficient is also an indicator of the relative amount of measurement error in test scores. Thus, a reliability coefficient of .80 would suggest that 80% of the observed score variance on a test is due to true score variance, and 20% is due to measurement error.

Assessing Test Reliability

Depending on whether measurement error is considered more a consequence of factors that vary over time (i.e., *time of measurement* error) or across test forms (i.e., *content sampling* error), estimates of reliability may be obtained in a variety of ways. For this reason, a distinction is made between various reliability coefficients. The *coefficient of stability* is estimated by correlating test scores obtained by administering the same test on two different occasions (called the test-retest method). It is therefore sensitive to time-dependent errors in test performance, but provides no information on the presence of content-sampling errors. The *coefficient of equivalence* is estimated by correlating two forms of the same test during one time period (alternate forms method). It attends to the effects of content sampling in the construction of forms but provides no information on time of measurement errors. Both sources of error variance are considered when assessing a *coefficient of stability and equivalence,* which is estimated by correlating scores obtained from two forms of the same test at different times (test-retest with alternate forms method) (Crocker & Algina, 1986). Because each of these methods takes into account different sources of random error, the coefficients should be expected to differ. Specifically, the coefficient of stability and equivalence should be smallest because it subsumes the sources of error variance included in each of the other two.

In contrast to these reliability methods, however, psychometric interest in reliability theory most commonly relates to the *precision* of the measurement instrument. The *coefficient of precision* (Coombs, 1950) can be thought of as the hypothetical correlation that would be observed between test scores if individuals could be readministered the same test items at the same point in time. Because many tests are only administered once to a population of individuals, the coefficient of precision must often be estimated from a single test administration. Methods appropriate for this condition have received a considerable amount of attention in psychometrics. Feldt and Brennan (1989) provided an overview of various *internal consistency coefficients,* which are measures of the interrelatedness, or homogeneity, of a set of test items. All are based on the notion of dividing the test into subtests (often just the individual items) to estimate content sampling error. Then estimates of the variances and covariances of the subtests (e.g., the individual test items) are used to construct an estimate of the coefficient of precision. Historically, the split-half reliability coefficient (computed by Spearman-Brown, Rulon, or other formulas) was used for this purpose. However, Cronbach's α and related coefficients have largely replaced split-half methods for estimating measurement precision. This has been largely due to the fact that Cronbach's α can be interpreted as the mean of all possible split-half correlations on a test and thus might be expected to provide a more stable estimate of precision than single split-half estimates based on arbitrarily defined test halves. Cronbach's α, however, is also known to yield a biased estimate of reliability and is frequently misinterpreted. We turn to these issues next.

The accuracy of a reliability coefficient as an estimate of the proportion of observed score variance attributable to true score variance depends on the degree to which the assumptions of the estimation method are satisfied. Cronbach's α assumes that the items are *essentially τ-equivalent* (Lord & Novick, 1968), meaning that the difference in true scores for any pair of items is constant across all examinees, although the items may have different variances. Because of the prevalence with which α is reported as an estimate of test reliability, its interpretation and statistical performance have received considerable attention in the psychometric literature. It is known, for example, that because essential τ-equivalence will in practical cases not hold true, α is in actuality an underestimate of the coefficient of precision. Raykov (1997) recently investigated the degree to which α underestimates reliability when this condition is violated and suggests a possible correction for α "slippage" that brings it closer to the true coefficient of precision.

Despite the routine manner in which it is reported in psychological research, α is also frequently misinterpreted (Cortina, 1993). For example, it has been common to regard α as a measure of the degree to which a test is unidimensional. Cronbach's α is sensitive to the magnitudes of subtest (item) covariances and variances, but it is not sensitive to patterns in the covariance matrix, which determine dimensionality. Another way of saying this is that α provides an estimate of the proportion of observed score variance that is due to common variance. High levels of α could, therefore, be due to the shared variance of several related dimensions or to a single dimension. There is, unfortunately, no way to tell which is the case on the basis of α. Thus, it is very possible for tests having the same α to vary with respect to their dimensionality (see discussion in Cortina, 1993).

It is also a common misconception that α be of a certain magnitude for the test to be considered "reliable." Schmitt (1996) suggested that tests intended to measure a broad content domain may contain low α only because they are performing as intended. For these and other such tests, corrections for attenuation can provide a means by which the low reliability of a measure need not detract from meaningful use of the test in assessing relationships between the construct measured and other variables. Other frequently overlooked factors also require consideration in the context of interpreting α, including the variance of test scores in the population in which it is estimated and the number of items on the test (Crocker & Algina 1986). In particular, the same test will produce lower α values when administered to a population having a smaller true-score variance, as error variance will remain the same and thus occupy a larger proportion of the observed score variance. On the other hand, α will increase when more items of equal quality to those already in the test are added. Thus, α taken by itself should not be regarded as a measure of the quality of items on the test.

It is important to note that issues of reliability and measurement precision can also be explored in the context of latent variable modeling, and in many cases will be more effectively examined in this context. McDonald (1985) has shown when using a common factor model that for tests measuring one common factor, the coefficient ω, computed as the square of the sum of the estimated item factor loadings divided by test variance, theoretically provides a better lower bound to the coefficient of precision than α. A similar approach is discussed by Raykov (1997). Conceptually, ω represents the square of the correlation between test score and the underlying common factor measured by the test items. Although practically speaking the process of fitting a factor model solely for the purpose of obtaining a reliability estimate may not be worthwhile (in most cases ω is only slightly larger than α), there are other good reasons for fitting a latent variable model to the test, such as to explore its dimensional structure, or to investigate the modeling features of individual items.

Assessing Measurement Error

Reliability coefficients provide information concerning the amount of error variance relative to true score variance and can be useful in comparing different measures. Often the amount of error variance itself is of most interest, however, especially in the context of interpreting and using test scores. For example, the square root of measurement variance, the *standard error of measurement,* is often used to describe the expected variation of observed scores about an examinee's true score. Recently, increased attention has been directed toward considering standard errors conditional on true score. Such approaches emphasize the fact that in many cases standard error is unlikely to be constant across the entire score scale. We have already noted how IRT supplies a measure of standard error, conditional on θ, that is based on the test information function. However, several methods for computing conditional standard errors (CSEs) have also been developed in the context of CTT that do not require the IRT modeling assumptions (for a discussion and comparison of these methods, see Feldt, Steffen, & Gupta, 1985; Qualls-Payne, 1992). It is important to keep in mind, however, that in CTT conditional standard errors are dependent on the score scale of the test for which they are computed. That is, if the scale on which scores are reported is different than the raw score scale, different conditional standard errors apply. Conditional standard errors can be useful in determining a scale on which to report scores, as it may be desirable to have a scale in which conditional standard errors are close to equal at all score levels. Kolen, Hanson, and Brennan (1992) analyzed the effects of transforming a score scale on the resulting conditional standard errors.

The need to correct for measurement error in test use has been a frequently overlooked and commonly misunderstood practice. Schmidt and Hunter (1996) provided an overview of a variety of research scenarios in which dealing with measurement error has been problematic, including cases in which researchers have failed to recognize the existence of measurement error, have used the wrong reliability coefficient to correct for it, or have misinterpreted the resulting unattenuated coefficient. Other methods of controlling for measurement error, such as structural equation modeling, provide a framework in which research hypotheses are investigated with respect to latent variables.

Reliability for Criterion-Referenced Tests

The applications of reliability considered thus far relate most appropriately to measurements that are *norm-referenced,* meaning score interpretations are based on a relative standard in which test performances of examinees are compared in the context of other examinees. Over the past couple of decades, increased psychometric attention has been directed toward measurements that are *criterion-referenced,* meaning that the scores are interpreted according to an absolute standard. Examples include the use of scores for inferences about mastery of particular skills, such as a credentialing examination, or when evaluating the effectiveness of an instructional program. In this case, attention is focused on the particular score(s) for which the test has special meaning, say the cut-off score between a "Pass" and a "Fail."

In reliability theory, there is usually a distinction drawn between investigations of reliability applied to norm-referenced conditions and those based on criterion-referenced tests. The latter often focus on the consistency of classification across test administrations as opposed to score variance. These methods also have applications to conditions involving multiple raters and are therefore sometimes also used for interrater reliability assessment. An example of a coefficient used for this purpose is Cohen's κ. Cohen's κ is computed as the proportion of individuals classified consistently across two administrations (or raters) corrected for the expected number of consistent classifications that would occur by chance. Statistical characteristics of this index have been discussed extensively in the literature (see, for example, Cantor, 1996; Lee & Fung, 1993; Rae, 1997).

Although κ is simple to compute and easily interpreted, it also assumes the availability of more than one test administration. Alternative methods for estimating κ based on a single test administration have been presented by Subkoviak (1976) and Huynh (1976). Subkoviak's method uses the individual's proportion correct score, the mean test score, and an internal consistency reliability estimate to estimate a proportion correct true-score for the examinee on the test. This true-score is then used to compute the probability of exceeding a particular cut-score (e.g., the Pass/Fail threshold), assuming a binomial test score distribution for the individual. Huynh's method is a little more complicated. It assumes that the population scores follow a negative hypergeometric distribution and estimates the joint density of the observed test scores with a hypothetical test. Livingston and Lewis (1995) have recently developed a similar method for conditions where the test items are polytomously scored. An overview of these and other criterion-referenced reliability methods was recently provided by Hambleton and Slater (1997).

The previously described methods are based strictly on the consistency with which scores are classified—that is, whether the scores are above or below a particular cut-score of interest. Alternative indices that can be used for criterion-referenced tests consider the scores themselves and their distances from the cut-score. Essentially these indices combine a consideration of classification error with measurement error. Livingston (1972) proposed an index based on the CTT reliability coefficient definition, but considers the variation of scores about the cut-score (rather than the mean score) in computing true-score variance and observed-score variance for estimating a reliability coefficient. Brennan and Kane (1977) considered a similar index that uses a different error variance component.

Indices such as κ can also be used to assess interrater agreement. Klauer and Batchelder (1996) have more recently provided a general modeling framework for the analysis of interrater agreement in which each rating is expressed as a function of an agreement component (or the "true" categorization of the observation) and an error component consisting of both within-rater inconsistencies as well as consistent judgments that are unique for the particular rater. The degree to which ratings are determined by the agreement component determines the reliability of the measurement. An advantage of this approach is that the model allows for distinct assessment of reliability, rater bias, and the true distribution of rater categories, which is corrected for rater bias. It also provides a good example of how test and item score modeling is playing a growing role in reliability assessment.

Generalizability Theory

Cronbach, Gleser, and Rajaratnam (1963) and Cronbach, Gleser, Nanda, and Rajaratnam (1972) provided an introduction to *generalizability theory,* which is an extension of reliability theory that separately analyzes the relative effects of multiple sources of score variance through analysis of variance procedures (Feldt & Brennan, 1989). Increasing interest in generalizability theory might be attributed in part to the growth of areas such as performance assessment, where testing not only involves an evaluation of multiple different tasks (e.g., essays written on different topics), but is also based on the scoring of multiple raters. In such a case, we can attribute the variability in scores for an individual on each essay with respect to two sources (called *facets* in generalizability theory)—essay type and rater.

In generalizability theory, there is typically a distinction made between two types of analyses—a G-Study (or Generalizability Study) and a D-Study (Decision Study). In a G-Study, the investigator identifies the *universe of admissible observations,* determined by what facets and what conditions of each facet define permissible measurement conditions, followed by estimation of the magnitudes of the various sources of score variation. In our example, permissible measurement conditions might include a particular set of possible essay topics and a particular group of individuals who could serve as raters. Sources of score variation would include not only main effects attributed to the individual, rater, and essay-type facets, but also all interactions between individuals, raters, and essay types. A further consideration in a G-Study is whether the conditions of a facet are fixed (e.g., the number of potential raters is finite) or random (e.g., the number of potential raters is infinite).

Practically speaking, it will often not be possible in the design of a measurement procedure to completely cross all conditions of each facet, especially as the number of facets becomes large. As a result, we might have the same rater evaluate the same subset of essay questions for each subject. In such a case, we say that the questions are *nested* within raters. In the context of a G-study, this results in a confounding of certain variance elements that otherwise (in the context of a crossed design) were estimable. Figure 5.8 provides an illustration of the consequence of the nesting of items (essay type) within raters, where each enclosed region in the Venn diagram corresponds to a variance component that can be estimated. Because the items are nested, it is impossible to distinguish between item variance and item-rater interaction variance, and likewise between variance attributed to the person-item and person-item-rater interactions. By contrast, when the facets are fully crossed, all sources of variance can be estimated. In designing a G-study, it is therefore important to keep in mind potential D-study designs so as to ensure that relevant sources of variance that will be needed are estimable. In our essay example, if our D-Study had as its goal an evaluation of the difficulty variation across essay types, the G-Study represented in Figure 5.8 does not supply the relevant variance estimate, as item variance (what we would need) is confounded with variance due to item-rater interaction.

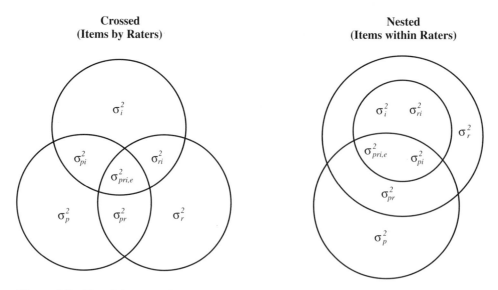

**Crossed
(Items by Raters)**

**Nested
(Items within Raters)**

Figure 5.8   Venn Diagrams Illustrating Sources of Score Variance in Generalizability Study.
Facets = items (*i*), raters (*r*); (*p* = persons)

A D-Study makes use of the results of a G-study in constructing a particular procedure for measurement. A first consideration in constructing a D-Study is the *universe of generalization,* which is the number of facets and conditions of each facet over which measurements will be generalized. The results of a G-study can be used to evaluate the effectiveness of various designs for minimizing the effects of measurement error and thus maximizing reliability. A further consideration in the design of a D-Study is whether the decision is relative—that is, the measurement is used to order individuals—or absolute, where the measurement is intended to infer an individual's universe score. In the absolute case, variance attributed to essay type enters into computation of the standard error of measurement even when all individuals are administered the same set of items; in the relative case, this does not occur, at least when all individuals are administered the same items.

One distinction from reliability assessment in CTT is the replacement of the concept of true score (which corresponded to expected performance on the test) by the concept of universe score, which corresponds to a subject's expected performance on a universe of permissible observations. In our example, each observation corresponds to a unique essay type-rater combination. Analogous to a reliability coefficient, we can compute a *generalizability coefficient,* defined as the ratio of universe score variance to observed score variance. Estimation of the generalizability coefficient is naturally dependent on what sources of error variance are identified (as is the reliability coefficient), and can be computed based on results from an ANOVA. A second distinction is that the concept of test parallelism in CTT is also replaced by a more realistic one based on sampling assumptions with respect to the universe of admissible observations (see de Gruijter & van der Kamp, 1991).

More specialized topics in the area of generalizability theory include multivariate generalizability, which is the case in which scores for multiple levels of a fixed facet are considered separately, as well as estimation of the variability of the estimated variance components (Feldt & Brennan, 1989). Good introductory sources to the area of generalizability theory are provided in de Gruijter and van der Kamp (1991), Shavelson and Webb (1991), and Shavelson, Webb, and Rowley (1989).

VALIDITY

Informally, test validity refers to the degree to which a test measures what it is intended to measure. As with reliability, we regard validity not as an inherent property of the test itself, but rather with respect to a particular interpretation or use of the test. In many cases, the same test can be interpreted or used in more than one way. For example, a mathematics test may be used to assess a student's mastery of a particular domain of mathematical concepts, to inform decisions in a competition for college scholarships, to identify a particular program of remedial instruction, to determine advanced placement in a college course, or any of a variety of other purposes. It is likely that the test will be "valid" for some of these uses but not others, despite the fact that we might claim that the test in all cases measures "mathematics ability." As a result, responsibility for investigating test validity often lies more with the test user than the test developer, especially in cases where test use departs from the intended or implied purpose for which it was developed. From this perspective, the practitioner carries the heavy responsibility not only for understanding previous validation evidence collected for a given test, but also for determining the relevance of that evidence for the particular purpose for which the test is to be administered.

Test validation is the process of collecting evidence that supports a particular use or interpretation of the test. It includes a variety of different kinds of evidence that are sometimes categorized as being *content, criterion,* and *construct related.* Content-related evidence is evidence that supports inferences from test performance to a larger domain of items similar to those on the test itself and from which the test items are considered a sample. Evidence of this kind therefore requires both a well-specified domain providing a detailed description of test content and expert judgment concerning the content relevance and representativeness of the sample (Messick, 1989). Such evaluations may require consideration both of the relative importance of certain elements of the domain and the degree to which more superficial aspects of the test (e.g., item wording, response format) coincide with the domain.

Criterion-related evidence refers to evidence supporting inferences from the test to external variables. Often we think of this type of evidence as relating to the usefulness of the test in the context of prediction, either with respect to a criterion at a later point in time (such as job performance) or concurrently (such as diagnosis of a psychological disorder). Finally, construct-related evidence suggests the test can be used to make inferences to a set of performances under the label of a particular psychological construct (Crocker & Algina, 1986). There are a variety of evidence types that are often considered to fall under this category, including information related to the internal structure of the test (i.e., the relative difficulties and dimensionality of the test items), relationships with other variables, relationships with other measures of the same construct, the consistency of response processes on the test with what is theoretically known about the construct, and an observed differentiation between groups known or suspected to differ on the measured construct, for example, in the context of an experimental treatment.

As we consider shortly, there has been considerable attention directed toward refining what is meant by validity. Increasingly the purpose of this threefold categorization (i.e., content, criterion, and construct validity) appears to be more in assisting in the organization and communication of validity research than of suggesting distinct validity "types." Alternative forms of categorization (e.g., Messick, 1994) have recently been proposed that may be more consistent with evolving conceptions of test validity as a unified concept, and it appears the proposed revision to the APA Standards for educational and psychological testing will further downplay this threefold distinction.

A large number of practical issues are currently of interest in the area of test validity. For example, with the increased use of computer-based tests, issues have emerged as to whether the trait or ability being measured is the same when administered in this format versus the conventional paper and pencil format (Green, 1988). The relationship between validity and other test evaluation concepts, such as reliability and test bias, is also an area requiring further clarification (Moss, 1995). Likewise, the question of who is primarily responsible for test validation, test developer or user, remains an important but largely unresolved issue (Shepard, 1993). A more comprehensive discussion of issues in validity theory might cover these topics in more detail. Instead, we focus our attention on some recent developments both in the development of validity as a psychometric concept and on statistical tools that may be relevant for its evaluation.

Concept of Test Validity

As validity has traditionally been somewhat of an elusive term (in contrast, for example, to the more quantifiable concepts of reliability and measurement error), much attention in psychometrics has been focused on what it means for a test to be considered valid. For example, since the discussion of construct validity by Cronbach and Meehl (1955), it has become increasingly popular to unify all "types" of validity under the rubric of construct validity. Moreover, investigations of construct validity are increasingly understood as occurring within the context of a theoretical framework that specifies hypothesized relations between the measured attribute and other variables (including other measures of the same construct) that ultimately serve to define the construct. Construct theory provides the basis for selecting test content at the stage of test construction, for expecting certain consistencies among item responses, and for predicting score relationships (Messick, 1989). From this standpoint, content- and criterion-related evidence of validity also relate to aspects of this network of relationships and are not always distinguishable from construct validity, as historically emphasized.

This way of thinking has several other implications for investigating test validity. First, it likens test validation to the process of hypothesis testing (Landy, 1986). More specifically, test validation becomes driven in large part by an attempt to rule out alternative hypotheses providing different explanations for test scores than that provided by the construct (Cronbach, 1989; Kane, 1992; Shepard, 1993). Second, it unifies the validation process. Investigations of test validity should not follow the common checklist mentality in which disjointed investigations are reported independently and without an overall judgment based on their connections to the common theoretical framework defining the construct. Rather, validity results should be transformed into an evaluative argument that integrates validity evidence in support of the proposed interpretation or use of the test (Cronbach, 1989). Third, and finally, the emphasis on construct theory increases the relevance of statistical tools such as structural equation modeling to addressing issues that are relevant to test validity. In a later section, we discuss some advances, for example in confirmatory factor analysis, that may help to provide the evidence needed to evaluate hypotheses relevant to test validity.

In the context of evaluating competing theoretical hypotheses, Messick (1989) considered the validity concerns of *construct underrepresentation* and *construct irrelevant variance*. Construct underrepresentation refers to the condition in which the test fails to cover the full breadth of the construct intended to be measured. For example, a measure may assess academic and social aspects of self-concept but not a physical aspect. If the physical aspect is theoretically considered to be part of the construct of self-concept, the construct is said to be underrepresented by the test. By contrast, construct irrelevant variance refers to elements measured by the test that are unrelated to the construct. Although some variance of this kind is perhaps inevitable in testing applications, the goal in test construction should be one of limiting its capacity to contaminate test scores. Examples of sources of construct-irrelevant variance include, for example, "test-wiseness," or the ability for some individuals to answer items based on subtle unintended hints in the wording of the items, and social desirability, which is relevant on self-report inventories where certain individuals can identify and prefer to report the desirable rather than the most accurate response (see McCrae & Costa, 1983, for another perspective on social desirability). Construct-irrelevant variance becomes especially problematic on achievement tests, for example, when they discriminate against members of a minority group, an issue we discuss later in the context of measurement invariance and test bias.

Much current debate in validity theory centers on the proposed consideration of the consequences of test interpretation and use as a component of test validity. Messick's (1989) frequently cited chapter on validity devotes considerable attention to what he refers to as the *consequential basis* of test validity, a facet of test validity that is to be distinguished conceptually from its *evidential* basis. Because validity is a feature of a test interpretation rather than of the test itself, Messick suggested that validity considerations carry over to an investigation of the implications of actions based on test use, in addition to the previously described assessment of whether the test satisfies its intended purpose. These consequences would include, for example, whether a remedial training program in which test participants are enrolled is successful, as well as unintended effects of testing, such as the disproportionate selection of members of a particular ethnic or gender group and subsequent social ramifications.

Although all test practitioners agree that the consequences of testing are an important concern, the notion that such consequences should in some way relate to what is meant by test validity has had many detractors. Their counterclaim is that validity as a term should relate only to the accuracy with which a trait is measured, rather than imply some judgment about actions based on test scores (Mehrens, 1997). Conceptually, it is possible to distinguish between the case in which a test measures what it should but is put to poor use versus the case in which a test fails to measure what is intended. The interested reader is referred to recent discussions of consequential validity in the Summer, 1997 and Summer, 1998 issues of *Educational Measurement: Issues and Practice.*

Validity Generalization

We have already noted the significance of test score use in the investigation of test validity, as well as the enormous burden it seemingly places on counselors in evaluating test validity. A related set of issues revolves around understanding the influence of situational factors on the validity of a test when correlating it with an external variable. Previously, the occurrence of widely fluctuating validity coefficients (i.e., the correlation of the test with an external variable) across studies was taken as evidence that the validity of the test should be investigated "locally"—that is, with respect to the specific context in which it is applied. More recently however, methods for investigating *validity generalization* have been proposed, and their results suggest that such fluctuations can be largely (if not exclusively) attributed to sampling error, range restriction, or unreliability in the test or criterion. Schmidt and Hunter (1977) proposed a method by which the true distribution of sample validity coefficients is approximated. According to their approach, if the mean of the distribution of validity coefficients is large enough and the standard deviation small enough, a generalizability of validity is said to exist. In such cases, the test can be thought of as equally valid across all contexts included in the domain of contexts considered. In the case of job selection, for example, a meta-analysis of validity coefficients across a variety of job settings might demonstrate that almost all variability in validity coefficients can be explained as artifacts of the sampling conditions previously mentioned.

Schmidt and Hunter's (1977) results have some important implications. Besides suggesting a reconsideration of situational specificity in validity investigations, their results also suggest a reconsideration of how the investigator should look at the validity of a test in a given context. If the particular test-criterion relationship being investigated is one for which there exists an extensive literature, a validity coefficient based on meta-analysis may be more accurate than one uniquely constructed for the situation itself, where small sample size is likely to result in inaccuracy. The task of the investigator is thus one of determining whether the unique characteristics of the measurement setting necessitate a local validation study, keeping in mind the limited accuracy that will be obtained due to the smaller sample size.

An alternative method discussed by Hedges (1988) is an *empirical Bayes method* that is useful when a "perfect" generalization of validity does not hold. The empirical Bayes approach provides a compromise between a validity coefficient estimated from a generalization procedure and one obtained from a local validation study. The attractiveness of this method is its capacity to make use of, and appropriately weight, both sources of information concerning the test's validity for the given situation. One can think of this method as being an adjustment of the situation specific coefficient in light of its sampling error and lack of reliability, according to what is known about the test-criterion relationship from previous studies.

Factor Analysis

As mentioned, an important way the validity of a test is investigated is through postulating and confirming hypotheses about the relation of one construct with other constructs. Historically, factor analysis has been a useful tool for describing systematic patterns in a correlation or covariance matrix that are relevant for investigating test validity. *Exploratory factor analysis* can use either type of matrix to derive a set of underlying component variables, or common factors, upon which each variable is assigned a particular weight (or factor loading). Often the derived factors are interpreted with respect to some common task element or experience shared by the variables that have large loadings. From a validity perspective, factor analysis is a useful way of investigating the degree to which a test possesses convergent and discriminant validity, a topic we return to shortly. However, because the goal in test validity is usually one of evaluating previously developed hypotheses, *confirmatory factor analysis* (CFA) is typically a more useful way of testing whether a given test's patterns of association with other variables correspond to what is expected. In CFA, hypotheses are investigated by imposing constraints on certain factor loadings so as to define more precisely the expected nature of the associations between variables in the matrix.

Factor analysis of test items (as opposed to tests) presents a unique challenge especially when items are scored dichotomously or use a small number of score categories. For example, it is commonly known that the correlation coefficient between two dichotomous items (called a *phi coefficient*) is affected by differences in difficulty among items. Application of factor analysis to a phi-coefficient matrix can result in the extraction of "difficulty factors" (McDonald & Ahlawat, 1974) that are artifacts of these effects. One way of addressing this problem is through *item-level factor analysis.* Item-level factor analysis methods use correlation coefficients called tetrachoric and polychoric coefficients for dichotomously and polytomously scored test items, respectively. Essentially these coefficients are based on the assumption that the observed item responses can be thought of as a manifestation resulting from discretizing an underlying normally distributed random variable at a particular threshold value (or values, in the case of polytomous scoring) unique to each item. A method for factor analyzing tetrachoric correlations (which also uses the mean item responses) was proposed by Christofferson (1975), using a method of estimation called generalized least squares (GLS); it was simplified by Muthen (1978) in the program LISCOMP.

A different approach to item factor analysis is a maximum-likelihood method proposed by Bock, Gibbons, and Muraki (1988) and implemented in the TESTFACT program. In contrast to the GLS method, TESTFACT uses the complete item response matrix rather than the matrix of correlation coefficients. Mislevy (1986) provided a comparison of the two methods and suggested that the computational algorithms used by each make the TESTFACT method preferable for cases involving a small number of factors and a large number of items; GLS is preferred when there are a large number of factors but the test has fewer items. Item-level factor analysis provides an important way of investigating whether the internal structure of a test conforms to what is hypothesized based on knowledge about the construct. For example, life satisfaction may consist of a past, present, and future component so that a factor analysis of a test measuring life satisfaction results in the extraction of three factors where items based on a similar time-reference have their largest loadings on the same factor.

Measurement Invariance

As educational and psychological tests are increasingly applied to members of different cultures and as sensitivities toward test bias against racial, ethnic, and gender groups have grown, an important issue in psychometrics has become that of determining whether a test measures the same trait or ability across identifiable subpopulations of individuals. The goal behind such investigations is one of attempting to ensure a comparability of test scores for individuals across groups or, from another perspective, to understand differences in the nature of the construct across groups. It is said that a test demonstrates *measurement invariance* when it measures the same trait across groups and in such a way that the measurement scales have the same numerical interpretation (Drasgow, 1987). There is a distinction sometimes made between measurement invariance and *predictive invariance,* the latter referring to the performance of the test in terms of its prediction of an external variable. The concepts are related, and we focus on just the first due to space limitations. (For a discussion of predictive invariance, see Cole and Moss, 1989, or Linn, 1984; for a consideration of its relation to measurement invariance, see Millsap, 1995, 1997.)

In the context of cross-cultural research, Van de Vijver and Leung (1997) made a distinction between *construct bias, method bias,* and *differential item functioning.* Construct bias occurs when the trait intended to be measured by the test has a different meaning across groups and cannot be adequately assessed using the same test in both groups. It is consequently more a feature of what is being measured than of the test itself, but nevertheless clearly has implications for test use. An example might be the construct of intelligence, which may consist of different components in Western as opposed to non-Western cultures as different skills are required to adapt to each environment (Van de Vijver & Leung, 1997). Method bias, by contrast, occurs when the construct is the same, but the test also measures some other unintended difference between groups. This type of bias can be examined, for example, by correlating the test with other known measures of the construct not suspected to vary across groups. We often think of sources of method bias as affecting the test as a whole rather than only a small subset of test items. A test intended to measure only mathematics ability, for example, but for which test instructions and all items are written in English may demonstrate method bias against Spanish-speaking students. Finally, DIF focuses on differences at the level of individual test items. It can be assessed by examining differences in the internal structure of the test across groups. An item on a reading comprehension test based on a passage dealing with the subject of auto mechanics may be relatively more difficult for women than men, for example (assuming that knowledge of auto mechanics tends to be greater among men than women).

In a study evaluating the measurement invariance of the Sexual Experiences Questionnaire (Fitzgerald et al., 1988), a measure of sexual harassment in the workplace, Donovan and Drasgow (1997) compared the item responses of workers in different work settings (a public utility company, a food distribution company, and a university) and from different cultures (Brazil and Italy). In such comparisons, it becomes important to consider each of the forms of bias described above. We should initially consider construct bias, that is, whether the concept of sexual harassment means the same thing across these various contexts (i.e., Are the same behaviors equally interpreted as harassment in foreign countries?). Further, it is likely that in some contexts there may be a greater reluctance among workers (possibly for fear of negative consequences) to acknowledge harassment experiences that have occurred, resulting in a possible method bias due to underreporting. A possible source of DIF may be due to poor translation of an item. Several of the items, for example, involved descriptions of specific behaviors (e.g., "told suggestive stories and jokes," "was staring or leering at you") that may have subtly different meanings, even when the most appropriate translation is chosen. Donovan and Drasgow (1997) found the more specific behaviorally based items (e.g., "told suggestive stories or offensive jokes," "made crude and offensive sexual remarks," "was staring or leering at you," and "touched you,") to demonstrate the largest amounts of DIF. They discuss a variety of potential cultural factors that may contribute to DIF for these items.

Cole and Moss (1989) defined test bias as occurring when a test is differentially valid across groups. As a result, one aspect of investigating test bias may involve an independent evaluation of the validity of the test for each group. From this standpoint, all methods relevant to evaluating construct validity discussed earlier become relevant. For example, demonstrating that the relative difficulties of items correspond to theoretical expectations is one way of suggesting the test is valid within the group.

Although a necessary component of measurement invariance, simply evaluating the validity within each group may not be sufficient for demonstrating measurement invariance, especially when the test is used for the purpose of comparing individuals from different groups (Van de Vijver & Leung, 1997). The most statistically developed approaches for investigating intergroup differences in test performance are based on analyzing the internal structure of tests, including DIF detection methods. One example of an IRT-based approach for assessing measurement invariance is described by Reise, Widaman, and Pugh (1993). They compared G^2 values (representing the likelihood of the observed data) for the case in which the item parameters for an IRT model are constrained to be the same across groups to one in which they are free to differ across groups. The difference in fit between the two cases can be approximated by a χ^2 distribution. Measurement invariance occurs to the degree that the model allowing the parameters to vary across groups provides a better fit. Reise et al. further assessed the implications of a lack of measurement invariance by comparing person fit statistics in the constrained model with the unconstrained model.

In addition to the IRT model-based DIF methods described earlier, an alternative class of DIF detection methods are nonparametric in that no specific form is assumed for the item response function. An example of such a method is the procedure SIBTEST, which evaluates the difference between nonparametrically estimated ICCs for two groups that are linked using a regression-correction procedure (Shealy & Stout, 1993). An attractive feature of SIBTEST is its capacity to evaluate how DIF accumulates against a group of individuals over multiple test items (Nandakumar, 1993).

One characteristic of these DIF methods is that by comparing performances across groups conditioned on the trait or ability measured by the test, they only assess differences in item performance that are due to features other than what the test is intending to measure. Historically, the distinction between whether differences in item performance were due to differences in what is supposed to be measured by the test (called "impact") versus construct-irrelevant sources has often been ignored.

If a factor analysis is performed in each group, a comparison of the resulting factor solutions is another way of assessing item-level differences across groups. Because factor solutions are rotationally indeterminant, this requires finding an appropriate rotational transformation of one solution to another so as to maximize their congruence. The similarities of the resulting factor loadings are then compared to evaluate the similarity of the test's dimensional structure across groups. Tucker (1951) proposed a commonly used index called the *coefficient of agreement* for this evaluation, although other related indices have also been proposed. Solutions obtained using other multidimensional data reduction methods, such as multidimensional scaling, can be compared in similar ways to evaluate differences in test structure across groups (e.g., Day & Rounds, 1998).

Another approach uses confirmatory factor analysis to test for measurement invariance. The idea here is similar to the IRT approach discussed previously in that we compare the fit of a more restricted model in which factor loadings are constrained to be equal across groups versus the fit of a model in which groups can have different loadings on the items. Such constraints can be easily imposed, for example, using software such as the LISREL program. The difference in χ^2 values for the two models is itself a χ^2 variable because the restricted model is nested within the full model, and can thus be used to test for the existence of differences between groups. Similarly, alternative models in-between the restricted and full models can be considered by restricting some of the items to have the same loadings across groups while others are permitted to vary. If such a model can be found to fit the data, it is said that *partial measurement invariance* holds (Reise et al., 1993).

Multitrait Multimethod Matrices and Convergent/Discriminant Validity

Part of determining the construct validity of a test or collection of tests often involves a demonstration of their *convergent* and *discriminant* validity. By convergent validity, we mean the tendency for the test to correlate highly with other measures of the same construct. By contrast, discriminant validity is evidenced by the low correlations between the test and measures of other distinct constructs. Campbell and Fiske (1959) proposed a commonly used experimental design for investigation of convergent and discriminant validation referred to as the multitrait multimethod (MTMM) approach. The MTMM approach requires the measurement of at least two different traits, using at least two different types of measures so that each trait is measured using each of the measurement types. The correlation matrix among all of the measures is called an MTMM matrix.

The coefficients in an MTMM matrix are often characterized as being of three different types. *Reliability coefficients* appear along the diagonal and represent correlations between measures of the same construct using the same measurement type. *Convergent validity coefficients* are the correlations among different measurements of the same construct. *Discriminant validity coefficients* include both correlations of different constructs using the same method (called heterotrait-monomethod coefficients) and correlations of different constructs using different methods (called heterotrait-heteromethod coefficients). Campbell and Fiske's approach to assessing the existence of construct validity relies largely on a visual inspection of the relative magnitudes of these coefficients. In general, the convergent validity coefficients should be larger than the discriminant validity coefficients for the test to be considered valid. If, for example, the heterotrait monomethod coefficients are larger than the convergent validity coefficients, it suggests the occurrence of method effects, implying that test scores are more affected by the method used than by the construct being measured.

Although Campbell and Fiske's qualitative criteria for evaluation of MTMM matrices have been found to be practically useful and simple to implement, they have the potential to be misleading, especially when measures differ in their reliability (Wothke, 1984). Thus, they may be better replaced by methods that make use of latent variables. There have been different models proposed that may provide a more descriptive explanation of the MTMM matrix, which also supply convergent and discriminant validation evidence (for a review, see Marsh & Grayson, 1995; Millsap, 1995; Wothke, 1996). The most popular approaches are those based on confirmatory factor analysis. Using CFA, the investigator specifies which measures have non-zero factor loadings on a given factor and then constrains each of the remaining loadings to be zero for that factor. In such a way, method and trait factors can be defined.

Marsh and Grayson (1995) provided an overview of four CFA models. A highly restrictive model in the context of MTMM is one that assumes that the intertest correlations are completely accounted for by the traits measured. This model, called the CFA correlated-traits model, assumes that there are no effects attributable to the methods and that the observed correlations are only a function of the correlations between traits and reliabilities of the measures. A second model, the CFA correlated traits/uncorrelated methods model, assumes that method factors exist but are not correlated across different methods. Such a model would provide a better fit for cases where heterotrait monomethod coefficients are large compared with heterotrait heteromethod coefficients. A less restrictive model, the CFA correlated traits/correlated methods model permits the existence of factors attributable to methods but also permits the method factors to be correlated across method. Finally, a fourth model for assessing method effects, the correlated traits/correlated uniquenesses model, allows method effects to vary depending on the trait being measured, but assumes no correlation between the different methods. One advantage of CFA in the analysis of MTMM matrices is the unambiguous evaluation of convergent validity, discriminant validity, and method effects by examining the size of factor loadings on factors corresponding to each type of effect. Comparing the fit of these confirmatory models also allows one to investigate more carefully the nature of method effects (when the models are nested, a statistical test for improvement in fit can be constructed).

Two less-known alternative approaches to CFA are *direct product models* (DP) and *covariance component analysis* (CCA; see Wothke, 1996). Although CFA implies that trait and method factors combine additively to affect test performance, DP models assume that they combine multiplicatively. An example of such a model is discussed by Swain (1975) and extended by Browne (1984) to the analysis of correlation matrices. CCA uses a multivariate random effects model to decompose an individual's score profile into a general component, trait profiles, and method profiles. It is most useful for cases where planned contrasts of trait and method effects are specified.

Finally, Kane (1982) suggested a method based on generalizability theory. In Kane's approach, each measurement is taken to represent a random sample from a universe of possible measurements that could have been administered. A validity coefficient, interpreted as an average convergent validity coefficient over all possible samples of measurement methods, is computed as variance due to persons over the sum of variances due to persons, the interaction of persons and method, and all other unexplained sources of variance.

PSYCHOMETRICS AND COGNITIVE PSYCHOLOGY

Many of the previously described efforts in modeling for the purpose of diagnosis, especially in the context of education, can be traced to a more general interest in redesigning test theory in ways that are consistent with current thinking in cognitive psychology. A frequent criticism of psychometrics is that it tends to be disproportionately influenced by developments in the field of statistics compared with psychology. Snow and Lohman (1989) contrasted psychometric models of the type in IRT and classical test theory, which serve primarily to order individuals with respect to an underlying trait or ability, with cognitive information processing (CIP) models, which serve primarily to develop and test substantive psychological theory. Snow and Lohman suggested that psychometric models typically have little or no substantive psychological justification, make overly simplistic assumptions about the psychology of items (such as local independence), and remove psychology as a whole from the test model, leaving psychometric issues such as test validity, for example, largely to investigations external to the model.

By contrast, CIP models are designed to provide more detailed descriptions of item performance according to sequences of cognitive operations that are performed on incoming or stored information. CIP models attempt to "explain the internal workings of the human cognitive system, the mental events and processes that connect stimulus and response in an item, test, or task performance, and thus to penetrate the black box of educational and psychological measurement models" (Snow & Lohman, 1989, p. 269). Snow and Lohman suggested that models that combine the strengths of psychometric and CIP models may prove to be the most valuable for future test analysis. Others suggest the potential of cognitive theory for test construction and development (Embretson, 1985). Given the influential role of differential psychology in the construction of mental ability tests and models, an important question is whether cognitive psychology provides a theoretical framework that converges or diverges with underlying psychometric theory (Sternberg, 1991).

One step to bringing test theory more in line with cognitive theory is to consider methods used by cognitive theorists. Sternberg (1991) provided an overview of various approaches for the measurement of intelligence based on cognitive theory, described as *cognitive-correlates, cognitive-components, cognitive-contents,* and *cognitive-training* based methods. Related categorizations have been discussed by Pellegrino and Glaser (1979) and Snow and Lohman (1989). The cognitive-correlates approach is concerned with the performance of simple information processing tasks, such as in letter matching or memory scanning experiments. Usually the speed with which these tasks are performed is the dependent variable of interest. Individual differences in the rate at which such tasks are performed has demonstrated significant but relatively low correlations with measures of intelligence, perhaps because the tasks are considerably different from those usually measured on intelligence tests.

Cognitive-components investigations study performances on tasks of the kind usually measured on the test itself, such as verbal analogies, mental rotations, or syllogisms. The goal of such studies is to formulate and test models for test performance and to examine how the cognitive components correlate across subjects, tasks, and with overall performance on the test. Cognitive-contents approaches relate to the nonprocess-related aspects of knowledge and not only include the knowledge elements themselves, but how they are organized and used in the context of test performance. Interest here often lies in studying expert-novice differences and the ways in which knowledge of a particular area is mentally represented, including what aspects of a problem each group pays attention to when attempting to solve a problem and how they make use of skills in problem solving. Some examples of methods by which this is investigated are discussed by Britton and Tidwell (1995), Johnson, Goldsmith, and Teague (1995), and Naveh-Benjamin, Lin, and McKeachie (1995). Finally, cognitive training approaches seek to provide evidence for cognitive theory by demonstrating an improvement in performance for participants that are trained in ways consistent with the theory. In the context of evaluating participants, cognitive training researchers might be interested, for example, in relating intelligence to a participant's potential for learning new material.

Although the goal of the psychometrician is different from that of the cognitive theorist, it seems to be increasingly recognized that a meaningful assessment of an individual's ability level must be based on tools that are consistent with what is known about the trait or ability being investigated. Even though much work in this area remains to be done, there are some important ways in which psychometrics is attempting to incorporate approaches more consistent with those used in cognitive psychology. There are some recent examples of models in psychometrics that relate more directly to the types of cognitive investigations just described. Embretson (1985) has introduced a class of multicomponent IRT models that describe item or task performance as a function of the cognitive components required and incorporate individual differences with respect to abilities in successfully executing each component. An example is the multicomponent latent trait model (Whitely, 1980), which models the probabilities of successfully executing each component through an IRT model using a component-specific ability parameter. Model estimation not only requires data related to the final response on the test item, but also to the success in executing each of the subtasks in each item (Embretson, 1993). Other examples include models that attempt to decompose the item difficulty parameter in IRT according to the cognitive components required for each item, such as Fischer's (1973) linear logistic model described earlier. Embretson (1984) has extended the MLTM model to include a similar representation for the subtasks on an item. This model, called the general component latent trait model, assesses both the relationship of the components to the total item and the relationship of stimulus features of items to the component outcomes.

A further consequence of the attention to cognitive theory has been an increased interest in response variables other than test or item scores. For example, the speed of test response is increasingly understood as an important reflection of cognitive process and ability (Berger, 1982; Roskam, 1997; Scheiblechner, 1985). Strategy selection, including how individuals adapt strategies over the course of the testing process, can provide important insight into the thinking and learning processes of individuals (Mislevy & Verhelst, 1990). Protocol analyses, in which individuals provide detailed descriptions of their thinking processes over the course of testing, are useful both for understanding the cognitive demands of items as well as differences in strategy selection among examinees. In many cases, the types of psychometric measures currently used can be supplemented with other types of tasks that more directly assess aspects of knowledge such as organizational structure. For example, one way of assessing a student's knowledge structure might involve a task that requires the student to evaluate the similarity of pairs of terms within a particular domain of knowledge. Tools such as multidimensional scaling and cluster analysis become relevant in such a context in their capacity to construct a spatial representation of such knowledge structures that can be compared with an expert knowledge structure (Nichols, Chipman, & Brennan, 1995).

Likewise, cognitive theory should enhance awareness of aspects of test items that have traditionally received less attention in psychometrics. Examples include the attentional requirements of test items, the effects of practice over the course of testing, the relevance of personality variables, and so on. It can also lead to the implementation of *faceted tests* that systematically manipulate item or test characteristics so as to permit experimental contrasts among parts of the test. Faceted tests can be put to use for diagnostic purposes or for identification of cognitive differences resulting from different methods of instruction (Snow & Lohman, 1989).

In the context of cognitive training, it becomes important to integrate assessment with instruction. Some considerations for designing tests so as to make them useful in the context of instruction have been discussed by Nitko (1989). Also, the integration of psychometric theory into the use of "intelligent tutors" provides a mechanism by which assessment takes place in the context of learning (Gitomer, Steinberg, & Mislevy, 1995).

CONCLUSION

Given many of the recent advances in psychometrics and the resulting tools for test construction and evaluation, the testing process appears to be rapidly becoming a more efficient and informative process. The development of new technology should continue to spur both new opportunities and new advances. Future counseling psychologists may one day experience the luxury of testing instruments that provide even more specific feedback to clients and that occupy an even greater role as psychoeducational tools than at present. Such innovations may have the unfortunate effect of enticing counseling psychologists away from their own roles as assessors, evaluators, and diagnosticians. However, these developments place even greater demands on the counselor, both because of the need to be familiar with new measurement methods and the availability of more information from which clients need to make decisions. For research, psychometrics provides an ever-expanding set of highly relevant tools for theory building and evaluation. Methods such as confirmatory factor analysis will likely grow in popularity within the counseling literature, and modeling frameworks such as IRT and generalizability theory will find further extensions to the wide range of tests used in counseling.

REFERENCES

American Educational Research Association, American Psychological Association, & National Council on Measurement in Education. (1985). *Standards for educational and psychological testing.* Washington, DC: American Psychological Association.

Andrich, D., & Luo, G. (1993). A hyperbolic cosine latent trait model for unfolding dichotomous single-stimulus responses. *Applied Psychological Measurement, 17,* 253–276.

Baker, F.B. (1992). *Item response theory: Parameter estimation techniques.* New York: Marcel Dekker.

Baker, J.G., Zevon, M.A., & Rounds, J.B. (1994). Differences in positive and negative affect dimensions: Latent trait analysis. *Personality and Individual Differences, 17,* 161–167.

Berger, M. (1982). The scientific approach to intelligence: An overview of its history with special reference to mental speed. In H.J. Eysenck (Ed.), *A model for intelligence* (pp. 13–43). New York: Springer-Verlag.

Birnbaum, A. (1968). Some latent trait models and their use in inferring an examinee's ability. In F.M. Lord & M.R. Novick (Eds.), *Statistical theories of mental test scores* (pp. 397–472). Reading, MA: Addison-Wesley.

Bock, R.D. (1972). Estimating item parameters and latent ability when responses are scored in two or more nominal categories. *Psychometrika, 37,* 29–51.

Bock, R.D., Gibbons, R., & Muraki, E. (1988). Full-information item factor analysis. *Applied Psychological Measurement, 12,* 261–280.

Brennan, R.L., & Kane, M.T. (1977). An index of dependability for mastery tests. *Journal of Educational Measurement, 14,* 277–289.

Britton, B.K., & Tidwell, P. (1995). Cognitive structure testing: A computer system for diagnosis of expert-novice differences. In P.D. Nichols, S.F. Chipman, & R.L. Brennan (Eds.), *Cognitively diagnostic assessment.* Hillsdale, NJ: Erlbaum.

Browne, M.W. (1984). The decomposition of multitrait-multimethod matrices. *British Journal of Mathematical and Statistical Psychology, 37,* 1–21.

Campbell, D.T., & Fiske, D.W. (1959). Convergent and discriminant validation by the multitrait-multimethod matrix. *Psychological Bulletin, 56,* 81–105.

Cantor, A.B. (1996). Sample-size calculations for Cohen's kappa. *Psychological Methods, 1,* 150–153.

Christofferson, A. (1975). Factor analysis of dichotomized variables. *Psychometrika, 40,* 5–32.

Cole, N.S., & Moss, P.A. (1989). Bias in test use. In R.L. Linn (Ed.), *Educational measurement* (3rd ed., pp. 201–219). Washington, DC: American Council on Education and National Council on Measurement in Education.

Coombs, C.H. (1950). The concepts of reliability and homogeneity. *Educational and Psychological Measurement, 10,* 43–56.

Cortina, J.M. (1993). What is coefficient alpha? An examination of theory and applications. *Journal of Applied Psychology, 78,* 98–104.

Crocker, L., & Algina, J. (1986). *Introduction to classical and modern test theory.* Orlando, FL: Harcourt Brace.

Cronbach, L.J. (1989). Construct validation after thirty years. In R.L. Linn (Ed.), *Intelligence: Measurement, theory, and public policy: Proceedings of a symposium in honor of Lloyd G. Humphreys* (pp. 147–171). Champaign: University of Illinois Press.

Cronbach, L.J., Gleser, G.C., Nanda, H., & Rajaratnam, N. (1972). *The dependability of behavioral measurements.* New York: Wiley.

Cronbach, L.J., Gleser, G.C., & Rajaratnam, N. (1963). Theory of generalizability theory: A liberalization of reliability theory. *British Journal of Mathematical and Statistical Psychology, 16,* 137–173.

Cronbach, L.J., & Meehl, P.E. (1955). Construct validity in psychological tests. *Psychological Bulletin, 52,* 281–302.

Day, S.X., & Rounds, J. (1998). Universality of vocational interest structure among racial and ethnic minorities. *American Psychologist, 53,* 728–736.

de Gruijter, D.N.M., & van der Kamp, L.J. (1991). Generalizability theory. In R.K. Hambleton & J.N. Zaal (Eds.), *Advances in educational and psychological testing: Theory and applications* (pp. 45–68). Boston: Kluwer.

Donovan, M.A., & Drasgow, F. (1997). *Establishing the measurement equivalence of a measure of sexual harassment across five samples: A multiple group comparison of differential item functioning.* Unpublished manuscript, University of Illinois at Urbana-Champaign.

Drasgow, F. (1987). Study of the measurement bias of two standardized psychological tests. *Journal of Applied Psychology, 72,* 19–29.

Embretson, S.E. (1984). A general latent trait model for response processes. *Psychometrika, 49,* 175–186.

Embretson. S.E. (1985). *Test design: Developments in psychology and psychometrics.* Orlando, FL: Academic Press.

Embretson, S.E. (1993). Psychometric models for learning and cognitive processing. In N. Fredricksen, R.J. Mislevy, & I.I. Bejar (Eds.), *Test theory for a new generation of tests* (pp. 125–150). Hillsdale, NJ: Erlbaum.

Embretson, S.E. (1996). The new rules of measurement. *Psychological Assessment, 8,* 341–349.

Feldt, L.S., & Brennan, R.L. (1989). Reliability. In R.L. Linn (Ed.), *Educational measurement* (3rd ed., pp. 105–146). Washington, DC: American Council on Education and National Council on Measurement in Education.

Feldt, L.S., Steffen, M., & Gupta, N.C. (1985). A comparison of five methods for estimating the standard error of measurement at specific score levels. *Applied Psychological Measurement, 9,* 351–361.

Fischer, G.H. (1973). The linear logistic test model as an instrument in educational research. *Acta Psychologica, 37,* 359–374.

Fischer, G.H. (1987). Applying the principles of specific objectivity and of generalizability to the measurement of change. *Psychometrika, 52,* 565–587.

Fitzgerald, L.F., Shullman, S., Bailey, N., Richards, M., Swecker, J., Gold, A., Ormerod, A.J., & Weitzman, L. (1988). The incidence and dimensions of sexual harassment in academia and the workplace. *Journal of Vocational Behavior, 32,* 152–175.

Fox, C.M., & Jones, J.A. (1998). Uses of Rasch modeling in counseling psychology research. *Journal of Counseling Psychology, 45,* 30–45.

Gitomer, D.H., Steinberg, L.S., & Mislevy, R.J. (1995). Diagnostic assessment of troubleshooting skill in an intelligent tutoring system. In P.D. Nichols, S.F. Chipman, & R.L. Brennan (Eds.), *Cognitively diagnostic assessment* (pp. 73–101). Hillsdale, NJ: Erlbaum.

Gray-Little, B., Williams, V.S.L., & Hancock, T.D. (1997). An item response theory analysis of the Rosenberg Self-Esteem Scale. *Personality & Social Psychology Bulletin, 23,* 443–451.

Grayson, D.A. (1986). Latent trait analysis of the Eysenck Personality Questionnaire. *Journal of Psychiatric Research, 20,* 217–235.

Green, B.F. (1988). Construct validity of computer-based tests. In H. Wainer & H.I. Braun (Eds.), *Test validity* (pp. 77–86). Hillsdale, NJ: Erlbaum.

Gulliksen, H. (1950). *Theory of mental tests.* New York: Wiley.

Hambleton, R.K., & Slater, S.C. (1997). Reliability and credentialing examinations and the impact of scoring models and standard-setting policies. *Applied Measurement in Education, 10,* 19–38.

Hammond, S.M. (1995). An IRT investigation of the validity of non-patient analogue research using the Beck Depression Inventory. *European Journal of Psychological Assessment, 11,* 14–20.

Harvey, R.J., & Thomas, L.A. (1996). Using item response theory to score the Myers-Briggs Type Indicator: Rationale and research findings. *Journal of Psychological Type, 37,* 16–60.

Hattie, J. (1985). Assessing unidimensionality of tests and items. *Applied Psychological Measurement, 9,* 139–164.

Hedges, L.V. (1988). The meta-analysis of test validity studies: Some new approaches. In H. Wainer & H.I. Braun (Eds.), *Test validity* (pp. 191–212). Hillsdale, NJ: Erlbaum.

Hoitink, H. (1990). A latent trait model for dichotomous choice data. *Psychometrika, 55,* 641–656.

Hulin, C.L., Drasgow, F., & Parsons, C.K. (1983). *Item response theory.* Homewood, IL: Dow Jones-Irwin.

Huynh, H. (1976). On the reliability of decisions in domain-references testing. *Journal of Educational Measurement, 32,* 179–197.

Johnson, P.J., Goldsmith, T.E., & Teague, K.W. (1995). Similarity, structure, and knowledge: A representational approach to assessment. In P.D. Nichols, S.F. Chipman, & R.L. Brennan (Eds.), *Cognitively diagnostic assessment.* Hillsdale, NJ: Erlbaum.

Kane, M.T. (1982). A sampling model for validity. *Applied Psychological Measurement, 6,* 125–160.

Kane, M.T. (1992). An argument-based approach to validity. *Psychological Bulletin, 112,* 527–535.

Kelderman, H., & Rijkes, C.P.M. (1994). Loglinear multidimensional IRT models for polytomously scored items. *Psychometrika, 59,* 147–177.

Kindlon, D.J., Wright, B.D., Raudenbush, S.W., & Earls, F. (1996). The measurement of children's exposure to violence: A Rasch analysis. *International Journal of Methods in Psychiatric Research, 6,* 187–194.

King, D.W., King, L.A., Fairbank, J.A., & Schlenger, W.E. (1993). Enhancing the precision of the Mississippi Scale for combat-related posttraumatic stress disorder: An application of item response theory. *Psychological Assessment, 5,* 457–471.

Klauer, K.C., & Batchelder, W.H. (1996). Structural analysis of subjective categorical data. *Psychometrika, 61,* 199–240.

Kolen, M.J., Hanson, B.A., & Brennan, R.L. (1992). Conditional standard errors of measurement for scale scores. *Journal of Educational Measurement, 29,* 285–307.

Landy, F. (1986). Stamp collecting versus science: Validation as hypothesis testing. *American Psychologist, 41,* 1183–1192.

Lee, J., & Fung, K.P. (1993). Confidence interval of the kappa coefficient by bootstrap resampling. *Psychiatry Research, 49,* 97–98.

Linn, R.L. (1984). Selection bias: Multiple meanings. *Journal of Educational Measurement, 21,* 33–47.

Linn, R.L., & Drasgow, F. (1987). Implications of the golden rule settlement for test construction. *Educational Measurement: Issues and Practice, 6,* 13–17.

Livingston, S.A. (1972). Criterion-referenced applications of classical test theory. *Journal of Educational Measurement, 9,* 13–26.

Livingston, S.A., & Lewis, C. (1995). Estimating the consistency and accuracy of classifications based on test scores. *Journal of Educational Measurement, 32,* 179–197.

Lord, F.M. (1974). Estimation of latent ability and item parameters when there are omitted responses. *Psychometrika, 39,* 247–264.

Lord, F.M. (1977). Practical applications of item characteristic curve theory. *Journal of Educational Measurement, 14,* 117–138.

Lord, F.M., & Novick, M.R. (1968). *Statistical theories of mental test scores.* Reading, MA: Addison-Wesley.

Mackinnon, A., Jorm, A.F., Christensen, H., Scott, L.R., Henderson, A.S., & Korten, A.E. (1995). A latent trait analysis of the Eysenck Personality Questionnaire in an elderly community sample. *Personality and Individual Differences, 18,* 739–747.

Marsh, H.W., & Grayson, D. (1995). Latent variable models for multitrait-multimethod data. In R.H. Hoyle (Ed.), *Structural equation modeling* (pp. 177–198). Thousand Oaks, CA: Sage.

Masters, G.N. (1982). A Rasch model for partial credit scoring. *Psychometrika, 47,* 149–174.

McCrae, R.R., & Costa, P.T. (1983). Social desirability scales: More substance than style. *Journal of Consulting and Clinical Psychology, 51,* 882–888.

McDonald, R.P. (1967). Nonlinear factor analysis. *Psychometric Monographs, 15.*

McDonald, R.P. (1981). The dimensionality of tests and items. *British Journal of Mathematical and Statistical Psychology, 34,* 100–117.

McDonald, R.P. (1985). *Factor analysis and related methods.* Hillsdale, NJ: Erlbaum.

McDonald, R.P., & Ahlawat, K.S. (1974). Difficulty factors in binary data. *British Journal of Mathematical and Statistical Psychology, 27,* 82–99.

Mehrens, W.A. (1997). The consequences of consequential validity. *Educational Measurement: Issues and Practice, 16,* 16–18.

Meijer, R.R. (1995). Person-fit research: An introduction. *Applied Measurement in Education, 9,* 3–8.

Meiser, T. (1996). Loglinear Rasch models for the analysis of stability and change. *Psychometrika, 61,* 629–645.

Messick, S. (1989). Validity. In R.L. Linn (Ed.), *Educational measurement* (3rd ed., pp. 13–103). Washington, DC: American Council on Education and National Council on Measurement in Education.

Messick, S. (1994). The interplay of evidence and consequences in the validation of performance assessments. *Educational Researcher, 23,* 13–23.

Millsap, R.E. (1995). Measurement invariance, predictive invariance, and the duality paradox. *Multivariate Behavioral Research, 30,* 577–605.

Millsap, R.E. (1997). Invariance in measurement and prediction: Their relationship in the single-factor case. *Psychological Methods, 2,* 248–260.

Mislevy, R.J. (1986). Recent developments in the factor analysis of categorical variables. *Journal of Educational Statistics, 11,* 3–31.

Mislevy, R.J., & Verhelst, N. (1990). Modeling item response when different subjects employ different solution strategies. *Psychometrika, 55,* 195–215.

Mokken, R.J. (1971). *A theory and procedure of scale analysis with applications in political research.* New York: Mouton.

Moss, P.A. (1995). Themes and variations in validity theory. *Educational Measurement: Issues and Practice, 14,* 5–13.

Muraki, E., & Carlson, J.E. (1996). Full-information factor analysis for polytomous item responses. *Applied Psychological Measurement, 19,* 73–90.

Muthen, B. (1978). Contributions to factor analysis of dichotomized variables. *Psychometrika, 43,* 551–560.

Nandakumar, R. (1993). Simultaneous DIF amplification and cancellation: Shealy-Stout's test for DIF. *Journal of Educational Measurement, 30,* 293–311.

Naveh-Benjamin, M., Lin, Y.G., & McKeachie, W.J. (1995). Inferring students' cognitive structures and their development using the "fill-in-the-structure" (FITS) technique. In P.D. Nichols, S.F. Chipman, & R.L. Brennan (Eds.), *Cognitively diagnostic assessment* (pp. 279–304). Hillsdale, NJ: Erlbaum.

Nichols, P.D., Chipman, S.F., & Brennan, R.L. (1995). *Cognitively diagnostic assessment.* Hillsdale, NJ: Erlbaum.

Nitko, A.J. (1989). Designing tests that are integrated with instruction. In R.L. Linn (Ed.), *Educational measurement* (3rd ed., pp. 447–474). New York: Macmillan, and American Council on Education.

Pellegrino, J.W., & Glaser, R. (1979). Cognitive correlates and components in the analysis of individual differences. *Intelligence, 3,* 187–214.

Petersen, N.S., Kolen, M.J., Hoover, H.D. (1989). Scaling, norming, and equating. In R.L. Linn (Ed.), *Educational measurement* (3rd ed., pp. 221–262). New York: Macmillan, and American Council on Education.

Qualls-Payne, A.L. (1992). A comparison of score level estimates of the standard error of measurement. *Journal of Educational Measurement, 29,* 213–225.

Rae, G. (1997). Sampling behaviour of kappa and weighted kappa in the null case. *British Journal of Mathematical and Statistical Psychology, 50,* 1–7.

Ramsay, J.O. (1991). Kernel smoothing approaches to nonparametric item characteristic curve estimation. *Psychometrika, 56,* 611–630.

Rasch, G. (1960). *Probabilistic models for some intelligence and attainment tests.* Copenhagen: Danish Institute for Educational Research.

Raykov, T. (1997). Scale reliability, Cronbach's coefficient alpha, and violations of essential tau-equivalence with fixed congeneric components. *Multivariate Behavioral Research, 32,* 329–353.

Reckase, M.D. (1985). The difficulty of items that measure more than one ability. *Applied Psychological Measurement, 9,* 401–412.

Reise, S.P., Widaman, K.F., & Pugh, R.H. (1993). Confirmatory factor analysis and item response theory: Two approaches for exploring measurement invariance. *Psychological Bulletin, 114,* 552–566.

Roskam, E.E. (1997). Models for speed and time-limit tests. In W.J. Van der Linden & R.K. Hambleton (Eds.), *Handbook of modern item response theory* (pp. 187–208). New York: Springer.

Samejima, F. (1969). Estimating of latent ability using a response pattern of graded scores. *Psychometrika Monograph, No. 17.* Psychometric Society. Frediction, New Brunswick, Canada.

Scheiblechner, H. (1985). Psychometric models for speed-test construction: The linear exponential model. In S.E. Embretson (Ed.), *Test design: Developments in psychology and education* (pp. 219–244). New York: Academic Press.

Schmidt, F.L., & Hunter, J.E. (1977). Development of a general solution to the problem of validity generalization. *Journal of Applied Psychology, 62,* 529–540.

Schmidt, F.L., & Hunter, J.E. (1996). Measurement error in psychological research: Lessons from 26 research scenarios. *Psychological Methods, 1,* 199–223.

Schmitt, N. (1996). Uses and abuses of coefficient alpha. *Psychological Assessment, 8,* 350–353.

Shavelson, R.J., & Webb, N.M. (1991). *Generalizability theory: A primer.* Newbury Park, CA: Sage.

Shavelson, R.J., Webb, N.M., & Rowley, G.L. (1989). Generalizability theory. *American Psychologist, 44,* 922–932.

Shealy, R., & Stout, W.F. (1993). A model-based standardization approach that separates true bias/DIF from group ability differences and detects test bias/DTF as well as item bias/DIF. *Psychometrika, 58,* 159–194.

Shepard, L.A. (1993). Evaluating test validity. *Review of Research in Education, 19,* 405–450.

Snow, R.E., & Lohman, D.F. (1989). Implications of cognitive psychology for educational measurement. In R.L. Linn (Ed.), *Educational measurement* (3rd ed., pp. 263–331). Washington, DC: American Council on Education and National Council on Measurement in Education.

Steinberg, L., & Thissen, D. (1996). Uses of item response theory and the test let concept in the measurement of psychopathology. *Psychological Methods, 1,* 81–97.

Sternberg, R.T. (1991). Cognitive theory and psychometrics. In R.K. Hambleton & J.N. Zaal (Eds.), *Advances in educational and psychological testing: Theory and applications* (pp. 367–393). Boston: Kluwer.

Stout, W.F. (1987). A nonparametric approach for assessing latent trait unidimensionality. *Psychometrika, 55,* 293–325.

Subkoviak, M. (1976). Estimating reliability from a single administration of a criterion-referenced test. *Journal of Educational Measurement, 13,* 265–275.

Swain, A.J. (1975). *Analysis of parametric structures for variance matrices.* Unpublished doctoral dissertation, University of Adelaide, Adelaide, Australia.

Sympson, J.B. (1977). A model for testing with multidimensional items. In D.J. Weiss (Ed.), *Proceedings of the 1977 Computerized Adaptive Testing Conference* (pp. 82–98). Minneapolis: University of Minnesota.

Tatsuoka, K.K. (1983). Rule space: An approach for dealing with misconceptions based on item response theory. *Journal of Educational Measurement, 20,* 345–354.

Tatsuoka, K.K. (1993). *Proficiency scaling based on conditional probability functions for attributes* (ETS Tech. Rep. RR-93–50-ONR). Princeton, NJ: Educational Testing Service.

Thissen, D., & Steinberg, L. (1986). A taxonomy of item response models. *Psychometrika, 51,* 567–577.

Tucker, L.R. (1951). *A method for synthesis of factor analysis studies* (Personnel Research Section Report No. 984). Washington, DC: Department of the Army.

Van der Linden, W.J., & Hambleton, R.K. (1997). *Handbook of modern item response theory.* New York: Springer.

Van de Vijver, F., & Leung, K. (1997). Methods and data analysis of comparative research. In J.W. Berry, Y.H. Poortinga, & J. Pandey (Eds.), *Handbook of cross-cultural psychology, Vol. 1: Theory and method.* Boston: Allyn & Bacon.

Wainer, H., Dorans, N.J., Green, B.F., Steinberg, L., Flaugher, R., Mislevy, R.J., & Thissen, D. (1990). *Computerized adaptive testing: A primer.* Hillsdale, NJ: Erlbaum.

Whitely, S.E. (1980). Multicomponent latent trait model for ability tests. *Psychometrika, 45,* 479–494.

Wothke, W. (1996). Models for multitrait multi-method matrix analysis. In G.A. Marcoulides & R.E. Schumacker (Eds.), *Advanced structural equation modeling: Issues and techniques* (pp. 7–56). Mahwah, NJ: Erlbaum.

Yen, W. (1981). Using simulation results to choose a latent trait model. *Applied Psychological Measurement, 5,* 245–262.

Zickar, M.J., & Drasgow, F. (1996). Detecting faking on a personality instrument using appropriateness measurement. *Applied Psychological Measurement, 20,* 71–87.

Zwinderman, A.H. (1991). A generalized Rasch model for manifest predictors. *Psychometrika, 56,* 589–600.

CHAPTER 6

Issues in the Analysis and Interpretation of Quantitative Data: Deinstitutionalization of the Null Hypothesis Test

TERENCE J.G. TRACEY

A weaker man might be moved to re-examine his faith, if in nothing else at least in the law of probability.

—Stoppard, 1967, p. 8

The scientific approach to the examination of phenomena is a defense against the pure emotion of fear.

—Stoppard, 1967, p. 12

These quotes are from the opening scene of the play, *Rosencrantz and Guildenstern Are Dead* (Stoppard, 1967), where the protagonists are tossing a coin and the improbable event of getting 90 heads in a row occurs. Guildenstern speaks these lines in his struggle to understand how such an event can occur. In some ways, the criticism of the ubiquitous null hypothesis testing strategy seems equally unnerving. Several methodologists have called for the eschewal of all null hypothesis tests. The null hypothesis test has been the mainstay of the field for years, and it may be hard to imagine the "improbability" of life without the null hypothesis. What will we do if we cannot use the null hypothesis? The purpose of this chapter is to review many of the problems associated with the null hypothesis testing strategy and then to present some recommendations regarding ways of ameliorating many of these problems.

CRITICISM OF THE NULL HYPOTHESIS TESTING STRATEGY

Several members of the profession of psychology have bemoaned the sad state of affairs with respect to the science of applied psychology (e.g., Guttman, 1985; Hunter, 1997; Meehl, 1967, 1978, 1991; Rosenthal, 1993). The most frequent criticism is that there is relatively little accumulation of knowledge. The culprits suggested for this purported lack of cumulation in applied psychology are many and often diverse (e.g., our research ignores the context of behavior, is too uncontrolled and vague, is too molecular and trite, and focuses only on the convenient by using only readily available measures and samples). However, recently some scholars, buttressed by advances in quantitative methods of research synthesis, have argued convincingly that cumulative knowledge does exist in many areas of psychological investigation (e.g., Hedges, 1987). The problem of the apparent lack of cumulation is attributable to our inability to recognize when

Appreciation is expressed to Cynthia Glidden-Tracey for her helpful comments on this manuscript.

cumulative knowledge exists because of our historical focus on null hypothesis significance testing in interpreting results of single studies and in determining consistency of results across studies. The assessment of the "true" presence of a specific finding is typically conducted using the "box-score" method of tallying the number of significant and nonsignificant results across studies and looking for clear superiority of one conclusion. The typical conclusion of such tallying approaches is one of equivocal results and thus little cumulation. However, Hedges has demonstrated that the knowledge base across several areas of psychological research is as cumulative as that of the physical sciences if the consistency of effect sizes is examined rather than tabulating the number of significant results across studies.

My purpose is to review many of the problems associated with the application of the null hypothesis inference test in counseling psychology research and to present some of the remedies that have been proposed. Even though psychology is more self-reflective about its methodology than most other sciences (Meehl, 1986), it does not appear that our current self-reflection can be entirely dismissed as just a typical phase of circumspection. The problems with the null hypothesis inference test have often been noted in the wider psychological literature, but they have been minimally heeded in most applied psychological areas, especially counseling psychology. Such lack of attention to the problem areas of null hypothesis testing could be attributable to a lack of knowledge of the issues (e.g., relatively few counseling psychologists read the methodological literature) or a lack of viable alternatives to null hypothesis testing. In this chapter, I (1) review the specific problems with standard approaches to null hypothesis testing; (2) present the major null hypothesis testing alternatives proposed in the conduct of quantitative research (i.e., replacing the null hypothesis test with point estimation, and exploratory data analysis); and (3) make some recommendations regarding research in counseling psychology (i.e., increasing the appropriateness of null hypothesis test applications, increasing theoretical specification of hypotheses, and using structural data description).

Although the problems of the null hypothesis testing strategy have been long known, there has been an accelerating condemnation of this strategy as an appropriate methodology for psychology (e.g., Bakan, 1966; Carver, 1978; Cohen, 1990, 1994; Guttman, 1985; Hunter, 1997; Loftus, 1991, 1993; Meehl, 1967; Oakes, 1986; Rozenboom, 1960; Schmidt, 1996). The use of the null hypothesis inference testing strategy has become institutionalized in psychology (Gigerenzer, 1993; Scarr, 1997), where the perception among researchers, practitioners, journal editors, and students is that there is no conclusion possible without a significant result (at least at the $p < .05$ level). The use of the null hypothesis testing strategy has become so basic to psychological research that it is hard to imagine a study without null hypothesis statistical tests.

It is understandable why the inference testing strategy has become so common; it has the appeal of bringing clarity to an otherwise ambiguous area. The discrete "yes/no" result of inference testing enables the researcher and reader to have some comfort in the presence or lack of presence of a result. Without the dichotomous nature of the test, the researcher, editor, and reader have to resort to the quality of the argument proposed, and this is harder to evaluate. How much of something is needed before one can say it is present at an important level? The inference testing strategy became the norm for making such claims and is so central that it has become institutionalized. However it is not without its flaws, and many claim it is so flawed as an institutionalized approach that psychology should abandon it all together (e.g., Hunter, 1997; Schmidt, 1996).

As noted in the literature, there are a variety of problems with the null hypothesis testing strategy as used in psychology, and I will highlight some of the major ones, including:

1. the improbability of the null hypothesis,
2. misperception of meaning of rejection of null,
3. misperception of meaning of failure to reject the null,
4. arbitrary basis of discrete decision-making,

5. confusion of significance level and importance,

6. ignoring Type II error,

7. inappropriate confirmatory nature of hypothesis testing,

8. overuse of omnibus testing,

9. bias against non-significant results,

10. confirmatory bias, and

11. failure to account for measurement error.

Clearly there are many problems with the institutionalization of the null inference strategy in psychology, but only one is inherent. Only the first problem listed—the improbability of the null hypothesis—is inherent in the null inference strategy. The other problems are really those of inappropriate application. It is difficult to separate the inherent problem of the null inference testing strategy from the application errors.

Improbability of the Null Hypothesis

As noted by many (e.g., Cohen, 1994; Meehl, 1978), the null hypothesis is rarely true. Cohen has labeled the null hypothesis the "nil hypothesis" to accentuate this characteristic. With a large enough N, the null hypothesis will almost always be rejected. It is rare that there would be absolutely no differences between two groups or that two variables are completely unrelated. Further, Meehl (1967, 1986) claims that there is a "crud factor" (i.e., the error variance that all psychological variables share) that floats throughout all psychological research, which alone accounts for the failure of the null hypothesis.

Misperception of the Meaning of the Rejection of the Null Hypothesis

The rejection of the null hypothesis is often erroneously interpreted as an indication of the extent to which research results can be replicated (Cohen, 1994; Schmidt, 1996; Zuckerman, Hodgins, Zuckerman, & Rosenthal, 1993). The significance test of the null hypothesis is a test of the probability that the observed data resulted given that the null hypothesis of no difference is true. Rejection of the null then implies that the observed data are unlikely if the null is true. Interpreting that the null hypothesis is an indication of study replicability is an example of confusion over reverse conditional probability. The idea of study replicability is one of the probability of the null hypothesis being true given a data set. The erroneous implication of rejection of the null is that because the null is unlikely, the p value reflects the probability that the same result will be replicated. This misperception is common (Cohen, 1994; Guttman, 1985; Schmidt, 1996) and understandable given the difficulty humans have in deciphering reverse conditional probabilities (Dawes, 1988) and the greater desirability involved in being able to claim replicability.

Misperception of the Meaning of Failure to Reject Null Hypothesis

It is not uncommon for researchers to interpret the failure to reject the null hypothesis as indicating that the null hypothesis is true and that there are no differences between groups, or that the relation between variables is zero. This interpretation is not warranted or supported by the null hypothesis testing strategy. The null hypothesis testing strategy involves an examination of the likelihood of the data given the null hypothesis being true. Null hypothesis testing does not involve examination of whether the null is indeed true. Failure to reject the null does not prove that no differences or relations exist, but that within the confines of the power of the test, they were of insufficient magnitude to reject the null. Future research employing more powerful tests (i.e., larger sample sizes, more reliable measures, more potent treatments, and greater control over error) may lead to the conclusions that the null is indeed false. Power (to be discussed later) is therefore important for two reasons: high power increases the likelihood that a false null will be detected, and high power increases one's confidence in null results and in the believability of the inference of no differences or relations. However, it bears repeating that one can never prove the null hypothesis to be true through conventional null hypothesis testing strategies. Increasing power only improves confidence in inferring from the data that the null *may be* true when it is not rejected.

Arbitrary Basis of Discrete Decision Making

The adoption of the $p = .05$ as the cutoff of significance was arbitrary. Results with p values of .06 and .051 are banished to the netherworld of nonresults. In an extreme case, is it possible to claim that a result of $p = .049$ is qualitatively different from a result with a $p = .051$? In Robert Rosenthal's (1991) words, "God loves the .06 nearly as much as the .05" (p. 220), so why is such a distinction made between the two values?

Confusion of Significance Level and Importance

This confusion takes two somewhat related forms. The first is to confuse statistical significance with importance (Scarr, 1997). If a relation or difference is found to be significant, it means that it is important and worthy of attention. Clearly there are many statistically significant results that are not earth shattering. Importance comes out of theory and practical application, not out of a statistical test.

Second, it is also not uncommon to see researchers overtly or covertly interpret the p value as an indication of strength of relation or degree of difference (e.g., $p < .000001$ is "Highly" significant). Given the same relation between two variables (say a correlation of $r = .15$), small samples could result in a $p = .25$, moderate samples might result in a $p = .08$, large samples would result in a $p = .001$, and huge samples would result in a $p = .0000001$. If these probabilities are interpreted as indicators of the magnitude of a difference, the researcher will make different conclusions about the same relation, depending on the size of the sample. However, the correlation has not changed at all, but the improved power attributable to the increasing sample size has enabled the investigator to conclude that a correlation of this magnitude (.15) is highly unlikely if the null hypothesis was true. When researchers interpret the value of p as indicative of magnitude, they are confusing probability with effect size. If researchers wish to discuss magnitude of effects, they should highlight effect size indicators, not significance levels. Cohen (1988) suggested level labels for relative effect sizes in the social sciences: Correlations of .10 are reflective of small effect sizes, .30 are reflective of medium effect sizes, and .50 are reflective of large effect sizes. Usage of effect sizes and Cohen's labels will better enable readers to understand the magnitude of the results.

Ignoring Type II Error

Hunter (1997) has noted that most researchers view the error rate in psychological research as being 5% (the standard alpha level used in null hypothesis testing—Type I error rate). However, Sedlmeier and Gigerenzer (1989) demonstrated that the average error rate in the psychological literature was actually 60%. This large error rate occurs almost entirely due to ignoring Type II error, the probability of failing to reject the null hypothesis when it should be rejected. As noted long ago by Cohen (1962), Type II error rate has been exceedingly high in most social science research and should be attended to in research design. However, Type I error rate has received almost exclusive focus; the result is that conflicting conclusions are drawn from studies with similar effect sizes but differing sample sizes.

Inappropriate Confirmatory Nature of Hypothesis Testing

Using a null hypothesis testing strategy involves looking for certain differences or relations. In a two-way analysis of variance design, the researcher looks for differences on variable A and on variable B and on their interaction. It is often true that many other potentially important variables may be related to the variables, but these were not examined because they could not be incorporated into the research design (e.g., the sample size was not large enough to add variable C as the third factor). What occurs is that the researcher examines only the ANOVA results and then, depending on the significance levels, rejects the null or not. The study is then over. Few attempts are made to move beyond the hypothesis testing strategy to see where important unaccounted variance may lie (e.g., variance attributable to variable C or its interaction with variables A or B from above). The null hypothesis testing strategy is used in too much of a lock-step fashion. Its blind adoption precludes potentially important hypothesis building through data inspection. This problem with the practice of null hypothesis testing can be summarized as "test, confirm or disconfirm, then get out." Often the underlying theory is not strong enough to support such a strict confirmatory approach.

Overuse of Omnibus Testing

Frequently, many factors or variables are examined in a study, and the null hypothesis test is applied to help the researcher determine where the important relations or differences lie. This is typically done in a "shotgun" fashion, where the investigator uses omnibus tests to determine where in a large set of relations some differences may lie (e.g., an analysis of variance examining any differences that may exist anywhere among five different groups). If the omnibus test yields significance, the researcher typically adopts a fairly atheoretical, post-hoc testing strategy, such as comparing each group with each other group. The null hypothesis testing strategy is being used in this case to winnow the relations and is thus a pseudoconfirmatory approach. However, this approach is problematic for theoretical and statistical reasons. Too often such a shotgun approach is adopted even when the researcher expects specific differences or relations in the data. Using the omnibus strategy decreases the probability (i.e., it has lower power) that actual differences will be found. The power of such tests is low. Further, the omnibus testing strategy may also not test the actual differences that the author may anticipate (e.g., a curvilinear result). Such applications of omnibus testing result in poor approximations of underlying theoretically defined differences and low power.

More specified focused tests involving single degrees of freedom in the numerator are more powerful and more tied to underlying theory because they must be specified a priori (Rosenthal & Rosnow, 1985). Using the above example of an analysis of variance conducted on five groups, a better test would result if the researcher specified what group mean(s) should be greater than what other group's means and then tested only these hypothesized differences. The specific tests would more closely fit the researcher's purposes than an ill-defined omnibus test, and the power of the specific tests would be greater, resulting in a greater chance of rejecting the null.

This problem of poorly defined contrasts resulting in poor confirmation appears to disagree with the previous problem of overadherence to confirmation testing strategy. Paradoxically, both, however, are true. The null hypothesis testing strategy of using poorly defined omnibus tests is really a pseudoconfirmatory approach. Certain effects are tested but only in a general, atheoretical manner. The narrowed focus of looking only at certain mean differences in a diffuse manner makes it only somewhat confirmatory. Many other patterns are not examined (differences due to factors not part of the design, or nonlinear relations), so there is no real exploration of how the data vary. Thus, current hypothesis testing involves a combination of the worst of both the confirmatory and exploratory approaches: weak testing of only a few ill-defined differences coupled with no data exploration to see if important, unspecified variation exists.

Bias against Nonsignificant Results

Greenwald (1975, 1993) has documented that there is a bias in the journal review process regarding nonsignificant results. Clearly, nonsignificant results are often attributable to poor research designs and low power, but editors and reviewers are less likely to view studies with nonsignificant results as appropriate for publication, regardless of the other qualities in the study. Rosenthal (1979) has argued that nonsignificant results are important for the field to build its cumulative knowledge base. Omission of such results in literature reviews can provide a deceptively rosy picture of certain relations or differences found significant in other research. Rejection of research with adequate power solely for nonsignificant results does not advance our knowledge.

Confirmatory Bias

Meehl (1978) pointed out another problem in the lack of cumulation in applied psychology, besides the application of the null hypothesis test: the confirmatory approach of most researchers. Meehl was not condemning the focus on testing explicit theoretical propositions; indeed, he recommended that more of these confirmation examinations be done. He was, however, criticizing the confirmatory information collection methods—looking only for information that confirms the hypotheses, rather than looking for information that would disconfirm the hypotheses. Confirmatory information collection approaches, with respect to either individual decision making or the design of research, are biased in favor of what the researcher already believes or expects. Disconfirmatory approaches are more productive because they provide a fairer test of the research question at hand.

It has been well documented in the realm of human decision making (Dawes, 1988; Tracey & Rounds, 1999) that a confirmatory approach results in many more inference errors than a disconfirmatory approach. Looking for confirmation overly restricts the information that is considered and, thus, a great amount of information salient to the decision is often missed. Individuals tend to see only the information that confirms expectations and to miss the information that calls the expectations into question. As individual information processors, we would all be better off to eschew a confirmatory approach to decision making but, regrettably, we do not. When presented with issues that need to be resolved, humans are most prone to adopt a confirmatory search strategy. We need to guard against this human tendency both as researchers and clinicians (Tracey, 1991a; Tracey & Rounds, 1999).

Failure to Account for Measurement Error

It is a rare researcher who does not know that it is important to attend to the reliability of the measures involved in any study, although many may not know why this is important (Zuckerman et al., 1993). The days of viewing measures as isomorphic with our constructs are gone (Campbell, 1990). All measurement involves error, which is that part of the observed score variance that is unrelated to the construct of interest. For theoretical reasons, it is important to obtain data that are as near to the construct of concern as possible. Measures with high proportions of error variance (i.e., poor reliability), will be poor approximations of the construct of concern, and any examinations of relations will include error variance masked as construct variance. Measures with poor reliability have two particularly pernicious effects on the research employing them. First, the correlation obtained between any measure with poor reliability and any other measure (highly reliable or not) will be lower than it would be if a more reliable measure were employed. Measurement error results in correlations that underestimate the "true" relations between the constructs they are intended to measure. Second, because they result in reduced (underestimated) correlations, the power of the significance tests on these relations will be compromised. Schmidt and Hunter (1996) estimate that the amount of measurement error variance in psychological research is often in the neighborhood of 50%. Given this high value, it is likely that many of the results in the literature are erroneous, adding to the difficulty of finding cumulative evidence of psychological findings.

SUGGESTED REMEDIES

As noted earlier, several prominent researchers (Hunter, 1997; Meehl, 1978; Schmidt, 1996) have argued that the null hypothesis testing strategy has masked the accumulation of knowledge in psychology. Our research does not appear to build on itself. All the above problems noted earlier have resulted in a conflicting morass of findings that are difficult, if not impossible, to understand. Hence the call for the overthrow of the institutionalized null hypothesis test.

In response, the American Psychological Association (APA) established a task force on statistical inference. The conclusions reached in the Initial Report (APA Task Force on Statistical Inference, 1996) noted four themes: (1) approaches to enhance the quality of data usage and to protect against misrepresentation of quantitative results, (2) the need for theory generating studies, (3) the use of minimally sufficient designs and analytic strategies, and (4) issues with computerized data analysis. The theme of enhancing data quality requires the researcher to provide extensive data (including means, standard deviations, sample sizes, complete distribution descriptions, graphic representations of data, and missing data description) and analytic description (e.g., mean differences, confidence intervals, and effect-size estimates). Further, researchers need to use techniques that assure that results are not attributable to anomalies in the data (e.g., inspection of outliers and the presence of nonrandom missing data, selection effects, and attrition effects).

The theme of theory generating studies focuses on the inappropriately confirmatory nature of exploratory research. More attempts should be made to explore the data. The theme of minimally sufficient designs and analytic strategies relies on the principle of parsimony. Minimally sufficient designs and analyses have the fewest and least restrictive assumptions and are more easily understood by the reader. In essence, the call is to use the simplest design appropriate to one's research question.

Finally, the task force recognized that computers make analysis easier but that problems arise with respect to researchers' understanding of what is being done in the analyses and/or relying on results without independent verification. These four themes are fairly general and attempt to cover many of the flaws noted by the task force.

Several more specific, and somewhat overlapping, solutions have been offered in the literature regarding research methodology, including point estimation and error specification, exploratory data analysis, improved standards regarding appropriate usage of null hypothesis testing, increased theoretical specification of hypotheses, and structural data description. These will be elaborated next.

Replacing Null Hypothesis Testing with Point Estimation

Those in favor of complete rejection of the null hypothesis testing strategy (e.g., Hunter, 1997; Loftus, 1991, 1993; Schmidt, 1996) have argued for a greater focus on point estimation with confidence intervals and presentation of data in the form of graphical error bar charts (also called bar graphs, box plots, and plot-plus-error-bar or PPE). Instead of testing the null hypothesis that the difference between two groups is zero, this approach would involve the specification of the magnitude of the difference (i.e., effect size), and then graphically represent the confidence interval about this point (e.g., 95% confidence interval). Such a presentation is easier for most people to grasp. Further, the presentation of effect sizes and confidence intervals would make for easy translation into meta-analytic studies.

Abelson (1997) supports the value of including point estimation and confidence intervals, but he is less sanguine regarding the extent to which this requirement obviates the problems with the null hypothesis. Providing point estimates and confidence intervals provides information to enable a conclusion to be made about the null hypothesis (e.g., Is the mean of one group outside the confidence interval of the other?). Mistakes associated with null hypothesis testing may still be made (and probably will) if point estimation and confidence intervals are used.

Another issue involving the application of point estimates with error information is that it can still present confusing information (Wilkinson, 1999). Presenting error information in terms of error bars around the point estimates can mislead readers into thinking that the data are symmetric, even if they are not. Also there is some disagreement regarding the types of error bars used. It is most common to call for the use of means and confidence intervals as the data for presentation in error bar charts. However, confidence intervals are easily confused with standard deviations and standard errors. It is not always clear what type of error the error bars are representing or what type should be presented (Morrison & Weaver, 1995). Given these problems with point estimations and error bars, several researchers advocate their increased use and inclusion in research publications but as supplemental to traditional testing, not as a replacement (e.g., Abelson, 1997; Bakeman & McArthur, 1996; Morrison & Weaver, 1995).

Exploratory Data Analysis

Exploratory approaches and statistics in psychology have been advocated for quite some time (Mulaik, 1984), but perhaps the most eloquent proponent has been John Tukey, who has proposed a fairly comprehensive alternative to traditional hypothesis testing, which he labeled exploratory data analysis (EDA; Tukey, 1977). The approach embodies many of the recommendations of the APA Task Force. EDA is comprised of a variety of statistical tools (e.g., graphical analysis, stem-and-leaf plots, and analysis of residuals), but mainly it represents an attitude or theory of research and knowledge discovery. Behrens (1997) summarized the EDA approaches as:

> (a) emphasis on the substantive understanding of the data that address the broad question of "what is going on here?" (b) emphasis on graphical representation of the data, (c) focus on tentative model building and hypothesis generation in an iterative process of model specification, residual analysis, and model respecification, (d) use of robust measures, re-expression, and subset analysis, and (e) positions of skepticism, flexibility and ecumenism regarding which methods to apply. (p. 132)

Behrens and Smith (1996) used the metaphor of the justice system to clarify how EDA is different from traditional null hypothesis testing. The traditional null hypothesis testing researcher serves as the prosecutor wherein a case is made very strongly for one specific outcome (i.e., rejection of the null hypothesis). The data serve as the trial proceedings, and the analysis is the jury, deciding if indeed the null is rejected or not. As noted above, such confirmatory approaches can blind the researcher to understanding what really is going on in the data because only one option is considered; the one option is either correct or it is not. The role of the analysis in EDA would be more that of the detective, who is less concerned with the guilt or innocence of an individual for a crime but in determining what occurred. Such an approach is more exploratory and potentially fruitful in discovering what has occurred.

EDA is not solely an exploratory approach. Tukey makes it clear that both exploration and confirmation are important but that they should occur in an iterative sequence, with exploratory approaches used first to develop models of the data and then confirmatory approaches to evaluate their accuracy. The EDA researcher not only builds models from exploratory analysis, but also then tests them. This testing process of necessity involves examination of different samples than the one used in the exploration. Thus the EDA process is an iterative one where a model is proposed, tested, altered, retested, realtered, and so on until the model proposed fits the data well. A key cornerstone in the process is that the researcher allows the data to tell their own story prior to constraining them. Perhaps the primary tools of the EDA researcher are the use of (1) robust measures, (2) graphical representations, and (3) residual analysis to better understand the data. Each of these tools will be discussed.

The goal of EDA is to explore and describe the data. EDA's focus is on understanding basic patterns in the data, and on identifying certain observations that deviate from this pattern (Smith & Prentice, 1993). The focus is on robust statistics that are insensitive to gross deviations of a few data points and minor deviations of many data points. EDA uses the median and a variety of nonparametric statistics. Most psychological research focuses on the mean as the primary representation of central tendency. The mean, however, is highly affected by the presence of outliers. Rank-based statistics such as the median are much less affected by distribution anomalies and thus provide a more robust representation of central tendency. Using nonparametric or distribution-free statistics also is favored because they involve no assumptions about underlying distributional properties. It does not matter if the data distribution deviates from a normal one when using these statistics. Such robust approaches have been developed for application in analysis of variance designs (Hoaglin, Mosteller, & Tukey, 1991).

The EDA researcher places importance on understanding the distributional properties of the data. Because the EDA researcher does not use the mean, the researcher does not use the standard deviation for the same reason: lack of robustness. Tukey (1977) proposed that the data distribution be understood using the median, the hinges, and the extremes. The hinges are defined as the data points halfway between the extremes and the median. He further suggested the hingespread as a robust measure of dispersion, which can be used in identifying outliers. An outlier is a data point that falls more than one and one-half hingespreads outside of a hinge. Values that fall more than three hingespreads outside a hinge are severe outliers. Outliers can be examined more closely to determine if they have responded accurately, for example. The question would be why did this person or these people score at this level? This could then provide key information in hypothesis generation or in data analysis (e.g., perhaps this individual should be omitted).

Graphical representations of the data can be extremely useful in understanding variation and generating hypotheses, and are relatively easy for readers to understand, but yet are used relatively infrequently in psychology as compared with other sciences (Wilkinson, 1999). Graphical analysis is especially useful in helping the researcher find aspects of the data that were unexpected. There is nothing like a picture! Common graphical representations used in EDA are the scatter plot, stem-and-leaf plots, dot plots, and box-plots. Each of these graphical depictions provide information about the data and can be used to examine the shape of the data, the dispersion, the distribution, presence of clusters or subsets, and presence of outliers. Advocates of EDA argue that it is rare that researchers know what the data look like, and thus they neglect some key information. Graphical representation provides a means of understanding the data. For example, by using any of the above graphical methods, the researcher can detect patterns in the data that were unexpected. Traditionally, graphical representations focused only on univariate or bivariate data description, but recent advances in graphic modeling cover multivariate data representation also (see Jacoby, 1998; Wainer & Thissen, 1993). Space precludes presentation of the various graphical representations. See Behrens (1997), Jacoby (1998), Smith and Prentice (1993), Wainer and Thissen (1993), Wilkinson (1999), and Tukey (1977) for examples.

A related graphical approach to data analysis is dynamic graphics (or active display methods; Cleveland & McGill, 1988). Dynamic graphics involve the interaction of the researcher and the graphs. The researcher actively manipulates the display to learn as much as possible from the data. This typically involves the three techniques of linking, brushing, and spinning. Linking involves examining several displays together in an attempt to better understand variation. Brushing entails highlighting certain data points to better see relations, and spinning refers to the rotation of the graphic depictions to better understand depth and distribution. The dynamic graphics approach fits well within EDA as it focuses on exploratory understanding of the data. The drawback to dynamic graphics are their inability to be used in traditional publication outlets where the authors can only choose certain graphic displays for the reader. Until research is presented in a computer mode that allows the reader to interact directly with the data, such dynamic graphics are reserved for the researcher. However, using such active approaches to understanding the data does enable the researcher to choose how to represent results.

A major part of EDA is the analysis of residuals, the unexplained aspects of data variation. In most studies, the researcher has a model that he or she is examining (either generated from the literature or from previous exploratory work), and this model is evaluated with regard to the extent that it is appropriate in explaining the data. In traditional research, the researcher typically stops at this point, concluding whether the model was supported. In EDA, the researcher readopts an exploratory approach and attempts to understand what patterns exist in the unexplained variance (i.e., above and beyond what is explained by the model tested). The exploratory researcher applies his or her techniques to the residuals.

To illustrate this process, take the example of the preference for women therapists found in the counseling literature. The researcher conducts a test and finds that, indeed, clients prefer women counselors at intake. The researcher using the typical null hypothesis testing strategy is done with data analysis. An EDA approach would be to examine the residuals after accounting for the gender differences. These residuals would be the data for examination, and patterns would be sought. In inspecting the graphic representations of the data, the researcher may find that there appear to be two clusters of individuals, for example. These clusters could be more closely examined for variables that may differentiate them, and it could be that the researcher finds that their presenting problems were different. One group might have had more interpersonal problems and the other group less interpersonal problems, such as academic- or career-related issues. Further examining preference using this problem type variable, the researcher may find that much more variation in preference for female therapists is taken into account when the variable of presenting problem is included. The EDA researcher would then add presenting problems to general preference for women therapists in the model, generate the residuals, and reexamine these for new hints at substantive variance. This iterative residual reexamination process is conducted until relatively little unexplained variance remains. The key difference in EDA is that the researcher keeps mining a data set as long as new residuals remain to be examined. However, hypotheses generated through residual analysis still require replication and/or cross-validation in new (or holdout) samples before they can be accepted as reasonable explanations. Sampling error is a plausible rival hypothesis for "findings" generated through this EDA post-hoc testing and theory-generating strategy.

The EDA approach embodies many of the recommendations of the APA Task Force. It focuses on using the simplest and most robust statistics, and on approaching the data both in a confirmatory mode and an exploratory mode. It is important to realize, however, that the EDA approach focuses on the sequential interplay between exploration and confirmation. Confirmatory examinations are made first, and then the residual data are explored. Results of residual analyses then become hypotheses to be tested in future investigations.

Increasing Appropriateness of Applications of Null Hypothesis Testing

This specific recommendation also encompasses many of the recommendations made by the APA Task Force, encouraging researchers to use the simplest designs and analyses appropriate to the research questions. Although there are many aspects of statistical inference that require attention, there are several areas that seem most frequently misunderstood and misused. Zuckerman et al. (1993) reviewed the methodological literature and found four areas frequently misrepresented: effect of reliability on Type I and Type II errors, contrast analysis, interpretation of interaction, and roles of power and effect size in successful replications. They developed questions regarding each of these areas, and then used them to survey 551 first authors of APA journal articles. The sampled psychologists got only 59% correct (compared with a chance correct rate of 46%). Thus, a very select and presumably knowledgeable group of elite researchers knew surprisingly little about inference testing. This lack of knowledge about some important aspects of analysis has led Estes (1997) and Meehl (1991) to recommend not a change in the methodological approach but better grounding of students and researchers in the mathematics underlying the methodology. Each of the specific areas covered in the Zuckerman et al. study will be discussed next.

Effect of Reliability on Type I and Type II Errors

The particular effect of poor reliability is that it will increase the probability of failing to reject the null hypothesis when it should be rejected. Unreliability increases the probability of Type II error by increasing error variance and producing a sample effect size (i.e., correlation or difference) that underestimates the population effect size. Thus, the power of the significance test is much lower than the researcher is aware. Power tables (e.g., Cohen, 1988) implicitly assume perfect measurement, so any estimation of the power of a study obtained from these tables is a maximal estimate. Given that there are no perfect measures in the psychological literature, and that most are far from perfect, the actual power is much lower than estimated. Thus, the already low power estimated for applied psychological research (Hunter, 1997) can be viewed as an overly optimistic estimate. The sad state of affairs regarding the power of our psychological research is even worse if one takes account of the unreliability of our measures. Researchers using measures with low reliability are more likely to fail to reject the null hypothesis and to provide sample effect sizes that badly represent the population effect size to which the researcher wants to generalize.

However, as Cohen and Cohen (1983) demonstrated, there is no associated change in the Type I error as a result of using unreliable measures. "Unreliability is a sufficient reason for low correlations; it cannot cause correlations to be spuriously high" (p. 70). If a researcher finds a significant result with an unreliable measure (and therefore with low power also), the researcher can conclude that the effect or relation exists (i.e., is different from zero). However, the researcher must also be aware that the correlation or difference obtained in the sample is an underestimate of the corresponding population parameter, and inferences about effect magnitude are in error. Besides concluding that effects exist, researchers need also to provide accurate estimation of the sizes of effects in order to better understand phenomena and contribute to our knowledge base.

Given the problems associated with unreliable measures, it is important that researchers use the most reliable measures of their constructs to cut down on the occurrence of erroneous results. However, this recommendation is often hard to follow. Many measures are just not that reliable. In many applied settings, measures need to be fairly brief, otherwise few will participate. Such brief measures will include much more error variance than will longer measures. Also not all constructs lend themselves to easy measurement because they are less overt and often "fuzzier" in nature. In these cases also, there will be greater amounts of error variance. One potential remedy to this issue of poor reliability is to correct for biases of imperfect measurement by using various corrections for attenuation. Schmidt and Hunter (1996) used a number of case examples to demonstrate how this can be done in a variety of situations with several different estimates of reliability, and their article should be consulted for some good practical advice to the researcher grappling with these issues.

Contrast Analysis

Researchers are overly prone to using omnibus tests and atheoretical post-hoc tests to examine data sets. Such procedures are rarely appropriate for theoretical, statistical, and pragmatic reasons. It is very rare that the researcher has no specific directional hypotheses in mind when designing a study. The substantive theory underlying the investigation should include specific contrasts between groups that should be obtained if the theory is true. To adopt a testing strategy that is a poor representation of the substantive theory guiding a study almost always ensures a poor test of the theory. The substantive theory driving the study should be congruent with the research design, measurement, and analysis to provide an adequate assessment (Tracey & Glidden-Tracey, 1999). Generating specific contrasts requires that the researcher tie the theory to the research methodology more explicitly.

Using specific contrasts also increases the power of the analyses. Omnibus tests are very general, indicating that somewhere there is a significant result. The researcher may be uninterested in some differences and, thus, why should they be tested? More importantly, it is possible that the effect the researcher desires to examine may not be supported in an omnibus test but would be in a much more focused test. Contrast analysis, consisting of focused a priori tests of one degree of freedom, have greater power than do general omnibus tests with global atheoretical post-hoc tests (Rosenthal & Rosnow, 1985; Rosnow & Rosenthal, 1988). Finally, focused contrasts can be used to examine relations that may not be revealed in more simple examinations generated by many atheoretical post-hoc procedures. Many effects will not be discerned unless explicitly examined (e.g., curvilinear effects and particular interactions).

McClelland (1997) took the idea of focused specific contrasts further by arguing that researchers should take additional steps to *optimize* the chance of examining the specific effects of interest. McClelland argued that equally assigning participants to conditions is inefficient and not powerful in many research designs. Research participant assignment should be done according to the specific hypotheses of the study. For example, if the researcher hypothesizes a linear effect in the data (e.g., older groups will manifest more cognitive complexity) and has taken the steps of specifying the appropriate focused contrasts, then the researcher should sample in a manner to ensure an adequate test of the linear hypothesis. In this example, the standard practice would be to sample equally across the five age groups of interest. This strategy is inefficient because the main differences of interest are at the extremes of age. McClelland recommended that in this case, the researcher should oversample in the extreme cases and then have smaller samples in the middle-age cases. Such a procedure would optimize the power of finding the linear effect as more individuals would be allocated in the cells that really matter to the hypothesis. Given that including subjects in studies often has associated costs, McClelland is advocating for a priori thinking also with regard to the sampling and allocation of subjects so as to maximize the power of specific contrasts. Adopting an a priori, focused set of contrasts and optimizing the research design would improve the quality of research in that studies would be better tied to the underlying substantive theory and would provide more powerful tests of the effects of interest.

Interpretation of Interaction

Interaction effects are often of concern to researchers but frequently poorly examined or interpreted. The major problems here concern inappropriate interpretation of interaction effects and poor specification of the interaction itself.

As noted by Rosnow and Rosenthal (1995, 1996), many interpretations of interaction effects are inappropriately conducted. They demonstrated that in the general linear model, which is the basis of multiple regression and analysis of variance models, the interaction is tested after the main effects are removed. As such, it is a further breakdown of the residual that remains after the main effects have been accounted. Once the omnibus test of the interaction test has been conducted and the investigator needs to know where the effects are, it is most common to compare the simple cell means in a post-hoc test. As Rosnow and Rosenthal note, this post-hoc interpretive strategy has been advocated and recommended by many, but it is inappropriate as it can lead to inaccurate conclusions. Comparing simple means confounds main effects with interactions and, depending on the particular configuration of main and interaction effects, very erroneous conclusions can be drawn.

A more appropriate practice for the interpretation of interaction effects is to examine the residualized means (i.e., the means obtained by removing the grand mean and main effects), instead of using the simple means. In cases where the interaction effect consists of only one degree of freedom, as in the case of a two by two ANOVA, such residualized means can be "eyeballed" to give the appropriate interpretation of the interaction effect. In cases where the interaction has more than one degree of freedom (i.e., where at least one of the ANOVA factors has more than two levels as in a 2×3 design), these residualized means should be used in the post-hoc statistical testing of effects. Only then will an accurate picture of the interaction result.

The method of specifying and testing interactions has also been questioned (Abelson & Prentice, 1997; Rosnow & Rosenthal, 1995, 1996). Typically, the researcher uses an omnibus test that focuses on all possible interaction effects. Such a test is not powerful (Abelson, 1997), nor does it reveal any information about where the differences exist. Abelson and Prentice advocated using both a theoretically derived confirmatory approach and an exploratory approach to the analysis of interaction effects. First, they advocate that the researcher specify a priori the form that the interaction should take. Such specifications require theoretical grounding and/or past empirical support; but often, even when such basis for a priori specification exists, it is rarely adopted.

Abelson and Prentice (1997) proposed three common interaction hypotheses that have been posited or observed in the psychological literature: the matching, the opposed concavities of profile, and the differential trend hypotheses. The matching hypothesis is perhaps the most common interaction hypothesis (e.g., person-environment fit), and it posits that maximal scores should exist in cells where the level on one factor matches the level on the other factor.

The opposed concavities of profile hypothesis involves a different pattern of scores across level. A common example would be for the researcher to expect that the means for one group would show a low-high-low pattern over different conditions or stimuli, whereas a second group would show a high-low-high pattern; the concavity of profiles of the first group is opposite that of the second group. This hypothesis can be used to describe any opposing pattern among groups. For example, Tracey (1993) has proposed that successful therapy manifests a pattern of high-low-high complementarity over the course of treatment and that this pattern is absent in less successful therapy.

The third common interaction hypothesis is the differential trends hypothesis, which involves repeated measurement on some variable (hence time is one of the effects in the design). This hypothesis addresses the question: "Do the groups have the same trend over time"? One group could, for example, remain constant while another shows a decreasing trend, a third shows an increasing trend, and a fourth group shows a highly accelerating increasing trend. The typical approach to test such a hypothesis is to apply polynomials in an exploratory fashion. Abelson and Prentice viewed this as limiting and less powerful than adopting a contrast model.

As discussed, these three interaction hypotheses cover most of the interactions of interest in psychology, and researchers would be well advised to adopt explicitly the one they consider most appropriate in an a priori manner. The three interaction hypotheses are very general and can be adapted to fit almost any model. The specification of the exact hypothesis tested can vary with the degree of specificity, from very basic hypotheses covering only a very general pattern, leaving much to vary, to very specified hypotheses where exact order of means is specified for each and every cell. For example, there are several forms that the matching hypothesis can take, ranging from those that only examine exact matching, to those that consider degree of match.

An example of the matching hypothesis in counseling psychology may make the issue of testing interactions clearer. The dominant model in vocational psychology is the person-environment fit model of John Holland (1985). People and environments can each be viewed as being adequately described by the six RIASEC types. The person-environment fit assumption (or matching hypothesis) is that individuals will be most represented in, satisfied with, and productive in an environment with characteristics similar to their own. A typical examination of this is to use a two-way

ANOVA, conduct an omnibus test on the interaction, and then test for differences in simple means to interpret the interaction. As suggested earlier, this strategy has problems both with the use of simple means and the omnibus test of interaction.

The use of the omnibus interaction test and atheoretical post-hoc tests (even if they are done on residualized means) cannot prove very enlightening. Given Holland's (1985) model, there can be little doubt about the form that the interaction should take. The researcher should specify contrasts to capture exactly this variation. The precision of the matching tests can be varied, from weak matching, where only exact matching is examined, to more specified tests, where an order among the means is specified: Highest means are those with an exact match; next are means of cells where the match is only one type off from perfect given Holland's hexagonal model; then the next highest means should be those with a match two types off; and finally those with a match three types off. More exact specification by the researcher would result in a test that more closely asks what the researcher wishes to know, and allows for a more powerful examination of the hypothesis.

Following the test of the interaction, there may still be a fair amount of interaction variance unaccounted for, and this case is where the exploratory approach could be adopted. The researcher could use some of the graphical approaches proposed by Tukey (1977) or Emerson (1991) to examine the residual scores (these new residual scores are the scores obtained after removing the main effects and the interaction contrasts). The examination of the residuals would reveal if there were patterns in the data that would warrant further examination. Adopting the approach advocated by Abelson in this case of person-environment matching would lead to better grounded and more theoretically valuable results, as well as a more powerful test.

Another example of interaction analysis that could be beneficial to counseling psychology is the increased application of aptitude-treatment interactions (ATI; Cronbach & Snow, 1977). ATI refers to the explicit examination of how individual differences variables (labeled here as aptitude, but only in the most general sense) interact with a manipulatable situation variable, such as type or setting of a treatment intervention, or even gender of the therapist. This design was originally proposed with educational interventions in mind (e.g., what type of instruction works best with what students?), but it clearly can be applied to much of the content of counseling psychology, given our focus on intervention and individual differences (Dawis, 1992).

ATI designs are examples of explicit interaction examinations that can provide detailed information about how services should be delivered to specific individuals. Dance and Neufeld (1988), Snow (1991), and West, Aiken, and Krull (1996) have presented clear descriptions of the specifics and values of such designs with respect to psychological interventions, but it is rare to see such designs adopted in the literature. ATI research focuses on the explicit examination of specific a priori interaction terms, and is thus a much more powerful approach to the examination of interaction than the omnibus evaluation of interaction. A quick perusal of the counseling literature in the fairly recent past yielded only one study explicitly using an ATI approach: Glidden-Tracey and Wagner (1995) examined how gender salient problem attributions (individual difference variable) moderated the favorability ratings of different treatment gender attributions. Given the integration of individual differences and treatment interventions, it is surprising that such designs are not used more frequently.

Role of Power and Effect Size in Successful Replications

It would not be difficult to peruse the research literature and find common examples of overinterpretation of probability levels at the expense of effect size (cf. Haase, Ellis, & Ladany, 1989; Haase, Waechter, & Solomon, 1982). The first study with a large sample (say 500 individuals) finds a correlation of .10 as significant, whereas the second study with a much smaller sample size will find a correlation of .30 not significant. One study will laud the importance of .10; the other one will ignore .30. As Cohen (1962) pointed out years ago, more focus needs to be placed on the effect size expected and found. In planning studies, researchers need to attend to the magnitude of the phenomena of interest. How large a difference or relation is expected? Such specification requires familiarity with the theory and past empirical research. Once the researcher has an expected effect size, then the researcher has the information to design an appropriate test of such an effect size.

The institutional application of the null hypothesis test dictates that the author needs to protect against Type I error rate (probability that the null is spuriously rejected) such that it is no greater than .05. However, in automatically adopting a Type I error rate of .05, many researchers are not fully aware that this greatly affects the probability of Type II error (i.e., the probability of failing to reject the null when it should be rejected). Estimates of the Type II error rate in psychological literature are around .60 (Sedlmeier & Gigerenzer, 1989). The easiest solution to this low power problem is to use only large samples. This is a wonderful recommendation in principle, but clearly one that cannot always be feasibly used. Some research contexts dictate a focus on smaller samples. Studies requiring intensive data collection of extremely sensitive materials are almost precluded from study. An example is the area of psychotherapy research, where it is very hard to gain information given the sensitivity and confidentiality of the information and process. Small sample sizes are the norm. Given these sample sizes, the power will be extremely low. Thus, even if the researchers find the result expected (e.g., a moderate effect size of $r = .30$), the test would not be powerful enough to find this effect size significant at .05. The researcher would conclude that the results were not supportive when, indeed, they might have been had a larger sample been employed.

Cohen (1988) recommended a power of .80 be considered the goal. With a power of .80, the Type II error is thus .20. The ideal study would thus have a Type II to Type I error ratio of 4 (.20/.05). Rosnow and Rosenthal (1988) have demonstrated that in most cases, the ratio is much higher. The ratio is especially high in cases where there is "low" sample size. For moderate effect sizes (i.e., $r = .30$), samples of 20 and 40—which are common for many therapy studies—have Type II/Type I ratios of 15 and 10, respectively. Thus, supportive results are unlikely in such studies.

I would like to argue for more planful thinking about statistical testing in general (Tracey & Glidden-Tracey, 1999), but specifically with respect to the selection of Type I and Type II error rates and sample size. In some contexts, it is just not feasible to get the large sample sizes needed to obtain a Type II/Type I error ratio of 4. If the sample size is limited, the researcher can only compromise on the error ratio. Traditionally, psychology has refused to compromise on the Type I error rate (.05 is set in stone), so researchers have had to suffer debilitating Type II error rates. The researcher should think less about Type I error rate and more about the ratio of errors. What this will involve is removing some of the shackles constraining alpha to .05. If the alpha level can be varied in consideration of the available power, then find such cases of extremely low power will be unlikely.

I am not advocating that the researcher set alpha at any level. The process of alpha specification needs to be tied to theory and past empirical results. First, the author needs to be able to specify and justify the expected effect size of the study. To be able to do this requires close integration of extant literature. If this effect size is well justified, then the researcher can design a study to examine it, ideally trying to approximate the error ratio of 4 (as a starting guide). Such an effect size and error ratio determine the minimum sample size. If this sample size is unlikely for such a context, which requires justification, then the researcher needs to think about how to modify the design. What is the maximal sample size reasonably obtainable? Given this sample, what is the error ratio? If the error ratio is too high, the only thing that can get changed is the alpha level. In such contexts, well-planned argument for changing the alpha level from the institutionalized .05 standard to one higher would bring the error ratios in line with interpretable contrasts.

This recommendation is so obvious that it is surprising that it is rarely done. In my perusal of the literature, I have seen it done only once (Tracey, 1985), but I must admit my search process was somewhat biased. However, to argue against the alpha level of .05 requires several conditions, which typically are not met in the literature. First, the authors need to attempt to cover as many bases as possible in an attempt to increase power. The authors need to (1) use the most reliable measures possible, (2) use corrections for attentuation, (3) make sure that the interventions, if any, are as potent as possible, (4) try to control as much experimental error as possible, and (5) use focused, a priori contrast tests rather than omnibus tests. After adequately attending to these issues affecting power, the researcher then needs to specify a priori the expected effect size, desired error ratio (what is the reasonable level for this study?), and the obtainable sample size. To do this requires clear justification on the researcher's part. As argued repeatedly by the critics of null hypothesis testing noted above, such a priori specification rarely occurs.

Increasing Theoretical Specification of Hypotheses

Meehl (1978) noted the slow progress of applied psychology, and also blamed the application of the null hypothesis inference strategy for much of the current state of affairs. One of the remedies he advocated was the increased testing and examination of well-specified effects. Meehl noted the overpreponderance of inference tests of zero effects. Besides the null hypothesis of zero effects being almost always false, it adds little theoretically to the literature. He advocated the adoption of specific tests of point values, pattern shapes, and/or order relations. Instead of testing if some effect is different from zero, a much stronger and more valuable test would be if the effect is of a certain magnitude (Wampold, Davis, & Good, 1990).

Repeated testing of zero effects does not optimally add to our knowledge, but if theory or past research could specify a certain value, we could build much more support for our theories and our research could build better on past results. As an example, if one were to design a study to examine the effectiveness of an intervention, the common approach would be to test the null hypothesis of zero effect. However, there is a wealth of research, from both individual studies and meta-analyses, which provides effect sizes of similar interventions. Would not a more valuable and stronger test be one examining if the intervention differed from the value found in past studies (e.g., ES = .75) rather than if it differed from zero? Such a test would tell us much more about how these results compare with the results of other studies, and would build on the literature.

Meehl (1967) also recommended similar specification of pattern shapes and order relations. If one were comparing the effectiveness of four interventions, the common approach is to use an analysis of variance design, apply an omnibus test of differences, and then if the omnibus test is significant to apply some post-hoc, atheoretical examination of where the differences might exist. As noted above in the section on criticisms of the null hypothesis testing strategy, this omnibus testing strategy is flawed because it lacks power, and it does not build on theory or previous knowledge. The power of such an omnibus testing strategy is less than that of more specific contrasts. Is the researcher really interested in whether all four interventions are different from zero, or is a more appropriate question one of which intervention is best? If this question of best intervention is important, does not the researcher have the theory or past research to make specific predictions about what the specific differences should be (i.e., to specify an ordering of the outcome effects across the four groups)? Would it not then be a more powerful examination of the researcher's hypothesis to test the order effects specifically with a priori contrasts? This recommendation requires that the researcher be much more specific about what is expected, as well as it being tied more closely to theory and extant empirical literature.

Omnibus testing can be valuable in exploratory contexts, but I believe that such contexts are exceedingly rare. Much more of the phenomenon of interest is known than is manifest in the research. Several authors have argued that much of applied psychological research does not use underlying theory or past empirical research, and that more attempts must be made to integrate substantive theory, research design, measurement, and analysis (Tracey, 1991a; Tracey & Glidden-Tracey,

1999; Wampold, 1998; Wampold et al., 1990). One aspect of integrating these components is to use theory and past research to specify effects. The more detail included in these effects, the better.

At first glance, what Meehl is calling for (i.e., increased theoretical specification and testing in our research) runs counter to the recommendation for more exploratory research. The current, institutionalized research model of adopting a fairly atheoretical examination of the null hypothesis does not serve the field well because it is neither exploratory nor confirmatory. As argued earlier, the practice of testing the null hypothesis often implies that once the test is conducted, no more examination of the data is carried out. As a result, data are not subsequently examined for hints that might enhance underlying theory. However, at the same time, the null strategy is not well implemented in a confirmatory manner either. The hypotheses tested are not well tied to theory or empirical literature, and the power of tests for ambiguous effects is weak. The resulting picture is of a researcher who has a fuzzy concept of differences that may exist and then only looks for these differences in a very weak manner. More specification and exact testing is needed to tie the research to the literature, followed with more exploratory examination of data variation to look for potentially rewarding future research foci.

This increased theoretical specification includes the adoption of a disconfirmatory data collection strategy, as advocated by Popper (1959). Popper argued that there is no means of proving that a theory is true, but that it is possible to prove a theory is untrue by demonstrating counterexamples. A disconfirmatory approach requires that the researcher specify what conditions need to exist for the theory to be proven false, and then the researcher attempts to see if these conditions exist. Instead of looking for confirmatory evidence of a set of theoretical propositions, the researcher would be better served to look for evidence that would disconfirm the theory. The search for disconfirming evidence is valuable in that it is less likely that important information will be overlooked; as noted above, searching for confirmatory evidence results in missing a great deal of salient information. Of course such a disconfirmatory approach requires that the researcher explicitly state, a priori, the conditions that need to exist to prove the theory unworthy. Such specifications require explicit theoretical grounding. The disconfirmatory approach to research is recommended given the increased chances of detecting novel information, the theoretical grounding required to apply it, and the greater potential contribution to the validity of the models used in the field.

Structural Data Description

Given some of the issues involved in null hypothesis testing, one alternative is to focus less on determining differences and more on establishing and understanding relations. A key question of many researchers is, What are the major dimensions or themes that underlie certain phenomena? The approaches to examining such a question are many, and include introspection based on personal experience, asking others and trying to look for consensus, and a priori specification of dimensions or themes with attempts to confirm these. Regardless of approach, I would like to advocate for the increased application of clustering techniques and multidimensional scaling (MDS) to understanding the dimensions and themes underlying phenomena. Both of these techniques are very general; can be used with a great variety of data types (including qualitative and quantitative, group and individual, and precise and fuzzy); can be applied in an exploratory or confirmatory manner; involve no statistical inference (hence obviating many of these problems); are simple and straightforward; involve few assumptions about the data; and provide easily understood results. Clustering approaches focus on defining the groups that exist in the data (i.e., clusters of similarity), and as such are very useful in defining the underlying content themes in a data set. MDS focuses on understanding the underlying dimensions that characterize the relations in the data. The dimensions are analogous, in some ways, to the factors in factor analysis and represent a reduced set of information that can summarize the data. MDS provides a spatial representation of how the data vary, and thus helps represent complex relations in a very easy to understand format. A review of the technical aspects of each technique is beyond the scope of this article, but I will review some possible applications in counseling. Readers are referred to Jones and Koehly (1993), Carroll and Arabie (1980), and Arabie, Carroll, and DeSarbo (1987) for thorough descriptions of each technique.

All that is required to conduct a cluster or MDS analysis is a matrix of similarity or dissimilarity ratings among objects. Examples of such ratings are co-occurrence data for categorical data (i.e., number of times two things occur together), ratings of (dis)similarity of stimuli, and correlations or agreements among stimuli. Hence, these techniques can be used with a wealth of data sets. MDS and clustering can be used on correlation matrices to yield information about structure, as exemplified by Tracey and Rounds's (1993) examination of the structure of vocational interests, or Tracey's (1991b) examination of the structure of power in therapy interaction. Wampold and White (1985) used clustering of citations to describe themes in counseling psychology. Fitzgerald and Rounds (1989) used clustering to determine the content themes of vocational psychology. Although there are some good examples of these techniques in the literature with respect to data description, the techniques appear to be underused.

Perhaps one of the most potent applications of clustering and MDS in counseling psychology is individual assessment. Many of the interventions used by counseling psychologists are geared toward helping clients think about, construe, or understand differently themselves and their world. Interventions are typically done on an individual level. Rather than adopting standard measures, assessment could be done on an individual basis. Clients could be asked to provide information on the similarity of key events/individuals in their lives or aspects of occupational choice, and these responses could be subjected to clustering or MDS. These analyses could identify the themes or dimensions that the *specific* client uses in thinking about the stimuli of interest. The counseling psychologist could then use these themes/dimensions to design an individualized intervention.

For example, if a client were asked to list current interpersonal relationships and problems and then rate the similarity of these with each other, an MDS may reveal that the client experiences trouble in all relationships where there is an interpersonal power differential. The therapist could then help the client understand how these relationships are different and not all solely characterized by power and that there are other aspects involved in relationships. Further, the same information could be gathered later and used as an assessment of change in thinking. Following treatment, the therapist could again assess the similarity among the client's issues and interpersonal relationships, and determine if the client is still using power as the main organizing principle in viewing relationships. For example, it may be that the client is now also using intimacy to characterize relationships, having developed a new means of thinking about involvement with others. Such an application is well suited to individual intervention, as it focuses on the unique construal process of each client, rather than adopting a model that is based on large samples of representative clients.

Another valuable application of clustering and MDS is in qualitative research. Qualitative research often focuses on "fuzzier," harder to define constructs; indeed, this is one of the benefits of such approaches. However, one of the drawbacks of qualitative research is that the results are highly dependent on the specific investigator, as the investigator culls through all the information and attempts to summarize the data in an accurate yet understandable form. One of the truisms that has been garnered from the literature on human and expert decision making (see Dawes, 1988; Dawes, Faust, & Meehl, 1989, 1993; Tracey, 1991a; Tracey & Rounds, 1999, for reviews of this extensive literature) is that humans and experts are excellent at evaluating key variables, but they are not good at combining the information. Clustering and MDS could be used as simple information combination techniques to reveal the themes and dimensions in the data. Thus, the qualitative researcher could focus on what he or she does best—gathering and evaluating specific information in its context; yet the weakest aspect, integration of information, would be bolstered by such techniques as MDS and clustering.

Structural data description techniques are very general and have great potential but have been underused (Jones & Koehly, 1993). The simplicity and generality of the approaches and the variety of data to which they can be applied augur well for their promise; however, such applications cannot supplant the importance of strong theory (Wampold, 1998).

CONCLUSIONS

I have discussed the problems with the null hypothesis testing strategy and presented many of the recommendations aimed at rectifying, avoiding, or ameliorating these problems. Although it does not appear that null hypothesis significance testing will be abandoned in the near future, the current debate surrounding its use has highlighted many issues that, if heeded, will go a long way toward improving psychological research. I have enumerated and discussed many of these in this chapter to provide a preliminary information source.

Beyond information, though, the researcher needs to approach the research in a more planful manner. I have argued elsewhere (Tracey & Glidden-Tracey, 1999) for viewing research as a reasoned argument. The researcher explicitly needs to provide a cogent case for argument support. A reasoned argument involves the congruent integration of the four components of substantive theory, research design, measurement, and analysis. All these components must agree for a reasoned case to be made. Uncritically adopting a null hypothesis testing strategy almost ensures that there will be little congruence across the components of a reasoned argument. The researcher needs to be aware of the issues involved in null hypothesis testing and to make decisions about how to resolve these issues relative to the other aspects of the research. Many of the problems associated with the null hypothesis test are really tied to other aspects of the research. For example, the null hypothesis problems of overuse of omnibus tests, confirmatory bias, and inappropriate confirmatory nature of the test really relate to inadequately specified substantive theory (Wampold et al., 1990). Better specified and articulated theory and related hypotheses would result in more appropriate applications of the null hypothesis. There are problems with the null hypothesis testing strategy. It should not be "required" for publication, nor should it be institutionalized. However, to argue for its abandonment does not remedy poor choices made in our research. Better specification and integration of substantive theory, design, measurement, and analysis would go much further than adopting a new form of institutionalized research that would not include the null hypothesis.

REFERENCES

Abelson, R.P. (1997). On the surprising longevity of flogged horses: Why there is a case for the significance test. *Psychological Science, 8,* 12–15.

Abelson, R.P., & Prentice, D.A. (1997). Contrast tests of interaction hypotheses. *Psychological Methods, 2,* 315–328.

American Psychological Association Task Force on Statistical Inference. (1996). *Initial Report.* Washington, DC: American Psychological Association.

Arabie, P., Carroll, J.D., & DeSarbo, W.S. (1987). *Three-way scaling and clustering.* Beverly Hills, CA: Sage.

Bakan, D. (1966). The test of significance in psychological research. *Psychological Bulletin, 66,* 423–437.

Bakeman, R., & McArthur, D. (1996). Picturing repeated measures: Comments on Loftus, Morrison, and others. *Behavior Research Methods, Instruments, and Computers, 28,* 584–589.

Behrens, J.T. (1997). Principles and procedures of exploratory data analysis. *Psychological Methods, 2,* 131–160.

Behrens, J.T., & Smith, M.L. (1996). Data and data analysis. In D. Berliner & B. Calfee (Eds.), *The handbook of educational psychology* (pp. 945–989). New York: Macmillan.

Campbell, J.P. (1990). Modeling the performance prediction problem in industrial and organizational psychology. In M.D. Dunnette & L.M. Hough (Eds.), *Handbook of industrial and organizational psychology* (Vol. 1, 2nd ed.). Palo Alto, CA: Consulting Psychologists Press.

Carroll, J.D., & Arabie, P. (1980). Multidimensional scaling. In M.R. Rosenzweig & L.W. Porter (Eds.), *Annual review of psychology* (Vol. 31, pp. 607–649). Palo Alto, CA: Annual Review.

Carver, R.P. (1978). The case against statistical testing. *Harvard Educational Review, 48,* 378–399.

Cleveland, W.S., & McGill, M.E. (Eds.). (1988). *Dynamic graphics for statistics.* Belmont, CA: Wadsworth and Brooks/Cole.

Cohen, J. (1962). The statistical power of abnormal-social psychological research. *Journal of Abnormal and Social Psychology, 65,* 145–153.

Cohen, J. (1988). *Statistical power analysis for the behavioral sciences* (2nd ed.). Hillsdale, NJ: Erlbaum.

Cohen, J. (1990). Things I have learned (so far). *American Psychologist, 45,* 1304–1312.

Cohen, J. (1994). The earth is round. *American Psychologist, 49,* 997–1003.

Cohen, J., & Cohen, P. (1983). *Applied multiple regression/correlation analysis for the behavioral sciences* (2nd ed.). Hillsdale, NJ: Erlbaum.

Cronbach, L.J., & Snow, R.E. (1977). *Aptitudes and instructional methods: A handbook for research on interactions.* New York: Irvington.

Dance, K.A., & Neufeld, R.W.J. (1988). Aptitude-treatment interaction research in the clinical setting: A review of attempts to dispel the "patient uniformity" myth. *Psychological Bulletin, 104,* 192–213.

Dawes, R.M. (1988). *Rational choice in an uncertain world.* San Diego, CA: Harcourt Brace.

Dawes, R.M., Faust, D., & Meehl, P.E. (1989). Clinical versus actuarial judgement. *Science, 243,* 1668–1674.

Dawes, R.M., Faust, D., & Meehl, P.E. (1993). Statistical prediction versus clinical prediction: Improving what works. In G. Keren & C. Lewis (Eds.), *A handbook for data analysis in the behavioral sciences: Vol. 1, Methodological issues* (pp. 351–367). Hillsdale, NJ: Erlbaum.

Dawis, R.V. (1992). The individual differences tradition in counseling psychology. *Journal of Counseling Psychology, 39,* 7–19.

Emerson, J.D. (1991). Graphical display as an aid to analysis. In D.C. Hoaglin, F. Mosteller, & J.W. Tukey (Eds.), *Fundamentals of exploratory analysis of variance.* New York: Wiley.

Estes, W.K. (1997). Significance testing in psychological research: Some persisting issues. *Psychological Science, 8,* 18–20.

Fitzgerald, L.F., & Rounds, J.B. (1989). Vocational behavior, 1988: A critical analysis. *Journal of Vocational Behavior, 35,* 105–163.

Gigerenzer, G. (1993). The superego, the ego, and the id in statistical reasoning. In G. Keren & C. Lewis (Eds.), *A handbook for data analysis in the behavioral sciences: Vol. 1, Methodological issues* (pp. 311–340). Hillsdale, NJ: Erlbaum.

Glidden-Tracey, C.E., & Wagner, L. (1995). Gender salient attribute x treatment interaction effects on ratings of two analogue counselors. *Journal of Counseling Psychology, 42,* 223–231.

Greenwald, A.G. (1975). Consequences of prejudice against the null hypothesis. *Psychological Bulletin, 82,* 1–20.

Greenwald, A.G. (1993). Consequences of prejudice against the null hypothesis. In G. Keren & C. Lewis (Eds.), *A handbook for data analysis in the behavioral sciences: Vol. 1, Methodological issues* (pp. 419–448). Hillsdale, NJ: Erlbaum.

Guttman, L. (1985). The illogic of statistical inference for cumulative science. *Applied Stochastic Models and Data Analysis, 1,* 3–10.

Haase, R.F., Ellis, M.V., & Ladany, N. (1989). Multiple criteria for evaluating the magnitude of experimental effects. *Journal of Counseling Psychology, 36,* 511–516.

Haase, R.F., Waechter, D.M., & Solomon, G.S. (1982). How significant is a significant difference? Average effect size of research in counseling psychology. *Journal of Counseling Psychology, 29,* 58–65.

Hedges, L.V. (1987). How hard is hard science, how soft is soft science: The empirical cumulativeness of research. *American Psychologist, 42,* 443–455.

Hoaglin, D.C., Mosteller, F., & Tukey, J.W. (Eds.). (1991). *Fundamentals of exploratory analysis of variance.* New York: Wiley.

Holland, J.L. (1985). *Making vocational choices: A theory of vocational personalities and work environments* (2nd ed.). Englewood Cliffs, NJ: Prentice-Hall.

Hunter, J.E. (1997). Needed: A ban on the significance test. *Psychological Science, 8,* 3–7.

Jacoby, W.G. (1998). *Statistical graphics for visualizing multivariate data.* Thousand Oaks, CA: Sage.

Jones, L.E., & Koehly, L.M. (1993). Multidimensional scaling. In G. Keren & C. Lewis (Eds.), *A handbook for data analysis in the behavioral sciences: Vol. 1, Methodological issues* (pp. 95–160). Hillsdale, NJ: Erlbaum.

Loftus, G.R. (1991). On the tyranny of hypothesis testing in the social sciences. *Contemporary Psychology, 36,* 102–105.

Loftus, G.R. (1993). A picture is worth a thousand p values: On the irrelevance of hypothesis testing in the microcomputer age. *Behavior Research Methods, Instruments, and Computers, 25,* 250–256.

McClelland, G.H. (1997). Optimal design in psychological research. *Psychological Methods, 2,* 3–19.

Meehl, P.E. (1967). Theory testing in psychology and physics: A methodological paradox. *Philosophy of Science, 34,* 103–115.

Meehl, P.E. (1978). Theoretical risks and tabular asterisks: Sir Karl, Sir Ronald, and the slow progress of soft psychology. *Journal of Consulting and Clinical Psychology, 46,* 806–834.

Meehl, P.E. (1986). What social scientists don't understand. In D.W. Fiske & R.A. Shweder (Eds.), *Metatheory in social sciences: Pluralisms and subjectivities* (pp. 315–338). Chicago: University of Chicago Press.

Meehl, P.E. (1991). Why summaries of research on psychological theories are often uninterpretable. In R.E. Snow & D.E. Wiley (Eds.), *Improving inquiry in social science: A volume in honor of Lee J. Cronbach* (pp. 13–60). Hillsdale, NJ: Erlbaum.

Morrison, G.R., & Weaver, B. (1995). Exactly how many p values is a picture worth? A commentary on Loftus's point-plus-error-bar approach. *Behavior Research Methods, Instruments, and Computers, 27,* 52–56.

Mulaik, S.A. (1984). Empiricism and exploratory statistics. *Philosophy of Science, 52,* 410–430.

Oakes, M.L. (1986). *Statistical inference: A commentary for the social and behavioral sciences.* New York: Wiley.

Popper, K.R. (1959). *The logic of scientific discovery.* New York: Basic Books.

Rosenthal, R. (1979). The "file-drawer problem" and tolerance for null results. *Psychological Bulletin, 86,* 638–641.

Rosenthal, R. (1991). Cumulating psychology: An appreciation of Donald T. Campbell. *Psychological Science, 2,* 213, 217–221.

Rosenthal, R. (1993). Cumulating evidence. In G. Keren & C. Lewis (Eds.), *A handbook for data analysis in the behavioral sciences: Vol. 1, Methodological issues* (pp. 519–551). Hillsdale, NJ: Erlbaum.

Rosenthal, R., & Rosnow, R.L. (1985). *Contrast analysis: Focused comparisons in the analysis of variance.* Cambridge, England: Cambridge University Press.

Rosnow, R.L., & Rosenthal, R. (1988). Focused tests of significance and effect size estimation in counseling psychology. *Journal of Counseling Psychology, 35,* 203–208.

Rosnow, R.L., & Rosenthal, R. (1995). "Some things you learn aren't so": Cohen's paradox, Ash's paradigm, and the interpretation of interaction. *Psychological Science, 6,* 3–9.

Rosnow, R.L., & Rosenthal, R. (1996). Contrasts and interactions redux: Five easy pieces. *Psychological Science, 7,* 253–257.

Rozenboom, W.W. (1960). The fallacy of the null-hypothesis significance test. *Psychological Bulletin, 57,* 416–428.

Scarr, S. (1997). Rules of evidence: A larger context for the statistical debate. *Psychological Science, 8,* 16–17.

Schmidt, F.L. (1996). Statistical significance testing and cumulative knowledge in psychology: Implications for training researchers. *Psychological Methods, 1,* 115–129.

Schmidt, F.L., & Hunter, J.E. (1996). Measurement error in psychological research: Lessons from 26 research scenarios. *Psychological Methods, 1,* 199–223.

Sedlmeier, P., & Gigerenzer, G. (1989). Do studies of statistical power have an effect on the power of studies? *Psychological Bulletin, 105,* 309–316.

Smith, A.F., & Prentice, D.A. (1993). Exploratory data analysis. In G. Keren & C. Lewis (Eds.), *A handbook for data analysis in the behavioral sciences: Vol. 2, Statistical issues* (pp. 340–390). Hillsdale, NJ: Erlbaum.

Snow, R.E. (1991). Aptitude-treatment interaction as a framework for research on individual differences in psychotherapy. *Journal of Consulting and Clinical Psychology, 59,* 205–216.

Stoppard, T. (1967). *Rosencrantz and Guildenstern are dead: A Play in three acts.* New York: Samuel French.

Tracey, T.J.G. (1985). Dominance and outcome: A sequential examination. *Journal of Counseling Psychology, 32,* 119–122.

Tracey, T.J.G. (1991a). Counseling as an applied science. In C.E. Watkins & L.J. Schneider (Eds.), *Research in counseling* (pp. 3–31). Hillsdale, NJ: Erlbaum.

Tracey, T.J.G. (1991b). The structure of control and influence in counseling and psychotherapy: A comparison of several definitions and measures. *Journal of Counseling Psychology, 38,* 265–278.

Tracey, T.J.G. (1993). An interpersonal stage model of the therapeutic process. *Journal of Counseling Psychology, 40,* 1–14.

Tracey, T.J.G., & Glidden-Tracey, C.E. (1999). Integration of theory, research design, measurement, and analysis: Toward a reasoned argument. *The Counseling Psychologist, 27,* 299–324.

Tracey, T.J.G., & Rounds, J.B. (1992). Evaluating the RIASEC circumplex using high-point codes. *Journal of Vocational Behavior, 41,* 295–311.

Tracey, T.J.G., & Rounds, J.B. (1993). Evaluating Holland's and Gati's vocational interest models: A structural meta-analysis. *Psychological Bulletin, 113,* 229–246.

Tracey, T.J.G., & Rounds, J.B. (1999). Inference and attribution errors in test interpretation. In R.K. Goodyear & J.W. Lichtenberg (Eds.), *Test interpretation: Integrating science and practice* (pp. 113–131). Boston: Allyn & Bacon.

Tukey, J.W. (1977). *Exploratory data analysis.* Reading, MA: Addison-Wesley.

Wainer, H., & Thissen, D. (1993). Graphical data analysis. In G. Keren & C. Lewis (Eds.), *A handbook for data analysis in the behavioral sciences: Statistical issues* (pp. 391–457). Hillsdale, NJ: Erlbaum.

Wampold, B.E. (1998). Necessary (but not sufficient) innovation: Comment on Fox and Jones (1998), Koehly and Shivy (1998), and Russell, Kahn, Spoth, and Altmeier (1998). *Journal of Counseling Psychology, 45,* 46–49.

Wampold, B.E., Davis, B., & Good, R.H., III. (1990). Hypothesis validity of clinical research. *Journal of Consulting and Clinical Psychology, 58,* 360–367.

Wampold, B.E., & White, T.B. (1985). Research themes in counseling psychology: A cluster analysis of citations in the process and outcomes section of the *Journal of Counseling Psychology. Journal of Counseling Psychology, 32,* 123–126.

West, S.G., Aiken, L.S., & Krull, J.L. (1996). Experimental personality designs: Analyzing categorical by continuous variable interactions. *Journal of Personality, 64,* 1–48.

Wilkinson, L. (1999). Graphs for research in counseling psychology. *The Counseling Psychologist, 27,* 384–407.

Zuckerman, M., Hodgins, H.S., Zuckerman, A., & Rosenthal, R. (1993). Contemporary issues in the analysis of data: A survey of 551 psychologists. *Psychological Science, 4,* 49–53.

CHAPTER 7

Qualitative Research for Counseling Psychology

SUSAN L. MORROW
MARY LEE SMITH

Despite deep roots in traditional research methodology, counseling psychology researchers have called for an expanded methodological repertoire for more than 20 years (Gelso, 1979; Goldman, 1976). The mid-1980s saw numerous calls for the inclusion of qualitative methods in counseling psychology (Gelso, 1984; Hill & Gronsky, 1984; Howard, 1983; Neimeyer & Resnikoff, 1982), arguing that these methods more clearly capture the complexity and meaningfulness of human behavior and experience. Polkinghorne (1984, 1991a, 1991b) persistently identified the "need for multiple systems of inquiry in counseling psychology" (1984, p. 424). Hoshmand (1989) proposed alternate research paradigms "characterized by an emphasis on understanding or the illumination of meanings" (p. 13). Throughout the 1990s, *The Counseling Psychologist* and *Journal of Counseling Psychology* published slowly increasing numbers of qualitative investigations, as well as special issues dedicated to qualitative methods. This willingness to broaden the scope of methodology mirrors the growing pluralism in the theories and practices of counseling psychology as a whole.

In this chapter, we present an overview of qualitative research methods and their application. First, we provide an overview of theoretical, definitional, and methodological issues in qualitative research. Next, we examine the various paradigms that underlie qualitative methods across disciplines and briefly sketch several approaches to qualitative research. The second section of the chapter addresses more practical issues related to conducting qualitative research: data gathering and analysis, standards of credibility, communicating results of qualitative research, and ethical considerations. Finally, we address the integration of science and practice in, and identify future directions for, qualitative research in counseling psychology.

THEORETICAL AND METHODOLOGICAL ISSUES AND STANCES IN QUALITATIVE RESEARCH

The disciplinary forebears of qualitative research include anthropology, sociology, and linguistics. Each discipline introduced constructs, methods, assumptions, research roles, and standards of practice, resulting in a complex field that defies simple description. Qualitative research is grounded in a variety of theories of research. Approaches to qualitative inquiry are virtually countless. Qualitative research also goes by a variety of names, including interpretive research, naturalistic research, fieldwork, participant observation, ethnography, and anthropological research. It is thus important to define qualitative research as it applies to counseling psychology and to identify its parameters.

Definitions and Parameters

Qualitative research is defined, first of all, by its emphasis on qualities or essences or the categories of the phenomenon of study. Data are verbal and visual rather than statistical. Researchers gather data by observing in detail what people do, by listening to their words, and by observing the artifacts they produce; they make accurate verbal and visual records of and form inferences from these nonnumeric data. The results of qualitative inquiry are typically presented in the form of words, descriptions, theoretical or conceptual frameworks, pictures, and diagrams rather than formal models and statistics. Researchers construct accounts and make knowledge claims, including case descriptions, narratives, theories, models, or statements of conclusions or assertions. The power of a qualitative presentation lies in the words of the participants and the analysis of the researcher. Quantitative data may be used secondarily to supplement or support the inferences made primarily from verbal data.

Qualitative research focuses on particular units of study, in and for themselves, as wholes. That is, the researcher studies and produces knowledge claims about one or a very few individuals, groups, or institutions. This is *idiographic* research. In contrast, *nomothetic* research aims to produce knowledge claims about large groups of individuals. Typically, the latter research collects data in the form of standardized measures from a large sample of individuals, reporting data on the averages or frequency counts of the grouped data and making generalizations to the respective traits of a population of similar individuals.

The second defining characteristic is the researcher's use of field methods to collect data. The researcher enters the life world of research participants, studying firsthand and over extensive periods of time what people do and say, how they categorize the events and phenomena of everyday life, and what they produce. Observation checklists and protocols are ordinarily not used, because the researcher is interested in the categories that evolve from the people studied (*emic* categories) rather than categories from theory that have been operationalized by the researcher (*etic* categories). For the same reason, interviews are not of the psychometrically standardized varieties employed in conventional psychological research. The researcher aims to uncover the stories and categories of participants, in their own words, and therefore uses a variety of open-ended procedures that differ from study to study. Regardless of the research paradigm, qualitative researchers acknowledge that methods are fallible and provide only a partial view of the phenomenon. Thus, it is essential to employ multiple methods in any study. In addition, the researcher is the instrument. That is, the collection method is not independent of the researcher, and the researcher's knowledge mediates information from any source of data.

Qualitative research may also be characterized by its purpose or aim. Whereas conventional research in counseling psychology aims to develop universal and generalizable principles of behavior, qualitative research aims to understand participants' actions within a particular social context. From this understanding, the investigator develops theoretical constructs that may serve as principles or models that will contribute to the knowledge base about the phenomenon under investigation. These principles are not seen as generalizable, however; rather, they remain bound to the context in which the research is conducted, and the audience decides how the findings may transfer to another context. Context, often addressed as mediating variables in quantitative research, tends to be treated more integrally and holistically by qualitative researchers and seen by them as inseparable from the individual and the individual's experience. Regardless of paradigm, social life is seen as complex, contingent, and mediated by individual interpretations and meanings of events and phenomena.

Qualitative research aims to understand and explain participant meaning. Polkinghorne (1991a) identified the purpose of qualitative research as producing "full and integrated descriptions of an experience or situation under study" (p. 164). Qualitative methods provide the strategies needed to address questions that may not be answered by quantitative methods alone, specifically the investigation of complex human phenomena and the meanings given by people to their life experiences (Hill, Thompson, & Williams, 1997; Polkinghorne, 1991b). Qualitative research, like quantitative, also allows the investigator to study sequential events (Hill et al., 1997) and presumed causal linkages (Erickson, 1986).

Because the aim of qualitative research is to understand participant actions in context, the researcher must be present in participants' natural worlds and everyday lives and close enough, spatially and psychologically, that participants will reveal the meanings they make of their experiences. Thus, the conventional distance between researcher and participants must be bridged, for example, by becoming a member of the group that is the object of study, inviting participants to become involved in some aspect of the research, or by negotiating access with the people they want to study in such a way that those people are fully informed and empowered.

Qualitative research also acknowledges the researcher as instrument. Subjectivity is considered inevitable and indeed the only way, through *verstehen* or interpretive understanding, that one person can understand the actions of another (Dilthey, 1977). Therefore, researcher subjectivity is brought to the fore through such reflexive processes as a self-reflective journal, a self-interview (Polkinghorne, 1991a), peer reviewers, or a research team. Bringing to light one's expectations, biases, assumptions, and feelings about the research enables the investigator to notice how subjectivity affects the research process. Whereas conventional researchers use this awareness to "bracket" or attempt to eliminate subjective influences on the investigation, constructivists hope to identify, for themselves and their audience, the "lens" through which the research is conducted.

Modern methodologists believe that all forms of social research have elements of subjectivity (Gergen & Gergen, 1991; Peshkin, 1988; Phillips, 1992). Experiments freeze and conceal subjectivity by choosing certain research questions and variables and ignoring others; making judgment calls in data recording, analysis, and interpretation; and the like. Notions of objectivity, although they are maintained by positivists and postpositivists as a "regulatory ideal" (Guba & Lincoln, 1994), have given way to notions of intersubjective confirmability and bounded rationality in qualitative research.

In conventional research, variables and hypotheses are grounded in existing theory, are singular (or few), and are stated prior to data collection and later tested by the data. In contrast, qualitative research assumes that meanings are multiple and diverse and that the social world is complex and contingent. Given the assumptions and aims delineated above, it would be inconsistent for the researcher to operationalize constructs in advance. Instead, the investigator allows categories of meaning to emerge from the data. This is called *inductive* logic. However, it is an overly simplistic view of the qualitative research process to view it as solely inductive, for such a position implies that the researcher enters the field tabula rasa, a blank slate on which the data write themselves. To the contrary, a theoretical understanding of the broad scope of the phenomenon enables the researcher to approach the study with an informed and open mind.

Broad research questions and working hypotheses guide and focus the inquiry process, organizing the observation process and underlying interview questions. The researcher cycles between the *inductive* process of immersion in the field and discovery of categories and themes, and the *deductive* process of testing those themes and categories against existing and newly collected data. Thus, qualitative research involves an *abductive* process (Behrens & Smith, 1996) that loops as often and as long as needed to bring the analysis to a coherent conclusion. Induction and deduction work in dialogue (Erickson, 1986).

Qualitative research is also characterized by its emergent design (Eisner, 1998; Glaser & Strauss, 1967; Smith, 1987). Thus, the research proposal identifies what the investigator intends to do in the course of the research (which Eisner, 1998, termed prefigured focus), but the original design is often modified as the investigation progresses.

Paradigms and Theoretical Foundations

Borgen (1992) noted the importance of asking what our "assumptions, world views, and meta-goals" (p. 112) are as we engage in the research process. The reader may ask why this attention to paradigms and theories is important. Typically, quantitative research has been either explicitly or implicitly grounded in a positivist or postpositivist paradigm, in which researchers rarely confront or reveal the theoretical underpinnings of practice. However, in qualitative research, the underlying paradigm influences data gathering, analysis, and standards by which the investigation is judged. Therefore, qualitative research reports frequently indicate, implicitly or explicitly, the paradigms and social theories that influence the research.

Paradigms are the basic belief systems, both formal and informal, that guide our inquiries both in scholarly research and in everyday life. Kuhn (1970) defined "paradigm" as "the entire constellation of beliefs, values, techniques, and so on shared by the members of a given community" (p. 175). A formal paradigm provides a theoretical framework to answer questions concerning ontology (the nature of reality), epistemology (how we know or understand reality), axiology (what is valued), and methodology (how we find out about knowledge or reality) (Guba, 1990). Formal paradigms described by various theorists include positivism, postpositivism, interpretivist/constructivist paradigms, and postmodern perspectives, including poststructural and ideological (critical, feminist, ethnic, and cultural) theories (Carr & Kemmis, 1986; Denzin & Lincoln, 1994; Guba, 1990; Hoshmand, 1994; Lincoln & Denzin, 1994).

Positivist Paradigm

The positivist paradigm is based on the ideas of Compte and others that definitive social knowledge is attainable (see discussion in Hamilton, 1994). It posits a realist ontology (i.e., that a single reality exists separate from anyone's perception of it). Constructs such as anxiety are just as real as kitchen tables, and apprehending their nature follows the same epistemological principles. Social reality is lawful, and the function of social scientists is to discover the universal forces that determine it. Objectivity is both possible and necessary in social science. Methods are perfectible, in the sense that the more research procedures can reduce error and control context and bias, the closer their findings are to the truth. To be considered scientific, knowledge must be public, reproducible, and impersonal. Research is assumed to be "dualist" in that researcher and "subject" are independent. Both researchers and the methods they use are assumed to be neutral and free of values. The guiding ideas of positivism demand particular research strategies and regulatory ideals (Guba & Lincoln, 1994), such as reliability checks, experimentation and manipulation, and verification of hypotheses. The standard of a study's validity is the extent to which its findings correspond to a single external reality. The positivist paradigm is antithetical to qualitative methods, although not all quantitative methods are founded in positivist ideas (Behrens & Smith, 1996).

Postpositivist Paradigm

The postpositivist paradigm is based on a critical realist ontology (reality exists but cannot be apprehended), sees objectivity as a regulatory ideal, and adheres to modified experimental or quasi-experimental, time-series, single-subject, and path analysis methodologies (Cook & Campbell, 1979; Guba, 1990; Kazdin, 1992). Research may be conducted in more natural settings, and discovery is introduced into the inquiry process. Researcher perspectives and built-in fallibilities of particular methods preclude the possibility that any one study can produce definitive conclusions. These ideas require that researchers employ multiple methods, including qualitative methods, and triangulation procedures to test the convergence of findings across methods and investigators.

Interpretive/Constructivist Paradigm

The interpretive/constructivist paradigm aims "to replace the scientific notions of explanation, prediction and control, with the interpretive notions of understanding, meaning and action" (Carr & Kemmis, 1986, p. 83). In contrast to the conventional realist perspective, the interpretivist/constructivist ontology is relativist, emphasizing understanding of "local and specific constructed realities" (Guba & Lincoln, 1994, p. 109). Individual meanings and, therefore, "realities" are particular to individuals but may be shared among individuals, that is, constructed within a social context.

The interpretivist/constructivist epistemological stance is transactional and subjectivist in that, in contrast to positivist/postpositivist perspectives, the investigator and investigated are "interactively linked" in such a way that the findings are mutually constructed (Guba & Lincoln, 1994, p. 110). The methodology of interpretivism/constructivism is grounded in the seventeenth-century German tradition of hermeneutics, an approach to interpretation of biblical text, later expanded by sociologists to provide a social science research method based on "interpretive understanding" as an alternative to the natural sciences paradigm. An important focus of this method was *verstehen*, or understanding, of text, social action, culture, or individual meaning-constructions (Carr & Kemmis, 1986; Schwandt, 1994). Interpretivist ideas suggest research procedures that are long term, direct, and in the context of participants' everyday lives. Meanings are not observed directly or measured indirectly. Instead, the researcher develops accounts of meanings-in-action (Erickson, 1986) based on studying sequences of participants' actions and language within a social context. Methods, however, are less important than the aims and assumptions of the researcher. Research methods are assumed to be fallible and partial, so that multiple methods are necessary to understand meanings-in-action fully. According to Schwandt (1994), "To understand this world of meaning one must interpret it. . . . To prepare an interpretation is itself to construct a reading of those meanings" (p. 118). The interpretation (account) meets standards of coherence, comprehensiveness, and reader credibility rather than abstract truth.

The Postmodern Paradigm

The postmodern paradigm, including poststructural and ideological (critical) perspectives, is characterized by a concern for the meanings of participants within a cultural context. Lather (1991) defined postmodernism as "the larger cultural shifts of a post-industrial, post-colonial era" and poststructuralism as "working out of those shifts within the arenas of academic theory" (p. 4). Although Lather and others used the terms interchangeably, we use the term postmodernism to refer to the larger context of postinterpretive paradigms (indeed, an entire societal movement), whereas poststructuralism is used more specifically to refer to a paradigm that deconstructs conventional beliefs about what is and challenges dominant meaning systems (Lather, 1991). Both poststructuralism and ideological paradigms are concerned with power; however, the poststructuralist views power as a function of language or "discourse" which originates in and re-creates hierarchies of power, whereas the ideological theorist views capitalism, racism, misogyny, heterosexism, and other oppressive institutions as the source of power imbalance.

The nature of reality (ontology) is relativist for the poststructuralist, whereas it is critical realist for the ideological theorist. That is, the poststructuralist position posits that there is no objective reality and is characterized by multiplicities of meanings; the ideological theorist, though acknowledging the constructed nature of personal meanings, points to a social reality that oppresses and colonizes particular groups of people. The two perspectives may be distinguished primarily by axiology. The poststructuralist "recognize[s] the unavailability of any transcendental trump or universal measure of good" (Flax, 1993), whereas ideological positions stress the harm to individuals and society that arises from unequal distribution of power and have as an explicit goal to empower. Poststructuralists and ideological theorists believe that knowledge is constructed in a social context; however, ideological theorists go further to address power and oppression.

Epistemologically, postmodern theorists recognize the futility of a dualistic, researcher-participant distinction and emphasize the joint construction of meaning. Further, the ideological theorist examines the power relationship between researcher and participant. Methodologically, postmodern theorists deconstruct accepted discourses through dialogue with participants. Research methods are less important than social theory and the aims of the researcher. The poststructuralist attempts to bring marginalized perspectives to the center, transforming arenas of power; the ideological theorist further endeavors to address power directly by affecting the consciousness of those who are disempowered and working with them to change oppressive power structures. For a general treatment of critical paradigms, see Kincheloe and McLaren (1994).

Whether a researcher articulates a formal paradigm, that research is influenced by personal, often crude, mental models (Phillips, 1996). Smith (1997) argued that these mental models "matter more than formal philosophical systems in explaining how [researchers] practice" (p. 84). In designing a study of, for example, empathy in counseling groups, one researcher insists on having two observers present to record process variables, believing implicitly in the importance of interobserver agreement checks and that research validity depends on prior demonstration of reliability. The second researcher takes for granted that validity depends on authenticity, refusing even to consider having a second observer present, as such an arrangement would likely increase observer effects. Each acts from habits of mind that assume certain truths about the nature of reality, knowledge, and methodology. In sum, research methods do not exist in a vacuum.

Selected Approaches to Qualitative Research

The qualitative genre encompasses many approaches—styles of working toward particular aims, with paradigms, methods, products, and standards consistent with those aims. We describe a few of these approaches that have particular relevance for counseling psychology.

Grounded Theory

Grounded theory was first articulated by Glaser and Strauss (1967). Based in a symbolic interactionist social framework and interpretivist or postpositivist theories, its aim is "the discovery of theory from data systematically obtained from social research" (p. 2) about the phenomenon of interest. Methods of data collection are eclectic. The research process is highly inductive, as the researcher begins analysis early in the data-collection process. Initial data analysis is used to organize subsequent data collection, as the researcher begins to define categories and flesh out their properties using "constant comparison analysis" in which concepts in the data are compared with one another. The researcher seeks to relate categories to one another, looking for an overarching core category or basic social process and propositional hypotheses about action sequences, causes and consequences, typologies, taxonomies, and the like.

The researcher then enters a deductive phase in which the emerging conceptual model is tested against extant data and data collected through theoretical (purposive) sampling. At all stages, the researcher monitors her or his thought processes, as well as evolving category definitions and propositions, through the use of analytic memos. The results may be presented in the form of a story, a model, a theoretical or conceptual statement, or a combination of any of these formats (Strauss & Corbin, 1990). Standards applied to the product are coherence, how well the data fit the categories and theory, and whether the theory works as an adequate explanation for the phenomenon.

Narrative Research

Narrative research has achieved an important place in qualitative research in counseling psychology. A narrative is "a story with a beginning, middle, and end that reveals someone's experiences" (Manning & Cullum-Swan, 1994, p. 465), or a "special type of discourse production" in which "events and actions are drawn together into an organized whole by means of a plot" (Polkinghorne, 1995, p. 7). This approach assumes that knowledge is constructed in the context of social life (Cooper & Heck, 1995; Hoshmand, 1994). Research inquiry, as a result, is imbedded in both personal and cultural contexts, with participants as cocreators of meaning with investigators (Hoshmand, 1994). Humans are active, storytelling agents who "represent the world and our lives to ourselves via stories" (Howard, 1989, p. 121); we are "storytelling organisms who, individually and socially, lead storied lives" (Cooper & Heck, 1995, p. 196).

The narrative research approach presents itself in one of two different forms: analysis of narratives or narrative analysis (Polkinghorne, 1995). In other words, "[n]arrative functions as both phenomenon and method" (Cooper & Heck, 1995, p. 196). In the analysis of narratives, stories may form the data corpus, or body of data, that is analyzed using any of a number of methods of analysis (Hoshmand, 1994; Polkinghorne, 1995). Mishler (1986) noted that interviews can either suppress or enhance participants' stories. Therefore, interviews should be framed in such a way that they "become occasions in which we ask for life stories" (Chase, 1995). Narrative analysis includes attention to themes, principal metaphors, and defining structures of stories. It consists of taking data that may not occur naturally in storied form and ending up with a narrative by composing the elements into a story (Polkinghorne, 1995). The presentation of narrative research may be dramatic, poetic, artistic, or metaphoric (Manning & Cullum-Swan, 1994). According to Eisner (1998), the standards to be applied to narrative inquiry include structural corroboration and referential adequacy. Objectivity and reliability are of less importance than coherence, plausibility, and the persuasiveness of the writer's perspective.

Case Study

A case study is the investigation of a "bounded system," whether an individual, group, or institution (Creswell, 1998). Stake (1994) identified three types of case studies. An *intrinsic case study* is the investigation of a particularly interesting case. In an *instrumental case study,* a particular case is examined for the purpose of better understanding a particular issue or refining a theory. Finally, in a *collective case study,* the investigator studies a number of cases in order to better understand a phenomenon across sites. Multiple data sources contribute to the rigor of a qualitative case study, including observations, interviews, documentary evidence, media, and artifacts (Creswell, 1998; Yin, 1989).

Case study data may be analyzed using any of a number of paradigmatic processes or analytic approaches. It is important that the case study be grounded historically and contextually and examined as holistically as possible. Case studies are not the same thing as single-subject designs but represent a concerted effort to integrate empirical data and theoretical ideas. Campbell (1975) argued that a case study consisted of hundreds of observations, thus degrees of freedom, from which causal claims might be made. Although bounded in time and place at the time of the study, results from case studies can be extrapolated to other cases (Cronbach, 1982).

Conversation Analysis

Conversation analysis (CA) is "the study of how ordinary talk accomplishes social identities and social order" (Gale, 1996, p. 109). Its roots lie in sociology and are part of the tradition known as ethnomethodology, or the study of ordinary reasoning (Potter & Wetherell, 1987). Although CA can comfortably be integrated with any paradigmatic perspective, it is similar to social constructionism in that "knowledge of reality arises from social interaction mediated through language" (Gale, 1996, p. 109; McNamee & Gergen, 1992). Words are seen not merely as symbols but as tools to accomplish specific goals. CA is based on three assumptions: (1) interaction follows structured patterns ("Conversations are meticulously organized phenomena," Gale, 1996, p. 109); (2) all interactions are contextually oriented ("Every action both shapes . . . and is constrained by the context," p. 109); and (3) "no order of detail can be dismissed, a priori, as disorderly, accidental or irrelevant" (Heritage, 1984, p. 241). CA has been used extensively in family therapy and creates the possibility of investigating what therapists actually *do* in practice, as well as *how* therapy and other types of communication are accomplished. Therefore, it is particularly applicable to counseling process research in that, by knowing the precise components of process, researchers can draw better conclusions. CA treats events in natural sequences, assuming that understanding the meaning of an interactional event depends on what happened both before and after that event.

Data include any naturally occurring conversational interaction and may consist of purposefully selected segments of conversation as well as transcriptions of entire interactions. Analysis during transcription is seen as a crucial step, contributing to immersion in the data. A detailed notational system is transcribed and analyzed, including verbal, paraverbal, and nonverbal communications;

turn-taking; structured aspects of grammar; cohesion (how lines and stanzas are linked); contextualization cues and prosody (rise and fall, speed, overall rhythm); and organization of language and themes (Gale, 1996; Gee, Michaels, & O'Connor, 1992; Labov & Fanshel, 1977; Sacks, Schegloff, & Jefferson, 1974). The credibility of CA lies in immersion in the data, peer review, an audit journal, negative case examples, and multiple examples used to demonstrate a theme.

Erickson's Approach

Erickson (1986) based his approach on the interpretivist paradigm and interactionist theories of social life. This approach aims to produce credible accounts of meanings and action within a social context. It assumes that (1) the validity of an interpretive (qualitative) study rests on "the immediate and local meanings of actions, as defined from the actors' point of view" (p. 119); (2) the meanings of participants form and are situated in the social context in which they live; and (3) meanings and events are interactive, that is, they evolve in the context of human interaction. Erickson described his research as "an attempt to combine close analysis of fine details of behavior and meaning in everyday social interaction with analysis of the wider social context" and to be "empirical without being positivist; to be rigorous and systematic in investigating the slippery phenomena of everyday interaction and its connections, through the medium of subjective meaning, with the wider social world" (p. 120).

This approach begins with the researcher's perspective and conceptual frame, as well as her or his best guesses about the phenomenon of study, and monitors that perspective as it is challenged by emerging evidence and analysis. The researcher casts a wide net, using as many methods as possible, to capture the full range of data, including those data likely to challenge the researcher's perspective. The research is governed by the idea of bounded rationality—that pure objectivity is impossible. Nevertheless, one tries to be as even-handed, precise, thorough, and careful as possible about collecting and making sense of the evidence.

Analysis overlaps data collection. In this approach, the mode of analysis is called modified analytic induction. In the inductive phase, the researcher generates assertions from the data as a whole. In the deductive phase, the researcher tests the warrant of each assertion by weighing positive and negative empirical instances. The reader is treated as a co-analyst; the researcher presents the full range of data and displays his or her methods and analytic process so that the reader can follow. The report is a compilation of warranted assertions and analytic vignettes that represent the connection between data and inferences. It is judged by standards of coherence, plausibility, and completeness.

Miles and Huberman's Systematic Approach

Miles and Huberman's (1994) approach is founded in realist assumptions about reality and knowledge. It assumes that reality exists independent of one's interpretations, and that dependable knowledge claims, including claims of causality, can be made from systematically gathered and analyzed qualitative data. At the same time, participant meanings and contextual effects must be taken into account. This approach begins with well-structured conceptual frameworks. That is, the researcher develops and defines categories and working hypotheses before going into the field, then proceeds more deductively than is common in other approaches to qualitative research. Some categories and hypotheses are allowed to emerge as the researcher becomes familiar with the local context, however. The researcher designs the study, purposively samples cases (multiple cases and observers are widely used), prestructures certain collection methods, and collects the data. Data analysis takes place in three parts: (1) data reduction (coding data according to a list of categories), (2) data display (organizing coded data in heuristic graphs and tables), and (3) conclusion drawing and confirmation. A variety of procedures are used to verify conclusions, including triangulation, participant checks, and audit trails. The standards against which the accounts are judged include confirmation across data sources and observers.

Action Research

Also referred to as participatory or collaborative research, action research involves research participants in many or all phases of the research, from initial design through use and presentation of results (Whyte, 1991). In a participatory model, the investigator acts more as a consultant than an expert (O'Neill, Small, & Strachan, 1999). Action research is a form of participatory investigation conducted by researchers whose purpose is to engage those with whom they conduct research (participants) in understanding and making changes in social situations. For example, consumers of psychological services may be involved in participatory action research to make changes in systems that will bring about a more positive environment (O'Neill et al., 1999). The accounts that result from action research are judged according to how well participants are able to make use of the knowledge produced to change or improve the situation or their own practice.

Ideologically Based Approaches

Counseling psychologists have increasingly drawn on sociocultural factors to explain psychological function and dysfunction, identity, and personal and vocational development. Ideological perspectives acknowledge the value-ladenness of all science, and politics and values are an integral part of all ideologically based methods. Ideological approaches are particularly suited to research with marginalized populations. Three perspectives—critical, feminist, and ethnic—will be addressed here. Action research and participatory or collaborative approaches are often integral to these perspectives. All these approaches overlap significantly, so a researcher may take both a critical and a feminist perspective, and most critical researchers engage in action research, just as many feminists engage in collaborative and participatory methods.

In all of these approaches, data-gathering and data-analysis methods assume lower priority relative to questions of social theory. For the critical researcher, the question is how societal structures, particularly related to socioeconomic class, disempower people and how the researcher can contribute to change and to empowerment of those who are being studied. The feminist researcher, too, is concerned with power and empowerment, often with a central focus on gender. In addition, feminist researchers have addressed power in the researcher-participant relationship (Fine, 1992; Lather, 1991; Olesin, 1994). Ethnic models are based on indigenous theories and methods and a critique of the hegemony (dominance) of Euro-American methodological stances (Scheurich & Young, 1997; Stanfield, 1994). Critical, ethnic, and feminist researchers extend their analyses of power to include a broad focus on race, class, gender, and often other variables such as sexual orientation. Ethnic models go a step further as they attempt to establish "novel indigenous paradigms grounded distinctly in the experiences of people of color" (Stanfield, 1994, p. 183).

CONDUCTING QUALITATIVE RESEARCH

Earlier we set the stage for conducting qualitative research by introducing the basic premises underlying qualitative research (i.e., paradigms, theories, and mental models that influence one's approach to conducting a qualitative investigation) and selected approaches to qualitative research. In this section, we examine conceptualization and design, the social context of data collection, and strategies of gathering and analyzing qualitative data.

Conceptualization and Design

Each qualitative study is grounded in the investigator's research paradigm and theories of social life—from one's theory about reality, knowledge, and the categories that explain social life. The researcher's attention is directed toward those aspects of social life that she or he deems most powerful as explanatory factors. For example, if one believes, as do the structural functionalists

(Merton, 1967) or conflict theorists, that the broad abstract categories of culture, society, or institution explain the actions of persons within them, one will design research methods to reveal indicators of those categories (e.g., social class). The researcher who believes, as do the symbolic interactionists (e.g., Blumer, 1969), that the causal elements of social life are revealed in what people do together in the course of particular transactions, will design a study to reveal incidents (talk, gestures, metalanguage) of those microlevel interactional categories. In either case, the design follows an implicit or explicit conceptual framework that sensitizes the researcher to certain kinds of data and relegates others to the background. Depending on one's paradigm, these initial conceptual frameworks may persist through the study or be modified or overturned as the study proceeds.

Research design encompasses the researcher's choice of relevant units of study—those places where the phenomenon of interest resides. Units may be synonymous with cases such as persons, schools, hospitals, or offices. Units may also be classes of events, such as the process of referral, diagnosis, and treatment assignment of psychiatric patients. Units may also refer to classes of events defined by location, such as street corners where needles are exchanged or reception desks where potential clients are processed. Research questions and paradigms suggest whether one case or more than one would best achieve the aim of understanding the phenomenon in its context. Single case study designs allow the most intense scrutiny of particular contexts. Dual or multiple case study designs permit examination of comparative elements of more than one case and, perhaps, promote broader interpretive perspectives (Miles & Huberman, 1994).

Choice of a particular case or cases takes place by sampling. Because it is rare for qualitative researchers to make statistical generalizations from the case studied to a population (rather providing the reader with sufficient information to make decisions about how the findings transfer to her or his own context), sampling strategies are nonprobabilistic. Instead, the common principle underlying them all is purposefulness (Patton, 1990). *Intensity sampling* consists of selecting participants who "manifest the phenomenon of interest intensely (but not extremely)" (p. 171). *Extreme or deviant case sampling,* which selects participants based on their uniqueness or specialness in some way, is based on the assumption that something important can be learned that will benefit the mainstream by studying extreme cases. In *critical case sampling,* one looks for cases that "make a point quite dramatically or are . . . particularly important in the scheme of things" (p. 174).

Maximum-variation sampling seeks to investigate a very heterogeneous group of cases to represent most of the possibilities. A combination of both typical case and maximum variation sampling is *stratified purposeful sampling,* in which one samples above-average, average (typical), and below-average cases. *Snowball or chain sampling* is a strategy in which well-situated people are asked to recommend participants who are particularly knowledgeable about the phenomenon or who represent less-accessible perspectives. *Criterion sampling* consists of setting predetermined criteria for selection of participants to gain an information-rich sample. One type of criterion sampling is *theory-based or operational construct sampling,* in which participants are selected on the basis that they can best illustrate the construct under investigation.

Some sampling strategies are integral to the emerging design of the study. *Confirming and disconfirming case sampling* strategies are conducted after data collection and analysis have been in process over time. Cases are deliberately sought to test emerging theory or categories and enhance the rigor of a study. In addition, *opportunistic sampling,* consisting of "on-the-spot decisions about sampling to take advantage of new opportunities during actual data collection" (Patton, 1990, p. 179), can enable the investigator to pursue unanticipated sources of data.

Sometimes, pragmatic considerations also drive the selection of cases. For example, *random sampling* may enhance the credibility of the investigation for audiences who are more comfortable with a conventional model of research. In addition, *samples of convenience* are sometimes used, with the researcher justifying the particular choice and explaining how its characteristics and the mechanisms of its choice must be taken into account in reading the report. Finally, it is common for the researcher to use *mixed purposeful sampling,* combining various purposeful sampling methods defined above.

Data Collection in Social Context

Qualitative research acknowledges that the process of data collection is interactive and dependent on the person of the researcher and whether researchers can position themselves in such a way that participants in the world they seek to understand will interact with them and "coproduce" (Graue & Walsh, 1998) the data. Just as a photographer must select a physical vantage point to take a picture of the Grand Canyon, so a researcher has to select a social vantage point from which to access the data of interest. This social vantage point refers to institutional access, social access, and social role.

Access to the Context in Which Action Occurs

At the heart of qualitative research lies an understanding of the sociocultural context of people's lives. Therefore, to develop understanding of action in context, the researcher enters the social world of participants and spends significant time in the field absorbing the culture of interest. This is true even if observational strategies are not the central data-gathering processes of a study. Immersion in the setting enables the researcher to form relationships with participants, frame interview questions that are relevant and understandable, give background from which to view subsequent data, and add complexity to the understanding of the phenomenon.

In qualitative research, the processes of attaining access to the field are an important part of the context of the study; therefore, the investigator identifies the social environment in which observation will take place and the issues related to entering the field. The selection of a site for observation is guided by many factors, such as what kind of setting will shed the most understanding on the phenomenon, how the setting can complement other data, and what setting can best illustrate the social interactions in which human meanings are constructed.

The investigator also articulates issues of site accessibility, including traditional issues of access (e.g., gaining permission, informed consent), as well as those peculiar to qualitative research. The formation of a relationship with the "gatekeeper" is essential to build the kind of rapport and trust that will ensure high-quality data. Spradley (1980) suggested six strategies for locating a social situation that can increase the investigator's chances for a successful study: simplicity, accessibility, unobtrusiveness, permissibleness, frequently recurring activities, and participation.

Researcher Stances and Roles

How and what one observes depends in part on the investigator's status as insider or outsider to the population and phenomenon, as well as the choices the investigator makes about personal placement on a continuum of participant-observation. The investigator's positioning as either an insider or an outsider affects the research design, what the researcher notices or fails to notice in the setting, the kinds of questions asked in interview, what data are accessible and how they are interpreted, and, consequently, the coherence of the eventual account. The insider perspective enhances the likelihood that individuals will agree to participate and increases trust and openness, thereby eliciting more and better data. However, because of shared culture and experience, both investigators and participants may fall prey to shared assumptions and taken-for-granted meanings, leading the researcher to fail to go into sufficient depth to understand participant meanings or to allow events in the field to go unnoticed or unquestioned because of their familiarity. The outsider is often in a position to view the situation from a broader, more distanced perspective, thereby noticing things the insider or participants experience as ordinary. However, the outsider may have more difficulty gaining entry into the field, establishing rapport and trust, and learning the more intimate aspects of the culture.

The other area of consideration related to researcher stances and roles is the continuum of participant-observation. In addition to insider-outsider concerns, the investigator must also make decisions about where to stand on the participant-observer continuum, from peripheral to complete membership (Adler & Adler, 1987) or nonparticipation to complete participation (Spradley, 1980). As noted above, there is no perspective-free view of the social world. Neither is there an ideal role. Each choice of role depends on the researcher's aim, paradigm, social theory, and research question.

Strategies for Gathering Data

Observational Strategies

Fieldwork observation has long been the central data-gathering strategy for anthropological and sociological researchers. Observation is part of almost all qualitative research, but the extent and nature of its use varies across disciplines. Its most obvious use in counseling psychology research is in individual and group therapy processes, where sessions are videotaped, transcribed, and analyzed. Observation should consist of "intensive, long-term participation in a . . . setting" (Erickson, 1986, p. 121) or prolonged engagement, as well as persistent and focused observations (Guba & Lincoln, 1989). The purpose of this kind of immersion is to familiarize the investigator with the everyday occurrences and meanings of participants and to understand their tacit knowledge, as well as to gather explicit information that will serve as data for the investigation. The primary data from observation are the concrete particulars, or fine-grained details of action in context, which the researcher painstakingly and accurately records.

Banister, Burman, Parker, Taylor, and Tindall (1994) suggested that the *context* be described with specificity and concreteness to give accurate meaning to phenomena and to capture the details of the situation. In keeping with the idiographic intent of qualitative research, *participants* are described concretely, in context of their lives and institutions, as whole and real people. Information about the *observer* is important so that the reader can understand how the researcher might have affected what was seen or recorded. Both verbal and nonverbal *actions* of participants are described to more fully depict them in a way that readers can both hear and see. The observer's *interpretations* of the situation become part of the data record. Specific reasons for interpretations of participant meanings are essential, that is, what behavioral data contributed to the observer's interpretation? Considering alternative interpretations of the situation is important to expand the possibilities for understanding the data. Erickson (1986) recommended searching for disconfirming evidence to challenge the observer's assumptions or "confirmatory bias" (Mahoney, 1991), thereby increasing the credibility of the interpretation. Finally, exploring one's *feelings* as an observer helps to highlight ways in which one can affect the study. The researcher's goal is to notice things the casual observer does not normally notice, to rigorously record every possible aspect of the situation, and then to communicate those data in a holistic manner that brings the reader into the social setting in which the phenomenon of interest occurs (Graue & Walsh, 1998).

Field notes are a time-honored method for preserving careful records of observational data (Emerson, Fretz, & Shaw, 1995). Notes may be complemented by audiotapes or sometimes must suffice if taping is not possible or advisable. Occasionally, in the case of mechanical failure, the investigator will be forced to recall from memory as much verbatim information as possible; generally the text of these notes is shorter and less detailed than the tape would have been. These records become more complete and accurate with practice. Field journals are not used only to record conversation, however. A primary function of field notes is to record those things that occur in the setting besides talk—the "stuff of the senses." The practiced field observer works to use every available sense—sight, sound, smell, touch, taste—as well as intuition. Therefore, impressions gained by the researcher about the site are recorded, as well as observable behavior. Reasonable inferences are also made about intentions and emotions related to what is observed (Graue &

Walsh, 1998; Spradley, 1980). Generally, field notes written on site are condensed accounts of what actually happened. As soon as possible after leaving the field, this condensed account should be expanded as the investigator fills in details and recalls things that were missed during the data-gathering session (Spradley, 1980). Field journals also contain analytic and self-reflexive entries that facilitate the interpretation of data.

Interviews

Counseling psychologists are in a good position to conduct interviews, as many of the same skills (e.g., active listening) that underlie the counseling process are essential to qualitative interviewing. However, the two enterprises have vastly different aims—to produce knowledge claims or to produce therapeutic benefits. Therefore, procedures differ between the two domains.

Depending on the paradigm within which the investigator is working, along with other considerations such as length and number of meetings with participants, interviews may be more or less standardized or structured. An informal interview is open-ended and provides the flexibility to follow the participant's lead, as well as to ask questions and probe replies that enhance the details of the participant's story. Thus, interviews with participants will, to some extent, be different from one another. The advantage to this type of interview is that the interviewer has the opportunity to be responsive to each participant (Patton, 1990). In addition, the open-ended interview has the greatest potential to elicit the participant's story in the participant's own words.

Ideally, the qualitative interview design is flexible, iterative, and continuous (Rubin & Rubin, 1995), in keeping with the emergent nature of qualitative research. Flexibility implies that "adjusting the design as you go along is a normal, expected part of the qualitative research process" (p. 44). The investigation is iterative in that, as the interviews progress, questions move from broad, explorative explorations to those that are more theme-based and deductive. Allowing the interview questions and process to change based on the evolving demands of the data and analysis will add to the depth, complexity, and richness of the constructs, themes, or theory that result from the investigation.

The quality of an interview can vary based on the experience and style of the interviewer, the types of questions asked, and the personal characteristics of the interviewee. Kvale (1996) identified six quality criteria for an interview. First, the answers should be "spontaneous, rich, specific, and relevant" (p. 145). Second, the interviewer's questions should be short and, correspondingly, the interviewee's responses long. Third, the interviewer should follow up and clarify participant meanings. Next, "the ideal interview is to a large extent interpreted throughout the interview" (p. 145); that is, the interviewer is engaged throughout the interview in analyzing and interpreting what is being heard. As a result, the interviewer is able to verify those interpretations within the interview context. Finally, the interview is " 'self-communicating'—it is a story contained in itself that hardly requires much extra descriptions and explanations" (p. 145).

Interviews can be conducted by one or more interviewers with one or more interviewees. Many of the basic premises of individual interviewing extend to dyads and groups. Focus-group interviews may be used alone or to complement other forms of data. Focus groups are used by researchers to take advantage of the interactive social processes of participants to examine the phenomenon in depth. The collective meaning-making process can add depth and richness to an interview-based study. A single- or two-session focus group with interview participants may help to clarify or confirm the researcher's emerging model, whereas an ongoing focus group (8 to 10 sessions or more) may produce a significant amount of additional data for analysis and take it to greater depth. A focus group may also engage in data analysis with the investigator.

Electronic Data

Electronic data can be used in a number of ways, including interviews, participant checks, and discussion groups. Murray and Sixsmith (1998) argued that e-mail interviews have the advantage of crossing the barriers of time and space and providing an environment in which participants may be more inclined to share sensitive information under the guise of some degree of anonymity. E-mail interviews may either take the place of or complement face-to-face interviews. Of course, e-mail interviews vastly simplify data management, as transcription is not required. Murray and Sixsmith (1998) addressed both advantages (unique linguistic characteristics of the medium; the development of relationship, convenience, clarification of concepts, involvement and empowerment over time, and cross-fertilization of ideas) and disadvantages (flow of information, loss of contextual information, absence of nonverbal information, and invisibility and presentation of self) of e-mail interviewing.

Collecting Documents and Artifacts

Physical data may be primary source material for a qualitative investigation, or they may supplement observational or interview data. Physical data consist of documents, art, media, and physical objects. These sources are incorporated into the researcher's data record. When documentary or archival data form the core of the data gathered in an investigation, it is sometimes because access to observational or interview data is limited in some way. Biographies and autobiographies can form the basis of important psychological information (e.g., on adolescent development or other topics). Where legitimate access to clinical case notes exists, these data may shed light on certain psychotherapy processes. Particularly in investigations where time and money may limit numbers of participants, documentary and other physical evidence can contribute to the quality of the investigation by providing multiple data sources at very little cost. Miles and Huberman (1994) provided useful procedures for collecting, indexing, and analyzing archival and documentary data such as those described here.

Analytic and Reflexive Memos

The common procedures of data generation in qualitative studies—including observation, interviews, and physical data—represent a starting point only, as researchers often invent or adapt methods that suit their particular questions or contexts. A further consideration for generating data involves analytic and reflexive or self-reflective memos. The analytic journal consists of interpretive memos, sudden insights, questions to ask during follow-up interviews, hunches, informal categories or themes, and countless other ideas that occur during the course of the investigation. The reflexive journal is used to track the investigator's personal thoughts and feelings during the investigation. These entries may be used in a number of ways, depending on the paradigms guiding the research and the investigator's personal leanings. In practice, observational entries, interpretations, and reflexive memos often flow from one to the other; therefore, many investigators keep a single journal to accomplish these multiple purposes.

Multiple Data Sources

One of the ways qualitative investigators enhance the credibility of their work is to use multiple data sources, also referred to as triangulation in both qualitative and quantitative research. Denzin (1978) identified four types of triangulation: by data, investigators, theory, and method. Data triangulation consists of using multiple data sources in an investigation, such as interviews plus focus groups. Investigator triangulation involves multiple investigators; the research team concept in which several investigators are involved in observations, interviews, and data analysis can provide investigator triangulation. Theory triangulation involves engaging multiple theoretical perspectives in the conduct of the research, particularly in the analysis; this may be enhanced by using a multidisciplinary team. Finally, methodological triangulation uses several approaches to investigating phenomena and analyzing data; for example, a researcher may complement a basic grounded-theory approach with an ideological analysis that foregrounds power.

Triangulation is a set of tactics that strengthen qualitative research. Single methods each have fallibilities and present one view of the phenomenon. For postpositivists, multiple methods balance out the weakness of any single one. In contrast, interpretivists practice triangulation so they will have multiple lines of sight on the phenomenon of interest, without the expectation that convergence will be attained (Mathison, 1988). Finally, we emphasize that, although we have presented suggestions about how methods might be used to generate data, correct methods—even when multiple data sources are employed—do not equate to true conclusions.

Analyzing Qualitative Data

Although the literature identifies several modes of analyzing qualitative data, analysis cannot be mechanistic or formulaic. Qualitative data analysis is the process of discovering or constructing meaning from data. So-called methods are mere heuristics or aids to the researcher's thinking. Behrens and Smith (1996) noted four attributes common to all modes of qualitative data analysis. First, data collection, analysis, and writing are inseparable and integral; the various research activities often occur simultaneously and cause the investigator to circle back to additional research steps. Second, data analysis is construction, not discovery. The researcher is the instrument of the research, and "perfect objectivity and replicability are neither possible nor worth pursuing as a research strategy" (p. 979). Next, qualitative researchers are involved in managing overwhelming amounts of complex data; despite various guidelines for analyzing data, the process cannot be reduced to a set of rules. All data analysis is a process of breaking down and building up again, of breaking apart data from their original context in time and space and reordering them in the form of categories, themes, stories, propositions, or theories. Finally, analysis rests on a foundation of rich description: "of context, site, actors, and action" (p. 979).

Grounded Theory Analysis

Grounded theory, first described by Glaser and Strauss (1967) and later expanded by Glaser (1978), Strauss (1987), and Strauss and Corbin (1990), is built on the idea that the investigator's purpose is to generate theory grounded in data. Data analysis begins with coding of initial data sets. *Open coding* (Strauss & Corbin, 1990) consists of a focused analysis of transcribed data in which the analyst examines the text in detail, making marginal notes and memos about each category or unit of meaning. A meaning unit may refer to pieces of data as small as a word or as large as a paragraph but should be able to be described by a code for a specific category or concept that reflects the basic idea of that incident or portion of text. The section of data is called an incident, or concrete referent to the abstract category. The researcher aims to define and flesh out the category by finding its properties or aspects (who participates in the phenomenon; under what circumstances; what proceeds and follows it; levels of duration, intensity, and frequency of the phenomenon; and the like).

The analysis proceeds through constant comparison, in which every instance of data referring to the phenomenon is compared with every other one to define the category in a cohesive and internally consistent way. The process of making connections between categories is known as *axial coding*. In axial coding, comparison is again used to identify the properties of various categories and explicate their relationships to one another and to the subcategories that fall under them.

Finally, *selective coding* consists of reaching for even higher levels of abstraction to identify a core category that integrates all other categories that have emerged from the data. The core category or basic social process is inclusive of all relevant data, and from it emerges "the story line" (Strauss & Corbin, 1990, p. 116)—a description of the findings in narrative form or a midlevel theory. In the deductive phase of analysis, the researcher engages in theoretical sampling to probe the story, theory, or emergent hypotheses by purposively selecting cases or incidents or by collecting new data. By this means, the story or theory is bounded or elaborated. The process ends when the categories and propositions are saturated; that is, no new properties of the categories are found by collecting new data, and the data and analytic results are brought into fit.

Through all of these processes of data analysis, the researcher makes use of memoing. Memos are analytic notes taken throughout the investigation and consist of the process and products of the analysis. Examples include the actual labels given to emerging concepts, codes, and categories; process descriptions of the investigation; theoretical statements about the emerging findings; descriptions of the relationships among various aspects of the data and analysis; ideas for further investigatory activity; diagrams related to the emerging theoretical model; and the like. Memos also keep track of the researcher's analytic process and prepare the way for the reader to judge the credibility of the account.

Narrative Analysis

Polkinghorne (1995) distinguished between two types of narrative inquiry: paradigmatic-type narrative inquiry and narrative-type narrative inquiry. The paradigmatic approach uses participants' stories as data, then analyzes those data using a particular analytic procedure (e.g., grounded theory). The narrative type "gathers events and happenings as its data and uses narrative analytic procedures to produce explanatory stories" (p. 5). Thus, a narrative or story may be data, an analytic approach, a product, or all three.

"In research that employs narrative analysis as distinguished from analysis of narratives, the result is an emplotted narrative" (Polkinghorne, 1995, p. 15). In this case, the investigator begins with "eventful data" and unifies those data into a coherent story "that unites and gives meaning to the data" (p. 15). Polkinghorne, based on Dollard (1935), recommended seven steps in developing a narrative. The first step in the analysis is to describe the cultural context in which the phenomenon of interest takes place and in which the participant makes meaning. Second, the researcher locates the participant (protagonist) spatially and temporally as an "embodied" being, including physical descriptions of the individual; the protagonist should be described in sufficient detail that she or he "lives" for the reader. Third, the investigator must attend to the participant's relationships with significant others. Next, the researcher focuses on the participant's meanings, goals, plans, purposes, motivations, interests, inner struggles, emotional states, and actions, as well as interactions with others. Fifth, the investigator must take into account the historical experiences of characters in the story. Sixth, the researcher creates a story with a beginning, a middle, and an end, including a focus on the uniqueness of individual participants in the process and outcome of the story. Finally, the resulting narrative must be plausible, understandable, and meaningful; data must support the conclusions, and the conclusions must be clearly identifiable within the narrative. As Polkinghorne (1995) noted, "The purpose of narrative analysis is not simply to produce a reproduction of observations; rather, it is to provide a dynamic framework in which the range of disconnected data elements are made to cohere in an interesting and explanatory way" (p. 20).

The narrative researcher attends to metaphors and their significance; how poetry is used in the language of participants; evidence for historic self-awareness and change in self-perceptions; themes, structure, plot, and moral to the story; action, setting, and character; ways time and chronology are used; conflicting narratives and changes in the story on retelling; and purposes of the story (e.g., to manage distress; to dramatize everyday events or, conversely, to make dramatic events appear ordinary; to teach a moral or lesson) (Manning & Cullum-Swan, 1994; Morrow, 1992; Riessman, 1993).

Erickson's Analytic Induction

According to Erickson (1986), analysis of data cannot be separated from data collection or writing. Erickson recommended that the investigator write expanded field notes and reflective notes following each foray into the field and before returning to gather additional data. Additionally, he suggested that time spent writing and reflecting should equal the time in the field; this will stimulate analytic induction, as well as reflection on extant theory and research. As part of the interplay between data collection and analysis, the investigator returns to the field with emerging theory to deliberately search for disconfirming evidence.

During analysis, the investigator immerses in the data through repeated readings and listenings, generating preliminary empirical assertions about the phenomenon of interest. An assertion is a statement of a general finding from the data about the phenomenon. Behrens and Smith (1996) noted that "it is useful to think of this process [of generating assertions] as an intuitive grasping of the entire set of data and committing to paper the answer to the question, 'What 10 (or so) things seem to be true about the phenomenon?'" (p. 980). These assertions, which "vary in scope and in level of inference" (p. 146), are first generated inductively during data collection as described above, then tested and retested through repeated forays into the data. After this phase of analysis, the researcher changes focus, adopting an attitude of skepticism in the warranting phase of analysis. The researcher searches the data for confirming evidence of each assertion, paying special attention to data collected through multiple methods. Having assembled these, the researcher looks again for any evidence that disconfirms the assertion. These are weighed against confirming data, and the assertion is accepted, deleted, or modified accordingly. The investigator not only may search for disconfirming evidence within the existing data, but may seek out discrepant cases in order to discover subtleties and complexities that might otherwise go unnoticed.

Next, the investigator searches for key linkages, or general and unifying patterns, among assertions in order to connect the various items of data. The subsequent integration of data analysis and writing is seen in the use of four elements: the analytic narrative vignette, particular description, general description, and interpretive commentary. The analytic narrative vignette is considered by Erickson (1986) to be "the foundation of an effective report of fieldwork research" (p. 149). It is a "vivid portrayal of the conduct of an event of everyday life" (p. 151) that will ultimately give the reader the experience of "being there" and provide convincingness of the investigator's arguments. As an analytic tool, it is "not simply a description; it is an analysis" (p. 151). Vignettes are tied to assertions; that is, each assertion should be accompanied by a vignette, and vignettes do not stand by themselves. Interview quotes and direct quotes from field notes accompany analytic narratives and are referred to as particular description. "Without particular description to instance and warrant one's key assertions, the reader must take the author's assertions on faith" (p. 149). General description includes synopses of patterns and support particular description. Finally, interpretive commentary helps the investigator make connections between particular and general description. Erickson illustrated the importance of integrating analysis and writing, so that even during the writing of the results and conclusions of an investigation, the investigator continues to reanalyze the data and make changes in the overall analysis.

Miles and Huberman's Three-Part Analysis

Miles and Huberman (1994) referred to the construction of an initial conceptual framework as "anticipatory data analysis." The categories generated from theories or preliminary empirical work act as "bins" that are then filled with data. In the *data-reduction phase* of analysis, the completed data record is coded, with the categories functioning as a kind of template. Thus, the data as a whole are "fractured," that is, reduced or organized into coded data. In the *data-display phase,* the researcher makes sense of the coded data by various techniques that help her or him see patterns or relationships in the coded data. For example, the researcher attempts to see how some codes seem to be related to other codes in temporal sequences or hierarchical classifications. This is accomplished through graphing and plotting the data or otherwise organizing it in displays, much as quantitative data are arranged visually in, say, a box plot or scatter plot. In the *conclusion-drawing/verification phase* of analysis, the researcher makes tentative propositional statements about the relationships of categories, testing them through triangulation across data sources and observers, examination of confirming and disconfirming evidence, study of outliers, and scrutiny by peer and participant review. The researcher also uses memos for the same purposes as grounded theorists do.

The Role of Computers in Qualitative Data Analysis

Researchers accustomed to conducting statistical analyses with the aid of computers often hold the mistaken impression that, as in quantitative research, the computer will actually do the analysis for the investigator. Although computers can be a useful tool to assist analysis, it is the researcher who does the thinking. The purpose of computer-assisted qualitative data analysis is to use various text-management functions to make the analyst's work more efficient (Tesch, 1990). In addition, Weitzman and Miles (1995) noted that computers provide the opportunity to analyze data more systematically without missing important information that could be lost through other methods. They identified six basic types of computer programs commonly used by qualitative researchers: (1) word processors, (2) text retrievers, (3) textbase managers, (4) code-and-retrieve programs, (5) code-based theory-builders, and (6) conceptual network-builders. Each of these types of programs is described briefly below.

Word processors are programs capable of writing field notes and memos, transcribing interviews, preparing files for coding and analysis, and writing reports. Most have search-and-retrieve functions that allow the investigator to cut and paste data into coded files in much the same way as one would physically cut and sort portions of text into different envelopes. In addition, some also use hypertext links, macros, and other functions that can enhance the analytic process.

Text retrievers are sophisticated, dedicated text-search programs that can find words, phrases, or other strings in one or more files. Some of these programs can also link data and perform other tasks characteristic of more advanced programs. In addition to search-and-retrieval functions, *textbase managers* provide a systematic way of "organizing, sorting, and making subsets" (Weitzman & Miles, 1995, p. 17) of text. These programs are not necessarily designed for qualitative data analysis, but their text management capabilities are extremely useful in analyzing data. Some also include hypertext, coding, and memoing functions.

Most *code-and-retrieve programs* were developed by qualitative researchers specifically for qualitative data analysis. They assist the investigator in dividing data into segments, attaching codes to segments, and retrieving all text associated with a particular code. Some have memoing capabilities as well. Programs in this category are considered aids to theory-building.

Code-based theory-builders were also primarily developed by qualitative researchers for qualitative data analysis. These programs provide code-and-retrieve functions, as well as having special additional features to support theory-building, such as helping to make connections between codes, developing higher order classifications, testing propositions, and other special functions. Some have very sophisticated search routines and are organized around complex sets of rules and logic.

Finally, *conceptual network-builders* build graphic networks, with categories arranged in graphic form and linked to other categories with arrows illustrating the specific relationships among categories. These links are based on "semantic networks" developed from the data.

Writing Qualitative Research

The purpose of the qualitative research report, whether in written or verbal form, is twofold: to report on the process and results of the particular investigation being reported and, frequently, to educate the audience about qualitative research (Polkinghorne, 1989, 1994). Even if the audience is familiar with qualitative methods, the author has a responsibility to identify her or his theoretical orientation and assumptions and to describe and justify the particular methods used (Fischer, 1999; Stiles, 1993). In addition, researchers explain how subjectivity and bias were managed.

Guba and Lincoln (1989) recommended describing the internal processes of the investigation, including changes in design and interpretation.

In qualitative research, the participants, the researcher, and the research project itself should be situated, socially, historically, and culturally (Elliott, Fischer, & Rennie, 1999; Smith, 1987; Stiles, 1993). This "situating" both contextualizes the research and makes it possible for the audience to judge how transferable the results may be to their own settings (Elliott et al., 1999).

All the steps and the rationale for one's choices should be specified, including sampling procedures (Polkinghorne, 1989). A detailed description of the type of interview format used and questions asked should also be provided (Polkinghorne, 1989; Ponterotto, 1994). Full details of the method, step by step, enable others to follow the same process. The order of research activities, including whether data were analyzed during data collection or after (Polkinghorne, 1989, 1994), should be delineated. All procedures that add to the rigor of the study (e.g., triangulation, checking transcriptions, immersion in data) should be elaborated (Elliott et al., 1999; Polkinghorne, 1989; Ponterotto, 1994). Because of confidentiality concerns, the investigator may not be able to make the data available to the "community of scholars" as recommended by Polkinghorne (1989); however, the audit trail should be available to scholars and included as an appendix in a thesis or dissertation. Finally, data analysis should be described in depth, including steps followed, data management procedures preparatory to and during analysis (e.g., transcription, transcription checks, manual or computer strategies), and how analysis proceeded during writing.

Results will represent a mix of contextual description, data from the data record, and the researcher's interpretation and analysis. The relative mix differs from approach to approach. One expects that interpretations will be firmly grounded in data (Glaser & Strauss, 1967; Stiles, 1993) through the use of supporting quotes. However, in most cases (with the exception of poststructuralist genres), the reader should not be taxed to form interpretations from an interminable catalog of direct quotations. Nor should readers be asked to trust the integrity of the investigator's analysis without strong supporting data. A balance of interpretive commentary and supporting quotes provides the most effective form of communicating results. Results (or a summary, in the concluding section or chapter) may be supported by forms of data display in addition to text: matrices, graphs, figures, charts, maps, or networks (Erickson, 1986; Miles & Huberman, 1994). Finally, "thick description" characterizes the research report. Thick description (Geertz, 1973) is not simple "observation and description, but the inscription [writing, fashioning meaning] . . . of these meanings of human action" (Schwandt, 1994, p. 123). It presents detail, context, emotion, social relationship, and the insertion of history into experience in such a way that the reader experiences "being there."

THE "GOODNESS" OF QUALITATIVE RESEARCH

In this section, we consider issues of rigor in qualitative research and how rigor or credibility is defined and approached. In furthering the question of the value of the enterprise, we also address issues of ethical relationships between researchers and participants.

Defining and Attaining Rigor

How one defines validity depends on one's research paradigm—what one assumes about the nature of reality and knowledge. In qualitative research, conventional standards of reliability and internal and external validity give way to different criteria. Lincoln and Guba (1985) argued for "parallel criteria" for qualitative research—credibility, transferability, dependability, and confirmability as counterparts to traditional criteria. However, the use of isomorphic criteria further reinforces the tendency, within a field that has traditionally been bound by conventional standards of rigor, to apply those standards inappropriately. Consequently, in this section we address standards of rigor or credibility that have emerged directly from qualitative paradigms. Eisner (1998) offered *coherence* as an appropriate standard:

> One criterion . . . is the coherence or tightness of the argument it presents. Does the story make sense? How have conclusions been supported? To what extent have multiple data sources been used to give credence to the interpretation that has been made? Are the observations congruent with the rest of the study? Are there anomalies that cannot be reconciled? Are there other credible interpretations? If so, what leads one to accept the interpretation offered? How well does the study relate to what one already knows? (p. 53)

To the coherence criterion, Eisner (1998) added the idea of structural corroboration—"confluence of multiple sources of evidence or the recurrence of instances that substantiate a conclusion" (p. 55)—and referential adequacy, or one's ability to point to specific instances in the data to support an interpretation.

Erickson (1986) expressed the view that the researcher must consider validity from the beginning of the research process. He identified three types of evidentiary inadequacy that have bearing on adequacy of amount, type, and variety of data: (1) inadequate amounts of evidence, (2) inadequate variety in kinds of evidence, and (3) faulty interpretive status of evidence. A safeguard against these inadequacies is to immerse oneself in the field. Immersion can be applied to time spent in a particular setting, length and numbers of interviews, pages of documentary evidence, and so forth. There are no simple answers as to how much time is enough. Prolonged engagement, described by Lincoln and Guba (1985), consists of spending enough time in the field to understand the culture, build trust, and become aware of distortions (of either investigator or participants) that may creep into the data. The process of immersion in the field is one of learning new information, having that information become familiar, beginning to understand that information, and finally "complexifying" one's understanding. A signal that one is sufficiently immersed in the field is that one gains no new information or insights that would add to the data or help to complexify one's analysis.

Many times qualitative researchers under the pressures of theses, dissertations, or the need to publish search for "the magic number" of interviews that will make their research credible. As Patton (1990) noted, "There are no rules for sample size in qualitative inquiry. Sample size depends on what you want to know, the purpose of the inquiry, what's at stake, what will be useful, what will have credibility, and what can be done with available time and resources" (p. 184). Lincoln and Guba (1985) recommended sampling to the point of informational redundancy, where no new information is forthcoming despite continued interviews. Hill et al. (1997) recommended a sample size of 8 to 15 participants to better understand whether findings are rare (applying to only one or two people) or more common (applying to several people); they discouraged larger samples because of the time involved in analysis and because "additional cases typically add minimal new data" (p. 532). We take the stance, however, that true redundancy is never possible due to the complexity of human experience. Even when new information per se is not forthcoming, additional data lend depth and complexity to the investigator's analysis.

A sample size less than a dozen participants may be justified if a large amount and variety of data are collected from each participant. Other factors, too, may influence the investigator to use a small sample. A single-participant (or single-dyad or single-site) case study, for example, may consist not only of interviews but additional corroborating data that enlarge the data corpus. When there are a very small number of individuals in the group of interest (e.g., women or ethnic minority presidents of the American Psychological Association), of course the total number may legitimately be quite small. Finally, when the sample is extremely homogeneous, redundancy may be achieved quite naturally with a small sample.

On the other hand, many factors warrant a much larger sample size: an extremely variable, heterogeneous sample; a broad, sweeping research question that aims at understanding very complex constructs; limited data available from each participant; and practical concerns about what will appear credible to a given audience. In addition to prolonged engagement or immersion in the phenomenon, the investigator must also exercise persistent observation (Lincoln & Guba, 1985); that is, one must pursue in depth the concepts that arise through prolonged engagement. Amount of data is not the sole concern, but whether the researcher can cast a wide net to encompass the full range of participant actions and meanings, as well as theoretical explanations for them. Although objectivity is not a goal, bounded rationality is, which for Erickson (1986) meant that the researcher records data precisely, carefully, and completely.

One must attend not only to concerns about amount of data, but to variety of data. As noted earlier, multiple data sources or triangulation will enhance the rigor of a qualitative investigation. As Berg (1995) suggested, "By combining several lines of sight, researchers obtain a better, more substantial picture of reality; a richer, more complete array of symbols and theoretical concepts; and a means of verifying many of these elements" (pp. 4–5). An interview study may be strengthened through the use of documentary evidence. The investigator should ask what data sources should be sought to fully understand the phenomenon of interest.

Finally, faulty interpretive status of data relates to the quality of the data collected. The quality of data may be affected by faulty information generated by participants because of lack of trust in the researcher or other reasons. It may also be due to inadequately designed research questions or inadequate time in the field in which the investigator caught only a portion of what would be otherwise available, as well as to the investigator's interpretive filter that can affect every aspect of the research, from design through analysis and writing.

Attending to the Personal Equation

Investigator bias and subjectivity are not viewed negatively in qualitative research. They are presumed to be a normal aspect of conducting research where the researcher is the tool of the investigation. However, the ways in which bias and subjectivity are viewed and managed are crucial. There are two types of bias that affect qualitative research.

The first type of bias is the potential for confirmatory bias common to all humans in the meaning-construction process (Mahoney, 1991). We have frequently heard beginning researchers proclaim that they are avoiding the literature on their topic so as not to "bias" themselves prior to conducting their research. However, having an explicit conceptual framework and more information can expand the scope of possibilities, enabling the investigator to frame research questions in the broadest possible manner so as not to unduly bias the conduct or results of the investigation. In the conduct of the investigation, and particularly the analysis, the researcher can take steps to challenge confirmatory bias. An active and conscientious search for disconfirming evidence, as well as discrepant or negative case analysis, challenges the researcher's confirmatory bias and increases researcher sensitivity to the meanings of incoming data (Erickson, 1986). Erickson argued that, during the assertion-warranting part of analysis, the researcher should adopt an attitude of skepticism, looking for ways to hold the work suspect. In addition, he proposed that the researcher document her or his perspective and guiding ideas at the beginning and end of the study to show how that perspective changed.

Researcher subjectivity should be framed carefully in relation to the paradigm undergirding the research. It would be inappropriate to "control" subjectivity in a study that centralized the mutual construction of relationship and meaning between investigator and participants (e.g., Heshusius, 1994; Moustakas, 1990). In such an approach, the "story" of the research process, including investigator subjectivities and changes in perspectives of participants over the course of the research, is as integral to the research report as are the results. From a more conventional research perspective, the investigator may seek credibility by arriving at agreement among members of the investigatory team. Hill et al. (1997) proposed an approach to achieving agreement among team members using a consensual approach called Consensual Qualitative Research that is compatible with a postpositivist paradigm. However, it may not necessarily be the case, as Hill et al. suggested, that the rigor of a qualitative study is threatened simply because researchers "use themselves as the sole judge to collect and code all the data" (p. 518). Depending on one's paradigm, subjectivity is managed in different ways. It is the responsible attention to, management of, and disclosure of one's subjectivity and other kinds of bias that are key to rigor in interpretivist/constructivist and postmodern paradigms. These goals can be accomplished by rigorous self-reflection, the use of peer debriefers or research teams, or both.

Participant Checks

Member- or participant-checking is a powerful tool for enhancing the rigor of a qualitative study. Checking with participants begins even during the interview process, where the interviewer continually verifies what she or he believes the interviewee is saying for accuracy and for meaning. During transcription, the researcher makes notes of follow-up questions for the interviewee based on the need to clarify and understand in more depth what the participant is saying. In addition, the analysis will raise further questions for participants. Checks can be conducted through brief follow-up phone calls or e-mails, more extended follow-up interviews, or focus groups in which the emerging theoretical framework or narrative is shared with participants for individual or group feedback. Some investigators return transcripts to participants to check for accuracy or to generate additional information. A particularly powerful form of participant-checking involves an ongoing focus group in which the investigator and participants examine and revise the emerging analytic model or narrative. In this way, participants become co-analysts of the data.

Inquiry Audit Trails

Provided that confidentiality is preserved, the investigator can enhance the credibility of a study by keeping an audit trail that is subject to review by a peer. Audit trails are of two kinds. The *complete audit trail* is comprised of all of the products of the inquiry: tapes, field notes, analytic and self-reflective journals, transcripts, memos, documents, and the emerging analytic scheme. A more *condensed audit trail* is a chronological record compiled by the investigator, preferably over the course of the investigation, that chronicles the various research activities (early conceptualization, initial interview schedule, dates of interviews, and other contacts with participants), as well as changes as the study evolves. At different points, this audit trail can contain a listing of emerging codes, different levels of analysis, and reasons for changes in the method. The audit trail is often given to an independent researcher or peer debriefer for feedback on the research conceptualization and processes. Miles and Huberman (1994) suggested helpful forms for documenting qualitative analysis that could be used within an audit trail.

Writing

A final aspect of rigor or credibility in qualitative research is evident in the writing or presentation of the results. Whereas the power of a quantitative investigation comes from sample size, significance, and numerical data, in qualitative research the power lies in the words of participants. These verbal data serve as evidence for interpretations and conclusions drawn by the researcher (Glaser & Strauss, 1967; Polkinghorne, 1994). Through analytic processes of immersion in the data, searching for confirming and disconfirming evidence, and constantly comparing the emerging analysis with the data corpus, the investigator has increased the likelihood that the results reflect participants' realities and meanings. This final step is a carefully orchestrated process of writing narrative or interpretive commentary that is liberally and accurately exemplified by quotes from participants. This provides systematic evidence that the assertions made are warranted (Erickson, 1986).

The above strategies offer possibilities for seeking credibility in qualitative research. However, it sometimes happens that novice qualitative researchers vest too much faith in procedures, a possible carryover from conventional research. The fact of conducting (or not conducting) an audit trail or triangulation does not by itself make the account more true (nor impeach it). These procedures merely increase credibility and enlarge the interpretive perspective by casting more lines of sight on the phenomenon. Kvale (1996) described the process of validation as an ongoing, discursive process of checking (adopting a critical attitude toward one's interpretation and probing for bias and poorly supported findings), questioning (seeking corroboration and consensus), and theorizing (probing the theoretical significance of the phenomenon).

A further issue about rigor is generalization—that is, inferences about the extent to which observations made in the research site have wider applicability. In conventional paradigms, where cases are equated with sampling units, generalization from case studies is considered problematic. In survey research, for example, generalizing from sample to population is warranted by the similarity of the two (the findings that are true for the sample should also be true of the population from which the sample is drawn, given sufficient sample size and a probabilistic method of selection). However, there are many other forms of generalization. Naturalistic generalization is the sense made of the account by the reader. Because of the adequacy and vividness of the portrayal and the persuasiveness of the interpretation, the reader makes associations and implicit comparisons between the situation described by the researcher and some other case in the reader's experience.

Extrapolation (Cronbach, 1982; Erickson, 1986) occurs when the reader is able to make a point-by-point comparison between the case studied and some other case, based on the concrete particulars presented, to probe the applicability of the findings. Analytic generalization (Glaser, 1978) is analogous to construct validation, in which the concrete incidents or referents of categories, processes, and themes are examined for logical connection and consistency. Researchers examine further cases or sites to see if new incidents point to similar processes or categories (Becker, 1990). Probing for analytic generalization results in bounding the theory constructed in the original site or expanding its applicability to other sites.

Ethical Considerations

Qualitative researchers are bound by the same research ethics as quantitative researchers. Issues of the worthiness of the project; boundaries of competence; informed consent; benefits, costs, and reciprocity; harm and risk; honesty and trust; privacy, confidentiality, and anonymity; intervention and advocacy; research integrity and quality; ownership of data and conclusions; the use and misuse of results; and various conflicts, dilemmas, and trade-offs have all been addressed by Miles and Huberman (1994) as important ethical concerns. Many of these concerns have evolved from the qualitative research genre but are relevant to research as a whole. In this section, we address questions that are specifically oriented to the qualitative research process.

Typically in social science research, the informed consent addresses risks and benefits to participants. However, two processes in qualitative research may impact the participant in unique ways (Eisner, 1998). First, the emerging nature of a qualitative design may guide the investigator to pursue new avenues that were not anticipated nor part of the informed consent process originally. In this case, the investigator must decide whether the new directions are substantial enough to require additional approval from the institution's human subjects review committee. The investigator must also consider the best way to obtain truly informed consent from the participant, who agreed to a protocol based on the original informed consent. Second, given the in-depth interviewing process often employed in a qualitative study, participants are apt to experience intense affect that neither investigator nor participant had predicted (Cieurzo & Keitel, 1999). The investigator may reduce this possibility by careful piloting of the interview questions, by consulting with experts about potential risks in advance, and by including in the informed consent a full range of possibilities.

A related concern is whether participants feel free to withdraw from the study (Eisner, 1998). Frequently, the investigator forms a particularly close relationship with participants due to the nature of the phenomena being investigated and by spending significant time learning about and hearing the stories of participants. Just as in the therapeutic relationship, the process of telling the intimate details of one's life often leads to an intense bond. Therefore, the process of leave-taking for either participant or investigator must be dealt with thoughtfully. Participants may be reluctant to withdraw from a study, even when it is in their best interest to do so. In addition, termination of the study may be distressing to some participants. The investigator will do well to plan leave-taking with care.

Unique concerns arise when the investigator is also a clinician. On the one hand, investigators with clinical training are at an advantage in that basic counseling skills provide the basis for excellent interviewing. However, the clinician/researcher must also be clear about the boundaries between the two roles (Morrow, 1992). Particularly if the interview process has the potential to raise strong affect in the participant, the investigator must know what kinds of questions "cross the line" into therapy, how to manage a crisis if it arises, and how the investigator's role will be explained and clarified to participants.

E-mail interviews raise unique ethical concerns (Libutti, 1999; Murray & Sixsmith, 1998). A process for gaining legitimate informed consent is essential. Because some of the usual cues are absent in the e-mail interview, the investigator must develop means for discerning whether the participant may be disclosing information with which she or he is not comfortable, if the participant is able to withdraw if uncomfortable, and if the participant is experiencing undue distress. In terms of confidentiality, participants should be informed that although e-mail gives the illusion of privacy (Libutti, 1999), it is not a confidential medium; and measures to enhance confidentiality should be explained carefully. Particularly in psychological research, there is a potential for participants to become distressed by certain topics and questions. Because some issues, such as abuse, may become distressing, the researcher must think carefully about potential harm to participants when using a medium that may not allow the researcher to provide appropriate resources and supports to participants.

These and other concerns that arise in the investigative process should be approached thoughtfully and with particular care (Eisner, 1998). Once again, because of the emergent nature of the qualitative endeavor, issues are almost certain to arise that one has not predicted (e.g., Brzezinski, 1999). Some basic perspectives on participants and the research process, therefore, should serve to undergird decisions about ethical qualitative research. Hoshmand (1989) noted that qualitative research must "commit the researcher to an egalitarian stance and a nonexploitative relationship with the human subject" (p. 14). This goal can best be accomplished by considering the welfare of the participant as an overarching principle; safeguarding participant rights, interests, and sensitivities; communicating research goals clearly to participants; protecting participant confidentiality; and making reports available to participants (Spradley, 1979).

Erickson (1986) added that research participants "need to be (a) as informed as possible of the purposes and activities of research that will occur, and of any burdens (additional work load) or risks that may be entailed for them by being studied. . . . [and] protected as much as possible from risks" (p. 141). Additionally, the researcher must be culturally competent to approach the site and participants in it with sensitivity. The qualitative researcher also has ethical obligations to the scholarly and professional community to be honest and competent and to leave the site "clean" and open to researchers who might follow (Eisner, 1998).

Ethical relations cannot be reduced to formula or regulation. In each case, researchers must ask themselves the following questions: "What does it mean for an individual to share her or his life story, particularly around painful events or risky information?" "How does the researcher give back to the individual or the community?" (Suzuki, Prendes-Lintel, Wertlieb, & Stallings, 1999). "How are power and collaboration managed in the research endeavor?" "Whose voices are represented in the presentation of the research?" "Who benefits from the research?" "How does research disrupt current abuses, inequities, and injustices?" (Fine, 1992).

PROSPECTS AND FUTURE DIRECTIONS

Counseling psychology has come a long way since the initial calls for alternate methods. Yet as the discipline sits at the brink of a broader application of qualitative inquiry, many questions present themselves for consideration. Do we, as counseling psychology researchers, prefer to hold only to postpositivist standards of rigor that have confined our inquiry in the past, or can we be open to multiple approaches to rigor and credibility that will honor multiple paradigms? How do we forge the link between quantitative and qualitative methods? Can we embrace subjectivity in some new ways, particularly given the growing focus on constructivist approaches in the field? How can qualitative traditions from other fields such as education and sociology inform our own progress? What place do participatory and action research have in the field? How are researchers investigating marginalized populations and phenomena constrained by current thinking in the field? What are the possibilities for training in and publication of qualitative research in counseling psychology?

The prospects for qualitative research in counseling psychology depend, we believe, on whether the field can embrace multiple paradigms and standards of rigor. One of the limitations at the present time is a tendency to view qualitative research as merely a variation of methodology grafted onto the prevailing paradigm. This paradigm hegemony (Hoshmand, 1994; Rennie, 1999) is exposed most clearly when editors and other critics impose standards of rigor that are inappropriate for interpretivist and critical paradigms. Stories abound of qualitative scholars having articles rejected primarily based on the size of their samples or lack of control group. Instead, journal editors and editorial boards, in consultation with a variety of qualitative consultants, should develop standards for judging qualitative research.

In addition to embracing multiple paradigms within qualitative research, counseling psychology researchers can explore the use of multiple methods (qualitative-quantitative). Ponterotto and Grieger (1999) likened the development of a mixed-methods identity to learning to become bicultural, noting that the different worldviews underlying each methodological approach bring different perspectives to the research endeavor, each complementing the other. Indeed, becoming "bimethodological" may address some of the concerns noted earlier regarding the importance of qualitative methods for multicultural research while dealing with institutional pressures to conduct conventional research for the sake of professional credibility. However, as Behrens and Smith (1996) noted, "It is difficult to become an expert in a single paradigm. Working functionally in two is far more difficult" (p. 948).

It is not uncommon for conventionally trained researchers to misunderstand the underlying worldview of qualitative research and to "relegate qualitative approaches to the discovery phase of a study, as a means to specify a hypothesis or refine a treatment" (Behrens & Smith, 1996, p. 948). However, Kvale (1983) noted the complementarity of qualitative and quantitative methods, with no particular sequence of application. In addition, open-ended questions at the end of a survey do not alone constitute qualitative research, as the responses typically do not constitute sufficient data for immersion, and they are rarely analyzed with the rigor required of a qualitative study. Such research cannot be considered qualitative without attention to the social worlds of participants, the meanings they make of their experiences, and so on. Although "qualitative add-ons" (Ponterotto & Grieger, 1999) may "colorize" a quantitative study and, indeed, give deeper meaning to the responses of participants, they do not alone make that study multimethod. The merging of qualitative and quantitative methods can indeed paint a broader picture of the phenomenon of interest. The uses of mixed methods vary, of course, across paradigms, with the postpositivist using them for convergence, while interpretivists use multiple methods to look at all aspects of the problem. In neither paradigm is one form of data privileged over the other.

Although a few qualitative investigators in counseling psychology (e.g., Friedlander, Heatherington, Johnson, & Skowron, 1994; Morrow & Smith, 1995; Rennie, 1994a; Thompson & Jenal, 1994) have emphasized, rather than controlled, subjectivity, the predominance of published research either ignores or attempts to minimize the person of the researcher. Rennie's concept of "horizons of understanding" to frame researcher subjectivity is a step toward using subjectivity in an affirmative manner.

With regard to training and publishing in the qualitative arena, Rennie (1994b) offered what he called "sobering considerations" (p. 242). First, learning to do good qualitative research can be daunting, and the majority of counseling psychology programs do not offer qualitative research training. Rennie's second concern is the difficulty publishing qualitative research. Although both major counseling psychology journals (*Journal of Counseling Psychology* and *The Counseling Psychologist*) accept qualitative research and methodological articles, policies can still change under changing editorship; and the majority of avenues for publication remain resistant to qualitative research. If these two broad challenges—appropriate editorial criteria and adequate training— can be met, qualitative research presents significant opportunities for counseling psychology and vice versa.

Qualitative research provides a distinctively human method of inquiry to investigate human behavior and meaning. In an increasingly complex world, qualitative approaches can focus on multiple meaning-perspectives and contextual influences in ways that traditional research cannot or will not do. Psychological research is easily stripped of context because of the predominant intrapsychic lens through which it is viewed. Fortunately, systemic, constructivist, and sociopolitical perspectives provide a rationale for considering the individual in context. It is simply the case that in psychology, even qualitative research is easily decontextualized, thereby violating one of the basic historic premises of the qualitative endeavor, that of examining the experiences and meanings of individuals within social life (Marecek, Fine, & Kidder, 1997).

Among the diverse group of scholars conducting qualitative research, only a sprinkling are psychologists (Tolman & Brydon-Miller, 1997). Therefore, concern regarding greater context-sensitive research is crucial in counseling psychology. The lives of participants, as well as the research endeavor itself, are imbedded in a historico-sociopolitical context; thus, context-sensitive qualitative research will seek to highlight history, politics, and the social milieu of the participants and phenomena of interest, as well as the researcher and research activities (Marecek et al., 1997). The ways that power and voice are enacted in the research relationship will affect the data that are gathered and the ultimate results of a study. Research that is context-sensitive will address these issues. Context-sensitive research will also examine the social influences and interactions between client and therapist in counseling process research. For example, in addition to generic issues of power and authority that rest in the therapist by virtue of her or his role, what additional variables such as race/ethnicity/culture, class, gender, and other differences further affect the counseling dyad? Finally, the social-historical context of participants' lives and the phenomenon under investigation is important to provide a framework for participant constructions of the topic of interest. For example, examining the institutional context of people with serious mental illness can help to frame the cognitions, affect, and behavior of institutionalized individuals (Davidson, Stayner, Lambert, Smith, & Sledge, 1997).

Increasingly, counseling psychology researchers are addressing phenomena and populations affected by a sociopolitical overlay. In investigations of the experiences of people of color, women, lesbian/gay/bisexual people, and other marginalized populations, as well as phenomena of abuse, oppression, and systemic dynamics, privilege and power are crucial issues to address if one is to avoid context-stripping. Yet, by virtue of the controversial nature of many of these issues, some scholars feel constrained to the use of either quantitative or conventionally articulated qualitative paradigms. This experience is particularly unfortunate as critical, feminist, ethnic, and other ideological paradigms have great potential to contextualize participant experiences and uncover their meanings. In addition, participatory and action-oriented strategies can contribute to changing oppressive and marginalizing conditions.

In times of accountability demands, contemporary social and economic pressures in the practice arena make it increasingly important to identify empirically supported counseling and psychotherapy approaches and techniques. Qualitative research offers the opportunity to add new depth to investigations of both therapy process and outcome by adding the "meaning" questions to the "measurement" questions. Outcome research, which is typically "aimed to tell us whether psychotherapy worked, whether clients or patients got better" (Orlinsky, Grawe, & Parks, 1994, p. 273), may be expanded to answer such questions as what clients' experiences of improvement were and to uncover the multidimensional results (e.g., which things are better, which are worse) of psychotherapy. Process research, "aimed to 'group, classify, and correlate' measures delineating the events of treatment" (Orlinsky et al., 1994, p. 273), may be extended to investigate client and therapist constructions of therapy events. Qualitative investigations open up the black box of experimental treatments and help to explain not only *whether* therapy worked but *how* it worked (Maxwell, 1996). Qualitative approaches to counseling process research have been conducted by Elliott et al. (1994); Elliott and Shapiro (1992); Friedlander et al. (1994); Rennie (1994a); Rhodes, Hill, Thompson, and Elliot (1994); Thompson and Jenal (1994); and others.

Qualitative research bridges science and practice. The similarities between human science/ qualitative research and counseling practice are many (Rennie, 1994b). Counseling psychology researchers and practitioners are both interested in subjectivities and the meanings people make of their lives and experiences (Rennie, 1994b). Second, both counseling practice and qualitative research emphasize mutuality and empowerment of the client or participant (Rennie, 1994b). In addition, both emphasize the whole person in context (Rennie, 1994b). As Elliott (1983) noted, qualitative methods may contribute to narrowing "the practitioner-researcher gap" by "adopting new, more clinically relevant research methods and . . . by engaging in activities to increase communication and collaboration with clinicians" (p. 47).

A number of additional characteristics common to both qualitative inquiry and counseling practice are worth noting. First, reflexivity is a central activity of both the qualitative investigator and the clinician (Hoshmand, 1994; Howard, 1996). In addition, narrative and storytelling are integrative activities for both qualitative research and the counseling context. Finally, the growth of constructivist approaches in counseling psychology creates the necessity of constructing research methods that can adequately investigate human meaning-making.

It is almost a truism that practitioners are frequently unfamiliar with the research on counseling and psychotherapy; however, conventional research methods can tend to be intellectually sterile, irrelevant to practice, and not particularly informative to the clinician who is years away from her or his last statistics or research methods course. Qualitative research, however, has the potential to attract the clinician because of the accessibility and similarity to practice of their underlying premises (client/participant constructions are central), method (interview), and the communication of results (often narrative, or at least supported with participants' words). As an example, the majority of responses received concerning the Morrow and Smith (1995) article on survival and coping of sexual abuse survivors came from practitioners who indicated the importance of the findings to themselves and their clients; this science-practice link would be a worthy topic for future investigation. In addition, qualitative studies may stimulate the curiosity of clinicians about their own work, with the potential to encourage them to be involved, directly or indirectly, in the research endeavor. Collaboration between the academy and practice could particularly be enhanced by participatory approaches.

Finally, the integration of science and practice may be best captured by Lather's (1991) definition of *praxis*, the integration of theory and action, science and practice, "theory both relevant to the world and nurtured by actions in it" (p. 12). In praxis lies the potential to fully embrace a synthesis of science and practice by engaging in context-imbedded, personally and socially relevant research that centralizes the meanings of participants and engages them in an empowering inquiry process with the researcher. Many of the tenets of qualitative inquiry challenge counseling psychologists to go beyond a scientist-practitioner model consisting of science *plus* practice and to investigate the possibilities of a true synthesis.

REFERENCES

Adler, P.A., & Adler, P. (1987). *Membership roles in field research.* Newbury Park, CA: Sage.

Banister, P., Burman, E., Parker, I., Taylor, M., & Tindall, C. (1994). *Qualitative methods in psychology: A research guide.* Buckingham: Open University Press.

Becker, H.S. (1990). Generalizing the results of qualitative inquiry. In E.W. Eisner & A. Peshkin (Eds.), *Qualitative inquiry in education: The continuing debate.* New York: Teachers College Press.

Behrens, J.T., & Smith, M.L. (1996). Data and data analysis. In D.C. Berliner & R.C. Calfee (Eds.), *Handbook of educational psychology* (pp. 945–989). New York: Simon & Schuster.

Berg, B.L. (1995). *Qualitative research methods for the social sciences* (2nd ed.). Boston: Allyn & Bacon.

Blumer, H. (1969). *Symbolic interactionism: Perspective and method.* Englewood Cliffs, NJ: Prentice-Hall.

Borgen, F.H. (1992). Expanding scientific paradigms in counseling psychology. In S.D. Brown & R.W. Lent (Eds.), *Handbook of counseling psychology* (2nd ed., pp. 111–139). New York: Wiley.

Brzezinski, L.G. (1999). *Dealing with disparity: Identity development of gay and bisexual men raised in the LDS church.* Unpublished doctoral dissertation, University of Utah, Salt Lake City.

Campbell, D.T. (1975). "Degrees of freedom" and the case study. *Comparative Political Studies, 3,* 178–193.

Carr, W., & Kemmis, S. (1986). *Becoming critical: Education, knowledge, and action research.* London: Falmer.

Chase, S.E. (1995). Taking narrative seriously: Consequences for method and theory in interview studies. In R. Josselson & A. Lieblich (Eds.), *Interpreting experience: The narrative study of lives* (pp. 1–26). Thousand Oaks, CA: Sage.

Cieurzo, C., & Keitel, M.A. (1999). Ethics in qualitative research. In M. Kopala & L. Suzuki (Eds.), *Using qualitative methods in psychology* (pp. 63–75). Thousand Oaks, CA: Sage.

Cook, T., & Campbell, D.T. (1979). *Quasi-experimentation: Design and analysis issues for field settings.* Chicago: Rand-McNally.

Cooper, J.E., & Heck, R.H. (1995). Using narrative in the study of school administration. *International Journal of Qualitative Studies in Education, 8,* 195–210.

Creswell, J.W. (1998). *Qualitative inquiry and research design: Choosing among five traditions.* Thousand Oaks, CA: Sage.

Cronbach, L.J. (1982). *Designing evaluations of educational and social programs.* San Francisco: Jossey-Bass.

Davidson, L., Stayner, D.A., Lambert, S., Smith, P., & Sledge, W.H. (1997). Phenomenological and participatory research on schizophrenia: Recovering the person in theory and practice. *Journal of Social Issues, 53,* 767–784.

Denzin, N.K. (1978). *The research act: A theoretical introduction to sociological methods* (2nd ed.). New York: McGraw-Hill.

Denzin, N.K., & Lincoln, Y.S. (1994). Introduction: Entering the field of qualitative research. In N.K. Denzin & Y.S. Lincoln (Eds.), *Handbook of qualitative research* (pp. 1–17). Thousand Oaks, CA: Sage.

Dilthey, W. (1977). *Descriptive psychology and historical understanding* (R.M. Zaner & K.L. Heiges, Trans.). The Hague: Nijhoff.

Dollard, J. (1935). *Criteria for the life history.* New Haven, CT: Yale University Press.

Eisner, E.W. (1998). *The enlightened eye: Qualitative inquiry and the enhancement of educational practice.* Upper Saddle River, NJ: Merrill/Prentice-Hall.

Elliott, R. (1983). Fitting process research to the practicing psychotherapist. *Psychotherapy: Theory, Research and Practice, 20,* 47–55.

Elliott, R., Fischer, C., & Rennie, D. (1999). Evolving guidelines for publication of qualitative research studies. *British Journal of Clinical Psychology, 38.*

Elliott, R., & Shapiro, D.A. (1992). Client and therapist as analysts of significant events. In S.G. Toukmanian & D.L. Rennie (Eds.), *Psychotherapy process research: Paradigmatic and narrative approaches,* (pp. 163–186). Newbury Park, CA: Sage.

Elliott, R., Shapiro, D.A., Firth-Cozens, J., Stiles, W.B., Hardy, G.E., Llewelyn, S.P., & Margison, F.R. (1994). Comprehensive process analysis of insight events in cognitive-behavioral and psychodynamic-interpersonal psychotherapies. *Journal of Counseling Psychology, 41,* 449–463.

Emerson, R.M., Fretz, R.I., & Shaw, L.L. (1995). *Writing ethnographic fieldnotes.* Chicago: University of Chicago Press.

Erickson, F. (1986). Qualitative methods in research on teaching. In M. Wittrock (Ed.), *Handbook of research on teaching* (3rd ed., pp. 119–161). New York: Macmillan.

Fine, M. (1992). *Disruptive voices: The possibilities of feminist research.* Ann Arbor: University of Michigan Press.

Fischer, C.T. (1999). Designing qualitative research reports for publication. In M. Kopala & L. Suzuki (Eds.), *Using qualitative methods in psychology* (pp. 105–119). Thousand Oaks, CA: Sage.

Flax, J. (1993). *Disputed subjects: Essays on psychoanalysis, politics and philosophy.* New York: Routledge & Kegan Paul.

Friedlander, M.L., Heatherington, L., Johnson, B., & Skowron, E.A. (1994). Sustaining engagement: A change event in family therapy. *Journal of Counseling Psychology, 41,* 438–448.

Gale, J. (1996). Conversation analysis: Studying the construction of therapeutic realities. In D.H. Sprenkle & S.H. Moon (Eds.), *Research methods in family therapy* (pp. 107–124). New York: Guilford Press.

Gee, J.P., Michaels, S., & O'Connor, M.C. (1992). Discourse analysis. In M.D. LeCompte, W.L. Millroy, & J. Preissle (Eds.), *The handbook of qualitative research in education* (pp. 227–291). San Diego, CA: Academic Press.

Geertz, C. (1973). Thick description: Toward an interpretive theory of culture. In C. Geertz (Ed.), *The interpretation of cultures: Selected essays* (pp. 3–32). New York: Basic Books.

Gelso, C.J. (1979). Research in counseling: Methodological and professional issues. *The Counseling Psychologist, 8,* 7–36.

Gelso, C.J. (Ed.). (1984). Philosophy of science and counseling research [Special section]. *Journal of Counseling Psychology, 31,* 415–476.

Gergen, K.J., & Gergen, M.M. (1991). Toward reflexive methodologies. In F. Steier (Ed.), *Research and reflexivity.* Newbury Park, CA: Sage.

Glaser, B.G. (1978). *Theoretical sensitivity.* Mill Valley, CA: Sociology Press.

Glaser, B.G., & Strauss, A.L. (1967). *The discovery of grounded theory: Strategies for qualitative research.* New York: Aldine.

Goldman, L. (1976). A revolution in counseling research. *Journal of Counseling Psychology, 23,* 543–552.

Graue, M.E., & Walsh, D.J. (1998). *Studying children in context.* Newbury Park, CA: Sage.

Guba, E.G. (Ed.). (1990). *The paradigm dialog.* Newbury Park, CA: Sage.

Guba, E.G., & Lincoln, Y.S. (1989). *Fourth generation evaluation.* Newbury Park, CA: Sage.

Guba, E.G., & Lincoln, Y.S. (1994). Competing paradigms in qualitative research. In N.K. Denzin & Y.S. Lincoln (Eds.), *Handbook of qualitative research* (pp. 105–117). Thousand Oaks, CA: Sage.

Hamilton, D. (1994). Traditions, preferences, and postures in applied qualitative research. In N.K. Denzin & Y.S. Lincoln (Eds.), *Handbook of Qualitative Research* (pp. 60–69). Thousand Oaks, CA: Sage.

Heritage, J. (1984). *Garfinkel and ethnomethodology.* Cambridge, England: Polity Press.

Heshusius, L. (1994). Freeing ourselves from objectivity: Managing subjectivity or turning toward a participatory mode of consciousness? *Educational Researcher, 23,* 15–22.

Hill, C.E., & Gronsky, B.R. (1984). Research: Why and how? In J.M. Whitely, N. Kagan, I.W. Harmon, B.R. Fretz, & F. Tanney (Eds.), *The coming decade in counseling psychology.* Schenectady, New York: Character Research.

Hill, C.E., Thompson, B.J., & Williams, E.N. (1997). A guide to conducting consensual qualitative research. *The Counseling Psychologist, 25,* 517–572.

Hoshmand, L.T. (1989). Alternate research paradigms: A review and teaching proposal. Major contribution in *The Counseling Psychologist, 17,* 3–79.

Hoshmand, L.T. (1994). *Orientation to inquiry in a reflective professional psychology.* Albany, New York: State University of New York Press.

Howard, G.S. (1983). Toward methodological pluralism. *Journal of Counseling Psychology, 30,* 19–21.

Howard, G.S. (1989). *A tale of two stories: Excursions into a narrative approach to psychology.* Notre Dame, IN: Academic Press.

Howard, G.S. (1996). *Understanding human nature: An owner's manual.* Notre Dame, IN: Academic Press.

Kazdin, A.E. (1992). *Methodological issues and strategies in clinical research.* Washington, DC: American Psychological Association.

Kincheloe, J.L., & McLaren, P.L. (1994). Rethinking critical theory and qualitative research. In N.K. Denzin & Y.S. Lincoln (Eds.), *Handbook of qualitative research* (pp. 138–157). Thousand Oaks, CA: Sage.

Kuhn, T.S. (1970). *The structure of scientific revolutions.* Chicago: University of Chicago Press.

Kvale, S. (1983). The quantification of knowledge in education: On resistance toward qualitative evaluation and research. In B. Bain (Ed.), *The sociogenesis of language and human conduct* (pp. 433–447). New York: Plenum Press.

Kvale, S. (1996). *InterViews: An introduction to qualitative research interviewing.* Thousand Oaks, CA: Sage.

Labov, W., & Fanshel, D. (1977). *Therapeutic discourse: Psychotherapy as conversation.* Orlando, FL: Academic Press.

Lather, P. (1991). *Getting smart: Feminist research and pedagogy with/in the postmodern.* New York: Routledge & Kegan Paul.

Libutti, P.O. (1999). The internet and qualitative research: Opportunities and constraints on analysis of cyberspace discourse. In M. Kopala & L. Suzuki (Eds.), *Using qualitative methods in psychology* (pp. 77–88). Thousand Oaks, CA: Sage.

Lincoln, Y.S., & Denzin, N.K. (1994). The fifth moment. In N.K. Denzin & Y.S. Lincoln (Eds.), *Handbook of qualitative research* (pp. 575–586). Thousand Oaks, CA: Sage.

Lincoln, Y.S., & Guba, E.G. (1985). *Naturalistic inquiry.* Beverly Hills, CA: Sage.

Mahoney, M.J. (1991). *Human change processes.* New York: Basic Books.

Manning, P.K., & Cullum-Swan, B. (1994). Narrative, content, and semiotic analysis. In N.K. Denzin & Y.S. Lincoln (Eds.), *Handbook of qualitative research* (pp. 463–477). Thousand Oaks, CA: Sage.

Marecek, J., Fine, M., & Kidder, L. (1997). Working between worlds: Qualitative methods and social psychology. *Journal of Social Issues, 53,* 631–644.

Mathison, S. (1988). Why triangulate? *Educational Researcher, 17*(2), 13–17.

Maxwell, J.A. (1996). *Qualitative research design: An interactive approach.* Thousand Oaks, CA: Sage.

McNamee, S., & Gergen, K.J. (1992). *Therapy as social construction.* London: Sage.

Merton, R.K. (1967). *On theoretical sociology.* New York: Free Press.

Miles, M.B., & Huberman, A.M. (1994). *A expanded sourcebook: Qualitative data analysis* (2nd ed.). Thousand Oaks, CA: Sage.

Mishler, E.G. (1986). *Research interviewing: Context and narrative.* Cambridge, MA: Harvard University Press.

Morrow, S.L. (1992). *Voices: Constructions of survival and coping by women survivors of child sexual abuse.* Unpublished doctoral dissertation, Arizona State University, Tempe.

Morrow, S.L., & Smith, M.L. (1995). Constructions of survival and coping by women who have survived childhood sexual abuse. *Journal of Counseling Psychology, 42,* 24–33.

Moustakas, C. (1990). *Heuristic research: Design, methodology, and applications.* Newbury Park, CA: Sage.

Murray, C.D., & Sixsmith, J. (1998). E-mail: A qualitative research medium for interviewing? *International Journal of Social Research Methodology Theory and Practice, 1,* 103–121.

Neimeyer, G., & Resnikoff, A. (1982). Qualitative strategies in counseling research. *The Counseling Psychologist, 10*(4), 75–85.

Olesin, V. (1994). Feminisms and models of qualitative research. In N.K. Denzin & Y.S. Lincoln (Eds.), *Handbook of qualitative research* (pp. 158–174). Thousand Oaks, CA: Sage.

O'Neill, J., Small, B.B., & Strachan, J. (1999). The use of focus groups within a participatory action research environment. In M. Kopala & L. Suzuki (Eds.), *Using qualitative methods in psychology* (pp. 199–209). Thousand Oaks, CA: Sage.

Orlinsky, D.E., Grawe, K., & Parks, B. (1994). In A.E. Bergin & S.L. Garfield (Eds.), *Handbook of psychotherapy and behavior change* (pp. 270–376). New York: Wiley.

Patton, M.Q. (1990). *Qualitative evaluation and research methods* (2nd ed.). Newbury Park, CA: Sage.

Peshkin, A. (1988). In search of subjectivity—One's own. *Educational Researcher, 17*(7), 17–22.

Phillips, D.C. (1992). *The social scientist's bestiary: A guide to fabled threats to, and defenses of, naturalistic social science.* New York: Pergamon Press.

Phillips, D.C. (1996). Philosophical perspectives. In D.C. Berliner & R.C. Calfee (Eds.), *Handbook of educational psychology.* Old Tappan, NJ: Macmillan.

Polkinghorne, D.E. (1984). Further extensions of methodological diversity for counseling psychology. *Journal of Counseling Psychology, 31,* 416–429.

Polkinghorne, D.E. (1989). Communication of results: The qualitative research report. *Methods, 3,* 63–85.

Polkinghorne, D.E. (1991a). Qualitative procedures for counseling research. In C.E. Watkins & L.J. Scheider (Eds.), *Research in counseling* (pp. 163–204). Hillsdale, NJ: Erlbaum.

Polkinghorne, D.E. (1991b). Two conflicting calls for methodological reform. *The Counseling Psychologist, 19*(1), 103–114.

Polkinghorne, D.E. (1994). Reaction to special section on qualitative research in counseling process and outcome. *Journal of Counseling Psychology, 41,* 510–512.

Polkinghorne, D.E. (1995). Narrative configuration in qualitative analysis. *International Journal of Qualitative Studies in Education, 8,* 5–23.

Ponterotto, J.G. (1994, August). *The editorial review of qualitative research in counseling psychology: Reflections and some recommendations.* Paper presented at the annual meeting of the American Psychological Association, Los Angeles.

Ponterotto, J.G., & Grieger, I. (1999). Merging qualitative and quantitative perspectives in a research identity. In M. Kopala & L. Suzuki (Eds.), *Using qualitative methods in psychology* (pp. 49–62). Thousand Oaks, CA: Sage.

Potter, J., & Wetherell, M. (1987). *Discourse and social psychology: Beyond attitudes and behavior.* London: Sage.

Rennie, D.L. (1994a). Clients' deference in therapy. *Journal of Counseling Psychology, 41,* 427–437.

Rennie, D.L. (1994b). Human science and counselling psychology: Closing the gap between research and practice. *Counselling Psychology Quarterly, 7,* 235–250.

Rennie, D.L. (1999). Qualitative research: A matter of hermeneutics and the sociology of knowledge. In M. Kopala & L. Suzuki (Eds.), *Using qualitative methods in psychology* (pp. 3–13). Thousand Oaks, CA: Sage.

Rhodes, R.H., Hill, C.E., Thompson, B.J., & Elliott, R. (1994). Client retrospective recall of resolved and unresolved misunderstanding events. *Journal of Counseling Psychology, 41,* 473–483.

Riessman, C.K. (1993). *Narrative analysis.* Newbury Park, CA: Sage.

Rubin, H.J., & Rubin, I.S. (1995). *Qualitative interviewing: The art of hearing data.* Thousand Oaks, CA: Sage.

Sacks, H., Schegloff, E.A., & Jefferson, G. (1974). A simplest systematics for the organization of turn-taking for conversation. *Language, 50,* 696–735.

Scheurich, J.J., & Young, M.D. (1997). Coloring epistemologies: Are our research epistemologies racially biased? *Educational Researcher, 26,* 4–16.

Schwandt, T.A. (1994). Constructivist, interpretivist approaches to human inquiry. In N.K. Denzin & Y.S. Lincoln (Eds.), *Handbook of qualitative research* (pp. 118–137). Thousand Oaks, CA: Sage.

Smith, M.L. (1987). Publishing qualitative research. *American Educational Research Journal, 24,* 173–183.

Smith, M.L. (1997). Mixing and matching: Methods and models. *New Directions for Evaluation, 74,* 73–85.

Spradley, J.P. (1979). *The ethnographic interview.* New York: Holt, Rinehart and Winston.

Spradley, J.P. (1980). *Participant observation.* Fort Worth, TX: Harcourt Brace.

Stake, R.E. (1994). Case studies. In N.K. Denzin & Y.S. Lincoln (Eds.), *Handbook of qualitative research* (pp. 236–247). Thousand Oaks, CA: Sage.

Stanfield, J.H., II. (1994). Ethnic modeling in qualitative research. In N.K. Denzin & Y.S. Lincoln (Eds.), *Handbook of qualitative research* (pp. 175–188). Thousand Oaks, CA: Sage.

Stiles, W.B. (1993). Quality control in qualitative research. *Clinical Psychology Review, 13,* 593–618.

Strauss, A.L. (1987). *Qualitative analysis for social scientists.* Cambridge, England: Cambridge University Press.

Strauss, A.L., & Corbin, J. (1990). *Basics of qualitative research: Grounded theory procedures and techniques.* Newbury Park, CA: Sage.

Suzuki, L., Prendes-Lintel, M., Wertlieb, L., & Stallings, A. (1999). Exploring multicultural issues using qualitative methods. In M. Kopala & L. Suzuki (Eds.), *Using qualitative methods in psychology* (pp. 123–133). Thousand Oaks, CA: Sage.

Tesch, R. (1990). *Qualitative research: Analysis types and software tools.* New York: Falmer.

Thompson, C.E., & Jenal, S.T. (1994). Interracial and intraracial quasi-counseling interactions when counselors avoid discussing race. *Journal of Counseling Psychology, 41,* 484–491.

Tolman, D.L., & Brydon-Miller, M. (1997). Transforming psychology: Interpretive and participatory research methods. *Journal of Social Issues, 53,* 597–603.

Weitzman, E.A., & Miles, M.B. (1995). *Computer programs for qualitative data analysis: A software sourcebook.* Thousand Oaks, CA: Sage.

Whyte, W.F. (1991). *Participatory action research.* Newbury Park, CA: Sage.

Yin, R.K. (1989). *Case study research: Design and method.* Newbury Park, CA: Sage.

PART II

Career, Educational, and Psychological Development

CHAPTER 8

Advances in Vocational Psychology Theory and Research

JANE L. SWANSON
PAUL A. GORE, JR.

The emergence of vocational psychology as a field of study occurred in response to pressing social concerns early in the twentieth century: children's welfare and the resultant labor laws, the industrial revolution, population shifts from rural to urban areas, large-scale immigration, and preparing youth for labor force participation. Likewise, changing economic and social conditions fueled evolution of the field of vocational psychology throughout the remainder of this century. Vocational psychologists were, by definition, applied psychologists. An implication is that practice often preceded theory, as scholars and practitioners addressed real-world concerns of individuals, such as youth entering the workforce, returning veterans, or unemployed adults during economic depressions or recessions.

As we enter the new millenium, we are confronted by new challenges. The very nature of the workforce is changing—increasing diversity in terms of race/ethnicity, sex, and age, temporary versus permanent workers, and part-time versus full-time workers. Rapid technological changes make workers' skills obsolete. Moreover, global economic and market factors influence the nature of competition and job opportunities.

Few vocational psychologists would question the significant impact of Parsons's (1909/1989) work; we are now poised to make equally significant contributions to the twenty-first century. To retain a vital role, though, we need to address these concerns in a fashion worthy of our predecessors—that is, in a way that accounts for the complexity of human experience, across the variety of intersecting roles throughout the life span, and with a balance of theoretical insight and pragmatic solutions.

Our goal is to review theory and research regarding vocational psychology, keeping in mind the connections between our past and our future. We address two interconnected bodies of literature. First, we focus on established and emergent theories of career development and vocational behavior, emphasizing new theoretical formulations as well as recent empirical study. Second, we summarize theoretical and empirical literature regarding vocational interests. We decided to include the latter section based on the volume of work that has been conducted since the last major review of vocational interests in the first edition of the *Handbook* (Hansen, 1984). These two bodies of literature represent the scholarly traditions of vocational psychology: Theories of career development were proffered in an attempt to explain observed behavior regarding vocational choice and adjustment over the life span, and the sustained focus on vocational interests exemplifies the atheoretical, empirically driven origins of vocational psychology.

MAJOR THEORETICAL PERSPECTIVES

For many years, vocational psychology has been dominated by several enduring theoretical approaches. Hackett, Lent, and Greenhaus (1991) observed that the theoretical traditions within vocational psychology could be classified as trait-factor, developmental, or social learning/social cognitive. Most of the established theories have received considerable attention from researchers, including efforts at theoretical reformulation (e.g., Super, Savickas, & Super, 1996). Additionally, efforts are underway to explore possible points of convergence among career theories and to more clearly explicate the relationship between career theory and practice. In this section, we review and discuss recent theoretical advances and research on career theory, focusing specifically on theoretical and empirical developments that have occurred since the publication of the second edition of the *Handbook of Counseling Psychology* (Brown & Lent, 1992).

We chose to exclude theories that have received little recent empirical attention. For example, Krumboltz's social learning theory of career decision making continues to suffer from the same lack of empirical attention that was noted in the last edition of the *Handbook* (Hackett & Lent, 1992). On the other hand, Krumboltz has taken seriously the challenge of developing a theory of career counseling, and therefore of melding career theory with career practice. The learning theory of career counseling, developed from his theory of career development, is discussed in the chapter by Brown and Ryan in the current volume.

Holland's Theory

John Holland's theory continues to enjoy empirical attention as it celebrates its fortieth anniversary (Holland, 1959). Holland's person-environment typology and theory of career choice clearly is the most widely studied career theory in history. Moreover, the concepts that derive from this theory are integral to the vocabulary, tools, and processes of career counseling. Study of Holland's hypotheses shows no signs of diminishing, and the publication of a sixth major theoretical statement (Holland, 1997) attests both to the theory's and its author's vitality. Briefly, Holland suggests that (1) persons and environments can be categorized according to six types (realistic, investigative, artistic, social, enterprising, and conventional; RIASEC); (2) persons tend to seek environments that will allow them to implement the characteristics of their work personality; and (3) behavior is a product of the interaction between personality types and environments. Supplementing these basic notions are hypotheses regarding consistency, differentiation, identity, congruence, and calculus. The consistency, differentiation, and identity hypotheses outline the relationships between the clarity of person and environment definitions and important career outcomes, such as educational and vocational choice, stability, and achievement. Congruence, or the degree of fit between person and environment, is also hypothesized to predict similar career outcomes. Finally, Holland's calculus hypothesis describes the relationships among the six model person/environment types—relationships that are arranged according to a hexagonal structure.

Most empirical tests of Holland's theory during the last decade have focused on the calculus and congruence hypotheses and cross-cultural applications of Holland's theory. The empirical studies related to Holland's notion of calculus, and most of the cross-cultural work, has taken place in the context of interest measurement, and so these topics are covered in a later section. This section focuses on recent investigations of the congruence hypothesis and other direct tests of Holland's theory.

Empirical Support

Perhaps no other aspect of Holland's theory has generated as much empirical data and controversy as has Holland's congruence hypothesis. The crux of the controversy, often traced back to a review by Spokane (1985), surrounds the predictive validity of congruence. In his review, Spokane noted that correlations between congruence and predicted academic and career outcomes rarely exceeded .25. The evidence that congruence predicts important academic and career outcomes, even at this level, is still somewhat equivocal. Some investigators have reported significant relationships between congruence and outcomes. Sutherland, Fogarty, and Pithers (1995), for example, reported correlations between various congruence measures and occupational stress (rs ranging from .11 to .27) and personal strain (rs ranging from .04 to .30). Similarly, Oleski and Subich (1996) found significant relationships between congruence and current job satisfaction ($r = .33$) in a sample of career changers. In contrast, other authors failed to find significant relationships or reported inconsistent relationships between congruence measures and work satisfaction among employed adults. For example, Upperman and Church (1995) reported correlations ranging from .06 to .12 between congruence and job satisfaction in a sample of enlisted military men. Similarly, Young, Tokar, and Subich (1998) reported relationships between 11 different congruence measures and 2 measures of job satisfaction that did not exceed .09.

In a review of 41 congruence studies, Assouline and Meir (1987) reported average effect size estimates between congruence and achievement ($r = .06$), stability ($r = .15$), and satisfaction ($r = .21$). A more recent meta-analysis echoed those findings (Tranberg, Slane, & Ekeberg, 1993), reporting a mean correlation between congruence and satisfaction of .17. These authors also identified a number of variables that appear to moderate the relationship between congruence and satisfaction, including the type of satisfaction measured, quality of the empirical study, and type of congruence index used. Moderation of the congruence-satisfaction relationship continues to receive empirical attention (Carson & Mowsesian, 1993; Richards, 1993; Tokar & Subich, 1997; Young et al., 1998).

That the type of congruence index used moderates the relationship between congruence and criterion variables is not surprising given that the original congruence index (Holland, 1963) has been supplemented by a host of congruence measures over the last four decades (for reviews see Brown & Gore, 1994, and Camp & Chartrand, 1992). These indices range from the computationally simple to the mathematically complex and incorporate different elements of Holland's original theory.

In an interesting series of studies, several authors have examined the adequacy of congruence measurement. Camp and Chartrand (1992) used 13 different indices to calculate congruence between career interests and several academic and career variables. Consistent with many previous findings, they reported small to moderate relationships between congruence and outcome variables (rs ranging from $-.09$ to .44). Their results suggest that the relationship between congruence and academic and career outcomes is moderated by the type of index used. More interesting, perhaps, was the observed heterogeneity of index intercorrelations in this study. These findings have potentially serious ramifications in that measures of a unitary construct should relate highly to one another and should uniformly predict outcomes. Camp and Chartrand's findings may suggest that extant congruence indices are actually measures of more than one underlying construct.

In a related study, Brown and Gore (1994) simulated all possible person-environment combinations to characterize the distributional properties of congruence indices. They detected serious flaws in many of the measures of congruence with most measures generating distributions that were positively skewed, and some distributions that were noticeably incomplete. Like Camp and Chartrand (1992), intercorrelations among congruence measures varied widely (.14 to .92), suggesting that not all congruence measures are created equal. Brown and Gore proposed a new index (C-index) that yields a symmetrical distribution and closely adheres to Holland's theory.

There are clearly fundamental problems with a number of extant indices that may be alleviated by the use of more theoretically consistent and psychometrically sound measures (e.g., Brown & Gore, 1994; Kwak & Pulvino, 1982). Should investigators continue exploring the predictive utility of career congruence, they are well advised to use these more desirable indices and to attend to methodological recommendations on conducting congruence research (Brown & Gore, 1994; Camp & Chartrand, 1992; Holland, 1997). Further, it remains to be seen how researchers will integrate recent findings on the three-dimensional, spherical structure of interests (Tracey & Rounds, 1996) into calculations of congruence.

Holland's notion that people tend to inhabit work and leisure environments that match their personalities has received strong support (Hansen & Sackett, 1993; Miller, 1991; Oleski & Subich, 1996). Hansen and Sackett (1993), for example, reported that up to 70% of a sample of undergraduate students demonstrated a high degree of fit between their interest profiles and college majors. As some authors have pointed out, however, people's tendency to be attracted to environments that are congruent with their interests may not always be possible. Downes and Kroeck's (1996) findings suggest that there is a mismatch between the availability of jobs in today's society and the normative pattern of primary interests in the population of workers. To put it succinctly, we can't always get what we want.

In sharp contrast to the volume of research on congruence, considerably less attention has been focused recently on the constructs of differentiation, consistency, and identity. Holland (1997) outlined a number of limitations with studies that have attempted to explore these constructs in recent years, such as the use of small or homogeneous samples in studies designed to explore the predictive validity of differentiation. Moreover, he called for increased attention to the relationships among differentiation, consistency, and identity, with the understanding that these are secondary constructs and that their unique contribution to understanding vocational behavior should be assessed after controlling for more central factors.

Holland (1997) hypothesized that differentiation, consistency, and identity are related to degree of vocational clarity and stability of vocational goals. Moreover, differentiation and consistency are hypothesized to predict stability of vocational choice, vocational persistence, and overall satisfaction. Several research groups have explored these relationships. Carson and Mowsesian (1993), for example, calculated correlations between differentiation, consistency, vocational identity, and job satisfaction. Vocational identity was most highly related to job satisfaction ($r = .45$), whereas the relationships between satisfaction and differentiation and consistency were less robust ($rs = -.03$ and $-.12$, respectively). Leong, Austin, Sekaran, and Komarraju (1998) made similar observations in a sample of employed adults from India, reporting correlations between differentiation, consistency, and job satisfaction ranging from $-.18$ to $.04$.

As with the construct of congruence, researchers have focused attention on refining the measurement of consistency and differentiation. These efforts have resulted in a number of specific suggestions for improving the manner in which the constructs are operationalized, such as dealing with ties in primary codes to determine consistency (Strahan & Severinghaus, 1992) and using more profile information in calculating differentiation (Sackett & Hansen, 1995; Swanson & Hansen, 1986). Researchers seem to be embracing the utility of these constructs, and the newer indices may hold promise for future researchers. In addition, some evidence suggests that differentiation is related to personality factors (De Fruyt & Mervielde, 1997; G.D. Gottfredson & Jones, 1993; Holland, Johnston, & Asama, 1994), a finding that may provide new research directions.

Research regarding vocational identity has demonstrated convergent and discriminant validity between Holland's Vocational Identity scale and measures of other career-related constructs (Holland, 1997). For example, identity correlated strongly with career self-efficacy (.54) and career decision-making self-efficacy (.61) (Solberg, Good, Fischer, Brown, & Nord, 1995). However, some authors have concluded that the construct of vocational identity is "fuzzy" and does not reflect its rich developmental underpinnings (Leung, Conoley, Scheel, & Sonnenberg, 1992; Vondracek, 1992).

Finally, a number of authors addressed the practical applications of Holland's theory. Mobley and Slaney (1996) suggest that gay men and lesbian women may intentionally enter incongruent occupations as a result of either real or perceived discrimination and homophobia in society. Additionally, these authors speculated about how heterosexuals' perceptions of stereotypic gay and lesbian work environments may influence the career paths of gays in our society.

Mahalik (1996) noted differential patterns by Holland type in a study of the relationship between client interest patterns and perceptions of counselor intentions in counseling. For example, enterprising clients tended to interpret interventions as challenges, and investigative clients responded more positively to prescriptive interventions as compared with experiential interventions. Further, a group of investigators have observed differential preferences for activities in career counseling based on Holland personality type (Boyd & Cramer, 1995; Lenz, Reardon, & Sampson, 1993; Niles, 1993), although these preferences were not always in the expected direction. Clearly, additional research is needed in this area before counselors can begin to tailor their interventions to their client's work personalities. Nevertheless, well-documented relationships between work personality and perceptions of counselor intentions not only would have clear implications for traditional career counseling but also for personal counseling.

Summary

Holland's theory of career choice continues to influence research and practice. Hexagons abound and career centers frequently organize their materials using the RIASEC model. Holland's person and environment organizational schemes continue to receive explicit endorsement from counselors and from test publishers. Research supporting Holland's typology is extremely strong (see the later section on vocational interests), and counselors may feel confident in their use of the hexagon as an organizing scheme for clients. The perceived failure of other hypotheses seems only to result in more intense empirical effort or elucidation of measurement issues. At first glance, the weak support for some of Holland's fundamental hypotheses (e.g., consistency and differentiation) and the small correlations often obtained in congruence studies suggest that career counselors should exercise caution when using these concepts with clients. Alternatively, perhaps our research efforts have been misdirected, and our outcome expectations have been set too high.

Researchers are encouraged not to dismiss what might appear to be lackluster findings with respect to Holland's major theoretical tenets. There are a number of statistical and methodological issues to consider when interpreting bivariate correlations in any body of research. First, investigators often attempt to explain variance in complex and multidimensional constructs (e.g., job satisfaction). Some researchers might argue that explaining 4% to 8% of the variance in an outcome using only one predictor is remarkable given the multitude of direct and indirect influences on behavior. Although higher correlations would be encouraging, lead to a more parsimonious explanation of psychological processes, and perhaps simplify the career counseling process, they might also be reflective of high levels of shared method variance.

Traditionally, researchers have judged the adequacy of correlational data using either statistical or practical significance. Such interpretation, as has been the case with research on Holland's theory, often results in attacks on theory or attempts to improve measurement. Rosenthal and Rubin (1982), however, suggested that correlations may be interpreted as direct measures of predictive accuracy. For example, a correlation of .20 allows us to predict an outcome 20% more accurately than would be possible without the use of that predictor. In fact, biomedical researchers routinely terminate studies when effect sizes reach .10–.20 on the grounds that it would be unethical to withhold such an effective treatment from participants in the control group (Rosenthal, 1990). A 20% increase in our ability to predict important vocational outcomes would seem like a "significant" gain, and when applied to career counseling, could considerably improve the quality of many people's lives.

Range restriction is another important statistical constraint to consider when interpreting findings from Holland's theory. His theory suggests, and the data confirm, that people naturally gravitate toward congruent environments. Further, survey data consistently indicate that the vast majority of individuals are satisfied with their jobs. Thus, the "modest" relationships often observed in congruence research may simply reflect range restriction in predictors, criteria, or both sets of variables (e.g., in studies of employed adults, there may be so little variance in satisfaction to predict that small correlations are inevitable). Researchers are strongly encouraged to scrutinize their data for potential range restriction, and to employ corrections for such restriction when population variance estimates are available.

Although researchers have spent considerable effort on increasing the specificity of congruence measurement, we seem to have forgotten how coarse our measures of persons and environments really are. We are attempting to improve our description of the relationship between two extremely global typologies by tinkering with the finer points of congruence measures. In essence, we are examining the interaction between persons and environments as though under a high-powered microscope, yet our view of each individual entity, person, or environment is based on a low-resolution magnifying glass: We know the overall structure of each, but we do not know their specific characteristics. Moreover, the intensity of our focus on environments seems not to match the scrutiny with which we have examined the person side of the equation (Holland, 1997). Efforts to define carefully the structure underlying interests, described later in this chapter, have no parallel in structural representations of environmental types. Environments are defined by the people that inhabit them, a somewhat circular definition that prevents independent description and investigation.

Finally, recent evidence suggests that a spherical structure (Tracey & Rounds, 1996) may more adequately describe occupational interests. The added third dimension of occupational prestige might serve as an important component in the description of both persons and environments. How this dimension will be, or already is, incorporated into existing measures of work personality and environments remains to be described. Investigators are urged not only to attend to variability in prestige across Holland types but also to variability in prestige within types. Moreover, additional research is needed to characterize how prestige is incorporated into the measurement of congruence and how it may affect the relationship between congruence and important career and academic outcomes.

Theory of Work Adjustment

The Theory of Work Adjustment (TWA) first appeared in a monograph as part of the Minnesota Studies on Vocational Rehabilitation (Dawis, England, & Lofquist, 1964) and has been elaborated on and extended a number of times (Dawis, 1996; Dawis & Lofquist, 1984; Lofquist & Dawis, 1991). The theory describes the dynamic interaction that occurs between persons and their work environments, and was developed to describe aspects of individuals and work environments that influence vocational adjustment. TWA evolved from a series of empirical investigations, and has given rise to a number of sound instruments (e.g., Rounds, Henly, Dawis, Lofquist, & Weiss, 1981; Weiss, Dawis, England, & Lofquist, 1967).

According to the theory, people have certain requirements for their work environment (work needs) and offer the environment a certain set of skills or abilities. Similarly, work environments have certain requirements of their employees (ability requirements) and can meet certain worker needs (reinforcement system). Correspondence between an employee's abilities and the ability requirements of the job predict satisfactoriness (a perception of satisfaction from the perspective of the employer). Correspondence between an employee's needs and the reinforcement system of the employer, on the other hand, predict satisfaction (a perception from the perspective of the employee). Together, satisfaction and satisfactoriness predict the length of time spent with a given employer (tenure). When employer and employee needs are being met, there exists a state of equilibrium. In contrast, when the needs of either the employee or employer are not being met, adjustment styles come into play. TWA describes these adjustment styles as flexibility (tolerance for discorrespondence before enacting adjustment behaviors), activeness (the tendency to attempt to change the other), reactiveness (the tendency to attempt to change self), and perseverance (the duration of adjustment behaviors before terminating employment).

Some authors have argued that TWA suffers from a number of nonempirical shortcomings. For example, Holland (1994) argued that TWA suffered not so much from a lack of empirical support as it did from serious "marketing" deficiencies. Other authors have noted that the theory continues to evade the awareness of some researchers (Hackett et al., 1991; Tinsley, 1993). In a recent special issue of the *Journal of Vocational Behavior* (Volume 43), Brown (1993), Tinsley (1993), Tenopyr (1993), and Hesketh (1993) noted that TWA fails to incorporate concepts from recent work in the area of personality theory. In contrast, P.C. Morrow (1993) and Murphy (1993) concentrated on possible precision problems with several of TWA's constructs, and the weak links that exist between TWA and other relevant disciplines (e.g., industrial-organizational psychology). In short, TWA continues to suffer from empirical neglect. Other than the special issue described above, only a handful of direct empirical tests of TWA have appeared in the literature in the last decade.

Empirical Evidence

From counseling psychology's perspective, perhaps the most germane aspect of TWA is the hypothesis that job satisfaction is inversely related to job turnover, a hypothesis that has received considerable support from organizational psychology research (for example see Carsten & Spector, 1987) and research specifically focusing on TWA. Breeden (1993) gathered satisfaction and correspondence data immediately prior to and two years following an occupation change in a large sample of employed adults. Changes in satisfaction ranged from 1 to 1.3 standard deviations from the intake to follow-up conditions. Further, the increases in satisfaction observed in participants who changed occupations were not observed in participants who elected to make no change in their employment status. Hesketh, McLachlan, and Gardner (1992) also reported positive correlations between satisfaction and tenure (.17) and intentions to stay on the job (.35).

Other investigators have focused on the theoretical relationships between correspondence and tenure or correspondence and satisfaction. For example, Bretz and Judge (1994) gathered data on satisfaction, success, correspondence, and job tenure from a large sample of employed adults. They used indices of person-environment fit that included correspondence between abilities and ability requirements and between needs and the organizational reinforcement system. Bretz and Judge reported a correlation of .09 between person-organization fit and tenure and a correlation of .36 between person-organization fit and job satisfaction. Moreover, person-organizational fit accounted for a significant portion of the variance in both tenure (1% to 5%) and job satisfaction (5% to 22%) after other variables, such as type of industry, education and organizational attainment level, and demographics, had been partialed out.

Melchiori and Church (1997) reported correlations ranging from .08 to .27 when assessing the relationship between need-reinforcer correspondence and job satisfaction in dual samples of mentally retarded and nondisabled workers. The observed relationship between these variables was higher in absolute magnitude for disabled workers (.27) than for nondisabled workers (.11). In a large sample of bank employees, Hesketh et al. (1992) reported correlations of .44 to .58 between need-reinforcer correspondence and job satisfaction (correlations varied according to the measurement strategy employed). They also observed positive correlations between performance (satisfactoriness) and intentions to remain on the job (.23) and tenure (.06). In contrast, these investigators failed to find support for satisfactoriness as a moderator of the correspondence-satisfaction relationship—a finding echoed by Bizot and Goldman (1993).

One recent study that explored the theoretical relationship between ability-ability requirement correspondence and satisfactoriness deserves mention. Bizot and Goldman (1993) observed a correlation of .29 between satisfactoriness (as measured by the Minnesota Satisfactoriness Scale) and ability-ability requirement correspondence. It should be noted, however, that these authors used an indirect measure of correspondence limiting the generalizability of their findings. These authors failed to find support for satisfaction as a moderator of the correspondence-satisfactoriness relationship.

Summary

The bulk of research on TWA conducted by vocational psychologists has concentrated on elaborating the relationship between needs-reinforcer correspondence, satisfaction, and tenure—presumably due to our focus on the individual rather than the organization. To date, the data seem to support relationships between correspondence and satisfaction, and between satisfaction and job tenure. In contrast, there is clearly less evidence supporting satisfaction and satisfactoriness as moderators of the correspondence-satisfactoriness and correspondence-satisfaction relationships, respectively. Despite generally promising findings over the last 35 years, however, research specifically using constructs and measures from this theory has proceeded at a very slow pace.

Super's Life Span, Life Space Theory

Super's "segmental" theoretical system includes recognition of life span aspects (developmental constructs) and life space aspects (multiple contexts of individuals' lives) of career development, and the view of work as embedded within other life roles. The intersection of life span (longitudinal) and life space (latitudinal) dimensions of Super's life career rainbow describes the current status of an individual and predicts that individual's future career trajectory.

A hallmark of Super's theory is the view that vocational development is a process of making several decisions, which culminate in vocational choices that represent an implementation of the self-concept. Vocational choices are viewed as successive approximations of a good match between the vocational self and the world of work. Super proposed a series of stages over the life span, beginning with growth in early childhood, and moving through exploration, establishment, and maintenance of a career, into disengagement in later life. He also proposed that transition between stages or "maxi-cycles" was characterized by a "mini-cycle" or a recycling through the stages of growth, reexploration, and reestablishment.

Within each stage, Super proposed characteristic developmental tasks. Successful mastery of these tasks allows individuals to function effectively in their life roles within that stage, and prepares them for the next task. Successful coping with the requirements of each stage is dependent on the individual's career maturity. Career maturity—or readiness to master the developmental tasks of each stage—involves both attitudinal factors and cognitive factors.

A cadre of active researchers and theorists guarantee the continuation of Super's theoretical constructs despite his recent death (Blustein, 1997; Herr, 1997; Nevill, 1997; Phillips, 1997). For example, Savickas (1996, 1997) has advocated the modification of Super's construct of "career maturity" into "career adaptability," defined as "readiness to cope with changing work and work conditions" (Savickas, 1994, p. 58). Career adaptability may offer greater relevance for adult career development, may provide a bridging construct for integrating the diverse segments of Super's life span, life space theory (Savickas, 1997), and may connect Super's theory to the fields of industrial/organizational psychology (Goodman, 1994).

Empirical Evidence

Super's theory has received a great deal of attention and empirical support over the years, from Super and his colleagues, as well as a number of independent researchers. However, contemporary empirical attention has been scant (Osipow & Fitzgerald, 1996). One area of recent work is documenting the existence of career stages and their associated tasks, generally providing results that are concordant with earlier studies. Dix and Savickas (1995), for example, identified characteristic coping responses associated with each of the six developmental tasks in Super's establishment stage, in an occupationally diverse male sample. Smart and her colleagues have reported support for Super's stage-related propositions in samples of Australian employed adults. Smart and Peterson (1997) tested Super's idea of recycling, finding that adults in the midst of career changes indicated greater concern with exploration than nonchangers. Smart (1998) reported differential attitudes within career stages of Australian professional women; for example, pay satisfaction and job involvement were lowest among women in the exploration stage, and professional commitment and career involvement were highest among women in the maintenance stage.

Research regarding the construct of career maturity has waxed and waned since the 1970s, yet continues to occupy researchers' attention (Watkins & Subich, 1995). The use of the construct of "career adaptability" to supplant "career maturity" may infuse this line of research with some new energy (Goodman, 1994; Savickas, 1997). For example, a recent empirical study reported support for career adaptability by examining the interrelations among career concerns, values, and role salience in a sample of employed adult men (Duarte, 1995).

Super's theory also has spawned a body of research characterizing the process of career exploration (e.g., Blustein, 1997; Phillips & Blustein, 1994). Exploration has been linked to parental attachment (Ketterson & Blustein, 1997; Schultheiss & Blustein, 1994) and to college students' progress in career decision making (Blustein, Pauling, DeMania, & Faye, 1994). Further, adults exhibit varying patterns of exploratory behavior (Niles, Anderson, & Goodnough, 1998). These studies provide broader developmental underpinnings for Super's theoretical propositions, particularly as they relate to concepts from attachment theory (see Blustein, Prezioso, & Schultheiss, 1995, for a review of attachment theory and its relevance to career development).

In addition to recent empirical attention, a number of authors have written about applications or extensions of Super's theory, related to gender (Cook, 1994), sexual orientation (Dunkle, 1996), and self-efficacy research and Gottfredson's theory (Betz, 1994). Moreover, Super's theory has been applied extensively outside of the United States, for example, in South Africa (Stead & Watson, 1998), and Australia (Smart, 1998; Smart & Peterson, 1997).

Super's theory is intuitively appealing, and offers assistance in understanding the richness of an individual's career and life. Research on the theory, however, is plagued by the same difficulties inherent to all developmental models, including the overreliance on cross-sectional designs, insufficient attention to true longitudinal life span development, use of retrospective recall methodology, and circularity in definitions of stages. Although the theory's propositions are logical and have the potential to be clinically quite useful, they lack the operational specificity found in other theories.

Summary

Super's theory directed vocational psychologists' focus to life span career development, yet research has continued to focus primarily on the early adulthood stage of exploration. Even though evidence has accumulated about the antecedents and outcomes of exploration, there clearly is a need to further our knowledge about later stages of career development (Swanson, 1992; Watkins & Subich, 1995). Attention to tasks in Super's establishment and maintenance stages seems to have fallen to researchers interested in work adjustment, from the perspective of the TWA. Further, tasks related to the disengagement stage have received relatively little attention from vocational psychologists. Finally, Super's earliest stage of growth also has been virtually ignored by vocational psychologists (with the exception of Gottfredson, as noted in the next section). We continue to focus on the point of initial career choice, and not nearly enough on what precedes or follows it.

Gottfredson's Theory of Circumscription and Compromise

L.S. Gottfredson's (1981, 1996) theory seeks to explain why individuals' vocational expectations, even when they are children, vary by sex, race, and social class. "Circumscription" refers to the process by which children narrow their "zone of acceptable alternatives" by progressive and irreversible elimination of unacceptable alternatives, in an age-graded sequence.

Gottfredson's four-stage model of circumscription characterizes children as having an increasing capacity to think abstractly, and these cognitive changes are reflected in how children conceptualize the occupational world. In Stage One (ages three to five), children develop an orientation to size and power. They categorize people in simple ways, such as big versus little, and they recognize observable differences between men and women. This recognition increases in Stage Two (ages six to eight), when children develop an orientation to sex roles. They tend to use dichotomous thinking, and use sex appropriateness to define their vocational aspirations. In this stage, children construct their tolerable-sex type boundary.

Stage Three (ages 9 to 13) entails orientation to social valuation, or sensitivity to prestige and status. Adolescents establish their tolerable-level boundary to eliminate occupations that are unacceptably low in prestige, and their tolerable-effort boundary to eliminate occupations that are too difficult to attain. Finally, in Stage Four (ages 14 and older), individuals develop their orientation to the internal, unique self. Interests, values, and abilities are clarified, and occupational exploration occurs within the zone of acceptable alternatives as circumscribed in earlier stages. Stages One through Three are focused on rejecting unacceptable alternatives. Stage Four is focused on identifying which of the acceptable alternatives are most preferred (L.S. Gottfredson, 1996), and begins the process of compromise.

"Compromise" in this instance entails the modification of alternatives due to inaccessibility, leading to acceptance of less attractive alternatives. Gottfredson posited that sex type, prestige, and field of interest are the three dimensions considered in the process of compromise. She further specified an order of compromise such that sex type is least likely, and field of interest most likely, to be compromised. Most individuals will settle for a "good enough" choice rather than the best possible choice.

Gottfredson's theory seemed to address an important missing piece in the understanding of vocational behavior, and is useful in conceptualizing the compromises that individuals make, particularly related to sex-typed learning and experiences. However, the theory is quite difficult to examine empirically because of its focus on internal processes that occur early in childhood. Therefore, scrutiny of the evolving processes of circumscription and compromise is necessarily indirect. Most research has used retrospective methodology to assess circumscription, a procedure that is ultimately not at all satisfactory. Researchers have focused on instrumentation but, as L.S. Gottfredson and Lapan (1997) noted, no one has determined how to quantify the three-dimensional space required to fully depict an individual's occupational preferences.

Moreover, L.S. Gottfredson and Lapan (1997) discussed a conceptual shift inherent in Gottfredson's theory in comparison to other theories, namely, that early vocational development is a process of rejection or elimination, rather than one of selection or expansion. Although this view may be a more accurate picture of what occurs as individuals confront environmental barriers and limits, as a conceptual shift it may be somewhat antithetical to the philosophy underlying traditional vocational psychology theories.

Empirical Evidence

Published research regarding Gottfredson's theory has been sparse in the last few years, and, although it has been the focus of a number of unpublished doctoral dissertations, interest in examination of the theory seems to be in decline. Moreover, in contrast to other theories of career development, in which the theorists also conduct the majority of the relevant research, Gottfredson herself has conducted little empirical evaluation of the tenets of her theory. Two groups of researchers have served as the primary investigators of Gottfredson's theory: Hesketh and colleagues (e.g., Hesketh, Elmslie, & Kaldor, 1990; Hesketh & McLachlan, 1991); and Leung and colleagues (e.g., Leung, 1993; Leung, Conoley, & Scheel, 1994).

As with earlier research, the few recent published studies provide mixed results for Gottfredson's theoretical propositions. Lapan and Jingeleski (1992) provided support for the underlying dimensions of sex type and prestige levels, reporting a common perceptual map among eighth graders. Sex differences emerged along sex-typed lines in expected attainment, self-efficacy, and interest. Circumscription is predicted to be determined early and to remain stable, yet empirical results suggest that changes in occupational sex type and prestige occur through adolescence, and that the number of considered occupational alternatives increases (Hall, Kelly, & Van Buren, 1995; Leung, 1993). Leung et al. (1994) reported consideration of higher prestige occupations with increasing age, consistent with Gottfredson's theory, but also consideration of a wide range of prestige levels, contrary to the theory.

The process of compromise also has received equivocal support. Perhaps most notable is that the order in which compromise was predicted to occur has not been supported. Contrary to Gottfredson's prediction that interest would be compromised first, prestige compromised second, and sex type compromised last, several studies have reported that sex type is least important in compromise situations (Hesketh et al., 1990; Leung, 1993). In fact, Leung (1993) reported that choices were more likely to be in the center of the sex-type continuum at later ages, a finding that corresponds to Tracey and Ward's (1998) report that sex-typed dimensions in interest structure are apparent in childhood, but not later in adolescence.

The use of retrospective methodology to examine circumscription continues to be problematic. For example, Leung (1993) excluded data from the earliest life period (age eight and under) due to the infrequency of participants' responses, which serves as an indicator of the difficulty of retrospective recall of early occupational aspirations. L.S. Gottfredson and Lapan (1997) argued that the value of previous research regarding compromise is not in the questions that have been answered, but rather in the identified difficulties in conceptualizing and assessing the occurrence of compromise.

Summary

Gottfredson's theory offers an interesting framework to conceptualize the development of aspirations in childhood, and is one of the few attempts to study specifically the period corresponding to Super's growth stage. However, it essentially remains quite difficult to test the theoretical propositions, and, unfortunately, an untestable theory is not particularly useful. Recent discussions of self-efficacy have been more explicitly included with Gottfredson's theory (L.S. Gottfredson & Lapan, 1997; Lapan & Jingeleski, 1992), suggesting that future efforts might focus on the convergence of Gottfredson's concepts with the social cognitive career theory.

Social Cognitive Career Theory

Bandura's (1986) reformulation of social cognitive theory has been accompanied by a steady stream of empirical work on the important roles of self-efficacy beliefs and other social cognitive constructs in career development. Social cognitive theory (Bandura, 1986) hypothesizes that individuals' behaviors are a function of the dynamic interplay between belief systems and environmental conditions. It suggests that self-efficacy beliefs, or individuals' beliefs about their abilities to carry out actions to reach a specific goal, determine whether an action will be pursued, how much effort will be expended in carrying out that action, persistence in the face of obstacles, and ultimate performance level. Also influential in guiding behavior are an individual's perceptions of probable response outcomes (outcome expectations) and the formation of goal intentions. Bandura advocated the concept of triadic reciprocality, a proposition that assumes that person, environmental, and behavioral factors interact dynamically and bidirectionally.

Hackett and Betz (1981) were the first authors to describe the role of self-efficacy beliefs in the career domain. Their seminal work was followed by over a decade of research that clearly established the importance of self-efficacy beliefs in various stages of career development. To summarize this research, self-efficacy beliefs are related to career entry behaviors such as career interests and range of occupational considerations (Betz, Harmon, & Borgen, 1996; Bores-Rangel, Church, Szendre, & Reeves, 1990; Lapan, Boggs, & Morrill, 1989; Lenox & Subich, 1994; Lent, Larkin, & Brown, 1989; Rotberg, Brown, & Ware, 1987); academic and career performance and persistence (Bores-Rangel et al., 1990; Lent, Brown, & Larkin, 1984, 1986, 1987; Locke, Frederick, Lee, &

Bobko, 1984; Multon, Brown, & Lent, 1991); and other career-relevant behaviors such as the use of computers (Hill, Smith, & Mann, 1987).

Research on the role of social cognitive factors in career development intensified following the introduction of social cognitive career theory (SCCT; Lent, Brown, & Hackett, 1994). These authors proposed three interrelated and dynamic models of academic and career-related interest, choice, and performance. According to this theory, an individual's exposure to academic and career-related experiences is a function of environmental and personal factors (e.g., socioeconomic status, genetics, personality variables). The development of important social cognitive variables such as self-efficacy beliefs and outcome expectations is dependent on an individual's experience, and these factors develop according to mechanisms described by Bandura (1986). An individual's self-efficacy beliefs and outcome expectations, in turn, relate to the development of academic and career-related interests. In short, people will develop interests in activities for which they have strong positive self-efficacy beliefs and for which they perceive desirable and probable outcomes.

In the absence of environmental barriers and in the presence of environmental support, interests translate into academic or career goals and, ultimately, academic- or career-related behaviors (e.g., course enrollment, occupational information seeking activities, job search behaviors). Consistent with the dynamic nature of social cognitive theory, SCCT holds that the outcome of such behaviors will provide valuable feedback for the further development of self-efficacy beliefs and outcome expectations. Thus, interest development and choice behaviors are a function of lifelong exposure to experiences, cognitive appraisal of those experiences, and the presence or absence of environmental obstacles.

Empirical Support

Research on aspects of SCCT has been intense during the last decade. Evidence of this can be seen in the widespread application of this theory (e.g., Bishop & Bieschke, 1998; Brown, Lent, Ryan, & McPartland, 1996; Chartrand & Rose, 1996; Hackett & Byars, 1996; S.L. Morrow, Gore, & Campbell, 1996; O'Brien & Heppner, 1996; O'Brien, Heppner, Flores, & Bikos, 1997); the publication of a special issue of the *Career Development Quarterly* (Volume 44, Number 4) on the application of social cognitive career theory to career counseling; and the rapid growth of measures of theoretical constructs (Betz, Borgen, & Harmon, 1996; Fouad, Smith, & Enochs, 1997; O'Brien et al., 1997; Rooney & Osipow, 1992). SCCT yields a number of very specific and testable hypotheses, many of which have been explored empirically. Although a comprehensive review of the SCCT literature is beyond the scope of this chapter, we attempt to summarize those theoretical propositions that have received the most attention.

SCCT's assertion that interests are positively related to self-efficacy beliefs and outcome expectations has received a great deal of attention from researchers. Lent et al. (1994) reported effect size estimates for the relationship between interests and self-efficacy beliefs (.53) and outcome expectations (.52) in their outline of SCCT. Similar effect sizes have been reported in a number of additional studies (Betz, Harmon, et al., 1996; Bieschke, Bishop, & Garcia, 1996; Fouad & Smith, 1996; Lapan, Shaughnessy, & Boggs, 1996; Lenox & Subich, 1994; Lopez, Lent, Brown, & Gore, 1997). Fouad and Smith (1996), for example, used path analysis to explore the relations among measures of math and science self-efficacy, outcome expectations, interests, and intentions, in a large sample of ethnically diverse middle-school children. Both outcome expectations and self-efficacy beliefs were positively related to interests (path coefficients of .18 and .29, respectively) and intentions (path coefficients of .39 and .13, respectively). Moreover, self-efficacy beliefs and outcome expectations were highly intercorrelated (path coefficient = .55), and model fit statistics provided strong support for the exploratory utility of the SCCT model among different ethnic groups. In a related study, Lopez et al. (1997) found very similar relationships among interests, self-efficacy beliefs, and outcome expectations in a sample of high school students.

Although empirical evidence supporting the relationships among self-efficacy beliefs, outcome expectations, and interests is substantial, there are a number of hypotheses that derive from this observation that have not yet been fully explored. For example, SCCT hypothesizes that changes in self-efficacy beliefs or outcome expectations will lead to changes in interests, and that self-efficacy beliefs and outcome expectations stabilize in late adolescence or early adulthood—a finding consistently reported in the interest measurement literature (Swanson, 1999). Research on these topics would be invaluable as practitioners begin to implement the concepts outlined in SCCT.

Lent et al. (1994) proposed that (1) self-efficacy beliefs are positively related to academic and career performance, (2) the relationship between abilities and outcomes will be partially mediated by self-efficacy beliefs and goals, and (3) the relationship between abilities and interests will be fully mediated by self-efficacy beliefs. Evidence in support of the first hypothesis continues to accumulate. For example, Multon et al. (1991) reported the results of a meta-analysis of the relationship between self-efficacy beliefs and academic performance and persistence. They found positive relationships between self-efficacy beliefs and academic performance (.38) and persistence (.34). The relationships between self-efficacy beliefs and academic outcomes tended to be larger with increased academic experience and when outcomes were measured following an intervention designed to bolster self-efficacy beliefs. Finally, these authors reported a stronger relationship for low-achieving students. Findings from additional studies (Hackett, Betz, Casas, & Rocha-Singh, 1992; Lent, Brown, & Gore, 1997; Lent, Lopez, & Bieschke, 1993; Lopez et al., 1997; Pajares & Miller, 1995; Schaefers, Epperson, & Nauta, 1997) provide clear evidence in support of the relationship between academic self-efficacy beliefs and academic performance (average $r = .42$ for content-specific performance measures and .28 for nonspecific performance measures).

Studies focusing on the mediating role of self-efficacy in the relationship between abilities and interests, and abilities and performance, are far less common. Lent et al. (1994) reported effect sizes from a small number of studies. They observed a modest relationship between abilities and interests ($r = .20$) that was completely eliminated when the effects of self-efficacy beliefs were controlled. These results suggest that self-efficacy beliefs fully mediate the relationship between abilities and interests but only partially mediate the relationship between past achievement and performance. In addition to the mediating role of self-efficacy beliefs, some studies have observed circumstances in which self-efficacy may moderate the relationship between abilities and performance. Brown, Lent, and Larkin (1989), for example, described an interaction effect between ability level and self-efficacy beliefs for academic requirements. Specifically, academic outcomes of lower aptitude students were facilitated by high self-efficacy beliefs, whereas the academic outcomes of higher aptitude students were unaffected by self-efficacy beliefs.

Consistent with Bandura's (1986) theory, SCCT hypothesizes that self-efficacy beliefs and outcome expectations develop as a result of four mechanisms (personal performance accomplishments, social persuasion, vicarious learning, and physiological reactions or emotional arousal). Using confirmatory factor analysis procedures, Lent, Lopez, Brown, and Gore (1996) found strong support for a theoretically consistent four-factor model of mathematics self-efficacy sources in high school and college students (Comparative Fit Index = .99). Other investigators (Lent, Brown, Gover, & Nijjer, 1996; Lent et al., 1991; Lopez & Lent, 1992; Lopez et al., 1997; Matsui, Matsui, & Ohnishi, 1990) consistently report that personal performance accomplishments are the strongest predictors of mathematics self-efficacy. Four of these studies (Lent et al., 1991; Lopez & Lent, 1992; Lopez et al., 1997; Matsui et al., 1990) provided sufficient information to calculate simple effect sizes. Personal performance accomplishments accounted for, on average,

32% of the variance in self-efficacy belief scores, whereas vicarious learning, verbal persuasion, and emotional arousal accounted for less variance (4%, 9%, and 7%, respectively) across studies. Lent, Brown, et al. (1996) employed a qualitative approach to the study of sources of self-efficacy beliefs and found that most individuals list personal performance accomplishments as the primary factor influencing their self-efficacy beliefs. Respondents also listed vicarious learning and physiological arousal experiences but far less frequently. Interestingly, respondents failed to list any instances of social persuasion in this study.

Most experimental studies of the relationship between sources of self-efficacy and self-efficacy estimates have, not surprisingly, concentrated on the role of personal performance accomplishments (N.K. Campbell & Hackett, 1986; Hackett, Betz, O'Halloran, & Romac, 1990; Hackett & Campbell, 1987). Results from these studies suggest that self-efficacy beliefs can be enhanced through successful performance experiences. Similar support for the role of vicarious learning in the development of self-efficacy beliefs can be found in the educational psychology literature (Schunk & Hanson, 1985; Schunk, Hanson, & Cox, 1987).

In sharp contrast to the growing body of evidence supporting the sources of self-efficacy beliefs, empirical support for the sources of career-related outcome expectations is lacking. The paucity of specific investigations on the sources of outcome expectations and more general research on the role of outcome expectations in career processes may be attributable, in part, to measurement deficiencies. Whereas measures of occupational and task specific self-efficacy continue to surface, fewer measures of outcome expectations have been reported. The most recent measures of outcome expectations (Fouad & Smith, 1996; Lent, Lopez, & Bieschke, 1993) require participants to respond with an indication of agreement to statements of positive outcomes. One may argue that these measures only implicitly incorporate both value (valence) and expectancy elements—relatively independent conceptual components that career researchers and practitioners recognize as important determinants in career decision making (Locke & Henne, 1986; Mitchell & Krumboltz, 1984; Vroom, 1964). However, Brooks and Betz (1990) provide some evidence that suggests that expectancy estimates alone predict choice behavior, as well as the product of expectancy and valence. Most investigators would probably agree that a great deal of fundamental measurement work still remains before the assessment of outcome expectations attains the levels already achieved in measuring other social cognitive constructs such as self-efficacy beliefs and interests.

A number of investigators have focused on the construct validity of measures of self-efficacy beliefs. For example, Betz and Klein (1996) reported that various measures of self-efficacy beliefs (e.g., career decision making self-efficacy, Skills Confidence Inventory [SCI] scores, occupational self-efficacy) correlated more highly with one another than they did with a measure of self-esteem. In a confirmatory factor analytic study, Lent et al. (1997) reported that self-efficacy beliefs at various levels of measurement specificity (broad academic milestones self-efficacy, mathematics course–specific self-efficacy, and math problem solving self-efficacy) were empirically distinguishable from measures of academic self-concept and academic adjustment. Finally, Betz, Harmon, et al. (1996) reported bivariate correlations between Strong Interest Inventory General Occupational Theme (GOT) scores and scores on the recently developed SCI. Although they reported generally strong positive correlations between GOT and SCI scores within the same Holland dimension (average $r = .47$), the observed correlations were not so high as to suggest that the scales were measuring the same underlying dimension.

Given the wealth of empirical findings generated by researchers investigating social cognitive determinants of career development, choice, and performance, it is not surprising that a number of authors are now writing about the clinical utility of SCCT. Several authors have focused on the application of SCCT to the special issues faced by specific client populations (e.g., Chartrand & Rose, 1996; Hackett & Byars, 1996; S.L. Morrow et al., 1996). Brown and Lent (1996) outlined a number of specific strategies for assisting clients who are experiencing career choice difficulties and for working with clients who may fail to implement career-related interests or goals due to the presence of career barriers. Swanson and Woitke (1997) provided additional recommendations related to addressing perceived barriers. Finally, Brown and Lent encourage counselors to work with their clients to identify and engage in academic- and career-related experiences that will bolster self-efficacy beliefs and provide accurate outcome expectation information.

Summary

Social cognitive career theory has had a significant impact on vocational psychology in the last decade. Although clearly stressing the importance of social cognitive constructs, SCCT also adopts a constructivist perspective, acknowledges the role of personal and contextual variables on the career trajectories of individuals, and embraces the role of personal agency in the formation of cognitions and goals. It was developed in response to a decade of work on the role of self-efficacy beliefs in career and academic decision making and performance, and it has received a great deal of empirical attention—due in part to the precise elaboration of its propositions and hypothesis.

Empirical support for the propositions outlined by SCCT is strong and growing. Investigators continue to study the often complex relationships among important social cognitive constructs, and to explore the relationship between these variables and important career behaviors. Researchers continue to focus on important measurement issues and the developmental etiology of adult career constructs. Given the consistent empirical findings, it is not surprising that some vocational psychologists are now beginning to turn their attention to the application of this theory to career counseling practice.

Despite the literature that has accumulated since the publication of SCCT, a number of specific propositions and measurement issues have not yet received attention. Noticeably missing from the literature are studies that explore the role of early contextual influences. Although Lent et al. (1994) clearly emphasized the central role of self-efficacy beliefs, outcome expectations, interests, and goal behaviors in their model, they also stressed the important role of personal and contextual affordances. Research on the early influence of personal and contextual variables is likely to introduce career researchers to a previously underresearched population (namely, children) and to bodies of literature that speak to the development of self-percepts and the performance of younger children (developmental and educational psychology). Such research could significantly contribute to our understanding of the early development of academic self-efficacy beliefs, the origin of academic and career outcome expectations, and the agonistic or antagonistic effects of personal and environmental factors on children's early learning experiences (see Arbona, this volume).

Of equal importance are studies designed to investigate the moderating role of personal and contextual variables at a point more proximal to important academic and career choice points (e.g., late adolescence and early adulthood). SCCT describes the smooth translation of academic- and career-related interests into goal intentions, and goals into actions, but it also describes the moderating role of personal and contextual variables in this process. A number of authors have speculated on the role of active and passive discrimination at all stages of career development (Chartrand & Rose, 1996; Hackett & Byars, 1996; S.L. Morrow et al., 1996), yet few studies have explored the effects of social-environmental and personal factors on the translation of interests into goals and goals into actions.

A separate line of research has examined perceptions of career barriers (McWhirter, 1997; Swanson & Tokar, 1991a, 1991b). This research recently has been recast within the framework of SCCT (Swanson, Daniels, & Tokar, 1996; Swanson & Woitke, 1997), offering new directions in exploring the role of perceived barriers in the implementation of interests, choice, and performance. For example, Swanson et al. speculated that barriers may be construed as equivalent to self-efficacy beliefs, to outcome expectations, or as mediating the relationship among constructs within SCCT, depending on the type of barrier under consideration.

From a measurement standpoint, we know a great deal about the relationships among social cognitive constructs and career outcomes in the math and science realm. Far less, however, is known about the role of social cognitive variables in other domains. Several recent attempts at extending SCCT beyond the math and science boundary are worthy of the reader's attention (Bieschke et al., 1996; Bores-Rangel et al., 1990; Brown et al., 1996; Church, Teresa, Rosebrook, & Szendre, 1992; O'Brien & Heppner, 1996; O'Brien et al., 1997; Vasil, 1992). The successful application of self-efficacy belief measures to other career-relevant behavioral domains is likely to result in important recommendations for practicing career professionals.

Issues of Diversity in Career Development Theories

All behavior—including vocational behavior—occurs within a cultural context. Individuals are shaped through the differential exposure that occurs according to gender, race/ethnicity, sexual orientation, socioeconomic status, and disability—factors that help to form individuals' environments and their life experiences, as well as their responses to the environment. An understanding of human behavior would not be complete without acknowledgment of cultural context (see Fouad & Brown, this volume). Although a comprehensive review of the literature regarding issues of diversity in vocational psychology is beyond the scope of this chapter, it is crucial to acknowledge the important advances that have occurred in the past decade and to encourage further theoretical development and empirical study.

Research and theory regarding issues of diversity in vocational psychology seem to be undergoing a paradigmatic shift. Early work focused on between-group differences, such as comparing career maturity scores of African American and Caucasian students. The next stage of research focused more on within-group differences, and investigated variables such as racial-identity attitudes or perceptions of opportunity structure among African Americans. These dual foci are logical places to begin when little is known about a group of individuals who "deviate" from established theory or knowledge—that is, whose vocational behavior may be substantially different from the groups who have received the bulk of research attention (middle class, Caucasian, male, heterosexual, able-bodied) for a multitude of reasons.

There are, however, recent signs that issues of diversity are being increasingly integrated into the "mainstream" of vocational psychology (and counseling psychology); put another way, contextual issues surrounding vocational behavior are beginning to be fully considered. This shift is by no means universal or uniform: Some groups have received more consistent attention, and the resultant body of research has thus developed to a point where theoretical integration is possible. For example, years of research into women's career development has paved the way for a more fundamental consideration of the role of gender in career choice (Cook, 1994; Phillips & Imhoff, 1997).

An unresolved issue regarding vocational psychology of diverse populations is whether it is necessary to develop separate theories versus expanding existing theories or developing new theories that encompass diverse experiences of a wider range of individuals (Harmon, 1997; Leong & Brown, 1995; Meara, 1997). Some theories are more adaptable to the diversity of human experience, and some include constructs that provide explanation for differences in experience. A conference sponsored by the Division 17 Section on Women, held at Michigan State University in October 1998, endeavored to place gender, race/ethnicity, and sexual orientation squarely in the center of counseling psychology research and practice. Another landmark conference was held by the Society for Vocational Psychology at the University of Wisconsin-Milwaukee in May 1999 to consider the impact of contextual factors in career development.

Gender Issues

Research regarding women's career development continues to be in the forefront of scholarly inquiry, and has been characterized as "the most active and vibrant area of research in all vocational psychology (Fitzgerald, Fassinger, & Betz, 1995, p. 67). Newer research is beginning to fully consider the contextual impact of gender in women's and men's lives. For example, several recent studies examining the career development of highly achieving women provide rich descriptions of the complex intersection of work and personal aspects (Richie et al., 1997; Williams et al., 1998). Meara (1997) provided a cogent example of the way in which gender permeates *all* aspects of career development—from daily work decisions, to permeability of work and family boundaries, to issues of workplace justice—and, therefore, needs to be fully incorporated into career development theory.

Race/Ethnicity

Racial discrimination and economic conditions have strongly affected the career behavior of racial/ethnic minorities in the United States, but have not been taken into account in most traditional career development theories or career counseling practice (Fitzgerald & Betz, 1994; Leung, 1995). Such external issues as discrimination and poverty have a disproportionate effect on racial/ethnic groups, limiting the options that individuals may consider and restricting their access to a wide variety of opportunities (Fitzgerald & Betz, 1994). The strong relationships between socioeconomic status and educational attainment and occupational level have led to a continuous cycle of poor and poorly educated minority individuals.

No one theoretical framework has been developed to explain the career behavior of racial/ethnic minorities (Leong & Brown, 1995). Rather, writers have focused on the delivery of culturally appropriate career counseling, and some also have described models for appropriate intervention. Three complementary models have recently been developed to help counselors conceptualize ways to incorporate culture into career counseling. The most comprehensive model is Leong and Hartung's (1997) integrative-sequential conceptual framework for career counseling. Leung's (1995) model focuses on career interventions, and Fouad and Bingham's (1995) model delineates the career counseling process, identifying specific areas in which culture may play a role.

Future research regarding the influence of race/ethnicity in vocational behavior could benefit from the same ideas espoused earlier regarding gender issues. Namely, we need to move beyond studies of racial/ethnic differences in career choice to a fuller understanding of the academic and career experiences of racial/ethnic minorities.

Gay/Lesbian/Bisexual Issues

The past five years have witnessed a substantial growth in literature regarding career development and vocational behavior of gay/lesbian/bisexual (GLB) individuals, in contrast to previous reviews suggesting little attention (Watkins & Subich, 1995). Much of the literature has been conceptual in nature, discussing career development issues for GLB individuals (Chung, 1995; Elliott, 1993; Fassinger, 1996a, 1996b; Prince, 1995). Several authors have addressed issues related to career assessment (Prince, 1997) and career counseling interventions (Chojnacki & Gelberg, 1994; Croteau & Thiel, 1993; Pope, 1995).

A recent special issue of the *Journal of Vocational Behavior* provided much-needed theoretical and methodological framework for future study regarding GLB career issues (Croteau & Bieschke, 1996; Lonborg & Phillips, 1996), including articles describing the utility of existing theories of career development, as noted earlier (Dunkle, 1996; Mobley & Slaney, 1996; S.L. Morrow et al., 1996). In contrast to the conceptual and practice-based articles, there is a dearth of empirical evidence regarding the career behavior of GLB individuals (for exceptions, see Boatwright, Gilbert, Forrest, & Ketzenberger, 1996; Chung & Harmon, 1994). Some of the conceptual articles provided specific hypotheses derived from existing theories (e.g., Mobley & Slaney, 1996). It is important not to assume that career development issues are the same for lesbian women and gay men, given the overlay of gender issues with sexual identity issues.

Because attention to GLB issues is relatively recent, it is not as fully "evolved" as other research, and has not been fully integrated into consideration of cultural context. Betz and Fitzgerald

(1993) cited GLB research as an example of the trend from "pathology to diversity" in how issues are viewed within counseling psychology research.

Theory Convergence

The preceding sections attest to the health of theory-building and theory-testing efforts in the field of career psychology. The trait-factor career counseling theory of Frank Parsons has been joined by additional person-environment fit theories, as well as developmental theories and theories that emphasize learning mechanisms and cognitions. It is clear from conceptual and empirical work that the field can no longer ignore the role of gender, ethnicity, culture, and socioeconomics in the process of career development (e.g., L.S. Gottfredson, 1981; Lent et al., 1994; Richardson, 1993). Most counseling psychologists would probably agree that understanding of career development has benefited greatly from the diverse theoretical work already described and from the theories preceding them.

Some authors, however, have argued that theoretical diversity can outlive its usefulness (Goldfried & Padawer, 1982) and that there comes a time in the evolution of a field when the benefits of theory convergence outweigh those provided by healthy competition among theories. Writers in the areas of psychotherapy process research and those espousing a unificationist position in psychology are addressing these issues. More recently, a number of prominent vocational psychologists recognized the potential benefits of looking at extant career theories through a concave or convergent lens. As a result of several articles celebrating the twentieth anniversary of the *Journal of Vocational Psychology* (Borgen, 1991; Hackett et al., 1991; Osipow, 1990; Super, 1992), a special conference was convened at Michigan State University to address the prospects of career theory convergence. This conference was hosted by the Vocational Behavior and Career Intervention Special Interest Group of Division 17 of the American Psychological Association (now called the Society for Vocational Psychology).

The authors of leading career theories (John Holland, René Dawis, Donald Super, John Krumboltz, and Edward Bordin) were invited to attend and to outline their views on theory convergence, including a discussion of possible bridges among theories. The authors differed considerably in their endorsement of efforts toward theory convergence, but all identified a number of possible points of overlap. For example, Krumboltz (1994) noted similarities between self-observation generalizations and Super's notion of vocational self-concept, and Holland (1994) described how Krumboltz's theory might be used to understand the development of RIASEC work personalities. In short, although these authors were not generally in favor of the development of one unifying theory of career development, they were able to acknowledge substantive overlap among theories. The proceedings from this conference were published in a book (Savickas & Lent, 1994) that includes the papers delivered by the major theorists listed, in addition to thoughtful discussions of specific bridge-building constructs written by prominent vocational researchers.

This theory convergence conference was followed by a second conference, entitled "Toward the Convergence of Career Theory and Practice," hosted by the Society for Vocational Psychology. The second conference was convened to address the perceived lack of practical utility of career theory to practice. The conference proceedings were recently published (Savickas & Walsh, 1996) and address two primary questions: Can career theory adequately inform practice? Can there ever be a theory of career practice?

Despite the energy invested in debating the possibilities, to date there are remarkably few studies that directly compare constructs from competing or even complementary theories (e.g., Lent et al., 1987; Rounds, 1990). As noted in previous sections, there are clear points of overlap among theories, with specific areas in which researchers could forge conceptual and empirical bridges.

There appear to be several potentially beneficial linkages among theories of career development. For example, social cognitive career theory (Lent et al., 1994) describes several very specific mechanisms that influence the development of interests—mechanisms that were alluded to, but not fully elaborated on, in Holland's theory. These theories already have been merged in the form of inventories such as the SCI (Betz, Borgen, et al., 1996), where social cognitive constructs such as self-efficacy beliefs are organized using Holland RIASEC types. Our understanding of the nature of work personalities would certainly benefit from studies focusing on the acquisition of interests in early childhood and adolescence through the dual lenses of Gottfredson's theory of circumscription and Lent et al.'s SCCT. Social cognitive mechanisms such as vicarious learning, personal performance accomplishments, and persuasion would seem to be logical targets for such investigations, especially as they relate to how children establish tolerable-effort boundaries between the ages of 9 and 13. Social cognitive constructs such as self-efficacy beliefs and outcome expectations might also be investigated for their ability to predict variance in career choice and satisfaction beyond that predicted by occupational congruence. Finally, self-efficacy beliefs for a wide variety of different behaviors (e.g., coping, social anxiety) might help to explain important career outcomes, such as performance, persistence, and satisfaction, in Holland's theory.

Other potential overlaps also exist. For example, the TWA describes the importance of vocational needs and their reinforcement by work environments. The perception of need reinforcement might contribute to vocational satisfaction in a way that is entirely complementary to contributions made by congruence. Preliminary exploration of this idea has yielded promising results (Rounds, 1990). Finally, Gottfredson's developmental theory might be used to explore gender and socioeconomic influences on the development or manifestation of work personalities.

VOCATIONAL INTERESTS

The study of vocational interests has occupied a central role in counseling psychology research for nearly a century, and the past few decades are no exception. One reason for the recent flurry of activity is a major overhaul of the Strong Interest Inventory (Harmon, Hansen, Borgen, & Hammer, 1994), with the introduction of a companion instrument to measure self-efficacy, the SCI. A second reason is the work focused on describing the structural underpinnings of interests, typically vis-à-vis Holland's model. In addition to the empirical literature, in 1997 a conference sponsored by the Society for Vocational Psychology highlighted theoretical and practical issues in interest measurement (Savickas & Spokane, 1999). In this section, we provide an update of theory and research regarding vocational interests occurring since Hansen's (1984) chapter in the first edition of the *Handbook*.

Origin, Development, and Stability

A clear gap in the theoretical understanding regarding vocational interests is their origin and development over the life span. Barak (1981) proposed a model of interest development, in which three cognitive factors (perceived ability, expected success, and anticipated satisfaction) determine an individual's interests. Surprisingly, Barak's model has received relatively little attention, in spite of its convergence with Bandura's (1986) construct of self-efficacy, as well as with social cognitive career theory (Lent et al., 1994). Some empirical support has been reported by Barak and his colleagues. For example, in an experimental manipulation, preschool children expressed greater preference for activities when they were followed by cognitive restructuring, in comparison to behavioral reinforcement or no intervention (Barak, Shiloh, & Hauschner, 1992).

Tracey and Ward (1998) described an inventory to measure children's interests and perceptions of competence, providing the type of instrumentation necessary to begin to examine questions regarding the origin and development of interests and emergence of the circular RIASEC structure. Their results demonstrated differences in structure by age (using elementary, middle school, and college-aged cross-sectional samples), suggesting the importance of sex typing in the early years as theorized by Roe (1957) and L.S. Gottfredson (1981). In addition, they reported an age-related increase in fit of the circular RIASEC model to the data.

Concern about the long-term stability or "permanence" of interests began as early as the 1930s: "[I]f interests change from year to year, they are not trustworthy guides to the choice of a career" (Strong, 1931, p. 3). The accumulated evidence since that time suggests that interests are quite stable, at least when viewed from a group perspective. People in general have stable interests, as do members of specific occupations (D.P. Campbell, 1966; Strong, 1931). Using test-retest correlations as an indicator of stability reveals coefficients ranging from .54 to .84, over intervals ranging from 1 year to 23 years (Johansson & Campbell, 1971).

Despite the evidence for interest stability, there also are considerable individual differences in interest stability: Some individuals demonstrate remarkably stable interests over time, whereas others have interest profiles that show substantial change, as evidenced by intraindividual correlation coefficients ranging from −.31 to .98 when examined over 3- to 12-year intervals (Hansen & Stocco, 1980; Hansen & Swanson, 1983; Lubinski, Benbow, & Ryan, 1995; Rohe & Krause, 1998; Swanson & Hansen, 1988). We do not know, however, what leads to a change in vocational interests, nor whether interest stability or change can be predicted, although some of social cognitive career theory's hypotheses offer possibilities for future investigation. Further, little is known about individual differences in stability of interests beyond the end of the college years. Previous results have focused primarily on time intervals spanning the period of formal education, with less attention paid to posteducational stability of interests (Swanson, 1999).

Structure

Concern about the dimensionality underlying vocational interests also has been ongoing since the 1930s, when E.K. Strong gave interest data to Thurstone to factor analyze (Betsworth & Fouad, 1997; Hansen, 1996; Tracey & Rounds, 1995). The search for structural dimensions underlying interests has accelerated substantially in the last few years, presumably because of the theoretical and practical significance in understanding how interests are characterized. Two primary themes are evident in recent research: investigation of the degree to which models are universal across diverse groups, and rethinking the manner in which structural models are conceptualized.

Universality of Structural Models

The vast majority of research examining the structural properties of vocational interests has used Holland's model as a basis. Evidence of structural invariance has consequences for theoretical understanding of interests, but also for use of interest inventories with clients. Structural comparisons provide a different perspective than do examinations of mean differences in interests. For example, mean score sex differences in interests are well documented, yet such differences do not necessarily imply structural sex differences; thus, both types of investigation are necessary.

Studies of the adequacy of the fit of Holland's theory to the structure of interests distinguish between tests of the circular order model and tests of the equidistant hexagonal or circumplex model (Fouad, Harmon, & Borgen, 1997; Rounds & Tracey, 1996). The former requires that the six types be arranged in the order specified by Holland, with adjacent types more highly related than opposing types. The latter model is more stringent, adding a requirement that the six types be arranged with equal distances among them. Studies typically employ a comparative approach, with three primary foci of attention regarding structural invariance: sex, U.S. racial-ethnic minority groups, and international populations.

Although earlier research suggested differences in the way interests are structured across groups, evidence is now accumulating for considerable invariance in the structure of interests. In particular, several recent efforts have demonstrated remarkable invariance (Day & Rounds, 1998;

Day, Rounds, & Swaney, 1998), as evidenced by virtually identical multidimensional scaling analysis patterns across sex and racial/ethnic group membership. In contrast to previous results, these analyses suggest that although mean differences continue to be evidenced among groups, the theoretical models underlying interests seem to provide equally adequate representations for a variety of individuals.

Evidence of sex differences in the strength of interests has been among the most incontrovertible findings in vocational psychology (Hansen, 1984). These differences have been found at the level of items and scales, and are apparent within and across occupational groups. Examining evidence regarding structural differences by sex, however, reveals a different picture. Several studies documented differences between men and women in the underlying structure of interests (Fouad et al., 1997; Hansen, Collins, Swanson, & Fouad, 1993), whereas meta-analyses suggest minimal differences (Anderson, Tracey, & Rounds, 1997; Day & Rounds, 1998; Ryan, Tracey, & Rounds, 1996).

Hansen et al. (1993) used the reference samples from the 1985 revision of the Strong to demonstrate support for the hypothesized circular ordering of Holland's model (RIASEC), but not for the circumplex arrangement that entails equidistance between points. This deviation from the hexagonal shape was particularly noticeable for women, for whom the plotted points for realistic and investigative collapsed onto one another.

In contrast, several studies showed little evidence for sex differences in interest structure. Ryan et al. (1996) reported no differences by sex or race, but did find differences in interest structure when socioeconomic status was jointly considered with race and sex. Anderson et al. (1997) examined seven male/female pairs of general occupational theme correlation matrices collected from 1974 to 1994, concluding that there was no evidence to support differential fit. Tracey's (1997) comparison of a hypothesized three-dimensional spherical structure underlying three different types of data—preferences for occupations, preferences for activities, and self-efficacy expectations—revealed sex differences in mean scale scores, but not in the fit of the model to the data. He interpreted these results to suggest that observed sex differences in actual prestige in occupational attainment may be due to lack of opportunity rather than lack of interest.

As with sex differences, persistent and substantial racial/ethnic differences have been documented in mean scores on interest inventories (Carter & Swanson, 1990). However, the structure of interests was not investigated until recently, and, as with sex differences, mean group differences do not necessarily imply the existence of group structural differences. Initial studies that focused on structural invariance found discrepancies from Holland's circumplex model.

Similar to the research on sex differences, recent research using large and representative samples has shown that the structure of interests is also invariant across race and ethnicity. For example, Fouad et al. (1997) examined dimensions underlying four racial/ethnic groups (including over 38,000 individuals) collected as part of the 1994 revision of the Strong Interest Inventory. They reported support for the circular structure for all eight groups (race-ethnicity by sex), but no support for the equidistant hexagonal structure for any of the groups.

Two other recent studies presented strong evidence for the universality of interest structure among U.S. racial/ethnic minority groups (Day & Rounds, 1998; Day et al., 1998). In each case, the researchers examined UNIACT data from large samples (e.g., nearly 50,000 college-bound students) and reported virtually identical mapping of the data/ideas and people/things dimensions for 10 groups (5 ethnic groups by sex). They concluded that sampling may have been a factor in earlier studies that documented racial/ethnic differences in interest structure and that their results may differ from earlier studies because of the use of UNIACT items, which measure only activities (versus, for example, occupational titles, which are common to other inventories).

Structure of interests also has been investigated in international samples, including Bolivian college students (Glidden-Tracey & Parraga, 1996), Japanese college students (Tracey, Watanabe, & Schneider, 1997), and Mexican engineering and law students (Fouad & Dancer, 1992) with varying degrees of fit, some very poor. These cross-national studies are fraught with confounding problems that limit their generalizability, such as adequacy of translations of inventories and other language issues, potential variation in the content and opportunity in occupations in different countries, and sampling issues.

Organization of these studies by topical area (that is, sex, race/ethnicity, country of origin) suggests equivocal conclusions about the universality of interest structures. However, examining the literature chronologically suggests an emerging agreement about universality, particularly in large, representative samples. Methodological and psychometric advances provided new rigorous techniques for examining conformity of models to data. Most research has found support for the circular RIASEC arrangement of Holland types, but less support for the hexagonal or circumplex structure.

Most recently, researchers are beginning to call for a shift in attention from the relative utility of Holland's model to the antecedents and consequences of observed differences in interest structures (Anderson et al., 1997). This shift reflects a willingness to accept the universality of Holland's model as an adequate representation of interests (Day & Rounds, 1998; Day et al., 1998; Rounds & Day, 1999) and a desire to move beyond structural concerns to other issues. Observed differences in the strength of interests or in structural representations may be viewed as clues to differential perceptions and experiences of the world of work, or as a "source for theorizing about cultural influences on interests" (Haverkamp, Collins, & Hansen, 1994).

Thus, there has been substantial convergence on the universality of Holland's model as a representation of interests, although there remain some nagging questions about the extent of deviations and their meaning. In the context of sex differences, Anderson et al. (1997) suggested that future research should "focus on understanding the development or implications of those differences rather than on the relative validity of Holland's model" (p. 362).

New Perspectives

The second major theme in the past decade entails new directions regarding the structure of interests, which may be characterized as efforts to "think outside (and inside) the hexagon" (Subich, 1992). Several researchers have focused on further modifications of Holland's model. Prediger and colleagues (Prediger, 1982, 1996; Prediger, Swaney, & Mau, 1993; Prediger & Vansickle, 1992) have emphasized a two-dimensional structure underlying Holland's model, suggesting that data-ideas and people-things offer a parsimonious, and more complete, description of the vocational interest space. Others have suggested alternative two-dimensional arrangements, essentially rotations of orthogonal dimensions in the hexagonal space (Hogan, 1983; Rounds & Tracey, 1993; Tokar & Fischer, 1998).

By far, the most prolific team of researchers regarding structure of interests is led by Tracey and Rounds. They have examined all of the alternative theoretical models of the structure underlying interests, including Holland's hexagonal model, Gati's (1991) hierarchical model (Tracey & Rounds, 1993), and Roe's circular structure (Tracey & Rounds, 1994). They also have developed methodological advances for evaluating interest structures (Rounds, 1995; Rounds, Tracey, & Hubert, 1992).

Consequences of the efforts by Tracey and Rounds have been twofold. First, they called attention to the fundamental nature of the dominant model in vocational psychology (Tracey & Rounds, 1995). They convincingly argued that the number of points in Holland's circular model is arbitrary: The use of six categories may be no more than a convenient representation of the structure of individuals' interests and occupational environments. A six-category system, however, has become reified through the widespread application of Holland's theory. Use of a greater number of defined points may clarify the relation of interest types to underlying dimensions, such as those proposed by Prediger (1982) or Hogan (1983), or to interdomain relationships (see next section). This disarmingly simple idea has raised the possibility of deviating from the six-point circumplex while still maintaining its circular arrangement.

Second, they proposed the addition of a third dimension to Holland's theory—prestige. Incorporation of the prestige dimension results in an innovative three-dimensional spherical model of vocational interest space, essentially as the intersection of three separate circumplexes resulting from the three dimensions each paired with one another. Although not without its critics (cf. Borgen & Donnay, 1996), the spherical model has served a heuristic purpose and continues to undergo examination by its proponents. For example, Tracey (1997) examined the spherical structure of interests in combination with a measure of self-efficacy expectations, and concluded that the structures paralleled one another. He also reported parallel structures for items measuring preferences for occupations and items measuring preferences for activities. Although mean sex differences were reported, the spherical model fit data from men and women equally well. Tracey also concluded that self-efficacy differed from self-esteem, but may not be a distinct construct from interests.

Overlap of Models of Interests with Other Domains

The interconnections among interests and other domains have received considerable attention recently, most notably, personality attributes, abilities, and self-efficacy. Some of this attention is fueled by the emerging dominance of the five-factor model of personality. Ironically, Holland (1997) has consistently presented his model as one of personality, yet the personality components per se have not received as much attention as other aspects of his theory.

In the domain of personality, the five-factor model represents a widely recognized system for describing the basic dimensions of personality: neuroticism, extraversion, openness to experience, agreeableness, and conscientiousness (Digman, 1990). A large body of research suggests that the five-factor model provides a suitable structure in which other personality systems may be interpreted and organized (Costa & McCrae, 1992, 1995).

The association between Holland's typology and personality variables has generally been supported in empirical studies relating scores on measures of Holland types to a wide range of personality inventories, such as Cattell's 16 PF (Bolton, 1985; Peraino & Willerman, 1983), the Myers-Briggs Type Indicator (Dillon & Weissman, 1987; Martin & Bartol, 1986), and the Eysenck Personality Questionnaire (Goh & Leong, 1993), among others. In an effort to describe these associations in a more parsimonious manner, another approach has been to examine the structural overlap of the basic dimensions underlying personality and interests (Rounds, 1995; Tokar & Fischer, 1998; Tokar & Swanson, 1995).

There are consistent results connecting aspects of the five-factor model of personality to portions of Holland's model: Investigative and artistic interests are related to openness to experience, and social and enterprising interests are strongly related to extraversion, with agreeableness differentiating these two types (Costa, Fozard, & McCrae, 1977; Costa, McCrae, & Holland, 1984; De Fruyt & Mervielde, 1997; G.D. Gottfredson, Jones, & Holland, 1993; Schinka, Dye, & Curtiss, 1997; Tokar, Fischer, & Subich, 1998). Even more compelling evidence suggests that scores on measures of the five-factor model can predict concurrent membership in Holland's vocational interest categories: Openness to experience and extraversion, plus the addition of agreeableness for females, reproduced the Holland hexagon in two-dimensional data-ideas-people-things space (Tokar & Swanson, 1995). Moreover, Holland (1999) argued that the facet scales which accompany the Big Five may clarify differences between adjacent interest types; for example, enterprising and conventional share relations with competence, achievement, striving, and self-discipline, but not with order, dutifulness, and deliberation (De Fruyt & Mervielde, 1997).

In spite of these convergences, there also are demonstrated points of divergence between the two models: Neuroticism and conscientiousness do not appear to be well represented in the interest domain (G.D. Gottfredson et al., 1993), even though these constructs are clearly important to work satisfaction and performance (Tokar et al., 1998). There also is consistent evidence that the correspondence of interest and personality domains appears to be moderated by gender, with different patterns of relationships existing for men and for women (G.D. Gottfredson et al., 1993; Tokar & Swanson, 1995; Tokar, Vaux, & Swanson, 1995).

Models of personality other than the Big Five dimensions also have received attention. Wiggins's Interpersonal Circle (Kiesler, 1983; Wiggins, 1979) rests on two underlying dimensions: The power dimension is defined by two types, dominant versus submissive; the affiliation dimension also is defined by two types, hostile versus friendly. Some evidence suggests that the affiliation dimension links the interpersonal circle and Holland's schema, as translated through Prediger's (1982) people/things dimension (Schneider, Ryan, Tracey, & Rounds, 1996). As another example, Donnay and Borgen (1996) investigated the predictive power of the four personal style scales on the newest revision of the Strong Interest Inventory, suggesting that these scales represent "relevant personality constructs beyond Holland's six types" (p. 276). Although these scales were less predictive than other Strong scales, they did reproduce a hexagon when personal style scale scores for six occupational prototypes were mapped in two-dimensional space.

A recent reanalysis by Tokar and Fischer (1998) moved beyond Holland types to underlying dimensions. Specifically, they derived scores based on Prediger's (1982) and Hogan's (1983) dimensions underlying the Holland hexagon, then predicted these two sets of dimensions from Big Five personality scores. Data for males were better predicted than for females, and Hogan's model produced a more parsimonious explanation than did Prediger's model. Interestingly, many of Tokar and Fischer's results conform to a model offered by Ackerman and Heggestad (1997), discussed in the next section, suggesting the convergence that is beginning to emerge from disparate literatures.

A related body of literature includes behavior genetic studies, which provide estimates of the relative influence of genetic and environmental factors on interests and personality. There is consistent evidence to suggest that genetic factors strongly influence personality. In contrast, literature regarding heritability of vocational interests suggests that environmental influences, particularly nonshared environmental effects, exert more influence than do genetic effects (Betsworth et al., 1994; Moloney, Bouchard, & Segal, 1991). Heritability also has been documented for other career-related variables, such as job satisfaction (Arvey, Bouchard, Segal, & Abraham, 1989), work values (Keller, Bouchard, Arvey, Segal, & Dawis, 1992), and propensity to change jobs (McCall, Cavanaugh, Arvey, & Taubman, 1997), variables which may have stronger links to personality dimensions than do interests (Tokar et al., 1998).

The link between interests and abilities has been discussed since the advent of interest measurement, yet there have been relatively few studies examining this relation. Lowman, Williams, and Leeman (1985) reported structural similarity between primary abilities and vocational interests in college women, but little common variance between the domains; in other words, although they shared a common structure, they were relatively independent of one another. Randahl (1991) reached a substantially different conclusion in her high-point profile analysis of an adult sample seeking career counseling: "[T]he relations between interests and abilities are strong and are in accordance with theoretical predictions" (p. 346).

Ackerman and Heggestad (1997) discussed the theoretical and empirical overlap among domains of interests, abilities, and personality. Reviewing previous literature, they noted that (1) science and engineering interests (investigative and realistic) were positively associated with math, spatial, and mechanical abilities; (2) literary interests were positively associated with verbal ability; (3) social service interests were negatively associated with many abilities, particularly math and spatial; and, (4) depth and breadth of interests were related to intellectual ability (Ackerman, Kanfer, & Goff, 1995; Kanfer, Ackerman, & Heggestad, 1996; Rolfhus & Ackerman, 1996). Their final integrative model incorporated abilities, interests, and personality, as reflected in four trait complexes: social, clerical/conventional, science/math, and intellectual/cultural. These four clusters are arranged so that interest, ability, and personality components fall into the circular order corresponding to Holland's theory, suggesting the utility of Holland's model as a heuristic, integrative model to organize the domains, and supporting his basic typological formulations.

Inserting Tokar and Fischer's (1998) findings regarding the common dimensions underlying interests and personality into Ackerman and Heggestad's (1997) model suggests that Hogan's (1983) two orthogonal dimensions of sociability and conformity fit perfectly into the four trait complexes. Prediger's (1982) dimensions, on the other hand, are more difficult to visualize, primarily because they bisect the spaces between the four clusters. Taken together, these empirical observations and theoretical speculations are supportive of Holland's circular arrangement yet also consonant with Tracey and Rounds's (1995) argument regarding the arbitrary nature of the hexagon: The four trait complexes may be a sufficient number of types to adequately represent the intersection of ability, personality, and interest domains.

Ackerman and Heggestad (1997) speculated about the causal sequences of the three domains, suggesting that abilities, interests, and personality develop in tandem. Ability and personality may determine the probability of success in a particular task, whereas interests determine the motivation to attempt the task: Success increases interest and failure decreases interest. These propositions are congruent with social cognitive career theory (Lent et al., 1994).

The literature discussed thus far relates to objectively measured ability. A related area of research and theory focuses on perceptions or self-ratings of ability. Self-rated abilities have shown predicted relations with interests, and may be more directly related to interests than are objectively assessed abilities (Barak, 1981; Swanson, 1993). These self-ratings may be construed as self-efficacy expectations, although Betz (1999) argued for a conceptual distinction between these two constructs. Self-efficacy beliefs, as discussed earlier, emerged from social cognitive theory, and are typically assessed by asking individuals to rate their level of confidence in a task; self-rated abilities originated in trait-and-factor theories, and are assessed in a normative fashion by asking individuals to compare their abilities with those of other people.

Tracey (1997) examined the connections between ratings of self-efficacy and preferences for occupations and activities. He concluded that a spherical model (Tracey & Rounds, 1996) fit all three types of data, but questioned whether self-efficacy added much to data available from the interest items. On the other hand, he suggested that the close associations between interests and self-efficacy may be reflective of their causal relationship. A third interpretation is that shared measurement or method variance inflated the observed link between interests and self-efficacy. Other authors (Bandura, 1986; Betz, 1994; Lent et al., 1989) have also speculated that a threshold of self-efficacy was necessary before interest would develop, a speculation that received preliminary support as reported by Lenox and Subich (1994).

Development of the SCI (Betz, Borgen, et al., 1996) as a complement to the Strong Interest Inventory (Harmon et al., 1994) provided a method of examining interests and self-efficacy in tandem. Betz, Harmon, et al. (1996) reported that mismatches involving high interest and low confidence were more likely to occur for interest areas that were atypical for one's sex, such as realistic for women and social for men, whereas mismatches involving high confidence but low interest were more likely to occur for interest areas that were highly sex-typical, such as realistic for men and social for women. Evidence also suggests that self-efficacy adds incremental validity to predictions of occupational membership made from interest data alone (Donnay & Borgen, 1999).

CONCLUSIONS

Standing on the verge of a new millennium, it is tempting to comment on the past and the future of vocational psychology. Many writers have reflected on what vocational psychologists believed to be important at the beginning of the twentieth century (Super, 1983). Our review of the literature reflects what vocational psychologists believe to be important as we begin the next century. SCCT and Holland's theory clearly dominate the literature, whereas other theories seem to have generated more discussion than empirical inquiry. Vocational interests is one area of research that is receiving as much attention today as it did in the 1920s and 1930s. That we continue to investigate the nature of interests is testimony to their enduring role both in the theory and practice of vocational psychology. One can view the disproportionate distribution of research as indicative of the current status of career development theories. On the other hand, what researchers choose to investigate is not necessarily related to a theory's scholarly merit. Perhaps more troubling is that our review includes but a fraction of research published in the last decade; that is, the majority of published research is not explicitly tied to career development theory or to a systematic course of sustained research.

It is also tempting to speculate how vocational psychologists at the turn of the next century will evaluate where we are today. Our response to a rapidly evolving society will undoubtedly dictate their assessment. What challenges will we face in the future? The workforce will contend with ever-increasing technology and diversity. We will all be called on to fully recognize the impact of cultural and contextual factors in vocational behavior. Changes are likely to occur in the nature of work itself—increases in the contingent workforce, novel work structures (telecommuting, job sharing), and salience and balance of work versus other life roles. An additional challenge will result from the changing nature of the employment contract and the meaning of "career." Extant theories of career development were formulated at a time when job tenure was commonplace—when it was a desirable outcome. A theory's responsiveness to changes in the outcomes valued by individuals in society may determine its continued survival.

We contend that the historical roots underlying vocational psychology will serve us well in the future, as they have in the past, and will ensure that the field continues to contribute to understanding human behavior and to meeting clients' needs. These roots are what define vocational psychology as an applied science—namely, responsiveness to changes in society, the interdependence of theory and practice, and the commitment to quality measurement.

REFERENCES

Ackerman, P.L., & Heggestad, E.D. (1997). Intelligence, personality, and interests: Evidence for overlapping traits. *Psychological Bulletin, 121,* 219–245.

Ackerman, P.L., Kanfer, R., & Goff, M. (1995). Cognitive and noncognitive determinants and consequences of complex skill acquisition. *Journal of Experimental Psychology Applied, 1,* 270–304.

Anderson, M.Z., Tracey, T.J.G., & Rounds, J.B. (1997). Examining the invariance of Holland's vocational interest model across gender. *Journal of Vocational Behavior, 50,* 349–364.

Arvey, R.D., Bouchard, T.J., Segal, N.L., & Abraham, L.M. (1989). Job satisfaction: Environmental and genetic components. *Journal of Applied Psychology, 74,* 187–192.

Assouline, M., & Meir, E.I. (1987). Meta-analysis of the relationship between congruence and well-being measures. *Journal of Vocational Behavior, 31,* 319–332.

Bandura, A. (1986). *Social foundations of thought and action: A social cognitive theory.* Englewood Cliffs, NJ: Prentice Hall.

Barak, A. (1981). Vocational interests: A cognitive view. *Journal of Applied Psychology, 75,* 77–86.

Barak, A., Shiloh, S., & Hauschner, O. (1992). Modification of interests through cognitive restructuring: Test of a theoretical model in preschool children. *Journal of Counseling Psychology, 39,* 490–497.

Betsworth, D.G., Bouchard, T.J., Jr., Cooper, C.R., Grotevant, H.D., Hansen, J.C., Scarr, S., & Weinberg, R.A. (1994). Genetic and environmental influences on vocational interests assessed using adoptive and biological families and twins reared apart and together. *Journal of Vocational Behavior, 44,* 263–278.

Betsworth, D.G., & Fouad, N.A. (1997). Vocational interests: A look at the past 70 years and a glance at the future. *Career Development Quarterly, 46,* 23–47.

Betz, N.E. (1994). Self-concept theory in career development and counseling. *Career Development Quarterly, 43,* 32–42.

Betz, N.E. (1999). Getting clients to act on their interests: Self-efficacy expectations as a mediator of the implementation of vocational interests. In M.L. Savickas & A.R. Spokane (Eds.), *Vocational interests: Their meaning, measurement, and use in counseling.* Palo Alto, CA: Davies-Black.

Betz, N.E., Borgen, F.H., & Harmon, L.W. (1996). *Skills Confidence Inventory: Applications and technical guide*. Palo Alto, CA: Consulting Psychologists Press.

Betz, N.E., & Fitzgerald, L.F. (1993). Individuality and diversity: Theory and research in counseling psychology. *Annual Review of Psychology, 44,* 343–381.

Betz, N.E., Harmon, L.W., & Borgen, F.H. (1996). The relationships of self-efficacy for the Holland themes to gender, occupational group membership, and vocational interests. *Journal of Counseling Psychology, 43,* 90–98.

Betz, N.E., & Klein, K.L. (1996). Relationships among measures of career self-efficacy, generalized self-efficacy, and global self-esteem. *Journal of Career Assessment, 4,* 285–298.

Bieschke, K.J., Bishop, R.M., & Garcia, V.L. (1996). The utility of the research self-efficacy scale. *Journal of Career Assessment, 4,* 59–75.

Bishop, R.M., & Bieschke, K.J. (1998). Applying social cognitive career theory to interest in research among counseling psychology doctoral students: A path analysis. *Journal of Counseling Psychology, 45,* 182–188.

Bizot, E.B., & Goldman, S.H. (1993). Prediction of satisfactoriness and satisfaction: An 8-year follow up. *Journal of Vocational Behavior, 43,* 19–29.

Blustein, D.L. (1997). The role of work in adolescent development. *Career Development Quarterly, 45,* 381–389.

Blustein, D.L., Pauling, M.L., DeMania, M.E., & Faye, M. (1994). Relation between exploratory and choice factors and decisional progress. *Journal of Vocational Behavior, 44,* 75–90.

Blustein, D.L., Prezioso, M.S., & Schultheiss, D.P. (1995). Attachment theory and career development: Current status and future directions. *The Counseling Psychologist, 23,* 416–432.

Boatwright, K.J., Gilbert, M.S., Forrest, L., & Ketzenberger, K. (1996). Impact of identity development upon career trajectory: Listening to the voices of lesbian women. *Journal of Vocational Behavior, 48,* 210–228.

Bolton, B. (1985). Discriminant analysis of Holland's occupational types using the Sixteen Personality Factor Questionnaire. *Journal of Vocational Behavior, 27,* 210–217.

Bores-Rangel, E., Church, A.T., Szendre, D., & Reeves, C. (1990). Self-efficacy in relation to occupational consideration and academic performance in high school equivalency students. *Journal of Counseling Psychology, 37,* 407–418.

Borgen, F.H. (1991). Megatrends and milestones in vocational behavior: A 20-year counseling psychology retrospective. *Journal of Vocational Behavior, 39,* 263–290.

Borgen, F.H., & Donnay, D.A.C. (1996). Comment: Slicing the vocational interest pie one more time: Comment on Tracey and Rounds. *Journal of Vocational Behavior, 48,* 42–52.

Boyd, C.J., & Cramer, S.H. (1995). Relationship between Holland high-point code and client preferences for selected vocational counseling strategies. *Journal of Career Development, 21,* 213–221.

Breeden, S.A. (1993). Job and occupational change as a function of occupational correspondence and job satisfaction. *Journal of Vocational Behavior, 43,* 30–45.

Bretz, R.D., & Judge, T.A. (1994). Person-organization fit and the theory of work adjustment: Implications for satisfaction, tenure, and career success. *Journal of Vocational Behavior, 44,* 32–54.

Brooks, L., & Betz, N.E. (1990). Utility of expectancy theory in predicting occupational choice in college students. *Journal of Counseling Psychology, 37,* 57–64.

Brown, S.D. (1993). Contemporary psychological science and the theory of work adjustment: A proposal for integration and a favor returned. *Journal of Vocational Behavior, 43,* 58–66.

Brown, S.D., & Gore, P.A., Jr. (1994). An evaluation of interest congruence indices: Distribution characteristics and measurement properties. *Journal of Vocational Behavior, 45,* 310–327.

Brown, S.D., & Lent, R.W. (1992). *Handbook of counseling psychology* (2nd ed.). New York: Wiley.

Brown, S.D., & Lent, R.W. (1996). A social cognitive framework for career choice counseling. *Career Development Quarterly, 44,* 354–366.

Brown, S.D., Lent, R.W., & Larkin, K.C. (1989). Self-efficacy as a moderator of scholastic aptitude-academic performance relationships. *Journal of Vocational Behavior, 35,* 64–75.

Brown, S.D., Lent, R.W., Ryan, N.E., & McPartland, E.B. (1996). Self-efficacy as an intervening mechanism between research training environments and scholarly productivity: A theoretical and methodological extension. *The Counseling Psychologist, 24,* 535–544.

Camp, C.C., & Chartrand, J.M. (1992). A comparison and evaluation of interest congruence indices. *Journal of Vocational Behavior, 41,* 162–182.

Campbell, D.P. (1966). Stability of interests within an occupation over thirty years. *Journal of Applied Psychology, 50,* 51–56.

Campbell, N.K., & Hackett, G. (1986). The effects of math task performance on math self-efficacy and task interest. *Journal of Vocational Behavior, 28,* 149–162.

Carson, A.D., & Mowsesian, R. (1993). Moderators of the prediction of job satisfaction from congruence: A test of Holland's theory. *Journal of Career Assessment, 1,* 130–144.

Carsten, J.M., & Spector, P.E. (1987). Unemployment, job satisfaction, and employee turnover: A meta-analytic test of the Muchinsky model. *Journal of Applied Psychology, 72,* 374–381.

Carter, R.T., & Swanson, J.L. (1990). The validity of the Strong interest inventory for black Americans: A review of the literature. *Journal of Vocational Behavior, 36,* 195–209.

Chartrand, J.M., & Rose, M.L. (1996). Career interventions for at-risk populations: Incorporating social cognitive influences. *Career Development Quarterly, 44,* 341–353.

Chojnacki, J.T., & Gelberg, S. (1994). Toward a conceptualization of career counseling with gay/lesbian/bisexual persons. *Journal of Career Development, 21,* 3–10.

Chung, Y.B. (1995). Career decision making of lesbian, gay, and bisexual individuals. *Career Development Quarterly, 44,* 178–190.

Chung, Y.B., & Harmon, L.W. (1994). The career interests and aspirations of gay men: How sex-role orientation is related. *Journal of Vocational Behavior, 45,* 223–239.

Church, A.T., Teresa, J.S., Rosebrook, R., & Szendre, D. (1992). Self-efficacy for careers and occupational consideration in minority high school equivalency students. *Journal of Counseling Psychology, 39,* 498–508.

Cook, E.P. (1994). Role salience and multiple roles: A gender perspective. *Career Development Quarterly, 43,* 85–95.

Costa, P.T., Jr., Fozard, J.L., & McCrae, R.R. (1977). Personological interpretation of factors from the Strong Vocational Interest Blank scales. *Journal of Vocational Behavior, 10,* 231–243.

Costa, P.T., Jr., & McCrae, R.R. (1992). Four ways five factors are basic. *Personality and Individual Differences, 13,* 653–665.

Costa, P.T., Jr., & McCrae, R.R. (1995). Solid ground in the wetlands of personality: A reply to Block. *Psychological Bulletin, 117,* 216–220.

Costa, P.T., Jr., McCrae, R.R., & Holland, J.L. (1984). Personality and vocational interests in an adult sample. *Journal of Applied Psychology, 69,* 390–400.

Croteau, J.M., & Bieschke, K.J. (1996). Beyond pioneering: An introduction to the special issue on the vocational issues of lesbian women and gay men. *Journal of Vocational Behavior, 48,* 119–124.

Croteau, J.M., & Thiel, M.J. (1993). Integrating sexual orientation in career counseling: Acting to end a form of the personal-career dichotomy. *Career Development Quarterly, 42,* 174–179.

Dawis, R.V. (1996). The theory of work adjustment and person-environment-correspondence counseling. In D. Brown & L. Brooks (Eds.), *Career choice and development* (3rd ed., pp. 75–120). San Francisco: Jossey-Bass.

Dawis, R.V., England, G.W., & Lofquist, L.H. (1964). A theory of work adjustment. *Minnesota Studies in Vocational Rehabilitation, 15.*

Dawis, R.V., & Lofquist, L.H. (1984). *A psychological theory of work adjustment.* Minneapolis: University of Minnesota Press.

Day, S.X., & Rounds, J.B. (1998). Universality of vocational interest structure among racial and ethnic minorities. *American Psychologist, 53,* 728–736.

Day, S.X., Rounds, J.B., & Swaney, K. (1998). The structure of vocational interests for diverse racial-ethnic groups. *Psychological Science, 9,* 40–44.

De Fruyt, F., & Mervielde, I. (1997). The five-factor model of personality and Holland's RIASEC interest types. *Personality and Individual Differences, 23,* 87–103.

Digman, J.M. (1990). Personality structure: Emergence of the five-factor model. *Annual Review of Psychology, 41,* 417–440.

Dillon, M., & Weissman, S. (1987). Relationship between personality types on the Strong-Campbell and Myers-Briggs instruments. *Measurement and Evaluation in Counseling and Development, 20,* 68–79.

Dix, J.E., & Savickas, M.L. (1995). Establishing a career: Developmental tasks and coping responses. *Journal of Vocational Behavior, 47,* 93–107.

Donnay, D.A.C., & Borgen, F.H. (1996). Validity, structure, and content of the 1994 Strong Interest Inventory. *Journal of Counseling Psychology, 43,* 275–291.

Donnay, D.A.C., & Borgen, F.H. (1999). The incremental validity of vocational self-efficacy: An examination of interest, self-efficacy, and occupation. *Journal of Counseling Psychology, 46,* 1–16.

Downes, M., & Kroeck, K.G. (1996). Discrepancies between existing jobs and individual interests: An empirical application of Holland's model. *Journal of Vocational Behavior, 48,* 107–117.

Duarte, M.E. (1995). Career concerns, values, and role salience in employed men. *Career Development Quarterly, 43,* 338–349.

Dunkle, J.H. (1996). Toward an integration of gay and lesbian identity development and Super's life-span approach. *Journal of Vocational Behavior, 48,* 149–159.

Elliott, J.E. (1993). Career development with lesbian and gay clients. *Career Development Quarterly, 41,* 210–226.

Fassinger, R.E. (1996a). From invisibility to integration: Lesbian identity in the workplace. *Career Development Quarterly, 44,* 148–167.

Fassinger, R.E. (1996b). Notes from the margins: Integrating lesbian experience into the vocational psychology of women. *Journal of Vocational Behavior, 48,* 160–175.

Fitzgerald, L.F., & Betz, N.E. (1994). Career development in cultural context: The role of gender, race, class, and sexual orientation. In M.L. Savickas & R.W. Lent (Eds.), *Convergence in career development theories* (pp. 103–118). Palo Alto, CA: Consulting Psychologists Press.

Fitzgerald, L.F., Fassinger, R.E., & Betz, N.E. (1995). Theoretical advances in the study of women's career development. In W.B. Walsh & S.H. Osipow (Eds.), *Handbook of vocational psychology* (2nd ed., pp. 67–109). Mahwah, NJ: Erlbaum.

Fouad, N.A., & Bingham, R.P. (1995). Career counseling with racial and ethnic minorities. In W.B. Walsh & S.H. Osipow (Eds.), *Handbook of vocational psychology* (2nd ed., pp. 331–365). Mahwah, NJ: Erlbaum.

Fouad, N.A., & Dancer, L.S. (1992). Cross-cultural structure of interests: Mexico and the United States. *Journal of Vocational Behavior, 40,* 129–143.

Fouad, N.A., Harmon, L.W., & Borgen, F.H. (1997). Structure of interests in employed male and female members of U.S. racial-ethnic minority and nonminority groups. *Journal of Counseling Psychology, 44,* 339–345.

Fouad, N.A., & Smith, P.L. (1996). A test of a social cognitive model for middle school students: Math and science. *Journal of Counseling Psychology, 43,* 338–346.

Fouad, N.A., Smith, P.L., & Enochs, L. (1997). Reliability and validity evidence for the middle school self-efficacy scale. *Measurement and Evaluation in Counseling and Development, 30,* 17–31.

Gati, I. (1991). The structure of vocational interests. *Psychological Bulletin, 109,* 309–324.

Glidden-Tracey, C.E., & Parraga, M.I. (1996). Assessing the structure of vocational interests among Bolivian university students. *Journal of Vocational Behavior, 48,* 96–106.

Goh, D.S., & Leong, F.T.L. (1993). The relationship between Holland's theory of vocational interests and Eysenck's model of personality. *Personality and Individual Differences, 15,* 555–562.

Goldfried, M.R., & Padawer, W. (1982). Current status and future directions in psychotherapy. In M.R. Goldfried (Ed.), *Converging themes in psychotherapy* (pp. 3–49). New York: Springer.

Goodman, J. (1994). Career adaptability in adults: A construct whose time has come. *Career Development Quarterly, 43,* 74–84.

Gottfredson, G.D., & Jones, E.M. (1993). Psychological meaning of profile elevation in the Vocational Preference Inventory. *Journal of Career Assessment, 1,* 35–49.

Gottfredson, G.D., Jones, E.M., & Holland, J.L. (1993). Personality and vocational interests: The relation of Holland's six interest dimensions to five robust dimensions of personality. *Journal of Counseling Psychology, 40,* 518–524.

Gottfredson, L.S. (1981). Circumscription and compromise: A developmental theory of occupational aspirations. *Journal of Counseling Psychology, 28,* 545–579.

Gottfredson, L.S. (1996). Gottfredson's theory of circumscription and compromise. In D. Brown & L. Brooks (Eds.), *Career choice and development* (3rd ed., pp. 179–232). San Francisco: Jossey-Bass.

Gottfredson, L.S., & Lapan, R.T. (1997). Assessing gender-based circumscription of occupational aspirations. *Journal of Career Assessment, 5,* 419–441.

Hackett, G., & Betz, N.E. (1981). A self-efficacy approach to the career development of women. *Journal of Vocational Behavior, 18,* 326–339.

Hackett, G., Betz, N.E., Casas, J.M., & Rocha-Singh, I.A. (1992). Gender, ethnicity, and social cognitive factors in predicting the academic achievement of students in engineering. *Journal of Counseling Psychology, 39,* 527–538.

Hackett, G., Betz, N.E., O'Halloran, M.S., & Romac, D.S. (1990). Effects of verbal and mathematics task performance on task and career self-efficacy and interest. *Journal of Counseling Psychology, 37,* 169–177.

Hackett, G., & Byars, A.M. (1996). Social cognitive theory and the career development of African American women. *Career Development Quarterly, 44,* 322–340.

Hackett, G., & Campbell, N.K. (1987). Task self-efficacy and task interest as a function of performance on a gender-neutral task. *Journal of Vocational Behavior, 30,* 203–215.

Hackett, G., & Lent, R.W. (1992). Theoretical advances and current inquiry in career psychology. In S.D. Brown & R.W. Lent (Eds.), *Handbook of counseling psychology* (2nd ed., pp. 419–451). New York: Wiley.

Hackett, G., Lent, R.W., & Greenhaus, J.H. (1991). Advances in vocational theory and research: A 20-year retrospective. *Journal of Vocational Behavior, 38,* 3–38.

Hall, A.S., Kelly, K.R., & Van Buren, J.B. (1995). Effects of grade level, community of residence, and sex on adolescent career interests in the zone of acceptable alternatives. *Journal of Career Development, 21,* 223–232.

Hansen, J.C. (1984). The measurement of vocational interests: Issues and future directions. In S.D. Brown & R.W. Lent (Eds.), *Handbook of counseling psychology* (pp. 99–136). New York: Wiley.

Hansen, J.C. (1996). Comment: What goes around, comes around. *Journal of Vocational Behavior, 48,* 73–76.

Hansen, J.C., Collins, R.C., Swanson, J.L., & Fouad, N.A. (1993). Gender differences in the structure of interests. *Journal of Vocational Behavior, 42,* 200–211.

Hansen, J.C., & Sackett, S.A. (1993). Agreement between college major and vocational interests for female athlete and non-athlete college students. *Journal of Vocational Behavior, 43,* 298–309.

Hansen, J.C., & Stocco, J.L. (1980). Stability of vocational interests of adolescents and young adults. *Measurement and Evaluation in Guidance, 13,* 173–178.

Hansen, J.C., & Swanson, J.L. (1983). Stability of interests and the predictive and concurrent validity of the 1981 Strong-Campbell Interest Inventory for college majors. *Journal of Counseling Psychology, 30*(2), 194–201.

Harmon, L.W. (1997). Do gender differences necessitate separate career development theories and measures? *Journal of Career Assessment, 5,* 463–470.

Harmon, L.W., Hansen, J.C., Borgen, F.H., & Hammer, A.C. (1994). *Strong Interest Inventory: Applications and technical guide.* Palo Alto, CA: Consulting Psychologists Press.

Haverkamp, B.E., Collins, R.C., & Hansen, J.C. (1994). Structure of interests of Asian-American college-students. *Journal of Counseling Psychology, 41,* 256–264.

Herr, E.L. (1997). Super's life-span, life-space approach and its outlook for refinement. *Career Development Quarterly, 45,* 238–246.

Hesketh, B. (1993). Toward a better adjusted theory of work adjustment. *Journal of Vocational Behavior, 43,* 75–83.

Hesketh, B., Elmslie, S., & Kaldor, W. (1990). Career compromise: An alternative account to Gottfredson's theory. *Journal of Counseling Psychology, 37,* 49–56.

Hesketh, B., & McLachlan, K. (1991). Career compromise and adjustment among graduates in the banking industry. *British Journal of Guidance & Counselling, 19*(2), 191–208.

Hesketh, B., McLachlan, K., & Gardner, D. (1992). Work adjustment theory: An empirical test using a fuzzy rating scale. *Journal of Vocational Behavior, 40,* 318–337.

Hill, T., Smith, N.D., & Mann, M.F. (1987). Role of efficacy expectations in predicting the decision to use advanced technologies: The case of computers. *Journal of Applied Psychology, 72,* 307–313.

Hogan, R. (1983). A socioanalytic theory of personality. In M.M. Page (Ed.), *Nebraska symposium on motivation 1982. Personality: Current theory and research* (pp. 55–89). Lincoln: University of Nebraska Press.

Holland, J.L. (1959). A theory of vocational choice. *Journal of Counseling Psychology, 6,* 35–45.

Holland, J.L. (1963). Explorations of a theory of vocational choice and achievement. II. A four-year prediction study. *Psychological Reports, 12,* 547–594.

Holland, J.L. (1994). Separate but unequal is better. In M.L. Savickas & R.W. Lent (Eds.), *Convergence in career development theories* (pp. 45–52). Palo Alto, CA: Consulting Psychologists Press.

Holland, J.L. (1997). *Making vocational choices: A theory of vocational personalities and work environments* (3rd ed.). Odessa, FL: Psychological Assessment Resources.

Holland, J.L. (1999). Why interest inventories are also personality inventories. In M.L. Savickas & A.R. Spokane (Eds.), *Vocational interests: Their meaning, measurement, and use in counseling.* Palo Alto, CA: Davies-Black.

Holland, J.L., Johnston, J.A., & Asama, N.F. (1994). More evidence for the relationship between Holland's personality types and personality variables. *Journal of Career Assessment, 2,* 331–340.

Johansson, C.B., & Campbell, D.P. (1971). Stability of the SVIB for men. *Journal of Applied Psychology, 55,* 34–36.

Kanfer, R., Ackerman, P.L., & Heggestad, E.D. (1996). Motivational skills and self-regulation for learning: A trait perspective. *Learning and Individual Differences, 8,* 185–209.

Keller, L.M., Bouchard, T.J., Jr., Arvey, R.D., Segal, N.L., & Dawis, R.V. (1992). Work values: Genetic and environmental influences. *Journal of Applied Psychology, 77,* 79–88.

Ketterson, T.U., & Blustein, D.L. (1997). Attachment relationships and the career exploration process. *Career Development Quarterly, 46,* 167–178.

Kiesler, D.J. (1983). The 1982 Interpersonal Circle: A taxonomy for complementarity in human transactions. *Psychological Review, 90,* 185–214.

Krumboltz, J.D. (1994). Improving career development theory from a social learning perspective. In M.L. Savickas & R.W. Lent (Eds.), *Convergence in career development theories* (pp. 9–31). Palo Alto, CA: Consulting Psychologists Press.

Kwak, J.C., & Pulvino, C.J. (1982). A mathematical model for comparing Holland's personality and environmental codes. *Journal of Vocational Behavior, 21,* 231–241.

Lapan, R.T., Boggs, K.R., & Morrill, W.H. (1989). Self-efficacy as a mediator of investigative and realistic general occupational themes on the Strong Interest Inventory. *Journal of Counseling Psychology, 36,* 176–182.

Lapan, R.T., & Jingeleski, J. (1992). Circumscribing vocational aspirations in junior high school. *Journal of Counseling Psychology, 39,* 81–90.

Lapan, R.T., Shaughnessy, P., & Boggs, K. (1996). Efficacy expectations and vocational interests as mediators between sex and choice of math/science college majors: A longitudinal study. *Journal of Vocational Behavior, 49,* 277–291.

Lenox, R.A., & Subich, L.M. (1994). The relationship between self-efficacy beliefs and inventoried vocational interests. *Career Development Quarterly, 42,* 302–313.

Lent, R.W., Brown, S.D., & Gore, P.A., Jr. (1997). Discriminant and predictive validity of academic self-concept, academic self-efficacy, and mathematics-specific self-efficacy. *Journal of Counseling Psychology, 44,* 307–315.

Lent, R.W., Brown, S.D., Gover, M.R., & Nijjer, S.K. (1996). Cognitive assessment of the sources of mathematics self-efficacy: A thought listing analysis. *Journal of Career Assessment, 4,* 33–46.

Lent, R.W., Brown, S.D., & Hackett, G. (1994). Toward a unifying social cognitive theory of career and academic interest, choice, and performance [Monograph]. *Journal of Vocational Behavior, 45,* 79–122.

Lent, R.W., Brown, S.D., & Larkin, K.C. (1984). Relation of self-efficacy expectations to academic achievement and persistence. *Journal of Counseling Psychology, 31,* 356–362.

Lent, R.W., Brown, S.D., & Larkin, K.C. (1986). Self-efficacy in the prediction of academic performance and perceived career options. *Journal of Counseling Psychology, 33,* 265–269.

Lent, R.W., Brown, S.D., & Larkin, K.C. (1987). Comparison of three theoretically derived variables in predicting career and academic behavior: Self-efficacy, interest congruence, and consequence thinking. *Journal of Counseling Psychology, 34,* 293–298.

Lent, R.W., Larkin, K.C., & Brown, S.D. (1989). Relation of self-efficacy to inventoried vocational interests. *Journal of Vocational Behavior, 34,* 279–288.

Lent, R.W., Lopez, F.G., & Bieschke, K.J. (1991). Mathematics self-efficacy: Sources and relation to science-based career choice. *Journal of Counseling Psychology, 38,* 424–430.

Lent, R.W., Lopez, F.G., & Bieschke, K.J. (1993). Predicting mathematics-related choice and success behaviors: Test of an expanded social cognitive model. *Journal of Vocational Behavior, 42,* 223–236.

Lent, R.W., Lopez, F.G., Brown, S.D., & Gore, P.A., Jr. (1996). Latent structure of the sources of mathematics self-efficacy. *Journal of Vocational Behavior, 49,* 292–308.

Lenz, J.G., Reardon, R.C., & Sampson, J.P. (1993). Holland's theory and effective use of computer-assisted career guidance systems. *Journal of Career Development, 19,* 245–253.

Leong, F.T.L., Austin, J.T., Sekaran, U., & Komarraju, M. (1998). An evaluation of the cross-cultural validity of Holland's theory: Career choices by workers in India [Special issue]. *Journal of Vocational Behavior, 52,* 441–455.

Leong, F.T.L., & Brown, M.T. (1995). Theoretical issues in cross-cultural career development: Cultural validity and cultural specificity. In W.B. Walsh & S.H. Osipow (Eds.), *Handbook of vocational psychology* (2nd ed., pp. 143–180). Mahwah, NJ: Erlbaum.

Leong, F.T.L., & Hartung, P. (1997). Career assessment with culturally different clients: Proposing an integrative-sequential conceptual framework for cross-cultural career counseling research and practice. *Journal of Career Assessment, 5,* 183–202.

Leung, S.A. (1993). Circumscription and compromise: A replication study with Asian Americans. *Journal of Counseling Psychology. 40,* 188–193.

Leung, S.A. (1995). Career development and counseling: A multicultural perspective. In J.G. Ponterotto, J.M. Casas, L.A. Suzuki, & C.M. Alexander (Eds.), *Handbook of multicultural counseling* (pp. 549–560). Thousand Oaks, CA: Sage.

Leung, S.A., Conoley, C.W., & Scheel, M.J. (1994). The career and educational aspirations of gifted high school students: A retrospective study. *Journal of Counseling and Development, 72,* 298–303.

Leung, S.A., Conoley, C.W., Scheel, M.J., & Sonnenberg, R.T. (1992). An examination of the relation between vocational identity, consistency, and differentiation. *Journal of Vocational Behavior, 40,* 95–107.

Locke, E.A., Frederick, E., Lee, C., & Bobko, P. (1984). Effect of self-efficacy, goals, and task strategies on task performance. *Journal of Applied Psychology, 69,* 241–251.

Locke, E.A., & Henne, D. (1986). Work motivation theories. In C.L. Cooper & I.T. Robertson (Eds.), *International review of industrial and organizational psychology 1986* (pp. 1–35). Chichester, England: Wiley.

Lofquist, L.H., & Dawis, R.V. (1991). *Essentials of person-environment correspondence counseling.* Minneapolis: University of Minnesota Press.

Lonborg, S.D., & Phillips, J.M. (1996). Investigating the career development of gay, lesbian, and bisexual people: Methodological considerations and recommendations. *Journal of Vocational Behavior, 48,* 176–194.

Lopez, F.G., & Lent, R.W. (1992). Sources of mathematics self-efficacy in high school students. *Career Development Quarterly, 41,* 3–12.

Lopez, F.G., Lent, R.W., Brown, S.D., & Gore, P.A., Jr. (1997). Role of social-cognitive expectations in high school students' mathematics-related interests and performance. *Journal of Counseling Psychology, 44,* 44–52.

Lowman, R.L., Williams, R.E., & Leeman, G.E. (1985). The structure and relationship of college women's primary abilities and vocational interests. *Journal of Vocational Behavior, 27,* 298–315.

Lubinski, D., Benbow, C.P., & Ryan, J. (1995). Stability of vocational interests among the intellectually gifted from adolescence to adulthood: A 15-year longitudinal study. *Journal of Applied Psychology, 80,* 196–200.

Mahalik, J.R. (1996). Client vocational interests as predictors of client reactions to counselor intentions. *Journal of Counseling and Development, 74,* 416–421.

Martin, D.C., & Bartol, K.M. (1986). Holland's Vocational Preference Inventory and the Myers-Briggs Type Indicator as predictors of vocational choice among master's of business administration. *Journal of Vocational Behavior, 29,* 51–65.

Matsui, T., Matsui, K., & Ohnishi, R. (1990). Mechanisms underlying math self-efficacy learning of college students. *Journal of Vocational Behavior, 37,* 225–238.

McCall, B.P., Cavanaugh, M.A., Arvey, R.D., & Taubman, P. (1997). Genetic influences on job and occupational switching. *Journal of Vocational Behavior, 50,* 60–77.

McWhirter, E.H. (1997). Perceived barriers to education and career: Ethnic and gender differences. *Journal of Vocational Behavior, 50,* 124–140.

Meara, N.M. (1997). Changing the structure of work. *Journal of Career Assessment, 5,* 471–474.

Melchiori, L.G., & Church, A.T. (1997). Vocational needs and satisfaction of supported employees: The applicability of the theory of work adjustment. *Journal of Vocational Behavior, 50,* 401–417.

Miller, M.J. (1991). Accuracy of the leisure activities finder: Expanding Holland's typology. *Journal of Vocational Behavior, 39,* 362–368.

Mitchell, L.K., & Krumboltz, J.D. (1984). Research on human decision making: Implications for career decision making and counseling. In S.D. Brown, & R.W. Lent (Eds.), *Handbook of counseling psychology* (pp. 238–280). New York: Wiley.

Mobley, M., & Slaney, R.B. (1996). Holland's theory: Its relevance for lesbian women and gay men. *Journal of Vocational Behavior, 48,* 125–135.

Moloney, D.P., Bouchard, T.J., Jr., & Segal, N.L. (1991). A genetic and environmental analysis of the vocational interests of monozygotic and dizygotic twins reared apart. *Journal of Vocational Behavior, 39,* 76–109.

Morrow, P.C. (1993). Work adjustment theory: From a distance. *Journal of Vocational Behavior, 43,* 90–97.

Morrow, S.L., Gore, P.A., Jr., & Campbell, B.W. (1996). The application of a sociocognitive framework to the career development of lesbian women and gay men. *Journal of Vocational Behavior, 48,* 136–148.

Multon, K.D., Brown, S.D., & Lent, R.W. (1991). Relation of self-efficacy beliefs to academic outcomes: A meta-analytic investigation. *Journal of Counseling Psychology, 38,* 30–36.

Murphy, K.R. (1993). Integrating research on work adjustment with research on job performance and behavior in organizations: Perspectives from industrial/organizational psychology. *Journal of Vocational Behavior, 43,* 98–104.

Nevill, D.D. (1997). The development of career development theory. *Career Development Quarterly, 45,* 288–292.

Niles, S.G. (1993). The relationship between Holland types preferences for career counseling. *Journal of Career Development, 19,* 209–220.

Niles, S.G., Anderson, W.P., Jr., & Goodnough, G. (1998). Exploration to foster career development. *Career Development Quarterly, 46,* 262–275.

O'Brien, K.M., & Heppner, M.J. (1996). Applying social cognitive career theory to training career counselors. *Career Development Quarterly, 44,* 367–377.

O'Brien, K.M., Heppner, M.J., Flores, L.Y., & Bikos, L.H. (1997). The career counseling self-efficacy scale: Instrument development and training applications. *Journal of Counseling Psychology, 44,* 20–31.

Oleski, D., & Subich, L.M. (1996). Congruence and career change in employed adults. *Journal of Vocational Behavior, 49,* 221–229.

Osipow, S.H. (1990). Convergence in theories of career choice and development. *Journal of Vocational Behavior, 36,* 122–131.

Osipow, S.H., & Fitzgerald, L.F. (1996). *Theories of career development* (4th ed.). Boston: Allyn & Bacon.

Pajares, F., & Miller, M.D. (1995). Mathematics self-efficacy and mathematics performance: The need for specificity of assessment. *Journal of Counseling Psychology, 42,* 190–198.

Parsons, F. (1989). *Choosing a vocation.* Garrett Park, MD: Garrett Park Press. (Original work published 1909)

Peraino, J.M., & Willerman, L. (1983). Personality correlates of occupational status according to Holland types. *Journal of Vocational Behavior, 22,* 268–277.

Phillips, S.D. (1997). Toward an expanded definition of adaptive decision making. *Career Development Quarterly, 45,* 275–287.

Phillips, S.D., & Blustein, D.L. (1994). Readiness for career choices: Planning, exploring, and deciding. *Career Development Quarterly, 43,* 63–73.

Phillips, S.D., & Imhoff, A.R. (1997). Women and career development: A decade of research. *Annual Review of Psychology, 48,* 31–59.

Pope, M. (1995). Career interventions for gay and lesbian clients: A synopsis of practice knowledge and research needs. *Career Development Quarterly, 44,* 191–203.

Prediger, D.J. (1982). Dimensions underlying Holland's hexagon: Missing link between interests and occupations? *Journal of Vocational Behavior, 21,* 259–287.

Prediger, D.J. (1996). Alternative dimensions for the Tracey-Rounds interest sphere: Comment. *Journal of Vocational Behavior, 48,* 59–67.

Prediger, D.J. (1998). Is interest profile level relevant to career counseling? *Journal of Counseling Psychology, 45,* 204–211.

Prediger, D.J., Swaney, K., & Mau, W.C. (1993). Extending Holland's hexagon: Procedures, counseling applications, and research. *Journal of Counseling and Development, 71,* 422–428.

Prediger, D.J., & Vansickle, T.R. (1992). Locating occupations on Holland's hexagon: Beyond RIASEC [Special issue]. *Journal of Vocational Behavior, 40,* 111–128.

Prince, J.P. (1995). Influences on the career development of gay men. *Career Development Quarterly, 44,* 168–177.

Prince, J.P. (1997). Career assessment with lesbian, gay, and bisexual individuals. *Journal of Career Assessment, 5,* 225–238.

Randahl, G.J. (1991). A typological analysis of the relations between measured vocational interests and abilities. *Journal of Vocational Behavior, 38,* 333–350.

Richards, J.M. (1993). Career development: A ten year longitudinal study in a population of scientists. *Journal of Career Assessment, 1,* 181–192.

Richardson, M.S. (1993). Work in people's lives: A location for counseling psychologists. *Journal of Counseling Psychology, 40,* 425–433.

Richie, B.S., Fassinger, R.E., Linn, S.G., Johnson, J., Prosser, J., & Robinson, S. (1997). Persistence, connection, and passion: A qualitative study of the career development of highly achieving African American-black and white women. *Journal of Counseling Psychology, 44,* 133–148.

Roe, A. (1957). Early determinants of vocational choice. *Journal of Counseling Psychology, 4,* 212–217.

Rohe, D.E., & Krause, J.S. (1998). Stability of interests after severe physical disability: An 11-year longitudinal study. *Journal of Vocational Behavior, 52,* 45–48.

Rolfhus, E.L., & Ackerman, P.L. (1996). Self-report knowledge: At the crossroads of ability, interest, and personality. *Journal of Educational Psychology, 88,* 174–188.

Rooney, R.A., & Osipow, S.H. (1992). Task-specific occupational self-efficacy scale: The development and validation of a prototype. *Journal of Vocational Behavior, 40,* 14–32.

Rosenthal, R. (1990). How are we doing in soft psychology? *American Psychologist, 45,* 775–777.

Rosenthal, R., & Rubin, D.B. (1982). A simple general purpose display of magnitude of experimental effect. *Journal of Educational Psychology, 74,* 166–169.

Rotberg, H.L., Brown, D., & Ware, W.B. (1987). Career self-efficacy expectations and perceived range of career options in community college students. *Journal of Counseling Psychology, 34,* 164–170.

Rounds, J.B. (1990). The comparative and combined utility of work value and interest data in career counseling with adults. *Journal of Vocational Behavior, 37,* 32–45.

Rounds, J.B. (1995). Vocational interests: Evaluating structural hypotheses. In R.V. Dawis & D. Lubinski (Eds.), *Assessing individual differences in human behavior: New concepts, methods, and findings* (pp. 177–232). Palo Alto, CA: Consulting Psychologists Press.

Rounds, J.B., & Day, S.X. (1999). Describing, evaluating, and creating vocational interest structures. In M.L. Savickas & A.R. Spokane (Eds.), *Vocational interests: Their meaning, measurement, and use in counseling.* Palo Alto, CA: Davies-Black.

Rounds, J.B., Henly, G.A., Dawis, R.V., Lofquist, L.H., & Weiss, D.J. (1981). *Manual for the Minnesota Importance Questionnaire.* Minneapolis: University of Minnesota, Department of Psychology.

Rounds, J.B., & Tracey, T.J. (1993). Prediger's dimensional representation of Holland's RIASEC circumplex. *Journal of Applied Psychology, 78,* 875–890.

Rounds, J.B., & Tracey, T.J. (1996). Cross-cultural equivalence of RIASEC models and measures. *Journal of Counseling Psychology, 43,* 210–239.

Rounds, J.B., Tracey, T.J., & Hubert, L. (1992). Methods for evaluating vocational interest structural hypotheses. *Journal of Vocational Behavior, 40,* 239–259.

Ryan, J.M., Tracey, T.J.G., & Rounds, J.B. (1996). Generalizability of Holland's structure of vocational interests across ethnicity, gender, and socioeconomic status. *Journal of Counseling Psychology, 43,* 330–337.

Sackett, S.A., & Hansen, J.C. (1995). Vocational outcomes of college freshmen with flat profiles on the Strong Interest Inventory. *Measurement and Evaluation in Counseling and Development, 28,* 9–24.

Savickas, M.L. (1994). Measuring career development: Current status and future directions. *Career Development Quarterly, 43,* 54–62.

Savickas, M.L. (1996). A framework for linking career theory and practice. In M.L. Savickas & W.B. Walsh (Eds.), *Handbook of career counseling theory and practice* (pp. 191–208). Palo Alto, CA: Davies-Black.

Savickas, M.L. (1997). Career adaptability: An integrative construct for life-span, life-space theory. *Career Development Quarterly, 45,* 247–259.

Savickas, M.L., & Lent, R.W. (Eds.). (1994). *Convergence in career development theories.* Palo Alto, CA: Consulting Psychologists Press.

Savickas, M.L., & Spokane, A.R. (Eds.). (1999). *Vocational interests: Their meaning, measurement, and use in counseling.* Palo Alto, CA: Davies-Black.

Savickas, M.L., & Walsh, W.B. (Eds.). (1996). *Handbook of career counseling theory and practice.* Palo Alto, CA: Davies-Black.

Schaefers, K.G., Epperson, D.L., & Nauta, M.M. (1997). Women's career development: Can theoretically derived variables predict persistence in engineering majors? *Journal of Counseling Psychology, 44,* 173–183.

Schinka, J.A., Dye, D.A., & Curtiss, G. (1997). Correspondence between 5-factor and RIASEC models of personality. *Journal of Personality Assessment, 68,* 355–368.

Schneider, P.L., Ryan, J., Tracey, T.J., & Rounds, J.B. (1996). Examining the relation between Holland's RIASEC types and the interpersonal circle. *Measurement and Evaluation in Counseling and Development, 29,* 123–133.

Schultheiss, D.P., & Blustein, D.L. (1994). Role of adolescent-parent relationships in college student development and adjustment. *Journal of Counseling Psychology, 41,* 248–255.

Schunk, D.H., & Hanson, A.R. (1985). Peer models: Influence on children's self-efficacy and achievement. *Journal of Educational Psychology, 77,* 313–322.

Schunk, D.H., Hanson, A.R., & Cox, P.D. (1987). Peer-model attributes and children's achievement behaviors. *Journal of Educational Psychology, 79,* 54–61.

Smart, R.M. (1998). Career stages in Australian professional women: A test of Super's model [Special issue]. *Journal of Vocational Behavior, 52,* 379–395.

Smart, R.M., & Peterson, C. (1997). Super's career stages and the decision to change careers. *Journal of Vocational Behavior, 51,* 358–374.

Solberg, V.S., Good, G.E., Fischer, A.R., Brown, S.D., & Nord, D. (1995). Career decision-making and career search activities: Relative effects of career search self-efficacy and human agency. *Journal of Counseling Psychology, 42,* 448–455.

Spokane, A. (1985). A review of research on person-environment congruence in Holland's theory of careers. *Journal of Vocational Behavior, 26,* 306–343.

Stead, G.B., & Watson, M.B. (1998). Career research in South Africa: Challenges for the future [Special issue]. *Journal of Vocational Behavior, 52,* 289–299.

Strahan, R.F., & Severinghaus, J.B. (1992). Dealing with ties in Holland-type consistency measures. *Journal of Vocational Behavior, 40,* 260–267.

Strong, E.K., Jr. (1931). *Change of interests with age.* Palo Alto, CA: Stanford University Press.

Subich, L.M. (1992). Comment: Holland's theory: "Pushing the envelope" [Special issue]. *Journal of Vocational Behavior, 40,* 201–206.

Super, D.E. (1983). The history and development of vocational psychology: A personal perspective. In W.B. Walsh & S.H. Osipow (Eds.), *Handbook of vocational psychology* (pp. 5–37). Mahwah, NJ: Erlbaum.

Super, D.E. (1992). Toward a comprehensive theory of career development. In D. Montross & C. Shinkman (Eds.), *Career development: Theory and practice* (pp. 35–64). Springfield, IL: Thomas.

Super, D.E., Savickas, M.L., & Super, C.M. (1996). The life-span, life-space approach to careers. In D. Brown, L. Brooks, & Associates (Eds.), *Career choice and development* (3rd ed., pp. 121–178). San Francisco: Jossey-Bass.

Sutherland, L.F., Fogarty, G.J., & Pithers, R.T. (1995). Congruence as a predictor of occupational stress. *Journal of Vocational Behavior, 46,* 292–309.

Swanson, J.L. (1992). Vocational behavior, 1989–1991: Life-span career development and reciprocal interaction of work and nonwork. *Journal of Vocational Behavior, 41,* 101–161.

Swanson, J.L. (1993). Integrated assessment of vocational interests and self-rated skills and abilities. *Journal of Career Assessment, 1,* 50–65.

Swanson, J.L. (1999). Stability and change in vocational interests. In M.L. Savickas & A.R. Spokane (Eds.), *Vocational interests: Their meaning, measurement, and use in counseling.* Palo Alto, CA: Davies-Black.

Swanson, J.L., Daniels, K.K., & Tokar, D.M. (1996). Assessing perceptions of career-related barriers: The career barriers inventory. *Journal of Career Assessment, 4,* 219–244.

Swanson, J.L., & Hansen, J.C. (1986). A clarification of Holland's construct of differentiation: The importance of score elevation. *Journal of Vocational Behavior, 28,* 163–173.

Swanson, J.L., & Hansen, J.C. (1988). Stability of vocational interests over 4-year, 8-year, and 12-year intervals. *Journal of Vocational Behavior, 33,* 185–202.

Swanson, J.L., & Tokar, D.M. (1991a). College students' perceptions of barriers to career development. *Journal of Vocational Behavior, 38,* 92–106.

Swanson, J.L., & Tokar, D.M. (1991b). Development and initial validation of the Career Barriers Inventory. *Journal of Vocational Behavior, 39,* 344–362.

Swanson, J.L., & Woitke, M.B. (1997). Theory into practice in career assessment for women: Assessment and interventions regarding perceived career barriers. *Journal of Career Assessment, 5,* 443–462.

Tenopyr, M.L. (1993). Construct validation needs in vocational behavior theories. *Journal of Vocational Behavior, 43,* 84–89.

Tinsley, H.E.A. (1993). Special issue on the theory of work adjustment. *Journal of Vocational Behavior, 43,* 1–4.

Tokar, D.M., & Fischer, A.R. (1998). More on RIASEC and the five-factor model of personality: Direct assessment of Prediger's (1982) and Hogan's (1983) dimensions. *Journal of Vocational Behavior, 52,* 246–259.

Tokar, D.M., Fischer, A.R., & Subich, L.M. (1998). Personality and vocational behavior: A selective review of the literature, 1993–1997. *Journal of Vocational Behavior, 53,* 115–153.

Tokar, D.M., & Subich, L.M. (1997). Relative contributions of congruence and personality dimensions to job satisfaction. *Journal of Vocational Behavior, 50,* 482–491.

Tokar, D.M., & Swanson, J.L. (1995). Evaluation of the correspondence between Holland's vocational personality typology and the five-factor model. *Journal of Vocational Behavior, 46,* 89–108.

Tokar, D.M., Vaux, A., & Swanson, J.L. (1995). Dimensions relating Holland's vocational personality typology and the five-factor model. *Journal of Career Assessment, 3,* 57–74.

Tracey, T.J.G. (1997). The structure of interests and self-efficiency expectations: An expanded examination of the spherical model of interests. *Journal of Counseling Psychology, 44,* 32–43.

Tracey, T.J., & Rounds, J.B. (1993). Evaluating Holland's and Gati's vocational-interest models: A structural meta-analysis. *Psychological Bulletin, 113,* 229–246.

Tracey, T.J., & Rounds, J.B. (1994). An examination of the structure of Roe's eight interest fields. *Journal of Vocational Behavior, 44,* 279–296.

Tracey, T.J., & Rounds, J.B. (1995). The arbitrary nature of Holland's RIASEC types: A concentric-circles structure. *Journal of Counseling Psychology, 42,* 431–439.

Tracey, T.J., & Rounds, J.B. (1996). The spherical representation of vocational interests. *Journal of Vocational Behavior, 48,* 3–41.

Tracey, T.J., & Ward, C.C. (1998). The structure of children's interests and competence perceptions. *Journal of Counseling Psychology, 45,* 290–303.

Tracey, T.J., Watanabe, N., & Schneider, P.L. (1997). Structural invariance of vocational interests across Japanese and American cultures. *Journal of Counseling Psychology, 44,* 346–354.

Tranberg, M., Slane, S., & Ekeberg, S.E. (1993). The relation between interest congruence and satisfaction: A metaanlysis. *Journal of Vocational Behavior, 42,* 253–264.

Upperman, P.J., & Church, A.T. (1995). Investigating Holland's typological theory with army occupational specialties. *Journal of Vocational Behavior, 47,* 61–75.

Vasil, L. (1992). Self-efficacy expectations and causal attributions for achievement among male and female university faculty. *Journal of Vocational Behavior, 41,* 259–269.

Vondracek, F.W. (1992). The construct of identity and its use in career theory and research. *Career Development Quarterly, 41,* 130–144.

Vroom, V.H. (1964). *Work and motivation.* New York: Wiley.

Watkins, C.E., & Subich, L.M. (1995). Annual review, 1992–1994: Career development, reciprocal work/nonwork interaction, and women's workforce participation. *Journal of Vocational Behavior, 47,* 109–163.

Weiss, D.J., Dawis, R.V., England, G.W., & Lofquist, L.H. (1967). Manual for the Minnesota Satisfaction Questionnaire. *Minnesota Studies in Vocational Rehabilitation, 22.*

Wiggins, J.S. (1979). A psychological taxonomy of trait-descriptive terms: The interpersonal domain. *Journal of Personality and Social Psychology, 37,* 395–412.

Williams, E.N., Soeprapto, E., Like, K., Touradji, P., Hess, S., & Hill, C.E. (1998). Perceptions of serendipity: Career paths of prominent academic women in counseling psychology. *Journal of Counseling Psychology, 45,* 379–389.

Young, G., Tokar, D.M., & Subich, L.M. (1998). Congruence revisited: Do 11 indices differentially predict job satisfaction and is the relation moderated by person and situation variables? *Journal of Vocational Behavior, 52,* 208–233.

CHAPTER 9

The Development of Academic Achievement in School-Aged Children: Precursors to Career Development

CONSUELO ARBONA

One of the most demanding cognitive and motivational challenges children face is the development of their academic competencies. This immense task begins before children enter school, and it constitutes their predominant activity during childhood, adolescence, and into young adulthood. Attending to the learning needs of young children is of crucial importance in facilitating their academic development. Because learning deficits are cumulative, the effects of early lack of academic achievement are progressively more difficult to counteract as children grow (Arbona, 1994; Levin, 1986). Furthermore, school outcomes have immediate as well as long-term consequences for children and adolescents. Low school achievement predicts negative behaviors in adolescence, such as substance abuse, delinquency, and early sexual intercourse, which, in turn, interfere with school performance and persistence (Dryfoos, 1990). At the same time, the development of intellectual skills in children and adolescents is associated with competent functioning in other areas of life (Masten & Coatsworth, 1998). In adulthood, academic attainment determines, to a great extent, career pursuits and lifestyle choices.

The theoretical and research literature related to the development of academic competencies in children and adolescents is vast. However, this area has not received much attention in the counseling psychology field. The development of academic competencies is particularly relevant for the study of career development and choice. Various authors have noted that the concept of career is most meaningful for individuals who have access to educational opportunities leading to stable occupations that allow for progressive movement over time (Fitzgerald & Betz, 1994; Richardson, 1993). With the notable exception of theoretical and research efforts examining the relation of self-efficacy to academic competence (Lent, Brown, & Hackett, 1994), most of the career related theory and research in counseling psychology has emphasized issues of career choice, primarily among college students. However, in the absence of educational attainment, the range of career choices individuals have is very constrained (Arbona, 1996; Betz, 1994). For this reason, understanding the factors that influence the academic development of children and adolescents is most relevant for vocational and career psychology.

This chapter provides a review of selected theories and empirical investigations related to the development of academic achievement in school age children. Major emphasis is given to sociocognitive theories of achievement motivation that examine the role played by thoughts, emotions, and perceptions of self in students' academic performance and general adjustment to school (Wentzel & Wigfield, 1998). Research examining the influence of parents and peers on students' achievement strivings also is included. The purpose of the chapter is to illustrate theories and research in the field of educational psychology that have direct relevance to psychological aspects of human development which are of interest to counseling psychologists. The approaches in motivation theory and research emphasized in the chapter center around aspects of human functioning that are developmental in nature, predictive of academic behaviors and performance, and amenable to change through sociocognitive and psychoeducational interventions. For the most part, the theoretical and empirical work included in the chapter have emerged from extended programs of research that are still active, some of which have included longitudinal work.

The first section provides a brief overview of the multiple factors identified in the literature that influence academic achievement. Second, the theoretical and empirical literature regarding parental and peer influences in academic achievement are reviewed. In the third section, the following achievement motivation theories and related research are reviewed: attribution theory (Weiner, 1985), achievement goal orientation theory, (Dweck, 1986; Maehr & Meyer, 1997), self-efficacy theory (Bandura, 1986, 1997; Zimmerman, 1995), and expectancy-value theory (Eccles & Wigfield, 1995).

PREDICTORS OF ACADEMIC ACHIEVEMENT: AN OVERVIEW

Academic achievement results from the complex interaction of individuals' aptitudes, skills, motivational dispositions, and environmental influences. Several indices have been used to measure academic achievement. Scores on standardized achievements tests, grades in specific classes, and grade point average (GPA) are the most commonly used indices. In some cases, scores on standardized ability measures or IQ tests are used to measure achievement; however, most often these measures are considered precursors to school success. As may be expected, indices of academic achievement are associated with multiple individual and contextual factors. The theoretical and research literature has paid special attention to the following predictors of academic achievement in school-aged populations: (1) socioeconomic status (SES) of parents, (2) children and parental IQ, (3) quality of schooling, (4) parental and peer influences, and (5) motivational factors. Before examining parental, peer, and motivational influences on academic achievement, a brief overview of the literature regarding the relation of achievement to SES, IQ, and quality of schooling is provided.

Socioeconomic Status

It is commonly accepted that SES strongly influences academic achievement. However, reports of the strength of the relation between SES and academic achievement vary widely across studies (e.g., Cassidy & Lynn, 1991; Entwisle & Alexander, 1992; White, 1982). The different variables that have been used to assess SES and academic achievement may be partially responsible for these inconsistent findings. Results from a meta-analysis of 101 studies indicated that the relation between SES and academic achievement ranged from .10 to .80 (White, 1982). A large amount of the variation in effect size (75%) across studies was explained by four study characteristics, including unit of analyses, measure of SES, measure of academic achievement, and grade level of student.

Analyses based on an aggregated unit (e.g. school, school district), where both the individual achievement and the SES measures were averaged for the unit, produced a higher correlation between SES and academic achievement ($r = .73$) than when the individual was the unit of analyses ($r = .22$). At the individual level of analyses, the correlation between SES and IQ ($r. = 33$) was somewhat larger than between SES and grades ($r. = 24$). As students become older, the strength of these correlations seems to decrease. It is possible that the influence of schooling and other socializing agents may reduce the influence of SES on achievement. It is also possible that a sizable proportion of low-achieving students drop out of school as they grow older, lowering the variance in achievement and decreasing the magnitude of these correlations (White, 1982).

The variables most often used to measure SES have included household income, parental education and occupation, and characteristics of the home environment. White (1982) reported that, on average, the correlation between students' SES, as typically measured (income, occupation, or education of household heads) and students' academic achievement is $r = .22$. However, SES measured in terms of characteristics of the home environment, such as parents' attitudes toward education, parents' aspirations for their children, and cultural and intellectual activities of the family, were more highly correlated with achievement ($r = .55$) than the more traditional demographic indices. This is consistent with other studies that have indicated that parental affective states and parenting practices are the pathways by which parental income, occupation, and education influence children's academic achievement (Garmezy, 1991; Luster & McAdoo, 1994; Valencia, Henderson, & Rankin, 1985). Taken together, these findings imply that other factors, in addition to "social address" variables, play an important role in explaining school success and that the effect of SES on achievement may be indirect, through its influence on these factors. The meta-analysis also suggests that the sheer number of variables used as indicators of SES makes it very difficult to interpret the strength of the relation between SES and academic achievement. In the future, researchers might well avoid the term SES and, instead, refer to the specific variable measured in the study such as income, parental education, school resources, or home atmosphere (White, 1982).

Intelligence

There is consensus among researchers that intelligence, as traditionally measured, and the mental abilities that it entails, predict achievement in school and in life in general (Ceci & Williams, 1997). However, the definition, developmental course, and measurement of these abilities are areas of long-standing controversy. The importance given to this topic by psychology is evidenced by a report published in 1996 by the American Psychological Association's (APA) Board of Scientific Affairs, summarizing what is known and not known regarding intelligence (Neisser et al., 1996). The following year the *American Psychologist* dedicated a special issue to intelligence and lifelong learning (Sternberg, 1997b).

Some authors have defined intelligence in rather narrow terms. Brody (1997), for example, offered the following definition: "IQ may be thought of as an index of the ability to acquire knowledge that distinguishes individuals occupying common social positions in our society" (p. 1046). In this definition, Brody refers to thinking abilities, the more commonly measured aspect of intelligence (often described as g or a general intelligence factor). Analytical abilities, which primarily encompass peoples' capacity to remember abstract information, critique it, and decide on its value (Sternberg, 1997a), is the aspect of intelligence most often examined in relation to academic achievement.

Other authors have proposed a broader definition of intelligence. For example, in Sternberg's (1997a) view, "Intelligence comprises the mental abilities necessary for adaptation to, as well as shaping and selection of, any environmental context" (p. 1030). Sternberg has developed a triarchic theory of intelligence that is based on the assumption that more than one type of ability is necessary for adaptation to environmental contexts. In addition to the analytical abilities measured by conventional IQ tests, he identified two other dimensions of intelligence—practical and creative abilities—that also are expected to contribute to success in school and in the world of work (Sternberg, 1993, cited in Sternberg, 1997a). Research findings using the Triarchic Ability Test have indicated that practical intelligence is relatively independent of analytical intelligence as measured by conventional tests. Practical intelligence also contributes to the prediction of school grades in elementary school when analytical intelligence is held constant (Sternberg & Clinkenbeard, 1995). Even though other authors also have endorsed a broader view of intelligence (e.g., Gardner, 1993), most of the existing research refers to intelligence as traditionally measured by IQ tests. These tests primarily assess mental abilities in terms of numerical reasoning, spatial analogies, vocabulary, and memory.

The relative contribution of heredity and environmental factors to individual differences in IQ scores is an area of heated debate (Neisser et al., 1996; Sternberg, 1997a). Even though it is estimated that in modern Western societies genetic factors contribute as much as 50% to 80% of the variance in IQ, differences in family contextual variables also contribute significantly to variations in IQ scores. On average, the relation of IQ scores to school grades ($r = .25$) and IQ and amount of schooling ($r = .55$) is moderate to strong (Neisser et al., 1996). It is generally believed that IQ acts as a causal factor in predicting academic achievement and school attainment, and, therefore, a person's IQ is not expected to be influenced significantly by years of schooling. From this perspective, it is reasoned that people who stay longer in school and achieve at higher levels do so because of their superior intelligence. However, in an extensive review of the literature, Ceci (1991) presented convincing evidence suggesting that IQ scores and amount of schooling received are reciprocally related. On the one hand, adults' educational attainment is predicted by their IQ scores as children, and, on the other, the amount of schooling a child receives exerts a substantial influence on the formation and maintenance of IQ, independent of parental education or socioeconomic factors. According to Ceci, the nature of IQ tests is in part responsible for this apparent circularity in the relation between IQ scores and school achievement. To a great extent, success on tests of intelligence depends on accumulated knowledge that is learned through schooling. At the same time, many of the skills and attitudes transmitted in the schooling process, including systematic-problem solving, abstract thinking, categorization, and sustained attention to material of little intrinsic interest, are also conducive to successful performance on standardized tests.

The authors of the APA Board of Scientific Affairs' report on intelligence concluded that intellectual competencies emerge from the complex interaction of both genetic and environmental factors, but that the pathways that mediate the relation between heritability and contextual factors to intellectual development are largely unknown (Neisser et al., 1996). Recent research in developmental neuroscience has demonstrated that both the structure and the function of the developing brain are profoundly responsive to experience (Nelson & Bloom, 1997). These findings are consistent with educational research indicating that in order to have long-lasting effects on intellectual ability and academic achievement, enrichment experiences provided to children at-risk need to start in early infancy and continue through the preschool years (Campbell & Ramey, 1994; Johnson & Walker, 1991). The implication here is that it may never be possible to tease out entirely the contributions of genetic and environmental influences in human development in general and in the development of academic competencies in particular. The relevant questions, then, seem to center around the discovery and understanding of the complex mechanisms by which nature and nurture interact in the process of human development.

School Opportunities

Much research has been conducted examining the effect of school organization and instructional practices on students' motivation and school achievement (Mac Iver, Reuman, & Main, 1995). Findings from this research have indicated that learning opportunities vary widely both across and within schools. In turn, these differences have a direct effect on students' academic achievement. In a comprehensive review of the literature, Mac Iver et al. identified four areas in which differences in students' learning opportunities have an impact on their school achievement: (1) access to the core curriculum for their grade level; (2) access to courses that promote the development of higher order knowledge; (3) access to college preparatory, accelerated, and advanced placement courses; and (4) access to information regarding the academic requirements and applications procedures regarding college.

As many as 26% of students in American schools receive academic instruction that emphasizes below–grade-level topics (Mac Iver & Epstein, 1994, cited in Mac Iver et al., 1995). This situation is exacerbated for students who are placed in lower ability groups, either within the classroom or in school tracks. These students tend to receive less demanding instruction in terms of content and skills than their peers (Fuligni, Eccles, & Barber, 1995). Their courses primarily emphasize basic skills and rote learning, rather than conceptual understanding. These differences are important because achievement and persistence in school is related to the content of the curricula to which students are exposed. Studies have shown that "tracking-up" middle school and high school students into college preparatory curricula has a positive long-term effect in students' academic achievement, school persistence, completion of college preparatory courses, and career expectations (Fuligni et al., 1995; Nyberg, McMillin, O'Neill-Rood, & Florence, 1997). This practice favors minority and majority students, as well as students of low and medium ability. On the other hand, students placed in low-achievement groups tend to do worse than their counterparts who are placed in heterogeneous classrooms (Fuligni et al., 1995). Therefore, it seems that tracking students according to ability level serves to amplify rather than diminish initial differences in academic achievement that result in different developmental trajectories.

In part as a product of tracking practices, students have differential access to college preparatory courses in high school, primarily in the areas of science and math. Many students who aspire to go to college do not get placed in high school courses that would enhance their chances of getting admitted to a four-year university. Similarly, many students do not pursue an accelerated sequence of math courses necessary to complete the introductory math college requirements that filters many students out of quantitative fields (Mac Iver et al., 1995). Even though lower achieving students are more adversely affected by these practices (Fuligni et al., 1995), studies have found that talented students are also affected. A study of four high schools in California indicated that 7% to 60% of students at the seventy-fifth national percentile in math achievement did not receive a college preparatory course in the tenth grade. Often times these mismatches occur because students and teachers ignore college requirements and because of flaws in schools' scheduling processes (Delaney, 1991).

In addition to influencing learning opportunities, aspects of school organization affect student-teacher relations and student motivation, which in turn influence academic achievement (Maehr & Midgley, 1991; Midgley, Anderman, & Hicks, 1995). Uguroglu and Walberg (1979) estimated that motivation measures typically account for 11% of the variance in achievement and ability measures (with a range of from 1% to 36%). This is consistent with findings from more recent research, indicating that self-efficacy beliefs account for 11% to 18% of variance in academic variables (Multon, Brown, & Lent, 1991; Schunk, 1989). As students become older, the correlation between SES and academic achievement decreases (White, 1982), whereas the relation between motivation and achievement increases (Multon et al., 1991; Uguroglu & Walberg, 1979). These findings suggest that motivational variables play an important role in the development of academic competencies in children and adolescents.

In sum, ability, socioeconomic status of the family, and schooling practices are associated with academic achievement in children and adolescents. However, research findings also have indicated that children with similar cognitive abilities and from similar socioeconomic backgrounds differ in their academic achievement and school success (e.g., Masten & Coatsworth, 1998; Neisser et al., 1996). It is, therefore, imperative to identify factors that may help explain these differences and to examine the pathways by which they exert their influence. Parental behaviors, peer influences, and motivational strivings have emerged as important variables in this regard.

PARENTAL AND PEER INFLUENCES

In recent years, research efforts have been directed at examining the role of the social context in the academic achievement and related behaviors of children and adolescents. Findings from this research have indicated that in addition to SES and schooling practices, parenting practices and relations with peers influence students' academic performance and achievement motivation (Steinberg, Lamborn, Dornbusch, & Darling, 1992; Wentzel & Wigfield, 1998). Parenting practices seem to influence the academic achievement of children and adolescents directly and indirectly. Parents can play a direct role in children's learning by providing them with educational opportunities and resources and by participating in school and learning activities. The number and type of educational resources available to children, such as the quality of the schools they attend and the number of books and educational resources available in the home, have been linked to academic achievement (Hess & Holloway, 1984). Similarly, parental involvement with young children's school related activities, such as helping with homework and reading to them, has been associated with positive academic outcomes (Hess & Holloway, 1984). Although few studies have examined these issues with adolescents, the available evidence suggests that parents' involvement in school related activities also enhances the academic performance of high school students (Steinberg, Lamborn, et al., 1992). Aspects of family functioning are also believed to influence children's academic achievement indirectly by facilitating the development of cognitive and social skills necessary for school success (Wentzel, 1994).

In a review of studies of preschool, elementary, and middle-school children, Hess and Holloway (1984) identified five processes linking parenting practices and school achievement: (1) verbal interaction between mother and child, (2) quality of the relationship between parent and children, (3) discipline and control strategies, (4) parental beliefs and attributions about the child, and (5) parents' achievement expectations. These parenting practices are believed to mediate the relation between SES and academic achievement. The most widely studied parenting-related variable seems to be parenting style, primarily defined in terms of the discipline and control strategies employed by parents.

School Grades

In her seminal work, Baumrind (1971) examined parenting styles in relation to children's cognitive and social competence. Based on observations of parent-child interactions, Baumrind identified three parenting styles—authoritative, authoritarian, and permissive—that differ in terms of the amount of parental responsiveness and control provided to children. The authoritative style is a democratic parenting style characterized by firm enforcement of rules and standards, open communication between parent and child, and encouragement of the child's independence and individuality. Authoritarian parents, on the other hand, tend to be overdemanding and controlling, expecting unconditional obedience and discouraging open communication between parent and child. Finally, permissive parents tend to exert little control over the child, make few demands for mature behavior, and allow considerable self-regulation by the child.

In studies with White, middle-class preschool and elementary school children, Baumrind (1978) found that these parenting styles were differentially related to children's social and cognitive skills. Authoritative parenting was associated with independent and socially responsible behaviors, as well as with high-cognitive competence. Authoritarian parenting, on the other hand, was associated with low independence, lack of socially responsible behaviors, and low-cognitive competence. Children of permissive parents were immature, lacked self-reliance and independence, and were low in cognitive competence. Baumrind's findings are consistent with other studies that have examined the relation between parental practices and children's school achievement, primarily among White, middle-class populations (Grolnick & Ryan, 1989; Hess & McDevitt, 1984).

Extending Baumrind's work, Dornbusch, Steinberg, and their associates have examined the relation of parenting styles to the academic achievement of high school students from various ethnic and socioeconomic groups (Dornbusch, Ritter, Leiderman, Roberts, & Fraleigh, 1987; Durbin,

Darling, Steinberg, & Brown, 1993; Lamborn, Mounts, Steinberg, & Dornbusch, 1991; Steinberg, Dornbusch, & Brown, 1992; Steinberg, Elmen, & Mounts, 1989; Steinberg, Lamborn, et al., 1992; Steinberg, Mounts, Lamborn, & Dornbusch, 1991). These researchers assessed parental styles from the perspective of the adolescents by asking them to report the frequency of certain parental behaviors that corresponded to Baumrind's parenting typology. Findings from Dornbusch and Steinberg's program of research have indicated that authoritative parenting is related to the school success of high school students contemporaneously and over time. Families with higher parental education tend to be higher in authoritative parenting and lower in authoritarian and permissive parenting. However, parenting authoritativeness seems to have a positive effect on adolescents' academic achievement across gender and socioeconomic groups.

In an initial study, Dornbusch et al. (1987) examined the relation between parental styles and students' grades (self-reported by students) among a large group of ethnically diverse high school students (approximately 8,000 White, Hispanic, African American, and Asian students). Multiple regressions within each ethnic group indicated that authoritarian parenting was negatively associated with grades among students from all ethnic groups. Authoritative parenting, on the other hand, was associated with higher grades for the White and Hispanic students, and it was unrelated to grades among Asian and Black students. Overall, the parental styles' typology best predicted grades for White students and seemed to be the least useful in explaining the academic achievement of Asian American students. Asian students reported both higher grades and higher levels of authoritarian parenting than White students.

The relation between parental authoritativeness and academic achievement seems to be mediated by other student and parental behaviors. In a path analytic study with White adolescents aged 10 to 16, Steinberg et al. (1989) found that students' report of authoritative parenting predicted, over a one-year period, students' work orientation which, in turn, was related to school grades. In a longitudinal study with high school students, Steinberg, Lamborn, et al. (1992) found that the relation between parental authoritativeness and grades obtained one year later was mediated by parental school involvement (attendance at school programs, help with course selection, and monitoring students' progress). Further analyses indicated that parental involvement was most highly correlated with school performance in authoritative homes, which suggests that nonauthoritative parenting may undermine the positive effects of parental involvement in school. Taken together, these findings indicate that, over time, adolescents from authoritative homes obtain better grades than their peers, in part because they develop a more positive attitude toward their work, and in part because their parents tend to be more involved in their schooling.

In subsequent studies, Steinberg and associates examined the relation of parental styles to adolescents' psychosocial development, psychological distress, problem behaviors, and academic achievement (Lamborn et al., 1991; Steinberg et al., 1991). In these studies, a large group of ethnically diverse adolescents (approximately 15,000 students in 9 high schools) was classified into four subgroups—authoritative, authoritarian, indulgent, or neglectful (the last two are types of permissive parenting)—according to the adolescents' ratings of their parents as high or low in two dimensions, strictness/supervision and acceptance/involvement. Findings indicated that adolescents from authoritative homes (high in both dimensions) fared the best in terms of all the indicators, whereas adolescents from neglectful homes (low on both dimensions) fared the worst (Lamborn et al., 1991). Further analyses (Steinberg et al., 1991) indicated that regardless of their ethnicity, social class, or parents' marital status, adolescents who described their parents as strict, accepting, and democratic (authoritative) also reported less anxiety and depression, and described themselves as more self-reliant and less likely to engage in delinquent behaviors than their peers. However, consistent with previous findings (Dornbusch et al., 1987), authoritativeness was associated with grades only among White and Hispanic adolescents (Steinberg et al., 1991). Regardless of parenting practices, Asian students outperformed and African American students underperformed their peers (Steinberg et al., 1991). These findings indicated that even though parenting styles were associated with emotional well-being in adolescents from all ethnic groups, ethnic differences in academic achievement could not be fully explained by differences in parental styles. In further analyses, Steinberg, Dornbusch, et al. (1992) identified three processes that helped explain the observed differences in academic achievement across the four ethnic groups: (1) students' work habits, (2) students' beliefs regarding the consequences of school failure for their occupational future, and (3) differences in parental and peer support for academic achievement.

In two separate questionnaire items (Steinberg, Dornbusch, et al., 1992), the adolescents were asked what consequences they expected for their future job prospects if they did or did not receive a good education in high school. Students from all ethnic groups endorsed the belief that a good education leads to good jobs, but holding this belief was not associated with students' attributions or behaviors regarding academic tasks. Asian American adolescents endorsed more than any other ethnic group the belief that educational failure will have negative occupational consequences. Hispanic and African American adolescents, on the other hand, indicated that lack of a good education would not hurt their job prospects. Results also showed that the belief in the negative consequences of school failure was highly correlated with students' engagement in academic activities (e.g., time spent on homework), and with their attribution of school grades to effort. In other words, Asian American students, who were the most pessimistic regarding school failure, reported spending more time doing homework and were more likely to attribute school success to effort than their African American and Hispanic counterparts. Because all groups valued education as a means of occupational attainment, these findings suggest that ethnic differences in grades had more to do with students' fears regarding the consequences of school failure and with their work habits and effort in school than with cultural values regarding the importance of education. This is consistent with other research that has indicated that work habits and school effort may affect school grades through their influence on learning and teacher grading practices (Jussim, 1991; Wentzel, 1993).

The relative influence of parents and peers also seems relevant in understanding ethnic differences in adolescents' grades. Adolescents who received support and encouragement for academic achievement from both parents and peers performed better than adolescents who only received support from one source and not the other, or those who received no support from any source (Steinberg, Dornbusch, et al., 1992). Among White students, those from authoritative homes reported belonging to a peer crowd more supportive of school achievement and engagement than did their peers from nonauthoritative homes (Durbin et al., 1993). These findings suggest that authoritative parenting was related to these students' school success directly, and also through its influence on peer crowd affiliation. It is possible that the lack of relation of authoritative parenting to peer affiliation (Steinberg et al., 1992) and to academic success (Dornbusch et al., 1987; Lamborn et al., 1991; Steinberg et al., 1991) among Asian and African American students is related to the characteristics of the peer groups these students generally have access to, given the level of ethnic segregation that characterizes most ethnically mixed high schools in the United States.

Consistent with other studies (e.g., Eaton & Dembo, 1997; Ogbu, 1992), Steinberg, Dornbusch, et al. (1992) found that, across social class groups, Asian Americans reported a great amount of peer support for academic achievement, whereas African Americans students found it very difficult to join a peer group that encouraged academic achievement. Taken together, these findings imply that the superior academic achievement of Asian American students is due, in part, to the strong support for academic activities they receive from their peers that seems to offset the negative implications of nonauthoritative parenting. African Americans, on the other hand, seem to be caught up in the bind between academic success and peer affiliation (Ogbu, 1992). To affiliate with peers who support and encourage academic achievement, many African American adolescents, especially in inner city settings, would have to cross ethnic boundaries, which is very difficult to do. Therefore, for many African American students the beneficial effects of authoritative parenting on academic achievement seems to be offset by lack of support from the peer group.

Similarly, the lower academic achievement among Hispanic students may be related to the greater prevalence of authoritarian parenting in their homes that is not offset by strong peer support for academic achievement (Steinberg, Dornbusch, et al., 1992).

Psychological Distress and Self-Restraint

The work by Steinberg and associates (Steinberg, Dornbusch, et al., 1992) suggests that students' work orientation, parental school involvement, and peer support mediate the relation between parenting styles and adolescents' academic achievement. Social and emotional adjustment also seem to play a role in linking parenting practices to the academic performance of children and adolescents (Wentzel, 1994). Studies have indicated that the quality of the parent-child relationship is related to children's emotional adjustment (Papini & Roggman, 1992) and to childhood social behaviors such as aggression and noncompliant behavior (Baumrind, 1978). At the same time, children's depressive affect (DuBois, Felner, Brand, Adan, & Evans, 1992) and inappropriate social behaviors (Wentzel, Weinberger, Ford, & Feldman, 1990) seem to be negatively related to school grades. For example, interest in school activities and emotional well-being predicted the classroom social behavior of middle-school students. In turn, adequate social behavior was positively associated with grades (Wentzel et al., 1990).

These findings imply that parenting practices are related to children's social and emotional behaviors and that these behaviors, in turn, are related to academic achievement. Wentzel and colleagues have conducted a series of studies examining these relations simultaneously. More specifically, they have investigated two aspects of social and emotional adjustment—emotional distress and behavioral restraint—in relation to parenting practices and to academic performance among sixth-grade boys (Feldman & Wentzel, 1990; Wentzel & Feldman, 1993; Wentzel, Feldman, & Weinberger, 1991). Self-restraint (students' self-regulatory behaviors directed at achieving long-term goals) involves four dimensions of socially competent classroom behavior: (1) impulse control, (2) suppression of aggression, (3) consideration of others, and (4) responsibility. In these studies, self-restraint was measured by students' self-reports and by a composite score of teachers and peer nominations of students' behaviors. Emotional distress was assessed by self-report measures of anxiety, depression, self-esteem, and emotional well-being.

An observational study revealed that qualities of the parent-son and parent-parent relationship predicted the child's social behavior and competence in school (Feldman & Wentzel, 1990). A series of multiple regression analyses indicated that proper parental control (autonomy with appropriate limits) and lack of parent-son and mother-father hostility predicted son's behavioral restraint in the classroom which, in turn, was associated with higher year-end grades. These findings suggest that children who grow up in families characterized by hostility and lack of adequate parental control have lower grades, in part, because they exhibit socially inappropriate behaviors in class. Similar findings were obtained when parenting practices were assessed in terms of sons' self-report of parental discipline style (Wentzel & Feldman, 1993; Wentzel et al., 1991). Parental discipline style, which was similar to the authoritarian parenting style described by Baumrind (1971) and Steinberg and associates (Steinberg et al., 1991), referred to parental practices that included harsh and inconsistent discipline and the use of severe punishment. Wentzel et al. (1991) found that fathers' discipline style was related negatively to their sixth-grade sons' self-restraint, whereas both mothers' and fathers' discipline style was related positively to the boys' emotional distress. In turn, self-restraint and emotional distress predicted students' year-end grades. Furthermore, parents' discipline styles at sixth grade predicted the students' self-restraint in class four years later. Students' self-restraint in tenth grade, in turn, was related positively to both their motivation to achieve and their grades (Wentzel & Feldman, 1993).

The studies by Wentzel and associates suggested that parenting practices influenced school grades by contributing to the sons' feeling of emotional well-being and to the development of appropriate classroom behaviors. Because of the correlational nature of these analyses, it is also possible that these findings reflect a reciprocal, rather than a unidirectional, relation between social and emotional adjustment, parenting practices, and academic achievement. For example, children's distress may be generated or exacerbated by their academic failure, and parenting practices may be influenced by parents' reactions to children's distress or misbehavior in school. Wentzel (1994) argued that, developmentally, it is expected that parenting practices would influence children's behavior and emotional adjustment, and that appropriate classroom behaviors would precede academic achievement. Some research findings have provided support for this argument.

The work by Baumrind (1978) described earlier indicated that parental practices influence the social competence of preschool children. This suggests that by the time children arrive at school the effect of parenting on social competence is already in place. Longitudinal studies have shown that nonaggressive and adaptive social behavior in elementary and middle school predicted grades and test scores in high school, when controlling for students' IQ (Feldhusen, Thurston, & Benning, 1970; Lambert, 1972). In addition, experimental studies have indicated that interventions designed to develop and enhance students' socially responsible behaviors often result in higher academic achievement (Coie & Krehbiel, 1984), whereas interventions implemented to increase academic skills generally do not result in improved social behaviors in the classroom (Hops & Cobb, 1974). Nevertheless, longitudinal work examining simultaneously the relation between parental practices, social behavior in the classroom, and academic achievement is needed to establish the causal directions of these effects.

Be that as it may, questions remain regarding the role of social behaviors and emotional adjustment in promoting academic achievement. It is important to note that in most of the studies conducted by Wentzel and associates, the relation between social and emotional adjustment and school success was much stronger when academic achievement was assessed by school grades than when it was assessed using scores on standardized achievement tests. These findings have added to an ongoing debate regarding what school grades actually measure (Jussim, 1989, 1991; Wentzel, 1991, 1993). Jussim (1989, 1991) contended that the discrepancy between teachers' grades and scores on standardized tests reflects, in part, teachers' attitudes and biases. Wentzel (1991, 1993), on the other hand, argued that this discrepancy is due to the different skills required to demonstrate competence on the classroom versus standardized achievement tests. School achievement requires both socially appropriate and academically competent behaviors, whereas scores on standardized tests primarily reflect intellectual skills. From this perspective, Wentzel (1991, 1994) has identified various pathways by which social responsibility may influence school success. Children who show appropriate social behaviors are likely to adhere to student-role requirements, such as paying attention and spending time on-task, that are consistent and positive predictors of academic performance. Inappropriate social behaviors, on the other hand, are likely to compete with learning and instruction. In addition, teachers may interpret socially responsible behaviors, such as showing interest and putting forth effort, as attempts to conform to expected classroom norms and reward them as aspects of academic achievement.

In summary, research findings by Steinberg, Wentzel, and their associates have indicated that parenting styles and family functioning are related to children's academic achievement directly, and indirectly, by way of their influence on students' work orientation, emotional distress, and restraint related behaviors. Parenting practices characterized by an adequate level of responsiveness and discipline are related to the development of a positive attitude toward work, a sense of emotional well-being, and appropriate social behaviors in children. These outcomes, in turn, predict students' school grades. At the same time, parenting practices characterized by overly demanding behaviors and harsh and inconsistent discipline are associated with more negative school outcomes. The work of Steinberg, Lamborn, et al. (1992) also indicated that the availability of school-oriented peers within the ethnic group interacts with parenting practices in the promotion of academic achievement, which underscores the importance of considering the multiple contexts that influence adolescents' behaviors. These findings suggest that enhancing the academic achievement of adolescents requires attention to both parental behaviors and peer norms.

ACHIEVEMENT MOTIVATION

The study of achievement motivation in the fields of education and psychology (Weiner, 1990) has a long and fruitful history. Maehr and Meyer (1997) have defined motivation as personal investment. They described the study of motivation as the study of "when and how do individuals invest time and energy in a particular activity" (p. 373). In the academic realm, this investment has been examined in terms of the direction of students' choices about what to do, the persistence they show in pursuing the choices made, and the intensity and quality of the behaviors students exhibit while pursuing their chosen activities. Of primary interest in education and career-related research has been the prediction and understanding of why students choose to pursue one course of action versus another (e.g., high school course selection, choice of major, career choice) (e.g., Wigfield, 1994). Persistence in educational tasks, or continuing motivation, also is considered an important aspect of motivation because long-term investment in learning is necessary for school success. Finally, in the last decade researchers have examined the quality of students' investment in educational activities. Quality of investment has been measured in terms of students' choice of challenging tasks, the use of strategic approaches to learning, and type and level of engagement in activities (Pintrich & De Groot, 1990). In summary, motivational research as it relates to education has examined both the factors that influence learning at one point in time and the factors that enhance long-term investment in learning.

Current paradigms conceptualize motivation as the product of the interaction between the person and the environment (Weiner, 1990). Maehr and Meyer (1997) have described the evolution of the concepts used in motivation research to signal the person and environment constructs in terms of three metaphors: person as machine, person as decision maker, and person as creator of meaning. Freud and Hull initially provided a mechanistic view of humans that described behavior as guided, inhibited, and enhanced by basic drives. Behavior was seen as motivated by social needs-based drives that, in some way, were related to basic physiological or innate affective needs (Weiner, 1990). From this dynamic framework emerged the "need for achievement" concept which linked academic motivation to a basic human need to establish competence.

Decision making first emerged as a major construct in motivation for schooling in the work of Atkinson (Atkinson & Birch, 1978). Consistent with a dynamic conception of motivation, Atkinson's work focused on motivational dispositions, such as the need for achievement, in explaining the choices students make. Atkinson defined motivation as the product of how important the outcome is for the person multiplied by the person's expected probability of attaining it. This conceptualization of motivation stressed the importance of thoughts about one's competencies and values in the decision-making process. According to Maehr and Meyer (1997), Atkinson's conception of motivation and the expectancy-value models of motivation it is associated with (e.g., Eccles's expectancy value model; Eccles & Wigfield, 1995) was more consistent with a view of the person as a "decision maker" than as a "reacting mechanism" (p. 384). Weiner (1985), a student of Atkinson, proposed that students' causal attributions regarding achievement outcomes, rather than their motivational dispositions, determined subsequent achievement strivings. Weiner's attribution perspective on achievement motivation emphasized the judgments people make regarding the perceived causes for their successes and failures and did not pay much attention to issues of importance or value. More recently, Eccles and Wigfield have examined in more depth the role of values in motivational strivings.

The observation that attributions of success and failure varied across persons (e.g., men and women) and situations (e.g., situations defined as play versus work) led to an interest in examining how people define success and failure and the purposes they have in trying to achieve one and avoid the other. In other words, the goals, self-beliefs, and values that people bring to situations emerged as important factors in understanding the nature of motivation. Issues of purposes and goals, examined in terms of achievement goal orientations (Dweck, 1986), self-efficacy beliefs (Bandura, 1986; Zimmerman, 1995), and subjective-task values (Eccles & Wigfield, 1995), ushered in the view of the person as "creator of meaning" (Maehr & Meyer, 1997). The goals and purposes the person has in a given situation not only seem particularly important in understanding the choices a person makes and the persistence in pursuing them, but the quality of the behaviors demonstrated.

Research examining the contribution of motivational variables to academic achievement has focused primarily on middle class populations. At the same time, a large proportion of the studies that have included ethnic minority students have been limited to comparing them with White students in terms of their endorsement of motivational variables. Because findings from such comparative studies do not say much about the process by which motivational variables influence academic achievement, it is not clear to what extent social class and ethnicity interact with, or relate to, achievement motivation in predicting academic achievement (Graham, 1994). Schultz (1993) examined the relation of social class and achievement motivation to academic achievement among African American and Hispanic elementary school students. Results indicated that both social class and achievement motivation explained unique variance in students' achievement scores. These findings suggest that achievement motivation contributes to academic achievement among more and less advantaged ethnic minority children. Studies that examine the relation of motivational variables to academic achievement among children from various social classes and ethnic backgrounds, as well as studies that examine within group differences in the relation between motivational constructs and achievement, are needed.

Attribution Theory and Research

Attribution theory, as formulated by Weiner (1985), primarily examines the reasons students give themselves to explain their experiences of success and failure and the cognitive, affective, and behavioral consequences that follow. These consequences include affective reactions to success and failure, evaluations of personal competency, expectations for the future, and persistence in the face of difficulties (Graham, 1991; Weiner, 1985). It appears it is more important for people to find the reasons why they have failed than it is to find an explanation for success. For example, students are more prone to ask themselves why they failed a class, or why they have difficulty solving math problems, than to wonder why things went well (Graham, 1991). In American culture, ability (including both aptitude and skills) and effort are the dominant perceived causes of success and failure. Other causes include personality, characteristics of the task, availability of resources, and luck. However, peoples' perceptions of their own competence and judgments regarding effort exerted seem to be the two most important reasons in explaining achievement outcomes (Weiner, 1985). In this section, the application of attribution theory to academic motivation is discussed.

Affective and Behavioral Consequences of Attributional Styles

Attributional styles, or peoples' interpretations of the causes that explain behavioral outcomes, may be described in terms of three dimensions: (1) locus, (2) stability, and (3) controllability. The locus dimension refers to whether the cause is perceived to be external or internal to the person. External causes include such things as luck, difficulty of the task, or teachers' judgments. Both ability and effort are considered internal causes because they refer to characteristics or behaviors of the person. The stability dimension describes causes as constant or varying over time. Ability is considered a stable cause that is not amenable to change, whereas level of effort exerted may change from situation to situation. Finally, the controllability dimension refers to the person's perceived control over the cause of the event, which is associated with personal responsibility. For example, effort is perceived to be under the control of the person who decides how hard to try in a given task. Ability, on the other hand, is considered a trait that a person either has or does not have and, therefore, is not controllable. In sum, ability is an internal, stable, uncontrollable cause whereas effort is internal, unstable, and controllable. Other possible causes such as luck and difficulty of the task also may described in terms of these three dimensions.

These conceptual distinctions about causes are important because each dimension is associated with specific affective responses that have implications for achievement related thoughts and behaviors (Weiner, 1985). The locus dimension is linked to self-esteem related feelings. Attributing outcomes to internal causes (e.g., ability) leads to feelings of pride when one experiences success, but to negative feeling about self in situations of failure. For example, children who attributed success to ability (internal cause) and failure to lack of effort or bad luck (external causes) reported higher self-esteem and academic self-competence than children who attributed success to luck (external cause) and failure to lack of ability (internal cause) (Kurtz, Betz, & Schneider, 1994; Watkins & Gutierrez, 1990a). Feelings of guilt and shame are associated with the controllability dimension. Guilty feelings are likely to emerge when controllable factors, such as lack of effort or lack of knowledge, are identified as the cause of failure. On the other hand, blaming failure on uncontrollable causes, such as lack of ability, leads to feelings of shame and helplessness. For example, fifth- and sixth-grade students who reported lack of academic competence and who perceived that they did not have much control over their academic outcomes, expressed more depressive symptoms after receiving unacceptable grades than did their peers without such cognitions (Hilsman & Garber, 1995). The stability dimension is associated with thoughts and feelings related to expectations for the future (Weiner, 1985).

Students' emotional reactions to different types of attributions for success and failure are important because they influence expectancies for success which, in turn, are believed to motivate future behavior (Weiner, 1985). Most of the research in attribution theory has examined the relation of attributional style to academic achievement motivation in situations of failure. Ascriptions of failure to effort, or other controllable causes, are considered adaptive attributions, whereas ascribing failure to causes that are out of the student's control is considered maladaptive. Attributing failure to unchangeable causes implies that one's behavior will not impact future outcomes, and it is likely to engender feelings of hopelessness that may lead to disengagement from academic tasks (Graham & Brown, 1988). On the other hand, attributing failure to unstable causes (e.g., lack of effort) that are amenable to change leads to more hopeful feelings and proactive behaviors (Weiner, 1985). Attribution retraining programs have been effective in increasing students' reported attributions to lack of effort, rather than to lack of ability (Forsterling, 1985). Adaptive attributions have been linked to task persistence and the academic performance of school-aged children (Andrews & Debus, 1978; Kurtz et al., 1994; Watkins & Gutierrez, 1990a).

Teachers' Behaviors and Students' Attributions

According to attribution theory, reactions to the success and failure of others is influenced by judgments regarding the perceived responsibility of the other person in causing the outcome (Graham, 1991). Controllable outcomes increase personal responsibility; therefore, they are judged with more severity than outcomes perceived as uncontrollable. Consistent with this view, teachers tend to react with pity or sympathy when they perceive students' failure as caused by low ability, and with anger when the perceived cause is lack of effort (Weiner, Graham, Stern, & Lawson, 1982). In turn, teachers' affective and behavioral reactions to students' experiences of success and failure provide students with indirect information regarding the causes of their achievement outcomes. This information may serve as the antecedents of students' self-ascriptions because it may help them determine if their performance in a school task is primarily due to effort or ability (Graham, 1991). As is discussed later in the chapter, students often perceive ability and effort as compensatory causes of achievement (Nicholls, 1984). That is, the more effort they need to exert on a task the less ability they believe they have, whereas achievements that require little effort imply high ability.

In a laboratory study, Graham (1984) found that sixth-grade students who had failed at a puzzle-solving task were more likely to blame their failure on lack of effort when the experimenter conveyed anger, and to lack of ability when the experimenter responded with pity. These findings suggest that teachers' behaviors that may be considered negative, such as anger and criticism, may communicate to some students the belief that they can do better, which implies that they have the ability to do so. Sympathy, on the other hand, may undermine students' strivings by communicating low-ability attributions. In other words, it is possible that well-timed and appropriate criticism may enhance students' motivational dispositions, whereas indiscriminate praise may be detrimental to students' motivation and achievement.

Attribution Theory and Cross-Cultural Populations

Weiner (1985) has suggested that attributional principles are universal. However, other researchers (Maehr & Nicholls, 1980) have noted that people adhering to worldviews that differ from American mainstream may not view ability and effort as the dominant causes of achievement, or they may vary in the extent to which they define specific causes, such as effort or ability, as controllable or uncontrollable. Research findings with international populations suggest similarities across cultural groups in the causes students identify for success and failure. For example, children from various European and Asian countries identified ability and effort as the most common explanations of success and failure at school (Oettingen, 1995; Singhal, 1988). Studies with international populations also have shown the expected theoretical relations between attribution beliefs and factors related to academic achievement. For example, Watkins and Gutierrez (1990b) found that, among Filipino high school students, attributions for high grades to either ability or effort mediated the relation between self-esteem and academic achievement in math and English.

Graham (1991, 1994) has argued that attribution theory provides a useful framework for understanding the academic motivation patterns of African American students. However, current and past research has mostly compared African American and White students in their causal attributions without examining the relation of causal thoughts and feelings to subsequent achievement behaviors among the African American students. Most studies conducted in the 1970s reported racial differences, indicating that African American students attached less value to effort as a cause for achievement and were more externally oriented in their attributions for their own outcomes. More recent findings, however, have shown no racial differences in attributional judgments about others (Whitehead, Smith, & Eichorn, 1982) or about the students themselves (Graham & Long, 1986; Hall, Howe, Merkel, & Lederman, 1986). Similarly, Duda (1985) found that White and Mexican American students did not differ in their attribution pattern regarding classroom success and failure.

Research examining the relation between causal attributions and motivational processes in African American and other ethnic minority students is needed. For example, attribution theory proposes that in the presence of academic failure, sympathy from others conveys a message of low ability. It seems relevant to examine to what extent African American and Latino children who experience academic problems are more likely to receive teacher sympathy than their White counterparts (Graham, 1994). In an analogue study comparing teacher's causal attributions for past performance of hypothetical students, teachers perceived the African American students' performance as more externally caused than identical performance ascribed to White students (Wiley & Eskilson, 1978). Because external causes often are out of the control of the student, such perceptions may lead to teacher sympathy and convey low-ability cues to ethnic and racial minority students.

In summary, attribution theory proposes that causal attributions influence students' affective reactions to academic failure, as well as their expectancies regarding future outcomes. Affective reactions and expectancies, in turn, are expected to influence students' persistence and performance in school tasks. Attribution research has mostly examined causal thoughts without paying much attention to the role of emotions in motivating achievement related behaviors. Findings have indicated that school age children who report adaptive attributions tend to persist longer in academic tasks and perform better than children with maladaptive attributions. However, there is no research that links achievement related emotions such as pride, shame, or guilt to changes in academic performance (Graham, 1991). Furthermore, most of this research has examined causal thoughts as they relate to experiences of failure. However, ascriptions for success may also be adaptive or maladaptive. For example, attributing success to good luck, an external and not controllable cause, may mitigate feelings of pride and lower the person's expectations for future success (Graham, 1991). There is evidence that children who feel helpless tend to attribute their success to external and uncontrollable causes (Diener & Dweck, 1980), which diminishes their expectations of experiencing success in the future. At the same time, attributing success to ability may enhance the students' self-efficacy, which may lead to improved academic outcomes.

Achievement Goal Orientation Theory and Research

Achievement goals are defined as students' reasons for engaging in academic work. Achievement goal orientation theory proposes that these reasons influence students' behaviors, cognitions, and feelings regarding school work. These behavioral and affective consequences, in turn, influence the level and quality of students' engagement in academic tasks. It is believed that individual and contextual factors determine the goals adopted by students. Because students tend to pursue similar goals across different achievement situations (Duda & Nicholls, 1992), to some extent these goals represent personal orientations they bring to the situation. At the same time, the psychological environment of the classroom and the school seem to influence the goals students adopt (Anderman & Maehr, 1994). Most of the research on achievement goals has focused on learning versus performance goals (Dweck, 1986). These two types of goals also have been labeled task versus ego involved (Nicholls, 1984) and mastery versus ability focused goals (Ames & Archer, 1988). In this chapter, the labels learning and performance goals are used.

In recent years, a growing body of empirical work examining the relation between students' achievement goal orientations and the quality of their engagement in academic tasks has accumulated. This research has primarily focused on three issues: (1) the definition of learning and performance goals, (2) the relation of learning and performance goals to aspects of academic motivation, and (3) the development and correlates of students' goal orientations.

Definition and Assessment of Learning and Performance Goals

A learning goal orientation is characterized by students' intrinsic interest in expanding their skills and mastering academic tasks. Students who adopt a learning goal orientation are likely to ask themselves, "How can I do this task?" and "What will I learn?" In contrast, students with a performance goal orientation are most interested in demonstrating their ability and outperforming their peers (Dweck, 1986). These students are mostly concerned with obtaining positive evaluations of their competencies and, especially, avoiding negative judgments. They ask themselves, "Can I do this task?" and "Will I look smart?" Achievement goals provide students with a cognitive framework from which they perceive and react to experiences of success and failure in academic tasks. Students with a learning goal orientation tend to attribute academic success to effort, and in situations of failure are expected to change strategies and increase effort. In contrast, students who have a performance orientation are likely to attribute academic success to ability, and to feel demoralized and give up in the face of failure (Dweck, 1986).

As children grow older, they increasingly distinguish between the roles of ability and effort in determining achievement. According to Nicholls (1984), children's goal orientations are related to their ideas about the relation between ability and effort and their beliefs regarding the causes of success and failure. When children consider that ability may be increased with effort, they tend to judge their abilities in relation to their previous performance and believe that with additional effort their abilities may increase. This conception of ability emphasizes mastery and improvement and, therefore, fosters a learning goal orientation. When children believe that ability is fixed, they tend to consider that it is inversely related to effort, so that having to put forth effort in an activity is interpreted as a lack of ability. These children tend to judge their abilities in comparison with their peers, and define success as performing better than others, which fosters a performance goal orientation. Nicholls's ideas regarding children's conceptualization of ability versus effort differ from the views of attribution theory (Graham, 1991; Weiner, 1985) in which ability is conceptualized as a stable trait that is not amenable to change.

Students' learning and performance goal orientations have been assessed from two perspectives: their personal goal orientations and the goal structure they perceive as salient in the classroom. The Motivational Orientation Scales developed by Nicholls and associates (Nicholls, Patashnick, & Nolen, 1985) have been frequently used to assess personal academic goal orientation. Items in these scales have been phrased in terms of feeling successful or pleased with certain behaviors. The sentence "I feel most successful when I do the work better than other students" is an example of an item designed to measure personal performance goal orientation (Nolen, 1988). In other scales, items have been phrased in terms of what the student wants to achieve. "I wanted to find out something new" is an example of a personal learning orientation goal (Meece, Blumenfeld, & Hoyle, 1988). According to Ames (1992), teacher practices, including the design of tasks and learning activities, evaluation of students' work, uses of rewards, and the distribution of authority and responsibility in the classroom, can make different goals salient. Examples of items measuring perceived classroom goals include "our teacher tries to find out what students want to learn about math" (learning goal) and "our teacher gets upset when we make mistakes in math" (performance goal) (Anderman & Midgley, 1997).

Goal Orientation and Academic Motivation and Achievement

Studies examining the relation between goals and academic motivational processes and behaviors have consistently shown that learning goals are associated with positive motivational behaviors and adaptive patterns of learning. Performance goals, on the other hand, tend to be associated with negative motivational strivings. However, these patterns of relations are not as consistent as those observed regarding learning goals (Ames, 1992). Midgley et al. (1998) have argued that this inconsistency is because researchers have failed to take into consideration the approach and avoidance components of performance achievement goals. In other words, performance oriented students may strive either to obtain positive evaluations or avoid negative evaluations of their capacities. A learning orientation, on the other hand, is considered an approach motivational pattern because students are striving to increase their knowledge and skills. The goal to avoid negative evaluations of one's abilities, rather than the goal to obtain positive evaluations, is expected to be associated with negative motivational consequences. A recent study that assessed the three goal orientations among sixth grade students—learning, performance approach, and performance avoid goals—provided support for this proposition (Middleton & Midgley, 1997). Midgley et al. (1998) reported on the development and validation of scales to measure task, ability approach, and ability avoid goal orientations (in their work, learning and performance goals are labeled task and ability goals, respectively).

Most of the empirical work in achievement goal orientation has focused on learning and performance avoidance goals. In most cases, studies have used either experimental laboratory or correlational designs. In laboratory studies, children's behaviors related to choice and completion of specific tasks are observed following experimental manipulations designed to foster a learning or a performance goal orientation. Results from these studies have shown that, compared with students in the performance goals condition, students in the learning goal condition spend more time on learning tasks (Butler, 1987), report higher levels of self-efficacy for the task (Schunk, 1996), report more intrinsic interest in learning activities (Butler, 1987; Stipek & Kowalski, 1989), prefer challenging tasks over easy ones, and persist longer when confronted with failure (Elliot & Dweck, 1988). In contrast, a performance goal orientation has been linked to negative affect following failure and judgments of lack of ability (Elliot & Dweck, 1988; Jagacinski & Nicholls, 1984) and lack of self-efficacy (Schunk, 1996). Elliot and Dweck (1988) found that students' perceived ability moderated the relation between performance goals and achievement behaviors. Under the performance goal condition, students with high-perceived ability exhibited adaptive learning behaviors, whereas students with low levels of perceived ability exhibited maladaptive patterns. However, correlational studies have not indicated a similar relation among performance goal orientation, ability, and achievement behaviors (Kaplan & Midgley, 1997; Miller, Behrenes, Greene, & Newman, 1993).

Correlational studies have examined personal achievement goal orientations, as well as students' perceptions of the goals that characterize the classroom learning environment in relation to students' cognitions and behaviors. These studies have shown that learning goals are positively associated with an adaptive attributional pattern (Ames, 1992; Nicholls et al., 1985) and with positive self-efficacy regarding academic tasks (Anderman & Midgley, 1997; Kaplan & Midgley, 1997; Middleton & Midgley, 1997; Midgley & Urdan, 1995; Wolters, Yu, & Pintrich, 1996). Goal orientation also is related to students' reported use of effective learning strategies (Ames & Archer, 1988; Meece et al., 1988; Middleton & Midgley, 1997). For example, compared with their performance oriented peers, students who placed greater emphasis on learning goals reported more active cognitive engagement in elementary school science activities (Meece et al., 1988), as well as a higher use of strategies requiring deep processing of information in middle school (Anderman & Young, 1994; Nolen & Haladyna, 1990) and in high school science tasks (Nolen, 1988). Similarly, Ames and Archer (1988) found that students who perceived a stronger emphasis on learning goals in the classroom also expressed a stronger preference for challenging tasks and a greater use of effective learning strategies than their peers.

Only two studies were found that examined the relation between goals and grades among school-aged children (Urdan, 1997; Wolters et al., 1996). These studies indicated a low to moderate relation between grades and learning goals (.14 and .25, respectively) and between grades and performance goals (.13 and .22, respectively). These findings suggest that goal orientation is related to both motivational variables and actual academic achievement. It is possible that third variables mediate the relation of goals to achievement. Urdan (1997), for example, found that goals were related to peer influences which in turn were related to grades.

Development and Correlates of Learning and Performance Goals

Students' goal orientation seems to be formed early on. Nicholls and associates have examined the degree to which students of various ages ascribe to learning and performance goal orientations in classroom settings (called by them task and ego goals, respectively). In cross-sectional, factor analytic studies of The Motivational Orientation Scales, they found that the two goal orientations formed two distinct factors among children in early and late elementary school (Nicholls, Cobb, Wood, Yackel, & Patashnick, 1990), as well as among high school students (Duda & Nicholls, 1992; Nicholls, Cheung, Laurer, & Patashnick, 1989). Goal orientation also seems to be consistent across domains. Factor analyses of The Motivational Orientation Scales' items indicated that high school students report similar goal orientations in the domains of academics and sports (Duda & Nicholls, 1992). In terms of developmental changes, findings from a cross-sectional (Midgley et al., 1995) and a longitudinal study (Anderman & Midgley, 1997) have indicated that children in upper elementary school are more learning (or task) oriented than children in middle school. Findings regarding performance (or ability) goals were mixed. One study found that middle school students were more oriented to performance (ability) goals than their elementary school peers (Midgley et al., 1995), whereas the other study showed no differences between students at the two levels (Anderman & Midgley, 1997).

Given the positive implications for students of adopting learning rather than performance goals in achievement situations, it seems important to examine the antecedents of goal orientation in children and adolescents. How is it that children come to adopt learning or performance goals? Even though it is expected that characteristics of the learner, such as self-perceptions of ability, influence goal orientation, no empirical research has examined these relations. However, findings from field-based studies have indicated that specific instructional practices are related to students' perceptions of goal saliency in the classroom. In classrooms where teachers emphasize doing the best or getting the highest grade by hanging up the best projects and posting grades, students tend to adopt performance goal orientations. On the other hand, in settings where instructional practices emphasize task-mastery, effort, and self-improvement, students are more likely to adopt learning-focused goals (Ames, 1992; Anderman & Young, 1993 cited in Anderman & Maehr, 1994; Nicols, 1996; Nolen, 1988). For example, high school students randomly assigned to a cooperative instruction learning program in geometry showed higher geometry achievement, as well as a higher endorsement of learning goals, than their peers who participated in a traditional instruction program (Nicols, 1996).

The school climate and culture (Anderman & Maehr, 1994), as well as students' interpretations of the goal structure of the classroom, influence the goals students adopt (Ames, 1992; Anderman & Midgley, 1997). In a one-year longitudinal study, Anderman and Midgley (1997) found that students perceived a greater emphasis on relative ability and less emphasis on effort and improvement in sixth grade than in fifth grade. Students also reported endorsing personal learning goals less after the transition to middle school, whereas their endorsement of personal performance goals did not change. These decreases in perceptions of learning goal stresses in the classroom are consistent with differences in the classroom environment in elementary and middle schools described by Eccles and associates (Eccles, Midgley, et al., 1993). Compared with elementary school practices, teachers in middle school classrooms tend to place greater emphasis on control and discipline and on public evaluation of students' work. Between classroom ability groupings are also more common in middle schools. These practices are likely to increase concerns about evaluation and social comparisons of students, concerns that are negatively associated with a learning goal orientation (see Eccles, Midgley, et al., 1993 for a review of this literature). The goal orientation fostered by general school policies also seems to contribute to students' goal orientations (Anderman & Maehr, 1994).

Anderman and Maehr (1994) described two projects, one at the classroom level and the other at the school level, that have used goal theory to enhance motivation in schools. In the first project, Ames and colleagues (Ames & Maehr, 1989, cited in Anderman & Maehr, 1994) worked with teachers in devising classroom experiences and suggestions for parents at home to increase the importance of learning goals. After one year, students who were exposed to these strategies showed motivational gains compared with students in the control group. Specifically, they perceived their classes to be more learning and mastery focused, reported a more positive attitude toward school, a higher self-concept of ability, a preference for more challenging work, and the use of more effective cognitive strategies than their peers (Anderman & Maehr, 1994). Maehr and Midgley (1991) developed a coalition project with a school district to implement schoolwide and classroom practices, procedures, and policies designed to emphasize task rather than ability goals. At the end of three years, various practices had been implemented in middle schools to change the learning environment, including eliminating ability groupings, restructuring the honor roll and the school's award programs, and increasing team-teaching and block scheduling. These two programs represent proactive and preventive interventions that provide classroom and school contexts designed to enhance positive growth and adaptive behaviors among all students.

In addition to schooling practices, peer behaviors also contribute to students' achievement orientation. Urdan (1997) found that among eighth grade boys and girls, associating with peers who support academic effort and achievement was a strong predictor of learning (task) goals, whereas lack of support from peers was a strong predictor of effort avoidance goals. It is likely that parenting practices are also associated with students' goal orientation. It is believed that authoritative parenting, by providing firm discipline and standards, and encouraging independent problem solving and critical thinking, prepares children for an educational environment that requires independent mastery and self-regulation (Hess & McDevitt, 1984; Steinberg, Dornbusch, et al., 1992). It is possible that by providing an adequate balance of discipline and support for the child's abilities and interests, authoritative parenting facilitates the development of a learning goal orientation in children. Authoritarian parenting, on the other hand, with its emphasis on rigid parental control is likely to discourage active exploration and independent behavior and foster a performance goal orientation. In other words, children who receive guidance and support from their parents are more likely to focus their efforts on the intrinsic rewards of learning, without being overly preoccupied with performance outcomes, whereas children whose parents are rigid and harsh are likely to be more concerned with performing well than with enjoying their learning experience. Permissive parents, on the other hand, may not provide adequate structure and guidance for children to develop the discipline and self-control necessary for academic achievement.

Achievement goal theory and related research has primarily emphasized two types of goals in academic situations: learning and performance goals. Because of the importance of peer concerns among adolescents, social goals, defined as the "perceived social purposes of academic achievement or failure" (Urdan & Maher, 1995, p. 224), also seem important in understanding school engagement for this age group. The relation of social goals to academic motivation and achievement is likely to be influenced by a number of factors, including the type of social goal pursued; how the student defines social goals and achievement (e.g., as a means of gaining approval from others, bringing honor to one's group, or showing that one is a good person); the beliefs and values of the targets of social goals; and the degree of conflict or coordination among goals (Urdan & Maehr, 1995). These factors, in turn, are likely to be influenced by parental and peer behaviors. As suggested by Steinberg, Dornbusch, et al. (1992), students who want to gain the approval of high-achieving peers will be motivated to put forth effort in academic pursuits, whereas students who want to get the respect of peers who do not value school work will not (Ogbu, 1992). Also, the extent to which students perceive that adults and peers converge in the importance given to school work will facilitate school attainment.

Self-Efficacy Theory and Research

Self-efficacy beliefs refer to expectations about one's ability to initiate and successfully execute courses of action. Bandura (1986) has proposed that these beliefs help determine individuals' willingness to initiate specific behaviors, their persistence in the face of obstacles or barriers, and their level of competence in executing the behaviors. Even though self-efficacy has received the most empirical attention, according to Bandura's theory (1986, 1997) other factors interact with self-efficacy beliefs in influencing behavior. These factors include skills, goals, expectations about the consequences of carrying out specific behaviors (outcome expectations), perceived values of possible outcomes, and environmental support. For example, in the absence of adequate skills, self-efficacy beliefs probably will not result in competent performance. Similarly, students are not likely to engage in behaviors they feel competent at unless they expect positive outcomes that are valued.

Self-efficacy theory (Bandura, 1986) has received empirical support from diverse fields including education, psychology, health, and sports (Pajares, 1996). Research in educational psychology has emphasized the contributions of self-efficacy to students' academic motivation and achievement (Bandura, 1993; Berry & West, 1993; Multon et al., 1991; Schunk, 1991; Zimmerman, 1995). Within counseling psychology, Betz and Hackett (1981) first used self-efficacy theory to explain gender differences in career choice. Many studies have subsequently examined the relation of self-efficacy beliefs to career choice and academic achievement in college students, particularly in the areas of math and science (Betz & Hackett, 1981; Brown, Lent, & Larkin, 1989; Hackett, 1995; Hackett & Lent, 1992; Lent, Lopez, & Bieschke, 1991, 1993). More recently, counseling psychologists have examined the relation of self-efficacy beliefs to academic outcomes among high school students (Lopez, Lent, Brown, & Gore, 1997). Research findings have provided support for the major tenets of Bandura's (1986) self-efficacy theory as they relate to educational outcomes.

Self-Efficacy and Academic Performance and Motivation

In the academic context, perceived self-efficacy refers to students' sense of competence regarding their abilities to organize and execute behaviors designed to achieve specific educational outcomes (Schunk, 1989; Zimmerman, 1995). Self-efficacy beliefs do not represent a global estimate of students' academic capabilities; rather, they are tied to specific domains and tasks. A student may express different levels of efficacy across domains (e.g., mathematics versus English courses) or across tasks within a domain (e.g., writing an essay versus writing a poem). According to Bandura (1986, 1997), the explanatory and predictive power of self-efficacy is enhanced when efficacy beliefs are assessed regarding circumscribed tasks that closely correspond to the outcome tasks with which they are compared. In these very specific and particularized assessments, self-efficacy instruments generally ask students to rate their competence in solving the same type of problems they are asked to solve or to choose from in the outcome assessment (e.g., Schunk, 1989). Even though acquired skills influence competency beliefs, self-efficacy is not just a reflection of these skills. Various studies have shown that children with similar levels of cognitive skills vary in their performance in academic tasks, depending on the strength of their self-efficacy beliefs for those tasks (Bandura, 1993). Researchers also have assessed self-efficacy perceptions at a higher level of abstraction by asking students to make judgments about their capabilities and choices in a domain, such as a specific course, subject area, or occupational area, without having a particular task or activity in mind.

Results from experimental studies have demonstrated that self-efficacy beliefs predict academic performance among school-aged children and adolescents (Multon et al., 1991; Schunk, 1989, 1991; Zimmerman, 1995). Schunk (1989, 1991) conducted a series of experimental investigations to examine the impact of instructional strategies on children's self-efficacy beliefs and skill attainment in basic math and language skills. The strategies included verbal modeling of cognitive strategies, proximal goal setting, ability and effort attributional feedback, positive incentives, and self-verbalization of task strategies. Self-efficacy beliefs were assessed in terms of discrete basic academic skills (subtraction, fractions) that corresponded highly to the outcome performance variables. Results consistently showed that the instructional strategies were effective in increasing students' competency beliefs, and that posttreatment self-efficacy beliefs, in turn, predicted success in performing the specified tasks. In a qualitative review of these experimental studies, Schunk (1989) reported that self-efficacy accounted for 11% to 18% of the variance in children's performance.

In a meta-analysis of published and unpublished studies conducted between 1977 and 1988 (including many of the studies conducted by Schunk and associates), Multon et al. (1991) reported that self-efficacy beliefs accounted for 14% of the variance in academic achievement (based on 38 studies). Multon et al.'s analyses revealed that the magnitude of the effect sizes in the relation of self-efficacy beliefs to academic achievement was related to four study characteristics: (1) timing of assessments, (2) achievement level, (3) age of participants, and (4) type of performance outcome measure used. In experimental studies, self-efficacy assessed at posttreatment yielded stronger effect sizes than when self-efficacy was assessed at pretreatment or from strictly correlational data. This finding suggests that, in addition to increasing self-efficacy beliefs, the instructional interventions used in the experimental studies also enhanced the relation between these beliefs and performance (Multon et al., 1991). The relation of self-efficacy to performance was stronger among lower achieving versus higher achieving students and among high school and college students than elementary school students. Finally, the type of performance measures used in the studies was related to the magnitude of the relation between competency beliefs and performance. Consistent with Bandura's (1986) propositions, studies that assessed efficacy beliefs and performance in the same discrete learning tasks, such as solving math problems, produced the strongest effect sizes. However, it is important to note that studies using broader academic self-efficacy measures and global performance assessments, such as grades and standardized achievement tests, also yielded statistically significant effects (Multon et al., 1991).

More recent correlational research also has indicated that self-efficacy beliefs, measured in terms of performance on discrete academic tasks, is related to students' academic achievement in writing and math problem-solving tasks. For example, in path analytic studies with high school and elementary school students, Pajares and associates found that gender and writing aptitude predicted students' self-efficacy beliefs which, in turn, had a direct effect on students' writing performance (Pajares & Johnson, 1996; Pajares & Valiante, 1997). Math self-efficacy also seems to influence math problem-solving performance among middle school students when controlling for the effects of math anxiety, cognitive abilities, mathematics grades, self-efficacy for self-regulatory learning, and gender (Pajares, 1996).

Domain-specific self-efficacy beliefs in math also exert a direct influence on global measures of academic achievement such as course grades. For example, Lopez et al. (1997) found that among high school students, perceived math ability and competence in math, assessed by a standardized achievement test, were related to math self-efficacy. Perceived math ability predicted grades via self-efficacy only, whereas math ability predicted grades directly, and indirectly through self-efficacy. In a longitudinal study, Meece, Wigfield, and Eccles (1990) found that students' perceived math ability at seventh grade was related to students' competency beliefs for math course performance. In turn, these competency beliefs predicted students' subsequent grades two years later. Math anxiety was related to competency beliefs but not to grades, which is consistent with studies with college students that have shown that self-efficacy beliefs are a better predictor of semester grades than is math anxiety (Siegel, Galassi, & Ware, 1985).

Consistent with theoretical propositions, self-efficacy beliefs also influence aspects of students' motivation to learn, including effort, persistence, and the use of self-regulatory strategies which, in turn, are related to academic performance. In terms of persistence, Schunk (1991) found that arithmetic skills training influenced children's performance and self-efficacy. In turn, self-efficacy exerted an indirect influence on math performance through its direct relation to persistence during the math task. In other words, students who performed better after the training did so, in part, because training-induced increases in their self-efficacy led them to persist longer during the posttest. Efficacy beliefs also seem to influence persistence and achievement in more global tasks, such as completing college courses. For example, in a one-year follow-up study, Lent, Brown, and Larkin (1984, 1986) found that college students' beliefs regarding their ability to pursue scientific and technical courses and occupations predicted their subsequent academic performance and persistence in science and engineering college courses. In their meta-analytic study, Multon et al. (1991) found that students' self-efficacy beliefs accounted for 12% of the variance in students' task persistence. In the 18 studies included in this meta-analysis, persistence in academic tasks was measured in terms of time spent on task (seven studies), number of tasks attempted (nine studies), and number of academic semesters completed in college (two studies).

Self-efficacy beliefs also have been related to choice behavior in discrete tasks and in global academic domains. Studies have found that in instructional contexts, interventions that enhance children's sense of self-efficacy also increase the children's intrinsic interest for the tasks learned.

Following the intervention, children who report higher self-efficacy for problem-solving tasks, such as mastery of subtraction, tend to choose on their own similar tasks more often than their peers who report lower self-efficacy (Bandura & Schunk, 1981; Zimmerman, 1995). Similarly, self-efficacy has been useful in predicting college students' interests and choice of college major in scientific and mathematics related careers (Hackett, 1995).

Self-regulated learning strategies refer to behaviors initiated and directed by students to acquire knowledge and skills independently of teachers or parents (Zimmerman & Martinez-Pons, 1990). These strategies include goal setting, self-evaluation, self-monitoring, time planning and management, and use of specific learning strategies (e.g., note taking, rehearsing, and memorizing). There is ample evidence to suggest that students' use of these strategies promote academic achievement. However, knowledge of the strategies alone does not seem to ensure that students will use them appropriately (Zimmerman, 1995). Research findings suggest that there is a reciprocal relation between students' academic self-efficacy and use of self-regulated learning strategies. Enacting self-regulatory behaviors, such as goal setting, leads to increases in self-efficacy. On the other hand, self-efficacy beliefs influence the implementation of such strategies (Berry & West, 1993; Pajares, 1996; Schunk, 1985; Zimmerman, 1995). These relations were illustrated in a path analytic study with high school students enrolled in social science classes (Zimmerman, Bandura, & Martinez-Pons, 1992). Students' confidence in their ability to implement self-regulated learning strategies was related to their confidence in academic subjects. Academic self-efficacy, in turn, predicted students' final grades directly and indirectly, through its influence on students' goals. In other words, students with a strong sense of self-efficacy regarding their self-regulatory and academic skills also set high goals for themselves, which lead to school success.

Research on self-efficacy and self-regulatory capabilities has implications for the development of instructional practices. For example, Schunk (1991) has found that just setting goals in instructional situations improves subsequent self-efficacy and skill acquisition, and that characteristics of the goal setting situation further enhance these gains. Specifically, proximal, specific, and difficult goals were more effective in enhancing self-efficacy, persistence, and performance in arithmetic tasks than were distal, general, and easy goals (Bandura & Schunk, 1981; Schunk, 1983b, 1983c). Self-set goals also lead to higher gains among middle school children than did teacher-set goals (Schunk, 1985). Other interventions, such as guided mastery, cognitive modeling, incentives, and challenges, also seem to facilitate the development of children's sense of self-efficacy and self-regulation in learning situations (Zimmerman, 1995).

Sources of Self-Efficacy

In light of the consistent relations demonstrated between self-efficacy and educational outcomes, identifying the antecedents of self-efficacy seems important for the development of interventions geared to enhance students' competency beliefs. According to Bandura (1986), self-efficacy beliefs emerge from a complex process of self-persuasion that involves the cognitive integration of diverse sources of information including (1) performance accomplishments, (2) vicarious (observational) experiences, (3) positive verbal persuasion and support from others, and (4) affective experiences and physiological arousal in the context of task performance. Personal performance is considered the most important source of self-efficacy information (Bandura, 1986). Observing others perform a task successfully (vicarious experiences) is likely to enhance self-efficacy only to the extent that those experiences are followed by successful personal accomplishments. The experience of stress or anxiety in relation to specific tasks is likely to lower self-efficacy at those tasks. Performance accomplishments and self-efficacy beliefs are reciprocally related in the sense that past performance influences efficacy beliefs, which, in turn, influence subsequent performance (Bandura, 1986).

Various studies have examined the hypothesized sources of self-efficacy in relation to mathematics self-efficacy beliefs among high school (Lopez & Lent, 1992; Lopez et al., 1997) and college students (Lent et al., 1991; Matsui, Matsui, & Ohnishi, 1990), and in relation to general academic self-efficacy in high school students (Hampton, 1998). These studies used researcher developed scales where students described retrospectively to what extent they had experienced the various sources of self-efficacy. Past performance emerged as a strong predictor of math self-efficacy in the five studies identified, whereas evidence for the importance of the other three self-efficacy sources was mixed. Only one other informational source added significantly to the prediction of math self-efficacy (beyond the effects of previous performance) among high school students in each of the three studies described: affective and physiological arousal (Lopez & Lent, 1992), social persuasion (Lopez et al., 1997), and vicarious learning (Hampton, 1998). In only one study, two sources of self-efficacy—vicarious learning and emotional arousal—contributed significantly, beyond previous performance, to the prediction of math self-efficacy for college students (Matsui et al., 1990). These correlational studies indicate that, as predicted by theory, past performance (either perceived by students or measured by grades or standardized tests) strongly influenced students' self-efficacy beliefs in the domains of math and academic learning. However, vicarious experiences, social persuasion, and emotional arousal did not seem to influence students' competency perceptions in a consistent manner.

In contrast, experimental studies conducted by Schunk and associates (Schunk, 1989, 1991) have indicated that instructional strategies that include vicarious learning experiences (modeling) and performance feedback consistently enhanced children's self-efficacy beliefs. For example, having elementary children observe peers, adults, or themselves demonstrate the basic arithmetic skills being taught (e.g., subtraction, fractions, division) resulted in enhanced self-efficacy beliefs (Schunk & Hanson, 1985, 1989; Schunk, Hanson, & Cox, 1987). Furthermore, some characteristics of the modeling situation (observing peers rather than teachers and optimistic rather than pessimistic models) resulted in greater increases in children's self-efficacy, persistence, and skill performance (Schunk & Hanson, 1985; Zimmerman & Ringle, 1981). In similar instructional situations, social and evaluative feedback also influenced self-efficacy beliefs. For example, providing students with encouraging information about their abilities (Schunk, 1983a), as well as feedback regarding their progress in meeting their goals, raised their self-efficacy beliefs (Bandura & Cervone, 1983). Feedback attributing success to effort or ability while students were engaged in academic tasks resulted in higher self-efficacy gains than with no feedback (Schunk, 1991). However, ability feedback for prior or early success promoted higher self-efficacy and skill acquisition than effort feedback (Schunck, 1983a). This last finding is consistent with Nicholls's (1984) proposition that children tend to interpret the need for effort in academic tasks as a sign that they lack ability. It is possible that attributing success to ability leads to higher self-efficacy because it communicates to students that they are capable of performing the task, whereas effort attributions may be interpreted by some students as lack of ability. Nevertheless, the fact that performance feedback (attributional or related to progress in meeting goals) enhances self-efficacy provides support for the importance of positive verbal persuasion and support from others as a source of self-efficacy (Bandura, 1986).

In sum, research findings provide support for the importance of the four informational sources of self-efficacy. As hypothesized by Bandura (1986), previous performance accomplishments have consistently emerged as the most important source of competency beliefs among children, adolescents, and young adults. Correlational studies have provided mixed findings regarding the influence of the other three self-efficacy sources among adolescents and college students. Methodological issues may help explain these findings. In all the correlational studies examined, the four informational sources were, for the most part, significantly and substantially intercorrelated, presenting multicollinearity problems (Lent et al., 1991). Also, it is possible that retrospective recollection of these informational sources is not adequate to capture their contribution to the development of self-efficacy beliefs. On the other hand, in experimental studies, instructional programs that included vicarious learning experiences and performance feedback consistently resulted in enhanced self-efficacy among children, suggesting that these experiences shape self-efficacy beliefs. Cross-sectional and longitudinal studies are needed to explore the contribution of developmental factors, family, and school experiences to changes in academic self-efficacy. Similarly, more information is needed regarding the importance of the various sources of efficacy information in the development of academic self-efficacy. Longitudinal studies are needed to examine changes in children's sense of competence as they grow older, and the contribution of these changes to their academic motivation, choice, and achievement.

Gender, Developmental, and Multicultural Perspectives on Self-Efficacy

Gender differences in the relation of self-efficacy beliefs to academic achievement and career interests has received some attention in educational and counseling psychology. Developmental and multicultural influences in self-efficacy have not received as much attention. Because of their specificity in terms of contexts and domains, self-efficacy beliefs provide a useful means for examining the relation of gender, age, and race to perceptions of competence, as well as the contributions of these perceptions to academic achievement (Pajares, 1996). These issues are discussed next.

Research findings related to gender differences in academic self-efficacy, particularly in math, show an equivocal picture. Many studies report higher math and science efficacy beliefs and achievement scores among males than females (Lent et al., 1991; Meece et al., 1990; Randhawa, Beamer, & Lundberg, 1993), whereas other studies have not found these differences (Lent et al., 1984, 1986; Lopez et al., 1997; Multon et al., 1991). However, the patterns of relations between self-efficacy and achievement behaviors seem to be similar for both genders. Most studies (with middle school, high school, and college students) have found that self-efficacy mediates the relation between gender and achievement related behaviors, which suggests that gender differences in enrollment and performance in math courses are, to a great extent, due to gender differences in math self-efficacy beliefs (Meece et al., 1990; Randhawa et al., 1993). At the same time, it seems that males and females have different experiences regarding the sources of self-efficacy, particularly as it relates to past performance (Lent et al., 1991). Taken together, these findings suggest that gender differences in efficacy-building experiences often lead to a lower sense of math self-efficacy among girls. Lower self-efficacy, in turn, results in lower interest and persistence in math activities. Longitudinal research is needed to explore these propositions.

There is practically no research examining age-related changes in self-efficacy beliefs or in the relation of efficacy beliefs to performance (Berry & West, 1993). However, existing findings suggest that level of academic self-efficacy, as well as the relation between self-efficacy beliefs and academic performance, increase with age. In a cross-sectional study, Zimmerman and Martinez-Pons (1990) found that for the most part, verbal and math self-efficacy increased with age in children in fifth, eighth, and eleventh grades. Increases in self-efficacy were related to a decrease in students' reliance on adults for assistance in school work, which suggests that academic self-efficacy develops in conjunction with children's growing independence from parents. The relation between self-efficacy and academic performance was stronger among older students. This suggests that older children have developed more accurate perceptions of their capabilities, and, therefore, they are able to make more accurate self-efficacy judgments than their younger counterparts (Multon et al., 1991). In contrast, Eccles and associates reported that with age children's perceived competency in academic domains decreases (Eccles, Wigfield, Harold, & Blumenfeld, 1993). Zimmerman and Martinez-Pons (1990) indicated that this discrepancy may be due to the fact that scales of perceived competence ask students to compare themselves with peers, whereas in measuring self-efficacy students are asked to make temporal comparisons regarding their own skills. In other words, as children become older they recognize improvements in their own competencies, but, as they become more aware of the performance of others, their evaluations of their competencies relative to peers tend to decrease.

A few studies have examined the strength of efficacy beliefs and their contributions to academic related behaviors among international and American ethnic minority students. In studies using item-specific efficacy assessments, African American and Hispanic students have reported lower self-efficacy beliefs in math (Pajares & Kranzler, 1995) and writing tasks (Pajares & Johnson, 1996) than their White counterparts. In a study comparing the level of academic self-efficacy among elementary school students in Los Angeles and three European countries, Oettingen (1995) found that children in Los Angeles and East Berlin were the most optimistic and the most pessimistic, respectively, with children from West Berlin and Moscow falling in between. Oettingen related these findings to cultural and political differences (collectivism-individualism, power differential, and tolerance for ambiguity) in the educational practices of the various countries.

Another question of interest is to what extent the contribution of self-efficacy beliefs to academic competence and career related behaviors are similar across cultural groups. Some studies suggest that they are. Research with Hispanic and White students of various educational levels has found that self-efficacy is a stronger predictor of academic achievement than is gender or ethnicity (Bores-Rangel, Church, Szendre, & Reeves, 1990; Hackett, Betz, Casas, & Rocha-Singh, 1992). Studies with Hispanic and Native-American students in the U.S., and Japanese students in Japan, have found the expected relations between self-efficacy and career aspirations (Bores-Rangel et al., 1990; Church, Teresa, Rosebrook, & Szendre, 1992; Lauver & Jones, 1991; Matsui, Ikeda, & Ohnishi, 1989). In contrast, Eaton and Dembo (1997) found that even though Asian American ninth graders reported lower levels of self-efficacy beliefs than their non-Asian counterparts in a novel achievement task, they outperformed the non-Asian students in the task. Fear of academic failure was the strongest predictor of performance for Asian American students and the weakest predictor for non-Asians. These findings suggest that the implications of self-efficacy beliefs seem to generalize across cultural groups, but that this cannot be taken for granted. Self-efficacy cognitions may elicit different responses in different cultural and ethnic groups.

Eccles's Expectancy-Value Model

Eccles's expectancy-value model emphasizes the social psychological reasons for students' choices and performance in achievement settings. In an extensive program of research that includes cross-sectional and longitudinal studies, Eccles and colleagues (Wigfield, 1994; Wigfield & Eccles, 1992) have examined the relation of students' expectancies and values to their school performance and choice of academic tasks, with particular interest in gender differences in these achievement behaviors. They have proposed that students' expectancies for success in an academic task and the value that they place on succeeding in the task (subjective task value) predict their achievement performance and persistence in the task, and their choice of similar tasks. These expectancies and values, in turn, are directly influenced by other achievement related beliefs, such as achievement goals, ability and task-difficulty perceptions, previous performance, and the beliefs, values, and behaviors of important persons in the students' life, such as parents and teachers (Eccles & Wigfield, 1995; Wigfield, 1994). The larger context, including cultural and historical factors, is also expected to influence the behaviors and beliefs of adults and children (Eccles, 1994).

In Eccles's expectancy-value model, competency beliefs refer to the students' judgments about their abilities in specific academic areas (e.g., math, music, sports), including comparing themselves with peers. These beliefs are assessed with items such as "How good at math are you?" and "If you were to order all the students in your math class from the worst to the best in math, where would you put yourself?" (Wigfield, 1994, p. 53). Expectancies for success are defined as students' beliefs regarding how well they will perform in the future in a specific academic domain. Sample items used to assess expectancies for success include "Compared with other students how well do you expect to do in math this year?" and "How well do you think you will do in your math course this year?" (Wigfield, 1994, p. 53). The concept of expectancies for success in Eccles's model is similar to Bandura's self-efficacy construct, which refers to the person's expectations of producing a given outcome. However, self-efficacy is measured in more specific, circumscribed terms that do not make reference to peer comparisons.

Subjective task value refers to the value or adequacy of the task in meeting the needs of the individual. It consists of four components: (1) attainment value, (2) interest value, (3) utility value, and (4) cost. Attainment value refers to how important it is for the person's sense of self to do well in a given task; interest value is the personal satisfaction experienced in doing the task (somewhat similar to intrinsic motivation); utility value refers to the usefulness of the task for the person's future plans (similar to extrinsic motivation); and cost is what the person needs to give up to complete a task, including the effort that will be required (Eccles & Wigfield, 1995).

The empirical work examining Eccles's model has been conducted with children and adolescents (from primarily White, middle-class backgrounds) in first through twelfth grades. In this work, three major issues have been examined: (1) the development of children's beliefs about their competencies, their expectations for success, and their values regarding specific subject areas (math, English, music, and sports); (2) the extent to which self-competency beliefs, expectancies, and values predict students' performance in specific academic areas, as well as their intentions and actual choices to continue taking courses in those areas; and (3) the application of the model to the understanding of gender differences in academic and occupational choices. The major findings of Eccles's program of research are discussed below.

Structure of Competency Beliefs, Success Expectancies, and Values

Eccles and colleagues have examined the structure of children's and adolescents' competency beliefs and values to determine to what extent these beliefs are distinguished in children's minds and how early the differentiation occurs (Eccles & Wigfield, 1995; Eccles, Wigfield, et al., 1993; Wigfield & Eccles, 1992). They found that among elementary school children (first through fourth grades), competency beliefs in the areas of math, reading, music, and sports formed clearly distinct factors (Eccles, Wigfield, et al., 1993; Wigfield & Eccles, 1992). Students ranging from first to twelfth grade also distinguished between competency-expectancy beliefs and values in the different academic areas. Results from confirmatory factor analyses showed that, across all grades and within each domain, the two-factor model, where expectancy-competency beliefs and values were posited as two separate factors, had significantly better fit indices than the one-factor model that included both competency beliefs and values (Eccles & Wigfield, 1995; Eccles, Wigfield, et al., 1993; Wigfield & Eccles, 1992).

Researchers also have examined whether children's competency beliefs and expectancies for success are different constructs and to what extent children differentiate between the various aspects of subjective task value. Findings indicated that, contrary to what was initially proposed in the Eccles expectancy-value model, children and adolescents do not seem to distinguish between their expectancies for success and their beliefs about their abilities in the domains of math, reading, music, and sports. Factor analyses of students' responses (first through twelfth grades) to items assessing competency beliefs, expectancy beliefs, and perceived level of performance yielded only one factor within each domain (Eccles & Wigfield, 1995; Eccles, Wigfield, et al., 1993; Wigfield & Eccles, 1992). Similarly, children in the early and middle elementary grades (first through fourth grades) did not differentiate, in the area of math, between three of the components of subjective task values: attainment, interest, and utility values (Wigfield et al., 1990, cited in Wigfield & Eccles, 1992). However, results of confirmatory factor analyses indicated that by early adolescence, students do distinguish between these three components of subjective task value (Eccles & Wigfield, 1995).

In summary, the research suggests that, in the domains of math, reading, music, and sports, as early as first grade children identify specific areas at which they are competent, and they also differentiate the areas they value from the "competent" areas. Children and adolescents, however, do not seem to differentiate between their competency beliefs, expectations for success, and perceived level of performance in these domains. In other words, students' beliefs about their academic performance and their abilities in a given domain are nearly identical to their expectations regarding future performance in the domain. In terms of math-related values, by early adolescence students reported differentiated ideas regarding how important math achievement is for them, how interested they are in it, and the utility of math for their future plans.

Age and Gender Differences in Competency Beliefs and Values

Several studies have examined age differences in children's expectancies for success, beliefs about their abilities, and subjective task values. Findings regarding students' expectancies and competency beliefs indicate that preschool children tend to have very optimistic expectations for success in academic tasks that often do not correspond to their actual level of achievement. Cross-sectional studies have shown that as children grow older, their competency beliefs and expectancies for success in academic tasks become more negative (Stipek & Mac Iver, 1989; Wigfield & Eccles, 1992). Results from a three-year longitudinal study also demonstrated that during the early elementary school years (from first, second, and third grade to fourth, fifth, and sixth grade) children's competency beliefs in reading, math, music, and sports declined (Wigfield et al., 1997). Developmental changes also have been observed in terms of children's values and interests regarding academic subjects.

Elementary school children tend to express positive values for different academic activities; however, as students progress through middle and high school their values and interests in some academic activities decline. In two cross-sectional studies with fifth through twelfth graders, older students reported lower value and interest in math and higher value and interest in English than their younger counterparts (Wigfield & Eccles, 1992). Similarly, findings from a longitudinal study indicated that across the transition from elementary to middle school, students' ratings of the importance and liking of math and English declined; during the seventh grade, students' ratings of the importance of math continued to decline, whereas importance ratings for English increased (Wigfield, Eccles, Mac Iver, Reuman, & Midgley, 1991). Findings with younger children also have indicated that as students progressed through elementary school, their valuing of math, reading, and music (assessed in terms of usefulness, importance, and interests) decreased (Wigfield et al., 1997). However, the relation between competency beliefs and values was positive and became stronger among the older children. Values and beliefs became more synchronous for many children during the second-grade year. These findings suggest that children and early adolescents tend to value those tasks in which they believe they can succeed. A remaining question is the causal direction of this relation: Do children value the tasks at which they think they are good or do they develop competencies in the tasks they value? (Wigfield et al., 1997).

The observed decline with age in children's competency beliefs, expectations for success, and valuing of academic subjects has been explained in terms of children's changing perceptions of ability (Nicholls, 1984). It is believed that as children grow older, they assess themselves more accurately and realistically, and, as a result, their beliefs become relatively more negative (Nicholls, 1984; Stipek & Mac Iver, 1989). Because older children tend to see ability as a stable characteristic that cannot be changed (Nicholls, 1984), in view of low performance they may protect their self-esteem by attaching less value to academic activities. However, these hypotheses do not explain why children who are doing well academically also report less value and interest in math as they grow older. Wigfield et al. (1991) have suggested that changes in the school environment from elementary to middle school that make competition among students more salient may explain, in part, these negative developmental changes in achievement expectations and values.

Eccles and colleagues have also examined gender differences in students' self-perceptions of ability and values in different academic domains (Eccles, Adler, & Meece, 1984; Eccles, Wigfield, et al., 1993; Wigfield et al., 1997). Findings indicate that as early as first grade boys and girls competency beliefs differ in gender stereotypic ways. For example, in Wigfield et al.'s (1997) three-year longitudinal study, at all grade levels (first through fourth) boys reported more positive competency beliefs than girls in math and sports, whereas girls reported more positive competency beliefs than boys in reading and instrumental music. These gender differences did not change much during the early elementary school years. Middle school and high school girls also reported lower competency beliefs in math than did boys (Eccles et al., 1984; Meece et al., 1990; Wigfield, 1994). Taken together, these findings imply that even before they have had much experience with schooling, boys and girls adopt stereotypical views about their capabilities that remain with them throughout the school years.

Findings regarding gender differences in the value attached to different academic domains vary across studies and age groups, with older students and higher achieving populations showing larger differences. Wigfield et al. (1997) found that among elementary school children (first through fourth grade), girls reported more interest in English and instrumental music and considered these academic activities more important and useful than did boys. On the other hand, boys considered sports more interesting, important, and useful than did girls. These gender differences remained constant throughout the elementary school years. Wigfield et al. (1997) also found that, in elementary school, boys and girls did not differ in their valuing of math, even though the boys had reported higher math ability self-concepts. Studies with high school students, however, have found gender differences in the value and importance attached to math and English, with females preferring English and males preferring math (Eccles et al., 1984).

The research described thus far suggests that as children become older, their expectations regarding academic tasks become more realistic, their competency self-perceptions in specific academic areas become more negative, and their interests and values in specific domains decrease. This research also points to gender differences in students' competency beliefs and values regarding specific academic areas. An important question in understanding the development of academic achievement in children is to what extent students' competency beliefs, expectancies for success, and values predict their academic performance and choice of academic activities (Wigfield, 1994).

Expectancy-Values and Academic Achievement and Choice

Eccles and colleagues have examined, longitudinally, the relation between students' beliefs and values and their performance in elementary, middle school, and high school math courses, as well as their intended and actual choices regarding math course enrollment. In path analytic studies with fifth through twelfth grade students (Eccles, 1984, cited in Wigfield & Eccles, 1992) and with middle school students (Meece et al., 1990), expectancy for success was the strongest predictor of subsequent math grades, whereas students' valuing of math was the strongest predictor of students' intentions to continue taking math courses. More recently, Wigfield (1992, cited in Wigfield, 1994) reported that competency beliefs assessed in fifth grade predicted students' grades as late as eight years later. They also have found that among eighth through tenth graders, the value attached to math predicted students' actual enrollment in advanced high school math courses, whereas their self-concept of ability was not strongly related to these enrollment decisions (Eccles et al., 1983, cited in Wigfield, 1994). Eccles and colleagues have not examined the relation between competency beliefs and academic achievement in early elementary school children. However, previous research has indicated that children's competency and expectancy beliefs show a stronger relation to grades with age (Stipek & Mac Iver, 1989). Young children tend to have an unrealistically positive view of their abilities, but as children grow older, their competency beliefs and expectancies for success correspond more closely with their performance.

Wigfield (1994) proposed that among young children, interest value would be a better predictor of choice of activities than the perceived importance or utility value of the activity. Utility values are expected to become stronger predictors of choice as students become older (Wigfield, 1994). This developmental change was suggested by Wigfield and Eccles (1989) who found that interests in math predicted intentions to continuing taking math courses for middle school students, whereas both interest and utility value of math predicted intentions for high school students. Additional work is needed to examine the causal relation between expectancies and values, and to determine the relation between young children's values and their choices for participating in different activities. This research could use measures developed by Eccles and colleagues for parents and teachers to rate children's interest and involvement in academic and nonacademic activities.

In summary, research findings have provided support for Eccles's contention that students' academic performance and choices are predicted by their competency beliefs and subjective task values. Particularly in the area of math, students' beliefs regarding their competencies and their expectations for success best predict their subsequent performance, whereas their subjective task values best predict their intended and actual decisions regarding enrollment in math courses. Eccles's expectancy-value model and related research also has provided insights regarding the motivational factors that help explain gender differences in achievement related choices (Eccles, 1994).

Expectancy Values and Women's Academic and Career Choices

Gender differences in academic and career choices are well documented (Betz, 1994; Farmer, Wardrop, Anderson, & Risinger, 1995). Despite recent efforts in educational and occupational settings to increase women's participation in nontraditional careers, women continue to be underrepresented in investigative and scientific occupations. Researchers in the career development field have noted that women's lack of interest and self-efficacy in math during the school years precludes them from considering investigative and scientific college majors and careers (Betz, 1994). Studies derived from expectancy-value theory have found that boys and girls generally differ in their competency beliefs and expectations for success in mathematics, music, and English (Eccles et al., 1984; Meece, Parsons, Kaczala, Goff, & Futterman, 1982; Wigfield et al., 1997). However, studies by Eccles and associates have shown that among high school students, subjective task values regarding math are a better predictor of subsequent enrollment in math classes than math competency and expectancy beliefs. Furthermore, some studies have not found gender differences in estimates of math ability among gifted elementary and high school students (Benbow & Stanley, 1982; Eccles, 1994). Therefore, it seems that gender differences in competency beliefs and expectations for success in mathematics do not solely explain gender differences in career choice among academically able and gifted students.

Eccles (1994) has proposed that, in addition to competency beliefs, the subjective value adolescent and young women attach to the options they perceive as available to them is an important predictor of their choice of academic activities. Research findings have provided support for these propositions among intellectually able and gifted women. In a longitudinal study with college-bound high school students, Eccles et al. (1984) observed that gender differences in values regarding mathematics mediated gender differences in students' decisions regarding enrollment in advanced math courses. Even though girls and boys did not differ in their expectations for success in mathematics, the girls were less likely to enroll in advanced math courses, primarily because they perceived math as less enjoyable, useful, and important than did the boys. School-aged children in gifted programs also have demonstrated gender differences in the value that they attach to different school subjects. Eccles and Harold (1992, cited in Eccles, 1994), for example, found that even though gifted school-aged girls did not differ from the boys in their expectations for success in mathematics, they considered math less important and less attractive than did the boys. The girls also reported more confidence in their reading ability than in their math ability. Similarly, among high school gifted students, women reported enrolling in math courses less often than the men because they preferred to take language courses instead (Benbow & Stanley, 1982).

Eccles (1994) provided evidence for the hypothesis that differences in women's preferences for various educational activities in high school predict their educational and occupational choices in college. In a longitudinal study with high school seniors, Eccles found that in addition to self-efficacy beliefs and expectancies for success, the values held by girls regarding characteristics associated with specific occupations were important predictors of their occupational plans in college. For example, valuing helping others predicted both planning to enter human services occupations and not planning to enter business or scientific fields. At the same time, valuing occupational prestige was related to not considering social services occupations. These findings indicated that self-efficacy beliefs and success expectations regarding specific career fields were important but not sufficient predictors of college women's occupational plans. Women's hierarchy of values regarding academic and occupational fields also were important in predicting their career choices.

In general, gender differences in the valuing of academic activities mirror cultural stereotypes regarding appropriate male and female roles. As was discussed earlier, these differences appear very early, before children have had extensive exposure to school, which suggests that early socialization practices at home and in school strongly influence children's beliefs and values. In a longitudinal study, Wigfield et al. (1997) found that among elementary school children competency beliefs and subjective task values in the areas of reading, math, music, and sports were related to teacher and parent ratings of children's competencies in all areas. The association between children's and adults' achievement beliefs seemed to be established during the first- and second-grade years and continued to become stronger with age. By the time children reach middle school and high school, parents' beliefs about their children's competencies seems to be more strongly related to students' competency beliefs than the students' own school grades (Jacobs & Eccles, 1992). Because some parents may distort their perceptions of girls' competencies in gender stereotypic ways, this developmental sequence is likely to dissuade girls from pursuing math related activities. Research findings have indicated that parents who endorse stereotypic views regarding gender differences in the distribution of talents and interests also tend to underestimate their daughters' talents in such typically male activities as sports, physics, and math (Eccles, Jacobs, & Harold, 1990; Jacobs & Eccles, 1992). Parents also make different attributions for daughters' and sons' academic successes and failures. Particularly in the area of math, parents tend to attribute girls' failures to lack of ability, whereas boys' failures are attributed to lack of effort (Yee & Eccles, 1988). These gendered messages may undermine women's beliefs in their math and science abilities, as well as their interest in and valuing of math and science related courses and career fields. The end result is that many capable women choose not to purse careers in these fields.

In summary, research findings show that boys and girls differ both in their expectations for success and values regarding the educational and occupational options available to them. In turn, these differences in expectations and values help explain gender differences (and individual differences within each gender) in educational and occupational choices. Furthermore, these findings also suggest that gender differences in achievement beliefs and in the valuing of activity domains mirror cultural stereotypes regarding appropriate male and female roles. However, not much is known regarding the antecedents of subjective task values in children and adolescents. A few studies have shown that the achievement beliefs of fifth- through twelfth-grade children are predicted by children's perceptions of their parents' beliefs (Wigfield & Eccles, 1992). It is necessary to study these links with younger children to examine to what extent these and other antecedents change with age. For example, it is likely that peer relations also influence the development of children's subjective task values; however, there is not much empirical information on peer influences in the development of children's values regarding academic tasks (Wigfield & Eccles, 1992).

SUMMARY AND INTEGRATION OF APPROACHES

Academic achievement is influenced by a myriad of personal and environmental factors. At the individual level, general abilities, motivational dispositions and beliefs (e.g., attributions, achievement goals, self-efficacy beliefs, expectancies for success, and subjective task values), affective states, and social skills constitute important influences on children's school achievement. At the same time, these individual variables interact in complex ways with aspects of the context in which students operate, including school organizational and instructional practices, family environment, and peer influences. At this point, it does not seem feasible to describe how all these factors simultaneously relate to each other, directly and reciprocally, to foster academic development. However, as evidenced in the literature reviewed in the chapter, teams of researchers have made important discoveries regarding parts of this complex puzzle. Furthermore, aspects of these theories may be integrated to increase our understanding of personal and contextual factors that relate to children's and adolescents' academic achievement.

Family resources and students' abilities (as measured by IQ tests) are predictive of academic success. However, children from similar socioeconomic background and ability groups show different levels of academic achievement that are related to school, family, and motivational variables. Research findings suggest that, regardless of socioeconomic and ethnic background, students of medium and low ability, who are taught demanding curricula, do much better academically, persist longer in school, and report higher career expectations than their peers who receive below–grade level instruction (Mac Iver et al., 1995). Instructional practices in the classroom and aspects of the school climate also seem to influence the attributional styles and the achievement goals adopted by students. Successful students tend to attribute their success and failure to controllable causes (e.g., effort) that are amenable to change (Graham, 1991), and their academic behaviors are primarily guided by a desire to master the academic material (Anderman & Midgley, 1997). Goal theory, in particular, has provided a conceptual framework for designing, implementing, and evaluating changes in classroom practices and schoolwide policies that contribute to the personal involvement of students in learning. School evaluation practices that tend to emphasize comparisons of relative ability rather than progress in learning are demoralizing to many students, particularly those who do not do very well as compared with their peers (Covington & Omelich, 1984). Often students do not put forth effort in challenging academic activities to protect themselves from concluding that they lack ability and, thus, protect their sense of worth (Nicholls, 1984). On the other hand, school evaluation practices that emphasize cooperative learning and the achievement of personal goals result in a higher level of students' engagement and effort in school activities, which enhances academic achievement.

Research related to sociocognitive theories of academic motivation has indicated that thoughts, emotions, and perceptions of self influence the achievement motivation strivings and the academic performance of children and adolescents. More specifically, Bandura (1986, 1997) has proposed that in the presence of adequate skills, positive outcome expectations, and personally valued outcomes, self-efficacy beliefs influence the choice, direction, and performance level of students' academic behaviors. Eccles's expectancy-value model has examined the influence of self-beliefs and subjective task values (attainment, interest, utility, and cost) on children's and adolescents' choice and performance in academic tasks. Recently, Lent et al. (1994) proposed an integrative model, primarily based on Bandura's (1986) social cognitive theory, that incorporates the contribution of self-efficacy beliefs, expected outcomes, values, and goals to choice and entry aspects of the career development process among adolescents and young adults. Specifically, Lent et al.'s model focuses on the interrelated processes of interest development, selection and choice of career options, and performance and persistence in educational and occupational pursuits. Even though Eccles's model and the Lent et al. model focus on somewhat differing age groups and also differ in how they operationalize certain constructs, there are conceptual similarities between them. Before discussing areas of convergence and dissimilarities in these models, Lent et al.'s integrative theory will be briefly described.

Lent et al. (1994) proposed that the interaction of personal and contextual characteristics in childhood and adolescence result in particular learning experiences that facilitate the development of a sense of personal self-efficacy and of expectations regarding the outcomes of one's performance. In turn, self-efficacy beliefs and outcome expectations jointly influence the formation of interests. In other words, adolescents and young adults are likely to develop interests in areas that they feel capable and in which they anticipate positive and valued outcomes. Self-efficacy, outcome expectations, and interests, in turn, lead to goals (e.g., aspirations, intentions, plans, decisions) for activity involvement. Once formulated, goals make it more likely for the person to select and become involved in particular activities. Activity involvement then leads to achievement experiences in particular performance domains. These achievement experiences (e.g., success, failure), which also are directly influenced by self-efficacy beliefs, influence, in a feedback loop, self-efficacy beliefs and outcome expectations. This process is likely to be repeated throughout the life span. However, it is expected to be most fluid until late adolescence or early adulthood when interests and ideas about one's competencies tend to crystallize.

Research related to self-efficacy theory and Eccles's expectancy-value theory have examined the relation of ability perceptions, expectancies, and subjective-task values to choice, persistence, and performance in academic activities. Self-efficacy beliefs refer to expectations for future performance, and, in this regard, self-efficacy resembles the expectancy construct in Eccles's expectancy-value theory. However, self-efficacy and expectancies differ in the way they are operationalized. Self-efficacy beliefs are assessed in terms of students' expectations regarding their ability to initiate and execute very specific tasks or behaviors in specific domains. Expectancies for success also refer to students' beliefs regarding how well they will do in an upcoming task, but, compared with self-efficacy beliefs, these expectancies are assessed in more global and peer-comparative terms.

In theory, both approaches (self-efficacy theory and expectancy-value theory) distinguish between students' general concept of ability in a domain (that is, how good they think they are) and their self-efficacy beliefs or expectations for future performance in that domain. However, in factor analytic studies, Eccles and Wigfield (1995) have found that children and adolescents do not seem to distinguish between competency beliefs and expectations for success as assessed in their program of research. On the other hand, research with college students has indicated that measures of academic self-concept (that assess relatively global self-perceptions of academic competence) and self-efficacy beliefs (assessed at different levels of domain-specificity) represent different, though related, latent constructs (Lent, Brown, & Gore, 1997). Findings with middle school and high school students also have indicated that the relation between a general concept of ability and school grades is mediated by self-efficacy beliefs, which suggests that perceived abilities and self-efficacy beliefs are distinct constructs (e.g., Lopez et al., 1997). The distinction between ability and self-efficacy perceptions is an important aspect of Bandura's (1986, 1997) self-efficacy theory which has been incorporated in Lent et al.'s (1994) model.

The concept of outcome expectations in Lent et al.'s (1994) model is conceptually similar to Eccles's subjective task value construct, particularly the components of utility and attainment value. Bandura (1986) defined outcome expectations as the expected consequences of enacting specific behaviors, including material, social, and self-evaluative outcomes. As defined by Eccles (Eccles & Wigfield, 1995), utility value refers to the usefulness of the activity for the person's future plans (which may include material and social outcomes), and attainment value refers to the importance for the person's sense of self of doing well in a given task (a type of self-evaluative outcome). Interests, an important aspect in Lent et al.'s (1994) model, is included as one of the components of subject task values in Eccles's model. At the same time, Lent et al. noted that, in their framework, the concept of outcome expectations incorporates the notion of values.

Most of the empirical work related to Bandura's theory has emphasized the self-efficacy construct. Findings from this research have indicated that self-efficacy is related both to choice and performance in academic pursuits. Research related to Eccles's expectancy-value model, however, suggests that competency beliefs and expectations for success are more strongly related to academic performance, whereas subjective task values are a stronger predictor of students' intentions and actual choices regarding academic tasks. Compared with the two other models (self-efficacy and expectancy-value theory), Lent et al. (1994) have described in more detail the intermediate mechanisms that link self-efficacy to choice and performance. Lent et al. have proposed that self-efficacy mediates the relation of abilities to interests, and goals mediate the relation of interests to choice or selection of activities. Consistent with Eccles's model, Lent et al. consider that interests are more highly related to choice of academic and career related activities than to performance, and that self-efficacy beliefs (competency beliefs in Eccles's model) directly influence performance attainments.

With the exception of the work of Eccles and associates, very little longitudinal work has been conducted regarding the developmental course of motivational beliefs and attitudes and their long-term effects on school grades and other measures of academic achievement. Research by Eccles and associates has indicated that as early as first grade children have distinct ideas about the academic subjects they like and those in which they think they are good. These ideas, which seem to remain fairly stable during the elementary school years, influence children's choice of and performance in academic tasks (Wigfield et al., 1997). The empirical literature has demonstrated that, independently of past performance or ability level, self-efficacy beliefs are related to students' academic performance and to their interest and choice of academic endeavors (Zimmerman, 1995). Taken together, these findings suggest that from an early age a positive sense of self-efficacy may be necessary for children to use their skills successfully in achievement situations. Therefore, it seems important that in working with low-achieving students, teachers distinguish between students who are not able to perform because of lack of skills and those who hold unrealistically low self-efficacy perceptions. Similarly, high-achieving students may avoid pursuing academic coursework in demanding areas because of lack of self-efficacy in the domain and not because of lack of skills. Ways of assessing students' competency beliefs, as well as interventions designed to enhance both academic skills and perceptions of efficacy, are needed.

Research conducted by Eccles and associates has demonstrated that, in addition to competency beliefs and expectancies for success (factors that have received most research attention), subjective task values are important in students' decisions and choices regarding academic activities (Wigfield et al., 1997). Because students' early choices have implications for later educational and career choices, Eccles's expectancy-value model and research is consistent with developmental career models (e.g., Super, 1990) that point to formative influences on later career related competencies and choices and with models that emphasize the role of interests in career choice (e.g., Holland, 1985). Attending to the development of competency beliefs and preferences for academic activities in young children seems important for career development for two reasons. First, these beliefs and values lead to decisions regarding engagement in academic areas, such as math and science, that have a lasting effect on the competencies children acquire. These competencies, in turn, are likely to influence the options children have available to them as they grow. Second, these early beliefs, values, and concomitant choices result in the development of personal hierarchies of values that may be resistant to change in late adolescence and early adulthood, when students are more likely to participate in career counseling activities. These issues seem to be most relevant for the career development of women, who, because of societal stereotypes, are at risk at an early age of becoming dissuaded from pursuing academic and career related activities in gender-typed fields such as math and science.

REFERENCES

Ames, C. (1992). Classrooms: Goals, structures, students and student motivation. *Journal of Educational Psychology, 84,* 261–271.

Ames, C., & Archer, J. (1988). Achievement goals in the classroom: Students' learning strategies and motivation processes. *Journal of Educational Psychology, 80,* 260–267.

Anderman, E.M., & Maehr, M.L. (1994). Motivation and schooling in the middle grades. *Review of Educational Research, 64,* 287–309.

Anderman, E.M., & Midgley, C. (1997). Changes in achievement goal orientation, perceived academic competency, and grades across the transition to middle-level schools. *Contemporary Educational Psychology, 22,* 269–298.

Anderman, E.M., & Young, A.J. (1994). Motivation and strategy use in science: Individual differences and classroom effects. *Journal of Research in Science Teaching, 31,* 811–831.

Andrews, G., & Debus, R. (1978). Persistence and the causal perceptions of failure: Modifying cognitive attributions. *Journal of Educational Psychology, 70,* 154–166.

Arbona, C. (1994). *First generation college students: A review of needs and effective interventions* (U.S. Department of Education, Office of Planning and Evaluation, Contract No. ea 93109001). Houston, TX: Decision Information Resources.

Arbona, C. (1996). Career theory and practice in a multicultural context. In M.L. Savickas & W.B. Walsh (Eds.), *Handbook of career counseling theory and practice* (pp. 45–54). Palo Alto, CA: Davies-Black.

Atkinson, J.W., & Birch, D. (1978). *An introduction to motivation* (2nd ed.). New York: Van Nostrand.

Bandura, A. (1986). *Social foundations of thought and action: A social cognitive theory.* Englewood Cliffs, NJ: Prentice Hall.

Bandura, A. (1993). Perceived self-efficacy in cognitive development and functioning. *Educational Psychologist, 28,* 117–148.

Bandura, A. (1997). *Self-efficacy: The exercise of control.* New York: W.H. Freeman.

Bandura, A., & Cervone, D. (1983). Self-evaluative and self-efficacy mechanisms governing the motivational effects of goal systems. *Journal of Personality and Social Psychology, 45,* 1017–1028.

Bandura, A., & Schunk, D.H. (1981). Cultivating competence, self-efficacy, and interest through proximal self-motivation. *Journal of Personality and Social Psychology, 41,* 586–598.

Baumrind, D. (1971). Current patterns of parental authority. *Developmental Psychology Monograph, 4,* 1–103.

Baumrind, D. (1978). Parental disciplinary patterns and social competence in children. *Youth and Society, 9,* 239–276.

Benbow, C.P., & Stanley, J.C. (1982). Consequences in high school and college of sex differences in mathematical reasoning ability: A longitudinal perspective. *American Educational Research Journal, 19,* 598–622.

Berry, J.M., & West, R.L. (1993). Cognitive self-efficacy in relation to personal mastery and goal setting across the life span. *International Journal of Behavioral Development, 16,* 351–379.

Betz, N.E. (1994). Basic issues and concepts in career counseling for women. In W.B. Walsh & S.H. Osipow (Eds.), *Career counseling for women* (pp. 1–41). Hillsdale, NJ: Erlbaum.

Betz, N.E., & Hackett, G. (1981). The relationship of career-related self-efficacy expectations to perceived career options in college women and men. *Journal of Counseling Psychology, 28,* 399–410.

Bores-Rangel, E., Church, A.T., Szendre, D., & Reeves, C. (1990). Self-efficacy in relation to occupational consideration and academic performance in high school equivalency students. *Journal of Counseling Psychology, 37,* 407–418.

Brody, N. (1997). Intelligence, schooling, and society. *American Psychologist, 52,* 1046–1050.

Brown, S.D., Lent, R.W., & Larkin, K.C. (1989). Self-efficacy as a moderator of scholastic aptitude-academic performance relationships. *Journal of Vocational Behavior, 35,* 64–75.

Butler, R. (1987). Task-involving and ego-involving properties of evaluation: Effects of different feedback conditions on motivational perceptions, interest, and performance. *Journal of Educational Psychology, 79,* 474–482.

Campbell, F.A., & Ramey, C.T. (1994). Effects of early intervention on intellectual and academic achievement: A follow-up study of children from low-income families. *Child Development, 65,* 684–698.

Cassidy, T., & Lynn, R. (1991). Achievement motivation, educational attainment, cycles of disadvantage and social competence: Some longitudinal data. *Journal of Educational Psychology, 61,* 1–12.

Ceci, S.J. (1991). How much does schooling influence general intelligence and its cognitive components? A reassessment of the evidence. *Developmental Psychology, 27,* 703–722.

Ceci, S.J., & Williams, W.M. (1997). Schooling, intelligence, and income. *American Psychologist, 52,* 1051–1058.

Church, A.T., Teresa, J.S., Rosebrook, R., & Szendre, D. (1992). Self-efficacy for careers and occupational consideration in minority high school equivalency students. *Journal of Counseling Psychology, 39,* 498–508.

Coie, J.D., & Krehbiel, G. (1984). Effects of academic tutoring on the social status of low-achieving socially rejected children. *Child Development, 55,* 1465–1478.

Covington, M.V., & Omelich, C. (1984). Effort: The double edged sword in school achievement. *Journal of Educational Psychology, 71,* 169–182.

Delaney, B. (1991). Allocation, choice, and stratification within high schools: How the sorting machine copes. *American Journal of Education, 99,* 181–207.

Diener, C., & Dweck, C. (1980). An analysis of learned helplessness II: The processes of success. *Journal of Personality and Social Psychology, 39,* 940–952.

Dornbusch, S., Ritter, P.L., Leiderman, P.H., Roberts, D.F., & Fraleigh, M.J. (1987). The relation of parental style to adolescent school performance. *Child Development, 58,* 1244–1257.

Dryfoos, J.G. (1990). *Adolescents at risk: Prevalence and prevention.* New York: Oxford University Press.

DuBois, D.L., Felner, R.D., Brand, S., Adan, A.M., & Evans, E.G. (1992). A prospective study of life stress, social support, and adaptation in early adolescence. *Child Development, 63,* 542–557.

Duda, J.L. (1985). Goals and achievement orientation of Anglo and Mexican-American adolescents in sports and in the classroom. *International Journal of Intercultural Relations, 9,* 131–150.

Duda, J.L., & Nicholls, J.G. (1992). Dimensions of achievement motivation in schoolwork and sport. *Journal of Educational Psychology, 84,* 290–299.

Durbin, D.L., Darling, N., Steinberg, L., & Brown, B.B. (1993). Parenting style and peer group membership among European-American adolescents. *Journal of Research on Adolescence, 3,* 87–100.

Dweck, C.S. (1986). Motivational processes affecting learning. *American Psychologist, 40,* 1040–1048.

Eaton, M., & Dembo, M. (1997). Differences in the motivational beliefs of Asian Americans and non-Asian students. *Journal of Educational Psychology, 89,* 433–440.

Eccles, J.S. (1994). Understanding women's educational and occupational choices: Applying the Eccles et al. model of achievement-related choices. *Psychology of Women Quarterly, 18,* 585–609.

Eccles, J.S., Adler, T., & Meece, J.L. (1984). Sex differences in achievement: A test of alternated theories. *Journal of Personality and Social Psychology, 46,* 26–43.

Eccles, J.S., Jacobs, J.E., & Harold, R.D. (1990). Gender role stereotypes, expectancy effects, and parents' socialization of gender differences. *Journal of Social Issues, 40,* 183–201.

Eccles, J.S., Midgley, C., Wigfield, A., Buchana, C.M., Reuman, D., Flanagan, C., & Mac Iver, D. (1993). Development during adolescence: The impact of stage-environment fit on young adolescents' experiences in schools and families. *American Psychologist, 48,* 90–101.

Eccles, J.S., & Wigfield, A. (1995). In the mind of the actor: The structure of adolescents' achievement task values and expectancy-related beliefs. *Personality and Social Psychology Bulletin, 21,* 215–225.

Eccles, J.S., Wigfield, A., Harold, R.D., & Blumenfeld, P. (1993). Age and gender differences in children's self- and task-perceptions during elementary school. *Child Development, 64,* 830–847.

Elliot, E.S., & Dweck, C.S. (1988). Goals: An approach to motivation and achievement. *Journal of Personality and Social Psychology, 54,* 5–12.

Entwisle, D.R., & Alexander, K.L. (1992). Summer setback: Race, poverty, school composition, and mathematics achievement in the first two years of school. *American-Sociological Review, 57,* 72–84.

Farmer, H.S., Wardrop, J.L., Anderson, M.Z., & Risinger, R. (1995). Women's career choices: Focus on science, math, and technology careers. *Journal of Counseling Psychology, 42,* 155–170.

Feldhusen, N.D., Thurston, J.B., & Benning, J.J. (1970). Longitudinal analyses of classroom behavior and school achievement. *Journal of Experimental Education, 38,* 4–10.

Feldman, S.S., & Wentzel, K.R. (1990). The relationship between family interaction patterns, classroom self-restraint, and academic achievement. *Journal of Educational Psychology, 82,* 813–819.

Fitzgerald, L.F., & Betz, N.E. (1994). Career development in cultural context: The role of gender, race, class, and sexual orientation. In M.L. Savickas & R.L. Lent (Eds.), *Convergence in career development theories: Implications for science and practice* (pp. 103–108). Palo Alto, CA: Davies-Black.

Forsterling, F. (1985). Attribution retraining: A review. *Psychological Bulletin, 98,* 495–512.

Fuligni, A.K., Eccles, J.S., & Barber, B. (1995). The long-term effect of seventh-grade ability grouping in mathematics. *Journal of Early Adolescence, 15,* 58–59.

Gardner, H. (1993). *Multiple intelligences: The theory in practice.* New York: Basic Books.

Garmezy, N. (1991). Resiliency and vulnerability to adverse developmental outcomes associated with poverty. *American Behavioral Scientist, 34,* 416–430.

Graham, S. (1984). Communicating sympathy and anger to black and white students: The cognitive (attributional) consequences of affective cues. *Journal of Personality and Social Psychology, 47,* 40–54.

Graham, S. (1991). A review of attribution theory in achievement contexts. *Educational Psychology Review, 3,* 5–39.

Graham, S. (1994). Motivation in African Americans. *Review of Educational Research, 64,* 55–118.

Graham, S., & Brown, J. (1988). Attributional mediators of expectancy, evaluation, and affect: A response time analyses. *Journal of Personality and Social Psychology, 55,* 873–881.

Graham, S., & Long, A. (1986). Race, class, and the attributional process. *Journal of Educational Psychology, 78,* 4–13.

Grolnick, W.S., & Ryan, R.M. (1989). Parent styles associated with children's self-regulation and competence in school. *Journal of Educational Psychology, 81,* 143–154.

Hackett, G. (1995). Self-efficacy in career choice and development. In A. Bandura (Ed.), *Self-efficacy in changing societies* (pp. 232–258). Cambridge, England: Cambridge University Press.

Hackett, G., Betz, N.E., Casas, M.J., & Rocha-Singh, I.A. (1992). Gender, ethnicity, and social cognitive factors predicting the academic achievement of students in engineering. *Journal of Counseling Psychology, 39,* 527–538.

Hackett, G., & Lent, R.W. (1992). Theoretical advances and current inquiry in career psychology. In S.D. Brown & R.W. Lent (Eds.), *Handbook of counseling psychology* (2nd ed., pp. 419–451). New York: Wiley.

Hall, V., Howe, A., Merkel, S., & Lederman, N. (1986). Behavior, motivation, and achievement in black and white junior high school science classes. *Journal of Educational Psychology, 97,* 108–115.

Hampton, N.Z. (1998). Sources of academic self-efficacy scale: An assessment tool for rehabilitation counselors. *Rehabilitation Counseling Bulletin, 41,* 260–277.

Hess, R.D., & Holloway, S.D. (1984). Family and school as educational institutions. In R.D. Parke (Ed.), *Review of child development research* (Vol. 7, pp. 179–222). Chicago: Chicago University Press.

Hess, R.D., & McDevitt, T.M. (1984). Some cognitive consequences of maternal intervention techniques: A longitudinal study. *Child Development, 55,* 2017–2030.

Hilsman, R., & Garber, J. (1995). A test of the cognitive diathesis-stress model of depression in children: Academic stressors, attributional style, perceived competence, and control. *Journal of Personality and Social Psychology, 69,* 370–380.

Holland, J.L. (1985). *Making vocational choices: A theory of vocational personality and work environments* (2nd. ed.). Englewood Cliffs, NJ: Prentice Hall.

Hops, H., & Cobb, J.A. (1974). Initial investigation into academic survival-skill training, direct instruction, and first grade achievement. *Journal of Educational Psychology, 66,* 548–553.

Jacobs, J.E., & Eccles, J.S. (1992). The influence of parents stereotypes on parent and child ability beliefs in three domains. *Journal of Personality and Social Psychology, 63,* 932–944.

Jagacinski, C.M., & Nicholls, J.G. (1984). Conceptions of ability and related affects in task involvement and ego involvement. *Journal of Educational Psychology, 76,* 909–919.

Johnson, D.L., & Walker, T. (1991). A follow-up evaluation of the Houston Parent-Child Development Center: School performance. *Journal of Early Intervention, 15,* 226–236.

Jussim, L. (1989). Teacher expectations: Self-fulfilling prophecies, perceptual biases, and accuracy. *Journal of Personality and Social Psychology, 57,* 469–480.

Jussim, L. (1991). Grades reflect more than performance: Comment on Wentzel (1989). *Journal of Educational Psychology, 83,* 153–155.

Kaplan, A., & Midgley, C. (1997). The effect of achievement goals: Does level of perceived academic competence make a difference? *Contemporary Educational Psychology, 22,* 415–435.

Kurtz, C., Betz, N.E., & Schneider, W. (1994). Self-concept, attributional beliefs, and school achievement. *Contemporary Educational Psychology, 19,* 199–216.

Lambert, N.M. (1972). Intellectual and non-intellectual predictors of high school status. *Journal of Special Education, 66,* 247–259.

Lamborn, S.D., Mounts, N.S., Steinberg, L., & Dornbusch, S.M. (1991). Patterns of competence and adjustment among adolescents from authoritative, authoritarian, indulgent, and neglectful families. *Child Development, 62,* 1049–1065.

Lauver, P.J., & Jones, R.M. (1991). Factors associated with perceived career options in American Indian, white, and Hispanic rural high school students. *Journal of Counseling Psychology, 38,* 159–166.

Lent, R.W., Brown, S.D., & Gore, P.A., Jr. (1997). Discriminant and predictive validity of academic self-concept, academic self-efficacy, and mathematics-specific self-efficacy. *Journal of Counseling Psychology, 44,* 307–315.

Lent, R.W., Brown, S.D., & Hackett, G. (1994). Toward a unifying social cognitive theory of career and academic interests, choice, and performance. *Journal of Vocational Behavior, 45,* 79–122.

Lent, R.W., Brown, S.D., & Larkin, K.C. (1984). Relation of self-efficacy expectations to academic achievement and persistence. *Journal of Counseling Psychology, 31,* 356–362.

Lent, R.W., Brown, S.D., & Larkin, K.C. (1986). Self-efficacy in the prediction of academic performance and perceived career options. *Journal of Counseling Psychology, 33,* 265–269.

Lent, R.W., Lopez, F.G., & Bieschke, K.J. (1991). Mathematics self-efficacy: Sources and relation to science-based career choice. *Journal of Counseling Psychology, 38,* 424–430.

Lent, R.W., Lopez, F.G., & Bieschke, K.J. (1993). Predicting mathematics-related choice and success behavior: Test of an expanded social cognitive model. *Journal of Vocational Behavior, 42,* 223–236.

Levin, H. (1986). *Educational reform for disadvantaged students: An emerging crisis.* West Haven, CT: National Education Association.

Lopez, F.G., & Lent, R.W. (1992). Sources of mathematics self-efficacy in high school students. *Development Career Quarterly, 41,* 3–12.

Lopez, F.G., Lent, R.W., Brown, S.D., & Gore, P.A., Jr. (1997). Role of social-cognitive expectations in high school students' mathematics-related interests and performance. *Journal of Counseling Psychology, 44,* 44–52.

Luster, T., & McAdoo, H.P. (1994). Factors related to the achievement and adjustment of young African American children. *Child Development, 65,* 1080–1094.

Mac Iver, D.J., Reuman, D.A., & Main, S.R. (1995). Social structuring of the school: Studying what is, illuminating what could be. *Annual Review of Psychology, 46,* 375–400.

Maehr, M.L., & Meyer, H.A. (1997). Understanding motivation and schooling: Where we've been, where we are, and where we need to go. *Educational Psychology Review, 9,* 371–409.

Maehr, M.L., & Midgley, C. (1991). Enhancing student motivation: A schoolwide approach. *Educational Psychologist, 26,* 399–427.

Maehr, M.L., & Nicholls, J. (1980). Culture and achievement motivation: A second look. In N. Warren (Ed.), *Studies in cross-cultural psychology* (pp. 192–216). New York: Academic Press.

Masten, A.S., & Coatsworth, J.D. (1998). The development of competence in favorable and unfavorable environments: Lessons from research on successful children. *American Psychologist, 53,* 205–220.

Matsui, T., Ikeda, H., & Ohnishi, R. (1989). Relations of sex-typed socialization to career self-efficacy expectations of college students. *Journal of Vocational Behavior, 35,* 1–16.

Matsui, T., Matsui, K., & Ohnishi, R. (1990). Mechanisms underlying math-self-efficacy learning of college students, *Journal of Vocational Behavior, 37,* 225–238.

Meece, J.L., Blumenfeld, P.C., & Hoyle, R.H. (1988). Students' goal orientation and cognitive engagement in classroom activities. *Journal of Educational Psychology, 80,* 514–523.

Meece, J.L., Parsons, J.E., Kaczala, C., Goff, S.B., & Futterman, E. (1982). Sex differences in math achievement: Toward a model of academic choice. *Psychological Bulletin, 91,* 324–348.

Meece, J.L., Wigfield, A., & Eccles, J.S. (1990). Predictors of math-anxiety and its consequences for young adolescents' course enrollment intentions and performance in mathematics. *Journal of Educational Psychology, 82,* 60–70.

Middleton, M.J., & Midgley, C. (1997). Avoiding the demonstration of lack of ability: An underexplored aspect of goal theory. *Journal of Educational Psychology, 89,* 710–718.

Midgley, C., Anderman, E., & Hicks, L. (1995). Differences between elementary and middle school teachers and students: A goal theory approach. *Journal of Early Adolescence, 15,* 90–113.

Midgley, C., Kaplan, A., Middleton, M.J., Maehr, M.L., Urdan, T., Anderman, L.H., Anderman, E., & Roesser, R. (1998). The development and validation of scales assessing students' achievement goal orientations. *Contemporary Educational Psychology, 23,* 113–131.

Midgley, C., & Urdan, T. (1995). Predictors of middle school students' use of self-handicapping strategies. *Journal of Early Adolescence, 15,* 389–411.

Miller, R.B., Behrenes, J.T., Greene, B.A., & Newman, D. (1993). Goals and perceived ability: Impact on students valuing, self-regulation, and persistence. *Contemporary Educational Psychology, 18,* 2–14.

Multon, K.D., Brown, S.D., & Lent, R.W. (1991). Relation of self-efficacy beliefs to academic outcomes: A meta-analytic investigation. *Journal of Counseling Psychology, 38,* 30–38.

Neisser, U. (Chair), Boodo, G., Bouchard, T.J., Jr., Bykin, W., Brody, N., & Ceci, S.J. (1996). Intelligence: Knowns and unknowns. *American Psychologist, 51,* 77–101.

Nelson, C.A., & Bloom, F.E. (1997). Child development and neuroscience. *Child Development, 68,* 970–987.

Nicholls, J.G. (1984). Achievement motivation: Conceptions of ability, subjective experience, task choice, and performance. *Psychological Review, 91,* 328–346.

Nicholls, J.G., Cheung, P.C., Laurer, J., & Patashnick, M. (1989). Individual differences in academic motivation: Perceived ability, goals, beliefs, and values. *Learning and Individual Differences,1,* 63–84.

Nicholls, J.G., Cobb, P., Wood, T., Yackel, E., & Patashnick, M. (1990). Assessing students' theories of success in mathematics: Individual and classroom differences. *Journal for Research in Mathematics Education, 21,* 109–122.

Nicholls, J.G., Patashnick, M., & Nolen, S.B. (1985). Adolescent's theories of education. *Journal of Educational Psychology, 77,* 683–692.

Nicols, J.D. (1996). The effects of cooperative learning on student achievement and motivation in a high school geometry class. *Contemporary Educational Psychology, 21,* 467–476.

Nolen, S.B. (1988). Reasons for studying: Motivational orientations and study strategies. *Cognition and Instruction, 5,* 269–287.

Nolen, S.B., & Haladyna, T.M. (1990). Motivation and studying in high school science. *Journal of Research in Science Education, 27,* 115–126.

Nyberg, K.L., McMillin, J.D., O'Neill-Rood, N., & Florence, J.M. (1997). Ethnic differences in academic retracking: A four year longitudinal study. *The Journal of Educational Research, 91,* 33–41.

Oettingen, G. (1995). Cross-cultural perspectives on self-efficacy. In A. Bandura (Ed.), *Self-efficacy in changing societies* (pp. 149–176). Cambridge, England: Cambridge University Press.

Ogbu, J.U. (1992). Understanding cultural diversity and learning. *Educational Researcher, 21,* 5–14.

Pajares, F. (1996). Self-efficacy in academic settings. *Review of Educational Research, 66,* 543–578.

Pajares, F., & Johnson, M.J. (1996). Self-efficacy beliefs in the writing of high school students: A path analysis. *Psychology in the Schools, 33,* 163–175.

Pajares, F., & Kranzler, J. (1995). Self-efficacy beliefs and general mental ability in mathematical problem solving . *Contemporary Educational Psychology, 26,* 426–443.

Pajares, F., & Valiante, G. (1997). Predictive and mediational roles of the self-efficacy beliefs of upper elementary school students. *Journal of Educational Research 90,* 353–360.

Papini, D.R., & Roggman, L.A. (1992). Adolescent perceived attachment to parents in relation to competence, depression, and anxiety: A longitudinal study. *Journal of Early Adolescence, 12,* 420–440.

Pintrich, P.R., & De Groot, E. (1990). Motivational and self-regulated components of classroom academic performance. *Journal of Educational Psychology, 82,* 66–78.

Randhawa, B.S., Beamer, J.E., & Lundberg, I. (1993). Role of mathematics self-efficacy in the structural model of mathematics achievement. *Journal of Educational Psychology, 85,* 41–48.

Richardson, M.S. (1993). Work in people's lives: A location for counseling psychologists. *Journal of Counseling Psychology 40,* 425–433.

Schultz, G.F. (1993). Socioeconomic advantage and achievement motivation: Important mediators of academic performance in minority children in urban schools. *The Urban Review, 25,* 221–232.

Schunk, D.H. (1983a). Ability versus effort attributional feedback: Differential effects on self-efficacy and achievement. *Journal of Educational Psychology,75,* 848–856.

Schunk, D.H. (1983b). Developing children's self-efficacy and skills: The role of social comparative information and goal setting. *Contemporary Educational Psychology, 8,* 76–86.

Schunk, D.H. (1983c). Goal difficulty and attainment information: Effects on children's achievement behaviors. *Human Learning, 2,* 107–117.

Schunk, D.H. (1985). Participation in goal setting: Effects on self-efficacy and skills of learning disabled children. *Journal of Special Education, 19,* 307–317.

Schunk, D.H. (1989). Self-efficacy and achievement behaviors. *Educational Psychology Review, 1,* 173–208.

Schunk, D.H. (1991). Self-efficacy and academic motivation. *Educational Psychologist, 26,* 207–231.

Schunk, D.H. (1996). Goal and self-evaluative influences during children's cognitive skill learning. *American Educational Research Journal, 33,* 359–382.

Schunk, D.H., & Hanson, A.R. (1985). Peer models: Influence on children's self-efficacy and achievement. *Journal of Educational Psychology, 77,* 313–322.

Schunk, D.H., & Hanson, A.R. (1989). Self-modeling and children's cognitive skill learning. *Journal of Educational Psychology, 81,* 155–163.

Schunk, D.H., Hanson, A.R., & Cox, P.D. (1987). Peer-model attributes and children's achievement behaviors. *Journal of Educational Psychology, 79,* 54–61.

Siegel, R.G., Galassi, J.P., & Ware, W. (1985). A comparison of two models for predicting mathematics performance: Social learning versus math-aptitude anxiety. *Journal of Counseling Psychology, 32,* 531–538.

Singhal, S. (1988). Children's attributions of perceived school success and failure. *Journal of Psychological Research, 32,* 5–16.

Steinberg, L., Dornbusch, S.M., & Brown, B.B. (1992). Ethnic differences in adolescent achievement: An ecological perspective. *American Psychologists, 47,* 723–729.

Steinberg, L., Elmen, J.D., & Mounts, N. (1989). Authoritative parenting, psychological maturity, and academic success among adolescents. *Child Development, 60,* 1424–1436.

Steinberg, L., Lamborn, S.D., Dornbusch, S.M., & Darling, N. (1992). Impact of parenting practices on adolescent achievement: Authoritative parenting, school involvement, and encouragement to succeed. *Child Development, 63,* 1266–1281.

Steinberg, L., Mounts, N.S., Lamborn, S.D., & Dornbusch, S.M. (1991). Authoritative parenting and adolescent adjustment across varied ecological niches. *Journal of Research in Adolescence, 1,* 19–36.

Sternberg, R.J. (1997a). The concept of intelligence and its role in lifelong learning and success. *American Psychologist, 52,* 1030–1037.

Sternberg, R.J. (1997b). Introduction to the special issue of intelligence and lifelong learning [Special issue]. *American Psychologist, 52,* 1029.

Sternberg, R.J., & Clinkenbeard, P. (1995). A triarchic view of identifying, teaching, and assessing gifted children. *Roeper Review, 17,* 255–260.

Stipek, D.J., & Kowalski, P.S. (1989). Learned helplessness in task-orienting and performance orienting testing conditions. *Journal of Educational Psychology, 81,* 384–391.

Stipek, D.J., & Mac Iver, D. (1989). Developmental change in children's assessment of intellectual competence. *Child Development, 60,* 521–538.

Super, D.E. (1990). A life-span, life-space approach to career development. In D. Brown & L. Brooks (Eds.), *Career choice and development* (pp. 197–261). San Francisco: Jossey-Bass.

Uguroglu, M.E., & Walberg, H.J. (1979). Motivation and achievement: A quantitative synthesis. *American Education Research Journal, 16,* 375–389.

Urdan, T.C. (1997). Examining the relation among early adolescent students' goals and friends' orientation toward effort and achievement in school. *Contemporary Educational Psychology, 22,* 165–191.

Urdan, T.C., & Maehr, M.L. (1995). Beyond a two goal theory of motivation and achievement: A case for social goals. *Review of Educational Research, 65,* 213–243.

Valencia, R.R., Henderson, R.W., & Rankin, R.J. (1985). Family status, family constellation, and home environmental variables, as predictors of cognitive performance of Mexican American children. *Journal of Educational Psychology, 77,* 323–331.

Watkins, D., & Gutierrez, M. (1990a). Attributional feedback and underachieving children: Differential effects on causal attributions, success, expectancies, and learning processes. *Australian Journal of Psychology, 43,* 625–631.

Watkins, D., & Gutierrez, M. (1990b). Causal relationships among self-concept, attributions, and achievement in Filipino students. *Journal of Social Psychology, 130,* 625–631.

Weiner, B. (1985). An attributional theory of achievement motivation and emotion. *Psychological Review, 92,* 548–573.

Weiner, B. (1990). History of motivational research in education. *Journal of Educational Psychology, 82,* 616–622.

Weiner, B., Graham, S., Stern, P., & Lawson, M. (1982). Using affective cues to infer causal thoughts. *Developmental Psychology, 15,* 1–20.

Wentzel, K.R. (1991). Classroom competence may require more than intellectual ability: Reply to Jussim (1991). *Journal of Educational Psychology, 83,* 156–158.

Wentzel, K.R. (1993). Does being good make the grade? Social behavior and academic competence. *Journal of Educational Psychology, 85,* 357–364.

Wentzel, K.R. (1994). Family functioning and academic achievement in middle school: A social-emotional perspective. *Journal of Early Adolescence, 14,* 268–291.

Wentzel, K.R. (1998). Parents' aspirations for children's educational attainments: Relations to parents' beliefs and social address variables. *Merill-Palmer Quarterly, 44,* 20–37.

Wentzel, K.R., & Feldman, S.S. (1993). Parental predictors of boys' self-restraint and motivation to achieve at school: A longitudinal study. *Journal of Early Adolescence, 13,* 183–203.

Wentzel, K.R., Feldman, S.S., & Weinberger, D.A. (1991). Parental child rearing and academic achievement in boys: The mediation role of social-emotional adjustment. *Journal of Early Adolescence, 11,* 321–339.

Wentzel, K.R., Weinberger, D.A., Ford, M., & Feldman, S.S. (1990). Academic achievement in preadolescence: The role of motivational, affective, and self-regulatory processes. *Journal of Applied Developmental Psychology, 11,* 179–193.

Wentzel, K.R., & Wigfield, A. (1998). Academic and social motivational influences on students' academic performance. *Educational Psychology Review, 10,* 155–175.

White, K.R. (1982). The relation between socioeconomic status and academic achievement. *Psychological Bulletin, 91,* 461–481.

Whitehead, G., Smith, S., & Eichorn, J. (1982). The effects of subject's race and other's race on judgments of success and failure. *Journal of Personality, 50,* 194–202.

Wigfield, A. (1994). Expectancy-value theory of achievement motivation: A developmental perspective. *Educational Psychology Review, 6,* 49–78.

Wigfield, A., & Eccles, J.S. (1989). Test anxiety in elementary and secondary school student. *Journal of Educational Psychology, 24,* 159–186.

Wigfield, A., & Eccles, J.S. (1992). The development of achievement task values: A theoretical analyses. *Developmental Review, 12,* 265–310.

Wigfield, A., Eccles, J.S., Mac Iver, D., Reuman, D., & Midgley, C. (1991). Transitions at early adolescence: Changes in children's domain specific self-perceptions and general self-esteem across the transition to junior high school. *Developmental Psychology, 27,* 552–565.

Wigfield, A., Eccles, J.S., Yoon, K.S., Harold, D., Abreton, A.J.A., Freedman-Doan, C., & Blumenfeld, P.C. (1997). Change in children's competency beliefs and subjective task values across the elementary school years: A 3-year study. *Journal of Educational Psychology, 89,* 451–469.

Wiley, M.G., & Eskilson, A. (1978). Why did you learn in school today? Teacher's perceptions of causality. *Sociology of Education, 51,* 261–269.

Wolters, C.A., Yu, S.L., & Pintrich, P.R. (1996). The relation between goal orientation and students' motivational beliefs and self-regulated learning. *Learning and Individual Differences, 8,* 616–622.

Yee, D., & Eccles, J.S. (1988). Parents perceptions and attributions for children's math achievement. *Sex Roles, 19,* 59–68.

Zimmerman, B.J. (1995). Self-efficacy and educational development. In A. Bandura (Ed.), *Self-efficacy in changing societies* (pp. 202–231). Cambridge, England: Cambridge University Press.

Zimmerman, B.J., Bandura, A., & Martinez-Pons, M. (1992). Self-motivation for academic achievement: The role of self-efficacy beliefs and personal goal setting. *American Educational Research Journal, 29,* 663–676.

Zimmerman, B.J., & Martinez-Pons, M. (1990). Students differences in self-regulated learning: Relating grade, sex, and giftedness to self-efficacy and strategy use. *Journal of Educational Psychology, 82,* 51–59.

Zimmerman, B.J., & Ringle, J. (1981). Effects of model persistence and statements of confidence on children's self-efficacy and problem solving. *Journal of Educational Psychology,73,* 485–493.

CHAPTER 10

Advances in Theory and Research on Subjective Well-Being

STEVEN B. ROBBINS
WENDY L. KLIEWER

Counseling psychology has a historic interest in the quality of people's lives, yet, our tendency is to focus on mental disorders and the causes and solutions to dysfunctional behavior and distress. In fact, within a 10-year window, for every 17 articles published on mental health and dysfunction in a psychology journal there is one on psychological well-being (D.G. Myers & Diener, 1995). Psychological well-being is an intriguing concept because it connotes so many different images. We frequently think of mental health, effective functioning in multiple domains (e.g., work, school, family), and coping and adaptation to stress and other life events. A recent special issue on "Wellness" engendered considerable reaction due to a lack of definitional consensus and to varying emphases on the processes and causes of psychological well-being (Stone, 1996).

Fundamental questions that must be addressed are, How do we know when we have psychological well-being, and who decides? We discuss the importance of conceptual and methodological clarity with the psychological well-being construct, and the need to distinguish between subjective and objective perspectives. Put another way, it is important to address the structure and meaning of well-being before moving to predictors and explanatory models. There is considerable confusion about the linkages between a range of demographic, psychological, and social factors when explaining well-being, which reflects the considerable debate currently raging on genetic, environmental, and psychological determinants of behavior (cf. Brown, Ryan, & McPartland, 1996; Diener, 1996; Lykken & Tellegen, 1996).

In this chapter, we discuss that most empirically based research has focused on subjective well-being, or an individual's own perception of happiness, quality of life, and other markers attributed to well-being. In this age of "consumerism" and self-determination, it makes sense that researchers' emphases are placed on one's own perspective. We can also speculate that models of psychological well-being, based on objective or "outside" perspectives, provoke considerable debate about the implied values when someone else determines what are the critical manifestations of well-being. Certainly Aristotle and the ancient Western philosophers spent considerable energy on this concept when they argued that happiness is the pinnacle of good (see Bradburn, 1969 for a discussion), and, as such, is the ultimate outcome we strive to achieve. In any case, empirical confirmation of nonsubjective models of psychological well-being is limited, whereas methodical, empirically based research on the subjective well-being construct is booming (Diener, 1984; Diener, Suh, Lucas, & Smith, 1999).

The last 15 years has witnessed considerable advance in our understanding of structure and meaning of subjective well-being. More recently, the move is toward a greater understanding of the determinants of well-being in adults, and to begin developing causal models linking environment, personality, adaptation, and well-being dimensions (Diener et al., 1999). Explanations for subjective well-being abound, with the historic conception that socioeconomic status, age, and race are critical determinants (Wilson, 1967). Yet, it is important to note that research refutes the "American ethos" that rich people are the happiest (cf. D.G. Myers, 1992).

The primary emphasis of this chapter is on connecting our knowledge of the subjective well-being construct to its possible determinants. We then turn to strategies that enable us to establish causal linkages and inform our heuristic models of psychological well-being and adjustment. These heuristic models are critical for establishing programmatic research and for guiding our applied interests. The goal of this chapter is to selectively review and integrate key research primarily within the last 10 years, with a focus on adult development. This is an enormous literature across many disciplines, with considerable conceptual and definitional confusion. The choice of emphasis here does not diminish the importance of associated topics, including physical health and well-being, mental health, or work and career development, many of which are covered elsewhere in this book.

STRUCTURE AND MEANING

The subjective well-being literature is a microcosm of the empiricism versus rationalism debate in psychology, and whether psychological constructs are best derived from empirically deduced strategies or theoretical models (see Nunnally, 1967 for review). Diener's (1984) classic review of the subjective well-being literature emphasized the empirical perspective, detailing scores of single item to multi-item psychological instruments that measure varying nuances of happiness, positive/negative affect, and general- and domain-specific life satisfaction. He found considerable empirical evidence to support a tripartite model of subjective well-being, referring to an individual's cognitive report of life satisfaction, the presence of positive affect, and the absence of negative affect. As summarized in Table 10.1, people's self-appraisals of satisfaction have both a global and a domain-specific component. In other words, people can provide judgments of their current, future, and past overall satisfaction level, but they can also provide judgments of such specific aspects of life as work, leisure, or family. These evaluations also connect to our affective states, whether described as pleasant or unpleasant. Thus, the three broad components of subjective well-being are highly interconnected, and cut across global and domain-specific dimensions.

Different self-report measures of life satisfaction are highly correlated, and tend to measure a unidimensional construct (Diener, 1984; Diener et al., 1999). A representative instrument is The Satisfaction with Life Scale (SWLS; Diener, Emmons, Larsen, & Griffin, 1985), which is a highly cited self-report measure of global life satisfaction. It asks for Likert ratings on five items. Examples are (1) How ideal is your life? (2) Have you obtained what is important? and (3) Would you change your life if it were to be lived over? Pavot and Diener (1993) reviewed the considerable research with the SWLS, finding it had substantial construct validity. Despite high construct validity, the SWLS and other global estimates of subjective well-being should not be held equivalent to the aggregate of daily ratings of life satisfaction. Kahneman and his research colleagues (Kahneman, 1999; Redelmeir & Kahneman, 1996) have found that single reports of global well-being are not equivalent to daily reports of well-being. These findings suggest that respondents' evaluations of specific life events or situations are not isomorphic with global ratings of life satisfaction.

Domain-specific measures are highly varied, and typically have emerged out of research related to the literature studying the adjustment process (e.g., Graziano, Jensen-Campbell, & Finch, 1997; Graziano & Ward, 1992) rather than the psychological well-being literature. Examples of domain-specific measures include the Student Adjustment to College Questionnaire (R.W. Baker & Siryk, 1984), the leisure satisfaction scale (Beard & Ragheb, 1980), the adult career concerns inventory (Super, Thompson, & Lindeman, 1987), and the global health rating scale (Wan, 1985).

Table 10.1   Components of Subjective Well-being from Empirical and Theoretical Perspective

Empirical/Subjective[a]			
Satisfaction		Affect	
Global	Domain Specific	Pleasant	Unpleasant
Desire to change life	Work	Joy	Guilt and shame
Life satisfaction	Family	Elation	Sadness
(current, past, future)	Leisure	Pride	Anxiety and worry
Significant others'	Health	Affection	Anger
views of one's life	Finances	Happiness	Stress
		Ecstasy	Depression
			Envy

Theoretical/Objective[b]	
First Order Factors	Second Order Factors
Self-acceptance	Environmental mastery
Environmental mastery	Self-acceptance
Positive relations with others	Control
Purpose in life	
Personal growth	
Autonomy	

[a] Modified from Diener (1999).
[b] Extracted from Ryff (1989).

As with the global life satisfaction scales, these measures are predominantly multi-item, self-report scales.

Domain-Specific versus Global-Subjective Well-Being

Evidence of the strength of relationships between domain-specific and general-subjective well-being estimates is contradictory. Despite the intuitive assumptions of a strong link, it turns out that the mean- and median-observed correlations between life and job satisfaction hover around .30 to .35 for men and .25 for women (Rice, Near, & Hunt, 1980). Moreover, when partialing out other facets of life satisfaction, such as marital and leisure satisfaction, Rice et al. found the correlations between work and life satisfaction drop into the teens. In a later meta-analytic review of the job and life satisfaction literature, Tait, Padgett, and Baldwin (1989) found a sizable overlap between work and nonwork experiences (average correlation = .44), especially when controlling for moderator effects (e.g., gender) and statistical artifacts (e.g., sampling and measurement error). R.A. Myers and Cairo's (1992) assessment of this empirical research supports the notion that the relationship between life and job satisfaction when controlling for moderator and statistical artifacts is nearly .50, or about 25% of the variance.

Several researchers (e.g., Diener, Smith, & Fujita, 1995; Izard, 1993) have found that long-term mean levels of specific emotions such as anger, anxiety, or sadness do not fully relate to global ratings of pleasant and unpleasant affect. In turn, Schwarz, Strack, and Mai (1991) found moderate correlations between life satisfaction and domain-specific ratings of work, leisure, and marital satisfaction (correlations ranging from .32 to .46). Causal linkages are also unclear. Robbins,

Lee, and Wan (1994) tested a multidimensional model of life and leisure satisfaction in older adults. They hypothesized that leisure satisfaction should directly influence life satisfaction, but found that the best fitting model kept these two constructs independent. As can be seen, both the strength and direction of relationships suggest that domain-specific and global-subjective well-being constructs are not equivalent, and at times surprisingly low.

Schwarz and Strack (1999) argue that the large discrepancy between domain and global ratings is due to the simplifying strategies we use when forming complex judgments. Domain-specific judgments are less complex to make, and comparison information is available. Schwarz and Strack further argue that it is not surprising that the relationship between objective events (e.g., dating frequency or work success) and subjective well-being is weak given the strong contextual influences (e.g., how, when, and where information is accessed) on subjective judgment making (see Sudman, Bradburn, & Schwarz, 1996 for a review). Several sources of bias include scale format (e.g., Schwarz, Knauper, Hippler, Noelle-Neumann, & Clark, 1991), item order (Schwarz et al., 1991), time frame (Winkielman, Knauper, & Schwarz, in press), and current mood (Moum, 1988).

Emotional Well-Being

Interestingly, the psychological study of affective states has a longer and more complex history than the study of self-appraised life satisfaction (e.g., M. Lewis & Haviland, 1998). As with life satisfaction, overall emotional well-being is not synonymous with specific affect states. For example, does being free from depression or anxiety mean I experience emotional well-being? We also know that global reports of emotional well-being are not equivalent to the accumulation of a series of situation-specific ratings of emotional well-being (Kahneman, 1999; Thomas & Diener, 1990). In turn, it is important to distinguish between the frequency and intensity of emotional experiences. Several studies (see Diener & Larson, 1993 for a review) have shown that the frequency of positive emotional experiences are more important determinants of global emotional well-being than the intensity of experience.

Although psychological measures of negative mood states primarily have emerged out of the clinical and mental health arena, there are several instruments developed for well-being research. An early measure of positive affect is Fordyce's (1977) happiness scale, which can be used as both a self-report and informant measure of happiness. A highly cited measure of affect state is the Positive Affect Negative Affect Schedule (PANAS; Watson, Clark, & Tellegen, 1988). The PANAS was constructed to measure enduring temperament, using a biological/genetic perspective. This scale contains 20 emotions adjectives which are rated on a five-point scale to indicate the amount of time spent experiencing each emotion. Its emphasis is on positive and negative arousal, or excitement and distress, respectively. A fuller description of pertinent measures of subjective emotional well-being may be found in Andrews and Robinson (1991).

Diener (1994) recommends that multimethod approaches be employed to measure subjective well-being. It is always desirable to obtain a broad spectrum of measurement strategies, and several nonself-report strategies are available. These include coding of nonverbal behavior (e.g., frequency of smiling), experience sampling, electrophysiological measures, written interviews, and informant report. Considerable evidence supports the convergence of nonself-report and self-report measures of well-being (Sandvik, Diener, & Seidlitz, 1993). Nonetheless, the primary emphasis has been on self-report instrumentation when measuring both emotional and cognitive markers of subjective well-being. Lack of significant relationships between self-reports of subjective well-being and social desirability (e.g., Diener, Sandvik, Pavot, & Gallagher, 1991) and the clear construct validity for global estimates support the continued use of subjective estimates.

A major concern with this tripartite model of subjective well-being is whether these constructs operate independently, and, if so, under what conditions. Current emotion theories (e.g., Ortony, Clore, & Collins, 1988) link cognitive appraisals to the experience of emotion, and argue that these two components are inseparable. The subjective well-being perspective assumes that our overall life evaluation is different from the amount of time spent in positive and negative mood states. To address this question, Lucas, Diener, and Suh (1996) used a multitrait-multimethod approach on three sets of data, using self-report and informant reports across time. They found that life satisfaction, positive affect, and negative affect could be reliably and independently measured, and that each of these constructs showed divergence from other psychological constructs (e.g., self-esteem and optimism). Moreover, they replicated previous research showing that negative and positive affect are not end points on the same continuum, but rather operate independently of each other (Watson et al., 1988). The orthogonality of positive and negative affect is not settled, as other researchers (e.g., Green, Goldman, & Salovey, 1993) have found that when controlling for measurement error, using structural equation modeling, high correlations were found between positive and negative affect.

ISSUES IN THE MEASUREMENT

Clear evidence supports the reliable and independent measurement of cognitive and affective self-appraisals of subjective well-being. Closer inspection of the underlying judgmental processes and their methodological implications reveals a more complex picture. Schwarz and Strack (1999) have drawn upon the judgment making and social psychological literatures to identify several key questions regarding the measurement of subjective well-being. They suggest that the context in which subjective well-being is queried will influence responses. For example, they found that the preceding questions to life satisfaction and affect items will raise and lower item scores. They also found that the nature of response alternatives will dictate response levels. These contextual findings are important because they raise the broader question of whether subjective well-being is stable, or if it is highly influenced by daily events and by current mood states. Frederickson and Kahneman (1993) also draw on the decision making and judgment literature when describing how the peak/end rule affects subjective well-being estimates. They proposed that people attend more to the ending of an event than to its longevity or its significance beforehand, finding initial evidence that supports this premise.

Another important question when measuring subjective well-being relates to "online," or immediate, versus "global," or long-term, ratings of subjective well-being. A random sampling of people's experiences over time result in online measures that capture the momentary experience of both pleasant and unpleasant affect. This approach is distinctively different than asking for retrospective, global evaluations as they are only moderately related (Schimmack, 1997; Thomas & Diener, 1990).

SUBJECTIVE VERSUS OBJECTIVE CONSTRUCTS

Objective approaches to understanding well-being are more theoretically driven than subjective approaches, and identify constructs often associated with effective psychological development. This alternative approach to the subjectivistic and empirical approach underlying subjective well-being is well represented by the theoretical work of Carol Ryff (Ryff, 1989, 1991; Ryff & Keyes, 1995) who proposes that psychological well-being encompasses six distinct dimensions: autonomy, environmental mastery, personal growth, positive relations with others, purpose in life, and self-acceptance (as summarized in Table 10.1). These dimensions are premised on social psychological and developmental perspectives, where a person's self-mastery, including environment, must be viewed from the perspectives of ideal, present, and past selves.

A fundamental assumption of Ryff's and others' work is that the criteria for well-being, and mental health, is dictated from outside rather than from the internal experience of the participant. Thus, additional characteristics besides subjective well-being are necessary to understand psychological health. It is easy to see why subjective well-being is not a necessary condition for psychological health: Schizophrenics are frequently "happy" and "manics" are often significant societal contributors despite considerable internal distress, in both cases subjective well-being and health are independent.

The broader psychological well-being concept is a "mixture" of internal and external perspectives, and various constructs fall along a continuum with well-being constructs used both as outcome variables and as process or mediating variables (Ryff, 1995). This lack of conceptual clarity complicates our understanding of psychological well-being, and further reinforces the need for carefully articulated models that test the linkages between the antecedents or determinants of well-being and global and domain-specific estimates of subjective well-being. In any case, instruments used to measure a broader psychological well-being construct have emerged from several theoretical disciplines, including the developmental (e.g., Ryff, 1989, 1991; six dimensions of psychological well-being), aging (e.g., Reker & Peacock, 1981; Reker, Peacock, & Wong, 1987, Meaning and Purpose of Life Scale) and counseling (e.g., Robbins, 1989, the self scales) literatures.

Ryff (1989) used a "construct-oriented" approach (see Wiggins, 1973 for a discussion) by writing theoretical definitions and items to correspond to her six dimensions of psychological health. She found preliminary evidence for the test-retest reliability and internal consistency of the six scales. Exploratory factor analysis of these six scales with eight other measures of subjective well-being and psychological adjustment produced three factors: Self-acceptance, environmental mastery, and control (Ryff, 1991). Ryff also found that these three factors were related but not equivalent to global measures of subjective well-being. In a later study (Ryff & Keyes, 1995), a confirmatory factor analytic procedure was used to test three alternative models: a single-factor model, a six-factor model, and a six-factor model with a higher order or latent construct. The results suggest that the six dimensions of psychological-being were independent, but also loaded onto a higher order factor. Considerable work is needed to establish the construct validity of these six dimensions, and to distinguish them theoretically from the tripartite model of subjective well-being.

Comparison of the subjective and objective approaches to the structure and meaning of psychological well-being serves to highlight a key difference in focus: research on subjective well-being emphasizes the subjective report of three relatively atheoretical and static outcome measures or constructs, whereas research on psychological well-being attempts to capture the underlying *meaning* of well-being. As a prototypical psychological well-being researcher, Ryff's approach is less concerned with empirically "validating" these six independent constructs than with describing a value- and culture-driven model of what the markers of quality of life should entail. Her approach emphasizes positive psychological functioning rather than subjective well-being (see Diener et al., 1999 for a discussion).

If the use of these two approaches was solely assessed by the quantity and quality of research support, the tripartite model of subjective well-being would win by a landslide. Ironically, Ryff's argument for examining the underlying meaning of well-being occurs at a time when we must move toward understanding the process by which individuals report or indicate well-being (i.e., life satisfaction and positive/negative affect as outcomes). In many ways, it is easier to test the process of psychological well-being when using clearly defined outcome measures that are temporally placed within a causal model, and that are conceptually distinct from underlying causes or determinants. Put another way, the strength of Ryff's theoretical model is also a weakness because it clouds the connections between antecedents and outcomes of psychological well-being. We discuss later in this chapter the importance of conceptually separating subjective well-being as an outcome or sign of quality of life from its antecedents or determinants.

CORRELATES OF SUBJECTIVE WELL-BEING

Early subjective well-being research focused on the strength of associations between a wide range of demographic, economic, social, health, and psychological variables and subjective well-being. These efforts were viewed as a necessary first step in beginning to understand a deceivingly simple question: What makes us happy? Wilson's (1967) seminal work on subjective well-being had a sweeping conclusion: "[A] happy person emerges as a young, healthy, well-educated, well-paid, extroverted, optimistic, worry-free, religious, married person with high self-esteem, high job morale, modest aspirations, of either sex and a wide range of intelligence" (p. 294). Unfortunately, the 700 studies published between this conclusion and Diener's (1984) exhaustive review did not substantiate this claim, with little variance accounted for between most demographic variables and subjective well-being. In a more recent review, Diener et al. (1999) point to several emerging emphases, including elaborating the connections between biopsychosocial determinants and specific components of subjective well-being, an elaboration of causal models that can be tested within sophisticated longitudinal designs, and understanding the processes underlying adaptation to life events.

The current status of our understanding of the correlates of subjective well-being yields considerable insight into faulty preconceptions and will provide important leads in developing a fuller understanding of the subjective well-being construct. This information is also important if we are to build models that test the causal linkages and temporal relationships between these correlates and subjective well-being. (See Argyle, 1987; Diener, 1984; Diener et al., 1999; D.G. Myers & Diener, 1995 for broad reviews of correlates of subjective well-being.) The current literature on correlates of subjective well-being reinforces several surprising findings since Wilson's (1967) seminal work on the root causes of happiness and well-being. Considerable evidence now suggests that money, age, gender, intelligence, and parenthood do not have significant associations with subjective well-being (see D.G. Myers & Diener, 1995 for summary). Factors moderately to strongly related to overall happiness are surprisingly limited, and include marital quality and social intimacy, work engagement and life-task participation, motivational factors such as goal striving and belonging, psychological resources such as positive illusions, control, generalized self-efficacy, and optimism, and temperament and other personality features. Factors having a somewhat weaker association with subjective well-being include health, social activity, and religion.

Demographic Factors

The significant positive relationship between money and happiness diminishes for those individuals who move beyond the poverty level (Argyle, 1987). Only those countries whose majority population is well below the poverty level (e.g., Bangladesh and India) report moderately strong relationships between economic security and well-being (Diener & Diener, 1996). A reason for this weak relationship may be due to the fact that most people around the world report themselves at the midpoint or above on life satisfaction and happiness estimates. After summarizing over 1,000 life satisfaction surveys conducted in 43 countries, Veenhoven, Ehrhardt, Ho, and deVries (1993) concluded that in 86% of the nations (both industrialized and nonindustrialized) respondents were above the neutral point (a typical scale is one where respondents are asked to rate their happiness from 0, most unhappy to 10, most happy). In fact, the mean rating for all nations was 6.33 (Veenhoven et al., 1993). Income may be related to subjective well-being more complexly, where people who emphasize materialistic goals have lower subjective well-being (Sirgy, 1998) than those who emphasize communal and self-actualizing goals (Scitovsky, 1976). In other words, in countries where threats to basic security needs are not prevalent, moderating factors such as goals and values may influence the connection between income and subjective well-being.

Education is also correlated at approximately .13 with both affective and cognitive measures of well-being (Diener et al., 1999; Witter, Okun, Stock, & Haring, 1984). Education becomes more important when individuals drop below a critical threshold of income (Diener & Larson, 1993) and in poor countries (Veenhoven et al., 1993). Interestingly, education may be indirectly related to subjective well-being, working through both occupational status and income. Witter et al. found in their meta-analysis of the research literature on education and well-being that the effect size for education on subjective well-being dropped from .13 to .06 when controlling for occupational status. This same finding holds true when controlling for income (Diener & Larson, 1993). Educational status may also influence expectations for success, which when frustrated, *lower* subjective well-being estimates. Clark and Oswald (1994) found that within groups of unemployed, more highly educated individuals reported higher levels of distress and lower levels of well-being. These findings point to establishing causal linkages between education, and critical mediators (e.g., goal seeking, work status, and "flow") when understanding the determinants of subjective well-being.

Age accounts for less than 1% of the variation in people's subjective well-being, and is another example where a discrete demographic factor alone does not directly relate to subjective well-being. Inglehart (1990) found that 80% of 170,000 people sampled across six age groups within 16 nations stated that they were satisfied with life. Although the average level of subjective well-being remains remarkably stable over the life span, the predictors of happiness change by cohort group: Older adults describe personal relations and health as more important (e.g., Herzog, Rogers, & Woodworth, 1982), and younger adults describe daily events as more directly influencing mood (e.g., Csikszentmihalyi & Larson, 1984). These findings suggest that adults readjust their expectations with age, so that income production becomes less important and social relations more important during the adult life course. It is clear that as the life span has lengthened, happiness levels are holding, perhaps because people are staying healthier (Fries, 1990) and engaged in activities in multiple life domains compared with earlier generations (Bass, 1995).

A paradox with gender is that the rates of *global* subjective well-being are roughly equivalent although specific vulnerability to varying psychiatric illnesses is highly gender bound (D.G. Myers & Diener, 1995; Nolen-Hoeksema & Rusting, 1999). Haring, Stock, and Okun (1984) found that less than 1% of the variance in subjective well-being was attributed to gender when conducting a meta-analysis of 146 studies. Interestingly, these findings hold across culture, where both Inglehart (1990) and Michalos (1991) found in 16 and 39 countries, respectively, that men and women had a comparably high report of global life satisfaction. Inglehart also found that 24% of women and 20% of men rated themselves as "Very Happy," whereas Lee, Secombe, and Shehan (1991) found that women were more likely than men to report being "very happy." Diener et al. (1999) propose that a higher incidence in the expression of negative and positive emotion in women balances itself out, which accounts for comparable scores on global subjective well-being between men and women.

This lack of overall gender differences in subjective well-being is misleading when one begins to look at domain-specific differences, primarily in mood expression. More specifically, women are twice as likely to report being depressed or anxious, and men are five times as likely to have alcoholism and violence problems (Kessler et al., 1994; Robins & Regier, 1991). In other words, women self-report more intense and frequent internally focused negative emotions than men. Although Fujita, Diener, and Sandvik (1991) found only 1% of the variance accounted for by gender when measuring happiness, they found over 13% of the variance accounted for when measuring the intensity of experiences.

The more important question with regard to gender relates to why women express or report a more intense emotional experience relative to men. Nolen-Hoeksema and Rusting (1999) review the extensive literature on gender and well-being, and conclude that inherent in the caregiving role women are socialized to identify and express their feeling states (e.g., Grossman & Wood, 1993; Wood, Rhodes, & Whelan, 1989). Less evidence is available to support genetic predispositions

(Blehar & Oren, 1995), although some findings suggest that in externalizing or acting out disorders such as alcoholism (McGue, Pickens, & Svikis, 1992), men have a genetic predisposition. Another study (Broderick, 1998) found that among fourth and fifth graders, girls ruminate more than boys. How much prescriptive social norms influence differences in emotional expression reflects the broader issue of biology versus learning when understanding gender.

The Traits of Happy People

As noted earlier, health, social activity, and religion are more strongly related to subjective well-being than are demographic factors. Health, income, and social or leisure activity not only were historically identified by Wilson (1967), but also by the retirement theorists as critical determinants of life satisfaction (see Tinsley & Schwendener-Holt, 1992 for a discussion). As with income, it appears that only moderate direct relationships exist between either health or social activity and subjective well-being. Health status, for example, has been found to correlate .15 with subjective well-being when controlling for measurement (i.e., self-report versus objective status; Watten, Vassen, Myhrer, & Syversen, 1997) and for emotional well-being such as positive or negative mood state (Hooker & Siegler, 1992). In other words, it appears that the importance of health status is inflated by self-appraisal and other personality factors. In a longitudinal study, Brief, Butcher, George, and Link (1993) found that only *subjectively* appraised health predicted global life satisfaction; these subjective health estimates were in turn influenced by negative emotionality and objective health. Within an aging population, Robbins et al. (1994) found that health and economic resources only indirectly influenced both life and leisure satisfaction, working through an individual's sense of goal continuity. Once again, these findings point to the importance of developing models that incorporate direct and indirect effects on global and domain-specific satisfaction.

An emergent area of psychological study is religion and mental health (Worthington, Kurusu, McCullough, & Sandage, 1996), which previously was plagued by conceptual confusion and contradictory findings (cf. Bergin, 1983). Research has moved beyond simple dichotomous measures of religious/nonreligious to assessing degree of involvement, commitment, and practice. These behavioral and certainty indices of religion consistently have shown a moderate relationship with global life satisfaction ($r = .26$), but a somewhat smaller positive relationship with emotional well-being ($r = .15$) (Ellison, 1991; Gartner, Larson, & Allen, 1991). Considerable speculation about the beneficial effects of religion appear centered on its role in creating feelings of control and optimism, cognitive constructs that would directly influence our cognitive view of the world (i.e., global life satisfaction), but not necessarily our positive and negative emotional appraisal of well-being (Diener et al., 1999; Ellison, 1991). Religion also may promote increased social benefits through improved social networks and shared purpose and meaning (D.G. Myers & Diener, 1995).

Marriage and other significant intimate relationships continue to be reported as either the cause of considerable joy, or, when dysfunctional, unhappiness (Glenn, 1990). Larger numbers of married adults (39%) than unmarried adults (24%) view themselves as "very happy" (Lee et al., 1991). Marital status is a highly intriguing correlate because of the common belief that marriage is a prime source of fulfillment, yet two thirds of all marriages end in divorce or separation (Bjorksten & Steward, 1984). Karney and Bradbury (1995) examined the findings of 115 longitudinal research studies examining marital quality and stability. They surmised that marital stability and marital satisfaction were not interchangeable, and that "enduring vulnerabilities" (p. 21), such as neuroticism and poor family histories, combined with an inability to adapt to stressful life events diminishes marital satisfaction, resulting in eventual instability. There also appears to be gender differences with women reporting more dissatisfaction across the life course (Gottman, 1994; Lowenthal, Thurnher, & Chiriboga, 1975), raising a question about whether benefits are comparable across the sexes.

What remains is a lack of critical information about the reciprocal nature of marital status and life satisfaction. Preliminary longitudinal evidence suggests that happy people are viewed as more desirable, and more likely to marry (Mastekaasa, 1995; Scott, 1991). How personality facilitates significant intimate relationships, and whether the existence of these relationships improves individual and dyadic well-being, thus ensuring the longer term relationship stability, must be further tested. Kwan, Bond, and Singelis (1997) used a structural equation model to test a cross-section of U.S. and Hong Kong citizens, finding that personality temperament worked through relationship harmony to predict life satisfaction. As Karney and Bradbury (1995) conclude, theoretical models are needed that test the mediating and moderating effects of background factors on marital satisfaction and stability so that the *process* by which couples create stable and satisfying relationships is fully understood. Gottman's (1994) work on the marital process is a potentially important start at using observational methods to assess marital interaction and conflict, which will be important for constructing causal models.

As detailed earlier, work satisfaction consistently correlates between .30 and .45 with global subjective well-being (e.g., Rain, Lane, & Steiner, 1991; Tait et al., 1989). We also know that unemployment status is linked to overall well-being estimates, where disabled (Mehnert, Krauss, Nadler, & Boyd, 1990) and unemployed (e.g., Oswald, 1997) individuals report higher levels of distress and lower levels of life satisfaction. The characteristics of work satisfaction have been extensively studied, and we know that it is a multidimensional construct, with both morale (affect) and satisfaction (cognitive) components (George & Brief, 1992). We also know that intrinsic and extrinsic rewards (e.g., Herzberg, 1968), multiple role conflict (Roxburgh, 1996), person-environment fit (Bretz & Judge, 1994), work overload, and supervisor support are important determinants of job morale and satisfaction.

Yet, the causal connections between work and life satisfaction are less clear (R.A. Myers & Cairo, 1992). For example, several researchers (e.g., Tait et al., 1989; Warr, 1999) have found that happier people perform better at work. These findings are counterintuitive in that we have assumed that work is an important determinant of life satisfaction. The correlational nature of this research may mask the importance of variables such as personality, which moderate the effects of life and domain-specific satisfaction (Diener et al., 1999). A significant program of research is beginning to test both the direction of effects and factors that moderate the relation between work and life satisfaction. In two separate studies, Judge and his colleagues (Judge & Hulin, 1993; Judge & Watanabe, 1993) used structural equation modeling to test the reciprocal relationships between work and life satisfaction. They found a reciprocal relationship at a single point in time, but when predicting life and job satisfaction after five years, they found that life satisfaction significantly predicted job satisfaction but not vice versa. These highly intriguing results suggest that those people who are generally satisfied with life will derive greater job satisfaction, and that specific work-related variables may have less influence on life satisfaction than previously thought.

The Emergent Role of Temperament and Personality Factors

The strong connection between a wide range of personality factors and subjective well-being is one good example of why tremendous attention is being paid to the role of personality across broad disciplinary areas of psychology, including social (Sarason & Sarason, 1982), biopsychological (McGue, Bacon, & Lykken, 1996), and developmental (Datan, Rodeheaver, & Hughes, 1987). Since the 1980s, the "Big Five" personality model has dominated the literature (Costa & McCrae, 1992; Goldberg, 1990). This model is intriguing because it incorporates both an empirically derived, trait approach to measurement and a biological perspective on the basic facets or structure of personality, in this case, neuroticism, extraversion, openness to experience, agreeableness, and conscientiousness. The NEO-PI was constructed to measure these traits, and is extensively used in research (Costa & McCrae, 1992; Costa, McCrae, & Dye, 1991). But other approaches to understanding personality, primarily motivational, that include such constructs as goal striving (Austin & Vancouver, 1996), life task participation (Harlow & Cantor, 1996), and self-mediators (Graziano et al., 1997) have also emerged. In an important theoretical work, Winter, John, Stewart, Klohnen, and Duncan (1998) look to integrate the trait and motive traditions in personality research. They argue that traits and motives interact in the prediction of behavior: Traits channel the behavioral expression of motives through the life course. Winter et al. present two longitudinal studies that connect extraversion (a trait) with affiliative and power motives, demonstrating that extraversion influences the need to affiliate, which in turn directly influences goal attainment in both work and relationship arenas.

Where does this revolution in personality leave us when understanding subjective well-being? For simplification sake, it is important to address the direct relationships between both temperamental and motivational personality constructs and subjective well-being before turning to more complex and reciprocal relationships. The two most commonly cited personality traits when predicting subjective well-being are extraversion (associated with high levels of energy and enthusiasm) and neuroticism (associated with high levels of negative mood and self-concept). Costa, McCrae, and Zonderman (1987) argued that psychosocial stressors were less central to psychological and physical adjustment than these temperamental factors. Neuroticism in particular was proposed to "represent a broad dimension of individual differences in the tendency to experience negative, distressing emotions and associated behavioral and cognitive traits" (p. 301).

Estimates of the relationship between extraversion and positive affect have consistently ranged in the low .70s (cf. Lykken & Tellegen, 1996). In a study of 40 nations, Lucas, Diener, Grob, Suh, and Shao (1998) found that extraversion consistently correlated strongly with positive affect even when excluding shared affect items in the instrumentation. Lucas et al. proposed that extraverts are more sensitive to positive reinforcement or "rewards," and demonstrate increased positive affect and prosocial behavior. In several analogue studies, extraverts were found to be more sensitive to positive mood induction (e.g., Rusting & Larsen, 1997).

Watson and Pennebaker (1989) explored the role of negative and positive affectivity when understanding the structure and meaning of subjective well-being. Their classic series of studies on health, stress, and distress revealed that negative and positive affect dimensions were surprisingly independent, correlating with different markers of health. Second, they found that although affectivity was associated with level of complaint, it was less predictive of long-term health status, suggesting that affectivity is a general "nuisance" factor that influences the "true association between stress and health" (p. 24). Watson and Pennebaker's study underscores two conceptual issues with the structure and meaning of emotional subjective well-being. First, are extraversion and neuroticism independent or do they represent a latent or underlying factor of global emotional well-being? Second, Watson and Clark (1984) argued that neuroticism and extraversion were best understood as markers of negative and positive emotionality, and relabeled these trait constructs as simply positive and negative affectivity. This approach creates considerable confusion with regard to what are determinants and what are measures of subjective well-being, especially with the case of neuroticism and negative affectivity.

In an attempt to clarify the conceptual issues between temperamental factors (i.e., Big Five), personality correlates, and subjective well-being, DeNeve and Cooper (1998) conducted a meta-analysis of 137 personality traits as correlates of subjective well-being. They examined 142 published research reports incorporating over 42,000 adult participants, and found that personality factors equally predicted life satisfaction, happiness, and positive affect but were less predictive of negative affect. When clustering personality correlates into the Big Five categories, they found that the personality variables associated with neuroticism were the strongest predictors of life satisfaction, happiness, and negative affect, whereas those variables associated with either extraversion or agreeableness were the strongest predictors of positive affect. There were several surprising findings, including the relatively low effect sizes between personality correlates and subjective well-being (ranging from .08 to .18), and the emergence of several personality variables with limited previous research (e.g. repressive-defensiveness, trust, loss of control, private self-esteem). It should also be noted that the researchers did not include self-esteem or dispositional optimism constructs because "these variables are often used synonymously with subjective well-being" (p. 199).

DeNeve and Cooper (1998) also compared effect sizes for composites of demographic, trait, and psychosocial variables on subjective well-being. They found that demographic variables accounted for less than 3% of the variance in each measure of subjective well-being; subjective health and role loss accounted for less than 5% of the variance; and extraversion and neuroticism together accounted for 6% of positive affect, 20% of negative affect, and 11% of life satisfaction. They speculated that personality plays an important background role in influencing such psycho-social factors as social activity, social support, coping style, goal striving, daily events, and resources. These factors, in turn, directly affect the various facets of subjective well-being (see Diener et al., 1999 and Diener, 1996 for similar conclusions).

The Baseline or Set Point

Heritability research has focused on the role biology plays in temperament. Lykken and Tellegen (1996) used behavioral genetics to argue that 40% to 55% of the variation in current subjective well-being and 80% of the variance in long term subjective well-being is due to genetic transmission. They also cited 10-year test-retest stability estimates of .50 for those in their twenties and .70 for those in middle age as additional evidence that subjective well-being remains stable despite critical life events and developmental factors. In further support of this latter point, Suh, Diener, and Fujita (1996) followed 115 individuals over two years, determining that only life events during the previous three months influenced life satisfaction and positive and negative affect. Studies such as these represent the behavioral genetic perspective that environmental factors may interplay with genetic factors, but have little independent value in understanding personality (cf. Tellegen, Lykken, Bouchard, & Wilcox, 1988). These findings suggest that individuals have to assess ability to change affect and satisfaction levels realistically, and that our understanding of the prevalence of both positive and negative affect rates is strongly determined by set point.

These behavioral genetics estimates are being contested in several ways. First, negative affect appears more stable than positive affect, with environmental factors having a strong influence on positive affect (L.A. Baker, Cesa, Gatz, & Mellins, 1992). Second, several other researchers have found much lower heritability estimates (e.g., McGue & Christensen, 1997 suggested .27), and have pointed to the strong influence of unique environmental conditions (e.g., Gatz, Pedersen, Plomin, & Nesselroade, 1992). Moreover, the causal ties between temperamental predispositions, life events, and subjective well-being are uncertain. Plomin, Lichtenstein, Pedersen, McClearn, and Nesselroade (1990) proposed that genetic factors are more likely to influence a person's behavioral response tendencies, which directly influence interpersonal and life experiences. This view is consistent with Costa and McCrae's (1980) "instrumental" view on the impact of temperament on subjective well-being.

Diener et al. (1999) argue that the heritability estimates of Lykken and Tellegen (1996) are based on predictions of affect over a 10-year period, and that when only the stable portion of affect is used to derive estimates (that is, estimates that are free of error), the rates are much lower. In any case, measures of subjective well-being show moderate to high temporal stability. Pleasant and unpleasant affect are stable across time (e.g., Costa & McCrae, 1988; Headley & Wearing, 1992), suggesting a set point for individuals that temporary fluctuations revolve around. At the same time, life satisfaction shows moderate stability over time, with Magnus, Diener, Fujita, and Pavot (1993) finding a .58 correlation over a four-year period. These estimates suggest that although affective and cognitive markers of well-being are influenced by daily events, there is considerable constancy over prolonged periods. It remains to be seen whether subjective well-being is a dispositional trait, and that fluctuations evolve around a set point. Even though the trait proponents (e.g., Costa et al., 1987) have provided compelling evidence, several other researchers maintain the importance of time and life events in understanding the "dynamics" of well-being (Veenhoven et al., 1993). As Diener (1996) eloquently argues, the relevant question may be the conditions under which personality traits strongly predict subjective well-being. He goes on to suggest that "a scientific understanding based on traits must be augmented by a process-orientation and a study of relevant situational factors" (p. 389).

Motivational Factors

Motivational factors have emerged as important correlates of subjective well-being. Perhaps most central to contemporary personality and social psychological theories of motivation are goal constructs (cf. Austin & Vancouver, 1996; Pervin, 1989), which assume teleology or purposefulness in behavior. Although goals are operationalized differently depending on the theoretical perspective, whether life tasks (Cantor & Kihlstrom, 1989), personal strivings (Emmons, 1986, 1991), or goal instability (Robbins & Patton, 1985), all hold in common that personal goals serve as central organizers of affect, cognition, and behavior. Considerable research has shown a strong relationship between various goal constructs and their qualities and subjective well-being estimates, including achieving valued goals and life satisfaction (e.g., Emmons, 1986), the presence of goal conflict and/or unachieved goals and negative affect (Elliot, Sheldon, & Church, 1997; King, 1996), and the level goal coherence/congruence and life satisfaction (Emmons & King, 1988; Sheldon & Kasser, 1995).

A conceptual distinction has been made between striving to obtain meaning and purpose in life through goal attainment and commitment as an *antecedent* to subjective well-being as opposed to being a central definition of well-being (see Ryff & Singer, 1998 for a discussion). Regardless of these conceptual distinctions, considerable evidence supports how goal-oriented, purposeful behavior predicts subjective well-being. A good example of this can be found in Cantor's (Cantor, 1994; Cantor & Fleeson, 1994) life task participation model, which posits that "sustained participation in personally- and culturally-valued tasks that change across the life course enhances well-being" (Cantor & Sanderson, 1999, p. 2). Cantor and Sanderson propose that intrinsically valued and autonomously chosen personal goals must be approached at a realistic level and with daily support. They also suggest that the presence of various social, personal, and tangible resources would facilitate goal attainment. We use Cantor and her colleagues' work later in the chapter to highlight a process model approach to understanding subjective well-being. Empirical findings are beginning to support this model. In one study, Harlow and Cantor (1996) studied 618 older adults, finding that satisfaction was connected to developmental stage-appropriate activities such as community service and social participation after controlling for a range of psychosocial and demographic factors.

The relationship of goals and subjective well-being is more complex than simply assuming goal attainment or purposeful behavior leads to increased well-being. Kasser and Ryan (1993, 1996) found that generative and communal goals such as community participation and affiliation were more strongly related to well-being than financial goals. Conversely, Lapierre, Bouffard, and Bastin (1997) examined negative states in elderly people, finding that those with goals that were related to security were less happy than those focusing on self-actualization. It is clear that the environmental context within which one strives for goal attainment dictates the processes by which goals influence subjective well-being (Diener et al., 1999). From a cultural perspective, research has shown that individual feelings of self-esteem and positive/negative affect are less important within collectivistic cultures than within individualistic cultures (cf. Markus & Kitayama, 1994; Suh, Diener, Oishi, & Triandis, 1998). In other words, culture may dictate the type of goals that are valued, the resources available to obtain these goals, and the way in which subjective well-being is expressed or understood.

Emergent research highlights the mediating roles goals play when understanding the influence of environmental resources and personality on subjective well-being. Robbins et al. (1994) found that goal continuity, defined as the degree to which older adults maintain a sense of coherence and purpose in their lives, directly predicted both leisure and life satisfaction while serving as a mediator for health, social support, and economic status. In a later study with older adults, Cook, Dougherty, and Robbins (1999) found that goal instability, defined as the inability to set purpose or direction and to provide energy to move on goals, served as a mediator of personality traits (as measured by the NEO-PI) when predicting marital satisfaction within a sample of older adults. Graziano et al. (1997) proposed that the "self" was "a mediating agent that translates personality into situated goal-directed activities and adaptation" (p. 392). They tested structural equation models that demonstrated that Big Five personality factors worked directly and indirectly through self-esteem when predicting school adjustment. In a similar vein, Elliot et al. (1997) found that neuroticism was positively related to adoption of avoidant goals, which were negatively related to long-term subjective well-being. Finally, there is also a reciprocal nature between goals and subjective well-being. Diener and Fujita (1995) demonstrated that happy people tended to select goals congruent with available resources, and successful goal attainment reinforces happiness.

Another emergent area within personality and social psychology is the role of belonging when understanding psychological development and subjective well-being. In a seminal article, Baumeister and Leary (1995) argued that belonging was a basic human need, which we all strive to fulfill. They argued that self-esteem is the positive by-product of belonging, and that an individual's ability to connect to the social world is fundamental in human nature. Myers (1999) elaborates this argument when reviewing the connection between "close relationships and the quality of life." He argues that close, supportive, intimate, connections are essential to human development and growth, and the experience of belonging underlies attachment, self-concept, and the well-being phenomena. In a recent series of studies, Lee and Robbins (1995, 1998) have found that social connectedness, a psychological marker of belonging, is directly related to life satisfaction, anxiety, and performance.

Psychological Resources

A conglomeration of individual difference factors that appear more directly related to "agency" rather than to temperament (see Lightsey, 1996 for an extensive review) are hypothesized as important determinants of subjective well-being. Several of these constructs relate to Ryff's (1989) notion of environmental mastery, control, and self-acceptance as central to psychological well-being. From a social cognitive theory perspective, all these constructs have cross-situational qualities, and organize how we respond to various stress and performance demand situations (Lightsey, 1996). *Generalized and domain-specific self-efficacy* refers to either broad or situation-specific beliefs that certain actions can be taken and successfully accomplished (Bandura, 1989). Lightsey argues that generalized self-efficacy is particularly instrumental in understanding subjective well-being, as it has been found to mediate coping and behavioral responses (e.g., Eden & Aviram, 1993), and to directly relate to decreased depression (e.g., Davis-Berman, 1990) and negative response tendencies (Smith & Petty, 1995). The relationship between generalized and domain-specific self-efficacy is still uncertain, and raises questions about the degree to which self-efficacy is a "learned" trait or a marker of underlying temperament (cf. Lightsey, 1996; Robbins, 1985).

Optimism-pessimism (Scheier & Carver, 1985) is another individual difference factor that contains both temperamental and agentic features (see Scheier, Carver, & Bridges, 1994 for an empirical attempt at distinguishing optimism from neuroticism). This factor refers to generalized positive and negative outcome expectancies, and measures stable individual differences that promote (or impede) psychological and physical well-being. Considerable research has connected optimism to psychological adjustment and well-being (e.g., Aspinwall & Taylor, 1997; Chang, 1996; Plomin et al., 1992). Scheier and Carver (1992) argue that increasing evidence points to the role of dispositional optimism-pessimism as an important causal determinant of psychological and physical well-being. As with the self-efficacy constructs, optimism is being employed in mediational models of adaptation and change. Chang (1998), for example, in a study with college students, tested how dispositional optimism directly predicted life satisfaction, depression, and physical well-being, as well as working indirectly through appraisal and problem-solving coping responses. In any case, considerable disagreement exists on the degree to which the constructs of optimism and pessimism are independent or bipolar, activate different emotional and coping responses, and are heavily determined by genetic influences (cf. Plomin et al., 1992; Schulman, Keith, & Seligman, 1993).

Two other constructs that fall under the general rubric of cognitive social learning are *personal control* and *positive illusions*. Personal control refers to an individual's belief that they can choose behavior that will result in positive outcomes while minimizing negative outcomes. This construct emerges out of the learned helplessness research (cf. Peterson, Maier, & Seligman, 1993), and countless studies have connected the learned helplessness paradigm to markers of mental health (Rodin, 1986). In a recent, representative study, Lachman and Weaver (1998) found that the sense of control moderated the relation between social class and other perceived constraints and health, life satisfaction, and depression. The related construct of positive illusions is premised on three assumptions: (1) our natural tendency is to view ourselves positively, (2) we assume greater control of the environment than is realistic, and (3) our view of the future has positive expectations beyond what is reasonable to predict (see Taylor & Brown, 1988, 1994 for discussion). In essence, research has shown that positive illusions are associated with improved response to postcancer treatment (Taylor, 1983) and other stressful events, but more recent researchers (cf. Colvin & Block, 1994) have challenged the premise that positive illusions underlie positive mental health.

As the above review indicates, although we know more about what does and does not influence subjective well-being than we did thirty years ago, substantial questions remain regarding how to measure subjective well-being, the stability of subjective well-being over the life course, critical contributors to subjective well-being, and the process by which those influences operate. In the remaining sections of this chapter, we highlight three promising theoretical models of subjective well-being, then discuss the strategies researchers need to employ to move the field of subjective well-being forward. We close with a summary of key findings to date, and identify some applied implications of this research.

THEORETICAL MODELS

A number of different models have been developed over the past thirty years to understand subjective well-being. The three models highlighted below differ in emphasis, and each have potential to clarify the critical determinants of subjective well-being and the processes accounting for individual differences in subjective well-being. The first type of model emphasizes the critical role of temperament and personality traits (Costa & McCrae, 1980), and exemplifies the "top down" approach described by Diener (1984). The second type of model focuses on the process of participation in goal-directed activity as central to subjective well-being (cf. Cantor & Sanderson, 1999). The third model emerges from the context of coping with stressful events or life circumstances, and highlights appraisal and coping processes (Holahan & Moos, 1994). Distinctions between these models are important because the models have different assumptions about what is critical to subjective well-being, and therefore shape the research questions asked and the designs employed to address those questions. The models are represented in Figure 10.1. We use the term "model" to refer to a broad framework for understanding subjective well-being, including the important influences on subjective well-being, the relationship of those influences to each other, and the direction of effects. One or more theories may be subsumed under a model.

Temperamental Model

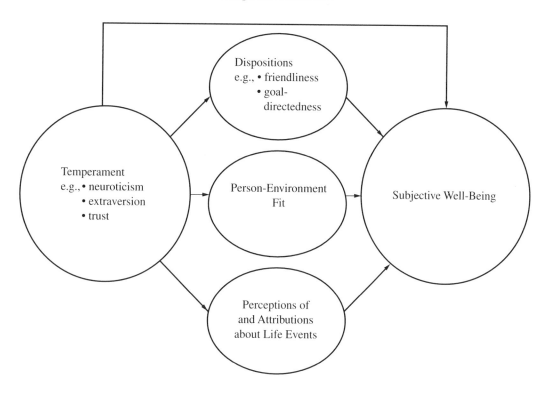

Process-Participation Model

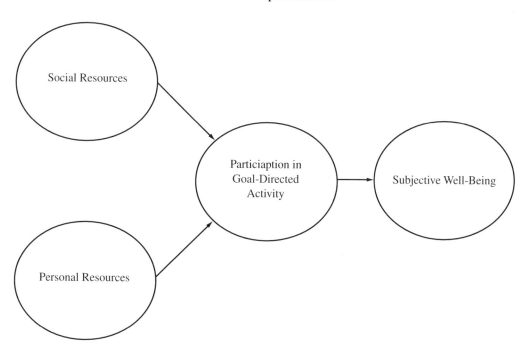

Figure 10.1   Illustrative Examples of Three Models of Subjective Well-Being

Coping Model

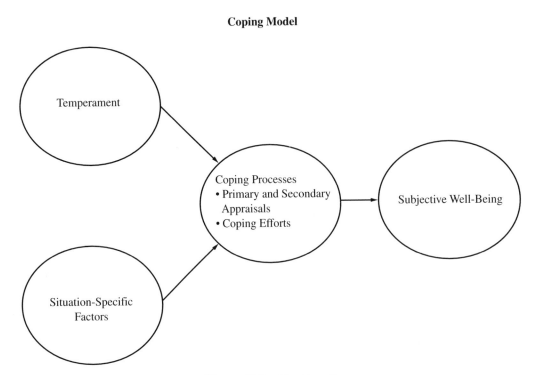

Figure 10.1   (Continued)

Temperament Model

The critical role of temperament and personality traits is the central feature of the first type of model (Costa & McCrae, 1980). In this perspective, temperament, which has a strong genetic component, has either direct effects on subjective well-being (the temperamental view; McCrae & Costa, 1991) or affects subjective well-being indirectly by influencing (1) the development of other stable dispositions such as goal directedness and coping style (the instrumental view; McCrae & Costa, 1991); (2) the degree of personality-environment fit (Diener, Larsen, & Emmons, 1984; Diener, Sandvik, Pavot, & Fujita, 1992); (3) one's perception of life events (Feist, Bodner, Jacobs, Miles, & Tan, 1995); (4) one's attributions regarding life events (DeNeve & Cooper, 1998); or (5) the types of life events one encounters (Magnus et al., 1993), which in turn influence subjective well-being. Whether the effects of personality on subjective well-being are direct or mediated, or a combination, the emphasis is on personality as the primary determinant of subjective well-being.

This personality approach to subjective well-being has garnered significant attention by researchers during the last 15 years for several reasons. First, as noted earlier existing models, which emphasized demographic correlates of subjective well-being, left much of the variance in subjective well-being unexplained (Wilson, 1967). Second, scientific advances in the field of behavioral genetics have enhanced interest in genetic contributions to individuals' mental health. The Big Five personality model that has dominated the literature during this period includes a strong biological component.

Models that emphasize the contribution of personality to subjective well-being have both advantages and disadvantages. One advantage is that they allow competing theories of why personality traits are associated with subjective well-being to be tested. Results of these studies can then be used to modify theory and to guide interventions promoting subjective well-being. For example, researchers can design studies to determine whether personality is associated with subjective well-being because of the influence of personality traits on a stable disposition such as goal-directedness, or because personality traits influence one's perception of life circumstances. Recommendations for intervention strategies would differ, depending on the results of such studies. For example, if researchers find that personality influences well-being because of its effect on perceptions of life events, then interventions might target individuals' appraisal processes. However, if researchers obtain more support for the notion that personality influences subjective well-being because of influences on goal-directedness, then interventions might take a more motivational approach. A shortcoming of the temperament model, however, is lack of attention to potential moderators. That is, the conditions under which personality traits affect subjective well-being, stable dispositions, perceptions and attributions about life events, the occurrence of life events, or other hypothesized mediators are not specified. One way of refining theories that emphasize the role of personality is to begin to identify the people, settings, or circumstances for which links between personality and hypothesized mediators are most and least likely to occur.

Research on determinants of subjective well-being operating from the personality perspective has taken several forms. In one form, dimensions of personality are correlated with dimensions of well-being using cross-sectional or longitudinal designs. For example, McCrae and Costa (1991), using a large, heterogeneous sample (ages ranged from 24 to 87) correlated the Big Five personality factors with measures of well-being. Notably, both self-ratings and ratings from spouses were used to assess personality. Consistent with previous research, neuroticism was negatively associated with well-being, and extraversion, agreeableness, and conscientiousness were positively related to well-being. Openness to experiences was not significantly correlated with well-being.

Although Diener has pointed out that an exclusive reliance on trait constructs in understanding subjective well-being is insufficient (Diener, 1996), his work also provides an example of research from the personality/temperament perspective. Using data from a large national probability sample ($N = 16,684$), Diener et al. (1992) examined the association between extraversion and subjective well-being. Data used in this study were collected at two time points, 10 years apart. As part of this study, Diener and his colleagues sought to account for association between extraversion and well-being, specifically by examining the concept of person-environment fit. This focus on potential mediators of the relation between personality and subjective well-being represents another form of the personality approach to subjective well-being, and is a logical development from purely descriptive work. Although extraverts in this sample worked in social occupations and lived in households with more persons significantly more often than introverts, Diener et al. did not find support for the contention that extraverts are happier because they spend more time in social environments relative to introverts. Thus, time spent in social environments does not seem to mediate or explain the relation between extraversion and subjective well-being.

Additional studies operating from the personality perspective have attempted to show associations between personality traits and the objective experience of life events, one's perception of life events, or the attributions one makes about the causes of life events as a way of explaining links between personality and subjective well-being. For example, Magnus et al. (1993) assessed the connections between the personality and objective life events using data from a four-year longitudinal study of young adults. They found that extraversion predisposed the participants in their study to experience more positive life events, and neuroticism predisposed participants to experience more negative events. Life events did not prospectively influence personality. Although this study did not assess subjective well-being, and therefore cannot demonstrate that life events mediated the relation between personality and subjective well-being, it does suggest one of the mechanisms through which personality might operate to influence well-being.

In a related vein, in DeNeve and Cooper's (1998) meta-analysis of 137 personality traits and subjective well-being, they suggest that what may be most critical to subjective well-being is the tendency to make either positive or negative attributions about one's emotions and life events, and even others' behaviors. This observation emerged from their findings that repressive defensiveness, trust, emotional stability, locus of control, desire for control, hardiness, positive affectivity, private collective self-esteem, and tension were the specific personality traits most strongly associated with subjective well-being. DeNeve and Cooper suggested that perhaps it is the tendency to appraise life events optimistically and to make control attributions, as well as optimistic attributions about others' motives, that is so meaningful for the experience of well-being. This is an intriguing hypothesis that has yet to be tested systematically.

As Diener et al. (1999) note, research has shown that the top-down influence of personality has a substantial influence on subjective well-being. What is less clear, however, are the reasons *why* personality traits are associated with subjective well-being, the direction of the personality-well-being relationship, and the conditions under which the association between personality and subjective well-being is most likely to be observed. Nonetheless, this theoretical model suggests many ways to explore both critical determinants of well-being and the processes by which those influences operate.

Process-Participation Model

The second type of model is a process approach to subjective well-being (Cantor & Sanderson, 1999). In this model, individuals' social, personal, and tangible resources increase their ability to pursue personal goals that are intrinsically valued, autonomously chosen, realistic, and that can be sought in the activities of daily life. Commitment to these goals leads to a sense of agency and purpose, to active engagement in their pursuit, and to a sense of meaning and social connectedness. Participation in goal-directed activity facilitates subjective well-being. Although this type of model acknowledges the role that resources play in individuals' pursuit of their goals (including personality traits), the model emphasizes the process of participation in goal-directed activity as central to subjective well-being, rather than resources.

Although the notion that what people are trying to do in their daily lives is critical to their well-being is not new (cf. Allport, 1937; Durkheim, 1933; Havighurst, 1960), renewed interest in the topic has emerged in the last 15 years (e.g., Brickman & Coates, 1987; Cantor, 1990, 1994; Sen, 1980). The advantage of this approach is that very specific tests of the relation between elements of goal-directed activity and subjective well-being can be conducted. For example, the questions "What is it about goal-directed activity that results in high subjective well-being?" or "When (under what conditions) does goal-directed activity result in high subjective well-being?" can be addressed. Both questions about process (e.g., Does goal-directed activity result in high subjective well-being because engagement in such activity produces a sense of meaning?) and questions about necessary and sufficient conditions (e.g., Do goals need to be both autonomously chosen and realistic to produce subjective well-being?) can be answered. The disadvantage of this model is that although resources are acknowledged as important influences on individuals' participation in life tasks, the focus on participation may underestimate the influence of resources and one's ability to access those resources on subjective well-being.

Research on subjective well-being operating from this model has examined facets of individuals' goals, as well as participation in goal-directed activity, and connections to general and domain specific to well-being. Emmons's (1986) study on personal strivings is a good example of early work focusing on goals. Emmons examined the relations between 40 undergraduates' personal goal strivings and subjective well-being using an experience sampling method over a three-week period. The importance of goal strivings and past attainment of goals was most predictive of positive affect; negative affect was predicted by low probability of future success, ambivalence about striving for goals, and goal conflict. Overall life satisfaction was best predicted by goal-striving importance and low conflict between goals. In a more recent study, Brunstein (1993) examined the extent to which goal commitment, goal attainability, and goal progress predicted the subjective well-being of students over a four-month period. Interactions between these dimensions of personal goals and their impact on well-being were studied. In prospective analyses, the impact of goal attainability on changes in subjective well-being was moderated by goal commitment. Students with a high level of goal commitment, coupled with favorable conditions to attain personal goals, showed moderate increases in subjective well-being from Time 1 to subsequent time points. Conversely, students with a high level of goal commitment, coupled with unfavorable conditions to attain person goals, demonstrated decreases in subjective well-being from Time 1 to subsequent time periods. Progress in goal attainment accounted for the interaction of goal commitment and goal attainability on subjective well-being. Robbins and his colleagues (Robbins et al., 1994) provide another example of a type of study linking goals to well-being. Robbins et al. used structural equation modeling techniques to test a model of adjustment to transition (in this case retirement) that included resources (perceived social support, health status, and SES), goal continuity (defined as the overall ability to set goals, the presence of a clearly established purpose, and the energy to take concerted action), leisure quality, and life satisfaction. Both interview and survey data was collected. Robbins et al. found that resources—social support, health, and SES—each affected goal continuity, which in turn affected leisure quality and life satisfaction.

A recent study by Harlow and Cantor (1996) provides an excellent example of research that emphasizes the process of participation and its influence on subjective well-being. Using data from 618 older adults in Terman's longitudinal study, Harlow and Cantor sought to determine if daily life participation predicts life satisfaction independently, and over and above the effects of broader personality and social-structural variables that promote well-being across contexts and time. Harlow and Cantor included measures of work participation and participation in 33 specific activities, change in participation, health and vitality, overall life satisfaction, as well as domain-specific satisfaction, social contacts, organizational affiliations, income, and data on life satisfaction, job satisfaction, income, and personality traits collected between 6 and 28 years earlier than the outcome variables. Participation, specifically participation in community service activities and social activities, and mass communication use, was associated with satisfaction with life as a whole after controlling for prior life satisfaction, health and vitality, marital status, social contacts, organizational affiliations, and work participation. Satisfaction in specific life domains was also predicted by participation in activities in those life domains, even after accounting for the control variables. Harlow and Cantor argue that these effects are observed because "participation directly represents the enactment of one's personal purposes within one's actual current living context, and thereby is a direct marker of a person's capacity to adjust to and find satisfaction in that particular life context." Cantor and Sanderson (1999) link research on goals and participation by arguing that the type of participation matters because the strength of the association between participation and well-being depends on the specific tasks on which individuals are working. They specifically posit that well-being should be enhanced when individuals are able to pursue "distinct personal goals in ways that are intrinsically-valued and autonomously chosen, approached at a feasible level, and facilitated in their daily life context" (p. 2). Consistent with findings of Robbins et al. (1994), Cantor and Sanderson point out that well-being also may depend on the presence of social, personal, and tangible resources, which increase the likelihood that individuals will participate in various tasks. As noted earlier, process-participation models of subjective well-being do not ignore the role of resources, but rather focus on participation in goal-directed activity as central to subjective well-being.

Coping Model

Embedded within a stress and coping framework, the third type of model, which we will call a coping model, focuses on coping processes that occur in response to stressful life events or circumstances that facilitate or impede subjective well-being. This model acknowledges the contribution of temperament and dispositional factors, as well as personal resources and situational factors, to individuals' appraisals of life events and the cognitive and behavioral efforts used to manage these life stressors (Holahan & Moos, 1994). However, the focus is on the coping processes (appraisals and coping efforts) involved in dealing with stressors, as it is these processes that are most proximal to subjective well-being.

A central difference between the coping model approach to subjective well-being and the models that emphasize personality and participation is that the coping model assumes a stressful context and the other models do not. In one sense, the question asked in the coping model approach is different: "Why do some individuals dealing with stressors report high subjective well-being, while others do not?" versus "Why do individuals vary in their level of subjective well-being?"

In their seminal 1984 book *Stress, Appraisal, and Coping,* Lazarus and Folkman identified a dual set of processes that affect individuals' adjustment to stressful life events and circumstances. One process, appraisal, involves both assessment of potential harm that could result from the stressful event (primary appraisal) and assessment of internal and external resources available to cope with the situation (secondary appraisal). The second process, coping, includes cognitive and behavioral efforts to manage affective responses to stressful situations or to change the situation. Lazarus and Folkman are careful to note that coping efforts are effortful attempts to manage stress responses, should not be equated with automatic responses, or with mastery of a situation. Thus, the term "coping" does not imply good adjustment or well-being. Numerous studies over the past two decades with college students and community samples have shown that the way in which individuals appraise situations and the coping efforts they employ to deal with them are linked to psychological and physical adjustment. In general, when individuals appraise stressors as less threatening, perceive more personal and social resources available to deal with stressors (e.g., social support, control, efficacy), and use a greater percentage of approach or active coping strategies (versus avoidance strategies), they report higher levels of subjective well-being, fewer psychological problems, and better physical health.

Although much of the work on stress, coping, and adjustment focuses on negative outcomes, both early (Antonovsky, 1979, 1987) and more recent (Carver, 1998; Epel, McEwen, & Ickovics, 1998; Ickovics & Park, 1998; Park, 1998; Saakvitne, Tennen, & Affleck, 1998) research has highlighted positive dimensions of adjustment. This body of research has sought to understand why some individuals, when faced with stressful circumstances, demonstrate growth and enhanced adjustment, while others demonstrate a return to normal functioning or psychopathology. In the preface to a recent special issue of the *Journal of Social Issues,* Ickovics and Park suggest that researchers in medicine and the social and behavioral sciences need to focus on thriving, rather than on pathology, as they study health. This shift in emphasis, they argue, can enhance our understanding of health and provide important opportunities for prevention and intervention.

Researchers emphasizing positive adjustment have concentrated on different characteristics important to this outcome. Antonovsky (1987), for example, has highlighted the protective role of a sense of coherence, demonstrating that individuals who are able to find meaning in the stressful events they encounter report good well-being and enjoy enhanced physical health. Maddi and Kobasa (1991) have focused on the concept of hardiness. Moos and his colleagues have taken a different tact by focusing both on appraisals of control and coping efforts (active and avoidant coping) in understanding adjustment. In a two-year longitudinal study of 175 freshmen who had moved away to attend college, Valentiner, Holahan, and Moos (1994) used causal modeling techniques to test the relationships among parental support, coping (the hypothesized mediator), control appraisals (the hypothesized moderator), and changes in psychological adjustment (assessed with measures of well-being and distress). As predicted, parental support was directly related to change in adjustment, as well as being partially mediated (explained) by use of approach coping. When control appraisals were examined as a moderator, approach coping fully mediated (explained) the relation between parental support and changes in adjustment for students dealing with a controllable event; however, there was only a direct association between parental support and change in adjustment for students dealing with an uncontrollable event. This study illustrates the use of coping concepts to understand *why* and *under what conditions* resources (parental support) affected well-being.

Other recent work which is conceptually consistent with the coping model approach to subjective well-being is Aspinwall and Taylor's (1997) description of the concept of proactive coping and its importance in warding off or offsetting potential stressors, and thus affecting well-being. One central implication of their framework is that by recognizing that many stressors are or can be avoided, coping, rather than stressors, becomes focal in models of adjustment.

As Diener and his colleagues note (Diener et al., 1999), the models described here are complementary rather than incompatible, and differ primarily in what they emphasize. Diener et al. suggest that process-participation and coping models will make the most progress if they incorporate people's dispositions and circumstances. However, merely including measures of dispositions and life circumstances in studies of subjective well-being will not advance the field scientifically unless attention is also paid to the types of research designs employed. In the following section, we address decisions about design, statistical technique, and choice of data that researchers must grapple with in planning studies of subjective well-being.

RESEARCH IMPLICATIONS

In this section, we argue that in order for the study of subjective well-being to advance, researchers must resolve questions about causality and test the assumptions of models against one another. Dealing with these two central issues will result in a clearer view of the antecedents and consequences of subjective well-being, and will provide researchers with direction for translating basic and generative research into prevention and intervention programs.

Causality Issues

The term causality refers to the notion that one variable (e.g., a personality trait) is responsible for, or contributes to, changes in another variable (e.g., subjective well-being). A necessary, but not sufficient, condition of causality is that the predictor variable (the cause) must temporally precede the outcome variable (the effect). Because most of the core elements in theories of well-being are not subject to random assignment, longitudinal designs, in which data are collected from participants at more than one point in time, are a better choice than cross-sectional designs, in which data are collected only once from participants, for beginning to establish causal associations. Thus, studies operating from each of the models discussed earlier should collect data on their predictor variables (e.g., personality traits, goal commitment, goal progress, participation, appraisals, coping) prior to collecting outcome variable data (e.g., subjective well-being). Although some studies collect predictor data at one time point and outcome data at another (e.g., Feist et al., 1995), an even stronger case for causality can be made when data on subjective well-being are also collected at the beginning of a longitudinal study. In this case, initial subjective well-being can be controlled in analyses predicting well-being at later time periods. If such analyses are planned, then the researchers must design their studies with enough time between data collection points to allow for change in subjective well-being. This is an interesting issue, given data suggesting that individuals have a well-being "set point" to which they return, and at least moderate stability in well-being across time.

In and of itself, longitudinal data, which in most cases involving subjective well-being is correlational, cannot establish causality. One statistical approach to this problem is to use structural equation modeling (SEM) techniques. Although some researchers maintain that causality can *never* be established using correlational data, others (Bentler, 1980) argue that in some cases SEM can be used to establish causal links among constructs.

To use SEM techniques most effectively, researchers must plan their studies at the outset to include adequate sample sizes, which are typically larger than those required when using regression analysis or analysis of variance (ANOVA) techniques, and multiple measures (indicators) of each construct in the model. Because multiple indicators of a construct are needed for SEM, this analytic technique provides an excellent opportunity to augment self-report data with data from others close to the participant, physiological indicators, or data from projective tests.

SEM techniques are not always the best choice, even when sample size and measurement issues have been addressed. Generally SEM techniques are best used (1) after a researcher has demonstrated that the indicators of the model constructs are reliable and valid; (2) when models are refined and parsimonious and variables that do not have strong associations with other variables in the model have been eliminated; and (3) when researchers are testing theories of *mediation* versus *moderation.* Although recent techniques have been developed to test moderation using LISREL (see Jaccard & Wan, 1996), these techniques are difficult when moderator variables are continuous, and converting a continuous variable to a categorical variable results in lost information. Regression analysis remains a good option for testing moderator effects (see Aiken & West, 1991), although regression analysis presumes that constructs are assessed with no measurement error, which is never the case. SEM techniques create error-free latent constructs using the measured indicators of each construct, and it is for this reason that researchers have argued that SEM strategies provide a less biased assessment of the significance of moderator effects (Jaccard & Wan, 1995; Peyrot, 1996; Ping, 1996).

Feist and his colleagues (1995) provide a nice example using SEM techniques to test causal relations between physical health, daily hassles, world assumptions, constructive thinking, and subjective well-being. Data on 160 participants were collected over four time periods spanning three months, although the SEM analyses were only conducted over a one-month period. (Analyses were conducted for Time 1→ Time 2 and replicated for Time 3 → Time 4.) Three indicators were used for each construct, except for world assumptions, which had two indicators. Confirmatory Factor Analysis indicated that the constructs were measured reliably. The structural models tested fit the data well. In the "bottom up" model Feist et al. tested, paths from physical health, world assumptions, and constructive thinking to subjective well-being were each significant. In addition, daily hassles had a direct influence on world assumptions and constructive thinking, and physical health had a direct influence on world assumptions.

A second design choice that can assist subjective well-being researchers in resolving questions about causality involves augmenting correlational data with experimental studies. This strategy will not be optimal for all subjective well-being researchers, but is particularly relevant for researchers using either a process-participation model or a coping model approach to subjective well-being. For example, after collecting correlational data on subjective well-being using a coping perspective (either cross-sectional or longitudinal designs may have been employed), researchers might design an intervention targeting appraisals or coping efforts. Participants could be randomly assigned to treatment and control groups, with or without matching them on the resources (e.g., personality traits, SES) that can affect coping processes, and assessed prior to and following the intervention. If participants in the intervention group, relative to controls, change their appraisals and coping efforts, and if these changes result in enhanced subjective well-being, then causality would be established. Another type of experimental intervention might involve increasing participants' level of realistic goals and self-efficacy. Again, participants could be randomly assigned to intervention and control groups, with or without matching them on the personality traits or other resources that can affect goal setting and efficacy. If participants in the intervention group, relative to controls, change their level of realistic goal setting as well as their self-efficacy, and if these changes result in increases in participation and subjective well-being, then causality would be established. Although many subdisciplines of psychology routinely use experimental designs to augment correlational research (this is a hallmark of action research, and research aimed at preventing mental health problems in children and adults), few examples of this strategy are available in the subjective well-being literature, particularly when looking at research conducted by counseling psychologists. This dearth of this research strategy may be partly a function of training and emphasis. In sum, using longitudinal designs or augmenting correlational studies with experimental tests, and, when appropriate, using sophisticated analytic techniques such as SEM, can help resolve issues of causality and thus advance the study of subjective well-being.

Testing Models

A second major way in which the study of subjective well-being can be advanced is to directly test the assumptions of models against one another. We discuss ways in which models differ that invite comparison, distinctions between mediation and moderation, which has implications for how models are described and tested, and the appropriate statistical strategies to test mediation and moderation.

Models of subjective well-being can posit differences in (1) the *direction* of associations between subjective well-being and other constructs (e.g., top down or bottom up approaches), (2) the relative strength of predictors influencing subjective well-being, (3) alternative paths of influence of predictors on subjective well-being (i.e., different mediational pathways), or (4) alternative models of influence on subjective well-being (e.g., mediation or moderation).

In the study described earlier, Feist et al. (1995) compared bottom up (subjective well-being was conceptualized as an effect) and top down (subjective well-being was conceptualized as a cause) models of subjective well-being using SEM techniques and found support for both perspectives. Feist et al. concluded that subjective well-being can be conceptualized as both a cause and an effect of one's physical health status, degree of daily hassles, assumptions about the world, and ability to cope constructively with life experiences, depending on where a researcher enters the causal chain.

Determining whether a variable acts as a mediator or moderator of influences on subjective well-being is another example of tests of competing models. Mediation refers to "the generative mechanism through which the focal independent variable is able to influence the dependent variable of interest" (Baron & Kenny, 1986, p. 1173); moderation refers to "a qualitative (e.g., sex, race, class) or quantitative . . . variable that affects the direction and/or strength of a relation between an independent or predictor variable and a dependent or criterion variable" (p. 1174). Moderator effects are interactions, and can take multiple forms. To complicate matters, some variables can be both mediators and moderators, depending on how they are conceptualized and when they are assessed. For example, if we hypothesized that persons high in trust have higher subjective well-being because they make positive attributions about others' motives (see DeNeve & Cooper, 1998), then making positive attributions about others' motives would be the hypothesized mediator. However, if we hypothesized that trust would be associated with higher subjective well-being only when individuals made positive attributions about others' motives, then making positive attributions would be the hypothesized moderator.

In general, subjective well-being researchers focusing on temperamental or personality traits have tested models of mediation versus moderation, and few subjective well-being researchers have tested competing models of influence. However, researchers studying outcomes related to well-being have tested competing models of influence. In a study of 173 college students' adjustment to chronic stress (crowding), Lepore, Evans, and Schneider (1991) used a longitudinal design to test how the role of social support in the chronic stress-distress relationship might change over time. Students were assessed two and eight months after exposure to the stressor. Support and distress were measured at each time point. At two months after exposure to the stressor, support *moderated* (buffered) the effect of crowding on psychological distress. Students with high levels of support showed little association between crowding and distress; students with low levels of support had a significant, positive association between crowding and distress. Consistent with their hypotheses, Lepore et al. found that over time exposure to the chronic stressor eroded support, and when the students were reinterviewed eight months after they were first exposed, there was evidence that support now *mediated* the chronic stress-distress relation. That is, chronic crowding eroded support, which in turn was associated with changes in distress.

Another example from the adjustment literature was a cross-sectional investigation of associations between hope, coping, and adjustment among children with sickle cell disease (H.A. Lewis & Kliewer, 1996). In this study, Lewis and Kliewer tested competing models of the influence of coping on the relation between hope and adjustment. One model tested the hypothesis that coping would mediate the relation between hope and adjustment. That is, hope would stimulate children to cope actively and to refrain from avoidance and denial behaviors, which in turn would be associated with better well-being. A second model hypothesized that coping would moderate the relation between hope and adjustment. That is, hope would be associated with better well-being only when children were engaged in high levels of active and support coping. Lewis and Kliewer found support for the second model. Hope was associated with better well-being when active coping, support coping, and distraction coping were high, but was unrelated to well-being when children did not employ those strategies. Determining the role of coping in this population was important in guiding prevention programs to enhance quality of life.

If progress is to be made in the study of subjective well-being, researchers need to be very precise about the language they use to describe their theories, and very careful in how they test their theories. Confusion over moderators and mediators is common (Holmbeck, 1997), and has hampered research progress in a number of areas. One point of confusion centers on which variables can be mediators versus moderators. As noted above, some variables can be both mediators and moderators, depending on how they are conceptualized and when they are assessed. However, other variables can only be moderators. Demographic variables (e.g., gender, age, race) are an example. Demographic variables can be moderators, but not mediators because they cannot explain *why* or *how* particular variables (e.g., temperament) influence subjective well-being, but they can explain *when* or *for whom* particular variables exert an influence on subjective well-being. For example, we might hypothesize that the influence of participation in goal-directed activity on subjective well-being might differ across the life span, with stronger associations observed in middle and late adulthood versus young adulthood. In this case, age is a hypothesized moderator, but age in and of itself does not explain why we might observe the pattern described above.

All three models of subjective well-being discussed earlier hypothesize mediational models of subjective well-being. Additionally, the process-participation and coping models of subjective well-being lend themselves particularly well to moderator analyses. For example, process-participation models can test the conditions under which having strong goal commitment is associated with subjective well-being. Is having a strong commitment to goals only associated with high subjective well-being when goals are autonomously chosen? When goals are enacted in the discourse of everyday life? When other personality traits are evident?

Although subjective well-being researchers who focus on personality rarely have tested moderator hypotheses, one way of refining theories that emphasize the role of personality is to begin to identify the people, settings, or circumstances for which links between personality and hypothesized mediators are most likely to occur. For example, work by Magnus et al. (1993) has shown that temperament is related to subjective well-being in part because temperament influences the type of life events one encounters. Assuming one had strong evidence that experiencing particular life events explained (mediated) the relation between temperament and subjective well-being, a next step might be to understand whether this explanation was conditional, that is, if it was more true for one group of people versus another.

The distinction between mediation and moderation is important for both theoretical and practical reasons. Theoretically, by specifying whether we hypothesize particular mediational paths or patterns of moderation, we can test our theories more carefully and advance our scientific knowl-edge about subjective well-being. Practically speaking, mediators and moderators have different implications for treatment, prevention, and public policy. Testing potential moderator effects may lead to the identification of subgroups that are more resilient or vulnerable under certain condi-tions, which has implications for counseling practice. For example, given limited resources, an in-tervention might only be offered to individuals who are at greatest risk for adjustment difficulties. Individuals could be screened (or identified, in the case of demographic variables) on the modera-tor identified in prior research. Moderator analyses might also suggest that different approaches are necessary for males versus females, or younger versus older clients. Additionally, such find-ings may guide future research on why or how the links between variables are conditional. Identi-fication of mediational variables offers a potential explanation of why an independent variable has an effect on subjective well-being, and such identification is important in the design and evalua-tion of intervention programs (Lewis & Kliewer, 1996). Specifically, clearly identifying media-tors shows a practitioner which variables should be targeted for change, and allows evaluators to build assessments of the mediator into the evaluation design.

Holmbeck (1997) provides a nice overview of the statistical strategies available for testing me-diation and moderation. As described by Holmbeck, mediation may be tested using regression or SEM techniques. ANOVA is also an appropriate analytic strategy when the predictor variable is categorical (Baron & Kenny, 1986). Moderation also may be tested using ANOVA, regression, or SEM techniques. However, as noted earlier, testing for moderator effects using LISREL when the moderator variable is continuous is complicated. The specifics of how one tests for mediation and moderation using these techniques may be found in Aiken and West (1991), Baron and Kenny (1986), Cohen and Cohen (1983), and Holmbeck (1997).

In sum, direct comparison of competing models about what influences subjective well-being, the process by which that influence operates, or the conditions under which that influence is most salient will advance research in subjective well-being by clarifying the research directions that are most promising. In testing competing models of subjective well-being, it is important to use ter-minology correctly, to be explicit about whether theories posit mediated or moderated effects, and to test for those effects appropriately. By doing so, subjective well-being research will avoid what Holmbeck (1997) calls terminological, conceptual, and statistical inconsistencies.

SUMMARY

Despite the fact that much is *not* known about subjective well-being, there are a number of key findings that can be summarized. First, subjective well-being has both cognitive and affective di-mensions which can be measured reliably, and both are important components of this construct. Thus, both assessments of life satisfaction and positive and negative affect should be obtained when studying subjective well-being. Second, individuals make both global and domain-specific judgments about their well-being, and global judgments are not merely a sum of the various domain-specific assessments of well-being. To understand an individual's self-rated well-being, one must understand which life domains are important to that person, and their evaluations of well-being in that domain. Third, demographic factors such as income, education, intelligence, age, and gender are only weakly correlated with subjective well-being, although some of these associations are complex. Fourth, in contrast to demographic variables, psychological resources, particularly self-efficacy, optimism, and control, are fairly strongly associated with subjective well-being. Fifth, motivational factors, specifically the pursuit of goals, also have strong associa-tions with subjective well-being. The process of participation in goal-related activity in the course of everyday living seems particularly critical to well-being. Sixth, personality traits also are strongly correlated with subjective well-being, with neuroticism and extraversion showing the most robust associations with well-being. These personality traits appear to operate by affecting individuals' views of themselves and others, how life events are perceived, or stable dispositions.

CONCLUSIONS

This chapter has highlighted the importance of explicating the processes and underlying mechanisms of subjective well-being (see Diener et al., 1999, for a discussion). In many ways, this is a daunting task given the emergence of so many psychological, social, environmental, demographic and biological factors. We have emphasized the importance of constructing multidimensional models that incorporate several facets of well-being, and that require careful conceptual and temporal (i.e., causal) delineation. This is especially critical given the current confusion over general versus domain-specific well-being estimates, and between psychological and subjective well-being conceptions.

The subjective well-being literature is a microcosm of the current zeitgeist in psychology: an absence of grand theories and the development of "models" that incorporate elements of a biopsychosocial perspective. Engel's (1977, 1980) call for a biopsychosocial model for understanding physical illness was a watershed event in that it integrated behavior into a biomedical perspective of physical illness. In essence, he developed a systems model that incorporated biological, psychological, and social determinants that interact in varying degrees to cause physical abnormality. It is fair to say that this effort to avoid reductionistic and exclusionary criteria pushed medicine, psychiatry, and psychology toward a broad context for understanding health and illness.

As the "biopsychosocial" perspective has increasingly been accepted (see Hoffman & Driscoll, this volume), the premium is on comparing and contrasting the relative role of biological mechanisms, psychological processes, and social influences. Kiesler (1999) vigorously argues for multicausal biopsychosocial theories that integrate "specific contributory causal (both vulnerability and protective) factors operative within each domain (biological, psychological, and social), their developmental onsets, and their historical and current interactions" (p. 238). Accordingly, single domain theoretical explanations are unacceptable for understanding the subjective well-being process.

Research on adjustment and well-being is moving in an analogous direction, with efforts at fusing theories by incorporating salient constructs and processes. The efficacy and parsimoniousness of these models must be determined. Lightsey (1996), for example, proposed a process model of psychological well-being that fuses concepts of generalized self-efficacy (cf. Bandura, 1989) and optimism (Scheier & Carver, 1992) into a cognitive-experiential processing model (Epstein, 1994). Within this framework, inherited appraisal response tendencies, emotion, behavior, and stress combine to predict well-being. In a critical review of this model, Scheier and Carver (1996) state that "the model has something of the feel of an attempt to link together all the specific theories that the author finds interesting, without regard to whether there is any real benefit in doing so" (p. 739).

Given what we currently know about subjective well-being, and of trends in the field of psychology generally, we offer several additional recommendations for advancing research on subjective well-being, and for applying what we currently know to the practice of counseling psychology.

First, counseling researchers must move between laboratory and field studies (see Forsyth & Strong, 1986, for a discussion of the unificationist view) to test both specific processes underlying subjective well-being under controlled conditions and multicausal-multidimensional models using field and other ecologically valid settings.

Two intriguing questions must be answered if we are to advance our understanding of the subjective well-being process in the lives of everyday people: What factors interact to affect behavior change? Can behavioral change result in significant adjustments to subjective well-being over time?

These interconnected questions are fundamental to our role as counseling psychologists. Once again, the answer to these questions reflect our current uncertainty with the relative importance of biopsychosocial factors. As Brown et al. (1996) insightfully speculate, a biologically driven set point may preclude significant improvement in subjective well-being. From this perspective, it is not personality change that should be the target for intervention efforts, but rather learning how to manage the affective and ideational consequences of one's personality that becomes critical.

A second, related recommendation is that counseling and preventive interventions must target realistic outcome goals, including designing protocols that effectively adjust dosing and frequency levels given participant attributes, for maximal cost-effectiveness. In other words, tailored prevention and intervention programs will be more effective from both clinical and cost-benefits points of view than universal prevention or intervention programs. Generative research that includes moderator analyses can help inform the design of these tailored interventions.

Third, given the research on the effects of participating in goal-related activities in one's daily life, counseling psychologists should assess the meaning of participation for their clients, the goals that clients seek to accomplish, and barriers to achieving those goals. More attention should be paid to addressing the types of goals clients have, and the barriers they face in working toward their goals in their day-to-day activities.

Lastly, the cultural determinants of subjective well-being need to be more fully integrated into our conceptual models, and tested to determine the nature and type of influence they contribute to the well-being process.

It is not clear how the biopsychosocial model integrates cultural determinants of subjective well-being, or directly addresses the issue of universal versus culture-specific psychological processes. Yet, culture may have a significant role, especially from a process model perspective. For example, the connection between goals and subjective well-being must be understood within the context of each individual's life story (McAdams, 1994), where culture is an important determinant of which goals are valued and attained. As we demonstrated, subjective well-being may be influenced by goal commitment and attainment (Cantor & Sanderson, 1999), which is highly culture bound because an individual's goal activity is reinforced or valued within the cultural and subcultural context.

A commonly cited cultural factor is individualism/collectivism (Triandis, 1989) or independent/interdependent self-conception (Markus & Kitayama, 1994). This refers to the degree to which autonomous, self-sufficient values versus relational harmony and collective values are preferred. Individuals in highly individualist cultures would derive self-esteem and goal satisfaction from individual achievement and distinction, whereas those from highly collectivistic cultures would value group achievement and relational goals. Interestingly, Suh et al., (1998) found that self-esteem only was correlated highly to happiness in individualistic cultures that placed a premium on the self. Happiness, then, may be highly culture bound depending on the fulfillment of individualistic or collectivist needs. Counseling psychologists should be aware of the cultural biases they bring into their prevention and intervention programs, and should explicitly ask about the values and cultural norms of the clients they are serving.

REFERENCES

Aiken, L., & West, S.G. (1991). *Multiple regression: Testing and interpreting interaction*. Newbury Park, CA: Sage.

Allport, G.W. (1937). *Personality: A psychological interpretation*. New York: Holt.

Andrews, F.M., & Robinson, J.P. (1991). Measures of subjective well-being. In J.P. Robinson, P.H. Shaver, & L.S. Wrightsman (Eds.), *Measures of personality and social psychological attitudes* (pp. 61–114). San Diego, CA: Academic Press.

Antonovsky, A. (1979). *Health, stress, and coping.* San Francisco: Jossey-Bass.

Antonovsky, A. (1987). *Unraveling the mystery of health: How people manage stress and stay well.* San Francisco: Jossey-Bass.

Argyle, M. (1987). *The psychology of happiness.* London: Routledge.

Aspinwall, L.G., & Taylor, S.E. (1997). A stitch in time: Self-regulation and proactive coping. *Psychological Bulletin, 121,* 417–436.

Austin, J.T., & Vancouver, J.F. (1996). Goal constructs in psychology: Structure, process, and content. *Psychological Bulletin, 120,* 338–375.

Baker, L.A., Cesa, I.L., Gatz, M., & Mellins, C. (1992). Genetic and environmental influences on positive and negative affect: Support for the two-factor theory. *Psychology and Aging, 7,* 158–163.

Baker, R.W., & Siryk, B. (1984). Measuring adjustment to college. *Journal of Counseling Psychology 31,* 179–189.

Bandura, A. (1989). Human agency in social cognitive theory. *American Psychologist, 44,* 1175–1184.

Baron, R.M., & Kenny, D.A. (1986). The moderator-mediator variable distinction in social psychological research: Conceptual, strategic, and statistical considerations. *Journal of Personality and Social Psychology, 51,* 1173–1182.

Bass, S.A. (1995). *Older and active: How Americans over 55 are contributing to society.* New Haven, CT: Yale University Press.

Baumeister, R.F., & Leary, M.R. (1995). The need to belong: Desire for interpersonal attachments as a fundamental human motivation. *Psychological Bulletin, 117,* 497–529.

Beard, J., & Ragheb, M. (1980). Measuring leisure satisfaction. *Journal of Leisure Research, 12,* 20–33.

Bentler, P.M. (1980). Multivariate analysis with latent variables. *Annual Review of Psychology, 31,* 419–456.

Bergin, A.E. (1983). Religiosity and mental health: A critical reevaluation and meta-analysis. *Professional Psychology: Research and Practice, 14,* 170–184.

Bjorksten, O., & Steward, T.J. (1984). Contemporary trends in American marriage. In C.C. Nadelson & D.C. Polonsky (Eds.), *Marriage and divorce: A contemporary perspective* (pp. 3–59). New York: Guilford Press.

Blehar, M.C., & Oren, D.A. (1995). Women's increased vulnerability to mood disorders: Integrating psychobiology and epidemiology. *Depression, 3,* 3–12.

Bradburn, N.M. (1969). *The structure of psychological well-being.* Chicago: Aldine.

Bretz, R.D., & Judge, T.A. (1994). Person-organization fit and the theory of work adjustment: Implications for satisfaction, tenure, and career success. *Journal of Vocational Behavior, 44,* 32–54.

Brickman, P., & Coates, D. (1987). Commitment and mental health. In P. Brickman (Ed.), *Commitment, conflict, and caring* (pp. 222–309). Englewood Cliffs, NJ: Prentice-Hall.

Brief, A.P., Butcher, A.H., George, J.M., & Link, K.E. (1993). Integrating bottom-up and top-down theories of subjective well-being: The case of health. *Journal of Personality and Social Psychology, 64,* 646–653.

Broderick, P.C. (1998). Early adolescent gender differences in the use of ruminative and distracting coping strategies. *Journal of Early Adolescence, 18,* 173–191.

Brown, S.D., Ryan, N.E., & McPartland, E.B. (1996, October). Why are so many people happy and what do we do for those who aren't? A reaction to Lightsey (1996). *The Counseling Psychologist, 24,* 751–757.

Brunstein, J.C. (1993). Personal goals and subjective well-being: A longitudinal study. *Journal of Personality and Social Psychology, 65,* 1061–1070.

Cantor, N. (1990). From thought to behavior: "Having" and "doing" in the study of personality and cognition. *American Psychologist, 45,* 735–750.

Cantor, N. (1994). Life task problem-solving: Situational affordances and personal needs. *Personality and Social Psychology Bulletin, 20,* 235–243.

Cantor, N., & Fleeson, W. (1994). Social intelligence and intelligent goal pursuit: A cognitive slice of motivation. In W. Spaulding (Ed.), *Nebraska Symposium on Motivation: 41. Integrative views of motivation, cognition, and emotion* (pp. 125–179). Lincoln: University of Nebraska Press.

Cantor, N., & Kihlstrom, J.F. (1989). Social intelligence and cognitive assessments of personality. In R.S. Wyer & T.K. Srull (Eds.), *Advances in social cognition* (Vol. 2, pp. 1–59). Hillsdale, NJ: Erlbaum.

Cantor, N., & Sanderson, C.A. (1999). Life task participation and well-being: The importance of taking part in daily life. In D. Kahneman, E. Diener, & N. Schwarz (Eds.), *Well-being: The foundations of hedonic psychology.* New York: Russell-Sage.

Carver, C.S. (1998). Resilience and thriving: Issues, models, and linkages. *Journal of Social Issues, 54,* 245–266.

Chang, E.C. (1996). Cultural differences in optimism, pessimism, and coping: Predictors of subsequent adjustment in Asian American and Caucasian American college students. *Journal of Counseling Psychology 43,* 113–123.

Chang, E.C. (1998). Dispositional optimism and primary and secondary appraisal of a stressor: Controlling for confounding influences and relations to coping and psychological and physical adjustment. *Journal of Personality and Social Psychology 74,* 1109–1120.

Clark, A.E., & Oswald, A.J. (1994). Unhappiness and unemployment. *Economic Journal, 104,* 648–659.

Cohen, J., & Cohen, P. (1983). *Applied multiple regression/correlation analysis for the behavior sciences* (2nd ed.). Hillsdale, NJ: Erlbaum.

Colvin, C.R., & Block, J. (1994). Do positive illusions foster mental health? An examination of the Taylor and Brown formulation. *Psychological Bulletin, 116,* 3–20.

Cook, D., Dougherty, L., & Robbins, S. (1999). *The contribution of personal qualities to perceived marital adjustment of older adults.* Manuscript submitted for publication, Virginia Commonwealth University, Richmond.

Costa, P.T., & McCrae, R.R. (1980). Influence of extraversion and neuroticism on subjective well-being: Happy and unhappy people. *Journal of Personality and Social Psychology, 38,* 668–678.

Costa, P.T., & McCrae, R.R. (1988). Personality in adulthood: A six year longitudinal study of self-reports and spouse ratings on the NEO Personality Inventory. *Journal of Personality and Social Psychology, 54,* 853–863.

Costa, P.T., & McCrae, R.R. (1992). *Revised NEO Personality Inventory (NEO PI-R) and NEO Five-Factor Inventory professional manual.* Odessa, FL: Psychological Assessment Resources.

Costa, P.T., McCrae, R.R., & Dye, D.A. (1991). Facet scales for agreeableness and conscientiousness: A revision of the NEO Personality Inventory. *Personality and Individual Differences, 12,* 887–898.

Costa, P.T., McCrae, R.R., & Zonderman, A.B. (1987). Environmental and dispositional influences on well-being: Longitudinal follow-up of an American national sample. *British Journal of Psychology, 78,* 299–306.

Csikszentmihalyi, M., & Larson, R. (1984). *Being adolescent: Conflict and growth in the teenage years.* New York: Basic Books.

Datan, N., Rodeheaver, D., & Hughes, F. (1987). Adult development and aging. *Annual Review of Psychology, 38,* 153–180.

Davis-Berman, J. (1990). Physical self-efficacy, perceived physical status, and depressive symptomatology in older adults. *Journal of Psychology, 124,* 207–215.

DeNeve, K.M., & Cooper, H. (1998). The happy personality: A meta-analysis of 137 personality traits and subjective well-being. *Psychological Bulletin, 124,* 197–229.

Diener, E. (1984). Subjective well-being. *Psychological Bulletin, 95,* 542–575.

Diener, E. (1994). Assessing subjective well-being: Progress and opportunities. *Social Indicators Research, 31,* 103–157.

Diener, E. (1996). Traits can be powerful, but are not enough: Lessons from subjective well-being. *Journal of Research in Personality, 30,* 389–399.

Diener, E., & Diener, C. (1996). Most people are happy. *Psychological Science, 7,* 181–185.

Diener, E., Emmons, R.A., Larsen, R.J., & Griffin, S. (1985). Satisfaction with Life Scale. *Journal of Personality Assessment, 49,* 71–75.

Diener, E., & Fujita, F. (1995). Resources, personal strivings, and subjective well-being: A nomothetic and idiographic approach. *Journal of Personality and Social Psychology, 68,* 926–935.

Diener, E., & Larson, R. (1993). The experience of emotional well-being. In M. Lewis & J.M. Haviland (Eds.), *Handbook of emotions* (pp. 405–413). New York: Guilford Press.

Diener, E., Larsen, R.J., & Emmons, R.A. (1984). Person X situation interactions: Choice of situations and congruence response models. *Journal of Personality and Social Psychology, 47,* 580–592.

Diener, E., Sandvik, E., Pavot, W., & Fújita, F. (1992). Extraversion and subjective well-being in a U.S. national probablity sample. *Journal of Research in Personality, 26,* 205–215.

Diener, E., Sandvik, E., Pavot, W., & Gallagher, D. (1991). Response artifacts in the measurement of subjective well-being. *Social Indicators Research, 24,* 35–56.

Diener, E., Smith, H., & Fujita, F. (1995). The personality structure of affect. *Journal of Personality and Social Psychology, 69,* 130–141.

Diener, E., Suh, E.M., Lucas, R.E., & Smith, H.L. (1999). Subjective well-being: Three decades of progress. *Psychological Bulletin, 125,* 276–302.

Durkheim, E. (1933). *The division of labor in society.* New York: Macmillan.

Eden, D., & Aviram, A. (1993). Self-efficacy training to speed reemployment: Helping people to help themselves. *Journal of Applied Psychology, 78,* 352–360.

Elliot, A.J., Sheldon, K.M., & Church, M.A. (1997). Avoidance, personal goals, and subjective well-being. *Personality and Social Psychology Bulletin 23,* 915–927.

Ellison, C.G. (1991). Religious involvement and subjective well-being. *Journal of Health and Social Behavior, 32,* 80–89.

Emmons, R.A. (1986). Personal strivings: An approach to personality and subjective well-being. *Journal of Personality and Social Psychology, 51,* 1058–1068.

Emmons, R.A. (1991). Personal strivings, daily events and psychological and physical well-being. *Journal of Personality, 59,* 453–472.

Emmons, R.A., & King, L.A. (1988). Conflict among personal strivings: Immediate and long-term implications for psychological and physical well-being. *Journal of Personality and Social Psychology, 54,* 1040–1048.

Engel, G.L. (1977). The need for a new medical model: A challenge to biomedicine. *Science, 196,* 129–136.

Engel, G.L. (1980). The clinical application of the biopsychosocial model. *American Journal of Psychiatry, 137,* 535–544.

Epel, E.S., McEwen, B.S., & Ickovics, J.R. (1998). Embodying psychological thriving: Physical thriving in response to stress. *Journal of Social Issues, 54,* 301–322.

Epstein, S. (1994). Integration of the cognitive and psychodynamic unconscious. *American Psychologist, 49,* 709–724.

Feist, G.J., Bodner, T.E., Jacobs, J.F., Miles, M., & Tan, V. (1995). Integrating top-down and bottom-up structural models of subjective well-being: A longitudinal investigation. *Journal of Personality and Social Psychology, 68,* 138–150.

Fordyce, M.W. (1977). Development of a program to increase personal happiness. *Journal of Counseling Psychology, 24,* 511–521.

Forsyth, D.R., & Strong, S.R. (1986). The scientific study of counseling and psychotherapy: A unificationist view. *American Psychologist, 41,* 113–119.

Frederickson, B., & Kahneman, D. (1993). Duration neglect in retrospective evaluations of affective episodes. *Journal of Personality and Social Psychology, 65,* 45–55.

Fries, J.F. (1990). Medical perspectives upon successful aging. In P.B. Baltes & M.M. Baltes (Eds.), *Successful aging: Perspectives from the behavioral sciences* (pp. 35–49). New York: Academic Press.

Fujita, A., Diener, E., & Sandvik, E. (1991). Gender differences in negative affect and well-being: The case for emotional intensity. *Journal of Personality and Social Psychology, 61,* 427–434.

Gartner, J., Larson, D.B., & Allen, G.D. (1991). Religious commitment and mental health: A review of the empirical literature. *Journal of Psychology and Religion, 19,* 6–25.

Gatz, M., Pedersen, N.L., Plomin, R., & Nesselroade, J.R. (1992). Importance of shared environments for symptoms of depression in older adults. *Journal of Abnormal Psychology, 101,* 701–708.

George, J.M., & Brief, A.P. (1992). Feeling good-doing good: A conceptual analysis of the mood at work-organizational spontaneity relationship. *Psychological Bulletin, 112,* 310–329.

Glenn, N.D. (1990). Quantitative research on marital quality in the 1980's: A critical review. *Journal of Marriage and the Family, 52,* 818–831.

Goldberg, L.R. (1990). An alternative "description of personality": The big-five factor structure. *Journal of Personality and Social Psychology, 59,* 1216–1229.

Gottman, J.M. (1994). *What predicts divorce? The relationship between marital processes and marital outcomes.* Hillsdale, NJ: Erlbaum.

Graziano, W.G., Jensen-Campbell, L.A., & Finch, J.F. (1997). The self as a mediator between personality and adjustment. *Journal of Personality and Social Psychology, 73,* 392–404.

Graziano, W.G., & Ward, D. (1992). Probing the big five in adolescence: Personality and adjustment during a developmental transition. *Journal of Personality, 60,* 425–440.

Green, D.F., Goldman, S., & Salovey, P. (1993). Measurement error masks bipolarity in affect ratings. *Journal of Personality and Social Psychology, 64,* 1029–1041.

Grossman, M., & Wood, W. (1993). Sex differences in intensity of emotional experience: A social role interpretation. *Journal of Personality and Social Psychology, 65,* 1010–1022.

Haring, M.J., Stock, W.A., & Okun, M.A. (1984). A research synthesis of gender and social class as correlates of subjective well-being. *Human Relations, 37,* 645–657.

Harlow, R.E., & Cantor, N. (1996). Still participating after all these years: A study of life task participation in later life. *Journal of Personality and Social Psychology, 71,* 1235–1249.

Havighurst, R.J. (1960). Life beyond family and work. In E.W. Burgess (Ed.), *Aging in western societies* (pp. 299–353). Chicago: University of Chicago Press.

Headley, B., & Wearing, A. (1992). *Understanding happiness: A theory of well-being.* Melbourne, Australia: Longman Chesire.

Herzberg, F. (1968). One more time: How do you motivate your employees? *Basic Human Needs and Rewards, 46,* 53–62.

Herzog, A.R., Rogers, W.L., & Woodworth, J. (1982). *Subjective well-being among different age groups.* Ann Arbor: University of Michigan, Survey Research Center.

Holahan, C.J., & Moos, R.H. (1994). Life stressors and mental health: Advances in conceptualizing stress resistance. In W.R. Avison & I.H. Gotlib (Eds.), *Stress and mental health: Contemporary issues and prospects for the future* (pp. 213–238). New York: Plenum Press.

Holmbeck, G.N. (1997). Toward terminological, conceptual, and statistical clarity in the study of mediators and moderators: Examples from the child-clinical and pediatric psychology literatures. *Journal of Consulting and Clinical Psychology, 65,* 599–610.

Hooker, K., & Siegler, I.C. (1992). Separating apples from oranges in health ratings: Perceived health includes psychological well-being. *Behavior, Health, and Aging, 2,* 81–92.

Ickovics, J.R., & Park, C.L. (1998). Paradigm shift: Why a focus on health is important. *Journal of Social Issues, 54,* 237–244.

Inglehart, R. (1990). *Culture shift in advanced industrial society.* Princeton, NJ: Princeton University Press.

Izard, C.E. (1993). Organizational and motivational functions of discrete emotions. In M. Lewis & J.M. Haviland (Eds.), *Handbook of emotions* (pp. 631–642). New York: Guilford Press.

Jaccard, J., & Wan, C.K. (1995). Measurement error in the analysis of interaction effects between continuous predictors using multiple regression: Multiple indicator and structural equation approaches. *Psychological Bulletin, 117,* 348–357.

Jaccard, J., & Wan, C.K. (1996). *LISREL approaches to interaction effects in multiple regression.* Thousand Oaks, CA: Sage.

Judge, T.A., & Hulin, C.L. (1993). Job satisfaction as a reflection of disposition: A multiple source causal analysis. *Organizational Behavior and Human Decision Processes, 56,* 388–421.

Judge, T.A., & Watanabe, S. (1993). Another look at the job satisfaction—life satisfaction relationship. *Journal of Applied Psychology, 78,* 939–948.

Kahneman, D. (1999). Objective happiness. In D. Kahneman, E. Diener, & N. Schwarz (Eds.), *Well-being: The foundations of hedonic psychology.* New York: Russell-Sage.

Karney, B.A., & Bradbury, T.N. (1995). The longitudinal course of marital quality and stability: A review of theory, method, and research. *Psychological Bulletin, 18,* 3–34.

Kasser, T., & Ryan, R.M. (1993). A dark side of the American dream: Correlates of financial success as a central life aspiration. *Journal of Personality and Social Psychology 65,* 410–422.

Kasser, T., & Ryan, R.M. (1996). Further examining the American dream: Differential correlates of intrinsic and extrinsic goals. *Personality and Social Psychology Bulletin, 22,* 280–287.

Kessler, R.C., McGonagle, K.A., Zhao, S., Nelson, C.B., Hughes, M., Eshelman, S., Wittchen, H., & Kendler, K.S. (1994). Lifetime and 12-month prevalence of *DSM-III-R* psychiatric disorders in the United States: Results from the National Comorbidity Study. *Archives of General Psychiatry, 51,* 8–19.

Kiesler, D. (1999). *Beyond the disease model of mental disorders.* Westport, CN: Praeger.

King, L.A. (1996). Who is regulating what and why? Motivational context of self-regulation. *Psychological Inquiry, 7,* 57–60.

Kwan, V.S.Y., Bond, M.H., & Singelis, T.M. (1997). Pancultural explanations for life satisfaction: Adding relationship harmony to self-esteem. *Journal of Personality and Social Psychology, 73,* 1038–1051.

Lachman, M.E., & Weaver, S.L. (1998). The sense of control as a moderator of social class differences in health and well-being. *Journal of Personality and Social Psychology, 74,* 763–773.

Lapierre, S., Bouffard, L., & Bastin, E. (1997). Personal goals and subjective well-being in late life. *International Journal of Aging and Human Development, 45,* 287–303.

Lazarus, R.S., & Folkman, S. (1984). *Stress, appraisal, and coping.* New York: Springer.

Lee, G.R., & Robbins, S. (1995). Measuring belongingness: Construction and validation of the social connectedness and Social Assurance Scales. *Journal of Counseling Psychology, 42,* 232–241.

Lee, G.R., & Robbins, S. (1998). A closer look at social connectedness: Its impact on adjustment and development. *Journal of Counseling Psychology, 45,* 338–345.

Lee, G.R., Secombe, K., & Shehan, C.L. (1991). Marital status and personal happiness: An analysis of trend data. *Journal of Marriage and the Family, 53,* 839–844.

Lepore, S.J., Evans, G.W., & Schneider, M.L. (1991). Dynamic role of social support in the link between chronic stress and psychological distress. *Journal of Personality and Social Psychology, 61,* 899–909.

Lewis, H.A., & Kliewer, W. (1996). Hope, coping, and adjustment among children with sickle cell disease: Tests of mediator and moderator models. *Journal of Pediatric Psychology, 21,* 25–41.

Lewis, M., & Haviland, D. (1998). *Handbook of emotions* (2nd ed.). New York: Guilford Press.

Lightsey, O.R., Jr. (1996). What leads to wellness? The role of psychological resources in well-being. *Counseling Psychologist, 24,* 589–759.

Lowenthal, M., Thurnher, M., & Chiriboga, D. (1975). Four stages of life. San Francisco: Jossey-Bass.

Lucas, R.E., Diener, E., Grob, A., Suh, E.M., & Shao, L. (1998). *Cross-cultural evidence for the fundamental features of extraversion: The case against sociability.* Manuscript submitted for publication, University of Illinois at Urbana-Champaign.

Lucas, R.E., Diener, E., & Suh, E.M. (1996). Discriminant validity of well-being measure. *Journal of Personality and Social Psychology, 71,* 616–628.

Lykken, D., & Tellegen, A. (1996). Happiness is a stochastic phenomenon. *Psychological Science, 7,* 186–189.

Maddi, S.R., & Kobasa, S.C. (1991). The development of hardiness. In A. Monat & R.S. Lazarus (Eds.), *Stress and coping: An anthology* (3rd ed., pp. 245–257). New York: Columbia University Press.

Magnus, K., Diener, E., Fujita, F., & Pavot, W. (1993). Extraversion and neuroticism as predictors of objective life events: A longitudinal analysis. *Journal of Personality and Social Psychology, 65,* 1046–1053.

Markus, H.R., & Kitayama, S. (1994). A collective fear of the collectives: Implications for selves and theories of selves. *Personality and Social Psychology Bulletin, 20,* 568–579.

Mastekaasa, A. (1995). Age variations in the suicide rates and self-reported subjective well-being of married and never married persons. *Journal of Community and Applied Social Psychology, 5,* 21–39.

McAdams, D.P. (1994). *The person: An introduction to personality psychology* (2nd ed.). New York: Harcourt Brace.

McCrae, R.R., & Costa, P.T. (1991). Adding Liebe und Arbeit: The full five-factor model and well-being. *Personality and Social Psychology Bulletin, 17,* 227–232.

McGue, M., Bacon, S., & Lykken, D. (1996). Personality stability and change in early adulthood: A behavioral genetic analysis. *Developmental Psychology, 29,* 96–109.

McGue, M., & Christensen, K. (1997). Genetic and environmental contributions to depression symptomatology: Evidence from Danish twins 75 years of age and older. *Journal of Abnormal Psychology, 106,* 439–448.

McGue, M., Pickens, R.W., & Svikis, D.S. (1992). Sex and age effects on the inheritance of alcohol problems: A twin study. *Journal of Abnormal Psychology, 101,* 3–17.

Mehnert, T., Krauss, H.H., Nadler, R., & Boyd, M. (1990). Correlates of life satisfaction in those with disabling conditions. *Rehabilitation Psychology, 35,* 3–17.

Michalos, A.C. (1991). *Global report on student well-being* (Vols. 1–4). New York: Springer-Verlag.

Moum, T. (1988). Yes-saying and the mood-of-the-day effects in self-reported quality of life. *Social Indicators Research, 20,* 117–139.

Myers, D.G. (1992). *The pursuit of happiness.* New York: Avon.

Myers, D.G. (1999). Close relationships and quality of life. In D. Kahneman, E. Diener, & N. Schwarz (Eds.), *Well-being: The foundations of hedonic psychology.* New York: Russell-Sage.

Myers, D.G., & Diener, E. (1995). Who is happy? *Psychological Science, 6,* 10–19.

Myers, R.A., & Cairo, P.C. (1992). Counseling and career adjustment. In S.D. Brown & R.W. Lent (Eds.), *Handbook of counseling psychology* (pp. 549–580). New York: Wiley.

Nolen-Hoeksema, S., & Rusting, C.L. (1999). Gender differences in well-being. In D. Kahneman, E. Diener, & N. Schwarz (Eds.), *Well-being: The foundations of hedonic psychology.* New York: Russell-Sage.

Nunnally, J. (1967). *Psychometric theory.* New York: Wiley.

Ortony, A., Clore, G.L., & Collins, N. (1988). *The cognitive structure of emotions.* New York: Cambridge University Press.

Oswald, A.J. (1997). Happiness and economic performance. *Economic Journal, 107,* 1815–1831.

Park, C.L. (1998). Stress-related growth and thriving through coping: The roles of personality and cognitive processes. *Journal of Social Issues, 54,* 267–278.

Pavot, W., & Diener, E. (1993). Review of the Satisfaction with Life Scale. *Psychological Assessment, 5,* 164–172.

Pervin, L.A. (Ed.). (1989). *Goal concepts in personality and social psychology.* Hillsdale, NJ: Erlbaum.

Peterson, C., Maier, S.F., & Seligman, M.E.P. (1993). *Learned helplessness: A theory for the age of personal control.* New York: Oxford University Press.

Peyrot, M. (1996). Causal analysis: Theory and application. *Journal of Pediatric Psychology, 21,* 3–24.

Ping, R.A. (1996). Latent variable interaction and quadratic effect estimation: A two-step technique using structural equation analysis. *Psychological Bulletin, 119,* 166–175.

Plomin, R., Lichtenstein, P., Pedersen, N.L., McClearn, G.E., & Nesselroade, J.R. (1990). Genetic influence on life events during the last half of the life span. *Psychology and Aging, 5,* 25–30.

Plomin, R., Scheier, M.F., Bergeman, C.S., Pedersen, N.L., Nesselroade, J.R., & McClearn, G.E. (1992). Optimism, pessimism and mental health: A twin/adoption analysis. *Personality and Individual Differences, 13,* 921–930.

Rain, J.S., Lane, I.M., & Steiner, D.D. (1991). A current look at the job satisfaction/life satisfaction relationship: Review and future considerations. *Human Relations, 44,* 287–307.

Redelmeir, D., & Kahneman, D. (1996). Patients' memories of painful medical treatments: Real-time and retrospective evaluations of two minimally invasive procedures. *Pain, 116,* 3–8.

Reker, G., & Peacock, E. (1981). The Life Attitude Profile (LAP): A multidimensional instrument for assessing attitudes toward life. *Canadian Journal of Behavioral Science, 13,* 264–273.

Reker, G., Peacock, E., & Wong, P. (1987). Meaning and purpose of life and well-being: A life-span perspective. *Journal of Gerontology, 42,* 44–49.

Rice, W.W., Near, J.P., & Hunt, R.G. (1980). The job-satisfaction/life-satisfaction relationship: A review of empirical research. *Basic and Applied Social Psychology, 1,* 337–364.

Robbins, S.B. (1985). Validity estimates for the Career Decision-Making Self-Efficacy Scale. *Measurement and Evaluation in Counseling and Development, 18,* 64–71.

Robbins, S.B. (1989). Validity of the superiority and goal instability scales as measures of defects in the self. *Journal of Personality Assessment, 53,* 122–132.

Robbins, S.B., Lee, R.M., & Wan, T.T.H. (1994). Goal continuity as a mediator of early retirement adjustment: Testing a multidimensional model. *Journal of Counseling Psychology, 41,* 18–26.

Robbins, S.B., & Patton, M. (1985). Self psychology and career development: Construction of the Superiority and Goal Instability Scales. *Journal of Counseling Psychology, 32,* 221–232.

Robins, L., & Regier, D. (Eds.). (1991). *Psychiatric disorders in America.* New York: Free Press.

Rodin, J. (1986). Aging and health: Effects of the sense of control. *Science, 233,* 1271–1276.

Roxburgh, S. (1996). Gender differences in work and well-being. *Journal of Health and Social Behavior, 37,* 265–277.

Rusting, C.I., & Larsen, R.J. (1997). Extraversion, neuroticism, and susceptibility to positive and negative affect: A test of two theoretical models. *Personality and Individual Differences, 22,* 607–612.

Ryff, C.D. (1989). Happiness is everything, or is it? Explorations on the meaning of psychological well-being. *Journal of Personality and Social Psychology, 57,* 1069–1081.

Ryff, C.D. (1991). Possible selves in adulthood and old age: A tale of shifting horizons. *Psychology and Aging, 6,* 286–295.

Ryff, C.D. (1995). Psychological well-being in adult life. *Current Directory of Psychological Science, 4,* 99–104.

Ryff, C.D., & Keyes, C.L.M. (1995). The structure of psychological well-being revisited. *Journal of Personality and Social Psychology, 69,* 719–727.

Ryff, C.D., & Singer, B. (1998). The role of purpose in life and personal growth in positive human health. In P.T.P. Wong & P.S. Fry (Eds.), *The human quest for meaning: A handbook of psychological research and clinical applications* (pp. 213–235). Hillsdale, NJ: Erlbaum.

Saakvitne, K., Tennen, H., & Affleck, G. (1998). Exploring thriving in the context of clinical trauma theory: Constructivist self development theory. *Journal of Social Issues, 54,* 279–300.

Sandvik, E., Diener, E., & Seidlitz, L. (1993). Subjective well-being: The convergence and stability of self-report and non-self-report measures. *Journal of Personality, 61,* 317–342.

Sarason, I.G., & Sarason, B.R. (1982). Social support as an individual difference variable: Its stability, origins, and relational aspects. *Journal of Personality and Social Psychology, 50,* 331–344.

Scheier, M.F., & Carver, C.S. (1985). Optimism, coping, and health: Assessment and implications of generalized outcome expectancies. *Health Psychology, 4,* 219–247.

Scheier, M.F., & Carver, C.S. (1992). Effects of optimism on psychological and physical well-being: Theoretical overview and empirical update. *Cognitive Therapy and Research, 16,* 201–228.

Scheier, M.F., & Carver, C.S. (1996). Psychological resources matter, no matter how you say it or frame it. *Counseling Psychologist, 24,* 736–742.

Scheier, M.F., Carver, C.S., & Bridges, M.W. (1994). Distinguishing optimism from neuroticism (and trait anxiety, self-mastery, and self-esteem): A reevaluation of the Life Orientation Test. *Journal of Personality and Social Psychology, 67,* 1063–1078.

Schimmack, U. (1997). *Frequency judgments of emotions: How accurate are they, and how are they made?* Unpublished doctoral dissertation, Free University, Berlin, Germany.

Schulman, P., Keith, D., & Seligman, M.E. (1993). Is optimism heritable? A study of twins. *Behavior Research and Therapy, 31,* 569–605.

Schwarz, N., Knauper, B., Hippler, H.J., Noelle-Neumann, E., & Clark, F. (1991). Rating scales: Numeric values may change the meaning of scale labels. *Public Opinion Quarterly, 55,* 570–582.

Schwarz, N., & Strack, F. (1999). Reports of subjective well-being: Judgmental processes and their methodological implications. In D. Kahneman, E. Diener, & N. Schwarz (Eds.), *Well-being: The foundations of hedonic psychology.* New York: Russell-Sage.

Schwarz, N., Strack, F., & Mai, H.P. (1991). Assimilation and contrast effects in part-whole question sentences: A conversational logic analysis. *Public Opinion Quarterly, 55,* 3–23.

Scitovsky, T. (1976). *The joyless economy: An inquiry into human satisfaction and consumer dissatisfaction.* Oxford, England: Oxford University Press.

Scott, C.K. (1991). *Marital status and well-being.* Unpublished doctoral dissertation, University of Illinois, Urbana-Champaign.

Sen, A.K. (1980). Equality of what? In S. McMurrin (Ed.), *Tanner lectures on human values* (pp. 195–220). Cambridge, MA: Cambridge University Press.

Sheldon, K.M., & Kasser, T. (1995). Coherence and congruence: Two aspects of personality integration. *Journal of Personality and Social Psychology, 68,* 531–543.

Sirgy, M.J. (1998). Materialism and quality of life. *Social Indicators Research, 43,* 227–260.

Smith, S.M., & Petty, R.E. (1995). Personality moderators of mood congruency effects on cognition: The role of self-esteem and negative mood regulation. *Journal of Personality and Social Psychology, 68,* 1092–1107.

Stone, G.L. (Ed.). (1996). Wellness [Special issue]. *The Counseling Psychologist, 24(4).*

Sudman, S., Bradburn, N., & Schwarz, N. (1996). *Thinking about answers: The application of cognitive processes to survey methodology.* San Francisco: Jossey-Bass.

Suh, E., Diener, E., & Fujita, F. (1996). Events and subjective well-being: Only recent events matter. *Journal of Personality and Social Psychology, 70,* 1091–1102.

Suh, E., Diener, E., Oishi, S., & Triandis, H.C. (1998). The shifting basis of life satisfaction judgments across cultures: Emotions versus norms. *Journal of Personality and Social Psychology, 74,* 482–493.

Super, D., Thompson, A., & Lindeman, R. (1987). *Manual for the ACCI.* Palo Alto, CA: Consulting Psychologist Press.

Tait, M., Padgett, M.Y., & Baldwin, T.T. (1989). Job satisfaction and life satisfaction: A reevaluation of the strength of the relationship and gender effects as a function of the date of the study. *Journal of Applied Psychology, 74,* 502–507.

Taylor, S.E. (1983). Adjustment to threatening events: A theory of cognitive adaptation. *American Psychologist, 38,* 1161–1173.

Taylor, S.E., & Brown, J.D. (1988). Illusion and well-being: A social psychological perspective on mental health. *Psychological Bulletin, 103,* 193–210.

Taylor, S.E., & Brown, J.D. (1994). "Illusion" of mental health does not explain positive illusions. *American Psychologist, 49,* 972–973.

Tellegen, A., Lykken, D.T., Bouchard, T.J., & Wilcox, K.J. (1988). Personality similarity in twins reared apart and together. *Journal of Personality and Social Psychology, 54,* 1031–1039.

Thomas, D., & Diener, E. (1990). Memory accuracy in the recall of emotion. *Journal of Personality and Social Psychology, 59,* 291–297.

Tinsley, D.J., & Schwendener-Holt, M.J. (1992). Retirement and leisure. In S.D. Brown & R.W. Lent (Eds.), *Handbook of counseling psychology* (pp. 627–662). New York: Wiley.

Triandis, H.C. (1989). Self and social behavior in differing cultural contexts. *Psychological Review, 96,* 269–289.

Valentiner, D.P., Holahan, C.J., Moos, R.H. (1994). Social support, appraisals of event controllability, and coping: An integrative model. *Journal of Personality and Social Psychology, 66,* 1094–1102.

Veenhoven, R., Ehrhardt, J., Ho, M.S.D., & deVries, A. (1993). *Happiness in nations: Subjective appreciation of life in 56 nations 1946–1992.* Rotterdam, The Netherlands: Risbo.

Wan, T.T.H. (1985). *Well-being for the elderly: Primary prevention strategies.* Lexington, MA: Lexington Books.

Warr, P. (1999). Well-being and the workplace. In D. Kahneman, E. Diener, & N. Schwarz (Eds.), *Well-being: The foundations of hedonic psychology.* New York: Russell-Sage.

Watson, D., & Clark, L.A. (1984). Negative affectivity: The disposition to experience negative affective states. *Psychological Bulletin, 96,* 465–490.

Watson, D., Clark, L.A., & Tellegen, A. (1988). Development and validation of brief measures of positive and negative affect: The PANAS Scales. *Journal of Personality and Social Psychology, 54,* 1063–1070.

Watson, D., & Pennebaker, J.W. (1989). Health complaints, stress, and distress: Exploring the central role of negative affectivity. *Psychological Review, 96,* 234–254.

Watten, R.G., Vassen, D., Myhrer, T., & Syversen, J.L. (1997). Personality factors and somatic symptoms. *European Journal of Personality, 11,* 57–68.

Wiggins, J.S. (1973). *Personality and prediction: Principles of personality assessment.* Reading, MA: Addison-Wesley.

Wilson, W. (1967). Correlates of avowed happiness. *Psychological Bulletin, 67,* 294–306.

Winkielman, P., Knauper, B., & Schwarz, N. (in press). Looking back at anger: The interpretation of emotion frequency questions depends on the time frame used. *Journal of Personality and Social Psychology.*

Winter, D.G., John, O.P., Stewart, A.J., Klohnen, E.C., & Duncan, L.E. (1998). Traits and motives: Toward an integration of two traditions in personality research. *Psychological Review, 105,* 230–250.

Witter, R.A., Okun, M.A., Stock, W.A., & Haring, M.J. (1984). Education and subjective well-being: A meta-analysis. *Education Evaluation and Policy Analysis, 6,* 165–173.

Wood, W., Rhodes, N., & Whelan, M. (1989). Sex differences in positive well-being: A consideration of emotional style and marital status. *Psychological Bulletin, 106,* 249–264.

Worthington, E.L., Kurusu, T.A., McCullough, M.E., & Sandage, S.J. (1996). Empirical research on religion and psychotherapeutic processes and outcomes: A 10-year review and research prospectus. *Psychological Bulletin, 119,* 448–487.

CHAPTER 11

Gender and Sexuality in Human Development: Implications for Prevention and Advocacy in Counseling Psychology

RUTH E. FASSINGER

It has become almost axiomatic to note that sex and gender have a profound impact on human emotion, cognition, behavior, interpersonal interactions, and cultural institutions. As such, they also have a critical influence on mental health issues and problems, as well as the formulation and delivery of counseling services (Gilbert, 1992; Gilbert & Scher, 1999). In a broadened conceptualization of sex and gender issues that includes sexuality and sexual orientation, it may be argued that sex—one's own sex as well as the sex of one's preferred intimate partners—"constitutes a primary organizing principle used by people in their interpretation of daily experiences and in their construction of attitudes and worldviews" (Fassinger & Richie, 1997, p. 84). Thus, "sex matters" to counseling psychologists, who must make sense of their own attitudes and behaviors regarding sex, gender, sexual orientation, and sexual expression, as well as deal appropriately and effectively with the gendered, sexualized worlds of their clients (Fassinger & Richie, 1997).

This expanded view of gender and sexuality follows the progression of scholarly thinking in these areas first noted by Gilbert (1992) in the second edition of this *Handbook*. There, Gilbert observed that the first edition of the *Handbook* had included a chapter on counseling women as a special population, but by the time of the second edition, gender issues were viewed as profoundly important to both men and women, and Gilbert's chapter on gender issues was included in a major section on counseling interventions, rather than considered relevant only as a "special" issue or population. The present chapter is positioned in the growing scholarly acknowledgment that all issues relating to sex and gender—including sexuality and sexual orientation—are inextricably linked, and that these aspects of human development cannot be considered in isolation. Thus, this chapter includes information on sex and gender (herein jointly referred to as gender), as well as sexuality and sexual orientation (jointly referred to as sexuality) in development.

Unfortunately, literature on sexual orientation and the experiences of lesbian, gay, and bisexual (LGB) people often is not available to, or accessed by, psychologists. The last five volumes of the *Annual Review of Psychology* contained either no references to lesbians, gay men, or homosexuality (1996), or two to four references only (1994, 1995, 1997, 1998), suggesting that LGB issues and populations are not yet being incorporated into mainstream psychological writing. In addition, there is ample documentation of ignorance, heterosexism, and homonegativity on the part of practicing psychologists (Garnets, Hancock, Cochran, Goodchilds, & Peplau, 1991), as well as inadequate training of graduate students in LGB issues (Buhrke & Douce, 1991), including trainees in counseling psychology (J.C. Phillips & Fischer, 1998). Thus, it seems particularly important to include attention to these issues in the present *Handbook*.

The first section of this chapter presents an overview of current scientific debates about gender and sexuality; subsequent sections address gender and sexuality within four general domains of

346

human development: (1) socialization during childhood and adolescence; (2) intimacy and family relationships; (3) education and work; and (4) aging and health. The chapter concludes with recommendations for prevention and advocacy in both science and practice, including implications for the training of counseling psychologists. It should be noted that detailed, comprehensive reviews of the extensive literatures in either gender *or* sexuality in development are far beyond the scope of this chapter. Thus, the chapter takes a more summational, issue-oriented approach, with research and theoretical writings used for illustrative purposes, rather than to provide exhaustive coverage. The overall goals are to stimulate thought by disrupting the present paradigm of counseling psychology as a primarily ameliorative endeavor, and to replace professional rhetoric regarding prevention and advocacy with concrete recommendations informed by contemporary theory and research.

DEFINITIONS AND DEBATES

Sex and Gender

Despite attempts to achieve consistency in the scientific terminology used to discuss gender and sexuality in psychology, there remains widespread misunderstanding and lack of consensus (Anselmi & Law, 1998; Deaux, 1998; Gentile, 1998; Gilbert & Scher, 1999; Unger & Crawford, 1998). Many scholars have noted that the primary barrier to appropriate language usage is rooted in Western culture's dichotomization of sex into two separate, distinct categories (male and female), and the linking—both conscious and nonconscious—of these biological categories with particular meanings, characteristics, and behaviors that are determined by sociocultural consensus to be associated with one sex or the other (Anselmi & Law, 1998; Unger & Crawford,1998). Thus, *sex* (a biological entity based on physiological, hormonal, reproductive, and genetic factors) has erroneously become equated with *gender* (a socially constructed set of ideas, beliefs, and values based on historical, economic, sociopolitical, and cultural factors). Assumptions about gender, in turn, lead to a host of prescriptions and proscriptions regarding "appropriate" male/female characteristics and behaviors (i.e., gender roles) and forms of sexual expression (i.e., sexual identity and orientation). Confusion over sex and gender is further compounded by scholars who use the term "gender" as a (perceived) more politically correct version of the term "sex," for example, in reporting the "gender" of the participants in a research study as 48% males and 52% females (Anselmi & Law, 1998; Gilbert & Scher, 1999).

The pervasive confusion over terminology is unfortunate, because it both reveals and perpetuates widespread gaps in collective understandings of sex and gender issues in both society and psychology. For example, the dichotomization of sex virtually ensures that most psychological research will treat sex as a subject variable and focus on articulating (and often exaggerating) sex differences (Anselmi & Law, 1998; Gilbert & Scher, 1999; Hare-Mustin & Maracek, 1990). Moreover, findings of sex differences—in kind or in degree—almost surely will be attributed to essential (usually biological) differences between females and males (Anselmi & Law, 1998; Hare-Mustin & Maracek, 1990). In an approach that maximizes differences and renders them relatively immutable, similarities are likely to be ignored and sociocultural influences related to gender overlooked (Gilbert & Scher, 1999; Hare-Mustin & Maracek, 1990). Finally, societal preoccupation with categorizing people as males or females suggests difficulty in making sense of those who do not fit neatly into these two categories (e.g., intersexed or transgendered individuals), and general resistance to viewing human sexuality on the continuum that is generally thought to characterize this trait (Bohan, 1996; Fausto-Sterling, 1998). Indeed, very little research has been undertaken in psychology on individuals who are not clearly or consistently male or female (Fausto-Sterling, 1998), and it is for this reason that transgender issues are not addressed in this chapter.

Even if one understands the distinction between sex and gender, there are conceptual traps to be avoided. An erroneous assumption may be made that sex differences cause gender differences, or that the causes of sex differences and effects are purely biological, and the causes of gender differences and effects are solely cultural. These assumptions are simplistic in light of contemporary thinking, which posits complex interplays of biological and cultural factors in the development and expression of both sex and gender (Anselmi & Law, 1998; Bohan, 1996; Breedlove, 1994; Bussey & Bandura, in press; Unger & Crawford, 1996). That is, there may be *essential* innate qualities that women and men possess as a result of biological and genetic endowments and evolutionary processes, but women's and men's characteristics and behaviors are profoundly *socially constructed* in that they arise out of cultural arrangements and transactions that shape experience very powerfully. Essentialists argue that the inborn nature of differences between women and men is demonstrated by similarities across cultures and species, and that observed differences in behavior are simply manifestations of internal differences in brains, hormones, and the like. Social constructionists, on the other hand, point to cross-cultural and cross-species variations, and argue that culturally determined ideologies and assumptions about gender so permeate individual and professional thinking—including approaches to scientific research—that it is difficult to "deconstruct" and recognize those assumptions. Many contemporary scholars consider the influences of both biology and culture on sex and gender to be interactive, subtle, complex, and not very well understood at present (Anselmi & Law, 1998; Bussey & Bandura, in press; Unger & Crawford, 1996).

Another difficulty in understanding sex and gender is that gender exists at many different levels of analysis, which can make comparisons across disciplines, or even research studies within a discipline, quite difficult (Anselmi & Law, 1998). Gilbert and Scher (1999) posit four levels of analysis regarding gender: (1) gender as difference, (2) gender as organizer or structurer, (3) gender as language and discourse, and (4) gender as interactive process. In terms of gender as difference, the problem in assuming that sex and gender are synonymous already has been noted, as well as the excessive focus on differences between females and males. Gilbert and Scher presented a particularly amusing example of the pervasiveness of gendered assumptions regarding men and women: The act of human conception—a relatively simple biological event—is widely portrayed (in medical texts as well as popular media such as children's books) as an event in which a patient, passive egg sits waiting for an energetic, aggressive sperm to penetrate and fertilize it, when actually the two cells fuse in a process that requires action from both.

Conceptualizing gender as organizer or structurer requires shifting attention to society and noting the implicit and explicit norms, policies, laws, and organizational structures that reflect assumptions about opportunities, rights, and roles for females and males. For example, schools and workplaces are both arenas in which males are encouraged and expected to achieve whereas females encounter numerous barriers to success and advancement. Similarly, the workplace is structured around norms and expectations that prevent men from participating fully in child care and home responsibilities, regardless of personal desire to do so.

In considering gender as language and discourse, the predominant theme is the use of language to reinforce societal notions of appropriate roles and behaviors for men and women. For example, to describe sexually active females and males as "sluts" or "studs," respectively, reflects strong societal ideologies prohibiting sexual exploration by women but encouraging it by men (of course, in a society also organized around heterosexuality, one might wonder with whom males are expected to be sexually active if females are prohibited from doing so). Similarly, the existence of a term such as "working mothers" without the parallel term "working fathers" implies a clash in cultural expectations for women that is not salient for men.

The last level of analysis of gender postulated by Gilbert and Scher (1999) is to view gender as an active, interactive process—not something that just happens to a passive recipient, but a process in which each person (re)enacts her or his internalized ideas regarding women and men in daily interactions with others. In recognition of the continual and active nature of this reinforcement of gendered assumptions and roles, scholars refer to this process as "doing gender" or "making gender"—that is, gender viewed as a dynamic process rather than a static attribute (West & Zimmerman, 1987). Gilbert and Scher pointed to numerous examples of doing gender: Leadership roles in male-female dyads, for example, are consistently assumed by men regardless of which member of the pair actually exhibits dominance behavior; and notions of superior male height and strength are maintained by consistent heterosexual pairings in which the woman is smaller or adjustments are made in shoes to preserve the illusion of greater height in men.

Regardless of the level of gender being considered, it seems clear that notions of gender exert powerful influence in everyday life. The problem, however, is not in gender per se—that we tend to see women and men as possessing different qualities, or even that scientific research may establish unequivocally that they do differ in some ways—but rather it is in the use of gender and gender differences to maintain systems of power and oppression that restrict people to narrow roles and opportunities. For example, psychological studies in which men exhibit greater field independence than women commonly have been invoked in arguments against women's involvement in positions of power, concluding that men are more capable of detachment and rational decision making and, therefore, more fit for positions of authority. Women, however, are considered to be too context-driven in their thinking, likely to make irrational (i.e., emotional) decisions, and therefore unfit for positions of responsibility. The sheer sexism of such labeling should be obvious (Why should "field independence" be more highly valued than "context sensitivity" as a human trait?), and the gendered assumptions that follow from this labeling clearly are disadvantageous to women (Gilbert & Scher, 1999).

Moreover, convictions regarding appropriate expressions of gender roles (based on one's biological sex) leave little tolerance or understanding for those who step outside those bounds; indeed, a woman who tested as "field independent" (and therefore presumably fit for positions of power) would likely be judged negatively for being too manly, suggesting the inescapable conundrum of doing gender. The restrictive nature of gender has unsettling implications for the view and treatment of LGB individuals, who often manifest nontraditional roles and behavior (Bohan, 1996). Indeed, many contemporary scholars believe that much societal homonegativity is rooted in disapproval of the violation of proscribed gender roles by LGB individuals, because what one does with one's sexual and intimate partners is rarely observable (myths about the conspicuousness of homosexuality notwithstanding) (Bohan, 1996).

Gender and Sexuality

Just as there is confusion in psychological science about the relationship between biological and cultural influences on the characteristics and behaviors of men and women, there exists considerable debate about biological and cultural factors in the development and manifestation of sexual orientation, that is, an individual's preferences for same-sex and/or other-sex intimate partners. Within the scholarly literature, there are essentialists who, like their counterparts in the literature on heterosexual development, search for biological, hormonal, and genetic explanations of same-sex preferences. From an essentialist point of view, sexual orientation is seen as an intrinsic aspect of an individual's identity, and sexuality, as expressed through the sex of one's partners, is seen as defining a person's being (Bohan, 1996). It is assumed that sexual orientation is a core quality of people that has existed across history and culture, and is thus seen as a "fundamental, essential form or manifestation of human experience" (p. 6). Scientific investigation, from an essentialist point of view, focuses on factors that influence the development, definition, and expression of sexual orientation, and Bohan noted that this has been the predominant point of view assumed by psychologists regarding sexual orientation.

However, just as current literature on the development of women and men has eschewed purely essentialist explanations in favor of more complex interpretations incorporating sociocultural phenomena, the literature on sexual orientation is beginning to evidence a recognition of the social construction of sexual orientation and sexual expression. Thus, constructionists argue that sexual orientation is not an intrinsic trait, but rather is a socially created notion that is grounded in our tendency to categorize human experience and imbue it with particular meanings. That is, we define people according to their erotic and emotional attachments, and then articulate categories (i.e., sexual orientations) to organize these attachments (Bohan, 1996). People come to define themselves based on the organizing principles or categories available to them, and society has effectively constructed experience by articulating a terminology to describe it. In an interesting language twist, experience comes to define individual identity, so that "homosexual" behavior comes to define what one is, "a homosexual" (Bohan). From a constructionist point of view, describing what is observed across history and cultures as manifestations of "sexual orientation" imposes a contemporary construct on behaviors that may have had very different meanings in other times or societies, and assumes attention to an aspect of identity deemed important in modern U.S. culture that may have little salience elsewhere (Bohan).

As with sex and gender, the problem in the social construction of sexual identity and sexual orientation is not the constructions per se, but the proscriptions assigned to them. Thus, sexual orientation as a concept becomes problematic when it ignores the complexity in human characteristics and behavior. For example, constraining sexual orientation to be defined by a limited number of choices (heterosexual, homosexual, or bisexual) obscures the complexity and fluidity of sexual desire, sexual identification, and sexual behavior (Bohan, 1996). Indeed, Kinsey and colleagues (e.g., Kinsey, Pomeroy, Martine, & Gebhard, 1953) established the inadequacy of a simple binary classification of sexual orientation almost a half century ago, and numerous modern scholars have articulated important dimensions of sexual identity, such as desire, fantasies, relationship history, community of support, attraction, preferences, patterns of intimacy, political commitments, and the like (e.g., Gonsiorek, 1995; Klein, 1993, Rothblum, 1994). Moreover, the empirical impossibility of clearly identifying discrete groups of people according to a highly complex dimension labeled simply "sexual orientation," coupled with the methodological problems in accessing populations whose sexual orientations are subject to malignant social prejudice, virtually ensure that our knowledge about LGB people will necessarily be inadequate and flawed (Bohan, 1996).

Another problem in the social construction of sexual orientation lies in the arbitrary linking of gender, particularly gender roles, with sexual orientation. Due to gendered notions of men and women and pervasive assumptions of heterosexuality as normative, society seeks to explain the mystery of same-sex sexual orientation in terms of constricted notions of gendered behavior—lesbians are believed to be like men (masculine), and gay men are assumed to want to be women (feminine). Indeed, it is not uncommon in psychological research for participants to describe lesbians and gay men in terms that typify the expected gender role behaviors of the other sex (Bohan, 1996; Kite, 1994). Moreover, any behavioral deviation from expected gender roles is regarded as evidence of homosexuality, which is to be scrupulously avoided in a society that denigrates LGB people. This leaves little room for gender role flexibility, or for understandings of interpersonal relationships and roles in any other terms but existing notions of gender—hence, beliefs that same-sex couples adhere to husband/wife roles or irrelevant questions about who is "dominant" during sexual activity. Indeed, Bohan noted that "rigid gender roles serve to maintain normative heterosexuality and to punish other sexual orientations; the heterosexual assumption, in turn, serves to reinforce gender roles by prescribing those behaviors that will protect against charges of deviance. Thus existing social structures are buttressed by our construal of gender and sexual orientation as coextensive" (p. 38).

Gender, Sexuality, and Identity

The rigid and nonconscious natures of current sociocultural ideologies regarding gender and sexuality create numerous obstacles in the development of coherent, healthy identities at the individual level. This is, of course, why these issues are important for practicing counseling psychologists, who typically work to prevent or ameliorate individual difficulties. The literatures on aspects of identity development related to race/ethnicity, gender, and sexual orientation are relatively recent, having emerged almost simultaneously during the past three decades out of political events (e.g., the civil rights, women's, and gay rights movements) that have cast those identities into sharp relief (Frable, 1997). From an essentialist point of view, these literatures seek to articulate phenomena critical to the development of a sense of self in relation to particular demographic locations (e.g., ethnicity, sex) and have produced numerous conceptualizations of identity development processes (Frable, 1997). Models of identity formation are potentially useful to counseling psychologists because they outline normative developmental trajectories that can be used to assess and understand individual difficulties, providing that they are used as general guides rather than rigid templates for behavior. In addition, developmental models can serve as heuristics for integrating diverse aspects of identity into coherent self-expressions, thereby supporting the mutually interactive, inextricably linked nature of ethnicity, gender, and sexuality in creating views of the self (Frable, 1997; Landrine, 1995).

From a social constructionist perspective, the recognition that identity is embedded in and influenced by sociocultural and political contexts is critically important in deconstructing essentialist ideologies that privilege some identities (e.g., heterosexual White male) over others (e.g., Black lesbian), based on faulty premises of inherent differences in intelligence, temperament, morality, and the like. As but one example, Collins (1998) pointed to historical attempts to prove biologically based race and sex differences that failed. Collins asserted that race and sex are largely social categories and cannot be separated from factors associated with "economic opportunity, cultural context, and the social meaning attributed to race and sex" (p. 6). Because an individual's sense of self is derived, in part, from encounters with systems of power and privilege in society (Collins, 1998), the specific ways that power and privilege are enacted become critically important in understanding individual identity development. Thus, counseling psychologists must maintain a vigilant awareness that, in a sociocultural milieu that establishes heterosexuality, Whiteness, and maleness as the norms or standards against which other identities are compared, individuals who do not comprise the norm will likely encounter predictable struggles in acquiring a positive sense of self. Moreover, when there are overt barriers built on virulent societal oppression, the role of the environment in creating individual difficulties cannot be dismissed in favor of purely intrapsychic or interpersonal explanations of human behavior. Such considerations are critically important in examining socialization processes regarding gender and sexuality in childhood and adolescence.

SOCIALIZATION IN CHILDHOOD AND ADOLESCENCE

Before discussing socialization processes in childhood and adolescence, it is worth noting that these periods in the human life span also are social constructions. That is, although there certainly are differences in the capabilities and characteristics of infants and adults, contemporary U.S. society's focus on children and adolescents as distinct social groups is the product of the relative affluence, availability of leisure time, decreasing infant mortality rate, and decreased need for a large, unskilled workforce during the last century, creating a surplus of youth and the concomitant need to create roles and expectations for this age group (Hollin, 1987). It is important to remember that all cultures (and even some subcultures within the United States) may not recognize these developmental periods and needs in ways typically addressed in the psychological literature, which is grounded in White, middle-class values and experiences. Moreover, some "problems" encountered by counseling psychologists exist because they are aberrations in culturally established social patterns that have been reified as proscribed behaviors; for example, teen pregnancy would not exist as a social problem in the absence of strong cultural expectations regarding female sexual behavior, single parenting, compulsory education, and financial independence. Thus, it is important to remain aware of the cultural embeddedness of psychological knowledge when examining what are assumed to be normative developmental processes in the lives of children and adolescents.

Gender Socialization

Perhaps the most consistent pattern to emerge from the past decade of scholarly work in gender and sexuality is the continued demonstration of the socialization of female and male youth into rigid, traditional gender and (hetero)sexual roles (Bohan, 1996; Brannon, 1999; Unger & Crawford, 1996). Moreover, the literature indicates that socialization practices persistently place females at a disadvantage relative to males, despite the well-documented harmful effects of traditional gender socialization on both sexes (Anselmi & Law, 1998). In addition, the linking of inflexible gender roles with heterosexist expectations regarding sexual identity places LGB youth in a particularly risky position for nonoptimal development (Bohan, 1996; Fassinger, 1996a).

In summarizing the vast literature on sex and gender socialization in childhood development, Unger and Crawford (1996) identified several overarching themes regarding persistent differential expectations of females and males:

1. Males are consistently viewed and treated as the more valued sex.
2. There is earlier and greater pressure for males to conform to gender roles than females, and this continues throughout childhood.
3. Parents remain largely unaware of their differential treatment of daughters and sons.
4. The different ways in which girls and boys are treated tends to produce patterns of nurturance, emotional sensitivity, and helplessness in girls, and efficacy and independence in boys.
5. Children are not passive recipients of socialization, but participate actively through expectations, behavioral choices, and views of the self.
6. People are generally unaware of sociocultural mandates that dichotomize sex, dictate conformity, and punish deviance from social norms.

Numerous examples illustrating these points are found in comprehensive discussions of gender socialization of children (e.g., Brannon, 1999), and in reviews of particular aspects of childhood socialization, such as gender segregation in childhood play (Maccoby, 1998) or the construction of masculinity through sports (Messner & Sabo, 1994).

Critical to the present discussion is the point that gender role socialization is an active, interactive developmental process—that children's ideas become molded by a complex interplay of cognitive, biological, motivational, and social learning processes, which evolve with the child's age and cognitive growth (Bussey & Bandura, in press). For example, a girl's ideas of what it means to be female change over time. This occurs in part because she becomes capable of increasingly complex cognitive representations of gender (e.g., progressing from judgments based on external factors, such as clothing, to an understanding of genitalia and the relative permanence of sex), but also because she experiences and reacts to shifting expectations from those around her (e.g., tolerance for being a tomboy in childhood, giving way to pressure to be more feminine during adolescence). Thus, children's gender role indoctrination becomes increasingly fortified over time, as their own gender schemas internalize and act on societal messages and thus become self-perpetuating. In essence, they develop greater sex bias over time to fit better into the sexist culture in which they live (Unger & Crawford, 1996).

The context of adolescence is one of increased freedom to make individual choices, as well as greater consequences of those choices (Lerner & Galambos, 1998). Optimal development depends on the adolescent's capacity to "adapt and adjust childhood behaviors to the adult forms that are considered acceptable in his or her culture" (Dusek, 1991, p. 4; cited in Wagner, 1996). Thus, societal messages regarding expected adult roles and behaviors intensify during adolescence, and the maturational changes associated with puberty serve to magnify gender socialization differences, bringing the disadvantaged position of adolescent females into sharper focus (Unger & Crawford, 1996). Fassinger (1996a) has suggested that current models of healthy adolescent development (e.g., Wagner, 1996) set standards of optimization that are unattainable by large segments of the adolescent population. If, for example, optimal emotional health includes affective awareness and self-confidence (Wagner, 1996), then gender socialization dramatically compromises the health of both males and females, the former in the blunting and denial of affect as the costs of independence and self-sufficiency, and the latter in poor self-esteem and low self-confidence as the consequences of training in helplessness and dependence on others (Fassinger, 1996a).

In addition to internalized negative attitudes that carry over from childhood gender socialization (Ward & Wyatt, 1994), there are many more contradictions in the cultural expectations of females than males during adolescence (Unger & Crawford, 1996). These are particularly evident in regard to physical appearance and sexual behavior, and these inconsistent and confusing messages can serve to reinforce girls' feelings of helplessness and inability to act. For example, societal secrecy and disgust regarding menstruation suggest that young women might greet this maturational event with ambivalence; this is, indeed, supported by research (see Stanton & Gallant, 1995).

Negative feelings about physical maturation are further exacerbated by the emphasis in U.S. culture on feminine thinness that makes normal pubertal increases in fat and weight a source of considerable anxiety and embarrassment for young women (see Brannon, 1999; Stanton & Gallant, 1995). Unlike adolescent males, who are growing *into* their expected adult physique (i.e., large, muscular), females are growing *out of* their societally prescribed body shape and size. It is little wonder that eating disorders and body image concerns are pervasive among women, including women of color (Brannon, 1999; Joiner & Kashubeck, 1996; Lester & Petrie, 1998), and that body image discontent is being documented in increasingly younger populations (Brannon, 1999). Recent research also demonstrates links between disordered eating and feminine gender role stress (Martz, Handley, & Eisler, 1995), self-objectification and body shame (Noll & Fredrickson, 1998), and lack of autonomy and self-esteem (Frederick & Grow, 1996). That eating disorders are strongly tied to gender socialization is further supported by findings that lesbians and feminists, who tend to demonstrate less internalization of sociocultural gender norms, exhibit lower rates of body dissatisfaction and disturbed eating (Bergeron & Senn, 1998).

The sexual arena also presents a conundrum for girls who are maturing into women. Unlike males, who are assumed to have uncontrollable urges that predispose them to engage in a great deal of sexual experimentation and behavior, females are expected to walk a fine line of maintaining attractiveness to males (and only males) at all times, while protecting themselves from actual sexual contact unless within the societally condoned confines of marriage. Thus, as Unger and Crawford (1996) have pointed out, societal regulation of adolescent sexuality focuses exclusively on girls, not boys, and emphasizes either sexual abstinence or marriage as the only alternatives. Young women are expected to be sexually seductive but asexual (because all but heterosexual outlets are denied), and they are not assumed to have sexual desires or needs apart from pleasing men. Indeed, recent social perception studies indicate the persistence of double standards for sexual behavior in young men and women, with young women judged more negatively than men when they provide a condom for protected sex or have sex outside of a committed relationship (Hynie & Lydon, 1995; Hynie, Lydon, & Taradash, 1997).

Because sex-negative attitudes do not entirely prevent sexual activity, females are, indeed, engaged in such activity (about half of those under age 19 are sexually active), and they are blamed when it occurs (Unger & Crawford, 1996). Sex-negative attitudes do discourage contraceptive use and, through pregnancy, females suffer the consequences of unprotected sexual intercourse to a greater degree than do males. It is estimated that each year in the United States, one million female adolescents become pregnant, and about half of those have babies; by age 18, about one-quarter of females in the United States have been pregnant at least once (Lerner & Galambos, 1998). Thus, attempting to regulate (hetero)sexual activity through the existing ideology of gender roles is not particularly effective.

The area of adolescent sexual behavior also provides a clear example of the complex interface between biological events and sociocultural processes. In boys' gender socialization, sexual maturation is associated with greater independence than in girls; given that physiological maturation occurs on average two years earlier for girls than boys, gendered societal patterns suggest the likelihood that females are actively discouraged from independent behavior, either by parental fears or the desire to keep girls' behavior parallel to that of boys (Unger & Crawford, 1996). In addition, the age of menarche has dropped from about 15 to 16 years of age a century ago to 12.5 years of age at present, resulting in shorter childhood and longer adolescence for young women. Thus, adolescent females are facing issues such as sexual choices at younger ages (with their less mature male peers) and are generally ill-prepared to do so, their antisexual socialization conflicting with the freedom and independence that their physical maturity might otherwise confer (Unger & Crawford, 1996).

Moreover, despite societal prohibitions against sexual activity in young women, prepubescent and adolescent females are, ironically, at extremely high risk for sexual abuse and sexual exploitation. Females are abused at a rate four times that of males, and although prevalence estimates vary (from about 25% to about 44% of females; Anselmi & Law, 1998), experts agree that substantial numbers of female youth will experience some form of severe sexual abuse or exploitation by age 18 (Knutson, 1995). In addition, abuse of girls is most likely to be perpetrated within the confines of the family (Anselmi & Law, 1998; Knutson, 1995), presumably sending confusing messages about males, authority, power, marriage, family, and personal safety. The alarmingly high rates of sexual exploitation of females, interacting with the repression of female sexuality, strong pressures to marry, and the changes associated with physical maturity, create a number of disturbing conflicts between biological maturation and cultural expectations for many young women. Such difficulties are likely to be exacerbated for young lesbian and bisexual women, who are struggling with unique developmental concerns related to sexuality.

Socialization and Lesbian, Gay, or Bisexual Youth

Youth who eventually become lesbian, gay, or bisexual often report feeling different from others during childhood, although the nature of their difference may not become clear until adolescence, by which time many have internalized a great deal of negativity regarding self-identity (Gonsiorek, 1993). Thus, for LGB youth, socialization is even more complex than for their heterosexual counterparts, because all developmental tasks related to gender and sexuality must be negotiated within a context of stigma and shame (Bohan, 1996; Ryan & Futterman, 1998; Savin-Williams, 1995). Stigma regarding sexual orientation often involves some combination of overt (even socially sanctioned) attitudinal and behavioral prejudice, pervasive invisibility and secrecy, inappropriate or nonexistent norms and role models, inadequate social resources, profound isolation, inaccurate information, temporary or permanent family upheaval, and interpersonal violence. Societal, institutional, and individual homonegativity virtually ensure that most LGB youth will experience and internalize some degree of conflict and shame regarding their minority sexual status, and will attempt to understand their own needs and preferences regarding gender and sexuality either in total isolation or with a limited number of others who also are likely to have internalized self-denigrating attitudes. It is little wonder that suicide risk and prevalence rates for psychological difficulties are particularly high among LGB youth (Bohan, 1996; Ryan & Futterman, 1998), despite a remarkable resiliency often exhibited in this population (Savin-Williams, 1995).

In identifying issues faced by LGB youth, it is important to distinguish between sexual identity and sexual behavior. The erroneous linking of these two characteristics is a common but particularly striking misunderstanding when considering adolescence, a time of much experimentation in regard to both identity and sexuality. It is well documented, for example, that many (perhaps most) individuals who eventually identify as LGB engage in heterosexual sex during adolescence, just as a substantial number of youth who identify clearly as heterosexual engage in homosexual behavior (Savin-Williams, 1995). There also are large numbers of youth who identify as heterosexual in the absence of any sexual activity at all, just as many youth realize same-sex attractions and identity without engaging in sexual behaviors. Indeed, most youth who report same-sex attractions, fantasies, and even sexual behavior are unlikely to label themselves as gay, lesbian, or bisexual (Savin-Williams, 1995). Thus, there appears to be a great deal of fluidity in adolescent sexuality, as well as reluctance to label oneself with a stigmatized identity.

Unfortunately, even tacit social acceptance of some sexual and identity experimentation during adolescence generally does not include LGB lifestyles and preferences, and LGB youth who do not fit in with their peers due to different interests and activities (gender roles) and different sexual attractions (sexual orientation) often experience a great deal of anxiety, depression, and chronic stress due to their differentness (Ryan & Futterman, 1998). For example, persistent stressors identified by LGB youth include coming out to others, having sexual orientation discovered by others, and being ridiculed for their sexual orientation. There also is evidence that normative distressing events of adolescence (e.g., arguments with parents, school difficulties) may be exacerbated by private concerns about sexual identity (Ryan & Futterman, 1998). Moreover, the social isolation experienced by many LGB youth means that they will lack resources for dealing with stress and may be more likely than their heterosexual peers to choose strategies that put their health and lives at risk, for example, alcohol and tobacco use, unprotected sex, delinquency, and running away (Bohan, 1996; Ryan & Futterman, 1998).

For those sexual minority youth who recognize and attempt to act on their same-sex feelings and attractions, there is very little opportunity for healthy dating experiences, despite their documented eagerness to establish close, loving, permanent relationships in the future (D'Augelli, 1991). In contrast to their heterosexual peers, for whom dating serves as an opportunity for erotic and emotional exploration of partner preferences, LGB youth seldom have the opportunity to date someone of the same sex who is both sexually attractive *and* socially and emotionally appropriate, producing a dichotomization of the erotic and the emotional/social aspects of dating (Savin-Williams, 1995). Thus, LGB adolescents may not perceive that emotional and sexual intimacy are even attainable in a same-sex relationship, and the effects of this dichotomy on males may be particularly damaging, as they learn that "they may have sex with other boys or men, but the two may never kiss because to do so would be too meaningful" (Savin-Williams, 1995, p. 179). Indeed, an oft-noted difference in the coming out experiences of lesbians and gay men is a more abrupt, sexualized process for males versus a more fluid and emotional-romantic course for females (Gonsiorek, 1993), which is born out of differential gender socialization patterns that emphasize sexual independence and relationship nurturance, respectively.

Frequent heterosexual dating by LGB adolescents, whether it occurs out of confusion over sexual orientation, pressure to conform, or desire to mask same-sex attractions and "pass" as heterosexual (Savin-Williams, 1995), is unlikely to meet the sexual and emotional needs of individuals whose preferences are for same-sex relationships. However, environmental constraints on same-sex dating suggest that it, too, will be unsatisfying, because it is likely to be of short duration, seldom includes emotional commitment and security, and often is secretive, invisible, and riddled with conflict (e.g., Sears, 1991). Although lesbians are more likely to have participated in a long-lasting, loving relationship during adolescence than are gay men (Savin-Williams, 1995), pervasive dating problems block many LGB adolescents from successfully negotiating an important developmental hurdle—the recognition of one's needs and desires regarding intimate partners. Thus, some LGB individuals may enter into the developmental task of achieving intimacy in adulthood with underdeveloped or inappropriate tools for negotiating this task.

INTIMACY AND FAMILY RELATIONSHIPS

Many of the issues highlighted in the previous section carry over into adulthood, when, for many (but not all), enduring intimate relationships are formed and some form of "family" or "home" life emerges. Couples and families may be seen as socially constructed entities, their acceptable forms and functions regulated both formally (e.g., in laws governing marriage and sexual expression) and informally (e.g., in religious and community beliefs about the place of women or men in the family), creating cultural scripts that are enacted by individuals in more or less similar ways (Unger & Crawford, 1996). In any kind of family, gender socialization and gender role issues are likely to be salient in defining the family structure, organizing tasks and roles in the home, influencing sexual patterns and behavior, determining power arrangements, and interfacing with the world outside the home. A general overview of unique issues faced by LGB couples and families is presented here, as this information may be new to many counseling psychologists. In addition, two especially salient issues (sex and multiple role demands) are highlighted in regard to heterosexual couples and families.

LGB Couples and Families

Same-sex couples attempting to establish a viable family life must contend with some of the same internalized gender messages as their heterosexual counterparts, and socialization patterns may be magnified in same-sex pairs due to presumably similar gendered learnings in both partners (Bohan, 1996). For example, socialization practices that train men to be independent and self-sufficient may lead to problems for gay male couples in achieving intimacy and interdependence. For lesbian couples, however, training in nurturance and helplessness may tend to produce struggles with independence and maintaining separateness, although scholars often point out that societal emphasis on independence is derived from androcentric norms that inadequately value women's relational styles (Bohan, 1996; Fassinger & Morrow, 1995). Most salient in the lives of same-sex couples, however, are issues related to stigmatization of identity and threats to lesbian and gay family structures created by societal heterosexism, homonegativity, and lack of support (Bohan, 1996).

Despite societal oppression, the realities of lesbian and gay relationships and families are beginning to be documented. In terms of longevity, studies suggest that about 75% of lesbians and 40% to 60% of gay men are in committed relationships at any given time, and these figures may actually underestimate the prevalence of committed relationships in these populations due to the absence of research on older LGB people or those not engaged in social or community activities (Bohan, 1996; Kurdek, 1995b; Peplau, 1991). Blumenstein and Schwartz (1983) indicated in their classic longitudinal study of homosexual and heterosexual couples that few couples who had been together for 10 or more years separated during the 18-month duration of the study (6% of lesbians, 4% of gay men, and 4% of heterosexual married couples); for couples who had been together for less than 10 years, breakup rates were similar for lesbian, gay, and cohabiting heterosexual couples (22%, 16%, and 17%, respectively), whereas the breakup rate for heterosexual married couples was 4%. These relatively minor differences in breakup rates are particularly interesting in light of the view of some relationship theorists (e.g., Kurdek, 1995a, 1995b; Peplau, 1991; Peplau & Cochran, 1990) that lesbian and gay couples face far more perceived barriers to relationship formation and far fewer impediments to relationship dissolution than do heterosexual couples. One might therefore expect high degrees of upheaval and termination in lesbian and gay relationships.

The fact that their breakup rates are not very dissimilar from heterosexual unions suggests the remarkable strength of such relationships in the face of adversity.

A more recent study (Bryant & Demian, 1994) of over 500 and 700 relatively young (mean age = 35) gay and lesbian couples, respectively, indicated that the average longevity of their relationships was about six years, with over 100 couples having been together for more than 15 years, and over 90% of the sample stating their expectation to remain in the relationship for a prolonged period of time or for life. In this sample, the median period of time between meeting and moving in together was less than four months, and the vast majority (approximately 90%) reported having lived together for at least part of the previous year. This study also found that about 25% of lesbian and 18% of gay male couples do not live together permanently. Bohan (1996) speculated that this pattern may be due to fears of disclosure or of being identified as lesbian/gay and therefore used as an identity management technique, or may be due to the rejection by lesbians and gay men of the traditional model of marriage, which typically involves high degrees of sharing of resources and sexual exclusivity. Certainly, this is an area in need of further study.

Lesbian and gay couples experience many of the same issues of daily living that face heterosexual families—raising children, dealing with extended family, negotiating financial matters, dividing up household chores, becoming accustomed to one another's habits and tastes, negotiating the home-work interface, and maintaining emotional and physical intimacy in the relationship. However, lesbian and gay couples must negotiate all these tasks within a context of stigma, isolation, and invisibility. For example, (1) they do not receive the same legal and fiscal supports as do heterosexual couples (e.g., medical and other insurance benefits, legal protections, tax benefits, child custody protections); (2) they often experience lack of support, denial, or censure from families-of-origin and communities (particularly in some racial, ethnic, cultural, or religious communities); (3) they must deal with the daily stress and conflicts of identity management and being out; (4) they must negotiate close same-sex friendships in the context of the primary same-sex relationship; and (5) they face pervasive and persistent denial of the legitimacy of their relationship, regardless of its longevity or their commitment to each other. Indeed, there are not even consistent labels to use to identify one's partner/lover/mate/significant other/boyfriend/girlfriend/domestic partner/housemate (Bohan, 1996). In addition, lesbians must contend with heteropatriarchal definitions of sexual activity that render much of their erotic life invisible or irrelevant (Fassinger & Morrow, 1995). Gay male couples and their communities face constant reminders of the presence of HIV/AIDS. Finally, both lesbians and gay men are forced to define their intimate commitments in sexual terms because there are no other avenues (e.g., legal, religious) open to them for doing so (Bohan, 1996; Fassinger & Morrow, 1995).

For those parenting children (2 to 8 million at present), there are additional obstacles to face (Patterson, 1995b). Partners who divorce their spouses from heterosexual marriages are likely to lose custody of children because of sexual orientation, and much damage can be done to their same-sex relationships out of denial, secrecy, and forced separation to maintain the illusion of heterosexuality before the courts. For those with custodial care of their children, who have managed to work through the normal transitions of step-parenting and blended families, pervasive societal heterosexism and homonegativity ensure that there will be some degree of disapproval to be dealt with in the schools, health system, and community. For same-sex couples attempting to acquire children through means other than previous heterosexual relationships (e.g., adoption, alternative insemination), legal and societal prohibitions, as well as high costs, make such efforts extremely difficult. Finally, same-sex couples who are parenting may feel isolated even in their lesbian and gay communities, which have tended not to be particularly focused on parenting roles.

How do same-sex couples and families weather these storms? Quite well, the research demonstrates. Studies indicate, for example, that lesbian and gay couples tend to express high levels of caring, intimacy, and attachment in their relationships, and that correlates of relationship satisfaction are very similar across all kinds of couples, regardless of sexual orientation—attachment, similarity in investment and commitment to the relationship, shared decision making and power in the relationship, similarity in backgrounds and attitudes, feeling that the relationship is high in rewards and low in costs, having at least one partner who is emotionally expressive, and harboring few dysfunctional relationship beliefs (Blumenstein & Schwartz, 1983; Eldridge & Gilbert, 1990; Kurdek, 1994, 1995b; Peplau & Cochran, 1990).

In addition, research indicates that most lesbian and gay couples—more so than their heterosexual counterparts—exhibit nonstereotypic gender role attitudes and behavior (stereotypes about "butches" and "femmes" notwithstanding), attempt to achieve equal power in their relationships, and are more satisfied with their relationships when they perceive them as egalitarian; the latter seems to be especially true of lesbian relationships (Bohan, 1996; see also Blumenstein & Schwartz, 1983; Eldridge & Gilbert, 1990; Kurdek, 1995a, 1995b; Peplau, 1991; Scrivner & Eldridge, 1995). Finally, heterosexual, gay, and lesbian couples report similar levels of satisfaction regarding sexual activity in their relationships, although frequency of sexual activity (defined according to hetero-patriarchal standards; Fassinger & Morrow, 1995) varies across the three groups (see Bohan, 1996, for a summary).

For same-sex couples with children, empirical studies of well-being typically focus on the children, arising from heterosexist societal concerns that growing up with same-sex parents will in some way harm children. Indeed, many studies focus on whether such children are more likely to grow up gay or lesbian. Bohan (1996) pointed out that simply posing this question itself suggests societal homonegativity in its implication that becoming lesbian or gay is a negative outcome to be avoided. Nevertheless, research suggests that children of lesbian or gay parents are not any more likely to exhibit a minority sexual orientation than children of heterosexual parents (Bohan, 1996); indeed, LGB people frequently point out that they were themselves raised by heterosexual parents, thus refuting assumptions of a causal link between parent and child sexual orientation. Much of the available research focuses on lesbian mothers, because they are most likely to encounter the courts in custody disputes (Bohan, 1996). Overall, studies indicate that children raised by lesbian or gay parents show no differences from heterosexually reared children in psychological adjustment (e.g., self-esteem, moral judgment, behavior problems) or social adjustment (e.g., popularity, peer group relations) (Patterson, 1994, 1995c).

There also is some evidence that children of lesbian or gay parents (compared with heterosexually reared children) demonstrate greater tolerance and flexibility (Bohan, 1996), that they may experience more stress but also a stronger sense of well-being (Patterson, 1994, 1995c), and that their postdivorce lesbian mothers are more likely than their heterosexual counterparts to foster the child's relationship with the father and positive relationships with men in general (Bohan, 1996). Interestingly, research on lesbian mothers also suggests that better adjustment of children occurs where the mother is accepting of her identity and lives openly with her partner, where she has disclosed her identity to her children and others in her life, and where child care is equally shared by both partners (Patterson, 1995a). The latter finding is relevant to many heterosexual women as well.

Issues for Heterosexual Couples/Families

In the previous edition of this *Handbook,* Gilbert (1992) outlined three key gender issues affecting both women and men: (1) men's socialized needs for power (including sex and violence against women); (2) beauty and women's self-concept (tied to women's socialization to be sexually pleasing to men); and (3) multiple role involvement for men and women (including dual-career issues and child rearing). These issues continue to create some of the most salient problems faced by heterosexual women and men, and their roots can be found in the socialization practices previously noted. In sum, for most individuals differential gender role socialization and expectations for females and males create patterns of adulthood functioning that can render heterosexual relationships difficult to negotiate (Gilbert & Scher, 1999; Unger & Crawford, 1996).

In terms of sexual activity and behavior, because females are taught to define themselves in terms of their attractiveness to males and also have the responsibility of regulating sexual interactions with males, the pressure to marry is often a very powerful force. Indeed, about 90% of American women marry by age 30 (although rates are somewhat lower for African American women, about 35% of whom remain unmarried by age 34), and cultural ideologies regarding motherhood continue to create intense demands on women to have children as well (Betz, 1994; Fitzgerald & Weitzman, 1992; Unger & Crawford, 1996). Because women are taught to assume nurturing roles, they also are likely to hold themselves accountable for maintaining the emotional bonds of couple and family relationships, and research that links the quality of marital relationships to depression and self-esteem in women supports the notion that many women may feel responsible for the condition of their relationships (Culp & Beach, 1998).

Socialization patterns create roles for males as sexual predators/initiators who define themselves in large measure by their sexual prowess, and roles for women as reluctant, passive, dependent recipients who are preoccupied with body-image concerns and focused on the emotional aspects of sex. These are firmly rooted ideologies by adulthood and can interfere with healthy intimacy in many couples. Research suggests that women often have minimal awareness of their own erotic needs and patterns, and they are more likely than men to experience guilt, fear, and anxiety about sex (Gilbert & Scher, 1999; Unger & Crawford, 1996). This is consistent with females' antisexual socialization, as well as the pervasive sexual exploitation of, and violence against, women (Unger & Crawford, 1996).

Moreover, socialized sexual scripts dictate focus on the pleasure of the male, and research indicates that many women in heterosexual relationships experience less pleasure and greater sexual dissatisfaction than do their male partners. In addition, the emphasis on men's pleasure prevents many women from insisting on safe sexual practices that protect them against unwanted pregnancy and sexually transmitted diseases (Unger & Crawford, 1996; Wyatt & Riederle, 1994). Men, on the other hand, may have difficulty understanding why their female partners seem reluctant to initiate or engage in sexual activity, or why the context of sexual activity (e.g., feeling emotionally connected, engaging in ritualized behaviors, such as deep conversation and romantic dinners) is so important to their partners. Also, it may be bewildering to many men to discover that what they accept as adequate sexual performance may, in fact, produce little pleasure (including orgasm) in their female partners (Gilbert & Scher, 1999).

Another area of common problems for heterosexual couples and families involves multiple role demands that fall disproportionately on women (Crosby, 1991; Gilbert, 1992; S.D. Phillips & Imhoff, 1997). Gender role socialization practices ensure that most women will have received implicit or explicit messages regarding their lack of worth and helplessness, as well as their need for males; in addition, they are likely to have received mixed messages concerning the importance of work and careers, as well as their capabilities of successfully pursuing careers, and many also plan to have children (Betz, 1994; Betz & Fitzgerald, 1987; Brannon, 1999). Men, on the other hand, typically are socialized to be efficacious and independent, and are likely to have prepared themselves for full-time, lifetime employment. It is thus unsurprising that men and women frequently enter into relationships with different motivations and needs. In fact, research indicates persistent differences in expectations of men and women regarding marital relationships, with women favoring flexibility, role sharing, and egalitarianism, and men preferring more traditional roles in which women bear the primary responsibility for home and children (Cook, 1993; Gilbert, 1992; S.D. Phillips & Imhoff, 1997).

Thus, when women try to form and maintain viable careers or simply engage in paid work to provide family income, they are far more likely than men to experience complex problems in multiple role management. Studies indicate that women spend about twice as much time as men engaged in housework and child care (Konicus, 1999), and that even where relationships are judged by both partners to be egalitarian, it is usually the woman who continues to carry most of the burden for planning and organizing home and family (Cook, 1993; Gilbert, 1992). Given that men's gender role socialization tends to be more rigid than that of women (and the gap widens with decreasing socioeconomic status), it is little wonder that patterns emerge of "overworked women and resistant to moderately involved men" (Unger & Crawford, 1996, p. 48). These patterns are consistent across cultural and ethnic groups, particularly those valuing traditional gender roles (Unger & Crawford, 1996).

It also is not surprising that (1) although multiple roles have considerable positive effects on the well-being of both women and men, current marital and workplace arrangements confer much more benefit on men than women, and more on middle- and upper-class women than working-class women (Crosby, 1991); (2) relationship dissatisfaction occurs more often in women than men, and women's relationship satisfaction is closely tied to the degree and kind of involvement of male partners in domestic work (Cook, 1993; S.D. Phillips & Imhoff, 1997); and (3) access to economic resources is a critical factor in women's management of multiple roles (Unger & Crawford, 1996; Wasserman, 1998). As one study noted, "For women, it's not having a job that's bad for your health, it's having a lousy job with inadequate support for at-home responsibilities" (Baruch, Barnett, & Rivers, 1983, p. 180).

Research also consistently suggests that the lop-sided nature of the division of household labor disadvantages women profoundly in the workplace. Interrupted careers, lower wages, missed promotions, and high-stress levels related to managing multiple roles are well-documented realities of work life for most married and unmarried women with children (e.g., Betz & Fitzgerald, 1987; Fitzgerald & Weitzman, 1992). For example, in a series of studies involving extensive interviews with more than 100 prominent, successful, culturally diverse women across a dozen career fields, most women with children reported that they felt positive about being mothers and content with choices they had made, but acknowledged negative effects on their careers; indeed, many also admitted that helpful and supportive male partners had not, for the most part, reduced their primary responsibility for home and children (Gomez & Fassinger, 1997; Hollingsworth, Tomlinson, & Fassinger, 1998; Noonan & Fassinger, 1998; Prosser, Chopra, & Fassinger, 1998; Richie et al., 1997).

Other recent studies support these findings. For example, a large study of faculty at 24 U.S. medical schools indicated that women with children were significantly less productive and less satisfied with their career progress than were men with children (averaging 18 published articles compared with 29 for men), and the investigators suggested that women's greater responsibility for children is one critical obstacle to their career progress (Carr et al., 1998). Similarly, a recent study of female scientists (in which many were married to scientists who presumably understood the demands of scientific careers) found that women with children shouldered most of the responsibility for child care, despite describing their spouses as "supportive" (Wasserman, 1998).

The point here is not to suggest that women stop marrying and bearing children to pursue careers (although this certainly ought to be an acceptable life path for those who choose it), but rather to note that the burden of managing a two-earner family (increasingly becoming normative) is borne disproportionately by women, and to their great disadvantage. Interestingly, although many of the scientists in the Wasserman (1998) study called for social or institutional solutions to multiple role problems (e.g., flextime, accessible day care), almost all of the prominent women in the studies by Fassinger and colleagues focused on their own individual strategies for coping (e.g., time management, hiring help, reorganizing priorities), suggesting that many women have internalized responsibility for problems that might be addressed more effectively through environmental change (Fassinger & O'Brien, in press).

Given just these two examples of potential difficulty for heterosexual couples, it is not surprising that the divorce rate now exceeds 50%, and a consequence of the rising divorce rate is an increasing number of single-parent households (a change that is especially apparent in middle- and upper-class families). Most single-parent families are headed by females, not only because women are more likely to gain custody of children in divorce settlements, but also because men are more likely than women to remarry (Unger & Crawford, 1996). The postdivorce standard of living increases for men and dramatically decreases for women—a 40% average decline in standard of living for women, although some studies have documented declines of over 70% (Unger & Crawford, 1996). Given that many divorced women also experience difficulty in collecting child support, the risk of financial strain is extremely high for female-headed families (Unger & Crawford, 1996). Indeed, Unger and Crawford described divorce as an "economic disaster" for women (p. 374), and pointed out that well over 25% of divorced women earn postdivorce incomes below the poverty level, with rates of poverty for African American women especially high. Much of the precipitous drop in the postdivorce standard of living for women is rooted in the persistent gap in earnings between women and men, and the greater likelihood that women will lack the job skills, training, and experience needed to obtain jobs that provide a viable income. These problems are related to pervasive patterns of disadvantage for women in education and the workplace.

EDUCATION AND WORK

Although education and work are covered in considerable detail in other chapters in this volume, it is worth highlighting a few of the issues related to gender and sexuality. This is particularly critical in regard to sexual orientation, where the scholarly literature is perhaps less known to the broad audience of counseling psychologists. It is also important to note that many of the issues related to gender and sexuality in couples and families also are related to vocational roles and pursuits, suggesting that work issues are inextricably linked to personal issues, especially for female and LGB populations.

Gender in Education and Work

Gender-related barriers to optimal educational and vocational development are well documented in the literature (e.g., Betz, 1994; Betz & Fitzgerald, 1987; Fassinger, in press; Fitzgerald & Weitzman, 1992). Frequent themes include the underuse of the talents and abilities of females, pervasive discrimination against females in schools and work settings, and the complexity for adult women of managing multiple roles. More specifically, external or environmental barriers, such as gender-role stereotypes, occupational stereotypes, bias in education (including higher education), lack of role models and mentors, biased career assessment and counseling, pay inequities, sexual harassment, barriers to advancement, and the null environment, give rise to internal barriers in individual women, such as math avoidance, home-career conflict, and low self-esteem, self-efficacy, and expectations for success (see Betz & Fitzgerald, 1987). Moreover, it has been pointed out that, for many contemporary women, the blatant educational and occupational discrimination of the past has been replaced by a benign tolerance that provides no real support or encouragement, and leaves girls and women even more subject to self-blame when educational/vocational goals are not met or are thwarted (Betz, 1989; Fassinger, in press; Fassinger & O'Brien, in press).

It can be argued that *all* barriers to women's vocational development be viewed as contextual or environmental, in that they arise out of societal structures such as norms, ideologies, practices, policies, and institutions that serve to limit access and options for females. Thus, although vocational interventions might continue to include traditional, individually focused activities such as counseling and career planning, it is also critical to target contextual, structural barriers directly to produce changes that can make work a more viable enterprise for women (Fassinger, in press; Fassinger & O'Brien, in press).

Sexuality in Education and Work

For LGB youth and adults, schools and work settings can be permeated with tensions and difficulties. Schools, for example, have been described as "unwelcoming and even hostile places" (Harris, 1997, p. xxi), where segregation by sex is practiced daily and overtly (note, for example, the common practice in elementary schools of lining up girls and boys separately); where rigid gender roles are taught and reinforced; where intractable heteronormativity and homophobia ensure that any kind of gender nonconformity will be quickly censured or punished, in teachers as well as in students; and where both overt and passive discrimination occur regularly, the former in open hostility and the latter in silence and invisibility (Fassinger, 1993; Harbeck, 1992; Harris, 1997). Indeed, Rofes (1997) asserted that schools have changed very little in the past decade of gay rights activism, and that "the school-based lives of lesbian, gay, and bisexual youth continue to be fraught with silences, denials, dangers, and omissions" (p. xiv).

Many specific problems have been documented in the literature (e.g., Fassinger, 1993; Harbeck, 1992; Harris, 1997). LGB teachers often are closeted because of (often realistic) fears of discrimination, ostracism, and job loss, and thus are rarely available as role models or change agents in schools. School counselors and administrators are likely to be uninformed about LGB issues and may fear supporting LGB students and teachers out of personal prejudice or institutional or community pressure. Academic and career counseling may be steeped in ignorance and occupational stereotypes. Curriculum content (including sex education) is unlikely to address LGB issues or people, and LGB youth probably will be isolated from interacting with other LGB youth. School activities are likely to be organized around promoting heterosexuality (e.g., dances and proms) and ghettoizing gender nonconformity (e.g, males in the drama club are seen as "fags" and "real men" are on the football team). Harassment and violence may be common practices in the school environment, and may go unreported and unrecognized because of victims' fears of revealing their homosexuality. In higher education, additional constraints may include the avoidance of LGB topics in research by faculty and students, denial of common benefits such as tuition remission and health insurance for domestic partners, discrimination in promotion and tenure, homophobic residence hall environments, and general social and collegial ostracism (Evans & Wall, 1991; Fassinger, 1993; McNaron, 1997).

Rofes (1997) noted that LGB youth are coming out at increasingly early ages (some in the later years of elementary school), suggesting that schools can no longer deny the existence of LGB students or teachers, and must begin to enact change more vigorously. He also suggested that gay activists largely have ignored educational institutions in their political and social change efforts, and that advocacy efforts have come primarily from LGB students themselves—a striking problem when one considers the relative lack of power held by students who occupy the lowest rung of the educational hierarchy. It also seems evident that social change efforts targeting young people in the institutions in which they spend the bulk of their waking hours have considerable preventive potential.

The workplace also can be a difficult place for many LGB people, and barriers to lesbian and gay vocational development are beginning to be consistently documented and studied (Croteau, 1996; Diamant, 1993). External challenges primarily are rooted in pervasive negative attitudes on the part of coworkers and superiors. Indeed, Gonsiorek (1993) noted that bigotry related to sexual orientation is one of the last bastions of societally sanctioned prejudice. Bigotry in the workplace may take the form of overt harassment and even physical violence, but is more likely to be masked in negative work evaluations, ostracism from social and professional networks, impediments to advancement, assignment to unattractive tasks, pay discrimination, termination attempts, and lack of support (Croteau, 1996; Fassinger, 1993, 1996b; Gonsiorek, 1993). Even where the worst that one experiences is a relatively benign ignorance on the part of one's peers, the pervasive organization of workplace norms around heterosexual lifestyles and activities can be both isolating and exhausting for LGB workers (Diamant, 1993).

Because of the largely intransigent homophobia and heteronormativity in the workplace, identity management becomes a key issue for many LGB workers. Strategies for identity management may include full disclosure of one's sexual orientation (and partner if relevant). However, many LGB workers choose, or are forced by oppressive environments, to adopt more indirect strategies such as keeping silent about one's personal life, avoiding social or conversational situations with coworkers, "passing" as heterosexual by maintaining a pretense of other-sex dating and partners, living long distances from the workplace to avoid chance discovery while engaged in lesbian or gay community activities, or even participating in homophobic jokes and slurs to avoid being detected (see Croteau, 1996; Fassinger, 1996b; Gonsiorek, 1993). Such identity strategies might be expected to take an obvious individual toll, and the potential for conflicts in couples where both are negotiating identity management on a daily basis is considerable (Fassinger, 1996b).

Internalized oppression also may make career pursuits difficult (Gonsiorek, 1993). A LGB worker may feel the need to work harder and achieve more than heterosexual coworkers as a protection against job loss or to achieve acceptance among coworkers and superiors. Some LGB workers may have internalized negative affect in terms of habituated self-defeating attitudes and behaviors that undermine their success. Internalized oppression also may cause many LGB workers to blame themselves when events occur that actually are rooted in external discrimination, for example, the lesbian worker who receives a negative work evaluation from a homophobic superior, but blames herself for allowing her lesbian identity to become known.

The developmental issues facing LGB people in even choosing a career or job are daunting. For example, it has been noted that career choice may be compromised in a number of ways by a gay or lesbian identity (e.g., Fassinger, 1996b; Gonsiorek, 1993; Morrow, 1997). Identity development for many LGB people takes place during high school, college, and young adulthood, precisely the time of life when the developmental task of choosing and implementing a career is supposed to occur. Career choice efforts may be delayed while immersion in sexual identity concerns takes precedence (Fassinger, 1996b; Morrow, 1997). Conversely, throwing oneself into educational pursuits and vocationally related activities may provide temporary distraction from the alarming throes of recognizing same-sex attractions and tendencies. Due to the self-esteem problems, depression, and anxiety that often accompany the sexual identity development process, career choices may be made hastily, with little knowledge, and without attention to the intersection of career and lifestyle (Fassinger, 1996b; Morrow, 1997). Thus, an individual may emerge from the vocational choice process in a career that is not suitable for her/his intended lifestyle (e.g., being in the military and wanting, but not being able, to live an openly gay lifestyle), or a person may choose a career as a way of stemming the tide of homosexual panic (e.g., choosing an abstinent religious vocation as a way of quelling unacceptable sexual feelings). Such inappropriate choices can result in a lifetime of occupational dissatisfaction and hidden identity for many LGB people, perhaps manifesting in physical and mental health problems as well.

AGING AND HEALTH

Due primarily to advances in medical technology and disease control, longevity has increased dramatically during the twentieth century, with current life expectancies for women and men of 80 and 73 years, respectively. The percentage of Americans over age 65 has more than tripled during this time, and the population of those over age 85 is the fastest-growing age group (American Psychological Association [APA], 1998). This suggests that aging is becoming an increasingly important and prolonged developmental period, and that counseling psychologists are likely to encounter larger numbers of older adults in their work. Moreover, longevity differences result in many more older women (especially women of color) than older men who eventually face poverty, ill-health, and other problems requiring intervention (Unger & Crawford, 1996). Research indicates that women are more likely to use physical and mental health services than men (see Gilbert & Scher, 1999; Strickland, 1988), and lesbians appear to exhibit particularly favorable attitudes toward seeking mental health intervention (Bradford & Ryan, 1987). Therefore, it is reasonable to expect increasing numbers of older women to seek the services of mental health professionals, and it is imperative that counseling psychologists are prepared to offer services—sensitive both to gender and sexuality—to this population.

Health and aging are inextricably linked in current day society, not only because of real changes in physical and mental health associated with aging, but because societal conceptions of old age represent it as a time of unrelenting deterioration in physical and mental capacities, thus creating a focus on health as the defining issue of aging. This serves as a reminder that experiences related to aging and mental and physical health/illness are powerfully socially constructed. That is, society inculcates its members with beliefs and values about what it means to be young, old, healthy, and sick, and these images are situated in a specific historical and sociopolitical context. Moreover, societal values which define the experiences of aging and health are quite specific in regard to gender and sexual orientation; consider, for example, the assumption that the "independence" of men is normal whereas women's "dependency" is pathological (note the subtle grammatical shift), or the belief that one must marry and have children to ensure having a caretaker when one is old, frail, and lonely. Thus, it is essential to consider issues of health and aging in conjunction with gender and sexuality.

Aging, Gender, and Sexuality

For purposes of illustration, consider closely the notion that marriage and children assure one of a protected old age, beginning with the obvious assumption that heterosexual marriage and childbearing are the sine qua non of a fulfilling family life. Apart from research findings clearly documenting successful family life for lesbian and gay people, it is also important to note that the focus on childbearing and child rearing for women interacts powerfully with the natural processes of aging. Nowhere is this more apparent than in the experience of menopause, which signals the end of the menstrual cycle and therefore woman's reproductive capacities. This normal biological process has intersected with negative images of older women found in the media, the medical profession, the helping professions, and other societal institutions, producing a view of older women as unattractive, used up, socially unnecessary, and mentally unstable due to hormonal processes that have run amok (Unger & Crawford, 1996).

Much has been written by feminist scholars about the medicalization of women's normal reproductive capacities and processes (including menopause) and the thriving drug industry spawned by treating natural hormonal changes in women (e.g., Tavris, 1992). One classic study (Goodman, 1982) found that over 50% of the women in a large sample had experienced surgery and 66% were taking medication for problems associated with menopause, but only 28% had indicated menopausal symptoms or problems on their medical history forms. A more recent study of medical and psychological writings on menopause found the predominance of a biomedical perspective and perjorative images of women (Rostosky & Travis, 1996). Although there are, of course, wide differences among women, research indicates that women do not suffer as profoundly and universally from menopausal problems as common beliefs and media hype suggest (Brannon, 1999; Stanton & Gallant, 1995). In fact, many women find the changes associated with menopause unnoticeable, quite tolerable, or even liberating where worries about pregnancy have been an ongoing source of stress (Unger & Crawford, 1996); indeed, one recent study found that 60% of midlife women reported no changes at all in their sexual responses (Mansfield, Koch, & Voda, 1998). Moreover, lesbians, as a group, appear to be the least concerned about menopause, perhaps due to less preoccupation with body image, less adverse effects of physiological changes associated with aging (such as vaginal dryness, which often compromises heterosexual women's comfort with intercourse), and less self-definition based on mothering roles (Fassinger & Morrow, 1995; Rothblum, 1994).

Scholars point to these apparent anomalies to emphasize the fact that the experience of menopause overlaps with a number of critical shifts in roles, responsibilities, and resources in many women's lives, and that difficulties associated with menopause have been found to be more clearly related to changes in life roles and societal perceptions, rather than physical symptoms associated with hormonal changes (Brannon, 1999). A now-classic study by Adelmann, Antonucci, Crohan, and Coleman (1989) demonstrated that cohorts of women who were socialized into adult roles during times in which motherhood was emphasized were found to have much more negative experiences related to the "empty nest syndrome" (children growing up and leaving home) than women for whom other life roles (e.g., employment) were available and acceptable. Moreover, there are ethnic, cultural, and class differences related to these issues. Women with greater economic resources, for example, are more likely to be able to enjoy the greater freedom conferred by the empty nest, and patterns within one's ethnic or cultural group also affect expectations about continuing close contact with children who live apart. Financial pressures also will be a consideration for women whose eligibility for public assistance ends with their children attaining the age of majority, and for women whose grown children are unable to adequately provide or care for children of their own (Unger & Crawford, 1996). Thus, research on middle-aged and older women suggests the profound effects of gender socialization on perceptions of family life.

A return to the earlier example reveals another explicit assumption that grown children actually will care for their aging parents. As longevity differences would predict, the aging parent is likely to be a woman; there are about 149 women for every 100 men over age 65, and 259 women for every 100 men over age 85 (Hatch, 1995). Many of these elderly women are living in poverty, and therefore do not have access to resources for daily living (e.g., medical care, transportation, recreation, day or permanent care facilities, meal delivery, in-home nursing, legal services). Older women are nearly twice as likely as older men to have incomes below the poverty level, and one in six elderly women is poor. Black and Latina women face higher levels of poverty than White women; for example, approximately 80% of elderly Black women and 50% of older Latinas are estimated to be living in poverty or near poverty (Padgett, 1988).

The income gap between retired women and men actually has widened during the past decade, due to intransigent earnings differentials compounded over a lifetime of paid work, as well as inadequate or nonexistent individual social security and pension benefits (or loss of spousal pension benefits) for older women (Unger & Crawford, 1996). Research suggests that lesbians may be at particular risk for poverty, due to longstanding financial disadvantage such as pay discrimination (due to being both female and lesbian), lack of support from families, and dual-career incomes that do not include the higher earnings of males. Indeed, in a large national sample of lesbians, whose education levels far exceeded those of the general female population, Bradford and Ryan (1987) found that over one-third had received public financial assistance in the past (e.g., welfare, food stamps), and that they were five times more likely than other women at midlife to experience financial difficulties.

Children caring for their aging parents are likely to be daughters or daughters-in-law, because a disproportionate number (about 71%) of family caregivers are women (Unger & Crawford, 1996). These women are likely to be working, bearing responsibility for their own teenage or young adult children, and (for many) tending ill or disabled spouses. These added burdens exacerbate multiple role conflicts and challenges for women. Such issues are likely to be more salient for working class women and for members of ethnic and cultural groups that emphasize extended family connections and support; not only is the expectation for elder care greater, but these women are less likely to have the job flexibility and comfortable income that allow them to meet elder-care demands without considerable strain (Unger & Crawford, 1996). Members of some ethnic minority groups also may age faster and suffer more precipitous health declines than their White peers, due to poverty and the cumulative stresses of oppression (Unger & Crawford, 1996). Moreover, advances in medical treatment are likely to exacerbate the elder-care problem as longevity continues to increase—indeed, some women now in their forties and fifties are engaged in caring for two generations above them. Research also suggests that sons are unlikely to provide elder care even where there are no daughters to assume this responsibility, and that when men do engage in elder care, they tend to do so through organizing and managing it, rather than actually being present (Coward & Dwyer, 1990; Montgomery & Kamo, 1989).

Another assumption embedded in the example above is that elderly people universally need caregiving, due to their helplessness and infirmity. It must be noted that many elderly people are capable of independent living well into old age (APA, 1998). Moreover, despite myths about loneliness and depression, most elderly maintain regular contact with families and appear to be quite content. Research indicates that community-dwelling older adults exhibit lower rates of diagnosable depression than younger adults (APA, 1998), and women, in particular, report sizable peer networks that provide support. Interestingly, the deprivation in income and health for many elderly people of color does not seem to predispose them to depression or lower life satisfaction; in fact, Black women have the lowest suicide rates of all age and ethnic groups (Padgett, 1988), and Blacks report greater life satisfaction in late middle age than their White counterparts (Carlson & Videka-Sherman,1990).

Also contrary to stereotypes, lesbian and gay elders typically appear to be well adjusted and living contentedly, especially those who are satisfied with their lesbian/gay identity and involved in the lesbian/gay community (Friend, 1990; Quam & Whitford, 1992). Although lesbian and gay elders face unique stressors stemming from their stigmatized identities (e.g., legal and medical barriers to caring for ill and aging partners, lack of gay-sensitive services and resources), some scholars (e.g., Friend, 1990; Reid, 1995) have pointed to uncommon strengths developed by LGB people in coping with stigma, and suggest that negotiating a lesbian or gay identity actually may prepare these elders more adequately than their heterosexual peers for the challenges of aging. This work posits that sexual minorities develop a kind of "crisis competency" (see Friend, 1990) during the difficult process of identity development, in which they are forced to learn many skills and attitudes that contribute to successful aging—forming supportive social networks outside the family, developing flexible gender roles and competence in a wide range of tasks necessary for daily living (e.g., cooking, handling finances), behaving assertively to obtain needed social and medical services, and coping with societal stigma and stereotypes.

It is also important to note cohort issues in defining the experiences of illness and aging (Unger & Crawford, 1996). Most of today's U.S. elderly were born at a time when the life expectancy was 49, and probably never expected to live so far into old age. Also, death was a common experience for this cohort—most had experienced the death of someone close by the time they were 15—and threats of disease and illness were constant. Most of this cohort did not receive much formal education, divorce was considered shameful, and reproduction could not be controlled legally. In contrast, succeeding generations are better educated overall, have had access to legal reproductive control, expect to live long lives, have had relatively infrequent encounters with illness and death due to advances in medical technology, and exercise greater choice in regard to marriage and intimate partners. It is a reasonable expectation that future elderly will experience the later stages of their lives very differently from contemporary older adults. It is critical for both research and the delivery of effective services to consider how these shifts will affect the way society reconstructs the experience of aging and illness in the next decades.

Mental Health Issues

Cohort effects noted in relation to physical health and aging also are likely to be salient in experiences of mental health and illness, not only due to very real differing life experiences related to stress, depression, and other mental health problems, but because beliefs about mental illness, which are socially constructed, change over time. One need only note examples of mental disorders that have been widely documented in the past to be reminded of this fact (e.g., "drapetomania," a nineteenth-century diagnosis applied to slaves who repeatedly escaped despite capture and punishment, or "hysteria" attributed to floating wombs in large numbers of repressed Victorian women whose dissatisfaction erupted into physical and emotional distress). Similarly, until the mid-1970s, homosexuality was viewed within psychology and psychiatry as a mental illness, as reflected by the *DSM-II.* However, in 1975 the APA dramatically reversed itself and declared homosexuality a viable lifestyle, urging psychologists to "take the lead in removing the stigma of mental illness long associated with homosexual orientations" (Conger, 1975), including advocacy efforts in enactment of civil rights legislation and elimination of societal discrimination. Homosexuality was subsequently removed from the *DSM,* although debate persists over the diagnosis of "persistent and marked distress about sexual orientation" (as encoded in *DSM-IV*), and research suggests that psychologists continue to exhibit heterosexist and homonegative attitudes and behaviors in their work (Garnets et al., 1991). Moreover, there is abundant documentation in the literature of mental health problems for LGB individuals stemming from societal oppression and invisibility (Atkinson & Hackett, 1998; Bohan, 1996; Fassinger, 1991). However, the APA continues to issue gay-affirmative legal and policy statements, such as the 1998 resolution against the use of therapies aimed at "conversion" of individuals from homosexuality to heterosexuality, and it must be acknowledged that fairly radical social and professional change has occurred in an area once universally accepted as a mental illness.

Volumes have been devoted to mental health issues related to sexual orientation, and a forthcoming handbook (which is edited and contains numerous contributions by counseling psychologists; Perez, DeBord, & Bieschke, 1999) promises to be an extremely useful resource for those working with these populations. A key point to be made here regarding mental health and sexual orientation returns to whether one views homosexuality as an innate, internal attribute (an essentialist position) or as a societally determined (and therefore arbitrary) category based on collective values and biases (a constructivist position). The former view would be more likely to posit problems related to homosexuality as intrapsychic or interpersonal deficits rooted in the individual, whereas the latter view would tend to attribute difficulties faced by sexual minority people as rooted in an environment of discrimination and stigmatization. The currently accepted interactive view—accepting sexual orientation as a core aspect of identity, but also acknowledging oppressive environmental conditions that lead to mental health problems—represents a clarion call to psychologists for prevention and advocacy efforts targeted at removing debilitating conditions that make sexual minority identities so difficult. Like gender identity (and racial/ethnic identity), sexual identity is deemed salient in contemporary U.S. society because of widely held, deeply ingrained social, political, economic, moral, and psychological beliefs that privilege and empower some groups over others. If such value systems did not exist, there might be less need to attend to these aspects of the self.

Acknowledging obvious societal contributions to the mental health problems of LGB people can serve to highlight similar processes regarding gender—processes that may be less evident due to more unconscious gendered ideologies. That is, well-documented sex differences in prevalence, diagnosis, and treatment of mental health problems are firmly grounded in cultural expectations and prohibitions regarding men and women, as well as societal belief systems about which behaviors are accepted or valued and which behaviors are considered unacceptable and therefore must be treated (Tavris, 1992). For example, women are diagnosed with and treated for psychological disorders in far greater numbers than are men, and there are several disorders (e.g., depression, anorexia, agoraphobia) that exhibit dramatically greater prevalence in women than men (Tavris, 1992; Unger & Crawford, 1996). Clearly, there are aspects of female gender role socialization that contribute to these differences—for example, societal messages that link thinness with attractiveness and that encourage dependence and passivity. Research also has found that sexist discrimination contributes significantly more than generic stressors to physical and psychiatric symptoms (e.g., depression) in women (Landrine, Klonoff, Gibbs, Manning, & Lund, 1995).

In addition, societal expectations often put women into a psychological double bind, in that they create opposing demands for behavior. Women are taught, for example, to be feminine (with all of the attendant passivity and dependence demanded by that role), but also are told that those behaviors are unhealthy; whatever choices a woman makes, she risks negative judgment, for violating expectations of womanhood, or for behaving in ways that are considered unhealthy. Given that cultural and gender taboos also largely prevent her from venting her frustration, anxiety, and anger, it is little wonder that the only acceptable avenue for dealing with problems open to many women is through the mental health system, in which they will be provided with a diagnosis of their individual deficits and prescriptions for behavioral changes that will allow them to better fit the untenable circumstances of their lives (Caplan, 1995; Tavris, 1992).

In addition, the medicalization of normal female functions such as reproduction virtually ensures that most mental health difficulties will be attributed to female anatomy and physiology. Research indicates, for example, that knowledge of the Premenstrual Dysphoric Disorder diagnosis increased perceptions of a woman's premenstrual difficulties in one sample, and participants were more likely to apply a psychiatric diagnosis to the woman if they believed it was related to her menstrual cycle (Nash & Chrisler, 1997). Moreover, the typical focus of psychotherapy on intrapsychic and personal solutions to difficulties reinforces the inexorable cycle of individual blame and responsibility for socially created problems. Thus, although it must be acknowledged that counseling and therapy provide effective help and support for many women, it is also important to direct preventive interventions and advocacy efforts at the sources of problems that women encounter.

RECOMMENDATIONS FOR PREVENTION AND ADVOCACY IN SCIENCE AND PRACTICE

Ameliorative interventions for difficulties associated with internalized roles and expectations regarding gender and sexuality may be of limited efficacy in the face of deeply entrenched, self-sustained belief systems and behavior patterns. A more effective approach might use preventive interventions that disrupt socialized beliefs and practices, allowing for more optimal development over the life span. This suggests that counseling psychologists turn their attention to advocacy efforts in science, schools, communities, workplaces, and the mental health arena targeting youth, families, educators, employers, community service providers, religious and political leaders, mental health professionals, and others who play a role in the formation and perpetuation of social constructions of gender and sexuality (Fassinger, in press; Fassinger & O'Brien, in press). Presented here are suggestions for prevention and advocacy that cut across the areas of socialization, couples and families, education and work, and aging and health, grouped according to the location or target of advocacy efforts (e.g., communities, workplaces).

Resistance to many of these recommendations is likely, especially in regard to gay-affirmative advocacy. In addition, some organizations (e.g., churches, schools) may be especially reluctant to attend to issues (e.g., date rape) or populations (e.g., gay youth) that are perceived as threatening to central ideologies or practices. To circumvent some of this resistance, counseling psychologists might begin change efforts in organizations in which they already are involved and respected personally or professionally (e.g., PTA, church, professional association), and to plan systematically for small changes over time. An alternative strategy is to support more sweeping change initiatives (e.g., enacting gay rights legislation), under the assumption that broad-based legal and policy changes will eventually filter down into individual organizations and people. Regardless of where they begin, the training that counseling psychologists receive in addressing client resistance can be put to effective use in advocacy activities. For example, assessing barriers to change in a group of teachers or employers is not very different from determining why an individual client is unable to move forward, and the skills that aid in helping clients (e.g., accurate reflection of client feelings and fears) also can be effective in preparing groups to embrace change. In addition, it is important for LGB counseling psychologists to make themselves visible in as many arenas as possible, so that they can serve openly as role models for those with whom they work.

The Scientific Arena

Scientific debates about identity definition and etiology in regard to gender and sexuality are areas where prevention and advocacy are easily implemented. Researchers can work toward clear, consistent terminology in their own work (both publications and presentations), and can educate others in this way as well. Researchers also might consciously articulate the policy and advocacy implications of their own studies, and work to develop journal publication practices that incorporate vigorous attention to policy and advocacy uses of research (Fassinger, in press; Fassinger & O'Brien, in press; Harmon & Meara, 1994).

Researchers also can contribute to theory development by shifting the predominant discourse in many areas included in this chapter. Gilbert (1992) pointed out, for example, that research which reframes dependence as a positive, relationship-enriching quality (for men in particular) could greatly enhance the well-being of both women and men. Similarly, counseling psychologists can help to shift the view of role strain as a "woman's problem" to a perspective that recognizes household work, child care, and family relationship maintenance as real labor that has clear economic and social value. They might, for example, study "working fathers," analyze the labor involved in managing a home, or document financial benefits accruing to workplaces which institute onsite child care. Counseling psychologists also might help to shift predominant views of loneliness in the elderly by studying networks and communities of older women for evidence of social and emotional support and intimacy. An example of how research can shift discourse is provided by Richardson (1993), who suggested that mothering be viewed as a legitimate vocational role by young disadvantaged women with limited occupational possibilities, emphasizing the importance of work, rather than occupation, in theorizing about vocational development.

Researchers also might undertake studies of prevention program design and evaluation in many of the areas previously discussed. For example, S.D. Phillips and Imhoff (1997) noted that, despite a great deal of attention to documenting problems in women's career development, very little research has explored career interventions for women. Studies that explore the effects of prevention programs in the career arena might be especially useful in providing direction for practitioners who develop and design interventions. Studies indicate, for example, that programs designed to reduce occupational stereotyping may result in immediate perceptual change in participants, but it is unclear whether such effects persist over time or function to expand actual occupational choices (S.D. Phillips & Imhoff, 1997). Similarly, research suggests that accurate information and contact with female coworkers decreases negative stereotypes regarding women workers, but it is not clear whether such attitudinal changes contribute to fairer treatment or a more positive workplace climate for women (S.D. Phillips & Imhoff, 1997). Researchers can provide these much-needed data from systematic study.

Schools

Involvement in schools (including nursery schools and day-care centers) through teacher in-service training and programming for parents and students is one avenue for change. In designing preventive interventions, a possible starting point is in the area of career development and occupational information. Not only is this an arena in which socialization forces operate forcefully, perniciously, and proscriptively to limit choices, but it also lends itself to educational efforts at any level, nursery school (e.g., reading books to toddlers about people in different jobs) through high school (e.g., organizing a guest speaker series featuring people in nontraditional jobs). In addition, it can seem helpful and nonthreatening, because its goal is to foster identity as a productive worker and increase future options for all youth. Activities can include speakers, books and films, field trips, and organized programs (e.g., Career Day), with parents and teachers being involved and educated along with the students.

Educational programming for students on such topics as healthy eating, body image, dating, sex and sexuality, gender roles, communication, and self-esteem also can help to promote the optimal development of young women and men. Counseling psychologists might offer training and in-service workshops and conferences for teachers, parents, and school personnel (especially those involved in sports, where homophobia and rigid gender roles tend to be rampant) in areas such as gender roles, sexual abuse, date rape, eating disorders, sexual orientation, harassment, and other important topics, using these opportunities to engage teachers and parents as allies in future efforts aimed at educating and supporting youth. For example, in-service training on eating disorders and body image or on the development of sexual orientation might lead to in-school programs or extracurricular activities (e.g., clubs) to support students in these areas, particularly if teachers and administrators who hold power are convinced of needs in these areas. Overall, thorough training of school personnel in gender and sexuality issues is likely to be critical to success in making educational environments fair and affirming for female and LGB youth.

In addition to preventive educational programming and in-service training in specific topic areas, counseling psychologists might engage in advocacy activities aimed at broader systemic change in schools (Fassinger, 1993, in press). For example, advocacy efforts might focus on: (1) implementing gay-affirmative sex education curricula; (2) recruiting and protecting LGB teachers and staff; (3) transforming the school curriculum to ensure that it is gender-fair, gay-affirmative, and nonageist (including deliberate focus on problem areas such as females' participation in math and science); (4) ensuring that schools have adequate resources regarding gender and sexual orientation (e.g., films, books, newspapers, magazines, female and gay-affirmative counselors); and (5) instituting policies and practices that affirm the basic rights of females and sexual minorities (e.g., including antidiscrimination clauses in contracts, protecting schools from the presence of antigay or antifeminist organizations).

Another way that counseling psychologists might contribute to changes in schooling is to become involved in college and university teacher preparation programs, helping to shape teacher preparation and certification requirements, and offering training in topics related to gender and sexuality. Neither new nor experienced teachers are likely to be well informed regarding the extensive social science literatures on gender and sexuality, and they might profit from knowledge that counseling psychologists can provide. Counseling psychologists in colleges of education not only are particularly well positioned for such interventions, but may reap the benefit of enhanced perceived relevance to the college through their involvement in programs of central importance to the college's mission and goals.

Communities

Within communities, counseling psychologists can offer educational programming and staff training in youth centers, religious institutions, and other local organizations. For example, programs on coping with chronic illness or negotiating the health system might be offered in churches, synagogues, or organizations for the elderly, and particular populations (e.g., older women, LGB elders) can be targeted for programming specific to their needs. Education regarding socialization and gender roles can be incorporated into parenting and childbirth classes, and programs on sexual choices and behaviors can be offered in youth organizations (e.g., Girl Scouts); again, prior connections with community organizations can help counseling psychologists gain entry and permission for activities that otherwise might be declined. Educational programming also might be directed toward religious and political leaders; for example, information on issues of sexual orientation, aging, women and work, or mental health can be provided, accompanied by offers of consultive support for educating their constituencies. Educational resource needs in community organizations also might be addressed, for example, through donations of books and magazines featuring LGB themes to local libraries or raising funds to create a women's resource room at a community center.

Other avenues of community advocacy in regard to gender and sexuality include writing letters to the editors of local and national newspapers, magazines, and professional newsletters, as well as activities targeting other media (e.g., petitions to support the inclusion of gay characters on television or to protest violence against women in pornographic films). Community-based support groups and chapters of national organizations (e.g., Gay and Lesbian Parents Coalition International and Parents and Friends of Lesbians and Gays) also can be established. Counseling psychologists interested in political advocacy might work toward repealing state sodomy laws and decriminalizing homosexuality, instituting antidiscrimination and civil rights legislation, and supporting same-sex marriage legislation. Important forensic efforts can be undertaken in providing expert witness testimony in court cases involving issues such as workplace discrimination, child custody, and sexual harassment, assault, and abuse.

The Workplace

It has been argued often in the literature on women's career development that the intersection between people's work lives and personal lives is inevitable and critical, and that counseling and other vocational interventions too often dichotomize spheres related to work and home (Fassinger, in press; Fassinger & O'Brien, in press; Harmon & Meara, 1994; Richardson, 1993). This may be especially harmful to LGB people, who already are struggling with hidden and invisible identities, where interventions that separate work and home widen the gap between private and public aspects of self and thus reinforce stigma and shame (Fassinger, in press). Interventions, whether ameliorative or preventive, should attend to work and home in an integrated way, with "vocational" interventions including attention to one's emotional and social life, and "psychosocial" interventions incorporating work issues.

There is great potential for prevention and advocacy efforts directed toward career issues and the workplace (Fassinger, 1993,1998, in press; Fassinger & O'Brien, in press). Targets for change might include (1) instituting mandatory onsite child care for working parents, with acute care for temporary illnesses and liberal family leave policies; (2) abolishing the rigid 40 to 60-hour in-house work week and creating more flextime and job-share arrangements; (3) requiring on-the-job training for employers and personnel specialists in gender-fair, gay-affirmative hiring and harassment policies and practices; (4) providing onsite educational programming on gender and sexuality issues for workers; (5) instituting domestic partner benefits for LGB couples and families; (6) ensuring antidiscrimination clauses in organizational documents (including employment contracts); (7) ensuring that vocational resources (e.g., books, brochures, films) used in schools and counseling centers portray female and openly gay workers across a variety of occupations; (8) establishing workplace and community networks that provide mentoring and cross-generational learning for women and LGB workers; (9) examining testing materials used in vocational intervention to ensure their applicability to women and LGB people; and (10) providing a sociopolitical analysis of contextual factors related to gender and sexual orientation in vocational decisions and behaviors (e.g., an educational presentation for workers that highlights ways in which gender socialization manifests itself in male and female behaviors in the workplace).

Mental Health Arena

In addition to educational programming regarding gender and sexual orientation in mental health that counseling psychologists might offer in schools, communities, and workplaces, there also is direct advocacy that can be done in the professional arena. Training activities targeted at other mental health professionals (e.g., social workers, counselors, family therapists) might be undertaken, as some may possess limited knowledge regarding gender and sexuality. Counseling psychologists also might participate actively in debates about diagnosis, and the radical approach taken by Caplan (1995) in proposing alternative diagnoses grounded in the harmful effects of gender roles can be instructive in this regard. Normal problems in living have been claimed as the therapeutic specialty of counseling psychologists, and it would seem that difficulties arising from socialized expectations regarding gender and sexuality fit within that purview. Because many counseling psychologists (willingly or reluctantly) use the *DSM-IV,* advocating for the inclusion of normal problems of living (currently the V-Codes in the *DSM-IV*) as reimbursable categories of treatment would help to ensure that clients could receive needed interventions without being overdiagnosed or overtaxed financially. Leaving diagnostic issues to be decided by clinical psychologists and psychiatrists does not well serve the interests of either clients or the counseling psychology profession. Finally, as a psychological specialty that claims a preventive focus, counseling psychology needs, as a field, to better train new professionals for prevention and advocacy roles. This implies rather extensive changes in graduate training programs.

Implications for Training

There is evidence that the current training of most counseling psychology graduate students in regard to gender and sexuality is inadequate or grounded in implicit sexist and heterosexist assumptions and practices (Atkinson & Hackett, 1998; Buhrke & Douce, 1991; Croteau, Bieschke, Phillips, & Lark, 1998; Mintz, Rideout, & Bartels, 1994; Nickerson & Kremgold-Barrett, 1990; J.C. Phillips & Fischer, 1998). For example, Mintz et al. found that over half of a national sample of advanced graduate students in clinical and counseling psychology had never heard of the Principles for the Counseling and Psychotherapy of Women (APA Division 17 Committee on Women, 1979), despite their publication 15 years before. Fifty-eight percent of the sample reported that no courses related to women or gender were offered in their programs, only about 15% had taken such a course, and most of the courses (83%) had been electives.

Similarly, a recent study (J.C. Phillips & Fischer, 1998) of the experiences of over 100 clinical and counseling psychology graduate students revealed that the modal number of hours of didactic training received in LGB issues, and LGB clients seen in practica, was zero. Almost three quarters of the sample reported never having had a supervisor with expertise in LGB issues, and half of the respondents had never been encouraged to explore their heterosexist biases in coursework or supervision. Although counseling psychology programs tended to provide more training in LGB issues than did clinical programs, the authors noted that much of the expertise students were developing arose from their own individual initiative (e.g., choosing LGB topics for papers), rather than from systematic training provided by their programs. Finally, the majority of the students in this sample reported that there were no visible LGB faculty or faculty with LGB expertise in their programs (J.C. Phillips & Fischer, 1998).

These data suggest the need for increased attention to gender and sexuality in graduate training, and many scholars have provided detailed suggestions for infusing these issues into training programs, including didactic courses, practica and supervision, research, and program climate (Atkinson & Hackett, 1998; Buhrke & Douce, 1991; Croteau et al., 1998; Fassinger, in press; Fassinger & O'Brien, in press; Fassinger & Richie, 1997). Also important in training new professionals for prevention and advocacy activities related to gender and sexuality is more deliberate integration of these roles into the scientist-practitioner model, fostering a science-practice-advocacy model of professionalism (Fassinger & O'Brien, in press). This may require inclusion of coursework and experiential training in policy, forensics, consultation, and program development and evaluation. In addition, the science-practice-advocacy model suggests that research be considered a sociopolitical activity—that is, a scientific endeavor that is embedded in cultural realities and thus has social and political consequences.

In conclusion, many counseling psychologists find themselves in professional activities focusing on the amelioration of individual and interpersonal problems, rather than the preventive, developmental interventions and social advocacy which would help to eliminate the sources of those problems. This may be due, in part, to the fact that training programs tend to emphasize counseling and therapy rather than prevention and advocacy activities. Restructuring the model of professional training to include advocacy roles might provide one avenue for counseling psychologists to fulfill the unique potential of our field—to work proactively to create a world in which *all* people can develop their full range of possibilities.

REFERENCES

Adelmann, P.K., Antonucci, T.C., Crohan, S.E., & Coleman, L.M. (1989). Empty nest, cohort, and employment in the well-being of midlife women. *Sex Roles, 20,* 173–189.

American Psychological Association, Division 17 Committee on Women. (1979). Principles concerning the counseling and therapy of women. *Counseling Psychologist, 8,* 21.

American Psychological Association, Working Group on the Older Adult. (1998). What practitioners should know about working with older adults. *Professional Psychology: Research and Practice, 29,* 413–427.

Anselmi, D.L., & Law, A.L. (1998). *Questions of gender: Perspectives & paradoxes.* Boston: McGraw-Hill.

Atkinson, D.R., & Hackett, G. (Eds.). *Counseling diverse populations* (2nd ed.). Boston: McGraw-Hill.

Baruch, G.K., Barnett, R.C., & Rivers, C. (1983). *Lifeprints: New patterns of love and work for today's women.* New York: New American Library.

Bergeron, S.M., & Senn, C.Y. (1998). Body image and sociocultural norms: A comparison of heterosexual and lesbian women. *Psychology of Women Quarterly, 22,* 385–401.

Betz, N.E. (1989). Implications of the null environment hypothesis for women's career development and for counseling psychology. *Counseling Psychologist, 17,* 136–144.

Betz, N.E. (1994). Basic issues and concepts in career counseling for women. In W.B. Walsh & S.H. Osipow (Eds.), *Career counseling for women* (pp. 1–42). Hillsdale, NJ: Erlbaum.

Betz, N.E., & Fitzgerald, L.F. (1987). *The career psychology of women.* Orlando, FL: Academic Press.

Blumenstein, P., & Schwartz, P. (1983). *American couples: Money, work, and sex.* New York: Morrow.

Bohan, J.S. (1996). *Psychology and sexual orientation: Coming to terms.* New York: Routledge & Kegan Paul.

Bradford, J., & Ryan, C. (1987). *The national healthcare survey: Final report.* Washington, DC: National Lesbian and Gay Health Foundation.

Brannon, L. (1999). *Gender: Psychological perspectives (2nd ed.).* Boston: Allyn & Bacon.

Breedlove, S.M. (1994). Sexual differentiation of the human nervous system. *Annual Review of Psychology, 45,* 389–418.

Bryant, S., & Demian, S. (1994). Relationship characteristics of American gay and lesbian couples: Findings from a national survey. *Journal of Gay and Lesbian Social Services, 1,* 101–117.

Buhrke, R.A., & Douce, L.A. (1991). Training issues for counseling psychologists in working with lesbian women and gay men. *Counseling Psychologist, 19,* 216–234.

Bussey, K., & Bandura, A. (in press). Social cognitive theory of gender development and differentiation. *Psychological Review.*

Caplan, P.J. (1995). *They say you're crazy: How the world's most powerful psychiatrists decide who's normal.* Reading, MA: Addison-Wesley.

Carlson, B.E., & Videka-Sherman, L. (1990). An empirical test of androgyny in the middle years: Evidence from a national survey. *Sex Roles, 23,* 305–324.

Carr, P.L., Ash, A.S., Friedman, R.H., Scaramucci, A., Barnett, R.C., Szalacha, L., Palepu, A., & Moskowitz, M.A. (1998). Relation of family responsibilities and gender to the productivity and career satisfaction of medical faculty. *Annals of Internal Medicine, 129,* 532–538.

Collins, P.H. (1998). Toward a new vision: Race, class, and gender as categories of analysis and connection. In D.L. Anselmi & A.L. Law (Eds.), *Questions of gender: Perspectives and paradoxes* (pp. 35–46). Boston: McGraw-Hill.

Conger, J. (1975). Proceedings of the American Psychological Association for the year 1974: Minutes of the annual meeting of the council of representatives. *American Psychologist, 30,* 620–651.

Cook, E.P. (1993). The gendered context of life: Implications for women's and men's career-life plans. *Career Development Quarterly, 41,* 227–237.

Coward, R.T., & Dwyer, J.W. (1990). The association of gender, sibling network composition, and patterns of parent care by adult children. *Research on Aging, 12,* 158–181.

Crosby, F.J. (1991). *Juggling: The unexpected advantages of balancing career and home for women and their families.* New York: Free Press.

Croteau, J.M. (Ed.). (1996). Career development of lesbians, gays, and bisexuals. *Journal of Vocational Behavior [Special issue], 48.*

Croteau, J.M., Bieschke, K.J., Phillips, J.C., & Lark, J.S. (Eds.). (1998). Lesbian, gay, and bisexual affirmative training. *Counseling Psychologist, 26,* 707–816.

Culp, L.N., & Beach, S.R.H. (1998). Marriage and depressive symptoms: The role and bases of self-esteem differ by gender. *Psychology of Women Quarterly, 22,* 647–663.

D'Augelli, A.R. (1991). Gay men in college: Identity processes and adaptations. *Journal of College Student Development, 32,* 140–146.

Deaux, K. (1998). Sorry, wrong number—A reply to Gentile's call. In D.L. Anselmi & A.L. Law (Eds.), *Questions of gender: Perspectives & paradoxes* (pp. 21–23). Boston: McGraw-Hill.

Diamant, L. (Ed.). (1993). *Homosexual issues in the workplace.* Washington, DC: Taylor & Francis.

Eldridge, N.S., & Gilbert, L.A. (1990). Correlates of relationship satisfaction in lesbian couples. *Psychology of Women Quarterly, 14,* 43–62.

Evans, N.J., & Wall, V.A. (Eds.). (1991). *Beyond tolerance: Gays, lesbians and bisexuals on campus.* Alexandria, VA: American College Personnel Association.

Fassinger, R.E. (1991). The hidden minority: Issues and challenges in working with lesbian women and gay men. *Counseling Psychologist, 19,* 157–176.

Fassinger, R.E. (1993). And gladly teach: Lesbian and gay issues in education. In L. Diamant (Ed.), *Homosexual issues in the workplace* (pp. 119–142). Washington, DC: Taylor & Francis.

Fassinger, R.E. (1996a). Adolescence: Options and optimization. *Counseling Psychologist, 24,* 491–497.

Fassinger, R.E. (1996b). Notes from the margins: Integrating lesbian experience into the vocational psychology of women. *Journal of Vocational Behavior, 48,* 160–175.

Fassinger, R.E. (1998, August). *Gender as a contextual factor in career services delivery: A modest proposal.* Paper presented at the annual meeting of the American Psychological Association, San Francisco.

Fassinger, R.E. (in press). Hitting the ceiling: Gendered barriers to occupational entry, advancement, and achievement. In L. Diamant & J. Lee (Eds.), *The psychology of sex, gender, and jobs: Issues and solutions.* Westport, CT: Greenwood Press.

Fassinger, R.E., & Morrow, S.L. (1995). OverCome: Repositioning lesbian sexualities. In L. Diamant & R. McAnulty (Eds.), *The psychology of sexual orientation, behavior, and identity: A handbook* (pp. 197–219). Westport, CT: Greenwood Press.

Fassinger, R.E., & O'Brien, K.M. (in press). Career counseling with college women: A scientist-practitioner-advocate model of intervention. In D.A. Luzzo (Ed.), *Career development of college students: Translating theory and research into practice.* Washington, DC: American Psychological Association.

Fassinger, R.E., & Richie, B.S. (1997). Sex matters: Gender and sexual orientation in training for multicultural counseling competency. In D. Pope-Davis & H. Coleman (Eds.), *Multicultural counseling competencies: Assessment, education and training, and supervision.* Thousand Oaks, CA: Sage.

Fausto-Sterling, A. (1998). The five sexes: Why male and female are not enough. In D.L. Anselmi & A.L. Law (Eds.), *Questions of gender: Perspectives & paradoxes* (pp. 24–28). Boston: McGraw-Hill.

Fitzgerald, L.F., & Weitzman, L.M. (1992). Women's career development: Theory and practice from a feminist perspective. In Z. Leibowitz & D. Lea (Eds.), *Adult career development* (2nd ed., pp. 124–160). Alexandria, VA: National Career Development Association.

Frable, D.E.S. (1997). Gender, racial, ethnic, sexual, and class identities. *Annual Review of Psychology, 48,* 139–162.

Frederick, C.M., & Grow, V.M. (1996). A mediational model of autonomy, self-esteem, and eating disordered attitudes and behaviors. *Psychology of Women Quarterly, 20,* 217–228.

Friend, R.A. (1990). Older lesbian and gay people: A theory of successful aging. *Journal of Homosexuality, 20,* 99–118.

Garnets, L., Hancock, K.A., Cochran, S.D., Goodchilds, J., & Peplau, L.A. (1991). Issues in psychotherapy with lesbians and gay men: A survey of psychologists. *American Psychologist, 46,* 964–972.

Gentile, D.A. (1998). Just what are sex and gender anyway? A call for a new terminological standard. In D.L. Anselmi & A.L. Law (Eds.), *Questions of gender: Perspectives & paradoxes* (pp. 14–17). Boston: McGraw-Hill.

Gilbert, L.A. (1992). Gender and counseling psychology: Current knowledge and directions for research and social action. In S.D. Brown & R.W. Lent (Eds.), *Handbook of counseling psychology* (2nd ed., pp. 383–418). New York: Wiley.

Gilbert, L.A., & Scher, M. (1999). *Gender and sex in counseling and psychotherapy.* Boston: Allyn & Bacon.

Gomez, M.J., Fassinger, R.E., & Prosser, J. (1997, August). *The career development of Latinas: An emerging model.* Paper presented at the annual meeting of the American Psychological Association, Chicago.

Gonsiorek, J.C. (1993). Threat, stress, and adjustment: Mental health and the workplace for gay and lesbian individuals. In L. Diamant (Ed.), *Homosexual issues in the workplace* (pp. 243–264). Washington, DC: Taylor & Francis.

Gonsiorek, J.C. (1995). Gay male identities: Concepts and issues. In A.R. D'Augelli & C.J. Patterson (Eds.), *Lesbian, gay, and bisexual identities over the lifespan: Psychological perspectives* (pp. 24–47). New York: Oxford University Press.

Goodman, M.J. (1982). A critique of menopause research. In A.M. Voda, M. Dinnerstein, & S.R. O'Donnell (Eds.), *Changing perspectives on menopause* (pp. 273–288). Austin: University of Texas Press.

Harbeck, K.M. (Ed.). (1992). *Coming out of the classroom closet: Gay and lesbian students, teachers, and curricula.* New York: Haworth Press.

Hare-Mustin, R.T., & Maracek, J. (1990). *Making a difference: Psychology and the construction of gender.* New Haven, CT: Yale University Press.

Harmon, L.W., & Meara, N.M. (1994). Contemporary developments in women's career counseling: Themes of the past, puzzles for the future. In W.B. Walsh & S.H. Osipow (Eds.), *Career counseling for women* (pp. 355–368). Hillsdale, NJ: Erlbaum.

Harris, M.B. (Ed.). (1997). *School experiences of gay and lesbian youth: The invisible minority.* New York: Haworth Press.

Hatch, L.R. (1995). Gray clouds and sliver linings: Women's resources in later life. In J. Freeman (Ed.), *Women: A feminist perspective* (5th ed., pp. 182–196). Mountain View, CA: Mayfield.

Hollin, C.R. (1987). Sex roles in adolescence. In D.J. Hargreaves & A.M. Colley (Eds.), *The psychology of sex roles* (pp. 176–197). New York: Hemisphere Press.

Hollingsworth, M., Tomlinson, M., & Fassinger, R.E. (1998, March). *Career journeys of highly achieving lesbians.* Presented at the annual conference of the Association for Women in Psychology, Baltimore.

Hynie, M., & Lydon, J.E. (1995). Women's perceptions of female contraceptive behavior: Experimental evidence of the sexual double standard. *Psychology of Women Quarterly, 19,* 563–581.

Hynie, M., Lydon, J.E., & Taradash, A. (1997). Commitment, intimacy, and women's perceptions of premarital sex and contraceptive readiness. *Psychology of Women Quarterly, 21,* 447–464.

Joiner, G.W., & Kashubeck, S. (1996). Acculturation, body image, self-esteem, and eating-disorder symptomatology in adolescent Mexican American women. *Psychology of Women Quarterly, 20,* 419–435.

Kinsey, A.C., Pomeroy, W.B., Martine, C.E., & Gebhard, P.H. (1953). *Sexual behavior in the human female.* Philadelphia: Saunders.

Kite, M.E. (1994). When perception meets reality: Individual differences in reactions to lesbians and gay men. In B. Greene & G.M. Herek (Eds.), *Lesbian and gay psychology: Theory, research, and clinical applications* (pp. 25–53). Thousand Oaks, CA: Sage.

Klein, F. (1993). *The bisexual option* (2nd ed.). New York: Harrington Park Press.

Knutson, J.F. (1995). Psychological characteristics of maltreated children: Putative risk factors and consequences. *Annual Review of Psychology, 46,* 401–431.

Konicus, J. (1999, January 23). Down and dirty: Leaving housework in the dust. *Washington Post.*

Kurdek, L.A. (1994). The nature and correlates of relationship quality in gay, lesbian, and heterosexual cohabiting couples: A test of individual difference, interdependence, and discrepancy models. In B. Greene & G.M. Herek (Eds.), *Lesbian and gay psychology* (pp. 133–155). Thousand Oaks, CA: Sage.

Kurdek, L.A. (1995a). Developmental changes in relationship quality in gay and lesbian cohabiting couples. *Developmental Psychology, 31,* 86–94.

Kurdek, L.A. (1995b). Lesbian and gay couples. In A.R. D'Augelli & C.J. Patterson (Eds.), *Lesbian, gay, and bisexual identities over the lifespan: Psychological perspectives* (pp. 243–261). New York: Oxford University Press.

Landrine, H. (Ed.). (1995). *Bringing cultural diversity to feminist psychology: Theory, research, and practice.* Washington, DC: American Psychological Association.

Landrine, H., Klonoff, E.A., Gibbs, J., Manning, V., & Lund, M. (1995). Physical and psychiatric correlates of gender discrimination: An application of the schedule of sexist events. *Psychology of Women Quarterly, 19,* 473–492.

Lerner, R.M., & Galambos, N.L. (1998). Adolescent development: Challenges and opportunities for research, programs, and policies. *Annual Review of Psychology, 49,* 413–446.

Lester, R., & Petrie, T.A. (1998). Physical, psychological, and social correlates of bulimic symptomatology among African American college women. *Journal of Counseling Psychology, 45,* 315–321.

Maccoby, E.E. (1998). *The two sexes: Growing up apart, coming together.* Cambridge, MA: Harvard University Press.

Mansfield, P.K., Koch, P.B., & Voda, A.M. (1998). Qualities midlife women desire in their sexual relationships and their changing sexual response. *Psychology of Women Quarterly, 22,* 285–303.

Martz, D.M., Handley, K.B., & Eisler, R.M. (1995). The relationship between feminine gender role stress, body image, and eating disorders. *Psychology of Women Quarterly, 19,* 493–508.

McNaron, T.A.H. (1997). *Poisoned ivy: Lesbian and gay academics confronting homophobia.* Philadelphia: Temple University Press.

Messner, M.A., & Sabo, D.F. (1994). *Sex, violence, and power in sports: Rethinking masculinity.* Freedom, CA: Crossing Press.

Mintz, L.B., Rideout, C.A., & Bartels, K.M. (1994). A national survey of interns' perceptions of their preparation for counseling women and the atmosphere of their graduate education. *Professional Psychology: Research and Practice, 25,* 221–227.

Montgomery, R.J.V., & Kamo, Y. (1989). Parent care by sons and daughters. In J.A. Mancini (Ed.), *Aging parents and adult children* (pp. 213–230). Lexington, MA: Heath.

Morrow, S.L (1997). Career development of lesbian and gay youth: Effects of sexual orientation, coming out, and homophobia. In M.B. Harris (Ed.), *School experiences of gay and lesbian youth* (pp. 1–16). New York: Haworth Press.

Nash, H.C., & Chrisler, J.C. (1997). Is a little (psychiatric) knowledge a dangerous thing? The impact of premenstrual dsyphoric disorder on perceptions of premenstrual women. *Psychology of Women Quarterly, 21,* 315–322.

Nickerson, E.T., & Kremgold-Barrett, A. (1990). Gender-fair psychotherapy in the United States: A possible dream? *International Journal for the Advancement of Counselling, 13,* 39–48.

Noll, S.M., & Fredrickson, B.L. (1998). A mediational model linking self-objectification, body shame, and disordered eating. *Psychology of Women Quarterly, 22,* 623–636.

Noonan, B., & Fassinger, R.E. (1998, March). *Empowering the challenged: A qualitative analysis of the career development of highly achieving women with physical and sensory disabilities.* Paper presented at the annual conference of the Association for Women in Psychology, Baltimore.

Padgett, D. (1988). Aging minority women: Issues in research and health policy. *Women & Health, 14,* 213–225.

Patterson, C.J. (1994). Children of the lesbian baby boom: Behavioral adjustments, self concepts, and sex role identity. In B. Greene & G.M. Herek (Eds.), *Lesbian and gay psychology* (pp. 156–175). Thousand Oaks, CA: Sage.

Patterson, C.J. (1995a). Families of the lesbian baby boom: Parents' division of labor and children's adjustment. *Developmental Psychology, 31,* 115–123.

Patterson, C.J. (1995b). Lesbian mothers, gay fathers, and their children. In A.R. D'Augelli & C.J. Patterson (Eds.), *Lesbian, gay, and bisexual identities over the lifespan: Psychological perspectives* (pp. 262–291). New York: Oxford University Press.

Patterson, C.J. (1995c). Sexual orientation and human development: An overview. *Developmental Psychology, 31,* 3–11.

Peplau, L.A. (1991). Lesbian and gay relationships. In J.C. Gonsiorek & J.D. Weinrich (Eds.), *Homosexuality: Research implications for public policy* (pp. 177–196). Newbury Park, CA: Sage.

Peplau, L.A., & Cochran, S.D. (1990). A relationship perspective on homosexuality. In D.P. McWirther, S.A. Sanders, & J.M. Reinisch (Eds.), *Homosexuality/heterosexuality* (pp. 321–349). New York: Oxford University Press.

Perez, R., DeBord, K., & Bieschke, K.J. (Eds.). (1999). *Handbook of counseling and therapy with lesbians, gays, and bisexuals.* Washington, DC: American Psychological Association.

Phillips, J.C., & Fischer, A.R. (1998). Graduate students' training experiences with lesbian, gay, and bisexual issues. *Counseling Psychologist, 26,* 712–734.

Phillips, S.D., & Imhoff, A.R. (1997). Women and career development: A decade of research. *Annual Review of Psychology, 48,* 31–59.

Prosser, J., Chopra, S., & Fassinger, R.E. (1998, March). *A qualitative study of the careers of prominent Asian American women.* Paper presented at the annual conference of the Association for Women in Psychology, Baltimore.

Quam, J.K., & Whitford, G.S. (1992). Adaptation and age-related expectations of older gay and lesbian adults. *Gerontologist, 32,* 367–374.

Reid, J.D. (1995). Development in late life: Older lesbian and gay lives. In A.R. D'Augelli & C.J. Patterson (Eds.), *Lesbian, gay, and bisexual identities over the lifespan: Psychological perspectives* (pp. 215–242). New York: Oxford University Press.

Richardson, M.S. (1993). Work in people's lives: A location for counseling psychologists. *Journal of Counseling Psychology, 40,* 425–433.

Richie, B.S., Fassinger, R.E., Linn, S.G., Johnson, J., Prosser, J., & Robinson, S. (1997). Persistence, connection, and passion: A qualitative study of the career development of highly achieving African American/black and white women. *Journal of Counseling Psychology, 44,* 133–148.

Rofes, E. (1997). Schools: The neglected site of queer activists. In M.B. Harris (Ed.), *School experiences of gay and lesbian youth: The invisible minority* (pp. xiii–xix). New York: Haworth Press.

Rostosky, S.S., & Travis, C.B. (1996). Menopause research and the dominance of the biomedical model 1984–1994. *Psychology of Women Quarterly, 20,* 285–312.

Rothblum, E. (1994). Transforming lesbian sexuality. *Psychology of Women Quarterly, 18,* 627–641.

Ryan, C., & Futterman, D. (1998). *Lesbian & gay youth: Care & counseling.* New York: Columbia University Press.

Savin-Williams, R.C. (1995). Lesbian, gay male, and bisexual adolescents. In A.R. D'Augelli & C.J. Patterson (Eds.), *Lesbian, gay, and bisexual identities over the lifespan: Psychological perspectives* (pp. 165–189). New York: Oxford University Press.

Scrivner, R., & Eldridge, N.S. (1995). Lesbian and gay family psychology. In R.H. Mikesell, D.D. Lusterman, & S.H. McDaniel (Eds.), *Family psychology and systems therapy: A handbook.* Washington, DC: American Psychological Association.

Sears, J.T. (1991). *Growing up gay in the south: Race, gender, and journeys of the spirit.* New York: Harrington Park Press.

Stanton, A.L., & Gallant, S.J. (Eds.). (1995). *The psychology of women's health.* Washington, DC: American Psychological Association.

Strickland, B.R. (1988). Sex-related differences in health and illness. *Psychology of Women Quarterly, 12,* 381–399.

Tavris, C. (1992). *The mismeasure of woman.* New York: Simon & Schuster.

Unger, R., & Crawford, M. (1996). *Women and gender: A feminist psychology (2nd ed.).* New York: McGraw-Hill.

Unger, R., & Crawford, M. (1998). Sex and gender—The troubled relationship between terms and concepts. In D.L. Anselmi & A.L. Law (Eds.), *Questions of gender: Perspectives & paradoxes* (pp. 18–20). Boston: McGraw-Hill.

Wagner, W.G. (1996). Optimal development in adolescence: What is it and how can it be encouraged? *Counseling Psychologist, 24,* 360–399.

Ward, L.M., & Wyatt, G.E. (1994). The effects of childhood sexual messages on African-American and white women's adolescent sexual behavior. *Psychology of Women Quarterly, 18,* 183–202.

Wasserman, E.R. (1998). Women in the National Academy: Their lives as scientists and as women. *Magazine of the Association of Women in Science, 27,* 6–10.

West, C., & Zimmerman, D.H. (1987). Doing gender. *Gender & Society, 1,* 125–151.

Wyatt, G.E., & Riederle, M.H. (1994). Reconceptualizing issues that affect women's sexual decision-making and sexual functioning. *Psychology of Women Quarterly, 18,* 611–626.

CHAPTER 12

Role of Race and Social Class in Development: Implications for Counseling Psychology

NADYA A. FOUAD
MICHAEL T. BROWN

What we know and what we need to know about the role of race and social class in human development is the focus of this chapter. The relevant body of knowledge is extensive and very diverse, representing the intersection of many disciplines. In addition to sociologists, anthropologists, geographers, and philosophers, psychologists have examined various aspects of the roles of race and class in human development; each discipline provides somewhat differing explanations. Most sociologists view race and class as components of social structure that determine, among other things, group membership, group identity, and human interaction (Chow, 1996). Some anthropologists view race and class as explanatory variables in understanding the organization, function, and cultural expressions of different societies (Ingham, 1996). Some geographers examine genetic differences and how differences in the physical environment give rise to different racial groups (Cavalli-Sforza, Menozzi, & Piazza, 1994), and some philosophers have expounded on the philosophic meaning of the word "race" (Lang, 1997; Zack, 1997). Common to the work of sociologists, anthropologists, and geographers is a group-level focus in which race and class are viewed as features of social group organization, rather than as individual difference variables.

As psychologists, and especially as counseling psychologists, we are primarily interested in the psychological influence of race and social class on the development and expression of individual behavior. We want to know, for example, the influence of race and class on the problems and issues that face our clients and on the processes and outcomes associated with helping to alleviate client distress. Our client may be a second-generation Mexican American male from a lower socioeconomic background whose family speaks Spanish in the home, and who is now the first in his family to attend college. We want to know how this client's racial and socioeconomic context have shaped his identity, perspectives, problems and challenges, behavioral repertoire, and options. We want to know if our perceptions of his behavior and manner of life influence our response to him as therapists. We also want to know to what extent his race and socioeconomic background frame his phenomenological perspective, and we want to know how his perspective interacts (positively and negatively) with our own. To be of optimal assistance to our clients, we want to know the extent to which race and socioeconomic status influence important developmental life roles and activities (e.g., playing, learning, working, and parenting). Of course, we also want to know how our client's race and class will affect our counseling with him. In short, we want to know the psychological, psychosocial, and psychotherapeutic consequences of racial background and socioeconomic context.

As counseling psychologists, it is critical that we understand that all of our clients are products of multifaceted cultural contexts. This is true of clients high or low in socioeconomic status, who come from European American backgrounds, as well as clients who are members of other racial or ethnic groups. Clients' cultural contexts are the contexts in which they have learned about themselves and the world around them. Those contexts have shaped their behavior and have influenced their perceptions of themselves and of others, as well as others' perceptions of them. Clients' cultural contexts have also helped to form their perceptions of the problems they bring to counseling and the resources on which they may draw.

Understanding the role that racial and socioeconomic context plays in human development ultimately helps us to be more effective as counseling psychologists. In this chapter, we advance the idea that the extent to which a person is (or is perceived) as being different in social standing from others affects psychological development and behavior. We have termed this concept "differential status identity."

In this volume, Ponterotto, Fuertes, and Chen discuss the implications of race and class for multicultural counseling. The focus of our chapter is on psychological development, and we have divided it into four major sections. In the first section, we examine how psychologists have conceptualized the variables of race and class, and we set forth the definitions of race, ethnicity, culture, and social class that we use throughout the remainder of the chapter. In the second section, we suggest that race and class are dynamic variables that influence the way personal and social identities are constructed. We believe that race and social class, in and of themselves, do not directly influence development, but, rather, they influence how individuals view themselves as the same or different from others in society. It is the perception of difference from others on salient dimensions, or their differential status identity, that has a direct influence on development.

In the third section, we examine new formulations of, and research on, racial identity theory that support our perspective on differential status identity. Finally, in the fourth section we evaluate empirical work on social class from the perspective of differential status identity, and we review literature on the role of social class in four life roles and activities: leisure, learning, parenting, and working. Influences of race and cultural variables are also considered in other chapters in this *Handbook* (for example, see Arbona; Blustein, Juntenen, & Worthington; and Swanson & Gore). Focused considerations of sex and gender issues are included in the chapters by Fassinger and Enns.

We reviewed relevant articles from a variety of sources. We identified articles through literature databases in psychology (Pyschinfo, Psychlit), as well as relevant books and chapters since the second edition of the *Handbook* to the present. In some cases, especially in the review of the social class literature, important early works are cited. Space precludes a review of all possible articles related to psychological influence of race and social class. Rather, we have identified articles that are particularly salient to the areas that we reviewed, as well as those that were particularly well conceived or theoretically important.

CONCEPTIONS OF RACE AND SOCIAL CLASS

Defining the terms race and social class is important to the reader's understanding of this chapter. There is, however, little general consensus about what "race" is and how race and social class should be indexed. With respect to the definition of "race," the lack of consensus in definition has led to confounding it with other terms, including "culture," "ethnicity," "ethnic group," and "cultural group."

Members of the general public appear to believe that U.S. citizens primarily comprise five racial groups (sometimes referred to as Asians, Blacks, Whites, Hispanics, and Native Americans). However, the terms employed to label these groups have resulted in a confusing mix of options that reflect race, ethnic group, national origin, and linguistic heritage (Betancourt & López, 1993). The use of racial categories is highly variable and arbitrary, reflecting historical precedent, law, politics, ancestry, emotions, racial physiognomy, and socioeconomic status (Beutler, Brown, Crothers, Booker, & Seabrook, 1996; Zuckerman, 1990). For example, individuals who were born in, or are descendants of people born in, Central or South America are commonly classified as

Hispanic or Latino. This connotes a heritage from Spanish conquerors, even though individuals may also have descended from Africa, from indigenous tribes, or from other European nationalities. Thus, the label Hispanic encompasses individuals from many countries, cultures, languages (e.g., Spanish, Portuguese, French), and backgrounds, and thus the label Hispanic cannot be used as a descriptor of any single set of psychological variables.

Although the scientific validity of the concept of race has been challenged (e.g., Beutler et al., 1996; Cavalli-Sfroza et al., 1994; Zuckerman, 1990), so much sociopolitical meaning has been tied to the term "race," with important psychological consequences for individuals, that it is virtually impossible to abandon it. Helms (1994, 1995) observed that although racial groups may not be biologically distinct, nonetheless they can be distinguished by pervasive and seemingly intractable conditions of domination and oppression. We define "race" as a social stratification construct based on visible physical features, as well as historical and political characteristics (Brown & Pinterits, in press). As a social stratification construct, race is construed to influence behavior. We share the view that, even though geneticists cannot find genotypic differences among different population groups, there are differential social and psychological consequences for individuals based on self- and other-perceived racial grouping. Perhaps, for that reason social scientists have looked for terminology to index the behavioral implications of variables such as race or racial group that have been used to differentiate among groups.

Some scholars have advocated the use of "ethnicity" or "culture" (as well as ethnic or cultural group) instead of race to connote the broader cultural context in which we develop and learn. The practice of substituting ethnicity (or culture) for race, however, has merely led to altering terminology without altering the operational definitions of these categories (Beutler et al., 1996). This problematic practice is most apparent in studies that classify subjects into racial or ethnic groups without knowing what race or ethnicity means to the individual, without knowing the salience of race or ethnicity to that individual, or without understanding the multiple contexts in which that individual has operated. Our examination of the controversy surrounding the definitions and terminology leads us to advocate that researchers stop this simplistic practice of racial or cultural group classification, and develop more meaningful ways to assess variance due to the influence of race or ethnic group on behavior.

We propose that it is best to think of race, racial group, and ethnic group as part of the learning context. In other words, identification with a particular group or groups is learned. "Ethnic group" membership derives from geographic place of origin and refers to a group of people who live, or once lived, in close proximity to one another and, as a consequence, share ways of thinking, feeling, and behaving learned from similar life circumstances shared over generations. "Ethnicity" refers to the ways of thinking, feeling, and behaving shared among people in close proximity who have had similar life circumstances over generations. Culture is an analogous but broader term than ethnicity in that it may not be tied to geography; it refers to the system of meanings, behaviors, and relationships acquired or learned from experiences in the environment that determine personal and social behavior, as well as relations to material and nonmaterial things. People who share culture are called a "cultural group." We are born into a cultural context that is the product of our parents' multiple contexts and that of necessity includes their race, geography, history, and other life circumstances, as well as their practices and beliefs that will influence our perceptions of ourselves as well as how others perceive us. The groups (racial, ethnic, and otherwise) to which the adults around us belong also partially shape our cultural context and learning. In addition, that context is shaped by the geographic location of the community in which we live, by our socioeconomic status, and by the structural interaction of those contexts with the larger societal group. Thus, we view culture as complex, multifaceted, and dynamic as it both influences and is influenced by individuals' behavior.

Turning from our discussion of race and culture to social class, review of the literature indicates that much less controversy surrounds its definition. However, we also found that socioeconomic status is typically indexed in a way that ignores the fact that status is a function of more than just level of educational attainment, income, or occupational prestige (Brown, Fukunaga, Umemoto, & Wicker, 1996; Rossides, 1997). Rather, we suggest that "social status" reflects one's relation to levels and types of economic resources, in addition to social valuation and access to societal control and influence (Brown et al., 1996; Rossides, 1997).

Contrary to our discussion, we have continued to use terms such as "member of a racial or ethnic minority" and "racial group" throughout this chapter. Our task was to review and critically evaluate the theoretical and empirical literature on race and social class. It was impossible to do this without adopting the language used by individuals conducting studies. We therefore have used these terms to convey the purpose and goal of individual studies or theoretical perspectives.

As we have noted, controversies about the definition of race, culture, and social class occurred as social scientists attempted to explain and predict the influences of these variables on behavior. However, although it is important to have common understanding of these concepts, we also need to understand how they influence development and behavior. How is it that people of similar cultural background evidence different behaviors or, conversely, that some groups of individuals exhibit similar behavior? Like others (e.g., Atkinson & Thompson, 1992), we believe that race and social class influence the development of one's identity, or self. For example, a Polish American woman's race or ethnicity may not appear to exert a strong influence on her psychological and social development. But if that same woman is born into a family of lower social standing, and goes to school with those of higher social position, that difference in social standing may have had a profound influence on her psychological development. A framework is needed to explain how this influence occurs.

NEED FOR AN INTEGRATIVE FRAMEWORK

Psychologists began to examine ways that people differ and the ways that culture influences behavior after they acknowledged that it is important to indicate the sex and racial makeup of their samples (see Jackson, 1995, and Sue & Sue, 1990, for historical perspectives specific to counseling psychologists). As a result, researchers began to find that categorizing individuals into racial groups was one way to explain the variance in their studies. However, they also found that racial grouping was too gross a measure to be reliable or even useful. Consequently, psychologists called for greater attention to within group differences, recognizing that individuals differed, even when they may have self-identified as belonging to a particular racial or ethnic group. In other words, psychologists acknowledged that all African Americans were not the same, and neither were all Hispanics, Native Americans, Asians, or European Americans. People in the same racial or ethnic group did not have the same racial or ethnic identity.

Studies examining within-racial group differences have been less prevalent than might be expected, but theories have abounded that propose mechanisms by which those differences occurred. Examples of the latter include racial identity theory (W.E. Cross, 1995a, 1995b; Helms, 1995), ethnic identity theory (Phinney, 1993), and acculturation models (Atkinson & Thompson, 1992). It has been accepted that these variables may have different and independent effects on development; however, it has also been recognized at times that their contributions are confounded.

We believe that race and socioeconomic status, in combination, constitute important features of one's cultural context. They influence one's perceived social status; this status is reflected in identity. As first steps in constructing an integrative framework to study the influence of race and social class, we drew on the intergroup relations literature, as well as on the literature on the construct of the self. We begin with a discussion of the self and integrate the intergroup relations literature as relevant in that presentation. We then discuss the self in the social context, discussing development of social standing. Finally, we propose the construct of differential status identity to describe the influence of differences in social standing; it is through this construct that we believe that race and social class influence the development of the self.

Self: Construct and Development

We examined the construct of the self because it is a powerful regulator of many aspects of human behavior, organizing and directing a wide variety of psychological and social phenomena (S.E. Cross & Madson, 1997). The self is a source of human agency and volition, regulating intentional behavior and permitting the person to function in the social world (Banaji & Prentice, 1994). As such, the self determines cognitions, emotions and motivations, and behaviors and behavioral intents. The self is a construct that is critically important to personality development and behavior (Banaji & Prentice, 1994; S.E. Cross & Madson, 1997).

Baumeister (1998) noted that the self represents three important elements or experiences: reflective consciousness, interpersonal being, and executive function. Reflective consciousness refers to self-awareness: the conscious attention turning back on itself. The element of interpersonal being expresses the idea that people exist in a social context. We learn who and what we are (and are not), in part, from other people, and this is reflected in membership in various social groups (i.e., ethnic, racial, and economic groups) and categories. Executive function expresses the idea that the self is not merely the passive consequence of environmental forces but, on the contrary, is an active agent and decision maker. It acts on its environment and on itself, taking a role in its own creation (or destruction).

The self is a dynamic cultural creation (Baumeister, 1998; Banaji & Prentice, 1994; Côté, 1996; S.E. Cross & Madson, 1997; Neisser, 1997; Vondracek, Lerner, & Schulenberg, 1986). Although we may be born with certain innate temperaments and behavioral predispositions, most scholars believe that the self continually and dynamically develops through reciprocal interaction within specific cultural settings. We participate in constructing the self via reflection and by our choice of social contexts and our social and material relations. Thus, the self is a product of our cultural world (or learning context) as much as it also shapes that world. The framework of that cultural world consists of ideals, values, events, geographies, histories, people, practices, symbols, and structures (physical and relational).

As the self develops, over time and experience, aspects of the self expand and become more complex, as do the number of social contexts in which the self participates (Baumeister & Sommer, 1997). Said another way, as we encounter new situations and roles, our "self" changes and develops (Demo, 1992; Vondracek et al., 1986). It is important to note that prevailing normative and social pressures shape the self. These circumscribe the options from which we execute behavioral choice (Côté, 1996); thus, for example, racism shapes the self, as does privilege. Behavioral patterns emerge to the extent that the self encounters and negotiates situations and roles that are similar over time (Markus, Mullally, & Kitayama, 1997).

Five of the central motivations directing the development of self are self-survival, self-improvement, self-enhancement, self-distinctiveness, and self-connectedness (Baumeister, 1998; Côté, 1996; S.E. Cross & Madson, 1997; Markus & Kitayama, 1991). The self seeks to maintain its existence (self-survival) and to further its movement toward an ideal self when possible (self-improvement). Self-enhancement refers to the desire to receive positive feedback about the self; and self-distinctiveness refers to the motivation to distinguish ourselves from others. Finally, we seek to maintain and increase connectedness with others (self-connectedness; Kemper, 1995).

Social Standing and Ordinant Groups

Scholars of the self and intergroup relations have generally not recognized that the social context of the self and the social groups to which a person may or may not belong are hierarchically ordered and arranged (Brewer & Miller, 1996; Kemper, 1995). All people in a given society are not equal, nor are the social groups to which they belong. The position of social groups relative to each other incorporate racial and socioeconomic information and result in differential resource access and influence. Furthermore, social positions are ranked differently in importance by the larger societal group and are rewarded accordingly.

Social positions, or social standings, are acquired by individuals and their families and are transmitted over generations, independent of biological or psychological attributes (Rossides, 1997). In the United States, social standing is based on economic resources, on educational and occupational status, as well as by sex, gender, race, religion, disability status, and physical appearance. Persons occupying similar social positions have similar life experiences and manifest similar psychological orientations and behaviors (Argyle, 1994; Brewer & Miller, 1996; Brown et al., 1996; Rossides, 1997). As a consequence, people in similar social positions form groups (Brewer & Miller, 1996).

Groups accorded higher social standing are "ordinant groups," connoting that they perceive themselves (and are perceived by others) to be of higher social standing in society (Brewer & Miller, 1996). There are ordinant groups in the larger society, as well as ordinant groups more proximal to the individual. Those in the larger societal group include Whites, males, Protestants, and those of higher social class, who have more economic resources, power, and prestige than others in society. Ordinant groups or persons more proximal to the individual may include family members, neighbors, or coworkers who have more economic resources, power, or prestige.

Social standings are hierarchically ordered such that there are ordinant and subordinate standings for individuals and the groups to which they ascribe or to which others ascribe them. Differences in social standings produce different selves, and this is reflected in different behavior (Brown et al., 1996; Côté, 1996; Rossides, 1997). The self can reflect multiple social standings with respect to economic, prestige, and power dimensions, and within these multiple standings, people develop characteristic ways of participating in their hierarchically ordered social and material worlds (Markus et al., 1997). White women in the United States, as an example, belong to both an ordinant group (Whites) and a subordinate group (women); if a White woman is poorly educated, she belongs to a subordinate group, but she belongs to an ordinant group if she is physically beautiful. Her belonging to both a subordinate and ordinate group will influence her psychological development, and the ways that she participates in society reflect selves that incorporates her multiple social standings.

People's assessments of their own social standing and the standing of others influence their behavior, and influence the behavior of others toward them (Centers, 1949; Rossides, 1997). For example, suppose that an upper middle-class White man's belief is that his social standing is superior to that of others. This may cause him to act in a particular way (such as expecting deference) and affect the behavior of others toward him (giving him deference). He may be gracious as a result of that deference; conversely, his behavior will be altered if he is not given "his due." His race and social class are incorporated within his social standing, and through that standing, influence the development of his "self."

Three categories of structural factors affect our social standing as well as the social standing of the groups to which we belong: economic factors, prestige, and power (cf. Brown et al., 1996; Rossides, 1997). Economic factors include indices of affluence, economic security and choice, and amount and degree of control over material and human resources. Such indices include but are not limited to income, wealth (e.g., liquid assets, personal property, real estate, stocks, bonds), occupational type, amount and type of education, family stability, and the education provided to children.

Prestige factors express how much an individual or group is prized or esteemed, or their degree of social valuation. Indicators of prestige include occupational prestige, subjective status, consumption behavior, group participation (including types of persons comprising the groups and the type of activities engaged in by the groups), and evaluations of racial, religious, and ethnic groups. It is noteworthy that race, ethnic group, and cultural behavior are considered prestige factors (Rossides, 1997). Racial physiognomy and cultural behavior elicit social reactions that indicate relative value, acceptance, and appreciation by the larger societal group (Brown & Pinterits, in press; Osipow & Fitzgerald, 1996).

Power factors include indices of control over the nature and distribution of social values, usually through political and legal institutions. Indicators of power factors include voting behavior and other types of political participation, political attitudes, and ability to influence public policy and legislation (including tax and education policies and laws). They also include access to and influence over government benefits (including entitlements for the rich and poor and housing ownership), and treatment by and influence over the legal system.

Research and theory on intergroup relations suggests that two pairs of the five central motivations of the self, discussed earlier, are proposed to operate antagonistically depending on level of social standing: self-enhancement versus improvement and distinctiveness versus connectedness. For example, a study by Hogg and Turner (1987) showed that when sex, a social stratifying variable, was made salient experimentally, males and females accentuated the sex-typicality of their self-perceptions. However, this was associated with lower self-esteem in the women as compared with conditions when sex was not made salient. In another study, Steele (1992) has shown that minority group members can embrace distinctive group identities though potentially at the cost of rejecting or defying majority group criteria for positive evaluation and achievement. These findings indicate that there can be self-enhancement value associated with self and social distinctiveness, but that this can be at the cost of self-improvement. The two studies also suggest that self-connectedness with ordinant group members may be associated with decreased self-enhancement and self-improvement.

As noted earlier, individuals can have multiple standings, based on their status with respect to each category of social structural factors (e.g., one can have high income and low prestige); thus, the influence of economic, prestige, and power factors can, theoretically, be independent of one another. However, a person's status in any one category can affect status in the other categories in significant ways. Consider what it means to be ascribed, by self or others, to the racial category of African American, which, as noted earlier, has been considered by the larger societal ordinant group to be a lower prestige factor (Rossides, 1997), but also has been related to economic and power factors. The history of African Americans in the United States has been one in which they have been valued as sources of entertainment and physical labor but not for their ability to manage and manipulate political and legal systems. Many currently have or control a small number of resources; in fact, many came here *as* economic resources. This disproportionate allocation of resources among racial groups in the United States is found despite research that has shown no relationship between behavior and racial physiognomy (Good, 1992; Rossides, 1997; Zuckerman, 1990).

Different races are perceived and valued differently, leading to differences in prestige and access to power and economic factors. A few findings reviewed by Rossides (1997) demonstrate these differences. The poverty rate of African Americans is three to four times higher than that of European Americans. In addition, African American unemployment is much higher and African American representation in top occupations is much lower. The amount and quality of higher education received by African Americans is much lower, and African American families are less stable. The rates of all serious diseases for African Americans are much higher, and received health care is generally inferior. Finally, African American arrest and imprisonment rates are much higher, as are the crime and legal system victimization rates.

This would indicate that the average social standing for African Americans is relatively low in prestige, as well as in accessability to economic resources and power. However, a particular individual may hold social standings very different from the modal standing for his or her group. Thus, for example, African Americans such as Oprah Winfrey or Colin Powell may have considerable affluence and educational attainment, provide the highest quality education for their children, and hold positions at the highest business and government levels. They receive considerable deference from others, associate with society's movers and shakers, evidence conspicuous consumption patterns, boast considerable political clout and influence over public attitudes and behavior, and receive beneficial governmental and legal treatment. This is quite different from the modal social standing for African Americans, and illustrates the considerable within-group differences in real and perceived social standing.

We believe that research findings of racial or ethnic group differences in behavior are due to the effect of racial or ethnic group membership on social standing. We also believe that social standings not only are multiple but multiply determined. Consequently, knowing an individual's ascribed racial or ethnic group status does not necessarily indicate that individual's real (or self- and socially perceived) social standing.

Salience of Social Standing

All dimensions of the self do not have equal significance. Just as the social and material world is hierarchically ordered and arranged, the various dimensions of the self are also arranged in such a way as to optimize satisfaction of the five motives: self-survival, self-improvement, self-enhancement, self-distinctiveness, and self-connectedness. Some dimensions of the self are more salient at times than others.

Salience depends on two factors: demands of the social and behavioral context and on the capacity of the person to satisfy those demands, real or perceived, and the relevance of the distinctions between in-groups and out-groups in a particular social situation (Brewer & Miller, 1996). Thus, the degree to which those distinctions differentiate the individual and the individual's in-group(s) from other individuals and out-groups also determines salience (see Brewer & Miller's, 1996, discussion of comparative fit).

We suggest that the most salient aspects of the self are those most relevant to the social and behavioral context in which a person is expected to function. It is also those on which the person (and the groups they represent) are either similar or different from those persons with more ordinant social standings. Thus, being of lower socioeconomic status is most salient when an individual associates with members of a higher socioeconomic status group. In our integrative framework, the more subordinate a person's social standing is and the more socially and behaviorally relevant the distinctions of individual and group characteristics are, the more salient are the dimensions of self on which the person is differentiated from the ordinant group. Distinctiveness from the ordinant group only operates for those areas that are salient to the individual. Thus, having less education than one's out-group is very salient in some contexts (e.g., being hired as a professor) and less salient in other contexts (being hired to play professional football). Differentiation from ordinant individuals and groups on salient dimensions is a powerful determinant of behavior and mediates the relationship between one's social standing and individual behavior.

The concept of salience has conceptual antecedents in counseling psychology, particularly in vocational psychology. As noted by Brown (Brown, 1995; Brown, Lum, & Voyle, 1997; Leong & Brown, 1995), over 40 years ago Anne Roe (Roe, 1956) suggested that social, as opposed to genetic, differences probably account for racial and ethnic group differences in personality development and career choice behavior. More recently, Roe (Roe & Klos, 1972; Roe & Lunneborg, 1990) argued that the determining issue for understanding the career choice behavior of a racial or ethnic group member is the extent to which an individual's social and experiential background differs from that of the social majority. Gottfredson (1986) also discussed the career choice behavior of "special groups" (including but not limited to racial and ethnic minority group members and women). She suggested that their choices likely depart from that of the general population to the extent that individual status on a number of risk factors markedly differentiates them from the general population and from their ascribed social groups. Differentiation from the ordinant cultural group and other racial and ethnic group referents might significantly affect career development (Brown, 1995; Brown & Pinterits, in press; Brown & Voyle, 1997) and other important aspects of psychological development.

To reiterate, construction of the self is a critical variable in psychological development. As it develops, the "self" is constituted of many different aspects, meaning it is multidimensional (S.E. Cross & Madson, 1997; Demo, 1992). For example, people develop conceptions of themselves and of themselves in relation to others, and others develop conceptions of them. A critical component of those conceptions of self and others is their internalized social standing. We argue that race and social class powerfully shape social standing. People with different social standings differentially learn what agency they have or do not have to shape the personal, interpersonal, and physical/material destinies of themselves and others in a society (the power factors). They learn standing-based methods for effecting such influence. They learn how important they are, or are not, and they learn what they are valued for (the prestige factors). In addition, they learn what standing-circumscribed resources they have, or do not have, access to for shaping their personal and social destinies. Such learning results in behavioral actions, efforts, and persistence (Bandura, 1997). Thus, the three structural dimensions of social standing are incorporated in and reflected by the self.

As an individual's social standing differs (or is perceived to differ) from that of a social group referent, that individual's psychological development evidences distinctiveness from that of the referent. In other words, we are proposing that being (or being perceived) as different from the general societal referent group shapes our psychological development differently than the development of those who are (or are perceived to be) less different. Thus, for example, if individuals' social standing does not (or is not perceived to) differ from that of White, middle-class males, they are likely to evidence behavioral patterns that are similar to them, even though they may not be White, middle-class, or male.

Differential Status Identity

We propose differential status identity (DSI) as a construct to understand and predict the psychological effects of race and social class. The concept is also useful for explaining within-racial, -ethnic, -social, and -class group differences. DSI is the identity derived from social standing differences from the ordinant group. It incorporates the psychological and psychosocial dimensions of race and social class that are social and behaviorally salient (real or perceived) and that differentiate individuals and their in-groups from members of ordinant out-groups. The influence of race and social class, however ascribed or achieved, operates through social stratification and the psychological consequences of such stratification. Thus, socioeconomic status will be a greater influence on the development of the poorest child in the class than it will be on the development of children closer to the modal socioeconomic status. Race will be a greater influence of the development of an African American than it will be for a White Anglo-Saxon in the United States, given the social distance between Blacks and Whites (Argyle, 1994) and the relatively higher social standing of Whites.

We are not suggesting that race and social class are not strong influences on the development of those belonging to ordinant groups, who may be less aware of their influence (i.e., privilege) on their development. Rather, we are suggesting that psychological consequences of social stratification operate more powerfully for those in the subordinate groups. We also note within-group differences among those presumed to be members of ordinant groups, as well. For example, Day, Cross, Ringseis, and Williams (1999) found that approximately 20% of Whites in their study of university library employees considered themselves to be part of an underrepresented group, due to religion, sexual orientation, job classification, or departmental affiliation. Day et al. termed this group the "nontraditional" underrepresented group; DSI would describe them as having affiliated with a subordinate group even though others may perceive them as belonging to the ordinant group.

The concept of DSI serves as a useful framework for understanding the impact of a host of cultural orientation variables, such as individual and collective selves (Turner, Hogg, Oakes, Reicher,

& Wetherell, 1987); independent and interdependent self-construals (Markus & Kitayama, 1991); individualism and collectivism (Kluckhohn & Strodtbeck, 1961; Singelis, Triandis, Bhawuk, & Gelfand, 1995; Triandis, McCusker, & Hui, 1990); racial identity (Atkinson & Thompson, 1992; Helms, 1990); ethnic identity (Baldwin, Duncan, & Bell, 1987; Landrine & Klonoff, 1994; Ruiz & Padilla, 1977); racial salience (Helms & Piper, 1994); acculturation (Padilla, 1980); cultural mistrust (Terrell & Terrell, 1981); and racism and discrimination (Howell, Frese, & Sollie, 1984; Landrine & Klonoff, 1996; McWhirter, 1997). A number of these concepts reflect the degree to which one affiliates, associates, or aligns with members of ordinant social groups and their members or to members of their ascribed social group (e.g., acculturation, cultural mistrust, racial identity, racial salience). DSI predicts that association with ordinant groups will be more predictive of behavior overall, but that in-group associations will be predictive of behavior in more parochial (in-group) contexts.

Other racial/cultural concepts address dimensions on which members of various social groups are expected to differ, especially ordinant and subordinate social groups, such as cultural values orientations and a number of other presumed culturally specific variables (e.g., face, Redding & Ng, 1982; Zane, 1993; or colorism, Brown, 1995). However, it should be noted that from the perspective of DSI, scholars would not expect simple status on supposedly culture-specific variables to differentiate among group members in terms of development and behavior. This would explain, for example, lack of differences found on coping strategies employed by Asian American and Caucasian students (Chang, 1996). Status on such variables would be expected to differentiate among groups only if the differentiating variable is (or is perceived to be) important to success in a given behavioral context and if members of the two groups differ in that success. If social groups differ on certain dimensions and if those dimensions are irrelevant to status differences between ordinant and subordinate groups, then the concept of DSI would lead us to suggest that such dimensions will not account for much variance in those dimensions.

We now turn to reviewing the theoretical and empirical literature related to one of the variables that has been proposed to explain the influence of race on psychological development, that is, racial identity. Racial identity theories were originally developed to help explain why some individuals depreciate their own racial or cultural group and others have a passionate allegiance to their group (e.g., Cross, 1995a; Helms, 1995). This literature is reviewed from the perspective of the differential status identity concept.

RACIAL IDENTITY AND DIFFERENTIAL STATUS IDENTITY

Theoretical Developments

The first racial identity theories focused on Black racial identity development (e.g., W.E. Cross, 1971, 1991; Helms, 1990). As W.E. Cross (1995a) put it, "Black researchers have been able to map out the four or five stages Black people go through when they tear down the 'old' identity and replace it with one that is more Black-oriented" (p. 53). More recently, theories have been developed to explain ethnic identity for Asians (Sodowsky, Kwan, & Pannu, 1995) and Mexican Americans (Bernal, Knight, Ocampo, Garza, & Cota, 1993), and racial attitudes of Whites (Helms, 1992), biracial individuals (Kerwin & Ponterotto, 1995), and ethnic adolescents (Phinney, 1993). Racial or ethnic group members are postulated to move from a depreciative perspective on their own racial or cultural group to a more appreciative perspective. They also are assumed to move from an appreciative perspective on the majority culture to a greater understanding of the role of the majority culture in oppressing their race or culture.

Central to conceptualizations of racial identity is that allegiance to one's own group is necessary for psychologically healthy functioning (Constantine, Richardson, Benjamin, & Wilson,

1998). In other words, moving from the ordinant group as the referent to the own group as referent is hypothesized to result in greater psychological health. This would suggest that greater identity with ordinant groups would be associated with greater stress, but also with better skills in coping with the ordinant group. Less salience of the ordinant group, and greater salience of the own in-group, would be associated with less stress, and better psychological health in terms of self-esteem—but all within a limited social context. With respect to a broader social and physical context, we would expect higher self-esteem, but lesser social comfort, lesser efficacy, and lesser achievement for those who do not identify with the ordinant group. In short, such individuals might feel very good about themselves and build a racial or ethnic enclave where they can function and achieve, but demonstrate greater disadvantage relative to individuals who are more broadly oriented.

W.E. Cross's (1971, 1995a, 1995b) theory was one of the first racial identity models (termed the Psychology of Nigrescence), and has recently been updated; DSI may play a role in explaining the findings that led to his revisions. The first of five stages in the Nigrescence Model, the preencounter stage, has been conceptualized as the stage in which African Americans are located before encountering themselves as Black individuals. Preencounter Blacks are hypothesized to move into the encounter stage when faced with a situation, or series of situations, that lead them to consider race as salient to their identity. Concomitantly, the individual experiences anger at White racism and the miseducation of White institutions. This stage is characterized by internal turmoil when individuals' concepts of their identity are challenged, as is their concept of the dominant culture.

The encounter stage gives way to the immersion/emersion stage, in which the Black individual is searching for a Black, or Afrocentric, identity. The immersion part of this phase refers to immersing the self in Black culture: literature, art, politics, history, and customs. This stage is an "immersion in Blackness and liberation from Whiteness," as the individual expresses rage at White institutions and people, and develops pride in being Black. In the emersion phase of this stage, the individual emerges from the turmoil and emotional upheaval to come to some resolution of the self in this newly shaped identity. The fourth phase of the Nigrescence model is the internalization phase, in which the individual internalizes the new identity. Blackness has a strong salience in that new identity. The reshaped new identity is not a new personality; rather, the individual's fundamental personality re-emerges. Finally, the last stage is the internalization-commitment stage in which Blacks develop a more sustained interest in Black concerns, translating their personal sense of Blackness into a long-term plan of action.

In W.E. Cross's initial model (1971), the preencounter stage was thought to be a stage in which Blacks hated all things associated with Black culture and, by extension, hated themselves. They were thought to have internalized White racism. In the revision to his theory, Cross acknowledged that there are individuals for whom the preencounter stage is characterized by a low perceived salience of race, as well as individuals who have an anti-Black perspective. He included individuals who view race as a problem, or as a social stigma, among those for whom race has low perceived salience. Although Cross originally suggested that Blacks in the preencounter phase were considered to be at risk for mental illness, his revised model posits that "the great majority of Pre-Encounter Blacks are probably as mentally healthy as Blacks in the more advanced stages of Nigrescence" (p. 104). In fact, he noted that in many cases Black success might have led to preencounter attitudes that minimize the impact of race or racism on identity.

Cross's latter point suggests that the role of differential status identity may operate in this stage in that some individuals with preencounter attitudes appear to have a desire to align with the ordinant group and a desire to differentiate from what they perceive as those in lower social standing. It also suggests that such individuals do not view themselves, and are not viewed by others, as different from the ordinant group. For those who are successfully differentiating from others in the more subordinate group (other Blacks) and aligning and affiliating with members of the more ordinant group (Whites), one would find relative advantage and life satisfaction though, perhaps, lower self-esteem if they also denigrate themselves as part of the subordinate group.

In the revised model, W.E. Cross (1995b) also recognized individual differences in the salience of Blackness to individuals in the internalized stage. For some, Blackness is central to the their self-definition, extending to a nationalistic perspective; others adopt a more multicultural focus. In this stage, "being Black is important to one's well-being, one's purpose in life, and one's sense of connection to other Blacks" (p. 119). However, in this stage, the individual may also bridge between Black culture and White culture, creating connections to non-Black individuals and organizations. Cross acknowledged that this may cause conflicts in the Black community between those who resist bridging between the two cultures, and others who want to create a more multicultural perspective. It may be that two groups of individuals with internalization attitudes have different referent groups. One group may see themselves as aligning with other groups to increase their relative social standing and decrease their differentiation from the ordinant group. The other group may continue to see their own racial group as the referent, and view the ordinant group as less desirable for alignment and affiliation.

Empirical Findings

We reviewed selected empirical tests of racial identity models and tests of the relationship between racial identity stages and various other constructs (e.g., achievement, tendency toward eating disorders, self-esteem). In our review of this literature, as well as in our review of the empirical research related to social class in the next section of this chapter, we wanted to be able to compare outcomes across studies. We also wanted to determine the magnitude of the effects of the studies, and, therefore, effect sizes were calculated for the quantitative studies we reviewed (Mullen, 1989). Following Cohen's (1988) recommendation, small, medium and large effect sizes relate to rs of .1, .3, and .5, respectively.

A premise of racial/ethnic identity theories is that race as a construct in the development of identity is more salient for those who identify themselves as African Americans or as another racial/ethnic group than for those who identify themselves as White. However, our concept of differential status identity suggests that the salience of race varies depending on how different one is (or is perceived to be), and with the importance of race to that difference. This was examined in three qualitative studies. Cunningham (1997) found that light-skinned African Americans, as opposed to dark-skinned African Americans, were concerned about being accepted by both European and African Americans. Jones (1997) discovered that women who felt different in visible and invisible ways incorporated those differences into their self-identity. Race mattered most explicitly for the Black women in her sample, and much less so for the White women. A.A. Young (1997) interviewed four low-income African American men, all in their early to mid-twenties, to examine the salience of race to their construction of their world. None of the men finished high school. Each had had little work experience, though all wanted to work and have a stable income. However, race was not viewed by two of the men as a factor in preventing that from occurring, whereas the other two viewed racial discrimination as an important factor in preventing them from economic success. The two who did not perceive racial discrimination as a barrier had significantly less interaction with the ordinant group, suggesting that differentiation from the ordinant group was not incorporated into their perspective of their social standing.

Racial identity theories also hypothesize that individuals who have internalized racial attitudes are more collectivistic (i.e., oriented toward the group) than individualistic (oriented toward self). It may be argued that within the United States, social standing of the ordinant group has been viewed as a result of individualistic traits (e.g., achievement or Protestant work ethic). As proposed in the differential status identity concept, for those high in social position, differentiation from others within or below one's ordinant group has survival, enhancement, and improvement value. However, for those lower in social position, alignment and affiliation with those within one's social position may have survival and enhancement value. Gaines et al. (1997) found no racial/ethnic differences in individualism, though they found a moderate to large effect size for the relationship between ethnic identity and collectivism ($r = .46$) and family orientation ($r = .54$).

Oyserman, Gant, and Ager (1995) also found a moderate effect size for the relationship between collectivism and ethnic identity for African Americans ($r = .42$), also finding that Whites were more likely to endorse the Protestant work ethic ($r = .21$). No differences were found across groups on individualism. It would have been useful to know if the African Americans and Whites in the Oyserman et al. study were comparable with respect to social class. As presented later, there are other studies showing that social class, a broader social status dimension than race, is positively associated with individualistic orientations and negatively associated with collectivistic orientations. Further, there is some suggestion that social class is a more powerful determinant of these orientations than is race.

Several studies found support for the hypothesized psychological health of the internalization stage, with rs ranging from .29 to .51, though some findings appear to be different for African American males relative to females. African Americans with internalized attitudes were found to have a sense of hope (for males, $r = .51$ and for females, $r = .32$). Females with internalized attitudes were also found to be higher on vocational identity ($r = .31$) (Jackson & Neville, 1998). Males with higher internalized attitudes were found to have a high student involvement in university activities compared with males in other identity stages ($r = .31$) (Taylor & Howard-Hamilton, 1995). Individuals in this stage were able to recognize and express their emotions (Dinsmore & Mallinckrodt, 1996), and had good problem-solving appraisal skills (Neville, Heppner, & Wang, 1997). Ford and Harris (1997) found a moderate effect size for achievement and internalized attitudes in a sample of gifted African American children; male underachievers had lower internalized racial attitudes than achieving boys, underachieving girls, or achieving girls. Internalized attitudes also have been consistently found to be related to self-esteem with effect sizes ranging from .17 to .45 (e.g., Goodstein & Ponterotto, 1997; Poindexter-Cameron & Robinson, 1997; Speight, Vera, & Derrickson, 1996). The findings with respect to the attitudes of internalization are, for the most part, consistent with the concept of differential status identity.

As noted earlier, Cross hypothesized that internalization attitudes would be related to greater mental health, and one of the features of the internalization stage is the motivation to, and facility for, making connections with others who are not Black. He called this a transcendant, or bridging function, connoting bridges with experiences, groups, organizations, and individuals who make up the non-Black world, particularly with White individuals, organizations, groups, and experiences. With respect to individuals with an internalized perspective, we might expect them to see themselves as less psychosocially differentiated from Whites, especially relative to Black individuals who would be characterized as being in the immersion-emersion stage.

In a study that used the African Self Consciousness Scale (Baldwin & Bell, 1985), a high African consciousness (corresponding to the internalization phase and immersion/emersion phase) and low stress cluster had the highest self esteem and perceived anger control (Chambers et al., 1998). This lends support to the positive health effects of the internalization stage. Phinney, Cantu, and Kurtz (1997), in a study of the relationship between ethnic identity and self-esteem, found that strong ethnic or American identity was the strongest predictor of self-esteem for all groups in their study (African American, Asian American, Latino, and White). This is consistent with the differential status identity concept. We would predict that, for individuals belonging to subordinate or perceived subordinate groups, affiliation with like others can have survival, improvement, and enhancement value, particularly when such persons anticipate negotiating ordinant culture institutions and systems that are perceived as antagonistic to subordinate group members. Together, these studies would suggest that differentiation of the self from members of the ordinant group and alignment with others at the same social standing have positive effects (e.g., self-enhancement and self-survival) for individuals, both psychologically and physically. However, we would also predict that such individuals would possess lower self-efficacy, but greater collective efficacy, for interacting with and influencing more ordinant groups and persons than individuals whose primary alignment is with the ordinant group.

Few studies specifically evaluated constructs related to the immersion/emersion or encounter stages, nor did studies that measure racial identity attitudes find significant relationships between attitudes related to these stages and other correlates. This may be related to concerns about the measures themselves (see Fischer, Tokar, & Serna, 1998; Tokar & Fischer, 1998; Yanico, Swanson, & Tokar, 1994). It may also be that individuals in these stages choose not to participate in university psychology class extra credit experiments and, thus, individuals in these stages were not well represented in these studies.

Consistent with the differential status identity concept, Goodstein and Ponterotto (1997) found that an orientation to other groups was inversely related to encounter attitudes ($r = -.43$). McCowan and Alston (1998) found small to moderate differences between senior and freshmen women in historically Black colleges (HBC) and predominantly White colleges (PWC) on racial identity. Freshmen women at the PWC endorsed more encounter and immersion/emersion attitudes than did senior PWC women ($r = .27$) though, overall, women at the PWC endorsed internalized attitudes more than did women at the HBC ($r = .21$). These findings lend some support for the hypothesis that encounters with the ordinant culture may lead to changes in attitudes. Those encounters may be beneficial in helping people develop race bridging or transcending attitudes and skills; they may also help in developing a consciousness of race.

Although limited support has been found for the relative lack of psychological health for those who endorse preencounter attitudes, the preencounter orientation is characterized by the lack of salience of race (W.E. Cross, 1995b). Consequently, the findings discussed above may reflect differing psychological phenomena. For some individuals, it may be that their real or perceived social standing is not that distinctive from ordinant groups. Indeed, we expect that for some, their perceived social position may be much higher than might be indicated by the sociostructural position of the racial or ethnic group to which they may be ascribed. For others, it may be that they are seeking alignment with ordinant groups rather than their own group. The latter case may have psychological implications for those aligned with ordinant groups who have been found to have lower self-esteem than those in other racial identity stages, with effect sizes ranging from .11 to .38 (Goodstein & Ponterotto, 1997; Poindexter-Cameron & Robinson, 1997; Speight et al., 1996). Students endorsing preencounter attitudes were more likely to self-designate as Other, American, or Black, though the effect was small (Speight et al., 1996). A small effect size was also found in a study by Arroyo and Zigler (1995), who examined the relationship between lack of salience of race and high achievement for both African Americans and European Americans and alienation from peers for both groups of low race–salient students. However, Arroyo and Zigler found that racelessness was related to anxiety and depression ($r = .22$ and .20, respectively) for African Americans. One way to view these findings is that African Americans and European Americans may be seeking alignment and affiliation with members of ordinant groups and not with like positioned or lower positioned persons (self-improvement), but that it may be at the expense of self-enhancement for African Americans.

As noted earlier, we would not expect culture-specific variables to explain differences among groups unless they are salient in differentiating them from ordinant groups. For example, if social groups do not differ in locus of control, it would not serve to differentiate among ordinant and subordinate groups, and thus would not be expected to account for differences among groups. That would explain why some studies have not found expected relations between racial identity and correlates. For example, Carter, DeSole, Sicalides, Glass, and Tyler (1997) found that neither psychosocial competence nor locus of control predicted racial identity attitudes. Carter et al. concluded that "one's capacity to be planful, and to cope in life is not directly associated with one's racial identity status." (pp. 68–69). Plummer (1996) did not find the expected pattern of attitude changes in racial identity due to cohort and age. Sanders Thompson (1996) did not find that racial identification mediated the impact of the experience of racism. In addition, Dinsmore and Mallinckrodt (1996) found no relationship between racial identity attitudes and eating disorders. Because racial identity status groups do not vary on these variables, we would assume that they are not related to salient distinctiveness from ordinant groups and, thus, to behavioral differences.

Measurement Concerns

One of the concerns with the literature on racial identity involves the measurement and meaning of key constructs. For example, do Helms's (1995) and W.E. Cross's (1995a, 1995b) concept of racial identity coincide with such variables as racial identity formation, racial identification, or racial socialization? Is racial identity the opposite of racelessness (Arroyo & Zigler, 1995) or the same as African self-consciousness (Chambers et al., 1998; Poindexter-Cameron & Robinson, 1997), or communal beliefs (Baldwin & Bell, 1985)? How do these concepts relate? Brookins (1994) examined the relationship among the Belief Systems Analysis Scale (BSAS; Montgomery, Fine, & James-Myers, 1990), the Racial Identity Attitude Scale (RIAS; Helms & Parham, 1990), and the African Self-Consciousness Scale (Baldwin & Bell, 1985), which tap components of an optimal worldview for African Americans. He found little correlation among constructs measured by the scales, concluding that each scale taps different constructs. Yet, many researchers who use the scales assume that they index racial identity. As we noted earlier, we would suggest that all of these constructs are reflections of affiliation with members of the ordinant or with the same social group.

Some researchers have expressed concerns about the psychometric properties of the scales, adding to the concerns about use of these instruments (e.g., Lemon & Waehler, 1996; Yanico et al., 1994). Others have developed new instruments to contribute to understanding of racial identity. Oyserman et al. (1995) added achievement as an African American to Helms's (1995) description of racial identity. They predicted that this component would be related to school persistence. This construct integrates appreciation for African American culture, awareness of prejudice and discrimination, and focus on individualism and achievement. We would also suggest that this construct indicates desire, intent, and ability to align and affiliate with real or perceived ordinants.

Smith and Brookins (1997) developed the Multi-Construct African American Identity Questionnaire to assess racial identity for adolescents. The measure taps orientation to own group, valuing own physical appearance, acceptance/rejection of African American stereotypes, and cooperative values. Landrine and Klonoff (1994, 1996) noted that one way to conceptualize within-group differences among African Americans is to use the construct of acculturation as a framework. To do so, they developed the African American Acculturation Scale (AAAS), with items designed to tap traditional African American religious beliefs, family structure and practice, socialization, traditionality of foods, preference for African American objects, interracial attitudes, superstitions, and health beliefs. High scores on the 74 item–scale indicate endorsement of traditional African American culture; moderate scores indicate bicultural orientation; and low scores indicate acculturation to the dominant culture (Landrine & Klonoff, 1994). We would suggest the AAAS reflects alignment and affiliation with a socially subordinate group. We would predict that it will successfully explain within-group differences among African Americans, but that it will be less useful in explaining the relationship of alignment with ordinant groups.

Finally, Sellers, Rowley, Chavous, Shelton, and Smith (1997) incorporated multiple dimensions of identity into their instrument, "Multidimensional Inventory of Black Identity," which was designed to reconcile inconsistencies in the racial identity literature. The authors began with the premise that the choices an individual makes are a function of the extent to which the choices are related to a salient role identity. There are many identities that an individual has, of which race is just one. Racial identity is presumed to have situational aspects, such as salience of race within the context. It is also presumed to have three stable aspects: (1) centrality of race to the individual's core self-concept; (2) the individual's beliefs about how African Americans should behave; and (3) the regard that the individual has toward African Americans (affective component). Their study found evidence for validity of the instrument measuring the three different constructs, lending support for the need to assess the diversity of experiences for African Americans.

Summary

Racial identity theory and its empirical literature are useful to our conceptualization of differential status identity, helping us to examine ways in which individuals perceive themselves as different from the ordinant group. However, effect sizes were generally small to moderate. Problems with measuring various racial identity constructs may account for some of the lack of support for the theoretical models. Another issue is that some measures may not adequately encompass differential status identity with the ordinant group.

The steady growth in instruments designed to assess aspects of social standing for members of subordinate groups is probably due to the inability of any one instrument to fully explicate the experiences of those groups. We would argue that existing measures have not fully incorporated the interaction between race and social class, nor have they captured the complexity of differential status identity.

SOCIAL CLASS AND PSYCHOSOCIAL DEVELOPMENT

Theoretical Developments

Psychologists have largely ignored the role of social class in individual behavior (Argyle, 1994; Brown et al., 1996; Frable, 1997). Although lacking depth and complexity, theorists in the area of vocational psychology have specifically addressed the role of social class. Brown et al. observed that most early vocational choice theorists noted the likely significance of socioeconomic status but failed to specify the nature, scope, and mechanism of its influence. Contemporary career choice theorists have been a little more explicit about the operation of social class in career choice and development, but such articulations require more development to be useful (Brown et al., 1996). In a promising development, Vondracek et al. (1986) emphasized the role of class-based resources and opportunities, and how the decision maker perceives them (a psychological variable) in affecting career development outcomes. However, such an emphasis ignores the role of social class in structuring the learning experiences of developing individuals. Another promising theoretical model was proposed by Lent, Brown, and Hackett (1994) to specify the learning experiences that socialize individuals to various educational and career orientations. However, Lent et al. did not specify how social class, specifically, might structure such experiences.

Also relevant to the domain of vocational behavior, sociologists (e.g., Sewell, Haller, & Portes, 1969) have proposed models of occupational attainment that show that families shape children's educational and occupational attitudes, leading to educational and, ultimately, occupational attainments. These models explicitly delineate the role of the family in social class. The reader will note that all these developments, sparse and under-developed as they are, have occurred in the vocational realm of psychology. Brown et al. (1996) and others (Argyle, 1994; Frable, 1997) have argued for the development of a psychology of social class that encompasses all areas of human behavior. We believe that the concept of DSI represents an important step in that development.

Empirical Findings

Sociologists have shown that many social problems are connected to lower social class, including crime, ill health, mental disorder, and political and social unrest (Argyle, 1994). As we will show, social class is also implicated in play and leisure behavior, education and learning, home life and parenting, and work-related behavior. However, the explanations for these associations remain elusive, perhaps because psychologists, whose province has been the explanation of individual behavior, have neglected social class in their theories, research, and practice (Argyle, 1994; Brown et al., 1996). Explanation of the relationship between social class and the various social ills already delineated is critical in the formulation of social policy, as well as in constructing interventions (Argyle, 1994). For example, if the relationship is due to biology and genetics, very little can be done to intervene to prevent crime, except to regulate mating, or to develop biogenetic interventions. If the associations are due to social structural inequities, then little short of social transformation or revolution will change matters for the socioeconomically subordinate. However, to the extent that the associations are due, at least partly, to socialization (e.g., learning), then psychologists, working with economists, sociologists, and policymakers, can craft and implement interventions to influence that socialization. Psychologists, particularly counseling psychologists, can play an important social role in that regard. We suggest that the concept of DSI provides a useful conceptual tool for construing the effect of social class on individuals and helping to formulate interventions to ameliorate its effects. We now present research findings regarding the DSI concept, turn then to research demonstrating the influence of social class on psychological and social behavior, and present important methodological issues that must be addressed to advance research relevant to the psychological implications of social class.

Research Relevant to the Differential Status Identity Concept

Sociologists have documented that people are conscious that they belong to a class (Centers, 1949; Jackman & Jackman, 1983), though they typically overestimate their status (Argyle, 1994; Rossides, 1997). Further, researchers have shown that social class is a more powerful predictor of worldview than are family structure, race, religion, national origin, income, or subjective class identification (Kohn, 1969; Kohn et al., 1983). Students from working class backgrounds attending elite academic institutions have been shown to be conscious of their relative social standing, interacting with others from a standpoint of relative social inferiority and feeling alienated (Stewart & Ostrove, 1993). Downwardly mobile divorced women report a conscious awareness of the need to reconcile their lower class reality with their former middle-class lives (Grella, 1991). It has also been shown that poor women who clean the homes of wealthy women don a "mask of deference" as they cross neighborhoods to those homes (Collins, 1991). In addition, for members of all status groups, styles of speech associated with ordinant social groups are seen as more prestigious than those associated with subordinate social groups, which are derogated (Brewer & Miller, 1996). When groups differ in status and power, there is a tendency to discriminate heavily in favor of fellow in-group members, especially by members of high-status or ordinant groups (Sachdev & Bourhis, 1991).

The concept of DSI assumes that persons with more ordinant social standings are more likely to be oriented toward independence and individualism as opposed to interdependence and collectivism, whereas the converse is proposed for persons who are relatively subordinate in social standing. Thus, contrary to the thinking of many racial and ethnic difference researchers, Marshall (1997) discovered that social class accounted for more variance in individualism than did national origin: Persons higher in social class evidenced greater individualism. Gurin, Miller, and Gurin (1980) found that persons lower in social class reported greater collectivistic orientations ($r = .28$), supporting the notion that persons with more ordinant social positions are oriented toward greater self-distinctiveness, whereas persons lower in social standing would evidence greater orientation toward self-connectedness, Willmott's study (1987) showed a greater preference for friends of the same class among persons of relatively low-social class. Relatedly, Cornfield and Kim (1994) reported substantially more prounion attitudes among the lower than higher social classes.

These findings are also reflected in the reports of Argyle (1994), Bronfenbrenner (1958), and Kohn (1969), indicating greater conformist orientations among the lower classes and greater independence and autonomy orientations among the more ordinant classes. Higher socioeconomic status has also been shown to be associated with greater locus of control, internality, and self-efficacy for a variety of tasks, including negotiation of graduate and professional school systems, investment of large sums of money and economic resources, management of the perceptions of others about oneself, ability to successfully relate to influential individuals in society, and ability to mobilize political and legal institutions to achieve goals (Argyle, 1994; Rossides, 1997; Veroff, Douvan, & Kulka, 1981).

Consistent with the DSI concept, research findings also indicate that people are aware of their relationship to persons holding more ordinant statuses and hold more hostile attitudes toward such persons as a function of the degree of perceived relative deprivation (Runciman, 1966). Relatedly, Blacks who compare themselves with other Blacks report higher self-esteem than Blacks who compare themselves with Whites (Rosenberg & Simmons, 1972), and Blacks who attended segregated schools possess higher self-esteem than those in integrated schools (Argyle, 1994; Rossides, 1997). Before concluding that it is better for Blacks to avoid social comparisons with Whites, it is important to consider research that indicates that such social comparisons seem to have a positive effect on achievement, aspirations, and expectations. Specifically, youth attending predominately middle-class schools report greater levels of these variables, regardless of their race or social class origin (Argyle, 1994; Rossides, 1997).

Somewhat consistent with the concept of DSI, there appears to be greater interracial group conflict in the lower classes than in the higher classes (Gerard, 1985). It may be that race is not as salient an individual difference variable among the socially higher positioned as it is for those among the lower social status.

Social Class and Psychological/Social Behavior

A number of studies are available that are consistent with the view that social class is related to psychological and social behavior; however, these studies were not specifically designed to examine the concept of DSI. The following findings appear to hold across racial and ethnic groups and across both sexes.

Play and Leisure

The role of social class in the recreational behavior of children has rarely been studied. Nonetheless, one report shows that children of higher socioeconomic statuses have been found to perform better across a wide range of sports (Krombholtz, 1997), popular stereotypes to the contrary.

Across the life span, it has been found that persons among the lower classes report more involvement in visual-auditory hobbies (e.g., television, radio, stereoplayers) than persons among the higher classes (Argyle, 1994; Gibson, 1993; Hu, 1990). Persons from the higher classes have been shown to read, watch, and listen to more news and information programs than persons from the lower classes, who attend to more entertainment programs (Argyle, 1994). Relatedly, traveling and reading were more likely to be reported as hobbies among higher social status persons (Hu, 1990; Pohjolainen, 1991) although these effects were generally small. Higher social class individuals also participate in more organizational activity (e.g., clubs, volunteering) than do lower class individuals (Argyle, 1994; Gibson, 1993; Pohjolainen, 1991) (rs ranged from .22 to .43).

Regarding leisure behavior and adjustment, it is not surprising that those from the higher socioeconomic classes evidence better postretirement adjustment than do persons from the lower classes (Gibson, 1993; Morrison, 1988; Richardson & Kilty, 1991; Weis, Koch, Kruck, & Beck, 1994; Wilensky, 1961); they also retire later than do others (Choi, 1994; Fridlund, Hanson, & Ysander, 1992; Weis et al., 1994) (*r*s ranged from .58 to .74). Interestingly, the leisure preferences of men and women (Shinew, Floyd, McGuire, & Noe, 1996) and Blacks and Whites (Floyd, Shinew, McGuire, & Noe, 1994) evidence somewhat less distinction among individuals in the higher socioeconomic classes than in the lower classes.

Education and Learning

According to many sociologists, education is less a means of enhancing knowledge and ability than it is a means of transmitting class position. As evidence supporting this position, they note that educational performance appears not to translate into performance outside of school settings (Rossides, 1997; Sleeter & Grant, 1998). Socioeconomic status is related to educational variables, such as expenditure per pupil, school attendance, IQ and achievement test scores, years of school completed, grades, diplomas and degrees, benefit from remedial courses, level of educational attainment, and type of college attended and completed (Rossides, 1997). Furthermore, social class is related to pupil and teacher turnover, regular promotion in grade, school learning rates, enrollment in college preparatory classes and schools, club participation, receipt of scholarships, parent participation, school activities, and school board composition (de Lone, 1979; Persell, 1977; Rossides, 1997). Consistent with the concept of DSI, teachers have higher performance expectations of higher social class students (Plewis, 1997). This latter variable has been shown to be related to school achievement (Braun, 1976a, 1976b).

Students of higher social position evidence higher educational aspirations (Cook et al., 1996; Majoribanks, 1991a, 1991b; Solorzano, 1992) (*r*s ranged from .15 to .21); higher levels of achievement expectations (Triplett & Jarjoura, 1997); greater educational attainment (De Graaf & Huinink, 1992; Kasen, Ouellette, & Cohen, 1990; Nagoshi, Johnson, & Honbo, 1993; Pfeiffer, 1991; Poole, Langan-Fox, & Omodei, 1990; Sweeting & West, 1994); and greater academic achievement (Undheim & Nordvik, 1992) (*r*s ranged from .23 to .51). Such students have also been observed to evidence greater employment readiness (Rains, Bisley, & McAlees, 1992) and earlier work experiences relative to others (Mortimer, Finch, Owens, & Shanahan, 1990).

Home Life and Parenting

The greater educational advantage of children from higher social class backgrounds is likely linked, at least in part, to relative home-life advantages and the parenting they experience. For example, we know that people tend to marry within their social class (Brewer & Miller, 1996; Rossides, 1997), solidifying the socioeconomic experience of their children. Children from higher socioeconomic statuses are more likely to have parents who are married and fewer siblings with whom to compete for attention and resources (Argyle, 1994; Rossides, 1997). Their parents are likely to be more mature and stable, and will have approached parenthood more planfully (Reiss & Lee, 1988; Rossides, 1997).

In addition, the parents of children in the higher social classes are more likely to have companionate marriages; that is, they are more likely to share play/leisure activities, work, friends, and parenting tasks (Argyle, 1994; Reiss & Lee, 1988; Rossides, 1997). They also expect more out of a marital relationship than do others (Argyle, 1994; Reiss & Lee, 1988). The parents of children in the lower social strata are more likely to evidence marriages where the parents have separate leisure, work, friends, and parenting lives (LeMasters, 1975; Rubin, 1976, 1994), with more role segregation (Reiss & Lee, 1988).

It is worth noting that the home life of persons in the lower socioeconomic statuses is more likely to include extended family interactions (Argyle, 1994; Rossides, 1997; Veroff et al., 1981).

This may be due to the fact that they are more likely to live nearer to their family and to see them more often. However, persons of higher social position have many more friendship groups (Goldthorpe, 1987; M. Young & Willmott, 1973), and are less likely to have friendships confined to their current socioeconomic status (Willmott, 1987).

Regarding parenting practices, there are some distinctions among the classes. Parents of higher status tend to read more stories, sing more songs, express more positive affection (Eisenberg, 1996; Goudena & Vermeulen, 1997), and say more prayers at bedtime with their children than do other parents (effect sizes are small to moderate) (Argyle, 1994; Stuart, Dixon, Masterson, & Quinlan, 1998). Parents of higher social position also exhibit more child-centeredness, father involvement in child care, and effort at stimulating the child's intellectual development (Argyle, 1994; Stuart et al., 1998). Indeed, social class is highly related to the amount of literacy materials in the home (McCarthey, 1997), and parents from the higher classes are more likely to buy and read books of all types (Argyle, 1994).

Parents from the higher social classes demonstrate greater consistency in using reasoning and love-oriented discipline techniques, including appeals to guilt rather than corporal punishment, in the rearing of children (Najman, Shaw, Bor, O'Callaghan, et al., 1994; Newson & Newson, 1968, 1976). Higher social status parents set higher levels of aspirations and expectations for their children (Argyle, 1994; Hill, 1997; Kinlock, 1987; Reid, 1989; Rossides, 1997); they also are more likely to value independence and autonomy in their children (Kohn, 1969; Kohn, Slomczynski, & Schoenbach, 1986) relative to lower socioeconomic status parents (rs ranged from .10 to .20).

Work Behavior

Sociologists have long noted that the type and level of work in which people participate is tied to social position and not only reflects personality but shapes it (Rossides, 1997). Not surprisingly, higher level organizational positions have fewer ordinants (Argyle, 1994). In addition, persons in such positions tend not to be as highly or closely supervised, tend to include complex activities involving data and people rather than things, and tend to be intricately organized (Kohn, 1977). Persons in the higher statuses also have positions that involve high levels of autonomy, influence, and responsibility, and pass on these values to their children (Argyle, 1994).

Persons in the higher classes employ more creative functions and behave in ways that reflect a belief that they control their destinies (Rossides, 1997). Persons from the lower classes employ more adaptive functions in their jobs, behaving in ways that reflect a belief that they do not have much control over their destinies (Riverin-Simard, 1992). Relatedly, persons in the lower socioeconomic statuses tend to have jobs providing less occupational self-direction and control than persons in the higher statuses (Link, Lennon, & Dohrenwend, 1993; Marmot, Feeney, Shipley, North, & Syme, 1994) (rs averaged around .70). Given all of the relative advantages for workers from the higher statuses, when one also considers that they are also more likely to be advanced in their positions (Sweeting & West, 1994), it is not surprising that work is more likely to be central to the identity of such persons (Burris, 1991; Gecas & Seff, 1990) (rs ranged from .16 to .33). By contrast, persons from the lower classes exhibit more absenteeism (Lusk, Kerr, & Ronis, 1995) and higher turnover rates (Cohen & Hudecek, 1993), and lower organizational commitment (Cohen & Hudecek, 1993; Marmot, 1995) and job satisfaction (Argyle, 1994).

The social status of parents appears to translate into the career interests, goals, and choices of their offspring (Brown et al., 1996). This is reflected in more white-collar versus blue-collar aspirations (Jacobs, Karen, & McClelland, 1991) and higher prestige level occupational preferences (Mullet, Neto, & Henry, 1992). Higher status college women have more science and engineering occupational aspirations (Hesketh, Elmslie, & Kaldor, 1990; Mau, Dommick, & Ellsworth, 1995) (rs ranged from .29 to .33). Students from higher status backgrounds also evidence greater self-efficacy for predominately male occupations (Lauver & Jones, 1991) (rs ranged from .10 to .17), and higher perceived abilities relative to higher level occupations (McDonald & Jessell, 1992), along with higher levels of occupational expectations (Solorzano, 1992) compared with lower status persons.

Methodological Concerns

Besides the absence of a psychological or psychosocial conception of social class and the absence of an associated measurement tool or methodology, there are a number of methodological problems that challenge the scholar interested in understanding social class effects from a psychological viewpoint. First, except for studies conducted by macrolevel scholars such as sociologists, investigations either analyzed for social class effects as a descriptive or exploratory exercise or social class was employed as a control variable to eliminate it as a "nuisance" variable. Rarely was the variable the central focus of psychological investigators (Brown et al., 1996; Frable, 1997). As Brown et al. pointed out, scholars have not often been clear or consistent in indicating whether early developmental or current contextual aspects of social class were of interest. If the former are under study, social class of origin or background should be operationalized; if the latter, the social class of the subject at present should be indexed.

It is problematic that even sociological investigators have failed to consider the multidimensional nature of social class. The fact that it is comprised of three important, albeit sometimes interrelated, components was reflected rarely in how social class was operationalized (Brown et al., 1996). The most common method was to assess income levels or parent educational levels. Occupational prestige levels were also used but rarely was occupation type employed, as Kemper (1995) advocated.

Because most studies have been conducted by sociologists, most of the reports are qualitative in nature. As Frable (1997) observed, quantitative studies of social class, especially those having psychological relevance, have been rare. Perhaps relatedly, most of the studies conceptualize "social class" as existing in a few discrete categories (cf. Argyle, 1994). It is our view that class distinctions are subtler, existing on a continuous, ordinal gradient across the three dimensions of class. Finally, much of the research reviewed examines distinctions between working-class and middle-class individuals; the very poor and the very rich are not often studied nor do their frames of reference enter into most reports having psychological relevance. We believe that a psychological conception of class must, of necessity, avoid such methodological limitations to advance understanding of this powerful determinant of psychological and social behavior.

Summary

The extant social class literature supports our conceptualization of the DSI concept and its hypothesized role in psychosocial development. Given that the field lacks a psychological theory of social class, it may be that further development of the DSI concept will yield such a model. Antecedent empirical support exists for the concept. Our review shows that important life roles and activities are related to, if not determined by, social class. It may be that peoples' psychologies are shaped by the operation of social class. Support for DSI also comes from findings indicating greater class consciousness and class-based collectivism and affiliation tendencies among the lower classes, and greater individualism and superiority strivings among the higher classes. However, note that almost all investigators in this area exclude race and ethnicity from their conceptualizations of social class; they also rarely attend to all three dimensions of social standing: economic, prestige, and power.

In summary, we suggest that research concerning the psychological concomitants of social class should (1) operationalize economic, prestige, and power dimensions of social class; (2) make social class a central variable of investigation; (3) specify whether early developmental or current contextual aspects of social class were of interest; and (4) index social class as a quantitative, continuous variable rather than as a categorical variable. Of course, research directly measuring and testing the operation of DSI is needed.

CONCLUSIONS AND FUTURE RESEARCH

The concept of DSI offers the potential of advancing our understanding of the influence of race and socioeconomic status on psychological development. First, it offers a social psychological variable that embodies the interaction between individuals and their social, historical, political, geographic, and economic context (i.e., their ecology). Second, it avoids examining race and socioeconomic status in isolation from each other (Betancourt & López, 1993) and recognizes that they are inextricably interrelated aspects of social standing. Such an approach aids understanding of why racial and ethnic differences have been difficult to document. It also helps to explain why the influence of socioeconomic status, which is a more inclusive index of standing, has been easier to document (Betancourt & López, 1993; Rossides, 1997; as a special case of this phenomenon in the vocational psychology literature, see Slaney & Brown, 1983). Third, the concept is expected to assist scholars in integrating the wide array of constructs employed to understand the psychosocial development and behavior of culturally diverse persons.

The DSI concept suggests a number of hypotheses. First, we suggest that the construct of social standing, or social position, is quantifiable. To measure it, we would determine how similar (or different) individuals view themselves from some description of persons occupying a middle-social status with respect to the power, prestige, or economic resources. Thus, DSI, just as social standing, is a multidimensional construct. The simple sum of the elements of each dimension is viewed as representing one's social standing. As currently conceived, high status on any one dimension may compensate for low standing on some other dimension. Resources and fame are not superordinant considerations. All three dimensions are important.

Other hypotheses related to DSI seem supported by the literature reviewed in the race/racial identity and social class sections of this chapter. Because of the survival and improvement value associated with doing so, we propose that people seek appeasement of and connectedness with ordinant persons and social groups when possible. In addition, people will generally seek self-distinctiveness with respect to others within or beneath their social standing because of the survival, self-enhancement, and self-improvement importance of doing so. Further, we propose that as DSI from members of ordinant groups increases, survival and self-improvement decreases. Also, we expect that psychosocial stress increases with increasing DSI from ordinants.

Alignment, affiliation, and collective organizational activity with others at or below one's social standing (self-connectedness) occurs and is prized to the extent that it is viewed as instrumental in improving one's social standing, feeling positive about oneself, and decreasing DSI from ordinant groups and their members. Thus, for example, African Americans and Mexican Americans may evidence considerable collective action when engaging ordinants but considerable striving and competition for dominance when relating with one another. Finally, we expect that people who belong to the ordinant groups in this country will seek connection with the superordinant (e.g., persons and groups with international and global economic resources, prestige, and political-legal power).

At the beginning of this chapter, we suggested that understanding the psychological influence of race and social class on our clients' development helps us to understand how our clients view themselves, as well as understanding how we view our clients. We believe that race, culture, and social class are part of our clients' learning context. It is critical to understand the social groups to which our clients perceive themselves as belonging, to which they are perceived as belonging, and the salience of their difference from ordinant groups. Knowledge of their differential status identity helps us to gain an awareness of the ways that they have learned to operate within the ordinant society. It also helps us to understand the ways that the five central motivations of our clients' selves have operated. In other words, it helps us to know how our clients have sought self-survival, self-improvement, self-enhancement, self-distinctiveness, and self-connectedness, and ways that self-enhancement may have been gained at the expense of improvement, or how distinctiveness may have been secured at the expense of connectedness. Gaining an appreciation of the multiple social standings in which our clients operate may be an important clue to their coping skills, their resources, and the ways that those multiple standings may have influenced their developmental life roles. We offer these hypotheses as potential areas for future research.

REFERENCES

Argyle, M. (1994). *The psychology of social class.* London: Routledge & Kegan Paul.

Arroyo, C.G., & Zigler, E. (1995). Racial identity, academic achievement, and the psychological well-being of economically disadvantaged adolescents. *Journal of Personality and Social Psychology, 69,* 903–914.

Atkinson, D.A., & Thompson, C.E. (1992). Racial, ethnic, and cultural variables in counseling. In S.D. Brown & R.W. Lent (Eds.), *Handbook of counseling psychology* (2nd ed., pp. 349–382). New York: Wiley.

Baldwin, J.A., & Bell, Y.R. (1985). The African self-consciousness scale: An Afrocentric personality questionnaire. *Western Journal of Black Studies, 9,* 61–68.

Baldwin, J.A., Duncan, J.A., & Bell, Y.R. (1987). Assessment of African self-consciousness among black students from two college environments. *Journal of Black Psychology, 13,* 27–41.

Banaji, M., & Prentice, D. (1994). The self in social contexts. *Annual Review of Psychology, 45,* 297–332.

Bandura, A. (1997). *Self-efficacy: The exercise of control.* New York: Freeman.

Baumeister, R.F. (1998). The self. In D.T. Gilbert, S.T. Fiske, & G. Lindzey (Eds.), *The handbook of social psychology* (Vol. 1, 4th ed., pp. 680–740). Boston: McGraw-Hill.

Baumeister, R.F., & Sommer, K.L. (1997). What do men want? Gender differences and two spheres of belongingness: Comment on Cross and Madson (1997). *Psychological Bulletin, 122,* 38–44.

Bernal, M.E., Knight, G.P., Ocampo, K.A., Garza, C.A., & Côté, M.K. (1993). Development of Mexican-American identity. In M.E. Bernal & G.P. Knight (Eds.). *Ethnic identity: Formation and transmission among Hispanics and other minorities* (pp. 31–46). Albany, NY: SUNY.

Betancourt, H., & López, S.R. (1993). The study of culture, ethnicity and race in American psychology. *American Psychologist, 28,* 629–637.

Beutler, L.E., Brown, M.T., Crothers, L., Booker, K., & Seabrook, M.K. (1996). The dilemma of factitious demographic distinctions in psychological research. *Journal of Consulting and Clinical Psychology, 64,* 892–902.

Braun, C. (1976a). Teacher expectations: Sociopsychological dynamics. *Review of Educational Research, 46,* 185–213.

Braun, C. (1976b). Teacher expectations. In M.J. Dunkin (Ed.), *International Encyclopedia of Teaching and Teacher Education* (pp. 598–605). New York: Pergamon Press.

Brewer, M., & Miller, N. (1996). Intergroup relations. Buckingham: Open University Press.

Bronfenbrenner, U. (1958). Socialization and social class through time and space. In E.E. Maccoby, T.M. Newcomb, & E.L. Hartley (Eds.), *Readings in social psychology* (3rd ed.). New York: Holt.

Brookins, C.C. (1994). The relationship between Afrocentric values and racial identity attitudes: Validation of the Belief Systems Analysis Scale on African American college students. *Journal of Black Psychology, 20,* 128–142.

Brown, M.T. (1995). The career development of African Americans: Theoretical and empirical issues. In F.T.L. Leong (Ed.), *Career development and vocational behavior of racial and ethnic minorities* (pp. 7–36). Hillsdale, NJ: Erlbaum.

Brown, M.T., Fukunaga, C., Umemoto, D., & Wicker, L. (1996). Annual review, 1990–1996: Social class, work, and retirement behavior. *Journal of Vocational Behavior, 49,* 159–189.

Brown, M.T., Lum, J.L., & Voyle, K.M. (1997). Roe revisited: A call for the reappraisal of the Theory of Personality Development and Career Choice. *Journal of Vocational Psychology, 51,* 283–294.

Brown, M.T., & Pinterits, J. (in press). Basic issues in the career counseling of African Americans. In W.B. Walsh, S.H. Osipow, R.P. Bingham, M.T. Brown, & C.M. Ward (Eds.), *Career counseling for African Americans.* Mahwah, NJ: Erlbaum.

Brown, M.T., & Voyle, K.M. (1997). Without Roe. *Journal of Vocational Psychology, 51,* 310–318.

Burris, B.H. (1991). Employed mothers: The impact of social class and marital status on the prioritizing of family and work. *Social Science Quarterly, 72,* 50–66.

Carter, R.T., DeSole, L., Sicalides, E.I., Glass, K., & Tyler, F.B. (1997). Black racial identity and psychosocial competence: A preliminary study. *Journal of Black Psychology, 23,* 58–67.

Cavalli-Sfroza, L.L., Menozzi, P., & Piazza, A (1994). *The history and geography of human genes.* Princeton, NJ: Princeton University Press.

Centers, R. (1949). *The psychology of social classes.* Princeton, NJ: Princeton University Press.

Chambers, J.W., Jr., Kambon, K., Birdsong, B.D., Brown, J., Dixon, P., & Robbins-Brinson, L. (1998). Afrocentric cultural identity and the stress experience of African American college students. *Journal of Black Psychology, 24,* 368–396.

Chang, E.C. (1996). Cultural differences in optimism, pessimism, and coping: Predictors of subsequent adjustment in Asian American and Caucasian American college students. *Journal of Counseling Psychology, 43,* 113–123.

Choi, N.G. (1994). Racial differences in timing and factors associated with retirement. *Journal of Sociology and Social Welfare, 21,* 31–52.

Chow, E.N. (1996). Introduction: Transforming knowledgement: Race, class and gender. In E.N. Chow, D. Wilkinson, & M.B. Zinn (Eds.), *Race, class and gender: Common bonds, different voices* (pp. xix–1). Thousand Oaks, CA: Sage.

Cohen, A., & Hudecek, N. (1993). Organizational commitment-turnover relationship across occupational groups. *Group and Organizational Management, 18,* 188–213.

Cohen, J. (1988). *Statistical power analysis for the behavioral sciences* (2nd ed.). Hillsdale, NJ: Erlbaum.

Collins, P. (1991). *Black feminist thought: Knowledge, consciousness, and the politics of empowerment.* New York: Routledge & Kegan Paul.

Constantine, M.G., Richardson, T.Q., Benjamin, E.M., & Wilson, J.M. (1998). An overview of black racial identity theories: Limitations and considerations for future theoretical considerations. *Applied and Preventive Psychology, 7,* 95–100.

Cook, T.D., Church, M.B., Ajanaku, S., Shadish, W.R., Jr., Kim, J.R., & Cohen, R. (1996). The development of occupational aspirations and expectations among inner-city boys. *Child Development, 67,* 3368–3385.

Cornfield, D.B., & Kim, H. (1994). Socioeconomic status and unionization attitudes in the United States. *Social Forces, 73,* 521–532.

Côté, J.E. (1996). Identity: A multidimensional analysis. In G.R. Adams, R. Montemayor, & T.P. Gullotta (Eds.), *Psychosocial development during adolescence. Advances in adolescent development: An annual book series* (Vol. 8.). Thousand Oaks, CA: Sage..

Cross, S.E., & Madson, L. (1997). Models of the self: Self-construals and gender. *Psychological Bulletin, 122,* 5–37.

Cross, W.E., Jr. (1971). The Negro to black conversion experience. *Black World, 20,* 13–27.

Cross, W.E., Jr. (1991). *Shades of black.* Philadelphia: Temple University.

Cross, W.E., Jr. (1995a). The psychology of Nigrescence: Revisiting the Cross model. In J.G. Ponterotto, J.M. Casas, L.A. Suzuki, & C.M. Alexander (Eds.), *Handbook of multicultural counseling* (pp. 93–121). Thousand Oaks, CA: Sage.

Cross, W.E., Jr. (1995b). In search of blackness and Afrocentricity: The psychology of black identity change. In H.W. Harris, H.C. Blue, & E.E.H. Griffith (Eds.), *Racial and ethnic identity: Psychological development and creative expression* (pp. 53–72). New York: Routledge & Kegan Paul.

Cunningham, J.L. (1997). Colored existence: Racial identity formation in light-skinned blacks. *Smith College Studies in Social Work, 67,* 375–400.

Day, D.V., Cross, W.E., Jr., Ringeis, E.L., & Williams, T.L. (1999). Self-categorization and identity construction associated with managing diversity. *Journal of Vocational Behavior, 54,* 188–195.

De Graaf, P.M., & Huinink, J.J. (1992). Trends in measured and unmeasured effects of family background on educational attainment and occupational status in the Federal Republic of Germany. *Social Science Research, 21*, 84–112.

de Lone, R.H. (1979). *Small futures: Children, inequality, and the limits of liberal reform* (Report for the Carnegie Council on Children). New York: Harcourt Brace.

Demo, D.H. (1992). The self-concept over time: Research issues and directions. *Annual Review of Sociology, 18*, 303–326.

Dinsmore, B.D., & Mallinckrodt, B. (1996). Emotional self-awareness, eating disorders, and racial identity attitudes in African American women. *Journal of Multicultural Counseling and Development, 24*, 267–277.

Eisenberg, A.R. (1996). The conflict talk of mothers and children: Patterns related to culture, SES, and gender of child. *Merrill-Palmer Quarterly, 42*, 438–458.

Fischer, A.R., Tokar, D.M., & Serna, G.S. (1998). Validity and construct contamination of the Racial Identity Attitude Scale—Long Form. *Journal of Counseling Psychology, 45*, 212–222.

Floyd, M.F., Shinew, K.J., McGuire, F.A., & Noe, F.P. (1994). Race, class, and leisure preferences: Marginality and ethnicity revised. *Journal of Leisure Research, 26*, 158–173.

Ford, D.Y., & Harris, J.J., III. (1997). A study of the racial identity and achievement of black males and females. *Roeper Review, 20*, 105–110.

Frable, D.E.S. (1997).Gender, racial, ethnic, sexual, and class identities. *Annual Review of Psychology, 48*, 139–162.

Fridlund, B., Hansson, H., & Ysander, L. (1992). Working conditions among men before and after their first myocardial infarction: Implications for a rehabilitative care strategy. *Clinical Rehabilitation, 6*, 299–304.

Gaines, S.O., Jr., Marelich, W.D., Bledsoe, K.L., Steers, W.N., et al. (1997). Links between race/ethnicity and cultural values as mediated by racial/ethnic identity and moderated by gender. *Journal of Personality and Social Psychology, 72*, 1460–1476.

Gecas, V., & Seff, M.A. (1990). Social class and self-esteem: Psychological centrality, compensation, and the relative effects of work and home. *Social Psychology Quarterly, 53*, 165–173.

Gerard, D. (1985). Religious attitudes and values. In M. Abrams, D. Gerard, & N. Timms (Eds.), *Values and social change in Britain*. Basingstoke, England: Macmillan.

Gibson, R. (1993). The black American retirement experience. In J.S. Jackson, L.M. Chatters, & R.J. Taylor (Eds.), *Aging in black America* (pp. 277–297). Newbury Park, CA: Sage.

Goldthorpe, J.H. (with Llewellyn, C., & Payne, C.). (1987). *Social mobility and class structure in modern Britain* (2nd ed.). Oxford, England: Clarendon Press.

Good, B.J. (1992). Culture and psychopathology: Directions for psychiatric anthropology. In T. Schwartz, G.M. White, & C.A. Lutz (Eds.), *New directions in psychological anthropology* (Publication of the Society for Psychological Anthropology, pp. 181–205). Cambridge, England: Cambridge University Press.

Goodstein, R., & Ponterotto, J.G. (1997). Racial and ethnic identity: Their relationship and their contribution to self-esteem. *Journal of Black Psychology, 23*, 275–292.

Gottfredson, L.S. (1986). Special groups and the beneficial use of vocational interest inventories. In W.B. Walsh & S.H. Osipow (Eds.), *Advances in vocational psychology: Assessment of interests* (Vol. 1). Hillsdale, NJ: Erlbaum.

Goudena, P.P., & Vermeulen, M. (1997). Mother-child fantasy play and social status of young children. *Early Child Development and Care, 129*, 95–103.

Grella, C. (1991). Irreconcilable differences: Women defining class after divorce and downward mobility. *Gender in Society, 4*, 41–55.

Gurin, P., Miller, A.H., & Gurin, G. (1980). Stratum identification and consciousness. *Social Psychology Quarterly, 43*, 30–47.

Helms, J.E. (1990). *Black and white racial identity: Theory, research, and practice*. Westport, CT: Greenwood Press.

Helms, J.E. (1992). *A race is a nice thing to have*. Topeka, KS: Content Communications.

Helms, J.E. (1994). The conceptualization of racial identity and other "racial" constructs. In E.J. Trickett, R.J.Watts, & D. Birman (Eds.), *Human diversity: Perspectives on people in context* (pp. 285–311). San Francisco: Jossey-Bass.

Helms, J.E. (1995). An update of Helms's White and People of Color Racial Identity models. In J.G. Ponterotto, J.M. Casas, L.A. Suzuki, & C.M. Alexander (Eds.), *Handbook of multicultural counseling* (pp. 181–188). Newbury Park, CA: Sage.

Helms, J.E., & Parham, T.A. (1990). Black Racial Identity Attitude Scale. In J.E. Helms (Ed.), *Black and white racial identity* (pp. 245–247). Westport, CT: Greenwood Press.

Helms, J.E., & Piper, R.E. (1994). Implications of racial identity theory for vocational psychology. *Journal of Vocational Behavior, 44,* 124–138.

Hesketh, B., Elmslie, S., & Kaldor, W. (1990). Career compromise: An alternative account to Gottfredson's theory. *Journal of Counseling Psychology, 37,* 49–56.

Hill, N.E. (1997). Does parenting differ based on social class? African American women's perceived socialization for achievement. *American Journal of Community Psychology, 25,* 675–697.

Hogg, M.A., & Turner, J.C. (1987). Intergroup behaviour, self-stereotyping and the salience of social categories. *British Journal of Social Psychology, 26,* 325–340.

Howell, F.M., Frese, W., & Sollie, C.R. (1984). The measurement of perceived opportunity for occupational attainment. *Journal of Vocational Behavior, 25,* 325–343.

Hu, J. (1990). Hobbies of retired people in the People's Republic of China: A preliminary study. *International Journal of Aging and Human Development, 31,* 31–44.

Ingham, J.M. (1996). *Psychological anthropology reconsidered.* Cambridge, England: Cambridge University Press.

Jackman, M.R., & Jackman, R.W. (1983). *Class awareness in the United States.* Berkeley: University of California Press.

Jackson, C.C., & Neville, H.A. (1998). Influence of racial identity attitudes on African American college students' vocational identity and hope. *Journal of Vocational Behavior, 53,* 97–113.

Jacobs, J.A., Karen, D., & McClelland, K. (1991). The dynamics of young men's career aspirations. *Sociological Forum, 6,* 609–639.

Jones, S.R. (1997). Voices of identity and difference: A qualitative exploration of the multiple dimensions of identity development in women college students. *Journal of College Student Development, 38,* 376–386.

Kasen, S., Ouellette, R., & Cohen, P. (1990). Mainstreaming and postsecondary educational and employment status of a rubella cohort. *American Annals of the Deaf, 135,* 22–26.

Kemper, T.D. (1995). What does it mean social psychologically to be of a given age, sex-gender, social class, race, religion, etc.? In B. Markovsky, K. Heimer, & J. O'Brien (Eds.), *Advances in group processes* (Vol. 12, pp. 81–113). Greenwich, CT: Jai Press.

Kerwin, C., & Ponterotto, J.G. (1995). Biracial identity development: Theory and Research. In J.G. Ponterotto, J.M. Casas, L.A. Suzuki, & C.M. Alexander (Eds.), *Handbook of multicultural counseling* (pp. 199–217). Thousand Oaks, CA: Sage.

Kinloch, G.C. (1987). Social class and attitudes towards education. *Journal of Social Psychology, 127,* 399–401.

Kluckhohn, F.R., & Strodtbeck, F.L. (1961). *Variations in value-orientations.* Evanston, IL: Row, Peterson.

Kohn, M.L. (1969). *Class and conformity: A study in values.* Homewood, IL: Dorsey.

Kohn, M.L., Schooler, C., Miller, J., Miller, K.A., Schoenbach, C., & Schoenberg, R. (1983). *Work and personality: An inquiry into the impact of social stratification.* Norwood, NJ: ABLEX.

Kohn, M.L., Slomczynski, K.M., & Schoenbach, C. (1986). Social stratification and the transmission of values in the family: A cross-national assessment. *Sociological Forum, 1,* 73–102.

Krombholtz, H. (1997). Physical performance in relation to age, sex, social class and sports activities in kindergarten and elementary school. *Perceptual and Motor Skills, 84,* 1168–1170.

Landrine, H., & Klonoff, E.A. (1994). The African American Acculturation Scale: Development, reliability, and validity [Special section: Africentric values, racial identity, and acculturation: Measurement, socialization, and consequences]. *Journal of Black Psychology, 20,* 104–127.

Landrine, H., & Klonoff, E.A. (1996). *African American acculturation: Deconstructing race and reviving culture.* Thousand Oaks, CA: Sage.

Lang, B. (1997). Metaphysical racism. In N. Zack (Ed.), *Race/sex: Their sameness, difference and interplay* (pp. 17–28). New York: Routledge & Kegan Paul.

Lauver, P.J., & Jones, R.M. (1991). Factors associated with perceived career options in American Indian, white, and Hispanic rural high school students. *Journal of Counseling Psychology, 38,* 159–166.

LeMasters, E.E. (1975). *Blue-collar aristocrats.* Madison: University of Wisconsin Press.

Lemon, R.L., & Waehler, C.A. (1996). A test of stability and construct validity of the Black Racial Identity Scale, Form B (RIAS-B) and the White Racial Identity Attitude Scale (WRIAS). *Measurement and Evaluation in Counseling and Development, 29,* 77–85.

Lent, R.W., Brown, S.D., & Hackett, G. (1994). Toward a unifying social cognitive theory of career and academic interest, choice, and performance [Monograph]. *Journal of Vocational Behavior, 45,* 79–122.

Leong, F.T.L., & Brown, M.T. (1995). Theoretical issues in cross-cultural career development: Cultural validity and cultural specificity. In W.B. Walsh & S.H. Osipow (Eds.), *Handbook of vocational psychology* (2nd ed., pp. 143–180). Hillsdale, NJ: Erlbaum.

Link, B., Lennon, M., & Dohrenwend, B. (1993). Socioeconomic status and depression: The role of occupations involving direction, control, and planning. *American Journal of Sociology, 98,* 1351–1387.

Lusk, S., Kerr, M., & Ronis, D. (1995). Health promoting lifestyles of blue-collar, skilled trade, and white-collar workers. *Nursing Research, 44,* 20–24.

Majoribanks, K. (1991a). Adolescents' learning environments and aspirations: Ethnic, gender, and social-status group differences. *Perceptual and Motor Skills, 72,* 823–830.

Majoribanks, K. (1991b). Family human and social capital and young adults' educational attainment and occupational aspirations: Ethnic, gender, and social-status group differences. *Psychological Reports, 69,* 237–238.

Markus, H.R., & Kitayama, S. (1991). Culture and the self: Implications for cognition, emotion, and motivation. *Psychological Review, 98,* 224–253.

Markus, H.R., Mullally, P.R., & Kitayama, S. (1997). Selfways: Diversity in modes of cultural participation. In U. Neisser & D. Jopling (Eds.), *The conceptual self in context* (pp. 13–61). Cambridge, England: Cambridge University Press.

Marmot, M. (1995). Sickness absence as a measure of health status and functioning: From the UK Whitehall study. *Journal of Epidemiology and Community Health, 49,* 124–130.

Marmot, M., Feeney, A., Shipley, M., North, F., & Syme, S. (1994). Work and other factors influencing coronary health and sickness absence. *Work and Stress, 8,* 191–201.

Marshall, R. (1997). Variances in levels of individualism across two cultures and three social classes. *Journal of Cross-Cultural Psychology, 28,* 490–495.

Mau, W.C., Dommick, M., & Ellsworth, R.A. (1995). Characteristics of female students who aspire to science and engineering and homemaking occupations. *Career Development Quarterly, 43,* 323–337.

McCarthey, S.J. (1997). Making the invisible visible: Home literacy practices of middle-class and working-class families. *Journal of Cross-Cultural Gerontology, 6,* 109–117.

McCowan, C.J., & Alston, R.J. (1998). Racial identity, African self-consciousness, and career decision making in African American college women. *Journal of Multicultural Counseling and Development, 26,* 28–38.

McDonald, J.L., & Jessell, J.C. (1992). Influence of selected variables on occupational attitudes and perceived occupational abilities of young adolescents. *Journal of Career Development, 18,* 239–250.

McWhirter, E.H. (1997). Perceived barriers to education and career: Ethnic and gender difference. *Journal of Vocational Behavior, 50,* 124–140.

Montgomery, D.E., Fine, M.A., & James-Myers, L. (1990). The development and validation of an instrument to assess an optimal Afrocentric worldview. *Journal of Black Psychology, 17,* 37–54.

Morrison, B.J. (1988). Gerontological social work practice in long-term care: Sociocultural dimensions: Nursing homes and the minority aged. *Journal of Gerontological Social Work, 5,* 127–145.

Mortimer, J.T., Finch, M.D., Owens, T.J., & Shanahan, M. (1990). Gender and work in adolescence. *Youth and Society, 22,* 201–224.

Mullen, B. (1989). *Advanced basic meta-analysis.* Hillsdale, NJ: Erlbaum.

Mullet, E., Neto, F., & Henry, S. (1992). Determinates of occupational preferences in Portuguese and French high school students. *Journal of Cross-Cultural Psychology, 23,* 521–531.

Nagoshi, C.T., Johnson, R.C., & Honbo, K.A. (1993). Famil background, cognitive abilities, and personality as predictors of educational and occupational attainment across two generations. *Journal of Biosocial Science, 25,* 259–276.

Najman, J.M., Shaw, M.E., Bor, W., O'Callaghan, M., et al. (1994). Working class authoritarianism and child socialization: An Australian study. *Australian Journal of Marriage and Family, 15,* 137–146.

Neisser, U. (1997). Concepts and self-concepts. In U. Neisser & D. Jopling (Eds.), *The conceptual self in context* (pp. 3–12). Cambridge, England: Cambridge University Press.

Neville, H.A., Heppner, P.P., & Wang, L. (1997). Relations among racial identity attitudes, perceived stressors, and coping styles in African American college students. *Journal of Counseling and Development, 75,* 303–331.

Newson, J., & Newson, E. (1968). *Four-years old in an urban community.* London: Allen & Unwin.

Newson, J., & Newson, E. (1976). *Seven-years old in an urban community.* London: Allen & Unwin.

Osipow, S.H., & Fitzgerald, L.F. (1996). *Theories of career development.* Boston: Allyn & Bacon.

Oyserman, D., Gant, L., & Ager, J. (1995). A socially contextualized model of African American identity: Possible selves and school persistence. *Journal of Personality and Social Psychology, 69,* 1216–1232.

Padilla, A.M. (1980). *Acculturation: Theory, models, and some new findings.* Boulder, CO: Westview Press.

Persell, C.H. (1977). *Education inequality: A theoretical and empirical synthesis.* New York: Free Press.

Pfeiffer, D. (1991). The influence of socio-economic characteristics of disabled people on their employment status and income. *Disability, Handicapped, and Society, 6,* 103–114.

Phinney, J.S. (1993). A three-stage model of ethnic identity development in adolescence. In M.E. Bernal & G.P. Knight (Eds.), *Ethnic identity: Formation and transmission among Hispanics and other minorities* (pp. 61–80). Albany, NY: SUNY.

Phinney, J.S., Cantu, C.L., & Kurtz, D.A. (1997). Ethnic and American identity as predictors of self-esteem among African American, Latino, and white adolescents. *Journal of Youth and Adolescence, 26,* 165–185.

Plewis, I. (1997). Inferences about teacher expectations from national assessment at Key Stage One. *British Journal of Educational Psychology, 67,* 235–247.

Plummer, D.L. (1996). Black racial identity attitudes and stages of the life span: An exploratory investigation. *Journal of Black Psychology, 22,* 169–181.

Pohjolainen, P. (1991). Social participation and lifestyle: A longitudinal and cohort study. *Journal of Cross-Cultural Gerontology, 6,* 109–117.

Poindexter-Cameron, J.M., & Robinson, T.L. (1997). Relationships among racial identity attitudes, womanist identity attitudes, and self-esteem in African American college women. *Journal of College Student Development, 38,* 288–296.

Poole, M., Langan-Fox, J., & Omodei, M. (1990). Determining career orientations in women from different social class backgrounds. *Sex Roles, 23,* 471–490.

Rains, M.J., Bisley, D.P., & McAlees, D.C. (1992). Vocational decision making of Native American 14–21 year olds: Comparisons and predictors. *Vocational Evaluation and Work Adjustment Bulletin, 25,* 45–50.

Redding, S.G., & Ng, M. (1982). The role of "face" in the organizational perceptions of Chinese managers. *Organization-Studies, 3*(3), 201–219.

Reid, I. (1989). *Social class differences in Britain* (3rd ed.). London: Fontana.

Reiss, I.L., & Lee, G.R. (1988). *Family systems in America* (4th ed.). Fort Worth, TX: Harcourt Brace.

Richardson, V., & Kilty, K.M. (1991). Adjustment to retirement: Continuity vs. discontinuity. *International Journal of Aging and Human Development, 33,* 151–169.

Riverin-Simard, D. (1992). Career paths and socio-economic status. *Canadian Journal of Counseling, 26,* 15–28.

Roe, A. (1956). *The psychology of occupations.* New York: Wiley.

Roe, A., & Klos, D. (1972). Classification of occupations. In J.M. Whiteley & A. Resnikoff (Eds.), *Perspectives on vocational development.* Washington, DC: American Personnel and Guidance Association.

Roe, A., & Lunneborg, P.W. (1990). Personality development and career choice. In D. Brown & L. Brooks (Eds.), *Career choice and development* (2nd ed., pp. 68–101). San Francisco: Jossey-Bass.

Rosenberg, M., & Simmons, R.G. (1972). *Black and white self-esteem in the urban school child.* Washington, DC: American Sociological Association.

Rossides, D.W. (1997). *Social stratification: The interplay of class, race, and gender* (2nd ed.). Upper Saddle River, NJ: Prentice Hall.

Rubin, L.B. (1976). *Worlds of pain: Life in the working class family.* New York: Basic Books.

Rubin, L.B. (1994). *Families on the fault line: America's working class speaks about the family, the economy, race, and ethnicity.* New York: Harper Perennial.

Ruiz, R.A., & Padilla, A.M. (1977). Counseling Latinos. *Personnel and Guidance Journal, 55,* 401–408.

Runciman, W.C. (1966). *Relative deprivation and social justice: A study of attitudes to social inequity in twentieth century England.* Berkeley: University of California Press.

Sachdev, I., & Bourhis, R.Y. (1991). Power differentials in minority and majority group relations. *European Journal of Social Psychology, 21,* 1–24.

Sanders Thompson, V.L. (1996). Perceived experiences of racism as stressful life events. *Community Mental Health Journal, 32,* 223–233.

Sellers, R.M., Rowley, S.A.J., Chavous, T.M., Shelton, J.N., & Smith, M.A. (1997). Multidimensional inventory of black identity: A preliminary investigation of reliability and construct validity. *Journal of Personality and Social Psychology, 73,* 805–815.

Sewell, W.H., Haller, A.O., & Portes, A. (1969). The educational and early occupational attainment process. *American Sociological Review, 34,* 89–92.

Shinew, K.J., Floyd, M.F., McGuire, F.A., & Noe, F.P. (1996). Class polarization and leisure activity preferences of African Americans: Intragroup comparisons. *Journal of Leisure Research, 28,* 219–232.

Singelis, T.M., Triandis, H.C., Bhawuk, D., & Gelfand, M.J. (1995). Horizontal and vertical dimensions of individualism and collectivism: A theoretical and measurement refinement. *Cross-Cultural Research: The Journal of Comparative Social Science, 29,* 240–275.

Slaney, R.B., & Brown, M.T. (1983). Effects of race and socioeconomic status on career choice variables among college men. *Journal of Vocational Behavior, 23,* 257–269.

Sleeter, C.E., & Grant, C. (1998). Illusions of progress: Business as usual. In H.S. Shapiro, D.E. Purpel, et al. (Eds.), *Critical social issues in American education: Transformation in a postmodern world* (2nd ed.). Mahwah, NJ: Erlbaum.

Smith, E.P., & Brookins, C.C. (1997). Toward the development of an ethnic identity measure for African American youth. *Journal of Black Psychology, 23,* 358–377.

Sodowsky, G.R., Kwan, K.K., & Pannu, R. (1995). Ethnic identity of Asians in the United States. In J.G. Ponterotto, J.M. Casas, L.A. Suzuki, & C.M. Alexander (Eds.), *Handbook of multicultural counseling* (pp. 123–154). Thousand Oaks, CA: Sage.

Solorzano, D.G. (1992). An exploratory analysis of the effects of race, class, and gender on student and parent mobility aspirations. *Journal of Negro Education, 61,* 30–44.

Speight, S.L., Vera, E.M., & Derrickson, K.B. (1996). Racial self-designation, racial identity, and self-esteem revisited. *Journal of Black Psychology, 22,* 37–52.

Steele, C.M. (1992, April). Race and the schooling of black Americans. *The Atlantic Monthly,* 68–78.

Stewart, A., & Ostrove, J. (1993). Social class, social change, and gender: Working class women at Radcliff and after. *Psychology of Women Quarterly, 17,* 475–497.

Stuart, M., Dixon, M., Masterson, J., & Quinlan, P. (1998). Learning to read at home and at school. *British Journal of Educational Psychology, 68,* 3–14.

Sweeting, H., & West, P. (1994). The patterning of life events in mid-to-late adolescence: Markers for the future. *Journal of Adolescence, 17,* 283–304.

Taylor, C.M., & Howard-Hamilton, M.F. (1995). Student involvement and racial identity attitudes among African American males. *Journal of College Student Development, 36,* 330–336.

Terrell, F., & Terrell, S.L. (1981). An inventory to measure cultural mistrust among blacks. *Western Journal of Black Studies, 5,* 180–184.

Tokar, D.M., & Fischer, A.R. (1999). Psychometric analysis of the Racial Identity Attitude Scale-Long Form. *Measurement and Evaluation in Counseling and Development, 31,* 138–149.

Triandis, H.C., McCusker, C., & Hui, C.H. (1990). Multimethod probes of individualism and collectivism. *Journal of Personality and Social Psychology, 59,* 1006–1020.

Triplett, R., & Jarjoura, G.R. (1997). Specifying gender-class-delinquency relationships: Exploring the effects of educational expectations. *Sociological Perspectives, 40,* 287–316.

Turner, J.C., Hogg, M.A., Oakes, P.J., Reicher, S.D., & Wetherell, N. (1987). *Rediscovering the social group.* Oxford, England: Blackwell.

Undheim, J.O., & Nordvik, H. (1992). Socio-economic factors and sex differences in an egalitarian educational system: Academic achievement in 16-year-old Norwegian students. *Scandinavian Journal of Educational Research, 36,* 87–98.

Veroff, J., Douvan, E., & Kulka, R.A. (1981). *The inner American.* New York: Basic Books.

Vondracek, F.W., Lerner, R.M., & Schulenberg, J.E. (1986). *Career development: A life-span developmental perspective.* Hillsdale, NJ: Erlbaum.

Weis, J., Koch, U., Kruck, P., & Beck, A. (1994). Problems of vocational integration after cancer. *Clinical Rehabilitation, 8,* 219–225.

Wilensky, H.L. (1961). Orderly careers and social participation: The impact of work history on social integration in the middle mass. *American Sociological Review, 26,* 521–539.

Willmott, P. (1987). *Friendship networks and social support.* London: Policy Studies Institute.

Yanico, B.J., Swanson, J.L., & Tokar, D.M. (1994). A psychometric investigation of the Black Racial Identity Attitude Scale—Form B. *Journal of Vocational Behavior, 44,* 218–234.

Young, A.A. (1997). Rationalizing race in thinking about the future: The case of low-income black men. *Smith College Studies in Social Work, 67,* 432–455.

Young, M., & Willmott, P. (1973). *The symmetrical family.* London: Routledge & Kegan Paul.

Zack, N. (1997). Race and philosophic meaning. In N. Zack (Ed.), *Race/sex: Their sameness, difference and interplay* (pp. 29–44). New York: Routledge & Kegan Paul.

Zane, N.W.S. (1993). An empirical examination of loss of face among Asian-Americans. In R. Carter (Ed.), *Ninth annual Cross-Cultural Roundtable Proceedings.* New York: Columbia University.

Zuckerman, M. (1990). Some dubious premises in research and theory on racial differences: Scientific, social, and ethical issues. *American Psychologist, 45,* 1297–1303.

PART III

Preventive and Developmental Interventions

CHAPTER 13

Preventive Interventions with School-Age Youth

ELIZABETH M. VERA
LE'ROY E. REESE

Prevention has been a defining theme of the profession of counseling psychology (Conyne, 1987; Gelso & Fretz, 1992; Kiselica & Look, 1993; Myers, 1992). Despite its historical prominence, counseling psychologists have had a somewhat tentative commitment to prevention in their daily work (Conyne, 1987; McNeil & Ingram, 1983). However, for many of the contemporary problems facing children and adolescents, prevention strategies represent the most promising interventions for decreasing the occurrence of cases requiring remedial treatment.

As we consider the current state of prevention research and practice with children and adolescents, it is clear the field has developed unevenly. For example, the theoretical and empirical literature on pregnancy prevention in adolescents is much more advanced than that on violence prevention. We have longitudinal data on what works in drug prevention, but more rigorous evaluation and theory development is only recently occurring in social competence and resiliency research.

In this chapter, theoretical and conceptual issues involved in prevention work with children and adolescents are detailed. Then, a review of strategies for preventing substance abuse, risky sexual activity, and violence are presented, followed by a review of programs designed to foster resiliency and competence. Finally, issues of program design and evaluation are discussed, with implications for future prevention research and practice.

PREVENTION

Definitions

Before proceeding further, it is critical to establish a working definition of "prevention." Traditionally, prevention has been seen as a tripartite concept consisting of primary, secondary, and tertiary approaches. Primary prevention, according to Conyne (1987), refers to intentional programs that target groups of people who are currently unaffected by a particular problem for the purposes of helping them continue to function in healthy ways, free from disturbance. Secondary prevention targets populations exhibiting early stage problems to forestall the development of more serious difficulties (e.g., working with aggressive kindergartners to curb later violent episodes). Secondary prevention efforts typically rely on early detection methods to identify the target population (Durlak, 1997).

Tertiary prevention aims to reduce the duration or consequences of established problems or disorders (e.g., family planning programs designed for pregnant teenagers). In many instances, tertiary prevention interventions are difficult to differentiate from traditional psychotherapy or

Dr. Le'Roy Reese completed work on this chapter when he was a faculty member at Chicago State University. He currently is employed by the Centers for Disease Control and Prevention.

rehabilitation. The Committee on Prevention of Mental Disorders (Munoz, Mrazek, & Haggerty, 1996) recommended that the term prevention be reserved for only those interventions that occur prior to the onset of a diagnosable disorder. Interventions that occur after the onset are considered treatment.

History with Children

The foundations of prevention in counseling psychology are rooted in the vocational guidance movement and the mental health and hygiene efforts of the early 1900s. The vocational guidance movement involved matching the needs of prospective workers with those of society to allow workers to be more productive, personally satisfied, and in a better position to resolve pressing social problems (Conyne, 1987; Gelso & Fretz, 1992). The mental health and hygiene movements attempted to educate the public about mental illnesses and to encourage involvement in alleviating its sources, as well as to improve treatment facilities (Conyne, 1987; Durlak, 1997). One outgrowth of this movement was the development of prevention efforts with children through the creation of child guidance clinics. The primary objective of these clinics was to target high-risk children and families living in poor neighborhoods and to improve their quality of life through environmental and social change (Durlak, 1997). Another early setting that was used to implement concepts of prevention with children was the school. According to Horn (1989), in the 1920s special visiting teachers would educate other teachers about prevention concepts and would demonstrate ways to develop positive qualities in their students to promote positive social and academic functioning and development.

Although prevention with children is not a new concept, it has not necessarily been adequately represented in the daily work of counseling psychologists. Kiselica and Look (1993) argued that some of the reasons prevention has failed to be embraced to the same extent as remedial services may involve a lack of clarity about what prevention constitutes, societal demands for remedial services, and a lack of interest among trainees and professionals. McNeil and Ingram (1983) suggested that prevention may have fallen by the wayside in favor of more "valued" activities, such as individual remedial psychotherapy.

Whatever the reason for this ambivalence, prevention remains, in many cases, the best set of strategies we have for decreasing the overall incidence of many types of psychological problems. Prevention with children and adolescents is becoming particularly necessary given the increasingly earlier ages at which they are being exposed to harmful environmental stressors (e.g., poverty, neglect and abuse, community violence), and are becoming involved in such high-risk activities as alcohol and drug use and sexual activity.

CRITICAL ISSUES IN THE DESIGN AND EVALUATION OF PREVENTION PROGRAMS

Before planning and implementing prevention activities with school-age youth, a number of important conceptual issues must be addressed. The first of these is understanding risk and protective factors. Risk and protective factors refer to those characteristics of persons and their environments that influence an individual's chance of developing mental health problems (Reiss & Price, 1996). Risk factors have been more intensively researched than protective factors. Protective factors foster resilience to risk and promote competence and adaptive outcomes (Kazdin, 1993).

Generally speaking, it is assumed that most types of problems are multiply determined (Durlak, 1997) and that the greater the number of risk factors to which a child might be exposed, the greater the likelihood of developing problems (Reiss & Price, 1996). Such factors may include biological predispositions, personality traits, family processes, peer influences, school experiences, and community variables. Additionally, "risk" may be manifest in a behavior (e.g., having unprotected sex, engaging in binge drinking) or a belief (e.g., believing teenagers cannot get pregnant, or that alcohol is not a drug) (Durlak, 1997). Person-environment interaction is a critical mechanism in understanding risk, in that personal risk factors may be modified by salient environmental factors (Black & Krishnakumar, 1998; Reiss & Price, 1996; Rutter, 1987). For example, it is reasonable to assume that children living in communities devastated by chronic gang violence will be at-risk for certain negative outcomes, but positive environmental influences, including prevention programs, might offset this risk.

Understanding the various risk and protective factors involved in certain problems may guide the development of intervention strategies. Interventions can be categorized as either person or environment centered (Baker & Shaw, 1987; Durlak & Wells, 1997). Person-centered interventions offer services directly to the target population (e.g., communication skills training, self-esteem enhancement). Environment-centered interventions seek to modify the child's social context (e.g., programs that modify parental child rearing techniques, or teachers' classroom management techniques). Programs that contain both person-centered and environment-centered intervention strategies, versus either alone, are likely to be the most successful (e.g., community-centered drug prevention programs that focus on individual vocational training and community economic development) (Durlak, 1997; Munoz et al., 1996).

Knowledge of which groups of children are in greatest need of preventive intervention is another important issue. The field of epidemiology has attempted to determine the rate of incidence and precipitating factors involved in the emergence of specific health problems. Conceptually, epidemiological research attempts to characterize the challenges facing individuals and their success or failure in meeting those challenges (Reiss & Price, 1996). Research on risk/protective factors and epidemiological studies on the general population aged under 18 are critical to the advancement of prevention science in the area of child and adolescent disorders (Munoz et al., 1996).

Although this type of information is vital, there remains considerable debate about whether psychologists should focus on identifying and decreasing particular risk factors (e.g., behaviors and beliefs) for specific disorders. An alternative approach would be to focus on increasing social competencies and other general protective factors, which should reduce child and adolescent mental disorders across the board (Albee, 1996). Much of this debate is connected to the assumptions made about the functions of risk-behaviors in youth.

For example, Jessor and Jessor's (1977) problem behavior theory, a dominant theoretical view, suggests that diverse problem behaviors such as drug abuse, delinquent behavior, and sexual activity have similar functions (e.g., gaining peer acceptance, coping with stress). Because such behaviors tend to bring about similar rewards or serve common purposes, they tend to come in "packages." This does not necessarily mean that drug abuse and academic dysfunction, for example, always co-occur, but samples of youth with one behavior are more likely to have higher rates of other behaviors than a comparison sample similar in age and gender (Kazdin, 1993). Practitioners guided by this philosophy would argue that helping youth develop the skills and abilities to meet their needs in nondestructive ways would be more beneficial than developing programs aimed at specific risk behaviors.

A closely related conceptual issue is whether programs target specific problems (e.g., substance abuse, violence) or whether interrelated behavior "packages" are targeted. The former types of programs have been criticized for having a myopic focus (Jessor, 1993; Kazdin, 1993; Osgood, 1995; Tolan & Guerra, 1994). Farrell, Danish, and Howard (1992) investigated the relationship between five adolescent problem behaviors (cigarette smoking, alcohol use, marijuana use, delinquency, and sexual intercourse) in seventh and ninth graders and found positive relationships to exist among the behaviors. A confirmatory factor analysis also supported the hypothesis that a common factor underlies adolescent problem behaviors. Thus, there would seem to be support for programs that target interrelated problems in youth.

The New Haven Social Development Program is one prevention program that addressed the interaction of multiple-risk situations (e.g., how substance abuse affects sexual decision making) in preventing health-compromising behaviors and attitudes (Weissberg, Caplan, & Harwood, 1991). Allen, Philliber, and Hoggson (1990) also developed a successful program that addressed the issues of school dropout, teen pregnancy, and substance abuse. It is expected that such programs will gain in popularity with prevention specialists.

Another important conceptual issue in prevention work with children and adolescents is understanding developmental differences among youth (Brooks-Gunn & Paikoff, 1993). Varying cognitive-processing abilities, social maturity, and environmental risk-exposure levels can have a profound impact on the appropriateness of prevention strategies for different children (Kazdin, 1993). An equally salient issue is understanding sociodemographic and cultural (e.g., gender, ethnic, racial, religious, and socioeconomic) differences in the experiences of children and adolescents. Not only do mental health problems manifest differently and at differential rates in groups of children in various cultural contexts, but many prevention programs are based on a Western worldview and were initially developed in middle-class communities, potentially limiting their generalizability.

Programs that do not apply to the cultural context of the participants are likely to be ineffective (Dryfoos, 1990; Kazdin, 1993; Lerner, 1995). Central to appropriate developmental contextualism is the emphasis that successful programs must be relevant to the lives of the participants (Lerner, 1995). For example, important gender differences in sexual activity have been found (Brooks-Gunn & Paikoff, 1993), which may require different types of prevention strategies for boys and girls. Additionally, cultural values related to specific behaviors can be critical to include in preventive intervention (e.g., values regarding sex in Fundamentalist Christian communities, or drinking and drug use in Muslim communities). Thus, an important challenge to prevention researchers is to reconcile differences between the assumptions of their prevention models and the cultural values of the target communities.

Cultural and developmental contextual issues also have implications for the timing of preventive efforts. As children, adolescents, and their families develop, patterns of thinking and behaving become much more complex. Interventions occurring later in life often require more intensive efforts and involve more systems (e.g. family, school, community) than those occurring earlier in life (Lerner, 1995). Thus, the "best time" to prevent many problems is before youth become exposed to multiple-risk factors or become involved in risky-behaviors such as sexual activity and drug use, thus suggesting the critical role of primary prevention.

To summarize, several conceptual issues must be addressed in the design and implementation of prevention programs with school-age youth. One must begin with a thorough understanding of the risk and protective factors involved in the development of specific problems. Because risk and protective factors come from within the child as well as the social context, multiple-level interventions seem to hold the greatest promise. Also, the interrelatedness of many types of problematic behaviors must be considered and addressed in a systematic way. Cultural and developmental appropriateness are also critical to the design of successful prevention programs.

METHODOLOGICAL ISSUES

Although interest in prevention with children has a long history, evaluation of the efficacy of such programs has been a relatively recent phenomena. In their meta-analysis of primary prevention outcome studies, Durlak and Wells (1997) found that over half of all controlled outcomes studies have appeared since 1980. One might question why it is that prevention researchers have not made program evaluation an inseparable part of their efforts. After all, there are indeed strong ethical, scientific, and financial motivators to prove that what we do "works."

Part of the problem facing researchers may be that there are some logistical challenges in evaluation research on prevention programs. Primarily, true randomized assignment to prevention programs and control conditions may not be possible because such services frequently are delivered in group settings, such as schools where it is easier to work with children in preexisting units. Additionally, a no-intervention control group, per se, is not always available or acceptable to participants, especially if one's focus is on children in need. However, there are some quasi-experimental designs that can assist in designing controlled outcome studies.

For example, it may be possible to randomly assign entire classrooms to treatment and control conditions, especially if participants are assured that services will be delivered to all targeted children eventually (e.g., delayed-treatment control groups). However, because this does not always result in comparable groups, many prevention researchers have used control groups that are deliberately matched on relevant characteristics such as age, grade, gender, socioeconomic status, race, and so on. The samples might be drawn from the same or different settings.

For instance, one might work with two matched classrooms of students within the same school (one receiving the program prior to the other), whereby the delayed-treatment classroom would serve as the comparison group for the treatment classroom.

Alternatively, other prevention programs have used participants from multiple schools comparable on relevant characteristics and have used one school as the control group for the treatment-school. However one chooses to arrange for a comparison sample, it is critical that evaluators provide some evidence of internal validity or the effectiveness of our efforts will remain suspect. Statistical procedures such as analysis of covariance can also assist researchers in understanding how inconsistencies between control and treatment groups may affect participant responsivity to our prevention efforts.

Once samples are selected, there are still issues of appropriate outcome measures that must be addressed. Program evaluation researchers have more recently widened the objectives of their program evaluations to include proximal as well as distal goals. Sometimes there are considerable delays between the intervention itself and the time at which a problem would be expected to develop (e.g., the effectiveness of a sex education program in delaying the onset of sexual activity). Longitudinal studies which would track this kind of information can often be expensive, and keeping track of program participants is difficult. However, although long-term effects may be the ultimate goal, in the interim it is important to document short-term effects of the program (Durlak & Wells, 1997).

Outcome evaluation data have been underwhelming in a great number of prevention programs. In some cases, this may be due to the challenge of demonstrating that a negative outcome has not occurred, or that a clinical disorder has not developed (Durlak & Wells, 1997). There may also be decisions about measurement that are important in affecting the type of feedback we receive from program participants. Outcome has been assessed in a variety of ways, ranging from quantitative measurement of psychological variables (e.g., self-esteem, self-efficacy) to behavioral rating scales (e.g., number of arrests, age of first pregnancy, frequency of drug use) to surveys of participants' perceptions of program effectiveness. Decisions about what kind of data are needed should be directly tied to the goals of the program.

Durlak and Wells's (1997) meta-analysis included 177 prevention program outcome evaluations. The types of programs analyzed included both affective and behaviorally focused efforts that were aimed at children from every age group. They found that most programs showed a reduction in problems (e.g., anxiety measures, behavior problems, depressive symptoms) or an increase in competencies (e.g., assertiveness skills, feelings of self-confidence, skill performance). Most of the programs reviewed achieved significant positive effects (mean effect sizes ranged from .24 to .93). The average participant surpassed the performance of 59% to 82% of those in the control group. Durlak and Wells concluded that, in general, prevention efforts have been beneficial to children and adolescents and should be a part of the future concentration of psychologists.

In the following section, the prevention literature from four general areas will be reviewed: substance abuse prevention, the prevention of sexually transmitted diseases and pregnancy, the prevention of violence and aggressive behavior, and programs that promote resiliency and competency. Although prevention of such problems is relevant at any age, the majority of these efforts have targeted children and adolescents.

PREVENTIVE PROGRAMS

Substance Abuse Prevention

The incidence of substance abuse problems in children and adolescents (as well as adults) has been a long-standing concern of mental health professionals (Schmidt, 1994). Over the years, research has revealed that youths' choice of drugs periodically changes, patterns of use tend to vary by ethnic group (Boles, Casas, Furlong, Gonzalez, & Morrison, 1994), and widespread use has leveled off more recently. However, children are being exposed to alcohol and illicit drugs at earlier and earlier ages. Thus, substance abuse remains a concern for the counseling profession.

Epidemiological studies have suggested that occasional use of drugs by adolescents is a different phenomenon from drug abuse and may arise from different etiological roots (Hawkins, Lishner, Catalano, & Howard, 1986). Thus, it is important for prevention researchers to clarify their goals and to specify whether they are trying to delay the onset of first use, or prevent occasional use, regular use, or drug abuse.

The risk factors involved in child and adolescent substance abuse can be classified into two general categories: contextual factors, which provide the legal and normative expectations around drug-use behavior; and personal/interpersonal factors which lie within individuals or their immediate environments (i.e., families, peer groups, and schools). Although a detailed review of these factors is beyond the scope of this chapter, we summarize this work here. Hawkins, Catalano, and Miller (1992) and Hawkins et al. (1986) provide an extensive review of risk factors and predictors of adolescent substance abuse.

Contextual risk factors include high societal and community norms regarding drug use, increased availability and accessibility of drugs and alcohol to youth, residing in extreme economic deprivation, and residing within extreme neighborhood disorganization. The individual factors involved are physiological (e.g., how the body metabolizes certain drugs); low bonding to family; early, persistent problem behaviors; academic failure; low degree of commitment to school; peer rejection in elementary grades; alienation and rebelliousness; attitudes favorable to drug use; and early onset of drug use. Interpersonal factors include family and parental alcohol and drug behavior; family attitudes and norms regarding substance use; poor and inconsistent family management practices; high levels of family conflict; and association with drug-using peers.

Protective factors are less well studied (Mrazek & Haggerty, 1994). However, included among those that have been identified are membership in structured, goal-directed peer groups that do not abuse drugs, strong attachment and involvement between youth and their parents, and genetic factors that modify consumption and affect the expression of chemical dependency. Given the multitude of risk and protective factors identified in the research, identifying children and adolescents at "high risk" can be a complicated matter.

Regardless of how many risk factors to which a child is exposed, at some point engaging in specific behaviors determines whether a child will self-expose to harm (i.e., consuming a drug). A variety of models have been proposed to explain the behavioral mechanisms involved in drug-use behaviors. Among the most frequently cited models is social learning theory (Bandura & Walters, 1959), which emphasizes the process of modeling and reinforcement in the learning of alcohol- and drug-related attitudes and behaviors. Theoretically, susceptibility to social influences that promote substance abuse is affected by knowledge, attitudes, and beliefs (Botvin & Botvin, 1992).

Programs that are based on social learning theory tend to emphasize the importance of self-regulation and self-control, as well as altering norms and perceived rewards of substance use.

Social learning theory is important to conceptualizations of prevention strategies because of its focus on factors influencing the choices youth make about substance use. Although there is considerable discussion of physiological predispositions toward addiction in the literature, many adolescents may experiment with substance use which can put them at serious risk. Thus, focusing on decision making as a mechanism of prevention should be useful for intervening with adolescents, regardless of their genetic vulnerability to substance abuse problems.

Drug- and alcohol-abuse prevention programs have been used with general populations of children and adolescents (i.e., universal programs), as well as with those at higher risk. Many programs have been found to be equally beneficial for both populations (Johnson et al., 1990). However, substance abuse prevention programs have changed over the years, and the field has recently come to some consensus regarding the components of successful efforts.

Early person-centered prevention efforts sought to teach children the facts of drug and alcohol use or preached the benefits of "just saying no," which oversimplified the complexity of drug use and abuse. Serious limitations were found in these early approaches in that, although they increased knowledge and awareness in students, they rarely yielded overall changes in drug use (Battjes, 1985). These findings are not surprising given the lack of empirical evidence for the causal relationship between knowledge and actual behaviors (Bukoski, 1986; Kazdin, 1993). However, Olson, Horan, and Polansky (1992) suggested that the failure of information-based programming may be due to inadequacies in implementation and distorting the facts about drugs to youth (i.e., the use of "scare tactics").

In contrast, more contemporary programs have adopted a broader focus than solely imparting accurate information or relying on slogans. Examples of such programs feature teaching refusal/assertiveness skills (so that youth wanting to refrain from substance use will know how to communicate their intentions) and enhancing youth's coping abilities so that drugs become less of a temptation (Schmidt, 1994). Programs' goals usually involve fostering a greater sense of control, coping, and interpersonal self-efficacy in program youth. In addition to these person-centered ingredients, successful programs have added environment-centered components which attempt to alter normative values of families and peer-groups regarding drugs and alcohol or change media-driven messages about their use (Schilling & McAlister, 1990; Wallack, 1986). The most successful types of drug- and alcohol-abuse prevention programs seem to be those that attempt to affect multiple risk and protective factors at both person-centered and environment-centered levels of intervention.

Some of the most promising work in the field has been conducted by Botvin and his colleagues. Botvin, Baker, Dusenbury, Tortu, and Botvin (1990), following a cognitive-behavioral model, hypothesized that substance use onset is the result of the interplay of social and intrapersonal factors. As a learned behavior, substance use is mediated by cognitions, attitudes, expectations, and personality, but is modeled and reinforced by social influences from peers, family members, and the media. They also identified self-esteem and self-efficacy as being important intrapersonal factors in determining general susceptibility to social influence and motivation to engage in substance use.

The cognitive-behavioral skills training approach derived from this model was evaluated over a three-year period involving predominantly White ethnic (91%) seventh-grade students. The main purpose was to facilitate the development of personal and social skills (e.g., building self-esteem, resisting advertising pressure, managing anxiety, communicating effectively), with particular emphasis on the development of skills for coping with social influences to smoke, drink alcohol, or use drugs.

Significant treatment effects were found for the majority of substance use variables, substance-related knowledge, normative expectations regarding substance use, and interpersonal skill building

(Botvin, Baker, Dusenbury, et al., 1990). Although this program originated as a program to prevent smoking, it has been expanded to include other drugs and has been found to be consistently effective.

Another well-known program was developed by Pentz et al. (1990). The Midwest Prevention Project targeted predominantly White (78%) sixth and seventh graders for training in skills to resist social pressures to use drugs and to counteract peer, adult, mass media, and other environmental modeling influences. This program also included indirect training of parents, teachers, and community leaders in communication, support, and prevention practice skills. The intervention consisted of ongoing mass media programming combined with a 10-session school program. The effects of program exposure on drug-use change were found to be significant (Pentz et al., 1990) at a one-year follow-up.

Another program that combines person-centered and environment-centered interventions was developed by Perry et al. (1996). This school-based, behavioral training program used peers and teachers as leaders to assist students in resisting social pressures to use drugs. Home activities encouraged communication about alcohol and drug abuse between children and their parents. Community members also served as volunteers in organizing drug-free activities in the community. Finally, community task forces were organized with the goal of changing public policy about merchant practices of selling alcohol to minors. This program successfully altered drug use by heavily influencing community, peer, and family norms.

There have also been innovative programs that have delivered preventive interventions in nontraditional contexts (i.e., not school based and clinic based) given that traditional programs have failed to reach those youth at greatest risk—those who are not in school or receiving psychological services (Kumpfer & DeMarsh, 1986). For example, Szapocznik et al. (1989) attempted to enhance family effectiveness by intervening with Hispanic youth in their family settings, targeting the constellation of family factors that put adolescents at risk for developing drug problems. Manger, Hawkins, Haggerty, and Catalano (1992) sought to prevent drug abuse via community organization strategies whereby community leaders would develop and integrate alcohol- and drug-free activities into existing community programs.

Although these programs represent only a small sample of those attempting to prevent drug and alcohol abuse in children and adolescents, they were selected to illustrate some of the details involved in design, implementation, and evaluation of such work. Although curriculum details and outcome measures vary in many programs, experts agree that comprehensive social skills programs that combine person- and environment-centered components are the best practices for preventing substance abuse in youth (Olson et al., 1992).

Sexually Transmitted Disease and Pregnancy Prevention

Although sexual activity in adolescence is not a clinically diagnosable problem per se, it constitutes a major health risk with potentially life-changing consequences. Unsafe sexual behavior can result in unplanned pregnancy, early parenthood, and the transmission of a host of diseases, the most serious of which is HIV infection.

Sexual maturation is one of the hallmarks of adolescence, and sexual activity is strongly influenced by biological development (e.g., biological maturity, hormone levels, and sexual behavior) (Card, Peterson, & Greeno, 1992). Also, gender differences are highly salient in this area. Despite the fact that on average girls tend to physically develop earlier than boys, the sexual activity rates of boys exceed those of girls at all age levels (Card et al., 1992; Coley & Chase-Lansdale, 1998). This suggests important effects of socialization and norms regarding such activity for boys and girls.

Sexual behavior is also clearly influenced by peer, family, individual, and community factors. Sexual activity is less likely among adolescents who have high educational or career aspirations (see Arbona, this volume, for a discussion of factors related to educational and career aspirations), who have a greater confidence in their own abilities to affect their environment (i.e., internal locus of control), and who have a lower propensity to take risks (Card et al., 1992). Additionally, females living in poverty with poorly educated parents are more likely to face teenage pregnancy (Coley & Chase-Lansdale, 1998). The interpretation of this particular finding varies, but many scholars believe that perceptions of limited life options and choices may result from living in poverty (Wilson, 1987). Access to resources such as family planning programs and contraceptive devices may also be affected in economically depleted communities.

Regardless of these other correlates, contraceptive use and frequency of sexual activity are the primary factors determining whether adolescents ultimately become pregnant or contract sexually transmitted diseases (STDs; Coley & Chase-Lansdale, 1998). Survey data indicate that one third of teenagers do not use contraceptives at first intercourse (which is a prime determinant of later contraceptive use), and, despite the fact that contraceptive use is increasing, adolescents tend to use contraceptives ineffectively and sporadically (Coley & Chase-Lansdale, 1998). In one investigation of why adolescents fail to practice safer sex, Fraser, Minton, and Valiquette (1995) found that ignorance, peer pressure, trusting that one's partner is not infected, low perception of vulnerability to STDs, and failing to take personal responsibility were listed as primary reasons.

Pregnancy and contracting STDs have different consequences for youth. Although many STDs can be medically treated, they primarily constitute a health risk if they are left untreated or are, in fact, untreatable. Pregnancy and teenage parenthood, on the other hand, with its continual demands and responsibilities, can leave little time for normal aspects of adolescent development (e.g., dating, career exploration, educational achievement) (Coley & Chase-Lansdale, 1998).

One common dilemma that researchers inevitably confront is the question of whether abstinence or contraceptive use should be the goal of intervention efforts. It is largely a question of values in deciding whether programs should advocate absolute abstinence, safer sexual practices in adolescents, or both. Adolescents have been put in a double bind because of societal sexual prohibitions in that if it is unacceptable to be sexually active, then contraceptive advice and planning also become unacceptable (Brooks-Gunn & Paikoff, 1993). However, abstinence is the safest way to protect oneself against STDs and unplanned pregnancy. Hence, many programs have aimed to delay the onset of sexual activity and increase the use of contraceptives in those adolescents choosing to become sexually active.

The strategies of prevention programs, as was the case for substance abuse, have ranged in scope from providing knowledge (of sexual reproduction and contraceptives), to modifying peer group or community norms (around sexual activity of youth), to promoting decision making and communication skills. Also, similar to the substance abuse literature, some of the most effective programs have taken a multilevel approach to intervention, including person-centered and environment-centered strategies (B.C. Miller & Paikoff, 1992). However, analogies between substance abuse and sexual activity are quite limited. One could argue that never using drugs is always an appropriate goal in life, including adulthood. Few adults, however, would argue that never becoming sexually active is equally beneficial (B.C. Miller & Paikoff, 1992).

Prevention programs that are narrow in focus and that limit strategies to information dissemination have largely failed (Miller & Card, 1992). This is not to say that having accurate information is unimportant. Rather, it is just not sufficient to prevent pregnancy and STDs. Additionally, programs that only promote abstinence have generally been unsuccessful (Bandura, 1989; Coley & Chase-Lansdale, 1998). Although there is no question that abstinence is the best preventive strategy, it is probably not realistic to expect all youth to make such a choice. When one considers recent changes in federal and state policies that financially support only those programs advocating abstinence (with an active exclusion of strategies that address contraception), there is a great concern for those adolescents who are sexually active.

Durlak (1997) summarized the characteristics of successful pregnancy/STD prevention programs. Such programs address both abstinence and safer sex as prevention strategies, include training youth in behavior skills (e.g., decision making, assertive communication, correct use of contraceptives), provide youth with accurate information about sexual risks, enhance family communication, modify peer and community norms regarding sexual activity of youth, and address relevant cultural issues (e.g., gender, religious, sexual-orientation differences).

As was the case with substance use and abuse, decision-making models have also had an important role in developing prevention strategies for sexual decision making. Among the most frequently cited models are Ajzen and Fishbein's (1980) theory of reasoned action, the health belief model (Becker, 1974), protection motivation theory (Rogers, 1983), and Bandura's (1982, 1986) self-efficacy theory.

The theory of reasoned action posits that behaviors are directly linked to intentions, intentions are determined by one's attitude toward the behavior and subjective norms, and attitude is determined by the belief that behavior leads to certain outcomes. Thus, this theory outlines the connection between knowledge and action by suggesting that attitudes and subjective norms serve as intermediary determinants of behavior. This theory, which has been applied to health-related behaviors by Fishbein and Middlestadt (1989), highlights the role of peer group and family norms, as well as individual beliefs and attitudes in health-promoting behavior in youth.

The health-belief model is a cognitive model of health behavior and compliance comprised of four components: (1) personal susceptibility to a negative health condition, (2) the perceived severity of the condition, (3) the value of the health-related behavior, and (4) barriers to the action. Taken together, these elements produce some degree of psychological readiness to act (Kirscht & Joseph, 1989).

Protection motivation theory is a closely related model which posits that adolescents make behavioral decisions via two pathways: threat appraisal and coping appraisal. Threat appraisal involves balancing perceived intrinsic and extrinsic rewards of a behavior with the perceived severity of the negative outcomes and perceptions of personal vulnerability to the threat. At the same time, a coping appraisal (i.e., evaluation of a protective action) occurs by balancing the perceived likelihood that the protective action will reduce the threat (response efficacy), and the belief that the protective action can be performed (self-efficacy) with response cost (barriers to completing the action). These dual appraisal processes, then, in combination, determine whether the behavior in question will occur.

Self-efficacy theory posits that people's beliefs about their capabilities to exert control over their behavior and social environment affect what they choose to do, how much effort they mobilize, how long they will persevere in the face of difficulties, and how well they manage situations (Bandura, 1989). Self-inefficacious thinking creates discrepancies between what people know and what they actually do. Bandura's theory has been used to guide many prevention efforts in this area, especially those that emphasize skill building. Some of the components of these models are represented in programs we review.

Howard and McCabe (1992) described a 10-part information and skills approach program for use with younger teens. The program was based on the assumption that younger teens (under 16 years old) are not yet able to understand the implications of their actions, can get their social needs met in ways other than having sex, and are often pressured into situations in which they really do not want to participate. It was also assumed that young teens need to be taught to resist peer pressure. The goal of the program was postponing sexual involvement, using older teenagers as program leaders.

Half the curriculum presented factual information on reproductive health, including information on birth control and its use. The other half focused on skill building and, in particular, on how to resist pressure to have sex. Eighth graders from predominantly low-income families comprised the sample. The overall findings indicated that students who experienced the program were significantly more likely to postpone sexual involvement than those in a control condition; the former were also more likely to use contraceptives if they did have sex. Fewer pregnancies were recorded over a five-year follow-up for program participants versus controls. Unfortunately, youth who were sexually active prior to the program were not found to change the frequency of their sexual activity, and pregnancy rates of this subset of the sample were not statistically different from non-program youth. These data suggest that alternative preventive strategies may be needed for youth who are already sexually active.

Jemmott, Jemmott, Spears, Hewitt, and Cruz-Collins (1992) used self-efficacy theory to design and implement a prevention program for AIDS risk behavior. The strategy advocated condom use in sexually active, female, African American adolescents, 15 to 21 years old. The social cognitive intervention condition consisted of activities designed to increase participants' confidence in using condoms and to address fears that condom use would have adverse consequences on the experience of pleasure. Control conditions which were used for comparison included an information-only condition where participants learned about AIDS and how to prevent STDs, and a general health-promotion condition. The social cognitive condition was superior to the control conditions in increasing perceived self-efficacy to use condoms and in increasing hedonistic expectancies about sexual activity using condoms.

In a second study (Jemmott, Jemmott, & Fong, 1992), the theory of reasoned action was used to design a sexual risk-reduction program for African American male high school students. The risk-reduction conditions aimed to increase participants' knowledge about STDs and to weaken problematic attitudes toward risky behavior. A control condition consisted of career-exploration activities. Immediately following the interventions, participants in the risk-reduction condition were found to have greater knowledge about AIDS, expressed less favorable attitudes toward risky sexual behaviors, and reported weaker intentions to engage in such behavior than did their career-condition counterparts. Differences in knowledge and intentions were found to remain at a three-month follow-up.

These studies are particularly noteworthy in that they are theory driven, had appropriate control groups, and used single-gender samples. Single-gender programs may be appropriate given the significant gender differences that tend to exist with regard to active versus passive decision making regarding sexual behavior (Levinson, 1986) and contraceptive use self-efficacy (Joffe & Radius, 1993). Thus, prevention of sexual risk-taking seems to be one area in which gender is a critical variable; skills, information, and attitudes seem highly related to implementing safer sexual practices, and perception of norms of adolescent sexual behavior in varying sociocultural contexts are important issues in this prevention domain.

Violence Prevention

Over the past two decades, psychologists and other health care providers have become increasingly concerned about escalating rates of violence among children and adolescents. This concern has mirrored increased attention of the media and legal system in response to rising homocide and injury statistics. Violence prevention has become a priority of the federal government in the last decade, as evidenced by the Centers for Disease Control's establishment of a Division of Violence Prevention and a Youth Violence Prevention Team. Beyond direct physical and developmental costs of youth violence, violence-related injury and disability is estimated to be billions of dollars annually (T.R. Miller, Cohen, & Rossman, 1993).

Prior to discussing the prevalence of youth violence, it is important to distinguish between youth aggression and youth violence. Aggression, characterized by fistfights, physical pushing, or name calling, is frequently observed among young people and is considered normative (Tolan & Loeber, 1993). Violent behavior, which causes physical harm either intentionally or unintentionally to another person(s), is more serious and much less normative (Tolan & Guerra, 1994). This distinction is often omitted or unclear in many prevention programs, yet it is important to the design of programs, particularly when one considers that most violent behavior is committed by a relatively small minority of youth (Loeber & Stouthamer-Loeber, 1998; Tolan & Guerra, 1994).

Although violent behavior may be relatively less frequent than other forms of risky behavior (e.g., drug use, sexual activity), its consequences take a much greater toll on others. For example, homicide is the second leading cause of death for adolescents between the ages of 15 and 24, and the leading cause of death for Blacks and members of Latin ethnic groups of this age group (Centers for Disease Control, 1996). In 1994, 38% of all homicide victims in the United States were younger than 24, and 20% of all violent crimes were committed by juveniles under the age of 18 (Centers for Disease Control, 1996). Such statistics suggest the existence of a crisis situation and underscore the urgency of understanding the precursors of violent behavior.

A number of individual and sociocultural theories have been proposed as explanations for the development of violence in youth. Igra and Irwin (1996) reviewed more general theories of youth risk-taking behavior. We provide a selective review of some of the major theories regarding the etiology and development of youth aggression and violence.

One of the simplest and most predictive theories of violence in youth is social learning theory (Bandura & Walters, 1959). The theory asserts that young people learn aggression and violence through observation, direct experience, evaluation of the consequences of such behavior, and regulation of one's own behavior. This theory has been instrumental in a variety of prevention and intervention programs. Some examples include limiting children's exposure to media violence (e.g. television, music, video games), reinforcement of prosocial responses to conflict, use of extinction methods to reduce antisocial behavior, and efforts to enhance young people's social perspective taking and self-monitoring. An extension of social learning theory is Patterson's (1982) social interactional model, which suggests that the contexts in which social learning occurs are important to the acquisition and maintenance of violence in youth (Pepler & Slaby, 1994). According to this model, children who reside in families or communities in which they are exposed to violence are more likely to replicate that behavior.

There have also been a number of other social-cognitive models offered as explanations for youth violence. These models focus on the role that cognitive processes play in learning, the interpretation of social experiences, influences on a person's response to particular social experiences, and the extent to which these processes influence continued aggression or openness to reductions in aggression. Pepler and Slaby (1994) provide a comprehensive review of these models.

Entire bodies of literature have been derived from applications of these models, and a comprehensive review of them is clearly beyond the scope of this chapter. However, these models are used to guide the following review of prevention programs.

Many studies have suggested that the causes of violence exist within an individual, grow out of interpersonal relationships, are the by-product of the individual's social milieu, or result from some interaction of these factors (Tolan & Guerra, 1994).

These risk factors include exposure to violence in the home and community (Gorman-Smith & Tolan, 1998); deficits in social problem-solving skills and cognitive impairments (Dodge & Frame, 1982); the presence of beliefs and attitudes supportive of aggression and violence (Guerra, Huesmann, & Hanish, 1995); and early involvement in aggressive and violent behavior (Farrington, 1991). Loeber and Stouthamer-Loeber (1998) suggest that initial involvements in violent behavior at younger ages are more predictive of later violent episodes. These children may be at the greatest risk for engaging in more serious and persistent delinquent and violent behavior in adolescence and adulthood.

Family characteristics that place children at risk include a history of psychological maladjustment and deviance in the child's parents (e.g., parental substance abuse or dependency and criminal behavior). Additionally, Henggler, Melton, and Smith (1992) and Thornberry, Huzinga, and Loeber (1995) suggested that children who do not possess a positive emotional relationship with their parents are potentially at risk. Parents who possess ineffective parenting skills, such as poor communication, inappropriate supervision of their children's activities, or a general lack of involvement in their child's life, also have children at greater risk for violent behavior (see

Farrington, 1991; Loeber & Stouthamer-Loeber, 1998). Other influences that can create risk include chronic stress (e.g., poverty) or the absence of a positive parental support system, sometimes observed in single-parent families (McLoyd, 1998).

A child's nonfamilial environment can create risk conditions as well. Children who associate with peers involved in violent or delinquent behavior increase their risk for participating in similar types of behavior. Additionally, delinquent or violent behavior often tends to occur in the presence of peers, which can increase the reinforcement of the violent behavior (Masten & Coatsworth, 1998).

Peers who are involved in violent behavior can also create problems within particular institutional environments (e.g. schools, community organizations). Students report higher numbers of fights, weapons, and drugs in schools where there is a gang presence (National Center for Educational Statistics, 1995). Youth in communities where there are gangs also report fears about personal safety and a resulting need to be self-defensive as they seek to negotiate their neighborhoods (Reese, Vera, Reyes, & Thompson, 1998).

Environmental characteristics such as abject poverty may also create risk potential for violence in youth. Poverty is a complex and important factor, particularly in interpreting differences in epidemiological rates of victimization and perpetration among ethnic and racial minorities in the United States. Stiffman, Earls, Dore, Cunningham, and Farber (1996) noted that poor people in the United States who are disproportionately of minority status do not have equal access to health, educational, and economic resources and tend to be victims of oppression (i.e., social violence). These authors noted that such oppression can increase the liklihood of individual and community violence.

Children in urban communities, when compared with children residing in rural or suburban communities, are at greater risk for delinquency and participation in violent behaviors, particularly in communities characterized by poverty (Black & Krishnakumar, 1998). Although it is unclear exactly how urbanization influences this risk, there is a substantial literature documenting aggression (Guerra, Huesmann, Tolan, & Van-Acker, 1995) and violence in urban communities (DuRant, Getts, Cadenhead, & Woods, 1995). Efforts to understand how specific types of urban ecologies compromise the development of children have been advanced by Wandersman and Nation (1998) who have developed models based on neighborhood characteristics (e.g., high-density buildings, abandoned buildings) to explain psychological maladjustment.

Two other risk factors include the availability of firearms and the influence of alcohol and other drugs. Presently, youth are carrying firearms in greater numbers, (Kann et al., 1996), particularly inner-city youth who report carrying weapons for protection (Jenkins & Bell, 1994). The Centers for Disease Control (1996) has found a significant positive relationship between youth homicides and homicides committed by firearms. Drugs are also often present in a large number of violent acts and must be considered a risk factor for violent behavior (Osgood, 1995).

Clarification of multivariate models is needed to advance the field's understanding of violence prevention. Drug Strategies (1998), a Washington, D.C., policy group, which focuses on the prevention of drug abuse and other risk behaviors, noted that comprehensive and rigorous evaluation studies of violence prevention programs are rare, though several elements considered critical to promising programs were cited. Examples include skill-based training informed by relevant theory (i.e., social learning and social cognitive theories); approaches that are multifaceted and include family, peers, community, and the media; developmentally tailored interventions; teacher training; culturally sensitive material; and programs that have been empirically demonstrated to be effective (see also Tolan & Guerra, 1994).

To illustrate some of the typical approaches to violence prevention, we have reviewed programs that include both person- and environment-centered components. Evaluation in violence prevention is so new that it is difficult to say with certainty what is the most effective way to implement programs. However, the following represent some of the most well-known efforts.

Hammond's (1991) Positive Adolescents Choices Training (PACT) is an example of a skill-based prevention program focused on aggression and violence in African American familial and peer relationships. Using the Dealing with Anger videotapes that depict similar peers, this program highlights the process of violence escalation, social perspective taking, negotiation, and self-regulation skills in the prevention of aggressive and violent behavior in youth considered at-risk for such behavior. A preliminary outcome study of the 20-session program, using an experimental and control group, found that control group participants were referred to juvenile courts more frequently for violent offenses at a three-year follow-up (Hammond & Yung, 1993).

The Viewpoints Training Program (Guerra & Panizzon, 1986) is a treatment program that uses cognitive-behavioral methods for changing youth beliefs and attitudes about violent behavior by enhancing problem-solving skills. In a study with incarcerated youth, Guerra and Slaby (1990) found that program participants had greater decreases in aggression than control group participants. The decrease was directly related to the targeted variables of the treatment program, thus providing some support for its promise as an effective intervention for youth with a history of violent behavior.

The Providing Alternative Thinking Strategies (PATHS) is a school-based skills training program that addresses a number of youth development constructs (Greenberg, 1996). These constructs include emotional, social, behavioral and moral competencies, prosocial norms and behavior, and resiliency. The focus of this program is on enhancing participants' ability to self-manage emotions and behavior while using effective interpersonal problem-solving skills. The program is taught by classroom teachers three times a week for approximately 30 minutes each session.

Evaluations of the program using a quasi-experimental design (i.e., with intervention and control groups) with both normally adjusted and high-risk students are promising (Greenberg & Kusche, 1997) and included significant improvements in defining complex feelings, reasoning and social perspective taking, interpersonal problem solving, and decreases in aggressive solutions. Additionally, there were significant improvements in frustration tolerance, assertiveness, and social skills. Teachers also rated participants as demonstrating greater self-management skills, appropriately resolving peer conflicts, and identifying problems significantly better than controls (Catalano, Berglund, Ryan, Lonczak, & Hawkins, 1999).

A one-year follow-up showed a sustained effect of the program on problem-solving skills and social perspective taking. Lower aggression was also reported. A two-year follow-up showed that both the normally adjusted and high-risk participants reported lower rates of conduct problems.

In conclusion, it would seem that children and adolescents, especially those with histories of aggression, need to learn a number of skills related to nonviolence. They need to know how to solve their problems assertively and communicate with others nonaggressively. They need to be with families and peers who do not reinforce or model violence or abuse. However, with regard to environmental contexts, they need to be provided with safe, organized activities in which they can participate regularly. We address some specific recommendations for advancing violence prevention efforts and research at the end of this chapter.

Resiliency and Competency Promotion Programs

One of the major challenges, and greatest hopes, to the prevention field has been determining why some youth, in the face of adversity and risk factors, do *not* experience problems, but rather make healthy decisions and have high levels of self-esteem and confidence. Rutter (1987) noted the importance of understanding how some youth maintain self-esteem and self-efficacy when faced with the same stressful situations that cause others to lose hope, and how some youth have mentors or confidants to whom they can turn when others find themselves alone. Children who thrive in the midst of adversity are recognized as having much to teach professionals about healthy development in adverse conditions (Masten & Coatsworth, 1998).

Anthony and Cohler (1987) referred to such successful children as invulnerable, but in many ways it is misleading to think of these children as insulated from risk and stressors. It is not the case that these youth avoid stressful life situations. Rather, the central element seems to lie in their power of recovery and their ability to return to patterns of adaptation and competence that characterized them prior to the stress period (Garmezy, 1993). Terms that have been used to describe the characteristics or qualities of such children are competency and resiliency.

Competency generally refers to a pattern of effective adaptation to one's sociocultural environment that is influenced both by a child's capabilities and the nature of the contexts in which the child lives (Masten & Coatsworth, 1998). Resiliency is defined as demonstrated competence despite significant challenges to adaptation or development, which characterizes individual differences in people's response to stress and adversity (Garmezy, 1993; Masten & Coatsworth, 1998; Rutter, 1987).

Researchers have attempted to address prevention of mental health problems through understanding and enhancing protective factors related to competence and resiliency (Anthony & Cohler, 1987; Garmezy, 1983; Radke-Yarrow & Brown, 1993; Werner & Smith, 1989). Garmezy (1993) identified three categories of protective factors: dispositional/individual attributes of the child, family characteristics such as cohesion and warmth, and the availability and use of external support systems (e.g., youth organizations, schools). The first category has received a great deal of attention from researchers.

Dispositional/individual factors include temperament, intelligence, internal locus of control, humor (Luthar & Zigler, 1991), self-esteem, self-efficacy (Masten & Coatsworth, 1998; Rutter, 1987), and positive future expectations (Wyman, Cowen, Work, & Kerley, 1993). The presence of important "life skills" or interpersonal competency skills were also found to characterize resilient children. Life skills maximize a child's chance of obtaining positive rewards from their environment while minimizing costs to the self and others (Gilchrist, Schinke, & Maxwell, 1987). These skills are thought to allow adolescents to make and preserve relationships, cope with a constantly changing environmental context, and, in the end, to gain and maintain self-esteem (Gilchrist et al., 1987). Buhrmester, Furman, Wittenberg, and Reis (1988) defined interpersonal competence skills as consisting of five domains: initiating relationships, self-disclosure, asserting displeasure with other's actions, providing emotional support, and managing interpersonal conflicts.

In attempting to create a profile of resilient children, Parker, Cowen, Work, and Wyman (1990) used discriminant analysis to identify that, in combination, global self-worth, empathy, realistic control attributions, social problem-solving skills, and self-esteem predicted group membership of stress-resilient versus stress-affected children. In a 10-year longitudinal study, Radke-Yarrow and Brown (1993) found that resilient children elicited more positive reactions from teachers, family members, and had more positive self-perceptions.

Bernard (1991) suggested that the challenge for the 1990s was the implementation of prevention strategies that strengthen protective factors in children, families, schools, and communities. Programs have been designed to foster resiliency and enhance social competence in children and adolescence. An example of a social competency promotion program was designed and evaluated by Caplan et al. (1992). Social competency in this case described interpersonal effectiveness and included teaching youth developmentally appropriate skills and information, fostering prosocial and health-enhancing values and beliefs, and creating environmental supports to reinforce the real-life application of skills (Weissberg, Caplan, & Sivo, 1989). The 20-session program emphasized stress management, self-esteem, problem solving, general health and drug education, assertiveness, and the development of social networks.

Research participants were sixth and seventh graders from urban and suburban school districts who ranged in age from 11 to 14. In the urban sample, 90% of the students were African American, and in the suburban sample, 99% were White. The intervention was found to be associated with enhanced self- and teacher-reported social adjustment of youth in both urban and suburban settings. Program students also evidenced improved coping skills.

The Seattle Social Development Project is a school-based program which addresses teaching practices in classrooms (e.g., managing disruptive child behavior effectively and the use of group process techniques to encourage prosocial behavior among students), combined with student training in social skill development (e.g., cognitive, social, emotional, and behavioral competencies), and parent training (e.g., instruction in understanding developmental competencies, effective behavior management techniques). The program is designed for elementary and middle-school students living in poorer communities with high levels of crime (Hawkins, Von Cleve, & Catalano, 1991). Evaluation of the Seattle project used a quasi-experimental design with control groups (see Hawkins, Catalano, Kosterman, Abbott, & Hill, 1999). A six-year follow-up evaluation demonstrated positive effects for the intervention group when compared with the control group on indices of delinquency and sexual behavior outcomes. Participants in the intervention also reported greater school bonding, increases in self-reported achievement, and less school behavior problems than controls. Lastly, Hawkins et al. (1999) found evidence that the intervention was significantly more effective for poorer participants in promoting school attachment yet more effective for participants from higher income families in delaying pregnancy or fatherhood. Thus, this program not only demonstrated positive effects for reducing violence but promoting social competencies in other life areas.

Danish (1996, 1997) has developed an award-winning life-skills intervention for adolescents called "The Goal Program" which is designed to teach adolescents how to succeed in their various life domains. Program evaluation data revealed that participants had better school attendance, less involvement in health-compromising behaviors, decreases in violence, and other problem behaviors as compared with their control group counterparts. The approach to program evaluation has also included idiographic procedures that allow participants to measure their level of success in pursuing a stated goal. Danish (1996) emphasized the importance of measuring for different outcomes and including measures of positive health, as opposed to negative markers.

Taking a positive- versus deficit-based approach to prevention is clearly represented in the resiliency/social competency literature. Such an approach is consistent with counseling psychology's emphasis on strengths and enhancement. Additionally, comprehensive life-skills programs are tentatively becoming approaches of choice in multiple domains of prevention programming (e.g., substance abuse, violence prevention). Thus, we anticipate that resiliency and social competency programs will gain more and more attention from prevention specialists in the coming years.

The most current trends in the resiliency/competency promotion research are typified in the "positive youth development" movement described by Catalano et al. (1999). Positive youth development approaches to preventive interventions assume that though children and adolescents who are still in school, not sexually active or engaging in delinquent behavior, would be considered "problem free," they may still lack the skills and attitudes to be productive members of families or the workforce (Weissberg & Greenberg, 1997). Thus, prevention programs which use decreases in "problem" behaviors as focal points of outcome (or program content) may in fact be insufficient in truly maximizing the potential of youth.

The components of positive youth development programs focus on fostering skills, attitudes, and competencies, including fostering bonding between children, family, peers, school, community, and culture; fostering resiliency; promoting social competencies (e.g., reading social cues, problem solving, prosocial behavior); enhancing cognitive competencies (e.g., school achievement, decision making); fostering behavioral competencies (e.g., communication skills, refusal skills, conflict-resolution skills); developing emotional competencies (e.g., ability to deal with one's own and others' feelings); fostering self-determination; enhancing moral competencies (e.g., empathy, respect for self and others); fostering spirituality; fostering self-efficacy; and developing positive identities (Catalano et al., 1999).

Many of the aforementioned components have been empirically demonstrated to decrease youth's involvement in a variety of health-compromising behaviors and to increase hallmarks of positive development, such as academic achievement, positive family relationships, and self-esteem (Catalano et al., 1999). The future of the child/adolescent prevention field is likely to be greatly influenced by the positive youth development movement.

FUTURE DIRECTIONS IN PREVENTION WITH YOUTH

As the field continues to investigate the effectiveness of existing prevention programs and understand the risk and protective mechanisms involved in a variety of childhood and adolescent mental health disorders, we must address the question of how to reach youth who are most in need of such efforts. The true benefit of our prevention efforts will be realized when we take "what works" into our communities on a larger scale, and we begin to see a decrease in the need for remedial services in youth.

But how is this to happen? How can we incorporate successful programs into schools, community centers, or other settings on a long-term basis? Reiss and Price (1996) argued that successful programs are maintained in communities only when they are owned and supported by community members. For this reason, it is necessary to engage in the process of forming partnerships with community members to negotiate effective and lasting alliances.

Lerner (1995) has spoken at great length about the ways in which community collaborations can be mutually beneficial when based on the assumptions that community members themselves are powerful agents of change and have the knowledge to address many existing problems. Among his suggestions for collaborative program development are: start with understanding the needs and goals of the community by including community members in the process of organizing and implementing programs; develop trusting relationships between the university and the community by making long-term commitments; integrate issues of diversity and the sociocultural context of the community being served; foster relationships between the children, parents, teachers, and community members; use multiple methods of evaluation guided by the values, norms, and aspirations of the community; emphasize the existing strengths of the community (i.e., what *is* working); and use both environment-centered and person-centered strategies.

In every area of prevention programming and research, we must address the issue of providing services to youth most in need. Often these youth are not in school at all, or attend so infrequently that they do not benefit from such programs when they are offered through schools.

In the area of STD and pregnancy prevention programming, future prevention programs must attempt to extend services to underserved, underrepresented populations (e.g., school dropouts, poor, ethnic minority communities, gay, lesbian, and bisexual youth). Because nonheterosexual adolescents can be particularly difficult to identify, programs must be presented in ways that include a wider range of sexual activity than male-female sexual relations.

Additionally, contraceptive resources must be made more accessible to those youth who choose to engage in sexual activity. Nonabstinent adolescents should not be "punished" for their choices by withholding resources (i.e., not funding programs that provide contraceptives) because the consequences to both the youth and society can be staggering. Programs must also seek to incorporate the influences of drug and alcohol use and coercion (e.g., violence) on sexual decision making. In other words, in instances where refusing sexual activity may bring about dangerous consequences for youth, adolescents must be assisted in methods for protecting themselves (Vera, Reese, Paikoff, & Jarrett, 1996).

The single most critical impediment to effective violence prevention appears to be the lack of systematic longitudinal studies about program effectiveness. The Drug Strategies (1998) group noted that, while rigorous evaluation studies are underway, the current empirical literature is limited. Of the programs evaluated, none met all of the following standards: (1) publication in peer review journals with (2) true experimental designs, (3) adequate sample size and statistical evaluation, and (4) outcome data following participants for at least two years.

In developing models to explain violence, it must be recognized that violence does not occur in isolation from other risk behaviors or risk factors. Models must be multifactorial, consider the reciprocal influence that different risk behaviors and risk factors have on one another, and recognize that influences may be different as a function of the target group's developmental period. For example, Gorman-Smith and Tolan (1998) found that exposure to community violence was related to increased depression, and aggression and depression have been identified as risk factors for adolescent substance abuse. Because violence prevention is a complex issue, intervention should occur at multiple levels with greater emphasis placed on primary prevention.

Future research on the role of social competence and resiliency should attend to the development of life skills on a long-term basis. As children and adolescents develop toward adulthood, they are presented with opportunities to use their skills in a variety of specific situations. It must be demonstrated empirically that being assertive with peers generalizes across contexts (assertiveness with friends, intimate relationships, acquaintances), where the reactions to various styles of communication may differ. For example, children may have an easier time refusing drugs from an acquaintance than from a good friend or boyfriend/girlfriend. Also, role plays, while behavioral in nature, may not simulate the emotional arousal involved in real-life dramas. Thus, skills alone, when taken out of a real-life context, may not be used at important times in the life experience of youth.

More attention also must be paid to environment-centered aspects of resiliency (e.g., creating opportunities for adults to be available to children, fostering family cohesion) than has previously been the case. If we fail to incorporate such contexts, we inappropriately place all the responsibility for resiliency and competency within the realm of the child, despite the fact that families and communities are significant contexts for the child. Children do not possess such total control in the real world.

There has not yet been adequate investigation of cultural (e.g., ethnic, gender) differences in life-skill competencies. For example, girls may be socialized to seek out social support or help in ways that boys are not. Also, boys may be more comfortable with assertive communication or may weigh the consequences of loss of friendship in ways differently than do girls. Contextual differences must also be addressed. For example, for children who reside among community violence, there may be different consequences of assertive communication or perceived benefits of aggressive posturing than for children residing in less violent communities.

One final factor that deserves study is whether children who may have existing mental health problems can benefit appropriately from prevention program participation. Leith and Baumeister (1996) found that emotionally distraught individuals may bring failure or misfortune to themselves by making poor, nonoptimal choices, and by taking unwise risks. Thus, children who have emotional problems may need to be identified in universal programming efforts and be provided with appropriate referrals.

Another critical consideration for the future is the importance of evaluation, both in terms of testing the applicability of initially successful programs to diverse populations and the discontinuation of programs found to be unsuccessful. Evaluation should include both short- and long-term outcome measures that are meaningful to both scientist-practitioners and the community participants. This process of collaborative evaluation is known as Development-in-Context Evaluation (Lerner, 1995) or Participatory-Normative Evaluation (Weiss & Greene, 1992).

Methodological rigor balanced with respect for the needs of the target population is an important goal for future program evaluation. Although the use of control groups for comparison and the random assignment of participants to conditions have been hallmarks of methodological rigor, these approaches may require modification to fit the expectations of parents, school administrators, and community leaders. For example, a school may prefer a delayed-intervention comparison group, where different classrooms of children receive the prevention program at alternating times, to a traditional no-treatment control group. Such methodological compromises, and a reliance on quasi-experimental designs, may be important to maintaining positive future relationships with community groups.

Program evaluation must also attempt to determine what aspects of the programs are responsible for their impact. In many cases, and in violence prevention in particular, it is too soon to know conclusively what aspects of programs account for change in participants. However, moving closer to this goal will allow researchers to address issues of cost-effectiveness and efficiency.

What seems to be clear at this point is the need for investigators to look at multiple, interacting risk and protective factors in understanding prevention in youth. Because there is no single predictor of problems, it is unlikely that any "magic bullets" for prevention will be identified (Masten & Coatsworth, 1998). Thus, programs must continue to develop both person- and environment-centered strategies in combination.

Theory must become an inseparable aspect of prevention program design, implementation, and evaluation in the future. As models of risk-taking behavior have indicated, the relationships between knowledge, risk and protective factors, and behavior are complex, and programs that are theory-driven are more likely to address such complexities, as well as facilitate data interpretation (Black & Krishnakumar, 1998). Additionally, we must be able to articulate why successful programs work if we hope to influence public policy and the allocation of funding for prevention programs.

As was stated earlier, an emphasis on prevention is one of the defining features of counseling psychology's identity among mental health specialties. Because prevention efforts are most beneficial to individuals who are early in their development, less exposed to risk factors, and uninvolved in risk-taking behavior, it stands to reason that children and adolescents are in many ways our preferred constituents.

The training of future counseling psychologists should include an emphasis on prevention and opportunities to deliver prevention services to youth. Hanson, Skager, and Mitchell (1991) described a prototypical doctoral program emphasizing prevention and proactive interventions designed to expand the roles of counselors. Their program focuses on training, education, fieldwork, and research in five areas of study: theory and methods for identifying "at risk" populations, effective prevention strategies, planning and consultation, program implementation, and evaluation, program modification, and research.

Conyne (1997) identified 10 skill clusters that were essential to training counselors in preventive counseling: primary prevention education, personal attributes development (e.g., flexibility, creativity, organizational skills), the ethics of prevention, marketing skills, multicultural competencies, group facilitation skills, collaboration skills, organization and setting dynamic skills, political dynamics (i.e., knowing the implications of systemic change inherent in prevention work), and research/program evaluation skills. Although many existing counseling programs provide training in some of the cluster areas, Conyne (1997) notes that fewer programs provide attention to primary prevention perspectives, organizational, and political dynamic skills.

Yung, Hammond, Sampson, and Warfield (1998) described a doctoral training program in clinical psychology that has an emphasis in violence prevention. Students in this program are prepared to become violence prevention trainers and consultants, in addition to direct service providers. Training emphasizes epidemiological patterns of youth violence, risk factors, public health models of intervention, and conceptual bases of prevention. Students are also exposed to curricula in social skill competencies (e.g., conflict resolution, anger management) and cognitive-behavioral theory. Experiential training takes place in middle-school practicum, where students serve as program facilitators and consultants to teachers and school personnel.

Such models are very useful for training programs that currently do not include prevention as a major focus. Important, however, to advancing the skills of trainees in prevention practice and research will be renewed interest in this area among the professorate. It is our sincere hope that the training of future counseling psychologists will feature prevention strategies in research and practice, with special attention paid to working with children and adolescents.

REFERENCES

Ajzen, I., & Fishbein, M. (1980). *Understanding attitudes and predicting social behavior.* Englewood Cliffs, NJ: Prentice-Hall.

Albee, G.W. (1996). Revolutions and counterrevolutions in prevention. *American Psychologist, 51,* 1130–1133.

Allen, J.P., Philliber, S., & Hoggson, J. (1990). School-based prevention of teen-age pregnancy and school dropout: Process evaluation of the national replication of the Teen Outreach Program. *American Journal of Community Psychology, 18,* 505–524.

Anthony, E.J., & Cohler, B.J. (1987). *The invulnerable child.* New York: Guilford Press.

Baker, S., & Shaw, M. (1987). *Improving counseling through primary prevention.* Columbus, OH: Merrill.

Bandura, A. (1986). *Social foundations of thought and action: A social-cognitive theory.* Englewood Cliffs, NJ: Prentice-Hall.

Bandura, A. (1989). Perceived self-efficacy in the exercise of control over AIDS. In V. Mays, G. Albee, & S. Schneider (Eds.), *Primary prevention of AIDS: Psychological approaches.* London: Sage.

Bandura, A., & Walters, R.H. (1959). *Adolescent aggression.* New York: Ronald Press.

Battjes, R.J. (1985). Prevention of adolescent drug abuse. *International Journal of the Addictions, 20,* 1113–1134.

Becker, M. (1974). *The health belief model and personal health behavior.* Thorofare, NJ: Slack.

Bernard, B. (1991). *Fostering resiliency in kids: Protective factors in the family, school, and community.* Portland, OR: Northwest Regional Educational Laboratory.

Black, M.M., & Krishnakumar, A. (1998). Children in low-income, urban settings: Interventions to promote mental health and well-being. *American Psychologist, 53,* 635–646.

Boles, S., Casas, J.M., Furlong, M., Gonzalez, G., & Morrison, G. (1994). Alcohol and other drug use patterns among Mexican-American, Mexican, and Caucasian adolescents: New directions for assessment and research. *Journal of Clinical Child Psychology, 23,* 39–46.

Botvin, G.J., Baker, E., Dusenbury, L., Tortu, S., & Botvin, E.M. (1990). Preventing adolescent drug abuse through a multimodal cognitive-behavioral approach: Results of a 3-year study. *Journal of Consulting and Clinical Psychology, 58,* 437–446.

Botvin, G.J., & Botvin, E.M. (1992). Adolescent tobacco, alcohol, and drug abuse: Prevention strategies, empirical findings, and assessment issues. *Developmental and Behavioral Pediatrics, 13,* 290–301.

Brooks-Gunn, J., & Paikoff, R.L. (1993). Sex is a gamble, kissing is a game: Adolescent sexuality and health promotion. In S.P. Millstein, A. Petersen, & E. Nightengale (Eds.), *Promotion of health behavior in adolescence.* New York: Oxford University Press.

Buhrmester, D., Furman, W., Wittenberg, M.T., & Reis, H.T. (1988). Domains of interpersonal competence in peer relationships. *Journal of Personality and Social Psychology, 55,* 991–1008.

Bukoski, W.J. (1986). School-based substance abuse prevention: A review of program research. In S. Griswold-Ezekoye, K. Kumpfer, & W.J. Bukoski (Eds.), *Childhood and chemical abuse: Prevention and intervention.* New York: Hawthorn Press.

Caplan, M., Weissberg, R.P., Grober, J.S., Sivo, P.J., Grady, K., & Jacoby, C. (1992). Social competence promotion with inner city and suburban young adolescents: Effects on social adjustment and alcohol use. *Journal of Consulting and Clinical Psychology, 60,* 56–63.

Card, J.J., Peterson, J.L., & Greeno, C.G. (1992). Adolescent pregnancy prevention programs: Design, monitoring, and evaluation. In B.C. Miller, J.J. Card, R.L. Paikoff, & J.L. Peterson (Eds.), *Preventing adolescent pregnancy* (pp. 1–37). Newbury Park: Sage.

Catalano, R.F., Berglund, M.L., Ryan, J.A.M., Lonczak, H.C., & Hawkins, J.D. (1999). *Positive youth development in the United States: Research findings on evaluations of positive youth development programs.* Department of Health and Human Services, National Institute for Child Health and Human Development, Washington, DC.

Centers for Disease Control and Prevention. (1996). *National summary of injury mortality data, 1987–1994.* Atlanta: National Center for Injury Prevention and Control.

Coley, R.L., & Chase-Lansdale, P.L. (1998). Adolescent pregnancy and parenthood: Recent evidence and future directions. *American Psychologist, 53,* 152–166.

Conyne, R.K. (1987). *Primary preventive counseling.* Muncie, IN: Accelerated Development.

Conyne, R.K. (1997). Educating students in preventive counseling. *Counselor Education and Supervision, 36,* 259–269.

Danish, S.J. (1996). Interventions for enhancing adolescents' life skills. *Humanistic Psychologist, 24,* 365–381.

Danish, S.J. (1997). Going for the goal: A life skills program for adolescents. In T. Gullotta & G. Albee (Eds.), *Primary prevention works* (pp. 291–312). Newbury Park, CA: Sage.

Dodge, K.A., & Frame, C.L. (1982). Social cognitive biases and deficits in aggressive boys. *Child Development, 53,* 629–635.

Drug Strategies. (1998). *Safe schools, safe students: A guide to violence prevention.* Washington, DC.: Drug Strategies.

Dryfoos, J.G. (1990). *Adolescents at risk: Prevalence and prevention.* New York: Oxford University Press.

DuRant, R.H., Getts, A.G., Cadenhead, C., & Woods, E.R. (1995). The association between weapon-carrying and the use of violence among adolescents living in and around public housing. *Journal of Adolescence, 18,* 579–592.

Durlak, J.A. (1997). *Successful prevention programs for children and adolescents.* New York: Plenum Press.

Durlak, J.A., & Wells, A.M. (1997). Primary prevention mental health programs for children and adolescents: A meta-analytic review. *American Journal of Community Psychology, 25,* 115–152.

Farrell, A.D., Danish, S.J., & Howard, C.W. (1992). Relationship between drug use and other problem behaviors in urban adolescents. *Journal of Consulting and Clinical Psychology, 60,* 705–712.

Farrington, D.P. (1991). Childhood aggression and adult violence: Early precursors and later-life outcomes. In D.J. Pepler & K.H. Rubin (Eds.), *The development and treatment of childhood aggression.* Hillsdale, NJ: Erlbaum.

Fishbein, M., & Middlestadt, S.E. (1989). Using the theory of reasoned action as a framework for understanding and changing AIDS-related behavior. In V. Mays, G.W. Albee, & S.F. Schneider (Eds.), *Primary prevention of AIDS.* Newbury Park, CA: Sage.

Fraser, J.M., Minton, H.L., & Valiquette, L. (1995). *Adolescents' top ten reasons for having unsafe sex.* Poster presented at the 103rd annual convention of the American Psychological Association, New York.

Garmezy, N. (1993). Children in poverty: Resilience despite risk. *Psychiatry, 56,* 127–136.

Gelso, C., & Fretz, B. (1992). *Counseling psychology.* Fort Worth, TX: Holt, Rinehart and Winston.

Gilchrist, L.D., Schinke, S.P., & Maxwell, J.S. (1987). Life skills counseling for preventing problems in adolescence. *Journal of Social Service Research, 10,* 73–84.

Gorman-Smith, D., & Tolan, P.H. (1998). The role of exposure to community violence and developmental problems among inner-city youth. *Development and Psychopathology, 10,* 101–116.

Greenberg, M.T. (1996). *The PATHS project: Preventive intervention for children: Final report to NIMH.* Seattle: University of Washington, Department of Psychology.

Greenberg, M.T., & Kusche, C.A. (1997, April). *Improving children's emotion regulation and social competence: The effects of the PATHS curriculum.* Paper presented at the annual meeting of the Society for Research in Child Development, Washington, DC.

Guerra, N.G., Huesmann, L.R., & Hanish, L. (1995). The role of normative beliefs in children's social behavior. In N. Eisenberg (Ed.), *Review of personality and social psychology* (Vol. 15, pp. 140–158). Thousand Oaks, CA: Sage.

Guerra, N.G., Huesmann, L.R., Tolan, P.H., & Van-Acker, R. (1995). Stressful events and individual beliefs as correlates of economic disadvantage and aggression among urban children. *Journal of Consulting and Clinical Psychology, 63,* 518–528.

Guerra, N.G., & Panizzon, A. (1986). *Viewpoints training program.* Santa Barbara, CA: Center for Law-Related Education.

Guerra, N.G., & Slaby, R.G. (1990). Cognitive mediators of aggression in adolescent offenders: 2. Intervention. *Developmental Psychology, 26,* 269–277.

Hammond, R. (1991). *Dealin with anger: Given' it. Takin' it. Workin' it out: Leader's guide.* Champaign, IL: Research Press.

Hammond, R., & Yung, B. (1993). *Evaluation and activity report: Positive adolescent choices training.* Unpublished grant report, U.S. Maternal and Child Health Bureau, Washington, DC.

Hanson, C.E., Skager, R., & Mitchell, R.R. (1991). Counselors in at-risk prevention services: An innovative program. *Journal of Mental Health Counseling, 13,* 253–263.

Hawkins, J.D., Catalano, R.F., Kosterman, R., Abbott, R., & Hill, K.G. (in press). *Preventing adolescent health-risk behaviors by strengthening protection during childhood.*

Hawkins, J.D., Catalano, R.F., & Miller, J.Y. (1992). Risk and protective factors for alcohol and other drug problems in adolescence and early adulthood: Implications for substance abuse prevention. *Psychological Bulletin, 112,* 64–105.

Hawkins, J.D., Lishner, D.M., Catalano, R.F., & Howard, M.O. (1986). Childhood predictors of adolescent substance abuse: Toward an empirically grounded theory. In S. Griswold-Ezekoye, K. Kumpfer, & W.J. Bukoski (Eds.), *Childhood and chemical abuse: Prevention and intervention.* New York: Hawthorn Press.

Hawkins, J.D., Von Cleve, E., & Catalano, R.F. (1991). Reducing early childhood aggression: Results of a primary prevention program. *Journal of the American Academy of Child Adolescent Psychiatry, 30,* 208–217.

Henggler, S.W., Melton, G.B., & Smith, L.A. (1992). Family preservation using multi-systemic therapy: An effective alternative to incarcerating serious juvenile offenders. *Journal of Consulting and Clinical Psychology, 60,* 953–961.

Horn, M. (1989). *Before it's too late: The child guidance movement in the United States, 1922–1945.* Philadelphia: Temple University Press.

Howard, M., & McCabe, J. (1992). An information and skills approach for younger teens: Postponing sexual involvement program. In B.C. Miller, J.J. Card, R.L. Paikoff, & J.L. Peterson (Eds.), *Preventing adolescent pregnancy.* Newbury Park, CA: Sage.

Igra, V., & Irwin, C.E. (1996). Theories of adolescent risk-taking behavior. In R. DiClemente, W. Hansen, & L. Ponton (Eds.), *Handbook of adolescent health risk behavior.* New York: Plenum Press.

Jemmott, J.B., Jemmott, L.S., & Fong, G.T. (1992). Reductions in HIV risk-associated sexual behaviors among Black male adolescents: Effects of an AIDS prevention intervention. *American Journal of Public Health, 82,* 372–377.

Jemmott, J.B., Jemmott, L.S., Spears, H., Hewitt, N., & Cruz-Collins, M. (1992). Self-efficacy, hedonistic expectancies, and condom-use intentions among inner-city Black adolescent women: A social cognitive approach to AIDS risk behavior. *Journal of Adolescent Health, 13,* 512–519.

Jenkins, E.J., & Bell, C.C. (1994). Violence among inner-city high school students and post-traumatic stress disorder. In S. Friedman (Ed.), *Anxiety disorders in African Americans.* New York: Springer.

Jessor, R. (1993). Successful adolescent development among youth in high-risk settings. *American Psychologist, 48,* 117–126.

Jessor, R., & Jessor, S.L. (1977). *Problem behavior and psychological development: A longitudinal study of youth.* San Diego, CA: Academic Press.

Joffe, A., & Radius, S.M. (1993). Self-efficacy and intent to use condoms among entering college freshmen. *Journal of Adolescent Health, 14,* 262–268.

Johnson, C.A., Pentz, M.A., Weber, M.D., Dwyer, J.H., Baer, N., MacKinnon, D.P., Hansen, W.B., & Flay, B.R. (1990). Relative effectiveness of comprehensive community programming for drug abuse prevention with high-risk and low-risk adolescents. *Journal of Consulting and Clinical Psychology, 58,* 447–456.

Kann, L., Warren, C.W., Harris, W.A., Collins, J.L., Williams, B.I., Ross, J.G., & Kolbe, L.J. (1996). Youth risk behavior surveillance. *Centers for Disease Control and Prevention, CDC Surveillance Summaries, Morbidity and Mortality Weekly Report, 45,* No. SS-4.

Kazdin, A.E. (1993). Adolescent mental health: Prevention and treatment programs. *American Psychologist, 48,* 127–141.

Kirscht, J.P., & Joseph, S.E. (1989). The health belief model: Some implications for behavior change, with reference to homosexual males. In V. Mays, G. Albee, & S. Schneider (Eds.), *Primary prevention of AIDS: Psychological approaches.* London: Sage.

Kiselica, M.S., & Look, C.T. (1993). Mental health counseling and prevention: Disparity between philosophy and practice? *Journal of Mental Health Counseling, 15,* 3–14.

Kumpfer, K.L., & DeMarsh, J. (1986). Family environmental and genetic influences on children's future chemical dependency. In S. Griswold-Ezekoye, K. Kumpfer, & W.J. Bukoski (Eds.), *Childhood and chemical abuse: Prevention and intervention.* New York: Hawthorn Press.

Leith, K.P., & Baumeister, R.F. (1996). Why do bad moods increase self-defeating behavior? Emotions, risk taking, and self-regulation. *Journal of Personality and Social Psychology, 71,* 1250–1267.

Lerner, R. (1995). *America's Youth in Crisis: Challenges and options for programs and policies.* Thousand Oaks, CA: Sage.

Levinson, R.A. (1986). Contraceptive self-efficacy: A perspective on teenage girls' contraceptive behavior. *Journal of Sex Research, 22,* 347–369.

Loeber, R., & Stouthamer-Loeber, M. (1998). Development of juvenile aggression and violence: Some common misconceptions and controversies. *American Psychologist, 53,* 242–259.

Luthar, S.S., & Zigler, E. (1991). Vulnerability and competence: A review of research on resilience in childhood. *American Journal of Orthopsychiatry, 61,* 6–22.

Manger, T.H., Hawkins, J.D., Haggerty, K.P., & Catalano, R.F. (1992). Mobilizing communities to reduce risks for drug abuse: Lessons on using research to guide prevention practice. *Journal of Primary Prevention, 13,* 3–21.

Masten, A.S., & Coatsworth, J.D. (1998). The development of competence in favorable and unfavorable environments: Lessons from research on successful children. *American Psychologist, 53,* 185–204.

McLoyd, V.C. (1998). Socioeconomic disadvantage and child development. *American Psychologist, 53,* 185–204.

McNeil, B., & Ingram, J.C. (1983). Prevention and counseling psychology: A survey of training practices. *Counseling Psychologist, 11,* 95–96.

Miller, B.C., & Paikoff, R.L. (1992). Comparing adolescent pregnancy programs: Methods and results. In B.C. Miller, J.J. Card, R.L. Paikoff, & J.L. Peterson (Eds.), *Preventing adolescent pregnancy.* Newbury Park, CA: Sage.

Miller, T.R., Cohen, M.A., & Rossman, S.B. (1993). Victim costs of violent crime and resulting injuries. *Health Affairs, 112*(4), 186–197.

Mrazek, P.L., & Haggerty, R.J. (1994). *Reducing risks for mental disorders: Frontiers for preventive intervention research.* Washington, DC: National Academy Press.

Munoz, R.F., Mrazek, P.J., & Haggerty, R.J. (1996). Institute of medicine report on prevention of mental disorders: Summary and commentary. *American Psychologist, 51,* 1116–1122.

Myers, J. (1992). Wellness, prevention, development: The cornerstone of the profession. *Journal of Counseling and Development, 71,* 136–139.

National Center for Educational Statistics. (1995). *Gangs and victimization at school. Education policy issues: Statistical perspective.* Washington, DC: US Department of Education.

Olson, C.M., Horan, J.J., & Polansky, J. (1992). Counseling psychology perspectives on the problem of substance abuse. In S.D. Brown & R.W. Lent (Eds.), *Handbook of counseling psychology* (Vol. 2, pp. 793–822). New York: Wiley.

Osgood, D.W. (1995). *Drugs, alcohol, and adolescent violence.* Center for the Study of the Prevention of Violence, Institute of Behavioral Sciences, 1–59. Boulder, CO.

Parker, G.R., Cowen, E.L., Work, W.C., & Wyman, P.A. (1990). Test correlates of stress affected and stress resilient outcomes among urban adolescents. *Journal of Primary Prevention, 11,* 19–35.

Patterson, G.R. (1982). *Coercive family processes.* Eugene, OR: Castalia Press.

Pentz, M.A., Trebow, E.A., Hansen, W.B., MacKinnon, D.P., Dwyer, J.H., Johnson, C.A., Flay, B.R., Daniels, S., & Cormack, C. (1990). Effects of program implementation on adolescent drug use behavior: The Midwestern prevention project. *Evaluation Review, 14,* 264–289.

Pepler, D.J., & Slaby, R.G. (1994). Theoretical and developmental perspectives on youth and violence. In L. Eron, J. Gentry, & P. Schlegel (Eds.), *Reason to hope: A psychosocial perspective on violence and youth.* Washington, DC: American Psychological Association.

Perry, C.L., Williams, C.L., Veblen-Mortenson, S., Toomey, T.L., Komro, K.A., Anstine, P.S., McGovern, P.G., Finnegan, J.R., Forster, J.L., Wagenaar, A.C., & Wolfson, M. (1996). Project Northland: Outcomes of a community-wide alcohol use prevention program during early adolescence. *American Journal of Public Health, 86,* 956–965.

Radke-Yarrow, M., & Brown, E. (1993). Resilience and vulnerability in children of multiple-risk families. *Development and Psychopathology, 5,* 581–592.

Reese, L.E., Vera, E.M., Reyes, R., & Thompson, K. (1998). *A qualitative investigation of perceptions of environmental risk in low-income African American children.* Unpublished manuscript.

Reiss, D., & Price, R.H. (1996). National research agenda for prevention research: The National Institute of Mental Health Report. *American Psychologist, 51,* 1109–1115.

Rogers, R.W. (1983). Cognitive and physiological processes in fear appeals and attitude change. In J. Cacioppo & R. Petty (Eds.), *Social psycho-physiology: A sourcebook* (pp. 153–176). New York: Guilford Press.

Rutter, M. (1987). Psychosocial resilience and protective mechanisms. *American Journal of Orthopsychiatry, 57,* 316–331.

Schilling, R.F., & McAlister, A.L. (1990). Preventing drug use in adolescents through media interventions. *Journal of Consulting and Clinical Psychology, 58,* 416–424.

Schmidt, J.J. (1994). Substance abuse prevention and intervention: An expanded perspective for counselors. *Journal of Counseling and Development, 72,* 514–519.

Szapocznik, J., Santisteban, D., Rio, A., Perez-Vidal, A., Santisteban, D., & Kurtines, W.M. (1989). Family effectiveness training: An intervention to prevent drug abuse and problem behaviors in hispanic adolescents. *Hispanic Journal of Behavioral Sciences, 11,* 4–27.

Thornberry, T.P., Huzinga, D., & Loeber, R. (1995). The prevention of serious delinquency and violence: Implications from the program of research on the causes and correlates of delinquency. *Sourcebook on Juvenile Offenders* (pp. 213–237). U.S. Department of Justice.

Tolan, P.H., & Guerra, N.G. (1994). *What works in reducing adolescent violence: An empirical review of the field.* The Center for the Study and Prevention of Violence, Institute of Behavioral Sciences, University of Colorado, Boulder.

Tolan, P.H., & Loeber, R. (1993). Antisocial behavior. In P.H. Tolan & B.J. Cohler (Eds.), *Handbook of clinical research and practice with adolescents.* New York: Wiley.

Vera, E.M., Reese, L.E., Paikoff, R.L., & Jarrett, R.L. (1996). Contextual factors of sexual risk-taking in urban African American preadolescent children. In B.J. Ross Leadbeater & N. Way (Eds.), *Urban girls: Resisting stereotypes, creating identities.* New York: New York University Press.

Wallack, L. (1986). Mass media, youth, and the prevention of substance abuse: Towards an integrated approach. In S. Griswold-Ezekoye, K. Kumpfer, & W.J. Bukoski (Eds.), *Childhood and chemical abuse: Prevention and intervention.* New York: Hawthorn Press.

Wandersman, A., & Nation, M. (1998). Urban neighborhoods and mental health: Psychological contributions to understanding toxicity, resilience, and interventions. *American Psychologist, 53*(6), 647–656.

Weiss, H.B., & Greene, J.C. (1992). An empowerment partnership for family support and education programs and evaluations. *Family Science Review, 5,* 131–148.

Weissberg, R.P., Caplan, M., & Harwood, R.L. (1991). Promoting competent young people in competence-enhancing environment: A systems-based perspective on primary prevention. *Journal of Consulting and Clinical Psychology, 59*(6), 720–728.

Weissberg, R.P., Caplan, M., & Sivo, P.J. (1989). A new conceptual framework for establishing school-based social competence promotion programs. In L.A. Bond & B.E. Compas (Eds.), *Primary prevention and promotion in schools* (pp. 177–200). Newbury Park, CA: Sage.

Weissberg, R.P., & Greenberg, M.T. (1997). School and community—competence enhancement in prevention programs. In W. Damon (Series Ed.), I.E. Segal & K.A. Renninger (Vol. Eds.), *Handbook of child psychology: Vol. 5. Child psychology in practice* (5th ed.). New York: Wiley.

Werner, E.E., & Smith, R.S. (1989). *Vulnerable but invincible: A longitudinal study of resilient children and youth.* New York: Adams, Bannister, and Cox.

Wilson, W.J. (1987). *The truly disadvantaged: The inner city, the underclass, and public policy.* Chicago: University of Chicago Press.

Wyman, P.A., Cowen, E.L., Work, W.C., & Kerley, J.H. (1993). The role of children's future expectations in self-system functioning and adjustment to life stress: A prospective study of urban at risk children. *Development and Psychopathology, 5,* 649–661.

Yung, B.R., Hammond, W.R., Sampson, M., & Warfield, J. (1998). Linking psychology and public health: A predoctoral clinical training program in youth violence prevention. *Professional Psychology: Research and Practice, 29,* 398–401.

CHAPTER 14

The School-to-Work Transition:
Adjustment Challenges of the Forgotten Half

DAVID L. BLUSTEIN
CINDY L. JUNTUNEN
ROGER L. WORTHINGTON

One of the more promising movements in education and public policy in the recent decade has been the concerted effort to enhance the quality of the school-to-work (STW) transition for noncollege-bound youth (also known as work-bound youth) (Gray & Herr, 1998; Lewis, Stone, Shipley, & Madzar, 1998; Marshall & Tucker, 1992; Reich, 1991; Worthington & Juntunen, 1997). The underlying objective of this movement has been to offer the majority of adolescents an improved opportunity to traverse the often vast distance between high school and a rapidly changing labor market (Gysbers, 1997; O'Neil, 1997; Stone & Mortimer, 1998). The movement to understand and strengthen the STW transition emerges out of an awareness that the United States arguably has one of the least effective systems for preparing noncollege-bound youth for the workforce in the Western world (Olson, 1997; Resnick & Wirt, 1996a). Although the United States has some of the finest university training in the world, our educational preparation for those who move into the workforce directly after high school is far less systematic, empowering, and equitable (Marshall & Tucker, 1992).

Current programmatic and research efforts on the STW transition grew from a number of interrelated issues and problems; perhaps the most notable of these issues is the emergence of declining wages, beginning in the early 1970s, among skilled and semiskilled workers (Hamilton, 1990; Olson, 1997; Marshall & Tucker, 1992). The general consensus is that declining wages are a function of a number of convergent events. First, the increasing level of automation has reduced the need for many semiskilled and unskilled workers, whose jobs are now filled by more efficient computers and automated systems (Resnick & Wirt, 1996). Second, the quality of the workforce of our economic competitors has increased dramatically in recent decades, often outdistancing American workers in selected areas (Marshall & Tucker, 1992; Reich, 1991). As a result, the manufacturing arm of the American economy has become known for the unhealthy combination of low skills and high wages (Marshall & Tucker, 1992; William T. Grant Foundation, 1988a, 1988b). Whereas jobs with reasonably decent wages were traditionally available for high school graduates (and often dropouts) in industrial, manufacturing, and agricultural fields, these opportunities increasingly have become less available.

Other reasons for the interest in the STW transition emerged from moral concerns with the distribution of wealth and power in Western nations (Marshall & Tucker, 1992; Reich, 1991). The wage gap between college-educated and noncollege-educated individuals has grown markedly

The authors would like to thank the following individuals who assisted in the literature search for this chapter: Anne Capobianco, Josie Collier, Karen Hooper, Claudine Lochard, Norma Pol, LaNae Shelton, Jeff Tan, and Naitain Wang. The order of authorship for the second and third authors was determined randomly; their respective contributions to this chapter were equivalent.

since the early 1970s (Gray & Herr, 1998; Olson, 1997; Reich, 1991). In addition, the disparity of wealth is even more pronounced in the inner cities and in rural areas, where, for instance, the unemployment rate for African American high school graduates is nearly double that of their European American peers (Olson, 1997; Wilson, 1996). Moreover, the loss of employment opportunities in the inner city has been linked with a vast array of other social problems, engendering Third World–like conditions within the core of some of the wealthiest cities of the world (Reich, 1991; Wilson, 1996). As such, the concern with the transition from school to work for work-bound youth has vast moral implications.

Another major impetus for STW initiatives grew out of the ongoing debates about the quality of education within the United States (Olson, 1997; Resnick & Wirt, 1996). A prominent concern within the educational community has been the diminishing skill level among work-bound youth, which has been particularly evident in academic comparisons with other Western countries (Resnick & Wirt, 1996a). Moreover, questions regarding the relevance of the high school curriculum have been constant themes in educational reform debates (Olson, 1997). Work-based learning, which refers to educational experiences rooted in an occupational setting, has been proposed as one potential solution to enhance both relevance and rigor within high schools (Gray & Herr, 1998; Olson, 1997). Thus, although much of educational practice has been reassessed in recent years (Marshall & Tucker, 1992), one of the most notable areas meriting attention in reform efforts has been the STW transition of work-bound youth (Olson, 1997).

In this chapter, we review the literature related to the transition from school to work for work-bound youth. Our work attempts to bridge the broad-based STW literature, emerging from education, public policy, sociology, labor economics, developmental psychology, and career development/vocational psychology. Given the wide scope of our mission in this chapter, it is impossible to state that we have exhaustively reviewed the relevant literature. As such, our policy in deciding on the content for inclusion in this chapter is based on our intent to provide a representative review of theory, research, and practice trends that we believe are most important and most likely to influence policy, practice, and scholarship in the coming decades. In addition, the literature that we review has been selected because of its potential relevance to the expanding roles of contemporary counseling psychologists.

Consistent with the numerous policy statements of the last decade (e.g., Hamilton, 1990; Pautler, 1994), we use the term work-bound to denote those individuals who do not attend a four-year college immediately after high school. It is important to note that many of the current STW efforts are directed toward all students, including the college-bound (Stern & Finkelstein, 1995). However, our decision in this chapter is to focus on the work-bound due to the fact that this population has been so profoundly neglected in recent decades of scholarship within counseling psychology and career development. Thus, this chapter addresses the large majority of youth who face increasingly uncertain futures as the labor market shifts rapidly from manufacturing to information and service. The transition element of the chapter title also merits some definitional parameters. In accordance with contemporary views of developmental transitions, we define transition broadly to encompass the period of preparation for the shift, the actual movement between life roles and responsibilities, and the period of initial socialization into the new role (Graber, Brooks-Gunn, & Petersen, 1996; Vondracek, Lerner, & Schulenberg, 1986).

The overall plan of this chapter is to provide readers with a necessary conceptual framework by reviewing the historical and social antecedents of the STW movement. This is followed by an overview of the current status of existing policies, programs, assessment issues, and "best practices" within the STW arena. A focused summary of the theoretical framework of the STW process is presented next, followed by a review of the relevant empirical literature. We conclude with an overview of current controversies, recommendations for future research and theory, and implications for psychological practice.

HISTORICAL PERSPECTIVES

As with most "new" ideas, initiatives, and intellectual pursuits, the STW movement has many roots in various educational and policy-based ideas and programs over the past few decades. A careful analysis of educational trends within the past century designed to integrate school and work reveals that these movements essentially force one to confront fundamental questions about the very meaning of education in modern industrial and postindustrial or information-based societies.

In short, the role of high schools has undergone radical transformations at different points within the history of Western cultures (see Marshall & Tucker, 1992, for an insightful review of these issues). Toward the end of the nineteenth century, high schools focused on the core areas of languages, math, science, history, and classical education. However, some critics have suggested that the classical approach to secondary education benefited only the affluent and college-bound, thus leading to low rates of high school completion among work-bound students (Leighbody, 1972). Shortly after the turn of the twentieth century, high schools began to adopt more direct responsibility for training students for employment roles, as exemplified by the movement known as vocational education.

Vocational Education

Beginning in the early part of the twentieth century, the vocational education movement sought to expand the economic potential of high school students by providing practical skills that could lead to employment immediately after high school (G.I. Swanson, 1981). However, vocational education has been viewed by some as a covert attempt to meet the demands of industries for trained workers (Marshall & Tucker, 1992), thereby further reinforcing class boundaries. On the other side of this continuum are those scholars who have viewed vocational education as part of a broader reform movement designed to equip youth for changing social roles, with the intention of empowering all students (G.I. Swanson, 1981).

According to many educators and policy analysts, vocational education has not been a resounding success (Marshall & Tucker, 1992; Olson, 1997). Perhaps one of the most difficult problems (which in many ways still plagues some of the STW initiatives) is the bifurcation of academic training along a vocational education versus college-preparation track (Gray & Herr, 1998; Olson, 1997). Sensing the inherent danger of developing a dualistic set of tracks in American education, Dewey (1916) called for a more systematic integration of vocational education into the fabric of a curriculum that adequately trained students to be thoughtful and wise citizens. Although Dewey's concerns about equity and academic relevance foreshadowed the integrative scope that forms the essence of the more effective STW proposals, his appeals for a more integrative stance with respect to vocational and traditional academic secondary education did not prevail (Olson, 1997). Despite the best intentions of educators and policymakers, vocational education was viewed as a second-rate educational option, which generally appealed to less able students or to students who were marginalized due to social and economic factors (such as their impoverished backgrounds or visible racial and ethnic minority status).

Career Education

In an attempt to reduce the divisiveness between college preparation and vocational education programs, educators and policy analysts sought to design programmatic interventions to address a number of outstanding problems simultaneously. Career education emerged as a rubric for a wide array of programs that have a common link, based on two interrelated objectives: to enhance the occupational relevance of education and to reduce the social class distinctions between vocational and academic tracks (Hoyt & High, 1982; Reinhart, 1979). The major mechanism of career education was to enhance the relevance of education by infusing a career development and occupational focus into various elements of the curriculum (Reinhart, 1979). The career development aspect was implemented by applying some core concepts of vocational psychology to the curriculum, with the intention of helping students to make wise choices and meaningful career plans (Hoyt & High, 1982; Reinhart, 1979). The occupational focus was manifested by integrating work-based training with the broader scope of the educational enterprise (such as the development of cognitive and quantitative skills). In contrast to vocational education, career education sought to provide a career-based emphasis in the educational curriculum at all levels, not solely for the work-bound, a path that also has been adopted in the STW movement.

In the early 1970s, career education received considerable public attention and funding. Although the intellectual energy and financial resources behind the career education movement have dissipated considerably, many of the ideas were integrated into the schools and have formed part of the conceptual framework for the STW movement. For example, the discussion of the vast economic and moral implications of existing divisions between college-bound and noncollege-bound, which has been so well articulated in the career education movement (Reinhart, 1979), helped to set the stage for the debates that are currently taking place in policy circles.

Vocational Guidance and Career Counseling Antecedents

The historical perspective adopted by Savickas (1999) provides ample evidence that vocational guidance and career development scholars and practitioners have been key players in the STW movement. Beginning with Parsons's (1909) classic volume, career counselors have been deeply concerned with the initial transition to work from secondary and postsecondary institutions. Many of the early classics in vocational guidance dealt directly with the career challenges faced by work-bound youth (see Keller & Viteles, 1937, and Savickas, 1999).

In addition to the practice components of vocational guidance, research emerging from various investigators within applied psychology and occupational sociology established a foundation for school to work that is still relevant. Savickas (1999) reviewed a few exemplary studies (e.g., Bell, 1938; Landy, 1940; Super & Wright, 1941) that sought to identify effective antecedent conditions for the transition from school to work. As we shall see later in this chapter, many of the findings from recent studies parallel results that have emerged in STW research in the 1930s and 1940s. For example, Savickas's conclusion that high school students who are exploratory and planful will be successful in the transition is remarkably contemporary with respect to the current knowledge base (cf. Gysbers, 1997). As Savickas noted in his review, research on the STW transition for work-bound youth diminished in its scope and impact after World War II, leaving counseling professionals at the fringes of scholarly efforts. Yet, significant interventions have emerged from school counseling innovations in recent years that have direct relevance to STW practice and policy (Gysbers, 1997).

Concluding Comments

It would not be accurate to convey the historical framework of the STW movement without acknowledging the important and substantive contributions that have emerged from special education and rehabilitation counseling (Phelps & Hanley-Maxwell, 1997). Thus, the current STW movement has many antecedents and traditions in education, school counseling, and public policy. Despite the diverse lineage, the STW tradition has engendered a rich and coherent literature, which has direct relevance to the current and future roles of counseling psychologists.

THE CURRENT STATE OF AFFAIRS

Changing Standards

As noted previously, several factors have contributed to increasing concerns about employment and education in the 1970s and 1980s. The unemployment rate hit a critical high in the 1980s, adding a note of urgency to the reform efforts at that time. One response to the unemployment peak of the early 1980s, particularly the even higher unemployment for youth, was an appeal to return education to its previous (and presumably higher) standards.

In a critically important national report entitled "A Nation at Risk" (National Commission on Excellence in Education, 1983), the educational system was blamed for slipping standards and mediocrity. Proponents of reform assumed that the structure of the current system could work, but that educators were somehow ineffective, leading to highly vocal criticisms of teachers. Thus, the need to improve student performance was emphasized, via explicit changes in teaching and educational standards. There was also an assumption that all these changes could take place within the school; little attention was paid to the impact of family, community, employers, or others outside of the school system. However, these reformers failed to recognize that student performance had not, in fact, slipped significantly. Instead, students were performing at generally the same level as in the past, but were facing a different set of demands (Marshall & Tucker, 1992). In other words, the standards that had been set, and reinforced, for education over decades were no longer sufficient.

The need for new standards was acknowledged by conferences of the nation's governors and President Bush in 1989 and 1990, during which the National Governor's Association established a Task Force on Education (Task Force on Education, 1990). Goals and strategies for education were set during these conferences, including substantive change in the structure of the organizational system within education. Specifically, greater acknowledgment was given to the role of life-long learning, the need to include communities in education, and the importance of enhancing the autonomy given to educators and related professionals (Task Force on Education). In contrast to the recommendations outlined in "A Nation at Risk" (National Commission on Excellence in Education, 1983), the 1990 Task Force on Education report clearly indicated that the problem could be solved only by reaching targets to which the country had never before aspired.

Many Task Force goals included an emphasis on lifelong learning and the development of transferable skills. One goal specifically states that "every school in America will ensure that all students learn to use their minds well, so they may be prepared for responsible citizenship, further learning, and productive employment in our modern economy" (Task Force on Education, 1990, p. 12). One way of doing this is to provide training in those necessary skills that will transfer into the labor market, as well as other areas of adult life.

The Secretary's Commission for Achieving Necessary Skills (SCANS) was formed in 1990 with the goal of identifying those transferable skills (Resnick & Wirt, 1996b). SCANS produced a set of five competencies (characteristics and behaviors of effective work-based behavior that transfer across occupations) and a three-part foundation of skills deemed necessary for successful job performance. The five competencies include the ability to use productively (1) resources, (2) interpersonal skills, (3) information, (4) systems, and (5) technology. These five competencies, although generally not required for high school completion, are seen as essential "workplace know-how" (SCANS, 1992). The three foundation skills that were deemed necessary include (1) basic skills, such as reading, writing, mathematics, and listening; (2) thinking skills, such as the ability to learn, reason, and solve problems; and (3) personal qualities, including responsibility, self-esteem, and integrity. Although some are integral parts of the traditional educational experience, the Commission argued that the remainder of these skills could be integrated into current curriculum. The Commission also articulated a set of recommendations that emphasized reinventing schools to include SCANS know-how, fostering work-based learning and training, reorganizing the workplace to adopt high performance standards, and restructuring assessment of student achievement (SCANS, 1992).

The SCANS (1992) report reflected the need of the reform agenda to address ways in which both educational institutions and employers contribute to the success of youth. This was, again, an important change in focus for educational reform. Instead of emphasizing only the responsibility of the school for preparing youth, the SCANS report provided specific recommendations for industry; specifically, employers were encouraged to develop human resources in the work setting, the community, and the nation.

Other reports with similar messages also received attention during this time. The William T. Grant Foundation (1988a) asserted the need to more actively support the youth of the United States. This report pointed to a history of treating students and schools as scapegoats for economic downturns and included a significant emphasis on the role of industry and the broader social community (W.T. Grant Foundation, 1988b). Two major policy analysts (including Ray Marshall, a former U.S. Labor Department secretary) provided a compelling argument for fundamental change in the educational system and the workforce in a widely cited book entitled *Thinking for a Living: Education and the Wealth of Nations* (Marshall & Tucker, 1992). Building on economic and educational theory, Marshall and Tucker explicated the losses that can occur if we do not more actively support youth, particularly the noncollege-bound, by considering them an important source of human capital, rather than a drain.

Eventually, these reform efforts became part of President Clinton's political platform and were written into legislation as the School-to-Work Opportunities Act (STWOA) of 1994. (For additional information on this legislation, see U.S. Congress, 1994.) Another critical aspect of the changing standards was manifested in the growing call for more rigorous and standardized means of assessing student performance and validating training credentials.

Assessment Issues

Two recent volumes (O'Neil, 1997; Resnick & Wirt, 1996a) have detailed the rapidly intensifying efforts to produce assessment strategies for the standards set by SCANS and other reform-based reports. At the core of this new system of assessment is the notion that clearly defined standards of achievement will provide the foundation for conveying the capabilities of work-bound students to potential employers (Resnick & Wirt, 1996a). As a result, schools will teach to the standards; achievement of the standards will be assessed in a fair and transparent manner; and the results will provide prospective employers with objective evidence of achievement on which to make employment decisions (Resnick & Wirt, 1996a). However, as Oliver et al. (1997) pointed out, the skills defined by the SCANS report cannot be taught or assessed through traditional methods. Instead, new assessments are likely to include a combination of written material, simulations, monitored performance, and evaluations of past work experience (Bailey, 1997). One particularly compelling set of recommendations was articulated by Lesgold (1996), who outlined an innovative assessment system, including tests of work-readiness, media products simulating work in an actual job, mastery plans divided up into small incremental steps, and portfolio systems in which students construct a record of significant performances that can be directly observed and evaluated by prospective employers.

The development of "criterion-referenced assessments based on an empirically established taxonomy of workplace competencies" has become the overarching goal of these initiatives as a means of more clearly delineating their content, structure, and validity (Nash & Korte, 1997, p. 82). In 1992, the U.S. Department of Labor and Education contracted with American College

Testing (ACT) to develop assessments for the five SCANS competencies (Nash & Korte, 1997). The National Job Analysis Study (NJAS; cf. Nash & Korte, 1994) arose out of the ACT contract and was designed to identify the content requirements for the SCANS assessments. Although still under development, the NJAS and associated Behaviorally-Anchored Rating Scales (BARS) are intended to provide profiles of requisite behaviors, knowledge, skills, and abilities for occupational clusters that can be used to infuse workplace content into the K–12 educational system (Nash & Korte, 1997). O'Neil (1997) and his colleagues also have presented a set of assessments for workforce readiness competencies in the areas of foundation literacy skills, generic employability skills, interpersonal skills, information usage, negotiation, and teamwork.

As large-scale assessment development efforts proceed, a variety of obstacles and issues are confronting the developers. Among the most pressing issues and obstacles are concerns about (1) rigid adherence to traditional pedagogy (Elmore, 1996; Tucker, 1996); (2) adverse impact for students from underrepresented minority groups (Bishop, 1996); and (3) the development of assessments that demonstrate adequate reliability and validity (Bock, 1996; Guion, 1996; Herr & Niles, 1997; Linn, 1996). Strategies for addressing these potential problems include efforts to apply cross-national perspectives from the successes of our competitors abroad (cf. Jenkins, 1996; Vickers, 1996).

This brief summary suggests that concerns for standards within high schools and other training institutions have been associated with a concomitant flurry of activity in the design and delivery of varied assessment tools for work-bound youth. As the next section indicates, a similar level of activity has characterized the efforts of program developers and educators who have created a wide array of models to implement the goals of the STW initiative.

School-to-Work Models

Federal funding provided by the STWOA allowed numerous new STW programs to be developed, in addition to the existing pilot projects and local initiatives that were already instituted throughout the United States. Essentially, six major types of STW programs, supported by local and federal funding, have emerged in recent years; included in this array of interventions are career academies, occupational-academic cluster programs, restructured vocational education programs, tech prep programs, youth apprenticeship programs, and school-based enterprises. Because the STWOA has recommended that communities develop partnerships to best fit their own needs, the structure for each of the six types of STW programs varies by site (Riley & Herman, 1997). Therefore, the following definitions, derived from Pauly, Kopp, and Haimson (1995) and Stern, Finkelstein, Stone, Latting, and Dornsrife (1994), should be seen as evolving.

Career academies are "school-within-a-school" programs that focus on a specific industry, wherein a small number of students move as a cohort through most coursework and on-the-job training. Occupational-academic cluster programs are larger programs that allow all students in a given school to take introductory, career-related courses and then pursue work-based learning. Restructured vocational education programs tend to include more career exploration activities than traditional vocational education programs, and seek to involve a wider range of students. Students receive job-related training in school, then on-the-job training while continuing with school attendance. Tech prep programs (also known as 2 + 2 programs) emphasize technology-related instruction and occupations, generally by linking the last two years of high school with the first two years of community college. Youth apprenticeship programs use the workplace as a learning environment and link students to mentors in the workplace; the work is generally paid, and classroom instruction emphasizes the integration of academic and vocational learning. Finally, within school-based enterprises, schools operate a business, with students performing the activities necessary to produce goods or services, market and sell them, and manage other activities related to the business.

Within these broad categories of programs, of course, individual schools are likely to employ a variety of models and combinations of models. The following section will address some ways in which various models have been successfully implemented.

Best Practices and Program Evaluation

It is important to note that different types of STW programs will emphasize a wide range of activities and goals, although all are involved in the overarching goal of helping youth make the transition to work. Tech prep programs, for example, are more likely to emphasize the students' connection to local community colleges, whereas career academies will be more likely to develop mentoring relationships with individual local employers.

Despite these differences, some common themes are evident in successful STW programs. Information on successful programs has been collected by the Manpower Demonstration Research Corporation (Pauly et al., 1995), the Northwest Regional Educational Laboratory (Haynes & Blake, 1998), the Institute on Education and the Economy (Bailey, Hughes, & Barr, 1998; Hughes, 1996), and in several studies sponsored by the National Center for Research in Vocational Education (NCRVE; Urquiola et al., 1997). It is important to note that many of the evaluation studies have been conducted in a more exploratory or formative fashion as opposed to the rigor one might expect with a methodologically sound field study or summative evaluation. Nevertheless, initial findings and more global overviews of promising best practices do yield some consistent themes.

Ideas and Strategies

One of the key elements of successful STW programs is that they reflect the input of members of the local community (e.g., including school administrators, parents, teachers, or business leaders), responding to a perceived need of local students (Pauly et al., 1995). Programs that are implemented in response to mandates (i.e., with a top-down approach) are more likely to be neglected or resented (Pauly et al., 1995).

Once local needs have been identified, the program must be integrated into the environment and structure of the school (Fouad, 1997; Pauly et al., 1995). It is essential for teachers and school staff, including counselors, to be invested in the STW program for it to be effective; as such, staff need to be involved in the process from the earliest stages. Additionally, positive evaluations have been associated with programs that provide support and training to service delivery personnel (Charner, Fraser, Hubbard, Rogers, & Horne, 1995). The literature also suggests that integrating career counseling into academic and work-based learning is an essential aspect of success (Gray & Herr, 1998).

Similarly, when employers are involved in the early planning stages of a STW program, they are more likely to stay invested and to continue to provide training opportunities for students (Charner et al., 1995; Hughes, 1996). Preliminary research has indicated that employers who become involved recognize benefits, primarily in the reduction of training necessary for new employees and in the increased skills that high school graduates have following work-based learning (Hughes, 1996; National Employer Leadership Council [NELC], 1997). This translates into a higher quality workforce, lower training costs, and greater productivity.

Once the key parties are involved, other specific strategies may contribute to program success. First, it is important to begin career activities early. Programs funded by STWOA funds must begin career counseling activities by the seventh grade (U.S. Congress, 1994); however, many meaningful career-related exploration activities can begin in early elementary school (Gysbers & Henderson, 1994). Pauly et al. (1995) also found that most of the successful programs they reviewed were marketed to all students. Providing a curriculum that is strong enough for both two-year and four-year college preparation, as well as integrating work-based experience, will minimize stigma and increase the overall efficacy of the program (Charner et al., 1995; Stern & Finkelstein, 1995).

Inherent in the structure of STW programs is some integration of workplace experience with school-based learning. The more these experiences are oriented to help the student place learning activities in the context of real work expectations, the more likely STW activities are to be effective (Pauly et al., 1995). An ultimate goal may be to form clear connections between all courses and career activities, in which academic disciplines are connected in some way to career preparation or exploration programs (Haynes & Blake, 1998).

Evaluation Studies: Next Steps

As is evident from this review, a considerable need exists to develop comprehensive evaluation plans for STW programs. However, over the past few years a small body of evaluation research has been developing. One initial method of evaluating STW programs is to consider how many students, schools, employers, and other agencies are involved in or impacted by STW. In their annual report to the U.S. Congress, Riley and Herman (1997) noted that, as of June 1996, over 932 partnerships had been established in 41 states and Puerto Rico, involving approximately 23% of the elementary and secondary schools in the United States and 200,000 businesses providing 119,000 training positions.

Initial research on students' experiences of STW initiatives provides some promising findings. The authors of one qualitative study (Phelps, Hernandez-Gantes, Jones, Sanchez, & Nieri, 1995) concluded that students who participated in an organized STW program were better able to integrate theory, course work, and real-life applications, as well as integrate course work across the curriculum. Of particular importance to vocational psychology, students also linked work-based learning to career development, learning new and transferable skills, developing career aspirations, involvement in career guidance and exploration, and facilitating the transition to further education. These findings seem to contradict some of the fears that STW will track students into a noncollege-bound track. In fact, graduates of many STW programs enter college (Bailey & Merritt, 1997), although this is less likely to be true for students in cooperative education programs (Stern et al., 1994).

Another important preliminary evaluation finding is that employer involvement has been difficult to obtain and nurture. Employers who have participated in STW activities report philanthropic motives as being most important for their involvement, whereas those that have not participated report that bottom-line incentives need to be greater for them to become involved (Bailey et al., 1998). Reflective of this difference, for-profit employers have tended to be less involved than public sector and not-for-profit organizations (Bailey et al., 1998).

The opportunities for conducting evaluation research on the STW transition are numerous and varied. Each type of STW program is formed by a complex combination of staff, students, and community and environmental conditions. Current research has not even begun to sift through these factors to determine which are more or less predictive of success (Pauly et al., 1995; Urquiola et al., 1997). Additionally, diversity factors have been only minimally considered (Phelps & Hanley-Maxwell, 1997). Longitudinal research investigating the impact of STW programs on actual employment opportunities and patterns has not yet begun in earnest; such research may better identify what works, and also address the obstacles that remain in the STW transition.

Questions, Controversies, and Obstacles

Several questions about the STW transition remain unanswered at this point. Many programs currently depend on federal funding for their existence. The federal legislation may no longer be available in 2001 when the STW legislation sunsets; at that time, local partnerships are supposed to be self-supporting. How successful individual communities have been in moving toward this goal is not yet known. Also, it is possible that enthusiasm for the STW movement will fade as federal support disappears, thus relegating it to the status of a passing fad.

As in previous cycles of educational reform, the same fear that STW programs will limit students' capacity to go to a four-year college still exists (Pauly et al., 1995). Parents and students are still likely to think of STW initiatives as a form of vocational education, and also express concerns that tracking students into different high school programs might limit their chances for college. Educational tracking has also been accompanied by a history of discrimination (Oakes & Guiton, 1994), thus introducing specific concerns for students of color. The fact that so much of the literature in the area focuses on the noncollege-bound may reinforce this stigma, even if this focus is an attempt to provide better understanding of students who have been ignored. Essentially, this is a fundamental conundrum for the field—attempting to serve the underserved without increasing stigmatization or discrimination.

Furthermore, implementation questions persist regarding specific STW goals. First, students are expected to integrate school- and work-based learning; however, what is not clear is the optimal balance of school and work experience (Stern & Finkelstein, 1995; Stone & Mortimer, 1998). Students who work tend to perform better in school, but only if they work a moderate amount (Stone & Mortimer, 1998). Some schools have made concessions about students working greater hours to attract and keep employer partners (Hughes, 1996). The integration of work-based learning, in such instances, may be detrimental to students. In a related vein, teachers need to develop new skills to assist students in this integration. For example, in a review of an allied health apprenticeship, Stern et al. (1994) suggested that teachers might need to develop a better understanding of the hospital experience to develop an appropriate curriculum. Although this would further student goals, it places significant demands on teachers.

Another noteworthy issue is the emphasis on providing future employment to students who participate in a STW program. Although school and partnership personnel can clearly facilitate employment searches, this goal can be elusive. This is especially true in rural areas and inner-cities, where employers are limited in number, at a great distance, or limited in variety of employment types (Stone, 1996). It is possible that there are simply not enough jobs in the United States to support all the workers who would seek them—or at least, not enough to provide an adequate living (W.T. Grant Foundation, 1988a). This observation about the inherent limitations of the labor market has led to suggestions that we need interventions that focus primarily on the labor market, rather than education and training (Stone, 1996). Indeed, that may be the necessary next step for a true STW revolution.

THEORETICAL ISSUES IN THE TRANSITION PROCESS

In order for the STW system to become a fully integrated component of educational reform, broad-based programmatic research that produces positive findings regarding its efficacy will need to be established within a variety of societal sectors (e.g., schools, businesses, communities). Without theoretical groundwork, such research efforts are likely to produce a vast array of potentially misleading and contradictory findings that obfuscate the utility of STW programs. Counseling psychology has a rich tradition of generating vocational psychology theories, and considerable emphasis on theory-driven research, yet our early involvement in STW research dissipated almost completely by the late 1950s. This section provides a general overview of theoretical issues and an analysis of the major theoretical contributions of counseling psychologists to the recent STW movement.

Applying Vocational Psychology Theories

A number of authors have recently called for the application of traditional vocational psychology theories and research to the STW transition process (Lent, O'Brien, & Fassinger, 1998; Lent &

Worthington, 1999; Worthington & Juntunen, 1997). This renewed interest has culminated in a recent set of initiatives in which person-environment fit, developmental, learning theory, social cognitive theory, developmental contextualism, and sociological-economic perspectives have been considered in light of the challenges posed by the STW movement. In this section, we review the available literature on the application of vocational psychology theories to the STW transition process.

Person-Environment Fit Theories

Although career theories in the person-environment fit (P-E fit) tradition have been extensively criticized in the literature (e.g., Hackett, Lent, & Greenhaus, 1991; Krumboltz, 1994), they persist in theory, research, and practice as arguably the field's dominant paradigm for understanding the complex relationships between individuals and their work environments (Hackett et al., 1991). The two most prominent of these approaches, the theories of Holland (1997) and Dawis and Lofquist (1984), have been recognized for their practical use in efforts to enhance the STW transition process of employment-bound youth (Herr, 1995; Rojewski, 1994; Swanson & Fouad, 1999).

Swanson and Fouad (1999) pointed out that among the various paradigms in vocational psychology, P-E fit theories have the capacity to assist the STW movement in achieving balance in underscoring the importance of both person and environment. They argued, for example, that use of the theory of work adjustment (TWA; Dawis & Lofquist, 1984) can help to balance the current emphasis on quality work and contemporary skills among employers with youthful workers by focusing on employee satisfaction as a means of promoting greater work adjustment. The job satisfaction of youthful employees can be increased through the use of methods to enhance students' knowledge of themselves and the range of occupations to which their abilities, achievements, interests, and needs could be applied (Herr, 1995; Rojewski, 1994; Swanson & Fouad, 1999). Herr (1995) also suggested that the P-E fit paradigm has the capacity to assist youth in understanding the elasticity or transportability of their current knowledge or skills across jobs, occupations, and industries. Ultimately, employers are hypothesized to benefit from the application of the vast technology of assessment associated with P-E fit theories, because the ultimate outcomes are satisfactoriness among employers, satisfaction among youthful workers, and workforce stability (Rojewski, 1994; Swanson & Fouad, 1999).

Developmental Theories

Surveying theory and research dating back to the 1920s, Savickas (1999) defined the essence of the developmental perspective on the STW transition as follows: "Youth cope better with the STW transition if, as high school students, they developed awareness of the choices to be made and information and planning that bears on these choices" (p. 326–327). As summarized by Herr (1995), Rojewski (1994), and Savickas, a developmental perspective of the STW transition involves (1) clarifying and implementing an occupational self-concept; (2) developing an understanding of the various life roles and their relationship to and interaction with the role of work in an individual's life; (3) developing an understanding of the dimensions of vocational maturity, including knowledge of the patterns of work across the life span and the tasks associated with various stages of vocational development; (4) forming positive attitudes toward planning and exploring; and (5) increasing competence in making choices and formulating plans.

Savickas (1999) described four types of methods and materials for fostering career development: orienting, teaching, coaching, and role rehearsal. Orientation involves "anticipatory guidance" provided by counselors and teachers that is designed to foster awareness of tasks and decisions in preparing for work. Cognitive competencies and behavioral skills that students may use to advance their career, the central foci of the STW movement, are facilitated through teaching. Career coaching is used to assist workers in adapting to the social and practical expectations of a specific workplace commonly associated with the developmental task of "stabilizing" within one's occupational role (Super, Savickas, & Super, 1996). Role rehearsal involves "vicarious preparation for and practice at solving typical problems that arise on the job" (Savickas, 1999, p. 333).

Learning Theory

Similar to the developmental perspective, Krumboltz and Worthington (1999) suggested that persons working to promote the successful STW transition be seen as counselors, coaches, educators, and mentors. Their position relies heavily on the recognition that, under the STWOA, the provision of learning experiences is at the basis of the career preparation of youth. Central to their argument is the notion that the demands of the rapidly changing work world require youth to do more than what has been suggested by traditional approaches to career development. Krumboltz and Worthington proposed that vocational interests, values, beliefs, preferences, and skills are all learned, and amenable to interventions targeted toward growth and enhancement.

Through learning, individuals can achieve increased control over environmental barriers (e.g., sexism, racism, classism) and their impact on career decision making (Rojewski, 1994). STW enhancement efforts grounded in learning theory include (1) positive reinforcement, (2) providing opportunities for social modeling and vicarious learning, (3) job simulations, (4) structuring work experiences for success, and (5) individualizing learning experiences (Herr, 1995; Krumboltz & Worthington, 1999; Rojewski, 1994). Role playing, behavioral rehearsal, and feedback help students to accurately understand and learn desirable behaviors or skills for career planning, facilitate appropriate career choices, and improve work performance and adjustment (Herr, 1995; Krumboltz & Worthington, 1999).

Social Cognitive Career Theory

Lent, Hackett, and Brown (1996, 1999) considered social cognitive career theory (SCCT; Lent, Brown, & Hackett, 1994) as a vantage point from which to view the STW transition process by focusing on six developmentally linked themes that unfold throughout the school years: (1) formation of self-efficacy and outcome beliefs, (2) interest development, (3) interest-goal linkages, (4) translation of goals into actions, (5) performance skills, and (6) negotiation of transition supports and barriers. Lent et al. (1999) pointed out that although "these six processes are viewed as iterative and ongoing, some of them seem especially salient during the elementary and middle school years, while others typify the experiences of high school students facing the imminent prospect of work entry" (p. 300). Within that context, Lent et al. (1999) argued cogently for understanding the STW transition process as encompassing a wide span of developmental phenomena, extending from early childhood into adulthood.

Consistent with this developmentally graded perspective on the STW transition, Lent et al. (1999) recommended that interventions target these specific processes in ways that are consistent with theory and research on social cognitive theory, including (1) closely attending to the factors that promote vicarious learning; (2) structuring career exploration and information-gathering activities in ways that facilitate accurate efficacy and outcome expectations; (3) increasing the specificity and clarity of goals; (4) assisting students in developing barrier-coping strategies; (5) helping students to recognize and access environmental resources that may facilitate their transition; and (6) providing opportunities both for facilitating skill development and the efficacy percepts that enable skill use.

Developmental-Contextual Theories

There has been heightened recognition over the past two decades that career development occurs within social, economic, and political contexts (Vondracek et al., 1986). From a broad macroeconomic and social policy perspective, the primary concerns regarding the STW transitions of youth have focused on two converging trends: the increasing demands for technological sophistication among workers in the labor force, and the lack of educational achievement and workforce preparation among a large sector of youth in the U.S. population relative to other developed nations (Commission on the Skills of the American Workforce, 1990; U.S. General Accounting Office, 1991, 1993; William T. Grant Foundation, 1988a, 1988b). Moreover, continuing gender and racial disparities in wages and unemployment remain the focus of concern and debate (Olson, 1997; Reich, 1991; Wilson, 1996). Borrowing from the ideas first proposed by Vondracek et al. (1986), Worthington and Juntunen (1997) described the STW transition within the framework of developmental social ecology (cf. Bronfenbrenner, 1977), in which a variety of social contexts are operative in the lives of youth and impinge on their social and psychological development to produce opportunities and outcomes reflected in their STW transitions. They argued that racial, gender, and economic diversity must be incorporated into our understanding of, and attempts to address, the vocational development of youth in the United States.

Sociological-Economic Theories

Smith and Scoll (1995) described the STWOA as one of the central legislative components of the Clinton human capital agenda. Furthermore, in a report by the Committee on the Changing Nature of Work (1993), the key to assuring the future economic security of U.S. companies and workers was described as "strengthening the skills and capacities of America's 'human capital'" (p. 9). In brief, human capital theory (Becker, 1993) is characterized by the notion that employment opportunities and economic rewards are reserved for those with the most marketable attitudes, knowledge, and skills. The theory suggests that individuals and society derive economic benefits from investments in people in the form of time, energy, and money. Although types of human capital investment include health, nutrition (Schultz, 1963), and a variety of other products of human socialization, education and on-the-job training have been the central targets of most theoretical and empirical inquiry (Sweetland, 1996). Increasing the human capital resources (i.e., motivated, knowledgeable, and skilled workers) available to employers is hypothesized to increase the competitiveness of the United States in the global economy, with corollary improvements in job options and the accessibility of the labor market (Becker, 1993; Smith & Scoll, 1995; Sweetland, 1996). With this in mind, the ultimate objectives of the current STW system in the United States are essentially consistent with the economic theory of human capital (Worthington & Juntunen, 1997).

Theoretically, the context of investments in personal and vocational development affords work-bound youth with optimal access to the opportunity structure in which matching interests with occupations (Holland, 1997) or expressing one's self-concept in the realm of work (Super et al., 1996) can occur. Among the most impressive findings of human capital research is that "more highly educated and skilled persons almost always tend to earn more than others" (Becker, 1993, p. 2).

Conclusions

Concern has been expressed that the STW movement appears to be an atheoretical movement "driven by an amalgamation of macroeconomic necessity, social policy concerns, and educational reform" (Worthington & Juntunen, 1997, p. 325), in which the strongest theoretical foundation arises from the human capital theory of economics. With increasing calls for theoretical advances and integration (Savickas & Lent, 1994), some scholars have already begun supporting the development of new theoretical models that specifically attend to the STW transition (Blustein, Phillips, Jobin-Davis, Finkelberg, & Roarke, 1997; Lent et al., 1998; Worthington & Juntunen, 1997); in a similar vein, the call for the incorporation of contextual and diversity issues into theoretical accounts is gaining momentum (Blustein, 1995; Herr, 1995; Rojewski, 1994; Worthington & Juntunen, 1997). Furthermore, considering the potential scope of impact the STW transition process could have on the lives of youth, it is reasonable to expect that an interdisciplinary effort may be warranted to construct a fully integrative theory of the STW transition, in which interprofessional collaboration will be a key element (Brabeck, Walsh, Kenny, & Comilang, 1997).

REVIEW OF EMPIRICAL RESEARCH ON THE TRANSITION PROCESS

We focus this section of the chapter on a review of the STW transition process as opposed to intervention studies. (For reviews of research evaluating existing STW programs, see Pauly et al., 1995 and Urquiola et al., 1997.) The literature that seeks to understand how the STW process occurs represents a critical body of knowledge that has not benefited from a comprehensive and integrative analysis. In our view, two essential questions about the STW transition process may be illuminated by empirical research. The first of these questions seeks to discern how an adaptive transition is defined, and the second focuses on identifying the antecedents of variations in transition behavior. In this section, we attempt to address both of these issues by reviewing major studies on the STW transition along with promising investigations of a more circumscribed nature. Our mode of searching the literature included the exploration of various social science databases, including those from psychology, education, and sociology covering the past 15 years. In addition, we have reviewed the citation lists from many of the notable studies in this area for further leads on important bodies of research. Given space limitations, we could not include all the relevant studies in this review. Thus, we have elected to include only investigations that demonstrated a rigorous use of research methodology (including qualitative and/or quantitative methods), along with conclusions that have the potential to inform research, theory, policy, or practice. We also have made a concerted effort to include a number of highly innovative and thoughtful studies conducted outside the United States, particularly in Europe, where there has been a deep interest in youth transition research for the past several decades. Due to the complex ways in which cultural and economic factors influence the STW transition, we urge readers to be cautious in considering the generalizability of the studies reported in this review.

Post Hoc Observational Studies

To organize this review, we initially present post hoc studies that employ large data sets, wherein the focus has been to attain a macro-level perspective of a given phenomenon, followed by post hoc studies that employ a more micro-level of analysis, often relying on qualitative and exploratory methods.

Macro-Level Post Hoc Studies

One particularly rich set of investigations conducted by Way and Rossmann (1996a, 1996b) examined family influences in the STW process. These studies used a diverse sample of 1,266 high school seniors and 879 young adults in one and two year postsecondary training programs across four diverse regions of the United States (Way & Rossmann, 1996b). The first study investigated the nature of family relationship characteristics in the prediction of proximal outcomes (e.g., motivation for learning, academic and social integration into school), as well as more distal outcomes (readiness for the transition as defined by career decidedness, vocational identity, work-effectiveness skills, and post–high school plans). The second study explored a similar array of independent and dependent variables among young adult learners who were students or trainees in community college programs that emphasized occupational training. The third study employed a qualitative approach in learning about the impact of family issues in the work lives of 50 participants from the initial sample, who were interviewed a few months after leaving high school.

In integrating their findings, Way and Rossmann (1996a) found that a cluster of family characteristics, falling under a proactive rubric (as defined by cohesiveness, expressiveness, democratic decision making, and an active recreation orientation), were linked to important learning processes (such as motivated strategies for learning, self-efficacy, and critical thinking) and to transition readiness. Although the findings were modest (with respect to the effect sizes of the direct and indirect effects, which ranged from .10 to .27), the results were consistent with existing theory and research on the facilitative role of an active and supportive family system. In their qualitative findings, Way and Rossmann observed a notable trend of family communication, which seemed to function to help interpret the reality of the adult world for the adolescent who is preparing for or undergoing the transition to work.

Layder, Ashton, and Sung (1991) developed a questionnaire designed to assess various aspects of the individual's education, career, and life history and then surveyed a representative sample of 1,786 young adults in the United Kingdom ranging from 18 to 24 years old who were not university students or graduates. These authors found that individuals who entered the labor market at the professional (and to a lesser extent clerical) levels were better able to rely on their own individual characteristics (e.g., educational achievements, orientation toward the future) than did individuals who entered the labor market at a more modest level. Individuals entering the labor market at a lower socioeconomic level tended to seek out and accept jobs based on labor market availability, without much reliance on their own goals and preferences.

Another key European study by Reitzele, Vondracek, and Silbereisen (1998) explored significant elements of the social and economic context in their study of work-bound and non-university educated young adults from sections of former Western and Eastern Germany. Using a stratified sample of 355 participants from the West and 389 participants from the East who had already made the transition from school to work, Reitzele et al. assessed the timing of the initial vocational choice and financial self-support, as well as the ages of completion of school and vocational training. The independent variables included educational background, parental support behaviors, life events before age 17, maturational history, ego identity status, values orientation, and planfulness. The results indicated that the social context, as exemplified by the divergent systems governing East and West Germany until 1989, played an important role in determining the timing and quality of the transition. For example, in the Western Germany sample, endorsing post-materialistic values (i.e., valuing freedom, friendship, and variety) predicted later vocational choices, whereas planfulness was inversely associated with progress toward self-sufficiency. (Those who were planful seemed to make a decision to forestall becoming financially independent, perhaps as a means of furthering their training and education.) In contrast, the timing of the important transition events within the Eastern cohort was more difficult to predict with the aforementioned array of predictors, suggesting that other social and political factors may have contributed to the career development of these youth. The findings from this study also indicate that some of the typical predictors of adaptive career development outcomes (e.g., planfulness) may be helpful in providing young adults with the means of forestalling potentially premature vocational choices.

Claes and Quintanilla (1994) initiated a multinational project beginning with an exploration of the career patterns of two target groups of young adults (office technology workers and machine operators) across seven diverse countries. Claes and Quintanilla explored the contribution of the participants' activities (e.g., work, education, unemployment, military), work centrality, intrinsic work orientation, extrinsic work orientation, entitlement orientation, and obligation orientation to the prediction of psychological well-being. Using data culled from retrospective reports over the previous 2.5 years, Claes and Quintanilla identified six transition patterns, revealing that young adults who moved from employment to additional training exhibited the highest level of psychological well-being. In contrast, the lowest level of psychological well-being was associated with the transition pattern that began with military or civil service (frequently preceded by unemployment) followed by employment. Claes and Quintanilla also noted that there were more similarities than differences in the transition patterns across the seven northwestern and southern European countries.

Micro-Level Post Hoc Studies

Citing the vast differences in the social and economic context for college-bound versus work-bound students and the questionable relevance of existing theoretical statements and research findings to the vast majority of students and workers, Blustein et al. (1997) conducted an exploratory qualitative investigation of the STW transitions of 45 noncollege-educated workers (ranging from ages 18 to 29). In contrast to the reliance on economic-based indicators of transition behavior and outcomes that have characterized many of the research studies to date, Blustein et al. used congruence and job satisfaction as two psychologically oriented indices of an adaptive transition.

First, Blustein et al. (1997) identified three individual attributes that appeared to be associated with successful transitions among the workers in their sample: (1) an involved and purposeful approach to career options and tasks, (2) self and environmental exploration, and (3) a clear sense of self. Second, they found that the participants viewed institutional opportunities and supports within the contexts of school, work, and family as facilitative of adaptive transitions. Key elements of these institutional supports included active and tangibly helpful counselors and access to jobs that provide opportunities for growth and further skill development, along with an emotionally and encouraging relational environment. Third, Blustein and his colleagues identified a prominent striving on the part of the participants for enhanced access to educational and vocational training options, which seemed to function as a means to cope with the frustrations and obstacles of the transition from school to work.

Another exploratory investigation by Borman (1991) relied on a purely qualitative approach wherein 25 working-class youth from urban areas within the United States were interviewed and observed in their first jobs at various points within a year of leaving high school. Borman observed extensive diversity in the nature of the initial workplace; however, one of the themes of the narrative data was that those occupational settings that provided more challenge and autonomy were considered by the respondents to be more satisfying. In addition, Borman found that the men in her sample were given tasks that offered greater interest, autonomy, and potentially transferable skills than the women.

An innovative discovery-oriented study conducted by researchers in Britain and Germany (Evans & Heinz, 1994) examined narrative biographies of 40 work-bound youth to assess the proximal and distal context that frames the transition for the participants. The data analysis in this project was directed primarily by the narrative of the participants as opposed to an a priori selection of independent and dependent variables. One of the major findings of this study was the identification of an adaptive approach to the transition, known as active individualization, which is distinguished by self-initiated activity, clear-cut occupational goals, and seeking a means of finding a match for one's interests and values. In contrast, a far less agentic path, including less clearly articulated occupational goals and unfocused strategies for negotiating the transition, characterized the less adaptive approach, known as passive individualization. Evans and Heinz found that individuals with greater access to the opportunity structure, a history of achievement, and social support were more likely to engage in active individualization.

Longitudinal Studies

One of the major sources of knowledge about career development has historically emerged from longitudinal research. Consistent with the focus of this chapter, we review only those investigations that study primarily work-bound youth who are facing or experiencing a transition from school to work. We begin by highlighting two historically important studies that have direct relevance to the current review, even though their overt focus was not exclusively on work-bound youth (yet, in reality, most of the participants were in fact noncollege-bound). One of these bodies of work, Super's Career Pattern Study, followed high school boys across several transitions, including the one from high school to college, work, and military service (Jordaan & Heyde, 1979; Super

& Overstreet, 1960). The second of these investigations, the Career Development Study, by Gribbons and Lohnes (1968, 1982), followed a cohort of young people across a 20-year time frame. Although it is impossible to capture the complexity and richness of these studies in this brief space, a number of findings from these studies have been critically important to more recent investigations, some of which have relied, explicitly or implicitly, on these extensive longitudinal findings (e.g., Blustein et al., 1997; Way & Rossmann, 1996a). In relation to the questions that we have posed at the outset of this section, these early investigations highlighted the importance of planfulness, exploration, a future orientation, and active involvement with one's high school as particularly adaptive features of pretransition behavior. Moreover, the work by Super and his associates coupled with the Gribbons and Lohnes contributions underscored the importance of social class in career development, as participants in both of these investigations with greater access to the opportunity structure fared better in their careers than their less-affluent and less-educated peers.

Using the rich data base culled from the National Longitudinal Survey—Youth (NLS—Y) project sponsored by the U.S. Department of Labor, two groups of research teams (Klerman & Karoly, 1995; Veum & Weiss, 1993) examined selected aspects of the STW transition, with a particular focus on the question of how much floundering occurs within the late adolescent and young adult labor market. A high level of floundering refers to employment instability, with late adolescents and young adults moving from job to job or work to unemployment, often involving large shifts in occupational field. Although many scholars have raised serious questions about the psychological and economic costs of floundering (e.g., Hamilton, 1990; Marshall & Tucker, 1992), others have suggested that such movement functions as a means for individuals and organizations to maximize person-environment fit (e.g., Heckman, 1994). Although both of these research teams focused on primarily economic and sociological variables as opposed to psychological outcomes of the transition, these studies are highly informative in STW policy circles (Urquiola et al., 1997). Hence, we believe that these results need to be presented and clearly understood.

The initial NLS—Y sample consisted of 12,781 individuals ranging in ages from 14 to 21; the data reported by these research teams were based on annual data collections that began in 1979 and ended in 1990. The findings from the Klerman and Karoly (1995) analysis revealed that high school graduates, particularly the white men in the sample, tended to report fairly stable employment patterns (i.e., an average of six jobs in the eight years since high school with at least one of these jobs lasting three years). Klerman and Karoly concluded their important and widely cited analysis by noting that "these results contradict the stylized facts underlying current school-to-work initiatives, many of which are predicated on the belief that the school-to-work transition involves periods of milling around that last until the mid-twenties" (page xv). They did, however, acknowledge that the situation for visible racial and ethnic minorities, women, and high school dropouts is quite problematic and worthy of the attention of educators and policy makers. A similar set of findings characterized the Veum and Weiss (1993) report, which focused on a more diverse array of dependent variables, including number of jobs held, weeks employed, spells of unemployment, and weeks unemployed. Veum and Weiss reported that for young people without college degrees, a considerable amount of variance in work histories can be explained by race and gender, with women and youth of color experiencing significant difficulties in the labor market. However, these differences become less marked for those youth with more post–high school training and education.

Another large-scale longitudinal study by Haggstrom, Blaschke, and Shavelson (1991) reported an illuminating set of results culled from the High School and Beyond study (HSB). The HSB project, initiated in 1982, followed 26,000 high school seniors from the classes of 1980 and 1982, with follow-ups in 1984 and 1986. Although this sample included college-bound as well as work-bound youth, several of the Haggstrom et al. results are highly relevant to our discussion. One of the most important findings is that nearly one third of 1980 and 1982 graduating seniors in the top quartile of academic aptitude did not enroll in any postsecondary institution, suggesting that the cohort of work-bound students is quite heterogeneous with respect to ability level. The outcomes that Haggstrom et al. examined in their study fall under the rubric of the sorting-out process, which refers to the timing and selection of a pathway (work, college, military, homemaking) in the first five years out of high school. In contrast to Klerman and Karoly (1995), Haggstrom et al. concluded that the transition from high school to work for the work-bound was indeed quite problematic. They noted "that a substantial proportion of high school seniors in the 1980s lacked direction when they left school, and that their subsequent activities were marked by false starts and backtracking" (Haggstrom et al., 1991, p. vii).

Longitudinally based studies of the transition from high school to work in Europe have attracted psychologists and sociologists, as well as the economists and macro-level sociologists who have tended to dominate this line of inquiry within the United States. One particularly informative investigation by Feij, Whitely, Peiro, and Taris (1995) used an extensive data set from the Work Socialization of Youth study in deriving a model to predict career-enhancing strategies and job content innovation among a sample of 859 work-bound youth from eight European countries. The first round of data collection took place at the initial stage of the participants' employment (between three and nine months) with the second data collection occurring one year later. Using two relatively innovative indices of an adaptive transition (career-enhancing strategies and job content innovation), Feij et al. examined an array of independent variables, including work centrality, intrinsic work values, extrinsic work values, coworker relations, and supervisor relations. Feij et al. concluded from their structural equation models that work centrality, intrinsic values, and availability and use of frequent contact with superiors and coworkers were predictive of an adaptive transition to the work role across both time frames.

An extensive set of rigorous longitudinal studies has been conducted in the United Kingdom by Bynner and his colleagues (e.g., Bynner, 1997, 1998; Bynner, Ferri, & Shepherd, 1997), who are among the most active and creative of the European research teams. These studies used a very rich data set derived from the British Cohort Study, which has examined the entire population of citizens of Britain who were born during a particular week of 1970 (similar cohorts were studied in 1946 and 1958). Although Bynner et al. acknowledged that a failure to track one third of the sample (resulting in a sample of 9,003) may have influenced their findings, their cautious and database based interpretation of their results have yielded informative insights into the nature of the transitions facing youth in the United Kingdom. In a general overview of this extensive data set, Bynner et al. concluded that training and education represent important investments in one's own human capital, which helps individuals to adjust to unpredictable economic forces. However, the role of social class was still prominent in this relatively global analysis, with the offspring of well-educated parents faring the best in terms of their occupational attainment.

Bynner (1997, 1998) also furnished more precise analyses of this longitudinal data set in two remarkably sophisticated and theoretically evocative articles. In an attempt to define human capital in operational terms, Bynner (1997) provided compelling empirical evidence regarding the importance of basic skills (i.e., literacy and numeracy skills) in attaining continuity in employment after leaving school. Comparing the 1958 and 1970 birth cohorts, Bynner (1998) tested structural equations to assess the contribution of various psychological, cognitive, and socioeconomic factors in the prediction of employment across the two time frames represented by each cohort. In this particular study, Bynner only used those participants who left school directly after turning 16 (the natural school-leaving age for the majority of British students), thereby relying on a sample that represented only work-bound youth. One particularly informative finding was the vast difference in occupational opportunities for the two cohorts. Bynner's results indicated that for the 1958 cohort, none of the identity component variables (i.e., basic cognitive skills, labor market experience, family support, and psychological state) had any predictive power in determining employment, whereas the data from the 1970 cohort revealed that basic skills, educational attainment, and psychological health were significantly associated with employment (accounting for between 7% and 11% of the variance). In effect, for the 1958 cohort, inadequate education or poor basic skills did not make any difference in one's ability to obtain employment, reflecting perhaps the more accessible labor market of that era. However, with the loss of extensive numbers of production jobs, which have been replaced by jobs requiring more cognitive skills and flexibility, the 1970 cohort needed a more sophisticated array of psychological and cognitive attributes to move successfully into the world of work.

A Canadian study by Borgen, Amundson, and Tench (1996) sought to assess psychological well-being in a sample of 172 high school seniors from British Columbia who were followed at three intervals (prior to high school graduation and then 6 and 16 months following graduation). Borgen et al. found that employment and school continuation were not related to psychological well-being, which was defined by self-esteem and an absence of anxiety and depression. In contrast, difficulties with finances and the capacity to ward off boredom were associated with well-being.

Heinz and his colleagues (Heinz, 1987; Heinz, Kelle, Wirtzel, & Zinn, 1998) have also contributed longitudinally derived knowledge to the STW literature. In one study, Heinz (1987) used interviews to learn how 200 students from a Hauptschüler (the lowest level vocational training school in Germany) were experiencing their transition into a region that had recently faced an increase in unemployment. The rigorous qualitative analyses suggested that the participants were maintaining a particularly optimistic view of their options. More precisely, initiative and self-responsibility were associated with positive experiences in negotiating the transition, despite a reality that was not consistent with their self-perceptions. In a more recent study, Heinz et al. (1998) sought to identify the extent to which apprenticeships serve to reinforce social class distinctions. This elegant project, which relied both on qualitative and quantitative methods, reported initial findings from a panel study that was conducted in Bremen and Munich, with samples around 1,000 for each site and a smaller subset of over a hundred participants for the qualitative analyses. This study examined various indices of career behavior across a five-year period and found that the German system indeed does reproduce many aspects of gender and social class inequality. In deriving further inferences from the qualitative data, Heinz et al. noted that many of the workers in these semiskilled positions sought diverse ways to define their own futures in an attempt to overcome some of the obstacles of their social class. However, the researchers also observed that the occupational context gradually sets limits on individuals' constructions of their career development.

Empirical Studies of Marginalized Populations

Given the difficulties of negotiating the movement from school to work for work-bound youth in general, this life transition would seem to be even more complex for young people who are marginalized by virtue of membership in a cohort of youth who have even less access to the educational and economic opportunity structure. Three such groups that have received attention in empirical research are youth with disabling conditions, women, and youth who are members of a visible racial and ethnic minority group. In this section, we review selected studies, with the intention of understanding how membership in a marginalized group might influence the STW process.

Youth with Disabling Conditions

The research on the STW transition for individuals with disabilities is quite extensive and has recently been reviewed by Phelps and Hanley-Maxwell (1997). Rather than attempting to describe this rich literature in depth, we initially summarize the conclusions of the Phelps and Hanley-Maxwell review, followed by a focused exploration of three particularly important studies that have charted the transition from school to work for individuals with disabling conditions. Using a search method that is similar to the one employed in the present chapter (i.e., reviewing data bases in psychology and education), Phelps and Hanley-Maxwell examined the past 10 years of the relevant literature on the STW transition and disability; the definition of disability in this review includes learning disabilities, emotional disabilities, speech impairment, visual disabilities, and mild/moderate retardation. One of the major observations of the Phelps and Hanley-Maxwell review is that the integration of academic and vocational learning within schools, as exemplified by instruction that attempts to contextualize learning within an explicitly work-based framework, has been associated with positive transition outcomes (such as obtaining jobs, duration of postschool employment). The second of the positive educational interventions for youth with disabilities is the use of school-supervised work experience. Programs such as the ones summarized in Pauly et al. (1995) and in the work of Stern and his associates (Stern et al., 1994), which describes youth apprenticeships, cooperative education, and school-based enterprises, seem to be particularly helpful to youth with disabling conditions. Phelps and Hanley-Maxwell noted that the empirical research indicates that involving youth with disabilities in work-based programs in high school seems to promote a smooth transition to work and reduces high school dropout rates (e.g., Wagner, Blackorby, Cameto, & Newman, 1993).

Using a national sample ranging from 900 to 2,000 students (depending on the dependent variable in question), Blackorby and Wagner (1996) described the progress of high school youth within special education programs across the first five years out of school, based on data culled from the National Longitudinal Transition Study of Special Education students (NLTS). The dependent variables included employment, postsecondary education, and residential independence, thereby providing a wide-angle lens on the post–high school life of late adolescents and young adults with disabilities. The NTLS data revealed some progress with respect to employment rates, wages, postsecondary school enrollment, and residential independence as the youth progressed further into adulthood. However, the findings indicated that youth with disabilities achieved levels far lower than their peers without identifiable disabilities. In addition, Blackorby and Wagner reported women and individuals from visible racial and ethnic minority groups experienced more profound difficulties across the array of adjustment variables used in the NTLS.

Another particularly innovative study by Barone, Trickett, Schmid, and Leone (1993) described a brief longitudinal investigation wherein 234 high school seniors (of which 175 were from mainstream classes and 59 were from special education classes) were followed from the spring of their senior year up to a period of six months after leaving high school. Using a descriptive rather than inferential approach to their data analysis, Barone et al. defined transition behavior in terms of employment and/or educational status, assuming that greater engagement with either school or work is preferable to lack of engagement. Barone and his colleagues found that the students from special education classes were far less likely to be engaged in either employment or postsecondary education than were their counterparts from mainstream classes.

In a somewhat different vein, Benz, Yovanoff, and Doren (1997) reported a longitudinal study that ascertained the impact of some of the new programmatic interventions that have emerged from recent STW initiatives on two outcome variables: competitive employment (defined by working 20+ hours per week and earning the minimum wage or higher) and productive engagement (defined by a minimum of at least half-time work, school, or full-time involvement in the military). Using a sample of 327 students (including 218 students with disabilities and 109 students without identifiable disabling conditions), the Benz et al. study revealed the overall positive impact of many of the characteristic STW programs. In terms of school-based learning, Benz and his associates identified the importance of basic academic skills, particularly for students with disabilities; in contrast, career exploration and career awareness activities were viewed as less important by the students, which may be explained by the heavily economic outcome criterion that did not include an explicit psychological or vocational dimension. Work-based learning, which represents a hallmark of school to work (Olson, 1997; Urquiola et al., 1997), was found to be important for all of the students in the sample. One cautionary note in this study was the finding that female students with disabilities were at a particular disadvantage in attaining competitive employment when compared with male students with disabilities and females from the general student population. Consistent with other studies (cf. Phelps & Hanley-Maxwell, 1997), students with disabling conditions were two times less likely to attain any sort of productive engagement after high school than their peers without disabilities. Given the evident struggles of women in negotiating the STW transition, we next turn to studies that highlight the way in which gender functions in this critical developmental process.

Transition Experience of Young Women

Although women in higher socioeconomic statuses (SES) groups appear to be making significant gains in their participation in the labor force, significant concerns regarding the STW transitions of work-bound and working-class women have been expressed due to the lack of viable opportunities in male-dominated segments of the workforce and the likelihood that women without college education will pursue primarily female-dominated occupational paths (Gray & Herr, 1998; Wilson, 1996). The social consequences of these two trends are far-reaching, yet still less than adequately understood. Included in this brief review are three relevant investigations intended to demonstrate the variety of issues present in the STW transition for young women.

Citing research demonstrating that movement into male-dominated occupations is likely to be at the professional level and involve college-educated women, Hannah and Kahn (1989) pointed toward the need to investigate the occupational choices of work-bound women from lower SES status. In their investigation of the relationships of SES and gender to the occupational choices of grade 12 students, Hannah and Kahn found that SES was a more important predictor of nontraditional gender-typed occupational choices for girls than it was for boys. Although boys tended to select male-dominated occupations irrespective of SES and prestige of the focal occupation, high SES girls were less gender-typed in their job choices than low SES girls.

Hao and Brinton (1997) used 14 waves of data from the NLS—Y to investigate the determinants of single mothers' (aged 14 to 21 years in 1979; $N = 1,576$) entry into and exit from the workforce and school attendance. Hao and Brinton found that the longer a woman spends in single motherhood, the less likely she is to enter the labor force or school or to sustain participation if she starts. Variables that were positively associated with entry into and continuity of "productive activities" included the amount of child support, higher parental family income, and the labor force participation of the mother of the respondents. High poverty rates were associated with an impeded entry, but had no impact on continuity, and unemployment rates and receipt of Aid for Families with Dependent Children (AFDC) benefits were not related to either variable.

Another key study conducted by Hamilton and Powers (1990) examined the transition from high school to work for working-class women from a rural, primarily European American background. Using a sample of 76 seniors from two high schools and a vocational center, Hamilton and Powers interviewed students initially in June of their last year of high school and again in November of the same year. Although many of these students had considerable work experience and some reported significant career planning, Hamilton and Powers were surprised in observing the very difficult transition experiences within their sample. Using an elaborate coding procedure reflecting rigorous use of qualitative methodology, they found that 60% of the women were not doing what they had planned five months earlier. Hamilton and Powers also reported that vocational planning and work experience were not associated with employment after high school, which was inconsistent with expectations and previous research.

Youth of Color

An unfortunate axiom in the social sciences is that membership in a visible racial and ethnic minority group has been characterized by significant obstacles in attaining access to meaningful employment (Carter & Cook, 1992; Wilson, 1996). The situation with respect to the STW transition is no different. As many of the previously cited studies have indicated, minority youth experience far more difficulty in obtaining the sort of education and support systems that facilitate the transition from school to work (Klerman & Karoly, 1995; Veum & Weiss, 1993). Despite the clear obstacles faced by students of color, the amount of research conducted in this area is quite sparse. Yet a few creative studies have been conducted that provide an informative glimpse into the complex transition faced by work-bound students of color.

Perhaps the most exhaustive of recent studies on the plight of minority youth has been conducted as part of Wilson's (1996) extensive sociological analyses of the primarily minority inner-city population in Chicago. Combining quantitative and qualitative methods, Wilson's research team developed the Urban Poverty and Family Life Study (UPFLS), which studied the impact of work (or the lack thereof) on individual and family experiences of inner-city African American, Latino, and (to a far lesser extent) European American residents of Chicago's poor neighborhoods. The quantitative arm of the study included a random survey of 2,500 individuals, and the qualitative portion entailed a subsample of 175 UPFLS participants along with a survey of 179 employers in the area. Although this study did not focus specifically on the experiences of work-bound youth, the investigation has considerable relevance to the present discussion of the STW transition. In brief, Wilson's research identified the full gamut of obstacles facing poor youth from the inner city, including discrimination, poor schools, the lack of accessible jobs, inadequate job training, and disintegrating neighborhoods.

Using narratives from the inner-city sample to tell this painful story, Wilson concluded that both race and class intersect to form a powerful set of influences that sustain the aversive conditions of the inner-cities. One of the major aspects of Wilson's position is that the loss of skilled and semiskilled work in urban areas has led to a domino-like process where inner city youth, particularly African American males, find themselves with ever-increasing obstacles in transitioning to work. Wilson noted the importance of the high-skills, high-wage argument that has motivated much of the STW; however, he argued that the inner cities are in a crisis state that demands immediate solutions, such as contemporary federally funded job programs (like a modern-day Works Progress Administration).

In an ethnographic study of low-wage adolescent and young adult workers, Newman (1996) described life among selected adolescent workers within four fast-food restaurants in Harlem. Beginning with a broad sample of 200 participants, Newman then selected a stratified random sample of 60 workers for more in-depth interviews; she then followed a very small sample of these youth over the course of nine months. The young people in Newman's sample generally experienced very positive outcomes as a result of their jobs, as manifested by the capacity to disengage from aversive social pressures in their communities, earn money to help their families and fund their postsecondary training efforts, and connect to other workers, thereby establishing an adaptive social support system. Implicit in Newman's report is support for the sort of work-school linkages that are characteristic of some of the best STW programs (cf. Pauly et al., 1995).

D'Amico and Maxwell (1994) found that early unemployment among a large subset of African American youth accounts for the divergence in wages across the life span in their study of the impact of post-school joblessness on male African American versus European American earnings. The total sample of 508 included 144 African American and 364 European American participants. Specifically, D'Amico and Maxwell concluded that African American males who experienced the highest levels of joblessness during the STW period faced the greatest reduction in relative wages later in life. D'Amico and Maxwell concluded that "equalization of racial employment levels during the initial foray into the labor market would reduce subsequent differences in wages" (p. 195) between African Americans and European Americans. Their data demonstrate that the deficits associated with immediate post-school joblessness effects seem to endure over the life span.

Powers (1994) took a novel approach in an investigation of labor force attachment among European American, African American, and Latino youth. He used seven waves of the NLS—Y data to assess the determinants of entering *inactivity* (as defined by not working and not attending school) for 1,731 initially active young men. This investigation could be conceptualized as a study of floundering, a characteristic of youthful transitions that many of the STW initiatives are designed to combat. Combining school enrollment and employment into a single dimension to measure labor force attachment, Powers found that social context variables play a key role in explaining weak labor force attachment among young men of color, but are relatively less important for European American youth. Specifically, among African Americans, transitions into inactivity were predicted more by sociocontextual criteria (living in the urban northern United States, family structure, marital status, and influential others) than by human capital factors (ability tests). For Latinos, the transitions into idleness appeared to be determined by both sociocontextual (local unemployment rates, family structure, and South/West U.S. residence) and socioeconomic factors (i.e., adjusted family income and father's employment status). For European American youths, socioeconomic characteristics (parents' education, father's employment, welfare status, and family income) and the array of human capital factors (test scores of ability, educational attainment, work experience, and previous school or employment status) were the strongest predictors of weakened workforce attachment.

Although a number of authors (e.g., Blustein et al., 1997; Worthington & Juntunen, 1997) have questioned the use of some STW research due to its almost exclusive reliance on economic outcomes (to the exclusion of psychological outcomes), a study by Greenlee, Damarin, and Walsh (1988) is one exception to this trend. They investigated the hypotheses that (1) African Americans, more often than European Americans, settle for jobs that do not match their real vocational interests, making their interest profiles less congruent (i.e., Holland, 1997) than those of European American workers in the same setting; and (2) insofar as African Americans adapt their interests to the occupations they enter, their interest profiles become less consistent or less differentiated than those of comparable European Americans. Using relatively small samples of African American ($N = 40$) and European American ($N = 40$) male workers in two occupations that did not require a college degree (restaurant proprietors and hospital aides), Greenlee et al. found that (1) African American proprietors were less congruent than European American proprietors, (2) African American aides were less differentiated than European American aides, and (3) African American aides may have adapted more rapidly to their occupation than African American restaurant owners had to theirs. These findings support the notion that psychological sequelae, as well as economic ones, result from less than optimal transitions, and may impact youth of color more broadly than is typically believed.

When considering the studies on marginalized populations in light of other empirical investigations reviewed earlier (e.g., Borman, 1991; Klerman & Karoly, 1995), the available research suggests that disabling conditions, gender, and visible racial and ethnic minority status play a discernible and aversive, although not uniform, role in the STW transition. Although the actual role of these characteristics is difficult to describe based on such a small number of studies, the evidence suggests that the STW transition seems to offer even more pronounced challenges and struggles for these populations.

Conclusions

Adaptive Transitions

A broad examination of the literature reviewed thus far suggests that a wide array of definitions of an adaptive STW transition for work-bound youth have been used in research. In general, investigations from macro-level social scientists have tended to use global indices of employment and unemployment or level of occupational attainment achieved in the labor market (Klerman & Karoly,

1995; Veum & Weiss, 1993). In contrast, psychological investigations have pointed to a wide array of definitions, generally encompassing some internal or relatively proximal external characteristics of one's posttransition behavior, including readiness for the transition (Way & Rossmann, 1996a), job satisfaction and occupational choice congruence (Blustein et al., 1997), and development of adaptive coping skills on the job (e.g., Borman, 1991; Feij et al., 1995). As such, a clear consensus about what constitutes an adaptive transition is difficult to infer at this point.

An in-depth examination of the previously reported studies in relation to current public policy debates (e.g., Marshall & Tucker, 1992; Olson, 1997; Resnick & Witt, 1996b) reveals a more complex, yet subtle, set of issues with respect to the definition of an adaptive transition. In brief, the definition of an adaptive transition varies extensively, often in relation to the investigator's overt and more covert objectives. More precisely, the decision about how to define an adaptive transition clearly influences the direction of the investigation, often with a clear impact on the development of interventions and policy recommendations. The Klerman and Karoly (1995) study provides a particularly evocative example of this conundrum. As we indicated earlier, Klerman and Karoly concluded that the STW transition problem, which has attracted such national and international attention, was not all that pervasive except among youth from minority backgrounds and high school dropouts and, to a lesser extent, women. The Klerman and Karoly work, which has had a discernible impact on the public debate about the STW process (Urquiola et al., 1997), defined a successful transition by looking at variability in job floundering and job tenure. (The conclusion of the Klerman and Karoly study is similarly echoed in some economic and policy papers by conservative scholars who argue against broad, systemic government-based programs and suggest that some degree of floundering is good for both individuals and employers. See, for example, Heckman, 1994.) In short, we believe that the absence of a consensually agreed-upon definition of an adaptive transition allows investigators the means by which they can buttress their political agenda. No doubt, this sort of situation exists within other domains of inquiry. However, within the STW movement, such a dilemma has important and potentially dramatic consequences.

As a response to this dilemma, we propose that researchers and policy analysts need to focus their attention on developing a broad, yet commonly accepted, definition of an adaptive transition that clearly includes the psychological experience of work-bound youth, while also encompassing the sociological and economic definitions that have been used to date in much of the existing STW research. Examples of investigations that have employed such a wide-angle lens include the Way and Rossman (1996a, 1996b) project, as well as the transition studies conducted in both Britain and Germany (Bynner, 1997, 1998; Heinz et al., 1998). Interestingly, these studies also identified some of the richest findings about the complex interplay of relevant predictors of adaptive transitions. In effect, we propose that researchers return to the rich multivariate definitions of adaptive transitions that characterized some of the earliest studies in this field (e.g., Gribbons & Lohnes, 1968; Super & Overstreet, 1960). In these early studies of career development, researchers employed elaborate indices of adaptiveness, considering psychological, sociological, and economic variables that were rooted in the historical context of the study.

When considering the early notions of readiness for career choices (Phillips & Blustein, 1994) in relation to the literature reviewed in this chapter, it is possible to identify some common themes that may help to focus subsequent definitional analyses of adaptive transitions. First, it seems critical to include some internal psychological index of the degree of individual satisfaction one experiences with respect to work and nonwork roles (cf. Blustein et al., 1997; Borgen et al., 1996; Evans & Heinz, 1994). Second, we recommend that investigators incorporate more global and objective indices of how well the individual is faring in attaining access to opportunities for growth, advancement, and further training within their job settings and other educational venues (Borman, 1991; Feij et al., 1995). Third, although we believe that some of the economic and job stability indices may have been overemphasized in many of the existing studies, it is important to acknowledge that access to increased earnings and job stability yields greater access to other resources that promote individual effectiveness and success. We are not suggesting that scholars only initiate studies where they include all possible aspects of an adaptive transition. However, we urge researchers to exercise greater caution in deriving implications from their findings when they present a circumscribed portrayal of transition behavior.

Predicting an Adaptive Transition: The Current Construction of Identity Capital

The empirical literature also has yielded a number of important observations about the optimal array of predictors of an adaptive transition. As we have indicated, the wide variety of dependent variables coupled with the diversity of cultural contexts evident in the existing research creates some difficulty in conceptualizing the adaptive transitioner. Nevertheless, some prominent trends are evident in our review that may be useful to future researchers in the STW area. One of the key ingredients in predicting favorable outcomes is access to the educational and occupational opportunity structure (Bynner et al., 1997; Layder et al., 1991; Wilson, 1996). This finding, which echoes some of the historically most robust notions in career development and occupational sociology (e.g., Becker, 1993; Super, 1957), essentially confirms the adage that the "rich get richer" in the struggle for occupational attainment and job satisfaction. Against this evident backdrop of social forces, however, all is not lost for working class and poor youth. Indeed, the literature provides some clear and relatively consistent findings with respect to how individuals can maximize their opportunities to have a successful and smooth transition.

First, work-bound youth who develop competencies, both in the basic skills and in the more applied and vocationally relevant domains of knowledge, enhance their means of effectively negotiating the transition from school to work (Bynner, 1997, 1998; Evans & Heinz, 1994; Veum & Weiss, 1993; Way & Rossmann, 1996a). Second, a particular array of psychological factors, including self-initiative, flexibility, purposefulness, and agency, have been associated with favorable outcomes (Blustein et al., 1997; Bynner, 1998; Way & Rossmann, 1996a). Third, an active and supportive relational environment, including family of origin, supportive and engaged peers, teachers, counselors, and coworkers and supervisors, has emerged as an important feature of the STW transition (Blustein et al., 1997; Bynner et al., 1997; Feij et al., 1995; Way & Rossmann, 1996a). Fourth, although the advent of work-based learning on a wide scale is a relatively recent phenomenon, there is some suggestion that an adaptive transition can be facilitated by an educational environment that offers some clear and meaningful connection to the world of work (e.g., Phelps & Hanley-Maxwell, 1997; Urquiola et al., 1997).

Following Bynner's (1998) suggestion, we propose the use of Côté's (1996) notion of identity capital as an organizing rubric to capture the diverse elements that seem to be needed to promote adaptive transitions from school to work. According to Côté, identity capital includes traditional characteristics such as academic achievements and vocational qualifications and the development of a stable and clear sense of identity (cf. Erikson, 1968). Identity capital also includes such psychological characteristics as flexibility, the development of an extensive behavioral repertoire, and a keen sense of awareness of one's social context. As Bynner (1998, p. 46) suggested, individuals from middle-class families tend to have built-in "vocational insurance" based on their access to the facilitative nutrients (educational opportunities, supportive social conditions) that are associated with greater affluence. The difficult task, naturally, is to find effective means of providing such vocational insurance for the forgotten half of working-class and poor youth.

Without question, various elements of identity capital need to come from a social context that is both supportive and instrumentally helpful in allowing work-bound youth to attain the skills and psychological characteristics needed for an effective STW transition. As some of the studies in this review have concluded, work-bound women seem to be struggling more than men in attaining an effective transition to meaningful employment (Borman, 1991; Klerman & Karoly, 1995). Moreover, the literature that has pointed to more extensive obstacles for students of color and individuals with disabling conditions clearly implicates the social and economic context as critical factors in the STW transition process (e.g., Klerman & Karoly, 1995; Phelps & Hanley-Maxwell, 1997; Wilson, 1996). Thus, it seems that investments in the social fabric that nourish the development of work-bound youth's identity capital is critical to reduce the degree to which social and economic factors inhibit the STW transition process. Some of the investments in the social context are already an explicit part of many of the STW initiatives, such as the use of work-based learning, active and supportive counselors and teachers, and involved and committed employers. However, as many scholars have noted, the development of individual talents and abilities is contingent on more than reform of education; a major theme from some of the broader sociological analyses is that the nature of effective interventions needs to be far more expansive, including families, work environments, and other critical social systems (Bynner, 1998; Lewis et al., 1998; Marshall & Tucker, 1992; Wilson, 1996).

When considered collectively, the empirical studies of the STW transition process reveal a highly complex picture that belies simple formulas or solutions. The next section of this chapter seeks to provide a framework for future researchers and practitioners who seek to enhance the opportunities and life experiences of work-bound youth.

IMPLICATIONS FOR RESEARCH, THEORY, AND PRACTICE

A Guide to the Next Generation of Inquiry

In our view, the literature on the STW transition process, although clearly still emerging and crystallizing, offers some useful ideas for further inquiry and theory development. Interest in the STW transition for work-bound youth has been a central area of inquiry in Europe for some time and is gradually gaining a foothold in the United States. The legislation and position papers that have evoked such a dramatic surge in research, program development, and policy debates may fade from the landscape; however, the impact of this movement has had clear implications in career development and educational scholarship and practice (Gysbers, 1997; Lewis et al., 1998; Olson, 1997; Worthington & Juntunen, 1997). One of the most important implications of the STW movement is rather than considering poor and working-class students as an afterthought, recent discourse and research initiatives have placed this forgotten population at the forefront of our thinking.

As a by-product of this more pronounced focus on work-bound and working-class students, one of the more neglected aspects of career development theory and research, that of social class, has reemerged in bolder relief. The notion that one's socioeconomic class influences the direction and success of one's work life is clearly not a new idea; in fact, it has been a centerpiece in the occupational attainment literature (Brown, Fukunaga, Umemoto, & Wicker, 1996; Hotchkiss & Borow, 1996). Considerations of social class are clearly necessary in building effective theories and in designing research studies on the STW transition process. In addition to considering social class as a major variable, we need to examine our own implicit class biases in how we conceptualize work and in how we design interventions. The complexities of the STW transition for working-class youth suggests that concerted and creative research projects are needed to develop the sort of public policy, educational reform, and counseling practice that are culturally affirmative and effective.

Promising Research Directions

Given the challenges that are posed in considering the STW transition, what then are the next steps in future research? One methodological recommendation is that researchers seek to operationalize their variables very carefully, with particular attention to how an adaptive transition is defined. In addition, there are a growing number of sophisticated studies (e.g., Bynner, 1997, 1998; Evans & Heinz, 1994; Heinz et al., 1998; Way & Rossmann, 1996a) that provide researchers with some clear ideas about how to conduct rigorous, yet relevant studies. Thus, we see the need for research to test the ideas that have emerged in the literature to date, including some of the critical points that we outlined earlier, such as the need to develop some commonly accepted views of an adaptive transition. Some of the more promising trajectories for future research would be to examine the precise nature of family and relational influences in the STW process, following up on the research of Blustein et al. (1997) and Way and Rossmann (1996a). Additionally, the relationships between such well-known constructs as self-efficacy and the emerging notion of an active and agentic approach to one's transitional behavior, which was detailed in many of the more rigorous studies (e.g., Bynner et al., 1997; Evans & Heinz, 1994), would be quite informative. We also believe that it is critical to continue pursuing theory-building ideas, which would be constructed with an explicit awareness of previous research and theory.

As we have stated, the STW domain provides a highly vivid example of how social, cultural, economic, and historical factors influence the way in which individuals negotiate the boundaries between school and work. We applaud the efforts of those scholars who have explicitly sought to examine how culture affects the STW transition, as evident in the growing number of multicultural and international studies that have been conducted to date (e.g., Borman, 1991; Evans & Heinz, 1994; Way & Rossmann, 1996a). Moreover, we encourage studies that seek to identify elements of a transition that are unique to a given culture and time period, as well as elements that are more universal. For example, although we may find that the general notion of investing in one's identity capital seems to be important, the precise composition of identity capital may have some unique elements in a given culture and time frame. Another critical issue to explore is the trend found in our review that women seem to struggle more with their transitions than their male counterparts (Borman, 1991; Klerman & Karoly, 1995). Research that can identify the nature of the social and cultural factors that impinge most prominently in the STW transition for women would do much to enhance our knowledge while also informing critically needed systemic and counseling interventions.

In terms of theoretical developments, the STW movement offers career development three challenging opportunities to expand our conceptual and intellectual horizons. First, the STW inquiry presents the role of social class in the center stage of our thinking and theory development efforts. Although a number of notable career theories include some discussion of social class (e.g., Lent et al., 1996; Mitchell & Krumboltz, 1996; Super, 1957), there is a need to incorporate discussions of social class more overtly in our theoretical deliberations. It may be useful, for example, to further integrate the sociologically oriented models (e.g., Hotchkisss & Borow, 1996) into theory development efforts. Second, the STW movement encourages scholars to examine and integrate the broader social, economic, political, and historical context into existing and new theoretical formulations. The third opportunity presented by the STW movement is reflected in the theory development efforts of those scholars who have explicitly included the perspective of the participants in their conceptualizations of the transition (e.g., Blustein et al., 1997; Borman, 1991; Evans & Heinz, 1994; Newman, 1996). Because of the social distance between most scholars and the objects of our inquiry in STW research, it would seem prudent to include the narratives and other life experiences of the participants in subsequent inquiry to inform the sort of theoretical models of the STW transition that will be culturally affirming.

Psychological Intervention and Training

The question of how best to promote an adaptive STW transition has engendered a healthy debate in recent years, primarily focusing on the broader macro-level issues involved in educational reform, job training programs, and social policy (Marshall & Tucker, 1992; Reich, 1991). (Readers interested in reviewing compelling and well-argued recommendations for policy change with respect to STW are referred to Hamilton, 1990; Marshall & Tucker, 1992; Olson, 1997; Reich, 1991;

Worthington & Juntunen, 1997.) Rather than restate these issues here, we focus instead on a relatively neglected aspect of STW intervention, namely psychological counseling and broader career development practices. In fact, many counseling psychologists have bemoaned the often haphazard manner in which career and psychological interventions have been included in STW legislation and programmatic initiatives (e.g., Lent et al., 1998). Although the STW knowledge base is not sufficient at this point to support a comprehensive reassessment of accepted counseling practice, the existing empirical and theoretical literature, coupled with recent innovations in counseling practice, offer some clear suggestions for effective interventions. In this section, we develop key elements of an informed approach to facilitating the STW transition that are derived from our review, followed by a brief overview of training issues raised by the STW movement.

In our review of the theoretical and empirical literature, we identified an array of psychological, cognitive, familial, relational, educational, and vocational influences that would seem particularly useful in facilitating an adaptive approach to the STW transition. Although some of the targets of such broad-based interventions may be beyond the political and policy scope of traditional counseling practitioners, we believe that the empirical results support a number of counseling approaches and intervention strategies. Primary among this constellation of factors is the use of an active and assertive approach on the part of counselors. As some of the studies have indicated (e.g., Barone et al., 1993; Blustein et al., 1997), counselors who engage in consistent outreach to work-bound students and who help these students feel connected to their educational and vocational institutions are likely to be more effective than the more traditional office-based practitioner. The assets of counselors assuming active roles in their work are clearly not new in our field (Brooks & Forrest, 1994; McWhirter, 1994; Richardson, in press). As such, we believe that counselors will need to engage in a variety of helping roles along with systemic outreach attempts to connect with work-bound clients. In addition, given the broad-based political and social policy issues embedded in the STW movement, we suggest that practitioners become cognizant of these important debates and help their clients and colleagues learn about the critical socio-political context that frames the accessibility of options for students.

As we consider the role of an active, agentic practitioner in light of the major trends that have emerged in our review, a parallel constellation of psychological characteristics within clients can be identified as optimal outcomes of STW-related counseling interventions. One of the key findings from this review has been the important role of an internalized degree of active engagement with one's academic, vocational, and related contexts in helping students to overcome obstacles and negotiate challenging developmental tasks (Blustein et al., 1997; Bynner, 1998; Evans & Heinz, 1994). Following the rich literature from the self-efficacy and learning paradigms (Krumboltz & Worthington, 1999; Lent et al., 1996), an important component of a comprehensive treatment model would include psychoeducational interventions that provide students with both the skills and confidence to tackle the transition from school to work. When considering these contributions in light of the STW literature, we believe that it may be useful for counselors to engage in interventions that will ultimately *empower* their clients to be assertive and self-determined. In brief, the sort of counseling approach that may be effective parallels many of the attributes of feminist counseling, wherein the objective of the intervention is to help clients integrate an enhanced sense of power in a supportive setting while they also have an opportunity to deal with their feelings and beliefs about their current life circumstances (Brooks & Forrest, 1994). An important task for practitioners and scholars would be to flesh out an empowerment-based approach to counseling that is tailored for work-bound youth.

Another set of predictors of the STW transition is the development of work-based skills, including both basic skills and more generic problem-solving skills (Bynner, 1997; Marshall & Tucker, 1992). Given the central role of skills development in promoting an adaptive transition, counselors and other practitioners may find it helpful to become familiar with the evolving changes in workforce preparation and training (Gray & Herr, 1998; Urquiola et al., 1997), thereby serving as a resource for their clients. Additionally, the development of flexible and rigorous work behaviors has emerged as an important aspect of adaptive transition behavior (Borman, 1991; Feij et al., 1995). In this context, workshops and structured group experiences delivered by counselors may be quite critical in helping students develop the necessary work attitudes and skills to succeed in an increasingly competitive labor market.

An underlying theme in many of the theories and research studies is the close interconnections between the education and work domains and other aspects of life experience (Blustein et al., 1997; Bynner et al., 1997; Evans & Heinz, 1994; Way & Rossmann, 1996a). Given the integrative nature of development in late adolescence and early adulthood (Bynner et al., 1997; Côté, 1996), we believe that interventions ought to reduce artificial boundaries between career and noncareer interventions, culminating in the delivery of comprehensive psychological services. Our recommendation is that practitioners provide work-bound students with an opportunity to work on their full array of developmental tasks, including identity formation and their overall capacity to develop relationships and derive support from these relationships (including family and peers). In integrating the extensive scope of the interventions that we are suggesting, we believe that systematic programs in school counseling and in other settings (such as job training programs, dropout prevention programs) would be most useful. As we suggest below, the framework for such systematic programs has already been detailed to a significant extent in the school counseling literature.

As Gysbers (1997) noted, structured and semi-structured guidance programs emerged in the 1960s and 1970s to replace the various remedial and direct service tasks of school counselors with a more developmental and preventive focus. Perhaps the most thoroughly conceptualized program has been developed by Gysbers and his colleagues (Gysbers, 1997). The major elements of this program include (1) a focus on the whole person; (2) a focus on providing comprehensive services, including prevention (via a guidance curriculum), individual planning and crisis-oriented counseling; and (3) an awareness of the need for human and financial resources that can be directed toward supporting the guidance program. The advantages of the Gysbers program for work-bound youth is that this sort of intervention contains many of the elements outlined in the previous section in a structured format that is consistent with the formal and informal norms of school systems.

Other reviews of school counseling programs, such as the one conducted by the National Center for Research in Vocational Education (NCRVE; Cunanan & Maddy-Bernstein, 1997) essentially support the use of the sort of systematic program articulated by Gysbers and his associates. The NCRVE project was based on a national search of exemplary school counseling programs. Because the search and evaluation processes were so extensive, including site visits to the top-ranked programs, the findings of the Cunanan and Maddy-Bernstein report merit consideration. In relation to the needs of work-bound students, the results of the NCRVE search suggest that the most effective counseling programs offer explicit, community-based transition programs in conjunction with systematic career exploration and career planning components in the guidance curriculum. In addition, the exemplary programs were considered to be cost-effective and were able to include students from all backgrounds and ability levels. Finally, the programs described in the Cunanan and Maddy-Bernstein report included activities for students beginning at the latest in seventh grade, with some of the programs beginning their interventions in the elementary school years.

With the opportunities for practice in the STW transition come responsibilities for training. In a survey of counseling psychologists (Juntunen & Worthington, 1997), 75% of the respondents indicated that counselors and counseling psychologists should become involved in the STW movement. However, among 49 respondents responsible for teaching counseling and counseling psychology courses, 42 (86% of those responding to this item) indicated that they were not planning to add any STW-related information to their curriculum. Several respondents commented that there was no room in a given course for extra information. It is important to note that training in the issues raised by the STW transition may not require large amounts of additional information. Instead, faculty might address the issues raised herein by considering the potential for counselors to impact systems and institutions, as well as individuals.

Currently, much of the training provided in career counseling emphasizes individual intervention strategies. This is reflected in widely used textbooks (i.e., Osipow & Fitzgerald, 1996; Zunker, 1998), which place heavy emphasis on theories of individual career development and pay minimal attention to sociological theory. However, to provide exemplary services to work-bound youth, counselors and counseling psychologists need a greater understanding of class issues and the social context of work, as well as the ability to communicate with larger systems, such as school and industry. Integrating such an emphasis with traditional career development approaches will prepare new practitioners to assist a wider range of clients.

A final comment about practice and training merits some attention as we are aware that most of the readers of this chapter will be counseling psychologists, some of whom may be wondering how they can get involved in STW practice efforts. We concur with Gysbers (1997), who noted that counseling psychologists can be critical players in the delivery of counseling and psychological services to work-bound youth. In addition to the traditional roles of school counselor, other opportunities exist in providing leadership and direct client services in STW training programs and community colleges. Moreover, as the STW initiative is expanded into four-year colleges, counseling psychologists are well positioned to provide administrative support and counseling interventions to university students. One of the major avenues for involvement in the STW movement is in providing leadership to programs and initiatives. We believe that counseling psychologists' unique blend of skills in career development, psychological counseling, evaluation, and research would lend themselves well to STW applications.

CONCLUSION

As this chapter has demonstrated, the challenges faced by work-bound students as they transition from school to work are complex and even, at times, overwhelming. In contrast to the seemingly luxurious period of exploration and moratorium that defines college and university life for many youth in Western cultures, work-bound youth need to resolve very complex developmental tasks while also obtaining cognitive and work-related skills, all within a very short time frame. However, as our review has indicated, the literature is replete with examples of individuals, either in structured STW programs, or via their own initiative, who have effectively negotiated this hurdle (Blustein et al., 1997; Urquiola et al., 1997; Way & Rossmann, 1996a). Herein lies the opportunity that often coexists with imposing challenges. We believe that a great deal can be learned from the considerable talent and inventiveness of work-bound youth who have been able to transition successfully from school to work. In addition, a critical opportunity exists to learn about the struggles of those young people who have not been able to find a meaningful place in the world of work and who often are relegated to marginalized lives.

The literature that we have reviewed is clear in the observation that the full breadth of interventions for work-bound youth must necessarily encompass psychological, educational, social, economic, and policy-based dimensions. In this light, we believe that the challenges and opportunities presented by the STW movement may function as a sort of call to arms for counseling psychologists to once again become involved in highly relevant, rigorous, and change-oriented research and practice, which can inform social policy as well as our traditional domains of career development and mental health. As in career development scholarship devoted to gender (Brooks & Forrest, 1994) and racial and ethnic status (Carter & Cook, 1992), we view the STW movement as an opportunity for counseling psychologists to provide leadership and needed research to delineate the complex role of social class in human development. We hope that the literature that we have reviewed in this chapter provides a more clearly articulated road map for those scholars and practitioners who wish to join the journey in ensuring that our knowledge base informs the widest array of students and clients. As the resurgence of interest in work-bound youth and working-class adults suggests, scholars and practitioners can do a great deal to make sure that the forgotten half (as the work-bound were called in the late 1980s) not only are remembered, but affirmed as a key part of our richly layered social fabric.

REFERENCES

Bailey, T. (1997). Changes in the nature of work: Implications for skills and assessments. In H.F. O'Neil, Jr. (Ed.), *Workforce readiness: Competencies and assessment* (pp. 27–46). Mahwah, NJ: Erlbaum.

Bailey, T., Hughes, K., & Barr, T. (1998). *Achieving scale and quality in school-to-work internships: Findings from an employer study* (MR-902). Berkeley, CA: National Center for Research in Vocational Education.

Bailey, T., & Merritt, D. (1997). *School-to-work for the college bound* (MR-799). Berkeley, CA: National Center for Research in Vocational Education.

Barone, C., Trickett, E.J., Schmid, K.D., & Leone, P.E. (1993). Transition tasks and resources: An ecological approach to life after high school. *Prevention in Human Services, 10,* 179–204.

Becker, G.S. (1993). *Human capital: A theoretical and empirical analysis, with special reference to education.* Chicago: University of Chicago Press.

Bell, H.M. (1938). *Youth tell their story.* Washington, DC: American Council of Education.

Benz, M.R., Yovanoff, P., & Doren, B. (1997). School-to-work components that predict postschool success for students with and without disabilities. *Exceptional Children, 63,* 151–165.

Bishop, J.H. (1996). Signaling the competencies of high school students to employers. In L.B. Resnick & J.B. Wirt (Eds.), *Linking school and work: Roles for standards and assessments* (pp. 79–124). San Francisco: Jossey-Bass.

Blackorby, J., & Wagner, M. (1996). Longitudinal postschool outcomes of youth with disabilities: Findings from the National Longitudinal Transition Study. *Exceptional Children, 62,* 399–413.

Blustein, D.L. (1995). Toward a contextual perspective of the school-to-work transition: A reaction to Feij et al. *Journal of Vocational Behavior, 46,* 257–265.

Blustein, D.L., Phillips, S.D., Jobin-Davis, K., Finkelberg, S.L., & Roarke, A.E. (1997). A theory-building investigation of the school to work transition. *The Counseling Psychologist, 25,* 364–402.

Bock, R.D. (1996). Open-ended exercises in large-scale educational assessment. In L.B. Resnick & J.B. Wirt (Eds.), *Linking school and work: Roles for standards and assessments* (pp. 305–338). San Francisco: Jossey-Bass.

Borgen, W.A., Amundson, N.E., & Tench, E. (1996). Psychological well-being throughout the transition from adolescence to adulthood. *Career Development Quarterly, 45,* 189–199.

Borman, K.M. (1991). *The first "real" job: A study of young workers.* Albany, NY: SUNY.

Brabeck, M., Walsh, M., Kenny, M., & Comilang, K. (1997). Interprofessional collaboration for children and families: Opportunities for counseling psychology in the 21st century. *Counseling Psychologist, 25,* 615–636.

Bronfenbrenner, U. (1979). Toward an experimental ecology of human development. *American Psychologist, 32,* 513–532.

Brooks, L., & Forrest, L. (1994). Feminism and career counseling. In W.B. Walsh & S.H. Osipow (Eds.), *Career counseling for women* (pp. 78–134). Hillsdale, NJ: Erlbaum.

Brown, M.T., Fukunaga, C., Umemoto, D., & Wicker, L. (1996). Annual review 1990–1996: Social class, work, and retirement behavior. *Journal of Vocational Behavior, 49,* 159–189.

Bynner, J.M. (1997). Basic skills in adolescents' occupational preparation. *Career Development Quarterly, 45,* 305–321.

Bynner, J.M. (1998). Education and family components of identity in the transition from school to work. *International Journal of Behavioral Development, 22,* 29–50.

Bynner, J.M., Ferri, E., & Shepherd, P. (Eds.). (1997). *Twenty-something in the 1990s: Getting on, getting by, getting nowhere.* Brookfield, VT: Ashgate.

Carter, R.T., & Cook, D.A. (1992). A culturally relevant perspective for understanding the career paths of visible racial/ethnic group people. In H.D. Lea & Z.B. Leibowitz (Eds.), *Adult career development: Concepts, issues, and practice* (pp. 192–217). Alexandria, VA: National Career Development Association.

Charner, I., Fraser, B.S., Hubbard, S., Roger, A., & Horne, R. (1995). Reforms of the school-to-work transition: Findings, implications, and challenges. *Phi Delta Kappan, 77,* 58–59.

Claes, R., & Quintanilla, S.A.R. (1994). Initial career and work meanings in seven European countries. *Career Development Quarterly, 42,* 337–352.

Committee on the Changing Nature of Work. (1993). Human capital initiative: The changing nature of work. *APS Observer.* Washington, DC: American Psychological Society.

Commission on the Skills of the American Workforce. (1990). *America's choice: High skills or low wages.* Rochester, New York: National Center on Education and the Economy.

Côté, J.E. (1996). Sociological perspectives on identity formation: The culture-identity link and identity capital. *Journal of Adolescence, 19,* 491–496.

Cunanan, E.S., & Maddy-Bernstein, C. (1997). *1996 National exemplary career guidance programs: Making the connections* (MDS-1091). Berkeley, CA: National Center for Research in Vocational Education.

D'Amico, R., & Maxwell, N.L. (1994). The impact of post-school joblessness on male black-white wage differentials. *Industrial Relations, 33,* 184–205.

Dawis, R.V., & Lofquist, L. (1984). *A psychological theory of work adjustment.* Minneapolis: University of Minnesota Press.

Dewey, J. (1916). *Democracy and education: An introduction to the philosophy of education.* New York: Macmillan.

Elmore, R.F. (1996). Policy choices in the assessment of work readiness: Strategy and structure. In L.B. Resnick & J.B. Wirt (Eds.), *Linking school and work: Roles for standards and assessments* (pp. 53–78). San Francisco: Jossey-Bass.

Erikson, E.H. (1968). *Identity: Youth and crisis.* New York: Norton.

Evans, K., & Heinz, W.R. (Eds.). (1994). *Becoming adults in England and Germany.* London: Anglo-German Foundation.

Feij, J.A., Whitely, W.T., Peiro, J.M., & Taris, T.W. (1995). The development of career-enhancing strategies and content innovation: A longitudinal study of new workers. *Journal of Vocational Behavior, 46,* 231–256.

Fouad, N.A. (1997). School-to-work transition: Voice from an implementer. *The Counseling Psychologist, 25,* 403–412.

Graber, J.A., Brooks-Gunn, J., & Petersen, A.C. (Eds.). (1996). *Transition through adolescence: Interpersonal domains and context.* Mahwah, NJ: Erlbaum.

Gray, K.C., & Herr, E.L. (1998). *Workforce education: The basics.* Needham Heights, MA: Allyn & Bacon.

Greenlee, S.P., Damarin, F.L., & Walsh, W.B. (1988). Congruence and differentiation among black and white males in two non-college-degreed occupations. *Journal of Vocational Behavior, 32,* 298–306.

Gribbons, W.D., & Lohnes, P.R. (1968). *Emerging careers.* New York: Teachers College Press.

Gribbons, W.D., & Lohnes, P.R. (1982). *Careers in theory and experience: A twenty-year longitudinal study.* Albany, NY: State University of New York Press.

Guion, R.M. (1996). Evaluation of performance tests for workforce readiness. In L.B. Resnick & J.B. Wirt (Eds.), *Linking school and work: Roles for standards and assessments* (pp. 267–304). San Francisco: Jossey-Bass.

Gysbers, N.C. (1997). Involving counseling psychology in the school-to-work movement: An idea whose time has come. *468 Counseling Psychologist, 25,* 413–427.

Gysbers, N.C., & Henderson, P. (1994). *Developing and managing your school guidance program.* Alexandria, VA: American Counseling Association.

Hackett, G., Lent, R.W., & Greenhaus, J.H. (1991). Advances in vocational theory and research: A 20-year retrospective. *Journal of Vocational Behavior, 38,* 3–38.

Haggstrom, G.W., Blaschke, T.J., & Shavelson, R.J. (1991). *After high school, then what? A look at the post-secondary sorting-out process for American youth.* Santa Monica, CA: RAND, R-4008-FMP.

Hamilton, S.F. (1990). *Apprenticeship for adulthood: Preparing youth for the future.* New York: Free Press.

Hamilton, S.F., & Powers, J.L. (1990). Failed expectations: Working-class girls' transition from school to work. *Youth and Society, 22,* 241–262.

Hannah, J.S., & Kahn, S.E. (1989). The relationship of socioeconomic status and gender to the occupational choices of grade 12 student. *Journal of Vocational Behavior, 34,* 161–178.

Hao, L., & Brinton, M.C. (1997). Productive activities and support systems of single mothers. *American Journal of Sociology, 102,* 1305–1344.

Haynes, L., & Blake, A. (1998, March). *Balancing life and work: The humanities as an essential part of career exploration.* Portland, OR: Northwest Regional Educational Laboratory.

Heckman, J. (1994). Is job training oversold? *The Public Interest, 115,* 91–115.

Heinz, W.R. (1987). The transition from school to work: Coping with threatening unemployment. *Journal of Adolescent Research, 2,* 127–141.

Heinz, W.R., Kelle, U., Wirtzel, A., & Zinn, J. (1998). Vocational training and career development in Germany: Results from a longitudinal study. *International Journal of Behavioral Development, 22,* 77–101.

Herr, E.L. (1995). *Counseling employment bound youth.* Greensboro, NC: ERIC/CASS.

Herr, E.L., & Niles, S. (1997). Perspectives on career assessment of work-bound youth. *Journal of Career Assessment, 5,* 137–150.

Holland, J.L. (1997). *Making vocational choices: A theory of vocational personalities and work environments* (3rd ed.). Odessa, FL: Psychological Assessment Resources.

Hotchkiss, L., & Borow, H. (1996). Sociological perspective on work and career development. In D. Brown & L. Brooks (Eds.), *Career choice and development* (3rd ed., pp. 281–334). San Francisco: Jossey-Bass.

Hoyt, K., & High, S. (1982). Career education. In H. Mitzel (Ed.), *Encyclopedia of educational research* (Vol. 1, pp. 231–241). New York: Free Press.

Hughes, K.L. (1996, August). Employer motivations for providing work-based learning placements to students: Preliminary results from research in progress. In E.B. Bizot (Chair), *Employer involvement in school-to-work transitions.* Symposium conducted at the 104th annual convention of the American Psychological Association, Toronto, Ontario, Canada.

Jenkins, D. (1996). The role of assessment in educating for high performance work: Lessons from Denmark and Britain. In L.B. Resnick & J.G. Wirt (Eds.), *Linking school and work: Roles for standards and assessment* (pp. 381–427). San Francisco: Jossey-Bass.

Jordaan J.P., & Heyde, M.B. (1979). *Vocational maturity during the high school years.* New York: Teachers College Press.

Juntunen, C.L., & Worthington, R.L. (1997). *A survey of counseling psychology faculty attitudes toward the school-to-work transition movement.* Unpublished manuscript.

Keller, F.J., & Viteles, M.S. (1937). *Vocational guidance throughout the world: A comparative survey.* New York: Norton.

Klerman, J.A., & Karoly, L.A. (1995). *The transition to stable employment: The experience of U.S. youth in their early labor market career* (MR-564). Berkeley, CA: National Center for Research in Vocational Education.

Krumboltz, J.D. (1994). Improving career development theory from a social learning perspective. In M.L. Savickas & R.W. Lent (Eds.), *Convergence in career development theories: Implications for science and practice* (pp. 9–31). Palo Alto, CA: Consulting Psychologists Press.

Krumboltz, J.D., & Worthington, R.L. (1999). The school-to-work transition from a learning theory perspective. *Career Development Quarterly, 47,* 312–325.

Landy, E. (1940). Occupational adjustment and the school. *Bulletin of the National Association of Secondary School Principals, 24,* 1–153.

Layder, D., Ashton, D., & Sung, J. (1991). The empirical correlates of action and structure: The transition from school to work. *Sociology, 25,* 447–464.

Leighbody, G.B. (1972). *Vocational education in America's schools: Major issues of the 1970s.* Chicago: American Technical Society.

Lent, R.W., Brown, S.D., & Hackett, G. (1994). Toward a unifying social cognitive theory of career and academic interest, choice, and performance [Monograph]. *Journal of Vocational Behavior, 45,* 79–122.

Lent, R.W., Hackett, G., & Brown, S.D. (1996). A social cognitive framework for studying career choice and transition to work. *Journal of Vocational Education Research, 21,* 3–31.

Lent, R.W., Hackett, G., & Brown, S.D. (1999). A social cognitive view of school-to-work transition. *Career Development Quarterly, 47,* 297–311.

Lent, R.W., O'Brien, K.M., & Fassinger, R.E. (1998). School-to-work transition and counseling psychology. *The Counseling Psychologist, 26,* 489–494.

Lent, R.W., & Worthington, R.L. (1999). Introduction: Applying career development theories to the school-to-work transition process. *Career Development Quarterly, 47,* 291–296.

Lesgold, A. (1996). Quality control for educating a smart workforce. In L.B. Resnick & J.B. Wirt (Eds.), *Linking school and work: Roles for standards and assessments* (pp. 147–192). San Francisco: Jossey-Bass.

Lewis, T., Stone, J., Shipley, W., & Madzar, S. (1998). The transition from school to work: An examination of the literature. *Youth and Society, 29,* 259–292.

Linn, R.L. (1996). Work readiness assessment: Questions of validity. In L.B. Resnick & J.B. Wirt (Eds.), *Linking school and work: Roles for standards and assessments* (pp. 245–266). San Francisco: Jossey-Bass.

Marshall, R., & Tucker, M. (1992). *Thinking for a living: Education and the wealth of nations.* New York: Basic Books.

McWhirter, E.H. (1994). *Counseling for empowerment.* Alexandria, VA: American Counseling Association.

Mitchell, L.K., & Krumboltz, J.D. (1996). Krumboltz's learning theory of career choice and counseling. In. D. Brown & L. Brown (Eds.), *Career choice and development* (3rd ed., pp. 233–280). San Francisco: Jossey-Bass.

Nash, B.E., & Korte, R.C. (1997). Validation of SCANS competencies by a national job analysis study. In H.F. O'Neil, Jr. (Ed.), *Workforce readiness: Competencies and assessment* (pp. 77–102). Mahwah, NJ: Erlbaum.

National Commission on Excellence in Education. (1983). *A nation at risk: The imperative for educational reform.* Washington, DC: U.S. Department of Education.

National Employer Leadership Council. (1997, March). *NELC employer participation model* [On-line]. Available: http:// www.nelc.org/model.shtml

Newman, K.S. (1996). Working poor: Low wage employment in the lives of Harlem youth. In J.A. Graber, J. Brooks-Gunn, & A.C. Petersen (Eds.), *Transition through adolescence: Interpersonal domains and context* (pp. 323–343). Mahwah, NJ: Erlbaum.

Oakes, J., & Guiton, G. (1994). Matchmaking: The dynamics of high school tracking decisions. *American Education Research Journal, 32,* 3–34.

Oliver, K.M., Russell, C., Gilli, L.M., Hughes, R.A., Schuder, T., Brown, J.L., & Towers, W. (1997). Skills for success in Maryland: Beyond workplace readiness. In H.F. O'Neil, Jr. (Ed.), *Workforce readiness: Competencies and assessment* (pp. 47–76). Mahwah, NJ: Erlbaum.

Olson, L. (1997). *The school-to-work revolution.* Reading, MA: Addison-Wesley.

O'Neil, H.F., Jr. (Ed.). (1997). *Workforce readiness: Competencies and assessment.* Mahwah, NJ: Erlbaum.

Osipow, S.H., & Fitzgerald, L.F. (1996). *Theories of career development* (4th ed.). Needham Heights, NJ: Allyn & Bacon.

Parsons, F. (1909). *Choosing a vocation.* Boston: Houghton Mifflin.

Pauly, E., Kopp, H., & Haimson, J. (1995). *Homegrown lessons: Innovative programs linking school and work.* San Francisco: Jossey-Bass.

Pautler, A.J. (Ed.). (1994). *High school to employment transition: Contemporary issues.* Ann Arbor, MI: Prakken.

Phelps, L.A., & Hanley-Maxwell, C. (1997). School-to-work transitions for youth with disabilities: A review of outcomes and practices. *Review of Educational Research, 67,* 227–266.

Phelps, L.A., Hernandez-Gantes, V.M., Jones, J., Sanchez, D., & Nieri, A.H. (1995). Students' indicators of quality in emerging school-to-work programs. *Journal of Vocational Education Research, 20,* 75–101.

Phillips, S.D., & Blustein, D.L. (1994). Readiness for career choices: Planning, exploring, and deciding. *Career Development Quarterly, 43,* 63–73.

Powers, D.A. (1994). Transitions into idleness among white, black, and Hispanic youth: Some determinants and policy implications of weak labor force attachment. *Sociological Perspectives, 37,* 183–201.

Reich, R.B. (1991). *The work of nations.* New York: Vintage Books.

Reinhart, B. (1979). *Career education: From concept to reality.* New York: McGraw-Hill.

Reitzele, M., Vondracek, F.W., & Silbereisen, R.K. (1998). Timing of school-to-work transitions: A developmental-contextual perspective. *International Journal of Behavioral Development, 22,* 7–28.

Resnick, L.B., & Wirt, J.B. (1996a). *Linking school and work: Roles for standards and assessments.* San Francisco: Jossey-Bass.

Resnick, L.B., & Wirt, J.B. (1996b). The changing workplace: New challenges for educational policy and practice. In L.B. Resnick & J.B. Wirt (Eds.), *Linking school and work: Roles for standards and assessments* (pp. 1–19). San Francisco: Jossey-Bass.

Richardson, M.S. (in press). A new perspective for counsellors: From career ideologies to empowerment through work and relationship practices. In A. Collins & R. Young (Eds.), *Future of work.* Cambridge, England: Cambridge University Press.

Riley, R.W., & Herman, A.M. (1997, September). *Report to Congress: Implementation of the School-to-Work Opportunities Act* [On-line]. Available: http://stw.ed.gov/congres1/exsum.htm

Rojewski, J.W. (1994). Applying theories of career behavior to special populations: Implications for secondary vocational transition programming. *Issues in Special Education and Rehabilitation, 9,* 7–26.

Savickas, M.L. (1999). The transition from school to work: A developmental perspective. *Career Development Quarterly, 47,* 326–336.

Savickas, M.L., & Lent, R.W. (Eds.). (1994). *Convergence in career development theories: Implications for science and practice.* Palo Alto, CA: Books/Cole.

Schultz, T.W. (1963). *The economic value of education.* New York: Columbia University Press.

Secretary's Commission on Achieving Necessary Skills (SCANS). (1992). *Learning a living: A blueprint for high performance.* Washington, DC: U.S. Department of Labor.

Smith, M.S., & Scoll, B.W. (1995). The Clinton human capital agenda. *Teachers College Record, 96,* 389–404.

Stern, D., & Finkelstein, N. (1995, April/May). *Making the transition from school to career* [On-line]. Available: http://vocserve.berkeley.edu/CW61/MakingtheTransition.html

Stern, D., Finkelstein, N., Stone, J.R., III, Latting, J., & Dornsife, C. (1994, March). *Research on school-to-work transition programs in the United States* [On-line]. Available: http:/vocserve.berkeley.edu/MDS-771/

Stern, D., Stone, J., Hopkins, C., McMillion, M., & Crain, R. (1994). *School-based enterprise: Productive learning in American high schools.* San Francisco: Jossey-Bass.

Stone, J.R., III, & Mortimer, J.T. (1998). The effects of adolescent employment on vocational development: Public and educational policy implications. *Journal of Vocational Behavior, 53,* 184–214.

Super, D.E. (1957). Career patterns as a basis for vocational counseling. *Journal of Counseling Psychology, 1,* 12–20.

Super, D.E., & Overstreet, P.L. (1960). *The vocational maturity of ninth-grade boys.* New York: Teachers College Press.

Super, D.E., Savickas, M.L., Super, C.M. (1996). The life-span, life-space approach to careers. In D. Brown & L. Brooks (Eds.), *Career choice and development* (3rd ed.). San Francisco: Jossey-Bass.

Super, D.E., & Wright, R.D. (1941). From school to work in the depression years. *School Review, 43,* 17–26.

Swanson, G.I. (1981). *The future of vocational education.* Arlington, VA: American Vocational Association.

Swanson, J.L., & Fouad, N.A. (1999). Applying theories of person-environment fit to the transition from school-to-work. *Career Development Quarterly, 47,* 337–347.

Sweetland, S.R. (1996). Human capital theory: Foundations of a field of inquiry. *Review of Educational Research, 66,* 341–359.

Tucker, M. (1996). Skills standards, qualifications systems, and the American workforce. In L.B. Resnick & J.G. Wirt (Eds.), *Linking school to work: Roles for standards and assessment* (pp. 23–51). San Francisco: Jossey-Bass.

United States Congress. (1994). *School to Work Opportunities Act of 1994* (P.L. No. 103–239). Washington, DC: Author.

United States General Accounting Office. (1991, August). *Transition from school to work: Linking education and worksite training.* Washington, DC: Author.

United States General Accounting Office. (1993, September). *Transition from school to work: States are developing new strategies to prepare students for jobs.* Washington, DC: Author.

Urquiola, M., Stern, D., Horn, I., Dornsife, C., Chi, B., Williams, L., Merritt, D., Hughes, K., & Bailey, T. (1997). *School to work, college, and career: A review of policy, practice, and results, 1993–1997* (MDS-1144). Berkeley, CA: National Center for Research in Vocational Education.

Veum, J.R., & Weiss, A.B. (1993, April). Education and the work histories of young adults. *Monthly Labor Review,* 11–20.

Vickers, M. (1996). New directions in the assessment of high school achievement: Cross-national perspectives. In L.B. Resnick & J.B. Wirt (Eds.), *Linking school and work: Roles for standards and assessments* (pp. 341–380). San Francisco: Jossey-Bass.

Vondracek, F.W., Lerner, R.M., & Schulenberg, J.E. (1986). *Career development: A life-span contextual approach to career development.* Hillsdale, NJ: Erlbaum.

Wagner, M., Blackorby, J., Cameto, R., & Newman, L. (1993). *What makes a difference? Influences on postschool outcomes of youth with disabilities.* Menlo Park, CA: SRI International.

Way, W.L., & Rossmann, M.M. (1996a). Family contributions to adolescent readiness for school-to-work transition. *Journal of Vocational Education Research, 21*(2), 5–33.

Way, W.L., & Rossmann, M.M. (1996b). *Lessons from life's first teacher: The role of the family in adolescent and adult readiness for school-to-work transition* (MDS-725). Berkeley, CA: National Center for Research in Vocational Education.

William T. Grant Foundation Commission on Work, Family, and Citizenship. (1988a). *The forgotten half: Non-college youth in America.* Washington, DC: Author.

William T. Grant Foundation Commission on Work, Family, and Citizenship. (1988b). *The forgotten half: Pathways to success for America's youth and young families.* Washington, DC: Author.

Wilson, W.J. (1996). *When work disappears: The world of the new urban poor.* New York: Random House.

Worthington, R.L., & Juntunen, C.L. (1997). The vocational development of non-college-bound youth: Counseling psychology and the school-to-work transition movement. *The Counseling Psychologist, 25,* 323–363.

Zunker, V.G. (1998). *Career counseling: Applied concepts of life planning* (5th ed.). Pacific Grove, CA: Brooks/Cole.

CHAPTER 15

Prevention and Development in the Workplace

BERYL HESKETH

One aim of counseling is to help people acquire the knowledge, skills, and attitudes that will enable them to manage their lives and find satisfaction and well-being. Work is a major part of life, and much of adulthood is spent in the workplace. This chapter assumes that counseling psychologists are as concerned about this facet of their clients' lives as they are about relationships, family, personal growth, and well-being. The importance of work to well-being has been demonstrated both theoretically and empirically, with studies having found that it accounts for between 10% and 25% of the variance in overall life satisfaction (Near, Rice, & Hunt, 1978; Saffron, 1985). Interestingly, one way of recognizing the value of work is to examine what happens when people find themselves unemployed or out of work.

For purposes of this chapter, I have taken a broad definition of work, namely, goal-directed activity that involves the expenditure of energy, often associated with obligations and constraints, and that is usually carried out within an employment contract. It is important to note, however, that not all work is carried out under the guise of employment, and that in some circumstances employment may in fact involve comparatively little work in the sense of meaningful goal-directed activity. Unemployment can mean the loss both of work and an employment contract.

Jahoda (1979), whose ideas were derived from research on unemployment, distinguished between the latent and manifest functions of work. The manifest functions are the obvious reasons why people work, namely, for pay, enjoyable activities, to be able to use one's skills and abilities, and for recognition and esteem. The latent functions of work become more obvious in recognizing what is missing when out of work. Latent functions include the provision of a time structure to the day, being linked to goals and purposes beyond one's own, having personal status and identity, and enforced activity. Warr (1987), whose ideas also arose from research on unemployment, extended these functions to include opportunities for control, use of skills and abilities, goal-directed activity, variety, and feedback. More recently, we have witnessed a growing emphasis on the importance of work and family balance (Finney, 1996; Kossek & Ozeki, 1998; Vincola & Mobley, 1998). Counseling psychologists can help their clients identify and clarify the role that work can play in their lives (Sonnenberg, 1997; Townsend & Nelson, 1997).

Throughout this chapter, I emphasize the need for clients to be helped to take control of their own career management. With the rapid changes facing industry, organizations no longer want to be left feeling responsible for the careers of their employees (Ettington, 1998; Rousseau, 1997). Rather, individuals are now expected to take personal responsibility for their progress within organizations. Herriot, Rousseau, and others (e.g., Herriot, 1992; Rousseau, 1996, 1997; Rousseau & Parkes, 1993) have written extensively about new contracts at work. Hall and associates (1996) and Hall and Moss (1998) described the consequence of these new contracts as leading to protean careers in which individuals, not the organizations, direct careers. One aim of this chapter is to provide background

I wish to thank Gillian Considine, Mark Sabaz, and Karolina Ivancic for their bibliographic and editorial assistance.

information that counseling psychologists in all settings can use to equip their clients for the challenge of managing careers in the new organizational climate. This will involve reviewing constructs and research drawn from the broader field of industrial and organizational (I/O) psychology on such topics as work performance, selection, job design, training, satisfaction, emotion and well-being at work, and withdrawal behavior (turnover, absenteeism, and lateness behavior). Brief coverage will also be given to work and family issues. Although counseling psychologists can contribute to all aspects of their clients' working life, counseling expertise is particularly relevant to issues associated with work and family balance, and the management of emotions at work.

In summary, work in general, and transitions between work and unemployment, and between work and retirement, may be related to well-being in important ways, with implications for all counseling psychologists dealing with adults in and out of the workplace. The remaining sections of this chapter provide a framework that may assist counseling psychologists to understand factors related to the psychology of work, and hence to facilitate adjustment and growth in the workplace. First, career development theory and research relevant to adult working life are highlighted. Emphasis is placed on theories that help deal with the changing nature of career paths and work opportunities, and those that point to intervention strategies. Next, the Minnesota theory of work adjustment (Dawis, 1994; Dawis & Lofquist, 1984; Hesketh & Dawis, 1991) is used as an organizing framework for discussing relevant constructs and ideas from industrial and organizational psychology. The material reviewed can be used directly with clients in the process of helping them develop career management skills.

The changes that have occurred at work require innovative approaches and emphasis on the part of counselors. A recent special issue of the *British Journal of Guidance and Counselling* (Arnold & Jackson, 1997) highlights the need for a new perspective on careers. The third section will address this need, discussing the concept of "Me Incorporated," within the evolving contractual relations, and the importance of integrating training, career development, and coping skills into a counseling framework (Hesketh & Considine, 1998).

Finally, I present a competency profile that highlights the theoretical knowledge, assessment and interventions skills, and professional attitudes needed by counseling psychologists to facilitate the workplace adjustment and growth of their clients.

ORGANIZATIONAL CAREER DEVELOPMENT THEORY, RESEARCH, AND PRACTICE

Literature on organizational career development includes topics such as training and career development (Noe, 1986), women in management (Tharenou & Conroy, 1994), and organizational career paths (Rosenbaum, 1989). Although the focus of much of this literature is written from an organizational management perspective, broader topics, such as mentoring (Kram, 1986; Russell & Adams, 1997), and work and family (Aryee & Luk, 1996; Duxbury, Higgins, & Thomas, 1996; Parasuraman, Purohit, & Godshalk, 1996; Stroh, Brett, & Reilly, 1996), are increasingly popular.

Changes occurring in the nature of work have been well documented (Rousseau, 1997). Much has been written about the breaking of the psychological contract between employer and employee (Herriot, 1988, 1992; Rousseau & Parkes, 1993) and about the increasingly transitory nature of work. Changing work patterns include a reduction in lifelong employment, an increase in part-time and contract work (Feldman, Doerpinghaus, & Turnley, 1994; Sonnenberg, 1997), and a growth of telecommuting and the use of remote communications for work (Feldman & Gainey, 1997; Stanek & Mokhtarian, 1998). These changes point to a need for constant skill updating and retraining (Bassi, Cheny, & Vanburen, 1997; Hesketh & Bochner, 1994). The changing age patterns of Western societies (Feller, 1991; Warr, 1994) add to the complexity of managing change at both an individual and organizational level. From a career development perspective, these factors combine to suggest that individuals can no longer afford to relegate career planning to a background activity with only occasional attention given to "taking stock."

Although it is doubtful that linear career paths were ever the dominant pattern of career development, Hall and others (e.g., Hall & Associates, 1996; Nicholson, 1993; Nicholson & Arnold, 1991) have demonstrated that a wider range of career path options is needed. In particular, concerns surrounding the motivational consequences of plateauing (Nelson-Horchler, 1986; Schiska, 1991) have prompted a reconsideration of the traditional assumption of hierarchical progression within an organization (Bardwick, 1986, 1987).

Changing Nature of Career Paths and Stages

The starkest way of illustrating the changing nature of career paths is to review developments in the thinking of Donald Super, arguably the most well-known developmental career theorist, and that of other early researchers (Miller & Form, 1947). Miller and Form, for example, suggested that one could define career patterns in terms of combinations of initial, trial, and stable jobs. Initial jobs were classified as those held while the individual was still completing formal education; trial jobs existed for periods of three years or less (usually after finishing formal education); and a stable job typically lasted for more than three years. Given these definitions, a stable career pattern could be obtained by directly attaining stability or, alternatively, by following an initial-stable or trial-stable career. Miller and Form suggested a higher level dichotomy between secure and insecure career patterns. Secure patterns included a stable and conventional grouping, whereas insecure patterns included trial, disestablished, and multiple trial career patterns. Although there was an assumption that most careers were of the secure and stable kind, even at the time of Super's career pattern study and the research of Miller and Form, instability was evident in many careers.

Super's (1953, 1957) original conceptualization postulated reasonably traditional age-related stages such as growth, exploration, transition, maintenance, and decline, with decline later relabeled as disengagement. In the 1980s, the concept of renewal was introduced to accommodate an increasing incidence of midcareer change. Within the structure of stages, Super (1953) defined career patterns as the occupational level attained, and the sequence, frequency, and duration of trial and stable jobs. Men and women differed in their career patterns.

More recently, however, Super (1990, 1994) abandoned the concept of age-related definitions of stage, while also introducing a career pattern that involves recycling through the stages. The concept of predominant and cyclical career concerns has to some extent replaced the earlier focus on career paths. Smart and Peterson (1997) and Smart (1998) emphasized the stages of exploration, establishment, maintenance, and disengagement relevant to adult career development. In a study involving 226 Australian men and women, Smart and Peterson found that individuals in the midst of career change were more likely to express career concerns that are traditionally relevant to the exploration stage. Interestingly, they found that people who had completed their change, or who were stable, were more satisfied with their jobs and career development than were participants currently in the active stage of career change. Those who had managed a change were no less satisfied than those who remained in a stable career pattern. These data provide support for the greater acceptance and advantage of managing career change in the current climate. Recycling into a new career can be viewed as part of normal development (Super, 1990, 1994; Super, Savickas, & Super, 1996).

In contrast, however, Schneer and Reitman (1997) found that both salary level and promotion opportunities were affected for MBA students who had an interrupted career in early or midcareer stages. The early career interruption was slightly less negative for females, whereas midcareer interruptions were less negative for males. However, neither males nor females completely caught up following a career interruption. Although one might argue that salary and promotion are not necessarily the only criteria to consider, Schneer and Reitman found that career gaps also affected career satisfaction indirectly through their impact on salary and promotion. Whether such findings would generalize to other occupational groups remains to be tested. Their review of other relevant literature and Rosenbaum's (1989) "tournament view" of careers (missing out on one round means being out of the tournament) suggest that it would. Although Super attempted to avoid value judgments about career paths, the management perspective, as evidenced in the view of Rosenbaum, and Schneer and Reitman, continues implicitly to accept a linear career path as the desired norm for career development. This is illustrated in the discussion on plateauing.

Career Plateauing

Career plateauing is a concept that is based on the notion of a linear career path with hierarchical promotion. "Organizational plateauing" occurs when an organization cannot offer further opportunities for promotion despite having staff with the required skills. The recent trend toward flattened hierarchical structures has resulted in an increase in organizational plateauing. "Individual plateauing" relates to an employee having reached the level at which the employee performs best and where a lack of appropriate skills prevents further promotion.

Research on plateauing has been fraught with methodological difficulties and conflicting results. Some studies point to negative outcomes of plateauing, such as reduced satisfaction and performance (Bardwick, 1986), whereas other studies found no adverse effects (Gerpott & Domsch, 1987; Near, 1985). In part, because some studies confounded the definition of plateauing with outcomes (limited hierarchical moves within an organization leading to a "failed" linear career path), more recent research has stressed the use of objective criteria to define plateauing. Objective criteria include variables such as age, salary, position, job tenure, and varying combinations of these. However, when using objective criteria to define plateauing, the psychological aspect may well be missed, because a feeling of stagnation need not be age and time bound. A psychological definition of plateauing needs to capture the frustration of unmet expectations and desire for promotion. Unfortunately, including a psychological emphasis in the definition of plateauing can lead to confusion with other factors, such as negative affectivity, that might also influence job satisfaction and well-being measures.

Based on the work of Chao (1990) and that of Tremblay, Roger, and Toulouse (1995), Ettington (1998) used both objective (salary, age, and tenure) and subjective (perceived likelihood of promotion) definitions of plateauing, together with associated relevant constructs (e.g., career orientation, work challenge, and social support) and performance ratings by supervisors. Care was taken to divide the sample into plateaued and nonplateaued managers, using five years since promotion as a natural break point, but checking this against other objective and subjective data.

Results showed that both objective (e.g., time since last promotion) and subjective (e.g., perceived likelihood of promotion) measures of plateauing correlated negatively with performance, but only subjective indices correlated negatively with satisfaction. As discussed earlier, subjective indices may capture general negative affectivity, perhaps explaining the correlation with satisfaction. One of the key factors that differentiated plateaued employees who maintained performance and satisfaction from those who did not was a perception that supervisors supported them and continued to provide challenging assignments. Both these issues point to ways in which individuals and organizations can avoid some of the negative consequences of plateauing. Supervisors need training to identify tasks that challenge employees and then to provide them with such opportunities. Individuals also need to take responsibility for proactively seeking challenge. These findings (as well as those of Bardwick, 1986, who noted that supervisors tend to reduce the amount of feedback given to plateaued employees) highlight ideas for direct interventions. It should be comparatively easy to train supervisors not to neglect plateaued employees by providing feedback, and to provide challenge through project work (Hall, 1985).

Counselors working with clients who feel plateaued could encourage them to seek challenge. It would also behoove counselors to be aware of the antecedents and consequences of plateauing, although it must be emphasized that the direction of effects remains unclear in much of the research.

Deceleration

Another issue often associated with mid-to-late career is the planning of one's retirement, including deciding whether to accept early retirement packages. Decision making associated with deceleration has received surprisingly little attention. Currently many employees face options of voluntary early retirement, and many more have no option at all. Decision making in the preretirement years has taken on the level of complexity previously associated with adolescence, yet we have little theory or research to guide psychologists in the provision of help at this important stage. An example of a recent study on retirement decision making is reviewed below, although broader issues of retirement are relevant to the later discussion of organizational commitment and withdrawal behavior.

The article by Schultz, Morton, and Weckerle (1998) reported the results from initial interviews with 992 individuals aged 50 to 61 sampled across the United States. This study is a welcome addition to the small but significant body of research on withdrawal behavior in later career life (Hanisch, 1994; Hanisch & Hulin, 1991; see also Tinsley & Schwendener-Holt, 1992). Schultz et al. and others distinguish between push-and-pull factors in the decision. Push factors tend to include ill health, job dissatisfaction, limited career opportunities, or no job at all; pull factors are more positive, being associated with opportunities for leisure, recreation, or a greater degree of freedom to engage in work at a slower pace. Identifying factors as either positive or negative has consequences in its own right, and, not surprisingly, there is some indication that many early retirees interpret the pull factors so that they can perceive the decision as being one that they chose (Halvorsen, 1994; Maule, 1995). More research is needed mapping objective reasons onto subjective reasons to determine whether a form of cognitive restructuring or reframing of the reasons can facilitate transition.

Schultz et al. (1998) found that the key factors distinguishing voluntary and involuntary early retirees' decisions involved both push-and-pull factors, such as poor health and a desire to pursue other activities, particularly among those with good health and sufficient finance. The positive features included opportunities to relax, spend time with a spouse, and avoid pressure. The voluntary group were more satisfied with life and retirement, and had better self-rated physical and emotional health and lower depression, than those for whom retirement was involuntary. It should be noted that the voluntary group were better educated, had higher incomes, and were much more likely to have attended employer-sponsored retirement planning meetings. These socioeconomic factors will obviously need to be controlled and understood in future research.

Once retired, negative factors differentiated those whose retirement had been voluntary and those faced with involuntary retirement. These included concerns about illness, lack of money, and inflation. Schultz used discriminant function analysis, and commendably, included a hold out sample for cross-validation. More research of this sort is needed, perhaps within the broader theoretical framework of decision-theories and withdrawal behavior. Schultz et al. (1998) noted, "[U]nfortunately how these perceptions (of push and pull factors) inform the retirement decision, or affect retirement valence and ultimate retirement adjustment has not been clearly established" (p. 46).

Protean Careers

Old employment contracts are increasingly less common. Reciprocal expectations of loyalty and commitment in return for security are being replaced by a new career contract where commitment is to the self, not the organization. These protean careers (Hall & Associates, 1996; Hall & Mirvis, 1995) place an emphasis on the concept of "Me Incorporated" (Hesketh & Considine, 1998). According to Hall and Moss (1998), an analysis of employment trends suggests that only 3.4% of the U.S. workforce has a traditional lifetime employment contract. Key features of the new protean careers are that (1) they are managed by individuals, not organizations, (2) they entail a high level of self-awareness, (3) self-managed learning becomes important, and (4) the individuals have more autonomy (Hall & Mirvis, 1995).

Even though the organization is not seen to have responsibility in these careers, Hall and Moss (1998) suggested a series of strategies for organizations to follow that would help individuals foster protean careers among their employees. These include (1) recognizing that the individual does "own" their career; (2) creating information and support for the individual, including information about opportunities available in the organization, perhaps using the Internet; (3) recognizing that careers involve relationships in organizations, and that the organization plays an important role; (4) providing expert career assessment and career development programs; (5) maintaining good lines of communication with the employees about their careers and informing them about career services and resources; (6) promoting work planning, not career planning, with a focus on realistic jobs and work that might be available; and (7) creating new learning opportunities by helping organizations design jobs and tasks that are challenging.

Planning and Managing Transitions

The concept of a protean career inevitably leads to the need to plan and manage transitions or changes in employment status or the nature of work activities. All transitions involve changed requirements of the individual, and often disrupt the use of expectations and well-automated skills. Within the career development literature, there is a shift from an emphasis on career choice and planning to one that has a focus on the management of transitions. During the past two decades, many Western countries have attempted to find solutions for youth unemployment by emphasizing the school to work transition (see Blustein, Juntuen, & Worthington, this volume; Fouad, 1997; Gysbers, 1997; Szymanski, 1997). College graduate employment and the transition from university to work has also been studied extensively (e.g., Arnold & Nicholson, 1991; Hesketh & McLachlan, 1991; Nicholson & Arnold, 1991), with considerable emphasis placed on the concept of "met expectations" (Cooke, Sims, & Peyrefitte, 1995; Irving & Meyer, 1994; Major, Kozlowski, Chao, & Gardner, 1995). These authors assume that college or university graduates' dissatisfaction with work and the associated high levels of turnover among new graduates can be attributed to high expectations that are not met once on the job. The concern about graduates' adjustment not only is relevant and important within the career counseling arena, but has also been a major focus of selection research (Chao, O'Leary-Kelly, Wolf, Klein, & Gardner, 1994; Morrison, 1993; Nicholson & West, 1996).

Both individuals and organizations can do much to increase the success of any education-to-work transition. For example, an analysis of the patterns of reinforcement available to students highlights the extent to which their university experience is punctuated by goals to be met in the form of assignments and examinations, with constant feedback about their progress. Once on a job, many individuals face much less clear short-term goals, and certainly do not receive feedback as distinctively or regularly. The comparative lack of feedback often creates a degree of uncertainty for the new employee about progress at work; this is something that both the individual and organizations can address. Organizations can structure the early job environment of college or university graduates to increase project work and feedback, and individuals can proactively seek feedback (Ashford, 1993; Ashford & Tsui, 1991). However, care needs to be taken in "feedback seeking" behavior, because in some instances, it can be perceived as inability to cope, with adverse consequences for individual career progress.

Examples of other transitions that have typically been studied include the retirement process (Hansson, De Koekkoek, Neece, & Patterson, 1997; Schultz et al., 1998); job transfers (Kirschenbaum, 1991; Kramer, 1993; Lee & Johnson, 1994); foreign assignments (Black, 1992; Caligiuri, 1997); and mergers and takeovers (Burke & Nelson, 1998; Cartwright & Cooper, 1994; Gowing, Kraft, & Quick, 1998; Schweiger & Denisi, 1991; Terry, Callan, & Sartori, 1996). However the minitransitions that may occur unexpectedly throughout working life, which will be an ongoing part of career development, are more important in the current climate of technology and change. A core competency for effective career management includes the development of generic skills required to manage transitions. Another way of stating this is that clients need to develop the knowledge, skills, and attitudes (KSAs) that will equip them to manage transitions and cope with change (Watts, 1996).

Transitions can be seen as involving preparation, encounter, and adjustment stages (Nicholson, 1990), and KSAs relevant to these stages can be described. Although Nicholson included a stablization phase, I would argue that this phase is synonymous with preparation because effective career planners need to be alert constantly. In general, if one views each transition as involving the three stages, in keeping with stage theory, successful mastery of one stage makes it easier to survive the next. Adequate knowledge, appropriate skills, and helpful attitudes during the preparation stage of a transition allow an individual to maintain more control during the actual encounter. Effective transition management leads to improved posttransition adjustment, and this in turn feeds into appropriate anticipatory behaviors and attitudes in the next preparation stage.

Preparation

Knowledge

An alert career planner will keep informed about the standing of their organization, its financial viability, organizational politics, and any changes management or others may be planning. This awareness and knowledge is essential to avoid surprises. Many employees fail to detect that change is likely to occur, and hence find themselves ill prepared for it.

Skills

To maintain this level of knowledge, it may be necessary to develop skills that allow an analysis of financial statements, annual reports, and business generally. Political skills, including influence tactics, networking behavior, and a capacity to ask the right questions in a nonthreatening manner become important.

Attitudes

Perhaps most important, individuals need to have a constant state of readiness, accepting that change may be likely to occur. If attitudes toward change are negative, then status quo biases are likely to result in an inability to accept the possibility of change. However, if change can be viewed as either a challenge or an opportunity rather than a threat, anticipatory attitudes are more likely to be helpful.

Encounter

Knowledge

Employees cope with change more effectively if management has fully informed them of the circumstances. Information is needed about the reasons for the change, exactly what the new circumstances will be, what areas of work will be affected, which will remain the same, and whether expectations will be different as a result of the change. In short, the more information, the better. Organizations seldom manage this aspect well, and hence a proactive individual may need to seek out the necessary information. Counseling psychologists can help clients develop the skills to do this in a manner that does not jeopardize career options.

Skills

Those individuals who have developed flexible skills that they are able to apply in a range of situations, and who have a capacity to acquire new skills quickly, are most likely to succeed in the transition phase (Allworth & Hesketh, 1999). For example, being able to adapt to new people, being open to new experiences, and undertaking effortful training that may be required are skills that are associated with effective transition. The coping literature (Lazarus & Folkman, 1987, 1991) highlights the importance of positive coping skills and attitudes for managing change and stress.

Lazarus and Folkman (1987) distinguished between problem- and emotion-focused coping. Problem-focused coping involves managing the change through a focus on the external source of the stressor; emotion-focused coping involves regulating one's own emotional reaction to the stressor. Earlier research suggested that where events are controllable, problem-focused coping appears to be the most effective. However, if the events are completely outside the control of the individual, emotion-focused coping may be more effective (Callan & Terry, 1992; Terry, 1994). However, Masel, Terry, and Gribble (1996), in a longitudinal laboratory study, suggested that amount of coping resources positively influenced adjustment independent of event controllability. More field research of a longitudinal nature is essential.

Allworth and Hesketh (1999) also demonstrate the predictive validity of self-efficacy for coping. Employees who feel they have the confidence to manage transitions and cope with change obtain better ratings from their supervisors on adaptive performance.

Attitudes

Seligman's (1998) concept of learned optimism is relevant to the development of attitudes that may facilitate the transition. Individuals who are optimistic may have the types of attitudes that will better equip them to emerge from the transition with major life goals intact, perhaps even with increased opportunities. Although there is undoubtedly a strong trait contribution to individual differences in optimism, by placing the concept within a learning theory framework (as was done for learned helplessness; Seligman, 1975), it becomes apparent that learning experiences can provide the key to developing optimism (Seligman, Reivich, Jaycox, & Gillham, 1995). This provides a challenge to counseling psychologists, as previous positive client experiences contribute cumulatively to optimistic beliefs and hence to improved management of transitions occurring in the workplace. Several authors have used interventions to increase optimism (Marko & Savickas, 1998; Riskind, Sarampote, & Mercier, 1996), and the generic value of optimistic attitudes for career planning suggest that career interventions that also foster optimism may be effective.

Adjustment

Knowledge

Following transition, a person is in effect experiencing a minisocialization phase with at least some of the requirements associated with newcomer socialization (Bauer & Green, 1994). New contingencies, power structures, sets of expectations, and a host of other subtle and concrete sources of information have to be recognized. Organizations can do much to assist during this process through clear communication, the provision of effective training, and through being open to proactive behaviors on the part of employees who seek out the information they need. Bauer and Green provided a thorough analysis of the contribution of individual and organizational actions aimed at increasing newcomer adjustment. However, it is worth noting that proactive behaviors on the part of individuals were perhaps less positive than might have been expected, in part because such behavior may be construed as being too demanding.

Skills

Skills of adjustment relate predominantly to increasing expertise within a role, seeking out new challenges, and developing comfortable team and work relationships. Capacity to learn from the transition experience is critical. If errors were made during transition, subsequent analysis of what produced these errors can result in improved management of future change.

Attitudes

A key attitude during the adjustment phase relates to the need to maintain watchfulness. Specifically, having successfully mastered a recent transition should not be seen as a reason to relax watchfulness in the posttransition or adjustment phase. In the current climate, career planning cannot be relegated to a background activity; individuals need to constantly take stock and check that events are not changing around them without their awareness.

Unfortunately, these requirements highlight a major dilemma. Individuals need constantly to be watchful given that much career development consists of increasingly frequent minitransitions and change. However, active attention to one's career and associated relevant events requires effortful processing, which is not always pleasant. Smart and Peterson (1997) found lower levels of satisfaction among participants actively undertaking change than among those not experiencing change, despite a successful later resolution of the change. Further research is needed to understand this dilemma and to highlight ways of dealing with it. Such research may help provide detail about the types of counseling support that would facilitate the transition process. Counseling psychologists have the skills to undertake this research and to develop individual or structured programs to help prepare and maintain the necessary KSAs for effective transition.

Critique of Constructs, Measures, and Methods

A major dilemma in the organizational development literature revolves around the value for career development of constructs such as plateauing. These, in turn, rely on an acceptance that a linear career path is still valid, or whether careers should be reconceptualized in terms of minitransition cycles. Both have value because expectations for linear progression remain a priority for many clients, and such opportunities do exist, albeit in a much reduced form. Nevertheless, alternative ways of conceptualizing careers are needed. The narrower focus that follows a transitions perspective is helpful to research because it is much easier to conceptualize and measure minitransitions than it is to obtain good data on career paths and patterns over the whole of adult working life.

Nevertheless, the need for longitudinal research is no less urgent, although the periods over which the samples are taken can vary in length. Research such as that of Masel et al. (1996), based on elicitation of stressful events in a longitudinal framework, offers promise. Methodologies using an "event characteristics" approach may apply well to the study of minitransitions. That is, there is a need to identify and define events, transitions, or salient actions of others, and to document the antecedents, and longitudinal consequences of these across an array of cognitive, behavioral, and affective dimensions. More effort is needed to capture perceptions and feelings about events at the time they occur rather than relying on retrospective questionnaire measures where the passage of time may well have engendered a process of reframing or reconstruction. These postevent adjustive processes are interesting in their own right, but to fully understand them requires mapping the course of experiences occurring between the event and the time at which measures are obtained.

ORGANIZATIONAL THEORY AND RESEARCH RELEVANT TO CAREERS

The aim of this section is to review key ideas and research drawn from the I/O psychology literature. If counseling psychologists are to work effectively with clients in organizational contexts, it is important to be able to draw on this important body of knowledge. For those with a desire to pursue the topic more fully, the four-volume *Handbook of Industrial and Organizational Psychology* (Dunnette & Hough, 1990, 1991, 1992; Dunnette, Hough, & Triandis, 1993) can be consulted. In this chapter, the Minnesota theory of work adjustment (Dawis & Lofquist, 1984) is used as an organizing framework (Hesketh & Dawis, 1991) to review recent developments in areas of I/O psychology most relevant to organizational careers.

Minnesota Theory of Work Adjustment and Related Issues

The Minnesota theory of work adjustment (TWA; Dawis & Lofquist, 1984) provides one of the most useful frameworks for a broad range of human resource interventions in organizations as well as for career planning and decision making. In its original form, the TWA described people and work environments in terms of the requirements (KSAs) that each has for the other and posited that the mutual satisfaction of each party's requirements gives rise to increased satisfaction and higher levels of performance. Higher levels of satisfaction and performance contribute to an increased period of interaction between the parties (tenure). The theory argues specifically that individuals seek work that satisfies important work-related needs and values (e.g., for security, compensation, advancement). If an individual's work-related needs are satisfied by the provision of appropriate reinforcers in the environment, it is hypothesized that the person will report high levels of satisfaction. Similarly, organizations require certain types of abilities from their employees, and will judge the individual's performance based on the degree to which abilities possessed by the individual match the ability requirements of the environment. The organization's satisfaction with the employees (their performance or satisfactoriness) is, therefore, predicted by the correspondence between the individual's abilities and the ability requirements in the work environment. Employee satisfaction and satisfactoriness then predict tenure in the organization.

Stated in terms used in the I/O psychology literature, organizations seek specific levels of KSAs and individuals supply these to a greater or lesser extent, resulting in various levels of performance or productivity. Both parties strive over time to improve correspondence, or fit, using active and reactive modes of adjustment, often through negotiation about activities such as training and job redesign. The two parties cease the relationship (through voluntary or involuntary departures) when the mismatch between required and supplied KSAs becomes too large or when the requirements for interests, needs, and values diverge from the available outlets for these in work contexts.

Individuals and organizations differ in their levels of flexibility; if either party is highly flexible, tolerance of a mismatch is likely to be greater. Individuals and organizations also differ in terms of the perseverance with which they maintain efforts to achieve adjustment. Self-efficacy for change (Allworth & Hesketh, 1999), for example, should be associated with perseverance in actively seeking to foster adjustment or in reactively adjusting to a situation.

Component hypotheses of the Minnesota TWA have received extensive empirical support both within the traditional vocational psychology literature, and in organizational psychology where the general concept of fit has been studied. Employee selection (Hunter, 1986; Hunter & Hunter, 1984; Ree, Earles, & Teachout, 1994; F.L. Schmidt, Hunter, Outerbridge, & Goff, 1988) represents a major body of research relevant to the relationship between the required KSAs and those supplied by the individual, a major component of TWA (Hesketh & Dawis, 1991). Meta-analyses demonstrate repeatedly that tests of cognitive ability offer generalized validity to a wide range of jobs, although validities are higher in more complex jobs (P.C. Schmidt, Ones, & Hunter, 1992). More recently, selection research has used the five-factor personality model as an organizing framework. Meta-analyses have demonstrated moderate validity in predicting performance from conscientiousness across a range of jobs, although most writers stress the need to relate personality to job requirements before examining validity (Hough et al., 1990; Robertson & Kinder, 1993). Validity studies of ability or personality dimensions that take into account the job requirements component are more compatible with TWA than are those that focus exclusively on the relationship between predictors and performance without the moderating influence of job requirements.

Much vocational research has emphasized the match between individual needs, interests, and values and outlets for these, as a predictor of job satisfaction (Holland, 1987, 1996a, 1996b; Organ & Ryan, 1995; Spokane, 1985), and eventually of turnover (George & Jones, 1996; Rosin & Korabik,

1995). The counseling applications of this body of research are well known, with many instruments available to assist clients in developing an understanding of their personal attributes, and then relating these to occupations that fit or offer relevant outlets (see for example, Brown & Ryan Krane in this volume).

The most interesting methodological debate in person-environment (P-E) fit research relates to the need to examine main effects between individual difference factors and environmental factors, as well as their interaction (Blau, 1994; Edwards, 1991; Hesketh & Gardiner, 1993; Zeffane, 1994). Traditional approaches to P-E fit research have measured fit as a difference or squared difference between a person and their work environment across a range of attributes (e.g., Bretz & Judge, 1994; Rounds, Dawis, & Lofquist, 1987; Spokane, 1985). However, the use of composite indices in this research has both conceptual and measurement difficulties. The measurement problem relates to the use of a difference score as a predictor, without incorporating the component parts that contributed to the difference (person and environment) in the model (Edwards, 1991; Evans, 1991).

Conceptually, this approach obscures important information, namely, that some individuals are more satisfied irrespective of the work environment in which they find themselves, and some environments are simply more rewarding. Theoretical explanations for the direct effects lie in constructs such as neuroticism (Goldberg, 1990, 1992) and negative and positive affectivity (Watson & Pennebaker, 1989; Watson, Pennebaker, & Folger, 1986), and their pervasive influence on individual well-being. The research undertaken by Warr (1987), which identified the features of a good environment, also points to partial explanations for the direct effect of the environment. Methodologically, Evans (1991) and Edwards and colleagues (Edwards, 1991; Edwards & Van-Harrison, 1993) have raised major concerns about the traditional way in which fit theories, such as those of Dawis and Lofquist (1984) and Holland (1985), have been tested within the vocational literature. This means that future researchers would do well to examine direct effects as well as fit, and to control for direct effects when testing fit models.

An alternative approach to assessing fit involves a profile or pattern approach that departs from the traditional reliance on linear and noninteracting relations among dimensions. For example, Gustafson and Mumford (1995) have used a pattern approach to capture the nonlinear interacting effects in a way not possible when relying on individual differences in person and environment dimensions and standard multiple regression to predict outcomes. Gustafson and Mumford used cluster analysis of "whole" individuals and of "whole" environments, arguing that the clustering represented higher order interactions among dimensions. The clusters of people and environments were used to form types that they could then relate to outcome measures such as performance and satisfaction. For example, they found that the often reported negative influence of high rigidity on performance could be offset when combined with high-achievement motivation, high-job involvement, high-internal locus of control, high self-esteem, and low anxiety. Such a combination predicted job satisfaction and performance consistently across a range of environments.

Gustafson and Mumford (1995) also clustered environments and found that patterns of environments predicted outcomes. For example, job satisfaction was predicted more strongly in the structured-complex environment than in the unstructured-unsupported environment. Furthermore, they found different patterns of factors predicted job satisfaction, job performance, and job withdrawal, and that situations moderated the effectiveness of the prediction of the criteria from person subgroup patterns. This study is exemplary, and suggests a major advance on previous P-E fit research and theorizing. The implications arising from this study suggest the need for a pattern or cluster approach to studying fit, rather than a focus on single dimensions.

The Minnesota TWA uses three criterion or outcome measures: satisfactory performance (satisfactoriness), employee satisfaction, and tenure. These constructs are discussed as they are embedded within contemporary issues.

Performance Modeling

Understanding and measuring performance or satisfactoriness at work has long been a major challenge for I/O psychologists. Given its central role as a criterion in much I/O research and evaluation, obtaining good measures of performance is critical. Fortunately, this decade has seen considerable emphasis placed on partitioning and modeling the performance domain (W.C. Borman, 1991; M.R. Borman & Motowidlo, 1993; Campbell, 1990). Campbell suggested that there are eight components of performance that seem to be generalizable across jobs: (1) job-specific task proficiency, (2) nonjob-specific task proficiency, (3) written and oral communication, (4) demonstrating effort, (5) maintaining personal discipline, (6) facilitating peer and team performance, (7) supervision, and (8) management/administration.

M.R. Borman and Motowidlo (1993) have suggested that these areas could be grouped into *task* and *contextual* performance factors. Task performance refers to role prescribed behaviors that are required for successful completion of the job, and contextual performance refers to non-prescribed behaviors and voluntary efforts aimed at supporting broader organizational goals. Hesketh and Allworth (1997) have suggested the inclusion of a third dimension, namely, *adaptive* performance (Allworth & Hesketh, 1999). They argued that adaptive performance contains both a cognitive and noncognitive component. The cognitive component relates to evidence that a person can acquire and learn new skills on the job; the noncognitive dimension taps into coping skills, self-efficacy for change, and other attitudinal variables. Adaptive performance is relevant because contemporary organizations require employees to adjust to and cope with change, handle stress, demonstrate flexibility, and learn new tasks easily. Allworth and Hesketh present data demonstrating that construct-oriented biodata developed to document past coping behavior can be used to predict adaptive performance, and that it does so distinctively from task and contextual performance.

The inclusion of adaptive performance serves to remind organizations and individuals of the importance of coping with change. The predictive validity of construct-oriented biodata highlights the value of accumulating positive experience in managing change in personal and work-related life. Counseling psychologists can help their clients realize that effective management of change sets up a cycle of being better prepared to manage future change. Individuals who engage in ongoing learning and new skill development, and who develop good coping and transition management skills, are likely to be rated more highly on the adaptive performance dimensions. Recent field-work suggests that another component of adaptive performance relates to encouraging others to change. In a team environment, it is important that all members of the group accept the need to adapt to the future direction of a company, including the acceptance of new group norms. Groups can work to overcome attempts by members to sabotage or resist change, because some team members may maintain a status quo orientation (Hesketh, 1995).

Satisfaction and Well-Being, and Emotion at Work

Up until about five years ago, very little attention was paid to the topic of emotion at work. Although there was much research on job satisfaction (Abramis, 1994), emotion was not the focus of attention. Perhaps it was assumed that the workplace created an environment in which emotions were not important, or where emotions should be controlled. Recently, however, the spotlight has been put on the emotional side of work (Ashforth & Humphrey, 1995; Staw, Sutton, & Pelled, 1994; Wharton & Erickson, 1993). People do get angry at work, or feel disappointment, jealousy, shame, embarrassment, resentment, depression, frustration, excitement, or joy. Given that emotions can be strong, there is a need to understand the circumstances that produce such emotions, and to help workers develop competence in handling their own and others' emotions in the workplace. Whether constructs such as emotional intelligence are helpful in this regard (J.D. Mayer &

Geher, 1996; J.D. Mayer & Salovey, 1995; Salovey & Mayer, 1990) requires more research. Nevertheless, the training counseling psychologists receive should equip them to provide interventions aimed at managing emotions at work.

A useful approach that has emerged from this literature relates to affect event theory (Frijda, 1993; Weiss & Cropanzano, 1996), which sees emotions as reactions to discrete events at work. Future research will benefit from documenting emotional events at work, and tracing the impact of these events on career-related decisions. The emotional reactions to these events can often be disproportionate, and lead to withdrawal behavior that has negative consequences for careers. Timely intervention on the part of counseling psychologists might help avert withdrawal or other adverse reactions such as violence. Counseling psychologists have expertise in understanding and helping clients manage emotions in life, including emotions that emerge out of social interactions either in family or work contexts.

One emotionally demanding area of work is the field of customer service. Many customer service staff have to engage in "emotional labor" (Hochschild, 1983), where they must disguise their real emotions and reactions to present a consistent, unperturbed, and sympathetic front. In some respects, the management of their emotions has exchange value because they are paid to achieve this front. However, if the effort involved is not recognized, cumulatively it can contribute to feelings of dissatisfaction and stress.

Although research on emotional experience at work is in its infancy, related research on job satisfaction, stress, and well-being has a long and extensive history. Perhaps not surprisingly, one of the first attempts at broadening the role of emotion at work was to look at its contribution to job satisfaction. Necowitz and Roznowski (1994), for example, examined the impact of negative affectivity on job satisfaction. This approach fits with the attempt to examine a dispositional contribution to job satisfaction to counter the heavy emphasis on situational factors. Finding a relation between negative affectivity and job satisfaction is not surprising. However, understanding the causal links in the relation is important, and highlights a very current debate about the role of negative affectivity (NA) as a biasing factor or a direct contribution to stress. For example, do individuals high on NA tend to recollect only negative features and hence evidence a processing bias in reporting levels of dissatisfaction, or do they genuinely experience more dissatisfaction than low NA individuals? Longitudinal data are needed to gain insight into the mechanisms.

Necowitz and Roznowski (1994) used a longitudinal laboratory study for this purpose. They found that, when exposed to a very monotonous task in the laboratory, NA had no impact on satisfaction. However in an enriched task, those of high NA perceived the task as less satisfying. The individuals low on NA concentrated more on the task than on their feelings about the task, whereas high NA individuals were influenced by their internal states.

Wright and Staw (1999) address in detail the debate surrounding the role of negative and positive affectivity as either a direct effect or a biasing factor in research on stress. Much depends on the nature of the measures (objective or subjective) and whether longitudinal data are obtained. In cross-sectional studies using subjective measures, the generalized affect states are often found to be biasing factors. However, their real contribution can be teased out when research designs are used that include objective measures and longitudinal data collection. Several major European projects have taken this approach.

Another area highly relevant to employee satisfaction and well-being is the management of work and family balance. Family relations are central to the well-being of people, and concerns and worries about family cannot easily be left at home. Organizations that are family friendly, through the provision of flexible work arrangements, day care, family leave, and supportive supervision, are likely to have less stressed employees. As seen below, employees in these companies are also less likely to withdraw from work, either through absences, lateness, or turnover (Keith & Schafer, 1984; Reitzes, Mutran, & Fernandez, 1996; Van den Bout, 1986; Wharton & Erickson, 1993).

Withdrawal Behavior: Its Antecedents

Job satisfaction, lack of fit, and organizational commitment are frequently studied as predictors of absenteeism, lateness, turnover, and turnover intentions (George & Jones, 1996; Zeffane, 1994). Work and family issues are also relevant. Furthermore, voluntary retirement can be viewed within the literature on turnover, although factors associated with retirement planning are more complicated. Much depends on the extent to which retirement is perceived as voluntary, and whether it is taken early or at a preplanned point in life (Halvorsen, 1994; Maule, 1995). Retirement or job loss has a major impact on work and family (Dunlop, 1996), highlighting a need for professional attention (Townsend & Nelson, 1997).

Hanisch and Hulin (1990) captured neatly the value of treating actions such as turnover, voluntary retirement, absenteeism, and lateness under a general construct of withdrawal behavior. All involve orienting away from an organization and are visible indicators of an underlying level of dissatisfaction or personal conflicts, often related to work and family. Hulin (1991) saw these behaviors as typifying the actions of dissatisfied individuals who wish to avoid the work situation.

The Hanisch and Hulin (1990) study found that satisfaction correlated strongly and negatively with several organizational withdrawal behaviors, including retirement. Nevertheless, other research highlights that each set of behaviors is associated with quite specific measurement issues, and unique and distinctive meaning. For example, Sagie (1998) and Johns (1994a, 1994b) have reviewed and studied absence behavior in considerable detail, highlighting the varied ways in which it can be measured, and the consequences of each. Reported absence is not the same as objectively measured absence.

In recent years, additional constructs have been introduced to help describe and explain the sequence of thoughts and decisions that lead to an individual's decision to quit. Krausz, Koslowsky, and Eiser (1998) suggested a progression whereby components of withdrawal behavior, such as absence and lateness, can predict subsequent intentions to quit. In part, the early withdrawal behaviors incur negative social sanctions from management which might contribute to dissatisfaction and subsequent turnover. Findings such as this indicate a possible way in which organizations can intervene to reduce turnover by using early indicators (lateness and absenteeism) as signs of difficulty in need of remedial attention. If lateness and absenteeism are related to work-family conflicts, counseling psychologists can help their clients directly; or if working in an organization, they can help the company to develop family friendly policies.

More generally, turnover is often associated with stress, conflict, dissatisfaction, and lack of organizational commitment, all of which can be targets for preventive interventions. Earl (1993), for example, predicted expatriates' intentions to quit from both job satisfaction and organizational commitment. Iverson, Olekalns, and Erwin (1998) highlighted the complex way in which predisposing positive and negative affectivity influences perceptions of stress, job satisfaction, and various withdrawal behaviors. They emphasized the need for any interventions that aim to manage workplace stress and burnout to take into account individual differences in these positive and negative orientations.

An interesting issue for future research is whether turnover models tested under traditional tenurable employment conditions will generalize to contract employment. Saks, Mudrack, and Ashforth (1996) have examined turnover within shorter contract positions and found that a high work ethic predicts the decision to remain until the end of the contract. Here it seems that the more general work commitment, as distinct from organizational commitment, may be relevant.

A cluster of constructs are reported in the literature, including job involvement (S.P. Brown, 1996), work commitment (Morrow, 1993), employment commitment (Jackson, Stafford, Banks, & Warr, 1983), organizational commitment (Allen & Meyer, 1996; R.B. Brown, 1996; Mathieu & Zajac, 1990), and career commitment.

Commitment as a concept can be related to the job, work in general, a career, or an organization, and there is a need to understand the antecedents, correlates, and consequences of each. S.P. Brown (1996) suggested a useful framework in relation to job involvement. Antecedents of job involvement, according to S.P. Brown include job characteristics, supervisory variables, and individual difference factors. Correlates cover demographic factors as well as the family of commitment variables, such as work involvement and career commitment. Consequences include the commonly studied outcome variables (performance, withdrawal behavior, satisfaction), as well as impacts on work and family. S.P. Brown's meta-analytic review of the literature highlighted that job involvement acted as an antecedent to organizational commitment, satisfaction, and turnover. Designing "good jobs," ones that contain features known to be associated with well-being, is one way in which organizational interventions can help clients feel more attached.

Conceptually, it should be possible to distinguish between job involvement, organizational commitment, and employment commitment. In support of this, S.P. Brown (1996) found that different factors correlated with job involvement and organizational commitment. Specifically, participative decision making and job design factors correlated with job involvement, whereas supervisory communication, turnover, and facet satisfaction related to organizational commitment. However, distinctive measurement is often difficult (R.B. Brown, 1996), and this methodological problem is compounded by attempts to explore the dimensionality of commitment. For example, Allen and Meyer (1996) have suggested that it is possible to distinguish between affective commitment, continuance commitment, and normative commitment, and they reported results of studies using their scales that support this argument. Although their work relates to organizational commitment, the constructs of affective and continuance commitment could relate to jobs and careers as well. R.B. Brown (1996), however, suggested a slightly different approach, emphasizing goal commitment (agreement with organizational goals), membership commitment (intention to remain), and people commitment (preparedness to help others in the organization).

Methodologically, this area of research is difficult to interpret because so little quality longitudinal data are available, and because of considerable overlap in the constructs and measures. For example, continuance commitment is, conceptually, very similar to intentions to leave or stay, and there is sometimes overlap in the actual wording of items measuring the two constructs (Allen & Meyer, 1996; Blau, Paul, & St. John, 1993; J.P. Meyer & Allen, 1991; J.P. Meyer, Allen, & Gellatly, 1990). Difficulties arise because of the need for large sample sizes to undertake what has become the default method of analysis, namely, structural equation modeling. However, richer theorizing and data are likely to arise from more intensive longitudinal data collected from individuals over an extended period of time. Even longitudinal research that samples data about attitudes and intentions two to three times over a few years fails to capture the real events that might provoke changes in attitudes and stimulate decisions to initiate a transition. The need for more systematic and frequent sampling of individual thoughts and intentions over time is the major challenge for research in the next decade. More intensive research may facilitate theory development and the development of associated programs to assist people who are planning a transition.

Critique of Constructs, Measures, and Methods of Research

Three major concerns are evident in the earlier discussion. The first relates to the controversy surrounding the best way to measure fit. The second relates to the overlap and confusion of constructs, with the consequent difficulty in obtaining uncontaminated measures. The third concern, which exacerbates the second, is the heavy reliance on cross-sectional studies. Even where longitudinal research is undertaken, this tends to include two, or at most three, brief snapshots of static states, with extrapolation needed to piece together what has happened in the intervening periods of time.

What is needed is research with frequent time samples, for example, employing online data collection. Opportunities may exist through the increased use of technology. For example, Csikszentmihalyi and Csikszentmihalyi's (1988) impressive body of research on the concept of flow has used a wristwatch beeper to get participants to provide frequent information about their activities and feelings. It may also be possible to design studies where employees provide a daily e-mail log of their feelings about work and the key events to which they are linked. These data may help untangle the web and flow of emotions in the workplace and, in combination with traditional measures, provide the basis for richer theorizing and research about the antecedents and consequences of affect-laden events than are typically studied under the umbrella of job satisfaction and work stress.

ORGANIZATIONAL INTERVENTIONS AND NEW APPROACHES

Arnold (1997) has distinguished between organizational interventions that focus on day-to-day activities, such as appraisal and mentoring, and those that involve special workshops or courses, such as career counseling or career development programs.

Day-to-Day Interventions

This section briefly covers performance appraisal, goal setting, employee assistance programs, and executive coaching.

Performance appraisal systems serve many different purposes. They are used as a basis for promotions, pay raises, establishment of training needs, for research criteria, and in some cases for career development. Not surprisingly, given the many and varied purposes of appraisal, systems are not unanimously accepted by employees or even those having to do the ratings (Tharenou, 1995). Clayton and Ayres (1996) suggested that stripping performance appraisal of its association with salary increments and promotions, and using it for development purposes, may be effective. Clear feedback is necessary, even if it involves identifying problem areas of performance, but this feedback can be framed in terms of goals for improvement, turning what might otherwise be a negative process into a productive goal setting and development exercise. Integrating personal goal setting with performance development sessions is one of the simplest and most effective organizational career development interventions. Recent career development programs employ this idea (R.D. Brown, 1988). Kaufmann (1998) reported on General Electric's approach to assisting information technology managers with their career planning through quarterly goal-setting sessions.

As is discussed in several chapters in this volume, constructs, such as self-efficacy, goal setting, and self-management, are important outcomes of counseling. They are also important in any individual or organizational level interventions. The effectiveness of goal setting is widely recognized as a clinical intervention (Laben, Sneed, & Seidel, 1995; Peterson & Sobell, 1994; Zahara & Cuvo, 1984), and as an effective motivational intervention in organizational and sports contexts (Gilbourne & Taylor, 1998; Kingston & Hardy, 1997). Counseling psychologists can help clients develop effective goal setting skills for setting career goals, learning goals, and specific performance goals.

Although far from universal, there is a growing trend for organizations to take seriously issues associated with work-family balance (Finney, 1996; Vincola & Mobley, 1998), and to introduce health and fitness programs at work (Harrison & Liska, 1994; Kerr & Vos, 1993; Lechner & De Vries, 1995). Sometimes these fall within the general umbrella of employee assistance programs, a potential area of service delivery for counseling psychologists.

One new development is worthy of comment. The cost to organizations of inept management has resulted in considerable attention being given to management selection, training, and coaching.

Several organizations now make use of a management coach for very senior managers or chief executive officers. Coaches are usually independent consultants, not employed by the organization, who may have been involved in the original selection of the manager. As a result, they know what the likely weaknesses are of the manager/CEO, and what difficulties are likely to be encountered in the new role (Witherspoon & White, 1996). The coach works with the senior executive to deal effectively with these difficulties, challenges the executive where others may be too afraid to do so, and generally serves as an independent counselor and coach. Skills and approaches used by the "coach" draw from sports psychology, counseling psychology, and organizational psychology because of the need for a detailed understanding of the demands and requirements in work and organizational contexts (Levinson, 1996), as well as personal factors.

Specific Career Development Interventions

Examples of organizational interventions include those aimed at job seekers and career development programs. One of the better examples of an intervention program for the unemployed is described by Caplan, Vinokur, Price, and Van Ryn (1989) and Vinokur, Van Ryn, Gramlich, and Price (1991). This theoretically based program draws on research in areas such as self-efficacy and group support, and contains a strong skill development component. Caplan et al. and Vinokur et al. reported the results of a systematic longitudinal evaluation of the program. Outcomes from the program were exceptionally positive, including improved job search success and higher starting salaries.

Most organizational career development interventions use person-environment fit as an underlying model. For example, the Gillian Stamp program (Stamp, 1989; Stamp & Stamp, 1993), widely used in industry (Brookes, 1993), makes use of visual graphics to help individuals recognize the importance of achieving an appropriate level of challenge in a job to stimulate performance (Career Path Mapping; Stamp & Stamp, 1993). The underlying assumption is that too little challenge leads to boredom, whereas too much leads to anxiety. High levels of challenge, where an individual is appropriately engaged, give rise to the state of flow (Csikszentmihalyi & Csikszentmihalyi, 1988). Stamp and Stamp advocated the use of a career path appreciation interview and work journals to foster career path mapping. Little systematic evaluation exists of these career development programs although most do relate in part to underlying theoretical ideas.

Career development programs are increasingly integrated with training plans. Within the management literature, there is considerable discussion about the concept of learning organizations (DiBella, 1997), where learning is implicitly reinforced throughout the structure and where career development is linked to learning. A learning organization would tend to provide its employees with more opportunities for strategic investment in both their own skills and those that the company may need in the future. Underlying the link between training and career development (Hesketh & Bochner, 1994) is an assumption that individuals may need to engage in effortful processing if training and the acquisition of new skills are to lead to effective long-term retention and transfer (Hesketh, 1997). Another reason why career interventions in organizations have been blurred with training relates to the need for ongoing skill acquisition for career survival to avoid the obsolescence trap (Hesketh & Considine, 1998). Career programs linked to training do have a place in organizations. However, more traditional career interventions may be less easy to implement within the organizational context. Kidd (1998) raised doubts about the value of organizationally based career programs because employees are unlikely to be open about their plans, desires, and feelings.

"Me Incorporated"—Strategic Career Planning

Strategic decisions occur in strategic situations, which are typified by uncertainty, complexity, and a requirement to integrate a wide range of potential influences on outcomes. Strategic decisions are future oriented. The current context of change at the macroeconomic, enterprise, and individual job level means that all career decisions require a strategic component.

Another change that has been evident this decade is the growth of consultancy work, with an associated increase in the use of time or outcome limited contracts. This has resulted in an increase in self-employed individuals who run small consultancies (Peiperl & Baruch, 1997). In these instances, managing one's company strategically can be thought of as symbolically equivalent to managing one's career. Hesketh and Considine (1998) use the metaphor of "Me Incorporated" to capture this new role.

Me Incorporated may need to maintain current activities while also investing in skills to safeguard against future obsolescence. Counselors may need to work hard to help clients overcome the natural resistance to thinking beyond the short term. Delay or time discounting (Hesketh, Watson-Brown, & Whiteley, 1998) is an area of research that examines the way in which the perceived value of an outcome is reduced because of being delayed. Outcomes that are not immediate are usually perceived to be of less value than an immediate outcome even though objectively this may not be true. Goal setting, particularly if it involves proximal goals each with a minioutcome, is one way of helping to reduce the degree to which perceived value is reduced with delay.

Investment for the Me Incorporated individual might also include accumulating social capital (Langford, 1997) through increased networking and the development of a diverse array of social contacts. The greater the diversity of the networks, the better; close intense networks seem not to be as valuable as diverse ones (Burt, 1997). These and other ideas, including the adaptation of strategic planning ideas from the organizational literature to career management, are reviewed in Hesketh and Considine (1998).

In summary, in the current context a Me Incorporated metaphor might help people think about themselves as a "minicompany" where decisions to participate in training and other learning opportunities are thought of as investing in the future. A Me Incorporated view of careers does rely on the possibility of a strong sense of agency on the part of clients. However, many clients may need more direct help and intervention from counseling psychologists. A competency profile for counseling psychologists who may be involved in workplace development follows.

COMPETENCY PROFILE

Knowledge

Counseling psychologists may need a detailed understanding of I/O theory and research, including job analysis, performance measurement, selection, training, job design, and human factors. They may also need a more detailed understanding of the organizational career development literature, and research on the social psychology of work, including teams and team development. Perhaps most importantly, a thorough grounding in the affective side of work, including job satisfaction, work stress, and emotional reactions to interpersonal and other work events, would be of assistance.

In addition to the I/O literature, knowledge of counseling theory and research is critical, including the more specific career decision-making literature. The line between counseling and good communication is sometimes fine in the workplace, and the literature on conflict, conflict resolution, and negotiation is also relevant.

To operate within an empirical framework may require knowledge of research approaches and methods, including single-subject research designs (Kazdin, 1982), goal-attainment scaling (Kiresuk & Sherman, 1968), multiple regression, and structural-equation modeling. Ethical issues encountered in organizational contexts are sometimes different from those faced by a counselor in other contexts. Knowledge of relevant ethical codes, particularly those relating to "who is the client?" are therefore important.

Skills

A flexible range of communication and counseling skills are the most critical component of the counseling psychologist's repertoire in all roles, including workplace development. Counseling skills may be useful for dealing with emotional problems and severe distress, as well as more typical developmental counseling sessions including goal setting, assistance in the preparation of client-centered training plans, and coaching interactions. Given the multicultural nature of the workplace, cultural sensitivity is critical (Hesketh & Bochner, 1994).

Counseling psychologists may need to "give away" their own skills. This might mean teaching clients about models (e.g., TWA) that they can use in their own career planning, providing communication and negotiation skills training, and developing listening skills. In general, knowing how to pass on skills to clients will be exceptionally beneficial for a counselor whose role includes workplace development.

Attitudes

Individual and organizational goals are not always incompatible, and it is often in the interests of both parties to arrive at a set of agreed-upon goals. A helpful attitude for counselors is one that recognizes the need for negotiation and compromise, so that clients do not develop unrealistic expectations of what work can provide.

CONCLUSIONS

This chapter has emphasized the importance of helping clients proactively to manage their own workplace and general career development in adult life. Counseling psychologists need to be aware of the significance of work in the lives of their clients. This significance is often brought into sharp relief when clients experience a transition from work to unemployment or to retirement. Counseling psychologists can facilitate the workplace development of their clients in many ways. First, there are many direct individual interventions that can assist clients to clarify their values and interests, and make informed choices about areas of work. Direct individual interventions can also arise from assistance in managing conflicts and emotions at work. Second, counseling psychologists can run programs for clients, for those who are unemployed, planning retirement, wanting to improve their transition management skills, develop competencies in career management, and so on. Third, there is also a role for counseling psychologists in advising organizations on how best to create environments that facilitate workplace development. This may include advice on traditional areas of I/O psychology, as well as the development of family friendly policies and employee assistance policies.

A final and very important role for counseling psychologists is to contribute to new knowledge. Several issues covered in the current chapter highlight a research agenda. For example, there is a need for a greater understanding of the best ways to help clients manage unmet career expectations. The changing nature of work has resulted in many employees having to alter their expectations for promotions, secure employment, and lifelong work. The literature on plateauing illustrates this point. Transition management is one aspect of managing unmet expectations, but important research questions remain. Another important research area relates to retirement. In earlier decades, the majority of employees could rely on predictable retirement dates. This is no longer the norm with voluntary and involuntary redundancies often providing a trigger for early retirement. There is currently insufficient theory and research dealing with the transitions and decision making surrounding retirement, and counseling psychologists are well placed to fill this gap.

Methodologically, it would be useful to encourage an increase in studies that made use of alternative ways of measuring and conceptualizing fit (see for example, Gustafson & Mumford, 1995).

Greater use might be made of critical incident research or studies that elicit particular emotional and other events, with a careful mapping of the antecedents and consequences of the events. Technology offers an opportunity to think creatively about data collection and methodology. Stressing the need for longitudinal research is not new, but perhaps more frequent sampling of moods and attitudes, and the recording of events that trigger these, might be possible, for example, when turning on or switching off a computer at the start and end of a day.

This chapter has introduced relevant literature for the various possible contributions that a counseling psychologist can make to workplace development, while also suggesting a few new ideas and approaches. Combining the KSAs listed in the competency profile for workplace counseling with generic counseling and research skills will equip counseling psychologists well for an important role in assisting clients to manage their working lives.

REFERENCES

Abramis, D.J. (1994). Work role ambiguity, job satisfaction, and job performance—meta-analyses and review. *Psychological Reports, 75,* 1411–1433.

Allen, N.J., & Meyer, J.P. (1996). Affective, continuance, and normative commitment to the organization: An examination of construct validity. *Journal of Vocational Behavior, 49,* 252–276.

Allworth, E.A., & Hesketh, B. (1999). Construct-oriented biodata: Capturing change related and contextually relevant future performance. *International Journal of Selection and Assessment, 7,* 97–111.

Arnold, J. (1997). *Managing careers into the 21st century.* London: Chapman.

Arnold, J., & Jackson, C. (1997). The new career: Issues and challenges [Special issue]. *British Journal of Guidance and Counselling, 25,* 427–434.

Arnold, J., & Nicholson, N. (1991). Construing of self and others at work in the early years of corporate careers. *Journal of Organizational Behavior, 12,* 621–639.

Aryee, S., & Luk, V. (1996). Work and nonwork influences on the career satisfaction of dual-earner couples. *Journal of Vocational Behavior, 49,* 38–52.

Ashford, S.J. (1993). The feedback environment: An exploratory study of cue use. *Journal of Organizational Behavior, 14,* 201–224.

Ashford, S.J., & Tsui, A.S. (1991). Self-regulation for managerial effectiveness: The role of active feedback seeking. *Academy of Management Journal, 34,* 251–280.

Ashforth, B.E., & Humphrey, R.H. (1995). Emotion in the workplace: A reappraisal. *Human Relations, 48,* 97–125.

Bardwick, J.M. (1986). Counseling a plateaued employee. *Management Solutions, 31*(12), 5–10.

Bardwick, J.M. (1987). How executives can help "plateaued" employees. *Management Review, 76,* 40–46.

Bassi, L.J., Cheny, S., & Vanburen, M. (1997). Training industry trends 1997. *Training and Development, 51,* 46.

Bauer, T.N., & Green, S.G. (1994). Effect of newcomer involvement in work-related activities: A longitudinal study of socialization. *Journal of Applied Psychology, 79,* 211–223.

Black, J.S. (1992). Coming home: The relationship of expatriate expectations with repatriation adjustment and job performance. *Human Relations, 45,* 177–192.

Blau, G. (1994). Developing and testing a taxonomy of lateness behavior. *Journal of Applied Psychology, 79,* 959–970.

Blau, G., Paul, A., & St. John, N. (1993). On developing a general index of work commitment. *Journal of Vocational Behavior, 42,* 298–314.

Borman, M.R, & Motowidlo, S.J. (1993). Expanding the criterion domain to include elements of contextual performance. In N. Schmitt, W.C. Borman, & Associates (Eds.), *Personnel selection in organizations.* San Francisco: Jossey-Bass.

Borman, W.C. (1991). Job behavior, performance, and effectiveness. In M.D. Dunnette & L.M. Hough (Eds.), *Handbook of industrial and organizational psychology* (Vol. 2, pp. 271–326). Palo Alto, CA: Consulting Psychologists Press.

Bretz, R.D., & Judge, T.A. (1994). Person-organization fit and the theory of work adjustment: Implications for satisfaction, tenure, and career success. *Journal of Vocational Behavior, 44,* 32–54.

Brookes, D.V. (1993). Recruiting for potential should be based on work complexity. *Canadian Management, 18,* 22–28.

Brown, R.B. (1996). Organizational commitment: Clarifying the concept and simplifying the existing construct typology. *Journal of Vocational Behavior, 49,* 230–251.

Brown, R.D. (1988). Performance appraisal as a tool for staff development. *New Directions for Student Services, 43,* 110.

Brown, S.P. (1996). A meta-analysis and review of organizational research on job involvement. *Psychological Bulletin, 120,* 235–255.

Burke, R.J., & Nelson, D. (1998). Mergers and acquisitions, downsizing, and privatization: A North American perspective. In M.K. Gowing, K.J. Kraft, & J.C. Quick (Eds.), *The new organizational reality: Downsizing, restructuring, and revitalization.* Washington, DC: American Psychological Association.

Burt, R.S. (1997). A note on social capital and network content. *Social Networks, 19,* 355–373.

Caligiuri, P.M. (1997). Assessing expatriate success: Beyond just "being there." In Z. Aycan (Ed.), *New approaches to employee management, expatriate management: Theory and research* (Vol. 4 pp. 117–140). Greenwich, CT: JAI Press.

Callan, V.J., & Terry, D.J. (1992). Coping with stress and organizational change. In L. Still & A. Kouzman (Eds.), *Best of management research papers in Australasia.* Sydney, Australia: McGraw-Hill.

Campbell, J.P. (1990). Modeling the performance prediction problem in industrial and organizational psychology. In M.D. Dunnette & L.M. Hough (Eds.), *Handbook of industrial and organizational psychology* (Vol. 1, pp. 687–732). Palo Alto, CA: Consulting Psychologists Press.

Caplan, R.D., Vinokur, A.D., Price, R.H., & Van Ryn, M. (1989). Job seeking, reemployment, and mental health: A randomized field experiment in coping with job loss. *Journal of Applied Psychology, 74,* 759–769.

Cartwright, S., & Cooper, C.L. (1994). The human effect of mergers and acquisitions. In C.L. Cooper & D.M. Rousseau (Eds.), *Trends in organizational behavior* (Vol. 1 pp. 47–61). Chichester, England: Wiley.

Chao, G.T. (1990). Exploration of the conceptualization and measurement of career plateau: A comparative analysis. *Journal of Management, 16,* 181–193.

Chao, G.T., O'Leary-Kelly, A.M., Wolf, S., Klein, H.J., & Gardner, P.D. (1994). Organizational socialization: Its content and consequences. *Journal of Applied Psychology, 79,* 730–743.

Clayton, P., & Ayres, H. (1996). Performance appraisals or performance development? A tale of two schemes. *Australian Journal of Public Administration, 55,* 63–71.

Cooke, D.K., Sims, R.L., & Peyrefitte, J. (1995). The relationship between graduate students attitudes and attrition. *Journal of Psychology, 129,* 677–688.

Csikszentmihalyi, M., & Csikszentmihalyi, I.S. (1988). *Optimal experience: Psychological studies of flow in consciousness.* New York: Cambridge University Press.

Dawis, R.V. (1994). The theory of work adjustment as convergent theory. In M.L. Savickas & R.W. Lent (Eds.), *Convergence in career development theories: Implications for science and practice.* Palo Alto, CA: CPP Books.

Dawis, R.V., & Lofquist, L.H. (1984). *A psychological theory of work adjustment.* Minneapolis: University of Minnesota Press.

DiBella, A.J. (1997). Gearing up to become a learning organization. *Journal of Quality and Participation, 20,* 12–14.

Dunlop, T. (1996). Work and the family: The impact of job loss on family well-being. *Journal of Child and Youth Care, 11,* 71–75.

Dunnette, M.D., & Hough, L.M. (Eds.). (1990). *Handbook of industrial and organizational psychology* (2nd ed., Vol. 1). Palo Alto, CA: Consulting Psychologists Press.

Dunnette, M.D., & Hough, L.M. (Eds.). (1991). *Handbook of industrial and organizational psychology* (2nd ed., Vol. 2). Palo Alto, CA: Consulting Psychologists Press.

Dunnette, M.D., & Hough, L.M. (Eds.). (1992). *Handbook of industrial and organizational psychology* (2nd ed., Vol. 3). Palo Alto, CA: Consulting Psychologists Press.

Dunnette, M.D., Hough, L.M., & Triandis, H. (Eds.). (1993). *Handbook of industrial and organizational psychology* (2nd ed., Vol. 4.) Palo Alto, CA: Consulting Psychologists Press.

Duxbury, L.E., Higgins, C.A., & Thomas, D.R. (1996). Work and family environments and the adoption of computer-supported supplemental work-at-home. *Journal of Vocational Behavior, 49,* 1–23.

Earl, N. (1993). Antecedents and consequences of satisfaction and commitment among expatriate managers. *Group and Organization Management, 18,* 153–187.

Edwards, J.R. (1991). Person-job fit: A conceptual integration, literature review and methodological critique. In C. Cooper & I. Robertson (Eds.), *International review of industrial and organizational psychology.* Chichester, England: Wiley.

Edwards, J.R., & Van-Harrison, R. (1993). Job demands and worker health: Three-dimensional reexamination of the relationship between person-environment fit and strain. *Journal of Applied Psychology, 78,* 628–648.

Ettington, D.R. (1998). Successful career plateauing. *Journal of Vocational Behavior, 52,* 72–88.

Evans, M.G. (1991). The problem of analyzing multiplicative composites: Interactions revisited. *American Psychologist, 46,* 1–6.

Feldman, D.C., Doerpinghaus, H.I., & Turnley, W.H. (1994). Managing temporary workers: A permanent HR challenge. *Organizational Dynamics, 23,* 49–63.

Feldman, D.C., & Gainey, T.W. (1997). Patterns of telecommuting and their consequences—framing the research agenda. *Human Resource Management Review, 7,* 369–388.

Feller, R. (1991). Employment and career development in a world of change: What is ahead for the next twenty-five years? National Employment Counselors Association's twenty-fifth anniversary [Special issue]. *Journal of Employment Counseling, 28,* 13–20.

Finney, M.I. (1996). Companies help employees manage personal business. *HR Magazine, 41,* 59–61.

Fouad, N.A. (1997). School-to-work transition: Voice from an implementer. *Counseling Psychologist, 25,* 403–412.

Frijda, N.H. (1993). Moods, emotion episodes, and emotions. In M. Lewis & J.M. Haviland (Eds.), *Handbook of emotions* (pp. 381–403). New York: Guilford Press.

George, J.M., & Jones, G.R. (1996). The experience of work and turnover intentions: Interactive effects of value attainment, job satisfaction, and positive mood. *Journal of Applied Psychology, 81,* 318–325.

Gerpott, T., & Domsch, M. (1987). R&D professionals' reactions to the career plateau: An exploration of the mediating role of supervisory behaviors and job characteristics. *R & D Management, 17,* 103–118.

Gilbourne, D., & Taylor, A.H. (1998). From theory to practice: The integration of goal perspective theory and life development approaches within an injury-specific goal-setting program. *Journal of Applied Sports Psychology, 10,* 124–139.

Goldberg, L.R. (1990). An alternative "description of personality": A Big-Five factor structure. *Journal of Personality and Social Psychology, 59,* 1216–1229.

Goldberg, L.R. (1992). The development of markers for the "Big Five" factor structure. *Psychological Assessment, 4,* 26–42.

Gowing, M.K., Kraft, J.D., & Quick, J. (1998). *The new organizational reality: Downsizing, restructuring, and revitalization.* Washington, DC: American Psychological Association.

Gustafson, S.B., & Mumford, M.D. (1995). Personal style and person-environment fit: A pattern approach. *Journal of Vocational Behavior, 46,* 163–188.

Gysbers, N.C. (1997). Involving counseling psychology in the school-to-work movement: An idea whose time has come. *Counseling Psychologist, 25,* 413–427.

Hall, D.T. (1985). Project work as an antidote to career plateauing in a declining engineering organization. *Human Resource Management, 24,* 271–292.

Hall, D.T., & Associates. (1996). *The career is dead—long live the career: A relational approach to careers.* San Francisco: Jossey-Bass.

Hall, D.T., & Mirvis, P.H. (1995). The new career contract: Developing the whole person at midlife and beyond. *Journal of Vocational Behavior, 47,* 269–289.

Hall, D.T., & Moss, J.E. (1998). The new protean career contract: Helping organizations and employees adapt. *Organizational Dynamics, 26,* 22–37.

Halvorsen, K. (1994). Those who cannot have what they want must want what they can get: Experience with company-based early retirement pension schemes in Norway. *Scandinavian Journal of Social Welfare, 3,* 50–60.

Hanisch, K.A. (1994). Reasons people retire and their relation to attitudinal and behavioral correlates in retirement. *Journal of Vocational Behavior, 45,* 1–16.

Hanisch, K.A., & Hulin, C.L. (1990). Job attitudes and organizational withdrawal: An examination of re-tirement and other voluntary withdrawal behaviors. *Journal of Vocational Behavior, 37,* 60–78.

Hanisch, K.A., & Hulin, C.L. (1991). General attitudes and organizational withdrawal: An evaluation of a causal model. *Journal of Vocational Behavior, 39,* 110–128.

Hansson, R.O., De Koekkoek, P.D., Neece, W.M., & Patterson, D.W. (1997). Successful aging at work: An-nual review, 1992–1996. The older worker and transitions to retirement. *Journal of Vocational Behavior, 51,* 202–233.

Harrison, D.A., & Liska, L.Z. (1994). Promoting regular exercise in organizational fitness programs: Health-related differences in motivational building blocks. *Personnel Psychology, 47,* 47–71.

Herriot, P. (1988). Graduate recruitment: Psychological contracts and the balance of power. *British Journal of Guidance and Counselling, 16,* 228–241.

Herriot, P. (1992). *The career management challenge.* London: Sage.

Hesketh, B. (1995). Status quo effects in decision-making about training and career development. *Journal of Vocational Behavior, 48,* 324–338.

Hesketh, B. (1997). Dilemmas in training for transfer and retention. *Applied Psychology: An International Review, 46,* 317–339.

Hesketh, B., & Allworth, A. (1997). *Adaptive performance: Updating the criterion to cope with change.* Paper presented at the 2nd Australian Industrial and Organizational Psychology Conference, Mel-bourne.

Hesketh, B., & Bochner, S. (1994). Technological change in a multi-cultural context: Implications for train-ing and career planning. In M.D. Dunnette, L. Hough, & H. Triandis (Eds.), *Handbook of industrial and organizational psychology* (Vol. 4, pp. 191–240). Palo Alto, CA: Consulting Psychologists Press.

Hesketh, B., & Considine, G. (1998). Integrating individual and organizational perspectives for career de-velopment and change. *European Journal of Work and Organizational Psychology, 4,* 405–418.

Hesketh, B., & Dawis, R.V. (1991). The Minnesota theory of work adjustment: A conceptual framework. In B. Hesketh & A. Adams (Eds.), *Psychological perspectives on occupational health and rehabilitation.* Marrickville, Sydney: Harcourt Brace.

Hesketh, B., & Gardiner, D. (1993). Person-environment fit: A reconceptualization and empirical test. *Journal of Vocational Behavior, 42,* 315–332.

Hesketh, B., & McLachlan, K. (1991). Career compromise and adjustment among graduates in the banking industry. *British Journal of Guidance and Counselling, 19,* 191–208.

Hesketh, B., Watson-Brown, C., & Whiteley, S. (1998). Time-related discounting of value and decision-making about job options. *Journal of Vocational Behavior, 52,* 89–105.

Hochschild, A. (1983). *The managed heart.* Berkeley: University of California Press.

Holland, J.H. (1985). *Making vocational choices: A theory of vocational personalities and work environ-ments.* Englewood Cliffs, NJ: Prentice-Hall.

Holland, J.H. (1987). Some speculation about the investigation of person-environment transactions. *Journal of Vocational Behavior, 31,* 337–340.

Holland, J.H. (1996a). Exploring careers with a typology. What we have learned and some new directions. *American Psychologist, 51,* 397–406.

Holland, J.H. (1996b). Integrating career theory and practice: The current situation and some potential remedies. In M.L. Savickas & B.W. Walsh (Eds.), *Handbook of career counseling theory and practice* (pp. 1–11). Palo Alto, CA: Davies-Black.

Hough, L.M., Eaton, N.K., Dunnette, M.D., Kamp, J.D., et al. (1990). Criterion-related validities of person-ality constructs and the effect of response distortion on those validities. *Journal of Applied Psychology, 75,* 581–595.

Hulin, C.L. (1991). Adaptation, persistence and commitment in organizations. In M.D. Dunnette (Ed.), *Handbook of industrial and organizational psychology* (2nd ed.). New York: Wiley.

Hunter, J.E. (1986). Cognitive ability, cognitive aptitude, job knowledge, and job performance. *Journal of Vocational Behavior, 29,* 340–362.

Hunter, J.E., & Hunter, R.F. (1984). Validity and utility of alternative predictors of job performance. *Psy-chological Bulletin, 96,* 72–98.

Irving, P.G., & Meyer, J.P. (1994). Reexamination of the met-expectations hypothesis: A longitudinal analysis. *Journal of Applied Psychology, 79,* 937–949.

Iverson, R.D., Olekalns, M., & Erwin, P.J. (1998). Affectivity, organizational stressors and absenteeism: A causal model of burnout and its consequences. *Journal of Vocational Behavior, 52,* 1–23.

Jackson, P.R., Stafford, E.M., Banks, M.H., & Warr, P.B. (1983). Unemployment and psychological distress in young people: The moderating role of employment commitment. *Journal of Applied Psychology, 68,* 525–535.

Jahoda, M. (1979). The impact of unemployment in the 1930s and 1970s. *Bulletin of the British Psychological Society, 32,* 309–314.

Johns, G. (1994a). Absenteeism estimates by employees and managers: Divergent perspectives and self-serving perceptions. *Journal of Applied Psychology, 79,* 229–239.

Johns, G. (1994b). How often were you absent? A review of the use of self-reported absence data. *Journal of Applied Psychology, 79,* 574–591.

Kaufmann, A.J.S. (1998). Helping build careers. *Infoworld, 20*(28), 99–100

Kazdin, A.E. (1982, September). Single-case experimental designs in clinical research and practice. *New Directions for Methodology of Social and Behavioral Science,* (13), 33–47.

Keith, P.M., & Schafer, R.B. (1984). Role behavior and psychological well-being: A comparison of men in one-job and two-job families. *American Journal of Orthopsychiatry, 54*(1), 137–145.

Kerr, J.H., & Vos, M.C. (1993). Employee fitness programmes, absenteeism and general well-being. *Work and Stress, 7,* 179–190.

Kidd, J.M. (1998). Emotion: An absent presence in career theory. *Journal of Vocational Behavior, 52,* 275–288.

Kingston, K.M., & Hardy, L. (1997). Effects of different types of goals on processes that support performance. *Sport Psychologist, 11,* 277–293.

Kiresuk, T.J., & Sherman, R.E. (1968). Goal attainment scaling: A general method for evaluating comprehensive community mental health programs. *Community Mental Health Journal, 4*(4), 443–453.

Kirschenbaum, A. (1991). The corporate transfer: Origin and destination factors in the decision to change jobs. *Journal of Vocational Behavior, 38,* 107–123.

Kossek, E.E., & Ozeki, C. (1998). Work-family conflict, policies, and the job-life satisfaction relationship: A review and directions for organizational behavior-human resources research. *Journal of Applied Psychology, 83,* 139–149.

Kram, K.E. (1986). Mentoring in the workplace. In D.T. Hall (Ed.), *Career development in organizations.* San Francisco: Jossey-Bass.

Kramer, M.W. (1993). Communication and uncertainty reduction during job transfer: Leaving and joining process. *Communication Monographs, 60,* 178–198.

Krausz, M., Koslowsky, M., & Eiser, A. (1998). Distal and proximal influences on turnover intentions and satisfaction: Support for withdrawal progression theory. *Journal of Vocational Behavior, 52,* 59–71.

Laben, J.K., Sneed, L.D., & Seidel, S.L. (1995). Goal attainment in short-term group psychotherapy settings. Clinical implications for practice. In M.A. Frey & C.L. Sieloff (Eds.), *Advancing King's systems framework and theory of nursing.* Thousand Oaks, CA: Sage.

Langford, P. (1997). *The role of social capital and networking behavior in job and career success.* Unpublished PhD dissertation, Macquarie University, Sydney.

Lazarus, R.S., & Folkman, S. (1987). Transactional theory and research on emotions and coping. *European Journal of Personality, 1,* 141–169.

Lazarus, R.S., & Folkman, S. (1991). The concept of coping. In A. Monat & R.S. Lazarus (Eds.), *Stress and coping: An anthology* (pp. 189–206). New York: Columbia University Press.

Lechner, L., & De Vries, H. (1995). Starting participation in an employee fitness program: Attitudes, social influence, and self-efficacy. *Preventative Medicine, 24,* 627–633.

Lee, T.W., & Johnson, D.R. (1994). Reactions to job transfer by job type and career stage. *Journal of Business and Psychology, 8,* 377–390.

Levinson, H. (1996). Executive coaching. *Consulting Psychological Journal: Practice and Research, 48,* 115–123.

Major, D.A., Kozlowski, S.W.J., Chao, G.T., & Gardner, P.D. (1995). A longitudinal investigation of newcomer expectations, early socialization outcomes, and the moderating effects of role development factors. *Journal of Applied Psychology, 80,* 418–431.

Marko, K.W., & Savickas, M.L. (1998). Effectiveness of a career time perspective intervention. *Journal of Vocational Behavior, 52,* 106–119.

Masel, C.N., Terry, D.J., & Gribble, M. (1996). The effects of coping on adjustment: Re-examining the goodness of fit model of coping effectiveness. *Anxiety, Stress, and Coping: An International Journal, 9,* 279–300.

Mathieu, J.E., & Zajac, D.M. (1990). A review and meta-analysis of the antecedents, correlates and consequences of organizational commitment. *Psychological Bulletin, 108,* 171–194.

Maule, J.A. (1995). Early retirement schemes: Factors governing their success and how these differ across job categories. *Personnel Review, 24,* 6–11.

Mayer, J.D., & Geher, G. (1996). Emotional intelligence and the identification of emotion. *Intelligence, 22,* 89–113.

Mayer, J.D., & Salovey, P. (1995). Emotional intelligence and the construction and regulation of feelings. *Applied and Preventive Psychology, 4,* 197–208.

Meyer, J.P., & Allen, N.J. (1991). A three-component conceptualization of organizational commitment. *Human Resource Management Review, 1,* 61–89.

Meyer, J.P., Allen, N.J., & Gellatly, I.R. (1990). Affective and continuance commitment to the organization: Evaluation of measures and analysis of concurrent and time-lagged relations. *Journal of Applied Psychology, 75,* 710–720.

Miller, D.C., & Form, W.H. (1947). Measuring patterns of occupational security. *Sociometry, 10,* 362–375.

Morrison, E.W. (1993). Longitudinal study of the effects of information seeking on newcomer socialization. *Journal of Applied Psychology, 78,* 173–183.

Morrow, P. (1993). *The theory and measurement of work commitment.* Greenwich, CT: JAI Press.

Near, J.P. (1985). A discriminant analysis of plateaued versus nonplateaued managers. *Journal of Vocational Behavior, 26*(2), 177–188.

Near, J.P., Rice, R.W., & Hunt, R.G. (1978). Work and extra-work correlates of life and job satisfaction. *Academy of Management Journal, 21,* 248–264.

Necowitz, L.B., & Roznowski, M. (1994). Negativity affectivity and job satisfaction: Cognitive processes underlying the relationship and effects on employee behaviors. *Journal of Vocational Behavior, 45,* 270–294.

Nelson-Horchler, J. (1986). When the escalator stops . . . motivation becomes the challenge. *Industry Week, 231,* 58–62.

Nicholson, N. (1990). The transition cycle: causes, outcomes, processes and forms. In S. Fisher & C.L. Cooper (Eds.), *On the move: The psychological effects of change and transition* (pp. 83–108). Chichester, England: Wiley.

Nicholson, N. (1993). Purgatory or place of safety? The managerial plateau and organizational age grading. *Human Relations, 46,* 1369–1489.

Nicholson, N., & Arnold, J. (1991). From expectation to experience: Graduates entering a large corporation. *Journal of Organizational Behavior, 12,* 413–429.

Nicholson, N., & West, M. (1996). Men and women in transition. In J. Billsberry (Ed.), *The effective manager: Perspectives and illustrations.* London: Sage.

Noe, R.A. (1986). Trainees' attributes and attitudes: Neglected influences on training effectiveness. *Academy of Management Review, 11,* 736–749.

Organ, D.W., & Ryan, K. (1995). A meta-analytic review of attitudinal and dispositional predictors of organizational citizenship behavior. *Personnel Psychology, 48,* 775–802.

Parasuraman, S., Purohit, Y.S., & Godshalk, V.M. (1996). Work and family variables, entrepreneurial career success and psychological well-being. *Journal of Vocational Behavior, 48,* 275–300.

Peiperl, M., & Baruch, Y. (1997). Back to square zero: The post corporate career. *Organizational Dynamics, 25,* 7–22.

Peterson, L., & Sobell, L.C. (1994). Introduction to the State-of-the-Art Review series: Research contributions to clinical assessment. *Behavior Therapy, 25,* 523–531.

Ree, M.J., Earles, J.A., & Teachout, M.S. (1994). Predicting job performance: Not much more than g. *Journal of Applied Psychology, 79,* 518–524.

Reitzes, D.C., Mutran, E.J., & Fernandez, M.E. (1996). Does retirement hurt well-being? Factors influencing self-esteem and depression among retirees and workers. *Gerontologist, 36*(5), 649–656.

Riskind, J.H., Sarampote, C.S., & Mercier, M.A. (1996). For every malady a sovereign cure: Optimism training. *Journal of Cognitive Psychotherapy, 10,* 105–117.

Robertson, I.T., & Kinder, A. (1993). Personality and job competences: The criterion-related validity of some personality variables. *Journal of Occupational and Organizational Psychology, 66*(3), 225–244.

Rosenbaum, J.E. (1989). Organization career systems and employee misperceptions. In M.B. Arthur, D.T. Hall, & B.S. Lawrence (Eds.), *Handbook of career theory* (pp. 329–353). New York: Cambridge University Press.

Rosin, H.H., & Korabik, K. (1995). Organizational experiences and propensity to leave: A multivariate investigation of men and women mangers. *Journal of Vocational Behavior, 46,* 1–16.

Rounds, J.B., Dawis, R.V., & Lofquist, L.H. (1987). Measurement of person-environment fit and predictions of satisfaction in the theory of work adjustment. *Journal of Vocational Behavior, 31,* 297–318.

Rousseau, D.M. (1996). *The boundaryless career.* New York: Oxford University Press.

Rousseau, D.M. (1997). Organizational behavior in the new organizational era. *Annual Review of Psychology, 48,* 515–546.

Rousseau, D.M., & Parkes, J.M. (1993). The contracts of individuals and organizations. In L.L. Cummings & B.M. Staw (Eds.), *Research in organizational behavior* (Vol. 15, pp. 1–43). Greenwich, CT: JAI Press.

Russell, J.E.A., & Adams, D.M. (1997). The changing nature of mentoring in organizations: An introduction to the special issue on mentoring in organizations. *Journal of Vocational Behavior, 51,* 1–14.

Saffron, K. (1985). *Social Indicators Survey.* Wellington, NZ: Government Printer Department of Statistics.

Sagie, A. (1998). Employee absenteeism, organizational commitment, and job satisfaction: Another look. *Journal of Vocational Behavior, 52,* 156–171.

Saks, A.M., Mudrack, P.E., & Ashforth, B.E. (1996). The relationship between the work ethic, job attitudes, intentions to quit and turnover for temporary service employees. *Administrative Sciences, 13,* 226–236.

Salovey, P., & Mayer, J.D. (1990). Emotional Intelligence. *Imagination, Cognition and Personality, 9*(3), 185–211.

Schiska, A. (1991). Revitalizing the plateaued employees on your staff. *Supervisory Management, 36,* 1–2.

Schmidt, F.L., Hunter, J.E., Outerbridge, A.N., & Goff, S. (1988). Joint relation of experience and ability with job performance: Test of three hypotheses. *Journal of Applied Psychology, 73,* 46–57.

Schmidt, F.L., Ones, D.S., & Hunter, J.E. (1992). Personnel selection. *Annual Review of Psychology, 43,* 627–670.

Schneer, J.A., & Reitman, F. (1997). The interrupted managerial career path: A longitudinal study of MBAs. *Journal of Vocational Behavior, 51,* 411–434.

Schultz, K.S., Morton, K.R., & Weckerle, J.R. (1998). The influence of push and pull factors on voluntary and involuntary early retirees' retirement decision and adjustment. *Journal of Vocational Behavior, 53,* 45–57.

Schweiger, D.M., & Denisi, A.S. (1991). Communication with employees following a merger: A longitudinal field experiment. *Academy of Management Journal, 34,* 110–135.

Seligman, M.E.P. (1975). *Helplessness: On depression, development, and death.* San Francisco, CA: Freeman.

Seligman, M.E.P. (1998). *Learned optimism.* Address given to the International Congress of Applied Psychology, San Francisco.

Seligman, M.E.P., Reivich, K., Jaycox, L., & Gillham, J. (1995). *The optimistic child.* Boston: Houghton Mifflin.

Smart, R., & Peterson, C. (1997). Super's career stages and the decision to change careers. *Journal of Vocational Behavior, 51,* 358–374.

Smart, R.M. (1998). Career stages in Australian professional women: A test of Super's model. *Journal of Vocational Behavior, 52,* 379–395.

Sonnenberg, D. (1997). The "new career" changes: Understanding and managing anxiety. *British Journal of Guidance and Counselling, 25,* 463–472.

Spokane, A.R. (1985). A review of research on person-environment congruence in Holland's theory of careers. *Journal of Vocational Behavior, 26,* 306–343.

Stamp, G. (1989). The individual, the organization and the path to mutual appreciation. *Personnel Management, 21,* 28–31.

Stamp, G., & Stamp, C. (1993). Well-being at work: Aligning purposes, people, strategies and structures. *International Journal of Career Management, 5,* 3–36.

Stanek, D.M., & Mokhtarian, P.L. (1998). Developing models of preference for home-based and center-based telecommuting—findings and forecasts. *Technological Forecasting and Social Change, 57,* 53–74.

Staw, B.M., Sutton, R.I., & Pelled, L.H. (1994). Employee positive emotion and favourable outcomes at the workplace. *Organization Science, 5,* 51–71.

Stroh, L.K., Brett, J.M., & Reilly, A.H. (1996). Family structure, glass ceiling, and traditional explanations for the differential rate of turnover of female and male managers. *Journal of Vocational Behavior, 49,* 99–118.

Super, D.E. (1953). A theory of vocational development. *American Psychologist, 6,* 185–190.

Super, D.E. (1957). *The psychology of careers.* New York: Harper.

Super, D.E. (1990). A life span, life-space approach to career development. In D. Brown & L. Brooks (Eds.), *Career choice and development* (2nd ed). San Francisco: Jossey-Bass.

Super, D.E. (1994). A life span, life space perspective on convergence. In M.L. Savickas & R.W. Lent (Eds.), *Convergence in career development theories: Implications for science and practice.* Palo Alto, CA: CPP Books.

Super, D.E., Savickas, M.L., & Super, C.M. (1996). The life-span, life-space approach to careers. In D. Brown & L. Brooks (Eds.), *Career choice and development.* San Francisco: Jossey-Bass.

Szymanski, E.M. (1997). School-to-work transition: Ecological considerations for career development. In J.L. Swartz & W.E. Martin, Jr. (Eds.), *Applied ecological psychology for schools within communities: Assessment and intervention.* Mahwah, NJ: Erlbaum.

Terry, D.J. (1994). Determinants of coping: The role of stable and situational factors. *Journal of Personality and Social Psychology, 66,* 895–910.

Terry, D.J., Callan, V.J., & Sartori, G. (1996). Employee adjustment to an organizational merger: Stress, coping and intergroup differences. *Stress Medicine, 12,* 14–22.

Tharenou, P. (1995). The impact of a developmental performance appraisal program on employee perceptions in an Australian federal agency. *Group and Organization Management, 20,* 245–271.

Tharenou, P., & Conroy, D. (1994). Men and women managers' advancement: Personal or situational determinants? *Applied Psychology: An International Review, 43,* 5–31.

Tinsley, D.J., & Schwendener-Holt, M.J. (1992). Retirement and leisure. In S.D. Brown & R.W. Lent (Eds.), *Handbook of counseling psychology* (2nd ed., pp. 627–665). New York: Wiley.

Townsend, C., & Nelson, D. (1997). Family and relationship problems. In C. Feltham (Ed.), *The gains of listening: Perspectives on counselling at work.* Buckingham, England: The Open University.

Tremblay, M., Roger, A., & Toulouse, J.M. (1995). Career plateau and work attitude: An empirical study of managers. *Human Relations, 48,* 221–237.

Van den Bout, J. (1986). Attributional and irrational cognitions, depression and (threat of) job redundancy. *Psychological Reports, 59,* 951–954.

Vincola, A., & Mobley, N. (1998). Performance management through a work/life lens. *HR Focus, 75,* 9–10.

Vinokur, A.D., Van Ryn, M., Gramlich, E.M., & Price, R. (1991). Long-term follow-up and benefit/cost analysis of the jobs program: A preventive intervention for the unemployed. *Journal of Applied Psychology, 76,* 213–219.

Warr, P. (1987). *Work, unemployment, and mental health.* Oxford, England: Oxford University Press.

Warr, P. (1994). Age and employment. In M.D. Dunnette, L. Hough, & H. Triandis (Eds.), *Handbook of industrial and organizational psychology* (Vol. 4). Palo Alto, CA: Consulting Psychologists Press.

Watson, D., & Pennebaker, J.W. (1989). Health complaints, stress, and distress: Exploring the central role of negative affectivity. *Psychological Review, 96,* 234–254.

Watson, D., Pennebaker, J.W., & Folger, R. (1986). Beyond negative affectivity: Measuring stress and satisfaction in the workplace. *Journal of Organizational Behavior Management, 8,* 141–157.

Watts, A.G. (1996). Toward a policy for lifelong career development: A transatlantic perspective. *Career Development Quarterly, 45,* 41–53.

Weiss, H.M., & Cropanzano, R. (1996). Affective events theory: A theoretical discussion of the structure, causes and consequences of affective experiences at work. *Research in Organizational Behavior, 18,* 1074.

Wharton, A.S., & Erickson, R.J. (1993). Managing emotions on the job and at home: Understanding the consequences of multiple emotional roles. *Academy of Management Review, 18,* 457–486.

Witherspoon, R., & White, R.P. (1996). Executive coaching: A continuum of roles. *Consulting Psychology Journal: Practice and Research, 48,* 124–133.

Wright, T.A., & Straw, B.M. (1999, January). Affect and favorable work outcomes: Two longitudinal tests of the happy-productive worker thesis. *Journal of Organizational Behavior, 20*(1), 1–23.

Zahara, D.J., & Cuvo, A.J. (1984). Behavioral applications to the rehabilitation of traumatic head injury. *Clinical Psychology Review, 4,* 477–491.

Zeffane, R.M. (1994). Understanding employee turnover: The need for a contingency approach. *International Journal of Manpower, 15,* 2–37.

CHAPTER 16

Counseling Older Adults: Theoretical and Empirical Issues in Prevention and Intervention

ROBERT D. HILL
BRIAN L. THORN
TED PACKARD

It has been widely documented that the nature of the U.S. population has changed dramatically in the past 50 years. Trends most prominent in this changing demography include large increases in the number of individuals living into old and very old age. The number of adults 65 and older has increased dramatically since 1980, and will continue to increase at a rate faster than the general population for years to come (U.S. Bureau of the Census, 1996).

These issues were not unanticipated by counseling psychologists. In 1980, a major contribution in *The Counseling Psychologist,* which focused on identifying the most important issues in 2000 A.D., highlighted the psychological and social problems associated with the aging of the U.S. population. Of the many scholars in counseling psychology who contributed to this issue, John Whitely (1980) noted that "general and substantial increase in life expectancy" (p. 4) would be apparent by 2000 A.D. and that "[a]s human life expectancy is extended by advances in nutrition and medicine, counseling psychologists can help individuals master the challenges associated with aging" (p. 6).

This prediction has become a reality. The Census Bureau has documented that in 1990 the average life expectancy in the United States (from birth to death) was 75.4 years (National Center for Health Statistics, 1995), and it is projected to approach 80 years by the year 2000 (Takamura, 1998; U.S. Bureau of the Census, 1996). A major question concerns the extent to which increasing life expectancy will influence social issues and public policy. What follows is a brief summary of several important issues associated with increased aging of the population that likely will be relevant to counseling psychology.

First, and most obvious, is the fact that because people are living longer there will be a greater representation of older adults in our population. The percentage of individuals 65 years of age and older now makes up approximately 8% of the U.S. population. If current trends continue, this will increase to 15% by the year 2010, meaning that approximately 40 million U.S. citizens will be dealing with the physiological and psychological realities of old age. In addition, increasing life expectancy also means that the number of individuals living into very old age will increase. In contrast to the 16% increase in those between the ages of 65 and 74 years between 1990 and 2010, the number of persons who are 75 years of age and older is expected to increase by 50%, and the number of those 85 years and older will double (U.S. Bureau of the Census, 1992, 1996). Issues facing the very old include dealing with progressive increases in disability, changes in family structure, bereavement, and death and dying. Although there is some research examining quality of life and psychological functioning in very old adults (e.g., centenarians), we know relatively little about assessing and ameliorating the challenges facing these individuals (see Bäckman, Small, Wahlin, & Larsson, in press; Kropf & Pugh, 1995; Poon, Sweaney, Clayton, & Merriam, 1992).

What can be anticipated, however, is that addressing the needs of the very old will require counseling psychologists and other mental health specialists to provide services in a variety of contexts that have not been in their traditional domain of professional practice. These contexts likely will include adult day care, nursing home, and transitional residential care, as well as a range of assisted living contexts. Several articles by counseling psychologists have highlighted this issue as an important future trend for our specialty (see Crose & Kixmiller, 1994; Lopez, 1980; Myers & Salmon, 1984; Nagel, Cimbolic, & Newlin, 1988).

Second, the heterogeneity of the older population will be great in terms of individual and cultural diversity. It is well known, for example, that females currently make up the majority of the older adult population because they have a longer life expectancy than men (Atchley, 1997; Nathanson, 1990; U.S. Bureau of the Census, 1996). What is less well known, and may have even greater long-term social consequences, are the very rapid increases in older ethnic minority populations, including African Americans, Hispanics, and Asian Americans (Atchley, 1997; Schneider & Grueling, 1990). In their national survey of older adults, The American Association of Retired Persons (AARP) reported that in 1994 ethnic minority groups totaled 14% of all older adults residing in the United States (8% were African American, 4% were Hispanic/Latino/a, 2% were Asian or Pacific Islander, and 1% were Native American/Alaska Native). By 2030, AARP estimates that the total minority representation could become as high as 25% (AARP, 1998). In her overview of aging issues for the twenty-first century, Takamura (1998) noted that by 2020 "the number of elderly Hispanic Americans is expected to increase by 300% . . . the number of elderly African Americans is expected to increase by 102% . . . [and among] Asian and Pacific Islander[s] a 358% increase is anticipated" (p. 411).

Although there is a growing literature in counseling psychology examining the special issues facing individuals from ethnic minority groups, very few studies have examined the impact of aging on ethnic minorities. This oversight contrasts with the growing literature in other professional disciplines (e.g., social work, nursing, gerontology) examining the range of psychological issues facing older ethnic minority adults (for example, see Gelfand, 1994; Markides & Black, 1996; Sakauye, 1996; Thurmond, 1996).

Finally, the scientific literature clearly documents that as individuals age, the prevalence of chronic disease and age-related disability increases. Even though the quality of life in older adults has improved, the prevalence of age-related disability in this population remains high, especially as individuals progress into very old age. Nearly 25% of individuals 85 years and older report needing assistance to live independently, and 20% report needing assistance with daily self-care (Atchley, 1997). In this regard, some degenerative conditions, such as Alzheimer's disease, that have a differential diagnosis based on age are becoming more commonplace in contemporary society (e.g., with late onset after 65 years and early onset 65 years or less by *DSM-IV* diagnostic standards; American Psychiatric Association, 1994). The cost of age-related degenerative disease states is enormous, both in terms of economic impact and psychological demands (Alloul et al., 1998; Raskind & Peskind, 1992). The potential for counseling psychologists to serve the needs of older adults with disabling conditions is enormous but relatively unaddressed.

In sum, with individuals in our society living longer, it has become critical to understand the nature of aging and how counseling psychologists can play a role in helping old and very old adults negotiate the physical, social, and psychological challenges associated with the aging process. This chapter (1) examines the theoretical and empirical literature both within and outside counseling psychology, with the goal of elucidating a meaningful conceptualization of old age that is consistent with the framework of normative adaptation and change that has been associated historically with counseling psychology; (2) explores concerns that are consistent with the range of issues and problems that older individuals face as a result of the aging process; (3) highlights counseling strategies and treatment recommendations for addressing older adult issues that are grounded in theory and research; and (4) recommends essential competencies that will enable counseling psychologists to work effectively with older adult clients.

Because counseling psychology interventions have been defined typically within a normative as opposed to a pathological framework (see Gelso & Fretz, 1992), this chapter highlights issues in normal aging. Issues in pathological aging such as Alzheimer's disease and related dementias (Edwards, 1993; Hill, Bäckman, & Stigsdotter-Neeley, in press; Nordhus, VandenBos, Berg, & Fromholt, 1998); late-life chronic psychiatric illness (Birren, Sloane, & Cohen, 1992; Carstensen, Dornbrand, & Edelstein, 1996; Hersen & Van Hasselt, 1998; Woods, 1996); and chronic disability and issues in long-term care associated with pathological aging (Gatz, 1996; Gatz & Smyer, 1992) are addressed elsewhere in the literature. The goal of this chapter is to provide theoretically and empirically grounded information that can be applied to professional practice specifically geared to counseling psychologists. To achieve this goal, we use three case vignettes as examples of typical (or normative) problems older adults may face as part of the aging process. By revisiting these case examples at different points in the chapter, we hope to demonstrate how counseling psychologists can provide meaningful psychological services to older individuals.

CASE VIGNETTES

Cognitive Loss

Jim is a 76-year-old European American man who is concerned about his failing memory. He had a long career as an insurance salesman whose territory covered a large rural area of a western U.S. state. He prided himself on his ability to recognize and remember the names of seldom seen clients and acquaintances; consequently, he perceives himself as "very good with names and faces." Jim reports that he enjoyed his career. On retirement at age 65, he devoted time to volunteer work and church-related activities. Jim noted that in recent years he has had greater difficulty remembering peoples' names when he has encountered them in unexpected places. He says he has come to counseling because he is distressed over his memory problems that appear to have worsened significantly over the past few years. Recently, Jim could not remember the name of a familiar person in his church congregation until prompted. His wife who attended the session with Jim noted that in the past year she has not been able to rely on him for remembering phone numbers and important dates (e.g., grandchildren's birthdays) as she did in the past. His family physician, who works in the same multidisciplinary group practice where Jim sought counseling, suggested that Jim seek advice from the psychologist on staff. Jim says, "My family doctor told me you might be able to help me find some answers. She said something about medication and testing. I have this terrible fear that these memory losses may be the first sign of Alzheimer's disease."

Caregiving

Juanita is an 83-year-old Hispanic woman who has been caring for her 84-year-old husband, Antonio, for several years. Antonio was diagnosed with Alzheimer's disease five years ago. Juanita was referred for counseling by a social worker from a local community action agency which does in-home visits with very frail older adults as well as home-bound disabled people. Juanita says that she is very discouraged. She reports a happy marriage of 60 years with Antonio and that they have 4 children, 12 grandchildren, and 7 great grandchildren. She has two sisters and one brother who live nearby. Juanita states that her family is very supportive, especially her oldest unmarried daughter who offered recently to move in with them as a way to help. However, as Antonio's condition has worsened some of Juanita's other children have suggested that he be permanently placed in a nursing home. Taking their advice, Juanita met with the administrator of a local nursing home, but decided against pursuing this option because, according to Juanita, "When we were married by Father Santiago in the Holy Trinity Church, he said that our marriage was for better or worse and until death do us part, and that's how it has always been. I could never live with myself if I placed Antonio in there. And even though he is not able to talk with me right now, we've been through tough times before, and I think we can get through this one as well. It's just that I am very lonely and believe that Antonio is never going to be what he was once. I wish my old age with Antonio could be comfortable instead of all hard work and sadness. Maybe I should just give up and ask my daughter, Carlita, to move in and help me take care of Antonio, but she has her own life to live too."

Career Issues

John is a 54-year-old European American man who has worked for a manufacturing company for 27 years. He was referred for counseling by the employee-relations department. One month prior to John's first counseling session the company merged with another firm, and he was laid off in the process. John was unable to exercise the company's early retirement option because the minimum retirement age was 55 years. Further, John reported that he was "not ready to retire" and was anxious about the prospect of not being able to continue working to support his family. John met a few times with a benefits counselor who gave him several career inventories and said that his profile was a close match to "farmer." He reported that this score probably reflected his long-standing hobby of gardening. He reported that a lot of emphasis in his "exit" counseling was placed on getting his resume updated, working hard to develop a job information network, and developing strategies for using the newspaper and the Internet to identify prospective jobs quickly. John has become discouraged with prospects for finding a new job and angry that all of his years of service (e.g., employee of the year awards) were rewarded with an abrupt and unanticipated dismissal. He states, "I'm really discouraged because who is going to hire an old man when there are 10 younger and more up-to-date people looking for the same positions? I was counting on this job getting me to retirement."

These vignettes represent distinctly different issues that individuals may encounter in older age, with the likelihood of facing such problems increasing as the aging process progresses into very late life. It is noteworthy that such issues are not confined to certain persons or specifiable classes of people. Thus, in many respects the challenges highlighted in this chapter occur as part of the normal aging process. Models of aging that fully capture problems in everyday living, therefore, must focus on what happens to normal individuals as they age. The two models that are presented next elucidate underlying physical and psychological processes in normal aging.

DEVELOPMENTAL MODELS OF AGING

The process of aging in late life has been discussed by a number of authors and from a variety of conceptual and theoretical perspectives. These efforts have included focusing on theoretical conceptualizations, such as activity level, disengagement, abandonment, role involvement, and socioenvironmental influences (see Fry, 1992 for a general summary of these and other social theories of aging). These theoretical propositions differ with respect to their empirical support and direct use for counseling psychologists working with older adults. However, given that aging is a universal process, a theoretical model for professional practice with the aged should be flexible enough to allow for cultural variations, while at the same time provide a framework for understanding biological, social, and intrapersonal changes that are a predictable part of the aging experience. In addition, such a model should be practical enough to guide the development of remedial, preventive, and educative interventions that are distinguishing features of counseling psychology (see Gelso & Fretz, 1992).

In this section, two models of normal aging are presented that have direct bearing on the development of an approach to professional practice that is grounded in principles associated with counseling psychology. These are Paul Baltes's Selective Optimization with Compensation Theory (Baltes, 1987, 1993, 1997; Baltes, Dittmann-Kohli, & Dixon, 1984; Baltes, Staudinger, & Lindenberger, 1999) and Robert Atchley's Continuity Theory (Atchley, 1989, 1992, 1997). Both of these conceptual models address real-world issues facing older adults and have been supported by empirical research.

Selection, Optimization, and Compensation

Selection, optimization, and compensation (SOC) is a general theoretical framework for human development, described as a metatheory by P.B. Baltes (1997). It borrows heavily from concepts in human abilities research that have elucidated a two-process model of intellectual function: crystallized and fluid intelligence (Horn, 1968, 1978, 1982; Horn & Cattell, 1966). Crystallized intelligence is reflected in mental abilities that depend on sociocultural influences such as formal schooling or learning due to informal exposure to one's culture (e.g., reading, interacting with people). Components of crystallized intelligence are exemplified by vocabulary ability and language usage, as well as the retrieval, integration, and synthesis of factual knowledge. On the other hand, fluid intelligence reflects processes that are inherent within the individual and that are postulated to operate independently of acculturation. Fluid intelligence is commonly quantified through novel tasks designed to measure processing speed, reaction time, working memory, and pattern recognition, as well as perception of simple and complex relationships. The predominance of developmental research that has examined these two forms of intelligence in adulthood has consistently found that they are differentially affected by aging. Much of the early research reported that crystallized intelligence was relatively stable in adulthood and old age, whereas fluid intelligence tended to decline progressively with advancing age (Horn & Donaldson, 1976; Rabbitt, 1993; Salthouse, 1991). More recent research assessing very old cohorts has documented that even crystallized intelligence may show measurable age-related declines as early as 65 years of age (Giambra et al., 1995).

Baltes's reconceptualization of these constructs reflects two fundamental expansions of the fluid/crystallized dichotomy of human abilities across the life span: the two-process model extends beyond intellectual functioning to encompass the broader domain of adaptation, and these two processes may interact with one another, inasmuch as stability in crystallized processes may compensate for age-related losses in fluid processes.

To set his theory apart from the human abilities literature, P.B. Baltes (1997) relabeled the components of his two-process categorization scheme as crystallized pragmatics and fluid mechanics. Baltes describes these processes as follows:

> Using a computer metaphor, one can conceptualize the fluid mechanics as reflecting the neurophysiological "hardware" or cognitive primitives of the human brain as it was shaped by biocultural evolution . . . crystallized cognitive pragmatics can be understood as the culture-based "software" of the mind. They reflect the bodies of knowledge and information that cultures provide in the form of factual and procedural knowledge about the world, human affairs, socialization, and human agency. (p. 373)

A central feature of Baltes's model is that although there is inevitable decline across the life course, learning continues to occur throughout adulthood and even into very old age. This life span learning capacity is labeled as "plasticity" or the unused "reserve" capacity that is engaged when a person is confronted with a novel learning situation. The ability to change cognitive capability through plasticity interventions has been documented in a series of studies where older adults have improved their memory performance in response to systematic and intensive mnemonic strategy training (Kliegl, Smith, & Baltes, 1989, 1990). Even in these instances, however, older adults still perform substantially less well than skilled younger adults, with distributions of scores of younger and older subjects on standard memory training tasks often showing little or no performance overlap (P.B. Baltes & Kliegl, 1992). In other words, as long as there is some reserve capacity in fluid mechanics, there may be selective improvement in old age on some abilities. Pathological conditions, such as dementia, often are characterized by severe restrictions in plasticity, and it may be that variations across individuals on this latent variable could distinguish between normative and pathological processes in age-related decline (M.M. Baltes, Kuhl, Gutzmann, & Sowarka, 1995).

P.B. Baltes (1997) has noted that the decomposition of the "life span architecture" is not limited to physical function, but includes psychological and cultural processes as well. Although his conceptualization of inevitable decline is a relatively pessimistic view of aging, it is indeed a well-established fact that the ultimate end of the aging process is death, a normative process of complete decomposition (McCue, 1995). Although there is great variability among individuals in this process, the overall balance of developmental gains and losses inevitably shifts toward the loss side of the ledger in very late life.

A somewhat different picture has emerged, however, from an innovative series of studies by Baltes and his colleagues at the Max Planck Institute on the impact of crystallized culture-based pragmatics on intellectual functioning in old age (P.B. Baltes, 1993; P.B. Baltes, Lindenberger, & Staudinger, 1995; P.B. Baltes & Staudinger, 1993). In these studies, operational definitions of "wisdom" were developed, a construct related to factual and procedural knowledge that flows from sociocultural experience. In contrast to working memory and processing speed, performance curves of subject responses to wisdom tasks did not decline precipitously with advancing age but remained relatively level into the 70- and 80-year-old age range. An important generalization from this research is that, to a degree as yet unknown, crystallized culture-based pragmatics can offset, partially, the inevitable declines associated with biologically based fluid mechanics. As Baltes succinctly stated, "Better software can lead to higher performance even if the hardware is of lesser quality" (P.B. Baltes, 1993, p. 582). More information will be presented about the importance of "wisdom" as an acquired, meaning-based adaptive skill in older age in a later section of the chapter.

P.B. Baltes (1997) has identified three adaptive processes, *selection, optimization,* and *compensation* that are applicable across the life span and that older adults engage in to deal with the pervasive effects of age-related decline. These processes contribute to the high degree of individual variability in old age, particularly with regard to psychological and cognitive functioning. *Selection* refers to the processes by which individuals become more discriminatory in their choice of activities on which to expend time and energy. For example, it is well documented that in advanced age older adults tend to alter their overall social network and focus on relationships that are perceived to have higher potential satisfaction and value, such as with family and close relatives (Lansford, Sherman, & Antonucci, 1998; van Tilburg, 1998). Freund and Baltes (1998) have further decomposed the concept of selection into *elective selection* or *loss-based selection*. Elective selection involves life span regulative processes that are involved in selecting from a pool of alternative developmental pathways to maximize adaptation. In contrast, loss-based selection involves responses that are designed specifically to address the decline (or loss) of previously available capabilities. The goal of selection in this regard is to maximize adaptation by minimizing the complexity of options associated with a specific life task (e.g., simplifying one's finances to make them more manageable).

Optimization refers to processes by which individuals, including older persons, develop increased functional efficacy via learning, practice, and experience. A considerable body of research has focused on developmental processes of optimization through models of education and learning that are specific to older adults (Jenkins, 1979; Willis, 1985). Finally, *compensation* is the conscious effort employed to mitigate limitations and losses in functional ability associated with the aging process. Lifelong learning and cultural support facilitate the individual's strategic use of these three strategies, and it is noteworthy that the underlying processes are influenced by individual difference factors, such as educational level, intellectual capacity, and culture (Hill, Wahlin, Winblad, & Bäckman, 1995).

P.B. Baltes et al. (1999) provide an excellent example of how adaptation in normal aging involves the interaction of these processes. This example may also help to elucidate further the relative role of each component process within this larger synergistic phenomenon.

> When the concert pianist Arthur Rubinstein, as an 80-year-old, was asked in a television interview how he managed to maintain such a high level of expert piano playing, he hinted. . . . First, he played fewer pieces *(selection)*; he practiced these pieces more often *(optimization)*; and to conteract his loss in mechanical speed he now used a kind of impression management, such as playing more slowly before fast segments to make the latter appear faster *(compensation)*. (pp. 483–484)

This example highlights the superordinate premise that the components of SOC generally focus on facilitating personal agency and helping individuals to maintain or regain control over important aspects of their lives that may be compromised due to age-related declines. This premise is critical in the development of interventions in normal aging (and some aspects of pathological aging) because research has documented a positive relationship between a sense of personal control and quality of life in community as well as institutional contexts (Langer & Rodin, 1976; J. Rodin, 1986; J. Rodin & McAvay, 1992). SOC may represent a concrete articulation of specific mechanisms by which personal control is preserved across the adult life span and especially in old age where absolute functional capacity is diminished.

Throughout this chapter, SOC will be used as guiding principles underlying intervention approaches tailored to issues in normal aging. It is important to note that these constructs are consistent with the remedial, educative, and preventive roles that Gelso and Fretz (1992) recommend for counseling psychologists who intervene with adult developmental issues across the life span.

Continuity Theory

Continuity theory is a generic social-psychological theory of aging based on the premise that the sense of identity in older individuals is influenced substantially by how they perceive themselves in changing contexts and the extent to which altered circumstances influence their view of themselves. Continuity theory views enduring individual characteristics and external events or contexts as modifiers of personal change. Atchley (1989) summarized the theory as follows:

> Continuity Theory holds that, in making adaptive choices, middle-aged and older adults attempt to preserve and maintain existing internal and external structures, and they prefer to accomplish this objective by using strategies tied to their past experiences of themselves and their social world. Change is linked to the person's perceived past, producing continuity in inner psychological characteristics as well as in social behavior and in social circumstances. Continuity is thus a grand adaptive strategy that is promoted by both individual preference and social approval. . . . In middle and later life, adults are drawn by the weight of past experience to use continuity as a primary adaptive strategy for dealing with changes associated with normal aging. (p. 183)

Atchley distinguished between internal and external continuity. Internal continuity involves the extent to which the inner structures and processes of the person guide adaptation. In this regard, such characteristics as temperament, emotional lability, and personal energy tend to dictate adaptation or predict the degree of change that a person is able to make in a new context. Atchley (1989) noted that "[i]nternal continuity is a healthy capacity to see inner change as connected to the individual's past and to see the individual's past as sustaining and supporting and justifying the new self" (p. 184). External continuity, on the other hand, represents the extent to which the societal structures (e.g, one's social circle, cultural group, family, coworkers) influence the self by interacting with one's internal identity. Atchley explained, "Continuity of activities, skills, and environments [external continuity] is a logical result of . . . optimum satisfaction from life" (p. 184).

Both these sources of continuity work to stabilize one's sense of self and limit the extent to which change is possible. Thus, in the latter half of the adult life span internal and external continuity will be powerful moderating factors in determining how older adults approach new tasks in a familiar context (e.g., managing the household following the death of a spouse), adapt to a changing context (e.g., moving to a retirement community), or deal with personal challenges to the self that are part of the aging process (e.g., age-related disability).

This theory has strong use for counseling interventions in that it is based on the premise that individuals are not different fundamentally in old age from earlier points in the life cycle, and each person can be understood using developmental themes that are stable or invariant within the individual across the life span. This premise is supported by research that has documented the stability of individual characteristics, including personality style (Costa & McCrae, 1980, 1992), cognitive stylistics (Shapiro, 1965), and vocational and personal interests (Hansen, 1984). Counseling strategies that have been effective in helping to maintain well-being in old age, such as life review (Gatz et al., 1998), are based on principles of internal continuity, or maintaining a consistent sense of self in the face of age-related change.

FUNDAMENTAL CONCEPTS TO CONSIDER

Several fundamental concepts emerge that are important for building an approach to counseling tailored to fit problems and issues prominent in normal and even in pathological aging. We believe these concepts can be generalized across age cohort, sex, ethnic, and socioeconomic groups.

1. Aging involves normative developmental processes that are inherently destructive, but despite its inevitability, decline can be buffered by cultural factors.
2. Individuals cope with a wide variety of issues in older age. Coping is influenced by lifelong adaptive or maladaptive styles that involve intra- and interpersonal factors.
3. Change is critical in optimal adaptation to age-related problems and issues, and the nature of adaptation is influenced by characteristics of the individual and their social context.
4. Aging is associated with a set of acquired characteristics (e.g., wisdom, spirituality) that exert a stabilizing influence in the presence of age-related decline, and "successful aging" is associated with the cultivation of these qualities.

The Role of Age-Related Decline

Most issues facing older adults are associated with age-related decline. Noteworthy in the three vignettes presented earlier are issues of loss, including cognitive decline, deterioration of a meaningful relationship, and termination of a long-time job. In Table 16.1 these losses are included as part of a larger constellation of late-life issues classified according to whether they are normative or nonnormative and intra- or interpersonal. This list of issues is not exhaustive, but represents examples of common challenges facing older adults. For a more complete treatment of problems and issues of loss facing older adults, readers may consult Birren and Schaie (1996), Nordhus et al. (1998), and Carstensen et al. (1996).

Table 16.1   Issues Facing Older Adults

Intrapersonal	Cognitive loss	Alzheimer's disease
	Diminished stamina and dexterity	Cardiovascular disease
	Diminished sensory functioning	Arthritis
		Osteoporosis
		Stroke
Interpersonal	Caregiving of a parent	Divorce
	Maintaining friendships	Death of a child
	Retirement from work	Death of a younger sibling
	Death of a spouse (if female)	

Division of such issues into a 2 × 2 taxonomy may seem to oversimplify the wide array of problems and concerns that are part of the aging experience. However, this kind of schema can focus attention clearly on critical aspects of the aging experience that have great likelihood of enhancing quality of life. In the first vignette, with regard to Jim's concern that he might be in the early stages of Alzheimer's disease, the overriding issue is not the symptoms per se, but what they may mean in predicting Jim's future functioning. Helping Jim assess the qualitative nature of his experienced loss (e.g., distinguishing between what is normal memory loss in older age versus what is nonnormative loss due to disease) is an important first step in any effective intervention strategy (American Psychological Association, 1998).

Addressing initial issues of loss is paramount for building working relationships with older clients. Although it may seem unduly pessimistic to point out to an older client that cognitive loss in later life is a normal and expected process, knowing one's "baseline" capability, adjusted for age, helps to challenge the faulty assumption that any cognitive loss is due to disease processes. In fact, Alzheimer's disease, resulting in nonnormative cognitive loss, affects only 4% to 8% of the overall population of individuals aged 65 years and older (American Psychiatric Association, 1994; American Psychological Association, 1998; Raskind & Peskin, 1992).

Counseling psychologists working with older adults need to understand the kind of developmental loss that would be considered "normative" in old and very old age, as well as an estimated time interval when an individual might face such issues. A client, for example, who has concerns about caring for parents may benefit from knowing that decrements in memory are encountered frequently by older adults sometime between the ages of 50 and 70 years (Ostrosky-Solis, Jaime, & Ardila, 1998). Expecting such events to occur can help individuals develop anticipatory strategies to minimize negative impacts on them and their families.

The concept of age-related decline is seen most clearly in the experience of dying, which was described earlier as a normative process (McCue, 1995). Although physical death in old age often results from disease, the actual event is best viewed as a normal end state of very late life (Hill, Packard, & Lund, 1996; Ingebretsen & Solem, 1998).

Conceptualizing issues as intra- or interpersonal in nature raises the question of how much individual control one can have over problems associated with aging. In the first vignette, loss of cognitive function is primarily an individual issue, but it may also affect others. This is also the case in the third vignette where a long-term job is lost either through planned or unplanned processes. Such experiences most directly affect the aging individual, but there also may be indirect effects on the family system (e.g., loss of income may change the family's socioeconomic status).

Conversely, issues that are primarily interpersonal, such as Juanita's caring for a cognitively impaired spouse in the second vignette, may have interpersonal effects on the identified caregiver. In this regard, the caregiver's capacity to cope with the problem may be influenced by multiple intrapersonal factors such as the care receiver's mental or physical condition, or the premorbid relationship that the caregiver had with the care receiver (Cavanaugh, 1998). Identifying such factors for the caregiver, and in some instances the care receiver, will help to normalize some of the personal burdens that the caregiver will inevitably experience (Query & Flint, 1996; Robinson & Thurnher, 1979).

An important factor in conceptualizing and intervening in age-related issues or problems is the role of culture. The second vignette portrays a Hispanic woman who is caring for her elderly husband, and as noted in the vignette, church and family play large roles in guiding the caregiver's decisions about her future and the future of her spouse. It is critical that the counselor work to incorporate the unique characteristics of the older individual in relation to the issue of concern, as well as demonstrating sensitivity to the individual's cultural context. For example, to address Juanita's concerns adequately, the counselor may need to seek out additional information about the culture and traditions of this family system. It is likely that Juanita's dilemma can be addressed more effectively through culturally appropriate means, including, for example, collaborative meetings between local church leaders and the family. In this example, relevant literature sources, such as Atkinson and Hackett (1997), Daley, Applewhite, and Jorquez (1989), and Torres-Gil (1987), may aid the counselor in understanding the various cultural issues associated with caregiving.

The Role of Continuity

In this section, specific aspects of Atchley's (1989) continuity theory are highlighted that are central to the model we are suggesting for counseling older adults. The basic assumptions of this model include (a) adult identity as relatively consistent and stable across the life span, (b) older adults acting in ways that are consistent and reaffirming of their identity, and (c) older adults, more than other age groups, using past experiences to address current issues and problems.

Although there have been numerous studies documenting the stability of adult personality characteristics over time (McCrae & Costa, 1990, 1991, 1994), Atchley's theoretical proposition of continuity in adult life span development provides a heuristic vehicle for translating these concepts into intervention strategies for working with older adults. In response to a major contribution in *The Counseling Psychologist* by Fry (1992), Atchley noted:

> What promotes life satisfaction [in older age]? There is substantial support for the idea that life satisfaction is enhanced if aging people can continue the expression of lifelong values in familiar relationships and environments. Thus continuity theory offers a framework that can be used to discover how each person has historically produced life satisfaction for her/himself. It also provides clues to what sorts of changes might threaten the life satisfaction of a person. (p. 339)

This statement suggests that individual coping with the wide array of issues of old age is the product of the person's long-term adaptive style and involves both intra- and interpersonal factors. This highlights the role of long-standing characteristics and traits that are an integrated part of the individual, and the interaction of such individual traits with the immediate and extended family system. In other words, coping in old age generally involves accessing intra- or interpersonal resources that already exist as part of the earlier adult coping repertoire.

For counseling psychologists who work with older adults, developing treatment plans that focus on helping older clients actualize their existing coping repertoires to address specific problems likely will be more helpful than approaches that require the older adult to establish new mind-sets or use new approaches to problem solving (Brammer & Abrego, 1981; Smyer, 1984). This is not to say that older clients will not benefit from new ideas or treatment recommendations. However, maximizing the probability that counseling interventions will be perceived as useful requires a thorough understanding of the older client's developmental history and sensitivity as to whether the strategies will be perceived as consistent with the client's identity.

In the third vignette, John views himself as career-obsolete because of his age. However, he likely has acquired characteristics from his life experiences, including a stable sense of self (e.g., likes, dislikes, needs, preferences, personal strengths, and mastery of life tasks) that may be used in helping him access coping strategies for dealing with his job loss. For example, one task of the counselor may be to help John reframe the search for work as an opportunity to find employment that better fits his enduring sense of self. Such a model of counseling has been described in detail by Brammer and Abrego (1981) for developing skills to cope with normative transitions in middle adulthood. Their model has direct application for working with older adults facing career transition issues, such as job loss or retirement.

The Role of Change

As discussed, a sense of consistency is critical in helping older adults manage issues related to changing internal and external contexts. However, the notion of change is essential in balancing stability with needs for adaptation, personal growth, and self-improvement (Mahoney, 1991). This does not mean that older persons are not capable of making large changes with respect to their lifestyle behaviors and patterns; however, there are several aspects of the change process that may differentiate older from younger adults. For example, there is empirical support for the assumption in continuity theory that stable internal structures are more difficult to alter in old age (Atchley, 1989). Further, controlled interventions have documented the role of age-related processes in diminishing plasticity or learning potential in old age (P.B. Baltes, Dittmann-Kohli, & Kliegl, 1986; Lindenberger, Mayr, & Kliegel, 1993).

The counseling and clinical literature also has documented that adaptive attitudes and behaviors may no longer suffice, but previously useful behaviors practiced over longer time intervals are more resistant to change (see Schlossberg, 1981; Smyer, 1984). This is also documented amply by aversive health-related lifestyle behaviors, such as cigarette smoking and alcohol abuse, that have been shown to be highly resistant to change in older age (Ganzini & Atkinson, 1996; Hill, Campbell, Thomas, & Soo-Tho, 1998). In addition, as behavioral routines are rehearsed repeatedly over long periods of time, they become connected to a larger set of values and beliefs that form the underlying identity of the individual (Castro, Newcomb, McCreary, & Baezconde-Garbanati, 1989). This is demonstrated by instances in which adaptive behavior that was maintained in one context continues in a new context, even though its use may no longer exist.

Consistent across all age groups is the psychological reality that stable change usually occurs in small steps. Mahoney (1991) noted that "significant psychological change is rarely easy or rapid" (p. 283). With regard to older adults, the magnitude of change, in absolute terms, may be constrained substantially by the individual's relational and intrapersonal context. The qualitative nature of change may also be different for older adults, thus highlighting the development of a rationale for change, as well as the practice of involving the older individual's mature system of values and beliefs, especially those that have been supported throughout the life span (i.e., one's sense of internal continuity). Stated practically, the reason for change must be compelling enough to the older client that the client is willing to risk changing long-standing beliefs and values that have been a source of security and well-being in the past.

Change associated with inevitable decline is an integral part of aging. Although biological change is an undisputed reality in late adulthood, it is insufficient in and of itself to portray accurately the individual's experience of growing old. Smyer (1984) has noted that aging is multidimensional and can be conceptualized best by considering interactions among biological, personal/psychological, physical/environmental, and social/cultural processes that underlie individual differences in the aging individual. He noted that "while it is assumed that development continues throughout the life span, the pace of development varies across individuals, and within the same individual, different biological and psychological systems or functions age at different rates" (p. 25). Even though the aging process is biologically destructive, it is overly simplistic to stereotype aging as homogeneous decline. What is critical is the wide variations in individual differences in biological aging. For example, it is well known that individuals tend to live longer if they come from higher socioeconomic strata, are better educated, and have easier access to medical care (Takamura, 1998; Worldwatch Institute, 1994). Some research suggests that education may have a preventive effect on the emergence and course of degenerative disease states such as dementia (Mortimer & Graves, 1993). These sociocultural factors are just a few of the many variables that play a prominent role in the nature and the course of aging in any given individual.

Rowe and Kahn (1987) coined the term "successful aging" to highlight that some individual differences in the aging process may be associated with nonloss or gains when compared with the average or "usual" individual. For example, through exercise some may show gains in physical endurance in comparison to the typical loss experienced by the average adult in the same age cohort who does not exercise (Stones & Kozma, 1996). What this concept implies is that older adults not only differ with regard to aging, but are able to influence the aging process themselves. Such potential is an example of the concept of plasticity that was discussed in an earlier section of the chapter (P.B. Baltes, 1993; P.B. Baltes & Baltes, 1980) and, as implied by Mahoney (1991), the flexibility to alter the negative progression of aging through cultural, social, and economic factors adds to our uniqueness as human beings.

Meaning-Based Characteristics of Successful Aging

In their well-known MacArthur Foundation studies of aging, Rowe and Kahn (1998) drew several important thematic conclusions about the defining characteristics of successful aging: "If successful aging is to be more than the imitation of youth, however, we must also ask whether there are valued human attributes that increase with age, or that might do so under appropriate conditions of opportunity and encouragement" (p. 139).

This passage suggests that successful aging is associated with a set of acquired personal characteristics that exert a stabilizing influence on individuals in the presence of age-related decline. These characteristics are a highly personalized part of the fully developed self and are commonly identified by such terms as wisdom (Sternberg, 1990), self-actualization (Maslow, 1968), and spirituality (Worthington, 1989). It is important to note that although such attributes are personal in nature, they also are associated with the ability to integrate experiences across the life span into a comprehensive understanding about how to function effectively and meaningfully in the world. Because much of the empirical literature examining characteristics of successful aging has focused on wisdom, this section elaborates this construct and explores relationships between wisdom and successful adaptation to age-related change.

Despite the fact that researchers have developed elaborate definitions of what wisdom entails (see P.B. Baltes, 1993; P.B. Baltes & Smith, 1990; Clayton & Birren, 1980; Holliday & Chandler, 1986; Orwoll & Perlmutter, 1992; Sternberg, 1990) or is not (Meacham, 1992), it remains an elusive and difficult construct to define. Most existing knowledge about wisdom comes from examining implicit conceptualizations of what it means to be "wise." For example, Holliday and Chandler asked a wide range of people of all ages to nominate individuals who they considered wise and to generate descriptors of their nominees. The descriptions then were compared with terms extracted from the literature to yield a set of distinctive characteristics of wisdom, including (1) exceptional understanding (e.g., seeing things within a larger context); (2) superior judgment (e.g., thinking carefully before deciding); (3) general competence (e.g., curious, intelligent); (4) interpersonal skills (e.g., fair, reliable, mature); and (5) social unobtrusiveness (e.g., discreet, nonjudgmental). A noteworthy characteristic of individuals nominated as wise was that, for the most part, they were older than the nominators themselves, a finding that supported the researchers' postulated relationship between positive aging and wisdom.

In a related vein, P.B. Baltes, Staudinger, Maercker, and Smith (1995) defined wisdom as a set of complex skills for dealing with problems in everyday living and as "expert-levels of performance in the fundamental pragmatics of life" (P.B. Baltes, Staudinger, et al., 1995, p. 155). An implicit assumption of this conceptualization is that wisdom is manifested most fully in old age and can be acquired through actively developing skills in the planning, conduct, and interpretation of life. To test their assumption, the researchers identified "wise" individuals through a nomination procedure and asked them to respond to two standardized vignettes designed to test for wisdom-related skills (Staudinger, Smith, & Baltes, 1994). One vignette portrayed a life-planning issue (a woman attempting to reconcile conflict between her desire to begin a late-life career and her family responsibilities) and an existential life crisis (the threat of suicide by a friend who was despondent over the meaninglessness of life). P.B. Baltes, Staudinger, et al. also attempted to control for the relative effects of age by recruiting a young and old control group of individuals of similar socioeconomic status. They also controlled for wisdom-related knowledge by recruiting an older group of clinical psychologists who, as a professional group, were predicted to perform very highly on these two tasks. Individuals nominated for their wisdom outperformed the young and old control groups on both tasks. Their performance also was equal to the older clinical psychologists. Thus, P.B. Baltes, Staudinger, et al. concluded that (1) unlike physiological processes and cognitive functions that deteriorate with age, wisdom does not appear to decline but may be enhanced in some individuals as a consequence of the aging process; (2) there are specific life span conditions that facilitate the development of wisdom; and (3) it may be possible to identify specific skills that are markers of wisdom and amenable to training.

From this and related studies (Sternberg, 1990), several identifying characteristics of wisdom have been noted consistently. Specifically, wisdom can be defined as exceptional understanding and judgment, combined with superior ability to use such processes in competent ways and to communicate to others the hypotheses and conclusions reached. With regard to late-life adaptation, Labouvie-Vief (1992) noted that wisdom is the ability to integrate life experiences with rational thought in ways that facilitate an approach to life that may have adaptive advantages in coping with age-related change.

Thus, unlike the pessimistic view of age-related decline previously discussed, what is suggested here is the possibility that for some individuals aging may facilitate the acquisition of attributes that can increase the individual's capacity to cope in old and very old age. P.B. Baltes et al. (1995) noted that wisdom is a core construct that provides "insights into the quintessential aspects of the human condition and human life, including its biological finititude, cultural conditioning, and interindividual variations. At the center of this body of knowledge and its application are questions concerning the conduct, interpretation, and meaning of life" (p. 155).

Most research suggests that wisdom is more prevalent in older than in younger adults, even though there is much variability across individuals (P.B. Baltes & Staudinger, 1993). Although the ability to be wise is related to a number of factors, including intelligence and creativity (Sternberg, 1985), wisdom is a broad construct that is activated in situations requiring the management of existential issues of meaning, suffering, life, and death. Although research has not conceptualized wisdom as a member of a broader collection of maturationally based constructs, such as spirituality and self-actualization, for the purposes of this chapter these concepts are viewed as having a number of common features. They tend to develop as a part of the aging process, and include specific abilities that enhance coping with many negative aspects of aging. They can also be used to process problems of everyday living across the life span.

A body of research has identified spirituality as another important life span maturational construct that can be a core feature of internal continuity (Atchley, 1997). Although the elucidation of a spirituality construct that can be validated and used to assess quality of life or coping has been problematic (see Ellison, 1994; Weiland, 1995; Worthington, 1989), spirituality has been found to be a dynamic life span phenomenon. Intrinsic aspects of religiosity, such as one's personal convictions and internal belief structures, have been found to be positively associated with optimal mental health (Bergin, 1983; Bergin, Masters, & Richards, 1987). Within counseling psychology, Worthington has perhaps best articulated a life span view of the development and maintenance of religious values and beliefs. A central feature of his conceptualization is the integral role that religiosity plays in both normative and idiosyncratic life transitions. Using this conceptualization, Worthington highlighted a number of life span issues that might benefit from spirituality-based counseling, including dealing with death, sexuality, alcohol and drug abuse, career issues, interpersonal relationships, and parenting. Recent research has focused on examining the efficacy of counseling strategies that involve salient aspects of religiosity, such as hope and forgiveness, to address life span developmental issues (McCullough, Worthington, & Rachal, 1997; Worthington et al., 1997).

Thus, when working with older adults, it may be useful to identify such maturational characteristics to understand more fully how an individual may cope with the realities of aging. In the third vignette, John is unexpectedly released from his long-term job. His initial response to this loss is to focus narrowly on the job itself and his altered sense of meaning as a former employee. In John's words, "I'm discouraged because who is going to hire an old man when there are 10 younger and more up-to-date people looking for the same jobs? I was counting on this job to get me to retirement." The benefits counselor provided several suggestions that all were focused on helping John secure new employment as soon as possible. Although these suggestions may have some value, accessing larger meaning-based processes may encourage John to reinterpret his job loss in a way facilitative of more optimal long-term adjustment. For example, allowing John to explore more deeply his conceptualization of retirement may help him reframe his job loss as a transition to activities potentially more fulfilling given his relative stage in life.

This kind of approach to career counseling has been highlighted in a series of studies examining the importance of stable intraindividual constructs (e.g., personality factors, lifelong goals, relational structures, religiosity) in predicting optimal adjustment to late-life career transitions such as retirement (see Payne, Robbins, & Dougherty, 1991; Robbins, Lee, & Wan, 1994). From such research, it could be postulated that simply engaging in a job search without a life span oriented self-evaluation process may exacerbate disillusionment about the relationship between work and other activities that John may value as he progresses into old and very old age (e.g., family, other meaningful personal relationships, self-enhancement activities).

A GENERAL FRAMEWORK

The fundamental principles presented are critical in understanding the aging process and in developing meaningful counseling interventions tailored to older adults. Atchley (1992) noted that although continuity theory can explain the processes of normative psychosocial adaptation in late life, it also can be useful for designing counseling strategies for maintaining a sense of cohesiveness in the face of change due to unexpected discontinuities, such as disease or unanticipated economic change (e.g., job loss). Baltes's selective optimization with compensation theory provides a framework not only for understanding adult cognitive functioning during later years, but also the management of a range of developmental events in late life (Freund & Baltes, 1998). Integrating these theories with the defining principles of counseling psychology can produce a general framework for counseling psychologists' conceptualization of late life issues, as well as a practical guide for intervening with older adults.

Major Themes

A first step in developing a framework tailored to issues of older adulthood, and grounded in principles of counseling psychology, is to review the distinguishing features of counseling psychology described by Gelso and Fretz (1992). These features are both philosophical and practice oriented and, for the most part, are consistent with the developmental theories presented earlier.

Gelso and Fretz's first major theme states that counseling psychology approaches personal change from a normative, nonpathological perspective. Smyer (1984) highlighted this concept as follows: "Often, the counselor's initial task is to assist the older client in differentiating the normal aging process from pathological or abnormal processes" (p. 25). This concept also was elaborated earlier as a central feature of the theory of selective optimization with compensation as it relates to older age. Tailoring this nonpathological theme to older adults requires redefining normative processes in terms of the extent to which optimization is possible. Stated in more practical terms, a 60-year-old marathon runner cannot maintain the same objective race times she achieved when 25 years of age; however, it still may be possible to have the fastest marathon time among her peers in a 60-year-old age-cohort.

A second major theme highlighted by Gelso and Fretz (1992) is the idea that counseling psychologists focus on strengths and personal assets. With respect to older adults, this means using previously developed positive coping skills to address predictable, and even unpredictable, issues that arise as part of the aging process. This "strength" theme is a central feature of continuity theory as Atchley (1992) noted:

> The main difference between older clients and younger ones is that the older clients often come with a stronger sense of what coping strategy has worked well for them in the past, and if that approach is no longer working, then the counselor may want to deal first with why strict continuity is not adaptive in the current situation. (pp. 339–340)

Inherent in this theme is the notion that it may be possible to access meaning-based maturational characteristics (e.g., wisdom, spirituality) as an integral part of coping. This may be as simple as providing a context for the individual to explore a problematic issue within the framework of these processes as suggested by Worthington (1989). It also may be as proactive as identifying characteristics that may be brought to bear on new issues (e.g., the capacity to forgive others) and encouraging older clients to use their strengths in addressing problems (e.g., reconciling negative memories of a recently deceased spouse).

A third theme from Gelso and Fretz (1992) is the perspective that emphasizes person-environment interactions rather than an exclusive focus on either the person or the environment. Individuals are intertwined inextricably with their sociocultural environment and must be understood in this context. This concept is a fundamental premise of SOC theory, and for this reason can be important in developing a framework for counseling older adults. Smyer (1984) proposed a counseling model for older adults that involves examining stressors in later life related to changes in physical functioning and in the sociocultural context as well. He presented a range of age-related problems that often are viewed from a single perspective (e.g., sleep disturbance in old age) and recommended ways to address these issues more completely by using a broader, multidimensional paradigm of adaptation and coping consistent with the themes noted earlier.

Conceptualizing older adults from holistic perspectives and avoiding stereotypic notions (e.g., "to be old is to be physically sick"; Rowe & Kahn, 1998) has the potential of being viewed by older adults as more relevant and meaningful. In their review of outcome research with older adults, Wellman and McCormack (1984) noted the importance of using a multidisciplinary team counseling approach. This notion is consistent with viewing older adult issues from a person-environment perspective.

Interventions that focus on helping older adults increase their sense of personal control through either altering external conditions that limit personal control or maximizing their sense of control through use of SOC principles have great potential for enhancing quality of life in old age. A powerful example of such an intervention was demonstrated in an early study conducted by Langer and Rodin (1976), who altered a floor of a nursing home to maximize the extent to which individual residents on the floor could take responsibility for their care. Residents in this "in-creased-responsibility" group reported that they felt happier and were more active than those in the comparison control floor at posttesting and after three weeks. In a follow-up study, R. Rodin and Langer (1977) noted that this enhanced sense of well-being among the residents on the "increased responsibility" floor remained after 18 months. Given the benefits of such an intervention in nursing home residents for enhancing the quality of life, it is our contention that the role of personal control for facilitating well-being in normal aging may be enormous.

The Role of the Counseling Psychologist

The themes described in this chapter may be applied broadly to the remedial, preventive, and educative or developmental professional roles of counseling psychologists enumerated by Gelso and Fretz (1992). The next section describes how counseling psychologists can use these roles in intervening with older adults.

The Remedial Counseling Role

This role involves assisting older individuals or groups with the resolution of problems that have resulted from impaired functioning. With the knowledge that decline is part of normal aging but can be moderated to some extent through compensation and optimization, the concept of remediation takes on relativistic meaning. For example, research indicates that cognitive functioning, particularly episodic memory performance, declines in old age (Kausler, 1994; Salthouse, 1991). For the individual who is experiencing age-associated memory impairment, encoding and recall strategies that were employed as a younger person (e.g., rapid repetition of information) may not be an effective compensation strategy. Thus, it becomes critical to search for solutions that can optimize performance in a declining system. For example, writing information down (e.g., making a shopping list, recording appointments in a day planner) may compensate for the heavy burden of encoding and retrieving large amounts of data that are accessed only infrequently (see Intons-Peterson & Newsome, 1992). However, for information that cannot be accessed from written material such as names and faces and personal identification numbers, older adults may benefit from learning mnemonic strategies that facilitate encoding and retrieval (Intons-Peterson & Newsome, 1992; Plude & Schwartz, 1996; Yesavage, Lapp, & Sheikh, 1989).

The Preventive Counseling Role

This role involves anticipating potential problems and intervening to eliminate or minimize their occurrence in the future. Preventive interventions may involve imparting information in advance of an issue (e.g., preparing a living will) that helps to guide choices before the issue of concern arises. An excellent example of a preventive intervention is helping very old adults create safer living spaces to deal with predictable future mobility impairments (Sterns & Camp, 1998). This is highlighted by research examining the wide range of technologies, such as handheld environmental control units (e.g., light dimmers or remote VCR and television controls), in aiding performance and minimizing accidents associated with everyday tasks in the home. This research also suggests that technologies can help to extend functional independence into very advanced age (Czaja, 1997). For example, memory for prescription taking in older adults has been improved by converting text-based medication regimens (commonly found on pill bottles) to pictorial or iconic images (Morrell, Park, & Poon, 1989). This strategy has been shown to improve adherence to medication regimens in older adults by capitalizing on spatial memory processes that are more resistant to age-related decline than is verbal memory (Park, Puglisi, & Smith, 1986).

Preventive interventions involve (1) helping older clients identify conditions or situations that hinder the successful negotiation of important everyday tasks (e.g., moving around the house); (2) collaborating with clients in developing realistic strategies to deal with identified conditions or situations (e.g., the reorganization of furniture); and (3) dealing with psychological barriers that impede effective functioning (e.g., "Moving my furniture around so I won't fall is a sign that I am becoming more dependent."). Psychological barriers often arise around complex tasks, such as driving an automobile, that are connected to an individual's internal sense of continuity (e.g., independence), where the action itself has become dangerous because of sensory, motor, or cognitive deficits associated with advanced aging (Persson, 1993; Sterns & Camp, 1998).

The Educative and Developmental Counseling Role

This role includes interventions that are meant to provide skills that build resistance to maladaptive functioning. As noted by Gelso and Fretz (1992, p. 6), "the distinction between the developmental and preventive roles is often subtle—a matter of degree rather than kind." With regard to age-related education, it is important for counseling psychologists to provide relevant information to help older adults understand issues that arise as a consequence of the aging experience. As highlighted in the first vignette, John is concerned that his memory loss is due to Alzheimer's disease. In assessing John's cognitive performance, the counselor can explain the etiology and progressive nature of Alzheimer's disease. This may help to reassure John that his condition likely is not due to a degenerative disease, while at the same time educating him about more valid warning signs of Alzheimer's disease. Therefore, in addition to reducing current anxiety that his memory loss is a symptom of disease, education about the nature of Alzheimer's disease may also decrease the possibility that John will erroneously interpret normal memory lapses in the future.

The three basic counseling roles noted above are not mutually exclusive when working with older adults. In fact, it may be that counseling psychologists regularly assume all three roles while addressing issues or problems. As a way to demonstrate how this might occur, consider the case of a retired high school teacher who is referred to a counselor by a geriatric physician for psychological problems secondary to progressive vision impairment due to macular degeneration. This disease of the eye, more commonly experienced by older adults, involves degeneration of the central part of the retina (Schieber, 1992). Consequences include a progressive loss in the ability to distinguish fine visual details, which can significantly limit adaptation to one's living environment (Research to Prevent Blindness, 1994). In this example, the visual disability may be accompanied by affective symptoms such as those found in depression or anxiety.

To address this issue, the counselor can begin with a thoughtful assessment to clarify the range of the client's difficulties and their relationship to her symptoms of distress. Such an assessment will probably involve contacting and collaborating with the physician who diagnosed the client's visual impairment. The counselor assesses directly the extent to which the client's impairment is influencing her sense of well-being and provides the client with accurate information about the extent and nature of her disease *(educative role)*. Counseling may be employed to treat the client's experience of distress by encouraging greater acceptance of diminished visual capability, while at the same time helping her to learn ways to remain functionally independent in the presence of the impairment *(remedial* or *rehabilitative role)*. The counselor also may help the client to develop strategies to prevent additional problems due to her progressive vision impairment. For example, a retired high school teacher, who presumably is comfortable in a classroom setting, might be encouraged to enroll in a community program that provides adaptive living assistance for visually impaired adults *(preventive role)*. Such an intervention not only would serve an educative function, but also might assist the client in developing a support group sensitive to her needs and facilitative of her efforts to adapt to declining visual capability.

In this example, the depressed mood and anxious affect are not viewed as psychopathological symptoms but instead as normative psychological manifestations predictably experienced by an individual facing a progressive disability. Interventions would focus on helping the client to compensate for declining function by selectively emphasizing other assets from the client's own familiar repertoire of skills, activities, and contexts *(optimization)*. Such an approach would maximize external continuity and bolster a sense of internal continuity (e.g., "How have you learned to solve problems before?").

The reality of physical and cognitive decline in older age generally means that adjustments are needed when considering such questions as "What level of adaptive functioning is reasonable to expect from this person?" and "How does one build on strengths when formerly cherished abilities have deteriorated with age?" Such questions highlight the importance of having a comprehensive theoretical framework for understanding the developmental processes and critical issues of late life in contrast to earlier stages of adulthood.

APPLYING THE GENERAL FRAMEWORK TO ISSUES OF OLDER ADULTS

In this section, the three vignettes presented previously are used to illustrate how the framework we have described can be applied to the common problems in everyday living that face individuals advanced in age. Note that the organization of these vignettes focuses on (1) defining the problem, (2) assessing the situation, and (3) intervening for change. Potential roles and functions of counseling psychologists within these three broad categories will be illustrated.

Cognitive Loss

Defining the Problem

Jim is expressing fear of the future more than concern about current problems. He wants to know if his "trouble remembering things" (names and faces of acquaintances) is indicative of the onset of Alzheimer's disease. A basic issue is whether his forgetfulness is normative for a 76-year-old man. Jim and his wife are aware that he used to be able to retrieve information more readily from long-term memory. Extra concentration no longer results automatically in recalling the desired information. Jim realizes that this represents a decrement in his cognitive abilities and knows that forgetfulness is one of the signs of Alzheimer's disease. Baltes's theory, discussed previously, describes this type of cognitive loss as a decrease in plasticity, or reduced efficiency in fluid mechanics, and posits that it is normal for a man in his midseventies to experience diminished cognitive plasticity to some degree.

Another important dimension of Jim's presenting concern is fear of losing his identity and his connection to important relationships. Many older people experience fear of Alzheimer's disease to such an extent that it undermines their health and well-being (Centofanti, 1998). Here again is the underlying question of whether Jim's forgetfulness is normative. To understand the nature of Jim's fear, Atchley's (1989) continuity theory provides a useful heuristic. Losing one's identity, as is experienced in advanced Alzheimer's disease, represents a major disruption of internal continuity. Connections between one's internal and external world are lost. Family and friends experience disruptions in the continuity of their external worlds when familiar relational dynamics with the disabled loved one gradually shift to unpredictable and sometimes incomprehensible interactions. The intensity of people's fear of losing their identity in this way is evidence of the importance of maintaining continuity in our world.

In sum, although Jim's forgetfulness is problematic, he is experiencing intense fear that his difficulty retrieving names is symptomatic of a disease process that could ultimately rob him of his cognitive capabilities and disconnect him from the relationships that mean the most to him.

Assessing the Situation

An informed counselor likely will begin the assessment process with an understanding that epidemiological studies have found the prevalence of dementia of the Alzheimer's type in the adult population to be only 4% to 8% in individuals 65 years of age and over (*DSM-IV*, American

Psychiatric Association, 1994; American Psychological Association, 1998). Assessment procedures selected for this client should be comprehensive yet balanced with a focus on methods that are relevant to the client's presenting concerns. To address the issue of whether the memory problem is normative, one of the first questions is whether the forgetfulness is encountered when Jim is extending his reserve cognitive capacity (plasticity). In other words, is remembering names a routine process given ample memory cues?

Desirable appraisal techniques with Jim will include a clinical interview and a mental status exam to assess his overall cognitive functioning, as well as the nature of his memory complaint (American Psychological Association, 1998). With regard to overall cognitive functioning, the counselor might use the Dementia Rating Scale (DRS; Mattis, 1988), a brief screening instrument for dementia. This instrument is easy to administer and has well-developed norms for distinguishing cognitive performance that may or may not be indicative of dementia. Performance on such an instrument can be used to address whether the memory problems Jim is experiencing are due to disease processes (i.e., nonnormative) or normative changes associated with aging. It may be that Jim previously functioned well above normal in the area of name and face recollection but now has moved into the average range of functioning. This sort of change may be alarming to him but does not necessarily indicate the onset of dementia.

At a more specific level, the counselor also might administer the Memory Assessment Scales (MAS; Williams, 1991) which provide a comprehensive measure of memory functioning. This instrument is particularly appropriate for Jim because it includes measures that assess both immediate and delayed recall for names and faces. Jim states that his problems with recall have been primarily with infrequently encountered people and only recently with the name of a more familiar church associate. Therefore, the assessment inquiry can be directed toward the determination of whether this represents cognitive loss that is beyond what would be expected for someone of Jim's age and capability. The MAS also measures reserve capacity by comparing Jim's functioning with comprehensive age-based norms for individuals in his age range. Finally, the assessment process should include an inquiry into the typical strategies used by Jim for remembering names. Knowing how Jim approaches this task may be important in the design of remedial interventions.

Intervening for Change

If the results from the DRS were indicative of dementia, the counselor should refer Jim for a comprehensive neuropsychological assessment by a qualified neuropsychologist who has specialty skills for diagnosing dementia. If Jim's condition is diagnosed as dementia, the counseling psychologist could work cooperatively with Jim, his family, the diagnosing specialist, and other professionals in the community to develop a treatment plan to deal with the predictable cognitive loss and changes in everyday functioning that are associated with this disease state.

In the more likely event that Jim's memory problems are determined to be within the normal range, the counselor can intervene in several ways. First, Jim and his wife can be educated about normative memory changes and what it means to suffer typical cognitive losses associated with older age *(educative role)*. For many older individuals, the knowledge that problems are normative is an effective reliever of distress. As part of educating Jim about his name-face memory difficulties, it also might be important to acknowledge the relative difficulty of remembering names or faces. This task involves retrieving precise information with minimal verbal cues (i.e., you don't get credit for recalling only part of a first name). Thus, it likely will be important to convey that name recall is a difficult issue for people across the life span.

Second, counseling may be employed to help resolve persistent affective, spiritual, or existential issues, such as grief or fear associated with impending death or declining health. When Jim understands and accepts the normal functional declines he is experiencing, he is likely to reexamine his choices of daily activities in an effort to focus his energy and time on those endeavors which capitalize on his remaining strengths and maximize his sense of well-being. Doing so will help Jim to maintain internal continuity in the face of external change and discontinuity *(remedial role)*.

Finally, preventive interventions may be employed to help Jim learn to compensate for memory deficits by using other retained abilities. The counselor working with Jim may prescribe cognitive exercises that help to optimize or maintain, as much as possible, his extant memory skills. For example, a simple memory aid such as a cue card, and some additional focused concentration, may help Jim retrieve more easily the names of new people he meets at church or in his volunteer activities. Another possibly helpful strategy may be to use written lists and notes, something Jim has not needed to do in the past. Part of this training should help Jim better understand the nature of memory (e.g., effective encoding facilitates retrieval) so that he can use this new knowledge in developing compensatory strategies to offset his emerging deficits *(preventive role)*.

Caregiving

Defining the Problem

Juanita's presenting problem originates not from concerns about her own cognitive and adaptive functioning, but from the increasingly difficult task of caring for her husband who has had a diagnosis of Alzheimer's disease for several years. In terms of the theoretical models outlined previously, she is experiencing a serious disruption in external continuity. The husband who has been an important part of her life for at least 60 years is no longer able to reciprocate in the intimate interactions of their shared relationship. Juanita may be experiencing the loss of her husband even though he remains alive and physically present. Because external continuity helps us to maintain a sense of internal continuity, she likely is feeling a loss of identity and an impaired sense of self. Considering that Juanita is 83, it also is likely that she is experiencing some degree of physical decline that hinders her ability to provide 24-hour care for her husband.

The question of whether Juanita's experience is normative is also relevant here but in a somewhat different way. In this case, the question takes the form of "Is it a normative experience for an 83-year-old woman to be struggling with the difficulties of providing care to a husband with a severe cognitive disability?" Further, it is important to address Juanita's expressed concern regarding the future consequences of continuing the caregiving role into very late life.

Assessing the Situation

A competent assessment in this case is one that is both culturally sensitive and prescriptive with regard to potential intervention strategies. Juanita is not presenting with concerns about her own cognitive functioning, so the primary means of assessment would involve soliciting her help in developing a thorough and developmentally appropriate psychological and social history. Juanita's issues are likely best understood within the context of her cultural, familial, and economic situation. As part of this assessment, questions should explore Juanita's beliefs about aging, beliefs about her role as a spouse, the nature of her relationship with her children and other family members, and her understanding and level of use of available support resources (e.g., the role of her church).

Clarifying the extent and nature of her husband's functional deficits also will be important. This might be accomplished by obtaining measures of her husband's adaptive functioning or ability to care for himself. This activities of daily living assessment procedure will involve determining the extent to which her husband requires help in negotiating self-care behaviors (e.g., bathing, toileting, transferring, eating, dressing; Katz, 1983). It also may be useful to assess Juanita for depression by using an age-appropriate measure of her affective state (e.g., the Geriatric Depression Scale; Yesavage, 1986), keeping in mind that many older people will use words like "lonely" and "sad" in ways that essentially downplay a significant level of depression (Weiner, 1992).

Intervening for Change

Juanita clings to the hope that she and her husband will "get through this," implying that she may not have a comprehensive understanding of her husband's demented condition. This may be especially problematic if her husband is not able to engage in self-care behaviors, which would mean that Juanita carries an extra heavy caregiving burden. The counselor, therefore, may want to help Juanita understand that Alzheimer's is a degenerative disease and that her husband's condition predictably will worsen. Such information may help Juanita to feel less conflict about outside help, especially as the caregiver role becomes more difficult with her husband's continuing decline *(educative role)*. The counselor may intervene by helping Juanita deal with grief issues associated with the loss of her husband as a coequal companion. The counselor also can help Juanita explore culturally appropriate ways that she can be "comfortable" in old age even in the presence of her caregiving role *(remedial role)*. For example, an intervention involving her family could help Juanita find ways to meet her own needs by refocusing on alternative assets, such as relationships with other family members, to help rebuild her sense of external continuity. This could also involve exploring the potential benefits and costs associated with her daughter's plan to move in and share some of the caregiving responsibilities with Juanita for a period of time *(preventive role)*.

Career Issues

Defining the Problem

Using the conceptual models discussed earlier, the counselor might view John's issue as an unexpected turn regarding a major life event. Retirement from work often is a normative event; however, at age 54 John's job loss can be considered nonnormative because of his age and the unexpected and sudden change in his life. For these reasons, John's concern about maintaining a sense of well-being and financial stability are adaptive psychological responses. Referring again to Atchley's (1989) notion of continuity, we can describe John's concerns in terms of a major disruption in external continuity, while internal continuity (John's sense of himself) hopefully will remain intact.

John's reported anxiety and discouragement indicate that his sense of intrapersonal cohesiveness is threatened. Because he has worked with the same company for 27 years and planned to stay there until retirement, vocational stability has played an important role in maintaining John's sense of inner well-being by providing continuous external reinforcement for his self-concept as the breadwinner of the family.

John's concerns include doubt about his value as a potential employee in a job market where he is competing for jobs with younger and possibly less expensive candidates. In this context, John places a high value on youth. His concerns imply that he feels less able to learn new skills, and, from a practical standpoint, he may be correct. From the theories presented earlier, we predict that as people age they tend to focus selectively on activities and environments that are compatible with their inner cognitive structures and needs in an effort to optimize daily functioning. In addition, as people grow older they lose some of their ability to focus concurrently on multiple activities. Although this decline usually happens slowly during the middle adult years, it may be that at age 54 John has a subjective awareness of a somewhat decreased aptitude for retraining. John is faced with an unanticipated change in his external environment at a time when he likely feels less able to adapt to that change.

Assessing the Situation

An assessment of John's concerns might follow a twofold process: (1) determine what elements have served to maintain his internal and external continuity over the years with regard to career and (2) ascertain to what extent his identity and sense of self have been affected by his job loss.

The benefits counselor approached John's situation from a perspective more appropriate for someone in early adulthood. Results from the career inventories may provide a useful starting place for exploration and clarification of John's skills, interests, and values, but he probably already has a relatively clear understanding of what he does well, what he likes, and what he dislikes in a career (i.e., internal and external continuity).

It may also be important to understand how much of John's identity is centered around his career. To some degree, the weight given to the importance of one's career in maintaining personal identity is related to gender ideology and cultural factors. Men from some cultural and age-cohort groups place great emphasis on the importance of one's career in defining who and what they represent (Atchley, 1997). If family, friends, religion, and other activities outside of work are emphasized to an equal or greater extent, then John's sense of self likely will remain largely intact and his identified concerns may be confined to providing financial support for his family and saving for retirement. Conversely, if John's career is the primary foundation of his identity, then he may be vulnerable to prolonged anxiety or depression until he is able to reenter the workforce in a career that can maintain his sense of identity as an employed and "useful" individual.

Intervening for Change

Several intervention approaches may be helpful for John. First, he can be reminded about the value of his past experience and repertoire of functional skills that can be applied to a variety of work activities. His discouragement about his future employability may, in part, result from thinking too narrowly about career options. Such pessimism may have been reinforced by the benefits counselor. Thus, John may benefit from information about a wide range of work options available to him, given his accumulated talents and skills *(educative role)*. This type of counseling can encourage John to consider creatively many possibilities for future employment, including making use of his established network of friends, colleagues, and acquaintances. If, for example, John has been involved over the years with community clubs or civic activities, he may find that his best and most attractive employment leads come from contacts in those areas of his life.

Clarification of John's assets and skills may help him to evaluate better his strengths, abilities, and interests as the foundation for building a new career. Counseling may also help John to resolve issues of lower self-worth that may have emerged in the aftermath of his job loss. Therapy in this context may best be perceived as a variation on the theme of grief counseling. By grieving his lost job and lost youth, and then moving on, John may feel freer to refocus his energy and attention on a new area that is consistent with his values and self. Through this process, he may be more likely to look back on this point in his life as a painful yet important time for him in restructuring his values and priorities *(remedial role)*.

Successful counseling may include the provision of information, in a sensitive and supportive way, about the wisdom that can be gained through finding meaning in his loss. In spite of the economic uncertainty that comes with being unemployed, if John is able to turn his loss into an opportunity for personal growth, then he will likely look back and perceive this unexpected turn of life events as a positive milestone. For example, John's initial job loss could become the turning point which leads to an interesting new career that is more flexible with regard to his family interests and brings him increased life satisfaction during his later working years *(preventive role)*.

INTERVENTION COMPETENCIES

Our vignettes have illustrated that counseling psychologists already possess many skills necessary for intervening with older adults. A goal of this chapter not only has been to build a conceptual foundation descriptive of the adult aging experience but also to help in developing counseling interventions. However, adequate preparation for addressing the many mental health issues that are part of the aging experience necessitates counseling psychologists having: (1) comprehensive knowledge of the aging process, (2) expertise in assessment of older adults, and (3) skill in developing counseling strategies in a variety of older adult contexts.

Knowledge of the Aging Process

Modest amounts of relevant information about the aging process and professional practice with older adults have been published in counseling psychology specialty journals and texts. A quarter of a century ago, this fact was apparent to Sidney Pressey (Pressey, 1973; Pressey & Pressey, 1972), one of the founders of the specialty of counseling psychology who, as an 83-year-old resident in a nursing home, recommended ways for counseling psychologists to address issues of the old and very old. Pressey also expressed concern over the dearth of gerontological research in the counseling psychology literature and the general lack of awareness in the discipline about the kinds of psychological issues that are prevalent in old age. Pressey and Pressey noted that:

> An old-age counselor, especially if so functioning in an institution [nursing home] . . . has research opportunities now almost unrecognized. . . . Indeed, in the notable favorable environment of the best institutions it should be possible to investigate potentials regarding longevity, maintained ability, and personality as nowhere else. (p. 366)

Since these early writings, two major contributions have appeared in *The Counseling Psychologist* that have highlighted counseling strategies for older adults (Smyer, 1984), and contemporary theories of aging (Fry, 1992). However, as noted throughout this chapter, adequately addressing issues of old and very old clients requires integration of comprehensive developmental theories of aging and specialized counseling strategies and interventions.

Gerontological knowledge has expanded dramatically, especially in the past 10 years. Numerous journals now exist dedicated solely to issues of the old and very old (e.g., *Journal of Gerontology, Journal of Mental Health and Aging, Clinical Gerontologist, Educational Gerontology, Psychology and Aging, Journal of the American Geriatrics Society*). Active professional organizations have developed, such as the Gerontological Society of America, a multidisciplinary organization that addresses the broad spectrum of physical, psychological, and social issues of adult development and aging. Within the National Institutes of Health, the National Institute of Aging annually funds single and multidisciplinary research which examines diverse issues facing the old and very old. Developing a gerontological knowledge base from these various sources is an essential activity for counseling psychologists who desire to develop proficiency skills for working with older adults.

Within the American Psychological Association, members of Division 20 (Adult Development and Aging), working in concert with psychologists from Division 12 (Clinical Psychology), recently drafted a report enumerating qualifications for practice in clinical and applied geropsychology (APA Interdivisional Task Force on Clinical and Applied Geropsychology, 1998). From these guidelines, three levels of training in geropsychology were proposed. Level 1 (generic training in aging and adult development) is encouraged for all licensed psychologists, because it is likely that most will encounter older adult clients in their professional practice as the general population ages. Level 2 (specific training in the provision of psychological services to older adults) is recommended for psychologists who wish to include an older adult clientele as part of their professional practice. In addition to obtaining information about the aging process, Level 2 training involves developing proficiency in identifying and treating some of the more common psychological issues facing older adults. Level 3 (specialized training, including comprehensive supervised experience in the provision of psychological services to older adults) is for psychologists wishing to become specialists in the psychological treatment of older adults. Level 3 requires demonstrated competence in working with older or very old clientele. At all three levels of training, psychologists are expected to develop awareness of assessment instruments and procedures (Segal, Coolidge, & Hersen, 1998) and intervention strategies (Gatz et al., 1998; Myers, 1990) that are specific to older adults. The next two sections highlight each of these areas of gerontological practice.

Issues in Assessing Older Adults

Given that older adults experience normative and nonnormative problems and issues that are common in individuals across the life span (e.g., depression, anxiety) and unique to old age (e.g., Alzheimer's disease), it is critical to assess the extent to which psychological issues or problems can influence everyday functioning in older age. Even for those psychological issues common in younger cohorts, the presenting symptoms can differ significantly between younger and older adults, as is found in the role of impaired cognitive function as a symptom of depression (Poon, 1992; Woods, 1996). Counseling psychologists who desire to work with older adults need to develop competency in assessing cognitive, affective, and physical aspects of functioning in old and very old age. Thus, it is critical to have access to assessment instruments and procedures that have been standardized, validated, and normed on older populations. Fortunately, there are a number of useful references to guide the practitioner in this regard (American Psychological Association, 1998; Davies, 1996; Poon, 1986; Segal et al., 1998).

An assessment issue that is critical in geropsychology is the identification and gauging of age-related dementias of which Alzheimer's disease is the most prominent subtype. The most widely used definition of dementia can be found in the *DSM-IV* (American Psychiatric Association, 1994). Briefly, dementia is characterized by profound and global impairment in one or more areas, including speech and writing, fine and gross motor coordination, encoding and/or retrieving of familiar and unfamiliar objects and people, and the ability to plan, execute, and monitor purposeful behavior. In dementia, complex reasoning ability is severely impaired, as well as the ability to function independently in everyday contexts.

It is beyond the scope of this chapter to provide a comprehensive overview of dementia and its assessment; however, this disorder can have a dramatic impact on an individual's sense of personal control and the ability to use compensatory mechanisms (SOC) to deal with late-life issues. Atchley (1989) has noted that, with regard to continuity theory, deteriorative disease states such as dementia represent one of the more profound disruptions to a person's sense of internal continuity. Counseling psychologists who desire to work with older adults should be familiar with a range of screening examinations that have been normed on older populations and can identify individuals who have cognitive deficits sufficient to warrant more in-depth assessment for dementia-related disorders. These screening examinations should include methods for assessing mental status (e.g., Blessed Dementia Index; Blessed, Tomlinson, & Roth, 1968; Mini-Mental Status Exam; Folstein, Folstein, & McHugh, 1975; Dementia Rating Scale; Mattis, 1988), as well as measures of self-care and adaptive function (Activities of Daily Living; Katz, 1983). Several excellent resources are available that provide an introduction and guide to screening for dementia (Hill et al., in press; Nordhus et al., 1998; Poon et al., 1992; Woods, 1996).

In addition to identifying specific instruments for assessing particular issues facing older adults (e.g., memory function, functional independence), it is important to consider qualitative aspects of the testing context. To obtain useful performance measures from older clients, administration procedures must be adapted to the specific age-related characteristics of the client (e.g., hearing deficits, psychomotor slowing). Segal et al. (1998) provided a useful set of guidelines for assessing older adults:

1. Ensure that the testing environment maximizes sensory cues for the older client.
2. Relax time constraints to optimize performance in the presence of predictable behavioral slowing that occurs in old and very old age.

3. Ensure that the purpose and procedure of the assessment is presented clearly to older clients.

4. Show respect and understanding for older clients by openly discussing issues of concern (e.g., age differences between client and therapist).

5. Make use of ancillary sources of information that can help in understanding and interpreting the performance of older clients (e.g., involving family members in the assessment process, especially if the family is caring for the older client).

6. Maintain a therapeutic approach when evaluating older clients, such as showing concern for the client's well-being during the assessment.

7. Consider the client's related medical conditions or medication use as a source of variation that may influence the outcome of the assessment.

Thus, it is important to consider qualitative issues in the testing environment, as well as specific instruments for obtaining representative indicators of cognitive, affective, or physical functioning. Finally, because aging can interact with other individual difference variables (e.g., gender, ethnic background, socioeconomic status), the relevance of these sources of individual and cultural diversity should also be considered (e.g., assessing an individual for dementia who has very little formal education).

Tailoring Counseling Interventions to Older Adult Contexts

As described earlier, consideration of person-environment fit is important when intervening with older clients. This is particularly important because of the wide range of contexts in which older adults may reside, apart from traditional home environments. Such contexts include but are not limited to retirement communities, assisted living centers, and skilled nursing facilities. There are even specialized skilled nursing homes for older adults diagnosed with dementia that provide focused care tailored to the psychological and behavioral problems associated with this disorder (Alzheimer's disease care units; Ohta & Ohta, 1988). Although counseling psychologists can provide useful services to older adults in these settings, models of intervention within the field of counseling psychology, for the most part, have not been developed for many of these contexts.

In a cross-sectional survey of 124 nursing home administrators, Crose and Kixmiller (1994) reported that management of psychological issues facing their older residents was the most frequently cited concern. Problems related to depression, loneliness, anxiety, and withdrawal were identified repeatedly. A relatively low percentage of administrators reported employing psychologists or other mental health professionals to assist with these issues. Like Pressey (1973), the authors contended that nursing homes can be particularly fertile environments for counseling psychologists to address the needs of older adults, particularly as members of multidisciplinary teams. Because a primary goal of nursing homes is to enhance resident well-being, nonmedical approaches that focus on person-environment interactions likely will result in intervention efforts that are more responsive to the physical and psychological needs of nursing home residents (see Langer & Rodin, 1976; R. Rodin & Langer, 1977).

Impaired mobility is a significant barrier to obtaining health care services (Melcher, 1988). Other disciplines, such as social work, nursing, and medicine, have developed elaborate in-home procedures for treating the very old. Like these related disciplines, counseling psychologists must develop proactive models of assessment and intervention for older citizens limited in their ability to use traditional community mental health services.

Counseling psychologists have yet to develop models of care that address specifically issues facing older adults. Like others across the life span, older adults deal with transitions associated with the aging process, and there is a substantial knowledge base that has emerged from counseling psychology for negotiating transitional experiences in adulthood (Brammer & Abrego, 1981; Schlossberg, 1981). Hopefully, the unique life-transition issues that characterize older and very old adults will begin to be addressed systematically and comprehensively by counseling psychologists in the near future. With our traditional emphases on normative development, assets and strengths, and person-environment interactions, we are well positioned to make substantive contributions in this increasingly critical arena.

DIRECTIONS FOR FUTURE RESEARCH AND THEORY

As the number of older adults in our society increases relative to younger aged groups, the focus of science and public policy will place a greater emphasis on the range of psychological issues facing older adults. It is within this context that counseling psychologists may play an important role. This chapter has highlighted strategies for prevention and intervention for normative issues of adjustment and transition in old age. It also may be important for counseling psychology to focus on the generation of conceptual and empirical knowledge about the aging process. Several areas are highlighted below that are consistent with traditional research emphases in counseling psychology and relevant to the aging experience in our contemporary society.

1. There is a need to develop models of career development that better elaborate the nature of career transition in later adulthood. Although research from counseling psychology cited earlier in this chapter has examined factors that predict adjustment to retirement in old age (Payne et al., 1991; Robbins et al., 1994), traditional conceptualizations of retirement as the end of career are not reflective of contemporary vocational trends across the adult life span (Canaff, 1997). In addition, developing and validating counseling approaches that are consistent with the older adult career transition experience seem warranted.

2. As highlighted by Gelso and Fretz (1992), models of counseling have historically emphasized normative developmental issues, and the literature that has conceptualized the aging phenomenon within the field has focused predominantly on normal aging (see Fry, 1992; Schlossberg, 1981; Smyer, 1984). Models of aging that impact research and training should be more inclusive of nonnormative issues, such as chronic disease and disability (American Psychological Association, 1998; Gatz, 1996), dementias (Centofanti, 1998; Edwards, 1993), and issues of long-term care (Nagel et al., 1988; Ohta & Ohta, 1988). The need for counseling psychologists not only to possess appropriate skills, but to have expanded knowledge about nonnormative chronic conditions that are prominent among the old and very old is also necessary if counseling psychologists are to be perceived as relevant service providers to older consumers (Crose & Kixmiller, 1994).

3. As noted earlier in this chapter, the fastest growing segment of older adults are those who are 85 years of age and older (Bäckman et al., in press), and there is a growing body of research examining the special issues facing this very old group (Ritchie, 1998; Smith & Baltes, 1997). One example that highlights this phenomenon are issues related to death and dying which have been relatively unaddressed in counseling psychology. The extent to which counseling psychologists are able to address the needs of the very old will depend, in part, on development of a knowledge base that incorporates issues of death and dying within models of transition and change that are integral to counseling psychology.

4. The chapter highlighted preventive, remedial, and educative roles that counseling psychologists can adopt addressing normative issues in late life. Several examples were provided describing how these roles might be applied to specific late-life issues. Outcome research is needed that provides empirical support for the effectiveness of these interventions in addressing various

age-specific issues. To date, outcome research examining counseling psychology interventions with older adults lags far behind what is available in other mental health specialties, including clinical psychology and social work (American Psychological Association, 1998; Carstensen et al., 1996; Gatz, 1996; Gatz & Smyer, 1992; Nordhus et al., 1998).

5. As noted early in the chapter, the changing demographics of the aging population indicate that a substantial number of older adults will be from ethnic minority groups. Some of the issues facing older ethnic minority adults include dealing with the economic challenges of poverty in old age, transmission of culture to younger generations, and the impact of ethnicity on access to social services (Harris, 1998). Although models of counseling exist that are specific to ethnic minority populations, many of these do not address the interaction of age and ethnicity (Atkinson & Hackett, 1997; Sue, Zane, & Young, 1994). Future research is needed to elucidate counseling approaches that consider special issues facing older adults from ethnic minority groups.

SUMMARY

This chapter has highlighted two theoretical models well adapted to the development of prevention and intervention strategies for issues facing adults in later life. These models of aging are comprehensive, deal with the qualitative aspects of the aging experience, and are consistent with the defining characteristics of counseling psychology (cf. Gelso & Fretz, 1992). P.B. Baltes's (1997) selective optimization and compensation theory addresses the pervasive experience of loss related to growing older. Atchley's (1989) continuity theory provides explanatory mechanisms for maintaining consistency and a stable sense of self in old and very old age. Several fundamental principles were presented from these models that illuminate the aging experience, including physical and psychological decline, age-related change, continuity, and the role of maturationally acquired characteristics as resources for meaning and coping. We noted that although there is great variability in how individuals negotiate the aging experience, death is the end result of aging and the ultimate equalizer of humankind. Finally, we examined how counseling psychology as a professional specialty is well positioned to address many of the normative issues associated with the aging experience, as well as to assist older adults in negotiating many of the nonnormative events that occur in old age, such as loneliness and depression. We maintain that, if counseling psychology is to remain a strong and relevant professional specialty into the twenty-first century, addressing the psychological issues of the old and very old must be an integral part of its professional mission.

REFERENCES

Alloul, K., Sauriol, L., Kennedy, W., Laurier, C., Tessier, G., Novosel, S., & Contandriopoulos, A. (1998). Alzheimer's disease: A review of the disease, its epidemiology and economic impact. *Archives of Gerontology and Geriatrics, 27,* 189–221.

American Association of Retired Persons. (1998). *Profile of older Americans.* Washington, DC: Author.

American Psychiatric Association. (1994). *Diagnostic and statistical manual for mental disorders* (4th ed.). Washington, DC: Author.

American Psychological Association. (1998). *Interdivisional task force on clinical and applied geropsychology.* Washington, DC: Author.

Atchley, R.C. (1989). A continuity theory of normal aging. *Gerontologist, 29,* 183–190.

Atchley, R.C. (1992). What do social theories of aging offer counselors? *The Counseling Psychologist, 20,* 336–340.

Atchley, R.C. (1997). *Social forces in aging* (8th ed.). Belmont, CA:Wadsworth.

Atkinson, D.R., & Hackett, G. (1997). *Counseling diverse populations* (2nd ed.). Boston: McGraw-Hill.

Bäckman, L., Small, B.J., Wahlin, Å., & Larsson, M. (in press). Cognitive functioning in the very old. In F.I.M. Craik & T.A. Salthouse (Eds.), *Handbook of aging and cognition* (2nd ed.). Mahwah, NJ: Erlbaum.

Baltes, M.M., Kuhl, K-P., Gutzmann, H., & Sowarka, D. (1995). Potential of plasticity as a diagnostic instrument: A cross validation and extension. *Psychology and Aging, 10,* 167–172.

Baltes, P.B. (1987). Theoretical propositions of life-span developmental psychology: On the dynamics between growth and decline. *Developmental Psychology, 23,* 611–626.

Baltes, P.B. (1993). The aging mind: Potential and limits. *Gerontologist, 33,* 580–594.

Baltes, P.B. (1997). On the incomplete architecture of human ontogeny: Selection, optimization, and compensation as foundation of developmental theory. *American Psychologist, 52,* 366–380.

Baltes, P.B., & Baltes, M.M. (1980). Plasticity and variability in psychological aging: Methodological and theoretical issues. In G.E. Gurski (Ed.), *Determining the effects of aging on the central nervous system* (pp. 41–66). Berlin, Germany: Schering.

Baltes, P.B., Dittmann-Kohli, F., & Dixon, R.A. (1984). New perspectives on the development of intelligence in adulthood: Toward a dual-process conception and a model of selective optimization with compensation. In P.B. Baltes & O.G. Brim, Jr. (Eds.), *Life-span development and behavior* (Vol. 6, pp. 33–76). San Diego, CA: Academic Press.

Baltes, P.B., Dittmann-Kohli, F., & Kliegl, R.K. (1986). Reserve capacity of the elderly in age-sensitive tests of fluid intelligence: Replication and extension. *Psychology and Aging, 1,* 172–177.

Baltes, P.B., & Kliegl, R.K. (1992). Further testing of limits of cognitive plasticity: Negative age differences in a mnemonic skill are robust. *Developmental Psychology, 20,* 121–125.

Baltes, P.B., Lindenberger, U., & Staudinger, U.M. (1995). Die zwei gesichter der intelligenz in alter [The two faces of intelligence in old age]. *Spektrum der Wissenschaft, 10* 52–61.

Baltes, P.B., & Smith, J. (1990). The psychology of wisdom and its ontogenesis. In R.J. Sternberg (Ed.), *Wisdom: Its nature, origins, and development* (pp. 87–120). Cambridge, England: Cambridge University Press.

Baltes, P.B., & Staudinger, U.M. (1993). The search for psychology of wisdom. *Current Directions in Psychological Science, 2,* 75–80.

Baltes, P.B., Staudinger, U.M., & Lindenberger, U. (1999). Lifespan psychology: Theory and application to intellectual functioning. *Annual Review of Psychology, 50,* 471–507.

Baltes, P.B., Staudinger, U.M., Maercker, A., & Smith, J. (1995). People nominated as wise: A comparative study of wisdom-related knowledge. *Psychology and Aging, 10,* 155–166.

Bergin, A.E. (1983). Religiosity and mental health: A critical reevaluation and meta-analysis. *Professional Psychology: Research and Practice, 14,* 170–184.

Bergin, A.E., Masters, K.S., & Richards, P.S. (1987). Religiousness and mental health reconsidered: A study of an intrinsically religious sample. *Journal of Counseling Psychology, 34,* 197–204.

Birren, J.E., & Schaie, K.W. (Eds.). (1996). *Handbook of the psychology of aging* (4th ed.). San Diego, CA: Academic Press.

Birren, J.E., Sloane, R.B., & Cohen, G.D. (1992). *Handbook of mental health and aging* (2nd ed.). New York: Academic Press.

Blessed, G., Tomlinson, B., & Roth, M. (1968). The association between quantitative measures of dementia and of senile changes in the cerebral grey matter of elderly subjects. *British Journal of Psychiatry, 114,* 797–811.

Brammer, L.W., & Abrego, P.J. (1981). Intervention strategies for coping with transitions. *The Counseling Psychologist, 9,* 19–36.

Canaff, A.L. (1997). Later life career planning: A new challenge for career counselors. *Journal of Employment Counseling, 34,* 85–93.

Carstensen, L.L., Dornbrand, L., & Edelstein, B.A. (Eds.). (1996). *The practical handbook of clinical gerontology.* Thousand Oaks, CA: Sage.

Castro, J.G., Newcomb, M.D., McCreary, C., & Baezconde-Garbanati, L. (1989). Cigarette smokers do more than just smoke cigarettes. *Health Psychology, 8,* 107–129.

Cavanaugh, J.C. (1998). Caregiving to adults: A life event challenge. In E.H. Nordhus, G.R. VandenBos, S. Berg, & P. Fromholt (Eds.), *Clinical geropsychology* (pp. 131–135). Washington, DC: American Psychological Association.

Centofanti, M. (1998). Fear of Alzheimer's undermines health of elderly patients. *APA Monitor, 29,* 6. Washington, DC: American Psychological Association.

Clayton, V.P., & Birren, J.E. (1980). The development of wisdom across the life span: A reexamination of an ancient topic. In P.B. Baltes & O.G. Brim, Jr. (Eds.), *Life-span development and behavior* (Vol. 3, pp. 103–135). San Diego, CA: Academic Press.

Costa, P.T., Jr., & McCrae, R.R. (1980). Still stable after all these years: Personality as a key to some issues in adulthood and old age. In P.B. Baltes & O.G. Brim, Jr. (Eds.), *Life-span development and behavior* (Vol. 3, pp. 65–102). New York: Academic Press.

Costa, P.T., Jr., & McCrae, R.R. (1992). Trait psychology comes of age. In T. Sonderegger (Ed.), *Nebraska Symposium on Motivation, 1991* (pp. 169–204). Lincoln: University of Nebraska Press.

Crose, R., & Kixmiller, J.S. (1994). Counseling psychologists as nursing home consultants: What do administrators want? *The Counseling Psychologist, 22,* 104–114.

Czaja, S.J. (1997). Using technologies to aid the performance of home tasks. In A.D. Fisk & W.A. Rogers (Eds.), *Handbook of human factors and the older adult.* San Diego, CA: Academic Press.

Daley, J.M., Applewhite, S.R., & Jorquiez, J. (1989). Community participation of the elderly Chicano: A model. *International Journal of Aging and Human Development, 29,* 135–150.

Davies, S. (1996). Neurpsychological assessment of the older person. In R.T. Woods (Ed.), *The handbook of the clinical psychology of ageing* (pp. 441–474). New York: Wiley.

Edwards, A.J. (1993). *Dementia.* New York: Plenum Press.

Ellison, C.G. (1994). Religion, the life stress paradigm and the study of depression. In J.S. Levin (Ed.), *Religion in aging and health* (pp. 78–121). Thousand Oaks, CA: Sage.

Folstein, M.F., Folstein, S.E., & McHugh, P.R. (1975). Mini mental state: A practical method for grading the cognitive state of patients for the clinician. *Journal of Psychiatric Research, 12,* 189–198.

Freund, A.M., & Baltes, P.B. (1998). Selection, optimization, and compensation as strategies of life management: Correlations with subjective indicators of successful aging. *Psychology and Aging, 13,* 531–543.

Fry, P.S. (1992). Major social theories of aging and their implications for counseling concepts and practice: A critical review. *Counseling Psychologist, 20,* 246–329.

Ganzini, L., & Atkinson, R.M. (1996). Substance abuse. In J. Sadavoy, L.W. Lazarus, L.F. Jarvik, & G.T. Grossberg (Eds.), *Comprehensive review of geriatric psychiatry II* (2nd ed., pp. 659–692). Washington, DC: American Psychiatric Press.

Gatz, M. (1996). Aging and mental disorders. In J.E. Birren & K.W. Schaie (Eds.), *Handbook of the psychology of aging* (4th ed., pp. 365–382). San Diego, CA: Academic Press.

Gatz, M., Fiske, A., Fox, L.S., Kaskie, B., Kasl-Godley, J.E., McCallum, T.J., & Loebach, J. (1998). Empirically validated psychological treatments for older adults. *Journal of Mental Health and Aging, 4,* 9–46.

Gatz, M., & Smyer, M. (1992). The mental health system and older adults in the 1990's. *American Psychologist, 47,* 741–751.

Gelfand, D. (1994). *Aging and ethnicity: Knowledge and services.* New York: Springer.

Gelso, C.J., & Fretz, B.R. (1992). *Counseling psychology.* New York: Harcourt Brace.

Giambra, L.M., Arenberg, D., Zonderman, A.B., Kawas, C., & Costa, P.T. (1995). Adult life span changes in immediate visual memory and verbal intelligence, *Psychology and Aging, 10,* 123–139.

Hansen, J.C. (1984). The measurement of vocational interests: Issues and future directions. In S.D. Brown & R. Lent (Eds.), *Handbook of counseling psychology* (pp. 99–136). New York: Wiley.

Harris, H.L. (1998). Ethnic minority elders: Issues and interventions. *Educational Gerontology, 24,* 309–323.

Hersen, M., & Van Hasselt, V. (1998). *Handbook of clinical geropsychology.* New York: Plenum Press.

Hill, R.D., Bäckman, L., & Stigsdotter-Neeley, N. (in press). *Cognitive rehabilitation in old age.* New York: Oxford University Press.

Hill, R.D., Campbell, B.W., Thomas, L.A., & Kok Moon Soo-Tho. (1998). Perceptions of well-being in older smokers. *Journal of Mental Health and Aging, 4,* 271–280.

Hill, R.D., Packard, T., & Lund, D. (1996). Bereavement. In J.A. Sheikh (Ed.), *Treating the elderly* (pp. 45–74). San Francisco: Jossey-Bass.

Hill, R.D., Wahlin, Å, Winblad, B., & Bäckman, L. (1995). The role of demographic and life style variables in utilizing cognitive support for episodic remembering among very old adults. *Journal of Gerontology: Psychological Sciences, 50,* 219–227.

Holliday, S.G., & Chandler, M.J. (1986). Wisdom: Explorations in adult competence. In J.A. Meacham (Ed.), *Contributions to human development* (Vol. 17, pp. 1–96). Basel, Switzerland: Karger.

Horn, J.L. (1968). Organization of abilities and the development of intelligence. *Psychological Review, 75,* 242–259.

Horn, J.L. (1978). Human ability systems. In P.B. Baltes (Ed.), *Life-span developmental psychology* (Vol. 1). New York: Academic Press.

Horn, J.L. (1982). The theory of fluid and crystallized intelligence in relation to concepts of cognitive psychology and aging in adulthood. In F.I.M. Craik & S. Trehub (Eds.), *Aging and cognitive processes* (Vol. 8, pp. 237–278). New York: Plenum Press.

Horn, J.L., & Catell, R.B. (1966). Refinement and test of the theory of fluid and crystallized intelligence. *Journal of Educational psychology, 57,* 253–270.

Horn, J.L., & Donaldson, G. (1976). On the myth of intellectual decline in adulthood. *American Psychologist, 31,* 701–719.

Ingebretsen, R., & Solem, P.E. (1998). Death, dying, and bereavement. In I.H. Nordhus, G.R. VandenBos, S. Berg, & P. Fromholt (Eds.), *Clinical geropsychology* (pp. 177–181). Washington, DC: American Psychological Association.

Intons-Peterson, M.J., & Newsome, G.L., III. (1992). External memory aids: Effects and effectiveness. In D.J. Herrmann, H. Weingartner, A. Searleman, & C. McEvoy (Eds.), *Memory improvement: Implications for memory theory* (pp. 101–122). New York: Springer-Verlag.

Jenkins, J.J. (1979). Four points to remember: A tetrahedral model of memory experiments. In L.S. Cermak & F.I.M. Craik (Eds.), *Levels of processing in human memory* (pp. 426–446). Hillsdale, NJ: Erlbaum.

Katz, S. (1983). Assessing self-maintenance: Activities of daily living, mobility, and instrumental activities of daily living. *Journal of the American Geriatrics Society, 31,* 721–727.

Kausler, D.H. (1994). *Learning and memory in normal aging.* San Diego, CA: Academic Press.

Kliegl, R.K., Smith, J., & Baltes, P.B. (1989). Testing-the-limits and the study of adult age differences in cognitive plasticity of a mnemonic skill. *Developmental Psychology, 25,* 247–256.

Kliegl, R.K., Smith, J., & Baltes, P.B. (1990). On the locus and process of magnification of age differences during mnemonic training. *Developmental Psychology, 26,* 894–904.

Kropf, N.P., & Pugh, K.L. (1995). Beyond life expectancy: Social work with centenarians. *Journal of Gerontological Social Work, 23,* 121–137.

Labouvie-Vief, G. (1992). Wisdom as integrated thought: Historical and developmental perspectives. In R.J. Sternberg (Ed.), *Wisdom: Its nature, origins, and development* (pp. 52–83). Cambridge, England: Cambridge University Press.

Langer, E.J., & Rodin, J. (1976). The effects of choice and enhanced personal responsibility for the aged: A field experiment in an institutional setting. *Journal of Personality and Social Psychology, 34,* 191–198.

Lansford, J.E., Sherman, A.M., & Antonucci, T.C. (1998). Satisfaction with social networks: An examination of socioemotional selectivity across cohorts. *Psychology and Aging, 13,* 544–552.

Lindenberger, U., Mayr, U., & Kliegl, R.K. (1993). Speed and intelligence in old age. *Psychology and Aging, 8,* 207–220.

Lopez, M.A. (1980). Social-skills training with institutionalized elderly: Effects of a precounseling structuring and overlearning on skill acquisition and transfer. *Journal of Counseling Psychology, 27,* 286–293.

Mahoney, R. (1991). *Human change processes: The scientific foundations of psychotherapy.* Chicago: Basic Books.

Markides, K.S., & Black, S.A. (1996). Race, ethnicity, and aging: The impact of inequality. In R.H. Binstock & L.K. George (Eds.), *Handbook of aging and the social sciences* (4th ed., pp. 153–170). San Diego, CA: Academic Press.

Maslow, A. (1968). *Toward a psychology of being.* Princeton, NJ: Van Nostrand-Reinhold.

Mattis, S. (1988). *Dementia rating scale.* Odessa, FL: Psychological Assessment Resources.

McCrae, R.R., & Costa, P.T., Jr. (1990). *Personality in adulthood.* New York: Guilford Press.

McCrae, R.R., & Costa, P.T., Jr. (1991). Adding Liebe und Arbeit: The full five-factor model and well-being. *Personality and Social Psychology Bulletin, 17,* 227–232.

McCrae, R.R., & Costa, P.T., Jr. (1994). The stability of personality: Observations and evaluations. *Current Directions in Psychological Science, 3,* 173–175.

McCue, J.D. (1995). The naturalness of dying. *Journal of the American Medical Association, 273,* 1039–1043.

McCullough, M.E., Worthington, E.L., Jr., & Rachal, K.C. (1997). Interpersonal forgiving in close relationships. *Journal of Personality and Social Psychology, 73*, 321–336.

Meacham, J.A. (1992). The loss of wisdom. In R.J. Sternberg (Ed.), *Wisdom: Its nature, origins, and development* (pp. 181–211). Cambridge, England: Cambridge University Press.

Melcher, J. (1988). Keeping our elderly out of institutions by putting them back in their homes. *American Psychologist, 43*, 543–647.

Morrell, R.W., Park, D.C., & Poon, L.W. (1989). Quality of instruction on prescription drug labels: Effects on memory and comprehension in young and old adults. *Gerontologist, 29*, 345–345.

Mortimer, J.A., & Graves, A.B. (1993). Education and other socioeconomic determinants of dementia and Alzheimer's disease. *Neurology, 43*, 39–44.

Myers, J.E. (Ed.). (1990). Techniques for counseling older persons [Special issue]. *Journal of mental Health Counseling, 12*(3).

Myers, J.E., & Salmon, H.E. (1984). Counseling for older persons: Status, shortcomings and potentialities. *Counseling Psychologist, 12*, 39–53.

Nagel, J., Cimbolic, P., & Newlin, M. (1988). Efficacy of elderly and adolescent volunteer counselors in a nursing home setting. *Journal of Counseling Psychology, 35*, 81–86.

Nathanson, C.A. (1990). The gender-mortality differential in developed countries: Demographic and sociocultural dimensions. In M.G. Ory & H.R. Warner (Eds.), *Gender, health, and longevity: Multidisciplinary perspectives* (pp. 3–23). New York: Springer.

National Center for Health Statistics. (1995). *Vital Statistics of the United States, 1990, 2* (Pt. A). Washington, DC: U.S. Government Printing Office.

Nordhus, E.H., VandenBos, G.R., Berg, S., & Fromholt, P. (1998). *Clinical geropsychology,* Washington, DC: American Psychological Association.

Ohta, R.J., & Ohta, B.M. (1988). Special units for Alzheimer's disease patients: A critical look. *Gerontologist, 28*, 803–808.

Orwoll, L., & Perlmutter, M. (1992). The study of wise persons: Integrating a personality perspective. In R.J. Sternberg (Ed.), *Wisdom: Its nature, origins, and development* (pp. 160–177). Cambridge, England: Cambridge University Press.

Ostrosky-Solis, F., Jaime, R.M., & Ardila, A. (1998). Memory abilities during normal aging. *International Journal of Neuroscience, 93*, 151–162.

Park, D.C., Puglisi, J.T., & Smith, A.D. (1986). Memory for pictures: Does an age-related decline exist? *Journal of Psychology and Aging, 1*, 11–17.

Payne, E.C., Robbins, S., & Dougherty, L.M. (1991). Goal directedness and older adult adjustment. *Journal of Counseling Psychology, 38*, 302–308.

Persson, D. (1993). The elderly driver deciding when to stop. *Gerontologist, 33*, 88–91.

Plude, D.J., & Schwartz, L.K. (1996). Compact disc-interactive memory training with the elderly. *Educational Gerontology, 22*, 507–521.

Poon, L.W. (1986). *Clinical memory assessment.* Washington, DC: American Psychological Association.

Poon, L.W. (1992). Towards an understanding of cognitive functioning in geriatric depression. *International Psychogeriatrics, 4*, 241–266.

Poon, L.W., Sweaney, A.C., Clayton, G.M., & Merriam, S.B. (1992). The Georgia centenarian study. *International Journal of Aging and Human Development, 34*, 1–17.

Pressey, S.L. (1973). Old age counseling: Crises, services, potentials. *Journal of Counseling Psychology, 20*, 356–360.

Pressey, S.L., & Pressey, A. (1972). Major neglected need opportunity: Old-age counseling. *Journal of Counseling Psychology, 19*, 362–366.

Query, J.L., Jr., & Flint, L.J. (1996). The caregiving relationship. In N. Vanzetti & S. Duck (Eds.), *A lifetime of relationships* (pp. 455–483). Pacific Grove, CA: Brooks/Cole.

Rabbitt, P. (1993). Does it all go together when it goes? *Quarterly Journal of Experimental Psychology: Human Experimental Psychology, 46*, 385–434.

Raskind, M.A., & Peskind, E.R. (1992). Alzheimer's disease and other dementing disorders. In J.E. Birren, R.B. Sloane, & G.D. Cohen (Eds.), *Handbook of mental health and aging* (2nd ed., pp. 457–482). New York: Academic Press.

Research to Prevent Blindness. (1994). *Progress report.* New York: Author.

Ritchie, K. (1998). Mental health of the oldest old: The relevance of centenarian studies to psychogeriatric research. *International Psychogeriatrics, 10,* 7–9.

Robbins, S.B., Lee, R.H., & Wan, T.T.H. (1994). Goal continuity as a mediator of early retirement adjustment: Testing a multidimensional model. *Journal of Counseling Psychology, 41,* 18–26.

Robinson, B., & Thurnher, M. (1979). Taking care of aged parents: A family cycle transition. *Gerontologist, 19,* 586–593.

Rodin, J. (1986). Aging and health: Effects of the sense of control. *Science, 233,* 1271–1276.

Rodin, J. (1990). Control by any other name: Definitions, concepts, and processes. In J. Rodin, C. Schooler, & K.W. Schaie (Eds.), *Self-directedness cause and effects throughout the life course* (pp. 1–17). Hillsdale, NJ: Erlbaum.

Rodin, J., & Langer, E.J. (1977). Long-term effects of a control relevant intervention with the institutionalized aged. *Journal of Personality and Social Psychology, 35,* 897–902.

Rodin, J., & McAvay, G. (1992). Determinants of change in perceived health in a longitudinal study of older adults. *Journal of Gerontology, 47,* 373–384.

Rowe, J.W., & Kahn, R.L. (1987). Human aging: Usual and successful. *Science, 237,* 143–149.

Rowe, J.W., & Kahn, R.L. (1998). *Successful aging.* New York: Pantheon Books.

Sakauye, K. (1996). Ethnocultural aspects. In J. Sadavoy, L.W. Lazarus, L.F. Jarvik, & G.T. Grossberg (Eds.), *Comprehensive review of geriatric psychiatry* (2nd ed., pp. 197–221). Washington, DC: American Psychiatric Press.

Salthouse, T.A. (1991). *Theoretical perspectives on cognitive aging.* Hillsdale, NJ: Erlbaum.

Schieber, F. (1992). Aging and the senses. In J.E. Birren, R.B. Sloane, & G.D. Cohen (Eds.), *Handbook of mental health and aging* (2nd ed., pp. 252–306). San Diego, CA: Academic Press.

Schlossberg, N.K. (1981). A model for analyzing human adaptation to transition. *The Counseling Psychologist, 9,* 2–18.

Schneider, E.L., & Grueling, J.M. (1990). The aging of America: Impact on health care costs. *Journal of the American Medical Association, 263,* 2335–2340.

Segal, D.L., Coolidge, F.L., & Hersen, M. (1998). Psychological testing of older people. In I.H. Nordhus, G.R. VandenBos, S. Berg, & P. Fromholt (Eds.), *Clinical geropsychology* (pp. 231–257). Washington, DC: American Psychological Association.

Shapiro, D. (1965). *Neurotic Styles.* New York: Basic Books.

Smith, J., & Baltes, P.B. (1997). Profiles of psychological functioning in the old and oldest old. *Psychology and Aging, 12,* 458–472.

Smyer, M.A. (1984). Life transitions and aging: Implications for counseling older adults. *The Counseling Psychologist, 12,* 17–37.

Staudinger, U.M., Smith, J., & Baltes, P.B. (1994). *Manual for the assessment of wisdom-related knowledge [Materially NR. 46 Des Max-Plank-Instituts fur Bildungsforschung].* Berlin, Germany: Max Planck Insitute for Human Development and Education.

Sternberg, R.J. (1985). Implicit theories of intelligence, creativity, and wisdom. *Journal of Personality and Social Psychology, 49,* 607–627.

Sternberg, R.J. (Ed.). (1990). *Wisdom: Its nature, origins, and development.* Cambridge, England: Cambridge University Press.

Sterns, H.L., & Camp, C.J. (1998). Applied gerontology. *Applied Psychology: An International Review, 47,* 175–198.

Stones, J.J., & Kozma, A. (1996). Activity, exercise, and behavior. In J.E. Birren & K.W. Schaie (Eds.), *Handbook of the psychology of aging* (4th ed., pp. 338–364). San Diego, CA: Academic Press.

Sue, S., Zane, N., & Young, K. (1994). Research on psychotherapy with culturally diverse populations. In A.E. Bergin & S.L. Garfield (Eds.), *Handbook of psychotherapy and behavior change* (4th ed., pp. 783–820). New York: Wiley.

Takamura, J.C. (1998). An aging agenda for the 21st century: The opportunities and challenges of population longevity. *Professional Psychology: Research and Practice, 29,* 411–412.

Thurmond, D.P. (1996). *Choosing to meet the need: A guide to improve targeting of title III services to low-income minority elderly.* Washington, DC: National Association of Area Agencies on Aging.

Torres-Gil, F. (1987). Hispanics: A special challenge. In A. Pifer & L. Bronte (Eds.), *Our aging society: Paradox and promise* (pp. 219–242). New York: Norton.

United States Bureau of the Census. (1992, July). Growth of America's oldest old population. *Profiles of America's elderly, No. 2* Washington DC: U.S. Government Printing Office.

United States Bureau of the Census. (1996). *Current population reports, special studies, 65+ in the United States* (pp. 23–190). Washington DC: U.S. Government Printing Office.

van Tilburg, T. (1998). Losing and gaining in old age: Changes in personal network size and social support in a four-year longitudinal study. *Journals of Gerontology: Psychological Sciences and Social Sciences, 53,* 313–323.

Weiland, S. (1995). Interpretive social science and spirituality. In M.A. Kimble et al. (Eds.), *Aging, spirituality and religion: A handbook* (pp. 589–611). Minneapolis, MN: Fortress Press.

Weiner, M.B. (1992). Treating the older adult: A diverse population: Psychoanalysis of the midlife and older patient [Special issue]. *Psychoanalysis and Psychotherapy, 10,* 66–76.

Wellman, R.E., & McCormack, J.M. (1984). Counseling with older persons: A review of outcome research. *The Counseling Psychologist, 12,* 81–95.

Whitely, J. (1980). Counseling psychology in the year 2000 A.D. *The Counseling Psychologist, 8,* 2–8.

Williams, M.J. (1991). *Memory assessment scales.* Camberwell, Australia: Psychological Assessment Resources.

Willis, S.L. (1985). Towards an educational psychology of the older adult learner: Intellectual and cognitive bases. In J.E. Birren & K.W. Schaie (Eds.), *Handbook of the psychology of aging* (2nd ed., pp. 818–847). New York: Van Nostrand-Reinhold.

Woods, R.T. (1996). Mental health problems in late life. In R.T. Woods (Ed), *Handbook of the clinical psychology of aging,* New York: Wiley.

Worldwatch Institute. (1994). *Vital signs.* New York: Norton.

Worthington, E.L. (1989). Religious faith across the life span: Implications for counseling and research. *The Counseling Psychologist, 17,* 555–612.

Worthington, E.L., Jr., Hight, T.L., Ripley, J.S., Perrone, K.M., Kurusu, T.A., & Jones, D.R. (1997). Strategic hope-focused relationship-enrichment counseling with individual couples. *Journal of Counseling Psychology, 44,* 381–389.

Yesavage, J.A. (1986). The use of self-rating scales in the elderly. In L.W. Poon (Ed.), *Clinical memory assessment of older adults.* Washington, DC: American Psychological Association.

Yesavage, J.A., Lapp, D., & Sheikh, J.I. (1989). Mnemonics as modified for use by the elderly. In L.W. Poon, D.C. Rubin, & B.A. Wilson (Eds.), *Everyday cognition in adulthood and late life* (pp. 598–611). Cambridge, England: Cambridge University Press.

CHAPTER 17

Health Promotion and Disease Prevention: A Concentric Biopsychosocial Model of Health Status

MARY ANN HOFFMAN
JEANINE M. DRISCOLL

Health status is not simply the presence or absence of disease, acute or chronic. It also includes psychological well-being which results from perceptions and learned skills that we use to adapt to physical, emotional, and interpersonal challenges that emerge throughout life. In this chapter, we propose a modified view of Engel's (1977, 1980) classic biopsychosocial model. Unlike Engel's model, which posits that biological, psychological, and social factors interact to cause disease or deficits, we believe that these same factors can lead to positive health outcomes, as well as to negative ones.

To better reflect this continuum of health outcomes resulting from the complex interplay between objective health and subjective well-being, we will use the term "health status" rather than "disease" which implies negative outcomes. We believe that health status better captures the effects of multiple domains (biological, psychological, and social) that contribute to health outcomes, as well as the ever-present potential for shifts in the continuum of outcomes. Furthermore, recent research suggests that some health outcomes are better correlated with psychosocial factors than with the presence or absence of objective disease (e.g., Eiche & Hoffman, 1998; Slaven & Lee, 1997). Because of this, it may be informative for research, counseling, and policy perspectives to focus on health status rather than simply on the occurrence and management of a specific disease. This kind of focus allows health promotion to occupy a primary place and espouses a preventive model of care. Finally, our conceptualization of wellness moves away from a disease-deficit model toward a model that incorporates adaptation and proactive responding. This conceptualization means that an individual may have an acute or chronic disease, but be relatively well in the midst of the disease process. Similarly, this conceptualization acknowledges the influential role of health-promoting attitudes and behaviors in preventing disease or in reducing the psychosocial costs of disease.

Recognition of the important effect psychosocial factors have on health status is a relatively recent phenomenon. Until the past twenty years, health status, disease acquisition, and disease progression typically were viewed from a biological perspective (T.W. Smith & Nicassio, 1995). This is striking when one considers that there are over 400 million yearly visits to primary care doctors and clinics in the United States, and that in one third of these visits no organic cause for the patient's symptoms can be found (Barsky, 1981; Sobel, 1995). According to Sobel, nearly one third of patients who visit health care professionals have bodily symptoms that are an expression of psychological distress, and the symptoms of another third of patients are a result of behavioral factors, such as diet and smoking. For the remaining patients, the course of their illness can be strongly influenced by moods such as depression and anxiety, by coping skills, and by social support.

As psychologists and health care providers have begun to recognize the important role that psychosocial factors play in health status and the development of chronic diseases, there has been an important shift in realizing that there is more to living than simply not dying (Ware, 1984). In other words, research on health status is focusing on understanding the antecedents and effects of wellness, disease, and treatment. As the focus of health care has moved beyond the simple biomedical goal of survival, there has been a new emphasis on the importance of behavioral and psychosocial outcomes. Consequently, a shift in health care objectives is occurring with more attention to quality of life outcomes and the economic and psychological costs of disease effects (Ware, 1984). This may lead to a greater understanding of individual differences in treatment outcomes, even for the same disease. Despite this shift toward recognizing the importance of psychosocial factors, our review of the literature shows that research on health psychology continues to focus primarily on a disease or deficit model. In other words, far greater attention is focused on the correlates and causes of disease and disability than on the factors associated with positive health. It may be easier to conceptualize, measure, and describe the absence of health than the presence of positive health.

CURRENT STATUS OF HEALTH IN THE UNITED STATES

Being well is integral to a daily life lived vibrantly and productively. However, even with increases in longevity, there have been decreases in the years of quality, healthy life (U.S. Department of Health & Human Services, 1996a). This means that through scientific knowledge and technology the length of human life has been extended, but the quality of that life may be less than optimal. For instance, more Americans than ever are currently living with chronic diseases, many of which are disabling.

Chronic disease is the major health problem facing our nation and its prevalence is widespread (Taylor & Aspinwall, 1990). Chronic diseases are present in approximately 40% of the working population and nearly 80% of the geriatric population (Pope & Tarlov, 1991). It is the leading cause of death, as well as the primary source of health expenditures (T.W. Smith & Nicassio, 1995; U.S. Department of Health & Human Services, 1996a). This is in sharp contrast to the early part of this century when the majority of deaths were due to a single cause such as an acute disease (Speers & Lancaster, 1998). Today, the majority of deaths are due to multicausal chronic disease. Lifestyle factors such as smoking, diet, excessive alcohol intake, and physical inactivity play critical roles in the etiology of chronic disease (U. S. Department of Health & Human Services, 1996a). More recently, sexual behaviors leading to diseases such as HIV/AIDS have played an important role (Hoffman, 1996). In addition, moods, cognition, and social support are now recognized for their contribution to wellness. This significant change in the pattern of illness from acute diseases to multicausal chronic diseases has far-reaching implications for disease prevention, progression, and management.

Both the economic and psychosocial costs of chronic disease are enormous (T.W. Smith & Nicassio, 1995). Even when chronic disease is not life threatening there are costs such as pain, loss of self-image, loss of valued roles, and changes in lifestyle. Direct costs include the more obvious and tangible aspects of disease such as medical expenditures for diagnosis and treatment. In contrast, indirect costs are the value lost to society due to premature disability and, in many cases, death caused by chronic disease. Examples include reduced work productivity for persons with a chronic disease and their partners, friends, and family members who provide care. To illustrate, the indirect costs of HIV disease are estimated at over $23 billion for the first decade of this epidemic (Farnham, 1994). These types of indirect costs also affect individuals, their support networks, the workplace, and communities in intangible ways that are difficult to assess. The prevalence and cost of chronic disease make it imperative that social and medical scientists develop a greater understanding of what factors are associated with health problems, but even more importantly, those that predict positive health and wellness.

In an effort to promote and improve health, the Public Health Service has issued an initiative called Healthy People 2000 (U.S. Department of Health & Human Services, 1996a). This initiative is a national health agenda whose objectives evolved from previous national agendas involving health promotion and disease prevention. The objective of Healthy People 2000, to increase the health status of Americans by the year 2000, is subsumed under three overarching goals: (1) increasing the span of healthy life or healthy years lived for all Americans; (2) reducing health disparities among Americans; and, (3) achieving and providing access to preventive services for all Americans. Fundamentally, Healthy People 2000 is a wellness agenda that strives to establish "the vision of healthy people in healthy communities." Progress has been made toward many of the goals set by this initiative (e.g., childhood immunizations, fewer gonorrhea and syphilis infections). However, in some areas (e.g., preventive clinical services, number of individuals disabled by chronic conditions, newborns with low birthweights) there has been no improvement, and in some cases, declines. An important area where progress is lacking is in reversing the relationship between socioeconomic disparities and health status.

Healthy People 2000 is noteworthy for recognizing that the foundations of good health are multidimensional, and include psychological and social factors that are as critical to health status as are biomedical ones. Awareness of what is necessary to maintain health and be well, and developing competent skills to pursue health and well-being, are examples of important psychosocial aspects of health promotion. For instance, stroke and hypertension are, in large part, preventable. Although genetic factors may predispose individuals to higher risks of both, diet, exercise, and nicotine and alcohol intake can be strong predictors of these disease processes. Daily choices and actions can exert life-altering effects. Furthermore, these daily individual choices and actions occur within a psychological, social, economic, and political context, which may facilitate or hamper health promotion efforts. This has recently led researchers to consider psychological, social, and biomedical variables when examining health outcomes.

ENGEL'S BIOPSYCHOSOCIAL MODEL

Engel's (1977, 1980) biopsychosocial model was the first to consider systematically the impact of psychological and social factors in conjunction with biological factors in predicting health. Engel's (1977) biopsychosocial model represented a radical departure from the then prevailing view of chronic disease as due primarily to biomedical factors, to one that recognized the effect of psychosocial factors. To illustrate, prior to this model, health care professionals focused on biomedical approaches to manage chronic disease such as directing patients to take medications, quit smoking, lose weight, and make dietary changes. Biomedical interventions are typically viewed as having a direct link with a particular disease symptom. For example, a patient might be instructed to take a particular medication, without consideration of psychosocial factors that might affect implementation and maintenance of the regimen. Although such interventions can be effective, the fact that many patients do not comply with these recommendations, comply inconsistently, or relapse suggests that a biomedical perspective alone is insufficient. Psychological factors such as stress, personality characteristics, and motivation to change contribute to both the acquisition and progression of chronic disease. Moreover, the social context of the client's life situation, including relationships with partners and family members, friends, work environment, culture, and the community, are also important factors in understanding health status.

The premise of Engel's (1977, 1980) model is that health outcomes are based on an interplay between biological, psychological, and social factors. These elements are organized in terms of hierarchical units ranging from the least to the most complex. These hierarchical units range from cells, the most basic unit, all the way up to the broadest unit, which represents the individual's culture-subculture. Each of these units represents a system with distinct qualities, yet each component can have both downward and upward effects in the total system or model as they affect disease. In other words, any system or unit within the larger system cannot be understood alone but must be considered in terms of the entire system.

With the publication of Engel's biopsychosocial model of chronic disease in 1977, research on the role of psychosocial factors in disease prevention, acquisition, and progression began to grow. Yet, Taylor and Aspinwall (1990) noted that despite this broadened perspective, medical citations on health-related quality of life continued to outnumber psychological citations by a ratio of 10:1.

Few would disagree about the importance of considering biological, psychological, and social variables in understanding health status, yet it is our view that conceptualizing how these constructs interact remains problematic despite 20 years of research on the biopsychosocial model. It remains both intriguing and perplexing that it is so difficult to determine the contribution of biological, psychological, and social variables to a given individual's health status. Even when a disease has a strong genetic component, environmental or lifestyle factors are often necessary to trigger this potential (Gail & Benichou, 1992). This concept is best illustrated by studies of identical twins. One twin may have a chronic disease associated with a genetic predisposition or vulnerability, but the other twin either does not have this disease, has a less severe case, or acquires it at a much later point in time (Gottesman & Shields, 1982).

Although Engel's model has guided research in recognizing the interplay between biological, psychological, and social domains, one criticism of the model is that it provides a broad conceptual framework rather than a unifying theory (T.W. Smith & Nicassio, 1995). Another difficulty that we see with Engel's model is that it is hierarchical. Although it makes intuitive sense to create a hierarchical model based on the simplest to most complex unit, and despite its interactional nature, this hierarchical arrangement implies that certain units or systems are more important than others. In a similar vein, Sadler and Hulgus (1990) pointed out that as a multilevel systems approach, Engel's model obscures which system level (e.g., cellular, person) is most important at any point in time. Finally, we believe that a hierarchical model, even one that is interactional, may make it more difficult to understand the integration of biological and psychosocial processes and may, therefore, perpetuate the conventional dichotomy or schism between them.

We propose a model of health status based on concentric circles that we believe better captures the interactions and recursive nature between biological, psychological, and social factors. Furthermore, we propose that health status, which can range on a continuum from healthy to unhealthy, is more inclusive than the concept of disease alone. This conceptual change may encourage researchers to consider positive aspects of adjustment as well as disease and pathology.

A CONCENTRIC BIOPSYCHOSOCIAL MODEL

Health Status

At the center of our model depicted in Figure 17.1 is what we call health status. Our choice of health status, as opposed to disease, reflects our view that health outcomes result from an ongoing, developmental biopsychosocial process that can yield a range of positive or negative outcomes. Similar to Antonovsky's (1979, 1987) view, an individual's health status can be placed somewhere along a continuum of well-being ranging from total illness to total wellness. This placement can vary as biopsychosocial influences change. As such, health status is a dynamic process that requires ongoing adaptation to biological, psychological, and social challenges that emerge throughout life. In contrast, most recent conceptualizations of health view the presence of disease, disease symptoms, or illness as the outcome of biopsychosocial processes. We believe that this emphasis on disease as the key outcome inadvertently keeps these biopsychosocial models rooted in a biomedical perspective. Instead, we are more interested in what facilitates movement toward health-related well-being rather than what leads to disease.

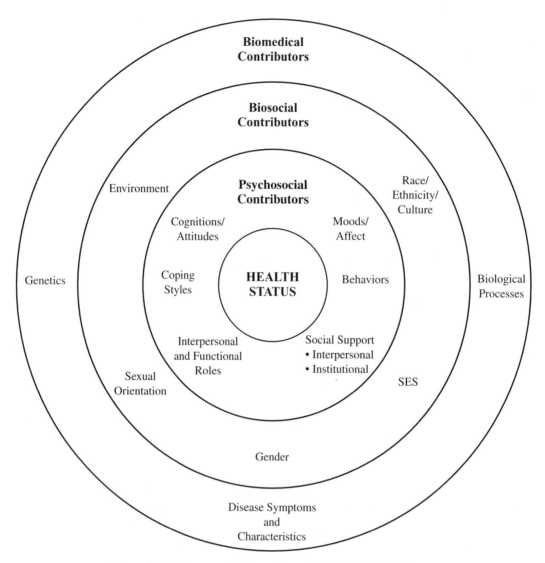

Figure 17.1   Concentric Biopsychosocial Model of Health Status

A second important aspect of our definition is that a higher level of health status, or wellness, is not wholly dependent on being free of disease or disability. Instead, we agree with Jensen and Allen's (1993) view of the dialectic relationship that exists between health-disease, and wellness-illness. Although distinct, health-disease and wellness-illness are neither mutually exclusive nor polar opposites. An individual can have a chronic disease, or disease symptoms, and report being relatively well because of that individual's subjective view of the objective evidence of illness or disease. In other words, health status consists both of states of psychological and of physical well-being. These aspects of health status are viewed as orthogonal, but related dimensions, rather than as a unidimensional construct. This is similar to Kaplan's (1990) view of health status as consisting of two essential elements: symptomatic complaints and health-related quality of life. He measures both of these constructs using his Quality of Well-being scale (Kaplan & Anderson, 1988; Kaplan, Sieber, & Ganiats, 1997).

We do want to note that we struggled with our choice of the term "health status." We wanted a phrase that conveyed a range of illness-wellness outcomes, that could include both physical symptoms and subjective views, and one that recognized that health represents a dynamic, ongoing process. We considered "wellness" but were influenced by Antonovsky's critique of this concept (Antonovsky, 1994) which was expanded by Levenstein (1994). They argued that the wellness perspective may downplay physiological causes of illness, and it may lead to blaming the individual for failing to be "well." Although our review of the literature showed that "disease" was by far the most common term used to designate health outcomes, we found that health status has been used to designate outcomes since at least 1946 when the World Health Organization (WHO) formulated its classic definition of health. This was perhaps the first definition to include psychological and social well-being (WHO, 1948).

Psychosocial Contributors

Our next concentric circle represents psychological and social variables. This circle is closest to health status because psychological and social variables often serve an indirect, mediating, or moderating role between biomedical and biosocial variables and health status. For example, social support that is consistent with what the individual needs (e.g., emotional, problem solving, financial) has been empirically shown to buffer the stress impact of some diseases (see Uchino, Cacioppo, & Kiecolt-Glaser, 1996).

Biosocial Contributors

Biosocial contributors, represented in the next concentric circle, are variables that have biological aspects, but are also, in part, defined by social constructions. For example, gender has a biological basis that in and of itself has implications for health status, but it is simplistic to ignore the social constructions of what it means to be a male or a female within one's culture. Similarly, health effects due to environmental factors can often be explained in biomedical terms (e.g., toxicity due to lead poisoning), but this relationship may be associated with social factors such as poverty.

Biomedical Contributors

What we call biomedical contributors are represented in the outer concentric circle. Until relatively recently, these variables were typically viewed as the direct and primary causes or predictors of health status. They represent more fixed constructs (e.g., genetics, a malignancy) than those represented in the other circles, and thus may be more difficult to modify directly through psychological interventions. Yet they are important to consider in terms of the direct effects they may have on health status, as well as the ways their impact might be modified through a focus on psychosocial variables. Furthermore, psychosocial interventions have the potential to reduce the incidence of these biomedical factors through interventions that focus on prevention. These include prevention strategies to reduce the likelihood of compromised health status due to diseases such as coronary heart disease, which has a biomedical aspect (e.g., atherosclerosis) and psychosocial and sociocultural correlates (Thoresen & Goldberg, 1998).

OVERVIEW OF RESEARCH

In this next section, we overview research that examines variables represented in each of the concentric circles. It is beyond the scope of this chapter to present an exhaustive review of the literature related to each aspect of our model. Therefore, we will focus on illustrative examples of these empirical connections. At the end of this section, we discuss the status of research that actually tests the biopsychosocial model by examining all three domains of the model.

Research on Biomedical Contributors

As previously noted, prior to Engel's publication of his biopsychosocial model, health status was primarily, even exclusively, defined biologically. Prescriptions for health relied on correcting or modifying biological processes that were malfunctioning. An interesting correlate of this conceptualization is "parentalism" within the health care system (i.e., the doctor knows best). Such an approach runs counter to the client or patient as a partner, collaborator, or even primary care provider (Sobel, 1995). Nevertheless, biology clearly influences health status even though often it is "nested" in layers of lifestyle, environment, and socioeconomic variables.

Biomedical factors (e.g., inherited characteristics) are estimated to cause only 20% of premature deaths in the United States (Foster, 1997). In terms of major causes of all deaths, heart disease accounts for nearly 40%, cancer malignancies for 20%, and stroke for 10% (Matarazzo, 1990). The remaining causes of death are attributed to a variety of such factors as diabetes, arteriosclerosis, and influenza. Although biological processes appear to be the primary cause of death for many of these diseases, it is important to note that these processes are often triggered by behavioral, psychological, and social factors. Thus, biological-type variables may represent a predisposing factor, but psychosocial variables may be necessary as mediating or cofactors, which accounts for the relatively low percentage of deaths directly attributable to biomedical factors alone.

Despite statistics showing the relatively small primary role that biological factors play in many negative health outcomes, the focus of interventions has been, and continues to be, on biomedical processes. Perhaps this is because most health care professionals become involved in care once a disease process has been established. In this case, biomedical approaches offer a necessary but often insufficient form of remedial treatment. However, a biomedical approach may be less effective than a psychosocial one for interventions that target prevention. Three types of biomedical variables are discussed: biological processes, disease symptoms and characteristics, and genetics.

Biological Processes

Biological processes refer to physiological events that affect health status. These include circulating hormones (e.g., cortisol), heart rate, and blood lipids (e.g., serum cholesterol). As mentioned previously, the vast majority of research on health has focused on biomedical variables and ignored psychosocial factors that play moderating and mediating roles in health outcomes. To investigate this phenomenon, Rostosky and Travis (1996) conducted a review of research on menopause over a 10-year time frame. Menopause is widely viewed as one of the most significant life passages for women, and one that has biopsychosocial causes and consequences. Yet an astounding 94% of the studies identified through Medline, and 70% of those found in PsychLit, were based on a biomedical perspective. In general, these studies treated menopause as a series of biological processes to be treated with hormone replacement therapies. In contrast, very few studies focused on psychosocial factors, such as the meaning of menopause in a woman's life, the role of exercise in alleviating symptoms, the relationship of menopause to mood, and decision making regarding hormone replacement therapy. Another example is the focus on serum cholesterol levels in research on correlates of heart disease. According to Thoresen and Goldberg (1998), this narrow focus on selected biological processes ignores the role of important human processes such as cognitions and behaviors. Although biological processes should be considered in understanding health outcomes, our view is that these processes are better understood by examining them within the context of psychosocial factors.

Disease Symptoms and Characteristics

Specific diseases have common symptoms that characterize them, although there are variations in the severity and course of diseases. In other words, there are commonalties within various diseases in terms of symptoms, medications, interventions, and disease outcomes. However, there may be vast differences in the impact of the disease in terms of factors such as perceptions of pain, changes in valued roles, and illness intrusion (Devins, 1994). Hoffman (1996) referred to "defining characteristics" of disease that affect all, or nearly all, persons with that specific disease and create some degree of universality among those affected. To illustrate, persons with HIV disease typically acquire this virus at a young age, which represents an off-time developmental event. HIV is a chronic disease managed by a rigid regimen of antiretroviral and protease inhibitors over the course of many years. The individual may be able to transmit the virus to others throughout his or her lifetime, and stigma continues to define this disease (Hoffman, 1996). Other examples include monitoring insulin levels and administering injections for diabetes, and managing muscle tremors and balance with Parkinson's disease. These defining characteristics, although stemming from biological factors, exert a profound psychosocial influence.

Genetics

According to the Centers for Disease Control and Prevention, 20% of premature deaths in the United States are attributable to inherited or genetic factors (McGinnis & Foege, 1993). Recent research is revealing the central role that genetic factors play in a number of diseases (Lee & Paxman, 1997). Genetics are the direct cause of some diseases such as sickle cell anemia. In other cases, genetics predispose people to diseases or complications from diseases (e.g., breast cancer, colon cancer, depression, alcoholism).

Because genetic links to various diseases are too numerous to delineate here, only a few examples will be given. A number of studies have shown a genetic component in obesity (e.g., Keesey, 1993), concluding that factors such as the number of fat cells and the body's metabolic set point are in part determined by genetics. Because closely related relatives of women with eating disorders have a significantly greater chance of having an eating or affective disorder, a genetic link is hypothesized to exist between eating disorders and depression (e.g., Gershon, Schreiber, & Hamovit, 1984). Evidence for a genetic contribution to smoking (Lerman et al., 1999) and alcohol (Peele, 1984) has also been found.

However, diseases often result from a complex and unknown combination of genetics and such other factors as lifestyle (Lee & Paxman, 1997). In other words, genetic vulnerabilities may be triggered by interpersonal, psychological, or environmental factors. Much of the recent progress in understanding the role of genes in various diseases is attributable to the Human Genome Project (Guyer & Collins, 1995).

Research on Biosocial Contributors

Contributors to health status that we have called "biosocial" have both a biological and physical basis, but often have socially constructed statuses. Yet these variables are often treated in research as if they only have biomedical aspects, and as if these biological aspects apply similarly to all groups of people. This concept can be illustrated by the history of medical research in the United States. Medical research, which forms the foundation for what we know about disease processes, takes place in social, economic, ethical, and legal contexts that shape and constrain health care and service delivery. Because scientific research reflects the culture and society in which it evolves, it is consequently permeated by the biases that operate in the dominant culture regarding gender, race, or ethnicity (Aday & Andersen, 1981; Mastroianni, Faden, & Federman, 1994). These demographic variables, ostensibly simple descriptive labels, yield complex psychosocial interactions and, in turn, affect what we know about the health of various groups of people. A stark example of this is the near exclusion of all but middle-class White men from clinical trials until recently (Mastroianni et al., 1994; Shavers-Hornaday, Lynch, Burmeister, & Turner, 1997). Consequently, relatively little is known about common disease processes, such as cardiovascular disease, for large groups of the population. This sociopolitical context may explain the differential treatment of men versus women, Whites versus racial minorities, and those of higher versus lower economic status within the health care system. Several biosocial variables will be discussed: race/ethnicity/culture, socioeconomic status, gender, sexual orientation, and environment.

Race, Ethnicity, and Culture

Although race can be viewed as a biological category in which certain biological traits such as skin color are passed through heredity (Young & Zane, 1995), there are multiple social constructions that have become interwoven with these biological aspects. Ethnicity may pertain to race, but it can be used to designate persons who share a common culture. According to Young and Zane, there are biological, cognitive, linguistic, psychological-emotional, and social factors to consider when addressing health issues with ethnically and culturally diverse persons. For example, biological differences based on physiological processes, such as lactose intolerance and drug metabolism, have been found (see Kalow, 1989). Researchers have concluded that in addition to differences in metabolism, there may be ethnic differences in brain receptor sensitivity (Cotton, 1990).

Cognitive differences due to ethnicity or culture include health schemas that organize beliefs about the causes of illness. Cultures may differ in terms of psychological and emotional variables, such as patterns of emotional expression, and in characteristics of social support networks. Furthermore, remedies that a given culture might use for health problems may be unknown to, or even discounted by, the formalized scientific health care community.

Racial and ethnic minorities are underrepresented in virtually all aspects of medical research (Shavers-Hornaday et al., 1997). Because there are racial/ethnic variations in responses to some medications and in the incidence of certain diseases, this underrepresentation has major implications for health promotion, prevention, and management. Moreover, many minorities have less trust in the medical and mental health community, and this may lead to underuse, less access to appropriate services, lower compliance, and limited knowledge about the health of many groups of people (Shavers-Hornaday et al., 1997). Several impediments to African American participation in medical research have been specified: distrust of the medical/scientific community, poor access to primary medical care, failure of researchers to actively recruit this population, lack of knowledge about clinical trials, and language and cultural variables (Shavers-Hornaday et al., 1997). However, at least some of these impediments may be more a function of socioeconomic status than race or ethnicity per se.

Socioeconomic Status

A recent report documents that a relationship exists between health status (i.e., progress toward health promotion, disease prevention) and income and education (U.S. Department of Health & Human Services, 1998). Less wealthy, less educated people are more likely to suffer various health problems and have limited or no access to preventive care. For instance, this report noted that alcohol use was 30% higher in people with less than a high school education than for those with college degrees. Sedentary lifestyle, hypertension, and cigarette smoking are similarly more prevalent in low-income, less-educated people, regardless of race. HIV infection is another example of a disease that is quickly becoming linked to socioeconomic status in the United States as more and more lower income persons, including a disproportionate number of African Americans and Latinos, become infected (Centers for Disease Control & Prevention, 1998; Krueger, Wood, Diehr, & Maxwell, 1990).

Relatedly, health status has been shown to improve with increasing socioeconomic status (Kunst, Guerts, & Berg, 1992). Specifically, the health status of each social class level within a given population is better than the classes below and worse than the classes above. This interesting finding challenges the notion that it is a simple matter of material deprivation that leads to poor health status because most segments of our society have access to the basic necessities, such as food and shelter (S. Kelly, Hertzman, & Daniels, 1997). Therefore, it is likely that the more specific conditions under which people live (such as everyday stressors), which may vary between social classes, affect health status over and above material deprivation.

Another factor to consider is the quality of health care linked to socioeconomic status (Ginzberg, 1991). Higher income often correlates with having adequate health insurance as well as access to care. However, it is not always possible to separate the effects of economic status from race in our country because of a long history of unequal opportunities and access to care (see Betancourt & López, 1993).

Gender

Little (1996) and Mastroianni et al. (1994) noted that male bias and male norms tend to be the lenses through which social and scientific reality is viewed. For example, the male body has become the norm for understanding most disease acquisition and progress. In terms of health care, this has meant that the "healthy person" has become synonymous with the "healthy male" (Little, 1996). This is due in part to underrepresentation of women in clinical medical trials, which has important implications for access to appropriate health care. One result is that health care providers know much less about disease acquisition and progression in women regarding diseases such as coronary heart disease (Gijsbers van Wijk, Van Vliet, & Kolk, 1996; Little, 1996; Mastroianni et al., 1994). Moreover, gender bias in the management and treatment of serious disease has led to such outcomes as women being less likely than men to receive a needed kidney transplant (Gijsbers van Wijk, Kolk, van den Bosch, & van den Hoogen, 1992).

Gender inequalities in health care reflect the basic inequality between men and women in most societies (Gijsbers van Wijk et al., 1996). It is important to note that both men's and women's health involves more than simple biology and includes their emotional, social, and physical well-being within a particular social, economic, and political context. In the United States, two major barriers that interfere with health care for women are attitudinal barriers that affect motivation to seek health care and organizational barriers that block access to and use of health services (Foster, 1997). Although many of the same health threats affect both men and women (e.g., coronary heart disease, stroke, cancer, lung-related diseases), domestic violence against women represents a major difference. According to Foster some 30% of visits by women to emergency services are caused by domestic violence; 90% of women who are physically abused do not discuss this violence with a health care provider.

In addition to a gender bias that permeates the health care system, there are biological and physiological differences between men and women that make one gender more vulnerable to particular disease states. Two common examples of gender differences in rates of disease acquisition are prostate cancer and breast cancer (men can get breast cancer but this occurrence is much lower than in women). When men and women have the same disease, progression and outcome may differ. For example, women who have a myocardial infarction are more likely to die earlier than men who do, and the prognosis for women who have undergone surgery for coronary heart disease is poorer (Wengner, Speroff, & Packard, 1993). Moreover, relatively little is known about the prevention and management of coronary heart disease in women because relatively few women have participated in clinical trials and in disease management programs.

Sexual Orientation

Sexual orientation is rarely discussed as a variable contributing to health status. Perhaps more than any other disease in history, HIV has focused attention on the interface between health and psychosocial and sociopolitical issues such as sexual orientation (Hoffman, 1996). HIV infection has shown that disease is not simply about the presence or absence of a virus or some other disease process. Rather, perceptions of disease often reflect the values, biases, and attributions of the cultural context in which they occur. It is likely that compassionate medical and political responses to HIV disease were delayed because of the stigma associated with the mode of transmission in the first wave of cases in this country (men having sex with men), and the fact that these men represented a marginalized group (gay men) (see Shilts, 1987). As illustrated by HIV disease, sexual orientation may also be a factor in willingness to seek health care, barriers to making health-protective changes, and access to appropriate care (Hoffman, 1996).

Environmental Factors

Environmental factors may affect both the acquisition and the outcome of diseases. Moreover, people living in urban areas, especially those of low socioeconomic status, are at a greater risk for poor health than all others (Speers & Lancaster, 1998). For example, exposure to smoke, asbestos, lead in paint, and similar substances can lead to various cancers and lung disorders. Asthma is an example of an illness that has increased dramatically in recent years. This has been primarily attributed to environmental factors, such as pollution and dust (Weiss & Wagener, 1990). Environmental factors have been implicated in respiratory, neurological, immunological, and developmental health effects (U.S. Congress, 1994). In addition, a number of environmental agents damage DNA, which may lead to various cancers and mutations (Huff, 1993)

Often it is difficult to assess what factors (e.g., physical aspects of the environment vs. other factors) are associated with a particular health outcome. For instance, low birthweights among African American inner city infants has often been blamed on maternal socioeconomic status. However, recent research suggests that an exaggerated neuroendocrine response to stress may be a likely factor in low birthweight infants (see Cotton, 1990). If so, then environmental stresses associated with the inner city, beyond economic status, may contribute to negative health outcomes. In a related vein, a regular exercise program, including such activities as walking or jogging, may be more difficult in some environments where safety and access are problematic.

In addition to physical health effects, the environment can be implicated in mental health issues. Thus, symptoms of mental health problems may not be due to intrapersonal difficulties per se but rather result from living within a dysfunctional environment. Finally, the environment affects, in large part, access to health care. For instance, middle-class urban areas often have an excess of health care providers, although poor urban centers and rural areas often have severe deficits and many hospitals in these areas have closed (Speers & Lancaster, 1998).

Research on Psychosocial Contributors

Psychosocial factors can be either important consequences of health status or contributing causes. In other words, the association between psychological and social phenomena and health is bidirectional. For example, thoughts, feelings, and moods can have significant effects on the onset of some diseases, the course of many, and the management of nearly all (Sobel, 1995). This is apparent from research that has shown that a large proportion of visits to physicians result from psychosocial distress (Barsky, 1981). Even in those patients with organic medical disorders, health status is strongly influenced by mood, coping skills, and social support. Yet the predominant approach in medicine is to treat people with physical and chemical treatments that ignore or minimize the mental, emotional, and behavioral dimensions of illness (Sobel, 1995).

Psychosocial factors can affect disease processes either directly of indirectly. Direct effects of psychosocial factors may be evident when there is a reliable association of such a variable with predicted changes in health outcomes or status. In other words, these effects do not require mediation by other processes and are essentially a closed loop between the psychosocial process and the particular health outcome (Smith & Nicassio, 1995). These types of psychosocial processes may either precede or follow a health outcome (e.g., anxiety leads to muscle tension; reporting that one is in pain leads to social reinforcement).

In contrast, indirect effects involve more complex relationships between psychosocial factors and health outcomes and require the contributions of mediational processes (T.W. Smith & Nicassio, 1995). Essentially this involves a series of sequences of relationships in which an initial factor contributes to another and these both lead to a third factor. For example, behavioral mediation occurs when avoidance coping leads to poor compliance with a medication regimen, such as taking beta blockers for hypertension. In turn, this leads to increased blood pressure, which puts the individual at risk for a stroke. Physiological mediation may occur when an individual experiences high levels of daily stress, which result in an increase in anxiety. This arousal is in turn associated with constriction of the peripheral blood vessels, resulting in elevated blood pressure. In both cases, blood pressure increases although the psychosocial mechanisms that indirectly mediate this outcome differ.

Finally, psychosocial processes may moderate the effects of other variables on health outcomes. In this case, they are not direct causal variables, rather they alter the relationship between a causal variable and a health outcome. Social support network and the coping mechanisms employed by the individual are common psychosocial moderators that frequently are the focus of psychotherapeutic interventions. These variables can moderate the impact of a stressful life event (e.g., divorce) and affect the likelihood of developing or exacerbating a chronic disease. For example, divorce is less likely to produce negative health consequences when people possess adequate coping resources. In this case, coping mechanisms moderate the relation of divorce to health status. Robbins and Kliewer's (this volume) discussion of the differences between mediator and moderator variables might be helpful in understanding the relationship of psychosocial processes to biological variables.

A relatively recent focus in the literature that provides support for the mediating and moderating effects of psychosocial variables is the field of psychoimmunology. Research in this area has shown the deleterious effects on immune functioning associated with stress and a number of other factors, such as exhaustion, nutrition, social supports, and coping mechanisms (Kiecolt-Glaser & Glaser, 1995). For example, greater distress is associated with poorer immune functioning (Kiecolt-Glaser & Glaser, 1992). This research highlights the important role that psychosocial variables play in relationship to health status. Moreover, psychosocial variables are modifiable through psychological and psychoeducational interventions, unlike many of the biomedical, and some of the biosocial variables described in our model. The following psychosocial contributors are discussed: behaviors, moods/affect, cognitions and attitudes, coping styles, social support, and life roles.

Behaviors

Engaging in health compromising behaviors and failing to practice health enhancing ones contributes to many chronic diseases. To illustrate, smoking is a risk factor for coronary heart disease, malignant neoplasms, and stroke which are the leading major causes of death (McGinnis & Foege, 1993). Eliminating smoking alone in the general population would reduce 25% of all cancer deaths (Taylor & Aspinwall, 1990). Tobacco use contributes to the most deaths per year in the United States (400,000), followed by diet (300,000), activity patterns (300,000), alcohol (100,000), firearms (35,000), sexual behavior (30,000), and illicit use of drugs (20,000) (McGinnis & Foege, 1993). These behavioral factors contribute to nearly half of all deaths. Other behaviors, such as Type A Behavior Syndrome, represent a constellations of behaviors and emotions (in this case, competitive drive, impatience, hostility, and rapid speech and motor movements) that have been associated with disease acquisition and progression (H.S. Friedman & Booth-Kewley, 1987).

Because most of the behaviors described are under voluntary control and therefore are viewed as having a high level of lifestyle involvement (e.g., smoking, diet, exercise), they represent areas where interventions can make significant changes. Biomedical approaches to these types of behaviors have obscured the importance of their occurrence within a social and interpersonal context. In other words, factors such as social support, self-efficacy, and coping-styles play important roles in facilitating or impeding behavioral changes. Thus, recognizing the importance of psychosocial factors in health-related behaviors places them in the psychosocial concentric circle.

Diet. Diet and physical activity represent the second leading cause of preventable deaths in the United States (McGinnis & Foege, 1993). In the United States, the major nutritional problem is "overnutrition" (Detels & Breslow, 1991). In addition to contributing to an increasing rate of obesity (U.S. Department of Health & Human Services, 1996a), diet contributes to cancers, diabetes mellitus, and cardiovascular disease. As many as 35% of cancer deaths are linked to diets implicating such factors as high-fat consumption, fried foods, and an inadequate intake of fruits, vegetables, and fibers (Detels & Breslow, 1991).

Smoking. Cigarette smoking is the leading cause of death in the United States among adults, resulting in 400,000 deaths or about 20% of all deaths (about 40% of all preventable deaths) (Foster, 1997). Shortly after the publication of the first surgeon general's report on smoking in 1964, tobacco use began to decline in adults, but this decline slowed in the 1980s (U.S. Department of Health & Human Services, 1996a). This report concluded that nearly all first tobacco use occurs during high school and that earlier use is associated with continued use as an adult. Moreover, health problems increase with both the quantity of cigarettes smoked and the number of years spent smoking.

Alcohol and Other Drugs. Alcohol use contributes to approximately 100,000 deaths a year or nearly 10% of preventable deaths (McGinnis & Foege, 1993). Alcohol use contributes to cirrhosis of the liver, cancers of the pancreas and liver, hypertension, and memory deficits (G.S. Smith & Kraus, 1988). In addition, alcohol contributes to accidents and is often paired with risky sexual behaviors (Hoffman, 1996). Greater attention to drunk driving has resulted in fewer motor vehicle deaths (Lee & Paxman, 1997).

Sedentary Lifestyle. Despite the acknowledged benefits of exercise, the level of physical activity among Americans has declined dramatically during this century. Research has shown that 25% of adults are not physically active at all and nearly 70% do not engage in physical activity on a regular basis (Caspersen, Christianson, & Pollard, 1986; U.S. Department of Health & Human Services, 1996b). In the past 20 years, inadequate physical activity has been recognized as playing a major role in the morbidity and mortality from cardiovascular disease, stroke, diabetes mellitus, and some forms of cancer (Kriska & Rexroad, 1998; U.S. Department of Health & Human Services, 1996).

A physically active lifestyle may well be public health's "best buy" for improving the overall health of individuals according to Van Mechelen (1997). One way of examining the effects of lifestyle variables, such as sedentary behavior on health outcomes, is through an assessment of the "population attributable risk" (PAR) due to that factor. Specifically, PAR is an estimate of the proportion of deaths from chronic diseases that would not occur if everyone in a population engaged, or did not engage, in specific health-related practices (Powell & Blair, 1994).

Research has shown that the PAR of a sedentary lifestyle for mortality from cardiovascular heart disease, colon cancer, and diabetes mellitus is 35%, 32%, and 35%, respectively, meaning that this percentage of these deaths could theoretically be prevented if everyone was vigorously active (Powell & Blair, 1994). To place this in a context relative to other health-related behaviors, the overall PARs for smoking, saturated fatty acid intake, and obesity (body mass index greater than 30) are 43%, 13%, and 14% in comparison to an overall PAR for sedentary lifestyle of 40%. It is striking that the public health burden caused by a sedentary lifestyle is of the same magnitude as that caused by such obviously harmful behaviors as smoking. Van Mechelen (1997) aptly noted that it may be more effective to encourage a physically active lifestyle than to put so much emphasis on further improvement of diet or reduction of body weight. Moreover, a physically active lifestyle helps maintain weight, may lead to favorable dietary and smoking habits, and has been associated with improvement in mood (Sime, 1984).

Moods/Affect

Emotional reactions play a role in remaining well and in disease acquisition. Moreover, emotional distress is common in people who are coping with chronic disease because nearly every aspect of their lives has the potential to change (Hoffman, 1996). There are numerous studies that document a correlation between mood status and various medical conditions. Common emotional reactions include denial, anxiety, depression, hope, and anticipatory grief. Many of these same emotional processes have been shown to be both a common response to coping with a disease and also to play a role in disease acquisition and progression. For example, negative affective styles marked by depression, anxiety, and hostility may both cause disease and occur as a response to disease (Taylor & Aspinwall, 1990). This is more likely to occur when negative affect is present over an extended period of time. Harmful health outcomes occur largely because of the effects of emotional distress on immune functioning (Kiecolt-Glaser & Glaser, 1995).

In contrast, some positive emotional states play a potentially protective role in disease acquisition, progression, and management. Yet the majority of the health psychology books that we reviewed for this chapter made no reference to the role of positive emotions in health status. Optimism is an example of a positive emotional and cognitive state that increasingly is being linked to positive health outcomes such as immune functioning (Segerstrom & Taylor, 1998). This variable has been associated with psychological and physical well-being, as well as positive adaptation to disease (Scheier, Carver, & Bridges, 1994; Seligman, 1990). Optimism may protect health through its relation with the use of effective, problem-focused coping strategies (e.g., Scheier, Weintraub, & Carver, 1986). This link between emotional and cognitive states illustrates one of the difficulties in determining the exact role of emotions in health status.

Anxiety.   High levels of anxiety can hamper physical and psychosocial functioning, and, conversely, persons with chronic disease often experience anxiety (J.E. Hughes, 1987; Popkin, Callies, Lentz, Cohen, & Sutherland, 1988). In understanding the role of anxiety in health status, the individual's propensity for anxiety must first be considered. For example, recent research has shown that individuals who react to stressful events with intense emotions such as anxiety (high reactors) experience two to three times the heart rate increase, and their endocrine systems respond more sharply to stressors than do low reactors (Cacioppo, 1998). One outcome of this high level of reactivity is a significantly weakened immune system, which puts them at higher risk for disease.

Although premorbid propensity for anxiety needs to be considered, there is evidence that medical interventions and the physical and psychosocial consequences of disease also can produce high levels of anxiety. In a study of persons with cancer, Welch-McCaffrey (1985) found that many aspects of the disease process and treatment produced high levels of anxiety, including waiting for test results, invasive procedures, side effects of treatment, and changes in lifestyle. Uncertainty about disease and treatment outcomes has been associated with anxiety in a number of other studies (e.g., Thompson, Webster, Cordle, & Sutton, 1987). However, the nature of the relationship between anxiety and health status is complex. Anxiety disorders occur in up to 40% of patients with Parkinson's disease, which is higher than in other disease comparison populations (Richard, Schiffer, & Kurlan, 1996). This suggests that anxiety may be both a psychological and neurobiological reaction to a particular illness or disease.

Depression.   One prevalent biopsychosocial disease is depression, which affects about 7% of the population on a lifetime basis (Nurnberger & Gershon, 1992). Depression can both cause disease and be a consequence of disease (Taylor & Aspinwall, 1990). The common symptoms of depression (e.g., disruption in sleep, lack of energy, changes in appetite, and loss of pleasure in usually satisfying activities) can have a pervasive influence across all dimensions of health status. For instance, depression decreases an individual's quality of life and can severely restrict that person's functional status. Recent estimates indicate that nearly half of visits to primary care physicians are related to depressive symptoms. Moreover, depression is common in persons with chronic disease (Rodin & Voshart, 1986). As such, depression, dysthymia, and various depressive symptoms can impede one's sense of well-being (see Wells, Golding, & Burnam, 1989).

The deleterious effects of depression as a chronic disease are well documented. In one study, various kinds of functioning (physical, occupational, social) were compared in persons with eight chronic medical conditions (e.g., diabetes, advanced coronary disease, arthritis) with persons with depression (Hays, Wells, Sherbourne, & Rogers, 1995). Individuals who met all criteria for major depression were more physically limited than people with other chronic medical conditions, except for heart disease patients. Occupational role functioning was significantly worse for patients with depressive symptoms than for those with most other medical conditions. The relationship between aspects of role functioning and depression was shown in another study of HIV-infected men (Griffin, Rabkin, Remien, & Williams, 1998). In this study, degree of physical limitation predicted depression irrespective of disease stage, physical symptoms, and CD4 cell counts. These studies point to the substantial costs of depression.

Anticipatory Grief.   Emotional responses to chronic disease may be understood using the concept of anticipatory grief. This type of grief is a cycle of feelings of loss and anguish over the expectation of major physical changes and possibly a premature death. This process often begins as soon as a diagnosis of a life-threatening illness is made, even before significant changes have occurred (Welch, 1982). Anticipatory grief may recur at each significant stage of disease progression. Anticipatory grief may focus on a general sense of loss of oneself as one once was, or may focus on more specific aspects of self, such as the loss of physical fitness, aspects of one's sexuality, energy, and dreams of a long life achieving expected and valued goals.

Hope.   Hope is essential to maintaining quality of life because it allows one to make plans, set goals, manage painful or complex health procedures or regimens, and use all the material and psychological resources one has at one's disposal. Without hope, the most basic aspects of health prevention, maintenance, and promotion become threatened. Hope is closely linked to the belief that what one does can make a difference in health outcomes. Hope is also closely linked with the positive aspects of denial in the case of potentially devastating health news and may be one of the mechanisms that allows people to be optimistic about the future (Hoffman, 1996).

Cognitions and Attitudes

Cognitive factors such as appraisals, thoughts, self-talk, and beliefs are typically excluded from biomedical models of health status which tend to view the link between changes in health behaviors and resultant effects on health as direct. Simply telling someone to take their medication, follow a low fat diet, or give up smoking ignores the powerful influence of factors such as appraisal and attitudes that influence health through mechanisms other than the usual behavioral risk factors. Cognitive factors have been shown to play an important role in the acquisition and progression of many diseases such as coronary heart disease (Jenkins, 1982).

Cognitions affect health status in several ways. For example, they often act as determinants of health behaviors which, in turn, influence health status. They may also have a direct effect on physiological processes (for example, fear about what it means to have a particular disease may lead to heart palpitations). Finally, aspects of the disease process itself may lead to changes in beliefs or attributions about oneself. For example, acquiring a disease or illness may be viewed as a failure, loss, challenge, punishment, or gain.

In their seminal work on coping, Lazarus and Folkman (1984) noted that the manner in which an individual construes an event shapes the emotional and behavioral responses to that event. This phenomenon accounts in part for the wide variations in how individuals coping with the same disease experience vastly different responses and outcomes. According to Lazarus and Folkman (1984), primary appraisal is the evaluation of what is at stake in a particular situation, and secondary appraisal is the assessment of what options exist to reduce perceived threat or harm. Appraisals about stressful events, in this case health-related events, include three components: harm/loss, threat, and challenge. Learning that one has a disease represents harm or loss. The expected and actual progression of the disease represents the threat of anticipated future losses.

Challenge, or the individual's perception of the potential for gain or growth, determines which coping mechanisms will be mobilized.

This model is very useful in understanding the great variation people show in response to threatening health events, ranging from prevention efforts such as changing one's diet to efforts to manage the effects of a disease, such as taking medications. To be successful, accurate appraisals must be made, the level of threat (e.g., emotional reactions) must be managed so as not to overwhelm the individual, and the challenges must appear to be manageable given the individual's resources.

Similar to cognitive appraisal, attribution theories posit that people form hypotheses about the meanings and causes of significant events that happen to them, and that these attributions have an impact on emotional reactions to these events. Attributions can assist in adjustment to disease if they are emotionally protective and create a sense of understanding and control; or, the converse can be true. For example, Moulton, Sweet, Temoshok, and Mandel (1987) found that for gay men, self-attributions of responsibility for becoming HIV positive had a negative effect on mood, whereas external attributions such as bad luck had an emotionally protective role. These findings fit well with studies about the effect of attributions on situations that can be modified (e.g., health practices, managing emotions) versus those that cannot (e.g., having already acquired HIV disease).

Other research on the role of cognition in health status suggests that having a sense of personal responsibility for one's health and the belief that one can influence health outcomes is related to longevity (e.g., Solomon, Temoshok, O'Leary, & Zich, 1987). However, feeling responsible for health outcomes is different than feeling responsible for disease acquisition. In one study, people with medically documented disease did better when they viewed themselves as being "healthy" rather than "ill" (Sobel, 1995). Such studies suggest that cognitions may at times contribute more to health status than do specific health behaviors.

Self-Efficacy.   Self-efficacy refers to the belief that one can exert control over one's behaviors and motives and the social environment. Beliefs about capabilities affect effort, choices, perseverance, cognitive patterns, mood, and stress (Bandura, 1989). Research on prevention and risk behaviors has often linked self-efficacy to health-promoting and health-impairing behaviors. For example, self-efficacy has been related to a number of health-related variables such as condom use (Wulfert & Wan, 1993), managing stress (Bandura, Cioffi, Taylor, & Brouillard, 1988), and pain perception (Turk, Meichenbaum, & Genest, 1983).

It is important to note that self-efficacy is typically viewed as situation specific in the health literature. In other words, an individual may have a high sense of efficacy regarding some types of health-promoting behaviors, but low efficacy in other areas. Furthermore, some health-protective behaviors, such as wearing a seat belt, can usually be accomplished by an individual without support from others. Other behaviors, such as practicing safer sex, are often dependent on complex interpersonal negotiations and require different efficacy beliefs.

Coping Styles

An important aspect of many chronic diseases is that they frequently prevent sustained and consistent problem solving on the part of the individual. This is due in part to the often unpredictable and erratic course of the disease. For example, diseases such as HIV, Parkinson's, and multiple sclerosis may have common or typical symptoms, but the course of the disease may dramatically differ between those afflicted. Moreover, the physical and psychosocial effect of a disease can challenge and overwhelm the coping strategies an individual may have employed to manage other life events. Coping involves managing emotions, cognitions, and behaviors.

Coping can be defined as "constantly changing cognitive and behavioral efforts to manage specific external and/or internal demands that are appraised as taxing or exceeding the resources of the person" (Lazarus & Folkman, 1984, p. 141). The literature on coping has distinguished two broad types of coping approaches: problem solving and emotional regulation (Lazarus & Folkman, 1984). Appraisals that result in perceptions of threat lead to the initiation of coping efforts or strategies (Lazarus & Folkman, 1984).

The literature is replete with support for the use of coping in moderating the effects of chronic disease. However, research has not yet definitively answered the question of which specific coping strategies help prevent, or facilitate adjustment to, chronic disease (Taylor & Aspinwall, 1990). The complexity of this issue is captured in a study of persons with cancer conducted by Sobel (1995). Those using active coping styles had a better rate of survival than those who used avoidance coping, which supports the findings of a number of previous studies. A finding that initially seems paradoxical was that patients who showed higher levels of emotional distress at the time of diagnosis and treatment had lower rates of cancer recurrence and death. Perhaps distress is an appropriate response at this point of the disease cycle, serving to activate appropriate coping. However, maintaining a high level of distress over time may lead to immune suppression and poorer outcomes (Cohen et al., 1998).

Methods designed to assist clients in learning problem-specific, coping responses that are tailored to a particular situation seem most effective. Coping effectiveness training (CET) emphasizes "fitting" the chosen coping strategy to the specific characteristics of the stressful situation (Chesney & Folkman, 1994). This approach is effective in reducing distress and enhancing overall quality of life.

Social Support

Social support often acts as a buffer when people are in distress and positively affects psychosocial adjustment to a variety of major life events, including health-related issues (Green, 1993). In a landmark nine-year study of men and women, death rates were twice as high for the most socially isolated persons as for those with strong social ties (Berkman & Syme, 1979). For example, socially isolated survivors of heart attacks were more than twice as likely to die as those who were less isolated. They were five to six times more likely to die if they were also in situations that led to additional isolation such as stressful occupations, divorce, exposure to violence, or retirement (Ruberman, Weinblatt, Goldberg, & Chaudhary, 1984). In addition, marital status has been associated with social isolation in that single men aged 45 to 54 die at twice the rate of married men of the same age (M.A. Davis, 1992).

There are many definitions of social support (Tardy, 1985), with the majority focusing on both the quantity and quality of support available. Quantity refers to the number of support sources available and quality refers to whether these supports are accessible and satisfying for the individual. Empirical support has been established for both the direct effect and buffering effect of social support (Cohen & Syme, 1985).

Lack of social support has been associated with poor health outcomes, including death, for a number of diseases such as myocardial infarctions (Berkman, Leo-Summers, & Horwitz, 1992) and coronary heart disease (Williams et al., 1992). For example, research has shown a relationship between HIV-infected persons' perceptions of social support and their reports of physical and psychological symptoms (e.g., Turner, Hays, & Coates, 1993). However, the effects of social support differ across various disease (Penninx et al., 1998) suggesting that varying health-related stressors result in different support needs.

An important aspect of social support that often is ignored in the health literature is what Kahn and Antonucci (1980) referred to as institutional sources of support. These supports include health and mental health clinics, schools, religious institutions, places of employment, and other community resources. These relationships are typically role-specific. That is, if the individual loses health insurance, moves, or loses a job because of disease progression, these sources of support may be lost. Institutional supports are critical in the lives of persons with chronic diseases because of the important resources they can provide, ranging from structure to disease-specific medical and psychosocial services. These supports affect the health of networks of people, not just the individual. Yet, there is a paucity of research on the role of institutional social supports in preventing disease and in buffering or moderating the effects of chronic disease.

Support groups can be viewed as a type of institutional support when they offer health-related expertise and support that cannot be acquired from individuals' interpersonal social networks. Support groups have long been viewed as an important psychosocial intervention for persons with a variety of chronic and acute diseases such as HIV infection (Hoffman, 1996). Group interventions have several advantages over individual counseling strategies: Being in a group with others who face the same disease provides a sense of community and support and ameliorates a sense of isolation; group members can serve as role models for each other as they share solutions to common dilemmas; and members benefit from helping each other (D. Spiegel, Bloom, & Yalom, 1981).

Changes in Interpersonal and Functional Roles

Life roles provide a sense of meaning and structure to life. Chronic disease often means that these roles are disrupted or changed and this can lead to a profound sense of threat and loss for the individual. One shortcoming we see in the health literature is the focus on the effects of chronic disease on functional life roles, to the near exclusion of whether the disease process has changed valued interpersonal roles. Functional status can be defined as the degree to which an individual is free of physically or mentally related limitations that affect the ability to perform socially allocated roles (Bowling, 1991). In other words, it is a measure of disease effects on basic day-to-day activities. Examples include self-care behaviors such as feeding, bathing, and dressing oneself, mobility, and physical activities such as housework.

Because this definition's focus on basic self-care activities is so narrow, a relatively small proportion of the general population (about 0.5%) report limitations in these functional areas (Bowling, 1991). In adults aged 40 and over, Huang et al. (1998) found that 7.5% reported at least one functional limitation in daily or household activities. The prevalence was higher among women than men, and physically fit and active participants reported less functional limitation. Moreover, this narrow definition fails to capture a wide array of roles that lie at the core of an individual's identity. For example, changes in social, interpersonal, work, and cognitive functioning are more common and, most likely, more distressing than changes in functional abilities. Hoffman's review of the literature on the effect of HIV disease on work and employment concluded that this disease was frequently associated with disruptions in jobs and careers (Hoffman, 1997).

Interface between Biological, Social, and Psychological Factors

In the previous section, we presented evidence for the relationship of the various domains of a biopsychosocial perspective to health status. How, then, does an interface occur between the biological, psychological, and social elements? We identified a number of empirical applications of the biopsychosocial model in the health literature. For example, a biopsychosocial model has been shown to predict disease activity in persons with rheumatoid arthritis (Parker, Smarr, Walker, & Hagglund, 1991), to be associated with level of treatment-related pain in persons with cancer (Syrjala & Chapko, 1995), and to predict adjustment to asthma (Eiche & Hoffman, 1998). For example, Eiche and Hoffman found that biological, social, and psychological variables predicted nearly 40% of the variance for health adjustment in a sample of adults with asthma. However, we noted that a number of the studies we reviewed failed to test all three domains of the biopsychosocial model. Furthermore, we could find no review of empirical studies of this perspective when we searched Psychinfo and Medline. Although the biopsychosocial model has been embraced in the health literature in recent years, a number of writers have commented about the ongoing mind-body segregation present in the field (e.g., Carr, 1996), and the need to dismantle the model to understand the interface between its three elements (Melamed, 1995).

Interventions to Enhance Health Status

It is beyond the scope of this chapter to present a comprehensive review of research on health interventions. Instead, we focus on several components or types of interventions that illustrate biopsychosocial perspectives that are especially relevant to counseling psychologists. Unlike biomedical interventions that target specific diseases or narrow behavioral risk factors, psychosocial interventions typically operate by influencing underlying shared determinants of health such as attitudes, beliefs, and moods that predispose toward health in general. They often address psychosocial processes such as barriers to change, adherence to treatment, and psychosocial competence that may increase long-term benefits.

At the heart of health interventions with a psychosocial focus is the role of the counselor as a facilitator of change and the role of the client as an active participant in change. This contrasts with the more passive role of the patient in an intervention where the doctor, as expert, "prescribes" a medication or a regimen. There is emerging evidence that empowering individuals to manage their biopsychosocial needs and become active participants in their health care can be both health and cost-effective. Related to constructs such as self-efficacy and mastery is the notion of learning effective self-care strategies to prevent health problems and to manage disease symptoms. For example, at least 25% of physician visits are for problems that could be self-managed. This includes behaviors such as noncompliance with medication, which then results in a medical crisis. If self-care increased in even a small number of these cases, the demand for expensive medical diagnostic and remedial services could be reduced by nearly 25% (Sobel, 1995). This means that simply helping people become active partners in their health care can reduce health care costs. By helping them manage not only their disease but also common underlying needs for psychosocial support, coping skills, and sense of control, health outcomes can be significantly improved (Sobel, 1995).

In this next section, we first describe research on the nonspecific effects of treatment. Next, we describe interventions that can enhance health status by engaging clients in everyday health promotion activities that activate and integrate biological, psychological, and social components. These involve the client as an active participant in learning self-care strategies to enhance health status. These include stress management, increasing positive cognitions, and becoming physically active. Finally, we discuss treatment or change adherence. The areas of intervention we describe can be used to address health status in general. That is, they may be used to maintain health, to prevent disease, or to lessen the physically and psychologically deleterious effects of disease progression.

Interventions That Address Nonspecific Aspects of Treatment

In the psychotherapy literature, much has been written about nonspecific therapeutic factors (Frank & Frank, 1991). Similar constructs emerge when considering health status. Three examples of this type of construct will be discussed: (1) readiness to change, (2) the placebo effect, and (3) the nocebo effect. These constructs are important because they reflect the mind-body relationship and the roles of beliefs and expectations in wellness and illness. Furthermore, they emphasize the importance of the relationship between client and counselor, and represent an important component of all interventions.

Readiness to Change

Health promotion and changes in attitudes and behaviors related to health status requires both an awareness that change is needed and a commitment and readiness to make changes. There are a number of continuum and stage theories in health psychology that are used to investigate health-protective behaviors including the theory of reasoned action, health belief model, and the protection motivation model (see Weinstein, Rothman, & Sutton, 1998). According to Weinstein et al., the transtheoretical model of behavior change (DiClemente & Prochaska, 1982; Prochaska, DiClemente, & Norcross, 1992) is presently the most widely used stage model in health psychology. It has been applied to a range of health behaviors, such as smoking cessation, safer sex adoption, and exercise adoption. Behavior change is classified into five discrete categories or stages based on past behavior and plans for future action or change. The "processes of change" are a second major dimension of this model, and these describe how changes occur (as opposed to when). Change processes are defined as 10 covert and overt activities (e.g., consciousness raising, reinforcement management, helping relationships) that individuals engage in when they are trying to change their behaviors (Prochaska et al., 1992).

Readiness to change is viewed as an important and necessary component of health prevention, promotion, and maintenance interventions. According to Prochaska et al. (1992), health behavior change is a complex process, which depends on an individual's awareness that behavioral change is necessary. This model describes phases of awareness ranging from an individual having no awareness that change is necessary, or that the current repertoire of behavior is unhealthy (precontemplation), to a nascent awareness that behavioral change is necessary. Next, this new awareness gives way to a more tentative, deliberate recognition of what the individual needs to change and a set of strategies and parameters for accomplishing such change. In turn, this awareness is translated into actions representing attempts at behavior change.

Action, the next phase, involves an awareness of what strategies and behaviors are effective and which are ineffective. It is an evaluative awareness that informs increasingly refined actions. These refined adaptive actions comprise the maintenance, or final, phase of the model. Prochaska and colleagues include relapse as a phase illustrating that behavioral change follows a spiral pattern, rather than a linear one, with mistakes and lapses. These mistakes and lapses become opportunities for learning, growing, and readapting. Based on research with thousands of participants who were trying to modify various addictive behaviors, such as smoking, alcohol abuse, and overeating, Prochaska et al. (1992) concluded that the evidence supported a transtheoretical model, a cyclical pattern of movement through specific stages of change, a common set of processes of change, and an integration of the stages and processes of change.

Four important implications of this research emerge for counseling interventions: (1) the need to assess a client's readiness to change, (2) the importance of tailoring interventions based on readiness, (3) accepting that relapse is the rule rather than the exception in most efforts to change, and, (4) being prepared to modify interventions to create a better match between readiness and treatment characteristics. Client success, or lack of success, provides the feedback to reassess readiness to change, or to modify the intervention.

Placebo and Nocebo Effects

The placebo effect is broadly defined as an aspect of treatment that promotes health but is not attributable to any specific intervention, pharmacological or otherwise. Conversely, the nocebo effect is a nonspecific aspect of treatment or course of treatment that hinders health status. Benson (1996) reviewed studies on the placebo and nocebo effects and concluded that both are comprised of three components: (1) the beliefs and expectations of the patient regarding given health problems and prescribed treatment; (2) the beliefs and expectations of the health care provider regarding given health problems and prescribed treatment; and (3) the beliefs and expectations that are engendered by the relationship between the patient and the provider. Although the placebo effect involves beliefs and expectations that something positive will happen, the nocebo effect involves beliefs and expectations that something negative will happen, or that an intervention will be ineffective.

As an illustration of the placebo effect, two matched groups of preoperative patients were studied (see Benson, 1996). On the evening prior to surgery, one group of patients was visited by their anesthetists who simply introduced themselves, assured the patients that all would go well the next day, and then left. The same anesthetists visited the other group of patients. However in this treatment, the anesthetists met with the patients for five minutes while they overviewed the next day's events, spoke reassuringly, and either touched the patient's hand or shoulder. Following surgery, patients in the compassionately treated group requested half the amount of pain medication and were discharged an average of 2.6 days sooner than the other group. This simple five-minute compassionate intervention led to tangible results and appeared to affect positively the beliefs and expectations of this group about their surgery.

According to H. Spiegel (1997), there are at least three ways in which the nocebo effect is activated. First, negative provider attitudes or aspects of the health care environment can hinder a client's health status. Such negativity may contribute to the client or patient feeling diseased and may provoke maladaptive or illness-focused behaviors. Such behaviors may be attempts to obtain reassurance or connection but are often misperceived by the providers as excessive demands for attention. Second, negative messages from the client's social group or environment may create negative expectations about interventions or outcomes. Family and friends may blame the client for acquiring the disease, or doubt the client's ability to manage disease progression. Likewise, others may minimize the pain of the disease and the losses and fears that accompany it. Such subtle messages may result in the client feeling isolated or stigmatized. Finally, the third way that the nocebo effect may be activated is through the process of secondary gain. This powerful, usually insidious process develops when an individual recognizes that special attention is received because of the pain or disease. For some people, pain or disease becomes a negative reinforcer in that they are relieved from doing things that may be unpleasurable (e.g., dealing with difficult emotional or relationship issues; household responsibilities), or they learn that they can pull others into doing things for them. Nevertheless, secondary gain brings secondary loss (H. Spiegel, 1997). As this secondary loss develops, clients' lives become organized around their disease or pain. Instead of the disease and its consequences becoming a part of their lives and of their identities, it moves to the center and defines them.

The placebo and nocebo effects reflect how thinking and expectancy become translated into a living entity (i.e., "thinking makes it so"). Moreover, they indicate that it is not only the individual's beliefs and expectations that influence health status but also the beliefs and expectations of health care institutions, health care providers, and family and friends. For example, a study examining verbal and nonverbal communication between physicians and patients found that physicians showed signs of negative response to sicker or more emotionally distressed patients (Hall, Roter, Milburn, & Daltroy, 1996). Sicker patients also behaved in more negative ways than healthier patients. This suggests that both parties contribute to expectancies and behaviors that shape their relationship in ways that likely contribute to health outcomes. Helping these various parties to identify and modify their cognitive schema is an essential intervention for counselors.

Interventions in Everyday Health Promotion

In a review of empirical studies of wellness in the past 16 years, Watt, Verman, and Flynn (1998) included randomized controlled studies of interventions ranging from cognitive behavioral therapy to exercise and meditation. Although most interventions yielded some positive results, the authors noted that it was difficult to draw conclusions because of methodological issues. Nevertheless, many of the positive findings pointed to increases in participants' abilities to care for themselves, or to change one aspect of their lives via problem-solving skills, stress reduction, exercise, or the practice of meditation. As the participants' self-care and self-efficacy increased so did their positive health-related outcomes. The interventions that are discussed in this next section—stress management, increasing positive cognitions, and adopting a physically active lifestyle—all represent important life changes that can have effects far beyond the targeted behaviors, cognitions, or emotions.

Stress Management

Stress is one of the most compelling biopsychosocial aspects of illness and disease (Parker, 1995). It is a universal and daily phenomenon requiring ongoing efforts on the part of the individual to regulate and manage both expected and unexpected stressors. Moreover, it has diverse meanings in terms of health status. For example, stress can refer to external or environmental events (stressors) that summon the coping mechanisms of the individual, or it can refer to biological responses (stress responses) within the individual that are a result of these events (Parker, 1995).

Stressors can contribute to the development of chronic disease, and stress responses typically increase as a result of chronic disease. Approximately 20 million Americans experience chronic, stress-induced physical illnesses such as hypertension (Schaffer, 1982). In addition, as much as 75% of all medical problems may be directly attributable to stress (G.H. Hughes, Pearson, & Reinhart, 1984). Consequently, stress management is an important life skill for preventing disease, managing disease effects, and maintaining well-being and health status.

A framework to understand stress responses that is useful in guiding counseling interventions is Everly's (1989) six-stage model: Stage 1 is the stressor event (real or imagined); Stage 2 is cognitive appraisal and affective integration; Stage 3 is neurological triggering mechanisms; Stage 4 is the physiological stress response; Stage 5 is target-organ activation (e.g., impaired cardiovascular, metabolic, and immune functioning); and Stage 6 is coping activities. These six stages are interrelated. Cognitive and affective responses play a critical role in two stages of this model (appraisal and coping)—an important modification of earlier stress models, which focused primarily on physiological reactions to environmental stressors. Furthermore, because Everly viewed the coping process as occurring after physiological responses, coping is conceptualized as cognitive, emotional, and behavioral efforts to regain homeostasis. Therefore, this model lends itself well to counseling-based, stress-management interventions.

Parker (1995) proposed four broad categories of stress-management strategies based on Everly's (1989) model. The first strategy is to eliminate or reduce biological (e.g., uncomfortable surroundings) and psychological (e.g., time demands) stressors. A second strategy to manage stress is to modify the cognitive-affective mediation of stressful events (e.g., positive reframing). Reducing physiological and psychological arousal through the use of interventions such as meditation and biofeedback is a third stress-management strategy. Finally, stress can be managed through constructive expression of the stress response (e.g., ventilation of emotions). All these management strategies, involving psychosocial processes to manage or modulate physiological responses, have received substantial empirical support (e.g., Blankfield, 1991; Blenkhorn, Silove, Magarey, Krillis, & Coninet, 1992; Hyman, Feldman, Harris, Levin, & Malloy, 1989).

Increasing Positive Cognitions: Self-Efficacy and Optimism

The literature on health status primarily focuses on ineffective or deleterious responses to life stressors, with the subsequent negative outcomes of health problems and chronic disease. Positive personal characteristics and coping mechanisms have received far less attention. Yet much can be learned from the attitudes and behaviors of people who effectively navigate life's stressors. Two such positive characteristics are self-efficacy and optimism.

Promoting Self-Efficacy.   Sobel (1995) noted that helping an individual to identify an area of life that the individual wants to change and then helping that person to make the change, no matter how small the scale, can profoundly increase the individual's sense of self-efficacy regarding managing that problem. These kinds of changes may include maximizing daily functioning, dealing with emotional challenges, increasing problem-solving skills, and increasing confidence in managing a given disease. In turn, Sobel suggested that this increase in self-efficacy precipitates what might be considered a neurobiological cascade that translates into what he referred to as a "biology of self-confidence."

Similarly, Benson (1996) commented that remembering times when the individual was well can set in motion neurobiological events, which positively nurture health status. He referred to this as "remembered wellness." In these examples, relatively small-scale, simple interventions are posited to have large-scale impact or ripple effects across biopsychosocial domains, especially in the area of self-efficacy.

Self-efficacy refers to the belief that one can exert control over one's behaviors and motives and the social environment. Beliefs about capabilities affect effort, choices, perseverance, cognitive patterns, mood, and stress (Bandura, 1989). Research on prevention and risk behaviors has often linked self-efficacy to health-promoting and health-impairing behaviors (e.g., Bandura, et al., 1988). Although self-efficacy typically is viewed as being specific to a given task (see Bandura, 1986), positive effects associated with specific skills and tasks may generalize (see Lightsey, 1996). As such, individuals become more confident and aware of how they have control and can use the control and power they have to optimize their health status. For example, helping an individual develop a routine for maximizing compliance to a complex medication regimen—one that requires taking pills at certain times of the day with certain foods and liquids—can generalize to helping this individual see that he or she has positive control over other aspects of life, such as nutrition and time-management. Similarly, for a client who is ambivalent about taking an antidepressant medication because that client wants to remain in control, a simple reframe would be to help the client see that control is maintained via the process of decision making.

Promoting Optimism. Optimism, the expectation of positive outcomes, has been associated with more effective coping with health challenges and better health outcomes (Carver et al., 1993). Dispositional optimism is defined as an individual holding generalized positive outcome expectations. In contrast, situational optimism is holding positive expectancies about a specific situation or outcome. A number of positive health outcomes have been associated with dispositional optimism. For example, individuals who are higher on this characteristic report better physical health (Scheier & Carver, 1992), less mood disturbance when faced with stressors (Aspinwall & Taylor, 1992), and slower immune decline when HIV-infected (Kemeny, Reed, Taylor, Visscher, & Fahey, 1998).

Hypothesizing that level of optimism would be associated with changes in immune functioning and mood state in individuals facing a stressful life situation, Segerstrom and Taylor (1998) studied a sample of first-year law students. They speculated that three different pathways (affect, coping, and health habits or behaviors) might mediate the effect of optimism on immune functioning and negative mood. Their findings showed that optimism was related to better mood and immune functioning. Coping partially accounted for the relationship between optimism and mood. Although optimism accounted for a relatively small amount of the variance in immune functioning, this study is noteworthy because it was the first published study to relate optimism to immune functioning in a healthy sample.

This study, along with other research on optimism, suggests that interventions that increase optimism are promising areas for counseling interventions and research. Although twin studies show a significant heritability estimate of about 25%, there is evidence of an environmental influence on optimism as well (Plomin, Scheier, Bergeman, & Peterson, 1992). One way this might work is through increasing positive expectations through the mechanism of effective coping. Optimists tend to use more problem-focused coping strategies than do pessimists (e.g., Stanton & Snider, 1993). When this is not possible or effective, they use more adaptive emotion-focused strategies such as acceptance and positive reframing. Teaching clients to use effective, problem-specific coping strategies might especially increase situational optimism. Because of the beneficial effects of optimism on psychological and physical well-being and its role in promoting a healthy personality, this is an important area for counseling research and interventions.

Increasing Exercise

Physical activity, along with diet and smoking, is one of the most important behavioral determinants of premature, preventable death in the United States. Although physical exercise has a number of direct physiological effects on health status, such as altering heart rate, increasing bone mass, and improving circulation, it also affects important psychosocial variables such as mood and self-efficacy (Marcus, Eaton, Rossi, & Harlow, 1994). Surprisingly, only 15% of sedentary adults visiting their physicians for routine checkups were advised to exercise more (C. Friedman, Brownson, Peterson, & Wilkerson, 1994). We could find no research that examined how often psychologists routinely recommended to sedentary clients that they increase their exercise levels. However, our clinical experience is that promoting physical exercise change is more successful than diet change because adoption of an exercise regimen typically results in healthy diet changes, whereas the opposite often is not the case. Other benefits of exercise include stress reduction and positive mood activation.

The Activity Counseling Trial (ACT) represents the first large scale behavioral intervention study of physical activity counseling in a randomized sample of sedentary adults conducted in a clinical setting (Dunn et al., 1998; King et al., 1998). Specifically, the goal of ACT is to evaluate three research conditions over a period of 24 months. Each condition (conditions A, B, and C) includes the advice to accumulate 30 minutes of moderate physical activity (e.g., brisk walking, climbing stairs) at an intensity of 70% to 80% of maximal heart rate for most days of the week. Condition A, the basic treatment, consists of this advice only. In conditions B and C (lifestyle and structured group, respectively), behavior change strategies are also provided to help participants increase their physical activity level to meet these recommendations. The ACT interventions both for the lifestyle and the structured groups were drawn from social cognitive theory, which examines the complex reciprocal influences among the person, the behavior being targeted for change, and aspects of the physical and social environment. The intervention strategy in both of these conditions was to alter key mediators of physical activity such as cognition, self-monitoring, and goal setting.

The major difference between conditions B and C is the type and frequency of contact delivered by health educators. Participants in the structured group received a free membership to a state-of-the-art fitness center where they worked under the supervision of a trained exercise leader at least three times a week. In contrast, participants in the lifestyle group met in small groups once a week with a facilitator experienced in conducting behavior change groups. Although the ACT study is not yet completed, preliminary results after 6 months of intervention show that both the lifestyle and structured groups (conditions B and C) achieved significant, comparable increases in physical activity and fitness. This finding was not found for the group that only received the exercise recommendations with no further interventions (condition A).

These early results suggest that educational directives to exercise more, even those that are explicit about how often, how long, and at what intensity, are not likely to be sufficient to change exercise habits in people with a sedentary lifestyle. The success of both the lifestyle and the structured groups suggest that psychosocial mediators such as incentives, social support, and self-efficacy play an important role in bringing about change. What ACT has not yet identified are the specific mediators responsible for the success of the lifestyle and structured groups.

Other research also supports the preliminary findings of the ACT study that psychosocial mediators play an important role in changing sedentary behavior and maintaining a physically active lifestyle. For example, Kriska and Rexroad (1998) identified several factors that promote or impede physical activity: supportive surroundings (e.g., family, friends, community); the physical environment (e.g., safety, accessibility of places to exercise); economics; time; and cultural variables. An important role for counseling psychologists is to promote a physically active lifestyle by helping clients to identify barriers and mediators that affect physical activity.

Adherence to Interventions and Regimens

Adherence to treatment is a process that should be assessed in all health-related interventions that rely on self-management and monitoring. Relief from symptoms or improvement does not necessarily mean that the client is adhering to the treatment. According to a review of the literature by Dunbar-Jacob, Burke, and Puczynski (1995), up to 80% of patients with chronic disease do not follow their treatment program well enough to attain therapeutic benefit. Poor results, continuation of symptoms, and increased cost are among the outcomes of lack of adherence to treatment. On a more serious level, lack of adherence can lead to the prevalence of treatment-resistant tuberculosis (Bloom & Murray, 1992) and to new strains of HIV disease that do not respond to existing medication regimens (Malow et al., 1998). Moreover, noncompliance kills 125,000 Americans a year, rehospitalizes thousands more, and runs up more than $100 billion a year in direct and indirect health-related costs (Drug Topics, 1992).

Adherence to medication has been the most frequent type of adherence study (Dunbar-Jacob et al., 1995). Results across studies, settings, and diseases show that just over half of patients adhere to medication regimens sufficiently to obtain therapeutic benefit. Adherence to diet regimens is lower than for medications (e.g., McCann, Retzlaff, Dowdy, Walden & Knopp, 1990). Even lower adherence rates are found for exercise (e.g., Perkins & Epstein, 1988). Thus, as the psychosocial requirements increase, adherence appears to decrease. In other words, it is generally much easier to meet the requirements of fairly simple medication regimens. Yet, a large percentage of people find adherence difficult even in this situation.

Several key factors have been associated with low adherence, although relatively few of these have been patient characteristics (Dunbar-Jacob et al., 1995). One exception has been adherence to medications among HIV-infected persons where a number of studies have found that gender, race, socioeconomic status, and substance abuse affect adherence (e.g., Mehta, Moore, & Graham, 1997; Sorensen et al., 1998). However, self-efficacy expectations (Ewart, 1989), satisfaction with medical care (Nagy & Wolfe, 1984), social support, and barriers to implementation of the regimen (Robertson & Keller, 1992) have all been associated with adherence. Characteristics of the regimen also have an effect on adherence, with the complexity of the treatment being most important (Hayes-Bautista, 1976). Other important regimen characteristics are frequency and duration of the regimen (McCann et al., 1990). Finally, provider characteristics, such as communication skills and warmth, increase compliance (M.S. Davis, 1978).

In keeping with these findings, Southam and Dunbar (1986) suggested that interventions to increase adherence focus on the following areas: (1) successfully initiating the regimen (early adherence is predictive of long-term adherence); (2) remediating adherence problems (e.g., identifying barriers, simplifying regimens); (3) maintaining adherence (e.g., long-term monitoring by health care professionals); (4) educational interventions (e.g., educating and involving family members); (5) modeling strategies (using videotapes); (6) behavioral strategies (e.g., self-monitoring, goal-setting); (7) social support; and (8) self-efficacy enhancement. Many of these recommendations rely heavily on psychosocial factors that may be ignored by physicians. Thus, they represent potential areas of intervention for counseling psychologists.

Despite the great importance of adherence to health-related regimens, there is a paucity of randomized, controlled intervention research in this area (Dunbar-Jacob et al., 1995). Furthermore, most of these studies have relied on self-report, which tends to overestimate adherence. Another important limitation of this body of research is that most studies have followed people for short periods of time (Dunbar-Jacob et al., 1995). Compliance over time, especially for diseases such as

HIV that require very complex medication regimens over many years, is another needed area for future research.

CRITIQUE AND SUGGESTIONS FOR FUTURE RESEARCH

Conceptualizing health status as a biopsychosocial process is a relatively recent perspective. This focus in the literature is growing rapidly as research moves beyond a biomedical model to one that recognizes the important interface between biological, psychological, and social factors. Our review of the literature suggests that despite this proliferation of research, there are still important research advances to be made. We discuss recommendations in the following areas: (1) conceptual issues about the manner in which biological, psychological, and social variables influence health status; (2) methodological issues; (3) understudied psychosocial variables; and (4) expanding the locus of intervention from the individual to include a systems focus.

Limitations of Current Biopsychosocial Conceptualizations

Despite the logical appeal of a biopsychosocial perspective, research on health status continues to be dominated by an emphasis on biomedical rather than psychosocial variables. In part, this may be because health outcomes typically are viewed as the presence or absence of disease, which reflects a deficit or pathogenic perspective. We believe that this emphasis needs to shift from its present focus on symptom reduction, to one that routinely includes health-related quality of life variables, and consideration of a range of outcomes including wellness. Another outcome of this conceptual shift might be greater attention to finding effective ways to anticipate and prevent problems through health promotion, rather than remediating illness and disease when it occurs.

Despite the health field's embrace of a biopsychosocial perspective, a number of writers have commented about the ongoing mind-body segregation (e.g., Carr, 1996). We previously noted that a number of the studies we reviewed on the biopsychosocial model failed to test all three domains of this framework. We believe that these limitations reflect difficulties in conceptualizing the interface between biological, psychological, and social variables, despite the intuitive appeal that they must "fit" together. Research is needed that dismantles the model to understand the interface between its three elements. Furthermore, we could find no reviews of empirical studies of the biopsychosocial perspective. A review of randomized, controlled studies might begin to address the importance of each of the domains of the model to health outcomes, and the interface between these elements.

Methodological Limitations

Our review of the research identified two areas, sampling and design, that we believe research efforts should address. Compared with White men, women and racial minorities have been underused as participants in health research. This is especially the case in clinical trials of new medications and treatment regimens to treat or prevent specific diseases. This has important implications for what we know about pharmacological and behavioral interventions as well as disease prevention, acquisition, and progression in many groups of people. In addition, sociodemographic variables such as race, income, and educational level are frequently not reported in health psychology research (see Park, Adams, & Lynch, 1998). Yet these variables have been shown to be related to health outcomes. Furthermore, socially constructed variables such as ethnicity and culture are important. However, these variables are rarely discussed in the literature, and the influence of these variables may be missed when demographic-type variables are simply dichotomized.

We noted several design limitations in our review. Much of the research in this area has been descriptive and cross-sectional. Longitudinal studies would allow for the exploration of causal relationships among variables and outcomes over time. This would allow important variables to be studied, such as changes in health status resulting from the shifts in the interface between biopsychosocial variables. Robbins and Kliewer's (this volume) review of the literature on subjective well-being concluded with several recommendations about design issues that could be applied to the biopsychosocial literature. For example, they recommended that longitudinal data be collected and analyzed with structural equation modeling techniques to establish some causal links among constructs. A second design choice they recommended is augmenting correlational data with experimental studies. Finally, we suggest that researchers consider qualitative methodologies to add valuable perspectives to quantitative approaches.

One area of strength we observed in our review was the large number of assessment instruments that exist, many of which are based on a substantial amount of evidence of reliability and validity. However, the vast majority are based on self-report. Although self-report measures are essential in capturing subjective assessments of experiences, measuring the same phenomenon using multiple assessment approaches would be optimal. In other cases, instruments focus on narrow definitions of the construct of interest. For example, measures of changes in carrying out life roles typically focus on functional roles (e.g., dressing oneself), or behaviors such as being able to return to work. Often excluded are valued life roles, such as changes in the ability to interact effectively on an interpersonal level or to do complex cognitive tasks at one's job.

Understudied Psychosocial Variables

There are several topics that we would like to see addressed to a greater extent in the literature. Because stress-coping frameworks dominate research on health and chronic disease, there is an underlying assumption that the disease process consists only of negative aspects. Research is needed on the ways in which disease or illness can have a transformative influence on the individual's life and, subsequently, on health outcomes. For example, learning that one has a disease may lead to positive life changes as one develops new skills and perspectives in coping with this challenge. In a related vein, positive emotional states play a protective role in health promotion and in disease management. Yet the majority of the health psychology books and studies we reviewed made no reference to the role of positive emotions in health status (e.g., optimism), or to correlates of the healthy personality. Our model reflects our belief that health status can be positive, as well as negative, as an effect of the interplay between biopsychosocial factors.

Work may also play an important role in health outcomes. In most models and theories of psychosocial development, the capacity to work occupies a central place. Within the field of counseling psychology, capacities to work and career development are important topics of research. Interestingly, few studies within counseling psychology have examined the relationships between health status and work, or more broadly, career development. From the perspective of our model, these relationships exist and may have implications for health status. For instance, how does stress or support in the workplace environment affect health status?

Spirituality also may influence health outcomes throughout the life span (see Koenig, 1998). Moreover, spirituality may be related to the attributions one makes regarding the meaning or role of adverse life events such as health crises. This, as well as how spirituality might be addressed in psychotherapy, are promising areas for research.

Expanding the Focus of Intervention from Individual to Systems

Although health change is typically directed at and effected by individuals, health behaviors (as well as health behavioral messages) occur within a sociopolitical and socioeconomic context. These contexts affect peoples' health beliefs and health status (see Lee & Paxman, 1997). Integral to effective health promotion strategies are assessments and interventions that attend to multicontextual, cultural variables. Furthermore, health occurs in a system that includes the individual, institutions such as clinics, and the community (Elliott & Shewchuk, 1996). In a study that intervened on a community, clinic, and individual level, peer-identified opinion leaders who frequented gay clubs were taught HIV information and trained to initiate conversations with other club patrons in which they discussed safer sex messages (J.A. Kelly et al., 1991). This resulted in a significant reduction in risk behavior when compared with a control group, an effect attributed to the effectiveness of opinion leaders to produce or accelerate change in community norms leading to individual change. More research is needed that moves beyond the individual as the unit of focus to the larger system.

IMPLICATIONS FOR COUNSELING PSYCHOLOGY

Health concerns, even those that are not life threatening, often profoundly affect people's emotional, social, sexual, and vocational functioning and cause disruptions in life goals and roles. Counseling psychology's core emphasis on enhancing optimal development across the life span is especially helpful when considering the interaction of disease with normal developmental processes and the long-term course of chronic disease. Counseling psychology's preventive focus is useful in facilitating interventions that promote health, prevent disease, and optimize wellness when chronic disease is present. For example, understanding the unfolding of biopsychosocial events that lead to wellness, or to illness, is essential and matches counseling psychology's notion of developmental processes and emphasis on maximizing adaptation to handle developmental transitions.

Counseling psychology's concept of the healthy personality, rather than the medical model of a person with deficits, provides a much-needed perspective in the ongoing development of the field of health psychology. Enhancing health through the potentially protective role of positive emotional states such as optimism and perceived control fits well with counseling psychology's view of the healthy personality.

We believe it is generally more important for counseling psychologists to focus on the psychosocial variables associated with health status (e.g., role change, adherence to treatment, barriers to change) rather than to direct interventions at specific biogenic symptoms. For instance, psychosocial variables are modifiable through psychological and psychoeducational interventions, unlike many of the biomedical and some of the biosocial variables described in our model. Collaborating with clients to increase their self-efficacy, sense of control, and optimism are natural roles for counseling psychologists. An important role for counseling psychologists is delivering psychoeducational interventions to facilitate self-care and collaborating with clients so they become active, informed partners in that care.

Effective collaboration requires a thorough psychosocial assessment with special attention to what is particularly motivating for the client and what has been motivating in the past to bring about change. Moreover, it requires a unique blending of educating and tailoring the intervention to fit the lifestyle, schedule, and personality of the client. Such collaboration rests on the foundational belief of counseling psychology that even in the midst of pain and distress, there are opportunities to be well and to become better.

Another aspect of collaboration is openness to working with other health professionals (Altmaier & Johnson, 1992; Thoresen & Eagleston, 1984). As a matter of fact, the biopsychosocial model of health status often requires that counseling psychologists avail themselves of physicians, nurses, and other health care providers to coordinate and evaluate care. In a similar way, counseling psychologists can serve as consultants to other health care providers, helping them to understand the manner in which psychosocial processes affect health. Counseling psychologists can also help other providers regarding difficulties and tensions these individuals experience working with particular clients, especially those who have a dual or triple diagnosis (e.g., affective disorder and lupus), or whose diseases stimulate reactions such as stigma and homophobia (Driscoll & Hoffman, 1997). Similarly, researchers and clinicians could collaborate in studying clinically meaningful and empirically sound research questions.

Counseling psychology has much to offer those with chronic disease and those who are at risk for disease. Traditional psychotherapeutic techniques, skills, and conceptual models can be creatively and systematically applied to enhancing health status. For instance, acute and chronic health problems can be viewed as life events or developmental tasks. Coping and adherence can be viewed as functions of personality style, emotional state, and quality of social support. Moreover, counseling psychology training should routinely acknowledge the importance of biological processes in psychosocial functioning by providing coursework and practica related to health psychology.

Throughout this chapter, we viewed health status as encompassing both physical symptoms and the adaptive skills used by the individual to respond to health threats. As a skill, well-being involves learning and practice in self-care and in viewing oneself as the primary care provider. At differing points in life span development, different skills are necessary because health challenges vary. As a process, health status involves a dynamic way of viewing life events, including disease, as opportunities for learning, growing, and healing. We view being well as an unfolding of biopsychosocial events related to optimizing health status.

The concentric biopsychosocial model of health status we proposed conceptualizes variables that influence this unfolding as well as the relational contexts in which these variables operate. Clinically, the model we proposed guides counselors in conceptualizing a given case or aspects of a case. Similarly, counselors can use the model to help educate clients, their families, health care providers and institutions, and communities in optimizing health status.

We previously noted that a number of the studies we reviewed failed to test all three domains of the biopsychosocial model. Although the biopsychosocial model has been embraced in the health literature in recent years, a number of writers have commented about the ongoing mind-body segregation present in the field (e.g., Carr, 1996). This suggests to us that biopsychosocial models have intuitive appeal, but they pose methodological challenges. Furthermore, because we could find no review of randomized controlled studies on this model, the contributions of the various domains is unclear. What is needed are studies that dismantle the model to understand the interface between its three elements (Melamed, 1995).

Despite these limitations, the biopsychosocial perspective has made an important contribution by focusing attention on the necessity of considering psychosocial factors that contribute to health status along with biomedical ones. This model has shown that subjective experiences such as grief and appraisals are not "soft signs," but essential aspects of the individual's experience that contribute to health status. As Engel (1980) noted, the manner in which health care professionals approach patients, and the problems they present, is influenced by the conceptual models they use to organize their knowledge. This model has brought a richness and complexity to the manner in which health-related problems are viewed.

Well-being and health status are integral to a life lived vibrantly in which one is connected to love, work, and play. Our role as counselors and researchers is to facilitate people's ability to respond adaptively to health tasks and challenges and to know that every life event holds an opportunity for using one's psychosocial resources to be well. We hope that our conceptualization of health status and the concentric biopsychosocial model stimulate research and clinical applications by promoting a view of health as a lifelong developmental process.

REFERENCES

Aday, L.A., & Andersen, R.M. (1981). Equity of access to medical care: A conceptual and empirical overview. *Medical Care, 19*(No. 12, Suppl.), 4–27.

Altmaier, E.M., & Johnson, B.D. (1992). Health related applications of counseling psychology: Toward health promotion and disease prevention across the life span. In S.D. Brown & R.W. Lent (Eds.), *Handbook of counseling psychology* (2nd ed., pp. 315–347). New York: Wiley.

Antonovsky, A. (1979). *Health, stress, and coping.* San Francisco: Jossey-Bass.

Antonovsky, A. (1987). *Unraveling the mystery of health: How people manage stress and stay well.* San Francisco: Jossey-Bass.

Antonovsky, A. (1994). A sociological critique of the "well being" movement. *Advances, 10,* 6–12.

Aspinwall, L.G., & Taylor, S.E. (1992). Individual differences, coping, and psychological adjustment: A longitudinal study of college adjustment and performance. *Journal of Personality and Social Psychology, 63,* 989–1003.

Bandura, A. (1986). *Social foundations of thought and action: A social cognitive theory.* Englewood Cliffs, NJ: Prentice-Hall.

Bandura, A. (1989). Self-efficacy mechanisms in physiological activation and health-promoting behavior. In J. Madden, IV, S. Math, & J. Barchas (Eds.), *Adaptation, learning, and affect.* New York: Raven Press.

Bandura, A., Cioffi, D., Taylor, C.B., & Brouillard, M.E. (1988). Perceived self-efficacy in coping with cognitive stressors and opioid activation. *Journal of Personality and Social Psychology, 55,* 479–488.

Barsky, A.J. (1981). Hidden reasons why patients visit doctors. *Annals of Internal Medicine, 94,* 492–498.

Benson, H. (1996). Harnessing the power of the placebo effect and renaming it "remembered wellness." *Annual Review of Medicine, 47,* 193–199.

Berkman, L.F., Leo-Summers, L., & Horwitz, R.I. (1992). Emotional support and survival after myocardial infarction. *Annals of Internal Medicine, 117,* 1003–1009.

Berkman, L.F., & Syme, S.L. (1979). Social networks, host resistance and mortality: A nine-year follow-up study of Alameda County residents. *American Journal of Epidemiology, 109,* 186–204.

Betancourt, H., & López, S.R. (1993). The study of culture, ethnicity, and race in American psychology. *American Psychologist, 48,* 629–637.

Blankfield, R.P. (1991). Suggestion, relaxation, and hypnosis as adjuncts in the care of surgery patients: A review of the literature. *American Journal of Clinical Hypnosis, 33,* 172–186.

Blenkhorn, A., Silove, D., Magarey, C., Krillis, S., & Coninet, H. (1992). The effect of a multimodal stress management program on immune and psychological functions. In A.J. Husband (Ed.), *Behavior and immunity* (pp. 189–209). Boca Raton, FL: CRC Press.

Bloom, B.R., & Murray, C.J.L. (1992, August 21). Tuberculosis: Commentary on a reemergent killer. *Science, 257,* 1055–1061.

Bowling, A. (1991). *Measuring health: A review of quality of life measurement scales.* Philadelphia: Open University Press.

Cacioppo, J.T. (1998). Somatic responses to psychological stress: The reactivity hypothesis. *Advances in Psychological Science,* 87–112.

Carr, J.E. (1996). Psychology and mind-body segregation: Are we part of the problem? *Journal of Clinical Psychology in Medical Settings, 3,* 141–144.

Carver, C.S., Pozo, C., Harris, S.D., Noriega, V., Scheier, M.F., Robinson, D., Ketcham, A., Moffat, F., & Clark, K. (1993). How coping mediates the effect of optimism on distress: A study of women with early stage breast cancer. *Journal of Personality and Social Psychology, 65,* 375–390.

Caspersen, C.J., Christenson, G.M., & Pollard, R.A. (1986). Status of the 1990 physical fitness and exercise objectives: Evidence from NHIS 1985. *Public Health Report, 101,* 587–592.

Centers for Disease Control and Prevention. (1998). HIV/AIDS surveillance report. *HIV/AIDS Surveillance Report, 10*(1), 1–15.

Chesney, M.A., & Folkman, S. (1994). Psychological impact of HIV disease and implications for intervention. *Psychiatric Clinics of North America, 17,* 163–173.

Cohen, S., Frank, E., Doyle, W.J., Skoner, D.P., Rabin, B.S., & Gwaltney, J.M., Jr. (1998). Types of stressors that increase susceptibility to the common cold in healthy adults. *Health Psychology, 17,* 214–223.

Cohen, S., & Syme, S.L. (1985). *Social support and health.* New York: Academic Press.

Cotton, P. (1990). Examples abound of gaps in medical knowledge because of groups excluded from scientific study. *Journal of the American Medical Association, 263,* 1051–1052.

Davis, M.A. (1992). Living arrangements and survival among middle-aged and older adults in the NHANES 1 Epidemiological Follow-Up Study. *American Journal of Public Health, 81,* 401–406.

Davis, M.S. (1978). Variations in patients' compliance with doctor's advice: An empirical analysis of patterns of communication. *American Journal of Public Health, 58,* 274–288.

Detels, R., & Breslow, L. (1991). Current scopes and concerns in public health. *Oxford Textbook of Public Health, 3,* 49–65.

Devins, G.M. (1994). Illness intrusiveness and the psychosocial impact of lifestyle disruptions in chronic life-threatening disease. *Advances in Renal Replacement Therapy, 1,* 251–263.

DiClemente, C.C., & Prochaska, J.O. (1982). Self-change and therapy change in smoking behavior: A comparison of processes of change in cessation and maintenance. *Addictive Behaviors, 7,* 133–142.

Driscoll, J.M., & Hoffman, M.A. (1997). Exploring attitudes of white dental students regarding willingness to treat people with HIV. *Journal of Dental Education, 61,* 717–726.

Drug Topics. (1992, August 17). Noncompliance: The invisible epidemic. *Drug Topics,* pp. 3–8.

Dunbar-Jacob, J., Burke, L.E., & Puczynski, S. (1995). Clinical assessment and management of adherence to medical regimens. In P.M. Nicassio & T.W. Smith (Eds.), *Managing chronic illness: A biopsychosocial perspective* (pp. 314–349). Washington, DC: American Psychological Association.

Dunn, A.L., Garcia, M.E., Marcus, B.H., Kampert, J.B., Kohl, H.W., & Blair, S.N. (1998). Six-month physical activity and fitness changes in Project Active, a randomized trial. *Medicine and Science in Sports and Exercise, 30,* 1076–1083.

Eiche, K.D., & Hoffman, M.A. (1998, August). *Exploring asthma adjustment within a biopsychosocial framework.* Paper presented at the Annual Meeting of the American Psychological Association, San Francisco.

Elliott, T.R., & Shewchuk, R.M. (1996). Defining health and well being for the future of counseling psychology. *Counseling Psychologists, 24,* 743–750.

Engel, G.L. (1977, April 18). The need for a new medical model: A challenge for biomedicine. *Science, 196,* 129–136.

Engel, G.L. (1980). The clinical application of the biopsychosocial model. *American Journal of Psychiatry, 137,* 535–544.

Everly, G.S., Jr. (1989). *A clinical guide to the treatment of the human stress response.* New York: Plenum Press.

Ewart, C.K. (1989). Psychological effects of resistive weight training: Implications for cardiac patients. *Medicine and Science in Sports and Exercise, 21,* 683–688.

Farnham, P.G., (1994). Defining and measuring the costs of the HIV epidemic to business firms. *Public Health Reports, 109,* 311–319.

Foster, H.W., Jr. (1997). Women's health care for the coming millennium. *Journal of Florida Medical Association, 84,* 358–363.

Frank, J.D., & Frank, J.B. (1991). *Persuasion and healing: A comparative study of psychotherapy* (3rd ed.). Baltimore: Johns Hopkins Press.

Friedman, H.S., & Booth-Kewley, S. (1987). The "disease-prone" personality: A meta-analytic view of the construct. *American Psychologist, 42,* 539–555.

Friedman, C., Brownson, R.C., Peterson, D.E., & Wilkerson, J.C. (1994). Physician advice to reduce chronic disease factors. *American Journal of Preventive Medicine, 10,* 367–371.

Gail, M.H., & Benichou, J. (1992). Assessing the risk of breast cancer in individuals. In V.T. DeVita, Jr., S. Hellman, & S.A. Rosenberg (Eds.), *Cancer prevention* (pp. 1–15). Philadelphia: Lippincott.

Gershon, E.S., Schreiber, J.L., & Hamovit, J.R. (1984). Clinical findings in patients with anorexia nervosa and affective illness in their relatives. *American Journal of Psychiatry, 141,* 1419–1422.

Gijsbers van Wijk, C.M.T., Kolk, A.M., van den Bosch, W.J., & van den Hoogen, H.J. (1992). Male and female morbidity in general practice: The nature of sex differences. *Social Science and Medicine, 35,* 665–678.

Gijsbers van Wijk, C.M.T., Van Vliet, K.P., & Kolk, A.M. (1996). Gender perspectives and quality of care: Towards appropriate and adequate health care for women. *Social Science and Medicine, 43,* 707–720.

Ginzberg, E. (1991). Access to health care for Hispanics. *Journal of the American Medical Association, 265,* 238–241.

Gottesman, I.I., & Shields, J. (1982). *Schizophrenia: The epigenetic puzzle.* Cambridge, England: Cambridge University Press.

Green, G. (1993). Social support and HIV [Editorial review]. *AIDS Care, 5,* 87–103.

Griffin, K.W., Rabkin, J.G., Remien, R.H., & Williams, J.B., (1998). Disease severity, physical limitations and depression in HIV-infected men. *Journal of Psychosomatic Research, 44,* 219–227.

Guyer, M.S., & Collins, F.S. (1995). How is the Human Genome Project doing, and what have we learned? *Proceedings of the National Academy of Science, USA, 92,* 10841–10848.

Hall, J.A., Roter, D.L., Milburn, M.A, & Daltroy, L.W. (1996). Patients' health as a predictor of physician and patient behavior in medical visits: A synthesis of four studies. *Medical Care, 34,* 1205–1218.

Hayes-Bautista, D. (1976). Modifying the treatment: Patient compliance, patient control, and medical care. *Social Science and Medicine, 10,* 233–238.

Hays, R.D., Wells, K., Sherbourne, C.D., & Rogers, W. (1995). Functioning and well-being outcomes of patients with depression compared with chronic general medical concerns. *Archives of General Psychiatry, 52,* 1–39.

Hoffman, M.A. (1996). *Counseling clients with HIV disease: Assessment, intervention, and prevention.* New York: Guilford Press.

Hoffman, M.A. (1997). HIV disease and work: Effect on the individual, workplace, and interpersonal contexts. *Journal of Vocational Behavior, 51,* 163–201.

Huang, Y., Macera, C.A., Blair, S.N., Brill, P.A., Kohl, H.W., & Kronenfeld, J.J. (1998). Physical fitness, physical activity, and functional limitation in adults aged 40 and older. *Medicine and Science in Sports and Exercise, 30,* 1430–1435.

Huff, J.E. (1993). Chemicals and cancer in humans: First evidence in experimental animals. *Environmental Health Perspectives, 100,* 201–210.

Hughes, G.H., Pearson, A.A., & Reinhart, G.R. (1984). Stress: Sources, effects, and management. *Family and Community Health, 7,* 47–58.

Hughes, J.E., (1987). Psychological and social consequences of cancer. *Cancer Surveys, 6,* 455–475.

Hyman, R.B., Feldman, H.R., Harris, R.B., Levin, R.F., & Malloy, G.B. (1989). The effects of relaxation training on clinical symptoms: A meta-analysis. *Nursing Research, 38,* 216–220.

Jenkins, C.D. (1982). Psychosocial risk factors for coronary heart disease. *Acta Medica Scandinavia, 660,* 123–136.

Jensen, L., & Allen, M. (1993). Wellness: The dialectic of illness. *IMAGE: Journal of Nursing Scholarship, 25,* 220–224.

Kahn, R.L., & Antonucci, R.C. (1980). Convoys over the life course: Attachment, roles, and social support. In P.B. Baltes & O.C. Brim (Eds.), *Life-span development and behavior.* New York: Academic Press.

Kalow, W. (1989). Race and therapeutic drug response. *New England Journal of Medicine, 320*(9), 588–590.

Kaplan, R.M. (1990). Behavior as the central outcome in health care. *American Psychologist, 45,* 1211–1220.

Kaplan, R.M., & Anderson, J.P. (1988). The Quality of Well-Being Scale: Rationale for a single quality of life index. In S.R. Walker & R. Rosser (Eds.), *Quality of life: Assessment and application* (pp. 51–77). London: MTP Press.

Kaplan, R.M., Sieber, W.J., & Ganiats, T.G. (1997). The Quality of Well-Being Scale: Comparison of the interviewer-administered version with a self-administered questionnaire. *Psychology and Health, 12,* 783–791.

Keesey, R.E. (1993). Physiological regulation of body energy: Implications for obesity. In A.J. Stunkard & T.A. Wadden (Eds.), *Obesity theory and therapy* (2nd ed., pp. 77–96). New York: Raven Press.

Kelly, J.A., St. Lawrence, J.S., Brasfield, T.L., Kalichman, S.C., Smith, J.E., & Andrew, M.E. (1991). HIV risk behavior reduction following intervention with key opinion leaders of population: An experimental analysis. *American Journal of Public Health, 8,* 168–171.

Kelly, S., Hertzman, C., & Daniels, M. (1997). Searching for the biological pathways between stress and health. *Annual Review of Public Health, 18,* 437–462.

Kemeny, M.E., Reed, G.M., Taylor, S.E., Visscher, B.R., & Fahey, J. (1998). *Negative HIV-specific expectancies predict immunologic evidence of HIV progression.* Unpublished manuscript.

Kiecolt-Glaser, J.K., & Glaser, R. (1992). Psychoneuroimmunology: Can psychological interventions modulate immunity? *Journal of Counseling and Clinical, 60,* 569–575.

Kiecolt-Glaser, J.K., & Glaser, R. (1995). Psychoneuroimmunology and health consequences: Data and shared mechanims. *Psychosomatic Medicine, 57,* 269–274.

King, A.C., Sallis, J., Dunn, A., Simons-Morton, D., Albright, C., Cohen, S., Rejeski, W.J., Marcus, B., & Coday, M. (1998). Overview of the activity counseling trial (ACT) intervention for promoting physical activity in primary health care settings. *Medicine and Science in Sports and Exercise, 30,* 1086–1096.

Koenig, H.G. (1998). Religious attitudes and practices of hospitalized medically ill older adults. *International Journal of Geriatric Psychiatry, 13,* 213–224.

Kriska, A.M., & Rexroad, A.R. (1998). The role of physical activity in minority populations. *Women's Health Issues, 8,* 98–103.

Krueger, L.E., Wood, R.W., Diehr, P.H., & Maxwell, C.L. (1990), Poverty and HIV serpositivity: The poor are more likely to be infected. *AIDS, 4,* 811–814.

Kunst, A.E., Guerts, J.J.M., & Berg, K. (1992). *International variation in socio-economic inequalities in self-reported health.* The Hague: Netherlands Central Bureau of Statistics.

Lazarus, R.S., & Folkman, S. (1984). *Stress appraisal and coping.* New York: Springer.

Lee, P., & Paxman, D. (1997). Reinventing public health. *Annual Review of Public Health, 18,* 1–35.

Lerman, C., Caparaso, N.E., Audrain, J., Main, D., Bowman, E.D., Lockshin, B., Boyd, N.R., & Shields, P.G. (1999). Evidence suggesting the role of specific genetic factors in cigarette smoking. *Health Psychology, 18,* 14–20.

Levenstein, S. (1994). Wellness, health, Antonovsky. *Advances, 10,* 26–29.

Lightsey, O.R. (1996). What leads to wellness? The role of psychological resources in well-being. *Counseling Psychologist, 24,* 589–759.

Little, M.O. (1996). Why a feminist approach to bioethics? *Kennedy Institute of Ethics Journal, 6,* 1–18.

Malow, R.M., McPherson, S., Klimas, N., Antoni, M.H., Schneiderman, N., Penedo, F.J., Ziskind, D., Page, B., & McMahon, R. (1998). Adherence to complex combination antiretroviral therapies by HIV-positive drug abusers. *Psychiatric Services, 49,* 1021–1022.

Marcus, B.H., Eaton, C.A., Rossi, J.S., & Harlow, L.L. (1994). Self-efficacy, decision-making, and stages of change: An integrative model of physical exercise. *Journal of Applied Social Psychology, 24,* 489–508.

Mastroianni, A.C., Faden, R., & Federman, D. (1994). Women's participation in clinical studies. In A.C. Mastroianni, R. Faden, & D. Federman (Eds.), *Women and health research: Ethical and legal issues of including women in clinical studies* (Vol. 1, pp. 36–74). Washington, DC: National Academy Press.

Matarazzo, J.D. (1990). Behavioral health: A 1990 challenge for the health sciences professions. In J.D. Matarazzo, N.E. Miller, S.M. Weiss, J.A. Herd, & S. Weiss (Eds.), *Behavioral health: A handbook of health enhancement and disease prevention.* New York: Wiley.

McCann, B.S., Retzlaff, B.W., Dowdy, A.A., Walden, C.E., & Knopp, R.H. (1990). Promoting adherence to low-fat, low-cholesterol diets: Review and recommendations. *Journal of the American Dietetic Association, 90,* 1408–1414.

McGinnis, J.M., & Foege, W. (1993). Actual causes of death in the United States. *Journal of the American Medical Association, 270,* 2207–2212.

Mehta, S., Morre, R.D., & Graham, N.M. (1997). Potential factors affecting adherence with HIV therapy. *AIDS, 11,* 1665–1670.

Melamed, B.G. (1995). The interface between physical and mental disorders: The need to dismantle the biopsychosocialneuroimmunological model of disease. *Journal of Clinical Psychology in Medical Settings, 1,* 225–231.

Moulton, J.M., Sweet, D.M., Temoshok, L., & Mandel, J.S. (1987). Attributions of blame and responsibility in relation to distress and health behavior change in people with AIDS and AIDS-related complex. *Journal of Applied Social Psychology, 17,* 493–506.

Nagy, V.T., & Wolfe, G.R. (1984). Cognitive predictors of compliance in chronic disease patients. *Medical Care, 22,* 912–921.

Nurnberger, J.I., & Gershon, E.S. (1992). Genetics in affective disorders. In E.S. Paykel (Ed.), *Handbook of affective disorders* (2nd ed., pp. 131–142). New York: Guilford Press.

Park, T.L., Adams, S.G., & Lynch, J. (1998). Sociodemographic factors in health psychology research: 12 years in review. *Health Psychology, 17,* 381–383.

Parker, J.C. (1995). Stress management. In P.M. Nicassio & T.W. Smith (Eds.), *Managing chronic illness: A biopsychosocial perspective* (pp. 285–312). Washington, DC: American Psychological Association.

Parker, J.C., Smarr, K.L., Walker, S.E., & Hagglund, K.J. (1991). Biopsychosocial parameters of disease activity in rheumatoid arthritis. *Arthritis Care and Research, 4,* 73–80.

Peele, S. (1984). The cultural context of psychological approaches to alcoholism: Can we control the effects of alcohol? *American Psychologist, 39,* 1337–1351.

Penninx, B.W., van Tilburg, T., Boeke, J.P., Deeg, D.H., Kriegsman, K.M., & van Eijk, J.T. (1998). Effects of social support and personal coping resources on depressive symptoms: Different for various chronic diseases? *Health Psychology, 17,* 551–558.

Perkins, K.A., & Epstein, L.H. (1988). Adherence to exercise programs. In R.K. Dishman (Ed.), *Exercise adherence: Its impact on public health* (pp. 399–416). Champaign-Urbana, IL: Human Kinetics Books.

Plomin, R., Scheier, M.F., Bergeman, C.S., & Pedersen, N. (1992). Optimism, pessimism, and mental health: A twin/adoption analysis. *Personality and Individual Differences, 13,* 921–930.

Pope, A.M., & Tarlov, A.R. (1991). *Disability in American: Toward a national agenda for prevention.* Washington, DC: National Academy.

Popkin, M.K., Callies, A.L., Lentz, R.D., Cohen, E.A., & Sutherland, D.E. (1988). Prevalence of major depression, simple phobia, and other psychiatric disorders in patients with long-standing Type-1 diabetes mellitus. *Archives of General Psychiatry, 45,* 64–68.

Powell, K.E., & Blair, S.N. (1994). The public health burden of sedentary living habits: Theoretical but realistic estimates. *Medical Science Sports Exercise, 26,* 851–856.

Prochaska, J.O., DiClemente, C.C., & Norcross, J.C. (1992). In search of how people change: Applications to addictive behaviors. *American Psychologist, 47,* 1102–1114.

Richard, I.H., Schiffer, R.B., & Kurland, R. (1996). Anxiety and Parkinson's disease. *Journal of Neuropsychiatry and Clinical Neurosciences, 8,* 383–395.

Robertson, D., & Keller, C. (1992). Relationship among health beliefs, self-efficacy, and exercise adherence in patients with coronary heart disease. *Heart and Lung, 21,* 56–63.

Rodin, G., & Voshart, K. (1986). Depression in the medically ill: An overview. *American Journal of Psychiatry, 143,* 696–705.

Rostosky, S.S., & Travis, C.B. (1996). Menopause research and the dominance of the biomedical model 1984–1994. *Psychology of Women Quarterly, 20,* 285–312.

Ruberman, W., Weinblatt, E., Goldberg, J., & Chaudhary, B. (1984). Psychosocial influences on mortality after myocardial infarction. *New England Journal of Medicine, 311,* 552–559.

Sadler, J.Z., & Hulgus, Y.F. (1990). Knowing, valuing, acting: Clues to revising the biopsychological model. *Comparative Psychiatry, 31,* 185–195.

Schaffer, M. (1982). *Life after stress.* New York: Plenum Press.

Scheier, M.F., & Carver, C.S. (1992). Effects of optimism on psychological and physical well-being: Theoretical overview and empirical update. *Cognitive Therapy and Research, 16,* 201–228.

Scheier, M.F., Carver, C.S., & Bridges, M.W. (1994). Distinguishing optimism from neuroticism (and trait anxiety, self-mastery, and self-esteem): A reevaluation of the Life Orientation Test. *Journal of Personality and Social Psychology, 67,* 1063–1078.

Scheier, M.F., Weintraub, J.K., & Carver, C.S. (1986). Coping with stress: Divergent strategies of optimists and pessimists. *Journal of Personality and Social Psychology, 51,* 1257–1264.

Segerstrom, S.C., & Taylor, S.E. (1998). Optimism is associated with mood, coping, and immune change in response to stress. *Journal of Personality and Social Psychology, 74,* 1646–1655.

Seligman, M. (1990). *Learned optimism.* New York: Knopf.

Shavers-Hornaday, V.L., Lynch, C.F., Burmeister, L.F., & Turner, J.C. (1997). Why are African Americans under-represented in medical research studies? Impediments to participation. *Ethnicity and Health, 2,* 31–45.

Shilts, R. (1987). *And the band played on.* New York: St. Martin's Press.

Sime, W.E. (1984). Psychological benefits of exercise training in the healthy individual. In J.D. Matarazzo, et al. (Eds.), *Behavioral health: A handbook of health enhancement and disease prevention* (pp. 488–508). New York: Wiley.

Slaven, L., & Lee, C. (1997). Mood and symptom reporting among middle-aged women: The relationship between menopausal status, hormone replacement therapy, and exercise participation. *Health Psychology, 16,* 203–208.

Smith, G.S., & Kraus, J.F. (1988). Alcohol and residential, recreational, and occupational injuries: A review of the epidemiological evidence. In L. Breslow, J.E. Fielding, & L.B. Lave (Eds.), *Annual review of public health* (Vol. 9). Palo Alto, CA: Annual Reviews.

Smith, T.W., & Nicassio, P.M. (1995). Psychological practice: Clinical application of the biopsychosocial model. In P.M. Nicassio & T.W. Smith (Eds.), *Managing chronic illness: A biopsychosocial perspective* (pp. 1–32). Washington, DC: American Psychological Association.

Sobel, D.S. (1995). Rethinking medicine: Improving health outcomes with cost-effective psychosocial interventions. *Psychosomatic Medicine, 57,* 234–244.

Solomon, G.F., Temoshok, L., O'Leary, A., & Zich, J. (1987). An intensive psychoimmunologic study of long-surviving persons with AIDS. *Annals of the New York Academy of Sciences, 496,* 647–655.

Sorensen, J.L., Mascovich, A., Wall, T.L., DePhilippis, D., Batki, S.L., & Chesney, M. (1998). Medication adherence strategies for drug abusers with HIV/AIDS. *AIDS Care, 10,* 297–312.

Speers, M.A., & Lancaster, B. (1998). Disease prevention and health promotion in urban areas: CDC's perspective. *Health Education and Behavior, 25,* 226–233.

Spiegel, D., Bloom, J.R., & Yalom, I. (1981). Group support for patients with metastatic cancer: A randomized prospective outcome study. *Archives of General Psychiatry, 38,* 527–533.

Spiegel, H. (1997). Nocebo: The power of suggestibility. *Preventive Medicine, 26*(pt. 5), 616–621.

Stanton, A.L., & Snider, P.R. (1993). Coping with a breast cancer diagnosis: A prospective study. *Health Psychology, 12,* 16–23.

Syrjala, K.L., & Chapko, M.E. (1995). Evidence for a biopsychosocial model of cancer treatment-related pain. *Pain, 61,* 69–79.

Tardy, C.H. (1985). Social support measurement. *American Journal of Community Psychology, 13,* 187–201.

Taylor, S.E., & Aspinwall, L.G. (1990). Psychosocial aspects of chronic illness. In P.T. Costa, Jr., & G.R. VandenBos (Eds.), *Psychological aspects of serious illness: Chronic conditions, fatal diseases, and clinical care* (pp. 7–60). Washington, DC: American Psychological Association.

Thompson, D.R., Webster, R.A., Cordle, C.J., & Sutton, T.W. (1987). Specific sources and patterns of anxiety in male patients with first myocardial infarction. *British Journal of Medical Psychology, 60,* 343–348.

Thoresen, C.E., & Eagleston, J.R. (1984). Counseling, health, and psychology. In S.D. Brown & R.W. Lent (Eds.), *Handbook of counseling psychology* (pp. 930–955). New York: Wiley.

Thoresen, C.E., & Goldberg, J.H. (1998). Coronary heart disease: A psychosocial perspective on assessment and intervention. In S. Roth-Roemer, S.E. Robinson Kurpius, & C. Carmin (Eds.), *The emerging role of counseling psychology in health care* (pp. 94–136). New York: Norton.

Turk, D., Meichenbaum, P., & Genest, M. (1983). *Pain and behavioral medicine: A cognitive behavioral perspective.* New York: Guilford Press.

Turner, H.A., Hays, R.B., & Coates, T.J. (1993). Determinants of social support among gay men: The context of AIDS. *Journal of Health and Social Behavior, 34,* 37–53.

Uchino, B.N., Cacioppo, J.T., & Kiecolt-Glaser, J.K. (1996). The relationship between social support and physiological processes: A review with emphasis on underlying mechanisms and implications for health. *Psychological Bulletin, 119,* 488–531.

U.S. Congress, Office of Technology Assessment. (1994). *Researching health risks* (OTA-BBS-570). Washington, DC: US Government Printing Office.

U.S. Department of Health and Human Services. (1996a). The health of the nation: Highlights of the Healthy People 2000 goals (chapter 1). *Healthy People 2000: Midcourse Review and 1995 Revisions.* Sudbury, MA: Jones and Bartlett.

U.S. Department of Health and Human Services. (1996b). *Physical activity and health: A report of the Surgeon General.* Atlanta, GA: U.S. DHHS, Centers for Disease Control and Prevention, National Center for Chronic Disease Prevention and Health Promotion.

U.S. Department of Health and Human Services. (1998). *Health in America tied to income and education.* Atlanta, GA: U.S. DHHS, Centers for Disease Control Prevention and Health Promotion.

Van Mechelen, W. (1997). A physically active lifestyle—public health's best buy? *British Journal of Sports Medicine, 31,* 264–265.

Ware, J.E. (1984, May 15). Conceptualizing disease impact and treatment outcomes. *Cancer,* (Suppl.), 2316–2326.

Watt, D., Verman, S., & Flynn, L. (1998). Wellness programs: A review of the evidence. *Canadian Medical Association Journal, 158,* 224–230.

Weinstein, N.D., Rothman, A.J., & Sutton, S.R. (1998). Stage theories of health behavior: Conceptual and methodological issues. *Health Psychology, 17,* 290–299.

Weiss, K.B., & Wagener, D.K. (1990). Changing patterns of asthma mortality: Identifying target populations at high risk. *Journal of the American Medical Association, 264,* 1683–1684.

Welch, D. (1982). Anticipatory grief: Reactions in family members of adult patients. *Issues in Mental Health Nursing, 4,* 149–158.

Welch-McCaffrey, S. (1985). Cancer, anxiety, and quality of life. *Cancer Nursing, 8,* 151–158.

Wells, K.B., Golding, J.M., & Burnam, M.A. (1989). Affective substance use and anxiety disorders in persons with arthritis, diabetes, heart disease, high blood pressure, or chronic lung conditions. *General Hospital Psychiatry, 11,* 320–327.

Wells, K.B., Stewart, A., & Hays, R.D. (1989). The functioning and well-being of depressed patients: Results from the Medical Outcomes Study. *Journal of the American Medical Association, 262.* 914–930.

Wenger, N.K., Speroff, L., & Packard, B. (1993). Cardiovascular health and disease in women. *New England Journal of Medicine, 329*(4), 247–256.

Williams, R.B., Barefoot, J.C., Califf, R.M., Haney, T.L., Saunders, W.B., Pruor, D.B., Hlatky, M.A., Siegler, I.C., & Mark, D.B. (1992). Prognostic importance of social and economic resources among medically treated patients with angiographically documented coronary artery disease. *Journal of the American Medical Association, 267,* 520–524.

World Health Organization. (1948). Constitution of the World Health Organization. In *Basic Documents.* Geneva, Switzerland: Author.

Wulfert, E., & Wan, C.K. (1993). Condom use: A self-efficacy model. *Health Psychology, 12,* 346–353.

Young, K., & Zane, N. (1995). Ethnocultural influences in evaluation and management. In P.M. Nicassio & T.W. Smith (Eds.), *Managing chronic illness: A biopsychosocial perspective* (pp. 163–206). Washington, DC: American Psychological Association.

PART IV

Counseling Interventions

CHAPTER 18

Advances in Theories of Change and Counseling

SERINE WARWAR
LESLIE S. GREENBERG

As we approach the millennium, it seems timely to reflect on the changes in the theory and practice of counseling over the past several years. Most differential treatment studies have still not found differences in outcome despite reports of over hundreds of different approaches to counseling and psychotherapy (see Wampold, this volume). This suggests that certain common or nonspecific change factors are important across therapeutic modalities. It also highlights the difficulty of defining and measuring change, and the need for theory and research that reconceptualizes change in counseling to simplify this complexity.

Change is the most striking and pervasive feature of existence. That nothing is permanent is almost a truism. Yet because of certain inherent philosophical puzzles about how it is possible for something to change and yet maintain its identity, change is not well understood. Before we can discuss therapeutic change processes, we need to understand what is meant by change. If we take a common dictionary definition of change, "to make or become different," or "to alter," the elusive nature of the concept of change is evident. Many questions arise if we apply this definition to counseling. What constitutes a clinically meaningful difference in the client? What are the important factors that need to change? From whose perspective should change be examined, the client's, the counselor's, or a third party's? Do we think of change within sessions, from session to session, or across therapy? How frequently do we measure change? As counselors, we need to have an understanding of what it means to change if we are to effect change in our clients.

In recent years, there has been an increasing recognition of the need for a different way of conceptualizing change. This has resulted in a shift in counseling research and practice from focusing only on the examination of final indices of change (i.e., gross comparisons of pre- and postchange) to an examination of the client's moment-by-moment change process in conjunction with indices of outcome at many points throughout therapy (Greenberg, 1986, 1991). This shift reflects our recognition that merely knowing that change has occurred simply is not enough, but instead we need to look at *how* that change has occurred. As counselors it is important that we study the process of change in a way that allows us to apply our knowledge of it in practice so that we can know how to facilitate change in our clients. To do this, we need to specify the key processes that lead to change in different approaches to counseling. What is most needed in counseling theory and research to enhance practice is the identification and specification of client change mechanisms and the articulation of the counseling interventions that set these processes in motion.

Recently proposed strategies for studying how people change in counseling involve identifying meaningful key events or episodes in counseling approaches to discover client-counselor interactions that produce specific types of change. For example, Rice and Greenberg's (1984) change events paradigm focuses specifically on isolating therapy segments in which predefined change events can be analyzed as an alternative to randomly sampling segments or describing entire counseling sessions (Greenberg, 1991). Similarly, the Core Conflictual Relationship Theme Method (CCRT; Luborsky & Crits-Christoph, 1990) breaks down counseling sessions into meaningful relationship episodes. When change is studied by investigating meaningful episodes, key events, or moments, the samples are either chosen by theoretically guided sampling or by client or counselor reports. By studying actual in-session phenomena, theory building is meaningfully concrete as it stays grounded in the phenomenon being studied.

Greenberg and Newman (1996) argue for an approach to change process research that views "the steps of science to be recursive with the initial step of observation and description." The first step of description should be exploratory and discovery-oriented. The next step is the development of an explanatory model of what was observed. Following this, the accuracy of the model is tested. This strategy was demonstrated in a study on resolving unfinished business with a significant other (Greenberg & Foerster, 1996). It used a task analytic approach for studying change that involves an iterative process of observation, description, and model building until an explanatory model for resolving unfinished business was well-constructed and validated. Similarly, Joyce, Duncan, and Piper (1995) used task analysis to develop and evaluate a conceptual model of client "working" responses to interpretation in brief dynamic individual therapy. This task-analytic research method is useful for building empirically based models of the specific steps needed to effect change for particular client processes.

Following an approach to studying change even more grounded in the data, a number of researchers (Elliot & Shapiro, 1992; Lietaer, 1992; Llewelyn, Elliot, Shapiro, Firth, & Hardy, 1988; Mahrer & Nadler, 1986) have asked clients and counselors to select moments or events in treatment that were most helpful and have built taxonomies of helpful moments. Elliot and Shapiro (1992) found that using a qualitative method to engage clients and counselors in analyzing clients' significant events elucidated client-counselor misunderstandings, and indicated that resolving misunderstandings in counseling can be extremely beneficial to building the working alliance. They suggested that if the counselor is aware of client-counselor misunderstandings, the counselor can use this awareness to develop ways of strengthening the alliance.

In Lietaer's (1992) study, which asked clients to report on helpful moments in client-centered counseling, he found that both clients and therapists perceived self-exploration and experiential insight as prominent helpful factors in counseling. Moreover, clients placed an emphasis on the importance of a safe and empathic environment in which they felt accepted by the counselor. Theory and practice are closely tied together, as these findings suggested that many of the change processes hypothesized by client-centered theory to be important were in fact what clients experienced as being beneficial in counseling.

We have introduced this chapter by defining change, and discussed the complexity of specifying and measuring the key processes that lead to change. We continue by reviewing important theoretical and empirical advances, and address their implications for counseling practice. In addition, we specify mechanisms of change in major approaches to counseling: dynamic, humanistic, and cognitive-behavioral. This chapter concludes with an overview of where the field of counseling stands in general, and a discussion of future directions. Although the focus of this chapter is on specific mechanisms of change, we first consider some empirically validated general therapeutic factors and measures of client change processes that can be applied to all counseling approaches.

COMMON THERAPEUTIC FACTORS AND FRAMEWORKS

There long has been a tension among researchers who argue that it is specific technical factors or mechanisms that produce change and those researchers who argue for common or nonspecific agents of change (Garfield, 1991, 1992; Stiles, Shapiro, & Elliot, 1986). However, as Goldfried, Castonguay, and Safran (1992) have pointed out, acknowledging that there are common factors across therapies does not eliminate the need to specify variables that are unique to counseling approaches. In fact, it is our opinion, that it is useful to conceptualize some therapeutic variables as involving both common and specific factors. For example, even though the alliance is a common factor in counseling, it also encompasses specific factors, as is evident in the notion that collaboration between the client and counselor on the unique goals and tasks of different therapeutic modalities is a critical part of establishing a working alliance. Thus, the working alliance is itself a relational variable, comprised of the specific technical factors in the different tasks and goals (Bordin, 1994).

General factors that have gathered a great deal of empirical support and have stood the test of time are the alliance and indices of clients' experiential involvement (Garfield & Bergin, 1994). These are briefly reviewed below. In addition, other common change variables and promising measures of change in counseling are discussed. Specifically, Stiles and colleagues' recent assimilation model, Orlinsky and colleagues' generic systems framework, and Goldfried's common ingredients are considered.

Therapeutic Alliance

As different approaches have increasingly been shown to result in similar client outcomes, there has been an increasing focus on different elements of the counseling relationship that are common to all approaches (Bordin, 1994; Gelso & Hayes, 1998; Henry & Strupp, 1994; Horvath & Greenberg, 1994; Pinsof, 1994; Raue & Goldfried, 1994; Watson & Greenberg, 1994). There is a consistent finding in the literature that a good therapeutic alliance is related to positive outcomes across various counseling modalities (Horvath & Greenberg, 1994; Luborsky, 1994; Safran & Muran, 1996). Client reported alliance appears to be the strongest predictor of outcome (Horvath & Greenberg, 1994). There is also some evidence that the task and goal components of the alliance are better predictors than the bond (Horvath & Greenberg, 1994). In addition, Safran and colleagues (Safran & Muran, 1996; Safran, Muran, & Samstag, 1994), in a move toward specifying interventions that help build or maintain a working alliance, have studied alliance ruptures and established the importance of responsive, nondefensive listening to client complaints as a means of healing strains in the relationship.

Rennie's (1992) qualitative work, which explored clients' experiences of counseling, using a grounded theory methodology, illuminated covert processes that contribute to the working alliance. He found that clients reported often concealing negative reactions from their counselors and deferring to their counselors' suggestions. Although the clients were cooperative and pleasant on the surface, they sometimes felt irritated with, and mistrustful of, their counselors, and were hesitant to express these negative reactions. Rennie labeled this concept as "client deference." Similarly, Hill and colleagues (Hill, Nut-Williams, Heaton, Thompson, & Rhodes, 1996; Hill, Thompson, Cogar, & Denman, 1993) have examined client and counselor reports of their covert processes in long-term therapy and found that clients had a tendency to hide negative feelings, thoughts, and reactions more frequently than positive reactions toward therapists. Furthermore, they found that counselors rarely were aware of what clients were keeping to themselves.

Dealing with client deference, alliance ruptures, and misunderstanding has emerged as an important change process variable in the last decade. Hill and colleagues (Hill et al., 1996; Hill, Thompson, & Corbett, 1992) suggest that becoming aware of interpersonal problems in counseling relationships is the answer to resolving clients' negative feelings toward their counselors. They advise that counselors need to be sensitive to client deference and create opportunities for clients to express their reactions. One way of doing this is by checking frequently with clients regarding their feelings about therapy so that counselors can intervene before a difficult situation reaches a point of crisis. Counselors also need to be aware that when they feel frustrated with clients or when things are not going well, clients also may be experiencing similar reactions (Hill et al., 1996). Another suggestion for counselors is to monitor the alliance closely by having clients fill out working alliance measures regularly to communicate to clients that their feelings about alliance issues are important, and to give the counselor information about specific aspects of the alliance (Hill et al., 1996).

Client Involvement

Measuring the degree of client involvement in counseling has been an important emerging trend in counseling process research (Greenberg & Pinsof, 1986). The "experiencing" construct has been used by counseling researchers in the past to assess client emotional involvement (Gendlin, Beebe, Cassens, Klein, & Oberlander, 1968), and was shown consistently to predict outcome, especially for client-centered counseling (Orlinsky & Howard, 1986). Experiencing is defined by Gendlin (1962) as our preconceptual, preverbal, bodily sense of being in interaction with our environment. It includes our experience of somatic events, feelings, sensations, reflexive awareness, and cognitive meanings that comprise our phenomenological field (Gendlin, 1962). The concept of experiencing as a common factor has recently been reinvestigated by Bohart and Wugalter (1991) who contend that change in "experiential knowing" is an important aspect of the counseling process in many approaches. More recently, experiencing is viewed as a means for clients in counseling to engage in an affective problem-solving process (Greenberg, Rice, & Elliot, 1993).

Experiencing is now reemerging as a general factor related to change in many counseling approaches (Castonguay, Goldfried, Wiser, Raue, & Hayes, 1996). Recent research has demonstrated that client experiencing is an important therapeutic variable that is related to outcome in dynamic, cognitive, and experiential counseling modalities (Castonguay et al., 1996; Goldman, 1997; Mahrer & Fairweather, 1993; Silberschatz, Fretter, & Curtis, 1986; Wiser & Goldfried, 1993). For example, it has recently been found that high experiencing and a strong alliance were the two factors that predicted improvement of depressive symptomology in cognitive therapy (Castonguay et al., 1996).

There has been an ongoing debate on whether experiencing is a change process in itself, or an individual difference variable that allows clients to become involved in treatment. Goldman (1997) investigated this issue and found that both early depth of experiencing and increase in depth of experiencing over treatment predicted outcome. This provided evidence supporting both points of view. Goldman not only showed that higher depth of experiencing predicted improvement in depression and other outcome variables, such as interpersonal problems and self-esteem, but also that increase in depth of experiencing on core themes over therapy, was the best predictor of outcome, better than either alliance or early experiencing. This is the first study to demonstrate that change in depth of experiencing over the course of counseling is related to outcome, supporting the claim that increased depth of experiencing is related to change. Of particular interest is the fact that early session experiencing also predicted outcome. This suggests that experiencing is both a trait variable, that indicates a capacity to do well in counseling, and a change process, that captures the process of emotional problem solving, in that, those who deepen experiencing in counseling sessions, in relation to core issues, have the most successful outcomes.

Another promising measure of the client change process is Stiles and colleagues' model of assimilation which defines a sequence of cognitive/affective levels through which problematic experiences are assimilated into a schema during successful therapy (Honos-Webb, Stiles, Greenberg, & Goldman, 1998; Stiles et al., 1990; Stiles, Meshot, Anderson, & Sloan, 1992). In this model, change occurs as a client progresses through seven stages evaluating the degree of awareness of the problematic experience, beginning with no awareness in stage 1, moving to an understanding of the problematic experience in stage 4, and ending in stage 7 with the client's application of that understanding as the client creates novel solutions in new situations (Honos-Webb et al., 1998). This model has been measured by the Assimilation of Problematic Experiences Scale (APES; Stiles et al., 1990, 1992). Using this scale, a number of good outcome cases have been shown to attain high degrees of problem assimilation, whereas client processes in poor outcome cases have been found to be blocked at various levels of the assimilation sequence (Honos-Webb et al., 1998; Stiles et al., 1990, 1992). Stiles and colleagues' have reconceptualized the assimilation process as a changing relationship between internal voices. One voice is that of an unwanted problematic experience, such as "I feel sad and lonely." This is in conflict with a dominant community of voices such as "it's important to be strong, independent and achieve," which disavows the less dominant voice. Assimilation occurs by means of an integration of these voices.

Generic Systems Framework

In addition to the alliance and experiential involvement, a number of other general factors have been proposed and studied. Orlinsky and his colleagues (Orlinsky, Grawe, Parks, 1994; Orlinsky & Howard, 1986, 1987) have proposed a generic systems framework for conceptualizing change in counseling, which they have developed from their reviews of empirical studies relating process to outcome in therapy. Their model considers relationships between contexts, processes, and outcomes that are common to all counseling modalities. They specify six characteristics of the counseling process found in all approaches: the therapeutic contract, counselor operations, therapeutic bond, self-relatedness, in-session impacts, and sequential flow which is a temporal aspect. Studies empirically testing this model provide support for its validity (Kolden, 1991; Kolden & Howard, 1992). Its use as an effective framework for evaluating change processes in counseling is highlighted by Kolden's (1996) study in which he used the generic systems framework to articulate a model of change for early sessions in dynamic therapy.

Goldfried (1982) has also made a comprehensive attempt to capture certain common ingredients across approaches. He has suggested the following common principles: (1) the facilitation of client expectations that treatment will help, (2) the existence of an optimal relationship, (3) feedback for promoting awareness, (4) corrective experiences, and (5) continued reality testing. These formulations have led to great interest in integrative approaches to treatment which attempt to incorporate a variety of change processes into one treatment. There has even been an increasing assimilation of techniques from many approaches into the major schools of counseling. In the next section we review advances in the specific change mechanisms within each major school of counseling.

CHANGE PROCESSES AND ADVANCES

Psychodynamic Approaches

Within the psychoanalytic school, as well as in the emerging brief psychodynamic counseling approaches, the key change process is the classical one of promoting client insight through interpretation. Increased specification and study of the use of interpretation has emerged in the last decade, particularly the investigation of the interpretation of transference through the Core Conflictual Relationship Theme method (CCRT; Luborsky & Crits-Christoph, 1990). Luborsky and Crits-Christoph developed the CCRT Method to extract a client's underlying pattern of conflictual themes. The main uses of the CCRT are to help guide the therapist in determining a treatment focus and in making interpretations (Luborsky, 1990). Each CCRT formulation includes the wishes toward other people, expected responses of others, and responses of the self. The CCRT has been shown to be reliable among counselors in making formulations (Luborsky & Crits-Christoph, 1990). Establishing the CCRT as a treatment focus can be beneficial to the client because it makes explicit the "target of change" and helps establish a goal that the client and counselor can work toward achieving (Luborsky, 1990). In his observations of interpretations made by effective counselors, Luborsky recommended that in choosing interpretations, the counselor should select the part of the CCRT to which the client is the most responsive and pertains the "most" to the client's suffering and symptoms. Luborsky also suggested that when making interpretations, the theme to be interpreted must be experienced by the client, and interpretation is most effective when this theme is seen to be impeding the treatment. Although there has been some criticism of the CCRT, suggesting that the use of this uniform method may distort the counseling process by overly specifying it, it seems that the gains of the method in promoting thematic meaningfulness, outweigh the risk of making an interpretation that is not focused on a core issue, or that is not meaningful to the client.

Strupp and Binder (1984) have identified a similar phenomena, the maladaptive interpersonal cycle as the key target of change in brief dynamic counseling. Their work has led them to highlight the importance of teaching counselors to deal with "the difficult client," who is generally withdrawn, or hostile and attacking, by not engaging in escalatory interactional cycles. They suggested that the empathic relationship and the provision of corrective emotional experiences are key in promoting change. Similarly, Henry and Strupp (1994) view the management of therapeutic alliance as a means of changing the interpersonal process. How the counselor behaves interpersonally toward the client becomes an important change mechanism in and of itself because it creates the opportunity for new interpersonal experiential learning (Henry & Strupp, 1994; Levenson, 1995; Levenson & Strupp, 1997). Within this more interpersonal dynamic counseling framework, a numbers of authors have demonstrated that the interpersonal stances taken in counseling are central to change (Levenson, 1995; Levenson & Strupp, 1997; Tracey, 1993). These stances have been shown to vary differentially over time in good and in poor outcome cases (Benjamin, 1993, 1996; Henry, 1996; Tracey, 1993; Wampold, 1995).

Interpersonal models assume that the counseling relationship is similar to other relationships in the client's life, and that the client will engage the counselor in a way that validates self-presentation. From this interpersonal perspective, treatment is viewed as the "delineation and the alteration of clients' relationship negotiation styles" (Tracey, 1993). The counselor's task is to engage the client in a relationship that is similar to the client's outside relationships, and to modify the client's behavior, so that the client learns alternative ways of interacting in relationships and adopts a more varied set of responses to people and situations.

Tracey (1993) has investigated a three stage interpersonal model of successful counseling process. The counseling process in this model is conceptualized by means of the construct of "complementarity," the degree to which the behaviors of the client and counselor complement each other (Tracey, 1993). The first stage in the beginning of counseling involves establishing rapport with the client and is characterized by high complementarity. This is achieved by the therapist's "adherence" to the client's definitions of the relationship. The second stage occurring in the middle of counseling involves changing a client's maladaptive behavioral pattern by having the counselor move away from the way that the client defines the relationship. Low complementarity is indicative of this second stage as it is considered to be conflictual. The third stage is one of high complementarity as it involves establishing a new way of interacting based on the client's amended concepts of self and others. Tracey proposed a revision to this model which split the middle conflictual stage of low complementarity into the dissatisfaction substage, comprising of high negative complementarity, and the unstable substage, characterized by low complementarity. This three-stage model of "high complementarity, low complementarity, high complementarity" has been found to be related to successful therapy, and divergence from the high-low-high pattern of complementarity has been associated with poorer outcomes (Tasca & McMullen, 1992; Tracey & Ray, 1984).

Attachment Theory and Client Change

In recent years, attachment has been viewed as more than just a stage-specific developmental issue in infancy, but as affecting adult relationships. Counselors have started to recognize the importance of using attachment theory to understand and treat clients in counseling. Attachment theory emphasizes the enduring desire for closeness and relations with a preferred other or others (Ainsworth, 1989). In biological terms, it can be defined as "a hardwired, neurologically-based behavioral system that has evolved to promote proximity to a caregiver" (Lyddon, 1995a). From a psychological viewpoint, it involves "internal working models" which are general guiding rules, established early in life, about self and others in interpersonal relationships (Lyddon, 1995a).

Using Bowlby's (1982, 1988) attachment theory, Gelso and Hayes (1998) propose that attachment theory provides the counselor with valuable information in understanding transference relations. They argue that early experiences with childhood attachment figures lead to the development of internal working models for relating to others. These internal models function as schemas that influence a person's perceptions and behaviors so as to produce current experiences that are consistent with these models. Thus, these early developed internal models operate as prototypes for adult relationships (Farber, Lippert, & Nevas, 1995).

Transference occurs when clients inaccurately perceive the client-counselor relationship, or the actions of the counselor, due to internal working models that have been developed in infancy (Gelso & Hayes, 1998). Recent empirical studies have shown that clients develop transference patterns toward their counselors that are similar to the attachment styles they formed in infancy, as well as the attachment styles they exhibit in their current relationships (Gelso & Hayes, 1998; Mallinckrodt, Gantt, & Coble, 1995). Securely attached individuals would develop positive transferences, whereas those individuals who formed insecure attachments with their caregivers would form negative transferences. For example, a client who is insecurely attached may perceive their counselor's cancellation of an appointment due to illness as a rejection because it is consistent with the rejection the client felt in childhood due to a primary caregiver's inconsistency. In contrast, in the same example, a securely attached individual may feel cared for by the counselor because the counselor was apologetic in cancelling the appointment.

The client-counselor relationship can be used to change clients' attachment organizations by focusing on clients' internal working models which are maintained by "attachment-related cognition, affect, and behavior" (Pistole & Watkins, 1995). By differentiating and understanding clients' early attachments, counselors can anticipate transferences that arise in therapy, and be prepared to deal with them. Through an attitude of curiosity about the meaning of the client's behavior and emotional responses, the counselor can help the client clarify attachment information, identify the elements of the client's working models, and interrupt the internal mechanisms that maintain dysfunction. More specifically, to facilitate change, counselors can direct attention to questions regarding beliefs and feelings about the self, the availability and trustworthiness of partners, and the appropriateness of reactions in present relationships.

Pistole and Watkins (1995) argue that clients can change the way their attachment system functions by using the counselor as a secure base for exploring past and present attachment-related memories, feelings, or interactions. By exploring these experiences, clients can articulate their understanding of their behavior and attachments, attain new viewpoints on negative attachment experiences, and alter their internal working models of attachment, with the aim of moving toward more adept behavior. The main premise is that although the client's dysfunctional attachment-related behavior is not effective in the present, it was practical and sensible in an earlier context. Consequently, the counselor's role is to provide the client with a safe and secure foundation to explore issues.

Matching Counseling Interventions to Needs

A theme that has been emerging more strongly in recent years in the study of therapeutic change is that individual differences are important and that the type of interventions used need to be matched to client characteristics. For example, Silberschatz et al. (1986) argue that the suitability of a counseling intervention to the particular needs of the client is more important than the intervention itself. Furthermore, they criticize therapies for failing to assess how well-suited interventions are in relation to the client's problems and treatment goals. In their research, they examined how interpretations influence the counseling process, and describe a new approach for assessing the suitability of counselor interpretations in brief psychodynamic therapy. To do this, they used Weiss and colleagues' (Weiss, Sampson, & the Mount Zion Psychotherapy Research Group, 1986) theory of psychopathology, which states that psychopathology arises from unconscious pathogenic ideas or false beliefs that are usually based in traumatic childhood experience. Moreover, clients enter counseling with a *plan* for disconfirming these false beliefs by testing them in the relationship with the counselor (Weiss et al., 1986). Thus, Silberschatz et al. (1986) contended that the counselor's interventions will be most effective when they are compatible with the client's plan. Their findings indicated that the suitability of interpretations is a better predictor of immediate progress than the kind of interpretation made (Silberschatz et al., 1986). Similarly, Piper and colleagues (Piper, Joyce, McCallum, & Azim, 1993) have demonstrated the importance of both the type of technique and its appropriateness for the client, in predicting client immediate response and counseling outcome.

Joyce and Piper (1996) also have specified variables that can influence the manner in which change occurs. In their study, they found that transference interpretations that fostered positive counseling outcome were mediated by the quality of object relations (QOR) between the client and counselor. Clients with high QOR differed from those with low QOR with respect to their reactions to transference interpretations. This highlights the importance of considering individual difference variables in matching specific treatments to particular clients, and of creating models that allow us to do so.

Joyce et al. (1995) developed a model of "working" responses to interpretation in brief dynamic individual counseling. They used a task-analytic method (Rice & Greenberg, 1984) to evaluate a conceptual model of "working" responses to dynamic interpretation episodes from 60 cases of brief dynamic therapy. Their model illustrated that working responses to interpretation develop from a complex collaboration between the client and counselor. They articulated three main phases of working responses to interpretation: (1) precondition operations, (2) interpretation operations, and (3) response operations.

In the precondition phase, they found that during "signaling" the client identified a need or concern. Following this, "awareness of discomfort" occurred, in which the client specified and gave examples of the uneasiness associated with the articulated concern. The next step of the model was "therapist focal emphasis," which required the counselor to ask orienting questions that helped direct and differentiate the client's experience, often evoking affect in the process. Therapist focal emphasis was found to lead back to a cycle of "signaling," this time a more concrete clarification of the need, and "awareness of discomfort," a clearer and more differentiated expression of the discomfort. Subsequently, an "invitation to interpret" by the client was made. This was demonstrated by the client's rearticulation of the difficulty, in a questioning manner, asking for help, often indirectly. In the last phase before counselor interpretation occurred, the role of the counselor was to "facilitate affect" by the use of silence, empathy, or focusing in on specific thoughts, feelings or behaviors of the client.

During the interpretation phase, the counselor began by "addressing" the client's specified concern or conflict. Next, the counselor's role involved "labeling and connecting" the concern by identifying it and linking it with affect, possibly making connections inside and outside of the counseling milieu. The counselor then gave the client "an invitation to respond," often by summarizing or repeating the interpretation. Transference was attended to either during labeling and connecting or during an invitation to respond.

Finally, the response resulted in "direct confirmation, partial confirmation, or direct disconfirmation" of the counselor's interpretation. Following this, the therapist's intervention was to "encourage work" by trying to promote application of the interpretation. Therapist tasks depended on the extent to which the client had confirmed the interpretation. Subsequently, client "expanding" occurred when clients expressed awareness of links between affect, behavior, and thoughts, or past and present experiences, or between their feelings and the expressed concern. Another part of the response involved "deepening" in which the client specified the conflict, and demonstrated insight or expressed a greater interest in wanting to change. Next, the counselor was found to once again "encourage work," leading to another cycle of "expanding," this time involving expression of responsibility for problems, and "deepening," the specification of client concerns in need of more exploration. Some clients increased the interpretation stage by inviting the "next round" of interpretation, which was made when "expanding" or "deepening" faded out.

Theoretical Developments

Kernberg and Clarkin (1993) have made important advances in specifying elements in the psychodynamic treatment of clients with borderline personality organization (BPO). They maintain that prominent features of BPO are a lack of integration of concepts of self and significant others, as well as the existence of primitive defense mechanisms, particularly splitting. They have based their treatment on diagnosing and resolving the lack of integration of the concept of self and the concept of significant others. The goal is to resolve primitive defense mechanisms and resolve internalized "part" object relationships into "total" object relationships (Kernberg & Clarkin, 1993).

Over the last decade, the modern psychodynamic view of countertransference and its role in the process of change has altered significantly. Rather than being considered countertherapeutic, it has come to be seen as useful and a fundamental component in the change process. The classical position argues that countertransference is an expression of the counselor's unresolved conflicts which are provoked by the client, but are not a part of the working relationship. Furthermore, countertransference was considered to impede the counselor's objectivity, and it was regarded as necessary for the counselor to work out his or her own conflicts in personal counseling. More modern dynamic approaches view countertransference as inevitable, as the client is viewed as having a dysfunctional manner of relating that the counselor will respond to accordingly (Binder, Strupp, & Henry, 1995; Butler & Strupp, 1991; Henry, Strupp, Schacht, & Gaston, 1994; Levenson, 1995; Mitchell, 1988). Furthermore, in the more modern therapies, countertransference is considered to be therapeutic as it allows the counselor to know experientially what it is like to interact with the client, and it can guide the counselor in knowing what the pattern of relating is like and what needs to be done to change it (Levenson, 1995; Levenson & Strupp, 1997).

Major theoretical developments within psychodynamic approaches have involved a move from drive to relational models. According to this view, people are portrayed not as a conglomeration of biologically based urges, but as comprehensible only within a tapestry of past and present relationships (Mitchell, 1988). These theoretical views have strongly influenced the role and the function of the counselor. Client responses are seen primarily as having to do with the real relationship with the counselor, and not as transferences from the past onto the counselor. Therefore, counseling is viewed as progressing by means of the development of an authentic intimate relationship in which client and counselor progressively make contact as real people (Frank, 1997). The major change process is thus a relational one, more akin to a corrective emotional experience than to insight.

Kohut (1995), in his self-psychological theory, proposed an empathic stance as being fundamental to psychoanalytic cure. He regarded the counselor's empathic attunement as serving a crucial soothing function which is internalized and leads to greater self-coherence and a strengthening of the self. Mitchell (1988), in his interpersonal approach, proposes a two-person psychology in which the relationship is viewed as the fundamental source of development and of therapeutic change. Thus, the counselor's countertransference is viewed as an important source of experiential information on what is occurring between client and counselor, and as an important basis for intervention. Recently, Stolorow and colleagues (Stolorow, 1994; Stolorow, Atwood, & Brandschaft,

1994) have proposed an even more radical intersubjective approach in which subjective experience is viewed as having no reality independent of the relationship in which it occurs. In this approach, they emphasize the importance of empathy in helping clients regulate their affective experience. These new dynamic approaches are all promoting a much more genuine relationship between counselor and client, and a greater emphasis on the counselor's empathic attunement to client affect (Bohart & Greenberg, 1997a).

These more relational psychodynamic approaches to counseling were somewhat anticipated by feminist views, particularly those from the Stone Centre, which advocated that it is the relational connection between the counselor and client that helps break women's sense of isolation (Jordon, 1997; Jordan, Kaplan, Miller, Stiver, & Surrey, 1991; Miller, 1986; Miller, Jordan, Kaplan, Stiver, & Surrey, 1997). These feminist approaches proposed a highly empathic stance and emphasized counselor self-disclosure. They were also highly sensitive to the influence of dominant culture on women. By focusing on the role of women in society, they have helped highlight the role of culture and diversity in psychological problems (Jordan, 1997).

Humanistic Approaches

The humanistic paradigm is composed of a number of distinct approaches to therapy, mainly client-centered therapy, Gestalt therapy, and recently emerging experiential therapy. Transactional, transpersonal, and existential counseling approaches can also be classified under the humanistic paradigm (McLeod, 1996b). Humanistic approaches emphasize the importance of the client-counselor relationship in promoting therapeutic changes (Bozarth, 1990; Polster & Polster, 1973; Rogers, 1959; Watson & Greenberg, 1994; Wheeler, 1991), and have come to see the counselor's presence as being highly therapeutic (Rogers, 1980; Watson, Greenberg, & Lietaer, 1998). In addition, one of the primary tasks in many humanistic therapies is to facilitate client experiencing, particularly in relation to problematic client concerns (Gendlin et al., 1968; Greenberg et al., 1993; Rennie, 1998; Toukmanian & Rennie, 1992).

Process-Experiential Approach

A recent trend in humanistic counseling has been the emergence of experiential approaches that have combined the relational stance of person-centred therapy with more active interventions, often from other counseling modalities. The development of these mixed modalities implies that on their own, the person-centered relationship conditions may not be as efficient in effecting change. However, these more active approaches do view the relationship conditions as an important ingredient of change and a necessary requirement for the active interventions to be effective.

This trend is exemplified by Greenberg et al.'s (1993) process-experiential approach which is aimed at deepening experience by integrating Gestalt interventions, such as empty-chair or two-chair work, cognitive and emotion theory, and aspects of Gendlin's (1981, 1996) experiential therapy into a person-centered relationship. In this approach, different interventions have been devised to promote specific change processes for specific in-session cognitive-affective problems. Counselor interventions are informed by the different process markers of opportunities for intervention, demonstrated by clients at different moments in the counseling session. The interventions and markers specified include empty-chair dialogue to resolve unfinished business with a significant other, two-chair dialogue to resolve self-evaluative or self-interruptive internal splits, systematic evocative unfolding for problematic reactions, focusing for an unclear felt sense, empathic affirmation at a marker of intense vulnerability (Elliot & Greenberg, 1995; Greenberg et al., 1993), and the provision of new interpersonal experience when the counselor feels the "pull" of clients' maladaptive interpersonal styles (van Kessel & Lietaer, 1998). These techniques are aimed at bringing into awareness and heightening particular aspects of clients' inner experiences at particular times so that they can be symbolized and used to create new meaning (Clarke, 1996; Toukmanian, 1990, 1992; Watson, 1996).

One of the major developments in the decade has been the empirical demonstration of the effectiveness of humanistic treatments. Greenberg, Elliot, and Lietaer (1994) conducted a meta-analysis of 37 outcome studies of experiential therapies from 1978 to 1994. They examined whether experiential therapies were as effective as nonexperiential treatments and found that there were no differences between treatments. However, when seven studies comparing the directive experiential treatments (process-experiential and Gestalt) with cognitive and behavioral treatments were examined, the results suggested that posttreatment gains of clients receiving directive experiential therapies were on the average .4 standard deviations higher than those obtained by clients in cognitive and behavioral counseling approaches. Although, this finding is not statistically significant as it is limited by the small sample sizes, it highlights the necessity for more extensive research with larger samples comparing experiential therapies with other approaches.

Recently, Greenberg and Watson (1998) compared the efficacy of process-experiential therapy with client-centered therapy in a study of 34 clients suffering from major depression. This study found large effect sizes in the alleviation of depressive symptomology at termination for both treatments (ES Pre-Post = 2.82 for the process-experiential treatment and ES Pre-Post = 2.60 for the client-centered treatment), demonstrating the effectiveness of these humanistic treatments in treating moderate depression. Although the counseling approaches did not demonstrate any differences in reduction of depressive symptomology at the end of counseling and six-month follow-up, the process-experiential approach had significantly better midtreatment, and termination outcomes on measures of self-esteem, interpersonal problems, and global symptoms. Both the empathic client-centered treatment and the process-experiential approach appeared to empower clients to find their own voice and helped them create new meaning, whereas the process-experiential approach, in addition, promoted deeper experiencing and emotional processing.

Focusing Approach

Focusing is a method of attending inwardly to bodily sensations to facilitate experiencing and emotional healing (Cornell, 1996; Gendlin, 1981, 1996). In recent years, Gendlin (1996) has placed an emphasis on using focusing to advance therapy during times when clients are at an impasse. Specifically, it is particularly useful for clients who seem stuck in therapy, or when counselors are having ongoing discussions with clients that do not seem to lead anywhere. In these cases, focusing can be used by having clients focus inwardly on physical sensations in their bodies following a therapeutic activity to discover if the intervention had an impact on the person's internal experience (Gendlin, 1996). For example, the counselor may make an empathic reflection to a client, such as, "I imagine that it must be scary for you not to know where your marriage stands," and the client may respond with, "I'm not sure how I feel about this." In this situation, the counselor can direct the client to "pay attention to any physical sensations that occur inside your body as you think about your marriage." The client may respond with, "I feel a strong shaky feeling in my chest. Lately, the shakiness is always there, but I have been avoiding it. I *am* scared that I will end up alone." Another potential client response might be, "I feel hot inside my stomach. I don't think I'm scared, but I think it's anger. Yeah, that really fits. I'm angry that I don't have a say in the outcome of my marriage."

Focusing is particularly useful when feelings remain unchanged in counseling despite the fact that they are repeatedly discussed (Gendlin, 1996). Gendlin proposes that these "dead-end" feelings remain unchanged because they seem final and there is no ambiguous experiential frontier onto which the client might venture. Therefore, the role of the counselor is to help the client "sense an unclear edge" of experience from feelings that are unchanging by focusing on them until further movement arises or new meaning is created (Gendlin, 1996). The assumption in this view is that elements in the mind and body can be in the center of awareness (figural) or can be at the edge of awareness (background). New meaning is then created by attending to the periphery of awareness and bringing material into the foreground. Thus, all experiences and events contain more than is currently in awareness, and provide the potential for growth. Change occurs by the counselor assisting the client in making the implicit, at the edge of awareness, explicit (Gendlin, 1996).

Focusing has also been found to be useful for clients who have difficulty facing painful feelings that have been deeply buried for a long time, and are in need of further processing. For example, Bierman's (1997) use of focusing-guided emotional processing in treating incarcerated domestically violent men who have been physically and emotionally abused themselves, in a once-a-day, twelve-week counseling group called Relating Without Violence, has shown very promising results. These men buried painful internal feelings of shame that resulted from early childhood maltreatment by responding with rage whenever these feelings were triggered. The use of focusing in Bierman's Relating Without Violence treatment program allowed the men to confront and process primary emotions which were too painful to face in childhood. This led to a reduction in defensiveness so they no longer had to ward off anticipated threats or mask shame by expressing rage, which resulted in "a decrease in the use of destructive responses to conflict, both physical and psychological, reduced, irritability and readiness for anger, and reduced defensiveness" (Bierman, 1997). Thus, as Bierman's Relating Without Violence program demonstrates, focusing can be used as a tool to help people face and deal with primary emotions that seemed too aversive to confront in childhood.

Gestalt Therapy

The most important advance in Gestalt counseling practice has been the development of a dialogic approach in which there is a much greater emphasis on contact in the client-counselor relationship as a key change process (Hycner & Jacobs, 1995; Wheeler, 1991; Yontef, 1995, 1998). This is a shift from traditional Gestalt therapy in which the experiments and techniques assumed center stage.

Gestalt counseling is currently seen as being based on three fundamental principles: field theory, phenomenology, and dialogue (Resnick, 1995). The main objective of dialogic Gestalt counseling is to make "contact" with the client. This is done by beginning counseling empathically, with a focus on the client's perspective (Yontef, 1998). This notion of contact involves an awareness of self and other. In dialogic contact, there is no expected goal or outcome outside of the contact, and contact is an ongoing goal throughout counseling. Dialogic therapy is based on the premises that beginning in early childhood an individual develops in relation to other people, that relational support is important, and that a lack of it can produce shame (Wheeler, 1995). Therefore, a positive sense of self can be fostered through dialogic relating in counseling (Yontef, 1998). Gestalt counseling has thus added the relationship as the important context for its original experiential orientation in which change was seen as coming about through action, through trying something new and letting awareness emerge from the new experimental behavior. This new emphasis on dialogue and contact as key change processes parallels the shift in psychodynamic counseling, from insight to a focus on the importance of interpersonal change processes.

Plummer (1997) has introduced a Gestalt model for the mental health treatment of culturally diverse populations. This model focuses its attention on counselor self-awareness as it is based on the premise that if counselors understand the effect of cultural influences on their own lives, then they can provide their clients with counseling that is culturally appropriate (Plummer, 1997). The model is comprised of four components: (1) "awareness/attitude" includes the beliefs, attitudes, and stereotypes that a counselor has about his or her own culture and other cultures; (2) "behaviors" refers to the counselor's external expression of cultural influences on an interpersonal level; (3) "cultural competence" is the counselor's demonstration of proficient skills that are culturally specific, and engagement in interventions that are suitable for particular cultures; and (4) "data" involve the acquisition of multicultural information, be it experientially or through reading (Plummer, 1997). This model has important implications for multicultural counseling as it proposes that difficulties in counseling with individuals from diverse cultures reside in the counselor and not in the client or the client's cultural background. Furthermore, it provides counselors with a model to enable them to deal with their cultural attitudes, behaviors, and stereotypes in a way that is therapeutically helpful to the client.

Empathy and Change

There has been a renewed interest in the role of empathy in counseling over the past few years, leading to its revitalization as an important change producing process. There is increasing openness and creativity in the manner that empathy is communicated (Bozarth, 1997). Barrett-Lennard (1997) has articulated a new aspect of the function of empathy in his discussion of the integral role of counselor empathy in promoting client self-empathy, as well as empathy for others as "the person who is at home with the subjective stirrings of his or her own inner being tends to be sensitive to the inner felt world of others and is not afraid of responding from this awareness" (p. 111). A process-experiential approach views empathy as being more selective than reflective, as well as more exploratory and evocative, directed at future growth possibilities, highlighting client strengths, and picking up implicit needs and desires of clients (Greenberg & Elliot, 1997). Specific targets of empathy (Greenberg & Elliot, 1997) and different functions and goals have been more clearly specified (Bohart & Greenberg, 1997a).

Although all the definitions of empathy in psychotherapy concur that an individual is "trying to sense, perceive, share, or conceptualize how another person is experiencing the world," more recently, empathy has been reconceptualized as a multidimensional construct involving understanding, validation, an experiential component, an active dimension, and a relational aspect (Bohart & Greenberg, 1997b). Three different forms of therapeutic empathy with specific functions have been identified, each consistent with a particular theoretical orientation. First is the view of empathy as rapport. This is most consistent with the cognitive-behavioral view of the empathic relationship as a context for intervention. Second, is the humanistic view of empathy as here and now, moment-by-moment attunement to the client's felt experience and meaning. In this view, empathy is seen as an important change process in itself leading to strengthening of the self, and promoting exploration and discovery. Third, in the more psychodynamic form, empathy is seen as the "there and then" understanding of the client's history, development, and internal dynamics, so as to help the counselor build an internal model of a client's internal functioning for use in later interpretation. Here, empathy is a means to the end of promoting understanding.

The humanistic approaches, by emphasizing process in the here and now, and seeing people as basically healthy, have been criticized for their lack of a differential treatment perspective, adopting more of a one size fits all approach, and for lack of attention to context and developmental history. Humanistic therapies have also been criticized for being useful only for the "worried well." These criticisms have recently started to be addressed by the development of differential treatments in which different in-session problems and processes, and ways of intervening with them, have been specified for different disorders (Greenberg, Watson, & Lietaer, 1998). Gestalt therapists have also gone beyond the here and now to take history and diagnosis into account in helping specify what change processes best fit a particular person (Melnick & Nevis, 1994; Yontef, 1995).

Importance of Emotion in Change

In recent years, emotion has been playing an increasingly important role in the theory and practice of counseling. It has emerged as important in cognitive-behavioral (A.T. Beck, 1996; J.S. Beck, 1996; Foa & Kozak, 1991; Linehan, 1993, 1996; Teasdale, 1993, 1996, 1997) and psychodynamic approaches to counseling (Kohut, 1995; Levenson, 1995; Stolorow et al., 1994), but has been particularly prominent in the experiential-humanistic therapies. Specifically, Greenberg and his colleagues (Greenberg, Korman, & Paivio, in press; Greenberg & Paivio, 1997; Korman & Greenberg, 1996) have articulated different types of emotional processes and specific interventions for different subtypes of emotions, and have demonstrated how to work in-session with specific emotions such as anger, sadness, fear, and shame (Greenberg & Korman, 1993; Greenberg & Paivio, 1997).

From this perspective, emotion serves an adaptive function as it alerts people to what is meaningful and what is harmful or beneficial for their well-being (Greenberg et al., 1993, in press; Korman & Greenberg, 1996). A fundamental source of emotion arises from an individual's implicit appraisal of situations pertaining to needs or goals (Frijda, 1986; Greenberg & Korman, 1993; Greenberg & Safran, 1987, 1989; Safran & Greenberg, 1991). Because emotions organize people for action and give them information about what is significant in their lives, and what is negative or positive for them, when a person is not able to consider and integrate emotional experience, difficulties in emotional processing develop, and, consequently, human functioning is impaired. When one is unable to access action tendencies and emotional information, a person's ability to act and make meaning is compromised. Emotion is one of the crucial tools an individual needs to navigate through the personal world (Greenberg & Safran, 1987, 1989). As a result, experiential therapies have aimed their interventions at the emotional processing level (Elliot & Greenberg, 1995; Greenberg & Paivio, 1997; Greenberg et al., 1993).

Emotion Schemes

Greenberg and Paivio (1997) have proposed that the primary unit of change when working with emotions is the emotion scheme, which is defined as "a complex synthesis of affect, cognition, motivation, and action that provides each person with an integrated sense of him- or herself and the world, as well as with subjective felt meaning." Experience is created through the evocation of emotion-schemes that produce a bodily felt sense, as well as beliefs and action tendencies (Greenberg & Paivio, 1997). Adaptive emotions should be evoked and attended to in counseling to help clients to feel grounded and to facilitate problem solving, whereas dysfunctional emotion schemes need to be accessed to make them amenable to change. Active process-experiential interventions are designed to evoke dysfunctional emotion schemes and have clients attend to, reprocess, and restructure them. Four different types of emotional experiences have been described. Primary adaptive emotions are peoples' most basic healthy emotions, whereas primary maladaptive emotions are a main source of dysfunction in the emotion system. Secondary feelings are those feelings that obscure more primary feelings (anger) that is expressed when hurt is primary, and instrumental feelings are those feelings expressed to influence others ("crocodile" tears to get sympathy).

Therapeutic Interventions in Working with Emotions

Greenberg and Paivio (1997) have articulated three phases in counseling as a guide to working with emotions. The first phase is the bonding phase in which the counselor attends to, emphasizes, and validates the client's emotional experience. This type of bond is seen as crucial for helping clients access emotion. In addition, there is an attempt to identify the underlying determinants of the client's present state and to develop a collaborative focus on these (Greenberg & Paivio, 1997). The second phase, evoking, involves arousing emotional experiences related to the core themes in the counseling sessions. An important part of this phase involves an exploration and differentiation of emotional experience to access primary emotions and the thoughts and needs associated with them. The transformation takes place in the third-restructuring phase. This involves accessing both core maladaptive emotion schemes and primary adaptive emotional experience with which to restructure the maladaptive schemes.

Restructuring of activated core maladaptive emotion schemes occurs by a self-challenging of the beliefs embedded in them by means of newly accessed healthy emotions and needs. For example, the shame-based emotion scheme of worthlessness that results from abuse, once activated, is combated by tapping into currently accessible anger at violation, or sadness at the loss associated with the abuse. This dialectical confrontation between the previously dominant maladaptive voice, saying, "I'm worthless," and the newly empowered adaptive voice in the personality, saying, "I'm worthwhile," provides the foundation for the development of a new self-organization. The counselor then supports and validates the client's new self-validating position, and helps the client reflect on this new emotional experience. This helps to create a new narrative that characterizes the new meanings developed in the dialectical synthesis of the dominant and subdominant voices. Supporting the claim that counseling leads to change in emotional organization, Korman (1998) has demonstrated that there were significantly more changes in the types of clients' in-session emotions expressed, from early to late sessions of process-experiential therapy, more often in cases with successful outcomes than in those with unsuccessful outcomes.

Cognitive-Behavioral Therapy

Cognitive theory maintains that an individual's emotional and behavioral responses to a situation are largely determined by how that individual perceives, interprets, and assigns meaning to that event. The cognitive theory of psychopathology is based on an information-processing perspective in which there are systematic information-processing biases that maintain psychopathology (J.S. Beck, 1995; A.T. Beck, Rush, Shaw, & Emery, 1979). Psychopathology occurs as a result of enduring dysfunctional schemas which manifest as negative automatic thoughts in the individual. The main change goals of cognitive counseling are to teach clients how to correct their faulty thinking and to alter the dysfunctional beliefs that make clients vulnerable to distorting their experiences (J.S. Beck, 1995; Greenberger & Padesky, 1995). A large amount of outcome research has been done demonstrating the effects of cognitive counseling, but questions remain concerning the specific change processes involved.

Therapeutic change is facilitated by challenging a client's beliefs by using behavioral experiments to engage in hypothesis testing with the client. Cognitive therapy is usually a structured, time-limited approach in which the counselor takes an active role in collaborating with the client to change clients' dysfunctional beliefs. Recently, counseling interventions have been more specifically tailored to particular client difficulties as there is a new emphasis on the role of specific types of dysfunctional beliefs for different presenting problems (A.T. Beck, 1993, 1996).

Castonguay and his colleagues (Castonguay et al., 1996) examined the relationship between process variables and final counseling outcome. One factor examined, the impact of distorted thoughts on client's mood, was specific to cognitive therapy, and two other factors, the therapeutic alliance and depth of experiencing, were regarded as being common to all approaches. They found that client outcome was related to both common variables, the working alliance and depth of experiencing. Surprisingly, however, there was a negative correlation between the counselor's focus on the impact of distorted cognitions on depressive symptoms and final outcome. It was hypothesized that counselors who experienced the counseling relationship as being strained focused more on implementing cognitive therapy tasks to deal with the lack of collaboration. Some counselors viewed the rupture as an indication of the client's distorted thoughts and proceeded to challenge them. The implications of this study are that difficult client states that produce problems like alliance strains may require deviating from a protocol for a specific approach, and from a cognitive perspective, may involve incorporating interpersonal and experiential interventions.

Although A.T. Beck et al. (1979) have stated that the primary mechanism of change in cognitive-behavioral counseling involves changing core cognitive schemas, there have been some challenges to this argument. Jacobson and his colleagues (1996) suggest that because there are many aspects involved in the treatment of cognitive-behavioral therapy, factors other than changing core schemas may play a role in alleviating depression. They propose two alternative hypotheses. The first hypothesis is the activation hypothesis that maintains that cognitive-behavioral therapy is efficacious because it makes clients active again, and encourages the initiation of contact with existing sources of reinforcement. The second alternative hypothesis about why cognitive-behavioral therapy might be effective is the coping skills hypothesis that contends that the new set of skills that clients acquire to cope with depressing events and thoughts, in addition to activation, accounts for the alleviation of depressive behavior. This hypothesis argues that it is not the altering of core cognitive schemas that improves depression, but that clients are learning effective strategies for coping with automatic thoughts and stress.

The hypotheses proposed by Jacobson et al. (1996) raise the question of whether changing core schemas in counseling is necessary in alleviating depression. To address this, Jacobson et al. tested the theory of change proposed by A.T. Beck et al. (1979) to explain the efficacy of cognitive-behavioral counseling for depression. They compared three psychotherapeutic modalities by randomly assigning 152 outpatients with major depression to one of the following treatment groups: (1) a treatment that focused only on behavioral activation; (2) a treatment that involved both behavioral activation and teaching the client how to change automatic thoughts, while excluding the components of cognitive counseling that focused on changing core schemas; or (3) a complete treatment in cognitive-behavioral therapy (Jacobson et al., 1996). Based on the cognitive theory of depression, it would be expected that a complete treatment of cognitive-behavioral counseling would be more effective than a treatment that only involved behavioral activation and automatic thoughts, which in turn would be more effective than behavioral activation by itself. Surprisingly, the findings of this study indicated that all of the treatments were equally effective in altering negative thinking and pathological attributional styles (Jacobson et al., 1996). These findings call into question the importance of changing core schemas in alleviating depression and have implications for the practice of cognitive counseling. Specifically, this study suggests that interventions should not be solely aimed at modifying dysfunctional interpretations or beliefs, and that other aspects of cognitive-behavioral counseling, such as teaching coping skills and the initiation of contact, should be emphasized in the interventions.

In his original theory to explain disordered thought processes in depression, A.T. Beck (1996) initially proposed that "the activation of certain idiosyncratic schemas represented the core problem in depression and could be assigned a primary role in the production of the various cognitive, affective, and behavioural symptoms." However, the view that core organizing beliefs based on a single cognitive schema, or that the automatic thoughts they produce, causes psychopathology, still lacks clear empirical support. For example, Teasdale (1993) and others have argued that automatic thoughts maintain rather than cause dysfunction. Because the core beliefs emerge only after numerous emotionally laden experiences, they have been viewed as only a part of a more emotionally laden scheme (Greenberg & Paivio, 1997), and it is this scheme that needs to be changed, rather than the core belief alone. Furthermore, it has been argued that dysfunction needs to be viewed as occurring by constructive meaning creation processes (Guidano, 1991, 1995a; Mahoney, 1991, 1993; R.A. Neimeyer, 1995b, 1995c) or by a complex process of the synthesis of many schemes and levels of processing (Greenberg & Paivio, 1997; Greenberg & Pascual-Leone, 1995; Teasdale, 1993), rather than by dysfunctional beliefs.

A further challenge to the view that changing core schemas is the mechanism of change in cognitive counseling comes from A.T. Beck (1996) himself. He has recently noted those aspects of his original cognitive theory that have not gathered empirical support. Three decades after his initial contributions in a paper entitled "Beyond Belief," he has amended his cognitive model to include the concepts of "modes," much like moods, and "charges" or "cathexes," to explain more fully how beliefs and thoughts are activated and influence functioning (A.T. Beck, 1996). According to A.T. Beck, modes are integrated systems of personality that include cognitive, affective, motivational, and behavioral components. These are much like the earlier proposals of emotion schemes (Greenberg & Paivio, 1997; Greenberg & Safran, 1987), and implicational levels of meaning, as the primary sources of meaning (Teasdale, 1993). A.T. Beck and Teasdale view these systems as being made up of structures or "schemas," or different levels of processing. These systems are designed to deal with certain demands or difficulties. A.T. Beck also introduces the terms, charges or cathexes, to account for changes in the intensity gradients of cognitive structures.

Along with Teasdale (1993), A.T. Beck (1996) now argues that some preconscious processing without thought activates a variety of cognitive-affective and physiological processes. His new position, that what is activated is a primal mode relevant to danger, is tantamount to acknowledging the importance of an affective process of fear of danger, or as Beck calls it, a phobic mode. The activation of this mode leads to cognitive, affective, motivational, and physiological responses. Although not yet clear, this view, to its credit, is a changing response to the lack of empirical evidence for cognitive therapy's simpler views on the primacy of cognition in human functioning and therapeutic change. Thus, there seems to be a major shift in cognitive counseling toward the recognition of the importance of emotionally influenced processes in therapy (A.T. Beck, 1996; Greenberg & Paivio, 1997; Greenberg & Safran, 1987; Guidano, 1991; Mahoney, 1991).

Cognitive Approaches for Specific Concerns

Within the cognitive-behavioral paradigm, it is suggested that each of the emotional disorders has a particular cognitive content, which can be assessed with self-report measures with varying degrees of reliability. In the 1990s, we have seen that cognitive counseling has increasingly been applied to personality disorders (A.T. Beck, 1993; Beck, Freeman, & Associates, 1990; J.S. Beck, 1996; Linehan, 1993), partly because these disorders coexist with other disorders, such as depression or anxiety, and make it more difficult to treat the latter. In working with personality disorders, cognitive counseling tends to be longer term, emphasizes the importance of the counseling relationship, and looks at how early learning plays a role in the development of schemas (A.T. Beck, 1993; A.T. Beck et al., 1990).

The development of particular treatment programs for particular client problems is exemplified by Linehan's (1993) highly successful integrative cognitive-behavioral approach called dialectical behavioral therapy (DBT) for women with BPO who have a history of self-injurious and suicidal behaviors. Her approach can be also applied to men, as well as borderline patients who do not have suicidal histories. Some distinctive features of her approach include an emphasis on dialectics which involves trying to reconcile opposites in an ongoing process of synthesis. The most important dialectic in DBT is the acceptance of clients as they are, while at the same time teaching them how to change. Linehan (1993, 1996) emphasizes acceptance as being necessary to maintain equilibrium while at the same time facilitating change. Her approach requires the counselor to think dialectically to change the client's dichotomous and rigid thinking. It combines efforts by the counselor to reframe suicidal and dysfunctional behaviors as problem-solving strategies that have been learned, and involves the client in active problem solving, while at the same time validating the client's current emotional, cognitive, and behavioral responses just as they are. Counseling addresses both the client's in-session and out-of-session problematic behaviors systematically by analyzing the client's behavior in consultation with the client, figuring out reasons for the client's behavior, coming up with different ways of responding, and having the client try out these solutions. DBT counseling also teaches the client how to regulate emotions and interpersonal skills. Another emphasis of DBT is having the client actively face threatening situations both in and outside of counseling.

Linehan (1993) contends that DBT is different from standard cognitive-behavior counseling because it accepts the present behavior and experiences of the client as they are. In addition, there is a focus in counseling on behaviors that interfere with the counseling process, which is similar to the psychodynamic concept of transference. There is also an emphasis placed on having a collaborative therapeutic relationship, especially because of the tendency for borderline patients to engage in self-harmful behaviors. Part of Linehan's "dialectical" component to this approach is due to the focus on process as opposed to structure. In addition, she focuses on emotion, particularly on teaching emotional regulation skills and on relational validation.

DBT is one of the few psychosocial treatments for BPO that have provided empirical support for its efficacy (Linehan, 1993). Linehan's study compared 24 subjects assigned to DBT, and 23 subjects who received a treatment-as-usual control condition for one year. Assessments were conducted every four months during treatment, and following treatment, two assessments were conducted at six-month follow-up intervals. Clinical trials conducted on DBT show that compared with "treatment-as-usual" controls, subjects assigned to DBT were significantly less likely to engage in parasuicide behaviors at all during the treatment year, reported fewer parasuicide episodes at each assessment point, and had less medically severe parasuicides over the year. This was in spite of the fact that DBT was no better at improving self-reports of hopelessness, suicidal ideation, or reasons for living. DBT was also more effective at limiting treatment dropout, and subjects assigned to DBT were less likely to enter psychiatric units than the control group. Results favoring DBT were found in each of the target areas (Linehan, 1993).

In recent years, cognitive models describing the development and maintenance of a disorder, as well as treatment procedures that focus on the main pathology of the disorder, have been developed for the treatment of different anxiety disorders. This is demonstrated in the work of researchers who have developed specific cognitive treatments for anxiety (Brown, O'Leary, & Barlow, 1993; Clark, 1996, 1997; Craske & Barlow, 1993). For example, in the last decade Clark (1996, 1997) has developed specific treatments for panic disorder and social phobia. Although there are commonalities between the treatments for the two disorders, such as helping clients identify and change faulty thoughts and beliefs that are anxiety provoking, and reversing the maintaining factors in the cognitive models, each treatment procedure is different because it caters specifically to the unique dysfunctional processes in each disorder.

Clark's (1997) model for anxiety disorder describes the sequence of a panic attack. First there is an internal or external stimulus that triggers the attack, which leads to the perception of this stimuli as dangerous; this in turn results in a state of apprehension, which is comprised of different bodily sensations. For panic disorder, the first step involves going over a recent panic attack with the client and identifying the symptoms and the negative thoughts that are related to the symptoms. The client is carefully questioned about the sequence of events to determine the client's idiosyncratic panic cycle. The next step is to reach an agreement with the client that the cause of the panic attacks is due to an interaction between bodily sensations and negative thoughts about the sensations. Cognitive interventions are aimed at having the client challenge misinterpretations of the physical sensations.

Often, the symptoms of a panic attack are misinterpreted by the client as a physical condition. For these clients, Clark (1997) recommends trying to identify triggers for unexpected panic attacks which are often slight bodily changes. The main cognitive intervention involves having the counselor point out inconsistencies between past events and the client's negative beliefs to help the client realize that his or her beliefs are irrational. Asking clients questions allows them to come to this understanding on their own (Clark, 1997). Educating clients about the physiological nature of anxiety is important for clients who are worried about fainting or believe they are having cardiac problems. Another cognitive procedure involves treating negative images about the outcome of anxiety attacks as negative thoughts (Clark, 1997). If the negative images are too threatening, the image can be changed by having the client visualize realistic outcomes of anxiety attacks to provide the client with less threatening images of the feared outcome. Advances in the treatment of trauma have also been made in other anxiety based treatments such as posttraumatic stress disorder (Calhoun & Resnick, 1993; Foa & Jaycox, 1998), health anxiety and obsessions (Salkovskis, 1996), and obsessive-compulsive disorder (Salkovskis & Kirk, 1997). In addition, eye movement desensitization and reprocessing (EMDR) has shown great promise in the treatment of trauma (Shapiro & Forrest, 1997).

Constructivist Therapy

The constructivist movement has begun to have an impact on traditional cognitive theory and practice, and has important implications for treating clients in counseling. Although constructivist counseling is an outgrowth of cognitive counseling, as meaning is seen as playing a prominent role in both approaches, there are notable differences in the theoretical and epistemological assumptions of constructivist counseling and traditional cognitive approaches to counseling. One of the fundamental epistemological assumptions of constructivism is that a universal, objective reality does not exist; conceptions of reality and truth are governed by language, and there are no immediate entrance ways into "realities" that are independent of language (R.A. Neimeyer, 1995b). Consequently, reality and truth are subjective, infinite, and determined by the language of a culture (R.A. Neimeyer, 1995b).

In traditional cognitive counseling, a major change process involves correcting dysfunctional thinking and changing maladaptive core beliefs. In contrast, the constructivist approaches to counseling emphasize facilitating change through meaning-making. Rather than "correcting" thinking or beliefs, constructivist therapy promotes creativity and the coconstruction of meaning in the therapy hour as it focuses on redeveloping the main metaphors that are a part of the client's story (G.J. Neimeyer, 1995). Therefore, change in constructivist counseling is accomplished through "a collaboration in the construction and reconstruction of meaning" between the client and counselor (R.A. Neimeyer, 1995b).

A main principle of constructivism is that human beings actively create their own realities as opposed to being passive recipients of their environments (R.A. Neimeyer & Mahoney, 1995; Spence, 1982). Moreover, human beings order their experience by being attuned to certain patterns or themes (Angus, 1992; Gonçalves, 1994a, 1994b). Given that reality and truth are actively fashioned by human beings and are not something "out there" to be discovered, for constructivists, a universal, veridical knowledge is not attainable, but more importantly, is not a goal. Instead of striving for a universal truth, R.A. Neimeyer (1995b) advises us that "we can and must draw on the symbolic resources of our place and time in formulating viable theories or useful fictions that enable us to negotiate our social world." Thus, knowledge is viewed as being personal, and rather than trying to evaluate its "accuracy," we should assess its "adequacy" in helping a person navigate his or her social world. Therefore, change occurs by the construction of more viable meanings.

The constructivist notion of "adequacy" to measure knowledge is an extremely useful criterion for counselors to help guide clients in therapy; it serves as a means to gauge clients' progress in therapy as counselors can assess whether clients' new understandings and reconstruals of their experiences are helpful in guiding them through their social world. Having a personal and subjective way to evaluate knowledge is a particularly crucial consideration for counselors when dealing with people of cultural backgrounds different from their own. A construction of meaning or specific knowledge that might seem unimportant or even irrational to a counselor may be highly meaningful to a client from a diverse cultural background because of its use in the client's social system.

Greenberg and Pascual-Leone (1995, 1997) have proposed a dialectical constructivist framework to help explain how people construct new meaning. This involves demonstrating that knowing is a progressive approximation to reality rather than a representation of it, and that novelty occurs by dynamic syntheses. They argued that knowing comes from a synthesis of many levels of processing, including, at the highest level, the integration of two streams of consciousness. One stream, that of experiential knowing, is rooted in biologically based emotion, whereas another stream of conceptual knowing is rooted in cultural and language based learning. As Guidano (1995a) asserts, knowing results from a dialectical interplay of explaining and experiencing. Basseches (1997) has also recently laid out a dialectical constructivist view of human development and counseling. He proposed three major processes to promote change: (1) supporting greater attentional allocation to specific experience to promote schematic reorganization; (2) offering new material in novel linguistic representations of experience; and (3) the enacting of novel experience in the relationship.

One of the fundamental tasks in constructivist counseling is self-observation (Guidano, 1995b). When engaging the client in self-observation, the main responsibility of the counselor is to distinguish between immediate experiencing and explanations of present experiencing (Guidano, 1995a; G.J. Neimeyer, 1995). Explaining involves the "symbolic reordering" of present experiencing as it is verbalized into linguistic form (Guidano, 1995a). This self-reflective process allows for the creation of new ways to represent experience. Similarly, R.A. Neimeyer (1995c) also emphasizes the importance of vacillating in-session between experiential processing and trying to conceptually understand experience, as being essential to changes in self-understanding.

One of the most essential characteristics of the interventions in constructivist counseling is that they introduce novelty into the therapeutic exploration (R.A. Neimeyer & Mahoney, 1995). Interventions that facilitate new experiences are an important aspect of the meaning-making that occurs in counseling (R.A. Neimeyer, 1995a). This newness fosters reconstructions and creations of meanings in therapy. It also directs the client's attention to new aspects of experience that were not previously considered or attended to, and challenges current ways of knowing and being. Constructivist therapy has yet to specify methods that distinguish it from other approaches. Given that what it offers is a theoretical view of how people know, this may not be where its major contribution lies.

Guidano (1995b) however has developed a "movieola technique" that stands as an example of one constructivist self-observation method that promotes meaning-making in counseling. It involves having the client re-create scenes sequentially from an incident that is being discussed in counseling. The counselor teaches the client to slowly "zoom in" and "out" of the scenes in the event as if the client were the producer, centering in on specific elements of the scenes from different angles, revising the scenes, and reinserting the scenes back into the narrative with the new components. This movieola technique is like shining a light to previously unattended aspects of events and experience with the intention of discovery. An enactment is another intervention used in constructivist therapy which involves different forms of interpersonal role plays. Enactments foster the creation of new meanings by introducing unique and original ways of self-observation (G.J. Neimeyer, 1995).

In a constructivist approach, the counselor accepts and respects the client's meaning system. Furthermore, the counselor uses and validates the client's frame of reference in counseling, although the counselor does not have to be tied to it. The counselor collaborates with the client to explore and try out new ideas, meanings, and feelings that may be too threatening for the client to express in the outside world. Moreover, while at the same time respecting the client's current viewpoints, new meanings are treated as hypotheses to be tested out and can be rejected if the client does not resonate with them. This experimental and exploratory attitude establishes a sense of safety and security and helps to eliminate clients' fears of having their current meaning systems abolished (G.J. Neimeyer, 1995).

Narrative Approaches

In recent years, constructivist counselors of different orientations have been using narrative approaches to assist clients in meaning-making (Gonçalves, 1994a, 1994b; Lyddon, 1995b; McLeod, 1996a, 1997; Spence, 1982; White & Epston, 1990). "Narrative (or narration), seen as activity, is the representation of the flow of events in a meaningful sequence," and "a narrative, as the product of narrative activity, is a representation of a sequence of events linked by plot (a storyline)" (Vogel, 1994). Other fundamental characteristics of narrative include its multiplicity, complexity, changingness, and ability to place human action in a particular time frame (Vogel, 1994). Narrative also gives meaning to life as it organizes human action (Lyddon, 1995b; Vogel, 1994). Change in this view comes from restorying our lives.

Narrative counseling approaches emphasize the role that narrative plays in shaping personal identity (Angus, 1992; Gonçalves, 1994a, 1994b; Lynch, 1997; R.A. Neimeyer, 1995a). Given that it is through language that we communicate, and that language emerges out of social context, the narrative view argues that it is language that shapes human experience (Gonçalves, 1994a, 1994b; Lynch, 1997). Furthermore, identity grows out of the linguistic statements that an individual ascribes to himself or herself, and a main linguistic tool in constructing identity is through narrative

(Lynch, 1997). R.A. Neimeyer (1995a, p. 233) asserts that client stories "have a vital intrapersonal function, namely *to establish continuity of meaning in the client's lived experience.*" Narratives are also an important vehicle for greater self-development (R.A. Neimeyer, 1995a). Efran (1994) views the function of narrative therapy as twofold. First, it merely proposes new stories or reconstructions which can alter assumptions held by the client. Second, it can help the client examine the nature of assumptions as the therapist brings in a different way of "reflecting, selecting, and deflecting" experience (Efran, 1994).

Narrative counseling can be viewed as a "(re)formation of the client's narratives about him or herself" (Lynch, 1997). Lynch presents a narrative theory of the counseling process which argues that counselors engage in therapeutic relationships seeking the "(re)formation of their client's self-narratives according to certain normative resources (such as macronarratives, beliefs, and a vision of the good life)." There is an emphasis on the social negotiation of self-narratives as they are not solely made up by a person, but are contingent on people in our environment who may agree or disagree with how we have characterized ourselves. This leads to rethinking (social negotiation) self-narratives so as to avoid "social isolation and censure" (Lynch, 1997). Personal identity may be seen not as the pure expression of some inner consciousness, but as the product of social interaction. In fact, Lynch (1997) identifies the counseling relationship as being "one specific form of the social negotiation of personal identity."

Lynch (1997) draws our attention to what the counselor brings to the therapeutic process and identifies the counselor's resources as "macronarratives, beliefs and vision of the good life that the therapist has drawn from a particular community of therapeutic belief." It is important for counselors to be aware of the frames of reference that they bring to therapy, particularly when working with people of different cultures who have diverse values and beliefs. For example, in North American culture, independence is desired and valued, whereas in other cultures such as the Filipino culture, independence is viewed as a rejection of family and community, and instead it is interdependence that is valued and revered. This narrative approach, based as it is in language and culture, is highly sensitive to cultural differences and cultural practices.

The major criticisms of constructivist approaches to counseling are that interventions are too abstract and complicated to manualize and replicate, and that there are no clear indications of when it is appropriate to engage clients in particular tasks (Mahoney, 1993). These criticisms are not surprising given that "[c]onstructivists are wary of an exclusive dedication to technique, preferring instead to empathize the critical role of the therapeutic relationship in enabling and initiating human change" (G.J. Neimeyer, 1995, p. 112). Moreover, change in constructivist therapy transpires through meaning-making, and there are an infinite number of ways that meaning can be created and reconstructed in counseling, consequently making it difficult to specify appropriate tasks.

Constructivist counseling does seem to emphasize certain types of interventions, such as exploring personal narratives and attending to self-processes; however, there are no specific techniques or interventions that are universal to constructivists. As long as there is an adherence to epistemological assumptions, the approach is considered to be constructivist. Thus, certain dynamic and humanistic approaches can be viewed as constructivist. Although, critics of constructivist approaches may consider this lack of procedure and specificity a weakness, it can be regarded as a strength of this approach. In constructivist counseling, the counselor is aspiring not only to uncover the specific concerns and difficulties of clients, but the idiosyncratic meanings and nuances of a client's issues (R.A. Neimeyer, 1995c). The counselor conducts this search for meaning collaboratively with the client in an exploratory manner, with curiosity, while suspending any preconceived notions about the client's issues. This lack of devotion to specific techniques promotes an atmosphere of openness, creativity, and new possibilities that might not be viable in other counseling approaches which permit only certain conceptualizations of a client's problem.

FUTURE DIRECTIONS

Consistent with research, the theory of how people change in counseling has been growing more specific, resulting in counseling practice that is more differentiated. We have seen a growing emphasis on interventions that have been developed for particular client problems. Although we have seen that each approach has its own unique mechanisms of change, in recent years there has been an evolution toward integration, as specific counseling approaches have started to assimilate features from other therapeutic orientations. Complete integration of different approaches may be complicated and difficult, however, assimilation of aspects of one approach into another will continue to occur. This is seen in (1) Linehan's (1993) assimilation of the humanistic concept of validation in her cognitive-behavioral treatment of clients with borderline personality disorder; (2) the newly emerging emphasis of emotion in cognitive counseling (A.T. Beck, 1996; Efran & Fauber, 1995; Teasdale, 1993, 1997) and psychodynamic approaches (Levenson, 1995: Levenson & Strupp, 1997); and (3) the assimilation of cognitions into humanistic therapies (Greenberg et al., 1993). These advances occur in conjunction with an emphasis on the importance of interpersonal factors and a strong alliance in all counseling approaches.

Increased specification of how people change seems essential in the new millennium, in tandem with the development of integrative models of treatment that help us combine these different change processes into more effective treatments. One point is clear: there are many ways that people change. Gone are the days of three-flavor ice cream, as well as three singular and opposing views of change: behavioral, dynamic, or humanistic. With greater specification of client change processes, the field will be in a better position to integrate different sets of interventions in combined packages that fit the idiosyncratic needs of particular clients. In the new millennium, we will increasingly see (1) greater specification of different kinds of client problem states that emerge in counseling as targets of change; (2) manualization of interventions that seem to be most appropriate, and effective, at these problem markers (such as the interpretation of Core Conflictual Themes, empty chair intervention for unfinished business, two-chair dialogue for splits, and challenging automatic thoughts); and (3) increased understanding of the change processes induced by particular interventions at these specific problem states. This will lead to practice that is guided by what interventions work best, when, for which specific client populations, and for which client concerns.

As the field moves to greater specification, some of the more general change processes still require further study. The working alliance needs to be investigated as a dependent variable through empirical studies that attempt to understand what helps to create a positive alliance. In addition, empathy is an elusive, yet crucial ingredient of the counseling process that still needs to be more clearly understood. In response to this, Bohart and Greenberg (1997b) have recently called for a new research effort on empathy, suggesting that it should be studied in multiple ways with different methodologies. Furthermore, attachment processes (Bowlby, 1988) and meaning construction processes (Mahoney, 1991; Power & Brewin, 1997), so central in human change, are still in great need theoretical and empirical development.

Two of the most salient findings in the counseling field to keep us humble in our study of human change processes indicate that it is the client that accounts for most of the outcome variance (Lambert & Hill, 1994), followed by the counseling relationship. The type of intervention used is a distant third. Thus, a client's capacity or readiness for change is a crucial factor. These findings are borne out by observations from our recent research program on the treatment of depression. We are finding that it is relatively easy to predict the course of treatment from early indications of clients' willingness to engage in the treatment process. It is clear that it is the clients who are most determining of the early alliance. Clients who rate the alliance very high after the first session are often destined to do well in the treatment. In contrast, clients who rate the alliance low after the first session are usually far more difficult to engage in treatment, and, consequently, often do not benefit from treatment as much as clients who easily form a strong alliance. Moreover, it is those clients who can trust easily, are easily able to establish a relationship, and can set up a good working alliance early in therapy who attain the most benefit from counseling. Thus, we need to learn more about how to work with clients who have more difficulty forming an alliance to develop strategies to set up a helping relationship.

More work is necessary to understand the type of in-session problematic client states, such as dominant attacking, or silent withdrawal, that make it challenging for the counselor to set up a good alliance and engage the client in the counseling process. Alliance-promoting interactional processes need to be further studied and more effectively specified. For example, Benjamin (1993) has indicated particular interactional stances in response to these difficult states that may produce beneficial effects on the alliance. Similarly, problematic moments that require intervention but do not necessarily invite them, such as clients declarations of desperate hopelessness, or clients' chronic avoidance of emotion, need to be described, and helpful ways of promoting change at these moments need to be specified. In the new millennium, change will continue to occur both by relational factors and technical change processes specific to particular problem states. We will be most effective as counselors if we provide both.

REFERENCES

Ainsworth, M.D.S. (1989). Attachments beyond infancy. *American Psychologist, 44,* 709–716.

Angus, L.E. (1992). Metaphor and communication interaction in psychotherapy. In S.G. Toukmanian & D.L. Rennie (Eds.), *Psychotherapy process research* (pp. 187–210). Newbury Park, CA: Sage.

Barrett-Lennard, G.T. (1997). The recovery of empathy—toward others and self. In A.C. Bohart & L.S. Greenberg (Eds.), *Empathy reconsidered: New directions in psychotherapy* (pp. 103–124). Washington, DC: American Psychological Association.

Basseches, M. (1997). A developmental perspective on psychotherapy process, psychotherapists' expertise, and "meaning-making conflict" within therapeutic relationships: A two part series. *Journal of Adult Development, 4*(1), 17–33.

Beck, A.T. (1993). Cognitive therapy: Past, present, and future. *Journal of Consulting and Clinical Psychology, 61*(2), 194–198.

Beck, A.T. (1996). Beyond belief: A theory of modes, personality, and psychopathology. In P.M. Salkovskis (Ed.), *Frontiers of cognitive therapy* (pp. 1–25). New York: Guilford Press.

Beck, A.T., Freeman, A., & Associates. (1990). *Cognitive therapy of personality disorders.* New York: Guilford Press.

Beck, A.T., Rush, A.J., Shaw, B.F., & Emery, G. (1979). *Cognitive therapy of depression.* New York: Guilford Press.

Beck, J.S. (1995). *Cognitive therapy: Basics and beyond.* New York: Guilford Press.

Beck, J.S. (1996). Cognitive therapy of personality disorders. In P.M. Salkovskis (Ed.), *Frontiers of cognitive therapy* (pp. 165–181). New York: Guilford Press.

Benjamin, L.S. (1993). *Interpersonal diagnosis and treatment of personality disorders.* New York: Guilford Press.

Benjamin, L.S. (1996). An interpersonal theory of personality disorders. In J. Clarkin & M. Lenzenweger (Eds.), *Major theories of personality disorders.* New York: Guilford Press.

Bierman, R. (1997). Focusing in therapy with incarcerated domestically violent men. *The Folio: A Journal for Focusing and Experiential Therapy, 15*(2), 47–58.

Binder, J.L., Strupp, H.H., & Henry, W.P. (1995). Psychodynamic therapies in practice: Time-limited dynamic psychotherapy. In B.M. Bongar & L.E. Beutler (Eds.), *Comprehensive textbook of psychotherapy: Theory and practice* (pp. 48–63). New York: Oxford University Press.

Bohart, A.C., & Greenberg, L.S. (1997a). Empathy: Where are we and where do we go from here? In A.C. Bohart & L.S. Greenberg (Eds.), *Empathy reconsidered: New directions in psychotherapy* (pp. 393–418). Washington, DC: American Psychological Association.

Bohart, A.C., & Greenberg, L.S. (1997b). *Empathy reconsidered: New directions in psychotherapy.* Washington, DC: American Psychological Association.

Bohart, A.C., & Wugalter, S. (1991). Changes in experiential knowing as a common dimension in psychotherapy. *Journal of Integrative and Eclectic Psychotherapy, 10,* 14–37.

Bordin, E.S. (1994). Theory and research on the therapeutic alliance: New directions. In A.O. Horvath & L.S. Greenberg (Eds.), *The working alliance: Theory, research, and practice* (pp. 13–37). New York: Wiley.

Bowlby, J. (1982). *Attachment and loss: Vol. 1. Attachment* (2nd ed.). New York: Basic Books.

Bowlby, J. (1988). *A secure base: Parent-child attachments and healthy human development.* New York: Basic Books.

Bozarth, J.D. (1990). The essence of client-centered therapy. In G. Lietaer, J. Rombouts, & R. Van Balen (Eds.), *Client-centered therapy and the person-centered approach: New directions in theory, research and practice* (pp. 59–75). New York: Praeger.

Bozarth, J.D. (1997). Empathy from the framework of client-centered theory and the Rogerian hypothesis. In A.C. Bohart & L.S. Greenberg (Eds.), *Empathy reconsidered: New directions in psychotherapy* (pp. 81–102). Washington, DC: American Psychological Association.

Brown, T.A., O'Leary, T.A., & Barlow, D.H. (1993). Generalized anxiety disorder. *Clinical handbook of psychological disorders: A step-by-step treatment manual* (pp. 137–188). New York: Guilford Press.

Butler, S.F., & Strupp, H.H. (1991). Psychodynamic psychotherapy. In M. Hersen, A. Kazdin, & A. Bellack (Eds.), *The clinical psychology handbook* (2nd ed., pp. 519–533). New York: Pergamon Press.

Calhoun, K.S., & Resick, P.A. (1993). Post-traumatic stress disorder. In D.H. Barlow (Ed.), *Clinical handbook of psychological disorders: A step-by-step treatment manual* (pp. 48–98). New York: Guilford Press.

Castonguay, L.G., Goldfried, M.R., Wiser, S., Raue, P.J., & Hayes, A.M. (1996). Predicting the effect of cognitive therapy for depression: A study of unique and common factors. *Journal of Consulting and Clinical Psychology, 64*(3), 497–504.

Clark, D.A. (1996). Panic disorder: From theory to therapy. In P.M. Salkovskis (Ed.), *Frontiers of cognitive therapy* (pp. 318–344). New York: Guilford Press.

Clark, D.A. (1997). Panic disorder and social phobia. In D.M. Clark & C.G. Fairburn (Eds.), *Science and practice of cognitive behavior therapy* (pp. 119–154). New York: Oxford University Press.

Clarke, K.M. (1996). Change processes in a creation of meaning event. *Journal of Consulting and Clinical Psychology, 64*(3), 465–470.

Cornell, A.W. (1996). *The power of focusing: A practical guide to emotional self-healing.* Oakland, CA: Hew Harbinger.

Craske, M.G., & Barlow, D.H. (1993). Panic disorder and agoraphobia. In D.H. Barlow (Ed.), *Clinical handbook of psychological disorders: A step-by-step treatment manual* (pp. 1–47). New York: Guilford Press.

Efran, J.S. (1994). Mystery, abstraction, and narrative psychotherapy. *Journal of Constructivist Psychology, 7,* 219–227.

Efran, J.S., & Fauber, R.L. (1995). Radical constructivism: Questions and answers. In R.A. Neimeyer & M.J. Mahoney (Eds.), *Constructivism in psychotherapy* (pp. 295–304). Washington, DC: American Psychological Association.

Elliot, R., & Greenberg, L.S. (1995). Experiential therapy in practice: The process-experiential approach. In B.M. Bongar & L.E. Beutler (Eds.), *Comprehensive textbook of psychotherapy: Theory and practice* (Vol. 1, pp. 123–139). New York: Oxford University Press.

Elliot, R., & Shapiro, D.A. (1992). Client and therapist as analysts of significant events. In S.G. Toukmanian & D.L. Rennie (Eds.), *Psychotherapy process research: Paradigmatic and narrative approaches* (pp. 163–186). Newbury Park, CA: Sage.

Farber, B.A., Lippert, R.A., & Nevas, D.B. (1995). The therapist as attachment figure. *Psychotherapy, 32*(2), 204–212.

Foa, E.B., & Jaycox, L.H. (1998). Cognitive-behavioral treatment of posttraumatic stress disorder. In D. Spiegel (Ed.), *Psychotherapeutic frontiers: New principles and practices.* Washington, DC: American Psychiatric Press.

Foa, E.B., & Kozak, M.J. (1991). Emotional processing: Theory, research, and clinical implications for anxiety disorders. In J.D. Safran & L.S. Greenberg (Eds.), *Emotion, psychotherapy and change* (pp. 21–49). New York: Guilford Press.

Frank, K. (1997). The role of the therapist's inadvertent self-revelations. *Psychoanalytic Dialogues, 7,* 281–314.

Frijda, N.H. (1986). *The emotions.* Cambridge, England: Cambridge University Press.

Garfield, S.L. (1991). Common and specific factors in psychotherapy. *Journal of Integrative and Eclectic Psychotherapy, 10,* 5–13.

Garfield, S.L. (1992). Eclectic psychotherapy: A common factors approach. In J.C. Norcross & M.R. Goldfried (Eds.), *Handbook of psychotherapy integration* (pp. 169–201). New York: Basic Books.

Garfield, S.L., & Bergin, A.E. (1994). Introduction and historical overview. In A.E. Bergin & S.L. Garfield (Eds.), *Handbook of psychotherapy and behavior change* (4th ed., pp. 3–18). New York: Wiley.

Gelso, C.J., & Hayes, J.A. (1998). *The psychotherapy relationship: Theory, research, and practice.* New York: Wiley.

Gendlin, E.T. (1962). *Experiencing and the creation of meaning.* New York: Free Press of Glencoe.

Gendlin, E.T. (1981). *Focusing* (2nd ed.). New York: Bantam Books.

Gendlin, E.T. (1996). *Focusing-oriented psychotherapy: A manual of the experiential method.* New York: Guilford Press.

Gendlin, E.T., Beebe, J., Cassens, J., Klein, M., & Oberlander, M. (1968). In J.M. Shlien (Ed.), *Research in psychotherapy* (Vol. 3, pp. 217–241). Washington, DC: American Psychological Association.

Goldfried, M.R. (1982). *Converging themes in psychotherapy: Trends in psychodynamic, humanistic, and behavioral practice.* New York: Springer.

Goldfried, M.R., Castonguay, L.G., & Safran, J.D. (1992). Core issues and future directions in psychotherapy integration. In J.C. Norcross & M.R. Goldfried (Eds.), *Handbook of psychotherapy integration* (pp. 593–616). New York: Basic Books.

Goldman, R.N. (1997). *Theme-related depth of experiencing and change in experiential psychotherapy with depressed clients.* Unpublished doctoral dissertation, York University, Toronto.

Gonçalves, O.F. (1994a). Cognitive narrative psychotherapy: The hermeneutic construction of alternative meanings. *Journal of Cognitive Psychotherapy, 8,* 105–126.

Gonçalves, O.F. (1994b). From epistemological truth to existential meaning in cognitive narrative psychotherapy. *Journal of Constructivist Psychology, 7,* 107–118.

Greenberg, L.S. (1986). Change process research. *Journal of Consulting and Clinical Psychology, 54,* 4–9.

Greenberg, L.S. (1991). Research in the process of change. *Psychotherapy Research, 1,* 14–24.

Greenberg, L.S., & Elliot, R. (1997). Varieties of empathic responding. In A.C. Bohart & L.S. Greenberg (Eds.), *Empathy reconsidered: New directions in psychotherapy* (pp. 167–186). Washington, DC: American Psychological Association.

Greenberg, L.S., Elliot, R., & Lietaer, G. (1994). Research on experiential therapies. In A.E. Bergin & S.L. Garfield (Eds.), *Handbook of psychotherapy and behavior change* (4th ed., pp. 509–539). New York: Wiley.

Greenberg, L.S., & Foerster, F.S. (1996). Task analysis exemplified: The process of resolving unfinished business. *Journal of Consulting and Clinical Psychology, 64*(3), 439–446.

Greenberg, L.S., & Korman, L.M. (1993). Assimilating emotion into psychotherapy integration. *Journal of Psychotherapy Integration, 3*(3), 249–265.

Greenberg, L.S., Korman, L.M., & Paivio, S.C. (in press). Emotion in humanistic psychotherapy. In P. Cain & J. Seeman (Eds.), *Handbook of research and practice in humanistic psychotherapy.* Washington, DC: American Psychological Association.

Greenberg, L.S., & Newman, F.L. (1996). An approach to psychotherapy change process research: Introduction to the special section. *Journal of Consulting and Clinical Psychology, 64*(3), 435–438.

Greenberg, L.S., & Paivio, S.C. (1997). *Working with the emotions in psychotherapy.* New York: Guilford Press.

Greenberg, L.S., & Pascual-Leone, J. (1995). A dialectical constructivist approach to experiential change. In R.A. Neimeyer & M.J. Mahoney (Eds.), *Constructivism in psychotherapy* (pp. 169–191). Washington, DC: American Psychological Association.

Greenberg, L.S., & Pascual-Leone, J. (1997). Emotion in the creation of personal meaning. In M.P. Power & C. Brewer (Eds.), *Transformation of meaning in psychological therapies: Integrating theory and practice* (pp. 157–174). New York: Wiley.

Greenberg, L.S., & Pinsof, W.M. (1986). *The psychotherapeutic process: A research handbook.* New York: Guilford Press.

Greenberg, L.S., Rice, L.N., & Elliot, R. (1993). *Facilitating emotional change: The moment by moment process.* New York: Guilford Press.

Greenberg, L.S., & Safran, J.D. (1987). *Emotion in psychotherapy: Affect, cognition, and the process of change.* New York: Guilford Press.

Greenberg, L.S., & Safran, J.D. (1989). Emotion in psychotherapy. *American Psychologist, 44,* 19–29.

Greenberg, L.S., & Watson, J. (1998). Experiential therapy of depression: Differential effects of client-centered relationship conditions and process experiential interventions. *Psychotherapy Research, 8*(2), 210–224.

Greenberg, L.S., Watson, J., & Lietaer, G. (1998). *Handbook of experiential psychotherapy.* New York: Guilford Press.

Greenberger, D., & Padesky, C.A. (1995). *Mind over mood: A cognitive therapy treatment manual for clients.* New York: Guilford Press.

Guidano, V.F. (1991). *The self in process.* New York: Guilford Press.

Guidano, V.F. (1995a). Constructivist psychotherapy: A theoretical framework. In R.A. Neimeyer & M.J. Mahoney (Eds.), *Constructivism in psychotherapy* (pp. 93–110). Washington, DC: American Psychological Association.

Guidano, V.F. (1995b). Self-observation in constructivist therapy. In R.A. Neimeyer & M.J. Mahoney (Eds.), *Constructivism in psychotherapy* (pp. 155–168). Washington, DC: American Psychological Association.

Henry, W.P. (1996). Structural analysis of social behavior as a common metric for programmatic psychopathology and psychotherapy research. *Journal of Consulting and Clinical Psychology, 64*(6), 1263–1275.

Henry, W.P., & Strupp, H.H. (1994). The therapeutic alliance as interpersonal process. In A.O. Horvath & L.S. Greenberg (Eds.), *The working alliance: Theory, research and practice* (pp. 51–84). New York: Wiley.

Henry, W.P., Strupp, H.H., Schacht, T.E., & Gaston, L. (1994). Psychodynamic approaches. In A.E. Bergin & S.L. Garfield (Eds.), *Handbook of psychotherapy and behavior change* (4th ed., pp. 467–508). New York: Wiley.

Hill, C.E., Nutt-Williams, E., Heaton, K.J., Thompson, B.J., & Rhodes, R.H. (1996). Therapist retrospective recall of impasses in long-term psychotherapy: A qualitative analysis. *Journal of Counseling Psychology, 43*(2), 207–217.

Hill, C.E., Thompson, B.J., Cogar, M., & Denman, D.W., III. (1993). Beneath the surface of long-term therapy: Therapist and client report of their own and each other's covert processes. *Journal of Counseling Psychology, 40,* 278–287.

Hill, C.E., Thompson, B.J., & Corbett, M.M. (1992). The impact of therapist ability to perceive displayed and hidden client reactions on immediate outcome in first sessions of brief therapy. *Psychotherapy Research, 2,* 148–160.

Honos-Webb, L., Stiles, W.B., Greenberg, L.S., & Goldman, R. (1998). Assimilation analysis of process-experiential psychotherapy: A comparison of two cases. *Psychotherapy Research, 8*(3), 264–286.

Horowitz, M.J. (1991). States, schemas, and control: General theories for psychotherapy integration. *Journal of Psychotherapy Integration, 1*(2), 85–102.

Horvath, A.O., & Greenberg, L.S. (1994). *The working alliance: Theory, research, and practice.* New York: Wiley.

Howard, G.S. (1991). Culture tales: A narrative approach to thinking, cross-cultural psychology, and psychotherapy. *American Psychologist, 46*(3), 187–197.

Hycner, R., & Jacobs, L.M. (1995). *The healing relationship in Gestalt therapy: A dialogic/self psychology approach.* Highland, NY: Gestalt Journal Press.

Jacobson, N.S., Dobson, K.S., Truax, P.A., Addis, M.E., Koerner, K., Gollan, J.K., Gortner, E., & Prince, S.E. (1996). A component analysis of cognitive-behavioral treatment of depression. *Journal of Consulting and Clinical Psychology, 64*(2), 295–304.

Jordan, J.V. (1997). *Women's growth in diversity: More writings from the Stone Center.* New York: Guilford Press.

Jordan, J.V., Kaplan, A.G., Miller, J.B., Stiver, I.P., & Surrey, J.L. (1991). *Women's growth in connection: Writings from the Stone Center.* New York: Guilford Press.

Joyce, A.S., Duncan, S.C., & Piper, W.E. (1995). Task analysis of "working" responses to dynamic interpretation in short-term individual psychotherapy. *Psychotherapy Research, 5*(1), 49–62.

Joyce, A.S., & Piper, W.E. (1996). Interpretive work in short-term individual psychotherapy: An analysis using hierarchical linear modeling. *Journal of Consulting and Clinical Psychology, 64*(3), 505–512.

Kernberg, O.F., & Clarkin, J.F. (1993). Developing a disorder-specific manual: The treatment of borderline character disorder. In N.E. Miller, L. Luborsky, J.P. Barber, & J.P. Docherty (Eds.), *Psychodynamic research: A handbook for clinical practice* (pp. 227–246). New York: Basic Books.

Kohut, H. (1995). Introspection, empathy, and psychoanalysis: An examination of the relationship between mode and theory. *Journal of Psychotherapy Practice, and Research, 4*(2), 163–177.

Kolden, G.G. (1991). The generic model of psychotherapy: An empircial investigation of patterns of process and outcome in relationships. *Psychotherapy Research, 1,* 62–73.

Kolden, G.G. (1996). Change in early sessions of dynamic therapy: Universal processes and the generic model of psychotherapy. *Journal of Consulting and Clinical Psychology, 64*(3), 489–496.

Kolden, G.G., & Howard, K.I. (1992). An empirical test of the generic model of psychotherapy. *Journal of Psychotherapy Practice and Research, 1,* 225–236.

Korman, L.M. (1998). *Changes in clients' emotion episodes in therapy.* Unpublished doctoral dissertation, York University, Toronto.

Korman, L.M., & Greenberg, L.S. (1996). Emotion and therapeutic change. In J. Panksepp (Ed.), *Advances in biological psychiatry* (Vol. 2, pp. 1–22). Greenwich, CT: JAI Press.

Lambert, M., & Hill, C. (1994). Assessing psychotherapy outcomes and processes. In A.E. Bergin & S.L. Garfield (Eds.), *Handbook of psychotherapy and behavior change* (4th ed., pp. 72–113). New York: Wiley.

Levenson, H. (1995). *A guide to time-limited dynamic psychotherapy.* New York: Basic Books.

Levenson, H., & Strupp, H.H. (1997). Cyclical maladaptive patterns: Case formulation in time-limited dynamic psychotherapy. In T.D. Eells (Ed.), *Handbook of psychotherapy case formulation* (pp. 84–115). New York: Guilford Press.

Lietaer, G. (1992). Helping and hindering processes in client-centered/experiential psychotherapy: A content analysis of client and therapist postsession perceptions. In S.G. Toukmanian, & D.L. Rennie (Eds.), *Psychotherapy process research: Paradigmatic and narrative approaches* (pp. 134–162). Newbury Park, CA: Sage.

Linehan, M.M. (1993). *Cognitive-behavioral treatment of borderline personality disorder.* New York: Guilford Press.

Linehan, M.M. (1996). Validation and psychotherapy. In A.C. Bohart & L.S. Greenberg (Eds.), *Empathy reconsidered: New directions in psychotherapy* (pp. 353–392). Washington, DC: American Psychological Association.

Llewelyn, S.P., Elliot, R., Shapiro, D.A., Firth, J., & Hardy, G. (1988). Client perceptions of significant events in prescriptive and exploratory periods of individual therapy. *British Journal of Clinical Psychology, 27*(2), 105–114.

Luborsky, L. (1990). The everyday clinical uses of the CCRT. In L. Luborsky & P. Crits-Christoph (Eds.), *Understanding transference: The core conflictual relationship theme method* (pp. 221–221). New York: Basic Books.

Luborsky, L. (1994). Therapeutic alliance as predictors of psychotherapy outcomes: Factors explaining the predictive success. In A.O. Horvath & L.S. Greenberg (Eds.), *The working alliance: Theory, research, and practice* (pp. 38–50). New York: Wiley.

Luborsky, L., & Crits-Christoph, P. (1990). *Understanding transference: The core conflictual relationship theme method.* New York: Basic Books.

Lyddon, W.J. (1995a). Attachment theory: A metaperspective for counseling psychology. *Counseling Psychologist, 23*(3), 479–483.

Lyddon, W.J. (1995b). Forms and facets of constructivist psychology. In R.A. Neimeyer & M.J. Mahoney (Eds.), *Constructivism in psychotherapy* (pp. 69–92). Washington, DC: American Psychological Association.

Lynch, G. (1997). The role of community and narrative in the work of the post-modern theory of the therapist's engagement in the therapeutic process. *Counselling Psychology Quarterly, 10*(4), 353–363.

Mahoney, M.J. (1991). *Human change processes.* New York: Basic Books.

Mahoney, M.J. (1993). Introduction to special section: Theoretical developments in the cognitive psychotherapies. *Journal of Consulting and Clinical Psychology, 61*(2), 187–193.

Mahrer, A., & Fairweather, D.R. (1993). What is "experiencing?" A critical review of meanings and applications in psychotherapy. *Humanistic Psychologist, 21,* 2–25.

Mahrer, A., & Nadler, W.P. (1986). Good moments in psychotherapy: A preliminary review, a list, and some promising research avenues. *Journal of Consulting and Clinical Psychology, 54,* 10–16.

Mallinckrodt, B., Gantt, D.L., & Coble, H.M. (1995). Attachment patterns in the psychotherapy relationship: Development of the Client Attachment to Therapist Scale. *Journal of Counseling Psychology, 42*(3), 307–317.

McLeod, J. (1996a). The emerging narrative approach to counselling and psychotherapy. *British Journal of Guidance and Counselling, 24*(2), 173–184.

McLeod, J. (1996b). The humanistic paradigm. In R. Woolfe & W. Dryden (Eds.), *Handbook of counselling psychology* (pp. 133–155). London, England: Sage.

McLeod, J. (1997). *Narrative and psychotherapy.* London, England: Sage.

Meichenbaum, D. (1993). Changing conceptions of cognitive behavior modification: Retrospect and prospect. *Journal of Consulting and Clinical Psychology, 61*(2), 202–204.

Melnick, J., & Nevis, S.M. (1994). Intimacy and power in long-term relationships: A Gestalt therapy-systems perspective. In G. Wheeler & S. Backman (Eds.), *On intimate ground: A Gestalt approach to working with couples* (pp. 291–308). San Francisco: Jossey-Bass.

Miller, J.B. (1986). *Toward a new psychology of women* (2nd ed.). Boston: Beacon Press.

Miller, J.B., Jordan, J.V., Kaplan, A.G., Stiver, I.P., & Surrey, J.L. (1997). Some misconceptions and reconceptions of a relational approach. In J.V. Jordan (Ed.), *Women's growth in diversity: More writings form the Stone Center* (pp. 25–49). New York: Guilford Press.

Mitchell, S. (1988). *Relational concepts in psychoanalysis: An integration.* Cambridge, MA: Harvard University Press.

Neimeyer, G.J. (1995). The challenge of change. In R.A. Neimeyer & M.J. Mahoney (Eds.), *Constructivism in psychotherapy* (pp. 111–126). Washington, DC: American Psychological Association.

Neimeyer, R.A. (1995a). Client-generated narratives in psychotherapy. In R.A. Neimeyer & M.J. Mahoney (Eds.), *Constructivism in psychotherapy* (pp. 231–246). Washington, DC: American Psychological Association.

Neimeyer, R.A. (1995b). Constructivist psychotherapies: Features, foundations, and future directions. In R.A. Neimeyer & M.J. Mahoney (Eds.), *Constructivism in psychotherapy* (pp. 11–38). Washington, DC: American Psychological Association.

Neimeyer, R.A. (1995c). Limits and lessons of constructivism: Some critical reflections. *Journal of Constructivist Psychology, 8,* 339–361.

Neimeyer, R.A., & Mahoney, M.J. (1995). *Constructivism in psychotherapy.* Washington, DC: American Psychological Association.

Orlinsky, D.E., Grawe, K., & Parks, B.K. (1994). Process and outcome in psychotherapy—Noch einmal. In A.E. Bergin & S.L. Garfield (Eds.), *Handbook of psychotherapy and behavior change* (4th ed., pp. 270–376). New York: Wiley.

Orlinsky, D.E., & Howard, K.I. (1986). Process and outcome in psychotherapy. In A.E. Bergin & S.L. Garfield (Eds.), *Handbook of psychotherapy and behavior change* (3rd ed., pp. 311–381). New York: Wiley.

Orlinsky, D.E., & Howard, K.I. (1987). A generic model of psychotherapy. *Journal of Integrative and Eclectic Psychotherapy, 6,* 6–27.

Pinsof, W.M. (1994). An integrative systems perspective on the therapeutic alliance: Theoretical, clinical, and research implications. In A.O. Horvath & L.S. Greenberg (Eds.), *The working alliance: Theory, research, and practice* (pp. 173–198). New York: Wiley.

Piper, W.E., Joyce, A.S., McCallum, M., & Azim, H.F.A. (1993). Concentration and correspondence of transference interpretations in short-term psychotherapy. *Journal of Consulting and Clinical Psychology, 61*(4), 586–595.

Pistole, M.C., & Watkins, C.E. (1995). Attachment theory, counseling process, and supervision. *Counseling Psychologist, 23*(3), 457–478.

Plummer, D.L. (1997). A gestalt approach to culturally responsive mental health treatment. *Gestalt Review, 1*(3), 190–204.

Polster, E., & Polster, M. (1973). *Gestalt therapy integrated.* New York: Brunner/Mazel.

Power, M.J., & Brewin, C.R. (1997). *The transformation of meaning in psychological therapies: Integrating theory and practice.* New York: Wiley.

Raue, P.J., & Goldfried, M.R. (1994). The therapeutic alliance in cognitive-behavior therapy. In A.O. Horvath & L.S. Greenberg (Eds.), *The working alliance: Theory, research, and practice* (pp. 131–152). New York: Wiley.

Rennie, D.L. (1992). Qualitative analysis of the client's experience of psychotherapy: The unfolding of reflexivity. In S.G. Toukmanian & D.L. Rennie (Eds.), *Psychotherapy process research: Paradigmatic and narrative approaches* (pp. 211–233). Newbury Park, CA: Sage.

Rennie, D.L. (1998). *Person-centred counselling: An experiential approach.* London, Thousand Oaks: Sage.

Resnick, R. (1995). Gestalt therapy: Principles, prisms, and perspectives. *British Gestalt Journal, 1,* 3–13.

Rice, L.N., & Greenberg, L.S. (1984). *Patterns of change: Intensive analysis of psychotherapeutic process.* New York: Guilford Press.

Rogers, C.R. (1959). *Client-centered therapy: Its current practice, implications, and theory.* Boston: Houghton Mifflin.

Rogers, C.R. (1980). *A way of being.* Boston: Houghton Mifflin.

Safran, J.D., & Greenberg, L.S. (1991). *Emotion, psychotherapy and change.* New York: Guilford Press.

Safran, J.D., & Muran, J.C. (1996). The resolution of ruptures in the therapeutic alliance. *Journal of Consulting and Clinical Psychology, 64*(3), 447–458.

Safran, J.D., Muran, J.C., & Samstag, L.W. (1994). Resolving therapeutic alliance ruptures: A task analytic investigation. In A.O. Horvath & L.S. Greenberg (Eds.), *The working alliance: Theory, research, and practice* (pp. 225–258). New York: Wiley.

Salkovskis, P.M. (1996). The cognitive approach to anxiety: Threat beliefs, safety-seeking behavior, and the special case of health anxiety and obsessions. In P.M. Salkovskis (Ed.), *Frontiers of cognitive therapy* (pp. 48–74). New York: Guilford Press.

Salkovskis, P.M., & Kirk, J. (1997). Obsessive-compulsive disorder. In P.M. Salkovskis (Ed.), *Frontiers of cognitive therapy* (pp. 179–208). New York: Guilford Press.

Shapiro, F., & Forrest, M.S. (1997). *EMDR: The breakthrough therapy overcoming anxiety, stress, and trauma.* New York: Basic Books.

Silberschatz, G., Fretter, P.B., & Curtis, J.T. (1986). How do interpretations influence the process of psychotherapy? *Journal of Consulting and Clinical Psychology, 54*(5), 646–652.

Spence, D. (1982). *Narrative truth and historical truth.* New York: Norton.

Stiles, W.B., Elliot, R., Llewelyn, S.P., Firth-Cozens, J.A., Margison, F.R., Shapiro, D.A., & Hardy, G. (1990). Assimilation of problematic experiences by clients in psychotherapy. *Psychotherapy, 27,* 411–420.

Stiles, W.B., Meshot, C.M., Anderson, T.M., & Sloan, W.W., Jr. (1992). Assimilation of problematic experiences: The case of John Jones. *Psychotherapy Research, 2,* 81–101.

Stiles, W.B., Shapiro, D.A., & Elliot, R. (1986). Are all psychotherapies equivalent? *American Psychologist, 41,* 165–180.

Stolorow, R.D. (1994). The nature and therapeutic action of psychoanalytic interpretation. In R.D. Stolorow, G.E. Atwood, & B. Brandschaft (Eds.), *The intersubjective perspective* (pp. 42–55). Northvale, NJ: Aronson.

Stolorow, R.D., Atwood, G.E., & Brandschaft, B. (1994). *The intersubjective perspective.* Northvale, NJ: Aronson.

Strupp, H.H., & Binder, J.L. (1984). *Psychotherapy in a new key: A guide to time-limited dynamic psychotherapy.* New York: Basic Books.

Tasca, G.A., & McMullen, L.M. (1992). Interpersonal complementarity and antithesis within a stage model of psychotherapy. *Psychotherapy, 29,* 515–523.

Teasdale, J.D. (1993). Emotion and two kinds of meaning: Cognitive therapy and applied cognitive science. *Behavior Research and Therapy, 31,* 339–354.

Teasdale, J.D. (1996). Clinically relevant theory: Integrating clinical insight with cognitive science. In P.M. Salkovskis (Ed.), *Frontiers of cognitive therapy* (pp. 26–47). New York: Guilford Press.

Teasdale, J.D. (1997). The relationship between cognition and emotion: The mind-in-place in mood disorders. In P.M. Salkovskis (Ed.), *Frontiers of cognitive therapy* (pp. 67–94). New York: Guilford Press.

Toukmanian, S. (1990). A schema-based information processing perspective on client change in experiential therapy. In G. Lietaer, J. Rombauts, & R. Van Balen (Eds.), *Client-centered and experiential therapy in the nineties* (pp. 309–326). Leuven, Belgium: Leuven University Press.

Toukmanian, S. (1992). Studying the client's perceptual processes and their outcomes in psychotherapy. In S.G. Toukmanian & D.L. Rennie (Eds.), *Psychotherapy process research: Paradigmatic and narrative approaches* (pp. 77–108). Newbury Park, CA: Sage.

Toukmanian, S., & Rennie, D.L. (1992). *Psychotherapy process research: Paradigmatic and narrative approaches.* Newbury Park, CA: Sage.

Tracey, T.J. (1993). An interpersonal stage model of the therapeutic process. *Journal of Counseling Psychology, 40*(4), 396–409.

Tracey, T.J., & Ray, P.B. (1984). Stages of successful time-limited counseling: An interactional examination. *Journal of Counseling Psychology, 31,* 13–27.

van Kessel, W., & Lietaer, G. (1998). Interpersonal processes. In L.S. Greenberg, J.C. Watson, & G. Lietaer (Eds.), *Handbook of experiential therapy* (pp. 155–177). New York: Guilford Press.

Vogel, D. (1994). Narrative perspectives in theory and therapy. *Journal of Constructivist Psychology, 7,* 243–261.

Wampold, B.E. (1995). Analysis of behavior sequences in psychotherapy. In J. Siegfried (Ed.), *Therapeutic and everyday discourse as behavior change: Towards a micro-analysis in psychotherapy process research.* (pp. 189–214). Norwood, NJ: ABLEX.

Watson, J.C. (1996). The relationship between vivid description, emotional arousal, and in-session resolution of problematic reactions. *Journal of Consulting and Clinical Psychology, 64*(3), 459–464.

Watson, J.C., & Greenberg, L.S. (1994). The alliance in experiential therapy: Enacting the relationship conditions. In A.O. Horvath & L.S. Greenberg (Eds.), *The working alliance: Theory, research, and practice* (pp. 153–172). New York: Wiley.

Watson, J.C., Greenberg, L.S., & Lietaer, G. (1998). The experiential paradigm unfolding: Relationship and experiencing in therapy. In L.S. Greenberg, J.C. Watson, & G. Lietaer (Eds.), *Handbook of experiential psychotherapy* (pp. 3–27). New York: Guilford Press.

Weiss, J., Sampson, H., & the Mount Zion Psychotherapy Research Group. (1986). *The psychoanalytic process: Theory, clinical observations, and empirical research.* New York: Guilford Press.

Wheeler, G. (1991). *Gestalt reconsidered.* New York: Garder Press.

Wheeler, G. (1995). Shame in two paradigms of therapy. *British Gestalt Journal, 4*(2), 76–85.

White, M., & Epston, D. (1990). *Narrative means to therapeutic ends.* New York: Norton.

Wiser, S.L., & Goldfried, M.R. (1993). Comparative study of emotional experiencing in psychodynamic-interpersonal and cognitive-behavioral therapies. *Journal of Consulting and Clinical Psychology, 61*(5), 892–895.

Yontef, G.M. (1995). Gestalt therapy. In A.S. Gurman & S.B. Messer (Eds.), *Essential psychotherapies: Theory and practice* (pp. 261–303). New York: Guilford Press.

Yontef, G.M. (1998). Dialogic gestalt therapy. In L.S. Greenberg, J.C. Watson, & G. Lietaer (Eds.), *Handbook of experiential therapy* (pp. 82–102). New York: Guilford Press.

CHAPTER 19

Gender Issues in Counseling

CAROLYN ZERBE ENNS

During the early years of the women's movement, Weisstein (1968/1993) declared that "psychology has nothing to say about what women are really like, what they need and what they want, essentially, because psychology does not know" (p. 197). Weisstein was especially critical of psychology's exclusion and limited view of women's lives as reflected in the fields of personality and psychotherapy. Thirty years later, however, the body of research on women's lives has become so extensive that authors of psychology of women texts must be highly selective in choosing what information to include (Hyde, 1996; Matlin, 1996). During the early 1980s, psychologists also identified the inadequacy of traditional androcentric models for understanding men's lives, noting that traditional masculine gender roles are associated with substantial conflict and stress (e.g., O'Neil, 1981; Pleck, 1981). As a result, profeminist approaches to the psychology and counseling of men have become increasingly visible within psychology (e.g., Andronico, 1996; Kupers, 1993; Levant & Pollack, 1995). In fact, computer (PsycLIT) searches of journal articles for the 1990s yield substantially more titles related to men's gender role conflict and stress than women's experience of these issues.

The purpose of this review is to apply this large body of nonsexist, feminist, and profeminist literature to gender-related counseling issues. The frameworks I have chosen for organizing this review are the Division 17 Principles Concerning the Counseling/Psychotherapy of Women (American Psychological Association, [APA], 1979) and Fitzgerald and Nutt's (1986) elaboration of these principles. The Division 17 Principles represent an especially appropriate foundation for this chapter because they were endorsed unanimously by the Executive Committee of Division 17 in 1978 and were subsequently endorsed by Divisions 12 (clinical psychology), 16 (school psychology), 29 (psychotherapy), and 35 (psychology of women), as well as the APA Education and Training Board. The Division 17 Principles have provided a basis for considering gender-related counseling issues for over 20 years. Yoder's recent (1999) text uses these principles to organize the discussion of feminist practice, further demonstrating the enduring value of this document. Although originally written as a guide for counseling women, these principles have significant implications for working with both men and women. The original document contained 13 specific principles. For this chapter, however, I have organized the principles as they relate to three major categories: knowledge base (Principles 1, 2, and 3), counselor attitudes (Principles 4, 7, 11, and 12), and counseling process and skills (Principles 2, 5, 6, 7, 8, 9, 10, and 13). Because of the explosion of knowledge about gender during recent decades, it is impossible to address adequately the recent counseling literature on gender in a single chapter. Thus, this review is highly selective and incomplete. Given the artificial nature of addressing gender issues in isolation from other aspects of identity, this chapter emphasizes the diversity of men and women whenever possible.

Special thanks to Gail Hackett for creating the outline and organizational framework for this chapter.

COUNSELOR KNOWLEDGE BASE

The Division 17 Principles outline the centrality of the counselor's knowledge base, including the importance of familiarity with the biological, psychological, and social issues that influence women and men; knowledge about subgroups of men and women; and the manner in which life experiences may influence women and men in diverse ways. Much of the knowledge relevant to gender, development, and sexual orientation is summarized by Fassinger (this volume). This chapter builds on her framework by emphasizing counseling implications. Thus, this discussion of knowledge is limited to the articulation of key assumptions and an overview of three major gender-related counseling concerns: (1) interpersonal violence; (2) family, career, and multiple role issues; and (3) body image issues.

Basic Assumptions for Organizing Knowledge about Gender

This chapter is based on the assumption that "gender is what culture makes out of the 'raw material' of biological sex" (Unger & Crawford, 1996, p. 18; see also Fassinger, this volume). Gender behaviors are enacted at an individual level as gender roles, at the interpersonal level as cues that shape reactions and perceptions, and at the social structural level as a system of power relations between and among men and women. The literatures on the biological, psychological, and sociological issues associated with gender are extensive, and the integration of these multiple domains of knowledge supports an effective biopsychosocial approach to gender (Brown, 1994; McGrath, Keita, Strickland, & Russo, 1990).

Since Weisstein (1968/1993) voiced her criticisms some 30 years ago, psychologists have become more cognizant of the limitations of many traditional psychological theories and have made significant advances in adopting more inclusive models of mental health (Brown & Brodsky, 1992; Enns, 1993). It remains important, however, for counseling psychologists to be attentive to subtle biases that remain embedded in theory. Lerman's (1986) criteria for feminist personality theory provide a useful framework for assessing the adequacy of theoretical models that provide a foundation for our knowledge base. Gender-fair models (1) view both women and men positively and centrally; (2) avoid particularistic terminology associated with traditional gender roles (e.g., by using terms such as parenting instead of mothering); (3) encompass the diversity and complexity of women's and men's lives and identities; (4) recognize the inextricable connection between the internal and external worlds of women and men; (5) attend to the manner in which gender, sexual orientation, race, ethnicity, and ability influence internal self-constructions; and (6) support non-sexist and feminist approaches to counseling and psychotherapy (Lerman, 1986).

Discussions about gender within psychology have often been dominated by controversies regarding gender difference and similarity. Some popular research programs were built on an idealistic and "uncomplicated vision" (Eagly, 1995, p. 149) that methodologically sound studies would quickly dispel mythologies about sex and gender by revealing gender similarities. Other frameworks (e.g., Gilligan, 1982; Jordan, Kaplan, Miller, Stiver, & Surrey, 1991) have emphasized differences between men and women and have redefined previously undervalued or unacknowledged aspects of women's traditional experience as unique women's strengths. Hare-Mustin and Marecek (1988) identified the first approach to theory and research as contributing to beta bias, or the minimization of the impact of gender on women's and men's lives, and the second framework as contributing to alpha bias, or the exaggeration of difference between men and women. Both approaches to gender may prompt individuals to see gender as lodged within the person rather than as actively created within relationships and social structures; they may perpetuate the notion that "the categories of 'man' and 'woman' are natural, self-evident" and unitary (Marecek, 1995, p. 162). Both approaches may compel individuals to draw conclusions about "generic" men and women in isolation from other important aspects of social position and identity, such as race, culture, ethnicity, sexual orientation, and social class.

As noted by Morawski (1987), it is impossible for men and women to "operate (effortlessly) in a social vacuum where expectations for gender-related behavior . . . are noticeably absent" (p. 55). Gender involves "doing" or engaging in behavior (West & Zimmerman, 1987), and is "materialized" in social encounters (Deaux & LaFrance, 1998). Models and foundations of knowledge that focus on "how" gender is constructed and that attend to the diversity of human experience support an integrated biopsychosocial approach to counseling. Gender schema theory (Bem, 1993) and interactive models of gender (Deaux & Major, 1987) are consistent with these assumptions in that they conceptualize gender and gender-related attitudes as embedded in a complex set of cognitive beliefs that are shaped by social interactions and power structures.

Knowledge of Gender-Related Concerns

Whereas women are more likely to exhibit higher rates of many disorders such as depression, eating disorders, dissociative identity disorder, posttraumatic stress disorder, and many of the anxiety disorders (e.g., agoraphobia, specific and social phobias), men are more likely to experience many of the addictive disorders and antisocial behaviors (Nolen-Hoeksema, 1998). Most of these disorders are associated with a complex array of factors, including biology, cognitive styles, economic factors, and culture (see Yoder, 1999, for an extended discussion of these factors). A gender analysis of such psychological problems also suggests that these problems often reflect men's and women's efforts to escape gender-role prescriptions, contend with the double binds and contradictory demands related to gender roles, or subscribe more closely to gender role stereotypes than do typical men or women (Franks & Rothblum, 1983; Kaplan, 1983). Gaining knowledge about the specific types of gender role conflicts that men and women face as well as the manner in which these role issues are shaped by race, ethnicity, and sexual orientation is useful for (1) understanding the symbolic communication and coping function of symptoms; (2) differentiating between and conceptualizing the personal, interpersonal, and cultural/social components of distress; and (3) addressing these issues in an empathic and comprehensive framework. Methods for dealing with gender role issues and conflict are addressed more completely in the section on counseling process and skills. The following discussion of interpersonal violence, multiple role, and body image issues illustrates the type of knowledge that facilitates effective counseling regarding many gender-related issues.

Interpersonal Violence

The prevalence of interpersonal violence, especially violence against women, is extensive, and interpersonal violence of many kinds is related to psychological distress (Goodman, Koss, & Russo, 1993). Studies consistently find high levels of physical or sexual abuse histories in studies of psychiatric samples (e.g., Bryer, Nelson, Miller, & Krol, 1987; A. Jacobson, 1989). Carmen, Rieker, and Mills (1984) found that 43% of 188 psychiatric patients had histories of physical and/or sexual abuse, and 53% of female patients and 23% of male patients had experienced physical or sexual abuse. Koss (1993) concluded that between 40% and 60% of patients seeking psychiatric care have experienced physical or sexual abuse of some type.

Rape prevalence rates for women ranging from 14% to 25% have been reported in eight major studies (Koss, 1993). Acute posttraumatic stress disorder (PTSD) is experienced by up to 95% of rape survivors within two weeks following rape, and about 50% continue to meet the diagnostic criteria of PTSD three months after rape (Foa & Riggs, 1995; Nolen-Hoeksema, 1998). Studies also find that between one-fourth (Straus & Gelles, 1990) and one-half (Stark & Flitcraft, 1988) of women in marital or other intimate relationships are the victims of domestic violence, and roughly half of battered women meet the diagnostic criteria for PTSD (Saunders, 1994). These trauma symptoms often co-occur with a wide range of other psychological problems.

Most studies of domestic violence have focused primarily on heterosexual relationships, but it is also important for counselors to acknowledge the extent and seriousness of domestic violence in lesbian (Browning, Reynolds, & Dworkin, 1991; Renzetti, 1992) and gay male (Island & Letellier, 1991) relationships. Although the rates of domestic violence and consequences of battering appear to be similar in heterosexual and homosexual relationships, the social and relationship dynamics associated with battering may be unique (Renzetti, 1992). Renzetti's study of battering in lesbian relationships noted that the major correlates of abuse included issues of autonomy and dependency, jealousy, power imbalances, and substance abuse. Battered individuals in same-sex relationships often face additional obstacles because of the heterosexist assumptions that may underlie beliefs about violence (Letellier, 1994) and homophobic attitudes on the part of mental health service providers, shelter personnel, and legal personnel (Letellier, 1994; Renzetti, 1992).

The psychological impact of child physical and sexual abuse has received sustained attention during the past decade. A frequently cited national survey found that 27% of women and 16% of men disclosed a history of child sexual abuse (Finkelhor, Hotaling, Lewis, & Smith, 1990). One survey found that compared with individuals without a victimization history, male and female victims of sexual abuse were two times more likely to meet the criteria of a psychiatric disorder sometime during their lifetime (Stein, Golding, Siegal, Burnham, & Sorenson, 1988). Browne and Finkelhor's (1986) review concluded that approximately 40% of sexual abuse survivors experience a level of distress that may require psychotherapy. The sequelae of sexual abuse are diverse and include depression, PTSD, dissociation, sexual dysfunction, self-esteem problems, and eating disorders (Pruitt & Kappius, 1992; Roesler & McKenzie, 1994). A recent study found that approximately 50% of women who experienced adult abuse also reported a history of child abuse. The impact of interpersonal violence may be cumulative, as revealed by the finding that women who experienced abuse both as children and adults exhibited more physical symptoms and higher levels of psychological distress than did those who experienced abuse during a single stage of life (McCauley et al., 1997).

Although a history of abuse or interpersonal violence is related to psychological distress, the level of psychological distress is variable, depending on the nature of the sample, developmental factors, family climate factors, and the range and pervasiveness of traumatic events (Rind, Tromovitch, & Bauserman, 1998). For example, a meta-analysis of 59 studies of college samples (Rind et al., 1998) found that students with a history of child sexual abuse were "slightly less well adjusted" (p. 22) than those persons without such a history. Furthermore, family environment factors explained more of this lower level of adjustment than did sexual abuse. The meta-analysis also revealed that college men and women may have different feelings and perceptions about their personal sexual abuse, with female victims reporting more negative experiences and reactions than male victims. These findings point to the importance of studying patterns of resilience, as well as pathology, that are displayed by victims of abuse.

Although substantial data attest to the extensive negative consequences of intimate violence, therapists sometimes underplay the seriousness of such violence or do not address the violence (Harway & Hansen, 1993). As a foundation for working with interpersonal violence, it is important for counselors to be knowledgeable about violence statistics, research findings regarding the dynamics and types of interpersonal violence (including variations by sexual orientation, race, and culture), the diverse and variable psychological consequences of violence, and methods for assessing violence and trauma. Given the multidimensionality of violence, it is also important for interventions to attend to a range of influences, including intrapsychic factors, developmental factors, family influences, power dynamics, and the social context in which violence occurs. Familiarity with crisis intervention procedures, methods for addressing posttraumatic symptoms and reactions, the costs and benefits of conjoint therapy for couples dealing with recent abuse, and methods for working with perpetrators are also valuable assets (American Psychological Association, 1996; Gauthier & Levendosky, 1996; Harway & Evans, 1996; Koss et al., 1994; Philpot, Brooks, Lusterman, & Nutt, 1997; Tolman, Mowry, Jones, & Brekke, 1986; Walker, 1994).

Although women are more like to experience significant psychological and physical harm as a consequence of adult interpersonal violence in heterosexual relationships, adult women and men report engaging in similar amounts of physical and verbal aggression. Compared with men, however, it appears that women are more likely to report their own negative behaviors, use aggression for different reasons (e.g., self-defense versus sexual jealousy), use psychological or indirect aggression, and limit their aggression to domestic spheres (Koss et al., 1994; J.W. White & Kowalski, 1994). Men are more likely than women to perpetrate multiple, more severe, and more aggressive actions (Koss et al., 1994). The most significant risk factor associated with becoming a victim of violence in the home is being female (American Psychological Association, 1996). It should be noted, however, that there are also significant differences within groups of men and women with regard to motivation for and levels of violence. For example, N.S. Jacobson and Gottman (1998) found two distinctive patterns among men who used severe violence. The first pattern, which is marked by physiological arousal during violent episodes, was more characteristic of batterers who showed emotional attachment to their partners and who appeared to use violence to prevent abandonment. The second pattern, which is not associated with physiological arousal, was more frequently displayed by men who showed low levels of emotional attachment to partners and used violence as a form of control or an assertion of independence.

The findings described in this section point to the diversity of violence and the complexity of intervening effectively with individuals who experience and display violence. Working with violence issues is a challenge within a climate that is currently characterized by a general "backlash" against feminism and feminist research on the treatment of violence (Enns, 1996). Victims of violence have sometimes been described as suffering from "rape hype" (Roiphe, 1993) or "false memory" (False Memory Syndrome Foundation, 1992), and researchers have been accused of exaggerating claims about the prevalence of violence or the gendered nature of much interpersonal violence. Within this climate, a social constructionist perspective is helpful for examining the strengths and survival skills of victims, the manner in which and the reasons why women and men exhibit aggression, and the ways in which power is related to aggressive and abusive interpersonal acts.

Family, Career, and Multiple Role Issues

Counseling psychologists have made significant contributions to feminist perspectives in career psychology (e.g., L. Brooks & Forrest, 1994; Hackett & Lonborg, 1994), furthering knowledge of the specific career concerns of men and women, the balancing of career and personal roles, conflicts and discrepancies between these roles, and the diverse ways in which these roles are enacted. Gilbert's (1992) chapter on gender in the second edition of this *Handbook* and Fassinger's chapter (this volume) provide excellent overviews of many gender-related career and family concerns.

In general, a combination of work and family roles is normative during adulthood, and the combination of these roles is generally more satisfying than traditional alternatives (Barnett & Rivers, 1996). Although women have steadily increased their involvement in careers and men have increasingly acknowledged the psychological costs and gender role conflicts of a life that centers primarily on achievement and work (e.g., Kupers, 1993; Levant & Pollack, 1995), significant issues and inequities between men and women remain. Employed women earn 76% as much as men (compared with 63% in 1979); are more likely to experience poverty or to remain concentrated in lower-status jobs in clerical, service, and sales domains (Herz & Wootton, 1996); and assume substantially more household and family responsibilities than men (Steil, 1994). The consideration of these issues is crucial for helping individuals and partners create mutually acceptable agreements about work and personal lives.

Family and work arrangements are diverse, and many traditional models are inadequate for conceptualizing the gender-related concerns of partners and their families (Demo & Allen, 1996; Laird & Green, 1996). The psychological literature contains a paucity of information regarding feminist perspectives on fathering (Silverstein, 1996). Most research programs have tended to view the mother-child dyad as the primary context in which development occurs. As a result, research about positive fathering is underrepresented, and the assumption that the mother-child bond is central, exclusive, unique, and the most important factor for healthy child development is perpetuated (Silverstein & Phares, 1996). A second problem is that heterosexist assumptions underlie many dominant theories of family life (Demo & Allen, 1996). Although researchers have gathered a substantial body of knowledge about the dynamics and issues of lesbian and gay families, this material is rarely integrated with mainstream studies of the family (C.A. Parks, 1998). Recent research indicates, for example, that despite the difficult legal, fiscal, and societal barriers, lesbian couples establish well-functioning families that nurture socially tolerant and well-adjusted children (C.A. Parks, 1998; Patterson & Redding, 1996). Knowledge of this literature is helpful for challenging negative stereotypes and prejudices about, and ensuring equitable treatment of, lesbian and gay male families (see Fassinger, this volume, for further discussion).

Body Image, Objectification, and Mental Health

Gilbert's (1992) review of gender concluded that cultural beliefs and stereotypes about beauty contribute to many gender-related problems. An early content analysis of women's portrayal in the media (Courtney & Lockeretz, 1971) identified the following themes: women as homebound, women as dependent, women as engaging in unimportant activity, and women as sex objects. Recent content analyses (e.g., Plous & Neptune, 1997) have found that women are less likely to be depicted as homebound and more likely to be portrayed in work roles; however, they are also depicted more frequently as sex and decorative objects. This "objectification" of women in the media and throughout other cultural institutions may contribute to mental health risks marked by body image dissatisfaction and self-objectification.

Research reveals that disordered eating and body dissatisfaction are associated with exposure to body ideals presented in the media (e.g., Stice & Shaw, 1994). Objectification theory (Fredrickson & Roberts, 1997; Noll & Fredrickson, 1998) proposes that women learn to assume an observer's point of view and apply internalized cultural stereotypes of beauty when they view and evaluate their own bodies. This internalization of the culture may lead to habitual body monitoring or surveillance, which contributes to women's shame and anxiety, the reduction of peak motivational states or "flow," and decreased awareness of internal signals of hunger and satiation. Self-objectification may also place individuals at increased risk for a wide range of disorders such as anxiety states, depression, disordered eating, and sexual dysfunction. Several studies have found that self-objectification predicts shame and restrained eating in women (Fredrickson, Roberts, Noll, Quinn, & Twenge, 1998; McKinley & Hyde, 1996; Noll & Fredrickson, 1998). Compared with men, women were also found to engage in greater self-objectification and to perform worse on a math test after being exposed to a condition designed to elicit body self-objectification (trying on a swimsuit) (Fredrickson et al., 1998).

Issues related to body satisfaction, body image, and eating may be experienced in unique ways by heterosexual women, lesbian women (Beren, Hayden, Wilfley, & Grilo, 1996; Beren, Hayden, Wilfley, & Striegel-Moore, 1997), and women of color (Harris, 1995; Joiner & Kashubeck, 1996). Furthermore, although eating disorders and body dissatisfaction affect women disproportionately, recent studies also reveal body dissatisfaction and eating disturbances within subgroups of men, such as gay men (Beren et al., 1996; Siever, 1994).

Of particular interest have been recent findings that lesbians express less dissatisfaction about their bodies than heterosexual women (Bergeron & Senn, 1998; Herzog, Newman, Yeh, & Warshaw, 1992; Siever, 1994). Gettelman and Thompson (1993) found that compared with lesbians, heterosexual women were more appearance oriented, disclosed more problematic eating behaviors, and showed more concern about body image, weight, and dieting. Another study found that lesbians chose a heavier ideal weight, were less concerned about their current weight, and did not diet as frequently as heterosexual women (Herzog et al., 1992). Although there is substantial overlap between lesbian and heterosexual women's body image attitudes—for example, members of both groups feel overweight and concerned about appearance (Beren et al., 1997)—lesbian women may internalize oppressive societal norms about the body to a lesser degree and may be more adept at resisting these attitudes (Bergeron & Senn, 1998).

When both men and women were included in a study of body satisfaction, heterosexual women and gay men disclosed the highest levels of dissatisfaction with their bodies (Siever, 1994). Heterosexual men showed the least concern about their own bodies, but the most concern about the bodies of their partners. Some of the most adverse effects of body objectification for heterosexual men may be revealed in their susceptibility toward objectified images of women that permeate the culture. N.J. MacKay and Covell (1997) found that compared with men who viewed a "progressive" advertisement, men exposed to a sex image advertisement showed lower acceptance of feminism and more attitudes supportive of sexual aggression. In another study, men exposed to sexually objectifying advertisements chose more sexist questions for a female job candidate, and were rated as acting in more sexualized and inappropriate ways than were men exposed to non-objectifying advertisements (Rudman & Borgida, 1995).

As with other issues presented in this section, it is important for counselors to be attentive to the diversity of clients and to be knowledgeable about individual, psychological, and sociocultural factors that influence body satisfaction, dissatisfaction, and self-objectification.

COUNSELOR ATTITUDES

According to Principles 4, 7, 11, and 12 of the Division 17 Principles, self-knowledge is central to competent work with gender-related concerns. These principles suggest that counselors make efforts to understand the variety of oppressions that influence clients and examine their own personal attitudes to ensure that their practices support optimal counseling goals and outcomes (American Psychological Association, 1979). They also suggest that self-care activities support competent practice. The first major category in this section discusses counselor attitudes as they relate to sexism and gender bias, antigay bias and heterosexism, personal privilege associated with race, and the interactive effects of sexism, racism, classism, and heterosexism. The second major category discusses the relevance of self-care to the maintenance of positive counselor attitudes.

Self-Examination of Values and Biases

Sexism and Gender Bias

The literature on racism and sexism indicates that blatant forms of sexism and negative attitudes toward women have decreased substantially during recent decades (Campbell, Schellenberg, & Senn, 1997). Researchers have found, however, that contemporary sexism often assumes more subtle and clandestine forms, which have been labeled as (1) modern sexism (Swim, Aiken, Hall, & Hunter, 1995; Swim & Cohen, 1997); (2) neosexism (Campbell et al., 1997; Tougas, Brown, Beaton, & Joly, 1995); and (3) ambivalent sexism (Glick & Fiske, 1996, 1997). Many modern or current forms of sexism/bias are not marked by the open endorsement of inequality, and often go unnoticed because they are embedded within cultural and societal norms. It may be marked by attitudes such as discrimination is no longer an issue, women and minorities are asking for too much, and many of the gains made by women and minorities are not deserved (Tougas et al., 1995).

Tougas et al. (1995) described neosexism as a "manifestation of conflict between egalitarian values and residual negative feelings toward women" (p. 843), noting that this form of sexism may be associated with unintentional biases or opposition to social policies designed to benefit women or minorities (see also Dovidio & Gaertner, 1996). Swim et al. (1995) also found that individuals scoring high in modern sexism tended to endorse more individualistic values, and to overestimate the percentage of women in male-dominated jobs (e.g., airline pilots, physicians). Both ambivalent sexism and ambivalent racism may be associated with conflicts between the principle of egalitarianism, which leads people to embrace equality and express empathy for "underdogs," and individualism or a Protestant work ethic, which imply that people are responsible for their own fate. Thus, the person who holds subtle racist or sexist beliefs may praise minority group members and women who transcend many of the effects of racism or sexism and become high achievers, but harbor negative attitudes toward more ordinary individuals (Glick & Fiske, 1996).

It is possible that recent "kinder and gentler justifications of male dominance and prescribed gender roles" (Glick & Fiske, 1997, p. 121) may be no less virulent than some blatant biases. Given the subtle nature of contemporary sexism and racism, it may be more difficult for individual men and women who are targets of racist or sexist beliefs to recognize the presence of bias. Thus, some clients may be more likely to internalize subtly sexist or racist attitudes and have greater difficulty resisting the effects of bias. Furthermore, counselors are not immune from internalizing these biases, especially if they are subtle, unintentional, or nonconscious.

Heterosexism, Homophobia, and Antigay Bias

Negative attitudes toward lesbian, gay, bisexual, and transgendered (LGBT) people exist at both blatant and subtle levels. Antigay violence (Fassinger, 1991) reveals that blatant prejudice against LGBT persons is often tolerated and supported within the larger culture. Both blatant prejudice and subtle heterosexist values can have a negative impact on the self-esteem and well-being of gay clients (Phillips & Fischer, 1998). Rudolph (1988) concluded that counselors often hold contradictory attitudes toward homosexuality, often believing concurrently in "the psychological health *and* potential pathology of homosexuality" (p. 167). Counselors may simultaneously see LGBT clients as fully functioning yet "hampered in their performance in certain positions by the very fact of their sexual orientation" (p. 167).

Several analogue studies, which have conceptualized the subtle heterosexist or homophobic responses that counselors harbor as countertransference reactions, suggest that counselor attitudes toward LGBT people may not be as conflicted as some clinical literature suggests (Gelso, Fassinger, Gomez, & Latts, 1995; Hayes & Gelso, 1993). Hayes and Gelso found that male counselors did not appear to experience discomfort in reaction to a male client's sexual orientation per se, but did experience greater anxiety with HIV-positive than HIV-negative clients. Gelso et al. found that counselors did not show more countertransference reactions to a lesbian client than a heterosexual client. Compared with male counselors, however, female counselors showed greater difficulty recalling a lesbian client's problems. Male and female counselors showed similar levels of recall with a heterosexual client. Authors of both studies found that although participants revealed low levels of homophobia in general, higher levels of homophobia were associated with counselor avoidance of client's feelings and concerns. These studies point to the complexity of homophobia and the likelihood that when counselors hold stereotypes and fears about LGBT clients, they may avoid addressing or responding to important clinical issues.

Heterosexism is often marked by the lack of acknowledgment of the realities and experiences of LGBT clients, which renders their experiences invisible (Fassinger, 1991; Garnets, Hancock, Cochran, Goodchilds, & Peplau, 1991). This practice leads to omission bias, or the omission of circumstances and experiences that are relevant to a group of people (Chernin, Holden, & Chandler,

1997; Garnets et al., 1991). Heterosexuality is often assumed to be a "given"; the lives of LGBT individuals are then judged according to the "normative" experience of heterosexual people. A second problem is connotation bias, which involves using phrases with negative connotations when referring to a minority group (Chernin et al., 1997). For example, Morton (1998) noted that lesbian relationships are often characterized as fused or enmeshed when compared with heterosexual relationship norms. More appropriate and positive phrases for conceptualizing this dynamic include an "ability for empathic relating" or "self-boundary flexibility."

Personal Privilege and Racism

Counselors are not likely to be aware of subtle ethnocentric or androcentric beliefs unless they carefully examine their own experiences of privilege and become educated about the lives and histories of diverse people. McIntosh (1989) described White privilege as the "invisible package of unearned assets which I can count on cashing in each day, but about which I was 'meant' to remain oblivious" (p. 10). These unearned privileges resemble a "weightless knapsack" of "blank checks" that are accorded to people who have greater social and economic power. White privilege includes being able to count on skin color adding to rather than detracting from perceptions of personal reliability, being assured that educational materials will give ample attention to one's race, and being able to accept a job with an affirmative action employer without individuals being suspicious that the job was awarded on the basis of race versus competence.

Espin (1995) cautioned that even when White psychologists have good intentions, they often remain blinded by their privileges. Members of minority cultures generally learn a wealth of information about majority cultures to survive and cope in them, but as a consequence of their privileged status, members of the majority culture often remain ignorant about important aspects of nondominant cultures. Antiracism training, consciousness-raising activities, and efforts to educate oneself about nondominant cultures facilitate ongoing self-examination and conscious acknowledgment of subtle biases (Brown, 1993).

Intersections of Sexism, Racism, Classism, and Heterosexism

Feminist psychologists have been attentive to androcentric biases in psychological theory but have often been blind to their own ethnocentrism. Too frequently, the experiences of White women are seen as synonymous with the experiences of "women in general," or as the normative group to which all other groups of women are compared (Yoder & Kahn, 1993). Psychological research has also tended to focus on negative or dysfunctional behaviors of people of color rather than positive aspects of coping (Wyche, 1993). Furthermore, the behaviors of people of color are sometimes defined as "dysfunctional" because they are judged by the standards of middle-class, White society rather than alternative paradigms that have more relevance for people of color (Espin, 1995).

For many people of color, racism may be a far more visible, virulent, and frequent experience than sexism or heterosexism (Comas-Diaz & Greene, 1994; Kanuha, 1990). If the counselor believes, for example, that women of color have more in common with other women than men who experience a shared oppression, the counselor may deny the relevance of important bonds and sources of support that ethnic minority women form with men who experience racism and other forms of common oppression (Greene & Sanchez-Hucles, 1997). It is also important for counselors to be aware that people of color often experience sexism and heterosexism within their ethnic communities, which further limits their choices and adds to psychological stress (Comas-Diaz & Greene, 1994; Kanuha, 1990). Although gender oppression is one of the common experiences that women face, it is shaped by individual economic, social, historical, and ecological realities (Greene & Sanchez-Hucles, 1997).

Reid (1993) noted that middle-class biases also permeate current psychological theory and that "feminist psychology does not differ greatly in this respect from traditional psychology. Indeed, poor women are virtually unnamed in feminist work" (p. 134). They are "shut out" and silenced. Reid suggested that feminist psychologists have often held the simplistic and egocentric view that although poor women may experience more racism and sexism than others, this oppression is similar to that experienced by middle-class women.

Kanuha (1990) stated that "if racism functions to oppress non-White people, it interacts with sexism to deny the mere existence of lesbians of color" (p. 173). She suggested that lesbians of color have been virtually invisible, in part because of the subtle racism in White feminist scholarship, which has tended to identify heterosexism as the primary form of oppression that all gay people face. The assumption that all lesbians and gay men suffer equally from homophobia detracts from an understanding of how classism, ageism, and racism contribute to the complexity of gender-related concerns such as domestic violence. Leslie and MacNeill (1995) added that gay people of color must often contend with racism in the gay community as well as homophobia within communities of color. They must achieve a healthy identity in the midst of a minority community which is likely to be homophobic and a majority culture that is homophobic, sexist, and racist.

When gender, race, class, and sexual orientation aspects of identity are conceptualized as "additive" or factors that can be neatly separated from each other, people of diversity may feel forced to choose between or prioritize identities associated with gender, sexual orientation, race, and class. When this occurs, the unique and complex identities of individuals may be written out of existence. It is especially important for White middle-class psychologists to avoid "White solipsism," or the tendency to "think, imagine, and speak as if whiteness described the world" (Rich, 1979, p. 299); and to educate themselves about the myriad interactions of identities, "isms," and contexts that shape the lives of clients (Reid, 1993).

Personal Functioning and Self-Care

Coster and Schwebel's (1997) survey revealed that psychologists rated the following seven items as most central to well-functioning: self-awareness and self-monitoring, a personal value system, balance between personal and professional lives, relationships with family members and partners, vacations, relationships with friends, and personal therapy. Mahoney's (1997) survey found that emotional exhaustion/fatigue was the most frequently cited personal problem encountered by doctoral psychotherapists (43%), and roughly one-third of respondents reported anxiety or depression during the past year. Pope and Tabachnick's (1994) survey of therapists noted that 61% reported having experienced depression, and 29% had felt suicidal at some point. Eighty-eight percent of Mahoney's (1997) sample and 84% of Pope and Tabachnick's sample had participated in personal therapy at some point. The results of these recent surveys point to the importance of self-care for supporting competent professional practice. The next section focuses on two specific issues associated with self-care: vicarious traumatization and issues associated with overidentification or underidentification with clients.

Vicarious Traumatization

Counseling psychologists who have heavy caseloads of survivors of various forms of abuse and violence may be especially vulnerable to physical and emotional exhaustion, role strain, and vicarious traumatization (Pearlman & Saakvitne, 1995). Schauben and Frazier's (1995) study of female counselors who work with sexual violence revealed that compared with counselors who saw fewer victims of violence, those who worked with a higher percentage of survivors reported more PTSD symptoms, more disrupted cognitions about themselves and others, and more signs of vicarious traumatization. However, the same counselors did not experience higher levels of negative emotion such as depression or hostility, nor did they exhibit significant signs of burnout. Pearlman and MacIan's (1995) exploratory study found that therapists (136 women and 52 men) who were new to trauma work reported higher levels of distress and greater disruptions of basic schemas than seasoned professionals. Compared with those with no personal trauma history, therapists with a trauma history also reported more disruptions of basic schemas (e.g., safety, self-trust, self-esteem) and higher levels of distress. In general, those therapists with the highest levels of distress were not receiving supervision and had engaged in trauma work for less time.

Participants' responses to open-ended questions (Schauben & Frazier, 1995) reveal additional information about aspects of working with violence survivors that are especially difficult, including: (1) the difficulty of hearing stories of abuse and experiencing clients' pain; (2) the challenge of establishing trust with clients who have been victimized; and (3) the frustrations of working with other systems, such as legal and mental health systems, that often provide inadequate assistance to survivors. Although limited empirical data about vicarious traumatization exist, the results of these studies point to the value of self-care, professional training for working with violence, and supervision.

Overidentification or Underidentification with Clients

Providing psychotherapy to survivors of violence or clients who share similar life histories with the counselor may pose special challenges. Surveys of mental health practitioners reveal that roughly one-third report having experienced sexual or physical abuse as a child or adolescent (Little & Hamby, 1996; Polusny & Follette, 1996; Pope & Feldman-Summers, 1992). Pope and Feldman-Summers indicated that when the entire life span was considered, roughly two-thirds of female therapists and one-third of male therapists reported at least one form of physical or sexual abuse. Elliott and Guy (1993) found that women therapists reported higher levels of sexual abuse (43%) than did women in other professions, and Nuttall and Jackson's (1994) survey found that 21% of clinicians reported a history of child sexual or physical abuse. In general, female therapists report substantially higher levels of past abuse than do male therapists.

Although these abuse experiences have the potential to influence the emotional competence of therapists (Pope & Vasquez, 1998), studies have found no differences between traumatized and nontraumatized therapists with regard to their perceptions about how abuse issues should be treated (Badura & Stone, 1998), their perceived competence for working with abuse (Pope & Feldman-Summers, 1992), and the therapeutic practices (Polusny & Follette, 1996) and assessment practices and diagnostic formulations (Little & Hamby, 1996) they reported using. However, therapists with abuse histories reported having more concerns about countertransference, such as making boundary mistakes or crying with clients, and disclosed using more coping strategies to enhance or support their practice as psychotherapists (Little & Hamby, 1996). Compared with those with no trauma history, respondents with an abuse or trauma history also reported higher rates of personal trauma symptoms (Follette, Polusny, & Milbeck, 1994; Pearlman & MacIan, 1995), and greater reluctance to participate in long-term marital/intimate relationships (Nuttall & Jackson, 1994). Survey findings suggest that therapist abuse status is not related to therapists' practices and competence, and that therapists' child abuse experiences do not appear to affect the quality of treatment that clients receive. However, findings also suggest that compared with nonabused therapists, therapists with abuse histories may experience somewhat more challenging issues regarding emotional identification and boundaries.

Several studies suggest that psychotherapists with an abuse history are somewhat more likely to believe clients who disclose abuse (Nuttall & Jackson, 1994) or to believe that their memories of abuse are accurate (Polusny & Follette, 1996). Counselors with similar experiences to those of their clients may have a deeper understanding of clients' concerns, and may develop a deep empathy that facilitates growth and change. On the other hand, they may be vulnerable to restimulation of their own pain. If this occurs, counselors can lose objectivity or overgeneralize the relevance of their personal experience for understanding their clients' concerns. When counselors have personal histories similar to those of clients, self-care activities, consultation, and supervision may be especially beneficial (Pearlman & Saakvitne, 1995).

Therapist gender may also be related to issues of identification with clients. Jackson and Nuttall (1993) found that male mental health professionals were less likely than female mental health professionals to believe allegations of sexual abuse. Badura and Stone (1998) found that compared with females, male psychologists were less likely to predict positive prognoses for clients who had recently remembered abuse (there were no gender differences for always remembered abuse). Adams and Betz (1993) noted that male clinicians were less optimistic about a client's likelihood of overcoming problems associated with incest and defined incest more narrowly than did female clinicians. Little and Hamby (1996) found that female therapists were more likely than male therapists to report screening for abuse during assessment, to see the effects of abuse as long term and harmful, to believe that counseling survivors of abuse is difficult, and to use coping mechanisms to deal with the complexities of their work. With regard to countertransference concerns, female therapists were somewhat more likely than male therapists to report feeling strong emotions such as hopelessness, disgust, and anger; crying with clients; and making boundary mistakes in therapy. In contrast, male therapists were somewhat more likely to report being sexually turned on or placing some blame on the client (Little & Hamby, 1996). In general, these findings suggest that sexual abuse issues may be related to somewhat different emotional reactions on the part of male and female clinicians, and that female clinicians are more likely than male clinicians to identify sexual abuse issues as salient. Sexual abuse and other forms of interpersonal victimization are experienced more frequently by women than men (see previous section on interpersonal violence), and this gender-related reality may be related to male and female therapists' perceptions and emotional reactions.

In general, findings relevant to counselor gender or abuse status alone are associated with relatively modest or small effect sizes. Therapists' perceptions and practices appear to be related to a complex array of other factors, including the therapist's theoretical orientation and gender role attitudes and ideology (Adams & Betz, 1993; Little & Hamby, 1996). Results of studies suggest that it is desirable for all clinicians to receive education and training about the potential for overidentifying and underidentifying with clients.

COUNSELING PROCESS AND SKILLS

In the following sections, I address counseling skills for working with gender issues as they relate to the therapeutic relationship, assessment, theoretical approaches to intervention, facilitative therapeutic procedures, and social change (Principles 2, 5, 7, 8, 9, 10, and 13).

The Therapeutic Relationship

Gender-Related Process Issues

Issues of power permeate all human relationships, including psychotherapy relationships (Pope & Vasquez, 1998). Many clients have experienced a range of oppressive experiences, victimization, and abuses of power in their personal lives, and may be especially sensitive to the use of power or may have difficulty recognizing how power can be used effectively. Because of the differential levels of power that men and women have historically held, counselor modeling of the appropriate use of power may be especially important when counseling focuses on gender-related concerns. The principles therefore suggest that it is therapeutic for the counselor to form relationships with clients that model collaborative interaction (Hill & Ballou, 1998; Wyche & Rice, 1997).

The positive and respectful negotiation of power is facilitated through informed consent and the negotiation of counseling contracts or rights and responsibilities statements that outline the nature and goals of therapy, the counselor's theoretical orientation, the costs and benefits of counseling, expectations of client and counselor, and alternatives to counseling (Pope & Vasquez,

1998). These procedures demystify psychotherapy, demonstrate respect for clients' autonomy, and convey confidence about clients' ability to make judgments that are in their best interest (Hill & Ballou, 1998; Wyche & Rice, 1997).

Power differentials are also reflected in language and nonverbal behavior. The Division 17 Principles (American Psychological Association, 1979) highlight the importance of using non-sexist language. Research clearly demonstrates that when people use masculine nouns and pronouns as "generic" language, responses are "predominantly—and usually overwhelmingly—male" (Henley, 1989, p. 65). Use of masculine generics also has been shown to result in women's lower comprehension or recall of material (Crawford & English, 1984), and women's belief that material is less personally relevant (D.G. MacKay, 1980). An equally important but subtle use of biased language is reflected in the structure of language that is used to compare men and women on many psychological variables. Tavris (1993a) noted that the pervasiveness of "male as normative" standards are revealed in a sentence that reads "women are less self-confident than men" instead of "men are not as realistic as women in assessing their abilities." When language does not refer inclusively to activities and roles related to intimate partnerships and parents, heterosexist biases are also conveyed (Committee on Lesbian and Gay Concerns, 1991). Counselors must maintain awareness that language is central to conveying standards of normalcy within psychology and seek to avoid comparisons that reinforce existing power differentials.

One of the few well-established gender differences is women's greater sensitivity to nonverbal cues and greater accuracy in decoding nonverbal language (Hall & Halberstadt, 1997; LaFrance & Henley, 1997). In addition, psychological research reveals that men and women use nonverbal language in different ways. On average, men interrupt women more frequently than women interrupt men, men are more likely to talk more than women in mixed groups, men are more likely to use silence to control discussion, men are more likely to touch women than women to touch men, women smile more than men, and men use greater personal space than women (see Gilbert & Scher, 1999 for a review). Some authors indicate that gender differences in nonverbal behaviors, such as posture, personal space, touching, eye-contact, facial expression, speaking styles, and decoding skill, are consistent with an "oppression hypothesis" (e.g., LaFrance & Henley, 1997; Unger & Crawford, 1996). In other words, people with higher status use nonverbal skills to emphasize and demarcate power. Conversely, individuals with lower levels of power enhance their coping and survival by being able to discern the desires and intentions of those with greater power. The debate about why gender differences in nonverbal behavior exist is not yet resolved (Hall & Halberstadt, 1997; LaFrance & Henley, 1997). However, it is important for counselors to be aware that nonverbal expression can be used to emphasize one's position as a more powerful or subordinate person, and to make efforts to use nonverbal communication that supports egalitarian relationships.

Boundary Issues

Boundary violations and power imbalances assume many forms, ranging from blatant forms of sexual misconduct to less invasive but problematic behaviors such as using touch or self-disclosure inappropriately. This section focuses on boundary management as it relates to self-disclosure, touch, and sexual misconduct. Fitzgerald and Nutt (1986) indicated that self-disclosure is an important outgrowth of self-examination and self-awareness and is useful for creating "mutually responsible" (p. 206) relationships. Self-disclosure in counseling has been a popular area of research (Watkins, 1990), and studies consistently find that analytically or traditionally oriented therapists are less likely to use self-disclosure than are other counselors (e.g., Edwards & Murdock, 1994; Simi & Mahalik, 1997). Feminist therapists, who see the discussion of gender issues as central to achieving counseling goals, may view self-disclosure in distinctive ways. They tend to use self-disclosure to equalize the psychotherapy relationship, empower the client, and establish informed consent. Simi and Mahalik (1997) found that compared with other therapists, feminist therapists expressed greater willingness to share information about personal background, and were more likely to be open to client requests for self-disclosure. Compared with psychoanalytic/dynamic therapists, feminist therapists were more likely to believe that self-disclosure decreases power differentials, is useful for validating clients' feelings, and can be liberating or empowering for clients.

A recent qualitative study revealed that clients often described themselves as discussing important personal issues immediately preceding counselor self-disclosure (Knox, Hess, Petersen, & Hill, 1997). Counselor disclosures were typically about past (not immediate) personal experiences, and clients generally believed that therapists disclosed in order to normalize their experiences or to provide reassurance. Clients viewed the consequences of self-disclosure as equalizing the relationship, normalizing the client's concerns, and as facilitating insight. Another recent study (Simone, McCarthy, & Skay, 1998) found that counselors' primary reasons for using self-disclosure included promoting feelings of universality, encouraging the client and instilling hope, modeling coping strategies, fostering a therapeutic alliance, and increasing awareness of alternative views. Each of these counselor and client perceptions is consistent with the values and goals endorsed by feminist therapists.

A consequence of self-disclosure, especially of self-disclosure of personal experiences and attitudes, is that boundary management may be complex. Simone et al. (1998) found that the primary reasons why counselors choose not to disclose are to avoid the blurring of boundaries and to maintain a focus on the client. Because of the complexities of therapeutic boundaries, Wyche and Rice (1997) indicated that feminist therapists have not arrived at consensus regarding the use of self-disclosure, and urged therapists to engage in "constant self scrutiny" (p. 64) when considering self-disclosure. The Feminist Therapy Institute (FTI, 1990) code of ethics also indicates that self-disclosure should be used "with purpose and discretion in the interests of the client" (p. 39). Self-disclosure is inappropriate and potentially harmful when the counselor expects that the client should meet his or her needs for closeness and validation, holds assumptions that his or her personal experiences are indicative of the experiences of most women or men, or discloses inappropriately about current stresses or problems (Smith & Fitzpatrick, 1995). Knox et al.'s (1997) finding that helpful disclosure was associated with discussion about past personal issues may be especially pertinent. When counselors disclose about the past rather than the present, they are more likely to communicate about issues for which they have achieved significant closure, and are more likely to use self-disclosure in purposeful, thoughtful, organized, and client-affirming ways.

The use of touch in psychotherapy is also complex. The positive use of therapeutic touch can provide reassurance, acceptance, and comfort; reinforce or emphasize important verbal messages; decrease clients' anxiety and increase trust; convey the presence of a safety net within the psychotherapy relationship; and promote emotionally corrective experiences (Durana, 1998; Kertay & Reviere, 1993). On the other hand, touch may also be associated with sexualized behaviors and the invasion of boundaries. Furthermore, forms of touch that ordinarily seem rather benign may be experienced as frightening or intrusive by clients who have experienced victimization (Courtois, 1997; Phelps, Friedlander, & Enns, 1997).

A survey of clients' experiences of and attitudes about physical contact (Horton, Clance, Sterk-Elifson, & Emshoff, 1995) revealed that positive touch is associated with: (1) general clarity about boundaries in counseling and the meaning of touch; (2) the client's perception that she or he has control over initiating and sustaining contact; (3) the client's belief that touch is for his or her benefit rather than the therapist's; and (4) congruence between touch and the nature of the client's issues and the level of intimacy in the relationship. Positive evaluations of touch were also connected to the presence of a strong therapeutic alliance. Sixty-nine percent of respondents believed that touch supported greater openness and trust, and 47% indicated that touch was associated with enhanced self-esteem or self-acceptance.

Seventy-one percent of respondents who had been sexually abused reported that touch enhanced their sense of power, trust, and self-esteem (Horton et al., 1995). However, other qualitative data reveal that some clients who have been abused are ambivalent about touch or see it as inappropriate (Phelps et al., 1997). Pope (1994) recommended that counselors use five considerations to guide their ethical decision making about the use of touch: (1) whether physical contact is wanted by the client, (2) the meanings of touch for the client, (3) the degree to which touch is consistent with treatment planning and goals, (4) the likelihood that the client may feel exploited by touch, and (5) the potential impact of the client's unique history, such as physical or sexual abuse, on the client's perceptions of touch.

Sexual misconduct is the most blatant of boundary violations in psychotherapy. Pope (1994) reported that there is "substantial evidence that therapists who become sexually involved with patients are overwhelmingly, although not exclusively, male, and that patients who become sexually involved with therapists are overwhelmingly, although not exclusively, female" (p. 15). Studies reveal that sexual involvement between a male therapist and a former or current female client accounted for between 86% and 92% of the cases reported (reviewed in Pope & Vasquez, 1998). Holroyd (1983) labeled male sexual intimacies with female clients as "the quintessence of sex-biased therapeutic practice" (p. 285) and noted that sexual misconduct is related to role-power and role-vulnerability (see also Pope, 1994). Gilbert and Scher (1999) proposed that the common thread underlying sexual intimacy with clients is male entitlement. This sense of entitlement takes on different forms such as the therapist's desires become the focus of counseling, the therapist rationalizes any potential harm to clients, or the therapist fosters and then exploits the client's dependence (Gilbert, 1992).

Female therapists are not immune from sexual misconduct or other problematic boundary violations. As noted by Brown (1991), adopting the title "feminist therapist" and assumptions about egalitarianism does not eliminate the possibility that one might engage in ethically problematic behaviors, including the sexual exploitation of clients. If a therapist assumes that adopting an ethic of egalitarianism erases power issues, the therapist may be especially vulnerable to violating clients' boundaries.

A national survey revealed that approximately half of the psychologists who responded had seen at least one client who had experienced sexual intimacies with a therapist (Pope & Vetter, 1991), and that most of these clients had experienced significant harm. A second survey revealed that one-quarter of respondents had provided psychotherapy to at least one client who had been sexually involved with a prior therapist (Parsons & Wincze, 1995). Providing information to clients about appropriate therapist behavior may contribute to prevention as well as help clients clarify options if they have been abused (Committee on Women in Psychology, 1989). Thorn, Shealy, and Briggs (1993) found that compared with controls, potential clients who read a brochure about sexual misconduct showed greater knowledge about inappropriate therapist behavior and indicated greater likelihood of responding assertively to therapist behaviors that made them uncomfortable. Prevention of therapist abuse may also be facilitated by training about dealing with sexual feelings, which are reported by approximately four out of five psychologists (Pope, Sonne, & Holroyd, 1993; Pope & Vetter, 1991).

Gender of Counselor and Client

The Division 17 Principles indicate that counselors should be sensitive to circumstances when it is more desirable for clients to be seen by male or female therapists. Fitzgerald and Nutt's (1986) commentary on the principles indicated that research on client preferences for therapist gender is "sparse and inconclusive" (p. 198), and Nelson's (1993) later review concurred with this conclusion.

Some studies indicate that women tend to show a greater preference for women therapists or a higher level of willingness to disclose and discuss highly personal and relational concerns with women counselors (e.g., Pikus & Heavey, 1996; Snell, Hampton, & McManus, 1992). However, Nelson's (1993) review concluded that although "trends" suggest that women clients may experience greater success with women counselors, "most findings have been inconclusive" (p. 200).

Findings about gender-pairings as they relate to counseling have been inconsistent, perhaps because of the many complicated aspects of identity and social roles that may influence and modify client preferences, including counselor and client class, gender role identity, ethnicity, sexual orientation, and age (Nelson, 1993; Pikus & Heavey, 1996). For example, two surveys have found that gay or lesbian clients viewed gay male and female and heterosexual female counselors as more helpful than heterosexual male counselors (V.R. Brooks, 1981; Liddle, 1996), suggesting that knowledge of counselor gender alone is inadequate for predicting optimal client-counselor pairings.

Given the conflicting findings associated with research on gender pairings, the recommendations of Fitzgerald and Nutt (1986) remain sound and merit repetition. Multiple personal and environmental factors and complex intersections of identity influence the therapeutic endeavor. Open discussion and negotiation with clients about their preferences is likely to serve the best interests of clients. When clients' presenting issues are related to issues of violence, such as rape, sexual abuse, domestic violence, and sexual harassment (Enns, 1993; Fitzgerald & Nutt, 1986), sensitivity to counselor-client pairings is especially appropriate.

Knowledge of Gender Issues in Assessment

Gender Bias in Diagnosis and Assessment

Chesler's (1972) book, *Women and Madness,* was one of the first accounts of how diagnostic categories pathologized women and supported their subordination. In light of this critique, early writings on feminist therapy expressed reservation about using diagnostic labels, arguing that they reflect the inappropriate application of social power, minimize the impact of environmental factors on symptoms, and reduce therapists' respect for clients. Furthermore, feminist therapists contended that the use of traditional diagnostic labels encourages therapists to focus primarily on removing intrapsychic conflicts rather than addressing the communicative function and social change implications of symptoms (Rawlings & Carter, 1977).

Building on these initial critiques, a variety of authors pointed out ways in which the symptoms displayed by men and women are consistent with gender role stereotypes and that women's efforts to conform more closely to gender stereotypes were more likely to be labeled as forms of pathology than were exaggerations of men's stereotypes (Franks & Rothblum, 1983; Kaplan, 1983). Feminist psychologists and therapists have continued to express concern about gender bias in assessment and diagnosis, including the tendency for therapists to minimize the impact of environmental factors on behavior, the presence of gender bias in psychometric instruments, the use of different labels for similar behaviors in men and women, and therapist misjudgments about appropriate diagnoses due to stereotyped beliefs about gender (DeBarona & Dutton, 1997; Worell & Remer, 1992).

Due to recent efforts to decrease bias in diagnosis and to pay closer attention to the role of culture in shaping symptoms (Walsh, 1997), the most recent version of the *Diagnostic and Statistical Manual of Mental Disorders* (APA, 1994, *DSM-IV*) is generally seen as a substantial improvement over previous manuals (Kupers, 1997; Ross, Frances, & Widiger, 1997). However, Kupers argued that despite efforts to base diagnostic categories on empirical data and rigorous evaluation, the most recent version of the *DSM* has the potential to be used as a "more rigorous rationalization for pathologizing nonmainstream behaviors and attitudes" (p. 340).

Much of the controversy over bias in assessment and diagnosis during the last ten years has centered on the inclusion of three controversial categories that were included within the appendix of the revised version of the 3rd edition of the *Diagnostic and Statistical Manual Disorders* (*DSM III-R;* APA, 1987) and designated as diagnostic categories needing further study. These proposed diagnostic categories were named masochistic personality disorder (later renamed self-defeating personality disorder, SDPD); sadistic personality disorder; and late luteal phase dysphoric disorder (currently labeled premenstrual dysphoric disorder) (Caplan, 1995; Ross et al., 1997). Feminist critics were successful in influencing authors of the *DSM-IV*, arguing that 85% of normally socialized women exhibit many criteria of SDPD and that the label does not acknowledge the survival value of passive or pacifying behaviors in reducing the emotional impact of physical violence that accompanies abusive relationships. Furthermore, the criteria for SDPD overlapped substantially with other personality disorders, lacked diagnostic power, and was supported by limited empirical data (Caplan, 1995). As a result, SDPD was removed from the diagnostic manual. Sadistic personality disorder was also eliminated because of lack of research support and potential for misuse (e.g., for avoiding the acceptance of responsibility for interpersonal violence).

In contrast to this outcome, premenstrual dysphoric disorder (PMDD) is included in the *DSM-IV* (APA, 1994) as a diagnosable disorder, and is currently listed in the main text under Depressive Disorder Not Otherwise Specified. A list of symptoms for further study remains in the appendix. This disorder received the approval of the psychiatric community despite inadequate empirical evidence, controversies about methodological weaknesses of studies on PMDD, and lack of consensus about symptoms of PMDD, its prevalence, and its validity as a distinctive disorder (Caplan, 1995; Figert, 1996). Tavris (1993b) concluded that "the psychiatric Establishment feeds the prejudice that women's hormones, but not men's, are a cause of mental illness" (p. B7). Kupers's (1993) argument that men also experience mood cycles that could be diagnosed as "pathological arrhythmicity" was not seriously considered by authors of the *DSM-IV*. Although the long-term impact of this controversy is not clear, a recent study of college women revealed that the very knowledge of PMDD as a diagnostic category increased women's perceptions that women's premenstrual changes are a general problem for women (Nash & Chrisler, 1997).

Studies continue to reveal that the gender and race of clients may influence assessments of their symptoms. For example, Landrine's (1989) study found that college students associated descriptions of personality disorders (e.g., dependent, antisocial) with gender, class, and racial stereotypes. More recently, Becker and Lamb (1994) presented clinicians with a male or female version of a vignette depicting a person who met criteria of both borderline personality disorder (BPD) and posttraumatic stress disorder (PTSD). The person in the female version was more likely than the person in the male version to be categorized as borderline. Furthermore, female clinicians were more likely to see PTSD as relevant to both versions of the vignette than were male clinicians, suggesting the male practitioners may "underestimate the negative effects of the sexual abuse on both male and female clients, raising the question of whether abuse survivors of both sexes might receive less than optimal treatment at the hands of many male therapists" (p. 59). Becker and Lamb also explored other labels that clinicians found relevant to the vignette and found that male versions were more likely to be rated as antisocial and female versions as histrionic.

A recent review of gender and diagnosis (Hartung & Widiger, 1998) noted that subtle forms of bias in assessment may be supported by sampling biases in research studies and subtle biases within diagnostic criteria. Many gender prevalence rates cited in the *DSM-IV* may be inaccurate due to the differential treatment seeking behaviors and referral patterns for men and women, resulting in biased clinical samples. In addition, the inclusion of only men or women as participants in research on specific problems (e.g., conduct disorder, eating disorders) may result in biased representations of men and women in many empirical studies. Furthermore, diagnostic criteria that are designed to be gender neutral "may disproportionately favor the manner in which the disorder appears in one gender relative to the other" (p. 267). Hartung and Widiger suggested that it is difficult to create gender neutral descriptions of problems when the manifestations of these problems are influenced by gender socialization (e.g. some personality disorders, conduct disorder, somatization disorder, sexual disorders). Some disorders that are described in gender neutral terms may actually be expressed differently in men and women, and subcultures of men and women. The failure to consider how gender may influence the expression of distress "is likely to result in the development of diagnostic criteria that are not equally valid for the two sexes" (p. 272).

In contrast to early studies that revealed clinicians' double standard of mental health for men and women (e.g., Broverman, Broverman, Clarkson, Rosenkrantz, & Vogel, 1970), recent assessments suggest that practitioners' perceptions and evaluations are more neutral (Walsh, 1997). However, Becker and Lamb (1994) indicated that current forms of gender bias may "inhere in the current system of diagnostic classification itself, at times in association with sex of client, sex of clinician, and professional affiliation" (p. 59).

It is important for counseling psychologists to be aware of the subtle ways in which diagnostic categories may support inaccurate assessments of gender-related concerns. Some diagnoses, such as BPD, can be used to label persons who are experiencing gender-related problems (e.g., the consequences of sexual violence) in pejorative and intrapsychic terms (Brown, 1994; Chesler, 1997; Herman, 1992). The use of these categories may contribute to victim blaming attitudes, and decrease the practitioner's sensitivity to contextual factors that shape distress as well as the communication and coping function of symptoms. Commenting on the increased use of BPD in the recent past, Kroll (1988) suggested that BPD is becoming a "nondiscriminatory synonym for personality disorder" (p. 1025). Diagnostic categories that address contextual factors and power abuses that influence psychological distress (e.g., PTSD and complex PTSD, Herman, 1992) are likely to emphasize the adaptive role of symptoms and support positive treatment possibilities for both men and women.

In her 25-year reassessment of *Women and Madness,* Chesler (1997) proposed that clinical bias continues to be evident in a number of domains, significantly affecting the lives of women, and to a lesser extent, men. Counselors should be cautious about subtle ways in which assessment and diagnosis can lead to (1) the conceptualization of some medical illnesses as psychological or psychiatric problems; (2) the pathologizing of victims of sex discrimination and violence within clinical and legal systems; and (3) a lack of sensitivity to issues of diversity and concerns of people of color.

Assessing Gender-Related Concerns

Brown (1990) suggested that as a part of the assessment process, therapists should pay particular attention to (1) the meaning of gender in light of the client's family values, stage of life, culture of origin, and current social environments; (2) the degree to which the client complies with gender role injunctions, as well as the rewards and penalties the client has experienced for noncompliance or compliance; (3) the manner in which the client responds to the counselor's gender, as well as the therapist's reactions to the client; and (4) presenting issues that are often associated with gender. Assessment of gender-related issues also requires literacy regarding cultural, ethnic, and racial variations in prescribed gender roles, as well as subtle expressions of gender-related issues. Effective assessment of gender-related issues is facilitated by a cooperative and phenomenological approach in which the client's perspective is viewed as equally valid as the counselor's perceptions.

Central to assessment is the gathering of information about the client's strengths and coping capacities, which provide a foundation for developing new skills. In an effort to understand the ecological context and situational factors affecting the client, the counselor may also seek information about the client's support systems, level of social isolation or connection, and stressful experiences that may exacerbate gender-related issues (Brown, 1994).

In general, assessment is a shared and ongoing experience between the counselors and clients, and is integral to competent treatment. Whenever possible, clients should be encouraged to name the meaning of their experiences and problems. This is especially important when adult clients explore problems associated with sensitive issues, such as childhood abuse. If a counselor prematurely labels a client as an "abuse victim," the client may be less willing to disclose information, may experience the counselor as imposing an agenda, or may feel subtly disempowered. In contrast, when counselors ask questions that encourage clients to explore their experiences, feelings, and behaviors in a comprehensive manner, clients become respected collaborators who may feel empowered by naming their own difficulties (Brown, 1994).

Theoretical Perspectives on Counseling

The introduction to this chapter highlights the importance of a social constructionist perspective that emphasizes the role of context in shaping gender behaviors and perceptions of men's and women's behavior. Despite almost thirty years of research from a social constructionist perspective, Bem (1993) contended that much of psychological theory and research: (1) is androcentric, as evidenced by the fact that psychologists continue to frame women's experience as it measures up to "normative" male experience (e.g., "women have lower self-esteem than men" versus "men are more conceited than women"); (2) tends to conceptualize men and women in polarized terms and "superimposes a male-female dichotomy on virtually every aspect of human experience" (p. 233) (e.g., through research that emphasizes gender differences rather than similarities); and (3) supports biological essentialism, or the notion that any differences that do exist are the consequence of "the intrinsic biological natures of women and men" (p. 233). Marecek (1997) elaborated on these themes, suggesting that psychology in the 1990s has been increasingly influenced by biological foundationalism. She argued that "both in psychology and in the culture at large, biologism goes hand in hand with political and social conservatism" (pp. 135–136).

Popular conceptualizations of gender, bearing titles such as *Men Are from Mars, Women Are from Venus* (Gray, 1992), expand on these themes and promote traditional gender behavior as normal, natural, and as highly adaptive. Gray's book, which is the best-selling hardcover tradebook of the 1990s (Gleick, 1997), is not based on empirical data, but disseminates theory without evidence, one of the major problems about which feminist psychologists have expressed concern since the 1960s (e.g., Weisstein, 1968/1993). The establishment of "Mars and Venus Counseling Centers" based on Gray's approach (Gleick, 1997) suggests that gender stereotypes may be supported and reinforced in at least some therapeutic environments.

These trends point to the importance of basing clinical work with men and women on sound theory and research that challenge stereotypes. Despite some conservative trends, acceptance and recognition of feminist therapy has increased and is receiving greater visibility. Two general texts on counseling theory currently include or will include a chapter on feminist therapy (Corey, in press; Sharf, 1996), and several videotape training series feature feminist therapy (e.g., Brown, 1996). The publication of a variety of recent books on gender and counseling (Gilbert & Scher, 1999; Philpot et al., 1997) and feminist therapy (e.g., Brown, 1994; Comas-Diaz & Greene, 1994; Enns, 1997; Worell & Remer, 1992) also point to the vitality of feminist and gender aware therapies. In the following sections, I address three theoretical perspectives (nonsexist, feminist, and gender-aware therapy) that are designed to support the development of healthy gender identities.

Nonsexist and Feminist Therapy

Nonsexist therapy is based on the premise that human development and behavior are determined more significantly by being human rather than being male or female, and that the goals of counseling and therapy are human goals rather than gender-related goals. Collier (1982) described nonsexist counseling as emphasizing "the need for *all* human beings to be able to actualize themselves regardless of biological gender" (p. 12). Thus, the goals of counseling include power over one's life, self-esteem, spontaneity and openness, the unstereotyped appreciation of others, independence, and individual growth (Collier, 1982; Rawlings & Carter, 1977). Rawlings and Carter proposed that nonsexist therapy may be especially appropriate for individuals with more traditional values for whom a more activist or feminist approach may be threatening.

Nonsexist and feminist therapists share the assumption that egalitarian relationships are central to growth and the goals of alleviating client distress and helping to achieve growth that is free of stereotypes (Collier, 1982). Feminist therapists move one step beyond nonsexist therapy by endorsing the principle that the "personal is political" (Rawlings & Carter, 1977), which emphasizes the importance of increasing clients' awareness of the social and political contexts that influence their problems, and focuses on directly challenging gender role stereotypes and oppressive institutional/cultural structures. Another difference between feminist and nonsexist approaches is that feminist therapists are especially attentive to the manner in which so-called "nonsexist" goals, such as independence and assertiveness, may be incomplete because they are embedded in subtle androcentric aspects of psychological theory (Crawford, 1995; Gilligan, 1982). Feminist approaches also recognize that nonsexist behaviors such as independence and assertiveness may be differentially rewarded or punished, depending on the gender of the client who is enacting these behaviors and the gender stereotypes or egalitarian attitudes of those he or she encounters in the surrounding social environment.

A recent survey of 173 self-identified feminist therapists (Beardsley, Morrow, Castillo, & Weitzman, 1998) revealed that feminist therapy principles can be organized around five themes or factors: multicultural competency, multicultural awareness, awareness of multiple oppressions, the personal is political, and subversive practices. The subversive practices factor included items that referred to client-therapist collaboration about diagnosis, methods of increasing client access to services (e.g., through the use of a sliding-scale fees), and diagnostic practices for increasing client access to insurance coverage. In contrast to Beardsley et al.'s quantitative study of feminist therapists, Hill and Ballou (1998) gathered open-ended responses from 35 feminist therapists associated with the Feminist Therapy Institute. Their analysis revealed the following themes: attention to power differences, overlapping relationships, and therapist accountability; emphasis on the sociocultural causes of distress; the valuing of women's experience; the use of an integrated analysis of the multifaceted and interlocking aspects of oppression; and an emphasis on social change. The parallel findings from these two studies reveal that the original tenets of feminist therapy (the personal is political and the counseling relationship is egalitarian) remain important. As feminist therapy has matured, feminist therapists have also become increasingly attentive to multiple oppressions, diversity issues, and multicultural perspectives.

Initially proposed as a method for counseling women, feminist therapy is also of significant value for men. Ganley (1988) proposed that feminist therapy can be especially useful for helping men (1) learn to integrate relationship and achievement needs; (2) increase their capacity for intimacy, self-disclosure, and emotional expression; (3) create mutually rewarding, collaborative relationships; and (4) learn noncoercive problem-solving methods. Disagreement still exists about whether it is more appropriate for men to refer to themselves as "feminist therapists" or "profeminist therapists." However, a recent qualitative study of experienced feminist therapists revealed that 24 of 25 respondents believed that men can practice feminist therapy (Marecek & Kravetz, 1998a).

Ganley (1988) referred to the feminist activities of male therapists as profeminist therapy because this phrase affirms men's contributions to an egalitarian society while also acknowledging and preserving the uniqueness of women's therapeutic roles. Profeminist therapists encourage men to confront sexist behavior; redefine masculinity according to values other than power, prestige, and privilege; and actively support women's efforts to seek justice (Tolman et al., 1986). Profeminist treatment models may be especially useful for working with men who exhibit violent behaviors. A profeminist model for male batterers examines how men's controlling behaviors, such as battering, psychological abuse, and verbal intimidation, maintain power imbalances. Profeminist counselors actively interrupt men's efforts to devalue women and other less powerful individuals, confront their controlling behaviors, and help men and women work toward establishing egalitarian relationships. Anger management, communication skills training, stress management, and accountability training are also important (Harway & Evans, 1996; Tolman et al., 1986).

Gender-Aware Therapy

Good, Gilbert, and Scher (1990) indicated that feminist therapy has had a significant impact on the practice of psychotherapy. They noted, however, that many individuals have viewed feminist therapy as applicable to women alone. In light of social changes and research on the detrimental aspects of traditional male gender roles, they proposed gender aware therapy as a method for integrating the principles of feminist therapy with knowledge of gender. Therapists who practice gender-aware therapy: (1) view gender issues and roles as central components of mental health, (2) understand men's and women's problems in light of the social context (an extension of the principle that the personal is political), (3) challenge gender role injustices encountered by men and women, (4) work toward establishing collaborative therapeutic relationships, and (5) respect clients' ability to choose behaviors that clients perceive as right for themselves. G.R. Brooks (1990) elaborated on therapeutic goals for men that are consistent with gender-aware therapy. Therapists can help men (1) decrease emphasis on career and work-related aspects of identity, (2) develop interpersonal behaviors other than those that involve taking charge and asserting themselves, (3) facilitate emotional expression among men, and (4) explore new models of parenting and fathering.

Gender sensitive therapy (Philpot et al., 1997) is a variant of gender aware therapy designed for work with couples and consists of the phases of (1) reflection, which consists of the therapist's demonstration of empathy for both partners' positions; (2) psychoeducation about the social construction of gender; (3) confrontation of gender issues; and (4) brainstorming about solutions. Key components of this couples approach include the validation and normalization of gender role conflicts, the reframing of individual communication problems as products of conditioning, and the act of uniting against and defining the "gender ecosystem as the enemy" (Philpot et al., 1997, p. 179).

Gender aware therapy combines elements of both nonsexist and feminist therapy, but is distinctive in subtle ways. In contrast to nonsexist therapy, which seeks to provide equal treatment for men and women, gender aware therapy places emphasis on exploring gender issues and views this exploration as central to mental health. Gender aware therapy emphasizes the importance of altering gender injustices. Compared with feminist therapy, however, social action and the analysis of power dynamics and differentials appear to be less salient components of gender aware therapy.

Facilitative Therapeutic Procedures

Gender Role Analysis

Gender role analysis is a hallmark of feminist therapy, and involves exploring the impact of gender on psychological well-being or distress and using this information to make decisions about future gender role behaviors. Gender-related issues related to ethnicity, sexual orientation, class, and race may also be integrated within gender role analysis. The counselor and client explore how traditional gender behaviors are transmitted, how they serve a functional role within many contexts, how these behaviors are reinforced and maintained, and how they contribute to difficulties the client encounters (Philpot et al., 1997). The counselor and client also clarify ways in which traditional coping methods have become less successful over time and contribute to the person's distress as that person's attempts to meet life tasks that require a wider range of skills (Worell & Remer, 1992). Assessment of deviations from gender-role norms and the consequences of such noncompliance are also important. Questions about the client's current behaviors are also relevant, and may focus on how decisions are made (e.g., career and family relationships), how conflict is handled, how the client views and relates to his or her body, and how dependency needs are expressed. An exploration of any trauma history and related coping mechanisms is also relevant (Brown, 1986, 1990).

Gender role analysis, or gender inquiry (Philpot et al., 1997), is intended to help clients develop empathic rather than self-blaming attitudes toward themselves. Clients' gender-related problems are depathologized (e.g., "dependency") and understood within a social context (Brown, 1986, 1990). Techniques associated with a variety of theoretical orientations (e.g., cognitive behavior therapy, gestalt therapy) can be integrated with the goals of gender role analysis and used to challenge and change restrictive behavior patterns (Enns, 1997).

In recent years, substantial attention has been devoted to identifying the nature and consequences of gender role conflict and oppressive aspects of masculinity ideology for men. A variety of models have been proposed, including Pleck's (1995) gender role strain/conflict paradigm, O'Neil's (1981, 1990) model of gender role conflict, and Pollack's (1995) theory of men's developmental traumas. In general, these models propose that men's gender role socialization and the "masculine mystique" lead to the fear of femininity and a variety of negative consequences including (1) restrictive emotionality; (2) the overvaluing of control, power, and competition; (3) homophobia; (4) restricted ability to show affection and the sexualization of intimacy; (5) obsession with achievement and success; and (6) a variety of health care problems (O'Neil, 1981, 1990).

Many instruments are available for assessing masculine ideology and gender role conflict/ stress, and can be used to facilitate gender role analysis with men (see Thompson & Pleck, 1995, for a review). Research studies have linked gender role conflict to a range of consequences (Good et al., 1995; Good, Wallace, & Borst, 1994), such as depression (Good & Mintz, 1990; Sharpe & Heppner, 1991), lower psychological well-being (Sharpe & Heppner, 1991), physical strain marked by physical illness or poor self-care (Stillson, O'Neil, & Owen, 1991), and the use of immature psychological defenses such as turning against others (Mahalik, Cournoyer, DeFranc, Cherry, & Napolitano, 1998). The restrictive emotionality component of masculinity ideology appears to be a significant predictor of distress and gender role conflict (Fischer & Good, 1997; Good et al., 1994). As a result, counselors may need to pay special attention to male alexithymia, which involves a lack of words for emotion (Fischer & Good, 1997; Levant, 1995), and to facilitate men's expression of vulnerable emotions.

Gender, Power, and Power Analysis

Constructs such as gender role and gender role conflict focus primarily on differential socialization by gender, but do not include an analysis of power dynamics, institutional structures, and patriarchal family structures that reinforce gender role socialization and limit the capacity of individuals to initiate personal change. Power analysis is designed to help men and women make decisions about what forms of power they possess or desire to gain access to, and about how they can use or share power in ways that will optimize the likelihood that their efforts to change or influence others will be successful (Worell & Remer, 1992). Discussion of power and power abuses from the client's past may also reveal why clients feel devalued or powerless, freeing the person to "embrace unexpressed emotions and to confront dysfunctional power conflicts that inhibit growth" (O'Neil & Egan, 1993, p. 74). Although power analysis may lead to initial discouragement (one may become aware of the limited power of an individual), power analysis may also decrease a client's self-blame and internalization of external problems, and motivate the individual to influence creatively the institutional and interpersonal demands they face (Worell & Remer, 1992). By identifying potential sources of personal power, the client negotiates new ways of initiating change and influencing the environment (O'Neil & Egan, 1993). Power analysis and empowerment involve (1) the analysis of power structures in society; (2) discussion and awareness of how individuals are socialized to feel powerful or powerless; (3) clarification of how individuals can achieve power in personal, interpersonal, and institutional domains; and (4) use of advocacy to facilitate social change (Morrow & Hawxhurst, 1998).

Power analysis may be associated with different types of issues and outcomes for many women and men. Gilbert (1992) stated that "white men in our culture typically grow up with feelings of confidence and specialness granted them simply because they are born male. This specialness is an essential aspect of male entitlement, which encourages men to feel that what they do or want takes precedence" (p. 391, see also Pyke & Coltrane, 1996; Steil, 1994). The differential levels of men's and women's sense of entitlement are often exhibited in heterosexual intimate relationships, and Major (1993) noted that men and women in heterosexual relationships often construct a variety of myths and cognitive justifications that reinforce socialized power differences. For example, the female partner may identify herself as having fewer needs than her partner, which supports her internal justification of role overloads. Men are likely to compare their household contributions with those of other men, rather than women and female partners. Other comparison standards, such as feasibility comparisons (the likelihood of being able to negotiate change) and self-comparisons (comparisons of one's current contributions with past contributions), may also decrease one's awareness of justice issues and support continuing inequities (Major, 1993; Pyke & Coltrane, 1996; Steil, 1994). According to a power analysis perspective, power issues such as these are sometimes invisible to clients, but should be addressed whenever possible.

The Gender Role Journey and Feminist/Womanist Identity

A variety of authors have noted that the clarification of one's gender-related identity can be understood as a developmental process. Downing and Roush's (1985) model of feminist identity development proposed that women who identify themselves as feminist negotiate a series of stages beginning with the passive acceptance of sexism, moving into a crisis stage of revelation, and proceeding to an embeddedness stage marked by intense connections to other women. The process culminates with synthesis, which involves the formation of an authentic feminist identity characterized by gender role transcendence and the integration of unique personal attributes with feminist principles; and active commitment, which entails commitment to social change.

Assessment of feminist identity can be facilitated with two instruments designed to measure this construct (Bargrad & Hyde, 1991; Rickard, 1987). Henderson-King and Stewart (1997) found predicted relationships between feminist identity phases and women's attitudes toward men and women's sensitivity toward sexism. The phase of revelation was most strongly related to sensitivity toward sexism and negative feelings toward men, and the strength of these relationships was smaller for each of the subsequent stages of feminist identity. The synthesis stage, which involves making assessments of others based on their individual qualities rather than group membership, was unrelated to attitudes about men. Fischer and Good (1994) also found relationships between women's perceptions of the presence of sex bias and both revelation and embeddedness phases. Another study (Gerstmann & Kramer, 1997) found a positive relationship between passive acceptance and absolute or dualistic thinking (16% of variance), and consistent but somewhat smaller relationships between synthesis of an authentic, personal feminist identity and dialectical thinking (making commitments based on an evolving and pluralistic framework). In general, findings suggest that feminist identification is complex, and manifested by a variety of attitudes. Questions still remain about the degree to which these "stages" are sequential or reflect qualitatively different experiences of feminism (Gerstmann & Kramer, 1997; Henderson-King & Stewart, 1997).

The relationship between feminist identity development and problems that women bring to counseling is less clear, as revealed by two studies on body image. Snyder and Hasbrouck (1996) found that body dissatisfaction and drive for thinness were positively associated with passive acceptance and negatively related to the final stage of active commitment. They also noted a modest negative relationship between the synthesis phase and bulimic symptoms and feelings of ineffectiveness. A second study (Cash, Ancis, & Strachan, 1997) found only a few small significant relationships between feminist identity and body image, but discovered that traditional gender attitudes about men's and women's social interactions were related to traditional and potentially dysfunctional personal appearance standards.

The gender role journey model proposes stages that parallel the phases of the feminist identity model, with the exception that it is described in more gender neutral terms (O'Neil & Carroll, 1988; O'Neil & Egan, 1992). During phase 1, individuals accept traditional gender roles and hold stereotypic views of masculinity, and during phase 2, persons experience ambivalence and confusion about gender roles and sexism. As awareness increases (phase 3), individuals direct anger and negative emotions at institutions and people who promote stereotypes of gender. During the final phases, persons engage in activist responses to restrictive roles and experience greater gender role freedom and integration. The gender role journey questionnaire (O'Neil, Egan, Owen, & Murry, 1993) can be incorporated into gender role discussions that occur during counseling, workshops, and other psychoeducational programs.

Helms (1990) has also proposed a womanist model of identity development that draws on some features of the feminist identity model and integrates them with other models, such as Black women's development. According to this model, healthy development may or may not be connected to feminism or activism. A study of college women revealed that early phases of womanist identity were associated with perceptions of gender bias in the college environment and lower self esteem; later phases were related to higher self-esteem (Ossana, Helms, & Leonard, 1992). Another study found that for White women, earlier stages of development were associated with greater psychological distress, but more internalized forms of womanist identity were associated with more positive mental health (Carter & Parks, 1996). For Black women, no relationships between mental health and womanist identity emerged. A third study found that for Black women, womanist identity was associated with racial identity development; for White women, racial and womanist identity development were not related (Parks, Carter, & Gushue, 1996). A final study of African American women (A.M. White, Strube, & Fisher, 1998), which used Downing and Roush's (1985) feminist identity model and Cross's (1991) racial identity model to assess identity, found that early stages of "acceptance" were related to greater acceptance of rape myths, and later stages were associated with the rejection of rape myths. These studies point to the value of integrating material relevant to feminism and womanism with models of racial identity. In general, early and more externalized definitions of feminism and womanism are more likely to be associated with psychological distress than internalized definitions. Furthermore, Black and White women may experience and negotiate these aspects of identity in different ways.

In addition to the intersections of feminist, gender, and ethnic identity, other aspects of identity, such as gay or bicultural identity formation, are also relevant to counseling. Reynolds and Pope's (1991) multidimensional identity model proposes that multiple identities may be negotiated in four ways, including identification with (1) one aspect of identity in a passive manner, (2) one aspect of identity through conscious identification, (3) multiple aspects of the self in a segmented fashion, and (4) combined aspects of the self through identity intersection. Each of these possible options represents an acceptable method for resolving identity issues, but each is likely to have unique implications for counseling.

Identity development models have important implications for the type of psychoeducational or counseling interventions that may be optimal at different stages of development. During early stages of "passive acceptance," clients may prefer relatively traditional counseling relationships, and therapists may focus on raising awareness by gently asking questions that help clients discover the impact of sexism, racism, and homophobia on their development. During "revelation" phases, when clients are becoming aware of oppression and its impact, counselors may need to provide additional support and encouragement as clients gradually move from seeing themselves as victims of discrimination to active coping agents. Several studies have noted that awareness of sexism and discrimination are associated with lower self-esteem or higher levels of psychological distress (e.g., Carter & Parks, 1996; Ossana et al., 1992). Clients who see the larger environment as sexist, homophobic, or racist may also be especially aware of hostility that is directed toward them as individuals, and this awareness may be exhibited as psychological distress.

Intervention tools that are most closely associated with feminist therapy, such as power analysis, emotion-related work, and self-disclosure, may be most beneficial during middle stages of development that are marked by awareness of bias and discrimination and the desire to interact with similar others in a safe, supportive environment. Group work may be most useful during these middle stages, when individuals solidify an emerging identity with those who share their values. For persons with more consolidated identities, individual decision making and critical thinking skills may be especially important as clients enact identities that may diverge at times from other persons' definitions of "liberated" behavior (McNamara & Rickard, 1989).

A Challenge: Men and Counseling

One of the major challenges to therapists is men's help-seeking patterns. Several investigations reveal that traditional masculine beliefs and gender role conflict are associated with lower levels of willingness to seek psychological help (e.g., Good & Wood, 1995; Robertson & Fitzgerald, 1992; Wisch, Mahalik, Hayes, & Nutt, 1995). Mahalik et al. (1998) found that men's gender role conflict is related to the use of defenses that protect men from acknowledging painful ideas and emotions, activities that are central to many forms of counseling. Men scoring high in gender role conflict showed less willingness to seek counseling when they viewed emotion-focused rather than cognitively focused counseling sessions (Wisch et al., 1995). However, Robertson and Fitzgerald (1992) noted that traditional men expressed openness to alternatives to traditional counseling and concluded that "simply changing the way in which some services are described (e.g., using terms such as *classes, workshops,* and *seminars,* rather than *personal counseling*) may encourage men with more highly masculine attitudes to take advantage of services that may be helpful to them" (p. 245).

Psychoeducation designed to educate men about the benefits of emotion and disclosure for enhancing mental health may be useful for overcoming help seeking reluctance. In addition, if counseling is portrayed as an activity that calls for the development of personal strength, competence, and courage through the discussion of personal concerns, men's resistance to seeking help may also decrease (Fischer & Good, 1997; Good & Wood, 1995). Many of the tools described in this section, such as gender role analysis, the gender role journey, and power analysis, are compatible with psychoeducational approaches that may help overcome men's resistance to help seeking. Given the fact that traditional men may be more open to cognitive and skill development approaches, emotion-focused work may be most effectively implemented by using bridging techniques that move the client from more comfortable cognitive engagement to less comfortable emotional expression and engagement (Wisch et al., 1995).

Social Change

Social change has been a central component of feminist therapy since its inception 30 years ago. Coster and Schwebel (1997) proposed that social activism has benefits for all psychologists and is an important component of self-care and well-functioning. Nevertheless, social change activities are relatively uncommon, even for feminist therapists. Beardsley et al.'s (1998) survey found that the following activities represent common practices of experienced, self-identified feminist therapists: using gender analysis and power analysis, maintaining awareness of diversity, and emphasizing collaborative therapy. In contrast, uncommon practices included the use of political analysis and encouraging clients to be involved in social change. Low endorsement of involvement in social change was also revealed by Marecek and Kravetz's (1998a) qualitative study, which found that self-identified feminist therapists "privileged private meanings, feelings, and ideas" (p. 26) and did not encourage clients to challenge systems of power. Both studies found that self-identified feminist therapists often feel isolated and fear public self-identification as a feminist therapist because of the powerful backlash against feminism during the 1990s. These findings suggest that it is important for therapists to consider renewing their commitment to social change (Morrow & Hawxhurst, 1998).

Attitudes about gender have changed substantially during the past thirty years. Spence and Hahn's (1997) longitudinal study found a gradual liberalization of both men's and women's gender role attitudes. However, a gender gap still exists, with women endorsing more egalitarian values than men (Spence & Hahn, 1997). Twenge's (1997) meta-analysis also concluded that attitudinal changes also mark "women's increased endorsement of masculine-stereotyped traits and men's continued nonendorsement of feminine-stereotyped traits" (p. 305). The gender gap in attitudes about gender roles suggests that issues of power and equality have importance not only for counseling, but also for social change efforts.

FUTURE DIRECTIONS

In this final section, I briefly explore two important areas of theory and research that will be important to continued advances in our understanding of gender and counseling.

Theory and Research on Gender Role Conflict

Over the past 20 years, research on men's gender role conflict has established the presence and structure of gender role conflict and many of its psychometric properties (Good et al., 1995). Research also reveals that gender role conflict in men is complex, and at least modestly related to psychological distress. Good et al. found, for example, that 15% of the variance in men's psychological distress was predicted by gender role conflict. A series of studies have also found a rather strong relationship between gender role conflict or masculinity ideology and negative attitudes toward help seeking (e.g. Good, Dell, & Mintz, 1989; Good & Wood, 1995; Robertson & Fitzgerald, 1992; Wisch et al., 1995). Good and Wood found that 25% of the variance in men's help seeking behavior was explained by restriction-related aspects of gender role conflict. To date, limited research has examined male gender role conflict in gay men, clinical populations (Good et al., 1995), men of color (Doss & Hopkins, 1998; Stillson et al., 1991; Wade, 1996), and at different periods of the life span (Cournoyer & Mahalik, 1995). In the future, research on these topics as well as the impact of gender role conflict on the processes and outcomes of psychotherapy will be important (Cournoyer & Mahalik, 1995; Heppner, 1995). Further examination of gender role conflict as it relates to the types of presenting problems and the coping styles of different men will also be central to understanding the diversity and implications of gender role conflict in men (Heppner, 1995). Given the resistance of some men to traditional therapy, examination of the processes and outcomes associated with alternative forms of intervention (Andronico, 1996) will also be important.

During recent years, substantial theory and research have examined men's gender role conflict, and less attention has focused on women's gender role conflict. Future theory and research should further examine the similarities, differences, and interrelationships between men's and women's gender role conflicts (McCreary, Newcomb, & Sadava, 1998), as well as how gender role conflict is shaped by multiple aspects of identity, life circumstances, and important relationships. Exploration of the ways in which gender role conflict is moderated and shaped by specific relationships and by specific role demands and contexts will provide insight about the contexts in which gender role conflict is exacerbated and the contexts in which gender role conflict is less salient (Heppner, 1995).

One of the limitations of gender role conflict theory is that it focuses almost exclusively on individual manifestations of psychological distress and is infrequently integrated with knowledge of power dynamics, especially as they are manifested in abuse or violence (G.R. Brooks & Silverstein, 1995). A focus on gender roles alone provides limited insight about the social change implications of men's and women's problems because the language of gender roles tends to focus on individualistic manifestations of gender and gender-related conflict rather than on institutional and cultural analyses of gender and power (Messner, 1998). Second, emphasis on separate masculine and feminine gender role ideologies can inadvertently support the exaggeration of differences between men's and women's role-related conflicts. Third, although discussions of gender roles and gender role conflict help explain how roles are reinforced and reproduced, they do not provide insights about large-scale social change. Messner argued that an emphasis on individual gender roles alone "implies a false symmetry between the male role and the female role, thus masking the oppressive relationship between women and men" (p. 258). These concerns point to the importance of integrating the increasing literature on gender role and gender role conflict within more complex models that attend to social-contextual factors and that suggest road maps for social change.

Theoretical and Research Perspectives on Nonsexist and Feminist Interventions

Feminist and nonsexist therapy approaches are supported by diverse theoretical traditions that are influenced by liberal, radical, socialist, cultural, women of color, lesbian, and postmodern feminisms (Enns, 1997; Walsh, 1997). The relationships between these theories and the practice of counseling need further examination. In the past, a variety of analogue studies have examined reactions of individuals to radical feminist, liberal feminist, and nonsexist approaches (Enns & Hackett, 1990, 1993; Hackett, Enns, & Zetzer, 1992; Hackett et al., 1996). In general, feminist respondents, including male participants with profeminist values (Enns & Hackett, 1993), have shown more positive reactions to counselors in general than individuals who do not endorse feminist values. Research participants have accurately labeled feminist approaches as feminist and have expressed positive attitudes toward feminist therapists. Respondents have also rated liberal and radical feminist counselors as emphasizing similar goals, but have viewed radical feminist therapists as communicating these goals more strongly than liberal feminist therapists (Enns, 1997). The findings of these analogue studies need to be examined through psychotherapy process studies with greater ecological validity.

Although feminist and nonsexist therapies have gained increasing visibility and acceptance in recent years, there have been virtually no efforts to study key features of these therapies within actual psychotherapy relationships. Exploration of the counseling processes and outcomes associated with specific techniques such as self-disclosure, gender role analysis, and power analysis is important. See Enns (1993) for additional commentary about process research on feminist therapy.

As noted in the section on assessment, bias in diagnosis remains an important counseling issue. In recent years, researchers have attempted to study the problems and symptoms of individuals from a strength rather than a deficit perspective. For example, Morrow and Smith's (1995) study of sexual abuse survivors' coping and survival skills contributes to a deepened understanding of survivors as strong and resilient individuals rather than as individuals with pathologies. Conceptual models built on studies such as this hold much more promise than do traditional diagnostic systems for supporting feminist and gender aware therapy.

Recent studies have focused on examining the attitudes, values, and theoretical diversity of actual feminist therapists (Beardsley et al., 1998; Hill & Ballou, 1998; Juntunen, Atkinson, Reyes, & Gutierrez, 1994; Marecek & Kravetz, 1998a, 1998b). These efforts have been facilitated by the creation of instruments that are designed to measure feminist identity development (Bargrad & Hyde, 1991; Rickard, 1987), agreement with different theories of feminism (e.g., Henley, Meng, O'Brien, McCarthy, & Sockloskie, 1998), and feminist therapy principles (e.g., Beardsley et al., 1998). Efforts to examine the diversity of masculinity ideologies are also emerging and will be important for supporting the study of masculinities (e.g., Fischer & Good, 1997). Given the diversity of feminist thought and masculinity ideologies, it will be increasingly important for researchers and counselors to (1) clarify their theoretical assumptions, (2) examine the relationship between theoretical/political traditions and nonsexist/feminist practice, and (3) explore the degree to which the espoused theoretical perspectives of therapists are consistent with actual practice.

CONCLUDING THOUGHTS

Betz and Fitzgerald's (1993) review of current developments in counseling psychology concluded that the study of gender and its implications for counseling "may well be the fastest-growing area within counseling psychology today" (p. 346). This review has highlighted a small portion of the recent scholarship on gender as it relates to the Division 17 Principles. Perhaps the most significant change since the original publication of these principles 20 years ago is counseling psychologists' recognition of the diversity of gender effects and the highly complex manner in which gender intersects with other important aspects of identity. Weber (1998) suggested that central to understanding race, class, gender, and sexuality in an integrated framework is recognizing the common features of these constructs. All four constructs (gender, sexuality, race, and class) are socially constructed, embedded in complex systems of power relationships, manifest themselves at both social structural and social psychological levels, are expressed simultaneously, and have important implications for activism. In keeping with the characteristics of these commonalities, it is important for counselors to avoid simplistic generalizations about gender and to remain attentive to the diversity of gender effects within the complicated world of counseling.

REFERENCES

Adams, E.M., & Betz, N.E. (1993). Gender differences in counselors' attitudes toward and attributions about incest. *Journal of Counseling Psychology, 40,* 210–216.

American Psychiatric Association. (1987). *Diagnostic and statistical manual of mental disorders* (3rd ed., rev.). Washington, DC: Author.

American Psychiatric Association. (1994). *Diagnostic and statistical manual of mental disorders* (4th ed.). Washington, DC: Author.

American Psychological Association. (1979). Principles concerning the counseling and psychotherapy of women. *Counseling Psychologist, 8,* 21.

American Psychological Association. (1996). *American Psychological Association Presidential Task Force on Violence and the Family: Final report.* Washington, DC: Author.

Andronico, M.P. (Ed.). (1996). *Men in groups.* Washington, DC: American Psychological Association.

Badura, A.S., & Stone, G.L. (1998). Factors influencing counseling center staff's perceptions of treatment difficulty in relation to student child sexual abuse. *Journal of College Student Psychotherapy, 13*(1), 15–38.

Bargrad, A., & Hyde, J.S. (1991). A study of feminist identity development in women. *Psychology of Women Quarterly, 15,* 181–201.

Barnett, R.C., & Rivers, C. (1996). *She works/he works: How two-income families are happier, healthier, and better off.* New York: HarperCollins.

Beardsley, B., Morrow, S.L., Castillo, L., & Weitzman, L. (1998, March). *Perceptions and behaviors of practicing feminist therapists: Development of the feminist multicultural practice instrument.* Paper presented at the 23rd annual conference of the Association for Women in Psychology, Baltimore.

Becker, D., & Lamb, S. (1994). Sex bias in the diagnosis of borderline personality disorder and posttraumatic stress disorder. *Professional Psychology, 25,* 55–61.

Bem, S.L. (1993). *The lenses of gender: Transforming the debate on sexual inequality.* New Haven, CT: Yale University Press.

Beren, S.E., Hayden, H.A., Wilfley, D.E., & Grilo, C.M. (1996). The influence of sexual orientation on body dissatisfaction in adult men and women. *International Journal of Eating Disorders, 20,* 135–141.

Beren, S.E., Hayden, H.A., Wilfley, D.E., & Striegel-Moore, R.H. (1997). Body dissatisfaction among lesbian college students: The conflict of straddling mainstream and lesbian cultures. *Psychology of Women Quarterly, 21,* 431–445.

Bergeron, S.M., & Senn, C.Y. (1998). Body image and sociocultural norms. *Psychology of Women Quarterly, 22,* 385–401.

Betz, N.E., & Fitzgerald, L.F. (1993). Individuality and diversity: Theory and research in counseling psychology. *Annual Review of Psychology, 44,* 343–381.

Brooks, G.R. (1990). The inexpressive male and vulnerability to therapist-patient sexual exploitation. *Psychotherapy: Theory, Research, and Practice, 27,* 344–349.

Brooks, G.R., & Silverstein, L.B. (1995). Understanding the dark side of masculinity: An interactive systems model. In R.F. Levant & W.S. Pollack (Eds.), *A new psychology of men* (pp. 280–333). New York: Basic Books.

Brooks, L., & Forrest, L. (1994). Feminism and career counseling. In W.B. Walsh & S.H. Osipow (Eds.), *Career counseling for women* (pp. 87–134). Hillsdale, NJ: Erlbaum.

Brooks, V.R. (1981). Sex and sexual orientation as variables in therapists' biases and therapy outcomes. *Clinical Social Work Journal, 9,* 198–210.

Broverman, I.K., Broverman, D.M., Clarkson, F., Rosenkrantz, P., & Vogel, S. (1970). Sex-role stereotyping and clinical judgments of mental health. *Journal of Consulting and Clinical Psychology, 34,* 250–256.

Brown, L.S. (1986). Gender-role analysis: A neglected component of psychological assessment. *Psychotherapy: Theory, Research, and Practice, 23,* 243–248.

Brown, L.S. (1990). Taking account of gender in the clinical assessment interview. *Professional Psychology: Research and Practice, 21,* 12–17.

Brown, L.S. (1991). Ethical issues in feminist therapy: Selected topics. *Psychology of Women Quarterly, 15,* 323–336.

Brown, L.S. (1993). Antidomination training as a central component of diversity in clinical psychology education. *Clinical Psychologist, 46,* 83–87.

Brown, L.S. (1994). *Subversive dialogues.* New York: Basic Books.

Brown, L.S. (1996). *Feminist therapy* [Videotape]. (Available from American Psychological Association, 750 First Street, NE, Washington, DC 20002)

Brown, L.S., & Brodsky, A.M. (1992). The future of feminist therapy. *Psychotherapy, 29,* 51–57.

Browne, A., & Finkelhor, D. (1986). The impact of child sexual abuse: A review of the research. *Psychological Bulletin, 99,* 66–77.

Browning, C., Reynolds, A.L., & Dworkin, S.H. (1991). Affirmative psychotherapy for lesbian women. *Counseling Psychologist, 19,* 177–196.

Bryer, J.B., Nelson, B.A., Miller, J.B., & Krol, P.A. (1987). Childhood sexual and physical abuse as factors in adult psychiatric illness. *American Journal of Psychiatry, 144,* 1426–1430.

Campbell, B., Schellenberg, E.G., & Senn, C.Y. (1997). Evaluating measures of contemporary sexism. *Psychology of Women Quarterly, 21,* 89–102.

Caplan, P.J. (1995). *They say you're crazy.* Reading MA: Addison-Wesley.

Carmen, E.H., Rieker, P.P., & Mills, T. (1984). Victims of violence and psychiatric illness. *American Journal of Psychiatry, 141,* 378–383.

Carter, R.T., & Parks, E.E. (1996). Womanist identity and mental health. *Journal of Counseling and Development, 74,* 484–489.

Cash, T.F., Ancis, J.R., & Strachan, M.D. (1997). Gender attitudes, feminist identity, and body images among college women. *Sex Roles, 36,* 433–447.

Chernin, J., Holden, J.M., & Chandler, C. (1997). Bias in psychological assessment: Heterosexism. *Measurement and Evaluation in Counseling and Development, 30,* 68–76.

Chesler, P. (1972). *Women and madness.* New York: Doubleday.

Chesler, P. (1997, Nov./Dec.). Women and madness: A feminist diagnosis. *Ms., 8*(3), 36–41.

Collier, H.V. (1982). *Counseling women.* New York: Free Press.

Comas-Diaz, L., & Greene, B. (Eds.). (1994). *Women of color: Integrating ethnic and gender identities in psychotherapy.* New York: Guilford Press.

Committee on Lesbian and Gay Concerns. (1991). Avoiding heterosexual bias in language. *American Psychologist, 46,* 973–974.

Committee on Women in Psychology. (1989). If sex enters into the psychotherapy relationship. *Professional Psychology: Research and Practice, 20,* 112–115.

Corey, G. (in press). *Theory and practice of counseling and psychotherapy* (6th ed.). Pacific Grove, CA: Brooks/Cole.

Coster, J.S., & Schwebel, M. (1997). Well-functioning in professional psychologists. *Professional Psychology: Research and Practice, 28,* 5–13.

Cournoyer, R.J., & Mahalik, J.R. (1995). Cross-sectional study of gender role conflict examining college-aged and middle-aged men. *Journal of Counseling Psychology, 42,* 11–19.

Courtney, A.E., & Lockeretz, S.W. (1971). A woman's place: An analysis of the roles portrayed by women in magazine advertisements. *Journal of Marketing Research, 8,* 92–95.

Courtois, C.A. (1997). Guidelines for the treatment of adults abused or possibly abused as children with attention to issues of delayed/recovered memory. *American Journal of Psychotherapy, 51,* 497–510.

Crawford, M. (1995). *Talking difference: On gender and language.* Newbury Park, CA: Sage.

Crawford, M., & English, L. (1984). Generic versus specific inclusion of women in language: Effects on recall. *Journal of Psycholinguistic Research, 13,* 373–381.

Cross, W. (1991). *Shades of black: Diversity in African-American identity.* Philadelphia: Temple University Press.

Deaux, K., & LaFrance, M. (1998). Gender. In D. Gilbert, S. Fiske, & G. Lindzey (Eds.), *Handbook of social psychology.* New York: McGraw-Hill.

Deaux, K., & Major, B. (1987). Putting gender into context: An interactive model of gender-related behavior. *Psychological Review, 94,* 369–389.

DeBarona, M.S., & Dutton, M.A. (1997). Feminist perspectives on assessment. In J. Worell & N.G. Johnson (Eds.), *Shaping the future of feminist psychology* (pp. 37–56). Washington, DC: American Psychological Association.

Demo, D.H., & Allen, K.R. (1996). Diversity within lesbian and gay families: Challenges and implications for family theory and research. *Journal of Social and Personal Relationships, 13,* 415–434.

Doss, B.D., & Hopkins, J.R. (1998). The multicultural masculinity ideology scale: Validation from three cultural perspectives. *Sex Roles, 38,* 719–741.

Dovidio, J.F., & Gaertner, S.L. (1996). Affirmative action, unintentional racial biases, and intergroup relations. *Journal of Social Issues, 52,* 51–75.

Downing, N.E., & Roush, K.L. (1985). From passive acceptance to active commitment: A model of feminist identity development for women. *Counseling Psychologist, 13,* 695–709.

Durana, C. (1998). The use of touch in psychotherapy: Ethical and clinical guidelines. *Psychotherapy, 35,* 269–280.

Eagly, A.H. (1995). The science and politics of comparing women and men. *American Psychologist, 50,* 145–158.

Edwards, C.E., & Murdock, N.L. (1994). Characteristics of therapist self-disclosure in the counseling process. *Journal of Counseling and Development, 72,* 384–389.

Elliott, D.M., & Guy, J.D. (1993). Mental health professionals versus non-mental-health professionals: Childhood trauma and adult functioning. *Professional Psychology: Research and Practice, 24,* 83–90.

Enns, C.Z. (1993). Twenty years of feminist counseling and therapy: From naming biases to implementing multifaceted practice. *Counseling Psychologist, 21,* 3–87.

Enns, C.Z. (1996). Counselors and the backlash: "Rape hype" and "false memory syndrome." *Journal of Counseling and Development, 74,* 358–367.

Enns, C.Z. (1997). *Feminist theories and feminist psychotherapies: Origins, themes, and variations.* New York: Haworth Press.

Enns, C.Z., & Hackett, G. (1990). Comparisons of feminist and nonfeminist women's reactions to variants of nonsexist and feminist counseling. *Journal of Counseling Psychology, 37,* 33–40.

Enns, C.Z., & Hackett, G. (1993). A comparison of feminist and nonfeminist women's and men's reactions to nonsexist and feminist counseling: A replication and extension. *Journal of Counseling and Development, 71,* 499–509.

Espin, O. (1995). On knowing you are the unknown: Women of color constructing psychology. In J. Adleman & G. Enguidanos (Eds.), *Racism in the lives of women: Testimony, theory and guides to practice* (pp. 127–136). New York: Harrington Park Press.

False Memory Syndrome Foundation. (1992). *False memory syndrome* [Brochure]. Philadelphia: Author.

Fassinger, R.E. (1991). The hidden minority: Issues and challenges in working with lesbian women and gay men. *Counseling Psychologist, 19,* 157–176.

Feminist Therapy Institute. (1990). Feminist Therapy Institute code of ethics. In H. Lerman & N. Porter (Eds.), *Feminist ethics in psychotherapy* (pp. 37–40). New York: Springer.

Figert, A.E. (1996). *Women and the ownership of PMS: The structuring of a psychiatric disorder.* New York: Aldine De Gruyter.

Finkelhor, D., Hotaling, G., Lewis, I.A., & Smith, C. (1990). Sexual abuse in a national survey of adult men and women: Prevalence, characteristics, and risk factors. *Child Abuse and Neglect, 14,* 19–28.

Fischer, A.R., & Good, G.E. (1994). Gender, self, and others: Perceptions of the campus environment. *Journal of Counseling Psychology, 41,* 343–355.

Fischer, A.R., & Good, G.E. (1997). Men and psychotherapy: An investigation of alexithymia, intimacy, and masculine gender roles. *Psychotherapy, 34,* 160–170.

Fitzgerald, L.F., & Nutt, R. (1986). The Division 17 Principles concerning the counseling/psychotherapy of women: Rationale and implementation. *Counseling Psychologist, 14,* 180–216.

Foa, E.D., & Riggs, D.S. (1995). Posttraumatic stress disorder following assault: Theoretical considerations and empirical findings. *Current Directions in Psychological Science, 4,* 61–65.

Follette, V.M., Polusny, M.A., & Milbeck, K. (1994). Mental health and law enforcement professionals: Trauma history, psychological symptoms, and impact of providing services to child sexual abuse survivors. *Professional Psychology, 25,* 275–282.

Franks, V., & Rothblum, E.D. (Eds.). (1983). *The stereotyping of women.* New York: Springer.

Fredrickson, B.L., & Roberts, T.A. (1997). Objectification theory: Toward understanding women's lived experiences and mental health risks. *Psychology of Women Quarterly, 21,* 173–206.

Fredrickson, B.L., Roberts, T.A., Noll, S.M., Quinn, D.M., & Twenge, J.M. (1998). That swimsuit becomes you: Sex differences in self-objectification, restrained eating, and math performance. *Journal of Personality and Social Psychology, 75,* 269–284.

Ganley, A.L. (1988). Feminist therapy with male clients. In M.A. Dutton-Douglas & L.E. Walker (Eds.), *Feminist psychotherapies: Integration of therapeutic and feminist systems* (pp. 186–205). Norwood, NJ: ABLEX.

Garnets, L., Hancock, K.A., Cochran, S.D., Goodchilds, J., & Peplau, L.A. (1991). Issues in psychotherapy with lesbians and gay men: A survey of psychologists. *American Psychologist, 46,* 964–972.

Gauthier, L.M., & Levendosky, A.A. (1996). Assessment and treatment of couples with abusive male partners: Guidelines for therapists. *Psychotherapy, 33,* 403–417.

Gelso, C.J., Fassinger, R.E., Gomez, M.J., & Latts, M.G. (1995). Countertransference reactions to lesbian clients: The role of homophobia, counselor gender, and countertransference management. *Journal of Counseling Psychology, 42,* 356–364.

Gerstmann, E.Z., & Kramer, D.A. (1997). Feminist identity development: Psychometric analyses of two feminist identity scales. *Sex Roles, 36,* 327–348.

Gettelman, T.E., & Thompson, J.K. (1993). Actual differences and stereotypical perceptions in body image and eating disturbance: A comparison of male and female heterosexual and homosexual samples. *Sex Roles, 29,* 545–562.

Gilbert, L.A. (1992). Gender and counseling psychology: Current knowledge and directions for research and social action. In S.D. Brown & R.W. Lent (Eds.), *Handbook of counseling psychology* (pp. 383–416). New York: Wiley.

Gilbert, L.A., & Scher, M. (1999). *Gender and sex in counseling and psychotherapy.* Boston: Allyn & Bacon.

Gilligan, C. (1982. *In a different voice.* Cambridge, MA: Harvard University Press.

Gleick, E. (1997). Tower of psychobabble. *Time, 149,* 69–70, 72.

Glick, P., & Fiske, S.T. (1996). The ambivalent sexism inventory: Differentiating hostile and benevolent sexism. *Journal of Personality and Social Psychology, 70,* 491–512.

Glick, P., & Fiske, S.T. (1997). Hostile and benevolent sexism: Measuring ambivalent sexist attitudes toward women. *Psychology of Women Quarterly, 21,* 119–136.

Good, G.E., Dell, D.M., & Mintz, L.B. (1989). Male role and gender role conflict: Relations to help seeking in men. *Journal of Counseling Psychology, 36,* 295–300.

Good, G.E., Gilbert, L., & Scher, M. (1990). Gender aware therapy: A synthesis of feminist therapy and knowledge about gender. *Journal of Counseling and Development, 68,* 376–380.

Good, G., & Mintz, L.B. (1990). Depression and gender role conflict. *Journal of Counseling and Development, 69,* 17–21.

Good, G.E., Robertson, J.M., O'Neil, J.M., Fitzgerald, L.F., Stevens, M., DeBoard, K.A., Bartels, K.M., & Braverman, D.G. (1995). Male gender role conflict: Psychometric issues and relations to psychological distress. *Journal of Counseling Psychology, 42,* 3–10.

Good, G.E., Wallace, D.L., & Borst, T.S. (1994). Masculinity research: A review and critique. *Applied and Preventive Psychology, 3,* 3–14.

Good, G.E., & Wood, P.K. (1995). Male gender role conflict, depression, and help seeking: Do college men face double jeopardy? *Journal of Counseling and Development, 74,* 70–75.

Goodman, L.A., Koss, J.P., & Russo, N.F. (1993). Violence against women: Physical and mental health effects. Part 1: Research findings. *Applied and Preventive Psychology, 2,* 79–89.

Gray, J. (1992). *Men are from Mars, women are from Venus.* New York: HarperCollins.

Greene, B., & Sanchez-Hucles, J. (1997). Diversity: Advancing an inclusive feminist psychology. In J. Worell & N.G. Johnson (Eds.), *Shaping the future of feminist psychology* (pp. 173–202). Washington, DC: American Psychological Association.

Hackett, G., Enns, C.Z., & Zetzer, H.A. (1992). Reactions of women to nonsexist and feminist counseling: Effects of counselor orientation and mode of information delivery. *Journal of Counseling Psychology, 39,* 321–330.

Hackett, G., & Lonborg, S.D. (1994). Career assessment and counseling for women. In W.B. Walsh & S.H. Osipow (Eds.), *Career counseling for women* (pp. 43–85). Hillsdale, NJ: Erlbaum.

Hackett, G., Morrow, S.L., Forrest, L.U., McWhirter, E., Olson, C., & Polansky, J. (1996, August). *The influence of feminist counseling and counselor directiveness of perceptions of counselors.* Paper presented at the 104th annual convention of the American Psychological Association, Toronto, CA.

Hall, J.A., & Halberstadt, A.G. (1997). Subordination and nonverbal sensitivity: A hypothesis in search of support. In M.R. Walsh (Ed.), *Women, men, and gender: Ongoing debates* (pp. 120–133). New Haven, CT: Yale University Press.

Hare-Mustin, R.T., & Marecek, J. (1988). The meaning of difference: Gender theory, postmodernism, and psychology. *American Psychologist, 43,* 445–464.

Harris, S.M. (1995). Family, self, and sociocultural contributions to body-image attitudes of African-American women. *Psychology of Women Quarterly, 19,* 129–145.

Hartung, C.M., & Widiger, T.A. (1998). Gender differences in the diagnosis of mental disorders: Conclusions and controversies of the *DSM-IV. Psychological Bulletin, 123,* 260–278.

Harway, M., & Evans, K. (1996). Working in groups with men who batter. In M. Andronico (Ed.), *Men in groups: Insights, interventions, and psychoeducational work* (pp. 357–375). Washington, DC: American Psychological Association.

Harway, M., & Hansen, M. (1993). Therapist perceptions of family violence. In M. Hansen & M. Harway (Eds.), *Battering and family therapy: A feminist perspective* (pp. 1–12). Newbury Park, CA: Sage.

Hayes, J., & Gelso, C.J. (1993). Male counselors' discomfort with gay and HIV-infected clients. *Journal of Counseling Psychology, 40,* 86–93.

Helms, J.E. (1990). *"Womanist" identity attitudes: An alternative to feminism in counseling theory and research.* Unpublished manuscript.

Henderson-King, D., & Stewart, A.J. (1997). Feminist consciousness: Perspectives on women's experience. *Personality and Social Psychology Bulletin, 23,* 415–426.

Henley, N.M. (1989). Molehill or mountain? What we do know and don't know about sex bias in language. In M. Crawford & M. Gentry (Eds.), *Gender and thought* (pp. 59–78). New York: Springer-Verlag.

Henley, N.M., Meng, K., O'Brien, D., McCarthy, W.J., & Sockloskie, R.J. (1998). Developing a scale to measure the diversity of feminist attitudes. *Psychology of Women Quarterly, 22,* 317–348.

Heppner, P.P. (1995). On gender role conflict in men—future directions and implications for counseling: Comment on Good et al. (1995) and Cournoyer and Mahalik (1995). *Journal of Counseling Psychology, 42,* 11–19.

Herman, J.L. (1992). *Trauma and Recovery.* New York: Basic Books.

Herz, D.E., & Wootton, B.H. (1996). Women in the workforce: An overview. In C. Costello & B.K. Krimgold (Eds.), *The American woman: 1996–97* (pp. 44–78). New York: Norton.

Herzog, D.B., Newman, K.L., Yeh, C.J., & Warshaw, M. (1992). Body image satisfaction in homosexual and heterosexual women. *International Journal of Eating Disorders, 11*, 391–396.

Hill, M., & Ballou, M. (1998). Making therapy feminist: A practice survey. *Women and Therapy, 21*(2), 1–16.

Holroyd, J.C. (1983). Erotic contact as an instance of sex-biased therapy. In J. Murray & P.R. Abramson (Eds.), *Bias in psychotherapy* (pp. 285–308). New York: Praeger.

Horton, J.A., Clance, P.R., Sterk-Elifson, C., & Emshoff, J. (1995). Touch in psychotherapy: A survey of patients' experiences. *Psychotherapy, 32*, 443–457.

Hyde, J.S. (1996). *Half the human experience: The psychology of women* (5th ed.). Lexington, MA: Heath.

Island, D., & Letellier, P. (1991). *Men who beat the men who love them: Battered gay men and domestic violence.* New York: Hawthorne.

Jackson, H., & Nuttall, R. (1993). Clinician responses to sexual abuse allegations. *Child Abuse and Neglect, 17*, 127–143.

Jacobson, A. (1989). Physical and sexual assault histories among psychiatric outpatients. *American Journal of Psychiatry, 146*, 755–758.

Jacobson, N.S., & Gottman, J.M. (1998). *When men batter women.* New York Simon & Schuster.

Joiner, G.W., & Kashubeck, S. (1996). Acculturation, body image, self-esteem, and eating-disorder symptomatology in adolescent Mexican American women. *Psychology of Women Quarterly, 20*, 419–435.

Jordan, J.V., Kaplan, A.G., Miller, J.B., Stiver, I.P., & Surrey, J.L. (Eds.). (1991). *Women's growth in connection.* New York: Guilford Press.

Juntunen, C.L., Atkinson, D.R., Reyes, C., & Gutierrez, M. (1994). Feminist identity and feminist therapy behaviors of women psychotherapists. *Psychotherapy, 31*, 327–333.

Kanuha, V. (1990). Compounding the triple jeopardy: Battering in lesbian of color relationships. *Women and Therapy, 9*(1/2), 169–184.

Kaplan, M. (1983). A woman's view of *DSM-III. American Psychologist, 38*, 786–792.

Kertay, L., & Reviere, S.L. (1993). The use of touch in psychotherapy: Theoretical and ethical considerations. *Psychotherapy, 30*, 32–40.

Knox, S., Hess, S.A., Petersen, D.Z., & Hill, C.E. (1997). A qualitative analysis of client perceptions of the effects of helpful therapist self-disclosure in long-term therapy. *Journal of Counseling Psychology, 44*, 274–283.

Koss, M.P. (1993). Rape: Scope, impact, interventions, and public policy responses. *American Psychologist, 48*, 1062–1069.

Koss, M.P., Goodman, L.A., Browne, A., Fitzgerald, L.F., Keita, G.P., & Russo, N.F. (1994). *No safe haven.* Washington, DC: American Psychological Association.

Kroll, J.K. (1988). *The challenge of the borderline patient: Competency in diagnosis and treatment.* New York: Norton.

Kupers, T.A. (1993). *Revisioning men's lives: Gender, intimacy, and power.* New York: Guilford Press.

Kupers, T.A. (1997). The politics of psychiatry: Gender and sexual preference in *DSM-IV.* In M.R. Walsh (Ed.), *Women, men, and gender: Ongoing debates* (pp. 340–347). New Haven, CT: Yale University Press.

LaFrance, M., & Henley, N.M. (1997). On oppressing hypotheses: Or, differences in nonverbal sensitivity revisited. In M.R. Walsh (Ed.), *Women, men, and gender: Ongoing debates* (pp. 104–119). New Haven, CT: Yale University Press.

Laird, J., & Green, R. (Eds.). (1996). *Lesbians and gays in couples and families.* San Francisco: Jossey-Bass.

Landrine, H. (1989). The politics of personality disorder. *Psychology of Women Quarterly, 13*, 325–339.

Lerman, H. (1986). *A mote in Freud's eye.* New York: Springer.

Leslie, D., & MacNeill, L. (1995). Double positive: Lesbians and race. In J. Adleman & G. Enguidanos (Eds.), *Racism in the lives of women: Testimony, theory, and guides to antiracist practice* (pp. 161–169). New York: Haworth Press.

Letellier, P. (1994). Gay and bisexual male domestic violence victimization: Challenges to feminist theory and responses to violence. *Violence and Victims, 9*, 95–105.

Levant, R.F. (1995). The new psychology of men. *Professional Psychology: Research and Practice, 27*, 259–265.

Levant, R.F., & Pollack, W.S. (Eds.). (1995). *The new psychology of men.* New York: Basic Books.

Liddle, B.J. (1996). Therapist sexual orientation, gender, and counseling practices as they relate to ratings of helpfulness by gay and lesbian clients. *Journal of Counseling Psychology, 43*, 394–401.

Little, L., & Hamby, S.L. (1996). Impact of a clinician's sexual abuse history, gender, and theoretical orientation on treatment issues related to childhood sexual abuse. *Professional Psychology: Research and Practice, 27,* 617–625.

MacKay, D.G. (1980). Language, thought and social attitudes. In H. Giles, W.P. Robinson, & P.M. Smith (Eds.), *Language: Social psychological perspectives* (pp. 89–96). Oxford, England: Pergamon Press.

MacKay, N.J., & Covell, K. (1997). The impact of women in advertisements on attitudes toward women. *Sex Roles, 36,* 573–583.

Mahalik, J.R., Cournoyer, R.J., DeFranc, W., Cherry, M., & Napolitano, J.M. (1998). Men's gender role conflict and use of psychological defenses. *Journal of Counseling Psychology, 45,* 247–255.

Mahoney, M.J. (1997). Psychotherapists' personal problems and self-care patterns. *Professional Psychology, 28,* 14–16.

Major, B. (1993). Gender, entitlement, and the distribution of family labor. *Journal of Social Issues, 49,* 141–159.

Marecek, J. (1995). Gender, politics, and psychology's ways of knowing. *American Psychologist, 50,* 162–163.

Marecek, J. (1997). Feminist psychology at thirty something: Feminism, gender, and psychology's ways of knowing. In D. Looser & A. Kaplan (Eds.), *Generations: Academic feminists in dialogue* (pp. 132–150). Minneapolis: University of Minnesota Press.

Marecek, J., & Kravetz, D. (1998a). Power and agency in feminist therapy. In I.B. Seu & C. Heenan (Eds.), *Feminism and Psychotherapy* (pp. 13–29). London: Sage.

Marecek, J., & Kravetz, D. (1998b). Putting politics into practice: Feminist therapy as feminist praxis. *Women and Therapy, 21*(2), 17–36.

Matlin, M.W. (1996). *The psychology of women* (3rd ed.). Fort Worth, TX: Harcourt Brace.

McCauley, J., Kern, D.E., Kolodner, K., Dill, L., Schroeder, A.F., DeChant, H.K., Ryden, J., Derogatis, L.R., & Bass, E.B. (1997). Clinical characteristics of women with a history of childhood abuse: Unhealed wounds. *Journal of the American Medical Association, 277,* 1362–1368.

McCreary, D.R., Newcomb, M.D., & Sadava, S.W. (1998). Dimensions of the male gender role: A confirmatory analysis in men and women. *Sex Roles, 39,* 81–95.

McGrath, E., Keita, G.P., Strickland, B.R., & Russo, N.F. (Eds.). (1990). *Women and depression.* Washington, DC: American Psychological Association.

McIntosh, P. (1989, July/August). White privilege: Unpacking the invisible knapsack. *Peace and Freedom,* 10–12.

McKinley, N.M., & Hyde, J.S. (1996). The objectified body consciousness scale. *Psychology of Women Quarterly, 20,* 181–215.

McNamara, K., & Rickard, K.M. (1989). Feminist identity development: Implications for feminist therapy with women. *Journal of Counseling and Development, 68,* 184–189.

Messner, M.A. (1998). The limits of "the male sex role": An analysis of the men's liberation and men's rights movements' discourse. *Gender and Society, 12,* 255–276.

Morawski, J.G. (1987). The troubled quest for masculinity, femininity, and androgyny. In P. Shaver & C. Hendrick (Eds.), *Sex and gender* (pp. 44–69). Newbury Park, CA: Sage.

Morrow, S.L., & Hawxhurst, D.M. (1998). Feminist therapy: Integrating political analysis in counseling and psychotherapy. *Women and Therapy, 21,* 37–50.

Morrow, S.L., & Smith, M.L. (1995). Constructions of survival and coping by women who have survived childhood sexual abuse. *Journal of Counseling Psychology, 42,* 24–33.

Morton, S.B. (1998). Lesbian divorce. *American Journal of Orthopsychiatry, 68,* 410–419.

Nash, H.C., & Chrisler, J.C. (1997). Is a little (psychiatric) knowledge a dangerous thing? The impact of premenstrual dysphoric disorder on perceptions of premenstrual women. *Psychology of Women Quarterly, 21,* 315–322.

Nelson, M.L. (1993). A current perspective on gender differences: Implications for research in counseling. *Journal of Counseling Psychology, 40,* 200–209.

Nolen-Hoeksema, S. (1998). *Abnormal Psychology.* Boston: McGraw-Hill.

Noll, S.M., & Fredrickson, B.L. (1998). A mediational model linking self-objectification, body shame, and disordered eating. *Psychology of Women Quarterly, 22,* 623–636.

Nuttall, R., & Jackson, H. (1994). Personal history of childhood abuse among clinicians. *Child Abuse and Neglect, 18,* 455–472.

O'Neil, J.M. (1981). Patterns of gender role conflict and strain: Sexism and fear of femininity in men's lives. *Personnel and Guidance Journal, 60,* 203–210.

O'Neil, J.M. (1990). Assessing men's gender role conflict. In D. Moore & F. Leafgren (Eds.), *Men in conflict: Problem solving strategies and interventions.* Alexandria, VA: Association for Counseling and Development Press.

O'Neil, J.M., & Carroll, M.R. (1988). A gender role workshop focused on sexism, gender role conflict, and the gender role journey. *Journal of Counseling and Development, 67,* 193–197.

O'Neil, J.M., & Egan, J. (1992). Men's and women's gender role journeys: A metaphor for healing, transition, and transformation. In B. Wainrib (Ed.), *Gender issues across the life cycle.* New York: Springer.

O'Neil, J.M., & Egan, J. (1993). Abuses of power against women: Sexism, gender role conflict, and psychological violence. In E.P. Cook (Ed.), *Women, relationships, and power: Implications for counseling.* Alexandria, VA: American Counseling Association.

O'Neil, J.M., Egan, J., Owen, S.V., & Murry, V.M. (1993). The gender role journey measure: Scale development and psychometric evaluation. *Sex Roles, 28,* 167–185.

Ossana, S.M., Helms, J.E., & Leonard, M.M. (1992). Do "womanist" identity attitudes influence college women's self-esteem and perceptions of environmental bias? *Journal of Counseling and Development, 70,* 402–408.

Parks, C.A. (1998). Lesbian parenthood: A review of the literature. *American Journal of Orthopsychiatry, 68,* 376–389.

Parks, E.E., Carter, R.T., & Gushue, G.V. (1996). At the crossroads: Racial and womanist identity development in black and white women. *Journal of Counseling and Development, 74,* 624–631.

Parsons, J.P., & Wincze, J.P. (1995). A survey of client-therapist involvement in Rhode Island as reported by subsequent treating therapists. *Professional Psychology: Research and Practice, 26,* 171–175.

Patterson, C.J., & Redding, R.E. (1996). Lesbian and gay families with children: Implications of social science research for policy. *Journal of Social Issues, 52,* 29–50.

Pearlman, L.A., & MacIan, P.S. (1995). Vicarious traumatization: An empirical study of the effects of trauma work on trauma therapists. *Professional Psychology, 26,* 558–565.

Pearlman, L.A., & Saakvitne, K.W. (1995). *Trauma and the therapist.* New York: Norton.

Phelps, A., Friedlander, M.L., & Enns, C.Z. (1997). Psychotherapy process variables associated with the retrieval of memories of childhood sexual abuse: A qualitative study. *Journal of Counseling Psychology, 44,* 321–332.

Phillips, J.C., & Fischer, A.R. (1998). Graduate students' training experiences with lesbian, gay, and bisexual issues. *Counseling Psychologist, 26,* 712–734.

Philpot, C.L., Brooks, G.R., Lusterman, D.D., & Nutt, R.L. (1997). *Bridging separate gender worlds: Why men and women clash and how therapists can bring them together.* Washington, DC: American Psychological Association.

Pikus, C.F., & Heavey, C.L. (1996). Client preferences for therapist gender. *Journal of College Student Psychotherapy, 10*(4), 35–43.

Pleck, J.H. (1981). *The myth of masculinity.* Cambridge, MA: MIT Press.

Pleck, J.H. (1995). The gender role strain paradigm: An update. In R.F. Levant & W.S. Pollack (Eds.), *A new psychology of men* (pp. 11–32). New York: Basic Books.

Plous, S., & Neptune, D. (1997). Racial and gender biases in magazine advertising: A content-analytic study. *Psychology of Women Quarterly, 21,* 627–644.

Pollack, W.S. (1995). No man is an island: Toward a new psychoanalytic psychology of men. In R.F. Levant & W.S. Pollack (Eds.), *A new psychology of men* (pp. 33–67). New York: Basic Books.

Polusny, M.A., & Follette, V.M. (1996). Remembering childhood sexual abuse: A national survey of psychologists' clinical practices, beliefs, and personal experiences. *Professional Psychology: Research and Practice, 27,* 41–52.

Pope, K.S. (1994). *Sexual involvement with therapists: Patient assessment, subsequent therapy, forensics.* Washington, DC: American Psychological Association.

Pope, K.S., & Feldman-Summers, S. (1992). National survey of psychologists' sexual and physical abuse history and their evaluation of training and competence in these areas. *Professional Psychology: Research and Practice, 23,* 353–361.

Pope, K.S., Sonne, J.L., & Holroyd, J. (1993). *Sexual feelings in psychotherapy: Explorations for therapists and therapists-in-training.* Washington, DC: American Psychological Association.

Pope, K.S., & Tabachnick, B.G. (1994). Therapists as patients: A national survey of psychologists' experiences, problems, and beliefs. *Professional Psychology: Research and Practice, 25,* 247–258.

Pope, K.S., & Vasquez, M.J.T. (1998). *Ethics in psychotherapy and counseling* (2nd ed.). San Francisco: Jossey-Bass.

Pope, K.S., & Vetter, V.A. (1991). Prior therapist-patient sexual involvement among patients seen by psychologists. *Psychotherapy: Theory, Research, and Practice, 28,* 429–438.

Pruitt, J.A., & Kappius, R.E. (1992). Routine inquiry into sexual victimization: A survey of therapists' practices. *Professional Psychology: Research and Practice, 23,* 474–479.

Pyke, K., & Coltrane, S. (1996). Entitlement, obligation, and gratitude in family work. *Journal of Family Issues, 17,* 61–82.

Rawlings, E., & Carter, D. (1977). Feminist and nonsexist psychotherapy. In E.I. Rawlings & D.K. Carter (Eds.), *Psychotherapy for women* (pp. 49–76). Springfield, IL: Thomas.

Reid, P.T. (1993). Poor women in psychological research: Shut up and shut out. *Psychology of Women Quarterly, 17,* 133–150.

Renzetti, C. (1992). *Violent betrayal: Partner abuse in lesbian relationships.* Newbury Park, CA: Sage.

Reynolds, A.L., & Pope, R.L. (1991). The complexities of diversity: Exploring multiple oppressions. *Journal of Counseling and Development, 70,* 174–180.

Rich, A. (1979). *On lies, secrets and silence.* New York: Norton.

Rickard, K. (1987, March). *A model of feminist identity development.* Paper presented at the annual meeting of the Association for Women in Psychology, Denver, CO.

Rind, B., Tromovitch, P., & Bauserman, R. (1998). A meta-analytic examination of assumed properties of child sexual abuse using college samples. *Psychological Bulletin, 124,* 22–53.

Robertson, J.M., & Fitzgerald, L.F. (1992). Overcoming the masculine mystique: Preferences for alternative forms of assistance among men who avoid counseling. *Journal of Counseling Psychology, 39,* 240–246.

Roesler, T.A., & McKenzie, N. (1994). Effects of childhood trauma on psychological functioning in adults sexually abused as children. *The Journal of Nervous and Mental Disease, 182,* 145–150.

Roiphe, K. (1993). *The morning after: Sex, far, and feminism on campus.* Boston: Little, Brown.

Ross, R., Frances, A., & Widiger, T.A. (1997). Gender issues in *DSM-IV.* In M.R. Walsh (Ed.), *Women, men, and gender: Ongoing debates* (pp. 348–357). New Haven, CT: Yale University Press.

Rudman, L.A., & Borgida, E. (1995). The afterglow of construct accessibility: The behavioral consequences of priming men to view women as sex objects. *Journal of Experimental Social Psychology, 31,* 493–517.

Rudolph, J. (1988). Counselors' attitudes toward homosexuality: A selective review of the literature. *Journal of Counseling and Development, 67,* 165–168.

Saunders, D.G. (1994). Posttraumatic stress symptom profiles of battered women: A comparison of survivors in two settings. *Violence and Victims, 9,* 31–44.

Schauben, L.J., & Frazier, P.A. (1995). Vicarious trauma: The effects on female counselors of working with sexual violence survivors. *Psychology of Women Quarterly, 19,* 49–64.

Sharf, R.S. (1996). *Theories of psychotherapy and counseling: Concepts and cases.* Pacific Grove, CA: Brooks/Cole.

Sharpe, M.J., & Heppner, P.P. (1991). Gender role, gender-role conflict, and psychological well-being in men. *Journal of Counseling Psychology, 38,* 323–330.

Siever, M.D. (1994). Sexual orientation and gender as factors in socioculturally acquired vulnerability to body dissatisfaction and eating disorders. *Journal of Consulting and Clinical Psychology, 62,* 252–260.

Silverstein, L.B. (1996). Fathering is a feminist issue. *Psychology of Women Quarterly, 20,* 3–37.

Silverstein, L.B., & Phares, V. (1996). Expanding the mother-child paradigm: An examination of dissertation research 1986–1994. *Psychology of Women Quarterly, 20,* 39–53.

Simi, N.L., & Mahalik, J.R. (1997). Comparison of feminist versus psychoanalytic/dynamic and other therapists on self-disclosure. *Psychology of Women Quarterly, 21,* 465–483.

Simone, D.H., McCarthy, P., & Skay, C.L. (1998). An investigation of client and counselor variables that influence likelihood of counselor self-disclosure. *Journal of Counseling and Development, 76,* 174–182.

Smith, D., & Fitzpatrick, M. (1995). Patient-therapist boundary issues: An integration review of theory and research. *Professional Psychology, 26,* 499–506.

Snell, W.E., Hampton, B.R., & McManus, P. (1992). The impact of counselor and participant gender on willingness to discuss relational topics: Development of the relationship disclosure scale. *Journal of Counseling and Development, 70,* 409–416.

Snyder, R., & Hasbrouck, L. (1996). Feminist identity, gender traits, and symptoms of disturbed eating among college women. *Psychology of Women Quarterly, 20,* 593–598.

Spence, J.T., & Hahn, E.D. (1997). The attitudes toward women scale and attitude change in college students. *Psychology of Women Quarterly, 21,* 17–34.

Stark, E., & Flitcraft, A. (1988). Violence among intimates: An epidemiological review. In V.V. Hasselt, R.L. Morrison, A.S. Bellack, & M. Hersen (Eds.), *Handbook of family violence* (pp. 293–318). New York: Plenum Press.

Steil, J.M. (1994). Equality and entitlement in marriage: Benefits and barriers. In M.J. Lerner & G. Mikula (Eds.), *Entitlement and the affectional bond: Justice in close relationships* (pp. 229–258). New York: Plenum Press.

Stein, J., Golding, J., Siegal, J., Burnham, M., & Sorenson, S. (1988). Long-term psychological sequelae of child sexual abuse: The Los Angeles epidemiologic catchment area study. In G. Wyatt & G. Powell (Eds.), *Lasting effects of child sexual abuse* (pp. 135–154). Newbury Park, CA: Sage.

Stice, E.M., & Shaw, H.E. (1994). Adverse effects of the media portrayed thin-ideal on women and linkages to bulimic symptomatology. *Journal of Social and Clinical Psychology, 13*(3), 288–308.

Stillson, R.W., O'Neil, J.M., & Owen, S.V. (1991). Predictors of adult men's gender-role conflict: Race, class, unemployment, age, instrumentality-expressiveness, and personal strain. *Journal of Counseling Psychology, 38,* 3–12.

Straus, M.A., & Gelles, R.S. (1990). *Physical violence in American families.* New Burnswick, NJ: Transaction.

Swim, J.K., Aikin, K.J., Hall, W.S., & Hunter, B.A. (1995). Sexism and racism: Old fashioned and modern prejudices. *Journal of Personality and Social Psychology, 68,* 199–214.

Swim, J.K., & Cohen, L.L. (1997). Overt, covert, and subtle sexism. *Psychology of Women Quarterly, 21,* 103–118.

Tavris, C. (1993a). The mismeasure of woman. *Feminism and Psychology, 3,* 149–168.

Tavris, C. (1993b, March 4). You haven't come very far, baby. *Los Angeles Times,* p. B7.

Thompson, E.H., & Pleck, J.H. (1995). Masculinity ideologies: A review of research instrumentation on men and masculinities. In R.F. Levant & W.S. Pollack (Eds.), *A new psychology of men* (pp. 129–163). New York: Basic Books.

Thorn, B.E., Shealy, R.C., & Briggs, S.D. (1993). Sexual misconduct in psychotherapy: Reactions to a consumer-oriented brochure. *Professional Psychology: Research and Practice, 24,* 75–82.

Tolman, R.M., Mowry, D.D., Jones, L.E., & Brekke, J. (1986). Developing a profeminist commitment among men in social work. In N. Van Den Bergh & L.B. Cooper (Eds.), *Feminist visions for social work* (pp. 61–79). Silver Springs, MD: National Association of Social Workers.

Tougas, F., Brown, R., Beaton, A.M., & Joly, S. (1995). Neosexism: Plus ca change, plus c'est pareil. *Personality and Social Psychology Bulletin, 21,* 842–850.

Twenge, J.M. (1997). Changes in masculine and feminine traits over time: A meta-analysis. *Sex Roles, 36,* 305–325.

Unger, R., & Crawford, M. (1996). *Women and gender: A feminist psychology* (2nd ed.). New York: McGraw-Hill.

Wade, J.C. (1996). African American men's gender role conflict: The significance of racial identity. *Sex Roles, 24,* 17–33.

Walker, L.E.A. (1994). *Abused women and survivor therapy.* Washington, DC: American Psychological Association.

Walsh, M.R. (Ed.). (1997). *Women, men, and gender: Ongoing debates.* New Haven, CT: Yale University Press.

Watkins, C.E. (1990). The effects of counselor self-disclosure: A research review. *Counseling Psychologist, 18,* 477–500.

Weber, L. (1998). A conceptual framework for understanding race, class, gender, and sexuality. *Psychology of Women Quarterly, 22,* 13–32.

Weisstein, N. (1993). Psychology constructs the female; or the fantasy life of the male psychologist. *Feminism and Psychology, 3,* 195–210. (Original work published 1968)

West, C., & Zimmerman, D.G. (1987). Doing gender. *Gender and Society, 1,* 125–151.

White, A.M., Strube, M.J., & Fisher, S. (1998). A black feminist model of rape myth acceptance: Implications for research and antirape advocacy in black communities. *Psychology of Women Quarterly, 22,* 157–175.

White, J.W., & Kowalski, R.M. (1994). Deconstructing the myth of the nonaggressive woman: A feminist analysis. *Psychology of Women Quarterly, 18,* 487–508.

Wisch, A.F., Mahalik, J.R., Hayes, J.A., & Nutt, E.A. (1995). The impact of gender role conflict and counseling technique on psychological help seeking in men. *Sex Roles, 33,* 77–89.

Worell, J., & Remer, P. (1992). *Feminist perspectives in therapy: An empowerment model.* New York: Wiley.

Wyche, K.F. (1993). Psychology and African-American women: Findings from applied research. *Applied and Preventive Psychology, 2,* 115–121.

Wyche, K.F., & Rice, J.K. (1997). Feminist therapy: From dialogue to tenets. In J. Worell & N.G. Johnson (Eds.), *Shaping the future of feminist psychology* (pp. 57–71). Washington, DC: American Psychological Association.

Yoder, J.D. (1999). *Women and gender.* Upper Saddle River, NJ: Prentice-Hall.

Yoder, J.D., & Kahn, A.S. (1993). Working toward an inclusive psychology of women. *American Psychologist, 48,* 846–850.

CHAPTER 20

Models of Multicultural Counseling

JOSEPH G. PONTEROTTO
JAIRO N. FUERTES
ERIC C. CHEN

Up until the late 1980s, multicultural research had been characterized as in an "infancy period" relative to more mature areas within counseling psychology such as career development (Ponterotto & Casas, 1991). By the mid-1990s, however, the field was described as having left its infancy period and "begun the development into a mature subset of behavioral science" (Rowe, Behrens, & Leach, 1995, p. 218). Rowe et al. were referring to recent advances in the development and testing of racial identity theory as central to the counseling profession.

It is fair to say that from the early 1980s to the early 1990s, two comprehensive models of multicultural counseling dominated the conceptual and empirical literature—the D.W. Sue et al. (1982; D.W. Sue, Arredondo, & McDavis, 1992) cross-cultural (or multicultural) counseling competency model, and Helms's (1984b, 1990) racial identity development model. In fact, it was difficult during this time to pick up a major research or review article, a book chapter, or a textbook in multicultural counseling without seeing extensive attention devoted to one or both of these models. In the last half-decade or so, however, a number of new comprehensive conceptual models of multicultural counseling have appeared in the literature. The outpouring of multicultural-focused writing generally, and of model generation specifically, supports Rowe et al.'s (1995) observation regarding the growth and maturation of the multicultural counseling field.

Our purpose in this chapter is to review and critique both foundational and emerging models of multicultural counseling. The chapter is organized into two major parts. In Part 1 we review two longer-standing, more foundational models—those of D.W. Sue et al. (1982, 1992, 1998) and Helms (1984b, 1990, 1995). These models have been extant for over 15 years, have continuously undergone conceptual elaboration by their developers, and have been the focus of a good amount of empirical research. This section also integrates available research on the models, with the guiding question being: Does the weight of empirical evidence support the basic tenets proposed by the models?

Part 2 introduces and reviews five emerging models of multicultural counseling (Atkinson, Thompson, & Grant, 1993; Fischer, Jome, & Atkinson, 1998b; Leong, 1996; Ridley, Mendoza, Kanitz, Angermeier, & Zenk, 1994; Trevino, 1996b). Each of these models was published within the last six years and has been subject to only minimal empirical validation at best. Nonetheless, our view is that each model potentially represents a major conceptual breakthrough for understanding the mechanisms of effective multicultural counseling. In Part 2, we briefly review the basic tenets of these models along with available research, and we attempt to provide a balanced critique of each model. Our overriding goal in this endeavor is to stimulate further model elaboration and systematic empirical testing.

IDENTIFYING AND DEFINING "MODELS" OF MULTICULTURAL COUNSELING

Writing this chapter was quite a challenge given the explosion of multicultural literature in this decade (see conceptual and research reviews in Ponterotto, Casas, Suzuki, & Alexander, 1995). We define "multicultural counseling" rather narrowly to refer to counseling issues involving the four major American racial/ethnic minority groups, namely Native American/Alaskan Natives, African Americans, Asian Americans, and Hispanic Americans/Latinos. We also include in this definition White American groups when the focus is on racial issues (e.g., White racial identity models). This specific definition allows for focused coverage in this chapter, however, we acknowledge the importance of examining the intersection of race, age, sexual orientation, class, and gender when considering counseling issues (see Fouad & Brown, this volume; Pope-Davis & Coleman, in press).

Our initial literature review entailed manual searches of the following eight journals from 1991–1998: *Journal of Counseling Psychology, The Counseling Psychologist, Journal of Counseling and Development, Journal of Multicultural Counseling and Development, Professional Psychology: Research and Practice, American Psychologist, Psychotherapy,* and the *Journal of Consulting and Clinical Psychology.* Our goal in this broad review was to select research, theory, and practice journals specifically in counseling; to consider other intervention-focused journals; and to tap a broader vision of the field (via the *American Psychologist*). This task resulted initially in the identification of nine models of multicultural counseling; subsequent follow-up searches in other sources uncovered another two models fitting our model criteria. After reviewing the 11 models, we decided to focus on 7 that have a broad and expansive focus and that are generally comprehensive and integrative in nature.

For the purpose of this chapter, we define "models" broadly to refer to conceptualizations that address the "how to" component of counseling, providing an explication of how therapy is conducted, the role of the clients and counselors, and the mechanisms for client change and growth. The models we critique vary widely in scope and breadth, yet each concentrates in some way on counseling intervention across racial/ethnic client populations. We begin with a review of two older and highly visible models.

SUE ET AL.'S MULTICULTURAL COUNSELING COMPETENCY MODEL

Perhaps the longest standing model of multicultural counseling is the Cross-Cultural Counseling Competency model initially presented in a Division 17 Position Paper (D.W. Sue et al., 1982). This report specified 11 specific competencies for multicultural counseling practice. The competencies were organized into three broad areas focusing on Counselor Attitudes and Beliefs (Awareness), Knowledge, and Skills. In 1992, the original competency report was expanded to include 31 specific competencies organized into the following three categories: Counselor Awareness of Own Assumptions, Values, and Biases; Understanding the Worldview of the Culturally Different Client; and Developing Appropriate Intervention Strategies and Techniques (D.W. Sue et al., 1992). Within each of these broad categories, the specific competencies were again organized into Attitudes and Beliefs, Knowledge, and Skills.

Development and expansion of the multicultural competence construct continued in the mid 1990's with an attempt to operationalize the 31 competencies specified in D.W. Sue et al. (1992). In a comprehensive report, Arredondo et al. (1996) presented 119 explanatory statements detailing how each of the 31 competencies could be met within a training context. In addition, the authors presented strategies aimed at achieving the objectives and competencies specified in the explanatory statements.

The most recent and comprehensive work on multicultural counseling competencies was completed in 1998 when a joint Divisions 17 and 45 committee chaired by Derald Wing Sue published *Multicultural Counseling Competencies: Individual and Organizational Development* (D.W. Sue et al., 1998). The book expands the list of 31 competencies to 34, though the basic organization of the competencies follows the D.W. Sue et al. (1992) format. The D.W. Sue et al. (1998) work is more comprehensive and expansive than any of the previous works on the competency model. The full competency list can be found in D.W. Sue et al. (1998) or in Ponterotto and Casas (in preparation), who also delineate a new supplemental research-specific competency report.

Ponterotto and Casas (1999) noted that the D.W. Sue et al. (1998) competency model has content validity for three reasons. First, diverse multicultural scholars have been working with the competencies for two decades. Therefore, the competencies appear to be conceptually vibrant and to ring true with a broad group of counseling experts. Second, the competencies have been operationalized (by multiple teams working independently) as self-report and observer-report instruments and as detailed behavioral descriptions (cf. Arredondo et al., 1996). Finally, two separate American Psychological Association (APA) divisions (17 and 45) and six separate divisions of the American Counseling Association (ACA) have officially endorsed the competency list (note that these organizations were working originally from the 1992 version of the competencies).

Despite the impressive content validity evidence for the expanded D.W. Sue et al. (1992, 1998) model, direct empirical tests of the model's specific competencies is limited. A basic question remains unanswered: Do counselors who possess these competencies evidence improved counseling outcome with clients across cultures? Although we do not know the full answer to this question, a growing body of research has accumulated in recent years that provides indirect support for clusters of competencies in the model. This research can be organized into two broad areas: First is a cluster of studies that examined the effects of culturally responsive counseling on client evaluations of the counselor; second is a developing body of research that directly examines correlates of multicultural counseling competence as operationalized in paper-and-pencil instruments conceptually rooted in the D.W. Sue et al. (1982) model. We address each area in turn.

Effects of Culturally Responsive/Consistent Counselor Behavior

A number of the D.W. Sue et al. (1992, 1998) competencies speak to the counselor's ability to provide culturally responsive counseling. Atkinson and Lowe (1995) stated that cultural responsiveness "refers to counselor responses that acknowledge the existence of, show interest in, demonstrate knowledge of, and express appreciation for the client's ethnicity and culture and that place the client's problem in a cultural context" (p. 402).

As part of a larger integrative research review, Atkinson and Lowe (1995) located seven studies that examined the effects of counselors responding to cultural content in sessions (Atkinson, Casas, & Abreu, 1992; Gim, Atkinson, & Kim, 1991; Pomales, Claiborn, & LaFromboise, 1986; Poston, Craine, & Atkinson, 1991; Sodowsky 1991; Thompson, Worthington, & Atkinson, 1994; Wade & Bernstein, 1991). In this series of mostly analog studies, Atkinson and Lowe concluded that the overall results "provide a clear-cut case for cultural responsiveness as a counseling strategy for building credibility with ethnic minority clients. There is also evidence that culturally responsive counseling results in greater client willingness to return for counseling, satisfaction with counseling, and depth of self-disclosure" (p. 403).

We located two additional studies that examined the impact of counselors responding to clients in a culturally responsive or consistent manner. Sodowsky (1996) exposed 38 counseling students to one of two videotapes. The analog counseling videos portrayed a White male counselor conducting an intake interview with an Asian Indian international student. The "counselor" and "client" were actors unaware of the study's purpose. In the "culturally consistent" version of the video, the counselor (with the client no longer present) describes his counseling tasks in a manner consistent with the client's values and upbringings. Issues of external kinship, family honor, respect for elders, and indigenous support structures were covered in this version. In the "culturally discrepant" tape, the counselor specifies tasks more congruent with the European American worldview, such as individual assertiveness, personal responsibility, and not relying too strongly on extended family for personal decisions. Importantly, both tape versions had been considered equally plausible in an earlier study (Sodowsky & Taffe, 1991). Findings indicated that the counseling students, using an observer-report version of the Multicultural Counseling Inventory (MCI; Sodowsky, Taffe, Gutkin, & Wise, 1994), rated the culturally consistent counselor significantly higher on all four subscales of the MCI.

Thompson and Jenal (1994) used a modification of grounded theory analysis (Strauss, 1987) to examine the dialogue in 24 "race-avoidant" (i.e., counselor statements in which allusions to race are eliminated) quasi-counseling sessions that were developed in a previous study (Thompson et al., 1994, cited in Atkinson & Lowe, 1995 review). In these vignettes, two Black and two White female counselors worked with Black female college students who were instructed to discuss concerns of women on campus. The 24 sessions (six for each counselor) represented the "universal content" condition "whereby counselors were instructed to address aspects of the participants' presenting concern that could relate to others regardless of race. For example, if the participant commented that she felt isolated on campus as a Black student, the counselor would reflect this concern with a statement such as, 'So, as a student on campus, you have felt isolated and alone'" (Thompson & Jenal, 1994, p. 485).

Using open, axial, and core coding strategies of grounded theory analysis, Thompson and Jenal (1994) arrived at a core theme of "quality of interaction," which was manifested as either smooth, exasperated, constricted, or disjunctive. Axial categories subsumed under each type of interaction were race or race-related concerns, racial identity perspectives, and client affiliation with counselor based on race. The results of the study found that the majority of clients (17 out of 24) struggled and disengaged with the counselors during the sessions. Overall, the findings suggested that facing a race-avoidant counselor proved primarily arrhythmic (characterized by interactional disengagement) to the interactional process.

Interestingly, in the seven sessions characterized as "smooth" (five were interracial and two intraracial), clients appeared to concede or acquiesce to the counselors' race avoidant posture. Thompson and Jenal (1994) commented that some clients in the "smooth" interactions raised racial issues early in the sessions but soon ceased to converse on this topic, almost as if they were conforming to the counselors' universalism. One wonders what impact this "smooth" category of interaction would have on the ongoing counseling process? Would these clients return for sessions? If so, would they evaluate positively the outcome of counseling?

In summary, the results of the Atkinson and Lowe (1995) research review, coupled with the findings of Sodowsky (1996) and Thompson and Jenal (1994), lend strong support to the cluster of D.W. Sue et al. (1992) competencies that speak to counselors' ability to understand, acknowledge, and address culture and race-related issues in sessions. We want to briefly highlight two of the nine studies for their methodological strengths. First, Wade and Bernstein (1991) conducted a true experiment in which 80 Black female college counseling center clients were randomly assigned to one of four counselors (two Black and two White) who had received four hours of multicultural training, or to one of four counselors who received no training (control condition). The treatment group's training addressed how to "(1) articulate the client's problems within a cultural framework, (2) articulate and deal with client resistance, (3) recognize and deal with their own defensiveness as counselors, and (4) recover from mistakes made during the process of counseling" (Wade & Bernstein, 1991, p. 10). All four of these training goals are reflected in the specific D.W. Sue et al. (1992, 1998) competencies.

The results of the experiment, which covered three sessions, indicated that clients working with the multiculturally trained counselors "rated their counselor higher on credibility and relationship measures, returned for more follow-up sessions, and expressed greater satisfaction with counseling" than did clients assigned to "control condition" counselors (Wade & Bernstein, 1991, p. 9).

The Thompson and Jenal (1994) study is also noteworthy because of its descriptive, qualitative methodology. Using a grounded theory analysis of session transcripts, the authors documented the interactional impact of not addressing racial issues in the sessions. Although the study was not true grounded theory in the sense of theoretical sampling and extensive face-to-face interviews with clients (see Polkinghorn, 1994; Ponterotto & Casas, in preparation), the methods and results, nonetheless, shed a light on the process and flow of counseling in a "race-avoidant" condition.

Most of the studies cited in this section were analog in nature, and there is a strong need for more true experimental research on this topic. In addition, qualitative approaches are particularly useful in examining the subjective experience of the therapy process for both counselor and client. True grounded theory studies (Glasser & Strauss, 1967), as well as the more recently developed consensual qualitative research (Hill, Thompson, & Williams, 1997), would seem particularly worthwhile here.

Scale-Specific Multicultural Counseling Competency Research

The most relevant test of the D.W. Sue et al. competency model stems from research incorporating one of four instruments designed to operationalize the model. The first instrument published was the Cross-Cultural Counseling Inventory-Revised (CCCI-R; LaFromboise, Coleman, & Hernandez, 1991), which was designed as an observer-report instrument. Three self-report instruments soon followed: the Multicultural Awareness-Knowledge-Skills Survey (MAKSS; D'Andrea, Daniels, & Heck, 1991); the Multicultural Counseling Inventory (MCI; Sodowsky et al., 1994); and the Multicultural Counseling Awareness Scale (MCAS; Ponterotto et al., 1996), recently revised and renamed the Multicultural Counseling Knowledge and Awareness Scale (MCKAS: Ponterotto, Rieger, Gretchen, Utsey, & Austin, in preparation). This collective group of instruments has been subject to a number of critical reviews (see Constantine & Ladany, in press; Ponterotto & Alexander, 1996; Ponterotto, Rieger, Barrett, & Sparks, 1994; Pope-Davis & Dings, 1994, 1995; Pope-Davis & Nielson, 1996).

Competencies as Related to Demographic and Training Variables

A careful reading of the specific competencies, particularly those in the expanded reports (D.W. Sue et al., 1982, 1998), leads one to assume that both personal and education/training experiences with diversity will yield higher competency levels. A number of studies using one of the four instruments has addressed these hypothesized relationships. Although the findings are by no means conclusive, the weight of the evidence tends to support certain propositions emanating from the D.W. Sue et al. (1992, 1998) competency model. For example, a "Skill" competency in the "Understanding the Worldview of the Culturally Different Client" category (D.W. Sue et al., 1998) specifies that:

> Culturally skilled counselors become actively involved with minority individuals outside the counseling setting (community events, social and political functions, celebrations, friendships, neighborhood groups, and so forth) so that their perspective of minorities is more than an academic or helping exercise. (p. 40)

Part of another "Skill" competency in the "Counselor Awareness of Own Assumptions, Values, and Biases" category reads "Culturally skilled counselors seek out educational, consultative, and training experiences to enrich their understanding and effectiveness in working with culturally different populations" (p. 39).

Let us examine the related research addressing these two competencies. First, to the degree that counselors-of-color have personal experience with culturally diverse individuals and are likely to be more involved with minority individuals outside the counseling setting (e.g., their own nuclear and extended families, community, church), one might expect (extrapolating from the competencies) that counselors-of-color would score higher on multicultural competency measures. In fact, in the majority of studies that assessed racial/ethnic differences in competency scores, regardless of instrument, counselors-of-color scored significantly higher than did European American counselors across a number of subscales (Ponterotto et al., 1996; Pope-Davis, Dings, & Ottavi, 1995; Pope-Davis & Ottavi, 1994a; Pope-Davis, Reynolds, Dings, & Nielson, 1995; Sodowsky, 1996; Sodowsky, Kuo-Jackson, Richardson, & Corey, 1998).

Regarding the second competency, a number of studies also found a clear relationship between multicultural training variables and multicultural counseling competency scores across instruments and subscales. Specifically, multicultural coursework, clinical supervision of minority cases, multicultural workshops and seminars attended, number of minority client contact hours, and multicultural research experience contributed to higher competency scores across a number of instruments and subscales (Ottavi, Pope-Davis, & Dings, 1994; Ponterotto et al., 1996; Pope-Davis, Dings, et al., 1995; Pope-Davis, Prieto, Whitaker, & Pope-Davis, 1993; Pope-Davis, Reynolds, et al., 1995; Pope-Davis, Reynolds, Dings, & Ottavi, 1994; Sodowsky et al., 1994, 1998).

Another training component examined in the multicultural literature involves pretest-posttest group designs assessing the impact of multicultural courses on competency scores. A series of studies incorporating either the Multicultural Counseling Inventory (Sodowsky, 1996; Sodowsky et al., 1994), the Multicultural Awareness, Knowledge, and Skills Survey (D'Andrea et al., 1991; Neville et al., 1996; Robinson & Bradley, 1997) or the Multicultural Counseling Awareness Scale (Ponterotto et al., 1996) all report significant score gain over a semester's multicultural course.

Competencies Related to Case Conceptualization Skills

Interestingly, two recent studies (Constantine & Ladany, in press; Ladany, Inman, Constantine, & Hofheinz, 1997) found that scores across the various self-report competency measures were not related to counselors' (written) multicultural case conceptualization ability as evaluated by independent raters. Constantine and Ladany also found select subscales across various competency instruments to be significantly correlated to scores on a frequently used social desirability measure. Furthermore, Sodowsky et al. (1998) found a significant relationship between the total score on the Multicultural Counseling Inventory (Sodowsky et al., 1994) and a new multicultural-specific social desirability scale. These studies raise important concerns regarding the construct validity of the self-report competency measures.

Competencies Related to Hypothesized, Linked Constructs

Other competencies in the D.W. Sue et al. (1998) reports speak to anticipated relationships between the competencies and other psychological variables, such as racial identity development, expanded worldview, acknowledgment of oppressive conditions for some minority clients, and a general nonracist personal stance. Research has explored a number of these anticipated relationships using primarily correlational and regression analyses.

Four studies examined the relationship between multicultural counseling competencies and racial identity attitudes. Using the White Racial Identity Attitude Scale (WRIAS; Helms & Carter, 1990) and the Multicultural Counseling Inventory (Sodowsky et al., 1994) as their primary instruments, Ottavi et al. (1994) found that racial identity attitudes explained variance in competencies beyond that accounted for by demographic (age and gender) and educational/clinical variables (multicultural coursework, multicultural workshops, minority client hours, hours of multicultural supervision, and number of practica). Specifically, Pseudo-Independence (a high status of racial identity) attitudes contributed significant incremental variance to each of the four competency subscales, and Autonomy (another high status) attitudes contributed significant incremental variance to the Knowledge subscale.

Using the White Racial Identity Attitude Scale and Multicultural Awareness, Knowledge, and Skills Survey, Neville et al. (1996) found that Autonomy attitudes were positively and significantly correlated with multicultural Awareness; that Pseudo-Independence attitudes were positively and significantly correlated with multicultural Awareness, Knowledge, and Skills; that Disintegration attitudes were negatively and significantly related to multicultural Knowledge; and Contact attitudes were negatively and significantly correlated with multicultural Awareness and Skills.

Studying both White and minority supervisees, Ladany, Inman, et al. (1997) used the Cross-Cultural Counseling Inventory-Revised (CCCI-R, modified as self-report) to operationalize D.W. Sue et al.'s competencies, and the WRIAS and Cultural Identity Attitude Scale (CIAS) to operationalize racial identity statuses for Whites and persons-of-color, respectively (Helms, 1995). Results from White counselors indicated that Pseudo-Independence attitudes contributed uniquely and significantly to variance in multicultural competence scores. For counseling students-of-color, Dissonance and Awareness subscales contributed uniquely and significantly to variance in competence scores.

Finally, Ladany, Brittan-Powell, and Pannu (1997), again using the modified CCCI-R, the CIAS, and the WRIAS (among other instruments), found that when a supervisor held higher status racial identity than the supervisee (known as progressive interactions), and when both supervisor and supervisee were in similar high statuses of racial identity (known as parallel high interactions), then the supervisor's influence on the supervisee's multicultural development was significantly greater than in other supervisor and supervisee dyads—namely, when the supervisee was of a higher status (regressive interaction) or when both supervisor and supervisee were in parallel lower statuses (parallel low interactions).

In all four studies, the significant relationships between racial identity statuses (Helms, 1995) and levels of multicultural counseling competence as measured by different competency instruments were in directions predicted by the competency model (and by the Helms's model; to be discussed later). Initially, the finding in Ladany, Inman, et al. (1997) that Dissonance contributed to variance in multicultural competence scores was a bit surprising as this status is considered a lower level status for persons-of-color. However, as explained by the authors of the study, this status often describes individuals who begin to question issues of race, and therefore individuals with Dissonance attitudes may be better able to understand how racial issues are central to the counseling relationship.

The Sodowsky et al. (1998), Ponterotto et al. (1996), and Ponterotto, Burkard, et al. (1995) studies also provide support for the multicultural competency construct's relationship with other constructs. As would be predicted, Sodowsky et al. found a more flexible worldview (preference for externality and collectivism versus internality and individualism), a sense of personal adequacy (high sociability, self-concept, and self-esteem), and an external locus of race etiology (belief in the need for collective, societal combating of racism), to be predictive of higher multicultural competency scores. Finally, the Ponterotto, Burkard, et al. (1995; Ponterotto et al., 1996) studies found competency scores to be related in expected directions to self-report levels of discrimination and subtle racism.

Summary

In summary, studies linked to the D.W. Sue et al. competency model have tended to support some but not all predictions extracted from the framework. The D.W. Sue et al. (1998) competencies, as operationalized by various self-report instruments, tend to be related as expected to select demographic and training variables, as well as to the constructs of racial identity status, worldview, and levels of discrimination. Importantly, however, the various self-report instruments were not related to counselors' ability (in written form) to conceptualize cases adequately from a multicultural perspective. Furthermore, select subscales across various self-report competency measures (as well as the total score for the Multicultural Counseling Inventory) were significantly correlated to social desirability influences. Finally, with regard to the competency measures, the support for the model has tended to be indirect, and gathered through single time-point correlational studies. We still do not know whether counselors scoring higher on the competency scales actually evidence more success in multicultural counseling. It has also been challenging to test the model due to the lack of specific testable hypotheses within the framework. Although some competencies are quite specific and can be linked readily to research hypotheses, other competencies are more general and thus difficult to operationalize (particularly for quantitative research).

Further specification of testable research hypotheses for the D.W. Sue et al. (1998) model would provide an important direction for model development. For example, we were impressed with Arredondo et al.'s (1996) training operationalization of the 31 D.W. Sue et al. (1992) competencies. These authors generated 119 specific explanatory statements detailing how these competencies could be achieved and demonstrated. Building upon the Arredondo et al.'s elaborative framework for training, it would be helpful to generate a list a research hypotheses emanating from the newest D.W. Sue et al. (1998) set of 34 competencies. Such a delineation of research questions would stimulate numerous dissertations and research projects that could, over time, systematically test the model.

It is important as well to comment on the current status of instrumentation designed to operationalize the competencies. The instrument critiques cited earlier caution researchers that the collective group of instruments is still only in their infancy. Psychometric reviews of the instruments have focused in four areas. First, the internal consistency of the subscales has generally been satisfactory, falling above the minimum floor of .70 deemed desirable (cf. Ponterotto, 1996) for research instruments. Second, subscale intercorrelations *within* instruments have often been low to moderate, supporting the uniqueness and nonredundancy of the awareness, knowledge, skills, and relationship factors.

A third consideration for researchers concerns the relation of the subscales *between* instruments. Given that the separate subscales all emanate, at least in part, from the D.W. Sue et al. (1982) competency specification, one would expect the like-named subscales of the instruments to be highly correlated. In fact, the knowledge and skills subscales across instruments are highly correlated as would be expected; but the awareness subscales across instruments are generally not, indicating that each instrument is measuring distinct components of the awareness construct (see particularly Constantine & Ladany, in press; Ponterotto et al., 1999; Pope-Davis & Dings, 1994). Perhaps the awareness construct is more complex or more difficult to operationalize in self-report form than the other constructs tapped by the competency instruments. A final concern is that at least one subscale of each instrument has been found to correlate with a measure of social desirability (Constantine & Ladany, in press; Sodowsky et al., 1998).

It is clear that additional psychometric testing, and likely revision, of all the competency measures is in order. At present, only the Multicultural Counseling Awareness Scale (Ponterotto et al., 1996) has been revised (Ponterotto et al., 1999). Furthermore, the limits of paper-and-pencil self-report measures of multicultural competence not only are significant because of the danger of social desirability contamination, but also because respondents tend to overestimate their competence (Constantine & Ladany, in press).

At present, there is a strong need for field-based process and outcome studies using actual clients in diverse settings. Do counselors who possess the D.W. Sue et al. (1998) competencies, whether judged through self- or observer-report, evidence a stronger therapeutic alliance and more impactful outcome over the course of therapy? Furthermore, we see a strong need for more qualitative research on multicultural counseling competence. For example, interviewing clients (and counselors) after successful (and unsuccessful) counseling using phenomenological, grounded theory, or consensual qualitative research methods would yield important insights for researchers.

Participant observation or case studies of mental health clinics known for effective minority community practice would also yield fruitful information.

HELMS'S RACIAL IDENTITY THEORY AND INTERACTION MODEL

In the mid 1980s, Helms (1984b) published her landmark theory on the effects of race in counseling. Building upon the Nigrescence theory of Cross (1971), which concerned stages of Black racial identity development, and adding her own theory of White racial identity development, Helms outlined the potential role of race and racial identity in counseling. In a series of conceptual works, Helms has continued to elaborate and refine her theory (see particularly Helms, 1990, 1995, 1996; Helms & Cook, 1999). One recent refinement was to change the term racial identity "stage" to "ego status." This change was made to highlight that the "stages" are not pure, mutually exclusive constructs, and that individuals may exhibit attitudes, behaviors, and emotions characteristic of more than one "stage." Because stage implies a static place or condition that a person reaches, Helms (1995) dropped the term. A second extension of Helms's model was to combine Cross's original model and Atksinon, Morten, and Sue's (1989) Minority Identity Development model to form a new People of Color Model (Helms, 1995).

Below we present brief descriptions of the statuses that make up Helms's Black (and People-of-Color) Racial Identity Model and White Racial Identity Model (Helms, 1995). For detailed descriptions of the stages or statuses of racial identity, the reader is referred to Carter (1995, 1997), Cross (1991, 1995), Helms (1990, 1995, 1996), Helms and Cook (1999), and Ponterotto and Pedersen (1993).

Regarding the Black (or People-of-Color) racial identity model, Helms (1995) posited five statuses. *Preencounter* (or *Conformity*) is characterized by an external self-definition, a devaluing of one's own racial group, and an allegiance to White standards of merit. Common to this status is selective perception and obliviousness to racial concerns. Cross (1995; Cross, Fagen-Smith, Vandiver, Cokley, & Worell, 1999) indicated that there are multiple subtypes or levels to this status. *Encounter* (or *Dissonance*) attitudes are characterized by confusion and ambivalence regarding commitment to one's racial group. Persons with high levels of this status may be ambivalent about life decisions, and may exercise repression of anxiety-provoking race information.

The *Immersion/emersion* status is characterized by an idealization of one's own racial group and a denigration of all that is associated with the White majority culture. This status is related to a hypervigilance toward racial stimuli and dichotomous thinking. The *Internalization* status is aligned with a positive commitment to one's own racial group, coupled with a capacity to respond objectively to members of the dominant White culture. Persons with high levels of Internalization attitudes are believed to exercise flexible and analytic thinking. As with the Preencounter status, Cross et al. (1999) noted that there are multiple subtypes subsumed within the Internalization status. Finally, the Integrative Awareness status is characterized by a capacity to value one's multiple and collective identities, as well as to empathize with social justice issues generally. The cognitive style connected to this status is one of complexity and flexibility (see Helms, 1995).

Helms's (1995) White identity model consists of six statuses. Persons in the *Contact* status are satisfied with the racial status quo, are unaware of continuing subtle racism, and are generally oblivious to racial issues and concerns. The *Disintegration* status is characterized by anxiety over unresolved racial dilemmas, as persons in this status are torn between own-group loyalty and a newfound knowledge of racial inequality. In the *Reintegration* status, White persons lapse into an idealization of one's own racial group, and a denigration and intolerance for non-White groups. The *Pseudoindependence* status is characterized by an intellectualized commitment to one's own racial group and a deceptive tolerance of non-White groups.

During the *Immersion/emersion* status, White people search for an understanding of the personal meaning of racism. Individuals in this status examine the meaning of being White in a historically racist society, and they may involve themselves in racial activism and justice issues. Finally, in the *Autonomy* status, the White person commits to social justice issues, and sees the importance of relinquishing privileges of racism. Cognitively, these individuals are complex and flexible (see Helms, 1995).

Helms's theoretical writing has had a tremendous influence inside and outside the field of counseling. For example, Helms's conceptual work has been extended to elementary schools (Helms, 1994b), everyday social interactions and group dynamics (Helms, 1990; Helms & Cook, 1999), general education (Carter & Goodwin, 1994), vocational development (Helms, 1994a; Helms & Cook, 1999; Helms & Piper, 1994; Parham & Austin, 1994), and clinical supervision (Cook, 1994; Helms & Cook, 1999). Furthermore, her model has been adapted for widespread lay audiences (Helms, 1992; Tatum, 1997). The theoretical work of Cross and Helms has stimulated extensive empirical work, a select sample of which is reviewed in this section.

Research Testing Helms's Black and White Racial Identity Models

Major tenets of Helms's theory can be organized into two clusters. First, the theory holds that each racial identity "ego status" for Blacks (and People of Color) and Whites is associated with various psychological, behavioral, social, cultural, and vocational variables. These variables are manifested in attitudes, feelings, and perceptions that are likely to influence counseling process and outcome.

The second cluster of theoretical assumptions concerns the interactive impact of clients and counselors who are at similar or dissimilar identity statuses. Helms (1990, 1995) outlined four types of relationships. In *parallel* relationships, the counselor and client are at the same level ego status. In *progressive* relationships, the counselor is at a higher status of racial identity than the client. *Regressive* relationships are characterized by the client being of a higher identity status than the counselor. Finally, *crossed* relationships, which are now (Helms, 1995) considered to be subtypes of progressive and regressive relationships, relate to dyads where counselor and client are at conceptually opposite statuses. Helms (1990, 1995) hypothesized both process and outcome results in her interaction model.

Helms's conceptual work, and her success with colleagues in operationalizing her and Cross's constructs via popular paper-and-pencil self-report instruments, has stimulated a large body of empirical research. Instruments used to operationalize Helms's and Cross's constructs include the Black Racial Identity Attitude Scale (BRIAS; Helms, 1990), the Cultural Identity Attitude Scale (CIAS; see Helms, 1997), the White Racial Identity Attitude Scale (WRIAS; Helms & Carter, 1990), and the White Racial Consciousness Development Scale (WRCDS; Claney & Parker, 1988). Most recently, Cross et al. (1999) have operationalized Cross's (1995) revised Nigrescence theory in their development of the Cross Racial Identity Scale.

The majority of research using Helms's model as a conceptual base has tested the first cluster of theoretical assumptions specified earlier. There have been a host of studies examining the relationship of various racial identity statuses to any number of psychological variables. Direct tests of Helms's interaction model, that is, the impact of parallel, progressive, regressive, or crossed dyadic relationships on counseling process and outcome, have been fewer in number. We review both clusters of studies in this section.

Correlates of Black Racial Identity

We located roughly 20 studies that examined correlates of the Black Racial Identity Attitude Scale (BRIAS). The BRIAS assesses four statuses: Preencounter, Encounter, Immersion-emersion, and

Internalization. The studies can be organized into five content categories: psychological health, ethnic and womanist identity, attitudes toward counseling, university campus involvement, and vocational or career development. The majority of the studies used college student samples. For each content category, we summarize the findings related to each Black racial identity ego status. Unless otherwise specified, the samples were college or university students.

Psychological Health

Preencounter attitudes have been related to lower levels of self-esteem (Goodstein & Ponterotto, 1997; Poindexter-Cameron & Robinson, 1997; Pyant & Yanico, 1991); higher levels of anxiety, memory impairment, paranoid thoughts, auditory hallucinations, alcohol concerns, and global psychological distress (Carter, 1991); problems identifying, expressing, and examining feelings (Dinsmore & Mallinckrodt, 1996); lower psychological well-being and higher depression (in nonstudents) (Pyant & Yanico, 1991); and lower levels of academic autonomy, general autonomy, and mature interpersonal relationships (Taub & McEwen, 1992).

Encounter attitudes have been related to lower self-esteem and psychological well-being and higher depression in nonstudents (Pyant & Yanico, 1991); problems identifying and expressing feelings (Dinsmore & Mallinckrodt, 1996); greater perceived culture-specific stress (Neville, Heppner, & Wang, 1997); lower levels of academic autonomy, mature interpersonal relationships, and intimacy (Taub & McEwen, 1992); and subscription to a locus of control characterized by luck, chance, or fate (Martin & Hall, 1992).

Immersion-emersion attitudes have been characterized by greater perceived general stress, lower problem-solving appraisal ability, and greater avoidance of problem-solving activities (Neville et al., 1997); lower levels of academic autonomy, mature interpersonal relationships, and intimacy (Taub & McEwen, 1992); stronger external thinking orientation (lack of self-examination of feelings) (Dinsmore & Mallinckrodt, 1996); and fewer memory difficulties (Carter, 1991).

Internalization attitudes have been associated with higher levels of self-esteem (Goodstein & Ponterotto, 1997; Poindexter-Cameron & Robinson, 1997); stronger internal locus of control (Martin & Hall, 1992); higher sense of hope in achieving goals (Jackson & Neville, 1998); a tendency to rely on a rational (versus dependent or intuitive) decision-making style (Helms & Parham, 1990); lower levels of culture specific stress (Neville et al., 1997); and more comfort in examining internal emotional experience coupled with few problems in identifying and expressing feelings (Dinsmore & Mallinckrodt, 1996). Interestingly, Carter (1991) found this status related to higher levels of paranoid ideation.

Ethnic and Womanist Identity

Preencounter attitudes have been related to a lower sense of ethnic identity (Goodstein & Ponterotto, 1997), and to a preference for the racial self-designation of "negro" or "colored" (Martin & Hall, 1992). This status also correlated as expected with its parallel status of Helms's womanist identity model (Poindexter-Cameron & Robinson, 1997). Encounter attitudes have been related to negative views toward other racial and ethnic groups (Goodstein & Ponterotto, 1997). Immersion-emersion attitudes have been associated with both negative views of other racial/ethnic groups (Goodstein & Ponterotto, 1997) and more traditional attitudes toward women (Martin & Hall, 1992). Finally, internalization was related to a strong sense of ethnic identity (Goodstein & Ponterotto, 1997), and to its parallel status in Helms's womanist identity model (Parks, Carter, & Gushue, 1996).

Attitudes toward Counselors and the Counseling Process

Preencounter attitudes have been associated with perceiving psychotherapy as an unlikely source of help (Delphin & Rollock, 1995), whereas encounter attitudes were associated with higher satisfaction with counseling from White therapists (Bradby & Helms, 1990). Immersion-emersion attitudes have been associated with less awareness of available campus mental health services, a lower valuation of psychological counseling services, and a preference for an ethnically similar counselor (Delphin & Rollock, 1995). Internalization attitudes have been associated with both a preference for Black counselors and White male counselors, as well as a preference for a counselor of similar socioeconomic status (Helms & Carter, 1991). Internalization attitudes have also related to a greater awareness of available campus mental health services (Delphin & Rollock, 1995), and a higher level of satisfaction with counseling from White therapists (Bradby & Helms, 1990).

University Campus Involvement

Two studies have examined the relationship between racial identity status and involvement in various campus activities. Preencounter attitudes have been associated with lower levels of involvement in cultural campus organizations (Mitchell & Dell, 1992), whereas encounter attitudes have been associated with higher levels of such activities. Immersion-emersion attitudes have been associated with higher levels of involvement in campus cultural organizations (Mitchell & Dell, 1992) and with varied campus activities and greater affiliation with fraternity involvement (Taylor & Howard-Hamilton, 1995). Similarly, internalization attitudes have been associated with greater involvement in both campus cultural and noncultural organizations (Mitchell & Dell, 1992), and higher general campus activity and affiliation with fraternities (Taylor & Howard-Hamilton, 1995).

Vocational and Career Variables

Recently, investigators have begun to examine the relationship between Black racial identity development and varied career and academic-choice variables. For example, preencounter attitudes related positively to math interests and negatively to social persuasion (academic/career choice support from others) (Gainor & Lent, 1998). Encounter attitudes were inversely related to intention to select a math-related major (Gainor & Lent, 1998). Internalization attitudes were related to higher levels of vocational identity for women but not men (Jackson & Neville, 1998), and higher math related social persuasion (Gainor & Lent, 1998). Importantly the magnitude of the significant correlations in the Gainor and Lent study were low (explaining about 2% of the variance in most vocational variables), and the most salient findings of their study regarding racial identity attitudes were that such attitudes "are minimally related to social cognitive variables and that they do not appreciably affect the relation of the social cognitive variables to the interest or choice criteria" (Gainor & Lent, 1998, p. 410). Also highlighting the relative independence of career variables and racial identity status, Evans and Herr (1994) found no relationship between racial identity status and "traditional" (based on U.S. census-tracked percentage of Blacks in specific careers) African American career aspirations.

Correlates of White Racial Identity Development

Our literature review uncovered roughly 20 studies that examined correlates of the White Racial Identity Attitude Scale (WRIAS). The WRIAS version used in the majority of theses studies assessed only five statuses: Contact, Disintegration, Reintegration, Pseudo-independence, and Autonomy. These studies can be grouped into five categories: psychological health, racism and interracial comfort, counselor training and competence variables, attitudes and expectations toward counseling, and vocational variables.

Psychological Health

Contact status attitudes have been associated with lower levels of inner directedness and capacity for intimate contact (Tokar & Swanson, 1991); more dualistic thinking (characterized by dichotomous thinking and looking to authority for answers) (Steward, Boatwright, Sauer, Baden, &

Jackson, 1998); and less ability to combine past events and future goals with present state of affairs (Tokar & Swanson, 1991). Disintegration attitudes have been associated with less ability to combine past events and future goals in assessing present conditions (Tokar & Swanson, 1991) and with lower levels of mature interpersonal relationships (Taub & McEwen, 1992).

Reintegration attitudes have been associated with lower capacity for intimate contact (Tokar & Swanson, 1991); lower levels of mature interpersonal relationships (Taub & McEwen, 1992); and higher levels of dualistic thinking (Steward et al., 1998). Pseudo-independence was found to correlate with higher autonomy and higher levels of mature interpersonal relationships (Taub & McEwen, 1992), whereas Autonomy attitudes related to higher inner directedness (Tokar & Swanson, 1991) and higher autonomy (Taub & McEwen, 1992).

Racism, Interracial Comfort, and Womanist Identity

Contact attitudes have been associated with lower levels of racism in women (Carter, 1990), and more positive views of other racial/ethnic groups (Goodstein & Ponterotto, 1997). Disintegration attitudes related to negative views of other racial/ethnic groups (Goodstein & Ponterotto, 1997), and Reintegration attitudes were related to higher levels of racism (Carter, 1990; Pope-Davis & Ottavi, 1992, 1994b), and to negative views of other racial/ethnic groups (Goodstein & Ponterotto, 1997). Pseudo-independence attitudes related to lower levels of racism for women (Pope-Davis & Ottavi, 1994b) and positive views of other racial/ethnic groups (Goodstein & Ponterotto, 1997). Finally, Autonomy attitudes related to positive views of other racial/ethnic groups (Goodstein & Ponterotto, 1997). Interestingly, racial identity development and womanist identity development were found to be independent processes for White women (Parks et al., 1996), unlike for Black women as discussed in the previous section. Interestingly, Newswanger (1996) found no differences in racial identity status scores of White students who had or did not have an African American roommate during the first year.

Counselor Training and Competence Levels

A number of studies have focused on professional counselors and trainees and have examined the relationship between racial identity attitudes and self-report levels of multicultural counseling competence (awareness, knowledge, and skills), the perceived therapeutic alliance, and rater evaluated multicultural case conceptualization ability. Contact attitudes were related to lower levels of multicultural counseling awareness and skills (Neville et al., 1996), and Disintegration attitudes were related to lower multicultural counseling knowledge and negative perceptions of the working alliance in an analog study (regardless of race of the client) (Burkard, Ponterotto, Reynolds, & Alfonso, 1999; Neville et al., 1996). Reintegration attitudes were also related to lower counselor ratings of the therapeutic alliance regardless of client race (Burkard et al., 1999).

Pseudo-independence attitudes have been related to higher self-report indices of multicultural counseling awareness, knowledge, and skills (Ladany, Inman, et al., 1997; Neville et al., 1996; Ottavi et al., 1994) and more positive perceptions of the working alliance with a hypothetical client across race conditions (Burkard et al., 1999). This status has also been found to be sensitive to multicultural training; in two pretest-posttest studies, Pseudo-independence attitudes rose significantly after a one-semester experiential and didactic multicultural course (Brown, Parham, & Yonker, 1996; Neville et al., 1996). Note that in the Brown et al. (1996) study the significant increase occurred for women but not men.

The results for the Autonomy status paralleled those for the Pseudo-independence status. Specifically, this status has been related to higher multicultural counseling awareness and knowledge (Neville et al., 1996; Ottavi et al., 1994), and positively related to the perceived working alliance regardless of hypothetical client race (Burkard et al., 1999). Furthermore, Autonomy attitudes were also found to be sensitive to multicultural exposure and training as scores rose after a one-semester multicultural counseling course (Brown et al., 1996; Neville et al., 1996). Interestingly, in the

Brown et al. study the findings regarding gender followed the opposite pattern than in the Pseudo-independence status, as Autonomy scores rose significantly only for male counselor trainees. Importantly, Ladany, Inman, et al. (1997) found no relationship between counselor trainee racial identity status and observer-rated evaluations of trainees' multicultural counseling case conceptualization skills.

Counselor Preferences and Expectations

Helms and Carter (1991) found that Disintegration attitudes were related to preferences for White, White female, and White male counselors and were related to preference for same-gender (in females) and same-social class counselors. This study also found that Pseudo-independent attitudes related to preferences for White female and White counselors, and that Autonomy attitudes predicted weak preferences for White and White female counselors. Carter and Akinsulure-Smith (1996) found no pattern of relationships between White racial identity status and expectations about counseling.

Work Values and Relationships

Two studies employed canonical correlations to examine the pattern of relationships between racial identity status and work variables. Although Carter, Gushue, and Weitzman (1994) concluded that racial identity status and work values are largely independent, the authors did uncover one significant canonical root, which indicated that White students who exhibited a pattern consistent with high Reintegration and Disintegration attitudes, coupled with low Pseudo-independent and Autonomy attitudes, possessed work values consistent with a get-ahead work ethic normally associated with White middle-class values (Ponterotto & Casas, 1991). Block, Roberson, and Neuger (1995) found that MBA students who had a pattern of racial identity scores reflecting high Disintegration and Reintegration attitudes combined with low Autonomy attitudes reacted negatively toward interracial situations at work.

Summary of Correlates of the Black and White Racial Identity Attitude Scales

The 40 or so studies we reviewed that incorporated either the Black or White racial identity measures of Helms and colleagues tend to support certain propositions of the model. It is clear that various psychological, social, and attitudinal correlates of various statuses tend to appear in the direction posited by the models. Also, as predicted theoretically by the model, and psychometrically by some high subscale intercorrelations (to be discussed later), there is understandable overlap among some statuses.

Importantly, there were many expected relationships between racial identity statuses and select variables that were not supported in these studies. This underscores Cross's (1991) position that racial identity development does not transform personality. As Cross has often suggested, "a shy and withdrawn person at Pre-encounter is still shy and withdrawn at Internalization; a gregarious person at Pre-encounter is still gregarious at Internalization" (personal communication, April 12, 1994). Furthermore, some studies have found racial identity status to be fairly independent of other important life experiences and tasks, such as career development variables (Evans & Herr, 1994; Gainor & Lent, 1998). As expected by Cross (1991), the most consistent finding to date is that racial identity status is predictive of feelings, attitudes, and comfort with persons from one's own and other racial groups.

The precise utility of the Cross (1995) and Helms (1995) model cannot be ascertained at this time, even after 40 studies. First, there are understandable limits to paper-and-pencil self-report measures of racial identity (to be discussed later). Second, in at least half of the studies reviewed, no specific theory-driven hypotheses were tested. Many studies were exploratory in nature, simply examining correlations among variables. There is a strong need for more systematic hypothesis-testing studies to further evaluate the latest elaborations of the Cross and Helms models (Cross et al., 1999; Helms, 1999; Helms & Cook, 1999).

Studies Testing Helms's Interactional Model

We located four studies that specifically tested tenets of Helms's interactional counseling model; each study examined the impact of counselor and client being at similar or different racial identity statuses. As highlighted earlier, the model predicts specific process and outcome results for matched and mismatched identity status dyads. Given the few studies available, we review each one in turn.

Richardson and Helms (1994) exposed 52 Black male undergraduates to one of two audiotapes selected from an earlier Carter and Helms (1992) study. In both tapes, the Black client and White counselor represent parallel dyads. The Black clients had the highest status scores in Internalization, and the White Counselors had highest status scores in Autonomy. Manipulation checks documented that the study's participants understood that the two "clients" were Black and that the two "counselors" were White. Furthermore, the counselors in both vignettes were rated similarly on all of the dependent variables. In both vignettes, the clients were presenting with race-related issues, though the presenting stressors were different across vignettes.

Richardson and Helms (1994) found that racial identity attitudes contributed significantly to participant affective reactions to the session. Specifically, using Helms's (1984a) Counseling Reactions Inventory, the results indicated that Encounter attitudes were predictive of negative counseling reactions. There were no significant relationships found between racial identity attitudes and evaluation of the counselor on the Counseling Rating Form—Short Form (Corrigan & Schmidt, 1983) and the Cross Cultural Counseling Inventory—Revised (LaFromboise et al., 1991). The authors interpreted the negative Encounter-counseling reactions finding as resulting from the counselor's lack of focus on the confusion about racial identity commitment that is characteristic of this stage.

In an interesting methodological variation, and using supervision as the interactive context, Ladany, Brittan-Powell, et al. (1997) found that the ordinal nature of the parallel relationship affected supervisee ratings. Specifically, when both supervisor and supervisee were in similar high statuses of racial identity (parallel high interactions), the supervisor's influence on the supervisee's multicultural development was significantly greater than when both supervisor and supervisee were in parallel lower statuses (parallel low interactions) or when supervisor and supervisee were in regressive matches. This study also found, as predicted by theory, that when a supervisor held higher status racial identity than the supervisee (progressive interactions), supervisee multicultural development ratings were higher than in parallel low or regressive interactions.

Carter (1995; Carter & Helms, 1992) has conducted a series of studies examining the impact of various racial identity status matchings on counseling process variables. The general research question addressed was whether different combinations of racial identity status dyads exhibited characteristic sets of relationship dynamics. The sample for both studies consisted of participants attending multicultural training workshops of Carter and colleagues in New York, California, and Maryland. Sixty-six workshop attendees participated in 33 audiotaped or videotaped simulated 15-minute counseling sessions. Participants completed the BRIAS or WRIAS, the Therapists Intentions List, the Client Reactions List, the Session Evaluation Questionnaire, the State-Trait Anxiety Inventory, and the Hostility Dimension of the Symptom Checklist-90 Revised (see Carter, 1995; Carter & Helms, 1992). Dyads fell into one of two relationship pairs: Parallel or progressive.

Analysis of the data involved examination of numerous correlations related to counselor intentions, counselor intentions and client behavior, client reactions, and client reactions and counselor behavior across parallel and progressive relationship pairs. The findings are a little difficult to interpret because of the sheer number of correlations performed. However, overall general findings reveal that "the effects of racial identity on the therapeutic process vary, depending on the level of identity or the manner in which racial identity combines in the therapy dyad" (Carter, 1995, p. 194). In most instances, as far as we could discern, the significant correlations were consistent with model specifications.

Some specific findings in these studies indicate that in terms of various process and outcome variables, parallel relationships may be counterproductive when racial issues serve as the focus of discussion. Carter (1995) concluded that the parallel dyad may be unable to deal effectively with issues of race. However, Carter did not specify the nature of the parallel relationships, that is, whether they were high- or low-status matches. Such a distinction would be helpful as demonstrated in the Ladany, Brittan-Powell, et al. (1997) study.

With regard to progressive relationships, a more tense therapeutic environment is created, yet the heightened discomfort may be beneficial to therapy. Finally, during regressive relationships the counselor is attempting to maintain power in the relationship, while the client is struggling to deepen understanding of racial issues. In this final scenario, Carter (1995) concluded that "the counselor appears comfortable with racial issues only when they are discussed in terms of the client's dynamics and not the counselor's" (p. 194).

Summary of Interactional Studies

The series of studies we reviewed in this section were rather complex and sophisticated, and the diverse array of instruments used and variables examined make conclusions only tentative at this point. However, initial findings from these four studies appear to be consistent with model expectations, though it is clear that a number of follow-up studies are needed in this area. These interactional studies are quite significant because they examine a critical component of Helms's racial identity interaction theory, as well as Carter's (1995) variant, known as the "racially inclusive model" of psychotherapy. Carter and Helms underscored the complexity of counseling in a historically oppressive multicultural society where both counselor and client not only bring visible demographic characteristics to the therapy relationship, but also an invisible set of attitudes and feelings regarding race and racial interactions. How a counselor works with and processes this unspoken group of attitudes and emotions may represent a critical variable in counseling and psychotherapy in this country. Carter (1995) and Helms's (1990, 1995) conceptual breakthroughs and exploratory research, coupled with Cross's (1991, 1995) pioneering theoretical visions, have brought the status of multicultural counseling to a new plateau of sophistication.

Summary of Cross and Helms's Models

Cross and Helms's models have stimulated more research in multicultural counseling than has any other extant framework. We would characterize the models as vibrant and visionary. However, definitive testing of the models has been hampered by concerns regarding instrumentation, hypothesis specification, and research method variation. Importantly, the chief instruments used to operationalize the Cross (1971) and Helms (1984b, 1990) models of racial identity, the BRIAS and WRIAS, have undergone close psychometric scrutiny. A cluster of studies has raised important questions about the reliability and validity of both the 30-item and 50-item BRIAS (Fischer, Tokar, & Serna, 1998; Lemon & Waehler, 1996; Ponterotto & Wise, 1987; Tokar & Fischer, 1998; Yanico, Swanson, & Tokar, 1994). Concerns consistently expressed in these studies are that the claimed four-factor structure of the BRIAS is not supported (a more simple structure may be warranted); that internal consistency coefficients for some subscales (particularly the Encounter scale) are quite low; and that score distributions for some subscales are markedly skewed. Similar psychometric concerns have been raised regarding the factor structure and internal consistencies of the WRIAS. A particular concern is that some WRIAS subscale intercorrelations are very high, suggesting factor redundancy (Behrens, 1997; Pope-Davis, Vandiver, & Stone, 1999; Swanson, Tokar, & Davis, 1994).

Helms (1996, 1997, 1999) and Carter (1995, 1996) have responded to criticisms of their research instruments by highlighting the complexity of the theoretical models and the limits of attempting to validate the instruments (and model) by relying solely on traditional measurement criteria (e.g., internal consistency, subscale intercorrelation, and factor structure). These authors have called for more varied and sophisticated uses of racial identity instrument scores through the use of pattern, profile, and cluster scores. Any researcher considering using extant racial identity measures, or developing their own, should be well versed in the recent debates on the measurement of racial identity development.

At this time, we recommend further testing and perhaps revision of the Black and White racial identity scales. We urge careful scrutiny of Cross et al.'s (1999) new racial identity instrument that attempts to capture more effectively the complexity of Cross's (1995) revised Nigrescence model. Furthermore, we look forward to further testing of new measures of racial identity/consciousness, such as the Multidimensional Inventory of Black Identity (Sellers, Rowley, Chavous, Shelton, & Smith, 1997) and the Oklahoma Racial Attitude Scale (Choney & Behrens, 1996; Pope-Davis et al., 1999). Finally, we applaud continued efforts to operationalize Helms's White identity model in new instrument form, such as the White Racial Consciousness Development Scale (Choney & Rowe, 1994; Parker, Moore, & Neimeyer, 1998).

Particularly needed at this time are constructivist research approaches that more descriptively capture the experiences of everyday citizens, clients, and counselors. Qualitative research methods will be particularly fruitful in this regard, with some studies beginning to appear in the literature. Carter's (1995) case study descriptions and analysis, and Jones's (1997) grounded theory study are good examples of more constructivist approaches to the study of racial identity development. Kerwin, Ponterotto, Jackson, and Harris (1993) and Root (1998) used qualitative methods to examine the complexity and dynamics of biracial identity development. We are clearly at the juncture where a multimethod approach to studying racial identity is in order (see Ponterotto & Casas, in preparation).

EMERGING MODELS OF MULTICULTURAL COUNSELING

This section of our chapter presents descriptive overviews and critiques of five emerging models of multicultural counseling. We consider the models to be conceptually sophisticated and potentially fruitful to our understanding of counseling within a cultural context. We begin by reviewing the Atkinson et al. and Trevino models as they have begun to receive direct empirical scrutiny. The remaining models are presented in random order and reflect no preferences on our part.

Atkinson et al.'s Acculturation, Locus of Problem Etiology, and Goals of Counseling Model

Atkinson et al. (1993) introduced a three dimensional (3-D) model for counseling racial/ethnic minority clients. The specific dimensions central to the model are acculturation (low to high), goal of helping (prevention to remediation), and locus of problem etiology (internal to external). The focus of the model is on deciding appropriate roles for the counselor based on the client's position along all three dimensional continua.

Acculturation as conceptualized by the authors is defined as the extent to which the client has adopted the beliefs, values, customs, and institutions of the dominant culture. Understandably, recent immigrants generally score low on measures of acculturation, whereas individuals more removed from the immigration experience (e.g., third and fourth generation) score high. Locus of problem etiology can be internal or external. Symptoms such as weak impulse control, mood swings, and irrational fear are generally assumed to have an internal etiology, whereas symptoms such as posttraumatic stress, work discrimination, and sexual harassment are generally assumed to have an external cause. Recently, Atkinson, Kim, and Caldwell (1998) have noted that external etiology refers specifically to discrimination and oppression experienced by racial/ethnic minority individuals. Within the 3-D model, goals of counseling can include either prevention of problems or remediation of problems. Typically prevention goals are established by the counselor and remediation goals are established by the client.

According to Atkinson et al. (1993), the intersection of the client's standing on the three dimensions leads to one of eight recommended roles for the counselor: advisor, advocate, change agent, consultant, counselor, facilitator of indigenous healing methods, facilitator of indigenous support systems, and psychotherapist. For example, a client higher in acculturation, with an internal problem etiology, and needing remediation, would best be served by a counselor or psychologist in the traditional psychotherapist role. However, if this same client were low in acculturation, the intersection of the three dimensions would speak to the role of facilitator of indigenous healing methods.

The 3-D model has been cited frequently in the conceptual literature (e.g., Coleman, 1995; D.W. Sue, Ivey, & Pedersen, 1996; D.W. Sue et al., 1998; Wehrly, 1995) as multicultural scholars resonate to its thesis of expanded counselor roles in meeting the needs of a culturally diverse clientele. However, direct empirical support for the model is limited. We located only one study that directly tested hypotheses emanating from the 3-D model. Given that there is only one test of the model, and because we found the study to be highly creative and experimentally sophisticated, we review it in some detail.

Atkinson et al. (1998) conducted two surveys wherein the various roles recommended by the 3-D model were evaluated by 103 psychologists (Survey #1) and 183 university students (Survey #2). The psychologist sample consisted of APA members who expressed interest in multicultural issues on their APA membership form. This sample was culturally heterogeneous: 32% Hispanic American, 23% European American, 22% African American, 12% Asian American, and 2% Native American (remainder unspecified). The student sample in Survey #2 consisted of Asian American university students on the West Coast.

Atkinson et al. (1998) developed 8 one-to-two sentence vignettes tapping the interacting dimensions of the 3-D model. For instance, to represent a high-acculturated client with an internal locus of problem etiology and a remedial goal for counseling, the following vignette was presented: "A fifth-generation Chinese American college graduate is deeply depressed after the death of his or her mother" (p. 417). On the opposite end of the continuum, the authors presented a low-acculturated client with an external locus of problem etiology and a prevention goal for counseling:

> A newly immigrated Korean with limited English-speaking proficiency has applied for a job at a local bookstore. The person is unaware that the proprietor of the bookstore has taken advantage of recent immigrants in the past by overworking and underpaying them. (p. 417)

Appropriate manipulation checks were conducted on each of the prepared vignettes to verify that the proposed dimensions being manipulated were clear. The researchers also developed a Helper Activity Questionnaire consisting of three items per recommended helper role (thus a total of 24 items). The items were content validated and also subjected to a confirmatory factor analysis, the results of which indicated satisfactory goodness-of-fit for the eight-role structure.

The results of this study provided moderate support for the 3-D model. The culturally diverse sample of psychologists, all of whom had expressed interest in multicultural issues, rated six of the eight helper roles for matched vignette conditions significantly higher than the average of the nonmatched roles. For two helper roles—advisor and advocate—the mean of the unmatched helper activity clusters were significantly higher than for the hypothesized matched clusters.

In the second survey, Asian American students gave higher cluster ratings to only three of the recommended roles (facilitator of indigenous support systems, consultant, and change agent). In a secondary analysis, Atkinson et al. (1998) examined the preferred helper roles for the students across all vignettes. A strong finding of this analysis was that regardless of 3-D vignette, the students ranked consultant or facilitator of indigenous support systems first or second across all eight vignettes. Interestingly, for the four external etiology vignettes, the consultant role ranked first, and for all four internal etiology vignettes, facilitator of indigenous support systems was ranked first.

The authors offered several pertinent warnings and weaknesses of the model. They noted that the model does not take into account potentially important within-group variables, such as client's level of modernity, racial identity development, and other factors such as gender, age, income level, or involvement with extended family. They also warned that the model should not be viewed as a "prescriptive tool for identifying a single counseling role to employ" (Atkinson et al., 1993, p. 271). Furthermore, they cautioned that high acculturation does not mean a client is free from oppression and discrimination. Finally, they noted that although one counselor role may be a best fit for the client at any given point in time, it is quite likely that a combination of, or changes in, roles may be required as the client makes progress and acculturates to the environment.

Some additional limitations we see with this model include lack of clarity regarding how change occurs or proceeds from counseling and, consequently, how the counselor shifts in role to better serve the client at any given point. Also, it may be difficult to assess the client's standing along the three dimensions because of language difficulties, cultural values, or client expectations. We expect that further elaboration of the model will address these points. A more in-depth discussion of ethical issues arising from counselors "switching" to roles for which they lack preparation also seems in order. From a research perspective, it will be important to show that matching (or shifting) counselor role to the client's intersecting position along the three continua leads to greater client satisfaction and goal attainment in counseling.

Trevino's Model of Worldview and Change

Drawing on the anthropology and counseling process research literature, Trevino (1996b) proposed a model for conceptualizing the change process in multicultural counseling using worldview, defined as "our basic perceptions and understandings of the world" (p. 198), as a unifying and mediating construct. According to Trevino, the individual's worldview represents an internally coherent system that is derived from one's shared cultural and unique personal experiences, thus differing from other people's views in level of abstraction (e.g., general versus specific perceptions of human nature). The counseling process is conceptualized as consisting of two levels and two corresponding phases. First, counselor-client congruency or similarity in general perceptions, values, and attitudes about the world strengthens the therapeutic relationship because this congruency increases communication as well as counselor credibility and empathy. To this end, during the initial phase of counseling, the counselor should endeavor to increase his or her understanding of the client's view of the world and presenting concern(s). Second, dissimilarity or discrepancy at a specific cognitive content level or point of view may effect change because this difference prompts the client to consider alternative perspectives and solutions regarding the presenting concerns or issues. The counselor at this second or intervention phase focuses on identifying strategies that may help the client to explore alternative ways of conceptualizing problems and solutions. Counseling outcome is postulated as a change of the client's worldview at the specific level, while the overarching general understanding of the world remains unchanged.

Trevino's (1996a) study was the only one we could find that directly tested her (Trevino, 1996b) model. This study specified two hypotheses: (1) that client-counselor congruency in interpersonal orientation (general worldview) would enhance the therapeutic relationship, a counseling process variable; and (2) that client-counselor discrepancy in relationship problem conceptualization (specific worldview) would facilitate client change, a counseling outcome variable. Using a two by two factorial design, with interpersonal orientation (congruent, discrepant) and problem conceptualization (congruent, discrepant) as the independent variables, she examined data from a sample of 48 ethnic minority undergraduate students who received two counseling sessions from one of four White counselors. Results revealed that client-counselor congruency in interpersonal orientation affected the counseling outcome, rather than the counseling process as predicted. Moreover, client-counselor discrepancy in relationship problem conceptualization affected the counseling process, rather than counseling outcome as predicted. Though the findings of this study do not support the hypotheses presented, they were nonetheless interesting. Clearly, follow-up research is needed, and at present there is too little evidence to verify or disconfirm Trevino's model. Fertile areas for future research include additional studies of the discrepancy and congruency hypotheses in the context of longer-term actual counseling. In addition, empirical efforts should also focus on the application of Trevino's model to other configurations of counseling dyads, such as a minority counselor and White client, or counselors and clients from different ethnic backgrounds.

In spite of its potential use in describing and outlining the role of worldview in facilitating client change, the explanatory and predictive power of Trevino's model is limited in several ways. The primary limitation lies in the elusive, if not philosophical, nature of the worldview construct. A more precise definition of worldview, both conceptually and operationally, is needed. In a similar vein, the imprecise definition, conceptual and operational, of other constructs such as congruency and discrepancy in the model makes it difficult to assess the model's potential. The implications for practice are also diminished because counselors are left to wonder how to proceed in counseling to capitalize on congruencies and discrepancies in worldview.

Furthermore, Trevino's framework needs to be expanded through the specification of assumptions and hypotheses. Implicit in the model are several assumptions that merit careful scrutiny such as that for change to occur, it must occur within the client's specific worldview. As noted by Essandoh (1996), for many minority clients, the change may need to occur in the environment (e.g., due to racist, sexist, anti-immigrant, or homophobic attitudes and forces). For this reason, modification of the client's worldview via the therapist's own worldview may not be a wise prescription for the client.

Ridley et al.'s Perceptual Schemata Model of Cultural Sensitivity

Grounded in information processing theory, cultural sensitivity is defined by Ridley et al. (1994) as a distinct perceptual schema that alerts the "counselor to cultural variables in the context of counseling, organizes cultural stimuli in meaningful ways, and appropriately channels this information to initiate some type of culturally responsive action" (p. 131). Implicit in this definition is a sequence of cognitive processes based on a computer metaphor to examine the role of cultural sensitivity in the flow of information in the human cognitive system, beginning with input (e.g., cultural stimuli) and ending with output (e.g., culturally responsive action). Premised on the belief that all counseling is culturally contextualized, Ridley et al.'s model placed a premium on cultural sensitivity as a vital means to understanding the idiographic experience of the client. The significance of cultural sensitivity as a perceptual schema lies in the explicit hypothesis that the accuracy of processing cultural information through perceptual schemata increases the likelihood of the counselor's effectiveness with culturally different clients. It should be noted, however, that in an attempt to remedy the conceptual problems of cultural sensitivity in the literature, Ridley et al. deliberately limited the construct of cultural sensitivity to the pre-behavioral stage in the counseling process, asserting that it is a necessary but insufficient condition for effective counseling.

Five specific subprocesses were proposed to influence interactively the counselor's cultural sensitivity: (1) self-processing (the degree to which the counselor is open and active in examining personal experiences, beliefs, values, and expectations); (2) purposefully applying schemata (the counselor's ability purposefully to apply the cultural perceptual schema to gather and organize client information in gaining a meaningful understanding of the client's experience); (3) maintaining plasticity (the degree to which the counselor is able to maintain flexibility in the application of cultural schema and to avoid stereotyping clients); (4) active-selective attention (the counselor's ability to attend actively to select aspects of cultural stimulus material); and (5) motivation (the counselor's willingness to engage in the previous four subprocesses).

As asserted by Ridely et al. (1994), the earlier definitions of counselor sensitivity in multicultural counseling are often fraught with ambiguities and consequently have fallen into scientific disrepute. Extrapolated from the rigorous conceptual and empirical base in cognitive psychology, Ridley et al.'s definition of cultural sensitivity has set the stage for fruitful theoretical and investigative inquires. Their model, however, has not received any empirical attention since it was developed, perhaps due to shortcomings in the computer metaphor, conceptual ambiguities regarding perceptual schema or cultural sensitivity, or a lack of inclusion of other client variables that may come into play in the counseling process.

Ridley et al.'s attempts to describe cultural sensitivity as a mental structure and as a cognitive process seem to proceed on assumptions that may or may not be warranted. One basic assumption is that humans process information like computers. This passive, purposeless computer model for human cognition certainly has its limitations because information processing of the computer is analogous to, but quite different from, human processing. Equally questionable is a related assumption that a static, unidirectional influence exists in the counseling process. Moreover, clients are omitted from the model, and it is unclear what roles perceptual schemata play in processing information about themselves, their counselors, and the counseling process. If schemata are modified as a result of feedback, client and counselor schemata are likely interactive and, therefore, do not operate in isolation from one another, as this model seems to suggest.

In addition, cultural sensitivity as defined in the model suggests that it would influence the counselor's culturally appropriate and responsive behavior. But it is not clear who should judge the extent to which the counselor's response is sensitive. Ridley et al. argued that the counselor should endeavor to understand the client's idiographic experience, implying that the client is ultimately the source of validation of the counselor's responses. Future research should thus assess the relations among the perspectives of the counselor, client, and observers relative to counselor sensitivity.

Leong's Integrative Model of Cross-Cultural Counseling

Noting the inadequacy of existing approaches to multicultural counseling, Leong (1996) argued that an ideal multicultural counseling theory should be integrative, sequential, and dynamic. The integrative feature of the model should manifest itself not only in its recognition of human beings as complex adaptive systems but also in its simultaneous examination of various dimensions of personality. To be helpful to the counselor working with the culturally different client, this model should be sequential through its microanalysis of the moment by moment, temporal unfolding of the counseling process, and of the effects of these interpersonal encounters on the counseling outcomes. Finally, an ideal model is one that avoids static, stagelike formulations in favor of a more dynamic view of complex interactions within and between counseling participants over time. Incorporating literature from other areas of psychology, Leong thus proposed a model intended to exhibit these characteristics.

Underlying Leong's (1996) model is Kluckhohn and Murray's (1950) tripartite model of personality, which asserted that personality consists of three levels (universal, group, and individual) which interact in a dynamic manner to influence cognition, emotion, and behavior. Of particular importance to multicultural counseling among these three levels of personality is the group-level orientation of personality (which includes cultural variables such as ethnicity, age, sex, and social class). Interwoven into Leong's framework were the following principles or concepts: (1) outgoing homogeneity effect, (2) cultural schema, (3) complexity, (4) complementarity, and (5) mindfulness.

First, outgroup homogeneity effect refers to the tendency of human beings to perceive greater homogeneity in members of other groups than in members in their own groups. It is a barrier for the multicultural counselor to overcome because it often prevents the counselor from effectively shifting among these three levels of client personality, thereby limiting the counseling effectiveness. This cognitive tendency is often a result of lack of exposure and contact with a member of a different cultural group, and thus leads to a somewhat simplistic, if not biased, view of the client. To minimize the influence of the outgroup homogeneity effect during the course of counseling, the counselor's task is to undergo continual self- and other-examination.

In addition, parallel to Bem's (1981) gender schema, Leong (1996) underscored the crucial role of cultural schema in influencing the counselor's perception, understanding, and interpretation of the client's culture-based experience. A multiculturally competent counselor has developed an elaborate cultural schema and possesses a high level of cognitive complexity. It is important to note, however, that a culture-schematic counselor is not necessarily culturally sensitive or competent. Racism, for example, is a result of the counselor perceiving an ethnic minority member based on biased and discriminating schema. The nature and content of the cultural schema should thus be given vital consideration. Moreover, culture schema are formed out of dominant values in society and family socialization experience and thus develop along a complexity continuum. A counselor with more mature and more developed culture schemata is thus hypothesized, according to Leong, to be more effective in multicultural counseling than a counselor who is culturally aschematic or who possesses cultural schemata at a lower level of cognitive complexity and maturity.

Leong also argued that each individual is a complex adaptive system and operates primarily on the universal, group, and individual levels. Consequently, each counseling relationship develops as a result of the counselor and the client operating at these three levels in a nonlinear, open, pattern-forming fashion. In other words, the three levels interact in a dynamic way within each individual and also within each interpersonal relationship.

To help the counselor tackle the complexity of the interpersonal interactions in counseling, Leong extended the complementarity concept from Sullivan's (1953) interpersonal theory to his formulations. Complementary interactions are evident when the counselor matches the client at any of the three personality levels through assessment, techniques, and interventions. Leong hypothesized that high complementary interactions between the counselor and the client would lead to positive outcomes, while low complementarity would lead to negative counseling outcomes such as misunderstanding or premature terminations.

Finally, Leong suggested that the counselor should obtain a high sense of mindfulness, as described by Langer (1989), to overcome the homogeneity effect barrier, become culturally schematic, and achieve a high level of cultural complementarity in counseling. According to Langer, rather than operating in an automatic, habitual manner that may lead to problems or errors, mindful individuals are open to new information and sensitive to the context when performing a task. Without this sense of mindfulness counselors are likely to be limited by their simplistic cultural schemata, engage in automatic behavior, and assume a single perspective. More specifically, counselors who function mindlessly are not alert to the ever-changing position along the tripartite personality continuum within themselves and their clients as well as within the counseling relationship, and their subsequent assessment and intervention strategies are thus severely compromised.

Compared with other emerging proposed frameworks reviewed in this chapter, Leong's (1996) theoretical conceptualization may be more comprehensive in scope and is reflective of complex human experience that may be universal, group-specific, or individualistic. Unlike some models of multicultural counseling that focus on group-level conceptualization, and others in mainstream psychology that examine human behaviors without attention to individual differences, Leong's formulations recognize the complexity of human experience, particularly cross-cultural counseling encounters. His foray into other psychological literatures is also noteworthy.

In spite of its comprehensiveness, however, this framework lacks conceptual precision. The specific nature of the five elements, as well as their connections in the model, have yet to be clarified. The definition of culture and cultural variables as a whole need further refinement as well. Leong's (1996) conceptualization of complementarity differs from that in Sullivan's (1953) interpersonal theory, which holds that complementarity occurs when the needs of one individual is met by the other's behavior in the interaction, thereby contributing to the development of a harmonious relationship. In addition, there is some evidence in the literature supporting the high-low-high pattern of complementarity among successful counseling cases (see Hill & Williams, this volume). To the extent that this finding extends to the context of multicultural counseling as well, Leong's assumption that successful counseling consists of smooth or conflict-free interactions may not be warranted.

It would be useful for future research to determine how Leong's (1996) cultural schema is related to cultural sensitivity as defined by Ridley et al. (1994). Another important research area is to examine the application of mindfulness and lack thereof in multicultural counseling and the relation of mindfulness to counselor reflectivity (e.g., Neufeldt, Karno, & Nelson, 1996) and intentionality (e.g., Hill, Carter, & O'Farrell, 1983). Research in these areas may be useful in counselor and supervisor training.

Fischer et al.'s Common Factors Perspective

A very recent comprehensive perspective of multicultural counseling is that presented by Fischer, Jome, and Atkinson (1998a; Fischer et al., 1998b), which focuses on understanding culture in counseling within an already established framework of "common factors" in psychotherapy and healing as a universal phenomenon. The authors believe their perspective "(1) may serve as a framework for unifying the diverse body of multicultural counseling literature, (2) has some empirical support, and (3) may be useful in guiding future multicultural research, training, and practice" (Fischer et al., 1998b, p. 525). A major tenet of the Fischer et al. perspective is that there is empirical evidence (cf. Lambert & Bergin, 1994) to support the construct of successful common factors across therapeutic modalities—speaking to a more universal or etic approach to helping. The authors believed that counselors and clients will be better served if researchers can first isolate and understand therapeutic factors common to all conventional (e.g., Eurocentric and Western-based) and indigenous healing approaches, and then supplement this etic perspective with necessary contextual, and culture-specific (emic) knowledge. In effect, Fischer et al. attempted to provide a bridge between emic and etic approaches to multicultural counseling.

The four common factors selected by Fischer et al. (1998b) are the therapeutic relationship, a shared worldview between client and counselor, meeting client expectations, and the use of ritual or intervention that is perceived as appropriate by both client and counselor. The authors emphasized that the common factors are additive, building on one another. There are immediate implications for intervention inherent in the Fischer et al. framework. The authors provided the counselor with a heuristic for continuously monitoring the counseling process. For example, Fischer et al. suggested that counselors ask themselves:

> What do I know or need to know about this individual, about his or her culture(s), and about people in general that will likely help me (1) to develop a good therapeutic relationship with him or her; (2) to discover or construct with the client a shared worldview or plausible rationale for distress; (3) to create an environment in which the client's expectations will be raised; and (4) to plan a healing procedure in which my client(s) and I both have confidence? (pp. 542–543)

The Fischer et al. (1998b) perspective extends beyond Ponterotto and Benesch's (1988) combined etic-emic approach to understanding the role of culture in counseling, which built on the influential work of Frank (1961) and Torrey (1972). Ponterotto and Benesch identified five common factors that appeared to transcend culture (tapping both indigenous and Western-based forms of helping): accurately identifying the client's/helpee's problem, the personal qualities of the counselor/helper, meeting client/helpee expectations in the helping process, establishing counselor/helper credibility (cf. S. Sue & Zane, 1987), and the implementation of some form of counseling/helping intervention. Ponterotto and Benesch suggested that within each transcendent condition, the counselor must tap emic interpretations of the construct (e.g., the same behavior may be defined as a problem or a strength given the culture; helper credibility is established very differently across cultures; helping interventions can be directive or nondirective, verbal or quietly meditative, depending on the culture).

Fischer et al. (1998b) extended significantly beyond the Ponterotto and Benesch (1988) common factors framework and other combined emic-etic approaches (e.g., Leong, 1996; D.W. Sue, et al., 1996) through their thoughtful reorganization of the extant empirical literature to support their construct, and through their in-depth discussion of how the common factors facilitate the counseling relationship. Furthermore, the authors integrated a broad conceptual and empirical body of literature.

Generally speaking, common factors approaches to multiculturalism have been met with some skepticism by multicultural specialists. For example, D.W. Sue et al. (1996), though not speaking to the newer Fischer et al. (1998b) conceptualization, summarized two concerns with regard to common factors integrations. "First, attempts to extract commonalities may lead to an overly general and ambiguous characteristic that one cannot translate into practice. Second, such an approach must still deal with the multiplicity of differences among the systems of helping" (p. 11). Though we find D.W. Sue et al.'s (1996) points well taken generally, we believe Fischer et al. (1998b) adequately address these cautions. First, their model possesses enough depth and clarity so that useful implications for practice are inherent in the framework. Second, the model openly acknowledges that in addition to common characteristics of the helping process across cultures, counselors must still be culturally aware and sensitive and must consider culturally specific contexts in counseling.

Given their careful review and integration of extant research, the Fischer et al. (1998b) framework has some scientific support. One important area for research on the Fischer et al. model is to examine counseling outcome. For example, the authors integrate research evidence indicating "that ethnic minority participants tend to prefer, perceive most positively, and be most willing to self-disclose to, counselors who share their worldview" (p. 553), or would choose "a counselor with similar attitudes and values" (p. 552); however, research is still needed to assess the extent to which satisfaction of these preferences translates into superior counseling outcomes.

CONCLUSION

This chapter has reviewed two foundational models and five emerging models of multicultural counseling. We believe the models represent significant contributions to the literature, and it is our hope that this review will stimulate additional systematic testing of the models using both positivist (theory driven) and constructivist (theory generating) paradigms. We examined four additional models that we did not have space to review yet we believe have extensive promise in stimulating research on the counseling process. These models were Ho's (1995) perspective on internalized culture; D.W. Sue et al.'s (1996) theory of multicultural counseling; Gonzalez, Biever, and Gardner's (1994) social constructionist approach to multicultural counseling; and Coleman's (1995, 1997) coping with diversity counseling model. Like the foundational and other emerging models, these additional models are certainly worthy of more conceptual attention and systematic empirical testing. The last decade has witnessed rapid growth of more comprehensive and integrative models of multicultural counseling, and we look forward to intensified research efforts to uncover the critical elements of successful counseling for all clients.

REFERENCES

Arredondo, P., Toporek, R., Brown, S.P., Jones, J., Locke, D.C., Sanchez, J., & Stadler, H. (1996). Operationalization of the multicultural counseling competencies. *Journal of Multicultural Counseling and Development, 24,* 42–78.

Atkinson, D.R., Casas, A., & Abreu, J. (1992). Mexican-American acculturation, counselor ethnicity and cultural sensitivity, and perceived counselor competence. *Journal of Counseling Psychology, 39,* 515–520.

Atkinson, D.R., Kim, B.S.K., & Caldwell, R. (1998). Ratings of helper roles by multicultural psychologists and Asian American students: Initial support for the three-dimensional model of multicultural counseling. *Journal of Counseling Psychology, 45,* 414–423.

Atkinson, D.R., & Lowe, S.M. (1995). The role of ethnicity, cultural knowledge, and conventional techniques in counseling and psychotherapy. In J.G. Ponterotto, J.M. Casas, L.A. Suzuki, & C.M. Alexander (Eds.), *Handbook of multicultural counseling* (pp. 387–414). Thousand Oaks, CA: Sage.

Atkinson, D.R., Morten, G., & Sue, D.W. (Eds.). (1989). *Counseling American minorities: A cross-cultural perspective* (3rd ed.). Dubuque, IA: Brown.

Atkinson, D.R., Thompson, C.E., & Grant, S.K. (1993). A three-dimensional model for counseling racial/ethnic minorities. *Counseling Psychologist, 21,* 257–277.

Behrens, J.T. (1997). Does the White Racial Identity Attitude Scale measure racial identity? *Journal of Counseling Psychology, 44,* 3–12.

Bem, S.L. (1981). Gender schema theory: A cognitive account of sex typing. *Psychological Review, 88,* 354–364.

Block, C.J., Roberson, L., & Neuger, D.A. (1995). White racial identity theory: A framework for understanding reactions toward interracial situations in organizations. *Journal of Vocational Behavior, 46,* 71–88.

Bradby, D., & Helms, J.E. (1990). Black racial identity attitudes and white therapist cultural sensitivity in cross-racial therapy dyads: An exploratory study. In J.E. Helms (Ed.), *Black and white racial identity: Theory, research, and practice* (pp. 165–175). New York: Greenwood.

Brown, S.P., Parham, T.A., & Yonker, R. (1996). Influence of a cross-cultural training course on racial identity attitudes of white women and men: Preliminary perspectives. *Journal of Counseling and Development, 74,* 510–516.

Burkard, A.W., Ponterotto, J.G., Reynolds, A.L., & Alfonso, V.C. (1999). The impact of white counselor trainees' racial identity upon working alliance perceptions in same- and cross-racial dyads. *Journal of Counseling and Development, 77,* 324–329.

Carter, R.T. (1990). The relationship between racism and racial identity among White Americans: An exploratory investigation. *Journal of Counseling and Development, 69,* 46–50.

Carter, R.T. (1991). Racial identity attitudes and psychological functioning. *Journal of Multicultural Counseling and Development 19,* 105–114.

Carter, R.T. (1995). *The influence of race and racial identity in psychotherapy: Toward a racially inclusive model.* New York: Wiley.

Carter, R.T. (1996). Exploring the complexity of racial identity attitude measures. In G.R. Sodowsky & J.C. Impara (Eds.), *Multicultural assessment in counseling and clinical psychology* (pp. 193–223). Lincoln, NE: Buros Institute of Mental Measurements.

Carter, R.T. (1997). Is white a race? Expressions of white racial identity. In M. Fine, L. Weis, L.C. Powell, & L.M. Wong (Eds.), *Off white: Readings on race, power, and society* (pp. 198–209). New York: Routledge & Kegan Paul.

Carter, R.T., & Akinsulure-Smith, A.M. (1996). White racial identity and expectations about counseling. *Journal of Multicultural Counseling and Development, 24,* 218–228.

Carter, R.T., & Goodwin, A.L. (1994). Racial identity in education. *Review of Research in Education, 20,* 291–336.

Carter, R.T., Gushue, G.V., & Weitzman, L.M. (1994). White racial identity development and work values. *Journal of Vocational Behavior, 44,* 185–197.

Carter, R.T., & Helms, J.E. (1992). The counseling process as defined by relationship types: A test of Helms's interactional model. *Journal of Multicultural Counseling and Development, 20,* 181–201.

Choney, S.K., & Behrens, J.T. (1996). Development of the Oklahoma Racial Attitudes Scale Preliminary Form (ORAS-P). In G.R. Sodowsky & J.C. Impara (Eds.), *Multicultural assessment in counseling and clinical psychology* (pp. 225–240). Lincoln, NE: Buros Institute of Mental Measurements.

Choney, S.K., & Rowe, W. (1994). Assessing white racial identity: The White Racial Consciousness Development Scale (WRCDS). *Journal of Counseling and Development, 73,* 102–104.

Claney, D., & Parker, W.M. (1988). Assessing white racial consciousness and perceived comfort with black individuals: A preliminary study. *Journal of Counseling and Development, 67,* 449–451.

Coleman, H.L.K. (1995). Strategies for coping with cultural diversity. *Counseling Psychologist, 23,* 722–740.

Coleman, H.L.K. (1997). Conflict in multicultural counseling relationships: Source and resolution. *Journal of Multicultural Counseling and Development, 25,* 195–200.

Constantine, M.G., & Ladany, N. (in press). Self-report multicultural counseling competence scales and their relation to multicultural case conceptualization ability and social desirability. *Journal of Counseling Psychology.*

Cook, D.A. (1994). Racial identity in supervision. *Counselor Education and Supervision, 34,* 132–141.

Corrigan, J.D., & Schmidt, L.D. (1983). Development and validation of revisions in the Counselor Rating Form. *Journal of Counseling Psychology, 30,* 64–75.

Cross, W.E. (1971). The negro-to-black conversion experience: Toward a psychology of black liberation. *Black World, 20,* 13–27.

Cross, W.E. (1991). *Shades of black: Diversity in African American identity.* Philadelphia: Temple University Press.

Cross, W.E. (1995). The psychology of nigrescence: Revising the Cross model. In J.G. Ponterotto, J.M. Casas, L.A. Suzuki, & C.M. Alexander (Eds.), *Handbook of multicultural counseling* (pp. 93–122). Thousand Oaks, CA: Sage.

Cross, W.E., Fagen-Smith, P., Vandiver, B., Cokley, K., & Worell, F. (1999, February). *Development of a new nigrescence measure: Theory, development and application.* Paper presented at the annual meeting of the Winter Roundtable on Cross-Cultural Psychology and Education, New York.

D'Andrea, M., Daniels, J., & Heck, R. (1991). Evaluating the impact of multicultural counseling training. *Journal of Counseling and Development, 70,* 143–150.

Delphin, M.E., & Rollock, D. (1995). University alienation and African American ethnic identity as predictors of attitudes toward, knowledge about, and likely use of psychological services. *Journal of College Student Development, 36,* 337–346.

Dinsmore, B.D., & Mallinckrodt, B. (1996). Emotional self-awareness, eating disorders, and racial identity attitudes in African American women. *Journal of Multicultural Counseling and Development, 24,* 267–277.

Essandoh, P.K. (1996). Multicultural challenges in graduate counseling psychology programs: Timely reminders. *Counseling Psychologist, 24,* 273–278.

Evans, K.M., & Herr, E.L. (1994). The influence of racial identity and the perception of discrimination on the career aspirations of African American men and women. *Journal of Vocational Behavior, 44,* 173–184.

Fischer, A.R., Jome, L.M., & Atkinson, D.R. (1998a). Back to the future of multicultural psychotherapy with a common factors approach. *Counseling Psychologist, 26,* 602–606.

Fischer, A.R., Jome, L.M., & Atkinson, D.R. (1998b). Reconceptualizing multicultural counseling: Universal healing conditions in a culturally specific context. *Counseling Psychologist, 26,* 525–588.

Fischer, A.R., Tokar, D.M., & Serna, G.S. (1998). Validity and construct contamination of the Racial Identity Attitude Scale–long form. *Journal of Counseling Psychology, 45,* 212–224.

Frank, J.P. (1961). *Persuasion and healing.* Baltimore: Johns Hopkins University Press.

Gainor, K.A., & Lent, R.W. (1998). Social cognitive expectations and racial identity attitudes in predicting the math choice intentions of black college students. *Journal of Counseling Psychology, 45,* 403–413.

Gim, R.H., Atkinson, D.R., & Kim, S.J. (1991). Asian-American acculturation, counselor ethnicity and cultural sensitivity, and ratings of counselors. *Journal of Counseling Psychology, 38,* 57–62.

Glasser, B., & Strauss, A.L. (1967). *The discovery of grounded theory: Strategies for qualitative research.* Hawthorne, NY: Aldine de Gruyter.

Gonzalez, R.C., Biever, J.L., & Gardner, G.T. (1994). The multicultural perspective in therapy: A social constructionist approach. *Psychotherapy, 31,* 515–524.

Goodstein, R., & Ponterotto, J.G. (1997). Racial and ethnic identity: Their relationship and their contribution to self-esteem. *Journal of Black Psychology, 23,* 275–292.

Helms, J.E. (1984a). *Counseling Reactions Inventory.* Unpublished manuscript, University of Maryland at College Park.

Helms, J.E. (1984b). Towards a theoretical explanation of the effects of race on counseling: A black and white model. *Counseling Psychologist, 12,* 153–165.

Helms, J.E. (Ed.). (1990). *Black and white racial identity: Theory, research, and practice.* Westport, CT: Greenwood.

Helms, J.E. (1992). *Race is a nice thing to have.* Topeka, KS: Content Communications.

Helms, J.E. (1994a). Racial identity and career assessment. *Journal of Career Assessment, 2,* 199–209.

Helms, J.E. (1994b). Racial identity in the school environment. In P.B. Pedersen & J.C. Carey (Eds.), *Multicultural counseling in schools* (pp. 19–37). Boston: Allyn & Bacon.

Helms, J.E. (1995). An update of Helms's white and people of color model racial identity models. In J.G. Ponterotto, J.M. Casas, L.A. Suzuki, & C.M. Alexander (Eds.), *Handbook of multicultural counseling* (pp. 181–198). Thousand Oaks, CA: Sage.

Helms, J.E. (1996). Toward a methodology for measuring and assessing racial as distinguished from ethnic identity. In G.R. Sodowsky & J.C. Impara (Eds.), *Multicultural assessment in counseling and clinical psychology* (pp. 143–192). Lincoln, NE: Buros Institute of Mental Measurements.

Helms, J.E. (1997). Implications of Behrens (1997) for the validity of the White Racial Identity Attitude Scale. *Journal of Counseling Psychology, 44,* 13–16.

Helms, J.E. (1999, February). *Using personal-level analysis to study racial identity.* Workshop presented at the annual meeting of the Winter Roundtable on Cross-Cultural Psychology and Education, New York.

Helms, J.E., & Carter, R.T. (1990). Development of the White Racial Identity Inventory. In J.E. Helms (Ed.), *Black and white racial identity: Theory, research, and practice* (pp. 67–80). Westport, CT: Greenwood.

Helms, J.E., & Carter, R.T. (1991). Relationships of white and black racial identity attitudes and demographic similarity to counselor preferences. *Journal of Counseling Psychology, 38,* 446–457.

Helms, J.E., & Cook, D.A. (1999). *Using race and culture in counseling and psychotherapy: Theory and process.* Boston: Allyn & Bacon.

Helms, J.E., & Parham, T.A. (1990). The relationship between black racial identity attitudes and cognitive styles. In J.E. Helms (Ed.), *Black and white racial identity: Theory, research, and practice* (pp. 119–131). New York: Greenwood.

Helms, J.E., & Piper, R.E. (1994). Implications of racial identity theory for vocational psychology. *Journal of Vocational Psychology, 44,* 124–138.

Hill, C.E., Carter, J.A., & O'Farrell, M.K. (1983). A case study of the process and outcome of time-limited counseling. *Journal of Counseling Psychology, 30,* 3–18.

Hill, C.E., Thompson, B.J., & Williams, E.N. (1997). A guide to conducting consensual qualitative research. *Counseling Psychologist, 25,* 517–572.

Ho, D.Y.F. (1995). Internalized culture, culturocentrism, and transcendence. *Counseling Psychologist, 23,* 4–24.

Jackson, C.C., & Neville, H.A. (1998). Influence of racial identity attitudes on African American college students' vocational identity and hope. *Journal of Vocational Behavior, 53,* 97–113.

Jones, S.R. (1997). Voices of identity and difference: A qualitative exploration of the multiple dimensions of identity development in women college students. *Journal of College Student Development, 38,* 376–385.

Kerwin, C., Ponterotto, J.G., Jackson, B.L., & Harris, A. (1993). Racial identity in biracial children: A qualitative investigation. *Journal of Counseling Psychology, 40,* 221–231.

Kluckhohn, C., & Murray, H.A. (1950). Personality formation: The determinants. In C. Kluckhohn & H.A. Murray (Eds.), *Personality in nature, society, and culture* (pp. 35–48). New York: Knopf.

Ladany, N., Brittan-Powell, C.S., & Pannu, R.K. (1997). The influence of supervisory racial identity interaction and racial matching on the supervisory working alliance and supervisee multicultural competence. *Counselor Education and Supervision, 36,* 284–304.

Ladany, N., Inman, A.G., Constantine, M.G., & Hofheinz, E.W. (1997). Supervisee multicultural case conceptualization ability and self-reported multicultural competence as functions of supervisee racial identity and supervisor focus. *Journal of Counseling Psychology, 44,* 284–293.

LaFromboise, T.D., Coleman, H.L.K., & Hernandez, A. (1991). Development and factor structure of the Cross-Cultural Counseling Inventory-Revised. *Professional Psychology: Research and Practice, 22,* 380–388.

Lambert, M.J., & Bergin, A.E. (1994). The effectiveness of psychotherapy. In A.E. Bergin & S.L. Garfield (Eds.), *Handbook of psychotherapy and behavior change* (4th ed., pp. 143–189). New York: Wiley.

Langer, E.J. (1989). *Mindfulness.* Reading, MA: Addison-Wesley.

Lemon, R.L., & Waehler, C.A. (1996). A test of stability and construct validity of the Black Racial Identity Attitude Scale. Form B (RIAS-B) and the White Racial Identity Attitude Scale (WRIAS). *Measurement and Evaluation in Counseling and Development, 29,* 77–85.

Leong, F.T.L. (1996). Toward an integrative model for cross-cultural counseling and psychotherapy. *Applied and Preventive Psychology: Current Scientific Perspectives, 5,* 189–209.

Martin, J.K., & Hall, G.C.N. (1992). Thinking black, thinking internal, thinking feminist. *Journal of Counseling Psychology, 39,* 509–514.

Mitchell, S.L., Dell, D.M. (1992). The relationship between black students' racial identity attitude and participation in campus organizations. *Journal of College Student Development, 33,* 39–43.

Neufeldt, S.A., Karno, M.P., & Nelson, M.L. (1996). A qualitative study of experts' conceptualizations of supervisee reflectivity. *Journal of Counseling Psychology, 43,* 3–9.

Neville, H.A., Heppner, M.J., Louie, C.E., Thompson, C.E., Brooks, L., & Baker, C.E. (1996). The impact of multicultural training on white racial identity attitudes and therapy competencies. *Professional Psychology: Research and Practice, 27,* 83–89.

Neville, H.A., Heppner, P.P., & Wang, L. (1997). Relations among racial identity attitudes, perceived stressors, and coping styles in African American college students. *Journal of Counseling and Development, 75,* 303–311.

Newswanger, J.F. (1996). The relationship between white racial identity attitudes and the experience of having a black college roommate. *Journal of College Student Development, 37,* 536–542.

Ottavi, T.M., Pope-Davis, D.B., & Dings, J.G. (1994). Relationship between white racial identity attitudes and self-reported multicultural counseling competencies. *Journal of Counseling Psychology, 41,* 149–154.

Parker, W.M., Moore, M.A., & Neimeyer, G.J. (1998). Altering white racial identity and interracial comfort through multicultural training. *Journal of Counseling and Development, 76,* 302–310.

Parks, E.E., Carter, R.T., & Gushue, G.V. (1996). At the crossroads: Racial and womanist identity development in black and white women. *Journal of Counseling and Development, 74,* 624–631.

Parham, T.A., & Austin, N.L. (1994). Career development and African Americans: A contextual reappraisal using the nigrescence construct. *Journal of Vocational Behavior, 44,* 139–154.

Poindexter-Cameron, J.M., & Robinson, T.L. (1997). Relationships among racial identity attitudes, womanist identity attitudes, and self-esteem in African American college women. *Journal of College Student Development, 38,* 288–296.

Polkinghorne, D.E. (1994). Reaction to special section on qualitative research in counseling process and outcome. *Journal of Counseling Psychology, 41,* 510–512.

Pomales, J., Claiborn, C.D., & LaFromboise, T.D. (1986). Effects of black students' racial identity on perceptions of white counselors varying in cultural sensitivity. *Journal of Counseling Psychology, 33,* 57–61.

Ponterotto, J.G. (1996). Evaluating and selecting research instruments. In F.T.L. Leong & J.T. Austin (Eds.), *The psychology research handbook: A guide for graduate students and research assistants* (pp. 73–84). Thousand Oaks, CA: Sage.

Ponterotto, J.G., & Alexander, C.M. (1996). Assessing the multicultural competence of counselors and clinicians. In L.A. Suzuki, P. Meller, & J.G. Ponterotto (Eds.), *Handbook of multicultural assessment: Clinical, psychological, and educational applications* (pp. 651–672). San Francisco: Jossey-Bass.

Ponterotto, J.G., & Benesch, K.F. (1988). An organizational framework for understanding the role of culture in counseling. *Journal of Counseling and Development, 66,* 237–241.

Ponterotto, J.G., Burkard, A., Rieger, B.P., Grieger, I., D'Onofrio, A., Dubuisson, A., Heenehan, M., Millstein, B., Parisi, M., Rath, J.F., & Sax, G. (1995). Development and initial validation of the Quick Discrimination Index (QDI). *Educational and Psychological Measurement, 55,* 1016–1031.

Ponterotto, J.G., & Casas, J.M. (1991). *Handbook of racial/ethnic minority counseling research.* Springfield, IL: Thomas.

Ponterotto, J.G., & Casas, J.M. (In preparation). *Handbook of racial/ethnic minority counseling research* (2nd ed.). Springfield, IL: Thomas.

Ponterotto, J.G., Casas, J.M., Suzuki, L.A., & Alexander, C.M. (Eds.). (1995). *Handbook of multicultural counseling.* Thousand Oaks, CA: Sage.

Ponterotto, J.G., & Pedersen, P.B. (1993). *Preventing prejudice: A guide for counselors and educators.* Thousand Oaks, CA: Sage.

Ponterotto, J.G., Rieger, B.P., Barrett, A., Harris, G., Sparks, R., Sanchez, C.M., & Magids, D. (1996). Development and initial validation of the Multicultural Counseling Awareness Scale. In G.R. Sodowsky & J.C. Impara (Eds.), *Multicultural assessment if counseling and clinical psychology* (pp. 247–282). Lincoln, NE: Buros Institute of Mental Measurements.

Ponterotto, J.G., Rieger, B.P., Barrett, A., & Sparks, R. (1994). Assessing multicultural counseling competence: A review of instrumentation. *Journal of Counseling and Development, 72,* 316–322.

Ponterotto, J.G., Rieger, B.P., Gretchen, D., Utsey, S.O., & Austin, R. (1999). *A construct validity study of the Multicultural Counseling Awareness Scale with suggested revisions.* Manuscript in preparation.

Ponterotto, J.G., & Wise, S.L. (1987). Construct validity study of the Racial Identity Attitude Scale. *Journal of Counseling Psychology, 34,* 218–223.

Pope-Davis, D.B., & Coleman, H.L.K. (Eds.). (in press). *Intersection of race, class, and gender: Implications for multicultural counseling.* Thousand Oaks, CA: Sage.

Pope-Davis, D.B., & Dings, J.G. (1994). An empirical comparison of two self-report multicultural counseling competency inventories. *Measurement and Evaluation in Counseling and Development, 27,* 93–102.

Pope-Davis, D.B., & Dings, J.G. (1995). The assessment of multicultural counseling competencies. In J.G. Ponterotto, J.M. Casas, L.A. Suzuki, & C.M. Alexander (Eds.), *Handbook of multicultural counseling* (pp. 287–311). Thousand Oaks, CA: Sage.

Pope-Davis, D.B., Dings, J.G., & Ottavi, T.M. (1995). The relationship of multicultural counseling competencies with demographic and educational variables. *The Iowa Psychologist, 40*(1), 12–13.

Pope-Davis, D.B., & Nielson, D. (1996). Assessing multicultural counseling competence using the Multicultural Counseling Inventory: A review of the research. In G.R. Sodowsky & J.C. Impara (Eds.), *Multicultural assessment in counseling and clinical psychology* (pp. 325–343). Lincoln, NE: Buros Institute of Mental Measurements.

Pope-Davis, D.B., & Ottavi, T.M. (1992). The influence of white racial identity attitudes on racism among faculty members: A preliminary examination. *Journal of College Student Development, 33,* 389–394.

Pope-Davis, D.B., & Ottavi, T.M. (1994a). Examining the association between self-reported multicultural counseling competencies and demographic variables among counselors. *Journal of Counseling and Development, 72,* 651–654.

Pope-Davis, D.B., & Ottavi, T.M. (1994b). The relationship between racism and racial identity among white Americans: A replication and extension. *Journal of Counseling and Development, 72,* 293–297.

Pope-Davis, D.B., Prieto, L.R., Whitaker, C.M., & Pope-Davis, S.A. (1993). Exploring multicultural competencies of occupational therapists: Implications for education and training. *American Journal of Occupational Therapy, 46,* 838–844.

Pope-Davis, D.B., Reynolds, A.L., Dings, J.G., & Nielson, D. (1995). Examining multicultural counseling competencies of graduate students in psychology. *Professional Psychology: Research and Practice, 26,* 322–329.

Pope-Davis, D.B., Reynolds, A.L., Dings, J.G., & Ottavi, T.M. (1994). Multicultural competencies of doctoral interns at university counseling centers: An exploratory investigation. *Professional Psychology: Research and Practice, 25,* 466–470.

Pope-Davis, D.B., Vandiver, B.J., & Stone, G.L. (1999). White racial identity attitude development: A psychometric examination of two instruments. *Journal of Counseling Psychology, 46,* 70–79.

Poston, W.S.C., Craine, M., & Atkinson, D.R. (1991). Counselor dissimilarity confrontation, client cultural mistrust, and willingness to self-disclose. *Journal of Multicultural Counseling and Development, 19,* 65–73.

Pyant, C.T., & Yanico, B.J. (1991). Relationship of racial identity and gender-role attitudes to black women's psychological well-being. *Journal of Counseling Psychology, 38,* 315–322.

Richardson, T.Q., & Helms, J.E. (1994). The relation of the racial identity attitudes of black men to perceptions of parallel counseling dyads. *Journal of Counseling and Development, 73,* 172–177.

Ridley, C.R., Mendoza, D.W., Kanitz, B.E., Angermeier, L., & Zenk, R. (1994). Cultural sensitivity in multicultural counseling: A perceptual schema model. *Journal of Counseling Psychology, 41,* 125–136.

Robinson, B., & Bradley, L.J. (1997). Multicultural training for undergraduates: Developing knowledge and awareness. *Journal of Multicultural Counseling and Development, 25,* 281–289.

Root, M.P.P. (1998). Experiences and processes affecting racial identity development: Preliminary results from the biracial sibling project. *Cultural Diversity and Mental Health, 4,* 237–247.

Rowe, W., Behrens, J.T., & Leach, M.M. (1995). Racial/ethnic identity and racial consciousness: Looking back and looking forward. In J.G. Ponterotto, J.M. Casas, L.A. Suzuki, & C.M. Alexander (Eds.), *Handbook of multicultural counseling* (pp. 218–235). Thousand Oaks, CA: Sage.

Sellers, R.M., Rowley, S.A.J., Chavous, T.M., Shelton, J.N., & Smith, M.A. (1997). Multidimensional Inventory of Black Identity: A preliminary investigation of reliability and construct validity. *Journal of Personality and Social Psychology, 73,* 805–815.

Sodowsky, G.R. (1991). Effects of cultural consistent counseling tasks on American and international student observers' perception of counselor credibility: A preliminary investigation. *Journal of Counseling and Development, 69,* 253–256.

Sodowsky, G.R. (1996). The Multicultural Counseling Inventory: Validity and applications in multicultural training. In G.R. Sodowsky & J.C. Impara (Eds.), *Multicultural assessment in counseling and clinical psychology* (pp. 283–324). Lincoln, NE: Buros Institute of Mental Measurements.

Sodowsky, G.R., Kuo-Jackson, P., Richardson, M.F., & Corey, A.T. (1998). Correlates of self-reported multicultural competencies: Counselor multicultural social desirability, race, social inadequacy, locus of control racial ideology, and multicultural training. *Journal of Counseling Psychology, 45,* 256–264.

Sodowsky, G.R., & Taffe, R.C. (1991). Counselor trainees' analyses of multicultural counseling videotapes. *Journal of Multicultural Counseling and Development, 19,* 115–129.

Sodowsky, G.R., Taffe, R.C., Gutkin, T.B., & Wise, S.L. (1994). Development of the Multicultural Counseling Inventory: A self-report measure of multicultural competencies. *Journal of Counseling Psychology, 41,* 137–148.

Steward, R.J., Boatwright, K.J., Sauer, E., Baden, A., & Jackson, J.D. (1998). The relationships among counselor-trainees' gender, cognitive development, and white racial identity: Implications for counselor training. *Journal of Multicultural Counseling and Development, 26,* 254–272.

Strauss, A. (1987). *Qualitative analysis for social scientist.* New York: Cambridge University Press.

Sue, D.W., Arredondo, P., & McDavis, R.J. (1992). Multicultural competencies and standards: A call to the profession. *Journal of Multicultural Counseling and Development, 20,* 64–88.

Sue, D.W., Bernier, J.E., Durran, A., Feinberg, L., Pedersen, P., Smith, E.J., & Vazquez-Nutall, E. (1982). Position paper: Cross-cultural counseling competencies. *Counseling Psychologist, 10,* 45–52.

Sue, D.W., Carter, R.T., Casas, J.M., Fouad, N.A., Ivey, A.E., Jensen, M., LaFromboise, T., Manese, J.E., Ponterotto, J.G., & Vazquez-Nutall, E. (1998). *Multicultural counseling competencies: Individual and organizational development.* Thousand Oaks, CA: Sage.

Sue, D.W., Ivey, A.E., & Pedersen, P.B. (1996). *A theory of multicultural counseling and therapy.* Pacific Grove, CA: Brooks/Cole.

Sue, S., & Zane, N. (1987). The role of culture and cultural technique in psychotherapy: A critique and reformulation. *American Psychologist, 42,* 37–45.

Sullivan, H.S. (1953). *The interpersonal theory of psychiatry.* New York: Norton.

Swanson, J.L., Tokar, D.M., & Davis, L.E. (1994). Content and construct validity of the White Racial Identity Attitude Scale. *Journal of Vocational Behavior, 44,* 198–217.

Tatum, B.D. (1997). *"Why are all the black kids sitting together in the cafeteria?" And other conversations about race.* New York: Basic Books.

Taub, D.J., & McEwen, M.K. (1992). The relationship of racial identity attitudes to autonomy and mature interpersonal relationships in black and white undergraduate women. *Journal of College Student Development, 33,* 439–446.

Taylor, C.M., & Howard-Hamilton, M.F. (1995). Student involvement and racial identity attitudes among African American males. *Journal of College Student Development, 36,* 330–336.

Thompson, C.E., & Jenal, S.T. (1994). Interracial and intraracial quasi counseling interactions when counselors avoid discussing race. *Journal of Counseling Psychology, 41,* 484–491.

Thompson, C.E., Worthington, R., & Atkinson, D.R. (1994). Counselor content orientation, counselor race, and black women's cultural mistrust and self-disclosures. *Journal of Counseling Psychology, 41,* 155–161.

Tokar, D.M., & Fischer, A.R. (1998). Psychometric analysis of the Racial Identity Attitude Scale–Long Form. *Measurement and Evaluation in Counseling and Development, 31,* 138–149.

Tokar, D.M., & Swanson, J.L. (1991). An investigation of the validity of Helms's (1984) model of white racial identity development. *Journal of Counseling Psychology, 38,* 296–301.

Torrey, E.F. (1972). *The mind game: Witch doctors and psychiatrists.* New York: Emerson-Hall.

Trevino, J.G. (1996a). *Effects of worldview congruencies and discrepancies in cross-cultural counseling.* Unpublished doctoral dissertation, Arizona State University, Tempe.

Trevino, J.G. (1996b). Worldview and change in cross-cultural counseling. *Counseling Psychologist, 24,* 198–215.

Wade, P., & Bernstein, B.L. (1991). Culture sensitivity training and counselor's race: Effects on black female clients' perceptions and attrition. *Journal of Counseling Psychology, 38,* 9–15.

Wehrly, B. (1995). *Pathways to multicultural counseling competence: A developmental journey.* Pacific Grove, CA: Brooks/Cole.

Yanico, B.J., Swanson, J.L., & Tokar, D.M. (1994). A psychometric investigation of the Black Racial Identity Attitude Scale–Form B. *Journal of Vocational Behavior, 44,* 218–234.

CHAPTER 21

The Process of Individual Therapy

CLARA E. HILL
ELIZABETH NUTT WILLIAMS

What goes on in therapy? What works in therapy? What can therapists do to help clients? Therapists need to know the answers to these questions to be more effective with their clients. Educators need to know the answers to these questions so that they can train therapists. Hence, research is needed on the process of therapy to provide us with the answers to these questions.

Process refers to overt and covert thoughts, feelings, and behaviors of both clients and therapists during therapy sessions. Process can be distinguished from input variables, extratherapy events, and outcome. Input variables involve characteristics of the clients and therapists (e.g., personality, demographics, expectations, theoretical orientation/worldview) and setting (e.g., physical arrangement of the room, agency vs. private practice). Extratherapy events occur outside therapy sessions and can help or hinder the therapeutic process, such as the death of a relative or having a good support system. Outcome refers to changes that occur directly or indirectly as a result of therapy, as measured in terms of immediate effects (e.g., the client response to specific therapist interventions), intermediate effects (e.g., change that occurs as a result of a therapeutic event or session), or distal effects (change that occurs as a result of an entire treatment). Process overlaps somewhat with these other variables (e.g., client insight can be both a process and an outcome); therefore, the distinctions between variables are not clear cut.

In this chapter, we focus on research about the process of individual, face-to-face, personal-social therapy conducted by therapists or therapists-in-training with adult clients. We use the terms "therapy" to refer broadly to counseling and psychotherapy; we use the terms "therapist" and "client" to refer to the participants. We include sessions involving clients who actively sought therapy or who were recruited for research purposes as long as the interaction was therapeutic (i.e., a trained therapist helping a designated client). We include studies involving both quantitative and qualitative methodologies, observations of sessions and recollections of experiences in sessions, and simple descriptive data (what happens in sessions) and links between process and outcome (what process variables are related to outcome). We reviewed published empirical articles that met the above criteria for approximately 15 years (from 1984 to 1998 with a few additional studies appearing early in 1999, which is roughly the time period since the Highlen & Hill chapter appeared in the first edition of the Handbook) in the five journals that most often publish therapy process research (*Journal of Counseling Psychology, Journal of Consulting and Clinical Psychology, Journal of Counseling and Development, Psychotherapy, Psychotherapy Research*) as well as some studies published in other journals during the time period.

We did not include studies involving training of therapists, supervision, therapy with children, group therapy, career counseling, or family therapy. (These topics are covered elsewhere in this book.) In addition, we did not focus on the effects of time limits in therapy, length of therapy,

---

We want to thank Ian Kellems, Misty Kolchakian, Jon Mohr, Emilie Nakayama, Teresa Wonnell, and Jason Zack for their helpful comments on drafts of the manuscript.

pretherapy expectations of therapy, evaluations of sessions (e.g., depth or quality of sessions), or client perceptions of therapists (e.g., as being expert, attractive, and trustworthy) because these did not involve process as defined above. Moreover, analogue studies not involving face-to-face interaction (e.g., people reacting to audiotapes, videotapes, transcripts of therapy sessions, or descriptions of therapy sessions as if they were clients or therapists) were not included because we reviewed only studies in which a therapeutic interaction actually occurred. Finally, we did not include studies in which the only process variable was a manipulation check or a check for adherence to treatment protocols.

The first thing we learned from our literature review is that process research is alive and well. With literally hundreds of articles to draw from, we could not do an exhaustive review of all of the findings. Hence, we cite examples of research in areas that struck us as most exciting and visionary. We use a descriptive approach to summarize what we have learned from the research. In general, we do not comment on methodology in particular studies, although we only discuss studies in which the methodology appeared to be adequate. We refer readers to other sources for methods of doing process research (Heppner, Kivlighan, & Wampold, 1999; Hill, 1990, 1991; Lambert & Hill, 1994).

We begin by examining therapist and client contributions to therapy process. We then examine therapist-client interactions and the therapeutic relationship. We conclude by providing a general critique of methodology used to study therapy process.

THERAPIST CONTRIBUTIONS TO THE PROCESS

In this section, we first discuss research on taxonomies (i.e., systems) of therapist techniques, and then we discuss research on specific therapist techniques and covert therapist behavior.

Taxonomies of Therapist Techniques

One purpose for developing taxonomies of therapist techniques has been to describe profiles of therapist behavior (e.g., psychodynamic therapists tend to make greater use of interpretation than self-disclosure whereas the opposite is true for humanistic therapists). A second purpose has been to investigate the effects of therapist techniques relative to other variables (e.g., input variables, client process variables, outcome). The two most common ways of measuring therapist techniques have been molecular methods (which examine the presence or absence of therapist techniques on a phrase, sentence, or speaking-turn level) and molar or global methods (which examine therapist techniques globally across larger segments or sessions).

Molecular Methods of Assessing Therapist Techniques

The most typical molecular method for measuring therapist techniques is through verbal response modes (e.g., open question, reflection of feeling, interpretation, direct guidance), which refer to the type of therapist verbal response independent of the topic or content of the speech (Hill, 1986). Response modes are generally determined by trained judges for each sentence of transcripts of therapy sessions. In a comparison of six widely used response modes systems, Elliott et al. (1987) found some convergence across measures. Six response modes (question, information, advisement, reflection, interpretation, and self-disclosure) were included in all six measures, although the measures used different terms for these response modes and included additional response modes.

Several studies have shown that therapists use different amounts of the various response modes depending on theoretical orientation (e.g., Stiles & Shapiro, 1995), role (e.g., Nagel, Hoffman, & Hill, 1995), and client type (e.g., Cummings, 1989). In addition, research has shown that therapist response modes account for only a small proportion of the variance in immediate outcome. For example, Hill, Helms, Tichenor, et al. (1988) found that response modes had only a small (1%) albeit significant effect on immediate outcome (as defined by client and therapist ratings of helpfulness, client reactions, and client experiencing levels). Specifically, interpretation, self-disclosure, paraphrase (restatement and reflection), and approval were very helpful interventions; open question, confrontation, and information were moderately helpful; and direct guidance and closed question were relatively unhelpful.

Some researchers have investigated sequences of therapist response modes as well as sequences between therapist and client behaviors. For example, Mahrer, Nifakis, Abhukara, and Sterner (1984) found that therapists used predictable chains or microsequences of response modes. They found that Fagan, a Gestalt therapist, fluctuated between using information-gathering, explicit structuring, and interpretation in a first session. In contrast, they found that Rogers, the founder of client-centered therapy, fluctuated among reflection, simple acknowledgment, and interpretation.

Some models have been developed to describe sequences of therapist and client behaviors. Hill and colleagues (e.g., Hill & O'Brien, 1999) proposed a process model involving therapist intentions, therapist response modes, client reactions, and client behaviors. Hill, Helms, Tichenor, et al. (1988) found evidence that client experiencing levels in the turn preceding the therapist's intervention, therapist intentions (reasons for using the response modes), and therapist response modes were all important in predicting immediate outcome. Martin (1984) proposed a similar cognitive-mediational model. Martin and colleagues (e.g., Martin, Martin, & Slemon, 1989) have shown that session effectiveness is related to the appropriate linking of therapist intentions, therapist behaviors, client perceptions, client cognitive processing, and client behaviors. Further work is needed to define additional components of the Hill and Martin models (e.g., client intentions). We also need to compare the explanatory power of the two models for different clients, therapists, and situations.

In addition to coding general interventions (similar to therapist verbal response modes), Goldfried and his colleagues code several additional aspects of therapist interventions in their Coding System for Therapeutic Focus: intrapersonal links, interpersonal links, people involved, and time frame. Using this system, Wiser and Goldfried (1998) found that shifts toward more affective client focus were accompanied by therapist confrontation, nondirective statements, prolonged silence, and affectively focused questions. To maintain high client emotional experiencing, therapists used affiliative and noncontrolling interpersonal stances, reflections and acknowledgments, and minimal encouragers. Emotional experiencing was disrupted by affiliative but moderately controlling interventions (e.g., "What might be a different way of looking at that?").

Molar or Global Methods of Assessing Therapist Techniques

Some researchers have suggested that therapist techniques should be assessed more holistically through global ratings made after watching entire sessions. Hence, therapists or judges have estimated how frequently techniques were used in entire sessions using Likert scales (e.g., The Therapeutic Procedures Inventory-Revised; McNeilly & Howard, 1991) or Q-sort technologies of ranking how much each technique is used relative to other techniques (e.g, Q-Set; Jones, Cumming, & Horowitz, 1988). For example, in the Q-Sort methodology, judges estimate how often each of 100 events (e.g., "Therapist gives explicit advice or guidance," or "Therapist explains rationale behind his or her technique or approach or treatment") occurs relative to the other 99 events. This Q-sort methodology forces judges to rank some events as occurring more often than others. In contrast, when using Likert scales, all events can be rated as occurring equally often.

Comparing Molecular and Molar Methods of Assessing Therapist Techniques

Heaton, Hill, and Edwards (1995) compared the molecular (using the Hill Counselor Verbal Response Category System, HCVRCS) and molar session-level approaches (using the Therapeutic Procedures Inventory-Revised—TPI-R, and the Q-Set) on the same data set. They matched the specific response modes from the HCVRCS (e.g., interpretation) with specific items on the Q-Set and TPI-R that asked about these same interventions. Hence, they essentially examined response modes either from a sentence or session level. Heaton et al. found that the directive, paraphrase, and interpretation clusters of items on the Q-Set and TPI-R were significantly related to each other, but neither were related to corresponding HCVRCS categories. Thus, molar and molecular methods appear to assess different things. Molecular measures are advantageous because they describe specific interventions and allow researchers to study the immediate effects of interventions. In contrast, molar methods are advantageous because they require less time from judges and allow for the assessment of multidimensional variables that occur across longer periods of time than speaking turns. Further research is needed to determine the validity of the two types of measures and to compare how they relate to other process variables and outcome.

Specific Therapist Techniques

Rather than studying the effects of therapist techniques in general, several researchers have investigated specific techniques in more depth. In this section, we describe research on interpretation, self-disclosure, paradoxical interventions, and techniques to encourage compliance with homework assignments.

Therapist Interpretation

Hill and O'Brien (1999) defined interpretations as interventions that "go beyond what a client has overtly stated or recognized and present a new meaning, reason, or explanation for behaviors, thoughts, or feelings so that clients can see problems in a new way" (p. 205). Research has shown that therapists interpret sparingly (ranging from 6–8% of all therapist statements, Barkham & Shapiro, 1986; Hill, Helms, Tichenor, et al., 1988), and that psychodynamically-oriented therapists interpret more often than behavioral therapists (Stiles & Shapiro, 1995). Furthermore, clients and therapists rated interpretations as very helpful, and interpretations enabled clients to experience their feelings (Hill, Helms, Tichenor, et al., 1988). In addition, clients free associated more when therapists provided interpretations than other interventions (Spence, Dahl, & Jones, 1993).

Research has also shown that interpretations of moderate depth are better than those that are either too superficial or too deep (e.g., Claiborn & Dowd, 1985), which supports the psychoanalytic principle of interpreting just beyond the limits of client awareness (Fenichel, 1941). As an example, a client might say she is flunking out of college but express no feelings about it and then shift to talking about how her parents have high standards that she rarely meets. A moderate interpretation that the client might be able to use is that the client's lack of feelings might be a defense against feeling that she is disappointing herself and her parents. In contrast, the client might react poorly to a superficial interpretation that her concern is related to not knowing what she will do in the future, or to a deep interpretation that flunking out of college is an attempt to gain revenge on her parents for ignoring her as a child.

Several studies have found that transference interpretations (i.e., interpretations that relate a client's behavior or feelings toward the therapist to experiences with significant others) are not particularly effective (e.g., Hoglend, 1996; Piper, Joyce, McCallum, & Azim, 1993). However, McCullough et al. (1991) demonstrated that the client's affective response to transference interpretations significantly predicted improvement at outcome. In other words, if clients responded affectively to the transference interpretation (a relatively rare occurrence), this was a good predictor of outcome.

Compelling evidence also shows that interpretations tailored specifically to the beliefs and needs of the individual client are more effective than transference interpretations (e.g., Crits-Christoph, Cooper, & Luborsky, 1988; Messer, Tishby, & Spillman, 1992; Norville, Sampson, & Weiss, 1996). For example, if a client's core conflict is guilt about achieving more than her mother did, an interpretation related to the core conflict tends to be more effective than a standard transference interpretation (e.g., relating her anxiety in session with a female therapist to an unresolved Oedipal conflict). This type of research requires that judges determine a reliable conceptualization of the client's core conflict, code therapist speech for which units are interpretations, and then rate the interpretations for how closely they match the core conflict. As noted in the previous section, methods for coding therapist techniques are common, but valid and reliable methods for conceptualizing cases are relatively new and have made it possible to do research in this area.

In a case study, Hill, Thompson, and Mahalik (1989) examined the interpretations across therapy that related to an important theme in therapy (i.e., that the client's current difficulties were due to inadequate parenting). The interpretations were presented in a context of approval and support; were interwoven with questions, restatements, and reflections; were of moderate depth; occurred only in the second half of treatment; and seemed to be accurate. The therapist repeated the interpretation many times and applied it to different situations, which she referred to as "chipping away" at the client's defenses. The client not only accepted the interpretation but slowly began to incorporate it into her thinking (e.g., she changed from seeing herself as spoiled to seeing herself as neglected). The interpretations helped her disclose important secrets (e.g., her father's attempted suicide and subsequent hospitalization in a mental hospital). Toward the end of therapy, the therapist paired the interpretation with a directive that the client was a good parent to her children and hence could parent herself. The interpretations helped the client achieve more self-understanding and, together with direct guidance, enabled her to change in fundamental ways (e.g., become a better parent, obtain a job, and begin an intimate relationship).

A process analysis by Joyce, Duncan, and Piper (1995) found that interpretations were most effective (i.e., facilitated clients' movement toward clarity) when clients demonstrated a readiness for interpretation, indicated by a clear invitation to the therapist to interpret, and were able to tolerate the interpretations. The most effective interpretations were those at the level of the clients' immediate experience. Clients' ability to become engaged in therapeutic work was associated with the accuracy of the interpretation. Confirmation of the accuracy was indicated by a clear shift as clients turned their focus inward and provided personally significant material.

In summary, the research suggests that interpretations can be helpful interventions but need to be delivered with care when clients indicate readiness and invite therapists to use them. In addition, the research suggests that interpretations need to be of moderate depth, specifically formulated for the client, repeated often, and applied to different situations. Transference interpretations, on the other hand, did not seem to be particularly helpful, unless they were followed by affect on the clients' part. These results confirm that we cannot just look at the effectiveness of interpretations globally (as was done in studies in the previous section examining the overall effects of techniques), but we need to examine specific issues such as type of interpretation, type of client, manner of delivery, timing, and context.

Confrontation

Confrontations are interventions in which therapists point out a discrepancy or contradiction (Hill, 1986). For example, the therapist might say to a client, "You say that you're happy, but you're frowning." Confrontations have been used infrequently, accounting for approximately 1% to 5% of all therapist statements (Barkham & Shapiro, 1986; Hill, Helms, Tichenor, et al., 1988). Furthermore, although clients and therapists rated confrontations as moderately helpful, clients had negative reactions to confrontations (e.g., felt worse, stuck, or misunderstood) and did not explore their feelings after confrontations, and therapists viewed sessions in which they did many confrontations as not very smooth or satisfactory (Hill, Helms, Tichenor, et al., 1988).

Using a sample of people who had problems with procrastination, Olson and Claiborn (1990) tested a hypothesis from dissonance theory (Festinger, 1957) that arousal (e.g., being confronted by discrepancies) should lead to greater acceptance of "interpretations" (we put interpretation in quotes because the interventions they used are considered to be information and direct guidance by Hill & O'Brien, 1999). Essentially, cognitive dissonance theory postulates that clients would accept "interpretations" as a way of reducing arousal or dissonance. Olson and Claiborn first confirmed that confrontations led to greater arousal (as determined by galvanic skin response) than did reflections of feelings. Then, clients received one of three conditions: (1) a confrontation followed by an "interpretation," (2) a reflection followed by an "interpretation," or (3) no interview. Confrontations pointed out a discrepancy between the client's statement in the interview and their behavior outside the interview (e.g., "You've been telling me that you plan to do something about your procrastination, but your repeated procrastination at school shows that you're resisting change"). Reflections were listening responses that did not describe any discrepancy (e.g., "That sounds really frustrating"). "Interpretations" presented clients with a view of procrastination that was discrepant from their own and included a guidance component to link understanding to action (e.g., "You make a personal choice to procrastinate or not. Taking full responsibility for your own procrastination may be the key to actually doing something about it."). Participants in the high arousal condition (i.e., confrontation followed by "interpretation") responded more positively, had greater reductions in arousal, and had higher acceptance of "interpretations" than participants in the other two conditions, which led the authors to conclude that "interpretations" delivered under conditions of high arousal were more influential than interpretations delivered under conditions of low arousal.

In a study of confrontational therapy, Salerno, Farber, McCullough, Winston, and Trujillo (1992) found that clients responded with defensiveness to confrontation, and that therapists confronted when clients were defensive. Similarly, Miller, Benefield, and Tonigan (1993) found that in contrast to a client-centered style, a directive-confrontation style yielded more resistance from clients, which, in turn, predicted poorer outcome at a one-year follow-up for clients who were problem drinkers.

These studies suggest that therapist confrontation leads to negative client reactions and defensiveness, and that client defensiveness leads to therapist confrontation. Confrontation also yields high client arousal, which seems to make clients more open to subsequent persuasion. Further research is needed to clarify the influence of client type (e.g., substance abusers vs. compliant clients), therapist manner of delivery (e.g., presented with respect versus with blame or accusation), and timing (after establishing a therapeutic relationship versus prior to establishing a relationship) on the effectiveness of confrontation.

Self-Disclosure

Self-disclosure refers to any statement in which a therapist reveals something personal about herself or himself to a client (Hill & O'Brien, 1999). Therapists use self-disclosure infrequently (ranging from 1%–4% of all therapist statements; Barkham & Shapiro, 1986; Hill, Helms, Tichenor, et al., 1988). However, in a survey by Edwards and Murdock (1994), most therapists reported that they disclosed at least occasionally. Their disclosures were most often about professional qualifications and experience. Moreover, they reported that they typically disclosed to increase feelings of similarity between themselves and clients.

Interestingly, clients rated therapist self-disclosure as very helpful, enabling them to reach high experiencing levels; therapists, in contrast, rated the self-disclosures as not very helpful (Hill, Helms, Tichenor, et al., 1988). The authors speculated that therapists rated self-disclosures as not very helpful because they felt vulnerable after sharing their experiences. Furthermore, different types of disclosure seem to have different effects. For example, Hill, Mahalik, and Thompson (1989) found that reassuring self-disclosures (e.g., "I enjoyed our last session, too") were rated as more helpful than challenging self-disclosures (e.g., "When my father died, I was angry").

In a qualitative study, Knox, Hess, Petersen, and Hill (1997) asked clients currently in long-term therapy to describe their experiences of and reactions to therapist disclosures. Clients reported that therapist disclosures were very useful and had a positive impact on the therapy. Clients perceived that therapists gave disclosures to normalize client's feelings and reassure them. The disclosures typically involved personal historical information about the therapists. Clients indicated that disclosures led to new insight or perspective, made therapists seem more real and human, improved the therapeutic relationship, and resulted in clients feeling more normal or reassured. For example, in one case, a client who struggled with drug addiction had difficulty trusting her therapist and opening up to him. She thought that he could not understand her struggle with drugs and asked him if he had ever tried street drugs. The therapist disclosed that he had tried street drugs, which the client said shocked her, "stopped the argument cold," made her rethink her assumptions and stereotypes, allowed her to see the benefits of healthy disagreement, and enabled her to use the therapeutic relationship as a learning ground for other relationships. She thus became more assertive in expressing her needs and opinions rationally. The disclosure also changed her perspective of the therapist, making him seem more human and similar to her, allowing her to feel closer to him, increasing her respect for him, and providing more balance in the relationship.

In summary, the evidence indicates that therapist self-disclosure is often effective, resulting in high ratings of helpfulness, high levels of client experiencing, and new insight or perspective. Furthermore, self-disclosure can make therapists seem real and human, improve the therapeutic relationship, make clients feel more normal or reassured, lead to symptom relief, and lead to a greater liking of therapists. Across studies, self-disclosures were used infrequently, which may have made them seem especially significant to clients. Hence, when self-disclosures are used infrequently and judiciously by therapists to normalize and reassure clients, they seem to be helpful.

Definitions of self-disclosure have varied widely across studies, making it difficult to compare results across studies. Hill and O'Brien (1999) suggested that there are at least five different types of disclosures: disclosures of facts/credentials, feelings, non-immediate personal experiences, immediate reactions to client, and strategies. Researchers need to study the effects of these different types of disclosures. Although naturalistic research on self-disclosures is difficult because of their infrequent occurrence in therapy, we recommend that researchers study naturally occurring therapy rather than simulations of therapy (e.g., Andersen & Anderson, 1985). Simulations cannot recreate the experience that clients have within therapy after a relationship has been established. For example, a research volunteer might react negatively to a therapist disclosure on a videotape simulation, whereas a client might react positively to the same self-disclosure if he or she knows that the therapist means well and there is a good relationship. Furthermore, research is needed about timing of self-disclosures.

Paradoxical Interventions

In paradoxical interventions, therapists prescribe the symptom. The classic example is to tell the insomniac to stay up all night mopping the floor instead of sleeping. In other words, rather than telling a client to change, a therapist tells a client to remain the same. The theory is that if clients follow the paradoxical intervention, they demonstrate that they have some control over their behavior (which they often have previously denied having). If they do not follow the paradoxical intervention and change to spite the therapist, they also have "won" because they modify the undesirable behavior. Hills, Gruzkos, and Strong (1985) found that it was not helpful for clients to be told why paradoxical interventions were being given and, in fact, suggested that it might be better when paradoxical interventions were unexpected or disruptive.

Paradoxical interventions were developed by communications theorists to work with reactant (resistant) clients, who oppose being told what to do directly (Haley, 1976; Watzlawick, Weakland, & Fisch, 1974). Westerman, Frankel, Tanaka, and Kahn (1987) and Horvath and Goheen (1990) found support for the moderating effects of client reactance level on paradoxical interventions, but Swoboda, Dowd, and Wise (1990) found no effects for client reactance level.

Different types of paradoxical interventions, such as reframing and restraining, also have been investigated. Swoboda et al. (1990) found that clients made more gains after a paradoxical reframing directive ("Being alone and feeling down shows great tolerance for solitude and basic self-satisfaction") than a paradoxical restraining directive ("If your depression lifted, people would react to you more favorably and would put greater demands on you"). Furthermore, Kraft, Claiborn, and Dowd (1985), in a study with depressed clients who had negative emotions, found that positive reframing (e.g., anger is a strength) led to more reduction in negative emotions than no reframing, but they found no differences between paradoxical or nonparadoxical directives.

Differences between studies in definitions, measures, and procedures make it difficult to compare results of the studies on paradoxical interventions and reactance levels, but the results about the effects of paradoxical interventions raise intriguing questions for further research. It would be interesting to know more about how different types of clients react to paradoxical interventions, how they make sense of them, and how they use them to change.

Techniques to Encourage Compliance with Homework Assignments

Worthington (1986) found that clients complied with homework assigned early in therapy more than they did with homework assigned later in therapy. Furthermore, clients were more likely to comply with homework that involved completing standardized measures than homework that involved unstructured tasks, motor behaviors, or thoughts. Worthington speculated that clients were willing to aid with initial assessments but were more reluctant to do other types of homework assignments. Clients were also more likely to comply with later homework assignments if they had complied with earlier ones, if the therapist checked with them first about their attitude toward doing homework, and explicitly followed up in subsequent sessions about whether the homework had been done. They were less likely to comply if therapists stressed their power as the expert. Unfortunately, the measures did not have adequate psychometric evidence, and so the results need to be replicated.

Conoley, Padula, Payton, and Daniels (1994) found that clients were most likely to follow therapist recommendations for homework that matched the problem, were not difficult to implement, and were based on the client's strengths. For example, a depressed and angry client said in the session that he wished that he had written down instances when he felt bad during the previous week so that he could remember them to discuss them in therapy. For homework, then, the therapist asked the client to write down instances when he felt badly, recording what he was thinking, doing, feeling, and what the situation was. The therapist gave the rationale that the homework would help them discuss the problem more specifically in the next session. After the homework was presented, the client responded favorably, saying that he liked to write and that writing had helped him in the past. Thus, the recommendation was rated as not difficult because it involved only a small amount of time, was not anxiety-producing, and was clear. In addition, it was based on the client's strengths because he had indicated that he liked to write. Furthermore, it clearly matched the client's stated problem because it facilitated the client in remembering situations in which he was depressed and angry. During the next session, the client indicated that he had implemented the recommendation.

Mahrer, Gagnon, Fairweather, Boulet, and Herring (1994) found that therapists typically used a combination of different methods to get clients to the point where they said they would carry out post-session behaviors. To encourage clients to say that they were going to *reduce* maladaptive behaviors, therapists were concrete and specific about what changes were needed, provided rationales for why change was important or desirable, provided encouragement and pressure to make the changes, and assigned homework. To encourage clients to say that they would *increase* new ways to behave, therapists allowed clients to initiate the new behaviors, highlighted client readiness and control, were concrete and specific about what changes were needed, clarified the behavior and context involved in the change, and rehearsed the new behaviors in the session.

In summary, the type of homework that is recommended and the manner in which therapists present the homework seem to be important. Basing homework recommendations on existing strengths rather than trying to remove deficits, making sure that clients are motivated and ready to make changes, assigning homework early in therapy, assigning standardized tests rather than other types of homework, and not stressing the therapist's own power and expertise all seem to increase the acceptability of action recommendations. We need to know more, however, about how to produce increases versus reductions in behaviors with different types of clients. Furthermore, we need to know more about client's reactions to different therapist interventions to encourage clients to make changes. We also need to investigate how clients go about thinking about and implementing suggestions between sessions.

Therapist Covert Processes

Therapist covert processes refer to experiences that go on under the surface and hence cannot be captured by examining overt behaviors on tapes or transcripts of sessions. In this section, we discuss the research on therapist intentions, self-talk, and countertransference.

Therapist Intentions

Intentions are reasons or goals for interventions, or what therapists want to accomplish with their interventions. Hill and O'Grady (1985) postulated that therapist intentions are not necessarily apparent to clients but influence therapists' choice of verbal and nonverbal interventions. Hill and O'Grady developed a list of 19 intentions (e.g, to give information, to identify and intensify feelings, to meet therapist's needs), and later provided further evidence of validity and stability (Hill, O'Grady, et al., 1994). Therapist intentions are clearly linked to specific therapist response modes, although the same intention can be implemented through several different response modes with different results (Hill, Helms, Tichenor, et al., 1988). Psychodynamic therapists used more intentions aimed at feelings and insight, whereas behavioral therapists used more intentions aimed at examining behaviors and cognitions and promoting change (Hill & O'Grady, 1985; Stiles et al., 1996). K.R. Kelly, Hall, and Miller (1989) found that the clarity (i.e., articulateness and concreteness) of therapist intentions was positively related to clients' and judges' ratings of therapy outcome.

Therapist intentions have been investigated in a number of different contexts by Kivlighan and colleagues. Kivlighan (1989) found that therapists-in-training used fewer assessment intentions and more exploration intentions after training in interpersonal-dynamic therapy. Kivlighan (1990) found that when therapists intended to assess, explore, and support, the working alliance was low. Kivlighan and Angelone (1991) found that novice therapists more often intended to challenge and focus on cognitions and less often intended to support, deal with the relationship, and attend to their own needs with introverted than extroverted clients, suggesting that introverted clients "pull" therapists to challenge them instead of support them.

In a study by Fuller and Hill (1985), four experienced therapists each saw four volunteer clients for single sessions. In a postsession review, therapists indicated their intentions and clients attempted to guess the therapists' intentions. They found that clients were most accurate at perceiving the intentions of getting information, setting limits, and clarifying, but were less accurate at perceiving the intentions of dealing with the relationship, resistance, and therapist needs. Accuracy of perceptions was not related to session outcome, which suggested that clients did not need to know exactly what therapists meant to do.

Several other studies have also shown that client awareness of therapist intentions either is not related or is negatively related to outcome (Horvath, Marx, & Kamann, 1988; Martin, Martin,

Meyer, & Slemon, 1986; Martin, Martin, & Slemon, 1987). We do not have an adequate explanation for these results, although Hill (1990) postulated that when clients are trying to determine therapists' intentions they are distracted from involvement in their own tasks in therapy. Further investigations of the effects of transparency of intentions is needed so that we can determine when it is desirable for clients to know what therapists are intending to do. For example, it would be interesting to know if it is helpful for clients to know why therapists use some techniques (e.g., reflection of feelings) but not others (e.g., paradoxical intentions), and whether this helpfulness varies according to the type of client (e.g., compliant versus reactant).

Stiles (1987) argued that the present measures of intentions are problematic because they do not take into account that intentions occur on many different levels of awareness. More specifically, a therapist may be aware of his or her intention and intend for the client to be aware of it, the therapist may be aware of his or her intention but not intend for the client to be aware of it, or the therapist may not even be aware of his or her intention. Future research needs to examine therapists' awareness of their intentions and the effects of different levels of intentions.

In summary, the development of measures of therapist intentions is an exciting addition to process research because researchers can now examine the inner working of therapists' minds in relation to their interventions. Difficulties arise in measuring intentions, however, because assessing them as they occur during the session would distract therapists from being involved in the tasks of therapy. Hence, intentions are typically measured after sessions by having therapists watch videotapes of sessions and try to recall their thoughts during sessions. Although some effort has been made (e.g., Hill, O'Grady, et al., 1994) to validate the accuracy of recall, questions remain about the validity of retrospective recall for assessing something as fleeting and out of conscious awareness as intentions. Creative efforts are needed to address these concerns.

Therapist Self-Talk

Self-talk, or internal dialogue, refers to what therapists say to themselves during sessions. Several category systems have been developed to code self-talk (e.g., Borders, Fong-Beyette, & Cron, 1988; Fuqua, Newman, Anderson, & Johnson, 1986; Morran, 1986; Morran, Kurpius, & Brack, 1989; Nutt-Williams & Hill, 1996). For example, Morran et al. (1989) identified 14 categories of self-talk (e.g., behavioral observations, client-focused questions, summarizations, associations, inferences, self-instruction, anxiety). A few studies have linked self-talk to naturally-occurring therapy process. For example, Nutt-Williams and Hill found that when therapists reported more self-focused and negative self-talk, they rated their interventions as less helpful and thought their clients were reacting negatively.

To assess the impact of therapist self-talk on their therapeutic work, Williams, Judge, Hill, and Hoffman (1997) asked beginning graduate student therapists to describe their in-session reactions and strategies used to manage their reactions. The major in-session feelings and reactions were of being anxious and uncomfortable, distracted-unengaged, overly self-focused, empathic-caring, comfortable-pleased, frustrated-angry with client, and inadequate-unsure of self. Therapists also had concerns about their therapeutic skills and performance, the therapeutic role, how to work with difficult clients, conflict in the therapeutic relationship, and reactions to specific client content. Supervisors of the therapists noted the existence of problematic behaviors (e.g., avoidance of issues, ending sessions abruptly, offering opinions too often, and becoming overinvolved) that may have been related to the therapists' internal reactions. Therapists reported that they managed their feelings and reactions during sessions by focusing on the client, using self-awareness, and suppressing feelings and reactions.

Although some research has been conducted on how to categorize therapist self-talk (e.g., facilitative vs. distracting, positive vs. negative, self-focused vs. other-focused), more definitional work is needed. For example, does self-talk include all covert cognitive processes (such as intentions, intervention planning, and self-critical thoughts) or should we tease apart these covert processes and study them independently? We also need to understand the effects of awareness of self-talk. For example, does thinking about what one's supervisor would say distract from or enhance a novice therapist's performance? In addition, we need to know how self-talk and intentions influence the behavior of both inexperienced and experienced therapists. Although covert processes are difficult to study, more research is needed in this area.

Therapist Countertransference

The classic Freudian (1910/1959) definition of countertransference is the analyst's unconscious and distorted reactions to a client's transference. An alternate definition includes all of a therapist's reactions to a client (Fromm-Reichman, 1950). These two schools of thought have been debated hotly (Kernberg, 1965), but there remains a great deal of disagreement in the literature on how to define countertransference (Panken, 1981). Regardless of the exact definition used, however, many researchers agree that a lack of awareness of countertransference can have adverse effects on the therapy process, whereas an awareness of countertransference reactions can be a valuable therapeutic tool (Gelso & Carter, 1994; Singer & Luborsky, 1977).

There have been several notable attempts in the last 15 years to investigate countertransference in relation to therapy process. McClure and Hodge (1987), who operationalized therapist countertransference as a misperception of the client's personality as either more or less similar to themselves, found that strong feelings of liking or disliking a client were related to distortions in views of the client's personality. In other words, therapists viewed clients whom they liked as having personalities similar to their own, whereas they viewed clients whom they disliked as having dissimilar personalities. Although the study is commendable in being one of the few that examined countertransference naturalistically, it also highlights the problems in doing countertransference research. Operationalization of countertransference was not based on clinical theory and was circular in logic (e.g., Does evidence of liking or misperceptions of personality traits mean the same thing as countertransference? Are all misperceptions countertransference distortions?)

Hayes, Riker, and Ingram (1997) found that beginning therapists' empathy and self-integration were negatively related to their countertransference behaviors (as assessed by therapists and their supervisors on the Countertransference Factors Inventory-Revised). In addition, they found that for less successful cases, countertransference behavior was negatively related to treatment impact, which reflects the importance of successfully managing countertransference reactions, especially with more difficult cases.

Finally, using a qualitative approach, Hayes et al. (1998) studied interviews in which expert therapists were asked immediately after sessions about countertransference. They studied only those statements in which therapists described personal reactions to clients that emanated from unresolved intrapsychic issues. They found that the typical origins of therapist countertransference reactions were family issues (e.g., parenting) and the therapists' needs and values (e.g., grandiosity or need for control). The typical triggers of therapist countertransference were the content of client material (e.g., death or family issues) and changes in therapy structure/procedures (e.g., missed sessions or termination). The typical manifestations of therapist countertransference were avoidance (e.g., boredom or distancing self from client) and negative feelings (e.g., anger or inadequacy). Hayes et al. pointed out that countertransference is prevalent, countering the myth that good therapists are somehow free from countertransference feelings. They also noted that countertransference can be both helpful and hindering in the therapy relationship.

Researchers need to continue to struggle with defining and measuring countertransference, preferably "discovering" the elements of the definition from the data (e.g., how therapists act and what they report feeling when experiencing a little or a lot of countertransference). We also need to learn more about the components of countertransference (e.g, its origins, triggers, and manifestations) and distinguish countertransference from other cognitive phenomena such as self-talk and intentions. In addition, Hayes et al. (1998) noted the importance of examining the role of culture (e.g., race/ethnicity, gender, sexual orientation) in our understanding of countertransference because unresolved issues or unexamined biases may play a role in countertransference reactions. Researchers also need to compare covert cognitive experiences to outward in-session behaviors. How do internal countertransference reactions relate to overt displays of therapist behavior? Finally, further investigation of the strategies therapists use to manage countertransference seems particularly important.

Summary

Not surprisingly, given the historical emphasis in counseling psychology on training therapists in techniques (see Hill & Corbett, 1993), there has been substantial empirical interest in testing the effects of therapist techniques. We are beginning to gather information about some techniques such as interpretation, confrontation, self-disclosure, paradoxical interventions, and ways to encourage client action. Hopefully, this information can be used in training therapists. However, research is also needed on other frequently occurring interventions, such as closed and open questions, reflections of feelings, direct guidance, and information-giving.

We also need to know more about nonverbal behaviors and their relation to verbal behaviors. One of the reasons for the dearth of research recently may be that existing measures of nonverbal behavior are simplistic (e.g., arm movements, head nods) and need to be replaced with measures that capture more of the gestalt of the nonverbal communication.

Furthermore, we need to develop better methods of assessing therapist techniques that include judgments of quality (see also Schaffer, 1982; Thompson & Hill, 1993) and empathy (see also Duan & Hill, 1996). Ideally, we would have multidimensional measures that describe the total therapist intervention (including overt behavior, nonverbal behavior, intentions, self-talk, and countertransference) instead of just looking at individual components in isolation. However, we recognize that the complexity of the resulting data would make it difficult to use the information empirically except in individual cases.

An exciting addition to the research on therapist contributions has been the focus on covert behaviors such as intentions, self-talk, and countertransference. Clearly, much is going on for therapists "beneath the surface." More efforts are needed to assess covert behaviors accurately and to look at the influence of covert behaviors on overt behaviors.

CLIENT CONTRIBUTIONS TO THE PROCESS

In this section, we first describe research on taxonomies of client behavior and then describe research on specific overt and covert client behaviors (see also Elliott & James, 1989).

Taxonomies of Client Behaviors

Taxonomies of client behaviors usually involve molecular assessments of the presence or absence of behaviors in sentences or speaking turns. The Hill, Corbett, et al. (1992) taxonomy includes categories for resistance, agreement, appropriate request, recounting, cognitive-behavioral exploration, affective exploration, insight, and therapeutic changes. Hill, Corbett, et al. found that cognitive-behavioral exploration was the most frequent client behavior in middle sessions of brief psychodynamic therapy.

Researchers have also catalogued the topics clients discuss in therapy. Richards and Lonborg (1996) used the Counseling Topic Classification System (CTCS) to code topics (e.g., academics, career/life planning, interpersonal concerns, stress). In a comparison with other process measures, they found that the CTCS provided clinically important information in relation to other therapist intentions and client experiencing. Although the raters were not able to identify multiple topics consistently, they were able to identify main topic sequences. Richards and Lonborg suggested that the main topics (or topic episodes) likely reflect the type of core information to which skilled therapists attend (while tuning out peripheral topics or "noise").

Overt Client Processes

The research on client involvement and resistance typically involves judgments by external judges and is more descriptive than predictive.

Client Involvement

Client involvement is a generic term that encompasses experiencing, progress, assimilation, and cognitive complexity. All of these terms indicate that a client is actively and productively involved in the tasks of therapy. These measures all involve judges using interval rating scales to assess the client's level of involvement.

The Client Experiencing Scale (Klein, Mathieu-Coughlan, & Kiesler, 1986) charts client movement from impersonal, superficial, emotionally-absent discussion to emotionally-rich exploration of self, with experiencing used as a vehicle for problem resolution and self-understanding. Klein et al. reported that experiencing is related to self-exploration, insight, working through, absence of resistances, and high-quality free association.

Client involvement and progress in therapy also have been assessed with the Rutgers Psychotherapy Progress Scale (e.g., Holland, Roberts, & Messer, 1998), a psychodynamically-oriented measure that involves expression of significant material, development of insight, focus on emotion, collaboration, clarity and vividness of communication, and focus on the self. The compatibility of the therapist intervention to the client's underlying dynamics was positively related to client progress (Messer et al., 1992).

The Assimilation Scale, developed by Stiles and colleagues, tracks changes in processing problematic or painful experiences and assimilating these experiences into schemata developed in the therapeutic interaction. Stiles et al. (1990) postulated that problematic experiences go from being warded off, to entering awareness as unwanted thoughts, to becoming clarified as a problem, to being understood, to changing, and finally to being mastered and integrated into everyday life. The Assimilation Scale is an observer-rated measure that focuses on one central problem within therapy (e.g., how the client assimilates her angry feelings toward her mother). Evidence for the Assimilation Model has been found (e.g., Field, Barkham, Shapiro, & Stiles, 1994), although assimilation may not occur as linearly as was initially proposed.

Honos-Webb and Stiles (1998) recently reformulated the Assimilation Model and Scale in terms of "voices." They suggest that a problematic experience is a separate, active voice within the client that is not connected to the community of voices (i.e., the self). In therapy, the client moves to assimilate the isolated voice of the problematic experience into the community of voices. For example, a symptom could be understood as a manifestation of a warded-off voice that needs to be heard and assimilated into the self. Using a voices conceptualization, Honos-Webb, Surko, Stiles, & Greenberg (in press) reported a case study in which a client assimilated a voice of neediness and weakness into the more dominant "superwoman" voice.

Rather than examining *what* clients say, some researchers have been examining *how* clients communicate. McCarthy, Shaw, and Schmeck (1986) postulated that client dialogue could be described in terms of five dimensions (deep-shallow, elaborative-nonelaborative, conclusion oriented-description oriented, clear-vague, personal-impersonal) that represent cognitive complexity of thinking. Martin and Stelmaczonek (1988) found that client dialogue was higher on these five dimensions during important events than it was during control events. Diemer, Lobell, Vivino, and Hill (1996) found that when client dialogue was cognitively complex (as defined by ratings on the five dimensions), both clients and therapists rated dream interpretation sessions during brief therapy as beneficial.

A common dimension among these measures is a progression from limited involvement to deep involvement. Clearly, research is needed to determine the empirical relationship among these measures of client involvement. There may be just one general type of client involvement, or the type of desirable involvement might vary for different theoretical approaches or different therapeutic events. Furthermore, research is needed to determine whether client behavior is best represented on a single continuum as is suggested by these measures or is best shown in terms of discrete categories as is suggested by the taxonomies of client behavior. Finally, research is needed to compare clients' perceptions of involvement with judges' perceptions of involvement, given that the majority of this research has used judges to rate client involvement. Client involvement seems like an internal experience that is not possible for judges to ascertain accurately.

Client Resistance

The opposite of client involvement is resistance, which has been defined in a variety of ways that typically reflect researchers' theoretical orientations. For example, using a behavioral perspective, Chamberlain, Patterson, Reid, Kavanagh, and Forgatch (1984) defined resistance as the discrete behaviors of confrontation, challenge, complaining, disagreeing with therapist, self-blaming, tattling, defending others, pushing own agenda, sidetracking, not responding, not answering, and disqualifying. In contrast, Mahalik (1994), using a psychodynamic perspective, defined resistance as opposition to expression of painful affect, recollection of material, the therapist, change, or insight. The findings indicate that directive therapist behavior often leads to client resistance (Bischoff & Tracey, 1995; Mahalik, 1994; Patterson & Forgatch, 1985), suggesting that clients react against being told what to do.

Research is needed to compare the definitions and corresponding measures. Furthermore, it seems important to determine the extent to which bias impinges on whether a particular behavior is labeled as resistance by both judges and therapists. Research is also needed to relate resistance to involvement. If the two constructs are two ends of the same continuum, we need to combine them; if they are independent constructs, they need to be differentiated theoretically and empirically.

Covert Processes

Covert processes refer to feelings and reactions that cannot necessarily be observed by outsiders. The rationale for studying covert processes is that these feelings and reactions influence how clients respond in sessions. The covert processes that have been investigated include reactions, nondisclosures, and transference.

Client Reactions

Researchers have asked clients about their reactions through having them review tapes of sessions and recall how they felt during particular moments in the session. Hill, Helms, Spiegel, and Tichenor (1988) found that about 60% of the client reactions were positive (e.g., felt understood, learned new ways to behave), whereas about 40% were negative (e.g., felt worse, stuck, no reaction).

Client reactions have been associated with therapist interventions. For example, Elliott and colleagues, in results that were replicated across two studies (Elliott, 1985; Elliott, James, Reimschuessel, Cislo, & Sack, 1985), found that clients reacted with a sense of personal contact to therapist self-disclosure, whereas they did not feel understood when therapists asked questions.

Thompson and Hill (1991) found that therapists were more able to perceive positive than negative client reactions. Furthermore, when therapists were aware that clients had positive reactions, their next interventions were perceived as helpful. In contrast, when therapists were aware that clients had negative reactions, their next interventions were not perceived as helpful, suggesting that therapists had difficulty responding when they knew clients had negative feelings. In another study, when therapists were aware of the negative client reactions, clients perceived the next therapist interventions as less helpful than when therapists were unaware of the negative client reaction (Hill, Thompson, & Corbett, 1992).

In summary, reactions are an important way to gain access to clients' experiences in therapy. It would be interesting to know more about when reactions are consistent with or inconsistent with overt behavior. We also need to know more about the effects of therapist awareness of client reactions. Furthermore, as with therapist intentions, new methods are needed to assess reactions during sessions.

Nondisclosures in Therapy

Hidden reactions, things left unsaid, and secrets are all types of nondisclosures that have been investigated. Hidden reactions are feelings related to specific therapist interventions. Things left unsaid are hidden thoughts and feelings within sessions that may or may not be in response to specific therapist interventions. Secrets refer to major life experiences, facts, or feelings that clients choose not to share with their therapists.

Researchers have found that clients hide negative reactions from their therapists (Hill, Thompson, et al., 1992; Hill, Thompson, Cogar, & Denman, 1993; Rennie, 1994). Rennie suggested that clients might hide reactions out of fear of retaliation or out of deference to the therapist's authority. For example, clients who feel angry at or misunderstood by their therapists are not likely to reveal those feelings if they feel unsafe in therapy.

Clients also leave things unsaid in sessions (Heppner, Rosenberg, & Hedgespeth, 1992; Hill et al., 1993; Regan & Hill, 1992). For example, Regan and Hill (1992) found that when clients refrained from talking about behaviors or cognitions, they were dissatisfied with therapy, but when they refrained from talking about emotions, they were satisfied, suggesting that clients do not like to be too vulnerable in therapy. In Hill et al., clients indicated that they left things unsaid because the emotions were overwhelming, they wanted to avoid dealing with the disclosure, and they feared that the therapists would not understand.

In addition, some clients have reported that they keep secrets from their therapists. Hill et al. (1993) found that 46% of clients in long-term therapy reported keeping secrets from their therapists, typically about sex, failure, and mental-health issues. The most frequently listed reasons were that clients felt too ashamed or embarrassed to share their secrets. Similarly, A.E. Kelly (1998) found that over 40% of clients in brief therapy listed a relevant secret that they had kept from their therapists, most often because they were afraid to express their feelings. After adjusting for initial symptomatology, tendency to keep secrets in general, and social desirability, A.E. Kelly found that keeping secrets in therapy was related to reduced symptomatology. A.E. Kelly's results raise interesting questions about whether it might be desirable for clients to keep some secrets from therapists, and under what conditions and for what treatments clients might want to keep secrets from therapists.

These results are important because they remind us that therapists cannot "read" clients' minds and hence cannot assume that they know how clients are reacting. Therapists are limited to their own interpretations of clients' overt behaviors and reports of covert reactions. Given that clients have, and sometimes hide, negative reactions, it seems crucial to determine whether we can detect clues for when clients are hiding negative reactions. Hill and Stephany (1990) found that clients had fewer head nods when they were experiencing negative reactions. In other words, clients became more still and less animated when they reacted negatively to therapist interventions. Further research is needed to determine whether other signs can be detected of negative reactions or secrets being withheld from therapists. Moreover, research is needed to examine whether it is necessary for clients to reveal everything or whether keeping some secrets can actually be beneficial for some clients in therapy. If it is beneficial for clients to conceal some secrets, we need to know more about what types of secrets are better off concealed and when to encourage clients to reveal their secrets.

Transference

Transference, which has long been a key construct in psychoanalytic theory, has been defined as the manifestation of unconscious, unresolved, and conflicting patterns of interpersonal relationships in the therapeutic setting (e.g., Gelso & Carter, 1994). Freud (1912/1958) conceptualized transference as a person's mental representation of early interpersonal relationships and suggested that transference serves as a guide to perceptions of current relationships. Transference typically is thought to involve a distortion on the part of clients because they relate to their therapists as they have related to significant others in the past, rather than to the therapist as a real person (Gelso & Carter, 1985, 1994). Some have argued with this strictly intrapsychic definition, however, suggesting instead that transference reflects the interpersonal interaction between the client and therapist (Richardson, 1997).

Despite continuing clinical interest, it continues to be challenging to conduct empirical research on transference due to the lack of a clear definition, the complexity of the topic, and the difficulty of observing unconscious processes. Fortunately, several different methods have been used over the past 15 years to study transference, including the study of transference-related phenomena, therapists' ratings, standardized measures, and qualitative interviews.

Most of the work has been directed at studying transference-related phenomena rather than directly studying transference. The most commonly used transference-related measure is the Core Conflictual Relationship Theme (CCRT), which Luborsky (1984) based on Freud's view of transference. The CCRT explores clients' maladaptive interpersonal relationships via their narratives about relationship episodes (Luborsky, Popp, Luborsky, & Mark, 1994). Using transcripts, judges first search for relationship episodes. Judges then describe the specific episode in their own words in terms of specific wishes, responses from others, and responses of self, after which they code the episode using standard categories. Recent CCRT studies suggest that relationship narratives can be uncovered in short pretherapy interviews (Barber, Luborsky, Crits-Christoph, & Diguer, 1995) and that clients display multiple themes rather than one predominant theme (Crits-Christoph, Demorest, & Connolly, 1990).

From observations of changes in both valence and pervasiveness of narratives over the course of therapy, Luborsky, Barber, and Diguer (1992) concluded that "the curative factors in psychotherapy are intimately involved with the content of the relationship narratives" (p. 288). They also noted, however, that we still need to examine whether a person's *actual* interactions with other people are related to the person's narratives about the interactions. To address this issue, Connolly et al. (1996) examined clients' relationship themes in relation to narratives about their therapists. They found that clients generally display repetitive interpersonal patterns regarding the significant others in their lives (e.g., wishing that others in their lives would nurture and protect them). They also noted, however, that although one may be able to identify different themes in one person, there is typically one main pattern, which may or may not be the pattern that is displayed in the relationship with the therapist. Thus, a client may generally wish to be assertive with others but may wish to be approached more actively by his or her therapist.

Other researchers have developed more direct measures of transference, using therapists' ratings of transference. For example, Gelso, Kivlighan, Wise, Jones, and Friedman (1997), using single-item ratings of positive, negative, and total transference in sessions, found that the interaction of therapist-rated transference and client emotional insight predicted outcome (i.e., client improvement). Furthermore, they found that the course (i.e., gradual buildup with marked decline toward the end of treatment) and the overall amount of negative transference differentiated more from less successful cases, providing support for Mann's (1981) contention that negative transference increases and is productively worked through in successful cases. In addition, Multon, Patton, and Kivlighan

(1996) developed the Missouri Identifying Transference Scale, a multi-item therapist-rated measure of positive and negative transference. Using this measure, Patton, Kivlighan, and Multon (1997) found that overall level of transference was unrelated to outcome but that increasing levels of transference across therapy were associated with positive outcomes.

A qualitative approach was used by Gelso, Hill, Mohr, Rochlen, and Zack (1999) to analyze data from interviews psychodynamic therapists about how transference operated in successful cases of long-term therapy. They found no simple patterns, suggesting that transference operates idiosyncratically across cases. The sources of transference were both maternal and paternal. The initial valence was either positive, negative, or mixed. The valence fluctuated throughout therapy. The content typically pertained to projections both of the feared bad parent and the wished-for good, approving parent. Transference typically was affected both positively and negatively by structural changes in the therapy (e.g., fee changes, vacations) as well as by events in the clients' lives outside of therapy (e.g., death of a mother). Hence, the results suggested that transference is complex and develops differently for various clients and therapists.

There appears to be no solid conclusion on the best way to measure transference. We need clearer definitions of transference and criteria for identifying "distortions" (i.e., we need to define from whose perspective distortions are to be defined). Mallinckrodt (1996a) suggested that we first assess clients' interpersonal schema (e.g., perhaps using a method such as the CCRT); determine how the schemas apply to the therapist (Connolly et al., 1996); and then assess which aspects of the schemas are "reasonable" (i.e., part of the real relationship and not transferential, see Gelso & Carter, 1994) and which are inflexible, repetitive, and distorted transference patterns. He also noted the importance of using multiple sources to assess transference given that different perspectives reveal different aspects of the process. Furthermore, research is needed about the specific influence of transference on client behaviors and reactions in sessions.

Summary

Much work has been done in the area of client contributions to the therapy process, particularly with the development of promising measures of client involvement and progress in therapy (e.g., Holland et al., 1998; Stiles et al., 1990). More innovative research is needed in these areas as well as in other areas such as the attainment of insight, resolving transference, and making changes outside of sessions. We especially stress the need for more research using the client's perspective rather than external judges who cannot know exactly how clients react in therapy.

INTERACTIONAL DYNAMICS BETWEEN THERAPISTS AND CLIENTS

In this section, our focus is on the way therapists and clients relate to each other. Interactional dynamics has been studied primarily through the construct of complementarity, which has arisen both from interpersonal theory (Carson, 1969; Kiesler, 1986) and relational control theory (which combines interactional theory, Strong, 1982, and communication theory, Haley, 1963). Friedlander (1993a) has an excellent review of the assumptions of and current research on interpersonal and relational control theories. We do not review the theoretical debate within the literature about the definitions but simply note that confusion in the definitions of complementarity has led to confusing and often contradictory findings (see Friedlander, 1993a; Lichtenberg et al., 1998).

Interpersonal Complementarity

Interpersonal complementarity, based on interpersonal theory, refers to the degree of fit in transactional patterns between a client and therapist (Carson, 1969; Kiesler, 1986). Complementarity is "an interpersonal situation in which two participants' interpersonal behaviors endorse and confirm each other's self-presentation in regard to both control and affiliation" (Kiesler & Watkins, 1989, p. 184). In terms of control, complementarity involves reciprocity (e.g., the therapist is dominant and the client is submissive, or the client is dominant and the therapist is submissive). In terms of affiliation, complementarity involves correspondence (both therapist and client are friendly or both are hostile toward each other).

A considerable amount of research on complementarity has used the observer-rated Structural Analysis of Social Behavior (SASB; Benjamin, 1974), which can be judged using self-report or judges. The SASB can be coded on three different levels: (1) self, representing clients' interpersonal dispositions toward their therapists (i.e., how they felt they reacted to their therapists, such as protesting or disclosing); (2) other, representing therapists' dispositions (i.e., how they felt their therapist reacted to them, such as affirming or attacking); and (3) intrapsychic, which representing clients' self-directed dispositions (i.e., how the clients reacted to themselves, such as self-accepting or self-rejecting).

Quintana and Meara (1990) used the SASB to examine clients' internalization of therapeutic relationships. Results suggested that there was initial complementarity on the self and other levels after the first therapy session but that the degree of complementarity did not increase across sessions. In other words, clients who saw themselves as self-disclosing, trusting, and connecting with their therapists also saw their therapists as affirming, nurturing, and approaching with them, but this perception did not increase in intensity as counseling progressed. In contrast, client intrapsychic dispositions changed over the course of counseling (e.g., from self-monitoring toward self-accepting), suggesting that clients may have learned to provide themselves with more affirmation and self-empathy throughout the therapy relationship.

Svartberg and Stiles (1992), using short-term anxiety-provoking psychotherapy (STAPP; Sifneos, 1979), found that complementarity ratings on the SASB predicted client change over and above therapist competence. The higher the complementarity ratings were of the clients and therapists on the SASB, the more successful changes the clients reported. Svartberg and Stiles suggested that interpersonal complementarity may be considered a predictor of successful change in therapy. These results were stronger, however, for short-term change (relief from distress) than for long-term change (social adjustment and attitude change).

The Checklist of Psychotherapy Transactions (CLOPT; Kiesler, 1988), an observer-rated measure, has also been used to study control and affiliation. Researchers have examined the psychometric properties of the CLOPT (e.g., Thompson, Hill, & Mahalik, 1991) and the relationship of the CLOPT to other variables, such as working alliance (e.g., Kiesler & Watkins, 1989) and transference (e.g., McMullen & Conway, 1997). Kiesler and Goldston (1988) used the CLOPT to examine the three Shostrom (1966) "Gloria" films with Rogers, Perls, and Ellis. They found, counter to theory, that Gloria did not always match with the therapists on the control and affiliation aspects of complementarity. For example, although Gloria matched with Ellis on the control dimension, she did not match with either Rogers or Perls. She stayed submissive in relation to Rogers's submissiveness (the theory predicts that she should become dominant) and dominant in reaction to Perls' dominance (the theory predicts she should become submissive). As with other studies (see review by Orford, 1986), Kiesler and Goldston found that hostile-dominant behaviors pulled for hostile-dominant behaviors from others rather than pulling for the expected hostile-submissive behaviors. In addition, they found that the most deviations from complementarity occurred in the hostile hemisphere of the interpersonal circle, a finding echoed by Kiesler and Watkins (1989). Thus, complementarity seems to occur most often when both individuals are friendly, whereas deviations from complementarity seem to occur when individuals are hostile. In this regard, Hoyt, Strong, Corcoran, and Robbins (1993) indicated that negative complementarity (hostility begetting hostility) should never be equated with harmonious interaction. They suggested that only positive complementarity (reciprocity on the control dimension; both friendly on the affiliation dimension) promotes smooth and successful therapeutic interactions, and that hostility should never be viewed as a sign of high accord in the relationship.

The results of the studies on complementarity suggest that complementarity may be one piece of the therapeutic interaction that relates to outcome, although more work is needed to determine whether the effect holds for long-term as well as short-term changes (Quintana & Meara, 1990; Svartberg & Stiles, 1992). In addition, the research suggests that positive rather than negative complementarity may be associated with successful outcome. Further research is needed to assess the relationship of different forms of complementarity to other process variables (e.g., therapist intentions and techniques, client reactions and behaviors) and to outcome.

Relational Control

Relational control theory emphasizes only the control aspect of the therapeutic relationship. Relationship control is the "mutual influence and extent to which each member of the system is allowed to define, control, or determine what will occur in the transaction" (Highlen & Hill, 1984, p. 376). The concept of relational or relationship control plays a central role in interactional theories of counseling (Claiborn & Lichtenberg, 1989; Strong & Claiborn, 1982). Interactional theorists believe that therapists should prevent clients from continuing to act in interpersonally maladaptive ways and should encourage the development of healthier client relationships, and hence they believe that successful client outcome is determined by the therapists and is under the therapist's control.

One particular operationalization of relational control, that of topic control (Lichtenberg & Kobes, 1992), refers to observations of whether it is the client or therapist who initiates shifts in topics (e.g., a therapist exerts topic control when asking a question that shifts the client's focus). Friedlander and Phillips (1984), using stochastic analysis to identify patterns in topic initiation and adoption, found sequences of talk to be highly stable and predictable but topic shifts to be frequent and repetitive (suggesting a possible struggle for control in the client-therapist interaction). The most predictable sequence was an effort to engage the speaker so that he or she would elaborate on an established topic (rather than shift to a new topic).

Similarly, Tracey and colleagues have examined therapist-client interactions using a topic initiation/topic following scheme. For example, using the sequence of topic-following/topic-initiation as an index of complementarity, Tracey and Ray (1984) found moderate support for a pattern of high-low-high complementarity between the client and therapist. According to Tracey and Ray, this pattern of reciprocal communication suggests that the early and late stages of therapy (in which there is a higher degree of complementarity or agreement of roles) reflect a time of low conflict in which both client and therapist engage in symmetrical interaction (complementary topic initiation and following sequences). In the middle stage of therapy, conflict occurs when the therapist alters his or her behaviors away from the client's initial expectations, thus initiating client change by helping clients become more aware of their expectations regarding others and their own interpersonal responses. Tracey (1985), basing his ideas on Haley's (1963) assertion that the therapist's role should be dominant in successful dyads, found evidence for counselor dominance in the middle or "conflict" stage of therapy.

Tracey (1993) expanded his three-stage (high-low-high complementarity) interpersonal model of successful therapeutic process by adding two substages to the second stage of the model: a dissatisfaction substage (characterized by high negative or hostile complementarity) and an unstable substage (characterized by low complementarity). He also included consideration of social norms and roles, differential interpretation of hostile and friendly behaviors, manifest (i.e., overt) vs. latent (i.e., covert) communication, and individual differences in adjustment in the expanded model. Tracey proposed several specific hypotheses to be tested (e.g., that the complementary relationship the client establishes with the therapist mirrors the types of interpersonal relationships the client engages in outside of the therapeutic relationship) and suggested that research is needed to examine the proposed moderator variables (e.g., social norms and roles).

Friedlander (1993b) questioned some of the assumptions underlying Tracey's (1993) model. For example, in response to the hypothesis that the initial stage of the therapeutic relationship should be characterized by high complementarity, she suggested that sometimes the most helpful intervention is a *noncomplementarity* one. And, she noted that it would probably be more productive for therapists to be friendly rather than hostile with hostile clients. Like Hoyt et al. (1993), Friedlander questioned whether negative complementarity ever can be helpful in therapy.

Lichtenberg et al. (1998) studied the relationship between relational control and relationship congruence, based on Strong's (1982) theory that successful therapy involves a transition from incongruence to congruence in client expectations of the therapeutic relationship. Lichtenberg et al. found no differences in relational control among the various stages of therapy, which failed to support the findings of previous studies on topic control (e.g., Tracey, 1993; Tracey & Ray, 1984). In addition, they found that the client was in control of the interaction in both successful and unsuccessful cases, challenging the notion that it is the therapist's role to control the client's changes in interpersonal behavior (Haley, 1963; Strong & Claiborn, 1982). They did note, however, that clients had less control (although still more than the therapist) in successful cases, indicating perhaps some support for the importance of the therapist's influence. Finally, Lichtenberg et al. found only minimal support for the view that successful therapeutic change is a result of changes in client-therapist relational congruence, contrary to Strong's contention.

In a comparison of several major control-coding systems, Tracey (1991) found only moderate intercorrelations, suggesting a lack of agreement in what is meant by "control." Tracey proposed a model of therapeutic control composed of three independent dimensions (intrapersonal vs. interpersonal; form vs. effect; and behavior vs. perceptions) as a more complete way to operationalize the topic of control or dominance in counseling. A model that incorporates these different approaches could be a useful tool in further study of interactional and sequential processes between clients and therapists.

Summary

The overlapping definitions of control (e.g., topic control, relationship congruence) has led to confusion in the literature. We echo Friedlander's (1993a) recommendation that we need to establish more clearly what we mean by the term "control." In addition, more research is needed to explore the question of who *should* be in control—the client or the therapist—and whether the answer depends on other process variables, such as the strength of the alliance, types of therapist techniques used, or the existence of client secrets. Much of the research on therapist-client interactions has been theoretically driven; however, several, quite disparate models of complementarity and control have guided the research. Hence, work is needed at a theoretical as well as empirical level to clarify this area. Furthermore, discovery-oriented or qualitative research might be useful for studying control and complementary in sessions from both the client and therapist perspectives.

THE ALLIANCE

Researchers and clinicians agree that the alliance (or therapeutic relationship) is one of the most critical aspects of the therapeutic encounter (Gelso & Carter, 1994). We use the generic term "alliance" to refer to a variety of terms (e.g., therapeutic alliance, working alliance, and helping alliance) that have been used but have not always been distinguished empirically. Although its origins lie mainly in psychodynamic and psychoanalytic theory (Freud, 1912/1958; Greenson, 1967), the current concept of the alliance relies on a more pantheoretical formulation (Horvath &

Luborsky, 1993). The alliance is viewed as an important component of therapy regardless of theoretical orientation (Hartley & Strupp, 1983; Robbins, 1992). In this section, we describe research on the alliance in relation to outcome, phases in the alliance, therapist contributions to the alliance, client contributions to the alliance, ruptures in the alliance, and measurement issues.

Alliance in Relation to Outcome

A meta-analysis by Horvath and Symonds (1991) of 24 studies found a moderate effect size ($r = .26$) between alliance and outcome. Similar effect sizes have been found for the alliance-outcome relationship within specific therapeutic orientations (Gaston, Piper, Debbane, Bienvenu, & Garant, 1994; Krupnick et al., 1996). In contrast, Gaston, Marmar, Gallagher, and Thompson (1991) found no substantial association between alliance and outcome, but they did find that alliance accounted for increasing variance as therapy progressed, suggesting that alliance may predict outcome better over time. Horvath and Luborsky (1993) postulated that the results of the studies relating alliance and outcome depend on the type of outcome being assessed. Alliance seems to be a better predictor of specific client change (e.g., particular symptom relief) than of change in global functioning.

Phases in the Alliance

There is conflicting theory and empirical evidence about the "phases" or "stages" of the alliance. One view is that the alliance increases steadily over time (Gunderson, Najavits, Leonhard, Sullivan, & Sabo, 1997; Kivlighan & Shaughnessy, 1995). Another view is that the alliance remains relatively stable over time (Eaton, Abeles, & Gutfreund, 1993). Yet another view is that there is a high-low-high pattern of fluctuations in the alliance over time (Gelso & Carter, 1994; Golden & Robbins, 1990). We should note that all of the studies that have evaluated alliance across therapy have used session-level measures of alliance, rather than studying fluctuations of alliance within sessions. More research is needed to examine changes within sessions as well as over time in the alliance. Furthermore, we need to study the effects of the initial strength of the alliance on the course of the alliance (e.g., the alliance may stay steady if it starts at a high level) and of traumatic events within or outside of therapy on the alliance.

Therapist Contributions to the Alliance

Three dimensions of therapist contributions to the alliance have been investigated: therapist characteristics, therapist techniques, and therapist experience level. In terms of therapist characteristics, higher alliance ratings have been found when therapists were perceived as flexible (Kivlighan, Clements, Blake, Arnzen, & Brady, 1993); comfortable with close interpersonal relationships and low in hostility (Dunkle & Friedlander, 1996); sensitive to cultural differences (Wade & Bernstein, 1991); and challenging, thematically focused, and focused on the here-and-now (Kivlighan & Schmitz, 1992).

In terms of therapist techniques, clients rated the alliance higher when their therapists focused on the clients' nonverbal behavior, suggesting the importance of sensitivity to nonverbal cues (Grace, Kivlighan, & Kunce, 1995). In examining time-limited dynamic psychotherapy, Foreman and Marmar (1985) detected improvements in alliance when therapists addressed client defenses, client guilt and expectation of punishment, and client problematic feelings in relation to therapists. Similarly, Crits-Christoph et al. (1988) found interpretive accuracy to be related to the strength of the alliance. Kivlighan (1990) found that the therapist intentions of assessing, exploring, and supporting were negatively related to the strength of the working alliance.

Surprisingly, neither therapist experience (Dunkle & Friedlander, 1996) nor competence (Svartberg & Stiles, 1994) were correlated significantly with alliance. However, Mallinckrodt and Nelson (1991) found that experience was associated with agreement about the tasks of therapy and the goals of treatment (two aspects of the working alliance as defined by Bordin, 1979) but not with ratings of the emotional bond between the client and therapist.

Although the findings about therapist contributions to the working alliance are interesting, they currently represent a compilation of diverse factors (e.g., flexibility, immediacy, interpretive accuracy) and findings have not been replicated. A unifying theory of therapist contributions is needed to integrate the therapist contributions to the alliance in a more consistent manner. Furthermore, replications need to be conducted with better measures.

Client Contributions to the Alliance

The research indicate that the important client contributions to the alliance involve the clients' interpersonal strengths. For example, Muran, Segal, Samstag, and Crawford (1994) found that friendliness and submissiveness were positively related to the development of the alliance, whereas hostility and dominance were negatively related to alliance. Similarly, Kokotovic and Tracey (1990) found a relationship between clients' level of adjustment, past and current relationship quality, and both client and therapist ratings of the alliance. In this study, clients who had a history of strained interpersonal relationships and current difficulties with hostility had lower alliance. In addition, Tryon and Kane (1995) found that clients who were able to connect with others interpersonally and become involved early in therapy developed strong alliances.

Client attachment style has also been related to the alliance. For example, Mallinckrodt, Gantt, and Coble (1995) developed the Client Attachment to Therapist Scale to assess the relationship of client attachment to working alliance. The four types of client attachment they found were secure, reluctant, avoidant, and merger. Avoidant clients rated working alliance lower than did the other types. In addition, Mallinckrodt et al. found clients' attachment memories (particularly in relation to bonds with their fathers) to be significantly associated with the working alliance. Thus, clients who had warm and emotionally expressive bonds with fathers had high working alliance ratings, whereas clients whose relationships with fathers were characterized by intrusiveness and control had low working alliance ratings. Mallinckrodt et al. also found clients' current social competencies to be strongly related to the ratings of the alliance, such that clients who were able to form healthy attachments had strong alliances.

In addition, Satterfield and Lyddon (1995) found that clients who lacked trust in the dependability of others were likely to evaluate the counseling relationship negatively early on. They suggested that "the extent to which clients feel they can depend on the availability and dependability of the counselor may be more important to the formation of the working alliance in the early phases of counseling than the clients' comfort with closeness and intimacy or their fears of being abandoned" (p. 188).

Furthermore, Mallinckrodt (1991) found that clients' early parental bonds may be related to the *therapist's* ratings of the working alliance, whereas current social support was a stronger predictor of *client*-rated alliance. Mallinckrodt suggested that therapists and clients may actually use different information to form perceptions of the working alliance. Indeed, Kivlighan and Shaughnessy (1995) found that client and therapist perspectives on the alliance were not highly correlated. It also appears that client ratings of the alliance are more predictive of therapy outcome than are therapist ratings (Horvath & Symonds, 1991). However, in at least one study (Klee, Abeles, & Muller, 1990), client contributions to the alliance early in therapy were predictive of their later contributions but were not predictive of treatment outcome. Thus, clients and therapist(s) seem to have different perceptions of the alliance.

Moreover, not all clients perceive the alliance similarly. In her qualitative analysis, Bachelor (1995) identified three distinct types of client-perceived alliance: nurturant, insight-oriented, and collaborative. This study was important because it showed that clients have a broad view of what constitutes the therapy relationship (e.g., that it involves insight-oriented activities). Because "clients cannot be viewed as a homogenous group" (p. 330), Bachelor called for continued investigation of the possible subtypes of alliance.

In summary, clients have a unique perspective on what constitutes the alliance, and this perspective is more predictive of outcome than the therapist perspective. In addition, the client's interpersonal characteristics and attachment style may interact with both the development of the alliance and the client's perception of it. As with therapist contributions, however, more research is needed to identify within-session changes in client perceptions of the alliance.

Problems in the Alliance

Several researchers have investigated what happens to the alliance during therapeutic ruptures, misunderstandings, and impasses.

Ruptures

Echoing Bordin's (1979) suggestion about the importance of the tear and repair of the alliance, Safran, Crocker, McMain, and Murray (1990) suggested that ruptures in the alliance are common in psychotherapy and that they can be an important stimulus to client change. They also noted that certain forms of therapy may be at risk for certain types of ruptures. For example, they suggested that a client working with an active and challenging cognitive therapist may be at risk of feeling overly criticized, whereas a client working with a "neutral" psychodynamic therapist may be more likely to feel the therapist is emotionally unavailable.

Safran (1984, 1990) identified several "markers" for the existence of ruptures: overt expressions of negative sentiments (e.g., client attacks therapist's competence), indirect communication of negative sentiments or hostility (e.g., client becomes withdrawn or evasive), disagreement about the goals or tasks of therapy (e.g., client becomes frustrated because she or he wants more direct advice from the therapist), compliance (e.g., client reluctantly or begrudgingly agrees to try a therapist suggestion), avoidance maneuvers (e.g., client skips from topic to topic), self-esteem-enhancing operations (e.g., client overexplains herself or himself or boasts to the therapist), and nonresponsiveness to intervention (e.g., client continuously "forgets" to complete outside homework assignments).

Safran et al. (1990) suggested five principles for therapists in terms of how to deal with ruptures in therapy: (1) attend to ruptures (i.e., be on the lookout for the rupture markers); (2) be aware of one's own feelings (i.e., use oneself as a "barometer" for the quality of the therapeutic relationship); (3) accept responsibility for one's role in the interaction; (4) empathize with the client's experience (i.e., convey an understanding of the client's feelings, such as disappointment or anger); and (5) maintain the stance of the participant/observer (i.e., avoid the pitfall of repeating a pattern from the client's previous dysfunctional interpersonal experiences).

Safran et al. (1990) also proposed a model for the resolution of ruptures, which emphasizes client assertions (e.g., of fears, negative sentiments) and therapist empathy with client assertions. Safran and Muran (1996) tested the model and arrived at a four-stage model that is operationally defined by the Core Conflictual Relationship Theme (CCRT) method (Luborsky, Popp, Luborsky, et al., 1994) in terms of examining response of self, expected response of other, and wish. In the first stage, the therapist attends to the rupture marker. The therapist and client then explore the rupture experience, based on the response of self (e.g., I was feeling annoyed). The therapist facilitates an exploration of avoidance in which the response of self or expected response of other is examined (e.g., I was afraid you'd be angry with me). Finally, the client's underlying wish is expressed as a self-assertion (e.g., I want your help). Safran's ideas are clinically sound and based on observations and task analyses, but further research is needed to validate this four-stage model.

Misunderstandings

Using qualitative analyses of interview data, Rhodes, Hill, Thompson, and Elliott (1994) studied events in which clients felt misunderstood in therapy. In cases where the misunderstanding was resolved, clients told their therapists that they felt misunderstood, although this disclosure often occurred after a delay of time. When clients raised the topic, therapists and clients engaged in a mutual repair process in which they tried to understand and resolve the event. Both therapists and clients talked about their feelings in the immediate moment. In some cases, therapists apologized or accepted responsibility for their behavior.

Unresolved misunderstanding events, in contrast, progressed in one of two pathways. In one pathway, clients told their therapists about their negative feelings, but the therapists were unresponsive and unaccepting. Clients stayed in therapy despite having negative feelings about the unresolved misunderstanding event. In the second pathway, clients did not tell their therapists about their negative feelings about the misunderstandings and eventually dropped out of therapy, with therapists apparently remaining unaware of the client's dissatisfaction. Unfortunately, this study relied on written responses rather than interviews with clients, and used clients who were therapists or therapists-in-training, therefore, it needs to be replicated.

Impasses

Hill, Nutt-Williams, Heaton, Thompson, and Rhodes (1996) interviewed therapists about their perceptions of impasses (defined as a deadlock or stalemate that causes therapy to become so difficult that progress is no longer possible and termination occurs) in long-term therapy. Therapists typically reported having felt surprised when their clients unilaterally terminated from treatment. Therapists did not recall a specific glaring event that led to the impasse but said that they had been aware of pervasive problems in the relationship. Therapists cited several variables that might have led to the impasses: severe client pathology, disagreement over the tasks and goals of therapy, possible therapist mistakes (e.g., being too directive), triangulation (significant people interfered with the therapy), transference, personal issues of the therapists, and poor therapeutic relationships. Therapists reported having many negative feelings about the clients and themselves during the impasse as well as lingering feelings of rumination and self-doubt after the termination.

As with ruptures in the alliance, studying misunderstandings and impasses in therapy provides us with the opportunity to look at therapy when it does not work. Understanding more about the client and therapist characteristics as well as the sequence of these events as they unfold should provide important information about what therapists need to do in therapy. Qualitative methods seem particularly appropriate for studying these events since evidence of dissatisfaction is often hidden in therapy. Additional studies are needed, however, given that these studies involved small samples. Moreover, different types of misunderstanding and impasse events (e.g., hostility, withdrawal), different client types (e.g., avoidant, secure), and different therapist types (e.g., supportive, aggressive) could be identified to help us refine our understanding of the process when problems emerge in the alliance.

Measuring the Alliance

Both conceptual and empirical work on the alliance seem to be gaining ground currently. Much of this work, however, depends on the strength, accuracy, and usefulness of the measures of alliance. Tichenor and Hill (1989) found evidence of both high interrater reliability for several observer-rated measures as well as high intercorrelation among the measures. They found, however, that the observer-rated measures were not correlated significantly with either therapist-rated or client-rated measures, suggesting major differences in perspectives. In a factor analysis of client-rated alliance measures, Hatcher and Barends (1996) discovered a single general factor that correlated strongly with overall outcome. Similarly, Salvio, Beutler, Wood, and Engle (1992) also suggested that there may be a single general factor that best represents client-rated alliance. Hence, we have convincing evidence that the existing measures from the same perspective assess roughly the same construct.

Hatcher and Barends (1996) suggested that current alliance measures need to be revised to reflect a more general view of the alliance as incorporating the two major conceptual pieces of the bond between the therapist and client (e.g., therapeutic alliance; Greenson, 1967) and the collaborative agreement between the client and therapist (e.g., the working alliance; Bordin, 1979). In addition, we have evidence that the perspective of who rates the alliance makes a difference (e.g., client, therapist or outside observer) (Horvath & Symonds, 1991; Tichenor & Hill, 1989) and thus any revisions to the existing measures need to address this issue as well. Hatcher, Barends, Hansell, and Gutfreund (1995) have suggested that one solution would be to use a multimeasure approach to assess the alliance (e.g., client, therapist, and outside raters).

Although there is some evidence that the alliance may be globally stable over time (Eaton et al., 1993), we wonder whether this finding is an artifact of assessing the alliance across entire sessions. The alliance also seems to fluctuate within sessions, as Safran and colleagues have shown (Safran, 1984, 1990; Safran et al., 1990). Alternatively, it may be that the alliance is both generally stable over time as well as constantly fluctuating within sessions. Hence, it may be useful to examine further the process of the alliance within sessions.

THERAPEUTIC EVENTS

Events involve several sequences of therapist and client behaviors related to a specific focus. In this section, we examine taxonomies of helpful and hindering events and then discuss specific therapeutic events.

Helpful and Hindering Events

Under the assumption that psychological change is most likely to occur during key, critical, decisive, or auspicious moments, many researchers have focused on the events in therapy that clients experience as significantly helpful or hindering. For example, Elliott (1985) divided events into task (new perspective, problem solution, problem clarification, and focusing attention); interpersonal (understanding, reassurance, involvement, and personal contact); and hindering (misperception, negative therapist reactions, unwanted responsibility, repetition, misdirection, unwanted thoughts) categories. Llewelyn, Elliott, Shapiro, Hardy, and Firth-Cozens (1988) found that the most helpful events for clients were problem solution, awareness, and reassurance, whereas the most common hindering events were unwanted thoughts. Martin and Stelmaczonek (1988) found that therapists and clients both thought that the most important events in therapy were insight, personal material, exploration of feeling, and new way of being.

A few studies have focused on the process of therapeutic events. Mahrer, White, Howard, Gagnon, and MacPhee (1986) found that very good moments were most likely to occur when therapists were sensitive to the immediate client condition, were geared up to create the necessary conditions, and used specific techniques skillfully with clients who were willing and ready to profit from them. Wilcox-Matthew, Ottens, and Minor (1997) identified several three-step patterns in helpful therapeutic events involving the presenting issue, the therapist intervention, and the impact on the client. For example, one pattern involved clients avoiding, therapists confronting or asking introspective questions, and then clients reporting a new focus. Another pattern involved clients expressing progress, therapists providing reinforcement, and then clients feeling supported.

Specific Therapeutic Events

An event typically begins with a marker, which is an indication that the client is ready to work on a particular type of problematic experience (Greenberg, 1991). The event then progresses through several therapist interventions and client operations to the resolution of the problem. In this section, we cover several event types: problematic reaction points, insight, creation of meaning, central issue, dream interpretation, and metaphors.

Problematic Reaction Points

A problematic reaction point (PRP) is when clients are puzzled by their reactions to events because their reactions are inappropriate or out of proportion to the event (e.g., being furious when someone does something nice for them). Rice and Sapiera (1984) hypothesized that systematic unfolding of PRPs proceeds through four phases. The marker is when clients express puzzlement about their reactions. Therapists then elicit the problematic reaction through the use of evocative language. Clients respond by identifying the salient aspects of the event that triggered their reactions and exploring their affective reactions or perceptions of the stimulus to identify its impact. Finally, clients broaden or deepen their exploration to acquire a deeper understanding of initial problem and their functioning and to give them a sense of being able to change the situation. Using task analyses, Watson (1996), Watson and Rennie (1996), and Wiseman and Rice (1989) provided empirical support that the resolution process proceeds through these four steps. Further research is needed to determine whether other approaches follow a similar pathway in helping clients resolve PRPs.

Insight

Elliott (1984) posited that insight involves metaphorical vision, connections or patterns or links, suddenness, and newness. Using comprehensive process analysis of events in dynamic therapy, he proposed that the attainment of insight evolves through the three stages of processing, insight, and elaboration. On the basis of further research with more events from both cognitive-behavioral and psychodynamic-interpersonal therapies, Elliott et al. (1994) proposed a five-stage model. The first stage involves contextual priming, such that earlier sessions set the stage for insight. Specifically, the development of the alliance and revelation of important thematic information are important. Furthermore, the client needs to have recently experienced a painful problematic life experience. In the second stage, the therapist presents the client with an interpretation about the painful event. In the third stage, there is an initial processing, in which the client's immediate reaction is to mull the information over briefly and unemotionally while agreeing to its general accuracy. Insight occurs in the fourth stage when a clear sense of connection is conveyed to the therapist in an emotional expression of surprise indicating its newness. In the final or fifth stage, insight stimulates the client to explore further, elaborating the emotional implications of the insight.

Further work is needed on defining insight, particularly about whether it involves both awareness and understanding, whether it involves both cognitive and affective components, and whether it involves process (i.e., the work of attaining insight) or outcome (i.e., the insight attained). Furthermore, it would be interesting to study insights that develop outside of therapy, particularly when they are stimulated by something that occurred within the therapy session. Our clinical experience is that clients sometimes claim with delight that they had an insight on their own between sessions, which we clearly recall having delivered that exact interpretation during the previous session. Clients may need time to assimilate interpretations and incorporate them as their own discoveries. To investigate such events, we need to expand the scope of our research and develop methodologies to investigate what happens between sessions.

Creation of Meaning

The creation of meaning (which refers to constructing meaning from emotionally charged experiences) was studied by Clarke (1989, 1991). Whereas insight is often an intellectual event, creation of meaning involves developing language to help clients express what they feel. The markers for creation of meaning are strong emotional arousal; an indication of a cherished belief being challenged; and surprise, confusion, or a lack of understanding. Clarke (1989) found that interventions that symbolized the meaning for the client (e.g., metaphors or verbal symbolization of the emotional reaction to the discrepancy) led to higher levels of experiencing, more focus in the voice quality, and more clarity of understanding of the confusing event than did empathic reflections. Based on her 1989 findings, Clarke (1991) suggested a revised three-stage model for the creation of meaning. The first (specification) phase involves emotional arousal, a statement of discrepant experience, symbolization of the cherished belief, and symbolization of the emotional reaction to the discrepancy between the belief and experience. The second (exploration) phase involves a statement of exploration, hypothesizing as to the origin of the cherished belief, evaluation of the reliability of the cherished belief by comparison of past and present experiences, and judgment about the tenability of the cherished belief. The third (revision) phase involves an alteration or elimination of the cherished belief, specification of the exact changes needed to accommodate to the discrepant data, and reference to or plans for future behavior based on the revised belief. Further research is needed to verify these stages. It would also be interesting to determine the similarity of the process for insight and creation of meaning events.

Central Issue

Mann (1981), in his model of time-limited psychodynamic therapy, recommended that therapists formulate the central issue for the client's present and chronically endured pain (e.g., independence vs. dependence, resolved vs. delayed grief) at the beginning of treatment. For Mann, the therapist's formulation of the central issue becomes the pivot around which therapy evolves, assuming that the client accepts it. In studying this central issue event using task analysis, Wiseman, Shefler, Caneti, and Ronen (1993) found evidence for four steps. The marker is when the client brings up the central issue. For example, for a client who has an independence conflict, the marker might be the client stating that she is moving out to live on her own. The therapist then intervenes to focus the client on the central issue and raise awareness of the conflict through interpretation, exploration, uncovering additional aspects of the conflict, and connecting it to the past. The client explores feelings raised by the conflict, deals with them, and gains awareness of other aspects of the conflict. The outcome of a successfully resolved central issue event is when clients express awareness and acceptance of new aspects of conflicts and have new understanding, accompanied by indications that they have emerged from exploration with a more mature ability to cope with issues that brought them to therapy. This examination of central issues seems particularly important as an example of how theoretically meaningful tenets of psychotherapy can be investigated in a clinically meaningful way.

Dream Interpretation

Hill (1996) conceptualized dream interpretation as involving three stages (exploration, insight, action). In the exploration stage, therapists ask clients to describe images in greater detail, associate to the images, and make links to triggers in waking life. In the insight stage, therapists work with clients to understand the dream at one of four levels (the experience itself, waking life, childhood experiences, or parts of self). In the action stage, therapists encourage clients to change the dream, continue working on the dream, or do something different in their lives based on what they learned from the dream interpretation. Clients consistently have reported higher levels of insight, working alliance, and understanding in dream interpretation (e.g., Heaton, Hill, Petersen, Rochlen, & Zack, 1998; Zack & Hill, 1998) than in regular therapy. In an analysis of single sessions of dream interpretation (Hill, Diemer, & Heaton, 1997), clients reported that it was helpful to gain insight, link the dream to waking life, and gain another person's feedback. Hence, dream interpretation seems to be helpful, perhaps because it is a structured approach that helps clients feel that they have accomplished something specific by the end of a session. Researchers need to compare the results of the Hill dream interpretation model to other models of dream interpretation (e.g., Freudian, Jungian). In addition, it would be interesting to use task analysis to study the dream interpretation process to see if the three-stage model can be empirically validated.

Metaphors

Metaphors refer to a wide range of phenomena (e.g., simile, analogy) that use images or picturesque language to describe things or events more vividly (e.g., feeling "sick as a dog," "blinded by reality," or "scared of one's shadow"). Metaphors are thought to help clients express themselves more fully so that they communicate better and become more aware of their feelings. Clients can also, however, use metaphors to obscure and block therapeutic progress. For example, a client could talk vaguely about her "hang-up" without ever disclosing exactly what she means, which could block the therapist from completely understanding her.

Angus and Rennie (1988) found two distinctive patterns for working with metaphors. One was a discovery-oriented, collaborative process associated with the development of a shared understanding between therapist and client of the meaning of the client's metaphor. In this process, therapists listened and encouraged clients to describe their experience, and then therapists elaborated and offered new ways for clients to think about the metaphor. Both client and therapist tuned into their inner experiences and discovered their reactions as they spoke, which made for a spontaneous and creative method of exploring feelings. In contrast, the second pattern involved a lack of collaboration that frequently was associated with a joint misunderstanding of the meaning of the metaphor. In this pattern, therapists used Socratic dialogue to get clients to identify what the therapists had already decided was "true." The purpose seemed to be to have the client adopt the therapist's perspective. Clients did not explicate their covert, experiential responses to the metaphor, although the therapists assumed a shared understanding. Therapists then interpreted client confusion or puzzlement as resistance. Further investigation of metaphors seems merited, including examination of whether it is productive to attend to some metaphors more than others.

Summary

An events approach to studying psychotherapy is a major advance over simply considering therapy as an undifferentiated whole. It allows researchers to examine process within events rather than studying the global effects of different variables without regard to context. Because of this approach, we have a preliminary understanding of what occurs during some events. For example, we know something about using the systematic evocative unfolding approach for dealing with problematic reaction points (e.g., Rice & Sapiera, 1984). Future research needs to compare other approaches for dealing with these events. Furthermore, other key therapeutic events (e.g., test interpretation, career exploration) need to be studied.

We also need to examine the use of clearly defined therapist techniques within specific therapeutic events. For example, what is the effect of transference interpretations when clients present a clear transference issue versus when they do not? Or, what is the effect of challenging versus reassuring self-disclosures during the priming versus the elaboration stages of the development of insight? Furthermore, we need to compare results obtained using task analysis and qualitative methods, the two most commonly used methods in this area. Finally, we need to develop new methods specifically designed to study sequences and steps within events.

METHODOLOGICAL ISSUES

The two most common methods for studying therapy process in previous time periods were descriptive research and experimental-analogue research. From 1984 to 1998, the scope of potential methodologies was expanded to include discovery-oriented or exploratory approaches, task analysis, and qualitative approaches. These new and exciting methods have revitalized the field and allowed researchers to investigate important clinical phenomena in more meaningful ways. In this section, we discuss the different methodological approaches and end with a brief discussion of data analysis strategies.

Descriptive Research Using Established Measures

In this method, researchers observe and describe what occurs within therapy using established measures completed by clients, therapists, or observers. For example, researchers have described the types of therapist verbal response modes used by therapists of different theoretical orientations (e.g., Stiles & Shapiro, 1995; Wiser & Goldfried, 1996) or they have compared the working alliances in different types of therapy (e.g., Carroll, Nich, & Rounsaville, 1997; Krupnick et al., 1996). Methodological issues involved in conducting this type of descriptive research have been discussed thoroughly in Hill (1990) and Lambert and Hill (1994). The advantages of this approach are that researchers use measures that have been tested and have validity and reliability. A disadvantage is that the established measures may not assess what researchers want to know in a particular study.

The Experimental-Analogue Paradigm

In the experimental-analogue paradigm, researchers clearly define and manipulate the process variable, control extraneous variables, and test the effects of the process variable on other process variables or on immediate or distal outcome. Good examples of this method are studies conducted by Claiborn and colleagues on the effects of interpretation and paradoxical interventions (Claiborn & Dowd, 1985; Hanson, Claiborn, & Kerr, 1997; Kraft et al., 1985; Olson & Claiborn, 1990). These researchers preserved the natural flow of therapy but inserted scripted interpretations or paradoxical interventions after a relationship was established. The advantages of the experimental-analogue paradigm are that process variables can be rigorously defined and implemented consistently, that some of the extraneous variables can be controlled, and that there is good internal validity in studies. The limitations are that it is not typically possible to control all the extraneous variables, and that external validity is compromised because the parameters of interventions (when, where, why, and how used) are determined by the research protocol and not by client needs. In actual therapy, for example, therapist interventions are based on therapists' perceptions of what clients need at particular moments in therapy rather than on scripted interventions to be delivered at specific moments. Furthermore, we have minimal data about whether clients react in therapy as they do in analogue situations, which raises concerns about the generalizability of analogue findings.

Discovery-Oriented or Exploratory Approaches

In this approach, researchers adopt an attitude of openness to learning about the process from their observations (Elliott, 1984; Hill, 1990; Mahrer, 1988). Hence, rather than relying on existing theory or established scales to code data, researchers develop scales or categories to code occurrences in sessions or to describe the experiences of participants based on the data from that study. A team of researchers first goes through the data and develops categories based on their observations. They then train a new set of judges who assign the data to the categories after reaching high interrater reliability. Examples of discovery-oriented projects are Mahrer and Nadler's (1986) development of a taxonomy of good moments in therapy and Hill, Diemer, et al.'s (1997) categorization of more and less helpful events in dream interpretation. The advantage of this approach is that researchers develop measures that rely more directly on the data in a particular study and are thus responsive to the phenomena. The disadvantage is that the results might not be generalizable if the samples are biased. In addition, although researchers assess interjudge reliability from new judges who assign the data to categories, they do not know if their measurement is valid or whether another set of judges would code the data the same way. Finally, aggregating results across studies using different measures is not possible, which makes it difficult to accumulate meaningful results.

Task Analysis

Task analysis is a rational-empirical method in that researchers approach the phenomena with a rational model to guide the investigation and then find ways to test the rational model empirically (e.g., Greenberg, 1984, 1991). The rational model is first developed by asking expert clinicians to explicate the steps involved in specific important events in therapy (e.g., evocative unfolding with problematic reaction points, two-chair technique for working with polarities). Researchers then observe the process of a few carefully selected cases that demonstrate successful implementation of the technique and modify the model based on these observations. Once they feel confident about the model, the researchers specify how each step of the model would manifest itself empirically on process measures (e.g., the client might be at less than a level 3 on the Experiencing Scale during the first step but increases to a level 5 or above in the second step). Next, they test the steps of the model empirically using data from a number of cases. Based on the data, they revise the model and test it on yet another sample of cases. The model as a whole can also be tested in terms of immediate and longer-term outcome, both of which are often defined specifically for the task (e.g., immediate resolution of a polarity).

Advantages of task analysis are that researchers can develop models that fit what clinicians do in specific situations and clearly specify empirical criteria by which to test steps of the models. Limitations are that clinicians may not be aware of what they actually do in specific events, and it can be difficult to define empirical criteria and find measures to test the steps. Furthermore, events might not always proceed in clear steps and not all instances of events follow the same path. In addition, not all of therapy can be divided neatly into specific events for task analysis because therapy sometimes proceeds without a specific task being involved or the event proceeds in a different order than proposed for a particular client or situation.

Qualitative Approaches

Qualitative methods use participants' words rather than numbers to describe phenomena. Qualitative approaches have been advocated for some time in counseling psychology as a way to address many of the problems inherent in traditional research paradigms (e.g., Hoshmand, 1989; Polkinghorne, 1984), but adequate methods have only recently been developed to satisfy the rigor expected in psychological research (see also Morrow & Smith, this volume).

Grounded theory (Rennie, Phillips, & Quartaro, 1988; Strauss & Corbin, 1990), phenomenological approaches (Giorgi, 1970, 1985), comprehensive process analysis (Elliott, 1989), and consensual qualitative research (Hill, Thompson, & Williams, 1997) are all promising qualitative approaches. Exemplar studies are Rennie (1994), Bachelor (1995), Elliott et al. (1994), and Knox et al. (1997) respectively. These qualitative methods have several features in common: (1) data are gathered through open-ended questions so as not to constrain the participant's responses; (2) researchers rely on words instead of numbers to describe data; (3) a small number of cases is studied intensively; (4) context is used when analyzing individual cases; and (5) the process is inductive, with results developed from observations of the data rather than from imposing an a priori structure or theory on the data.

Advantages of qualitative approaches are that they provide a richness of detail, describe inner experiences and clinical phenomena, include context, and explain both simple and complicated sequences. Limitations are that small sample sizes (8–15 cases) can be nonrepresentative, results might not replicate across research teams, and the research process is very labor intensive. A further limitation is that qualitative methods are typically not standardized so that each different researcher has used slightly different methods, often with minimal attention to reliability of judgment. Methodological research is needed to investigate procedures used in qualitative studies (e.g., how many interviewers are needed, whether interviews should be conducted by telephone or face-to-face, how to compose a research team, how to assess validity and reliability).

Advances in Analytic Approaches

Several new statistical approaches have been developed for analyzing process data. Sequential analyses (e.g., Wampold & Kim, 1989), time-series analyses (e.g., Jones, Ghannam, Nigg, & Dyer, 1993), hierarchical linear modeling (e.g., Patton et al., 1997), and structural equation modeling (e.g., Mallinckrodt, 1996b) all allow researchers to investigate relationships among process variables as well as between process and outcome. Kivlighan (this volume) provides an introduction to hierarchical linear modeling in the context of group counseling research. Although it is beyond the scope of this chapter to review these strategies in detail, we encourage researchers to try new analytic strategies for making sense of process data.

Summary

The addition of new methods has led to a paradigm shift in process research. Researchers have opened themselves up to think about methodology in new and different ways that more closely approximate clinical practice. Of course, these new methods need to be refined to make them valid, reliable, manageable, and applicable to process research. Furthermore, although painstaking and not sensational, research is needed about methodology (e.g., establishing validity and reliability of methods, testing the effects of different numbers and types of judges, testing the effects of using audiotapes versus videotapes versus transcripts) to advance our methodological sophistication and the quality of our results.

We also need more studies that involve replications of findings across different types of methodologies. For example, Hill and colleagues (Hill, Thompson, et al., 1992; Hill et al., 1993; Thompson & Hill, 1991) used quantitative methods to replicate Rennie's (1994) qualitative study of things clients leave unsaid in therapy. Such replication across methods (i.e., "triangulation") provides compelling evidence for findings.

CONCLUSIONS

Kiesler (1973) lamented that the typical pattern was for researchers to develop a measure of an easily observed but often trivial process variable (e.g., head nods, speech dysfluency) and use it to test a hypothesis. They would become discouraged, however, because of the incredible amount of work required to produce minimal results and hence would abandon process research. Hence, there was minimal accumulation of results and much discouragement about the ability of process research to answer questions of interest (also see Hill & Corbett, 1993 for a review of this history). In contrast, during the 1984–1998 time period, researchers used measures that were more clinically relevant and used them in several studies (see Greenberg & Pinsof, 1986; Hill, Nutt, & Jackson, 1994), so that we can now compare results across studies and accumulate results about therapy process.

In addition, process research has become more relevant to clinical practice. Recent advances in discovery-oriented and qualitative methods have allowed process researchers to study questions that have relevance and applicability to practicing clinicians (e.g., research on how misunderstandings can be resolved). We need to continue the trend of making process research more relevant to the practitioner. Involving practitioners in discussions of clinical phenomena can be helpful. Input from practitioners ensures that we are studying relevant clinical questions and that we study questions in a clinically sensitive manner.

We also need to translate the findings from process research to research on training therapists, which in our opinion has been sadly neglected in recent years. In other words, when we know that something is effective in therapy, we need to study how to train therapists to use that intervention effectively. Research on training will likely in turn enhance research on therapy process because it will inform us about what we can teach and what we cannot.

In addition to using more discovery-oriented and qualitative methods, we also need to develop more and better clinically-relevant models for understanding how the therapy process operates and then use these models to guide our future research. Preliminary models have been developed by Hill and colleagues (e.g., Hill & O'Brien, 1999) and Martin (1984) about microsequences of process variables. Orlinsky and colleagues (e.g., Orlinsky, Grawe, & Parks, 1994) have developed a generic process-outcome model for the evaluation of universal change process in therapy. Gelso and Carter (1994) have developed a model of the therapy relationship. Tracey (1993) developed a model of the interpersonal dynamics. Just as Rogers' (1957) compelling hypotheses about the necessary and facilitative conditions for therapy stimulated a tremendous amount of research, clear process models could help to stimulate more and hopefully better process research in the future.

In sum, these are exciting times in process research. There is a lot of creative energy, and researchers are developing new ways to study process. We are beginning to make important advances and develop some ideas about effective processes in therapy. We anticipate that the next 15 years will bring even greater understanding of the therapy process.

REFERENCES

Andersen, B., & Anderson, W. (1985). Client perceptions of counselors using positive and negative self-involving statements. *Journal of Counseling Psychology, 32,* 462–465.

Angus, L.E., & Rennie, D.L. (1988). Therapist participation in metaphor generation: Collaborative and noncollaborative styles. *Psychotherapy, 25,* 552–560.

Bachelor, A. (1995). Clients' perception of the therapeutic alliance: A qualitative analysis. *Journal of Counseling Psychology, 42,* 323–337.

Barber, J.P., Luborsky, L., Crits-Christoph, P., & Diguer, L. (1995). A comparison of core conflictual relationship themes before psychotherapy and during early sessions. *Journal of Consulting and Clinical Psychology, 63,* 145–148.

Barkham, M., & Shapiro, D.A. (1986). Counselor verbal response modes and experienced empathy. *Journal of Counseling Psychology, 33,* 3–10.

Benjamin, L.S. (1974). Structural analysis of social behavior. *Psychological Review, 81,* 392–425.

Bischoff, M.M., & Tracey, T.J.G. (1995). Client resistance as predicted by therapist behavior: A study of sequential dependence. *Journal of Counseling Psychology, 42,* 487–495.

Borders, L.D., Fong-Beyette, M.L., & Cron, E.A. (1988). In-session cognitions of a counseling student: A case study. *Counselor Education and Supervision, 28,* 59–70.

Bordin, E.S. (1979). The generalizability of the psychoanalytic concept of the working alliance. *Psychotherapy: Theory, Research, and Practice, 16,* 252–260.

Carroll, K.M., Nich, C., & Rounsaville, B.J. (1997). Contribution of the therapeutic alliance to outcome in active versus control psychotherapies. *Journal of Consulting and Clinical Psychology, 65,* 510–514.

Carson, R.C. (1969). *Interaction concepts of personality.* Chicago: Aldine.

Chamberlain, P., Patterson, G., Reid, J., Kavanagh, K., & Forgatch, M. (1984). Observation of client resistance. *Behavior Therapy, 15,* 144–155.

Claiborn, C.D., & Dowd, E.D. (1985). Attributional interpretations in counseling: Content versus discrepancy. *Journal of Counseling Psychology, 32,* 186–196.

Claiborn, C.D., & Lichtenberg, J.W. (1989). Interactional counseling. *Counseling Psychologist, 17,* 355–443.

Clarke, K.M. (1989). Creation of meaning: An emotional processing task in psychotherapy. *Psychotherapy, 26,* 139–148.

Clarke, K.M. (1991). A performance model of the creation of meaning event. *Psychotherapy, 28,* 395–401.

Connolly, M.B., Crits-Christoph, P., Demorest, A., Azarian, K., Muenz, L., & Chittams, J. (1996). Varieties of transference patterns in psychotherapy. *Journal of Consulting and Clinical Psychology, 64,* 1213–1221.

Conoley, C.W., Padula, M.A., Payton, D.S., & Daniels, J.A. (1994). Predictors of client implementation of counselor recommendations: Match with problem, difficulty level, and building on client strengths. *Journal of Counseling Psychology, 41,* 3–7.

Crits-Christoph, P., Cooper, A., & Luborsky, L. (1988). The accuracy of therapists' interpretations and the outcome of dynamic psychotherapy. *Journal of Consulting and Clinical Psychology, 56,* 490–495.

Crits-Christoph, P., Demorest, A., & Connolly, M.B. (1990). Quantitative assessment of interpersonal themes over the course of psychotherapy. *Psychotherapy, 27,* 513–521.

Cummings, A.L. (1989). Relationship of client problem type to novice counselor response modes. *Journal of Counseling Psychology, 36,* 331–335.

Diemer, R.A., Lobell, L.K., Vivino, B.L., & Hill, C.E. (1996). Comparison of dream interpretation, event interpretation, and unstructured sessions in brief therapy. *Journal of Counseling Psychology, 43,* 99–112.

Duan, C., & Hill, C.E. (1996). Theoretical confusions in the construct of empathy: A review of the literature. *Journal of Counseling Psychology, 43,* 261–274.

Dunkle, J.H., & Friedlander, M.L. (1996). Contribution of therapist experience and personal characteristics to the working alliance. *Journal of Counseling Psychology, 43,* 456–460.

Eaton, T.T., Abeles, N., & Gutfreund, M.J. (1993). Negative indicators, therapeutic alliance, and therapy outcome. *Psychotherapy Research, 3,* 115–123.

Edwards, C.E., & Murdoch, N.L. (1994). Characteristics of therapist self-disclosure in the counseling process. *Journal of Counseling and Development, 72,* 384–389.

Elliott, R. (1984). A discovery-oriented approach to significant events in psychotherapy: Interpersonal process recall and comprehensive process analysis. In L.N. Rice & L.S. Greenberg (Eds.), *Patterns of change: Intensive analysis of psychotherapy process* (pp. 249–286). New York: Guilford Press.

Elliott, R. (1985). Helpful and nonhelpful events in brief counseling interviews: An empirical taxonomy. *Journal of Counseling Psychology, 32,* 307–322.

Elliott, R. (1989). Comprehensive process analysis: Understanding the change process in significant therapy events. In M.J. Packer & R.B. Addison (Eds.), *Entering the circle: Hermaneutic investigation in psychology.* Albany, NY: SUNY Press.

Elliott, R., Hill, C.E., Stiles, W.B., Friedlander, M.L., Mahrer, A.R., & Margison, F.R. (1987). Primary response modes: A comparison of six rating systems. *Journal of Consulting and Clinical Psychology, 55,* 218–223.

Elliott, R., & James, E. (1989). Varieties of client experience in psychotherapy: An analysis of the literature. *Clinical Psychology Review, 9,* 443–467.

Elliott, R., James, E., Reimschuessel, C., Cislo, D., & Sack, N. (1985). Significant events and the analysis of immediate therapeutic impacts. *Psychotherapy, 22,* 620–630.

Elliott, R., Shapiro, D.A., Firth-Cozens, J., Stiles, W.B., Hardy, G.E., Llewelyn, S.P., & Margison, F.R. (1994). Comprehensive process analysis of insight events in cognitive-behavioral and psychodynamic-interpersonal psychotherapies. *Journal of Counseling Psychology, 41,* 449–463.

Fenichel, O. (1941). *The psychoanalytic theory of neurosis.* New York: Norton.

Festinger, L. (1957). *A theory of cognitive dissonance.* Stanford, CA: Stanford University Press.

Field, S.D., Barkham, M., Shapiro, D.A., & Stiles, W.B. (1994). Assessment of assimilation in psychotherapy: A quantitative case study of problematic experiences with a significant other. *Journal of Counseling Psychology, 41,* 397–406.

Foreman, S.A., & Marmar, C.R. (1985). Therapist actions that address initially poor therapeutic alliance in psychotherapy. *American Journal of Psychiatry, 142,* 922–926.

Freud, S. (1958). The dynamics of transference. In J. Strachey (Ed. and Trans.), *The standard edition of the complete works of Sigmund Freud* (Vol. 12, pp. 99–108). London: Hogarth Press. (Original work published in 1912)

Freud, S. (1959). Future prospects of psychoanalytic psychotherapy. In J. Strachey (Ed. and Trans.), *The standard edition of the complete psychological works of Sigmund Freud* (Vol. 20, pp. 87–172). London: Hogarth Press. (Original work published 1910)

Friedlander, M.L. (1993a). Does complementarity promote or hinder client change in brief therapy? A review of the evidence from two theoretical perspectives. *Counseling Psychologist, 21,* 457–486.

Friedlander, M.L. (1993b). When complementarity is uncomplimentary and other reactions to Tracey (1993). *Journal of Counseling Psychology, 40,* 410–412.

Friedlander, M.L., & Phillips, S.D. (1984). Stochastic process analysis of interactive discourse in early counseling interviews. *Journal of Counseling Psychology, 31,* 139–148.

Fromm-Reichman, F. (1950). *Principles of intensive psychotherapy.* Chicago: University of Chicago.

Fuller, F., & Hill, C.E. (1985). Counselor and helpee perceptions of counselor intentions in relationship to outcome in a single counseling session. *Journal of Counseling Psychology, 32,* 329–338.

Fuqua, D.R., Newman, J.L., Anderson, M.W., & Johnson, A.W. (1986). Preliminary study of internal dialogue in a training setting. *Psychological Reports, 58,* 163–172.

Gaston, L., Marmar, C.R., Gallagher, D., & Thompson, L.W. (1991). Alliance prediction of outcome beyond in-treatment symptomatic change as psychotherapy processes. *Psychotherapy Research, 1,* 104–113.

Gaston, L., Piper, W.E., Debbane, E.G., Bienvenu, J., & Garant, J. (1994). Alliance and technique for predicting outcome in short- and long-term analytic psychotherapy. *Psychotherapy Research, 4,* 121–135.

Gelso, C.J., & Carter, J. (1985). The relationship in counseling and psychotherapy: Components, consequences, and theoretical antecedents. *Counseling Psychologist, 13,* 155–244.

Gelso, C.J., & Carter, J. (1994). Components of the psychotherapy relationship: Their interaction and unfolding during treatment. *Journal of Counseling Psychology, 41,* 296–306.

Gelso, C.J., Hill, C.E., Mohr, J., Rochlen, A.B., & Zack, J. (1999). The face of transference in successful, long-term therapy: A qualitative analysis. *Journal of Counseling Psychology, 46,* 257–267.

Gelso, C.J., Kivlighan, D.M., Wise, B., Jones, A., & Friedman, S.C. (1997). Transference, insight, and the course of time-limited therapy. *Journal of Counseling Psychology, 44,* 209–217.

Giorgi, A. (1970). *Psychology as a human science: A phenomenologically based approach.* New York: Harper & Row.

Giorgi, A. (1985). Sketch of a psychological phenomenological method. In A. Giorgi (Ed.), *Phenomenology and psychological research* (pp. 8–22). Pittsburgh: Duquesne University Press.

Golden, B.R., & Robbins, S.B. (1990). The working alliance within time-limited therapy: A case analysis. *Professional Psychology: Research and Practice, 21,* 476–481.

Grace, M., Kivlighan, D.M., & Kunce, J. (1995). The effect of nonverbal skills training on counselor trainee nonverbal sensitivity and responsiveness and on session impact and working alliance ratings. *Journal of Counseling and Development, 73,* 547–552.

Greenberg, L.S. (1984). Task analysis: The general approach. In L.N. Rice & L.S. Greenberg (Eds.), *Patterns of change: Intensive analysis of psychotherapy process* (pp. 124–148). New York: Guilford Press.

Greenberg, L.S. (1991). Research on the process of change. *Psychotherapy Research, 1,* 3–16.

Greenberg, L.S., & Pinsof, W. (Eds.). (1986). *The psychotherapeutic process: A research handbook.* New York: Guilford Press.

Greenson, R.R. (1967). *The technique and practice of psychoanalysis* (Vol. 1). Madison, CT: International Universities Press.

Gunderson, J.G., Najavits, L.M., Leonhard, C., Sullivan, C.N., & Sabo, A.N. (1997). Ontogeny of the therapeutic alliance in borderline patients. *Psychotherapy Research, 7,* 301–309.

Haley, J. (1963). *Strategies of psychotherapy.* New York: Grune and Stratton.

Haley, J. (1976). *Problem-solving therapy: New strategies for effective family therapy.* New York: Harper & Row.

Hanson, W.E., Claiborn, C.D., & Kerr, B. (1997). Differential effects of two test interpretation styles in counseling: A field study. *Journal of Counseling Psychology, 44,* 400–405.

Hartley, D.E., & Strupp, H.H. (1983). The therapeutic alliance: Its relationship to outcome in brief psychotherapy. In J. Masling (Ed.), *Empirical studies in analytic theories* (pp. 1–37). Hillside, NJ: Erlbaum.

Hatcher, R.L., & Barends, A.W. (1996). Patients' view of the alliance in psychotherapy: Exploratory factor analysis of three alliance measures. *Journal of Consulting and Clinical Psychology, 64,* 1326–1336.

Hatcher, R.L., Barends, A., Hansell, J., & Gutfreund, M.J. (1995). Patients' and therapists' shared and unique views of the therapeutic alliance: An investigation using confirmatory factor analysis in a nested design. *Journal of Consulting and Clinical Psychology, 63,* 636–643.

Hayes, J.A., McCracken, J.E., McClanahan, M.K., Hill, C.E., Harp, J.S., & Carozzoni, P. (1998). Therapist perspectives on countertransference: Qualitative data in search of a theory. *Journal of Counseling Psychology,* 468–482.

Hayes, J.A., Riker, J.R., & Ingram, K.M. (1997). Countertransference behavior and management in brief counseling: A field study. *Psychotherapy Research, 7,* 145–153.

Heaton, K.J., Hill, C.E., & Edwards, L. (1995). Comparing molecular and molar methods of judging therapist techniques. *Psychotherapy Research, 5,* 141–153.

Heaton, K.J., Hill, C.E., Petersen, D., Rochlen, A.B., & Zack, J. (1998). A comparison of therapist-facilitated and self-guided dream interpretation sessions. *Journal of Counseling Psychology,* 115–121.

Heppner, P.P., Kivlighan, D.M., Jr., & Wampold, B.E. (1999). *Research design in counseling* (2nd ed.). Pacific Grove, CA: Brooks/Cole.

Heppner, P.P., Rosenberg, J.I., & Hedgespeth, J. (1992). Three methods of measuring the therapeutic process: Clients' and counselors' constructions of the therapeutic process versus actual therapeutic events. *Journal of Counseling Psychology, 39,* 20–31.

Highlen, P.S., & Hill, C.E. (1984). Factors affecting client change in counseling. In S. Brown & R. Lent (Eds.), *Handbook of counseling psychology* (pp. 334–396). New York: Wiley.

Hill, C.E. (1986). An overview of the Hill counselor and client verbal response modes category systems. In L. Greenberg & W. Pinsof (Eds.), *The psychotherapeutic process: A research handbook* (pp. 131–160). New York: Guilford Press.

Hill, C.E. (1990). A review of exploratory in-session process research. *Journal of Consulting and Clinical Psychology, 58,* 288–294.

Hill, C.E. (1991). Almost everything you ever wanted to know about how to do process research on counseling and psychotherapy but didn't know who to ask. In C.E. Watkins & L.J. Schneider (Eds.), *Research in counseling* (pp. 85–118). Hillsdale, NJ: Erlbaum.

Hill, C.E. (1996). *Working with dreams in psychotherapy.* New York: Guilford Press.

Hill, C.E., & Corbett, M.M. (1993). A perspective on the history of process and outcome research in counseling psychology. *Journal of Counseling Psychology, 40,* 3–24.

Hill, C.E., Corbett, M.M., Kanitz, B., Rios, P., Lightsey, R., & Gomez, M. (1992). Client behavior in counseling and therapy sessions: Development of a pantheoretical measure. *Journal of Counseling Psychology, 39,* 539–549.

Hill, C.E., Diemer, R., & Heaton, K.J. (1997). Dream interpretation sessions: Who volunteers, who benefits, and what volunteer clients view as most and least helpful. *Journal of Counseling Psychology, 44,* 53–62.

Hill, C.E., Helms, J.E., Spiegel, S.B., & Tichenor, V. (1988). Development of a system for categorizing client reactions to therapist interventions. *Journal of Counseling Psychology, 35,* 27–36.

Hill, C.E., Helms, J.E., Tichenor, V., Spiegel, S.B., O'Grady, K.E., & Perry, E.S. (1988). The effects of therapist response modes in brief psychotherapy. *Journal of Counseling Psychology, 35,* 222–233.

Hill, C.E., Mahalik, J.R., & Thompson, B.J. (1989). Therapist self-disclosure. *Psychotherapy, 26,* 290–295.

Hill, C.E., Nutt, E.A., & Jackson, S. (1994). Trends in psychotherapy process research: Samples, measures, researchers, and classic publications. *Journal of Counseling Psychology, 41,* 364–377.

Hill, C.E., Nutt-Williams, E., Heaton, K.J., Thompson, B.J., & Rhodes, R.H. (1996). Therapist retrospective recall of impasses in long-term psychotherapy: A qualitative analysis. *Journal of Counseling Psychology, 43,* 207–217.

Hill, C.E., & O'Brien, K.M. (1999). *Helping skills: Facilitating exploration, insight, and action.* Washington, DC: American Psychological Association Press.

Hill, C.E., & O'Grady, K.E. (1985). List of therapist intentions illustrated in a case study and with therapists of varying theoretical orientations. *Journal of Counseling Psychology, 32,* 3–22.

Hill, C.E., O'Grady, K.E., Balenger, V., Busse, W., Falk, D.R., Hill, M., Rios, P., & Taffe, R. (1994). Methodological examination of videotape-assisted reviews in brief therapy: Helpfulness ratings, therapist intentions, client reactions, mood, and session evaluation. *Journal of Counseling Psychology, 41,* 236–247.

Hill, C.E., & Stephany, A. (1990). The relationship of nonverbal behaviors to client reactions. *Journal of Counseling Psychology, 37,* 22–26.

Hill, C.E., Thompson, B.J., Cogar, M.M., & Denman, D.W., III. (1993). Beneath the surface of long-term therapy: Client and therapist report of their own and each other's covert processes. *Journal of Counseling Psychology, 40,* 278–288.

Hill, C.E., Thompson, B.J., & Corbett, M.M. (1992). The impact of therapist ability to perceive displayed and hidden client reactions on immediate outcome in first sessions of brief therapy. *Psychotherapy Research, 2,* 143–155.

Hill, C.E., Thompson, B.J., & Mahalik, J.R. (1989). Therapist interpretation. In C.E. Hill, *Therapist techniques and client outcome: Eight cases of brief psychotherapy.* Newbury Park, CA: Sage.

Hill, C.E., Thompson, B.J., & Williams, E.N. (1997). A guide to conducting consensual qualitative research. *Counseling Psychologist, 25,* 517–572.

Hills, H.I., Gruzkos, J.R., & Strong, S.R. (1985). Attribution and the double bind in paradoxical interventions. *Psychotherapy, 22,* 779–785.

Hoglend, P. (1996). Analysis of transference in patients with personality disorders. *Journal of Personality Disorders, 10,* 122–131.

Holland, S.J., Roberts, N.E., & Messer, S.B. (1998). Reliability and validity of the Rutgers Psychotherapy Progress Scale. *Psychotherapy Research, 8,* 104–110.

Honos-Webb, L., & Stiles, W.B. (1998). Reformulation of assimilation analysis in terms of voices. *Psychotherapy, 35,* 23–33.

Honos-Webb, L., Surko, M., Stiles, W.B., & Greenberg, L.S. (in press). Assimilation of voices in psychotherapy: The case of Jan. *Journal of Counseling Psychology.*

Horvath, A.O., & Goheen, M.D. (1990). Factors mediating the success of defiance- and compliance-based interventions. *Journal of Counseling Psychology, 37,* 363–371.

Horvath, A.O., & Luborsky, L. (1993). The role of the therapeutic alliance in psychotherapy. *Journal of Consulting and Clinical Psychology, 61,* 561–573.

Horvath, A.O., Marx, R.W., & Kamann, A.M. (1988). Thinking about thinking in therapy: An examination of clients' understanding of their therapists' intentions. *Journal of Consulting and Clinical Psychology, 58,* 614–621.

Horvath, A.O., & Symonds, B.D. (1991). Relation between working alliance and outcome in psychotherapy: A meta-analysis. *Journal of Counseling Psychology, 38,* 139–149.

Hoshmand, L.L.S.T. (1989). Alternate research paradigms: A review and teaching proposal. *Counseling Psychologist, 17,* 3–79.

Hoyt, W.T., Strong, S.R., Corcoran, J.L., & Robbins, S.B. (1993). Interpersonal influence in a single case of brief counseling: An analytic strategy and a comparison of two indexes of influence. *Journal of Counseling Psychology, 40,* 166–181.

Jones, E.E., Cumming, J.D., & Horowitz, M.J. (1988). Another look at the nonspecific hypothesis of therapeutic effectiveness. *Journal of Consulting and Clinical Psychology, 56,* 48–55.

Jones, E.E., Ghannam, J., Nigg, J.T., & Dyer, J.F.P. (1993). A paradigm for single-case research: The time-series study of a long-term psychotherapy for depression. *Journal of Consulting and Clinical Psychology, 61,* 381–394.

Joyce, A.S., Duncan, S.C., & Piper, W.E. (1995). Task analysis of "working" responses to dynamic interpretation in short-term individual psychotherapy. *Psychotherapy Research, 5,* 49–62.

Kelly, A.E. (1998). Clients' secret keeping in outpatient therapy. *Journal of Counseling Psychology, 45,* 50–57.

Kelly, K.R., Hall, A.S., & Miller, K.L. (1989). Relation of counselor intention and anxiety to brief counseling outcome. *Journal of Counseling Psychology, 36,* 158–162.

Kernberg, O. (1965). Notes on countertransference. *Journal of the American Psychoanalytic Association, 13,* 38–56.

Kiesler, D.J. (1973). *The process of psychotherapy: Emperical foundations and systems of analysis.* Chicago: Aldine.

Kiesler, D.J. (1986). Interpersonal methods of diagnosis and treatment. In J. Cavenar (Ed.), *Psychiatry* (Vol. 1, pp. 1–24). Philadelphia: Lippincott.

Kiesler, D.J. (1988). *Therapeutic metacommunication: Therapist impact disclosure as feedback in psychotherapy.* Palo Alto, CA: Consulting Psychologists Press.

Kiesler, D.J., & Goldston, C.S. (1988). Client-therapist complementarity: An analysis of the Gloria films. *Journal of Counseling Psychology, 35,* 127–133.

Kiesler, D.J., & Watkins, L.M. (1989). Interpersonal complementarity and the therapeutic alliance: A study of relationship in psychotherapy. *Psychotherapy, 26,* 183–194.

Kivlighan, D.M. (1989). Changes in counselor intentions and response modes and in client reactions and session evaluation after training. *Journal of Counseling Psychology, 36,* 471–476.

Kivlighan, D.M. (1990). Relation between counselors' use of intentions clients' perception of working alliance. *Journal of Counseling Psychology, 37,* 27–32.

Kivlighan, D.M., & Angelone, E.O. (1991). Helpee introversion, novice counselor intention use, and helpee-rated session impact. *Journal of Counseling Psychology, 38,* 25–29.

Kivlighan, D.M., Clements, L., Blake, C., Arnzen, A., & Brady, L. (1993). Counselor sex role orientation, flexibility, and working alliance formation. *Journal of Counseling and Development, 72,* 95–100.

Kivlighan, D.M., & Schmitz, P.J. (1992). Counselor technical activity in cases with improving working alliances and continuing-poor working alliances. *Journal of Counseling Psychology, 39,* 32–38.

Kivlighan, D.M., & Shaughnessy, P. (1995). Analysis of the development of the working alliance using hierarchical linear modeling. *Journal of Counseling Psychology, 42,* 338–349.

Klee, M.R., Abeles, N., & Muller, R.T. (1990). Therapeutic alliance: Early indicators, course, and outcome. *Psychotherapy, 27,* 166–174.

Klein, M.H., Mathieu-Coughlan, P., & Kiesler, D.J. (1986). The Experiencing Scales. In L. Greenberg & W. Pinsof (Eds.), *The psychotherapeutic process: A research handbook* (pp. 21–72). New York: Guilford Press.

Knox, S., Hess, S., Petersen, D., & Hill, C.E. (1997). A qualitative analysis of client perceptions of the effects of helpful therapist self-disclosure in long-term therapy. *Journal of Counseling Psychology, 44,* 274–283.

Kokotovic, A.M., & Tracey, T.J. (1990). Working alliance in the early phase of counseling. *Journal of Counseling Psychology, 37,* 16–21.

Kraft, R.G., Claiborn, C.D., & Dowd, E.T. (1985). Effects of positive reframing and paradoxical directives in counseling for negative emotions. *Journal of Counseling Psychology, 32,* 617–621.

Krupnick, J.L., Sotsky, S.M., Simmens, S., Moyer, J., Elkin, I., Watkins, J., & Pilkonis, P.A. (1996). The role of the therapeutic alliance in psychotherapy and pharmacotherapy outcome: Findings in the National Institute of Mental Health Treatment of Depression Collaborative Research Program. *Journal of Consulting and Clinical Psychology, 64,* 532–539.

Lambert, M.J., & Hill, C.E. (1994). Assessing psychotherapy outcomes and processes. In A.E. Bergin & S.L. Garfield (Eds.), *Handbook of psychotherapy and behavior change* (4th ed., pp. 72–113). New York: Wiley.

Lichtenberg, J.W., & Kobes, K. (1992). Topic control as relational control and its effects on the outcome of therapy. *Psychological Reports, 70,* 391–401.

Lichtenberg, J.W., Wettersten, K.B., Mull, H., Moberly, R.L., Merkley, K.B., & Corey, A.T. (1998). Relationship formation and relational control as correlates of psychotherapy quality and outcome. *Journal of Counseling Psychology, 45,* 322–337.

Llewelyn, S.P., Elliott, R., Shapiro, D.A., Hardy, G., & Firth-Cozens, J. (1988). Client perceptions of significant events in prescriptive and exploratory periods of individual therapy. *British Journal of Clinical Psychology, 27,* 105–114.

Luborsky, L. (1984). *Principles of psychoanalytic psychotherapy: A manual for supportive-expressive treatment.* New York: Basic Books.

Luborsky, L., Barber, J.P., & Diguer, L. (1992). The meanings of narratives told during psychotherapy: The fruits of a new observational unit. *Psychotherapy Research, 2,* 277–290.

Luborsky, L., Popp, C., & Barber, J.P. (1994). Common and special factors in different transference-related measures. *Psychotherapy Research, 4,* 277–286.

Luborsky, L., Popp, C., Luborsky, E., & Mark, D. (1994). The core conflictual relationship theme. *Psychotherapy Research, 4,* 172–183.

Mahalik, J.R. (1994). Development of the Client Resistance Scale. *Journal of Counseling Psychology, 41,* 58–68.

Mahrer, A.R. (1988). Discovery-oriented psychotherapy research. *American Psychologist, 43,* 694–702.

Mahrer, A.R., Dessaulles, A., Nadler, W.P., Gervaize, P.A., & Sterner, I. (1987). Good and very good moments in psychotherapy: Content, distribution, and facilitation. *Psychotherapy, 24,* 7–14.

Mahrer, A.R., Gagnon, R., Fairweather, D.R., Boulet, D.B., & Herring, C B. (1994). Client commitment and resolve to carry out postsession behaviors. *Journal of Counseling Psychology, 41,* 407–414.

Mahrer, A.R., & Nadler, W.P. (1986). Good moments in psychotherapy: A preliminary review, a list, and some promising research avenues. *Journal of Consulting and Clinical Psychology, 54,* 10–16.

Mahrer, A.R., Nifakis, D.J., Abhukara, L., & Sterner, I. (1984). Microstrategies in psychotherapy: The patterning of sequential therapist statements. *Psychotherapy, 21,* 465–472.

Mahrer, A.R., White, M.V., Howard, M.T., Gagnon, R., & MacPhee, D.C. (1986). How to bring about some very good moments in psychotherapy sessions. *Psychotherapy Research, 2,* 252–265.

Mallinckrodt, B. (1991). Clients' representations of childhood emotional bonds with parents, social support, and formation of the working alliance. *Journal of Counseling Psychology, 38,* 401–409.

Mallinckrodt, B. (1996a). Capturing the subjective and other challenges in measuring transference: Comment on Multon, Patton, and Kivlighan (1996). *Journal of Counseling Psychology, 43,* 253–256.

Mallinckrodt, B. (1996b). Change in working alliance, social support, and psychological symptoms in brief therapy. *Journal of Counseling Psychology, 43,* 448–455.

Mallinckrodt, B., Gantt, D.L., & Coble, H.M. (1995). Attachment patterns in the psychotherapy relationship: Development of the Client Attachment to Therapist Scale. *Journal of Counseling Psychology, 42,* 307–317.

Mallinckrodt, B., & Nelson, M.L. (1991). Counselor training level and the formation of the psychotherapeutic working alliance. *Journal of Counseling Psychology, 38,* 133–138.

Mann, J. (1981). The core of time-limited psychotherapy: Time and the central issue. In S.H. Budman (Ed.), *Forms of brief therapy* (pp. 25–43). New York: Guilford Press.

Martin, J. (1984). The cognitive mediational paradigm for research on counseling. *Journal of Counseling Psychology, 31,* 558–571.

Martin, J., Martin, W., Meyer, M., & Slemon, A. (1986). An empirical test of the cognitive mediational paradigm for research on counseling. *Journal of Counseling Psychology, 33,* 115–123.

Martin, J., Martin, W., & Slemon, A. (1987). Cognitive mediation in person-centered and rational-emotive therapy. *Journal of Counseling Psychology, 34,* 251–260.

Martin, J., Martin, W., & Slemon, A. (1989). Cognitive-models of action-act sequences in counseling. *Journal of Counseling Psychology, 36,* 8–16.

Martin, J., & Stelmaczonek, K. (1988). Participants' identification and recall of important events in counseling. *Journal of Counseling Psychology, 35,* 385–390.

McCarthy, P.R., Shaw, T., & Schmeck, R.R. (1986). Behavioral analysis of client learning style during counseling. *Journal of Counseling Psychology, 33,* 249–254.

McClure, B.A., & Hodge, R.W. (1987). Measuring countertransference and attitude in therapeutic relationships. *Psychotherapy, 24,* 325–335.

McCullough, L., Winston, A., Farber, B., Porter, F., Pollack, J., Laikin, M., Vingiano, W., & Trujillo, M. (1991). The relationship of patient-therapist interaction to outcome in brief psychotherapy. *Psychotherapy, 28,* 525–533.

McMullen, L.M., & Conway, J.B. (1997). Dominance and nurturance in the narratives told by clients in psychotherapy. *Psychotherapy Research, 7,* 83–98.

McNeilly, D.L., & Howard, K.I. (1991). The Therapeutic Procedures Inventory: Psychometric properties and relationship to phase of treatment. *Journal of Personality Integration, 1,* 223–235.

Messer, S.B., Tishby, O., & Spillman, A. (1992). Taking context seriously in psychotherapy research: Relating therapist interventions to patient progress in brief psychodynamic therapy. *Journal of Consulting and Clinical Psychology, 60,* 678–688.

Miller, W.R., Benefield, R.G., & Tonigan, J.S. (1993). Enhancing motivation for change in problem drinking: A controlled comparison of two therapist styles. *Journal of Consulting and Clinical Psychology, 61,* 455–461.

Morran, D.K. (1986). Relationship of counselor self-talk and hypothesis formulation to performance level. *Journal of Counseling Psychology, 33,* 395–400.

Morran, D.K., Kurpius, D.J., Brack, C.J., & Brack, G. (1995). A cognitive-skills model for counselor training and supervision. *Journal of Counseling and Development, 73,* 384–389.

Morran, D.K., Kurpius, D.J., & Brack, G. (1989). Empirical investigation of counselor self-talk categories. *Journal of Counseling Psychology, 36,* 505–510.

Multon, K.D., Patton, M.J., & Kivlighan, D.A. (1996). Development of the Missouri Identifying Transference Scale. *Journal of Counseling Psychology, 43,* 243–252.

Muran, J.C., Segal, Z.V., Samstag, L.W., & Crawford, C.E. (1994). Patient pretreatment interpersonal problems and therapeutic alliance in short-term cognitive therapy. *Journal of Consulting and Clinical Psychology, 62,* 185–190.

Nagel, D.P., Hoffman, M.A., & Hill, C.E. (1995). A comparison of verbal response modes used by master's level career counselors and other helpers. *Journal of Counseling and Development, 74,* 101–104.

Norville, R., Sampson, H., & Weiss, J. (1996). Accurate interpretations and brief psychotherapy outcome. *Psychotherapy Research, 6,* 16–29.

Nutt-Williams, E., & Hill, C.E. (1996). The relationship between therapist self-talk and counseling process variables for novice therapists. *Journal of Counseling Psychology, 43,* 170–177.

Olson, D.H., & Claiborn, C.D. (1990). Interpretation and arousal in the counseling process. *Journal of Counseling Psychology, 37,* 131–137.

Orford, J. (1986). The rules of interpersonal complementarity: Does hostility beget hostility and dominance, submission? *Psychological Review, 93,* 365–377.

Orlinsky, D.E., Grawe, K., & Parks, B.K. (1994). Process and outcome in psychotherapy—Noch einmal. In A.E. Bergin & S.L. Garfield (Eds.), *Handbook of psychotherapy and behavior change* (4th ed., pp. 270–376). New York: Wiley.

Panken, S. (1981). Countertransference reevaluated. *Psychoanalytic Review, 68,* 23–44.

Patterson, G.R., & Forgatch, M.S. (1985). Therapist behavior as a determinant for client noncompliance: A paradox for the behavior modifier. *Journal of Consulting and Clinical Psychology, 53,* 846–851.

Patton, M.J., Kivlighan, D.M., & Multon, K.D. (1997). The Missouri Psychoanalytic Counseling Research Project: Relation of changes in counseling process to client outcomes. *Journal of Counseling Psychology, 44,* 189–208.

Piper, W.E., Joyce, A.S., McCallum, M., & Azim, H.F.A. (1993). Concentration and correspondence of transference interpretations in short-term psychotherapy. *Journal of Consulting and Clinical Psychology, 61,* 586–595.

Polkinghorne, D.E. (1984). Further extension of methodological diversity for counseling psychology. *Journal of Counseling Psychology, 31,* 416–429.

Quintana, S.M., & Meara, N.M. (1990). Internalization of therapeutic relationships in short-term psychotherapy. *Journal of Counseling Psychology, 37,* 123–130.

Regan, A.M., & Hill, C.E. (1992). An investigation of what clients and counselors do not say in brief therapy. *Journal of Counseling Psychology, 39,* 168–174.

Rennie, D.L. (1994). Clients' deference in psychotherapy. *Journal of Counseling Psychology, 41,* 427–437.

Rennie, D.L., Phillips, J.R., & Quartaro, G.K. (1988). Grounded theory: A promising approach to conceptualization in psychology? *Canadian Psychology, 29,* 138–150.

Rhodes, R., Hill, C.E., Thompson, B.J., & Elliott, R. (1994). Client retrospective recall of resolved and unresolved misunderstanding events. *Journal of Counseling Psychology, 41,* 473–483.

Rice, L.N., & Sapiera, E.P. (1984). Task analysis of the resolution of problematic reactions. In L.N. Rice & L.S. Greenberg (Eds.), *Patterns of change: Intensive analysis of psychotherapy process* (pp. 29–66). New York: Guilford Press.

Richards, P.S., & Lonborg, S.D. (1996). Development of a method for studying thematic content of psychotherapy sessions. *Journal of Consulting and Clinical Psychology, 64,* 701–711.

Richardson, M.S. (1997). Toward a clinically relevant model of counseling research: Comment on Patton, Kivlighan, and Multon (1997) and Gelso, Kivlighan, Wine, Jones, and Friedman (1997). *Journal of Counseling Psychology, 44,* 218–221.

Robbins, S.B. (1992). The working alliance. In M. Patton & N. Meara (Eds.), *Psychoanalytic counseling* (pp. 97–121). Chichester, England: Wiley.

Rogers, C.R. (1957). The necessary and sufficient conditions of therapeutic personality change. *Journal of Consulting Psychology, 21,* 95–103.

Safran, J.D. (1984). Assessing the cognitive-interpersonal cycle. *Cognitive Therapy & Research, 8,* 333–348.

Safran, J.D. (1990). Towards a refinement of cognitive therapy in light of interpersonal theory. *Clinical Psychology Review, 10,* 87–105.

Safran, J.D., Crocker, P., McMain, S., & Murray, P. (1990). Therapeutic alliance rupture as a therapy event for empirical investigation. *Psychotherapy, 27,* 154–165.

Safran, J.D., & Muran, J.C. (1996). The resolution of ruptures in the therapeutic alliance. *Journal of Consulting and Clinical Psychology, 64,* 447–458.

Salerno, M., Farber, B.A., McCullough, L., Winston, A., & Trujillo, M. (1992). The effects of confrontation and clarification on patient affective and defensive responding. *Psychotherapy Research, 2,* 181–192.

Salvio, M., Beutler, L.E., Wood, J.M., & Engle, D. (1992). The strength of the therapeutic alliance in three treatments for depression. *Psychotherapy Research, 2,* 31–36.

Satterfield, W.A., & Lyddon, W.J. (1995). Client attachment and perceptions of the working alliance with counselor trainees. *Journal of Counseling Psychology, 42,* 187–189.

Schaffer, N.D. (1982). Multidimensional measures of therapist behaviors as predictors of outcome. *Psychological Bulletin, 92,* 670–681.

Shostrom, E.L. (Producer). (1966). *Three approaches to psychotherapy* [Film]. Santa Ana, CA: Psychological Films.

Sifneos, P.E. (1979). *Short-term dynamic psychotherapy: Evaluation and technique.* New York: Plenum Press.

Singer, B.A., & Luborsky, L. (1977). Countertransference: The status of clinical versus quantitative research. In A.S. Gurman & A.M. Razdin (Eds.), *Effective psychotherapy: Handbook of research* (pp. 433–451). New York: Pergamon Press.

Spence, D.P., Dahl, H., & Jones, E.E. (1993). Impact of interpretation on associative freedom. *Journal of Consulting and Clinical Psychology, 61,* 395–402.

Stiles, W.B. (1987). Some intentions are observable. *Journal of Counseling Psychology, 34,* 236–239.

Stiles, W.B., Elliott, R., Llewelyn, S.P., Firth-Cozens, J.A., Margison, F.R., Shapiro, D.A., & Hardy, G. (1990). Assimilation of problematic experiences by clients in psychotherapy. *Psychotherapy, 27,* 411–420.

Stiles, W.B., & Shapiro, D.A. (1995). Verbal exchange structure of brief psychodynamic-interpersonal and cognitive-behavioral psychotherapy. *Journal of Consulting and Clinical Psychology, 63,* 15–27.

Stiles, W.B., Startup, M., Hardy, G., Barkham, M., Rees, A., Shapiro, D.A., & Reynolds, S. (1996). Therapist session intentions in cognitive-behavioral and psychodynamic-interpersonal psychotherapy. *Journal of Counseling Psychology, 43,* 402–414.

Strauss, A., & Corbin, J. (1990). *Basics of qualitative research: Grounded theory procedures and techniques.* Newbury Park, CA: Sage.

Strong, S.R. (1982). Emerging integrations of clinical and social psychology: A clinician's perspective. In G. Weary & H. Mirels (Eds.), *Integrations of clinical and social psychology* (pp. 181–213). New York: Oxford University Press.

Strong, S.R., & Claiborn, C.D. (1982). *Change through interaction: Social psychological processes of counseling and psychotherapy.* New York: Wiley.

Svartberg, M., & Stiles, T.C. (1992). Predicting patient change from therapist competence and patient-therapist complementarity in short-term anxiety-provoking psychotherapy: A pilot study. *Journal of Consulting and Clinical Psychology, 60,* 304–307.

Svartberg, M., & Stiles, T.C. (1994). Therapeutic alliance, therapist competence, and client change in short-term anxiety-provoking psychotherapy. *Psychotherapy Research, 4,* 20–33.

Swoboda, J.S., Dowd, E.T., & Wise, S.L. (1990). Reframing and restraining directives in the treatment of clinical depression. *Journal of Counseling Psychology, 37,* 254–260.

Thompson, B.J., & Hill, C.E. (1991). Therapist perceptions of client reactions. *Journal of Counseling and Development, 69,* 261–265.

Thompson, B.J., & Hill, C.E. (1993). Client perceptions of therapist competence. *Psychotherapy Research, 3,* 124–130.

Thompson, B.J., Hill, C.E., & Mahalik, J.R. (1991). A test of the complementarity hypotheses in the interpersonal theory of psychotherapy: Multiple case comparisons. *Psychotherapy, 28,* 572–579.

Tichenor, V., & Hill, C.E. (1989). A comparison of six measures of working alliance. *Psychotherapy, 26,* 195–199.

Tracey, T.J. (1985). Dominance and outcome: A sequential examination. *Journal of Counseling Psychology, 32,* 119–122.

Tracey, T.J. (1991). The structure of control and influence in counseling and psychotherapy: A comparison of several definitions and measures. *Journal of Counseling Psychology, 38,* 265–278.

Tracey, T.J. (1993). An interpersonal stage model of the therapeutic process. *Journal of Counseling Psychology, 40,* 396–409.

Tracey, T.J., & Ray, P.B. (1984). Stages of successful time-limited counseling: An interactional examination. *Journal of Counseling Psychology, 31,* 13–27.

Tryon, G.S., & Kane, A.S. (1995). Client involvement, working alliance, and type of therapy termination. *Psychotherapy Research, 5,* 189–198.

Wade, P., & Bernstein, B.L. (1991). Culture sensitivity training and counselor's race: Effects on black female clients' perceptions and attrition. *Journal of Counseling Psychology, 38,* 9–15.

Wampold, B.E., & Kim, K. (1989). Sequential analysis applied to counseling process and outcome: A case study revisited. *Journal of Counseling Psychology, 36,* 357–364.

Watson, J.C. (1996). The relationship between vivid description, emotional arousal, and in-session resolution of problematic reactions. *Journal of Consulting and Clinical Psychology, 64,* 459–464.

Watson, J.C., & Rennie, D.L. (1996). Qualitative analysis of clients' subjective experience of significant moments during the exploration of problematic reactions. *Journal of Counseling Psychology, 41,* 500–509.

Watzlawick, P., Weakland, J., & Fisch, R. (1974). *Change: Principles of problem formation and problem resolution.* New York: Norton.

Westerman, M.A., Frankel, A.S., Tanaka, J.S., & Kahn, J. (1987). Client cooperative behavior and outcome in paradoxical and behavioral brief treatment approaches. *Journal of Counseling Psychology, 34,* 99–102.

Wilcox-Matthew, L., Ottens, A., & Minor, C.W. (1997). Analysis of significant events in counseling. *Journal of Counseling and Development, 75,* 282–289.

Williams, E.N., Judge, A.B., Hill, C.E., & Hoffman, M.A. (1997). Experiences of novice therapists in prepracticum: Trainees', clients', and supervisors' perceptions of therapists' personal reactions and management strategies. *Journal of Counseling Psychology, 44,* 390–399.

Wiseman, H., & Rice, L.N. (1989). Sequential analyses of therapist-client interaction during change events: A task-focused approach. *Journal of Consulting and Clinical Psychology, 57,* 281–286.

Wiseman, H., Shefler, G., Caneti, L., & Ronen, Y. (1993). A systematic comparison of two cases in Mann's time-limited psychotherapy: An events approach. *Psychotherapy Research, 3,* 227–244.

Wiser, S., & Goldfried, M. (1996). Verbal interventions in significant psychodynamic-interpersonal and cognitive-behavioral therapy sessions, *Psychotherapy Research, 6,* 309–316.

Wiser, S., & Goldfried, M. (1998). Therapist interventions and client emotional experiencing in expert psychodynamic-interpersonal and cognitive-behavioral therapies. *Journal of Consulting and Clinical Psychology, 66,* 634–640.

Worthington, E.L. (1986). Client compliance with homework directives during counseling. *Journal of Counseling Psychology, 33,* 124–130.

Zack, J., & Hill, C.E. (1998). Predicting dream interpretation outcome by attitudes, stress, and emotion. *Dreaming, 8,* 169–185.

CHAPTER 22

Outcomes of Individual Counseling and Psychotherapy: Empirical Evidence Addressing Two Fundamental Questions

BRUCE E. WAMPOLD

Recently, the Library of Congress opened the exhibition "Sigmund Freud: Conflict and Culture." This exhibit initiated debate in the public media about the nature of psychotherapy and whether it is an effective means to address mental health issues in an era of health maintenance organizations (HMOs) and biological explanations of mental disorders. *Newsweek* noted, "In recent years the doctor [Freud] has been declared out, done in by a combination of Prozac, managed care and posthumous revelations that he willfully ignored patients' testimonials of child abuse, misstated some evidence, even fell asleep during sessions" (Leland & Kalb, 1998, p. 60). Although counseling and psychotherapy have evolved from Freud's talking cure, the public perception of individual psychotherapeutic intervention is not well grounded in modern conceptualizations or in empirical evidence for the efficacy of such activities.

The purpose of this chapter is to explore the evidence for the efficacy of counseling and psychotherapy. The first fundamental question we address is whether counseling and psychotherapy, as a general class of activities, lead to positive outcomes. The evidence convincingly supports the belief that psychotherapy is efficacious. Given this conclusion, the logical next step would be to identify the aspects, components, ingredients, or factors of counseling and psychotherapy that create the beneficial outcomes. In this regard, the counseling and psychotherapy communities are not in agreement, either conceptually or empirically. There are many conceptualizations of counseling and psychotherapy, variously referred to as modalities, theories, approaches, or systems, each with coherent and logical explanations for behavior and behavior change. Empirically, evidence can be found to support many approaches, which further complicates understanding. It is no small wonder that the public is confused about counseling and psychotherapy. An attempt to bring some clarity to the empirical evidence will be accomplished by differentiating common factor models and specific ingredient models. The second fundamental question is whether the general effects of counseling and psychotherapy are due to the commonalities that underlie most approaches or to the specific ingredients of each particular approach.

Before launching into the empirical evidence, a note is needed about what is convincing empirical evidence. It is impossible to collect and summarize the thousands of studies published on the process and outcome of counseling and psychotherapy. Moreover, given a relatively high frequency of Type I and II errors, there will inevitably be individual published studies supporting a multitude of conclusions, including contradictory conclusions. Consequently, whenever possible, syntheses of research will be cited in lieu of individual studies. Well-conducted meta-analyses, as a preferred method to synthesize research, provide a quantitative summary of the myriad of studies addressing a hypothesis. Use of meta-analysis avoids the problem of reconciling traditional narrative literature reviews that seem to reach different conclusions (e.g., some studies with statistically significant results and some with no statistically significant results; see, e.g., Hedges & Olkin, 1985).

ABSOLUTE EFFICACY OF COUNSELING AND PSYCHOTHERAPY: EVIDENCE REGARDING THE FIRST FUNDAMENTAL QUESTION

Freud, the originator of "talk therapy" and a central character in the development of counseling and psychotherapy, was convinced that psychoanalysis was a potent treatment for his patients (Strupp & Howard, 1992). However, this conclusion was made on data that would not be considered scientific from an empirical standpoint. In 1952, Eysenck roundly criticized psychotherapy, claiming that the proportion of those helped was equivalent to the proportion who experienced spontaneous remissions. Although based on a review of empirical research, in retrospect, Eysenck's conclusion appeared to be biased toward the conclusion that psychotherapy is ineffective (Bergin & Lambert, 1978). It took another 25 years before a systematic quantitative review of the outcomes of counseling and psychotherapy occurred. In 1977, Smith and Glass developed a statistical means to synthesize research outcomes, which they called meta-analysis, and applied it to outcome research in counseling and psychotherapy. They found that there was sufficient evidence to conclude emphatically that counseling and psychotherapy were effective means to help people with their problems; subsequent meta-analyses have consistently supported this conclusion. This abbreviated history serves to set the stage for discussing both the research methods and meta-analytic results related to the absolute efficacy of psychotherapy.

Research Methods to Establish Absolute Efficacy

Absolute efficacy refers to outcomes of psychotherapy vis-à-vis no treatment and answers the question, "How much better, in general, is a treated client than he or she would have been without treatment?" Absolute efficacy is best addressed by a between-group design in which participants are randomly assigned to a treatment group and a no-treatment group, the treatment group receives the designated intervention, and the functioning of the participants is assessed subsequently (at termination or some time thereafter). The scores of the participants who have been treated are assumed to be representative of the hypothetical population of persons who (1) meet the study criteria (e.g., are depressed) and (2) who receive the treatment. The scores of the participants who do not receive treatment (no treatment control or waiting-list control) are assumed to represent the hypothetical population of persons who (1) meet the study criteria and (2) do not receive treatment. If the null hypothesis of equivalent means is rejected (in favor of the treatment group), then it is concluded that treating similar persons results in a better outcome than would be the case if these persons were not treated. The randomized posttreatment only control group design (and the valid alternative, randomized pretest-posttest control group design—for instances in which it is deemed advantageous to administer a pretest) form the basis of what is referred to as *clinical trials*; the intricacies of these designs are discussed elsewhere (e.g., see Heppner, Kivlighan, & Wampold, 1999).

An important issue here is that the results of control group designs should not be construed to imply that any particular component of the treatment led to the outcome. In most control group studies in counseling and psychotherapy, as we shall see, treated persons are found to be more functional or less distressed than untreated persons as a result of treatment. However, the result may be due to (1) the specific actions of the therapist that are endemic to the treatment or (2) characteristics of the treatment that are similar to most treatments (e.g., the therapeutic relationship). As will be shown in this chapter, attributing effects of counseling and psychotherapy to specific versus common aspects of treatments is a particularly thorny issue; at this point, suffice it to say that the straightforward control group designs provide precious little information apart from the basic, but critical, question related to general efficacy.

Another aspect of the control group design is that the results are obtained in the context of a clinical trial, in which clients are selected based on strict inclusion and exclusion criteria. Treatments are delivered in a standard fashion (typically guided by a treatment manual), within a time limit, by therapists who are trained specifically for the study and are closely monitored and supervised. The term *efficacy* has been used to describe positive results of clinical trials, which have become "the 'gold standard' for measuring whether a treatment works" (Seligman, 1995, p. 966). However, the generalizability of the results of tightly controlled clinical research to practice settings largely is unknown but is clearly an important issue (see Howard, Krause, Saunders, & Kopta, 1997; Kazdin, Kratochwill, & VandenBos, 1986; Wampold, 1997; Weisz, Donenberg, Han, & Weiss, 1995). Seligman (1995) suggested that the term *effectiveness* be used to refer to the outcomes of counseling and psychotherapy as practiced in real-life clinical settings. The little evidence on effectiveness that exists will be included along with efficacy findings.

Given this brief discussion of the design issues, attention is turned to the empirical evidence related to whether counseling and psychotherapy produce superior positive results vis-à-vis no treatment.

Empirical Evidence for Absolute Efficacy

As mentioned, Smith and Glass (1977) quantitatively reviewed studies related to absolute efficacy. In their analysis, Smith and Glass reviewed all of the 375 studies that they could find that compared a counseling or psychotherapeutic treatment to a control group. The efficacy of the treatment was quantified by indexing the effect size of the treatment as the difference in the obtained sample means divided by the standard deviation of the control group. A positive effect size indicated the superiority of the treatment, in standard deviation units.

The 375 studies produced 833 indexes of effect size, due to use of multiple outcome measures. Over the studies, which included over 25,000 control group and 25,000 treatment group participants, the average effect size was .68; that is, the posttreatment means of the treated participants, on the whole, were superior to the posttreatment means of the control groups by .68 standard deviations. There are a few ways to get a practical sense of this effect. First, as noted by Smith and Glass (1977, pp. 754–755), assuming normal distributions, an effect of .68 can be interpreted as indicating that 75% of those treated were better than the average of those untreated. Second, according to Cohen's (1988) typology, effects can be classified as large, medium, and small—with Smith and Glass' effect size being between medium and large. A third way is to compare the psychotherapy effect size with the magnitude of effects produced by other types of interventions, such as aspirin as a prophylaxis for coronary disease (see Rosenthal, 1990), and the general efficacy of educational, psychological, and behavioral interventions (see Lipsey & Wilson, 1993). Such comparisons again support the efficacy of psychotherapy because the effects of such treatments are comparable to other psychological interventions, comparable to educational interventions, and superior to many medical interventions.

It would be difficult to overestimate the contribution of Smith and Glass' (1977) study. Until 1977, controversy reigned relative to the efficacy of counseling and psychotherapy; researchers were free to select studies that supported their position and to underestimate the importance of others. In 1977, the psychotherapy community was faced with a quantitative result derived from all of the available studies. At first, the meta-analysis was challenged by several camps (e.g., Eysenck, 1978; Wilson & Rachman, 1983). One of the ubiquitous criticisms was the "garbage-in, garbage-out" hypothesis, based on the possibility that many of the studies included were flawed and, consequently, the estimate of the effect size for a common hypothesis is flawed. However, Smith and Glass considered this possibility, coded various features of the studies that might affect outcomes (including internal validity of the study), so that threats to their conclusion could be ruled out; none of the features examined materially altered the basic conclusion that counseling and psychotherapy are efficacious activities.

Since 1977, there have been a proliferation of meta-analyses addressing the efficacy issue. The original 1977 database was expanded and reanalyzed by Smith, Glass, and Miller (1980), resulting in an average effect size of .85, which was larger than the previous effect size (viz., .68). This indicates that the average treated person has a better outcome than 80% of untreated persons. Critics of the Smith et al. meta-analysis reanalyzed the data and could find no basis to dispute the conclusion that psychotherapy is efficacious (Andrews & Harvey, 1981; Landman & Dawes, 1982).

So many meta-analyses of the effects of psychotherapy have now been conducted that reviews of meta-analyses have been conducted. Three comprehensive reviews (Grissom, 1996; Lambert & Bergin, 1994; Lipsey & Wilson, 1993) have confirmed that counseling and psychotherapy are efficacious. Based on 13 meta-analyses, Lambert and Bergin (1994) estimated the effect size for the efficacy of counseling and psychotherapy to be .82, a value very close to the .80 value found by Smith et al. (1980) established roughly two decades before! Given the error in estimation and the fact that the average did not account for the fact that the same studies were contained in some of the meta-analyses, nor for the fact that effect sizes were not weighted (as recommended by meta-analytic methodologists, e.g., Hedges & Olkin, 1985), the grand effect size of .82 likely is accurate to one decimal place, yielding a convenient and historic benchmark value of .80. Recall that an effect size of .80 is a profoundly large value, so that the conclusion can be amended, using a verbal description of a quantitative result: counseling and psychotherapy are remarkably efficacious.

Clearly, the global efficacy issue has been decided, but one has to wonder whether the result applies universally; that is, is counseling and psychotherapy effective for all problems or disorders? The answer appears to be that for problems and disorders that are thought to be appropriate for treatment and to which researchers have turned their attention, the answer is "yes." Reviews of meta-analyses reveal that large effect sizes are obtained across a variety of problems and disorders, including depression, anxiety, somatic symptoms, marital disorders, neuroticism, and many others (Lambert & Bergin, 1994; Lipsey & Wilson, 1993).

Does Efficacy Translate into Effectiveness?

Recall that efficacy refers to outcomes of clinical trials, an artificial context, and that the results of such trials (and meta-analyses of such trials) may not generalize to practice settings. However, effectiveness of counseling and psychotherapy, which refers to naturalistic outcomes, is enormously more difficult to establish, if for no other reason that random assignment to treatment and control groups is typically precluded in clinical settings. Nevertheless, there is evidence that counseling and psychotherapy are effective under common clinical conditions, although this evidence is necessarily weaker than was the efficacy evidence discussed previously.

Seligman (1995) reported the results of a survey of psychotherapy conducted by *Consumer Reports*. Approximately 180,000 readers of *Consumer Reports* were asked to complete the survey if they had experienced stress or emotional problems for which they had sought help from "friends, relatives, or a member of the clergy; a mental health professional like a psychologist or a psychiatrist; your family doctor; or a support group" (Seligman, 1995, p. 967). Approximately 7,000 readers responded, of which 2,900 saw a mental health professional. Overall, the conclusion was that counseling and psychotherapy was effective:

> Treatment by a mental health professional usually worked. Most respondents got a lot better. Averaged over all mental health professionals, of the 426 people who were feeling *very poor* when they began therapy, 87% were feeling *very good, good,* or at least *so-so* by the time of the survey. Of the 786 people who were feeling *fairly poor* at the outset, 92% were feeling *very good, good,* or at least

so-so by the time of the survey. These findings converge with meta-analyses of efficacy. (Emphasis in original, p. 968)

Clearly, the *Consumer Reports* study is flawed from the perspective of internal validity; not unexpectedly, it has been criticized for all of the obvious (and some not so obvious) reasons (e.g., Brock, Green, Reich, & Evans, 1996; Hunt, 1996; Kotkin, Daviet, & Gurin, 1996; Mintz, Drake, & Crits-Christoph, 1996). Nevertheless, it represents, by far, the most comprehensive study of consumers of counseling and psychotherapy ever conducted and the results, flawed as they may be, provide important information about consumers' perspectives on outcomes.

Meta-analytic attempts to estimate the effectiveness of counseling and psychotherapy have been attempted. In the most sophisticated of such attempts, Shadish et al. (1997) examined studies that were contained in 15 previous meta-analyses, categorizing the treatments in the studies contained in the meta-analyses according to their clinical representativeness. Shadish et al. found that of the total corpus of studies in the original meta-analyses (in excess of 1,000 studies), only 56 studies contained treatments that met criteria for being *somewhat similar* to clinic therapy, which was defined as treatments that (1) were conducted outside a university, (2) involved clients referred through usual clinical routes, and (3) used experienced professional therapists with regular caseloads. Only 15 studies contained treatments that met the additional criteria that the treatment did not rely on a manual or was not monitored, and only one study contained a treatment that passed the complete set of criteria for clinic representativeness. Several analyses were conducted on these data, yielding a general conclusion than those studies conducted in clinical settings did not produce smaller effects than produced by the original meta-analyses. Figure 22.1 contrasts the effect sizes for the 15 original meta-analyses with the effect sizes for the specific studies that were somewhat similar to clinic therapy. The outcomes of clinic therapy are not demonstrably inferior to the outcomes of therapy conducted in clinical trials, although this conclusion must be tempered by the extremely small number of studies that contained treatments similar to clinic therapy.

The optimism generated by the *Consumer's Reports* study (Seligman, 1995) and the Shadish et al. (1997) meta-analysis relative to effectiveness is tempered by findings of Weisz and colleagues (Weisz et al., 1995; Weisz, Weiss, & Donenberg, 1992) that child and adolescent psychotherapy delivered in clinics is either not effective or is less effective than comparable laboratory therapy. However, the Weisz analyses were plagued by problems as well, in that the clinic therapy studies examined were conducted many years ago, contained clients who (1) were more severely disordered than typical clients in clinical trials, and (2) had multiple disorders.

The analyses of clinic versus laboratory outcomes in the Weisz (Weisz et al., 1992, 1995) and in the Shadish (1997) analyses raise a critical methodological issue relative to the efficacy versus effectiveness contrast. In all cases, the contrast was made by comparing the effect size of laboratory studies (i.e., the difference between the mean of the laboratory therapy outcome minus the mean for the control group, expressed in standard deviation units) to the effect size of clinic studies (i.e., the difference between the mean of the clinic therapy outcome minus the mean for the control group, expressed in standard deviation units). However, as will be discussed later in this chapter, such contrasts are confounded because the therapy studies and the laboratory studies differ in many ways (other than the setting of the therapy), including type of outcome measures used, severity of the disorder, type of therapy delivered, prevalence of comorbidity, and so forth. No study could be found that directly compared laboratory and clinic-delivered versions of the same therapy.

A promising method to assess the generalizability of therapies validated in clinical trials to clinic settings is called *benchmarking,* which was used recently to assess the generalizability of cognitive-behavioral treatment (CBT) for panic disorder (Wade, Treat, & Stuart, 1998). CBT for panic disorder has been validated in two clinical trials; the researchers attempted to validate the

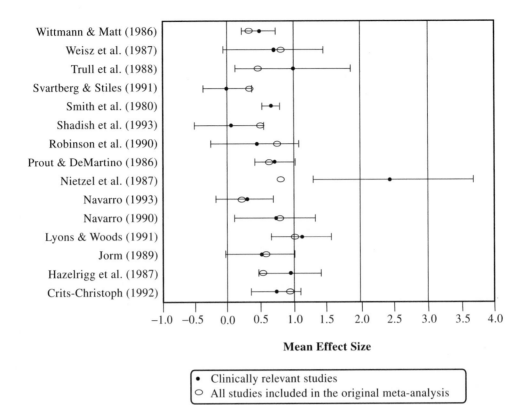

Mean Effect Size

•	Clinically relevant studies
○	All studies included in the original meta-analysis

Figure 22.1 Mean Effect Sizes and 95 Percent Confidence Intervals for Clinic Studies. Adapted with permission from W. R. Shadish et al. (1977). Evidence that therapy works in clinically representative conditions. *Journal of Consulting and Clinical Psychology, 65,* 355–365.

use of CBT in the clinic by comparing the results obtained in a community mental health center with the benchmark set by the two clinical trials, using the same set of outcome measures. Although the clinic participants were younger, had less education, were more likely to be taking psychotropic medications, and had a greater degree of agoraphobia, the results obtained in the clinic sample were comparable to the benchmark, providing evidence for the effectiveness of CBT for panic disorder. Unfortunately, one aspect of this study detracted from describing the treatment delivered in the community mental health center as "clinic" treatment. Although the therapists used in the study were selected from the clinic staff, they received extensive training and supervision in CBT for panic disorder. In this way, the treatment becomes more similar to the laboratory treatment and would meet only the minimal criteria for clinic therapy developed by Shadish et al. (1997).

RELATIVE EFFICACY OF COUNSELING AND PSYCHOTHERAPY: ACCUMULATING EVIDENCE REGARDING THE SECOND FUNDAMENTAL QUESTION

Having established empirically the efficacy (and most likely the effectiveness) of counseling and psychotherapy, it is important to identify the components of treatments that are responsible for the effects. At the most general level, the positive outcomes of the various treatments can be attributed to one of two sources: *specific ingredients* or *common factors*. Attributing causality to these two possible causal models has enormous implications for the practice of, and research into, counseling and psychotherapy. The first fundamental empirical question confronting the field was that of absolute efficacy and effectiveness. Having proved, by preponderance of the evidence, that counseling and psychotherapy are efficacious (and most likely clinically effective), attention must be turned toward the second fundamental question related to the factors that lead to the positive outcomes. The first part of this section will discuss the two competing models; the second part will discuss research strategies; and the third part will present the meta-analytic evidence.

The Competing Models of Causality

The terms *specific ingredients* and *common factors* adopted in this chapter are not unique. A cursory reading of the literature yields several other similar terms—active ingredients, nonspecific effects, generic factors, and placebo effects. Although the terms used in this chapter cannot be defined unambiguously, the models presented will be sufficient to make a differential prediction about outcomes of counseling and psychotherapy.

Common Factor Model

By the 1930s, approaches to psychotherapy had proliferated, with psychoanalysis evolving into forms espoused by, among many others, Horney, Adler, Jung, and Sullivan (Cushman, 1992). In 1936, Rosenzweig observed that the outcomes of the various psychotherapies were similar and suggested that the commonalities of the therapies were more important than the differences. Since that time, the emphasis on common factors has grown into a movement, which has become known as *psychotherapy integration.* Although, the decades of thinking about common factors cannot be presented here, some basic concepts and a particular model will be discussed.

Castonguay (1993) noted that there are three distinct meanings that can be applied to understanding common factors in psychotherapy. The first meaning refers to global aspects of therapy that are not specific to any one approach (or that are common across approaches), such as insight, corrective experiences, opportunity to express emotions, and acquisition of a sense of mastery. The second meaning pertains to aspects of treatment that are auxiliary to treatment and refer primarily to the interpersonal and social factors. This second meaning encompasses the therapeutic context and the therapeutic relationship (e.g., the working alliance). The third meaning of the term involves those aspects of the treatment that influence outcomes but that are not therapeutic activities or related to the interpersonal/social context. This latter meaning includes client expectancies and involvement in the therapeutic process.

In an attempt to bring coherence to the many theoretical discussions of common factors, Grencavage and Norcross (1990) reviewed publications that discussed commonalities and coded the commonalities into five areas: client characteristics, therapist qualities, change processes, treatment structures, and relationship elements. Table 22.1 presents the three most frequent elements in each category.

The three meanings discussed by Castonguay (1993) and the descriptors gleaned from the literature by Grencavage and Norcross (1990) convey a set of distinct and discrete elements that, taken together, comprise the common factors in counseling and psychotherapy. However, some well-known theorists in this area conceptualize commonalities as a meaning system that cannot be broken down into constituent parts. Probably the best-known and well-characterized system has been proposed by Frank in the various editions of his seminal book, *Persuasion and Healing* (Frank & Frank, 1991), "The aim of psychotherapy is to help people feel and function better by encouraging appropriate modifications in their assumptive worlds, thereby transforming the meanings of experiences to more favorable ones" (p. 30). Persons who present for psychotherapy are demoralized and have a variety of problems, typically depression and anxiety. That is, people seek psychotherapy for the demoralization that results from their symptoms rather than for symptom relief.

Frank and Frank described the components shared by all approaches to psychotherapy. The first component is that psychotherapy involves an emotionally charged, confiding relationship with a

Table 22.1   Common Factors Gleaned from the Literature

Category	Commonalities
Client characteristics	Positive expectation/hope or faith
	Client distressed or incongruent
	Client actively seeks help
Therapist qualities	General positive descriptors
	Cultivates hope/enhances expectations
	Warmth/positive regard
Change processes	Opportunity for catharsis/ventilation
	Acquisition and practice of new behaviors
	Provision of rationale
Treatment structures	Use of techniques/rituals
	Focus on "inner world"/exploration of emotional issues
	Adherence to theory
Relationship elements	Development of alliance/relationship (general)
	Engagement
	Transference

Note: Only the three most frequent commonalities found by Grencavage and Norcross (1990) are presented here. Adapted with permission from L.M. Grencavage and J.C. Norcross (1990). Where are the commonalities among the therapeutic common factors? *Professional Psychology: Research and Practice, 21,* 372–378.

helping person (i.e., the therapist). The second component is that the context of the relationship is a *healing setting,* in that the client presents to a professional, who the client believes can provide help and who is entrusted to work in his or her behalf. The third component is that there exists a rationale, conceptual scheme, or myth that provides a plausible explanation for the patient's symptoms and prescribes a ritual or procedure for resolving them. According to Frank and Frank, the particular rationale needs to be accepted by the client and by the therapist, but need not be "true." That is, the rationale can be a myth in the sense that the basis of the therapy has not been "scientifically" proven. The final component is a ritual or procedure that requires the active participation of both client and therapist and that is based on the rationale (i.e., the ritual or procedure is believed to be a viable means of helping the client).

Frank and Frank discussed six elements that are common to the rituals and procedures used by all psychotherapists. First, the therapist combats the client's sense of alienation by developing a relationship that is maintained after the client divulges feelings of demoralization. Second, the therapist maintains the patient's expectation of being helped by linking hope for improvement to the process of therapy. Third, the therapist provides new learning experiences. Fourth, the clients' emotions are aroused as a result of the therapy. Fifth, the therapist enhances the client's sense of mastery or self-efficacy. Sixth, the therapist provides opportunities for practice.

Although Frank and Frank discussed components common to all therapies, the healing context and the meaning attributed to it by the participants (therapist and client) are critical contextual phenomena. According to these authors, provision of new learning experiences, as an example, will not be therapeutic unless the client perceives the therapy to be taking place in a healing context in which he or she as well as the therapist believe in the rationale for the therapy, the therapist delivers therapeutic actions consistent with the rationale, the client is aroused and expects to improve, and a therapeutic relationship has been developed. In a meaning system conceptualization of common factors, specific therapeutic actions, which might be common across therapies, cannot be isolated and studied.

The outcome evidence to be reviewed in this chapter will be considered at the global level so that the validity of the general model of common factors will be examined. That is, the order of reduction will be at the most general level. Consequently, support for the general factor model will not provide evidence relative to the individual components of the model (such as those found in Table 22.1) or whether a meaning system model (e.g., Frank and Frank, 1991) is more explanatory than a collection of common elements. On the other hand, evidence for common factors supports the notion that contextual and component processes, taken as a system that is common across psychotherapies, is a determinant of therapeutic efficacy and effectiveness.

Specific Ingredients

All proponents of particular approaches to counseling and psychotherapy believe that the specific components that are unique to that approach are responsible for the therapeutic gains that result from its application. To return, for the moment, to the origins of psychotherapy, Freud believed that his therapeutic conceptualization and actions (e.g., free association, interpretation of dreams, transference) were responsible for the outcomes he witnessed and, moreover, that alterations in these aspects of therapy by those who followed in his footsteps would attenuate outcomes. In spite of Freud's belief in the specific ingredients, it has been the behaviorists who best articulated specific ingredient models. The behaviorists have proposed treatments containing components grounded in the scientific understanding of behavior (Fishman & Franks, 1992).

To understand what types of ingredients would be classified as specific, consider the four types of therapeutic components developed by Waltz, Addis, Koerner, and Jacobson (1993): (1) unique and essential, (2) essential but not unique, (3) acceptable but not necessary, and (4) proscribed. Table 22.2 gives examples of components of psychodynamic therapy and behavioral therapy. In this chapter, we will use the term *specific ingredients* to refer to those components of treatment that are considered to be unique to the treatment and essential (viz., Waltz et al.'s first category), according to the proponents of the treatment.

Descriptions of the specific ingredients and the rationale for their inclusion are found in treatment manuals. Treatment manuals were developed in the 1980s to standardize treatments in psychotherapy efficacy studies (Luborsky & DeRubeis, 1984; Waltz et al., 1993) and contain "a definitive description of the principles and techniques of [the] psychotherapy, . . . [and] a clear statement of the operations the therapist is supposed to perform (presenting each technique as concretely as possible, as well as providing examples of each)" (Kiesler, 1994). Those aspects of the treatment stipulated in the manual and which are unique to the particular treatment are considered specific ingredients. Treatments typically contain many specific ingredients, and each specific ingredient contains many related therapeutic actions. For example, cognitive-behavioral treatment for depression (Beck, Rush, Shaw, & Emery, 1979) contains three general classes of specific ingredients: behavioral activation; activation and modification of dysfunctional thoughts; and identification and modification of more stable patterns of thoughts (Jacobson et al., 1996). Each of these three classes contain various therapeutic actions with the same therapeutic goal (e.g., modifying dysfunctional thoughts).

The level of reduction supported by the empirical evidence here with regard to specific ingredients will be similar to that for the common factors. Because the evidence is presented at the meta-analytic level, evidence for a particular ingredient is precluded. The purpose of this review is to establish whether the outcome data generally support common factors or specific ingredients (or both) as determinants of the well-documented general efficacy of counseling and psychotherapy.

Common Factor and Specific Ingredient Hypotheses for Outcomes

There are a variety of ways to examine the common factor versus specific ingredient explanations for the efficacy of counseling and psychotherapy. Because this chapter is focused on outcomes, the

Table 22.2   Examples of Four Types of Components

Psychodynamic Therapy	Behavioral Therapy

Unique and Essential

1. Focus on unconscious determinants of behavior	1. Assigning homework
2. Focus on internalized object relations as historical causes of current problems	2. Practicing assertion in the session
3. Focus on defense mechanisms used to ward off pain of early trauma	3. Forming a contingency
4. Interpretation of resistance	

Essential but Not Unique

1. Establish a therapeutic alliance	1. Establish a therapeutic alliance
2. Setting treatment goals	2. Setting treatment goals
3. Empathic listening	3. Empathic listening
4. Planning for termination	4. Planning for termination
5. Exploration of childhood	5. Providing treatment rationale

Acceptable but Not Necessary

1. Paraphrasing	1. Paraphrasing
2. Self-disclosure	2. Self-disclosure
3. Interpreting dreams	3. Exploration of childhood
4. Providing treatment rationale	

Prescribed

1. Prescribing psychotropic medications	1. Prescribing psychotropic medications
2. Assigning homework	2. Focus on unconscious determinants of behavior
3. Practicing assertion in the session	3. Focus on internalized object relations as historical causes of current problems
4. Forming contingency contracts	4. Focus on defense mechanisms used to ward off pain of early trauma
5. Prescribing the symptom	5. Interpretation of resistance

Source: Reprinted with permission from J. Waltz, M.E. Addis, K. Koerner, and N.S. Jacobson (1993). Testing the integrity of a psychotherapy protocol: Assessment of Adherence and Competence. *Journal of Consulting and Clinical Psychology, 61,* 620–630.

research design that produces differential predictions for outcomes will be reviewed. There are two possible results that need to be examined to sort out the common factor versus specific ingredient issue. The first possible result is that treatments vary in their efficacy. That is, some treatments will be found to be immensely efficacious, some moderately efficacious, and some not efficacious at all. Presumably, the relative differences in outcomes would be due to the fact that the specific ingredients of some treatments were more potent than the specific ingredients of other treatments. Variance in outcomes may be due to other factors, such as therapist competence, therapist allegiance, and so forth, a point we will discuss later.

A second pattern of outcomes would be that all treatments produce about the same outcome. If the common factors were responsible for the efficacy of counseling and psychotherapy rather than specific ingredients, then the particular treatment delivered would be irrelevant with regard to the outcome. However, it could be argued that specific ingredients are indeed the causally important components, but that all specific ingredients are equally potent—a logically permissible hypothesis but one that seems implausible.

It is worth reiterating the differential hypothesis here. Important evidence relative to the common factor/specific ingredient issue is produced by data about the relative effectiveness of the various treatments that exist. If specific ingredients are responsible for outcomes, variation in effects is expected, whereas if common factors are responsible, homogeneity of effects (that is, general equivalence of treatments) is expected. Historically, the homogeneity of effects as evidence for common factors dates from 1936 when Rosenzweig proposed that common factors were responsible for the positive effects exhibited by the extant approaches to psychotherapy. To emphasize this conclusion, he used the Dodo bird's conclusion after a haphazard race in *Alice's Adventures in Wonderland* (Carroll, 1865/1962): "At last the Dodo said, 'Everybody has won, and all must have prizes'" (p. 412). The *Dodo bird effect* has become a mnemonic for the general equivalence of outcomes across psychotherapeutic approach.

Research Methods for Examining Hypotheses

As discussed by Wampold (1997), there are two primary means to establish the relative efficacy of various treatments: the comparative outcome design (Heppner et al., 1999) and meta-analyses of control-group designs and of comparative outcome designs. These research strategies will be discussed and the inferential ambiguities will be examined.

Comparative Designs for Determining Relative Efficacy

In the comparative design, subjects are randomly assigned to treatment A or treatment B, the treatments are delivered, and posttests are administered, rendering a design identical to the control-group design, except that two treatments are administered (rather than one treatment and a control group). Comparative designs typically contain a control group as well so that it can be determined whether the treatments are superior to no treatment.

There are two possible outcomes of comparative designs. One possible outcome is that the means of the outcome variables for the two treatments are not significantly different. Given the pervasive evidence for efficacy, assume that both treatments were superior to a no treatment control group. Thus, as administered and assessed, the two treatments appear to be equally efficacious. However, there is ambiguity around interpretation of this result. This result could be interpreted as support for the common factor model as both treatments presumably are delivered in the healing context as described by Frank and Frank (1991). However, it is difficult to rule out the possibility that the efficacy was due to the specific ingredients of the two treatments, where the specific ingredients have approximately equal potency. Moreover, it may be that one set of specific ingredients is more potent than the other, but that the statistical power to detect this difference is low, given that the effect is smaller than the treatment/no treatment effect (Kazdin & Bass, 1989).

It would appear that a less ambiguous conclusion could be reached by a comparative design that yielded a superior outcome for one of the treatments compared. Presumably, if Treatment A was found to be superior to Treatment B, then the specific ingredients constituting Treatment A are active, that is, these ingredients were responsible for the superiority of Treatment A. However, an example of such a finding will demonstrate that ambiguity remains even when superiority of one treatment is found.

Snyder and Wills (1989) compared the efficacy of behavioral marital therapy (BMT) to insight-oriented marital therapy (IOMT). At posttest and 6-month follow up, it was found that both BMT and IOMT were superior to no treatment controls, but equivalent to each other. The authors recognized that the finding could not disentangle the common factor/specific ingredient explanations, "Although treatments in the present study were relatively uncontaminated from interventions specific to the alternative approach, each treatment used nonspecific interventions common to both"

(p. 45). Four years after termination of treatment, an important difference between the treatments was found: 38% of the BMT couples were divorced whereas only 3% of the IOMT were divorced (Snyder, Wills, & Grady-Fletcher, 1991). This result would seem to provide evidence for the specific ingredients of IOMT, but Jacobson (1991), a proponent of BMT, argued otherwise, "It seems obvious that the IOMT therapists were relying heavily on the nonspecific clinically sensitive interventions allowed in the IOMT manual but not mentioned in the BMT manual. . . . To me, the . . . data suggest that in this study, BMT was practiced with insufficient attention to nonspecifics" (p. 143). Jacobson argued that the playing field was not level because there was an inequivalence in the potency of the common factors.

It should be noted that in any single study, the inequivalence of the common factors will always be a threat. One of the essential aspects of Frank and Frank's meaning model is that the therapist believe in the basis of the treatment being delivered. In most clinical trials comparing two treatments, the research is conducted in the laboratory of an advocate of one of the treatments and the therapists (typically graduate student therapists) are immersed in this treatment and learn the other treatment only to conduct the research. Thus, the meaning model is compromised for the alterative treatment, because the therapists are insufficiently invested in the alternate treatment and do not adequately believe in its efficacy. There is compelling evidence that this allegiance makes a difference in outcomes. Berman, Miller, and Massman (1985) reviewed studies that compared cognitive therapies to systematic desensitization and found differences in the effects produced by researchers who favored cognitive therapy and researchers who favored systematic desensitization. For the 10 studies reviewed that were conducted by researchers with allegiance to cognitive therapy, cognitive therapy was found to be superior to systematic desensitization (mean effect size of .27). On the other hand, in the 5 studies that were conducted by researchers with allegiance to systematic desensitization, systematic desensitization was found to be superior to cognitive therapy (mean effect size of .38). Allegiance not only created a difference in the size of the effect but in the direction of the effect.

Studies examining the relative efficacy of treatments for depression were similarly plagued by allegiance effects (Robinson, Berman, & Neimeyer, 1990). Allegiance effects cannot be estimated from a single study and thus Jacobson (1991) raised a valid criticism relative to the inequivalence of common factors. However, this criticism could be raised *ipso facto* for any comparative study that found that one treatment was superior to another treatment. On the other hand, when a study supports a researcher's position, the study will be described laudatorily; for example, Hollon and Beck (1994) described a study that showed the superiority of a cognitive-behavioral treatment to a behavioral treatment of anxiety as "elegantly crafted" (p. 438). As we shall see, meta-analyses of comparative studies can address allegiance and related issues. The allegiance effects detected by Berman et al. (1985) and by Robinson et al. (1990) provide evidence for the common factor model, as therapist belief in the treatment is a component of the common factor model.

There is another problem with interpretations of statistically significant differences between the outcomes of two treatments. Statistical theory predicts that by chance some comparisons of treatments will produce statistically significant difference (i.e., Type I errors). Although some comparative studies have produced differences between treatments (e.g., Butler, Fennell, Robson, & Gelder, 1991; Snyder et al., 1991), it may well be that these studies represent the few that would occur by chance. This problem is exacerbated by the fact that differences are often found only for a few of the dependent variables in a study (e.g., one variable, divorce rate, in the Snyder et al. study). Again, meta-analyses, which are discussed in the next section, can address the Type I error problem as well.

Meta-Analytic Methods for Determining Relative Efficacy

Meta-analyses can be used to examine the relative efficacy of treatments over many studies, thus testing the hypothesis that treatments are uniformly effective versus the alternative that they vary in effectiveness. Meta-analysis provides a quantitative test of the hypotheses and avoids conclusions based on salient, but unrepresentative studies. For example, Persons and Silberschatz (1998) cited a number of studies that have shown the superiority of one treatment over another but, as discussed above, each of these studies may be flawed (e.g., due to allegiance) or due to Type I error. As well, studies that failed to show differences were not cited by Persons and Silberschatz, leaving the questions about relative efficacy over the corpus of studies unanswered. Moreover, meta-analysis provides a quantitative index of the size of the effect that may be due to relative efficacy—if treatments are not equivalent in their effectiveness, then how different are they? Finally, meta-analysis can examine other hypotheses about relative effectiveness that cannot be answered easily by primary studies. For example, the allegiance hypothesis, discussed above, is easily examined in a meta-analytic context; in the discussion of the meta-analyses pertinent to relative efficacy, other hypotheses will be discussed.

There are two primary meta-analytic means to examine relative efficacy. The first method reviews control-group designs. According to this method, (1) treatments examined in studies are classified into categories (e.g., CBT; systematic desensitization), (2) the effect size is computed for each treatment vis-à-vis the control group, (3) the effect sizes within a category are averaged (e.g., the mean effect size for CBT is calculated over the studies that contain CBT and a control group), and (4) the mean effect sizes for the categories are compared (e.g., CBT versus systematic desensitization).

Making inferences based on the meta-analysis of control-group designs is problematic because the comparison between categories may be confounded by a number of variables. In the example used here, the studies that compared CBT with a control group and systematic desensitization with a control group may differ on a number of dimensions other than treatment, such as type of outcome variable used, severity of disorder treated, presence of comorbidity of participants, treatment standardization, treatment length, and allegiance of the researcher. One way to deal with the confounding variables is to meta-analytically model their mediating and moderating effects. Shadish and Sweeney (1991), for example, found that setting, measurement reactivity, measurement specificity, measurement manipulability, and number of participants moderated the relationship of treatment and effect size, and that treatment standardization, treatment implementation, and behavioral dependent variables mediated the relationship of treatment and effect size. Modeling meta-analytic confounds post-hoc is extremely difficult, with the same problems encountered in primary research, such as leaving out important variables, mis-specification of models, unreliability of measurements, lack of statistical power, and so forth.

A second way to test relative efficacy meta-analytically is to review studies that directly compared two psychotherapies. This strategy avoids confounds due to aspects of the dependent variable, problem treated, setting, and the length of therapy. Shadish et al. (1993) noted that direct comparisons "have rarely been reported in past meta-analyses, and their value for controlling confounds seems to be underappreciated" (p. 998). It should be noted that some confounds, such as skill of therapist and allegiance remain in the direct comparison strategy. If therapist skill or allegiance are not well controlled in the primary study, then meta-analysis of such studies will similarly be confounded, although these confounds can be modeled. As we shall see, there are a number of meta-analyses of direct comparisons in the area of psychotherapy outcome, some of which control and/or model remaining confounds.

Meta-analysis of direct comparisons of treatments raises an issue that must be resolved. To properly test the common factor hypothesis, it is important that the treatments compared adequately make use of the meaning model that underlies common factors. That is, (1) both treatments would need to appear to the participants to be efficacious, (2) the therapists would have to have confidence in the treatment and believe, to some extent, that the treatment is legitimate, (3) the treatment would have to be delivered in a manner consistent with the rationale provided, (4) the participants would have to perceive the rationale as sensible, and (5) the treatment would have to be delivered in a healing context. Studies often include treatments that are not intended to be therapeutic and which, to any reasonably well-trained psychologist, would not be legitimate. Such treatments are often called "alternative" treatments or placebo controls. An example of a treatment that would not be intended to be therapeutic (and hence would not meet a common factor meaning model test) was used by Foa, Rothbaum, Riggs, and Murdock (1991) to establish empirical support for cognitive-behavioral treatments. In the comparison treatment, supportive counseling for posttraumatic stress in women who had recently (within the previous year) been raped, (1) clients were taught a general problem-solving technique, (2) therapists responded indirectly and were unconditionally supportive, and (3) clients "were immediately redirected to focus on current daily problems if discussions of the assault occurred" (p. 718). This counseling would not be seen as viable by therapists, in all likelihood, because it contains no particular theoretical rationale or established principles of change and, in the absence of other components, "few would accept deflecting women from discussing their recent rape in counseling as therapeutic" (Wampold, Mondin, Moody, & Ahn, 1997, p. 227). Clearly, the supportive counseling treatment was not intended to be therapeutic and therapists would not deliver the treatment with a sufficient sense of efficacy. To provide a fair test of the common factors versus specific ingredients, the comparisons of treatments must involve treatments that are intended to be therapeutic.

In the next section, meta-analyses bearing on the question of relative efficacy will be reviewed. Additional problems with these analyses will be noted, where appropriate.

Meta-Analyses Producing Evidence for/against Relative Efficacy

There have been several meta-analyses that bear on the question of relative efficacy. The presentation of these meta-analyses will be chronological, with each correcting some problems of previous attempts and including current studies. Because the evidence has not been uniformly accepted by the psychotherapy community (e.g., see Crits-Christoph, 1997, Howard et al., 1997; Wilson & Rachman, 1983), the results of these meta-analyses will be presented in some detail.

Smith and Glass (1977)

Although Smith and Glass' (1977) meta-analysis of psychotherapy outcomes is best known for the evidence that it produced relative to absolute efficacy, it also produced evidence about relative efficacy of various approaches to treatment. Smith and Glass classified over 800 effects from control group studies into 10 types of therapy and calculated the average effect size for each type along with the number of effect sizes and the percentile of the median treated person vis-à-vis the control group (see Table 22.3). On average, 60% of those treated with Gestalt therapy were better than the average untreated person, whereas 82% of those treated with systematic desensitization were better than the average untreated person. Overall, the type of therapy accounted for about 10% of the variance in effects, indicating that there appears to be a small but significant amount of variance in outcome that is due to type of therapy. However, as discussed previously, the effect sizes for the various types of therapy were derived from treatment versus control group studies and these studies differed on a number of variables, including duration, severity of problem, type of outcome measure used, and so forth.

Smith and Glass (1977) adopted the following strategy to reduce the threats generated by these confounds. First, they created more general classes of therapy types by aggregating the 10 types into 4 classes: ego therapies (transactional analysis and rational-emotive therapy), dynamic therapies (Freudian, psychodynamic, Adlerian), behavioral (implosion, systematic desensitization, and behavior modification), and humanistic (Gestalt and Rogerian). The four superclasses were determined using multidimensional scaling of experts' ratings of similarity of the types. Smith and Glass then compared the behavioral therapies superclass to the nonbehavioral therapies superclass

Table 22.3   Effects of Ten Types of Therapy on Any Outcome Measure

Type of Therapy	Average Effect Size	No. of Effect Sizes	Median Treated Person's Percentile Status in Control Group
Psychodynamic	.59	96	72
Adlerian	.71	16	76
Eclectic	.48	70	68
Transactional analysis	.58	25	72
Rational-emotive	.77	35	78
Gestalt	.26	8	60
Client-centered	.63	94	74
Systematic desensitization	.91	223	82
Implosion	.64	45	74
Behavior modification	.76	132	78

Source: Adapted with permission from M. L. Smith and G. V. Glass (1977). Meta-analysis of psychotherapy outcome studies. *American Psychologist, 32,*752–760.

(all of the remaining, with the exception of Gestalt, which was omitted because there were few studies and because it fell in the same plane as the behavioral therapies). The difference in the effect sizes for these two superclasses was .2 standard deviations, but this small difference was still confounded by considerations such as outcome variables and latency of measurement after termination. When only the studies that contained a behavioral and a nonbehavioral treatment in the same study were compared (i.e., direct comparisons), the difference between the two superclasses shrunk to .07 standard deviations, which, given a standard error of .06, makes the difference between the behavioral and nonbehavioral treatments to be essentially zero (i.e., within 2 standard errors from zero).

Smith and Glass (1977) also modeled the confounds statistically. They regressed effect size onto study characteristics, including diagnosis, intelligence, age, the manner in which the client presented, latency to measurement of outcome, reactivity of outcome measure, as well as interactions, and found that about 25% of the variance in effects were due to study characteristics. Using these regressions, effect size for classes of treatments could be estimated (i.e., holding study characteristics constant). For example, for phobic clients, the following effects were found: psychodynamic, 0.92; systematic desensitization, 1.05; behavior modification, 1.12.

When study characteristics are considered, it appears that various types of therapy, broadly defined, produce generally equivalent outcomes, a conclusion reached by Smith and Glass, "Despite volumes devoted to the theoretical differences among different schools of psychotherapy, the results of research demonstrate negligible differences in the effects produced by different therapy types" (1977, p. 760). Historically, it is interesting to note that when Rosenzweig proposed in 1936 that common factors were responsible for therapeutic change, he "assumed . . . that all methods of therapy when competently used are equally successful" (p. 413). Smith and Glass provided the first meta-analytic evidence that Rosenzweig's assumption was correct.

Smith and Glass' (1977) support for the Dodo bird effect raised a torrent of criticism. To those interested in the specific ingredients of particular treatments, the Dodo bird effect was unacceptable:

> If the indiscriminate distribution of prizes argument carried true conviction . . . we end up with the same advice for everyone—"Regardless of the nature of your problem seek any form of psychotherapy." This is absurd. We doubt whether even the strongest advocates of the Dodo bird argument dispense this advice. (Rachman & Wilson, 1980, p. 167)

There are a number of features of the Smith and Glass (1977) analysis that create some caution in accepting the homogeneity of outcome effects for the various types of counseling and therapy. First, all of the studies reviewed appeared prior to 1977; hence, the findings may have been time bound. Since that time, the cognitive therapies have proliferated, treatments have been standardized with manuals, outcome measures have been refined, and designs have become more sophisticated. Stiles, Shapiro, and Elliott (1986), in their thoughtful discussion of why the Dodo bird effect may not be true, argued that true difference in treatment efficacy may have been obscured by poor research methods and that as the methods and treatments improve, differences will be detected. This argument implies that a conclusion made in 1977 should not be the last word. Wampold, Mondin, Moody, Stich, et al. (1997) tested the improving-methods hypothesis and this result will be discussed later.

A second issue is that to compare categories of treatments (such as cognitive-behavioral and psychodynamic), each treatment must be classified into one and only one of the categories. However, defining the categories and making classifications can be problematic. For instance, (Crits-Christoph, 1997) classified an "emotionally focused therapy" (Goldman & Greenberg, 1992) as cognitive-behavioral, even though the treatment assumed that "psychological symptoms are seen as emanating from the deprivation of unmet adult needs" and involves, in part, "identification with previously unacknowledged aspects of experience by enactment of redefined cycle" (p. 964). Moreover, classifying treatments assumes that the important differences are among classes of treatments, rather than among all treatments (Wampold, Mondin, Moody, Stich, et al., 1997). Often treatments within a category are compared in primary research studies to test hypotheses about the efficacy of specific ingredients. For example, a researcher interested in the specific ingredients of behavioral treatments for anxiety might compare *in vivo* to imaginal exposure. Ignoring within category comparisons omits important information about the common factor/specific ingredient issue as these comparisons typically are designed to demonstrate the efficacy of a particular ingredient. Finally, it appears that most direct comparisons of treatments are within category comparisons (e.g., see Shadish et al., 1993).

A final problem with the Smith and Glass (1977) analysis was that statistical theory of meta-analysis was not fully developed at the time. It was not until the mid-1980s that the distributional properties of effect sizes were derived and methods for testing meta-analytic hypotheses developed (e.g., see Hedges & Olkin, 1985). Although the issues are technical and will not be discussed here, recent meta-analyses (1) weight studies so that studies with greater sample size are more influential in calculation of the aggregate effect size, (2) derive standard errors for effect size for individual studies as well as the aggregated effect size over all studies, facilitating hypothesis testing, (3) test homogeneity to determine if the effect sizes are sampled from a common population, (4) model the dependence among the outcome variables in a study, and (5) alter the tests of effects due to moderating variables by taking into account that the standard deviation of individual effect sizes can be estimated (see Hedges & Olkin, 1985). These changes are technical, but can affect conclusions made from the analyses. As we shall see, the most current meta-analyses have addressed all of the technical problems endemic to the early meta-analyses.

Shapiro and Shapiro (1982)

In 1982, Shapiro and Shapiro addressed the problem related to confounds by conducting a meta-analysis of studies that directly compared two or more psychotherapies. They reviewed all studies published between 1975 and 1979 (inclusively) that contained two groups who received a psychological treatment and one group who received no treatment or minimal treatment (i.e., control groups); hence evidence about absolute as well as relative efficacy was obtained. Each treatment was classified into one of 15 categories, as shown in Table 22.4.

The first set of results from Shapiro and Shapiro (1982) are found in Table 22.4. Depending on a number of oddities of the database, the overall effect size for the treatments in comparison to

Table 22.4   Relative Advantage of Treatment Categories

Method	No. of Groups	No. of Studies	No. of Comparisons	Effect Size	Advantage
Behavioral	310	134	56	1.06	.32[b]
Rehearsal, self-control, and monitoring	38	21	16	1.01	.20
Biofeedback	9	9	9	.91	−.33
Covert behavioral	19	13	10	1.52	.22
Flooding	18	10	9	1.12	.11
Relaxation	42	31	27	.90	−.14
Systematic desensitization	77	55	50	.97	.04
Reinforcement	28	17	13	.97	.36
Modeling	11	8	6	1.43	.07
Social skills training	14	14	14	.85	.13
Study skills training	4	4	4	.26	−.75
Cognitive	35	22	20	1.00	.40[c]
Dynamic/humanistic	20	16	13	.40	−.53[b]
Mixed (mainly behavioral)	40	28	24	1.42	.52[b]
Unclassified (mainly behavioral)	18	14	14	.78	−.23[a]
Minimal	41	36	36	.71	−.56[c]

[a] $p < .05$
[b] $p < .01$
[c] $p < .001$

Note: Mixed treatments were those that contained features of more than one type of treatment; unclassified treatments were dissimilar to other types and were too infrequent to justify their own category; minimal treatments were treatments not intended to be therapeutic (e.g., placebo controls). Adapted with permission from D.A. Shapiro and D. Shapiro (1982) copyright by APA. Meta-analysis of comparative therapy outcome studies: A replication and refinement. *Psychological Bulletin, 92,* 581–604.

control groups was between .72 and .98, which is consistent with the .80 value mentioned earlier. Clearly, there seems to be some variance in the effect size by category. Indeed, from 5% to 10% of the variance in effect size was due to treatment category (depending on how it was calculated), values approximately equal to that determined by Smith and Glass (1977). However, the determination of variance due to treatment by this method does not take into account the confounds due to the studies differing in dependent variables, disorders treated, severity of disorder, skill of the therapists, and allegiance to the treatment, as discussed above. When some of these other variables were coded and analyzed, these variables accounted for 22% to 36% of the variance.

The last column in Table 22.4 lists the effect sizes of each treatment type with the treatments to which it was compared. That is, for each comparison of a treatment type with some other treatment, the mean of the comparison group was subtracted from the mean of the designated treatment group and the resulting difference divided by the standard deviation. Thus, positive values in this column indicate that the designated treatment was superior to the treatments to which it was directly compared in the primary studies. For example, the value of .40 for cognitive indicates that cognitive therapy was superior to the treatments to which is was compared and the average difference was .40 standard deviations. It appears that cognitive therapy and mixed therapies were superior to other therapies, and that, as a superclass, the same can be said of behavioral therapies.

As well, dynamic/humanistic, unclassified therapies, and (as expected) minimal therapies were inferior to other therapies. However, there are several issues to consider in interpreting these results. First, the comparison groups vary by category; for example, cognitive therapy comparisons were different than the comparisons for the dynamic/humanistic comparisons. Second, these comparisons included comparisons to minimal treatments, although Shapiro and Shapiro claimed that this did not affect the results greatly. Third, a preponderance of the dynamic/humanistic treatments contained no ingredients unique to the respective therapies and thus were not intended to be therapeutic, providing a poor test of the common factor model. Fourth, it should be realized that the significance levels of such comparisons are suspect because, at the time, the distributions of meta-analytic statistics had not been derived. Nevertheless, it is worth pointing out that the magnitude of the differences between treatments and comparisons (excluding minimal treatments) ranged from .04 to .53, significantly less than the .80 value related to absolute efficacy of psychological treatments.

Shapiro and Shapiro (1982) recognized the limitations of examining the relative advantage of therapies by the method represented in Table 22.4. The alternative used was to estimate the difference among the various pairwise comparisons of therapy types. Obviously, in the primary studies, not all therapies were compared to all other therapies. Shapiro and Shapiro provided estimates of the pairwise comparisons of therapy types if the two types of therapies were compared in at least four studies and yielded at least 10 effect sizes. These pairwise comparisons are presented in Table 22.5. As expected, when treatments were compared to minimal treatments, they were generally superior to these controls. Of the 13 remaining comparisons, only two reached statistical significance ($p < .05$), although these significance levels are flawed. Nevertheless, the general lack of differences seems to support the homogeneity of treatment efficacy.

Further perusal of Table 22.5 reveals that several of the differences with the largest magnitude involved comparisons with mixed treatments, which were defined as "methods that defied classification into any one of the categories because they contained elements of more than one" (Shapiro & Shapiro, 1982, p. 584), which certainly makes interpretation of these differences difficult. If the purpose of direct comparisons of treatments is to establish the potency of a specific ingredient, then comparisons to a treatment that is a "cocktail" of many ingredients provides little evidence for the specificity of a particular ingredient.

In Shapiro and Shapiro's (1982) analysis, the only pairwise difference that was statistically significant and that did not involve minimal treatments or mixed treatments was the superiority of cognitive therapy to systematic desensitization, which could be construed as evidence of the efficacy of cognitive ingredients vis-à-vis the conditioning mechanisms of systematic desensitization. Although this appears to be the first meta-analytic evidence for specific ingredients, the advantage of cognitive therapy may have been due to the allegiance of the researchers to cognitive therapy in the studies reviewed by Shapiro and Shapiro, as shown next.

The contribution made by Shapiro and Shapiro (1982) was that only studies that directly compared two treatments were meta-analyzed, eliminating the confounds discussed previously (e.g., dependent measures, disorder treated, severity). However, several other issues remain, including the need to classify treatments into categories (which eliminated analysis of direct comparisons within categories), unavailability of appropriate sampling theory for meta-analysis, and the date of the studies reviewed (viz., 1975 to 1980).

Berman, Miller, and Massman (1985)

Because the superiority of cognitive therapy to systematic desensitization was the only meta-analytic evidence against the Dodo bird effect and because their own research had not found significant differences between cognitive therapy and systematic desensitization (Miller & Berman, 1983), Berman et al. (1985) meta-analyzed all such comparisons, including those in the Shapiro and Shapiro (1982), their previous study, and an issue-by-issue search of relevant journals to July

Table 22.5   Pairwise Comparisons of Therapy Types

	Method B				
Method A	Relaxation	Systematic Desensitization	Social Skills Training	Mixed	Minimal
Rehearsal, self-control, and monitoring					.64[b] (6)
Biofeedback	−.20 (8)			−.72 (4)	
Covert behavioral					.54 (4)
Relaxation		−.24 (13)		−.59 (5)	.29 (4)
Systematic desensitization		.32 (5)		−.28[a] (7)	.50[a] (15)
Reinforcement					.14 (5)
Social skills training		.06 (5)			.37[a] (4)
Cognitive		.53[c] (9)	.28 (4)		.68[a] (7)
Dynamic/humanistic			.35 (4)	−.93 (4)	
Unclassified	−.16 (4)	.02 (6)			.46[a] (6)

[a] $p < .05$
[b] $p < .01$
[c] $p < .001$

Note: All comparisons are Method A–Method B differences based on 1 difference score per study and *N* of studies given in parentheses. Mixed treatments were those that contained features of more than one type of treatment; unclassified treatments were dissimilar to other types and were too infrequent to justify their own category; minimal treatments were treatments not intended to be therapeutic (e.g., placebo controls). Adapted with permission from D.A. Shapiro and D. Shapiro (1982) copyright by APA. Meta-analysis of comparative therapy outcome studies: A replication and refinement. *Psychological Bulletin, 92,* 581–604.

1983. They located 20 studies that directly compared cognitive therapy to systematic desensitization and found no evidence for the superiority of cognitive therapy. The mean effect size for the cognitive/systematic desensitization difference was only .06.

To reconcile the discrepancies between results, Berman et al. (1985) noticed that investigators appeared to have a preference for one of the treatments, as evidenced by the relative space used to describe the treatments, statement of directional hypotheses, and other features of the written report. Table 22.6 presents the results by allegiance. The results are astonishing! When conducted by investigators with allegiance to cognitive therapy, cognitive therapy was superior, but when conducted by investigators with allegiance to systematic desensitization, systematic desensitization was superior. However, from Frank and Frank's (1991) perspective, the results are consistent with predictions. Recall that according to their model, the therapist must necessarily believe in and present a therapy as viable for it to be effective. It would not be surprising to find the therapists used in studies to be trained by the investigator and to believe in the efficacy of the desired treatment; consequently, they would be expected to be more enthusiastic, involved, and loyal to that treatment.

Berman et al. (1985) recognized the importance of their findings for the common factor model, ". . . the evidence from this and other reviews suggest that our understanding of why psychotherapy works might be enhanced more from identifying factors common to all forms of treatment than from examining features specific to particular therapies" (p. 460). Nevertheless, Berman et al.'s

Table 22.6 Cognitive Therapy versus Systematic Desensitization, by Allegiance

Allegiance	Number of Studies	Effect Size
All direct comparisons	20	0.06
Allegiance to cognitive therapy	10	0.27
Allegiance to systematic desensitization	5	−0.38

Note: Positive effect sizes indicate superiority of cognitive therapy. Adapted with permission from J. S. Berman, C. Miller, and P. J. Massman (1985). Cognitive therapy versus systematic desensitization: Is one treatment superior? *Psychological Bulletin, 97,* 451–461.

results emanated from older studies, were specific to two treatment types, involved classification of treatments, and did not take full advantage of the emerging meta-analytic sampling theory.

Although the focus of this chapter is not on particular treatments for particular disorders, we next turn to a meta-analysis of psychotherapy for the treatment of depression. If differences between treatments are to appear, they have a good chance of appearing in this area given the intense efforts to design specific treatments for depression. The first manualized treatment in psychotherapy was designed for depression (Beck et al., 1979), providing the impetus for treatments in this area. In 1990, Robinson et al. conducted a comprehensive meta-analysis of controlled outcome research, and we now turn to that study.

Robinson, Berman, & Neimeyer (1990)

In 1989, Dobson found meta-analytic evidence for the superiority of Beck's cognitive therapy vis-à-vis other treatments. However, that meta-analysis suffered from two problems. First, the primary studies were restricted to those that used the Beck Depression Inventory (Beck, Ward, Mendelson, & Erbaugh, 1961), a measure that consistently favors a cognitive approach. Second, the allegiance of the investigators was not taken into account. Robinson et al. (1990) attempted to correct these and other problems in earlier meta-analyses in the area of depression.

Robinson et al. (1990) located 58 controlled studies of psychotherapy treatments for depression that were published in 1986 or before. The treatments in these studies were classified as (1) cognitive, (2) behavioral, (3) cognitive behavioral, and (4) general verbal therapy. The latter category was a collection of psychodynamic, client-centered, and interpersonal therapies. Although many analyses were reported in this meta-analysis, the direct comparisons of these four types are discussed here.

The meta-analysis of those studies that directly compared two types of therapy are reported in Table 22.7. Of the 6 pairwise comparisons, 4 were statistically significant and relatively large (viz., the magnitude of the significant comparisons ranged from .24 to .47). However, these differences could well be due to allegiance. Robinson et al. (1990) rated the allegiance, based on the nature of the report but also by prior publications of the investigators, and controlled for this variable. When allegiance was controlled, the estimate of the effect size disappeared, as shown in the last column of Table 22.7. Interestingly, the allegiance effects were not due to adherence to treatment protocols. That is, the less preferred treatments were not less efficacious because the specific ingredients in these treatments were not delivered as prescribed, leaving open the likelihood that the inferiority was due to aspects of the common factors, such as therapeutic relationship, providing a cogent statement of the rationale for treatment, and so forth.

The Robinson et al. (1990) study provides somewhat ambiguous evidence relative to the specific ingredients/common factor issue. At the most basic level, differences were found between treatment types, and this finding was based on direct comparisons, ruling out many confounds. However, these differences disappeared as a result of allegiance, raising a threat to the differences. Moreover, the allegiance effect did not seem to be related to adherence, giving additional

Table 22.7   Direct Comparisons between Different Types of Psychotherapy for Depression as Determined

Comparison	No. of Studies	Effect Size[a]		Estimate if No Allegiance
		M	SD	
Cognitive vs. behavioral	12	0.12	0.33	0.12
Cognitive vs. cognitive-behavioral	4	−0.03	0.24	−0.03
Behavioral vs. cognitive-behavioral	8	−0.24[b]	0.20	−0.16
Cognitive vs. general verbal	7	0.47[b]	0.30	−0.15
Behavioral vs. general verbal	14	0.27[b]	0.33	0.15
Cognitive-behavioral vs. general verbal	8	0.37[b]	0.38	0.09

[a] Positive numbers indicate that the first therapy in the comparison was more effective; negative numbers indicate that the second therapy in the comparison was more effective.
[b] $p < .05$.

Note: Means, standard deviations, and standard errors are based on weighted least-squares analyses in which effect sizes were weighted by sample size. Adapted with permission from L. A. Robinson, J. S. Berman, and R. A. Neimeyer (1990). Psychotherapy for the treatment of depression: A comprehensive review of controlled outcome research. *Psychological Bulletin, 108,* 30–49.

support to the common factor model. The classification of treatments into types, hypothesis testing strategies that did not use meta-analytic sampling theory, and, as we shall see, the inclusion of therapies that may not have been intended to be therapeutic, detract from the validity of the study. We now turn to a meta-analysis of all direct comparisons of bona fide psychotherapies that attempted to correct inadequacies in previous meta-analyses.

Wampold, Mondin, Moody, Stich, Benson, & Ahn (1997)

Wampold, Mondin, Moody, Stich, et al. (1997) sought to address the issues in previous meta-analyses to provide an additional test of the Dodo bird effect. They included all studies from 1970 to 1995, in six journals that typically publish psychotherapy outcome research, that directly compared two or more treatments intended to be therapeutic. Basing conclusions on direct comparisons eliminates many confounds, as discussed earlier. Treatments were restricted to those that were intended to be therapeutic (i.e., bona fide), so that treatments that were intended as control groups, or were not credible to therapists, would be excluded. This restriction is important because the meaning model (e.g., Frank & Frank, 1991) of psychotherapy stipulates that the efficacy of a treatment depends on therapist and client believing that the treatment is intended to be therapeutic. A treatment was determined to be bona fide provided (1) the therapist had at least a master's degree, developed a therapeutic relationship with the client, and tailored the treatment to the client; (2) the problem treated was representative of problems characteristic of clients, although severity was not considered (i.e., the diagnosis did not have to meet DSM criteria); and (3) the treatment satisfied two of the following four conditions: citation to an established treatment (e.g., a reference to Rogers', 1951, client-centered therapy); a description of the treatment was presented and contained reference to psychological mechanisms (e.g., operant conditioning); a manual was used to guide administration of the treatment, or the active ingredients of the treatment were specified and referenced.

A unique feature of the Wampold, Mondin, Moody, Stich, et al. (1997) meta-analysis was that treatments were not classified into therapy types. Classifying treatments into categories tests the hypothesis that there are no differences among therapy categories, whereas the Wampold, Mondin, Moody, Stich, et al. meta-analysis tested the hypothesis that the differences among all comparisons of individual treatments is zero. Besides testing the more general Dodo bird conjecture, this strategy avoided several problems encountered by earlier meta-analyses. First, as demonstrated by Shapiro and Shapiro's (1982) meta-analysis, there are many pairwise comparisons of treatment categories that contain no or few studies. Second, classification of treatments is not as straightforward as one would believe (Wampold, Mondin, Moody, & Ahn, 1997). Third, comparison of treatment types eliminates from consideration all comparisons within treatment types, of which there are many and of which many were designed to test the efficacy of specific ingredients. Finally, and importantly, pairwise comparisons of treatment types obviates an omnibus test of the Dodo bird conjecture—does the fact that 2 of 13 comparisons were significant in the Shapiro and Shapiro analysis indicate that there are few, but important differences, or that these 2 are due to chance?

Another feature of the Wampold, Mondin, Moody, Stich, et al. (1997) meta-analysis was that all statistical tests relied on meta-analytic distribution theory (Hedges & Olkin, 1985), which provides more valid tests of the Dodo bird conjecture. Meta-analyses conducted without such theory use standard errors that are incorrect because they do not take into account that the variances of effect sizes for individual studies are estimated. Moreover, Wampold, Mondin, Moody, Stich, et al. (1997) aggregated outcome variables within studies to eliminate the dependencies ignored when multiple effect sizes from studies are used.

The primary hypothesis tested in this meta-analysis was that the true differences among treatments intended to be therapeutic was zero. Two other hypotheses related to the Dodo bird conjecture were tested. Recall that Stiles et al. (1986) speculated that improving research methods, such as more sensitive outcome measures and manualized treatments, would detect true differences among treatments that had been obscured in the past. To test this hypothesis, Wampold, Mondin, Moody, Stich, et al. (1997) determined whether more recent studies, which would presumably use better research methods, produced larger differences than did more dated studies. The second hypothesis was related to classification of studies. If specific ingredients were causal to treatment efficacy, treatments within categories, such as cognitive behavioral treatments, which contain similar ingredients, would produce small differences, whereas treatments from different categories (cognitive behavioral and psychodynamic), which contain very different ingredients, would produce large differences. Wampold, Mondin, Moody, Stich, et al. (1997) tested this hypothesis by relating the size of treatment differences to treatment similarity. If the Dodo bird conjecture is not true (i.e., treatments differ in their efficacy), comparison of relatively dissimilar treatments would produce larger differences than comparisons of relatively similar treatments. On the other hand, if the Dodo bird conjecture was true, then treatment similarity would be irrelevant.

Avoiding classification of treatments into categories created a methodological problem. In previous meta-analyses of comparative outcome studies, treatments were classified into categories and then one category was (arbitrarily) classified as primary so that the algebraic sign of the effect size could be determined. For example, in Shapiro and Shapiro's (1982) comparison of various therapy types, cognitive (vis-à-vis systematic desensitization) was classified as primary so that a positive effect size indicated that cognitive therapy was superior to systematic desensitization. Wampold, Mondin, Moody, Stich, et al. (1997), however, had to assign an algebraic sign to each comparison of treatments (i.e., for each primary study). There are two options, both of which were used. First, a positive sign could be assigned so that each comparison yielded a positive effect size. However, this strategy would overestimate the aggregated effect size; however, the aggregate of the positively signed effects provides an upper bound estimate for the difference in outcomes of bona fide treatments. The second option, which is to randomly assign the algebraic sign to the effect size for individual comparisons, creates a situation in which the aggregate effect size would be zero, as the "plus" and "minus" signed effects would cancel each other out. However, if there are true differences among treatments (i.e., the Dodo bird conjecture is false and specific ingredients are producing effects in some treatments), then comparisons should produce many large effects, creating thick tails in the distribution of effects whose signs have been randomly determined, as shown in Figure 22.2. On the other hand, if there are truly *no* differences among treatments (i.e., the Dodo bird conjecture is true), then most of the effect sizes will be near zero and those further out in the tails of the distribution would amount to what would be expected by chance. Wampold, Mondin, Moody, Stich, et al.'s meta-analysis tested whether or not the effects were homogeneously distributed around zero, as would be expected if the Dodo bird conjecture were true.

The evidence produced by the Wampold, Mondin, Moody, Stich, et al. (1997) meta-analysis were consistent, in every respect, with the Dodo bird conjecture. First, the effects, with random signs, were homogeneously distributed about zero. That is, the preponderance of effects were near zero and the frequency of large effects was consistent with what would be produced by chance, given the sampling distribution of effect sizes. Second, even when positive signs were attached to each comparison, the aggregated effect size was small, roughly equal to .20, which compared to the effect size for the efficacy of psychotherapy (viz., .80) is quite small. Turning the groups around, an effect size of .20 indicates that 42% of the people in the inferior treatment are "better" than the average person in the superior treatment. The value of .20 is consistent with another meta-analysis of outcomes (Grissom, 1996) that used a similar method. Moreover, .20 is a gross upper bound (i.e., the true difference among treatments is at most .20) and that there is no evidence from this meta-analysis to reject the null hypothesis that the true difference among treatments is zero.

Wampold, Mondin, Moody, Stich, et al. (1997) found no evidence that the differences in outcome among treatments was related to either the year in which the study was published or the similarity of the treatments. Moreover, it does not appear that comparisons of treatments that are quite different produce larger effects than comparisons of treatments that are similar to each other, a result consistent with the Dodo bird conjecture. This indicates that improving research methods are not detecting differences among treatments. Rosenzweig's conjecture, made in 1936, empirically supported in the late 1970s and early 1980s (Shapiro & Shapiro, 1982; Smith & Glass,

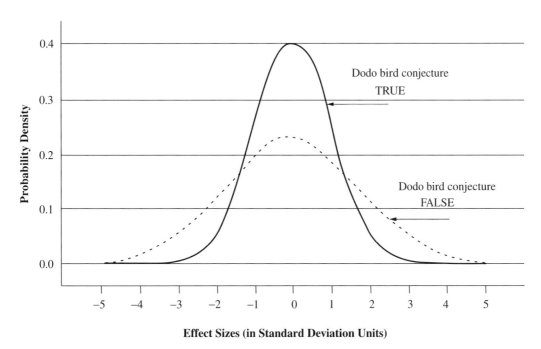

Effect Sizes (in Standard Deviation Units)

Figure 22.2 A Distribution of Effect Sizes (with signs determined randomly) When the Dodo Bird Conjecture Is True and When It Is False. Reprinted with permission from B. E. Wampold, G. W. Mondin, M. Moody, F. Stich, K. Benson, and H. Ahn (1997). A meta-analysis of outcome studies comparing bona fide psychotherapies: Empirically, "All must have prizes." *Psychological Bulletin, 122,* 203–215.

1977), has survived another test and thus must be considered "true" until sufficient evidence for its rejection is presented.

In spite of their correction of previous methodological flaws and the consistency of the results with previous findings, Wampold, Mondin, Moody, Stich, et al. (1997) conclusions were challenged on the basis of (1) counter examples, (2) alternative explanations for the results, (3) methodological problems, and (4) the inadequacy of randomized clinical trials (Crits-Christoph, 1997; Howard et al., 1997). Further analysis, however, ruled out these criticisms (Wampold, Mondin, Moody, & Ahn, 1997), although the uniform efficacy of treatments intended to be therapeutic is not a "comfortable" finding for advocates of particular treatments.

Placebo Controls

Researchers use placebo groups to purportedly control for common factors and consequently establish the efficacy of such ingredients. There have been many meta-analyses of outcome studies that involved placebo groups (e.g., Barker, Funk, & Houston, 1988; Bowers & Clum, 1988; Grissom, 1996; Prioleau, Murdock, & Brody, 1983). Generally, it has been found that bona fide treatments are superior to placebos and that placebos are superior to no treatment (see Lambert & Bergin, 1994). These results are cited as evidence that specific ingredients are responsible for outcome. However, the meaning model makes the same prediction as the specific ingredient model relative to placebo control groups. A critical component of the meaning model is that the therapist believe in the rationale of the treatment; placebos may be credible to the clients, but are never intended to be therapeutic by those who administer the treatment. In medicine, treatments are double-blinded (neither the patients or the administrator of treatments knows whether the "pill" is active or placebo). Because therapists can never be blinded, Seligman (1995) noted, "Whenever you hear someone demanding the double-blind study of psychotherapy, hold onto your wallet" (p. 965). The problems with placebos in psychological outcome studies are discussed elsewhere (e.g., Brody, 1980; Critelli & Neumann, 1984; Grunbaum, 1981; Horvath, 1988; Wampold, 1997; Wilkins, 1983, 1984). The point here is that both the specific ingredient and the common factor models make exactly the same prediction relative to placebos and consequently the results of such studies are uninformative relative to the specific ingredient versus common factor issue.

CONCLUSIONS

The answer to the first fundamental question about the absolute efficacy of psychotherapy is unambiguous: Psychotherapy generally produces positive outcomes and it appears that these benefits are not restricted to the research context. The answer to the second fundamental question about relative efficacy appears to be unambiguous as well: Treatments intended to be therapeutic are generally equivalent in terms of the benefits produced. What are the implications of these findings for research and practice of counseling and psychotherapy?

Theoretically, the evidence appears to support a model of psychotherapy in which the common factors are paramount. If specific ingredients in the various therapies were the important factors leading to the positive outcomes, then it would be expected that some treatments (viz., those with the "best" specific ingredients) would produce superior outcomes to others (viz., those with inferior specific ingredients). Little evidence for heterogeneity of outcomes for various therapies has been found.

Caution must be exercised about the implications of accepting a meaning model of counseling and psychotherapy. A necessary component of the Frank and Frank (1991) model is a therapeutic "ritual." The ritual is a set of procedures that are theoretically grounded and that the therapist and client believes are therapeutic. Simply, the therapist has to act strategically to assist the client. In this sense, the therapy must contain specific ingredients. Nothing in the argument constructed in this chapter implies that common factors are necessary and sufficient for therapeutic change. A working alliance between therapist and client, for example, must be formed around strategic and grounded interventions. The interventions might contain aspects of what are thought of as common ingredients (e.g., corrective experiences) but they might also involve activities unique to a treatment (e.g., contingency contracting).

The evidence reviewed in this chapter indicates that the specific ingredients are not the aspects of the therapy responsible for therapeutic change. Nevertheless, to the degree that these specific ingredients are necessary to construct a coherent treatment, in which therapists have faith and which provides a convincing rationale to clients, they are absolutely necessary in therapy. This point is cogently articulated by Jerome Frank, in the preface to the most recent version of his model (Frank & Frank, 1991):

> My position is not that technique is irrelevant to outcome. Rather, I maintain that, as developed in the text, the success of all techniques depends on the patient's sense of alliance with an actual or symbolic healer. This position implies that ideally therapists should select for each patient the therapy that accords, or can be brought to accord, with the patient's personal characteristics and view of the problem. Also implied is that therapists should seek to learn as many approaches as they find congenial and convincing. Creating a good therapeutic match may involve both educating the patient about the therapist's conceptual scheme and, if necessary, modifying the scheme to take into account the concepts the patient brings to therapy. (p. xv)

Nothing in the meaning model and the empirical evidence reviewed implies that all therapies should be embraced. As stated by Frank, therapists should utilize treatments that they find "congenial and convincing." As psychologists, only those treatments grounded in the science of psychology should be "congenial and convincing," and therefore practices based in alternative explanatory systems (e.g., the occult) will be necessarily proscribed. Indeed, the outcome studies that form the corpus meta-analyzed and reviewed in this chapter predominantly involve treatments that are based on psychological principles and the scientific study of behavior (Wampold, Mondin, Moody, Stich, et al., 1997, explicitly limited consideration to such treatments). Consequently, the conclusions reached herein are limited to *psychological* treatments and in no way should be construed as support for other types of treatments or "anything goes." It may be that for clients who ascribe to explanations of behavior that are not consistent with psychological principles might well benefit from nonpsychological treatments. Herbal remedies, rituals of indigenous populations, prayer, and so forth could produce beneficial effects when administered to believers by faithful practitioners trained in those modalities, but they are not contained in the set of psychological treatments; *these alternative treatments should not be "congenial and convincing" to psychologists.*

The support for the common factor model, as opposed to the specific ingredient model, has implications for counselor training and service delivery. These implications are briefly mentioned here.

In an effort to provide a scientific basis for psychological treatments, there has been a movement to create a set of treatments that are designated as empirically supported (Baucom, Shoham, Mueser, Daiuto, & Stickle, 1998; Chambless & Hollon, 1998; DeRubeis & Crits-Christoph, 1998; Kazdin & Weisz, 1998; Kendall, 1998). Although designation as an empirically supported treatment no longer requires that efficacy be attributed to the specific ingredients of the treatment (Chambless & Hollon, 1998), there is the presumption that not all psychological treatments are equally efficacious. Nevertheless, as shown in this chapter, there is good evidence to believe otherwise. Wampold (1997) suggested, somewhat tongue-in-cheek, that all psychological treatments should be designated as empirically supported and that a treatment be removed only if there is demonstrable evidence that it is less efficacious than others. Nevertheless, the empirically supported treatment movement has had, and will likely have increased, influence on training and service provision. The evidence strongly favors letting clients select a psychological treatment that makes sense to them and permitting therapists to adapt treatments to be consonant with the attitudes, values, and culture of the client, rather than having third-party payers or health maintenance organizations mandate a particular treatment. Whereas the specific ingredient model assumes that an empirically valid treatment is universally applicable for a disorder, a common factor model of the type proposed by Frank and Frank (1991) prescribes that the treatment be consistent with the meaning system of the client, which provides a persuasive rationale for culturally specific treatments. Henry (1998) and Wampold (1997) have discussed the ramifications of empirically supported treatment movement for science and practice.

With regard to training, the support for the common factor model suggests that generic training, emphasizing strategies to build the working alliance, is essential. However, generic training is not sufficient and counselors-in-training must build theoretically consistent intervention skills. Master therapists learn to weave interventions into the fabric of the psychotherapy process, creating a therapeutic context that permits the client to change. The failure to find support for specific ingredients suggests that focusing on the execution of empirically validated treatments, to the exclusion of other important aspects of the therapeutic process, is unjustified.

A final implication of the Dodo bird conjecture pertains to the allocation of research resources. If the Dodo bird conjecture is true, as it appears to be, then clinical trials focused on relative efficacy (i.e., comparative outcome studies) will result in only a few differences that are due to chance. Much attention will be given to these Type I errors. In makes little sense to fund comparative research trials or to have researchers spend their limited time on such research when the likelihood of finding true differences is small (Wampold, 1997). What appears to be a scientifically based endeavor, is an illusion (Henry, 1998).

As summarized by Wampold, Mondin, Moody, and Ahn (1997):

> It may be that continued research in psychotherapy will show that some treatments are slightly more effective than others, although the model of uniform effectiveness will fit these data better than a model that indicates that treatments vary in their effectiveness. We would cherish the day that a treatment is developed that is dramatically more effective than the ones we use today. But until that day comes, the existing data suggest that whatever differences in treatment efficacy exist, they appear to be extremely small at best. Although uniform efficacy may not be a popular finding for some, this empirical result should guide, rather than obstruct, research and practice. (p. 230)

REFERENCES

Andrews, G., & Harvey, R. (1981). A re-analysis of the Smith, Glass, & Miller data. *Archives of General Psychiatry, 38,* 1203–1208.

Barker, S.L., Funk, S.C., & Houston, B.K. (1988). Psychological treatment versus nonspecific factors: A meta-analysis of conditions that engender comparable expectations for improvement. *Clinical Psychology Review, 8,* 579–594.

Baucom, D.H., Shoham, V., Mueser, K.T., Daiuto, A.D., & Stickle, T.R. (1998). Empirically supported couple and family interventions for marital distress and adult mental health problems. *Journal of Consulting and Clinical Psychology, 66,* 53–88.

Beck, A.T., Rush, A.J., Shaw, B.F., & Emery, G. (1979). *Cognitive therapy of depression.* New York: Guilford Press.

Beck, A.T., Ward, C., Mendelson, M., & Erbaugh, J. (1961). An inventory for measuring depression. *Archives of General Psychiatry, 6,* 561–571.

Bergin, A.E., & Lambert, M.J. (1978). The evaluation of therapeutic outcomes. In S.L. Garfield & A.E. Bergin (Eds.), *Handbook of psychotherapy and behavior change: An empirical analysis* (2nd ed., pp. 139–190). New York: Wiley.

Berman, J.S., Miller, C., & Massman, P.J. (1985). Cognitive therapy versus systematic desensitization: Is one treatment superior? *Psychological Bulletin, 97,* 451–461.

Bowers, T.G., & Clum, G.A. (1988). Relative contributions of specific and nonspecific treatment effects: Meta-analysis of placebo-controlled behavior therapy research. *Psychological Bulletin, 103,* 315–323.

Brock, T.C., Green, M.C., Reich, D.A., & Evans, L.M. (1996). The Consumer Reports study of psychotherapy: Invalid is invalid. *American Psychologist, 51,* 1083.

Brody, N. (1980). *Placebos and the philosophy of medicine: Clinical, conceptual, and ethical issues.* Chicago: University of Chicago Press.

Butler, G., Fennell, M., Robson, P., & Gelder, M. (1991). Comparison of behavior therapy and cognitive behavior therapy in the treatment of generalized anxiety disorder. *Journal of Consulting and Clinical Psychology, 59,* 137–175.

Castonguay, L.G. (1993). "Common factors" and "nonspecific variables": Clarification of the two concepts and recommendations for research. *Journal of Psychotherapy Integration, 3,* 267–286.

Chambless, D.L., & Hollon, S.D. (1998). Defining empirically supported therapies. *Journal of Consulting and Clinical Psychology, 66,* 7–18.

Cohen, J. (1988). *Statistical power analysis for the social sciences* (2nd ed.). Hillsdale, NJ: Erlbaum.

Critelli, J.W., & Neumann, K.F. (1984). The placebo: Conceptual analysis of a construct in transition. *American Psychologist, 39,* 32–39.

Crits-Christoph, P. (1997). Limitations of the dodo bird verdict and the role of clinical trials in psychotherapy research: Comment on Wampold et al. (1997). *Psychological Bulletin, 122,* 216–220.

Cushman, P. (1992). Psychotherapy to 1992: A history situated interpretation. In D.K. Freedman (Ed.), *History of psychotherapy: A century of change* (pp. 21–64). Washington, DC: American Psychological Association.

DeRubeis, R.J., & Crits-Christoph, P. (1998). Empirically supported individual and group psychological treatments for mental disorders. *Journal of Consulting and Clinical Psychology, 66,* 37–52.

Dobson, K.S. (1989). A meta-analysis of the efficacy of cognitive therapy for depression. *Journal of Consulting and Clinical Psychology, 57,* 414–419.

Eysenck, H.J. (1952). The effects of psychotherapy. *Journal of Consulting Psychology, 16,* 319–324.

Eysenck, H.J. (1978). An exercise in meta-silliness. *American Psychologist, 33,* 517.

Fishman, D.B., & Franks, C.M. (1992). Evolution and differentiation with behavior therapy: A theoretical and epistemological review. In D.K. Freedman (Ed.), *A history of psychotherapy: A century of change* (pp. 159–196). Washington, DC: American Psychological Association.

Foa, E.B., Rothbaum, B.O., Riggs, D.S., & Murdock, T.B. (1991). Treatment of post-traumatic stress disorder in rape victims: A comparison between cognitive-behavioral procedures and counseling. *Journal of Consulting and Clinical Psychology, 59,* 715–723.

Frank, J.D., & Frank, J.B. (1991). *Persuasion and healing: A comparative study of psychotherapy* (3rd ed.). Baltimore: Johns Hopkins University Press.

Goldman, A., & Greenberg, L. (1992). Comparison of integrated systemic and emotionally focused approaches to couples therapy. *Journal of Consulting and Clinical Psychology, 60,* 962–969.

Grencavage, L.M., & Norcross, J.C. (1990). Where are the commonalities among the therapeutic common factors? *Professional Psychology: Research and Practice, 21,* 372–378.

Grissom, R.J. (1996). The magical number .7 ± .2: Meta-analysis of the probability of superior outcome in comparisons involving therapy, placebo, and control. *Journal of Consulting and Clinical Psychology, 64,* 973–982.

Grunbaum, A. (1981). The placebo concept. *Behaviour Research and Therapy, 19,* 157–167.

Hedges, L.V., & Olkin, I. (1985). *Statistical methods for meta-analysis.* San Diego, CA: Academic Press.

Henry, W.P. (1998). Science, politics, and the politics of science: The use and misuse of empirically validated treatments. *Psychotherapy Research, 8,* 126–140.

Heppner, P.P., Kivlighan, D.M., Jr., & Wampold, B.E. (1999). *Research design in counseling* (2nd ed.). Belmont, CA: Brooks/Cole.

Hollon, S.D., & Beck, A.T. (1994). Cognitive and cognitive-behavioral therapies. In A.E. Bergin & S.L. Garfield (Eds.), *Handbook of psychotherapy and behavior change* (pp. 428–466). New York: Wiley.

Horvath, P. (1988). Placebos and common factors in two decades of psychotherapy research. *Psychological Bulletin, 104,* 214–225.

Howard, K.I., Krause, M.S., Saunders, S.M., & Kopta, S.M. (1997). Trials and tribulations in the meta-analysis of treatment differences: Comment on Wampold et al. (1997). *Psychological Bulletin, 122,* 221–225.

Hunt, E. (1996). Errors in Seligman's "The effectiveness of psychotherapy: The Consumer Reports study." *American Psychologist, 51,* 1082.

Jacobson, N.S. (1991). Behavioral versus insight-oriented martial therapy: Labels can be misleading. *Journal of Consulting and Clinical Psychology, 59,* 142–145.

Jacobson, N.S., Dobson, K.S., Truax, P.A., Addis, M.E., Koerner, K., Gollan, J.K., Gortner, E., & Price, S.E. (1996). A component analysis of cognitive-behavioral treatment for depression. *Journal of Consulting and Clinical Psychology, 64,* 295–304.

Kazdin, A.E., & Bass, D. (1989). Power to detect differences between alternative treatments in comparative psychotherapy outcome research. *Journal of Consulting and Clinical Psychology, 57,* 138–147.

Kazdin, A.E., Kratochwill, T.R., & VandenBos, G.R. (1986). Beyond clinical trials: Generalizing from research to practice. *Professional Psychology: Research and Practice, 17,* 391–398.

Kazdin, A.E., & Weisz, J.R. (1998). Identifying and developing empirically supported child and adolescent treatments. *Journal of Consulting and Clinical Psychology, 66,* 19–36.

Kendall, P.C. (1998). Empirically supported psychological therapies. *Journal of Consulting and Clinical Psychology, 66,* 3–6.

Kiesler, D.J. (1994). Standardization of intervention: The tie that binds psychotherapy research and practice. In P.F. Talley, H.H. Strupp, & S.F. Butler (Eds.), *Psychotherapy research and practice: Bridging the gap* (pp. 143–153). Basic Books.

Kotkin, M., Daviet, C., & Gurin, J. (1996). The Consumer Reports mental health survey. *American Psychologist, 51,* 1080–1088.

Lambert, M.J., & Bergin, A.E. (1994). The effectiveness of psychotherapy. In A.E. Bergin & S.L. Garfield (Eds.), *Handbook of psychotherapy and behavior change* (4th ed., pp. 143–189). New York: Wiley.

Landman, J.T., & Dawes, R.M. (1982). Smith and Glass' conclusions stand up under scrutiny. *American Psychologist, 37,* 504–516.

Leland, J., & Kalb, C. (1998, October 12). Herr Dokter, what does it all mean? *Newsweek,* 60–61.

Lipsey, M.W., & Wilson, D.B. (1993). The efficacy of psychological, educational, and behavioral treatment: Confirmation from meta-analysis. *American Psychologist, 48,* 1181–1209.

Luborsky, L., & DeRubeis, R.J. (1984). The use of psychotherapy treatment manuals: A small revolution in psychotherapy research style. *Clinical Psychology Review, 4,* 5–14.

Miller, R.C., & Berman, J.S. (1983). The efficacy of cognitive behavior therapies: A quantitative review of the research evidence. *Psychological Bulletin, 94,* 39–53.

Mintz, J., Drake, R., & Crits-Christoph, P. (1996). Efficacy and effectiveness of psychotherapy: Two paradigms, one science. *American Psychologist, 51,* 1084–1085.

Persons, J.B., & Silberschatz, G. (1998). Are results of randomized controlled trials useful to psychotherapists? *Journal of Consulting and Clinical Psychology, 66,* 126–135.

Prioleau, L., Murdock, M., & Brody, N. (1983). An analysis of psychotherapy versus placebo studies. *Behavioral and Brain Sciences, 6,* 275–310.

Rachman, S.J., & Wilson, G.T. (1980). *The effects of psychological therapy* (2nd ed.). New York: Pergamon Press.

Robinson, L.A., Berman, J.S., & Neimeyer, R.A. (1990). Psychotherapy for the treatment of depression: A comprehensive review of controlled outcome research. *Psychological Bulletin, 108,* 30–49.

Rogers, C.R. (1951). *Client-centered therapy: Its current practice, implications, and theory.* Boston: Houghton Mifflin.

Rosenthal, R. (1990). How are we doing in soft psychology? *American Psychologist, 45,* 755–757.

Rosenzweig, S. (1936). Some implicit common factors in diverse methods of psychotherapy. *American Journal of Orthopsychiatry, 6,* 412–415.

Seligman, M.E.P. (1995). The effectiveness of psychotherapy: The Consumer Reports study. *American Psychologist, 50,* 965–974.

Shadish, W.R., Matt, G.E., Navarro, A.M., Siegle, G., Crits-Christoph, P., Hazelrigg, M.D., Jorm, A.F., Lyons, L.C., Nietzel, M.T., Prout, H.T., Robinson, L., Smith, M.L., Svartberg, M., & Weiss, B. (1997). Evidence that therapy works in clinically representative conditions. *Journal of Consulting and Clinical Psychology, 65,* 355–365.

Shadish, W.R., Montgomery, L.M., Wilson, P., Wilson, M.R., Bright, I., & Okwumabua, T. (1993). Effects of family and marital psychotherapies: A meta-analysis. *Journal of Consulting and Clinical Psychology, 61,* 992–1002.

Shadish, W.R., & Sweeney, R.B. (1991). Mediators and moderators in meta-analysis: There's a reason we don't let dodo birds tell us which psychotherapies should have prizes. *Journal of Consulting and Clinical Psychology, 59,* 883–893.

Shapiro, D.A., & Shapiro, D. (1982). Meta-analysis of comparative therapy outcome studies: A replication and refinement. *Psychological Bulletin, 92,* 581–604.

Smith, M.L., & Glass, G.V. (1977). Meta-analysis of psychotherapy outcome studies. *American Psychologist, 32,* 752–760.

Smith, M.L., Glass, G.V., & Miller, T.I. (1980). *The benefits of psychotherapy.* Baltimore: Johns Hopkins University Press.

Snyder, D.K., & Wills, R.M. (1989). Behavioral versus insight-oriented marital therapy: Effects on individual and interpersonal functioning. *Journal of Consulting and Clinical Psychology, 57,* 39–46.

Snyder, D.K., Wills, R.M., & Grady-Fletcher, A. (1991). Long-term effectiveness of behavioral versus insight oriented marital therapy: A 4-year follow-up study. *Journal of Consulting and Clinical Psychology, 59,* 138–141.

Stiles, W.B., Shapiro, D.A., & Elliott, R. (1986). "Are all psychotherapies equivalent?" *American Psychologist, 41,* 165–180.

Strupp, H.H., & Howard, K.I. (1992). A brief history of psychotherapy research. In D.K. Freedheim (Ed.), *History of psychotherapy: A century of change* (pp. 309–334). Washington, DC: American Psychological Association.

Wade, W.A., Treat, T.A., & Stuart, G.L. (1998). Transporting an empirically supported treatment for panic disorder to a service clinic setting: A benchmarking strategy. *Journal of Consulting and Clinical Psychology, 66,* 231–239.

Waltz, J., Addis, M.E., Koerner, K., & Jacobson, N.S. (1993). Testing the integrity of a psychotherapy protocol: Assessment of adherence and competence. *Journal of Consulting and Clinical Psychology, 61,* 620–630.

Wampold, B.E. (1997). Methodological problems in identifying efficacious psychotherapies. *Psychotherapy Research, 7,* 21–43.

Wampold, B.E., Mondin, G.W., Moody, M., & Ahn, H. (1997). The flat earth as a metaphor for the evidence for uniform efficacy of bona fide psychotherapies: Reply to Crits-Christoph (1997) and Howard et al. (1997). *Psychological Bulletin, 122,* 226–230.

Wampold, B.E., Mondin, G.W., Moody, M., Stich, F., Benson, K., & Ahn, H. (1997). A meta-analysis of outcome studies comparing bona fide psychotherapies: Empirically, "All must have prizes." *Psychological Bulletin, 122,* 203–215.

Weisz, J.R., Donenberg, G.R., Han, S.S., & Weiss, B. (1995). Bridging the gap between laboratory and clinic in child and adolescent psychotherapy. *Journal of Consulting and Clinical Psychology, 63,* 688–701.

Weisz, J.R., Weiss, B., & Donenberg, G.R. (1992). The lab versus the clinic: Effects of child and adolescent psychotherapy. *American Psychologist, 47,* 1578–1585.

Wilkins, W. (1983). Failure of placebo groups to control for nonspecific events in therapy outcome research. *Psychotherapy: Theory, Research and Practice, 20,* 31–37.

Wilkins, W. (1984). Psychotherapy: The powerful placebo. *Journal of Consulting and Clinical Psychology, 52,* 570–573.

Wilson, G.T., & Rachman, S.J. (1983). Meta-analysis and the evaluation of psychotherapy outcome: Limitations and liabilities. *Journal of Consulting and Clinical Psychology, 51,* 54–64.

CHAPTER 23

Four (or Five) Sessions and a Cloud of Dust: Old Assumptions and New Observations about Career Counseling

STEVEN D. BROWN
NANCY E. RYAN KRANE

Numerous reviewers of the career counseling and intervention literature have concluded that career interventions work, but beyond this basic conclusion have been much more circumspect about the state of knowledge in the area (e.g, Fretz, 1981; Lunneborg, 1983; Oliver & Spokane, 1988; Phillips, 1992; Spokane & Oliver, 1983; Swanson, 1995; Whiston, Sexton, & Lasoff, 1998). Most criticisms of the literature have focused on researchers' apparent failure to study the process of career intervention and to identify and study through appropriate attribute by treatment interaction designs important vocational problem, client, and treatment characteristics that might moderate the effects of career interventions. As a result, most reviewers conclude with the lament that although we know that career interventions are effective, we know little about how, why, and for whom they work. In the first part of this chapter, we hope to show that we may actually know more than we think about the workings of effective career interventions.

Another theme that seems to have emerged over the past several years has to do with the relation between career and personal counseling, with many contemporary writers suggesting that there is so much overlap between the two that they should be considered as identical activities (e.g., Betz & Corning, 1993; Manuele-Adkins, 1992; Subich, 1993; Swanson, 1995). Our reading suggests that the current flurry of writings on this topic has been stimulated, in part, by an attempt to make career counseling a more attractive career path for new and fledgling counseling psychologists. Swanson (1995, p. 221), for example, in a review of this literature, specifically stated that "the issue is being revisited with renewed vigor due to recent evidence that counseling psychologists are decreasing their involvement in career counseling and vocational psychology. . . . " Thus, it seems that some writers want to increase the attractiveness of career counseling activities by making career counseling synonymous with psychotherapy, urging trainees and practitioners to focus more on personal issues (regardless of client wishes and goals), and lengthening career treatment interventions to mirror psychotherapy (e.g., Gold & Scanlon, 1993; Rounds & Tinsley, 1984; Swanson, 1995). While we agree with the need to make career work more attractive to new professionals in our field given the important role that work satisfaction seems to play in overall life satisfaction and mental health (e.g., Diener, Suh, Lucas, & Smith, 1999; Robbins & Kliewer, this volume), we think that the effort to equate career counseling and psychotherapy may be premature and tends to focus more on the needs of our field than on the needs of our clients. We argue in this chapter that the important goals of career counseling involve helping people make goal-congruent work or career choices that will allow them to experience work, career, and life satisfaction in a changing society. When and whether we focus on noncareer issues, the types of personal issues that are important, and how intensive and extensive an intervention should be are data-based questions that deserve

740

careful examination. In the second part of this chapter, we elucidate client characteristics and vocational problems that might require different (perhaps psychotherapeutic) forms of intervention and suggest how attribute by treatment interaction studies may guide this effort.

We focus on research and theory related to helping clients make career choices. Other chapters in this edition of the *Handbook* discuss other important targets for career intervention, including the early development of aspirations (Arbona, this volume), the school-to-work transition process (Blustein, Juntunen, & Worthington, this volume), development and adjustment in the workplace (Hesketh, this volume), and issues of retirement (Hill, Thorn, & Packard, this volume). The chapter is not, however, limited to a specific age group. Rather, our interest is in reviewing research and theory and drawing implications for working with persons, regardless of age, whose primary concern is making or remaking a career choice.

We start by reviewing published meta-analyses of career intervention outcome (Oliver & Spokane, 1988; Spokane & Oliver, 1983; Whiston et al., 1998) and then present some new meta-analytic data focusing specifically on the process and outcome of career interventions designed to promote career choice (Ryan, 1999). We will, on the bases of these analyses, reiterate past conclusions (i.e., that career interventions are effective), but also suggest some new conclusions about the process and outcome of effective career-choice interventions. We conclude the first section by suggesting, in part, that Crites (1981) in his often cited, tongue in cheek, "three sessions and a cloud of dust" criticism of trait-factor counseling was only off by a session or two in describing the number of sessions needed to achieve highly successful career choice outcomes (hence our title), provided that certain critical ingredients are present in the intervention.

THE PROCESS AND OUTCOME OF CAREER-CHOICE INTERVENTIONS

Several meta-analytic investigations have been conducted over the past two decades that have examined the effectiveness of career interventions (Baker & Popowicz, 1983; Oliver & Spokane, 1988; Spokane & Oliver, 1983; Whiston et al., 1998). Spokane and Oliver, in the first large scale meta-analysis of the career intervention literature, included data from 52 studies published between 1950 and 1980, involving some 6,700 subjects, in which some form of career intervention was compared to a control condition on at least one career-related outcome. Overall, it appeared that the average client who received any type of career intervention obtained outcomes that exceeded 80% of the untreated controls ($d = .85$) and that the effects of group or class interventions were larger ($d = 1.11$) than either individual counseling ($d = .87$) or such alternative interventions as computer-assisted, self-directed, and career-education interventions ($d = .34$). Spokane and Oliver, however, were unable to identify any other moderators of treatment effects and urged caution in interpreting the differential effects of treatments due to the potential confounding influence of treatment intensity (e.g., number of sessions) on obtained differences. Nonetheless, this was the first integrative review to suggest quantitatively that career interventions were demonstrably effective, and it set the stage for future meta-analyses.

Oliver and Spokane (1988) subsequently added another nine studies published between 1980 and 1983 to their original database and conducted more fine-tuned analyses of factors that may contribute to effect-size variability. They again reported an average effect size of .82, which reduced to .48 when individual study effect sizes were weighted by sample size to give more weight to studies with larger samples. This weighted effect size increased to .69 when a study with 2,245 subjects that obtained an overall null effect ($d = 0.00$) was removed. Similar to the 1983 findings, the largest unweighted effect size was associated with class interventions ($d = 2.05$) followed by workshops ($d = .75$), individual counseling ($d = .74$), group counseling ($d = .62$), computer-assisted guidance programs ($d = .59$), and self-directed interventions ($d = .10$). A small number of studies ($k = 4$) employing group test interpretation interventions achieved an average effect size ($d = .76$) comparable to those obtained for individual and group counseling interventions but were much more highly variable ($sd = 1.54$ versus .65 and .79 for individual and group counseling, respectively). However, in a multiple regression analysis, only a treatment intensity variable (number of hours + number of sessions) accounted for significant variance in effect size variability, suggesting that length of treatment may be more important than type of intervention in maximizing client gains. Oliver and Spokane, therefore, concluded that (1) career interventions are generally effective, (2) class interventions appear to be the most effective but also the most expensive form of intervention, and (3) therefore, individual and structured group interventions represent the most cost-effective forms of intervention, with cost advantage going to structured groups on the basis of the number of clients that can be reached in a single intervention. Beyond this, Oliver and Spokane were unable to identify critical treatment ingredients that might aid the practitioner in designing effective interventions or critical client variables that might suggest differential treatment effectiveness.

Whiston et al. (1998) updated the Oliver and Spokane (1988) meta-analysis by selecting career intervention studies published between 1983 and 1995 and incorporating recent advances in meta-analytic methodology into their analyses. In relation to methodology, research has demonstrated that individual and average effect-size estimates tend to display a positive bias in small samples (i.e., they provide inflated estimates of effect size in small samples) that can be reduced by applying corrections to individual and overall estimates (see Hedges & Olkin, 1985). The result of this double correction procedure is less biased estimates of individual study and overall effect sizes in meta-analyses. It has also been shown (see Hedges & Olkin, 1985) that regular least squares regression procedures, such as those used in the earlier Oliver and Spokane (1988) meta-analysis, may yield biased parameter estimates and tests of significance. Thus, Hedges and Olkin (1985) advocated use of a weighted least squares regression procedure by which each individual effect size is weighted by the inverse of its variance before entering into the analysis.

Whiston et al. (1998) employed the double correction procedure in arriving at overall effect-size estimates and the weighted least squares regression procedure in analyzing their data for potential moderators of effect-size variability. Thus, the effect sizes that they reported for career interventions, although based on a different data set, are probably less biased estimates of intervention effectiveness than are those reported in the Oliver and Spokane meta-analyses and the regression analyses probably also yielded less biased parameter estimates and statistical tests. Finally, Whiston et al. employed a hierarchical regression strategy that allowed them to examine the independent effects of important client and treatment characteristics on effect-size variability after controlling for study characteristics and methodological factors.

The Whiston et al. (1998) meta-analysis was based on a set of 47 studies published between 1983 and 1995, employing 4,660 participants who received an average of 4.19 sessions ($sd = 4.23$) of career intervention lasting an average of 7.50 hours ($sd = 9.96$). The overall effect size obtained in this study ($d = .45$) was lower than those reported by Spokane and Oliver ($d = .85$) and Oliver and Spokane ($d = .82$), but was quite consistent with Oliver and Spokane's (1988) sample size weighted effect size ($d = .48$). Due to the relatively large number of studies that measured career maturity and career decidedness, Whiston et al. also conducted separate meta-analyses of the effects of career interventions on these two outcomes and found overall effect-size estimates of .53 for career maturity and .19 for decidedness, suggesting that the effects of career interventions on maturity may be somewhat more potent than their effects on decidedness.

Comparisons of effect sizes by type of treatment revealed that individual counseling yielded the highest overall effect size ($d = .75$), followed by group counseling ($d = .57$), computer interventions ($d = .41$), career workshops ($d = .22$), class interventions ($d = .15$), and self-directed interventions ($d = .11$). Thus, when the biasing effects of sample size are taken into consideration (i.e., when weighted versus unweighted effect sizes are examined), individual and group counseling interventions appear to continue to show strong and positive associations with career outcomes, and class interventions appear to be less effective than previously thought. The relatively low potency of totally self-directed interventions is consistent across all three meta-analysis.

However, weighted least-square regression analyses reported in Whiston et al. (1998) revealed that nearly all effect-size variability was accounted for by study characteristics and methodological factors. That is, in none of the three analyses did treatment (i.e., type of treatment, intensity of treatment) or participant (e.g., age, sex) characteristics account for significant unique variability in career outcomes over and above the variability accounted for by study (e.g., number of treatments—the more the better) and method (e.g., study quality—the more valid the better) characteristics.

Thus, the published meta-analyses confirm what a number of reviewers have already suspected and concluded about the career intervention literature; namely, that career interventions are effective (the average treated participant outscores the average control participant by about half a standard deviation when outcomes are globally considered), but how and why they work and for whom they are most (and least) effective is unknown. In fact, it appears from Whiston et al. (1998) that how an outcome study is conducted has more to do with the size of effects that are obtained than anything about the client or what is done within the intervention context.

Fortunately, a recently completed study by Ryan (1999) may allow us to revise these somewhat depressing conclusions. Ryan conducted a series of meta-analyses focusing specifically on career-choice outcomes and several other outcomes (i.e., congruence, vocational identity, career maturity, and career decision-making self-efficacy) suggested by prominent theories of career choice and development to be linked to one's ability to make and commit to satisfying career choices. Like Whiston et al. (1998), this study employed up to date meta-analytic methodology (i.e., unbiased, double-corrected effect-size estimates and weighted least-squares regression procedures) and entered study, method, participant, and treatment characteristics hierarchically into the weighted least-squares regressions to ascertain the unique contributions of participant and treatment characteristics to effect-size estimates after controlling for study and method characteristics.

Unlike Whiston et al. (1998), Ryan (1999) included all relevant studies from the Oliver and Spokane database as well as more recent studies. She also broadened the definition of career choice outcomes (based on Lent, Brown, & Hackett's, 1994 discussion of career choice goals) to include indices of decidedness, indecision, choice certainty, choice commitment, and choice satisfaction. Perhaps most importantly, unlike prior meta-analyses, Ryan coded for the presence or absence in each treatment of 18 codable intervention components (e.g., use of self-report inventories, written exercises, value clarification exercises, computer interventions, and card sorts) and entered these last in the regression analyses to examine the contributions of these specific intervention components to effect-size variability above and beyond that accounted for by study, method, participant, and treatment characteristics.

The results of these meta-analyses, which will be summarized only in aggregate here, were based on 62 studies, employing 7,725 participants. Gender data were reported in 73% ($k = 45$) of the studies. In these studies, 57% of the participants were female and 43% were male. Although only 21% of the studies identified participants by race and ethnicity, where race and ethnicity could be identified 68% were Caucasian, 21% were African American, 10% were Hispanic American, 1% were Asian American, and fewer than 1% were of other racial and ethnic backgrounds. Interventions averaged 7.49 sessions ($sd = 8.85$) over an average 5.36 weeks ($sd = 4.64$) and were fairly equally divided among self-directed (21%), group (16%), class (29%), and combined (26%) interventions (only 8% of the studies employed individual counseling interventions exclusively). Unbiased effect-size estimates across all of the analyses ranged from .21 for career decision-making self-efficacy beliefs to .63 for vocational identity as an outcome, with a mean (across analyses) effect size of .34. Although the latter effect size is somewhat lower than those reported in prior meta-analyses that employed a wider range of career outcomes, a very interesting pattern of results emerges when average effect size is plotted against the number of sessions of treatment.

This pattern, as illustrated in Figure 23.1, shows a clear, but nonlinear, relation that appears to peak at four to five sessions (mean effect size = 1.26) and thereafter drops rather dramatically to an average effect size of .35 for interventions of 12 sessions or more. Equally dramatic is the increase in effect size from .24 for a single session intervention to .47 for interventions employing two or three sessions.

The weighted least-squares regression analyses also yielded some interesting and clinically useful findings. First, consistent with all prior meta-analyses participant characteristics (e.g., age, educational level, motivation) failed to contribute unique variance to effect-size variability over and above that accounted for by study and method characteristics. Second, also consistent with prior meta-analyses, wholly self-directed interventions appeared to be less effective ($d =$ .23) than individual ($d = .41$), class ($d = .43$), and group ($d = .55$) forms of treatment for career choice difficulties. Third, and perhaps most important for practice and future research, specific intervention components (when entered as a block at the final step of the regression analyses) accounted for between 2% to 38% unique variance in effect sizes, and five specific components were identified as contributing significantly to effect-size variability in at least one of the analyses: (1) written exercises, (2) individualized interpretations and feedback, (3) world of work information, (4) modeling opportunities, and (5) and attention to building support for choices within one's social network.

These five intervention components not only appear to be individually important but, as illustrated in Figure 23.2, collectively seem to be associated with remarkable, almost linear, increases in (average, across analyses) career-choice effect sizes. Thus, interventions that used none of the critical components ($k = 11$) produced an average effect size of .22, with 27% of the individual effect sizes being negative. When only one of the components was included in the

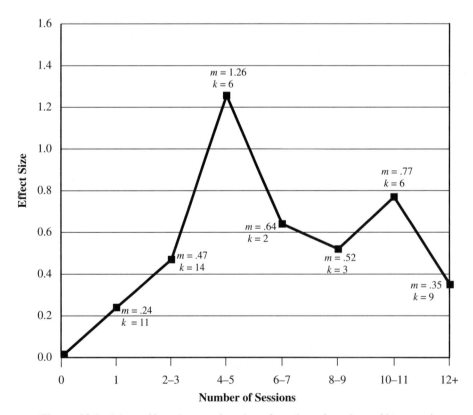

Figure 23.1   Mean effect size as a function of number of sessions of intervention

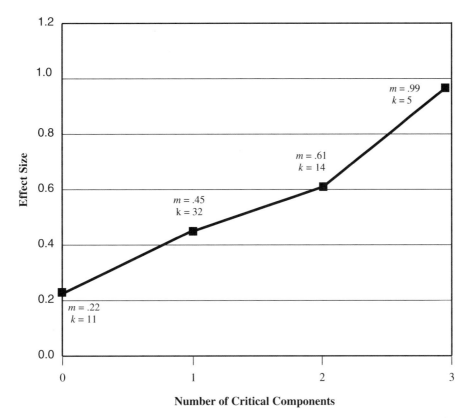

Figure 23.2 Mean effect size as a function of number of critical treatment ingredients

intervention ($k = 32$), the average effect size estimate increased to .45 (with 9% negative effect sizes), and when another component was added ($k = 14$) the average effect size increased to .61 (with 14% negative effect sizes). Adding a third critical component ($k = 5$) was associated with an even more dramatic effect size increase ($d = .99$) and the presence of negative effect sizes disappeared. Unfortunately, no studies employed more than three of the identified critical ingredients.

These results do not appear to be overly contaminated by treatment type. For example, the weak (and sometimes negative) effects associated with interventions that employed none of the critical components was not due to the presence of a disproportionate number of self-directed interventions in this category. Rather, interventions that used none of the critical components contained more class (45%) than self-directed (27%) interventions. How a semester-long career class could fail to use any of the five identified critical ingredients does admittedly strain the imagination, but some apparently do (according to what was reported in the studies) and these demonstrate extremely weak outcome effects.

It is important, however, not to misinterpret these findings. They do not, for example, suggest that other commonly employed (e.g., computer-guided assistance, tests and inventories, career exploration activities, values clarification exercises, card-sort procedures, outside readings) and less commonly used (e.g., anxiety-reduction procedures and efforts to help clients manage and overcome choice-related barriers) intervention components are ineffective or unnecessary. Rather, they simply suggest that the effectiveness of career interventions for choice-making difficulties can be improved (often dramatically) by ensuring that five components are included as part of the intervention: written exercises, individualized interpretations and feedback, information on the world of work, modeling, and building support.

Written Exercises

Written exercises were defined as exercises that prescribe activities for clients or encourage clients to record reflections, thoughts, or feelings concerning their career development (Ryan, 1999). Such exercises included journals, diaries, logs, and workbooks. For example, Simon, Howe, and Kirschenbaum (1972) used a values clarification manual to encourage participants to consider the extent to which work, jobs, and careers related to their life goals. Berman, Gelso, Greenfeig, and Hirsch (1977) used a personal class journal to encourage students actively to search for and reflect upon information that would be helpful in setting and reaching their career goals, and Powers (1978) had clients maintain a log on which primary occupational preferences and planning activities were recorded. Two additional examples of studies that produced relatively large effect sizes and employed written exercises included Brenner and Gazda-Grace (1979) and Glaize and Myrick (1984), who employed workbooks and other printed materials to help clients recognize personal occupational misperceptions and stereotypes. Although somewhat speculative (and deserving future research attention), two common themes appear to run through these written exercises and may represent critical issues to target in the development of written material: (1) helping people establish work and life goals and plan for their implementation, and (2) assisting clients to gain accurate, nonstereotypic information on occupational possibilities. We would further hypothesize that the effectiveness of the former type of written exercise may be due, in part, to the fact that clients are required to commit to their goals and plans in writing rather than merely to talk about them with others or a counselor.

Individualized Interpretations and Feedback

Individualized interpretations and feedback, regardless of modality, involved one-to-one dialogue between the counselor and client concerning vocational issues and career development (Ryan, 1999). Interventions that were coded in this category frequently involved the provision of test interpretation information, whether in a group or individual counseling context, that was individually tailored and provided to each participant (e.g., Kerr & Erb, 1991; Luzzo & Taylor, 1993-1994; Smith & Evans, 1973; Zytowski, 1977). Other interventions included providing, within a class or group context, individual attention on papers written about career plans (e.g., Babcock & Kaufman, 1976) or individualized feedback on participants' career decision-making strategies (e.g., Sherry & Staley, 1984). Given these data, it seems important for counselors engaged in group or class-based career interventions to provide direct, individually-focused interpretations of self-appraisal information gathered during the course of counseling. Direct and individually-focused feedback to clients on their career planning and decision-making strategies also appears to be valuable.

Given the number of persons who seek career services (see for example, Holland, 1996b), these data and those presented earlier might also suggest that relatively short (four to five session) group interventions may be treatments of choice for many clients, provided that more standard intervention activities are accompanied by individualized interpretations and feedback (along with the other four apparently critical treatment ingredients). Finally, a good deal has been written about the need to study career counseling process (e.g., Swanson, 1995) and the role of the working alliance in career interventions (e.g., Meara & Patton, 1994). It might be informative, therefore, to explore empirically the influence that individualized interpretations and feedback (and the other critical ingredients) have on the working alliance.

Information on the World of Work

This self-explanatory category, pertaining (Ryan, 1999) to the provision of practical information (via the counselor, a computer, other group members, or outside readings) on earnings, opportunities, outlook, work activities, advancement opportunities, and training requirements for a variety of career fields and types of jobs, is often organized around extant occupational classification systems (e.g., Roe, 1956). Thus, it appears that maximally effective career interventions not only provide opportunities to consider career goals and gain individualized self-appraisal information, but also provide participants with up-to-date information about the world of work and accurate information about skills, requirements, and likely outcomes of a particular set of occupational preferences. Arbona (1996) has specifically suggested that career practice could be improved (especially for low-income Hispanic Americans and other racial and ethnic group members) if counselors had more knowledge about, and could provide more information on, the training and other requirements of career and employment paths open to their clients. Ryan's data clearly support this contention.

Modeling

Modeling involves exposing clients to individuals who have attained success in the processes of career exploration, decision making, and implementation (Ryan, 1999). Potentially effective modeling activities can include guest speakers (e.g., Lent, Larkin, & Hasegawa, 1986); facilitator self-disclosure of Holland type, work history, and career development (e.g., Ganster & Lovell, 1978) or thinking processes (e.g., Hutchinson, Freeman, Downey, & Kilbreath, 1992); or video or film presentations (e.g., Luzzo, Funk, & Strang, 1996).

Attention to Building Support

Helping clients build support networks also appears to facilitate their career development and career choices (Ryan, 1999). The specific support-related interventions that were reported in the database ranged from including significant others (e.g., parents) in the career planning process (e.g., Palmer & Cochran, 1988) to employing facilitators who were familiar with and informed about the cultural contexts in which clients lived (Rodriguez & Blocher, 1988) to teach clients how to interact positively with their environments using social influence theory (Smith & Evans, 1973).

Intervention efforts designed to decrease career-related barriers did not account for significant unique variance in career intervention effect sizes in Ryan's (1999) meta-analysis, despite the attention that career barriers have received from theoreticians and researchers in recent years. For example, we know a great deal about the types of barriers that people experience as a function of their gender, race/ethnicity, and social class (e.g., Farmer, 1976; Luzzo, 1993; McWhirter, 1997; McWhirter & Luzzo, 1996; McWhirter, Torres, & Rasheed, 1998; Swanson & Tokar, 1991a; Swanson & Woitke, 1997) and have developed psychometrically sound ways to measure them (e.g., Swanson, Daniels, & Tokar, 1996; Swanson & Tokar, 1991b). Unfortunately, research employing these and other measures has not consistently found that perceived barriers are related to career choice and development outcomes (Luzzo, 1996; Luzzo & Hutcheson, 1996; McWhirter, Hackett, & Bandalos, 1998; Swanson et al., 1996), a finding that is clearly echoed in the intervention literature by Ryan's results.

On the other hand, supports and their relations to career development and choice outcomes have not received the same amount of theoretical and research attention as have barriers, but the few studies that are available point quite consistently to their importance in the career development process. For example, McWhirter, Hackett, et al. (1998) found that perceptions of support (but not barriers) were significantly related to the career aspirations and educational plans of a sample of Mexican-American high school girls, even through these young women reported a fairly large number of barriers. As another example, Richie et al. (1997), in a qualitative study of the career development of highly successful African American and Caucasian women, presented data to suggest that a primary factor accounting for the occupational success of these women was the impressive degree to which they felt supported by their families and other people (especially, but not exclusively, other women) in their social networks. All reported significant barriers associated with sexism and racism but were nonetheless successful owing in part, in their views, to the support they received from others. Other research has clearly documented the power that supportive peers (and family) can have on the aspirations of school age youth, the damage to aspirations that is produced by nonsupportive peer networks (e.g., Arbona, this volume; Steinberg, Dornbush, & Brown, 1992), and the important role of family, school, and workplace support in the school-to-work transition process (Blustein et al., this volume; Blustein, Phillips, Jobin-Davis, Finkelberg, & Roarke, 1997).

These data, as well as those presented in Ryan's (1999) meta-analysis, clearly suggest that career interventions need to focus on helping clients build networks of people who are supportive and facilitative of their career plans. While we would not suggest that career counselors abandon their focus on helping people overcome barriers to preferred career paths, the data suggest that it is imperative to help people find ways to build support for their plans. In fact, this may be a most powerful way to reduce the perceived limiting influences of barriers and to enable persons to overcome potential career-limiting environmental influences (e.g., Richie et al., 1997). Career interventions may simply not be as effective without such efforts and the help that they provide clients in turning their aspirations into reality may be seriously compromised. Particularly important would be research that (1) tests the comparative and combined effectiveness of different types of intervention strategies (e.g., teaching skills versus including families) and (2) investigates the role that counselor cultural awareness and knowledge plays in increasing the effectiveness of support-enhancing interventions.

Conclusions

The data that we have presented so far in this chapter clearly confirm the conclusions of prior reviews of the career intervention outcome literature; namely, that career interventions are effective, especially in helping people to make, commit to, and achieve short-term satisfaction with career and work choices. However, we may now be able to go beyond these conclusions by hypothesizing that brief (four to five session) group interventions can be made exceptionally effective if they (1) require clients to commit their career goals and plans in writing; (2) offer them individualized self-appraisal information and help on their goals, plans, and decision-making strategies; (3) provide up-to-date information that allows participants to gauge accurately the skills and education required and outcomes achievable by pursuing different career paths; (4) include models who demonstrate how to go about career planning; and (5) assist clients to identify and gain access to important sources of support in their environments who can facilitate their choices and help them overcome obstacles that might stand in their way.

We might even get more students interested in career work by communicating this and other information to them. For example, we might, first of all, present students with the clear and compelling data on the importance of work satisfaction to overall life satisfaction and subjective well-being as well as on the number of persons who desire career services (and, thus, the number of persons whose lives they can influence in a positive way). We might also let them know that the effects that are obtainable from short, well-designed career interventions are larger than those usually produced by psychotherapy, and that we may actually know more about how to produce these effects than do psychotherapy researchers (see Wampold, this volume). Finally, we could communicate to them that there is much interesting, challenging, and important research still to be done (and that they might actually get to do psychotherapy with some of their career clients). It is to the latter topic that we turn next.

FUTURE DIRECTIONS FOR RESEARCH AND PRACTICE

We have already suggested some questions for future research on career interventions, including investigating the degree to which the five critical components relate to the working alliance, exploring the central mechanisms through which written exercises influence outcomes, comparing the relative efficacy of support-enhancement methods, and assessing the additive contributions of counselor cultural knowledge and awareness to the effectiveness of support-enhancing interventions. Beyond these basic questions, there is a good deal of research that still needs to be done to increase knowledge of how best to work with persons experiencing career-choice difficulties. For one, we need outcome research that tests directly the influence of critical ingredients, incorporates and tests hypotheses derived from theoretical writings on the choice-making process, and explores the effects of career intervention on other types of choice-related outcomes. Also important is research that explores the degree to which specific client characteristics (e.g., sex, race/ethnicity, social class, sexual orientation, and presenting problems) moderate the outcome of well-designed career-choice interventions so that interventions can be modified to best meet the needs of the greatest number of users of career services.

Testing the Effects of Critical Ingredients on Counseling Outcome

One decided advantage of meta-analytic research is that questions can be addressed in meta-analyses that have not been previously tested directly in a body of literature. Such was the case in Ryan's (1999) identification of critical intervention ingredients. Although little research has addressed directly the comparative and combined effects of different intervention techniques, Ryan was able to explore such ingredients by combining and conducting between study comparisons. As should any new research finding, these aspects of Ryan's meta-analytic results should be treated as hypotheses to be replicated in subsequent primary investigations. There have been no studies conducted to date that have included all five critical ingredients. It would, therefore, be informative to test the outcome effects of interventions that include all five critical ingredients and compare the effect sizes obtained to those reported by Ryan.

Additionally, interventions might be systematically dismantled or constructed (see Heppner, Kivlighan, & Wampold, 1999) to test the unique and combined effects of the critical ingredients on intervention outcome. In following a dismantling strategy, an investigator would start with an intervention that included all critical ingredients and then compare its effects to interventions that include fewer of the critical components. From a constructive standpoint, one would start with an intervention that includes only one of the critical ingredients and then systematically add a component at a time, comparing outcome effects at each step. With the constructive strategy, it might be beneficial to start with a component that is likely to yield the largest effect and then assess the unique contribution to outcome variance that is obtainable from each added component. Individualized interpretations and feedback and building support appeared to yield the largest effect sizes, respectively, in Ryan's (1999) meta-analyses and, therefore, represent good candidates as the initial ingredients (i.e., individualized interpretations followed by supports) to be included when using a constructive research strategy. Written exercises seemed to yield the weakest effect sizes among the critical ingredients and, thus, should probably be the final component to explore with constructive strategies (and the first to be removed in dismantling designs). In fact, for power considerations, Ryan chose to use a liberalized alpha level ($p < .10$) to identify critical ingredients, and written exercises was the only component chosen whose beta weights in the regression analyses were not associated consistently with more conventional alpha levels. Thus, because choice of written exercises as a critical ingredient was associated with a higher type I error rate than is conventionally acceptable, direct tests of its contribution to career choice interventions are especially needed (along with research, to be discussed later, that attempts to improve the effectiveness of this component).

We and others (e.g., Holland, 1996b; Oliver & Spokane, 1988) have also suggested that group interventions represent the interventions of choice for cost as well as outcome considerations. However, this also represents an hypothesis for future investigation since no studies of the comparative effects of different types of interventions (e.g., group versus individual versus class versus self-directed) have been conducted in which the comparison conditions were equated on the numbers and types of critical ingredients. Thus, we need further research that directly compares the effects of different types of interventions that include all five critical treatment components.

We also wonder whether the effects of self-directed interventions could be substantially improved if all five critical ingredients could be incorporated into these types of interventions. This does not seem to be beyond the realm of possibility now that many self-directed interventions are computer-based (Holland, 1991a). Self-directed interventions already provide opportunities for persons to conduct self-assessments and to learn in some detail about different career options. It might also be possible to build computer-based, self-directed interventions that additionally (1) include opportunities for persons to think about and record their career and life goals, (2) give concrete individualized narrative interpretations of self-assessment exercises, (see, for example, Holland's, 1991b, Interpretative Report Option for the *Self-Directed Search*), (3) model effective decision-making strategies (e.g., Gati, 1996; Gati, Fassa, & Houminer, 1995), and (4) provide exercises through which individuals could identify potential sources of support in their environments and learn strategies to marshall support for their choices and overcome barriers. If research supports the effectiveness of such interventions and yields effect sizes nearly comparable to those that can be obtained by other forms of intervention, the impact on the number of clients who could benefit from effectively developed career services could be enormous.

Incorporating Career Theory to Improve Outcomes

Another important line of inquiry involves using extant career theories and research to refine further the critical counseling ingredients. Such a strategy might also allow us to identify other potentially important treatment components.

Goal Properties

Goal concepts, like those incorporated into written exercises, figure prominently in several theories of career choice and development (Holland, 1997; Lent et al., 1994; Super, Savickas, & Super, 1996; Vondracek & Kawasaki, 1995), and have been found to be important predictors of work performance (e.g., Locke & Latham, 1990) and life satisfaction (e.g., Diener et al., 1999). Collectively, the literature on goal setting indicates that (1) firmly held, (2) clear and specific, and (3) challenging but attainable goals are associated with high levels of work performance and strong motivational effects (see Lent et al., 1994; Locke & Latham, 1990).

Recent research from the life satisfaction and subjective well-being literatures suggests other important goal properties. Brunstein, Schultheiss, and Grässmann (1998), for example, found that progress toward need-congruent goals was related positively to subjective well-being, while commitment to need-incongruent goals was related negatively to estimates of well-being. Other research has suggested that goal commitment is positively associated with satisfaction when a person's goals across life roles are coherently organized, compatible, and nonconflictual (e.g., Emmons, 1986). Finally, goals seem to have positive effects on satisfaction and well-being only when appropriate resources are available for their attainment (see Diener et al., 1999).

We have already hypothesized that having clients record their goals and plans might increase the clarity of their goals and their commitment to them. The above research suggests that having clients also consider how compatible their career goals are to the goals they have in other roles, and to their needs and values may add to the effectiveness of goal-setting and planning exercises. [See Ford's (1992) Living Systems Framework for some suggestions about how these activities might be accomplished.]

Need and Ability Data

Another theory-into-practice lead involves the types of self-appraisal information that might be provided to clients through individualized interpretations to maximize outcome effects. For example, there are a wide variety of data supporting hypothesized (Dawis & Lofquist, 1984) relations between need-reinforcer correspondence and work satisfaction, and between ability-ability requirement correspondence and work satisfactoriness (see Swanson & Gore, this volume). Need-reinforcer correspondence has, in fact, been shown to be more strongly related to work satisfaction than interest congruence and the two (i.e., correspondence and congruence) additively do a better job of predicting satisfaction than either alone (Rounds, 1990). Unfortunately, our reading of the intervention literature suggests that these findings have not been well incorporated into career practice. Indeed, objective measures of ability and inventories of vocational needs are much less frequently incorporated into career interventions (even when individual interpretations are given) than are self-rated ability estimates and measures of interest and Holland (1997) type. The inclusion of need data may not only provide clients with more data with which to make satisfying career choices, but additionally may help them to develop need-congruent goals and to evaluate the degree to which their goals are need-congruent (see above).

Some writers have suggested that the case for ability tests may not be as compelling. Prediger (1999), for example, has argued that self-rated ability estimates may serve as substitutes for measures of objective abilities in career interventions because self-rated abilities demonstrate hit rates comparable to the hit rates of tested abilities when occupational choice and/or membership is used as a criterion (e.g., American College Testing [ACT], 1998). However, there are equally consistent data to indicate that when tested and self-estimated abilities do not agree, people more often aspire to, and ultimately choose, occupations that are congruent with self-estimates (e.g., Betsworth, 1999; Handschin, 1996). While there is nothing inherently wrong with clients choosing such occupations, we think that career interventions should not just perpetuate the status quo, but should expand real occupational possibilities for clients. Stated simply, a goal of career interverention is not simply to help persons make choices that they would have made without career assistance (although these may turn out to be good choices), but rather to help increase the probability that clients have made an optimum (i.e., satisfying and satisfactory) choice. Thus, we think that an exclusive reliance on self-estimated abilities, although less financially costly and time consuming than multi-aptitude test batteries, may come with a cost to clients—they simply may not consider some potentially rewarding occupations because they erroneously think that they do not have requisite talents. Thus, we suggest that objective measures of ability need also to be incorporated more frequently into career interventions. They may provide clients with a fuller understanding of their work personalities, and allow them to identify occupations that they may have already eliminated on the basis of faulty ability percepts. The yield would be a wider range of career and work possibilities from which to choose.

Identifying Foreclosed Options

Recent attempts to translate Lent et al.'s (1994) Social Cognitive Career Theory into a model for career practice have particularly hypothesized that efforts to broaden occupational possibilities for clients should include helping them to explore career paths and occupations that they may have prematurely eliminated on the basis of inaccurate self-efficacy beliefs and/or occupational information (see Swanson & Gore, this volume, for a review of research on the theory). S.D. Brown and Lent (1996), for example, described how objective ability, vocational need, and interest data can be used to help identify such foreclosed possibilities as well as how card sort procedures can be modified to accomplish the same ends. The *Skills Confidence Inventory* (SCI: Betz, Borgen, & Harmon, 1996), a self-efficacy measure developed as a companion for the new edition of the *Strong Interest Inventory* (SII: Harmon, Hansen, Borgen, & Hammer, 1994), provides measures of self-efficacy for each of the six General Occupational Themes on the SII, and can also be used to help clients identify areas where interests may have been compromised by low self-efficacy beliefs (e.g., Betz et al., 1996) or inaccurate occupational information (Harmon et al., 1996). Thus, practitioners might incorporate these procedures into their intervention efforts to ensure that prematurely foreclosed possibilities are considered. Research is needed that tests (1) the comparative effectiveness of these and other procedures for identifying prematurely eliminated occupational possibilities, and (2) the degree to which a focus on identifying foreclosed occupational possibilities may be associated with improved choice and (especially) satisfaction outcomes.

It should be pointed out, however, that Holland (1996b, p. 3) has chided such suggestions as being insensitive to clients' vocational aspirations, presumably on the basis of studies (see Holland, 1996a) showing strong correlations between aspirations and later choices ("Some counselors don't appear to listen to a client's goals and proceed instead to administer treatments designed to change a person's aspirations without getting informed consent or understanding"). Our response is the same as we made earlier to Prediger's claims about the predictive validity of ability self-estimates. That is, it is neither too surprising nor terribly interesting to us to know that people end up doing things in which they express an interest. What is more interesting and potentially more important is how well these expressed interests (i.e., aspirations) relate to the satisfaction that people feel about their choices. The purpose of exercises designed to help people more fully consider possible career paths (including ones in which they might not now express a strong interest) is not to ignore their goals and change their aspirations without consent, but rather to help them be more fully informed about potentially rewarding and satisfying career paths so that their aspirations are aimed as high as their abilities will take them.

Investigating the Effects of Career Interventions on Long-Term Work Satisfaction

Another critical topic for future career intervention outcome research is to explore whether career interventions are associated with long-term work and life satisfaction. Holland (1996b, p. 5) pointed out that clients do not "show up asking for maturity inventories or wanting to know the implications of their life stage." Rather, he suggested that clients seek counseling because they want to learn about the kinds of work that will bring them happiness and whether they can perform that kind of work well. We agree with Holland on this one and find it somewhat troubling that the effects of career interventions on long-term work and life satisfaction have been largely ignored as a topic of investigation in the intervention literature. While Ryan's (1999) meta-analysis suggests that well-designed career interventions can have a positive effect on short-term levels of choice satisfaction, there are virtually no follow-up data available on whether clients who use career services attain greater levels of later job satisfaction, work performance, and life satisfaction than do those who do not use career services (see Oliver & Spokane, 1988, Table 23.9, and Whiston et al., 1998, Table 23.10). Although collecting such long-term follow-up data is admittedly time consuming and difficult, it is critical if we are to understand fully the effectiveness of career interventions and influence public policy in any meaningful way.

In relation to public policy, career and vocational psychologists have, for example, recently lamented the apparent indifference of school-to-work initiatives to the contributions of career psychology theory (e.g., Lent, O'Brien, & Fassinger, 1998) and have endeavored to show how career theory and research can improve school-to-work programs (see Blustein et al., this volume). However, at the same time, we seem to have failed to appreciate how our intervention research may have contributed to this state of affairs. To reiterate and paraphrase Holland (1996b), clients do not seek counseling to become more career mature, and policymakers may not be overly impressed by our apparent ability to increase the career maturity, career decision-making self-efficacy beliefs, or short-term choice satisfaction of our clients. What they want to know is whether any of this makes a difference in the work (and nonwork) lives of people who use our services, especially in a contemporary world where large segments of society have to cope with unpredictable work opportunities and where job change is becoming the norm (Cascio, 1995; Holland, 1996b; Richardson, 1993; Savickas, 1993). As we indicated at the outset of this chapter, we define the important goals of career intervention to involve helping people make goal-congruent work or career choices that will allow them to experience work and life satisfaction in the future. To date, the field has learned a great deal about how to help people make choices that are associated with concurrent levels of satisfaction, commitment, and certainty, but relatively little about the power of its interventions to affect their future levels of work satisfaction, satisfactoriness, and happiness.

One immediate (but not wholly satisfactory) approach would be a consumer satisfaction study similar to the recent *Consumer Reports* study of the effectiveness of psychotherapy (Seligman, 1995). Such a study could survey large segments of the population about their life satisfaction, work satisfaction and career patterns, and additionally ask questions about whether respondents used career services, the types of services that were used, their satisfaction with the services, and the degree to which they felt that the services contributed to their current feelings of work satisfaction. The data that could be mined from such a survey would provide interesting information on the likely association of career services to work satisfaction and the types of services that may be related to long-range work and life satisfaction.

Other obvious forms of research would include collecting more long-range follow-up data from career clients and participants in career intervention research. Apart from the time-consuming nature of this challenge, such a strategy would need to contend with certain methodological conundrums. For example, detecting an effect of interventions on long-term work and life satisfaction may be exceptionally difficult primarily (but not solely) because satisfaction surveys (e.g., Andrews & Withey, 1976) have revealed that most people report that they are satisfied with their work and their lives. Although some suspect this trend to be changing with the changing nature of work in modern society (e.g., Savickas, 1993), it has been stable for so long that any real effect that career interventions may have on long-term satisfaction is probably small. Thus, we need to be careful to design follow-up research in such a way as to minimize Type II errors (e.g., by using psychometrically sound outcome measures and employing large samples). If multiple follow-up studies are conducted, we could also use meta-analyses to yield more powerful tests of follow-up effects than can be achieved through individual studies that are unable to employ samples of sufficient size to obtain powerful tests at the individual study level. We do not want to conclude erroneously (or have policymakers conclude erroneously) that career interventions have no long-term impacts on the work lives of clients simply because our research was unable to detect small but socially important effects.

We could also use the constructive research strategies once again to test whether additional intervention components suggested by the literatures on work satisfaction and the changing nature of work add significant unique variance to choice and later satisfaction outcomes (see Hesketh, this volume and Krumboltz, 1996 for some possibilities). Such research should not, however, start with the assumption that what we do well now will not continue to be effective in the twenty-first century and build completely new interventions. For example, it may be that the effects that the five critical intervention ingredients have on the (1) clarity, consistency, and congruency of clients' work and life goals, (2) accuracy of self-knowledge and vocational identities, (3) decision-making and planning strategies and corresponding self-efficacy beliefs, (4) and abilities to garner support for their plans and goals may be sufficient to allow clients to prosper occupationally and personally in a changing society. Our main point here is simply that research should, we think, start by adding new ingredients on to demonstrably effective career interventions, and then test empirically whether additional gains in short- and long-term effectiveness are attained with the additional ingredients. We will offer a similar conclusion regarding studies of attribute by treatment interaction—the topic to which we turn next.

Future Directions for Attribute X Treatment Research

A number of writers have commented on the need for research that considers client and vocational problem characteristics that might moderate the effectiveness of career interventions (i.e., outcome effects may be of a different magnitude or direction for certain types of clients). Fretz (1981, p. 77), for example, concluded that "Little progress can be made in improving the effectiveness of career interventions until more specific and systematic evaluative attention is given to (1) treatment parameters in myriad contemporary interventions; (2) the relationships of participant attributes to the effects of treatments. . . ." It appears that research over the ensuing years, when considered collectively and meta-analytically, has yielded some important insights into the types of treatment parameters that are most strongly associated with career intervention outcome. However, little progress seems to have occurred in identifying client or vocational problem characteristics that may moderate treatment effects.

Client Characteristics

Although much has been written about the unique career development needs of women; members of racial and ethnic minority groups; and gay, lesbian, and bisexual clients; surprisingly little research has tested whether the effects of career interventions are different for these groups. Ryan's (1999) database, for instance, yielded no studies where either race/ethnicity or sexual orientation was tested as a moderator of treatment effects. She also found that race/ethnicity and sexual orientation were so infrequently reported that the moderating influences of these variables could not be studied meta-analytically (see also Oliver & Spokane, 1988; Spokane & Oliver, 1983; Whiston et al., 1998).

There have been more studies of sex differences in treatment outcome, but few have found differential outcome effects for men and women. Ryan (1999), for instance, located eighteen studies that analyzed for sex differences; three of these (Amatea, Clark, & Cross, 1984; Myers, Lindeman, Thompson, & Patrick, 1975; Wilson, 1987) reported significant main effects of sex on treatment outcome (all showing that women obtained higher post-treatment career maturity scores than did men), but none found significant sex by treatment interactions on intervention outcome. However, once again, participant sex was so infrequently reported in primary investigations that the potential moderating effects of sex on outcome could not be tested with sufficient power in any of the meta-analyses.

One reason for the dearth of moderator studies may be that many writers appear to assume that extant career interventions will be ineffective (or significantly less effective) for women, racial/ethnic minority, and gay, lesbian, and bisexual clients. They, therefore, develop career interventions that are presumed to meet the unique needs of these groups (e.g., Atanasoff & Slaney, 1980; Berman et al., 1977; Brenner & Gazda-Grace, 1979; Kahn & Ward, 1983; Rodriguez & Blocher, 1988). While we do not disagree with the needs for such interventions, we do think that it is also important to test for (rather than assume the existence of) differential effects of interventions on the basis of sex, race/ethnicity, and sexual orientation, especially now that we may know more than we previously thought about the critical ingredients of effective interventions. Thus, we need research that tests explicitly for sex, race/ethnicity, and sexual orientation differences associated with interventions that focus, as the data indicate they probably should, on (1) helping clients develop, prioritize, and commit in writing to career and life goals that are clear, need-congruent, and coherently organized; (2) giving clients individualized self-appraisal information that also includes need and objective ability data so that need-congruent goals can be developed, accurate ability information can be gained, and prematurely foreclosed occupational options can be reconsidered; (3) providing them with access to occupational information on career pursuits that might be goal- and personality-congruent; (4) helping them develop strategies to build supportive networks that can facilitate aspirations and help overcome barriers to occupational pursuit; and (5) enlisting models who can demonstrate how they personally established goals, gained self-understanding, marshaled support, and chose their current career paths.

We have already suggested how mainstream career theory may improve the effectiveness of career interventions. We might also consider how the extant literature on the career development of women, racial and ethnic minorities, and gays, lesbians, and bisexuals can be used to flesh out and fine-tune the critical ingredients so that effectiveness can be maximized. First, there are a variety of data to suggest that modeling effects are maximized by employing models with whom clients can identify along multiple salient dimensions, including ethnicity, age, gender, social class, and sexual orientation. Thus, as Bowman (1995) and others (Fouad & Bingham, 1995; Hackett & Byars, 1996; Leong & Brown, 1995; Morrow, Gore, & Campbell, 1996) have suggested, inclusion of models of the same race, sex, and sexual orientation as clients may be critical. Credibility of modeling effects (see Lent, Brown, & Hackett, 1996) may also be enhanced by employing models who can demonstrate how they have coped with choice-making difficulties and how they struggled, but ultimately persevered, with the same factors with which clients are contending (or will have to contend). Such coping models may provide people with more useful information and elicit stronger motivational effects than mastery models (of the same sex, race, ethnicity, or sexual orientation) who have not had to contend with the difficult career development tasks.

Second, it may be that barrier identification and coping strategies have not been shown to account for remarkable amounts of variance in career intervention outcomes because persons who are likely to experience significant societal barriers (e.g., members of racial and ethnic minority groups) have not been included in great enough numbers in the career development outcome research. A number of writers have suggested that counseling efforts for women (e.g., Betz & Fitzgerald, 1987), racial/ethnic minorities (e.g., Bowman, 1995), and gay, lesbian, and bisexual clients (Pope, 1995) need to encourage clients to persevere in the face of obstacles, and to anticipate and learn to cope with choice barriers and potentially aversive work situations. Thus, the focus on building support networks may need to be complemented by specific attention to the types of barriers that clients may encounter. It may be found that an explicit focus on barriers, along with preventive and coping strategies, may account for more variance in the career intervention outcomes of women, minorities, and gays than for other groups.

Third, it may also be necessary to attend to stages of identity development of minority and gay, lesbian, and bisexual clients. Writers have discussed the need for counselors to be aware of, and understand the impact of, clients' racial/ethnic (Fouad & Bingham, 1995) and sexual (Pope, 1995) identity development and to incorporate this understanding into counseling. Although research on the relation of racial identity development to career development variables has not been particularly supportive of these suggestions (e.g., Gainor & Lent, 1998), this may be more an artifact of measurement than of theoretical deficiencies. For example, the most widely used measure of racial identity development (Racial Identity Attitude Scale; Helms & Parham, 1990) has consistently yielded quite marginal to poor internal consistency estimates across all of its subscales. As a result, correlations that have been obtained between these subscales and career development variables may have been attenuated to such an extent that the power of studies to detect real, non-null relations has been severely limited. Thus, there is still a good deal of important research to be done on racial identity development, including the development and refinement of scales that would more adequately measure key theoretical constructs.

Fourth, the multiple role conflicts experienced by women who work outside of the home have been well-documented and the influence of these conflicts on the career lives of women are clear (see Betz & Fitzgerald, 1987; Gilbert & Brownson, 1998). Thus, we would hypothesize that career interventions, perhaps as part of the goal-setting component, should help women anticipate multiple role conflicts that may be associated with their career pursuits and plan strategies to manage (and even prevent) them. A recent body of research that may help direct these efforts involves the role of multiple role self-efficacy beliefs in women's career development. Multiple role self-efficacy beliefs have been defined as the perceived ability to manage tasks related to career and family roles and have been hypothesized to relate positively to women's career development (e.g., Lefcourt & Harmon, 1992). Unfortunately, research has not been consistently supportive of these hypotheses. Multiple role self-efficacy beliefs have been found to predict women's choices of nontraditional versus traditional careers (Lefcourt & Harmon, 1992; Stickel & Bonett, 1991), but not such other outcomes as level, prestige, commitment to, or satisfaction with career choices (Dukstein & O'Brien, 1995). Another clear finding from this literature is that the samples that have been employed report rather high levels of multiple role self-efficacy and, therefore, yield very restricted ranges of observed scores.

Orput (1998) recently pointed out that most of the women employed in these studies were anticipating rather than actually engaging in multiple roles and that their responses may, therefore, have reflected a positive and unrealistic bias about their abilities to handle multiple roles. To test this assumption, Orput (1998) assessed the multiple role self-efficacy beliefs of women at different stages of career and family development, finding significant relations between multiple role self-efficacy beliefs and career commitment only among women who were concomitantly dealing with career and family issues. One implication of these findings is that women who are participating in career-choice interventions, but who have not yet had to engage simultaneously in work and family roles, may underestimate the level of work and family conflict that they may personally experience. As a result, they may overestimate their abilities to manage such conflict effectively. Thus, career interventions may need not only to help women develop stronger efficacy beliefs about their abilities to manage multiple role conflicts, but also to develop strategies to help women to preview more realistically, and to prepare for, multiple role conflicts that may occur later in their lives.

Vocational Problem Diagnostics

Rounds and Tinsley (1984), in the first edition of this *Handbook,* argued that future progress in understanding the process and outcome of career interventions would require increased attention to developing clinically useful and testable vocational problem diagnostic systems that can yield suggestions for differential treatments. While it does not appear that useful vocational problem diagnostic systems have been developed, research conducted over the past decade has yielded data that seem to suggest differential treatments. For example, a series of cluster analytic studies has been conducted that has sought to identify homogeneous subgroups of persons experiencing problems with career indecision (Chartrand et al., 1994; Larson, Heppner, Ham, & Dugan, 1988; Larson & Majors, 1998; Lucas, 1993; Lucas & Epperson, 1990; Multon, Heppner, & Lapan, 1995).

Although these studies have used samples drawn from diverse populations of undecided persons (e.g., college students who had not declared a major in a timely fashion, participants in career courses, gifted high school students, counseling center clients), and have employed different measures of factors thought to be predictive of indecision, they have yielded some remarkably consistent findings. First, studies that have included measures of need for occupational information have uniformly identified a cluster of persons whose choice problems primarily reflect only a need for occupational information. Second, measures of anxiety and negative affect have yielded another cluster of persons defined primarily by high levels of negative affect and general and choice anxiety. Third, this research has also identified a cluster of clients whose choice problems tend to be associated with high levels of general and choice-related anxiety and negative affect, low vocational identity, high needs for career information, and low feelings of efficacy over problem-solving and decision-making abilities. These clients have been labeled by all investigators as chronically indecisive (Holland & Holland, 1977; Salomone, 1982) and as needing more intensive forms of career intervention. Thus, it appears that at least three types of career clients have been consistently identified: (1) those who seem just to need additional occupational information and help with occupational exploration, (2) those whose career-choice problems are primarily anxiety-related, and (3) more severely impaired clients who present with a constellation of problems revolving around anxiety, poor vocational identity development, high perceived needs for occupational information, and low feelings of efficacy around their abilities to solve problems and make career decisions. Other client clusters have not been as well replicated across the various studies.

Before concluding, we would like to outline a heuristic and testable model of career indecision problems that we think can bring some additional clarity to the results of the cluster analyses, and suggest some hypotheses about differential treatments and potential moderators of career intervention effects that go beyond what has been revealed thus far by these studies. Specifically, we hypothesize that career indecision is a hierarchically arranged, tripartite construct consisting of a disposition to experience negative affect (i.e., negative affectivity), problems in vocational identity formation, and needs for occupational information as the higher order latent dimensions. The dispositional dimension has been repeatedly uncovered in studies of the structure of affect (Watson & Tellegen, 1985), and seems to be defined primarily by trait anxiety, a tendency to experience a wide variety of negative emotions across time and situation, and cognitive/perceptual tendencies to focus on, magnify the importance of, and ruminate about the negative aspects of self, others, and situations (Watson & Clark, 1984). Persons experiencing high levels of negative affectivity have been found to self-report lower levels of work and life satisfaction and to be less career certain than those with lower levels of negative affectivity (e.g., Chartrand, Rose, Elliott, Marmarosh, & Caldwell, 1993; Decker & Borgen, 1993; Meldahl & Muchinsky, 1997), presumably because of their heightened tendencies to experience negative emotions and to focus on what is wrong with their choices, careers, and life situations (S.D. Brown, 1993). Research (e.g., Nolen-Hoeksema, Parker, & Larson, 1994; Pierce et al., 1998) has also suggested that the ruminative tendencies characteristic of negative affectivity may have particularly powerful effects on persons' feelings of satisfaction and well-being, perhaps even stronger than other characteristics associated with this affective state. For example, Pierce et al. found that the predisposition toward rumination accounted for significant unique variance in cognitive interference beyond the effects of other traits associated with negative affectivity. Nolen-Hoeksema et al. found that bereaved adults with a ruminative coping style reported more depression six months after widowhood than did persons with lesser tendencies to ruminate. This effect even held after the effects on depression of gender, initial depression, and social support were controlled.

In light of these findings, we suggest that some clients may experience difficulties with choice making because of their affective and cognitive tendencies to experience negative emotions when thinking about their career lives and occupational choices, and their concomitant tendencies to focus on, exaggerate the importance of, and ruminate about, what might go wrong with their choices of careers and occupations. We further suggest that measures of trait anxiety (e.g., Spielberger, Gorsuch, & Lushene, 1968), negative affect (e.g., Watson, Clark, & Tellegen, 1988), and fear of commitment (Serling & Betz, 1990) may provide particularly good measures of the central components of negative affectivity, and may be able to be used alone or collectively as diagnostic indicators. Betz and Serling (1993), for example, reported correlations between their Fear of Commitment Scale and trait anxiety of .72 and .74 in two samples of college students. Measures of ruminative tendencies (e.g., Pierce et al., 1998) which have so far not been employed in the career literature might also be included in future research and as diagnostic markers in practice settings.

Vocational identity is a central construct in several theories of career choice and development (e.g., Holland, 1997; Vondracek & Kawasaki, 1995) and has been found to be a significant predictor of career choice and career decidedness (e.g., Blustein & Noumair, 1996; Carson & Mowsesian, 1993; Holland, 1996a). Further, correlations that we have observed among vocational identity scales (e.g., Holland, Daiger, & Power, 1980) and measures of career maturity attitudes, goal properties (e.g., stability), career decision-making self-efficacy beliefs, and problem-solving appraisals seem often to be so large to suggest that these measures are tapping into dimensions of the same latent construct, which we have tentatively labeled as vocational identity so that it can be embedded in the larger literature on identity development across the life span (see Skorikov & Vondracek, 1998). Thus, we suggest that some persons may experience career-choice difficulties because of a less than fully developed vocational identity (i.e., they have experienced some degree of difficulty in establishing stable, clear, and need-congruent career goals; display immature career attitudes; lack adequate knowledge about their interests, needs, values, talents, and personalities; or feel less than efficacious about their abilities to make effective career decisions).

Finally, we suggest that measures of vocational identity (e.g., Holland et al., 1980), career maturity attitudes (e.g., Crites, 1978), career decision-making self-efficacy (e.g., Betz, Klein, & Taylor, 1996; Taylor & Betz, 1983), problem-solving appraisal (e.g., Heppner & Petersen, 1982), and goal stability (e.g., Robbins & Patton, 1985) can serve as diagnostic markers of the major dimensions of vocational identity. Measures that tap into other critical aspects of goal constructs (e.g., clarity, need-congruence, and role consistency) but that have not been used in the career literature might also help us refine our understanding of vocational identity.

The third dimension, need for career information, seems to be self-explanatory. It is marked primarily by extant measures of need for occupational information (e.g., Chartrand, Robbins, Morrill, & Boggs, 1990; Holland et al., 1980; Jones, 1989) that may reflect more specifically on clients' felt needs for additional (1) practical and school-based experiences that would give them better ideas about potential career directions, (2) consultations with others about occupational possibilities, and (3) information on job opportunities, educational requirements, and other aspects of occupations they are considering (see Chartrand et al., 1990, Table 1).

Although there are no data that address directly the validity of this structural model, the results of two factor analyses can be interpreted through the model's lens. Fuqua and Newman (1989), in a study designed to explore latent dimensions associated with career indecision, conducted a principal component analysis (PCA) of thirteen measures from four primary scales that had previously been found to relate to career indecision: *Career Decision Profile* (CDP; Jones, 1989), *Career Decision Scale* (CDS: Osipow, 1980), *My Vocational Situation* (MVS; Holland et al., 1980) and the *Career Maturity Inventory* (CMI; Crites, 1978). A three-factor solution was chosen as best representing the underlying structure of the correlation matrix. Unfortunately, this solution was somewhat difficult to interpret since several scales showed substantial cross-factor loadings, several measures of career indecision (i.e., dependent rather than independent variables) were included in the component analyses, and a trait anxiety scale that was administered to subjects was not included in the primary analysis. Finally, Fuqua and Newman chose an analytic procedure (PCA) that is primarily a data reduction rather than an exploratory factor analytic strategy, and that has been shown to yield inaccurate solutions when there are fewer than 30 to 40 variables included in the analysis (see Gorsuch, 1990).

Because of these problems, we (along with Paul Gore) reanalyzed Fuqua and Newman's correlation matrix (see their Table 1) using a more appropriate analytic strategy (i.e., principal axis factoring) after eliminating measures of indecision and adding the trait anxiety measure to the correlation matrix that was factored. The resultant solution yielded three factors that were quite consistent with our model. The first factor was defined primarily by the CDP Occupational-Educational Information and Matching Self with Career subscales, and the MVS Occupational Information Scale, and seems clearly to reflect a need for occupational information latent dimension. The second factor was marked primarily by the MVS Vocational Identity Scale (this also had a secondary loading on the first factor), the CDP Self-Clarity, Choice-Work Importance, and Decisiveness subscales, the CDS Indecision subscale, and CMI Attitudes Scale (this scale also showed secondary loadings on the first factor). This factor bears a close resemblance to vocational identity as we have defined it. The third factor had only one salient loading and that was the trait anxiety scale which we hypothesized to be a primary marker of the Negative Affectivity dimension.

More recently, Larson and Majors (1998) conducted a principal components analysis that did not include measures of occupational information. Their analytic strategy (PCA) was probably less than optimal since only six variables were used and latent dimension exploration was the study's primary purpose (see our earlier comments). Nonetheless, the resultant two component solution yielded latent dimensions that Larson and Majors labeled Career and General Agency/Efficacy (component 1) and Career and General Distress (component 2). These components could also be considered as Vocational Identity and Negative Affectivity, respectively, on the basis of the markers of each component (e.g., problem-solving appraisal and career decision-making self-efficacy beliefs both loaded on the first factor, while negative affectivity was a major marker of the second factor).

Although two studies (especially our reanalysis of Fuqua and Newman's correlation matrix) provide indirect support for our tripartite model of career indecision, the model's validity needs to be tested in future research. Should such research support this hypothesized structure for vocational indecision problems, the model has clear counseling implications. For example, we would suggest that there may be at least four diagnostic clusters of persons who seek out vocational assistance, three of which have already been identified through prior cluster analyses. First are clients whose choice problems revolve mainly around needs for occupational information. These clients may benefit maximally from vocational guidance activities that help them to gain additional experiences and to acquire and use effectively information that would allow them to make a congruent career choice. The extensive and detailed occupational and school information available on most well-developed computer guidance systems as well as the opportunities provided for self-assessment (see Gati, 1996) suggest these as potentially cost-efficient and effective interventions for such clients. We would not, however, also hypothesize that clients primarily in need of career information would benefit significantly less from well-developed standard interventions, especially since the secondary loadings that were observed in our re-analysis of Fuqua and Newman's (1989) data suggest that vocational identity formation and attitudinal issues may be significant for some of these clients. We simply hypothesize that other, less intensive forms of intervention may be most cost-effective for some of these clients.

Second are clients whose indecision revolves primarily around problems in identity formation. These persons, we would hypothesize, are likely to represent the types of clients who have been studied most frequently in the career outcome literature and are, therefore, those who are likely to benefit most from the types of well-developed four- to five-session interventions that we described in the first part of this chapter. At least three of the five critical treatment components appear to be specifically useful to vocational identity development (i.e., goal development written exercises, individualized interpretations, and modeling activities), while the other two treatment ingredients (occupational information and support building) may facilitate clients' abilities to make and implement goal-congruent choices.

Third are clients with well-developed vocational identities and with little need for additional career information, but whose choice-making is impaired by dispositional tendencies to experience choice dissatisfaction and anxiety, and to focus on the negative aspects of their career options. We would hypothesize that these clients may not respond optimally to well-developed four- to five-session interventions, and will need help (individually or as an adjunct to standard interventions) gaining insight into how their affective tendencies affect their career decision-making abilities and learning to manage these tendencies in order to be able to arrive at and commit to a career direction (see Brown, Ryan, & McPartland, 1996).

The fourth (indecisive) type of client who combines difficulties on all three dimensions is the client at the career and personal counseling interface who will probably require more intensive psychotherapeutic-like interventions. Such interventions will need to focus on affect and anxiety management strategies as well as on techniques to promote vocational identity development. However, additional interventions may also be required. D. Brown and Brooks (1996) presented a richly detailed case description of a client (Joan) who, we think, closely resembles this type of client. The responses to this case provided by the various contributors to the Brown and Brooks text provide a number of interesting leads for future treatment-oriented research. Savickas (1996) also outlined a model for career service delivery that is consistent with many of our differential treatment hypotheses and may serve as a starting template for future work.

We hope that our structural and diagnostic model stimulates inquiry into its validity and clinical usefulness as well as aids in future research on questions of differential treatment efficacy. A crucial first question that should be addressed in such research is whether well-developed vocational interventions (like those described in this chapter) have differential effects on clients whose problems are defined primarily by negative affectivity or by the negative affectivity, vocational identity, and information constellation. It would, finally, also be informative to test whether problems in different areas of identity formation (e.g., problems in goal-setting versus more extensive vocational identity formation problems) might serve as moderators of standard treatment efficacy, and whether less intensive forms of intervention are effective for persons who seem only to need additional career information.

CONCLUSIONS

We have used a good deal of space in the second section of this chapter discussing research that needs to be done to improve the effectiveness of career interventions. However, we do not want recency effects to dilute the "take-home" message of the first section of the chapter; namely, that brief, four- to five-session, career interventions are demonstrably effective for a large number of clients, especially, if they (1) allow clients to clarify career and life goals in writing, (2) provide clients with individualized interpretations and feedback, (3) give up-to-date information on the requirements and likely consequences of considered career paths, (4) include models who demonstrate effective planning and coping strategies, and (5) help clients develop support networks that will facilitate their abilities to pursue their aspirations. Although the individual and collective effects of these five critical treatment ingredients still need to be verified empirically, we think that practitioners can use this information now to build or fine-tune interventions for their clients.

At the same time, the information that we presented in the second part of the chapter suggests that there is still much that we need to do to ensure that our counseling efforts meet the needs of the greatest number of clients. Specifically, we need research that explores the potential moderating effects of client sex, race/ethnicity, sexual orientation, social economic status, and vocational problem status on the short-term and long-range effectiveness of career interventions. This research must not only use appropriate attribute by treatment designs, but also must employ what we have learned about the content of effective interventions. Should such studies show that outcome effects are moderated by any or all of the above client characteristics, then we need to study further how interventions can be developed or modified to take into account the unique experiences and needs of these groups. We have made some suggestions about how extant career theories and theories that have been developed to explain the career development patterns and needs of specific groups may aid these efforts. We finally presented a tentative vocational-choice problem diagnostic system that may be empirically and clinically useful if moderator analyses demonstrate that, in fact, extant well-developed interventions do not have uniform effects on clients who present with different constellations of underlying choice problems.

REFERENCES

Amatea, E.S., Clark, J.E., & Cross, E.G. (1984). Life-styles: Evaluating a life role planning program for high school students. *Vocational Guidance Quarterly, 32,* 249–259.

American College Testing. (1998). *Interim psychometric handbook for the 3rd edition ACT Career Planning Program.* Iowa City, IA: Author.

Andrews, F.M., & Withey, S.B. (1976). *Social indicators of well-being: Americans' perceptions of life quality.* New York: Plenum Press.

Arbona, C. (1996). Career theory and practice in a multicultural context. In M.L. Savickas & W.B. Walsh (Eds.), *Handbook of career counseling theory and practice* (pp. 45–54). Palo Alto, CA: Davies-Black.

Atanasoff, G.E., & Slaney, R.B. (1980). Three approaches to counselor-free career exploration among college women. *Journal of Counseling Psychology, 27,* 332–339.

Babcock, R.J., & Kaufman, M.A. (1976). Effectiveness of a career course. *Vocational Guidance Quarterly, 24,* 261–266.

Baker, S.B., & Popowicz, C.L. (1983). Meta-analysis as a strategy for evaluating effects of career education interventions. *Vocational Guidance Quarterly, 31,* 178–186.

Berman, M.R., Gelso, C.J., Greenfeig, B.R., & Hirsch, R. (1977). The efficacy of supportive learning environments for returning women: An empirical evaluation. *Journal of Counseling Psychology, 24,* 324–331.

Betsworth, D.G. (1999). Accuracy of self-estimated abilities and the relationship between self-estimated abilities and realism for women. *Journal of Career Assessment, 7,* 35–44.

Betz, N.E., Borgen, F.H., & Harmon, L. (1996). *Skills Confidence Inventory applications and technical guide.* Palo Alto, CA: Consulting Psychologists Press.

Betz, N.E., & Corning, A.F. (1993). The inseparability of "career" and "personal" counseling. *Career Development Quarterly, 42,* 137–142.

Betz, N.E., & Fitzgerald, L.F. (1987). *The career psychology of women.* New York: Academic Press.

Betz, N.E., Klein, K.L., & Taylor, K.M. (1996). Evaluation of a short form of the Career Decision-Making Self-Efficacy Scale. *Journal of Career Assessment, 4,* 47–57.

Betz, N.E., & Serling, D.A. (1993). Construct validity of fear of commitment as an indicator of career indecisiveness. *Journal of Career Assessment, 1,* 21–34.

Blustein, D.L., & Noumair, D.A. (1996). Self and identity in career development: Implications for theory and practice. *Journal of Counseling and Development, 74,* 433–441.

Blustein, D.L., Phillips, S.D., Jobin-Davis, K., Finkelberg, S.L., & Roarke, A.E. (1997). A theory-building investigation of the school-to-work transition. *Counseling Psychologist, 25,* 364–402.

Bowman, S.L. (1995). Career intervention strategies and assessment issues for African Americans. In F.T.L. Leong (Ed.), *Career development and vocational behavior of racial and ethnic minorities* (pp. 137–164). Mahwah, NJ: Erlbaum.

Brenner, D., & Gazda-Grace, P.A. (1979). Career decision making in women as a function of sex composition of career-planning groups. *Measurement and Evaluation in Guidance, 12,* 8–13.

Brown, D., & Brooks, L. (1996). *Career choice and development* (3rd ed.). San Francisco: Jossey-Bass.

Brown, S.D. (1993). Contemporary psychological science and the theory of work adjustment: A proposal for integration and a favor returned. *Journal of Vocational Behavior, 43,* 58–66.

Brown, S.D., & Lent, R.W. (1996). A social cognitive framework for career choice counseling. *Career Development Quarterly, 44,* 354–366.

Brown, S.D., Ryan, N.E., & McPartland, E.B. (1996). Why are so many people happy and what do we do for those who aren't? A reaction to Lightsey (1996). *Counseling Psychologist, 24,* 751–757.

Brunstein, J.C., Schultheiss, O.C., & Grässmann, R. (1998). Personal goals and emotional well-being: The moderating role of motive dispositions. *Journal of Personality and Social Psychology, 75,* 494–508.

Carson, A.D., & Mowsesian, R. (1993). Moderators of the prediction of job satisfaction from congruence: A test of Holland's theory. *Journal of Career Assessment, 1,* 130–144.

Cascio, W.F. (1995). Whither industrial and organizational psychology in a changing world of work? *American Psychologist, 50,* 928–939.

Chartrand, J.M., Martin, W.F., Robbins, S.B., McAuliffe, G.J., Pickering, J.W., & Calliotte, J.A. (1994). Testing a level versus an interactional view of career indecision. *Journal of Career Assessment, 2,* 55–69.

Chartrand, J.M., Robbins, S.B., Morrill, W.H., & Boggs, K. (1990). Development and validation of the Career Factors Inventory. *Journal of Counseling Psychology, 37,* 491–501.

Chartrand, J.M., Rose, M.L., Elliott, T.R., Marmarosh, C., & Caldwell, S. (1993). Peeling back the onion: Personality, problem solving, and career decision-making style correlates of career indecision. *Journal of Career Assessment, 1,* 66–82.

Crites, J.O. (1978). *Career Maturity Inventory.* Monterey, CA: CTB/McGraw-Hill.

Crites, J.O. (1981). *Career counseling: Models, methods, and materials.* New York: McGraw-Hill.

Dawis, R.V., & Lofquist, L.H. (1984). *A psychological theory of work adjustment.* Minneapolis: University of Minnesota Press.

Decker, P.J., & Borgen, F.H. (1993). Dimensions of work appraisal: Stress, strain, coping, job satisfaction, and negative affectivity. *Journal of Counseling Psychology, 40,* 470–478.

Diener, E., Suh, E.M., Lucas, R.E., & Smith, H.L. (1999). Subjective well-being: Three decades of progress. *Psychological Bulletin, 125,* 276–302.

Dukstein, R.D., & O'Brien, K.M. (1995). *The contribution of multiple role self-efficacy and gender role attitudes to women's career development.* Unpublished manuscript.

Emmons, R.A. (1986). Personal strivings: An approach to personality and subjective well-being. *Journal of Personality and Social Psychology, 51,* 1058–1068.

Farmer, H.S. (1976). What inhibits achievement and career motivation in women? *Counseling Psychologist, 6,* 12–15.

Ford, M.E. (1992). *Motivating humans: Goals, emotions, and personal agency beliefs.* Newbury Park, CA: Sage.

Fouad, N.A., & Bingham, R.P. (1995). Career counseling with racial and ethnic minorities. In W.B. Walsh & S.H. Osipow (Eds.), *Handbook of vocational psychology* (2nd ed., pp. 331–365). Mahwah, NJ: Erlbaum.

Fretz, B.R. (1981). Evaluating the effectiveness of career interventions [Monograph]. *Journal of Counseling Psychology, 28,* 77–90.

Fuqua, D.R., & Newman, J.L. (1989). An examination of the relations among career subscales. *Journal of Counseling Psychology, 36,* 487–491.

Gainor, K.A., & Lent, R.W. (1998). Social cognitive expectations and racial identity attitudes in predicting the math choice intentions of black college students. *Journal of Counseling Psychology, 45,* 403–413.

Ganster, D.C., & Lovell, J.E. (1978). An evaluation of a career development seminar using Crites' Career Maturity Inventory. *Journal of Vocational Behavior, 13,* 172–180.

Gati, I. (1996). Computer-assisted career counseling: Challenges and prospects. In M.L. Savickas & W.B. Walsh (Eds.), *Handbook of career counseling theory and practice* (pp. 169–190). Palo Alto, CA: Davies-Black.

Gati, I., Fassa, N., & Houminer, D. (1995). Applying decision theory to career counseling practice: The sequential elimination approach. *Career Development Quarterly, 43,* 211–220.

Gilbert, L.A., & Brownson, C. (1998). Current perspectives on women's multiple roles. *Journal of Career Assessment, 6,* 433–448.

Glaize, D.L., & Myrick, R.D. (1984). Interpersonal groups or computers? A study of career maturity and career decidedness. *Vocational Guidance Quarterly, 32,* 168–176.

Gold, J.M., & Scanlon, C.R. (1993). Psychological distress and counseling duration of career and noncareer clients. *Career Development Quarterly, 42,* 186–191.

Gorsuch, R.L. (1990). Common factor analysis versus component analysis: Some well and little known facts. *Multivariate Behavioral Research, 25,* 33–39.

Hackett, G., & Byars, A.M. (1996). Social cognitive theory and the career development of African American women. *Career Development Quarterly, 44,* 322–340.

Handschin, B. (1996). *The role of self-estimated and tested abilities in vocational choice in adults at four time periods postcounseling.* Unpublished doctoral dissertation, University of Minnesota, Minneapolis.

Harmon, L.W., Borgen, F.H., Berreth, J.M., King, J.C., Schauer, D., & Ward, C.C. (1996). The Skills Confidence Inventory: A measure of self-efficacy. *Journal of Career Assessment, 4,* 457–477.

Harmon, L.W., Hansen, J.C., Borgen, F.H., & Hammer, A.L. (1994). *Strong Interest Inventory: Applications and technical guide.* Palo Alto, CA: Consulting Psychologists Press.

Hedges, L.V., & Olkin, I. (1985). *Statistical methods for meta-analysis.* New York: Academic Press.

Helms, J.E., & Parham, T.A. (1990). Black Racial Identity Attitude Scale (Form RIAS-B). In J.E. Helms (Ed.), *Black and white racial identity* (pp. 245–247). New York: Greenwood Press.

Heppner, P.P., Kivlighan, D.M., Jr., & Wampold, B.E. (1999). *Research design in counseling* (2nd ed.). Belmont, CA: Wadsworth.

Heppner, P.P., & Petersen, C.H. (1982). The development and implications of a personal problem-solving inventory. *Journal of Counseling Psychology, 29,* 66–75.

Holland, J.L. (1991a). *Self-Directed Search (SDS) Form CP: Computer Version.* Tampa, FL: Psychological Assessment Resources.

Holland, J.L. (1991b). *Self-Directed Search (SDS) Form CP: Interpretive Report.* Tampa, FL: Psychological Assessment Resources.

Holland, J.L. (1996a). Exploring careers with a typology: What we have learned and some new directions. *American Psychologist, 51,* 397–406.

Holland, J.L. (1996b). Integrating career theory and practice: The current situation and some potential remedies. In M.L. Savickas & W.B. Walsh (Eds.), *Handbook of career counseling theory and practice* (pp. 1–11). Palo Alto, CA: Davies-Black.

Holland, J.L. (1997). *Making vocational choices* (3rd ed.). Tampa, FL: Psychological Assessment Resources.

Holland, J.L., Daiger, D.C., & Power, P.G. (1980). *My vocational situation.* Palo Alto, CA: Consulting Psychologists Press.

Holland, J.L., & Holland, J.E. (1977). Vocational indecision: More evidence and speculation. *Journal of Counseling Psychology, 24,* 404–414.

Hutchinson, N.L., Freeman, J.G., Downey, K.H., & Kilbreath, L. (1992). Development and evaluation of an instructional module to promote career maturity for youth with learning difficulties. *Canadian Journal of Counselling, 26,* 290–299.

Jones, L.K. (1989). Measuring a three-dimensional construct of career indecision among college students: A revision of the Vocational Decision Scale—The Career Decision Profile. *Journal of Counseling Psychology, 36,* 477–486.

Kahn, S.E., & Ward, V.G. (1983). Evaluation of group vocational counseling for women. *Journal of Employment Counseling, 20,* 34–41.

Kerr, B., & Erb, C. (1991). Career counseling with academically talented students: Effects of a value-based intervention. *Journal of Counseling Psychology, 38,* 309–314.

Krumboltz, J.D. (1996). A learning theory of career counseling. In M.L. Savickas & W.B. Walsh (Eds.), *Handbook of career counseling theory and practice* (pp. 55–80). Palo Alto, CA: Davies-Black.

Larson, L.M., Heppner, P.P., Ham, T., & Dugan, K. (1988). Investigating multiple subtypes of career indecision through cluster analysis. *Journal of Counseling Psychology, 35,* 439–446.

Larson, L.M., & Majors, M.S. (1998). Applications of the Coping with Career Indecision instrument with adolescents. *Journal of Career Assessment, 6,* 163–179.

Lefcourt, L.A., & Harmon, L.W. (1992). *Self-efficacy expectations for role management (SEERM): Measure development.* Paper presented at the meeting of the American Psychological Association, Toronto, Canada.

Lent, R.W., Brown, S.D., & Hackett, G. (1994). Toward a unifying social cognitive theory of career and academic interest, choice, and performance [Monograph]. *Journal of Vocational Behavior, 45,* 79–122.

Lent, R.W., Brown, S.D., & Hackett, G. (1996). Career development from a social cognitive perspective. In D. Brown & L. Brooks (Eds.), *Career choice and development* (3rd ed., pp. 373–421). San Francisco: Jossey-Bass.

Lent, R.W., Larkin, K.C., & Hasegawa, C.S. (1986). Effects of a "focused interest" career course approach for college students. *Vocational Guidance Quarterly, 34,* 151–159.

Lent, R.W., O'Brien, K.M., & Fassinger, R.E. (1998). School-to-work transition and counseling psychology. *Counseling Psychologist, 26,* 489–494.

Leong, F.T.L., & Brown, M.T. (1995). Theoretical issues in cross-cultural career development: Cultural validity and cultural specificity. In W.B. Walsh & S.H. Osipow (Eds.), *Handbook of vocational psychology* (2nd ed., pp. 143–180). Mahwah, NJ: Erlbaum.

Locke, E.A., & Latham, G.P. (1990). *A theory of goal setting and task performance.* Englewood Cliffs, NJ: Prentice-Hall.

Lucas, M.S. (1993). A validation of types of career indecision at a counseling center. *Journal of Counseling Psychology, 40,* 440–446.

Lucas, M.S., & Epperson, D.L. (1990). Types of vocational undecidedness: A replication and refinement. *Journal of Counseling Psychology, 37,* 382–388.

Lunneborg, P.W. (1983). Career counseling techniques. In W.B. Walsh & S.H. Osipow (Eds.), *Handbook of vocational psychology* (pp. 41–76). Hillsdale, NJ: Erlbaum.

Luzzo, D.A. (1993). Ethnic differences in college students' perceptions of barriers to career development. *Journal of Multicultural Counseling and Development, 21,* 227–236.

Luzzo, D.A. (1996). Exploring the relationship between perception of occupational barriers and career development. *Journal of Career Development, 22,* 239–248.

Luzzo, D.A., Funk, D.P., & Strang, J. (1996). Attributional retraining increases career decision-making self-efficacy. *Career Development Quarterly, 44,* 378–386.

Luzzo, D.A., & Hutcheson, K.G. (1996). Causal attributions and sex differences associated with perceptions of occupational barriers. *Journal of Counseling and Development, 75,* 124–130.

Luzzo, D.A., & Taylor, M. (1993–1994). Effects of verbal persuasion on the career self-efficacy of college freshmen. *California Association for Counseling and Development (CACD) Journal, 14,* 31–34.

Manuele-Adkins, C. (1992). Career counseling is personal counseling. *Career Development Quarterly, 40,* 313–323.

McWhirter, E.H. (1997). Perceived barriers to education and career: Ethnic and gender differences. *Journal of Vocational Behavior, 50,* 124–140.

McWhirter, E.H., Hackett, G., & Bandalos, D.L. (1998). A causal model of the educational plans and career expectations of Mexican American high school girls. *Journal of Counseling Psychology, 45,* 166–181.

McWhirter, E.H., & Luzzo, D.A. (1996, August). *Examining perceived barriers, career interest-aspiration and aspiration-major congruence.* Paper presented at the meeting of the American Psychological Association, Toronto, Canada.

McWhirter, E.H., Torres, D., & Rasheed, S. (1998). Assessing barriers to women's career adjustment. *Journal of Career Assessment, 6,* 449–479.

Meara, N.M., & Patton, M.J. (1994). Contributions of the working alliance in the practice of career counseling. *Career Development Quarterly, 43,* 161–177.

Meldahl, J.M., & Muchinsky, P.M. (1997). The neurotic dimension of vocational indecision: Gender comparability? *Journal of Career Assessment, 5,* 317–331.

Morrow, S.L., Gore, P.A., Jr., & Campbell, B.W. (1996). The application of a sociocognitive framework to the career development of lesbian women and gay men. *Journal of Vocational Behavior, 48,* 136–148.

Multon, K.D., Heppner, M.J., & Lapan, R.T. (1995). An empirical derivation of career decision subtypes in a high school sample. *Journal of Vocational Behavior, 47,* 76–92.

Myers, R.A., Lindeman, R.H., Thompson, A.S., & Patrick, T.A. (1975). Effects of educational and career exploration system on vocational maturity. *Journal of Vocational Behavior, 6,* 245–254.

Nolen-Hoeksema, S., Parker, L.E., & Larson, J. (1994). Ruminative coping with depressed mood following loss. *Journal of Personality and Social Psychology, 67,* 92–104.

Oliver, L.W., & Spokane, A.R. (1988). Career-intervention outcome: What contributes to client gain? *Journal of Counseling Psychology, 35,* 447–462.

Orput, D. (1998). *The relationship between multiple role self-efficacy beliefs and career commitment based on a joint analysis of career and family development.* Unpublished doctoral dissertation, Loyola University, Chicago.

Osipow, S.H. (1980). *Manual for the Career Decision Scale* (2nd ed.). Columbus, OH: Marathon Consulting and Press.

Palmer, S., & Cochran, L. (1988). Parents as agents of career development. *Journal of Counseling Psychology, 35,* 71–76.

Phillips, S.D. (1992). Career counseling: Choice and implementation. In S.D. Brown & R.W. Lent (Eds.), *Handbook of counseling psychology* (2nd ed., pp. 513–547). New York: Wiley.

Pierce, G.R., Ptacek, J.T., Taylor, B., Yee, P.L., Henderson, C.A., Lauventi, H.J., & Bourdeau, C.M. (1998). The role of dispositional and situational factors in cognitive interference. *Journal of Personality and Social Psychology, 75,* 1016–1031.

Pope, M. (1995). Career interventions for gay and lesbian clients: A synopsis of practice knowledge and research needs. *Career Development Quarterly, 44,* 191–203.

Powers, R.J. (1978). Enhancement of former drug abusers' career development through structured group counseling. *Journal of Counseling Psychology, 25,* 585–587.

Prediger, D.J. (1999). Basic structure of work-relevant abilities. *Journal of Counseling Psychology, 46,* 173–184.

Richardson, M.S. (1993). Work in people's lives: A location for counseling psychologists. *Journal of Counseling Psychology, 40,* 425–433.

Richie, B.S., Fassinger, R.E., Linn, S.G., Johnson, J., Prosser, J., & Robinson, S. (1997). Persistence, connection, and passion: A qualitative study of the career development of highly achieving African American–Black and White women. *Journal of Counseling Psychology, 44,* 133–148.

Robbins, S.B., & Patton, M.J. (1985). Self-psychology and career development: Construction of the superiority and goal instability scales as measures of defects in self. *Journal of Personality Assessment, 53,* 122–132.

Rodriguez, M., & Blocher, D. (1988). A comparison of two approaches to enhancing career maturity in Puerto Rican college women. *Journal of Counseling Psychology, 35,* 275–280.

Roe, A. (1956). *The psychology of occupations.* New York: Wiley.

Rounds, J.B., Jr. (1990). The comparative and combined utility of work value and interest data in career counseling with adults. *Journal of Vocational Behavior, 37,* 32–45.

Rounds, J.B., Jr., & Tinsley, H.E.A. (1984). Diagnosis and treatment of vocational problems. In S.D. Brown & R.W. Lent (Eds.), *Handbook of counseling psychology* (pp. 137–177). New York: Wiley.

Ryan, N.E. (1999). *Career counseling and career choice goal attainment: A meta-analytically derived model for career counseling practice.* Unpublished doctoral dissertation, Loyola University, Chicago.

Salomone, P.R. (1982). Difficult cases in career counseling: II. The indecisive client. *Personnel and Guidance Journal, 60,* 496–500.

Savickas, M.L. (1993). Career counseling in the postmodern era. *Journal of Cognitive Psychotherapy: An International Quarterly, 7,* 205–215.

Savickas, M.L. (1996). A framework for linking career theory and practice. In M.L. Savickas & W.B. Walsh (Eds.), *Handbook of career counseling theory and practice* (pp. 191–208). Palo Alto, CA: Davies-Black.

Seligman, M.E.P. (1995). The effectiveness of psychotherapy: The Consumer Reports study. *American Psychologist, 50,* 965–974.

Serling, D.A., & Betz, N.E. (1990). Development and evaluation of a measure of fear of commitment. *Journal of Counseling Psychology, 37,* 91–97.

Sherry, P., & Staley, K. (1984). Career exploration groups: An outcome study. *Journal of College Student Personnel, 25,* 155–159.

Simon, S.B., Howe, L., & Kirschenbaum, H. (1972). *Values clarification.* New York: Hart.

Skorikov, V., & Vondracek, F.W. (1998). Vocational identity development: Its relationship to other identity domains and to overall identity development. *Journal of Career Assessment, 6,* 13–35.

Smith, R.D., & Evans, J.R. (1973). Comparison of experimental group guidance and individual counseling as facilitators of vocational development. *Journal of Counseling Psychology, 20,* 202–208.

Spielberger, C.D., Gorsuch, R.L., & Lushene, R. (1968). *State-Trait Anxiety Inventory.* Palo Alto, CA: Consulting Psychologists Press.

Spokane, A.R., & Oliver, L.W. (1983). The outcomes of vocational intervention. In W.B. Walsh & S.H. Osipow (Eds.), *Handbook of vocational psychology* (pp. 99–116). Hillsdale, NJ: Erlbaum.

Steinberg, L., Dornbush, S.M., & Brown, B.B. (1992). Ethnic differences in adolescent achievement: An ecological perspective. *American Psychologist, 47,* 723–729.

Stickel, S.A., & Bonett, R.M. (1991). Gender differences in career self-efficacy: Combining a career with home and family. *Journal of College Student Development, 32,* 297–301.

Subich, L.M. (1993). How personal is career counseling? *Career Development Quarterly, 42,* 129–131.

Super, D.E., Savickas, M.L., & Super, C.M. (1996). In D. Brown & L. Brooks (Eds.), *Career choice and development* (3rd ed., pp. 121–178). San Francisco: Jossey-Bass.

Swanson, J.L. (1995). The process and outcome of career counseling. In W.B. Walsh & S.H. Osipow (Eds.), *Handbook of vocational psychology* (2nd ed., pp. 217–259). Mahwah, NJ: Erlbaum.

Swanson, J.L., Daniels, K.K., & Tokar, D.M. (1996). Assessing perceptions of career-related barriers: The Career Barriers Inventory. *Journal of Career Assessment, 4,* 219–244.

Swanson, J.L., & Tokar, D.M. (1991a). College students' perceptions of barriers to career development. *Journal of Vocational Behavior, 38,* 92–106.

Swanson, J.L., & Tokar, D.M. (1991b). Development and initial validation of the Career Barriers Inventory. *Journal of Vocational Behavior, 39,* 344–361.

Swanson, J.L., & Woitke, M.B. (1997). Theory into practice in career assessment for women: Assessment and interventions regarding perceived career barriers. *Journal of Career Assessment, 5,* 443–462.

Taylor, K.M., & Betz, N.E. (1983). Applications of self-efficacy theory to the understanding and treatment of career indecision. *Journal of Vocational Behavior, 22,* 63–81.

Vondracek, F.W., & Kawasaki, T. (1995). Toward a comprehensive framework for adult career development theory and intervention. In W.B. Walsh & S.H. Osipow (Eds.), *Handbook of vocational psychology* (2nd ed., pp. 111–142). Mahwah, NJ: Erlbaum.

Watson, D., & Clark, L.A. (1984). Negative affectivity: The disposition to experience aversive emotional states. *Psychological Bulletin, 96,* 465–490.

Watson, D., Clark, L.A., & Tellegen, A. (1988). Development and validation of brief measures of positive and negative affect: The PANAS scales. *Journal of Personality and Social Psychology, 54,* 1063–1070.

Watson, D., & Tellegen, A. (1985). Toward a consensual structure of mood. *Psychological Bulletin, 98,* 219–235.

Whiston, S.C., Sexton, T.L., & Lasoff, D.L. (1998). Career-intervention outcome: A replication and extension of Oliver and Spokane (1988). *Journal of Counseling Psychology, 45,* 150–165.

Wilson, R.C. (1987). Career maturity gains of adult basic education students receiving career development education. *Adult Literacy and Basic Education, 11,* 23–31.

Zytowski, D.G. (1977). The effects of being interest-inventoried. *Journal of Vocational Behavior, 11,* 153–157.

CHAPTER 24

Process, Outcome, and Methodology in Group Counseling Research

DENNIS M. KIVLIGHAN, JR.
MADELYN N. COLEMAN
D. CRAIG ANDERSON

Group treatment is a fundamental aspect of the work of counseling psychologists. In a survey of 402 members of Division 17 (Counseling Psychology) approximately 47% of the respondents reported performing group counseling as a regular part of their professional practices. Further, respondents indicated that group counseling was an important aspect of their professional identity, with younger counseling psychologists especially emphasizing the importance of group counseling (Fitzgerald & Osipow, 1986). In addition, 5% of the articles published in the *Journal of Counseling Psychology* (JCP) address group counseling. These figures suggest that counseling psychologists have an important interest in group counseling and that a significant amount of empirical investigation has focused on this topic.

In this chapter, we will focus on three major areas of group counseling research and in each discuss not only the research findings but also draw implications for group counseling practice. The first part of the chapter will be devoted to the large body of literature addressing questions of group counseling outcome (e.g., Is group counseling effective? How effective is group counseling versus other modes of counseling? With whom is group counseling most effective?) To delimit this somewhat overwhelming task, we will attend primarily to the meta-analytic studies of outcome questions that have appeared over the past 10 or so years. In addition, prior reviews and theoretical writings will be used to complement the meta-analytic findings.

The second part of the chapter will then focus on research on group process, drawing primarily on research stimulated by, and derived from, Yalom's hypotheses about critical therapeutic factors in group counseling. The third, and final, section of the chapter will attend to some of the complexities involved in conducting research on group counseling process and outcome highlighting specifically four critical methodological issues and suggesting some design and statistical solutions.

GROUP COUNSELING OUTCOME

Historically, reviews of group counseling research have addressed questions of group counseling outcome by qualitatively summarizing the studies in this area. In the 1990s, reviewers of group counseling research began to use meta-analysis to review, quantitatively, group counseling outcome studies. Meta-analysis is "a general conceptual approach to problems of summarizing, integrating, and testing practical questions and theoretical issues with the results of previous research" (Mullen, Driskell, & Salas, 1998, p. 213). Using meta-analysis to test practical (Is design quality related to group counseling effect size?) and theoretical (Is the size of the group related to group counseling effect size?) questions represents a significant advantage over qualitative reviews of the group counseling literature.

Meta-analysts have addressed the following outcome questions: (1) Is group counseling effective? (2) What are the relative effects of group and individual counseling? and (3) Is group counseling effective with specific client populations? The eight meta-analyses of the group therapy outcome literature that we identified addressed each of these questions. All eight meta-analyses were published since 1990; six of the eight analyses were published between 1995 and 1998.

The most comprehensive study, a meta-analysis of group sensitivity training (GST) was conducted by Faith, Wong, and Carpenter (1995). The most current, and one of the most thoughtful studies, was a meta-analysis conducted by McRoberts, Burlingame, and Hoag (1998). These meta-analyses are, on the whole, current, and afford a good overview of group therapy outcome research. In many ways, these analyses represent an attempt to respond to Barrett, Hampe, and Miller's (1978) classic call for testing differential therapeutic treatments. In other words: Which means of treatment, provided by what kind of therapist(s), with which style of intervention, is most efficacious for what specific set of problems, with what specific population? This is an increasingly germane concern in the age of managed care, as the field attempts to discern specific forms of treatment that are both cost effective and clinically efficacious (Fettes & Petters, 1992; McRoberts et al., 1998; Tillitski, 1990).

The meta-analysis reviewed use the d statistic as a measure of effect size. Usually, this statistic is calculated by subtracting the mean of the treated participants (e.g., those in group treatment) from the mean of the control participants and dividing this difference by the pooled standard deviation of the treatment and control groups. A similar principal is used when comparing group and individual treatments. Specifically, the mean of the group counseling participants is subtracted from the mean of individual counseling participants and this difference is divided by the pooled standard deviation of the individual counseling and group counseling conditions. The interpretation of these effect-size calculations is done in relation to standard deviation units. For example, if group counseling has an effect size of 1.50 when compared to control conditions, this would mean that the average person in the group treatment condition scores 1.5 standard deviations higher than the average person in the control condition.

Tillitski (1990) opened the decade with a frequently cited, ground-breaking meta-analysis of group therapy outcome research. Because Tillitski only used studies that directly compared group, individual, and control treatments, only nine studies were involved in the meta-analysis. Prior to this study, meta-analysts used between-study comparisons (e.g., comparing the effect sizes of group and individual treatments from widely differing studies) whereas this study used a more compelling within-study approach to treatment comparison. The findings suggested that group (effect size = 1.35) and individual (effect size = 1.35) forms of treatment were both efficacious when compared to control groups and were equal in their effectiveness. Tillitski also found some indication that therapy groups were comparatively more efficacious with adolescents, with an opposite trend toward individual counseling being superior when children and adult subjects were involved.

In 1991, Gorey and Cryns conducted a meta-analysis of group therapy with depressed clients, 65 years and older, making use of 19 studies. The authors reported that group therapy appeared to have a statistically and clinically significant effect on the depressive symptoms of the clients studied, accounting for 32% of the variance in change in affective states. The findings also indicated that (1) small therapy groups (< 6 clients) were more efficacious with clients who live alone, or were only moderately depressed, and (2) brief group interventions were more efficacious than long-term group interventions with this population.

Fettes and Peters (1992) conducted a meta-analysis of research examining group therapy with clients presenting with bulimic symptoms. Forty studies were incorporated into this analysis. In summary, the results of the study indicated that group therapy for bulimic symptoms was moderately beneficial (effect size = 0.75), with treated groups improving significantly more than untreated control groups. The findings also suggested that treatment gains were sustained and even increased, for a year following group therapy termination, with effect sizes of 0.89 for measures taken three to six months after treatment and effect sizes of 1.17 for measures taken 9 to 12 months after treatment. The analysis also showed that group treatment was most effective when combined with other forms of treatment (effect size = 0.75). The magnitude of group effect did not appear to be associated with treatment type, study location, method of soliciting subjects, therapist gender, or experimental design. The findings were, however, equivocal regarding the comparative efficacy of group therapy versus individual and drug therapy for bulimia. Nevertheless, it does appear that group therapy is an efficacious form of treatment for bulimia, although the exact mechanisms of effect are still unclear.

Faith et al. (1995) conducted an important meta-analysis of group sensitivity training (GST). This was a comparatively large meta-analysis, incorporating 63 studies with a total of 3,238 participants. In addition to its large scope, this study also appears to be of importance in that it has been argued that the therapeutic processes used in sensitivity groups are quite similar to those used in a wide range of interpersonal therapy groups (Lieberman, 1976; Shaffer & Galinsky, 1989). As a result, the findings of this study have the potential to be generalized across a wide range of interpersonal group treatments. In summary, the findings of the analysis indicated that GST had a positive therapeutic effect (effect size = 0.62), and is comparable in its therapeutic effect size to other means of psychotherapeutic treatment. Other findings of the study suggested that effect sizes were positively associated with both the number of sessions and the size of the group. The authors speculated that more sessions and larger groups would increase the potential for feedback, and thereby increase the therapeutic effect of GST treatments. As with the other studies, Faith et al. suggested that further research is needed to more fully understand the process and the therapeutic mechanisms of GST.

De Jong and Gorey (1996) conducted a meta-analysis of short-term and long-term group therapy with female survivors of childhood sexual abuse. Seven studies were used in the analysis. Given the paucity of available studies in this domain, the results were equivocal. The findings suggested that both group counseling and individual counseling have an effect on the survivors' affect and self-esteem. However, the effects of short-term (effect size = 0.79) and long-term (effect size = 0.66) counseling were not statistically different. This suggests that both type of treatments are useful in working with this client population.

In 1997, Reeker, Ensing, and Elliott conducted a meta-analysis of group therapy with sexually abused children. The authors incorporated 15 studies in their analysis. The findings suggested that therapy groups for sexually abused children had a clinically significant treatment effect (effect size = 0.79), with a trend towards larger effects in exclusively female groups. The authors speculated that these groups might be efficacious because they address issues of isolation and stigmatization more effectively than individual therapy. Fettes and Peters (1992) made a similar observation about the possible therapeutic value of group therapy for bulimics.

Hoag and Burlingame (1997) conducted a very thorough meta-analysis of the effectiveness of child and adolescent treatment groups. Fifty-six studies were used in the analysis. What was of note about this study was the manner in which the authors tried to assess for both the general effectiveness of group therapy and a number of specific therapeutic factors. In this sense, the authors were pushing the literature toward a better understanding of the process of group therapy, as well toward a better response to Barrett et al.'s (1978) call for differential therapeutic treatments. The findings in the first part of the analysis indicated that children and adolescents in group therapy improved significantly more than controls or those treated with placebos (effect size = 0.61). Treatment provided in clinical settings (effect size = 1.13) was more efficacious than treatment provided in school settings (effect size = 0.53). Furthermore, counseling groups (effect size = 0.65) were found to be more effective than psychoeducational groups (effect size = 0.40). There were also positive associations found between therapist allegiance to the particular forms of treatments being studied and effect sizes. Finally, the findings indicated that the more recent studies seemed to report higher effect sizes than older studies.

The most recent, and one of the most thoughtful meta-analyses of the group therapy literature, was a study published by McRoberts et al. in 1998. What was of note about this study was the manner in which the authors tried to assess for both the general effectiveness of group therapy and a number of specific therapeutic factors. The McRoberts et al. study specifically examined the comparative effectiveness of individual and group psychotherapy. Unfortunately, as the authors commented, there were only 23 studies in the literature that qualified for their meta-analysis. Their findings were consistent with previous studies, in that both forms of treatment were found to be efficacious, without a clear advantage for either form of treatment. Both individual and group psychotherapy subjects performed significantly better than wait-list controls, with no statistical difference found for the effect size of either treatment. The effect size for the group versus individual comparison was 0.01. Nevertheless, a few important relationships did appear. McRoberts et al. examined a number of moderating variables to assess for possible relationships with effect size. The vast majority of these potential relationships were not significant. Only study year was reliably related to the difference between group and individual treatment effect sizes. Specifically, in early studies, group treatment was more effective than individual treatment (effect size = -0.22), while in later studies individual counseling had larger effect sizes (effect size = 0.11).

In summary, these eight meta-analyses represent an important break from the narrative tradition of earlier reviews, with each study attempting to advance the literature through various quantitative analyses, incorporating various statistical strategies. In doing so, each of the articles spoke to aspects of the differential treatment called for by Barrett et al. (1978), but a summary of the analyses suggests there is still much to learn. In this sense, some of the conflicts between study findings, give both researchers and practitioners alike, greater insight into the differential mechanisms of group therapy. For example, Gorey and Cryns (1991) found that small therapy groups were more efficacious with elderly clients who lived alone, and that brief group interventions were more efficacious than longer term group interventions with depressed elderly subjects. By contrast, Faith et al. (1995), in their analysis of group sensitivity training (GST), with nonclinical populations, found a positive association between number of sessions and group size and outcome. Finally, the findings from these meta-analyses were consistent with the findings of previous group outcome research, in that group therapy has been consistently found to be an efficacious form of therapy, with effect sizes similar to other forms of psychological and educational interventions (Faith et al., 1995). Although the field has much to learn, these meta-analyses did a good job of building upon one another, and in doing so, in advancing the field in an informed manner. Nevertheless, there is much to be determined about various client, therapist, group, methodological, and treatment variables. Quantitatively, there is a clear need for more group therapy outcome research; and differentially, there is a need for more specific group therapy outcome research (McRoberts et al., 1998).

GROUP COUNSELING PROCESS

Yalom (1995) is the single most influential theorist in the group counseling arena. His approach to group counseling is organized around 11 therapeutic factors or processes (see Table 24.1) and how these factors are hypothesized to be perceived as differentially important as a function of (1) type of group (out-patient versus in-patient), (2) stage of group development, and (3) individual differences among group members (Yalom, 1995).

Additionally, Yalom (1995) considered interpersonal learning and group cohesiveness to be "so important and complex" (p. 2) that he treated these two factors separately from the remaining therapeutic factors. Following Yalom's lead we review the research on the comparative perceived

Table 24.1   Description of Therapeutic Factors

Therapeutic Factors (Yalom, 1975)	Therapeutic Factors (Bloch & Crouch, 1985)	Definition
Instillation of hope	Instillation of hope	Member recognizes other members' improvement and that the group can be helpful; member develops optimism for his or her own improvement.
Universality	Universality	Member perceives that other members share similar feelings or problems.
Imparting information	Guidance	Advice giving by therapist or fellow members.
Altruism	Altruism	Member gains a positive view of himself or herself through extending help to others in group.
Corrective recapitulation of primary family group	_____	Member experiences the opportunity to reenact some critical familial incident with members of the group in a corrective manner.
Development of socializing techniques	Learning from interpersonal action	Group provides members with an environment that allows the member to interact in a more adaptive manner.
Interpersonal learning-input	Learning from interpersonal action	Member gains personal insight through other members' sharing his or her perception of the member.
Interpersonal learning-output	Learning from interpersonal action	Group provides members with an environment that allows the member to interact in a more adaptive manner.
Cohesiveness	Acceptance	Feeling of togetherness provided and experienced by the group.
Catharsis	Catharsis	Member releases feelings about past or here-and-now experiences; this release leads to member feeling better.
Existential factors	_____	Member ultimately accepts that he or she has to take responsibility for his or her own life.
Imitative behavior	Vicarious learning	Member learns through the observation of others learning experiences.
	Self-understanding	Member gains insight into his or her behaviors or cognitions.
	Self-disclosure	Member reveals personal information to other group members.

Table 24.2 Most Important Therapeutic Factors in Inpatient Versus Outpatient Counseling Groups

Author(s)	Type of Group	Inpatient/ Outpatient	Assessment	Factor System	Highest Ranked Factors
Bloch & Reibstein (1980)	Psychotherapy (neurotic & personality disorders)	Outpatient	Critical Incidents Questionnaire (QIC)	Bloch, Reibstein, Crouch, Holroyd, & Themen (1979)	1. Self-understanding 2. Self-disclosure 3. Learning from interpersonal actions
Bonney, Randall, & Cleveland (1986)	Former incest victims	Outpatient	Yalom Q-Sort	Yalom (1975)	1. Self-understanding 2. Cohesiveness 3. Family reenactment
Brabender, Albrecht, Sillitti, Cooper, & Kramer (1983)	Short-term psychotherapy	Inpatient	CIQ	Bloch et al. (1979)	1. Vicarious learning 2. Acceptance 3. Learning from interpersonal actions
Colijn, Hoencamp, Snijders, Van Der Spek, & Duivenvoorden (1991)	Long-term psychotherapy	Inpatient (41%) and outpatient (32% day treatment)	Dutch version of Yalom's 60-item questionnaire	Yalom (1975)	1. Catharsis 2. Interpersonal learning (input) 3. Self-understanding
Kahn, Webster, & Storck (1986)	Psychodynamic psychotherapy (awareness) & structured psychoeducational (focus)	Inpatient	Modified questionnaire	Modified system (Lieberman, Yalom, & Miles [1975])	Awareness: 1. Universality 2. Catharisis (general) 3. Altruism Focus: 1. Universality 2. Involvement 3. Instillation of hope
Kapur, Miller, & Mitchell (1988)	Long-term psychotherapy	Inpatient & outpatient	Modified version of Yalom's questionnaire	Yalom (1975)	Inpatient: 1. Identification 2. Family reenactment 3. Guidance Outpatient: 1. Identification 2. Altruism 3. Guidance
Macaskill (1982)	Borderline patients psychotherapy	Inpatient	Abbreviated version of Yalom's questionnaire	Yalom (1975)	1. Self-understanding 2. Altruism 3. Instillation of hope
MacDevitt & Sanislow (1987)	Offenders' personal growth group	Inpatient	Yalom's questionnaire	Yalom (1975)	
Marcovitz & Smith (1983)	Short-term psychotherapy	Inpatient	Q-Sort	Yalom (1975)	1. Catharsis 2. Cohesiveness 3. Altruism
McLeod & Ryan (1993)	Short-term therapy group for older women	Outpatient	Q-Sort	Yalom (1975)	1. Existential awareness 2. Cohesiveness 3. Instillation of hope

Table 24.2 (Continued)

Author(s)	Type of Group	Inpatient/ Outpatient	Assessment	Factor System	Highest Ranked Factors
Shectman, Bar-El, & Hadar (1997)	Counseling and psychoeducational groups for adolescents	Outpatient	CIQ	Yalom (1985)	Counseling: 1. Interpersonal learning 2. Catharsis 3. Socializing techniques Psychoeducational: 1. Interpersonal learning 2. Catharsis 3. Socializing techniques
Sherry & Hurley (1976)	Personal growth group	Outpatient	Q-Sort	Yalom (1975)	1. Interpersonal learning (input) 2. Catharsis

value of the therapeutic factors and then turn to studies that specifically address the effects of interpersonal learning and group cohesiveness.

The Influence of Group Type on Therapeutic Factors

By far, the majority of the therapeutic factors (TF) literature is concerned with Yalom's first hypothesis (i.e., that the importance that group members place on TFs will vary as a function of group type). Studies that have addressed this hypothesis are summarized in Table 24.2. A recent review of this research (Crouch, Bloch, & Wanlass, 1994) concluded that although findings varied somewhat on the basis of how TFs were assessed, self-understanding, learning through interpersonal interaction, and self-disclosure were rated as most important by out-patient group clients. On the other hand, in-patient clients tended to view cohesiveness, altruism, universality, and instillation of hope as most helpful. In addition, we located studies not reviewed by Crouch et al. (1994).

The MacDevitt and Sanislow (1987) study provides a good example of the complexities in trying to examine the comparative value of therapeutic factors. These authors examined groups conducted with offenders and found differences in helpfulness ratings as a function of restrictiveness of incarceration that are only partially consistent with the data summarized by Bloch and Crouch (1985). There were four levels of restriction ranging from probation (least restrictive) to segregation (most restrictive). Only those members who attended a minimum of four group sessions were included in the study. Although, it is not explicitly stated, it is assumed that the questionnaire (i.e., Yalom's 60-item Q-sort) was completed at the conclusion of the group therapy experiences.

Across the four groups, catharsis and existential awareness were among the top-rated therapeutic factors. The two least restricted groups (i.e., probation and minimum security) also highly endorsed instillation of hope, whereas members of the two most restricted groups (i.e., maximum security and segregation) rated interpersonal input highly. Across the four groups, guidance, family reenactment, and identification were all rated as the least helpful therapeutic factors. The high endorsement of catharsis and the low endorsement of guidance, family reenactment, and identification as therapeutic factors is consistent with other research (Yalom, 1975). However, MacDevitt and Sanislow's findings differed from those from the earlier research in some important ways.

For one, offenders placed a greater emphasis on instillation of hope than did participants in other studies. MacDevitt and Sanislow suggested that offenders may feel a "greater need to rely on hope as a way to deal with their situations" (1987). Logically, this makes a great deal of sense. Incarceration represents an environment in which an individual is stripped of most of his or her personal rights. Hope may be one of the few resources on which they can count. Existential awareness, was also ranked higher by offenders than other populations and may "reflect the extremity of their life circumstances and their powerlessness in the face of institutional controls" (MacDevitt & Sanislow, 1987). In this sense, existential awareness and instillation of hope seem to be both highly interrelated and important for this population.

In examining the studies recorded in Table 24.2, we were struck by the broad range of therapeutic factors that were seen as most helpful by members of both in-patient and out-patient groups. Despite Crouch et al.'s (1994) contention that out-patient groups tended to endorse self-understanding, learning from interpersonal action, and self-disclosure as most helpful; we could identify no discernable pattern in the present studies. We believe that the in-patient versus out-patient dimension proposed by both Yalom (1995) and Crouch et al. (1994) may not be useful for making sense of the studies examining the relative rankings of TFs. There does, however, seem to be some logical consistency in the TFs identified as most helpful by the participants in the various group settings. The in-patient versus out-patient distinction, however, does not seem to capture these fundamental differences.

There is a second more fundamental problem with studies examining the relative rankings of therapeutic factors in different types of groups. Researchers seem to be falling into the fallacy of the patient universality assumption (Kiesler, 1966). Specifically, these researchers are assuming that all group clients have a uniform experience of the group. Recently, Shaughnessy and Kivlighan (1995) attempted to address the client uniformity assumption through using cluster analysis. They argued that the use of simple rank-orderings typified in previous research may obscure the existence of possible differences within groups. These researchers used Bloch and Crouch's (1985) TFs paradigm and Critical Incidents Questionnaire (CIQ) in their assessment of therapeutic factors in personal growth groups. There were 10 groups that met for a total of 26 sessions and five groups that met for 13 sessions. After each session, each participant was asked to complete a CIQ.

Results indicate that there were four subgroups of clients that could be differentiated by the pattern of TFs that they endorsed: (1) broad-spectrum responders, (2) self-reflective responders, (3) other directed responders, and (4) affective responders. Broad-spectrum responders represented the largest subgroup and were characterized by having a fairly equal endorsement of all 10 therapeutic factors. In other words, they found all of aspects of their group experience helpful to some extent at some point in the life of the group. The second cluster, self-reflective responders, were characterized by endorsing a high number of critical incidents related to self-understanding, and placed a particular high emphasis on universality and learning through interpersonal actions. The third cluster (other directed responders) were so labeled because of their high endorsement of vicarious learning and altruism. Therefore, these members seemed to gain the most from giving to others, and learning from or observing others. The fourth cluster (affective responders) highly valued acceptance and catharsis and seemed to be characterized by their emotionality.

The results of this study imply that when more sensitive research techniques are employed, differences between therapy groups may not be as salient as differences among clients within groups. This suggests that "group leaders should be cautious about emphasizing a relatively small set of therapeutic factors" (Shaughnessy & Kivlighan, 1995, p. 265). If leaders choose to take this approach, they may inadvertently exclude a large subset of group members. In light of the large body of previous literature that posits different results, replication of this study is suggested. This is especially the case for those studies using out-patient group members as subjects.

Whereas a number of studies have examined the relative ranking of TFs in various types of group settings, there has been, as we indicated earlier, little evidence of consistent differences across these various types of settings. A major deficit in this area of research is the lack of theoretical conceptualization to guide the various comparisons. Researchers have compared relative rankings of TFs across various groups without specifying a theoretical rationale for why these groups may differ in the action of the therapeutic mechanisms. This has resulted in a literature composed of contradictory and atheoretical findings that has added little knowledge to the practice and theory of group counseling. As shown in Shaughnessy and Kivlighan (1995), the endorsement of TFs is not even consistent within a particular group. This suggests that endorsement of TFs is a more complex process than suggested by studies that simply examine endorsement within a particular type of group setting. Future research should, therefore, rely on planned theoretical comparisons and examine within group differences in the endorsement of TFs.

The Influence of Group Development and Individual Member Differences on Therapeutic Factors

As stated earlier, Yalom proposed two additional hypotheses regarding members' endorsement of therapeutic factors. Specifically, Yalom (1995) hypothesized that the value that members place on therapeutic factors will vary by stages of group development and member individual differences. Only two studies simultaneously addressed these hypotheses (Kivlighan & Goldfine, 1991; Kivlighan & Mullison, 1988). Results of both of these studies, when considered in concert with Shaughnessy and Kivlighan's (1995) cluster analytic findings, yield interesting and compelling implications.

Kivlighan and Mullison (1988) examined the relationships among the stage of group development, group members' interpersonal behavior, and members' rating of therapeutic factors. They used the TF system developed by Bloch, Reibstein, Crouch, Holroyd, and Themen (1979) and measured TFs by administering the CIQ after each group counseling session. The authors also administered the Check List of Interpersonal Transactions (CLOIT; Kiesler, 1984) to characterize the group members' interpersonal behavior. The CLOIT measures along the dimensions of affiliation (love versus hate) and control (dominance versus submission).

There were three interpersonal growth groups that met weekly for one and a half hours for 11 weeks. The group leaders completed the CLOIT after the third session and identified each member as affiliative ($N = 6$) or nonaffiliative ($N = 11$) and dominant ($N = 5$) or submissive ($N = 12$). The authors defined the first five sessions as early in group development and the last six sessions as late. The designations were made to maintain consistency with Yalom's original hypothesis.

There were significant differences found for the affiliative interpersonal behavior dimension but not for the control dimension. Results indicated that affiliative group members found self-understanding most helpful, while nonaffiliative members rated self-disclosure, learning through interpersonal action, and altruism as most helpful. Differences were also found between the early and late stages of group development, such that there appeared to be an overrepresentation of universality in the early stages of group development and more of an emphasis on learning through interpersonal actions in late sessions.

The authors proposed that perhaps the lack of significant results for the control dimension of interpersonal behavior may have been due to the small sample size included in the study. However, the results they found for the affiliative dimension were in line with previous theoretical suppositions. Both Yalom (1985) and Kiesler (1996) hypothesized that group members should be encouraged to behave in ways that are the opposite of their typical way of interacting (see Kivlighan & Mullison, 1988). Therefore, it makes sense that nonaffiliative participants would find self-disclosure as helpful. The reasoning for affiliative participants' endorsement of self-understanding is, however, not as clear.

Most of Yalom's hypotheses regarding members' rating of TFs and group development were supported. For example, Yalom predicted that universality would be rated as more important in early stages while learning through interpersonal actions would be perceived as more helpful in late stages. However, in contrast to Yalom's hypothesis, Kivlighan and Mullison (1988) did not find instillation of hope or guidance to be rated as more helpful in the early stages of group development. Kivlighan and Mullison suggested that a more sophisticated model of group development may yield more detailed and relevant data than the simple early-late model. For example, it may be that group development is not related to time but to events within the group's life. If this is the case, the early-late model of development would not be sensitive enough to measure differences in (or changes in) group members' rating of TFs.

Kivlighan and Goldfine (1991) conducted a similar study using a more refined model of group development. As in Kivlighan and Mullison (1988), the group participants' interpersonal style was assessed along the dimensions of affiliation and dominance. The Group Climate Questionnaire (MacKenzie, 1983) was used to identify engaged, differentiation, and individuation stages of group development. The results supported Kivlighan and Goldfine's hypothesis that affiliative participants would value cognitive therapeutic factors, while non-affiliative participants would value behavioral factors. Also as hypothesized, universality and hope decreased and catharsis increased across the three stages of group development. Contrary to Kivlighan and Mullison, learning through interpersonal action did not show an increase in importance during latter stages of group development.

Thus, it appears universality and instillation of hope are relatively more important in early group development, while catharsis increases in importance during later stages of group life. It is, however, less clear whether insight and learning through interpersonal action have a developmental component. Future research can build on the promising start in this area.

There has been less theoretical structure to guide the research examining the relationship between individual differences and member ratings of therapeutic factors. This lack of theoretical grounding has hampered research in this area. The one theoretical model that has been examined, interpersonal theory, shows promising results. Specifically, the research suggests that group participants benefit from a group experience that encourages them to interact in ways that are contrary to their normal interpersonal style. For example, non-affiliative group members may value factors like interpersonal learning and self-disclosure. Future research could use other theoretical models (e.g., attachment theory) in examining the relation of individual differences and group members' rankings of therapeutic factors.

Implications for Practice

Research on therapeutic factors should be readily applicable in practice settings. The research confirms what most practitioners suspect, that group clients do not have a uniform reaction to the group counseling experience. Clients differ in the therapeutic experiences that they will find the most helpful. In addition, the group counselor needs to modify his or her approach based upon the stage of group development or the individual differences of his or her group members.

In terms of stage of group development, it appears that group counselors should initially emphasize factors like universality and instillation of hope. In fact, universality and instillation of hope are the foundation for the development of group cohesiveness. Once cohesiveness is established, the group leader can emphasize factors like catharsis and insight. It is important, however, to temper these recommendations with the knowledge of client individual differences. It is clear from the Shaughnessy and Kivlighan typology and from the research examining the role of affiliation and endorsement of therapeutic factors that clients do not have a uniform experience in the group counseling situation. Group leaders need to be able to balance a nomeothetic approach to TFs based on stage of group development with an idiographic approach to TFs based on individual differences. Hopefully, future research will clarify the relative emphasis of these two models.

Interpersonal Learning /Interpersonal Feedback

One of the most widely researched therapeutic factors is interpersonal feedback. Yalom (1975) conceptualized this TF as interpersonal learning—input or output. Bloch and his associates

(Bloch & Crouch, 1985) have labeled this TF learning through interpersonal action. Theoretical conceptualizations are provided in Table 24.1. Two of the most prolific researchers in this area, Morran and Stockton, have operationalized this concept through their research. They describe interpersonal feedback as occurring when "one group member shares his or her perception of and reaction to another's behavior with that other person" (Morran, Robison, & Stockton 1985, p. 57).

Kivlighan (1985) reviewed the feedback literature and provided a conceptual model for integrating the studies on interpersonal feedback. He proposed that feedback is a multidimensional construct consisting of four interrelated dimensions. Two of these dimensions are concerned with the recipient of feedback and two are related to the deliverer of feedback. More specifically, he discussed the receiver dimension in terms of acceptance and effects of receiving the feedback. The deliverer dimension was discussed in terms of willingness to deliver feedback and "effects accorded to the deliverer" (Kivlighan, 1985, p. 380).

Along the receiver dimension, Kivlighan noted that there was little research that had examined the relationship between acceptance of feedback and characteristics of the feedback deliverer. Two studies, (Flowers, 1979; Morran et al., 1985), found that feedback from group members had a greater impact than feedback from the therapist. For example, Morran et al. included role status (leader versus member), session number, and feedback valence to "explore the possible differences in leader- versus member-generated feedback in terms of message content and acceptance by group member recipients" (p. 58). Morran et al. found that: (1) leader feedback was less accepted by group members even though it was rated as higher in quality, (2) negative feedback given in the fourth session was rated as more helpful than if it was given in the second session, (3) leader-member differences in quality diminished over time, and (4) there were no differences across time for the effectiveness of positive feedback.

Perhaps the most striking feature of this study was the finding that group members found feedback delivered by other group members as more helpful than feedback delivered by the group leader. It is not clear, however, why this phenomenon occurred. Differences in the quality of feedback can not account for differences in feedback acceptance because leaders delivered higher quality feedback than did group members. Future research should seek to identify the dimensions that account for the differences in acceptance of feedback from group leaders and group members.

Kivlighan (1985) found only one study that examined the relationship between acceptance of feedback and characteristics of the receiver (Morran & Stockton, 1980). Morran and Stockton looked at the effects of member self-concept on the acceptance of positive and negative feedback. Members with high self-concept rated negative feedback as more desirable than did members with lower levels of self-concept. In a more recent study, Robison, Morran, and Stockton (1986) examined the relationship between receiver level of defensiveness and acceptance of feedback, and found no relationship between these variables.

Research examining the relationship between acceptance of feedback and characteristics of the receiver is hampered by the lack of a theoretical model to aide in selection of receiver variables. Recently, however, Hawkins (1997) developed a model relating receiver characteristics to feedback acceptance. This model grew out of Dweck's (1986) theory of cognitive process in achievement motivation. In Dweck's model, goal processes mediate a learner's (group member's) approach to achievement situations. Learners (group members) with a learning goal orientation endeavor to acquire more knowledge or skill when they are in a learning situation. Group members with learning goals accept and seek out negative feedback because this type of feedback helps them approach and master the learning task. Learners (group members) with a performance goal orientation attempt to demonstrate how much they already know or try to keep others from seeing how little they know. Group members with a performance goal orientation reject negative feedback because they see this feedback as indicating their lack of ability. Hawkins argued that receiver characteristics influence the acceptance of feedback to the extent that these receiver characteristics relate to a group member's goal orientation. Groups members with learning goal orientations are likely to accept negative feedback, whereas those with a performance goal orientation are hypothesized to be less receptive of negative feedback. Hawkins (1997) research confirmed this model showing that students with a learning goal orientation were more likely to accept negative feedback than students with a performance goal orientation.

By far the area of interpersonal feedback that has been studied most extensively is the concept of valence. Valence refers to whether the feedback being delivered includes positive or corrective (negative) content. Most of the studies in this area include valence as a variable, typically as a qualifier of the type of feedback being examined. Kivlighan reported that across a number of studies, positive feedback has been consistently considered as more credible, desirable, and impactful than negative feedback. This appears to be the case considering more recent research (e.g., Robison et al., 1986).

The other area related to the receiver dimension Kivlighan mentions is the effects of feedback on the recipient. Studies in this area have recorded or manipulated the amount of feedback that a group member receives. Tschuschke and Dies (1994) examined feedback delivery in a long-term in-patient group experience and found that group members who received the highest level of feedback, particularly in early group sessions, benefited the most from their group experience. Rohde and Stockton (1992) manipulated the amount of feedback that group members received by randomly assigning group members to groups that did or did not use a structure feedback exercise. Members in groups using the structured feedback exercise had higher goal attainment ratings than members in the control groups. Results of these studies indicate that group leaders should seek out ways of promoting feedback exchange in their groups. Future research on the receipt of feedback should incorporate more specificity when examining feedback received. Specifically, researchers should examine how feedback valence and feedback type relate to group outcome.

Kivlighan discussed willingness and effects to the deliverer of feedback in counseling groups. Willingness is discussed in terms of group members' willingness, or conversely reluctance, to deliver negative feedback. Typically researchers require members to deliver positive and negative feedback and deliverers in these situations consistently rate the negative feedback as less accurate than the positive feedback. Deliverers also state that it is more difficult to deliver negative feedback. Kivlighan suggested the more relevant task is to examine how group leaders can facilitate members' delivery of negative feedback in more spontaneous ways.

Robison, Stockton, Morran, and Uhl-Wagner (1988) examined the anticipated consequences of communicating negative behavioral feedback in early group sessions. Factor analyses revealed seven dimensions related to anticipated consequences of delivering negative behavioral feedback: (1) effects on communicator' relationships, (2) effects on receiver/receiver's reactions, (3) effects on communicator's self-control, (4) effects on communicator's self-esteem, (5) effects on communicator's status/influence, (6) effects on others' understanding/acceptance, and (7) effects on others/group process. These results suggest that there are a number of different reasons why group members are reluctant to offer negative feedback, especially in early group development. Future research may want to replicate this study to find if the factor structure replicates across group types and members. In addition, research should address ways to ameliorate these anticipated consequences to enable a greater degree of natural feedback exchange in group counseling.

Finally, Kivlighan discussed the effects on the deliverer of feedback. Only Flowers et al. (1974) have conducted research in this area and found that group members who deliver a great deal of negative feedback tend to be less receptive to feedback of any kind from other members. Other studies (Flowers & Booarem, 1989, 1991) suggest that group members need to be flexible in their use (acceptance and delivery) of all types and levels of feedback. Specifically, those group members who had the highest levels of receiving and delivering both positive and negative feedback gained the most from the group experience.

Implications for Practice

Interpersonal feedback has held a prominent place in group counseling theory. A number of studies have examined both the antecedents and the consequences of feedback. The delivery and acceptance of negative feedback seems to be the crucial dimension in developing models of feedback delivery. We are beginning to understand why group members are reluctant to deliver negative feedback, but we have not as yet developed methods for helping them overcome this reluctance. Hawkins' model of feedback acceptance provides a promising approach for examining this phenomenon. Thus, group leaders need to pay attention to the type of learning goals group members have adopted and to develop methods for helping group members with a performance approach become more learning oriented.

Group Cohesiveness

Group cohesiveness has been the focus of numerous empirical investigations in the broad area of group dynamics. Specifically, group dynamics researchers have been interested in the relationship between group cohesiveness and performance. A meta-analysis of this research showed that group cohesiveness, especially measured as commitment to the group task, was positively and significantly related to performance (Mullen & Cooper, 1994), and that group cohesiveness enhances decision quality (Mullen, Anthony, Salas, & Driskell, 1994). These results suggest that group cohesiveness is a critical group process dimension that may have impacts on the process and outcome of diverse task groups.

Group cohesiveness is also seen as an important process aspect in group counseling/therapy. For example, Budman, Soldz, et al. (1989) described group cohesiveness as "one of the pivotal determinants of effective group therapy" (p. 340). Yalom (1995) defines group cohesiveness as "the condition of members feeling warmth and comfort in the group, feeling they belong, valuing the group and feeling, in turn, that they are valued and unconditionally accepted and supported by the other members" (p. 48). Despite a consensus on its importance, group counseling researchers have had an extremely difficult time operationalizing group cohesiveness. This situation has led reviewers to decry the poor state of group cohesiveness research (e.g., Bednar & Kaul, 1994).

Recently, Crouch et al. (1994) detected a growing consensus on the definition and measurement of group cohesiveness. This consensus has been stimulated by Yalom's (1995) formulation that group cohesiveness is the group therapy analogue of the working alliance in individual therapy and by findings that measures of cohesiveness and alliance are substantially related (Marziali, Munroe-Blum, & McCleary, 1997). Increasingly, group cohesiveness is seen as consisting of two components: (1) an emotional bond among the group members and group leaders, and (2) the group members agreement on, and commitment to, the goals and tasks of treatment (Bordin, 1979; Budman, Soldz, et al., 1989). A promising measure of these two components of group cohesiveness is the Harvard Community Health Plan Group Cohesiveness Scale (Budman, Demby, et al., 1989).

As in the general group dynamics area, the empirical studies in group counseling confirm the importance of group cohesiveness. These results also parallel the research in individual counseling showing a positive relationship between working alliance and treatment outcome (Horvath, & Symonds, 1991). Despite differences in measurement, a number of studies have shown that group cohesiveness is positively related to a wide range of treatment outcomes (Braaten, 1989; Budman, Demby, et al., 1989; Kapp, Gleser, & Brissenden, 1964; Kivlighan & Lilly, 1997; MacKenzie, Dies, Coche, Rutan, & Stone, 1987; Marziali et al., 1997; Phipps & Zastowny, 1988; Rugel, 1987; Tschuschke & Dies, 1994; Weiss, 1972; Yalom, Houts, Zimerberg, & Rand, 1967). Given these positive results, it is important to examine: (1) the development of group cohesiveness over time; (2) the consequences of group cohesiveness, specifically the variables that may mediate the group cohesiveness-treatment outcome relationship; and (3) the antecedents of group cohesiveness, especially the group leaders role in creating a cohesive group environment.

Most studies have adopted a static approach (see next section of this chapter for alternative approaches) when examining group dynamics. In regards to group cohesiveness, this involves measuring the level of group cohesiveness at a single point in time and correlating cohesiveness scores with measures of treatment outcome. Although this research has generally supported the importance of cohesiveness to group counseling outcome, other research suggests that more informative data is provided by examining cohesion as a dynamic construct that changes across the life of a counseling group. For example, a recent study (Kivlighan & Lilly, 1997) examined the relationship to treatment outcome of static and dynamic measures of group outcome. Whereas midtreatment group cohesiveness scores were found to account for approximately 40% of the variance in therapeutic gain, a high-low-high pattern of group cohesiveness development over time accounted for 79% of the variance in therapeutic gain.

Group cohesiveness appears to influence a number of positive group dynamics. In this way group cohesiveness can be seen as a primary condition that allows the group to function (Crouch et al., 1994). For example, group cohesiveness is correlated with group member empathy, self-disclosure, and feelings of acceptance and trust (Roarke & Sharah, 1989) and with liking the group, supporting and caring about other group members, and taking a dominant or active role in the group (Rugel, 1987). One study that used path analysis to examine time-lagged (i.e., causal) relationships found that group cohesiveness was related to greater ownership of group success but not to better attitudes about enacting constructive group behaviors (Fuehrer & Keys, 1988). This study provides the strongest evidence to date that group cohesiveness influences positive group interactions and not vice a versa. Finally, Budman, Soldz, Demby, Davis, and Merry (1993) examined differential effects of group cohesiveness early and late in group development. High cohesiveness early in the group was associated with an equal (as opposed to one or a few members monopolizing the group session) amount of group member participation and to a relatively high level of outside group statements. High cohesiveness late in the group was related to a relatively high level of inside group statements. Taken together, the results of these studies suggest that group cohesiveness plays an important catalytic role by potentiating a number of important interactional variables.

How do group leaders promote group cohesiveness? Researchers have attempted to answer this question by correlating measures of group cohesiveness and leader style (Antonuccio, Davis, Lewinson, & Breckenridge, 1987; Hurst, Stein, Korchin, & Soskin, 1978; McKenzie et al., 1987; Phipps & Zastowny, 1988). Leader warmth/caring showed a consistent positive relationship to group cohesiveness in each of these studies. In addition, Antonuccio et al. and MacKenzie et al. found that less controlling leaders had more cohesive groups. Further, one time-series study examined the time lagged (causal) relationships between leader styles (warmth/caring and conditionality) early and late in group development (McBride, 1995). McBride found that conditionality (setting and reinforcing clear norms) lead to higher levels of group cohesiveness in early group sessions, while warmth/caring lead to enhanced group cohesiveness in late group sessions.

A number of other studies examined the relationship between the use of structured exercises and early group cohesiveness. In general, tests of this model show that structured as opposed to unstructured conditions result in higher levels of group cohesiveness (e.g., Fuehrer & Keys, 1988; Robison & Hardt, 1992). The effects of structure on group cohesiveness may be particularly pronounced for group participants with a low risk-taking disposition (Robison & Hardt, 1992). It is not clear if cognitive or behavioral structure is more effective in producing group cohesiveness or if the type of structure may interact with group member risk-taking disposition to enhance group cohesiveness (Kaul & Bednar, 1994). Two studies (Kivlighan, McGovern, & Corazzini, 1984; Stockton, Rohde, & Haughey, 1992), however, suggest that group cohesiveness is enhanced when the content of the structure matches the stage of group development (e.g., asking group members to name the member to whom they are closest and most distant as a way to promote distinctions—an important component of the differentiation stage of group development). Taken as a whole, the results these studies suggest that group leaders can increase group cohesiveness through their judicious use of structure.

Structure of Therapeutic Factors

Three studies addressed the underlying dimensions that might characterize Yalom's therapeutic factors. Fuhriman, Drescher, Hanson, Henrie, and Rybicki (1986) argue that interpersonal learning, cohesion, catharsis, and insight were the primary dimensions in Yalom's typology. A factor analysis of a curative factors scale designed to tap these dimensions resulted in a three-factor model: cohesion, catharsis, and insight. Additional analysis revealed that cohesion and catharsis were more highly valued than insight. Furthermore, clients in a community mental health center placed a higher value on all three factors than did clients in a Veteran's Administration or university setting.

Stone, Lewis, and Beck (1994) factor analyzed a modified version of Lieberman, Yalom, and Miles' (1973) How Groups Work Scale. As in the Fuhriman et al. (1986) study, three factors emerged from this analysis. Stone et al.(1994) labeled these factors core elements in therapeutic group process, skill development, and insight, and receipt of guidance from group process. Obviously, there is little consistency in the dimensions identified in these two studies.

Kivlighan, Multon, and Brossart (1996) addressed the underlying structure of group therapeutic factors by factor analyzing responses to three measures of therapeutic impact: (1) Therapeutic Factors (Bloch et al., 1979) (2) Categories of Good Moments (Mahrer & Nadler, 1986) and (3) Taxonomy of Helpful Impacts (Elliott, 1985). Principle components analysis revealed four underlying factors that accounted for the variance in the items comprising these three inventories. These factors were labeled emotional awareness-insight, relationship-climate, other- versus self-focus, and problem definition-change. Validity analyses indicated that the emotional awareness-insight and problem definition-change factors were related to the technical aspects of leader behavior. When the leader provided more structure and cognitive input, group members reported a greater level of awareness and problem definition. In addition, the relationship and other- versus self-focus factors were related to the personal dimension of group leadership. When the leaders were more empathic and caring, group members reported a greater level of self focus and better within group relationships.

The Fuhriman et al. (1986) and Kivlighan et al. (1996) studies show some consistency in the structure of group therapeutic factors. Both studies identified insight/awareness and cohesion/relationship-climate factors. These similarities suggest that there may be two fundamental dimensions of therapeutic impact in group counseling. Unfortunately, there are relatively few studies that have examined the theoretically and empirically important nature of the structure of therapeutic impacts. Future research should continue to address this important question.

GROUP COUNSELING METHODOLOGY

As seen in the two preceding sections, group counseling presents a number of perplexing methodological and statistical issues for the counseling researcher to address. Since the inception of group counseling research, there has been a fairly steady stream of commentary concerning the methodological shortcomings in group counseling research. For example, between 1948 and 1992, approximately 60 articles examined methodological problems in group counseling research and made specific recommendations for addressing these problems (Burlingame, Kircher, & Taylor, 1994). In addition, Burlingame et al. have described a historical myopia, wherein commentators fail to consider or build on past methodological recommendations. While not wanting to contribute to this historical myopia, we nevertheless want to address four methodological issues that continue to plague group counseling research: (1) the nested nature of the data (i.e. members in the same group do not constitute independent units of observation); (2) tracking the mutual influences and mutual dependencies that exist in group counseling; (3) static versus dynamic measurement of group constructs, and (4) the power of the research. In this section, we will describe these four issues and provide recommendations for appropriate methodological and statistical solutions.

Nested Data

A researcher may want to study the relationship between the focus of the group leaders' interventions and the group members' perceptions of group climate. As the independent variable, the researcher can train group leaders to focus on either the cognitive or the affective dimensions of group process. The dependent variable in this design may be the Group Climate Questionnaire (GCQ; MacKenzie, 1983) filled out by each group member. How does the researcher analyze these data? She could average the GCQ scores for the members of a group and use these averaged scores in a *t*-test when comparing the leaders trained to focus on the cognitive or affective dimensions of group process. Unfortunately, this approach to data analysis ignores the variability in GCQ scores among the members of a group and also drastically reduces the *N* of the analysis. An alternative approach is to assign the same value of the independent variable (cognitive or affective) to each member of a group and use a *t*-test to compare individual group members that were in groups that were cognitively or affectivity oriented. Unfortunately, in this approach, the GCQ scores are not independent, which violates the independence assumption of the *t*-test. As pointed out by Morran, Robison, and Hulse-Killacky (1990), the violation of the independence assumption can lead to either an over-estimation or an under-estimation of the true effect.

A number of writers have addressed the problem of the nonindependence of observations when group members are in the same group (e.g., Bednar & Kaul, 1978). In addition, Morran et al. (1990) recommended that ANOVA designs with nested factors be used to analyze group designs with nonindependent nested data. Whereas nested ANOVA designs can successfully address the problem of nested data when the "independent" variable is categorical, they cannot be used when the "independent" variable is measured continuously. The example cited above and the examples in Morran et al. are limited to the case where one variable of interest is at the group level (e.g. the cognitive or affective focus of the leader's intervention) and one variable of interest is at the individual level (e.g., the individual group member's perception of group climate). It is possible to have nested data in group research and be interested in analyzing relationships at only one level of nesting.

An example of this second situation may clarify this type of analysis. A group researcher may what to examine Yalom's (1995) hypotheses about projection by having the group members rate both themselves and their group leader in terms of interpersonal style. The ratings of the group leader by members of the same group are not independent. In fact it would be important to know how much variance in members' ratings of leader interpersonal style is attributable to the leader and how much of this variance is attributable to the group members. In examining the relationship between group member ratings of self and the leader misleading results can occur if the variance attributable to the leader is not taken into account.

Multilevel analyses, of which Hierarchical Linear Models (HLM; Bryk & Raudenbush, 1992) are examples, address the problem of nested data by allowing the researcher to simultaneously model data at two (group and individual) levels. Unlike ANOVA designs with nested factors, HLM can be used with both categorical and continuous "independent" variables and can be used for both across level and within level analyses.

HLM address the problem of nested data by initially partitioning the variance in the data into within group (variance between group members) and between group (variance between groups) components. In the projection example given earlier, the variance in ratings of group leader interpersonal style would be partitioned into a within group component (the variance attributable to the differences among group members) and a between group component (the variance attributable to differences among group leaders). This partitioning of variance lets the researcher control for between leader differences when examining the relationship between group member self- and leader-ratings. When the researcher examines the relationship between group member self- and leader-ratings, member self-ratings are used to predict *only* the variance in leader ratings that is within group (variance between group members).

If the above study also had an experimental condition with leaders focusing either cognitively or affectivity and the researcher wanted to see how this focus affected group members' ratings of group leader interpersonal style, variance partitioning would again be important. As above, the variance in ratings of group leader interpersonal style would be partitioned into a within group component (the variance attributable to the differences among group members) and a between group component (the variance attributable to differences among group leaders). This time, however, the partitioning of variance lets the researcher control for differences between individual group members when examining the relationship between leader focus and group member ratings of the leader. When the researcher examines the relationship between leader focus and group member ratings of the leader, leader focus is used to predict *only* the variance in group member ratings of the leader that is between group (variance between group leaders).

Finally, HLM allows the group researcher to examine interactions between different levels of nesting. In the example above, the researcher may hypothesize that the relationship between self- and leader-ratings of interpersonal style will be stronger when the leaders uses an affective focus than when leaders use a cognitive focus. Once again the variance in ratings of group leader interpersonal style is partitioned into a within group component (the variance attributable to the differences among group members) and a between group component (the variance attributable to differences among group leaders). Next the within group variance (the variance in leader-ratings that is between group members) is partitioned into two parts, an intercept and a slope. The intercept represents the average level of member ratings of leader interpersonal style, while the slope is a regression coefficient depicting the within group relationship between group member self- and leader-ratings of interpersonal style. In other words, each group has a unique slope coefficient that describes the relationship between self- and leader-ratings of interpersonal style for that particular group. These slope coefficients will vary between groups, and it is this between group variance in self- and leader-ratings that the researcher will attempt to predict with the leader focus variable. When the researcher examines the relationship between leader focus and the relationship between group member ratings self and of the leader, leader focus is used to predict *only* the variance in the relationship between group member ratings of self and of the leader that is between group (variance between group leaders). Not only does HLM let the group researcher account for the non-independent structure of his or her data, it also, through analyzing interactions between levels, allows the researcher to ask questions impossible to examine when the data are examined at only the individual or group level of aggregation.

Unfortunately, there are no published examples of multilevel analyses in the group counseling literature. However, a reanalysis of Gehlert's (1994) data provides an illustration of the usefulness of multilevel analysis with group counseling data. Gehlert examined the relationship between group members' narcissistic vulnerabilities and their perception of group climate. Seventy-five members of 21 counseling groups filled out the Superiority Scale (Robbins & Patton, 1985), as a measure of narcissistic vulnerabilities and the Group Climate Questionnaire (MacKenzie, 1983), which measured group climate in terms of engagement, avoidance, and conflict. Gehlert analyzed these data at the level of the individual member without taking into account the dependency in group climate ratings for members of the same group. In his analyses, the Superiority scale showed no relationship to group climate, correlating $-.04$, $.09$, $.13$ (all nonsignificant at the $p < .05$ level) with the engagement, avoidance and conflict scales, respectively. When reanalyzed with

HLM, however, a different picture emerges. The relation between a member's narcissism and his or her perception of group climate was obscured in Gehlert's analyses because between group variance in group climate was confounded with between member variance in group climate in his correlational analyses. The HLM analyses reveals that 16%, 13%, and 15% of the variance in group member ratings of engagement, avoidance, and conflict, respectively, was between group variance. After controlling for this between group variance in group climate ratings, the correlations of superiority and group climate are $-.24$, $.31$, and $.36$ (all significant at the $p < .05$ level) for the engagement, avoidance, and conflict scales, respectively. By failing to take into accounted the nested structure of his data, Gehlert (1994) was not able to detect the real relationships that existed between group member narcissistic vulnerability and perceptions of group climate.

Burlingame et al. (1994) reviewed 192 studies of group counseling and found that only 11% used analyses that addressed the dependencies that existed in the group data. The failure to account for dependencies in group data is a serious problem for group researchers. As in the Gehlert (1994) study, results may lead to erroneous conclusions because of inappropriate analyses. Multilevel analyses with HLM provide a relatively simple means for analyzing group data. Good introductions to multilevel analyses can be found in Bryk and Raudenbush (1992) and Arnold (1992).

Mutual Dependencies

Closely related to the problem of nested data is the problem/opportunity of the mutual dependencies that exist in group data (Marcus & Kashy, 1995). Mutual dependencies exist in group counseling data because any rating made by group members is subject to multiple influences. For example, all the members of a group in which John and Jane are members are asked to rate each other in terms of warmth. According to Marcus and Kashy, Jane's rating of John's warmth is a function of five factors. At the group level, Jane's perception of John's warmth is a function of their group's general level of, or norms for, the expression and or perception of warmth. In some groups every member is rated as generally warm and in other groups all members are rated as generally cold. There are also two individual factors that influence Jane's rating's of John's warmth. The perceiver effect describes Jane's set (schema) for experiencing or perceiving warmth. That is Jane's tendency to rate all group members similarly in terms of warmth. The target effect describes John's general level of expressed warmth or the agreement that exists among all the group members when rating John's warmth. The dyadic effect describes the unique relationship between Jane and John in terms of warmth expressed and received. The dyadic effect is Jane's unique ratings of John's warmth which is not accounted for by Jane's perceiver effect or John's target effect. The final component of Jane's ratings of John's warmth is random error. To separate out the effect of random error from the dyadic effect it is necessary to obtain warmth ratings at several time periods.

When all members of a group rate each other along one or more dimensions (e.g., warmth in the example above), the obtained data are referred to as round-robin data. The social relations model (Kenny & La Voie, 1984) is a statistical technique for analyzing round robin data using the five components described above. Most group research ignores these different sources of variance in round-robin ratings and acts as if these rating are only an expression of the target's level of a characteristic (e.g., warmth). As pointed out by Marcus and Kashy (1995), however, understanding and analyzing the different sources of rating variance enables group researchers to ask and answer a number of interesting and theoretically meaningful questions. For example, Yalom's (1995) social microcosm theory predicts that the person's schema (perceiver effect) should be the most important source of variance in early group sessions. As groups develop, however, the person's schema should become less important in terms of perception of others. The social relations model (Kenny & La Voie 1984) allows group researchers to test theories like Yalom's social microcosm by partitioning rating variance into group, perceiver, target, dyadic, and error components. If Yalom's theory is correct, the perceiver effect should be significantly larger in early group sessions than it is in later group sessions.

Group members consistently report that member-to-member interactions are the most helpful aspect of group counseling (Dies, 1993). In social relations terms, member-to-member interactions are the dyadic effect. Dyadic effects are all but ignored in most group research (Marcus & Kashy, 1995). For example, research on interpersonal feedback has almost exclusively analyzed target effects (factors that influence a group members acceptance of feedback) or perceiver effects (do leader or group members give better feedback). Unfortunately, the results of the interpersonal feedback studies can be misleading because the various effects (group, target, perceiver, dyadic, and error) have not been disentangled. Marcus and Kashy outlined a series of questions that group researchers interested in interpersonal feedback could address with round-robin data and the social relations model.

There are few examples of social relations analyses in the group counseling literature. Marcus and Kashy (1995) provided a nontechnical description of the social relations model, while Marcus and Holahan (1994) provided an example of the analysis with therapy groups. In Marcus and Holahan, group members rated each other in terms of dominance, hostility, submission and friendliness. For all four dimensions there were significant target and perceiver effects, but no significant group and dyadic effects. Group member interpersonal ratings were almost exclusively a function of the person being rated and the person doing the rating. This finding fits with Yalom's social microcosm hypothesis. Unfortunately, Marcus and Holahan did not collect interpersonal ratings over time. Therefore, it was not possible to see if perceiver and target effects diminished over time (as predicted by theory).

As do Marcus and Kashy (1995), we believe that the social relations model holds great promise for group counseling researchers. We encourage group counseling researchers to collect round-robin type data and to analyze them with the social relations model. If this occurs, we can begin to answer some of the core questions in group counseling research.

Static versus Dynamic Measurements

Bennis and Shepard (1956) were among the first group researchers to describe stages of group development. Since this seminal work, hundreds of articles have described various stage models of group development (e.g., Tuckman, 1965). Paradoxically, the emphasis on time and process that undergirds the group development literature, has failed to be incorporated into the main stream of group counseling literature. Whereas group theorists and practitioners see groups as dynamic and evolving, most group researchers have measured group phenomena at single points in time. In taking these types of static measurements, group researchers miss the time dependent nature of group process. Even when group researchers gather multiple measures over time, they typically group the data into arbitrary time frames (e.g., early, middle, late as seen in Kivlighan & Goldfine, 1991).

Recently, two analytic strategies, Tuckerized growth curves and individual growth modeling, have been used to describe the process of stability and change in group processes over time. Brossart, Patton, and Wood (1998) used Tuckerized growth curves to identify patterns in conflict ratings over the course of a 26-session counseling group. Kivlighan and Lilly (1997) used individual growth modeling to link changes in group engagement, avoidance, and conflict to measures of group benefit.

Tuckerized Growth Curve Analysis

As described by Brossart et al. (1998), Tuckerized growth curves provide a method for simultaneously examining both intraindividual variability and interindividual variability. Specifically, Tuckerized growth curves are a form of T technique factor analysis (Cattell, 1966; Tinsley, 1992).

In other words, variables are held constant (one variable is examined at a time) and people and occasions are examined. The goal of a Tuckerized growth curve analysis is to identify groups of people who share a common pattern of change over time.

Brossart et al. (1998) provided an excellent description of the steps involved in a Tuckerized growth curve analysis. Typically the researcher begins by plotting the raw data (conflict ratings, in Brossart et al., 1998). These plots provide the researcher with an initial estimate of the number of growth curves that will be necessary to account for the intraindividual variability in the variable of interest. As in factor analysis, where the researcher must determine the number of factors to retain, the researcher using Tuckerized growth curve analysis has to decide on the number of reference curves to retain. The number of reference curves to retain is determined by examining the "mean square ratio" (similar to an eigenvalue in *R* technique factor analysis) for each component. In examining conflict ratings, Brossart et al. (1998) retained three reference curves with mean square ratio values of 26.21, 6.27, and 4.26 that accounted for 64%, 11% and 6%, respectively, of the variance in conflict ratings.

The next step in a Tuckerized growth curve analysis involves rotating the retained reference curves. Brossart et al. used two criteria for rotating their reference curves: (1) no negative loadings and (2) match to the raw data. Figure 24.1 depicts the three rotated reference curves from Brossart et al. (1998). The final step in a Tuckerized growth curve analysis is to interpret the reference curves. For example, Brossart et al. said that curve 3 in Figure 24.1 was a close match to MacKenzie and Livesly's (1983) theory of group development. The group members represented by this curve indicated a rapid early rise followed by a sharp decline in conflict. Brossart et al. interpreted this pattern as representing MacKenzie and Livesly's differentiation stage of group development.

Tuckerized growth curve analysis represents an exciting new tool for group counseling researchers. As illustrated by Brossart et al. (1998), Tuckerized growth curve analysis can be used

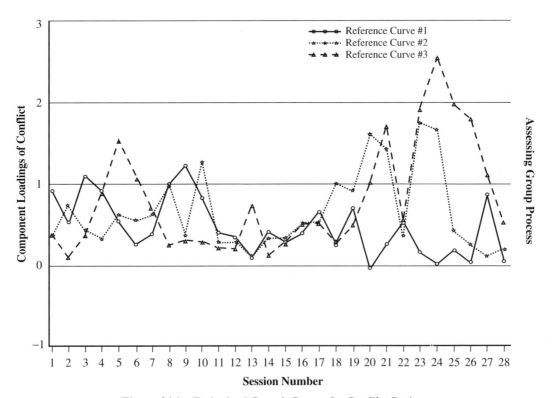

Figure 24.1 Tuckerized Growth Curves for Conflict Ratings

in an exploratory/descriptive manner. It is also possible to use Tuckerized growth curve analysis as an initial step in a predictive analysis. For example, Tuckerized growth curves could be used as a criterion variable in examining the effects of different group structuring techniques or as a predictor variable in connecting group process to group counseling outcome (e.g., how does membership in the three reference curves described by Brossart et al. relate to counseling outcome).

Individual Growth Modeling

One possible reason for the relative neglect of dynamic (versus static) analyses of group process variables is the methodological and statistical difficulties inherent in the analysis of change. Francis, Fletcher, Stuebing, Davidson, and Thompson (1991) propose that studies of change may benefit from the application of individual growth curve estimation. Using growth curve analysis, researchers may more precisely and fully estimate the structure of growth phenomena.

Until recently, there has not been a practical and powerful method for the statistical analysis of repeated measures type of process data. To represent these types of data, group researchers have used either: (1) nonstatistical graphical methods, coupled with visual inspection; or (2) arbitrarily divided data points into predetermined phases (i.e., early, middle, and late periods); and used repeated measures analysis of variance or repeated measures multivariate analysis of variance. As discussed by Willett, Ayoub, and Robinson (1991) and Francis et al. (1991) these methods have proven problematic from both a logical and statistical perspective. Growth modeling offers a powerful, alternative method for analyzing repeated measures, group process data.

In the first step of a growth curve analysis, a theoretical or heuristic growth model (e.g., linear or quadratic curve) is fit to the data from individual groups and to the sample of groups as a whole. The parameters from these initial models are then used in the second step of the modeling process as outcomes (i.e., dependent variables) on to which other variables are regressed. For example, if a linear growth model is used to model group cohesiveness, each group will have: (1) an intercept term that represents that group's average level of cohesiveness at a particular point in time; and (2) a slope term that represents the linear slope for change over time in the group's level of cohesiveness.

Growth modeling has been typically applied to outcome data. Only Kivlighan and Lilly (1997) have used growth modeling with group process data. They used hierarchical linear modeling (HLM) to estimate growth curves from Group Climate Questionnaire scores. The growth parameters from the estimated growth curves for the group climate data were related to the between group variable of group success.

Conceptually, HLM involves a two-stage analysis. In the first or *unconditional* model, a growth curve is fit for each individual group. This growth curve is described by two (intercept, linear slope) or more parameters. These sets of parameters are used in the second or *conditional* model as dependent variables in a series of regressions. Arnold (1992) has summarized this analytic technique by describing HLM as "regressions of regressions" (p. 61). Kivlighan and Lilly (1997) investigated how group climate growth curves were related to the amount of participant-rated benefit from the group experience.

Kivlighan and Lilly (1997) ran three HLM analyses modeling the Engaged, Conflict, and Avoiding dimensions of group climate. They examined the relationship among these group climate ratings and group benefit with a series of model building steps. Initially, they examined linear, quadratic, and cubic growth models for the Engaged, Conflict, and Avoiding dimensions of group climate. Once the appropriate growth model was determined, the relationship between this model and group benefit was assessed.

In the Kivlighan and Lilly study, the estimated engaged score suggested that group members saw their groups as moderately engaged at the midpoint of group counseling. For the engaged scores, neither the linear, quadratic, nor cubic growth models provided a good fit for the 14 groups in the study. In the conditional model Kivlighan and Lilly (1997) found that group benefit and mid-treatment engaged scores were significantly related. Group benefit accounted for approximately 40% of the variance in midtreatment engaged scores. The quadratic slope term was also significantly related to group benefit, with a high-low-high pattern of engaged scores related to group benefit. Group benefit accounted for approximately 79% of the variance in engaged scores. This result showed that the pattern, over time, of engaged scores was a better indicator of benefit than a one-time measure of group engagement. This supported Kivlighan and Lilly's hypothesis that the growth pattern for engaged scores would account for more of the variance in benefit that a static midtreatment measure of engaged.

Like Tuckerized growth curve analysis, individual growth modeling provides an exciting new analytic tool for group counseling researchers. We encourage group counseling researchers to begin or continue to collect longitudinal, repeated measures-type data. Most importantly, group counseling researchers should analyze this data with techniques that allow them to get the full power and richness that longitudinal data makes possible. Tuckerized growth curve analysis, individual growth modeling allow the group counseling researcher to get the most out of his or her longitudinal data.

The Power of the Research

Often group researchers do not study group-level phenomena (e.g., cohesiveness) because they cannot find enough groups to use a traditional research designs (e.g., between subject designs). For example, a researcher may want to test Yalom's hypothesis that therapist generated session summaries lead to more group cohesiveness. To test this hypothesis, with a between subjects (group) design, the group research would probably need to identify at least 24 groups (depending on the reliability of the measure of cohesiveness) and then randomly assign 12 of the groups to a treatment (receiving session summaries) condition and the other 12 groups to a control (not receiving session summaries) condition. Most group researchers do not have access to 24 or more counseling groups. This problem is usually addressed by studying individual group members and their attraction to the group rather than studying a group-level variable like group cohesiveness.

Robison, Morran, and Hulse-Killacky (1988) proposed an alternative way of handling this problem. They suggested that ABAB and multiple baseline designs, two types of single-subject research designs, could be used to address important group-level questions in one or a few groups. Robison et al. (1988) provided a description of the ABAB and multiple baseline designs and gave examples of how these designs can be used in group counseling research. We concur that these designs provide an exciting alternative for examining group-level phenomena. Unfortunately, since the publication of the Robison et al. article, there have been few single-subject designs published in the major counseling journals. In an effort to extend the thoughtful analysis of Robison et al., we present two additional single-subject designs, the randomized AB and time-series designs, that group counseling researchers can use to examine group-level phenomena.

The randomized AB design involves two phases (or treatments) that are repeated randomly. For example, Jauguet (1987) examined the effects of an agenda-go-round exercise on group cohesiveness. In her study, A represented sessions where the agenda-go-round was not used, and B represented sessions where this exercise was used. Randomized treatment order allowed Jauquet to use a randomization test (Edgington, 1987) to compare cohesiveness scores in the A and B sessions. In addition, Jauquet examined carryover effects using a 2 (agenda-go-round, non-agenda-go-round) times 2 (preceded by an agenda go-round, preceded by a non-agenda-go-round) factorial design.

The leader of a training group either did (B treatment condition) or did not (A treatment condition) begin group sessions with an agenda-go-round exercise, based on a random AB schedule. Cohesiveness at each meeting was measured by member ratings on the Engaged and Avoiding scales of the Group Climate Questionnaire (MacKenzie, 1983). A 2 by 2 ANOVA revealed no main effects for type of session phases or type of preceding session on the Engaged and Avoiding scales.

There was, however, a significant interaction effect on the Engaged and Avoiding scales. An examination of the means showed that non-agenda-go-round sessions that followed agenda-go-round sessions were rated by the group members as more engaged and less avoidant when compared to other treatment orders. This finding suggests that a periodic use of the agenda-go-round intervention may enhance members' perception of cohesiveness in groups.

Not only is Jauquet's study important in demonstrating the usefulness of a randomized AB design, it also demonstrates the usefulness of examining carryover effects. A simple *t*-test comparing the results during the A and B phases would have suggested that the agenda-go-round intervention did not have an effect on cohesiveness. The factorial analysis suggested that the simple question of whether or not to use an agenda-go-round is misleading. Rather Jauquet's study suggested that the more appropriate question is when and how often to use the agenda go-round. In a nonrandomized ABAB design, the researcher would never have been alerted to this possible interaction effect.

The defining characteristic of a time-series design is multiple observations over time (Cook & Campbell, 1979). There are two types of time-series designs: (1) interrupted time-series and (2) analysis of concomitance. In an interrupted time-series design, a treatment is administered at some point in the series of observations (the point at which the treatment takes place is called an interruption of the series). The logic of the interrupted time-series design involves comparing the observations before and after the interruption. If the treatment has an effect, there should be a difference in the observations prior to and following the interruption.

Unfortunately, the statistical analysis of interrupted time-series can be quite complicated, requiring considerable expertise (Crosbie, 1993). One of the main problems in analyzing time-series data is dealing with the problem of autocorrelation. Autocorrelation occurs when each score in a series of scores is more similar to the preceding score than it is to the mean score for the series. Recent advances in time-series analysis make the procedures more accessible to group counseling researchers. Specifically, Crosbie developed ITSACORR, a relatively simple procedure that can be used with data from short time series (as few as five observations pre and post interruption).

ITSACORR estimates and then statistically compares the slopes for the pre and post interruption observations. ITSACORR produces an overall *F*-test and two *t*-tests. The overall *F*-tests whether there is any overall difference between pre and post interruption observations. One of the *t*-tests is associated with the intercept, which tests whether or not the mean level of observations are different pre and post interventions. The other *t*-test is associated with the slopes, which tests whether or not the direction and or the rate of change in the observations differ for pre and post intervention periods.

ITSACORR has not been used in group counseling research. Daus (1995), however, used an interrupted time-series design to examine the effects of case presentations in group supervision on counselor self-efficacy. Daus had counselor trainees fill out the Counseling Self-Estimate Inventory (COSE; Larson et al., 1992) after each practicum class period. These COSE scores were the repeated observations in the time-series analysis. The case presentation served as the interruption in this series of observations. Daus used the ITSACORR program to see if the intercepts and the slopes of counselor self-efficacy changed from prior to the case presentation to subsequent the case presentation.

One counselor trainee in the Daus study had six COSE observations prior to her case presentation (interruption) and seven observations after the case presentation. The overall omnibus *F*-test for these data was significant showing an overall change in COSE scores from pre to post interruption (i.e., case presentation). In addition, both *t*-tests were significant. The significant *t*-test for the intercept showed that her average level of counselor self-efficacy was higher after the case presentation than it was before the presentation. The significant *t*-test for the slope showed that the rate of change for counselor self-efficacy was steeper after the case presentation than it was before the presentation. These results suggested that, for at least this one trainee, the case presentation resulted in an overall increase in self-efficacy.

At times, counseling researchers are interested not in examining the effect of a treatment in a time series, but whether changes in one variable in the time series cause subsequent changes in another variable in a time series. For instance, do changes in the group leader's level of self-disclosure affect the cohesiveness of the group? This type of analysis is referred to as an analysis of concomitance in time series. The researcher observes two variables over time.

Bivariate time-series analysis and spectral analysis are two sophisticated methods for answering questions about concomitance. Unfortunately, there are few examples of time-series analyses in the group counseling literature. According to Jones, Ghannam, Nigg, and Dyer (1993), in time-series analysis, the researcher attempts to infer a causal relationship between observations constituting one series of data points (e.g., group leader self-disclosure) and observations of a second series (e.g., group cohesiveness).

McBride (1995) used time-series analysis to examine the relationship between the personal and technical aspects of group leader behavior (Dies, 1993) and group climate ratings. She examined personal growth groups in which the group members rated leader behavior (Bolman, 1971) and group climate (MacKenzie, 1983) after each of 26 sessions. McBride divided her observations in to an early (sessions 1–13) and a late (sessions 13–26) period.

McBride computed the mean cross-correlation coefficients (CCC) for the personal or technical aspect of leader behavior and the engaged ratings from the Group Climate Scale (MacKenzie for both the early and late group sessions). In interpreting a CCC, a positive lag meant that the leader behavior led to engagement, while a negative lag meant that engagement led to leader behavior. Like a correlation coefficient, the sign of the CCC denoted the direction of the relationship while the absolute value indicated the magnitude of the relationship.

The CCC at lag 1 for the personal-engagement relationship for early group sessions was .05 (not statistically significant), while the CCC at lag 1 for the technical-engagement relationship for early group sessions was .20 (statistically significant). This result showed the importance of leader technical activity for early group development. Specifically, when group leaders were more technically oriented in an early group session, the group was more engaged in the following session.

Summary

There are a number of statistical and methodological issues that limit the conclusion that can be drawn from the published group counseling studies. In addition, group research is probably not conceived or carried out because of design and or statistical obstacles. Fortunately, there are a number of statistical and methodological advances that can allow group counseling researchers to overcome these design difficulties.

The feedback literature is an excellent example of the systematic progress that group process researchers can achieve when an area of study receives sustained empirical attention. Future group process studies can productively focus on the other group therapeutic factors specified in Yalom's (1995) influential model. The next decades can be an exciting and important time for group counseling process and outcome research.

CONCLUSIONS

Numerous forms of group counseling are practiced in a wide variety of settings with clients experiencing a multitude of clinical, educational, and social problems. In addition, researchers have examined many aspects of group counseling process and outcome. Research designs and statistical analyses have ranged from naïvely simple to elegantly complex. The conclusions that can be drawn from the numerous empirical examinations of group counseling are necessarily limited by the quality of the research designs used to study group counseling process and outcome. There are many complex methodological and statistical problems that group researchers have not consistently addressed in the outcome and process literature. Perhaps, the most important of these is the problem of nested data. It is impossible to determine the extent to which this one crucial issue has effected the results of the numerous process and outcome studies.

While acknowledging the design and statistical problems that are pervasive in the group counseling literature, it is possible to reach some relative firm conclusions about the process and outcome of group therapy. It is clear that group counseling is more effective than control or placebo treatments, and that the effect sizes for group counseling are equivalent to those of other recognized psychosocial and educational interventions. On the average, individual and group counseling have equivalent effects. However, group or individual treatments may be differentially effective with certain clients or certain problems. The exact nature of these potential-client-by-treatment and problem-by-treatment interactions cannot be determined from the present set of empirical findings. More sophisticated research designs will have to be consistently employed to answer these questions. There are no simple answers to questions about the effective structural features of group treatments. Sometimes more and sometimes fewer group sessions are related to better outcomes. Likewise, sometimes larger and sometimes smaller groups are associated with better outcomes. Only with sophisticated interactional designs can group researchers begin to sort out the answers to these complex structural questions.

Group researchers need to move beyond designs that simply examine the relative value of therapeutic factors or use gross distinctions like type of group to compare the relative value of therapeutic factors. Theoretical models need to be developed that link group or client type to endorsement of therapeutic factors. Researchers need to systematically examine therapeutic factors in addition to feedback and cohesiveness—group cohesiveness being the group equivalent of the working alliance in individual counseling. Group cohesiveness promotes positive group processes and leads to enhanced group counseling outcome. Group leader warmth and leader structuring are related to more cohesive groups. Outcome is enhanced when group members receive and deliver both positive and negative feedback. Structural interventions (feedback exercises) and group cohesiveness promote the receipt and delivery of positive and negative feedback.

REFERENCES

Antonuccio, D.O., Davis, C., Lewinson, P.M., & Breckenridge, J.S. (1987). Therapist variables related to cohesiveness in a group treatment for depression. *Small Group Behavior, 18,* 557–564.

Arnold, C.L. (1992). An introduction to hierarchical linear models. *Measurement and Evaluation in Counseling and Development, 25,* 58–90.

Barrett, C.L., Hampe, I.E., & Miller, L.C. (1978). Research on child psychotherapy. In S.L. Garfield & A.E. Bergin (Eds.), *Handbook of psychotherapy and behavior change: An empirical analysis.* (2nd ed., pp. 411–435). New York: Wiley.

Bednar, R.L., & Kaul, T.J. (1978). Experiential group research: Current perspectives. In S.L. Garfield & A.E. Bergin (Eds.), *Handbook of psychotherapy and behavior change* (2nd ed., pp. 769–815). New York: Wiley.

Bednar, R.L., & Kaul, T.K. (1994). Experiential group research: Can the cannon fire? In A.E. Bergin & S.L. Garfield (Eds.), *Handbook of psychotherapy and behavior change* (4th ed., pp. 631–663). New York: Wiley.

Bednar, R.L., Melnick, J., Kaul, T.J. (1974). Risk, responsibility and structure: A conceptual framework for initiating group counseling and psychotherapy. *Journal of Counseling Psychology, 21,* 31–37.

Bennis, W.F., & Shepard, H.A. (1956). A theory of group development. *Human Relations, 9,* 415–437.

Bloch, S., & Crouch, E. (1985). *Therapeutic factors in group psychotherapy.* Oxford, England: Oxford University Press.

Bloch, S., & Reibstein, J. (1980). Perceptions by patients and therapists of therapeutic factors in group psychotherapy. *British Journal of Psychiatry, 137*, 274–278.

Bloch, S., Reibstein, J., Crouch, E., Holroyd, P., & Themen, J. (1979). A method for the study of therapeutic factors in group psychotherapy. *British Journal of Psychiatry, 134*, 257–263.

Bolman, L. (1971). Some effects of trainers on their T groups. *Journal of Applied Behavioral Science, 7*, 309–325.

Bonney, W., Randall, D., Jr., & Cleveland, J.D. (1986). An analysis of client-perceived curative factors in a therapy group of former incest victims. *Small Group Behavior, 17*, 303–321.

Bordin, E.S. (1979). The generalizability of the psychoanalytic concept of the working alliance. *Psychotherapy: Theory, Research and Practice, 16*, 252–260.

Braaten, L.J. (1989). Predicting positive goal attainment and symptom reduction from early group climate dimensions. *International Journal of Group Psychotherapy, 39*, 377–387.

Brabender, V., Albrecht, E., Sillitti, J., Cooper, J., & Kramer, E. (1983). A study of curative factors in short-term group psychotherapy. *Hospital and Community Psychiatry, 34*, 643–644.

Brossart, D.F., Patton, M.J., & Wood, P.K. (1998). Assessing group process: An illustration using Tuckerized growth curves. *Group Dynamics: Theory, Research, and Practice, 2*, 3–17.

Bryk, A.S., & Raudenbush, S.W. (1992). *Hierarchical linear models: Applications and data analysis methods*. Newbury Park, CA: Sage.

Budman, S.H., Demby, A., Feldstein, M., Redono, J., Scherz, B., Bennett, M.J., Koppenaal, G., Daley, B.S., Hunter, M., & Ellis, J. (1989). Preliminary findings on a new instrument to measure cohesion in group psychotherapy. *International Journal of Group Psychotherapy, 37*, 75–93.

Budman, S.H., Soldz, S., Demby, A., Davis, M., & Merry, J. (1993). What is cohesiveness? An empirical examination. *Small Group Research, 24*, 199–216.

Budman, S.H., Soldz, S., Demby, A., Feldstein, M., Springer, T., & Davis, M.S. (1989). Cohesion, alliance and outcome in group psychotherapy. *Psychiatry, 52*, 339–350.

Burlingame, G.M., Kircher, J.C., & Taylor, S. (1994). Methodological considerations in group psychotherapy research: Past, present, and future practices. In A. Fuhriman & G.M. Burlingame (Eds.), *Handbook of group psychotherapy: An empirical and clinical synthesis* (pp. 41–80). New York: Wiley.

Cattell, R.B. (1966). The data box: Its ordering of total resources in terms of possible relational systems. In R.B. Cattell (Ed.), *Handbook of multivariate experimental psychology* (pp. 67–128). Chicago: Rand McNally.

Colijn, S., Hoencamp, E., Snijders, H., Van Der Spek, M., & Duivenvoorden, H. (1991). A comparison of curative factors in different types of group psychotherapy. *International Journal of Group Psychotherapy, 41*, 365–378.

Cook, T.D., & Campbell, D.T. (1979). *Quasi-experimentation: Design and analysis issues for field setting.* Boston: Houghton Mifflin.

Crosbie, J. (1993). Interrupted time series analysis with brief single subject data. *Journal of Consulting and Clinical Psychology, 61*, 966–974.

Crouch, E.C., Bloch, S., & Wanlass, J. (1994). Therapeutic factors: Interpersonal and intrapersonal mechanisms. In A. Fuhriman & G.M. Burlingame (Eds.), *Handbook of group psychotherapy* pp. 269–315. New York: Wiley.

Daus, J.A., III. (1995, August). *Changes in counseling efficacy across a semester of group supervision: A time series analysis.* Unpublished doctoral dissertation, University of Missouri, Columbia.

de Jong, T.L., & Gorey, K.M. (1996). Short-term versus long-term group work with female survivors of childhood sexual abuse; A brief meta-analytic review, *Social Work with Groups, 19*(1), 19–27.

Dies, R.R. (1993). Research on group psychotherapy: Overview and clinical applications. In A. Alonso & H.I. Swiller (Eds.), *Group therapy in clinical practice* (pp. 473–518). Washington, DC: American Psychiatric Press.

Dweck, C.S. (1986). Motivational processes affecting learning. *American Psychologist, 41*, 1040–1048.

Edington, E.S. (1987). Randomized single-subject experiments and statistical tests. *Journal of Counseling Psychology, 34*, 437–442.

Elliott, R. (1985). Helpful and nonhelpful events in brief counseling interviews: An empirical taxonomy. *Journal of Counseling Psychology, 32*, 307–322.

Faith S.M., Wong, F.Y., & Carpenter, K.M. (1995). Group sensitivity training: Update, meta-analysis, and recommendations. *Journal of Counseling Psychology, 42*(3), 390–399.

Fettes, P.A., & Peters, J.M. (1992). A meta-analysis of group treatments for bulimia nervosa. *International Journal of Eating Disorders, 11*(2), 97–110.

Fitzgerald, L.F., & Osipow, S.H. (1986). An occupational analysis of counseling psychology: How special is the specialty? *American Psychologist, 41,* 535–544.

Flowers, J.V. (1979). The differential outcome effects of simple advice, alternatives and instructions in group psychotherapy. *International Journal of Group Psychotherapy, 29,* 305–316.

Flowers, J.V. (1987). Client outcome as a function of agreement or disagreement with the modal group perception of curative factors in short-term, structured group psychotherapy. *International Journal of Group Psychotherapy, 37,* 113–118.

Flowers, J.V., & Booarem, C.D. (1989). Four studies toward an empirical foundation for group therapy. *Journal of Social Service Research, 13,* 105–121.

Flowers, J.V., & Booraem, C.D. (1991). A psychoeducational group for clients with heterogeneous problems: Process and outcome. *Small Group Research, 22,* 258–273.

Flowers, J.V., Booarem, C.D., & Seacat, G.F. (1974). The effect of positive and negative feedback on members' sensitivity to other members in group therapy. *Psychotherapy: Theory, Research and Practice, 11,* 346–350.

Francis, D.J., Fletcher, J.M., Stuebing, K.K., Davidson, K.C., & Thompson, N.M. (1991). Analysis of change: Modeling individual growth. *Journal of Consulting and Clinical Psychology, 59,* 27–37.

Fuehrer, A., & Keys, C. (1988). Group development in self-help groups for college students. *Small Group Behavior, 19,* 325–341.

Fuhriman, A., & Burlingame, G.M. (1994). Group psychotherapy: Research and practice. In A. Fuhriman & G.M. Burlingame (Eds.), *Handbook of group psychotherapy: An empirical and clinical synthesis* (pp. 3–40). New York: Wiley.

Fuhriman, A., Drescher, S., Hanson, E., Henrie, R., & Rybicki, W. (1986). Refining the measurement of curativeness: An empirical approach. *Small Group Behavior, 17,* 186–201.

Gehlert, K.M. (1994). *Narcissistic vulnerability and perception of climate in group counseling.* Unpublished doctoral dissertation, University of Missouri, Columbia.

Gorey, K.M., & Cryns, A.G. (1991). Group work as interventive modality with older depressed client: A meta-analytic review. *Journal of Gerontological Social Work, 19*(2), 137–157.

Hawkins, A.K. (1997). The effect of goal orientation on counselor trainees' acceptance of positive and negative feedback (Doctoral dissertation, University of Missouri, Columbia, 1997). *Dissertation Abstracts International, 57,* A5061.

Hoag, M.J., & Burlingame, G.M. (1997). Evaluating the effectiveness of child and adolescent group treatment: A meta-analytic review. *Journal of Clinical Child Psychology, 26*(3), 234–246.

Horvath, A.O., & Symonds, B.D. (1991). Relation between working alliance and outcome in psychotherapy: A meta-analysis. *Journal of Counseling Psychology, 36,* 139–149.

Hurst, A.G., Stein, K.B., Korchin, S.J., & Soskin, W.F. (1978). Leadership style determinants of cohesiveness in adolescent groups. *International Journal of Group Psychotherapy, 28,* 263–277.

Jauquet, C.A. (1987). *The effects of an agenda setting exercise on process involvement in a counseling training group.* Unpublished master's thesis, University of Missouri, Columbia.

Jones, E.J., Ghannam, J., Nigg, J.T., & Dyer, J.F.P. (1993). A paradigm for single-case research: The time-series study of a long-term psychotherapy for depression. *Journal of Consulting and Clinical Psychology, 61,* 381–394.

Kahn, E., Webster, P., & Storck, M. (1986). Brief Reports: Curative factors in two types of inpatient psychotherapy groups. *International Journal of Group Psychotherapy, 36,* 579–585.

Kapp, F.T., Gleser, G., & Brissenden, A. (1964). Group participation and self-perceived personality change. *Journal of Nervous and Mental Disease, 139,* 255–265.

Kapur, R., Miller, K., & Mitchell, G. (1988). Therapeutic factors within in-patient and out-patient psychotherapy groups: Implications for therapeutic techniques. *British Journal of Psychiatry, 152,* 229–233.

Kaul, T.J., & Bednar, R.L. (1994). Pretraining and structure: Parallel lines yet to meet. In A. Fuhriman & G.M. Burlingame (Eds.), *Handbook of group psychotherapy* (pp. 155–188). New York: Wiley.

Kenny, D.A., & La Voie, L. (1984). The social relations model. *Advances in Experimental Social Psychology, 18,* 141–182.

Kiesler, D.J. (1966). Some myths of psychotherapy research and the search for a paradigm. *Psychological Bulletin, 65,* 110–136.

Kiesler, D.J. (1984). *Check list of psychotherapy transactions (CLOPT) and check list of interpersonal transactions (CLOIT).* Richmond: Virginia Commonwealth University.

Kiesler, D.J. (1996). *Contemporary interpersonal theory and research: Personality, psychopathology, and psychotherapy.* New York: Wiley.

Kivlighan, D.M., Jr. (1985). Feedback in group psychotherapy: Review and implications. *Small Group Behavior, 16,* 373–385.

Kivlighan, D.M., Jr., & Goldfine, D.C. (1991). Endorsement of therapeutic factors as a function of stage of group development and participant interpersonal attitudes. *Journal of Counseling Psychology, 38,* 150–158.

Kivlighan, D.M., Jr., & Lilly, R.L. (1997). Developmental changes in group climate as they relate to therapeutic gain. *Group Dynamics: Theory, Research, and Practice, 1,* 208–221.

Kivlighan, D.M., Jr., McGovern, T.M., & Corazzini, J.G. (1984). The effects of the content and timing of structuring interventions on group therapy process and outcome. *Journal of Counseling Psychology, 31,* 363–370.

Kivlighan, D.M., Jr., & Mullison, D. (1988). Participants' perception of therapeutic factors in group counseling: The role of interpersonal style and stage of group development. *Small Group Behavior, 19,* 452–468.

Kivlighan, D.M., Jr., Multon, K., & Brossart, D. (1996). Helpful impacts in group counseling: Development of a multidimensional rating system. *Journal of Counseling Psychology, 43,* 347–355.

Larson, L.M., Suzuki, L.A., Gillespie, K.N., Potenza, M.T., Bechtel, M.A., & Toulouse, A.L. (1992). Development and validation of the Counseling Self-Estimate Inventory. *Journal of Counseling Psychology, 39,* 105–120.

Lieberman, M.A. (1976). Change induction in small groups. *Annual Review of Psychology, 27,* 217–250.

Lieberman, M.A., Yalom, I., & Miles, M. (1973). *Encounter groups: First facts.* New York: Basic Books.

Lovett, L., & Lovett, J. (1991). Group therapeutic factors on an alcohol in-patient unit. *British Journal of Psychiatry, 159,* 365–370.

Macaskill, N. (1982). Therapeutic factors in group therapy with borderline patients. *International Journal of Group Psychotherapy, 32,* 61–73.

MacDevitt, J., & Sanislow, C. (1987). Curative factors in offenders' groups. *Small Group Behavior, 18,* 72–81.

MacKenzie, K.R. (1983). The clinical application of a group climate measure. In R.R. Dies & K.R. MacKenzie (Eds.), *Advances in group psychotherapy: Integrating research and practice* (pp. 159–170). Madison, CT: International University Press.

MacKenzie, K.R., Dies, R.R., Coche, E., Rutan, J.S., & Stone, W.N. (1987). An analysis of AGPA Institute groups. *International Journal of Group Psychotherapy, 37,* 55–74.

MacKenzie, K.R., & Lively, W.J. (1983). A developmental model for brief group therapy. In R.R. Dies & K.R. MacKenzie (Eds.), *Advances in group psychotherapy: Integrating research and practice* (pp. 159–170). Madison, CT: International Universities Press.

Mahrer, A.R., & Nadler, W.P. (1986). Good moments in psychotherapy: A preliminary review, a list, and some promising research avenues. *Journal of Consulting and Clinical Psychology, 54,* 10–16.

Marcovitz, R., & Smith, J. (1983). Patients' perception of curative factors in short-term group psychotherapy. *International Journal of Group Psychotherapy, 33,* 21–39.

Marcus, D.K., & Holahan, W. (1994). Interpersonal perception in group therapy: A social relations analysis. *Journal of Consulting and Clinical Psychology, 62,* 776–782.

Marcus, D.K., & Kashy, D.A. (1995). The social relations model: A tool for group psychotherapy research. *Journal of Counseling Psychology, 42,* 383–389.

Marziali, E., Munroe-Blum, & McCleary, L. (1997). The contribution of group cohesion and group alliance to the outcome of group psychotherapy. *International Journal of Group Psychotherapy, 47,* 475–497.

McBride, L.C. (1995). Toward group process understanding: Leadership and group climate (Doctoral dissertation, University of Missouri, Columbia, 1994). *Dissertation Abstracts International, 55,* 5571.

McLeod, J., & Ryan, A. (1993). Therapeutic factors experienced by members of an out-patient therapy group for older women. *British Journal of Guidance and Counselling, 21,* 64–71.

McRoberts, C., Burlingame, G.M., & Hoag, M.J. (1998). Comparative efficacy of individual and group psychotherapy: A meta-analytic perspective. *Group Dynamics: Theory, Research and Practice, 2*(2), 101–117.

Morran, D.K., Robison, F.F., & Hulse-Killacky, D. (1990). Group research and the unit of analysis problem: The use of ANOVA designs with nested factors. *Journal for Specialists in Group Work, 15,* 10–14.

Morran, D.K., Robison, F.F., & Stockton, R. (1985). Feedback exchange in counseling groups: An analysis of message content and receiver acceptance as a function of leader versus member delivery, session, and valence. *Journal of Counseling Psychology, 32,* 57–67.

Morran, D.K., & Stockton, R. (1980). Effects of self-concept on group member reception of positive and negative feedback. *Journal of Counseling Psychology, 27,* 260–267.

Morran, D.K., Stockton, R., & Bond, L. (1991). Delivery of positive and corrective feedback in counseling groups. *Journal of Counseling Psychology, 38,* 410–414.

Mullen, B., Anthony, T., Salas, E., & Driskell, J.E. (1994). Group cohesiveness and quality of decision making: An integration of tests of the group-think hypothesis. *Small Group Research, 25,* 189–204.

Mullen, B., & Cooper, C. (1994). The relation between group cohesiveness and performance: An integration. *Psychological Bulletin, 115,* 210–227.

Mullen, B., Driskell, J.E., & Salas, E. (1998). Meta-analysis and the study of group dynamics. *Group Dynamics: Theory, Research and Practice, 2,* 213–229.

Phipps, L.B., & Zastowny, T.R. (1988). Leadership behavior, group climate and outcome in group psychotherapy: A study of outpatient psychotherapy groups. *Group, 12,* 157–171.

Reeker, J., Ensing, D., & Elliott, R. (1997). A meta-analytic investigation of group treatment outcomes for sexually abused children. *Child Abuse and Neglect, 21*(7), 669–680.

Roarke, A.E., & Sharah, H.S. (1989). Factors related to group cohesiveness. *Small Group Behavior, 20,* 62–69.

Robbins, S.B., & Patton, M.J. (1985). Self psychology and career development: Construction of the superiority and goal instability scales. *Journal of Counseling Psychology, 32,* 221–231.

Robison, F.F., & Hardt, D.A. (1992). Effects of cognitive and behavioral structure and discussion of corrective feedback outcomes on counseling group development. *Journal of Counseling Psychology, 39,* 473–481.

Robison, F.F., Morran, D.K., & Hulse-Killacky, D. (1998). Single-subject research designs for counselors studying their own groups. *Journal of Specialists in Group Work, 14,* 93–97.

Robison, F.F., Morran, D.K., & Stockton, R. (1986). Effects of valence and receiver defensiveness on acceptance of feedback in counseling groups. *Journal for Specialists in Group Work, 11,* 2–8.

Robison, F.F., Stockton, R., Morran, D.K., & Uhl-Wagner, A. (1988). Anticipated consequences of communicating corrective feedback during early counseling group development. *Small Group Behavior, 19,* 469–484.

Rohde, R.I., & Stockton, R. (1992). The effect of structured feedback on goal attainment, attraction to the group, and satisfaction with the group in small group counseling. *Journal of Group Psychotherapy, Psychodrama and Sociometry, 44,* 172–180.

Rugel, R.P. (1987). Achieving congruence in Tavistock groups: Empirical findings and implications for group therapy. *Small Group Behavior, 18,* 108–117.

Shaffer, J., & Galinsky, M.D. (1989). *Models of group therapy* (2nd ed.). Englewood Cliffs, NJ: Prentice-Hall.

Shaughnessy, P., & Kivlighan, D., Jr. (1995). Using group participants' perceptions of therapeutic factors to form client typologies. *Small Group Research, 26,* 250–268.

Shechtman, Z., Bar-El, O., & Hadar, E. (1997). Therapeutic factors and psychoeducational groups for adolescents: A comparison. *The Journal for Specialists in Group Work, 22,* 203–213.

Sherry, P., & Hurley, J. (1976). Curative factors in psychotherapeutic and growth groups. *Journal of Clinical Psychology, 32,* 835–837.

Stockton, R., Rohde, R.I., & Haughey, J. (1992). The effects of structured group exercises on cohesion, engagement, avoidance, and conflict. *Small Group Research, 23,* 1555–1568.

Stone, M., Lewis, C., & Beck, A. (1994). The structure of Yalom's curative factor scale. *International Journal of Group Psychotherapy, 44,* 239–245.

Tillitski, C.J. (1990). A meta-analysis of estimated effect sizes for group versus individual versus control treatments. *International Journal of Group Psychotherapy, 40*(2), 215–224.

Tinsley, H.E.A. (1992). Psychometric theory and counseling psychology research. In S.D. Brown & R.W. Lent (Eds.), *Handbook of counseling psychology* (2nd ed., pp. 37–70). New York: Wiley.

Tschuschke, V., & Dies, R.R. (1994). Intensive analysis of therapeutic factors and outcome in long-term inpatient groups. *International Journal of Group Psychotherapy, 44,* 185–208.

Tuckman, B.W. (1965). Developmental sequence in small groups. *Psychological Bulletin, 63,* 384–399.

Willett, J.B., Ayoub, C.C., & Robinson, D. (1991). Using growth modeling to examine systematic differences in growth: An example of change in the functioning of families at risk of maladaptive parenting, child abuse, or neglect. *Journal of Consulting and Clinical Psychology, 59,* 38–47.

Yalom, I.D. (1975). *The theory and practice of group psychotherapy* (2nd ed.). New York: Basic Books.

Yalom, I.D. (1985). *The theory and practice of group psychotherapy* (3rd ed.). New York: Basic Books.

Yalom, I.D. (1995). *The theory and practice of group psychotherapy* (4th ed.). New York: Basic Books.

Yalom, I.D., Houts, P.S., Zimerberg, S.M., & Rand, L. (1967). Prediction of improvement in group psychotherapy. *Archives of General Psychiatry, 17,* 159–168.

CHAPTER 25

Processes and Outcomes in Couples and Family Therapy

MYRNA L. FRIEDLANDER
MA. TERESA TUASON

When a couple seeks professional help for an ailing relationship, a positive outcome is by no means assured. Although the majority of couples do improve their marriages in counseling (Gurman, Kniskern, & Pinsof, 1986), some 50% of clients leave treatment still feeling dissatisfied with their partners (Prince & Jacobson, 1995). Often couples wait too long before seeking outside help. In some cases, one partner initiates counseling to leave the relationship. In other cases, the damage already done may simply be too extensive to repair. Memories of vicious or mean-spirited conflict can overshadow all attempts to build trust and recapture a feeling of joy.

Couple and family therapists—experiential as well as behavioral—tend to be active, direct, and forceful (e.g., Friedlander, Highlen, & Lassiter, 1985; Friedlander, Wildman, Heatherington, & Skowron, 1994; Pinsof, 1986). They need to advocate for relationships while expressing warm, patient concern for every individual. This is not easy when the stories they hear suggest villains and victims or when advocating for the well being of one family member means that others may suffer.

Indeed, providing treatment to distressed couples and families has challenges that can rattle even the most experienced and skillful therapist. It is common for one client to be highly resistant to accepting professional help. Ignoring the resistance will surely stagnate the therapy, if it does not end prematurely. On the other hand, trying too hard to be empathic to a resistant client can so alienate other family members that the end result is identical.

Some family therapists describe themselves as neutral parties in the family struggles (Selvini Palazzoli, Boscolo, Cecchin, & Prata, 1980). But neutrality in the absence of warmth and caring does not go far, and warmth can be misconstrued. Because most family problems involve interpersonal conflict of some kind or another, expressing warmth toward one client may be interpreted as betrayal by another. Neutrality can also be problematic when one family member clearly needs individual help. It is difficult to make a referral for that person when other family members view it as a vindication or a triumph. At times, even the most carefully worded recommendation can backfire, the result being that no one in the family receives help.

Most of these process concerns are unique to family therapy because of the complexity involved in working with several people simultaneously. Although therapists who work with individuals need to consider the effects of their work on clients' family ties, the challenges to those ties do not occur in the session itself. While the immediacy of change in the presence of a therapist is the *raison d'être* for family therapy, the risks clients take are not negligible. In family sessions, clients expose themselves to having secrets revealed without their consent. They risk finding out that a personal relationship they value is not valued by the other party. They risk being humiliated or attacked by the people closest to them. If the therapist is unable to stem the tide of blame and recrimination, the damage to the individual or the family may be long lasting, quite possibly irreversible.

797

This is by no means to suggest that there are no joys to be experienced in family therapy. To the contrary, it is not unusual for frightened, vulnerable people to learn to express their love and caring to one another for the first time. Brothers learn what it means to be a brother; sisters, to be a sister. When a husband and wife, living apart miserably, find renewed hope and pleasure in one another, this change can reverse the direction of their lives and those of their children. Many family therapists believe that dramatic outcomes like these are rarely achieved in individual therapy.

But how do such results come about? Who benefits from family therapy? Who does not? Indeed, what is a "good outcome" in couples and family therapy? Must everyone involved benefit for the outcome to be considered "good"?

Defining outcome is, clearly, a more formidable task for family therapy researchers than it is for researchers of individual therapy. Outcomes need to be considered for individuals as well as systemwide, and there is little agreement on how to diagnose systemic problems or assess their remediation. Conducting follow-up studies is problematic as well. Maintaining even the most positive treatment results is complicated by the rapid changes families experience as children grow and develop.

Process research is similarly challenged. Not only do multiple perspectives need to be assessed, but observable, in-session behaviors only tell part of the story, arguably less of the story than in individual therapy. Since each family develops a unique way of communicating, the latent messages in family members' interactions can be undetected or easily misunderstood by observers. Consider Father interrupting Mother, for example. This behavior may signify more than a simple bid to speak. It may mean that (1) he, not she, is the gatekeeper in the family, (2) she is about to reveal something he would prefer to keep hidden, (3) he views himself as the authority on that subject, (4) he does not respect her opinion or her right to voice it, and so forth. These private meanings—any or all of which the family members are acutely aware—can be lost to the researcher.

In the past 15 years, counseling psychologists have become increasingly interested in working with couples and families. This interest reflects the longstanding emphasis in our specialty on understanding developmental passages, person-environment fit, and system change. Indeed, traditional areas of interest in counseling psychology like career development as well as emerging areas like health psychology have consistently taken into account family influences on children, adolescents, and adults. Whereas few family therapy outcome studies have been conducted by counseling psychologists, counseling psychologists are leaders in the investigation of change processes in couples and family therapy. With the inclusion of this chapter in the *Handbook,* it is hoped that still more counseling psychologists will be attracted to this fertile area of investigation.

In this chapter, research on couples and family therapy is critically reviewed. (The term *couples therapy* is used rather than *marital therapy* so as to be inclusive. Unfortunately, few investigators have reported the percentage of nonmarried couples in their samples.) While an effort has been made to provide a thorough summary of this large body of literature, the review is representative, not exhaustive.

Manual and computer searches were used to locate comparative outcome studies as well as studies providing evidence of family therapy's efficacy for different client problems and diagnoses. The review of process research begins with studies that describe what happens in family therapy sessions, followed by those that highlight effective mechanisms of change. The chapter concludes with implications of the literature for building theory, informing practice, and guiding future investigative efforts.

HOW EFFECTIVE IS COUPLES AND FAMILY THERAPY?

Recent comprehensive reviews of the outcome literature (Baucom, Shoham, Mueser, Daiuto, & Stickle, 1998; Dunn & Schwebel, 1995; Pinsof, Wynne, & Hambright, 1996) clearly support the overall efficacy of couples and family treatments compared to no-treatment or wait-list controls. In a meta-analysis of 71 studies (Shadish, Ragsdale, Glaser, & Montgomery, 1995), for example, the effect size was $d = .51$, which means that, on average, the treatment groups did approximately half a standard deviation better than the untreated controls. Furthermore, couples and family therapy effect sizes are comparable to those of individual therapy; in 23 studies that directly compared family to individual treatment, the meta-analytic differences were negligible, $d = -.05$ (Shadish et al., 1995). Despite concerns about the clinical significance of the positive outcomes reported in many studies, there is little empirical evidence that couples and family therapies actually cause harm to clients (Pinsof et al., 1996). Controlled outcome studies are summarized next.

What Works for Couples?

Couples with Relationship Problems

The most thoroughly investigated approach to couples work, behavioral marital therapy (BMT), has been compared with wait-list (e.g., Baucom, Sayers, & Sher, 1990; Hahlweg, Revenstorf, & Schindler, 1982; Jacobson, 1977, 1984; Snyder & Wills, 1989; Turkewitz & O'Leary, 1981) and attention-placebo controls (e.g., Liberman, Levine, Wheeler, Sanders, & Wallace, 1976). Consistently, BMT has been found to be more efficacious than these comparison groups. Furthermore, a study (Jacobson, Schmaling, & Holtzworth-Munroe, 1987) with 34 couples showed that the comprehensive BMT approach was superior to two of its components, behavior exchange and problem-solving training.

In terms of clinically significant change, reviewers of the literature (Jacobson et al., 1984) have concluded that, on average, 50% of couples undergoing BMT treatment improved beyond measurement error and 35% of the couples were no longer distressed at posttest, compared with an improvement rate of 13.5% for wait-list couples. Although couples' gains tend to be maintained for 6 to 12 months, longer term follow-up studies (Jacobson et al., 1987; Snyder, Wills, & Grady-Fletcher, 1991) have shown substantial rates (30%–38%) of relapse or divorce.

Two approaches, cognitive marital therapy and brief couples therapy (BCT), focus on clients' cognitive processes. Whereas cognitive therapists work with the irrational standards, assumptions, and beliefs that influence couples' relationships, BCT therapists use restraining techniques and positive reframing. Both approaches have demonstrated improvements in relationship adjustment as compared with controls (Davidson & Horvath, 1997; Huber & Milstein, 1985); in Davidson and Horvath, 39% of the couples met reliable change criteria for clinically meaningful improvement. On the other hand, these authors found no differences in the specific cognitive processes targeted by BCT, and there was no association between changes in marital satisfaction and changes in relationship beliefs.

More exploratory approaches are insight-oriented marital therapy and emotionally focused therapy (EFT). In the insight approach, couples are helped to clarify, interpret, and express feelings, beliefs, and standards for themselves, their relationship, and each other. Snyder and Wills (1989) reported that the gains in marital adjustment by insight treatment were maintained for 6 months and in lengthier follow-ups. Similar to this approach, EFT focuses on couples' feelings, but without the emphasis on insight. Several studies comparing EFT with wait-list controls (Goldman & Greenberg, 1992; James, 1991; Johnson & Greenberg, 1985) support its efficacy, not only for relationship concerns but also for couples who are dealing with chronically ill children (Walker, Johnson, Manion, & Cloutier, 1996).

Despite an impressive number of studies supporting the benefit of couples therapy compared with no treatment (e.g., a meta-analytic effect size $d = .60$; Shadish et al., 1995), there is little evidence to support one approach over another. In 105 studies that directly compared theoretical orientations, nonsignificant differences were found in 81% of the comparisons (Shadish et al. 1995).

One exception is Johnson and Greenberg's (1985) comparison of BMT and EFT for moderately distressed couples. The relative effectiveness of EFT was demonstrated at posttest and 2 months later. On the other hand, no differences were found in a comparison of EFT with EFT plus communication skills (James, 1991). Likewise, comparisons of BMT and BMT combined with cognitive structuring, emotional expressiveness training, or both (e.g., Baucom et al., 1990) showed no significant treatment differences. Similar results were also obtained in a comparison of BMT with enhanced BMT (i.e., cognitive restructuring, generalization training, and exploration of feelings) (Halford, Sanders, & Behrens, 1993).

A lack of differences posttreatment does not mean, however, that the long-term benefits are identical. In a comparison of BMT and insight-oriented marital therapy (Snyder & Wills, 1989), the treatments were similar with respect to adjustment at posttest and 6 months later, but after 4 years, couples in the insight treatment reported significantly better adjustment. Far fewer of them (3%) had experienced divorce than the couples (38%) in the BMT sample. Similarly, no posttest differences were found in comparisons of EFT with systemic therapy (Goldman & Greenberg, 1992), but in a 4-month follow-up, therapeutic gains were maintained only in the systemic group. Evidence from this study also suggested that maintenance of treatment gains is likely to depend on problem severity. Whereas results favored EFT for moderately distressed couples at posttest and 2 months later, this difference was not obtained for seriously distressed couples, many of whom relapsed (Goldman & Greenberg, 1992).

Couples with Individual Problems

Apart from studies in which the target is the couple's relationship, there are numerous investigations of conjoint treatments for clients with specific diagnoses. One concern is how best to treat couples when one partner is depressed. In studies comparing BMT and individual cognitive therapy, no treatment differences were found among distressed couples (O'Leary & Beach, 1990), with both treatments producing improvement in depressive symptoms, but results favored the individual approach for nondistressed couples (Jacobson, Dobson, Fruzzetti, Schmaling, & Salusky, 1991). Authors have concluded that depression prompted by marital problems is best treated with BMT, but depression not linked with marital distress responds more favorably to individual cognitive therapy (Beach & O'Leary, 1992; O'Leary, Riso, & Beach, 1990; Prince & Jacobson, 1995).

Aside from this line of research, the majority of treatment studies for individual problems uses partner involvement to motivate clients to engage in therapy, change maladaptive habits, and maintain treatment gains over time. A large group of partner-assisted studies, not surprisingly, concern sexual dysfunction. In these studies, diagnosed sexual disorders are the focus of concern rather than more diffuse sexual concerns (e.g., infrequent or unsatisfying sexual interactions) that reflect distress in the relationship.

Partner-assisted interventions include education, self-exploration, directed masturbation, sensate focus, sexual fantasy, and imagery. Masters and Johnson's (1970) treatment for sexual dysfunctions, particularly women's orgasmic disorders, uses the partner as a coach and encourages couples to discuss difficulties surrounding sexual interaction. In addition to studies on the efficacy of this treatment program (e.g., Matthews et al., 1976), several investigations have compared it to communication-based couples therapy. Everaerd and Dekker (1981), for example, found that couples who underwent communication therapy improved their relationship, while those who had sex therapy acquired better sexual skills and maintained these gains for 6 months. In another research program, Hurlbert (1993; Hurlbert, White, Powell, & Apt, 1993) compared a package of partner-assisted sexual skills training, a general couples intervention, and orgasm consistency training with a women-only group for clients with hypoactive sexual desire disorders. The combined treatment package for couples was superior to both the wait-list group and the women-only group on measures of sexual compatibility, desire, and satisfaction.

Studies with heterogeneous samples have had more ambiguous results (e.g., Crowe, Gillan, & Golombok, 1981). The couple's level of functioning seems to be a contributing factor. Hawton and Catalan (1986), for example, reported poorer outcomes in sex therapy for couples with greater marital distress, a history of separation, and poorly motivated male partners. Similarly, MacPhee, Johnson, and van der Veer (1995) found that EFT was less effective for women with inhibited sexual desire if their marriages were distressed.

Another group of studies uses partner involvement in the treatment of alcoholism and drug abuse. It has long been recognized that, because alcohol abuse has debilitating effects on family members, partners should be involved early on in the treatment process (Edwards & Steinglass, 1995). Although most studies focus more on abstinence than relationship concerns, one study (O'Farrell & Choquette, 1991) demonstrated that BMT for alcoholic men and their wives effectively reduced the couples' patterns of violence.

Several behavioral treatment packages for alcoholism have been tested empirically, including the community reinforcement approach (Azrin, Sisson, Meyers, & Godley, 1982; Sisson & Azrin, 1986) and Project CALM (Counseling for Alcoholic Marriages; O'Farrell, Choquette, Cutter, Brown, & McCourt, 1993), which includes a BMT couples group. Results tend to support the efficacy of these approaches over individual treatment in terms of abstinence as well as marital adjustment. Notably, in one study, O'Farrell, Cutter, and Floyd (1985) found that, with respect to abstinence, the BMT group was more successful than an interactional couples group that focused on support, insight, feelings, and decreasing conflict. The results of these studies need to be considered cautiously, however, because only the BMT treatments in Project CALM included disulfiram (Antabuse).

The strongest evidence in couples alcohol treatment is for the motivating influence of spouses confronting their partners and educating themselves about alcoholism (Edwards & Steinglass, 1995). Less impressive are the long-term treatment results in terms of abstinence. While spouse involvement increases participation in after-care programs, treatment gains tend to diminish with time (Edwards & Steinglass, 1995).

Relatively fewer studies on couples treatments for drug abuse have been conducted, and the results are less positive than those for alcoholism (Liddle & Dakof, 1995). One important investigation by Fals-Stewart, Birchler, and O'Farrell (1996) compared BMT with individual treatment for men. In addition to significantly altered drug use, including fewer arrests and hospitalizations, the men's relationships with their partners improved for a year following treatment. Differences in the men's drug use were not, however, maintained over time.

Partner-assisted programs have also been shown to be effective in treating some physical problems (Campbell & Patterson, 1995), such as hypertension (Morisky et al., 1983), obesity (Pearce, LeBow, & Orchard, 1981), and adjustment to home peritoneal kidney dialysis (Hener, Weisenberg, & Har-Even, 1996), as well as anxiety-based disorders. A strictly behavioral approach to agoraphobia, in which partners function as coaches but relationship difficulties are addressed only if necessary, has been successful to some extent (e.g., Craske, Burton, & Barlow, 1989). There is, however, stronger evidence for combining couples' communication sessions with partner-assisted exposure (Arnow, Taylor, Agras, & Telch, 1985). Because couples' relaxation training was used as a control (Arnow et al., 1985), the superiority of the communication-based treatment is noteworthy.

Studies of partner-assisted treatments for obsessive compulsive disorder have been less favorable (Emmelkamp, de Haan, & Hoodguin, 1990; Emmelkamp & de Lange, 1983). Emmelkamp et al. found no differences between partner-assisted and nonassisted treatments, and results were comparable regardless of the client's level of marital distress.

In the studies reviewed previously, one member of a couple was diagnosed with a physical or emotional disorder. In the family therapy studies summarized next, the identified client is usually a child, although treatments for seriously disturbed young adults and their parents have also been studied.

What Works for Families?

Parent Management Training

For children's problems like oppositional and conduct disorders, behavior problems, delinquency, and attention-deficit hyperactivity disorder (ADHD), parent management training (PMT) has been the most widely used treatment, with demonstrated effectiveness (Estrada & Pinsof, 1995). This program, which targets specific problem behaviors using modeling, role playing, and home practice, has successfully changed the problem behaviors of children who are antisocial (Estrada & Pinsof, 1995) and reduced other behavior problems at home and at school (Forehand & Long, 1988) over an impressive, 14-year posttreatment interval (Estrada & Pinsof, 1995). Furthermore, a few studies have taken into account PMT's benefits to the family as a whole—in reducing family conflict, increasing cohesiveness and expressiveness within the family (Sayger, Horne, & Glaser, 1993), changing the behavior of parents, and alleviating stress (Peed, Roberts, & Forehand, 1977; Sayger et al., 1993).

Despite the strong evidence for PMT's efficacy, some studies indicate important exceptions. Estrada and Pinsof (1995), for example, pointed out that sizable numbers of families (30%–50%) do not maintain clinically significant gains, and attrition rates in excess of 50% are not uncommon. For children with ADHD, PMT can improve family relationships, alleviate parental stress, and reduce children's aggressiveness and other behavior problems, but this treatment does not seem to affect the essential elements of the disorder—impulsivity, distractibility, and excessive activity (Estrada & Pinsof, 1995). Furthermore, comparisons of PMT with other approaches are not conclusive. Barkley, Guevremont, Anastopoulos, and Flecher (1992), for example, found no significant differences in the treatment of ADHD when PMT was compared with family systems therapy and parent-child training in problem solving, and the clinical improvement rates (5%–30%) did not differ by approach (Estrada & Pinsof, 1995). Other studies suggest that PMT's success depends on client factors. When the parents are exceptionally stressed or depressed (Webster-Stratton, 1990) or when the families are disadvantaged and isolated (Miller & Prinz, 1990), treatment participation tends to be low, outcomes tend to be poor, and those who benefit from the program do not always maintain their gains over time (Estrada & Pinsof, 1995).

PMT has also been evaluated as part of larger treatment packages. Problem-solving training for children seems to be enhanced with PMT (Kazdin, Esveldt-Dawson, French, & Unis, 1987), and children's gains tend to be maintained (Estrada & Pinsof, 1995). Also, interventions that focus on marital communication have increased PMT's effectiveness with dysfunctional families (Dadds, Schwartz, & Sanders, 1987). Moreover, stimulant medication combined with PMT has been effective in treating children with ADHD (Horn et al., 1991).

Other Approaches

Behavioral programs other than PMT have also been evaluated empirically. Lovaas's (1987) well-known family treatment for children with autistic disorders has been widely studied (Birnbrauer & Leach, 1993). In this approach, intensive work with the child is combined with an education program in which parents are taught therapeutic techniques based on principles of social learning and operant conditioning. Similar to PMT, this family intervention seems to be less effective for children and adolescents who present with multiple symptoms or whose families are extremely distressed or disadvantaged (Chamberlain & Rosicky, 1995).

Other psychoeducational programs have been successful for families affected by chronic medical conditions (Satin, LaGreca, Zigo, & Skyler, 1989). These programs provide information and educate families with ways to cope with the child's medical condition and physical disabilities. Parent involvement that is congruent with the child's developmental needs tends to be effective for obese preadolescents (Campbell & Patterson, 1995). In-home programs seem to be beneficial for families with fewer social, economic, and emotional resources (Campbell &

Patterson, 1995). Results suggest improvements not only in the child's physical status and sense of independence, but also in the parents' ability to cope with stress and frustration (Campbell & Patterson, 1995).

Other behaviorally-focused programs have been successful in treating children's problems (Kazdin, 1987). Social learning (Patterson, 1982), structural and functional family therapy (Alexander & Parsons, 1982), and multitarget ecological treatments (Chamberlain & Reid, 1991) are effective treatments for conduct disorders in younger children and adolescent delinquency. Outcomes include improvement in behavior (Szapocznik et al., 1989) and decreased rates of incarceration (Bank, Marlowe, Reid, Patterson, & Weinrott, 1991) and hospitalization (Chamberlain & Reid, 1991).

Studies of family programs for adults with schizophrenia and bipolar disorder are among the best executed in the field. Whereas a psychodynamic family approach was shown to produce negative outcomes for families with schizophrenia (McFarlane, Link, Dushay, Marchal, & Crilly, 1995), short-term behavioral, educational, and family support models have demonstrated effectiveness. Even for high-risk families, these treatments tend to be more cost effective than inpatient care (Goldstein & Miklowitz, 1995). In a sizable study of 96 acutely-ill patients with schizophrenia (Goldstein, Rodnick, Evans, May, & Steinberg, 1978), for example, no patients who received a "moderate dose" of family therapy relapsed, whereas 48% of those who received neuroleptics without family therapy did so.

The psychoeducational model includes training in communication and problem solving along with information about symptoms, biological theories of etiology, warning signs of relapse, and medication and treatment issues. Benefits accrue not only for the identified client but also for the family, with lower rates of distress and improved self-efficacy (Abramowitz & Coursey, 1989; Birchwood, Smith, & Cochrane, 1992; Mills & Hansen, 1991). In a recent pilot study, Eakes, Walsh, Markowski, and Cain (1997), comparing a brief solution-focused family model to traditional outpatient therapy, found that clients reported improved family relations posttreatment. Whereas these short-term educational models have not consistently demonstrated long-term success with respect to relapse and rehospitalization (Glick et al., 1985), behavioral programs have been more successful in this regard (Falloon, Boyd, & McGill, 1984). Likewise, supportive family therapy has demonstrated effectiveness in follow-up studies (Leff, Kuipers, Berkowitz, & Sturgeon, 1985), as has a systems approach that combines psychoeducation with a focus on intergenerational boundaries (Hogarty et al., 1991).

Indeed, systems approaches like structural therapy (Minuchin, 1974) focus more than psychoeducational and behavioral approaches on general family relationships. Nonetheless, outcome studies on these approaches are concerned with treating specific diagnoses, predominantly psychosomatic disorders, eating disorders, and drug abuse, rather than the kinds of relational difficulties that bring many families to therapy.

With respect to eating disorders, structural family therapy tends to be more effective than individual therapy for younger children and adolescents who have had anorexia for three years or less, but success is limited for those with chronic anorexia, or for families with high levels of expressed emotion (Campbell & Patterson, 1995). In one study of clients with various eating disorders, (Russell, Szmukler, Dare, & Eisler, 1987), family therapy for bulimia was not more successful than individual treatment, but only 23 participants in the study were bulimic.

With respect to drug abuse, the structural approach has demonstrated effectiveness in engaging the adolescents and their families in treatment, reducing drug use, and improving family functioning (e.g., Alexander & Parsons, 1982; Liddle & Dakof, 1995; Szapocznik et al., 1988). Indeed, well-designed, controlled studies have shown that structural treatment for drug abuse can be effective even when only one family member is willing to engage in treatment (Szapocznik et al., 1988). Research on family involvement in treating adult drug abuse, however, is limited and inconclusive (Liddle & Dakof, 1995).

Finally, there are promising new programs of research on family approaches for children with internalizing disorders. Dadds, Spence, Holland, Barrett, and Laurens (1997) found that a family-based group intervention reduced anxiety at posttest and at the 6-month follow-up. Comprehensive family management rewards children's courageous behavior and extinguishes excessive complaining while helping parents to manage their own anxiety and to solve problems and communicate more effectively (Barrett, Dadds, & Rapee, 1996). A combination of family management with individual therapy for the child was more successful than the individual approach alone; after therapy, 84% of the children in the combined group and 57% in the individual therapy group no longer met the diagnostic criteria for anxiety disorder (Barrett et al., 1996). For depressed adolescents, Diamond and Siqueland (1995) are currently gathering outcome data on a brief family approach that combines systemic/structural therapy with a focus on parent-child trust and attachment. If effective, this approach will provide an alternative that is more supportive than confrontive.

In this large body of outcome research, many studies are flawed due to inadequate samples, a lack of validated instruments, and confounds in the design (Pinsof & Wynne, 1995). Even when the studies are well done and the findings across studies are consistent, questions remain. It is often impossible to determine what aspects of the treatment were responsible for the observed changes. It is likely that different treatments with similar efficacy rates achieve success differently. It is equally likely that these treatments are successful because of common factors (Stiles, Shapiro, & Elliott, 1986). For this reason, a thorough understanding of the research in this field requires a critical review of the process literature, which follows.

WHAT MAKES COUPLES AND FAMILY THERAPY EFFECTIVE?

Early on, family therapy researchers had the modest goal of describing what takes place in family sessions, particularly what therapists do. To date, the major questions have concerned the kinds of interventions family therapists use, the degree to which these interventions reflect theory, if (and how) therapists relate differently to different family members, and which therapist and client behaviors and interactional patterns predict successful outcomes. More recently, process researchers have turned their attention to the specific mechanisms of change—the effective ingredients—in family therapy. Various programs of research have focused on the therapeutic alliance, specific components of treatment, and therapeutic change episodes.

While recent interest in qualitative methods has resulted in a handful of such studies, the majority of work to date has relied on the observation of verbal behavior. Table 25.1 summarizes the most frequently used observational coding systems in the family therapy process literature. (See Friedlander, in press, for a more detailed account.) A glance at the coding dimensions listed in Table 25.1 shows that relatively few have to do with the actual content of family therapy sessions. Rather, the kinds of behaviors of interest to researchers emphasize the "report" aspect of communication (i.e., how verbal messages are delivered). In particular, most of the codes reflect interpersonal dynamics of authority, power, control, and conflict. This is not surprising, since most family difficulties have to do with issues of power and control and a critical aspect of the family therapist's role is to mediate conflict and facilitate compromise (Minuchin, 1974). It should be noted, however, that despite the theoretical emphasis on interpersonal behavior, only two coding systems, the Structural Analysis of Social Behavior (SASB; Benjamin, 1974; Benjamin, Foster, Roberto, & Estroff, 1986) and the Family Relational Control Communication Coding System (FRCCCS; Friedlander & Heatherington, 1989; Heatherington & Friedlander, 1987), explicitly operationalize reciprocal interactions or communication patterns.

In the sections that follow, descriptive studies of family therapy are reviewed, followed by research on the therapeutic relationship and on specific mechanisms of change.

Table 25.1   Most Frequently Used Observational Coding Systems

Coding System	Authors	Major Dimensions	Behavior Therapist	Client	Interaction
DSCIS	Alexander et al., (1976); Waldron et al., (1993)	Structuring	X		
		Defensiveness		X	
		Supportiveness	X	X	
SASB	Benjamin (1974); Benjamin et al., (1986)	Affiliation	X	X	
		Interdependence	X	X	
		Complementarity/ noncomplementarity			X
FTCS	Pinsof (1979, 1986)	Topic	X		
		Intervention	X		
		Temporal orientation	X		
		Interpersonal structure	X		
		System membership	X		
		Route	X		
		To Whom	X		
		Grammatical form	X		
		Event relationship	X		
HCVRCS-R	Friedlander (1982)	Verbal response modes	X		
TPCS	Chamberlain et al., (1984); Chamberlain et al., (1985)	Teach	X		
		Confront	X		
		Noncompliance/resistance		X	
		Cooperation		X	
FRCCCS	Friedlander & Heatherington (1989); Siegel et al., (1992)	One-up messages	X	X	
		One-down messages	X	X	
		Complementarity			X
		Symmetry			X
TICS	Shields et al., (1991)	Structuring	X		
		Joining	X		
		Collaboration		X	
		Conflict		X	
CCCS	Friedlander & Heatherington (1998)	Intrapersonal-interpersonal	X	X	
		Internal-external	X	X	
		Responsible-not responsible	X	X	
		Linear-circular	X	X	

Note: Table includes coding systems used in at least two empirical studies. DSCIS = Defensive and Supportive Communication Interaction System; SASB = Structural Analysis of Social Behavior; FTCS = Family Therapist Coding System; HCVRCS = Hill Counselor Verbal Response Mode Category System—Revised; Therapy Process Coding System; FRCCCS = Family Relational Control Communication Coding System; TICS = Therapeutic Interaction Coding System; CCCS = Cognitive Constructions Coding System.

How Do Therapists Behave?

Therapist Behavior with Couples

In a recent study assessing the relation of first-session behavior with treatment duration and clients' session evaluations, Odell and Quinn (1998) concluded that the most effective therapists deliberately restrained couples from "overparticipating" (p. 382). At times, however, the problem may be *underparticipation*. Brown-Standridge and Piercy (1988) studied how therapists respond to distancing behaviors by husbands versus wives. Observational coding indicated that therapists who used reflections when husbands were closed did not behave similarly with wives.

It seems reasonable that the degree of therapist activity depends on individual client differences. Cline, Mejia, Coles, Klein, and Cline (1984) tested the association between therapist directiveness, gender, client socioeconomic status (SES), and outcome in a marital study with 77 couples. Results showed that directiveness predicted increases in couples' positive behaviors (e.g., agreement, approval, accepting responsibility) only for those in the lower SES group, and more so for husbands than wives. In the middle SES group, therapist directiveness was inversely associated with outcome, particularly for husbands. These results need to be considered cautiously, however, because all the therapists were men. Furthermore, limited inferences can be made from correlational process-outcome research. A significant correlation between outcome scores Y and process variable X only indicates that more X tended to occur in successful treatments; it does not show a contingent relationship between X and Y. In other words, one cannot interpret Cline et al.'s results to mean that directive therapist interventions either led to or were followed by positive couple behaviors.

Therapist Behavior with Families

Far more studies have been conducted on therapist behavior than on any other aspect of family treatment. Results of several comparative studies of expert theorists representing different orientations suggest that (1) there are striking similarities across approaches, (2) therapists behave similarly with different families, and (3) technical differences are consistent with theoretical differences (Friedlander, Ellis, Raymond, Siegel, & Milford, 1987; Friedlander & Highlen, 1984; Friedlander et al., 1985; Heatherington, Marrs, & Friedlander, 1995). It should be noted that with one exception (Heatherington et al., 1995), these were analyses of demonstration interviews conducted in the 1960s and 1970s. Nonetheless, the findings are important because the work of these theorists—Salvador Minuchin, Carl Whitaker, Mara Selvini Palazzoli, Murray Bowen, and Nathan Ackerman, among others—have influenced the training and practice of subsequent generations of family therapists.

In brief, the structural, strategic-systemic, and experiential family therapists in the early studies tended to be active, present oriented, and directive, using questions, instructions, and informative interventions rather than reassurance, reflections of feeling, or interpretations. Frequently, they relied on indirectly routed interventions (i.e., addressing one family member about the experience of another, "Your father seems to be very concerned about your welfare"). Therapists directed their interventions to the parents and problem child more than to other family members (Friedlander & Highlen, 1984; Friedlander et al., 1987) and focused primarily on individuals and dyads within the family, particularly parent-child relationships (Friedlander et al., 1985, 1987). While there was remarkable consistency within therapists across families, the therapists seemed to modify their approach based on a judgment of the family's readiness and openness for change (Friedlander et al., 1987). Seven constructionist/narrative therapists studied more recently (Heatherington et al., 1995) tended to provide information to their clients and relied on questions and reflections rather than on confrontations or interpretations.

This is not to say that technical differences are not meaningful. Studies of four therapists (Murray Bowen, Nathan Ackerman, Don Jackson, and Carl Whitaker) interviewing the same family (Friedlander & Highlen, 1984; Friedlander et al., 1985) and two therapists (Salvador Minuchin and Carl Whitaker), each interviewing six different families (Friedlander et al., 1987), revealed differences that clearly reflected theory. Carl Whitaker, for example, used more self-disclosure and here-and-now references, reflecting his humanistic-experiential approach, and Murray Bowen referred more to the past and to the family of origin, reflecting his insight-oriented, historical approach.

Studies of highly experienced, skillful theorists conducting demonstration interviews cannot, however, provide information about what takes place in successful family therapy sessions conducted by actual practitioners in field settings. There are some studies that do provide this information. An early process-outcome investigation by Postner, Guttman, Sigal, Epstein, and Rakoff (1971) showed that, relative to the group with poor outcomes, in the good outcome group the therapists were more active and focused increasingly on one family member, usually the parent who was more verbal. Furthermore, they used relatively more "interpretive" than "drive" responses with these families over time. (A *drive* response is intended to stimulate interaction, provide support, or obtain information, whereas an *interpretive* response aims to clarify intentions, suggest alternatives, or further understanding.)

A more recent study by Shields, Sprenkle, and Constantine (1991) found that "completer" cases could be distinguished from "noncompleter" cases on the basis of therapist structuring following family disagreements. Active structuring was also predictive of (1) client ratings of session depth in Odell and Quinn's (1998) study of first sessions and (2) client outcome in Green and Herget's (1991) evaluation of therapist behavior by systemic/strategic team consultants. The importance of being active is further underscored by Pinsof's (1979, 1986) Family Therapy Coding System (FTCS) comparison of novice therapists and their supervisors. Consistent with Shields et al. (1991) and Green and Herget (1991) as well as the studies of expert therapists, Pinsof found that supervisors were more likely than trainees to use active, explicit interventions and to focus on family interactions and communication patterns.

Finally, the question of gender-based behavior has been a prominent feature of the family therapy process literature. Because questions have repeatedly been raised about the potentially damaging effects of therapists reinforcing traditional gender roles (e.g., Luepnitz, 1988), several investigators have sought to compare male and female therapists' responses to clients in family therapy. In two studies of functional family therapy, inexperienced student therapists did not behave in ways that are consistent with gender-role stereotyping. In Mas, Alexander, and Barton (1985), for example, female therapists spoke less in the affective mode of experience than did male therapists. In Newberry, Alexander, and Turner (1991), there were no differences in male versus female therapists' use of supportiveness or structuring (stereotypically feminine and masculine behaviors, respectively). In fact, the female therapists tended to respond to client supportiveness with structuring more frequently than did the male therapists. On the other hand, a study of more experienced therapists did provide evidence to support the gender traditionality hypothesis. Shields and McDaniel (1992) reported that, compared with female therapists, male therapists were more likely to take charge when family members asserted themselves or disagreed with them. (There were, however, no differences in the treatment retention rate by therapist gender.)

While these three studies suggest some differences in the behaviors of male and female therapists, they do not address the more important question of whether therapists respond differently to mothers versus fathers or to sisters versus brothers. Recent evidence showing that fathers introduce more topics (Werner-Wilson, Zimmerman, & Price, 1998) and mothers are interrupted far more frequently than fathers by therapists of both genders suggests that family therapy is characterized by the same power dynamics that occur in nontherapeutic settings (Werner-Wilson, Price, Zimmerman, & Murphy, 1999).

How Do Clients Behave?

Client Behavior in Couples Therapy

In their recent study of gender differences, Werner-Wilson et al. (1998) found that wives introduced more topics in marital therapy than did husbands (the opposite pattern being the case in family therapy). The authors suggested that this gender difference may, in part, be due to women's greater comfort discussing emotionally intimate topics. In another gender-based comparison

(Brown-Standridge & Piercy, 1988), 13 couples were treated by 6 experienced therapists, and client behaviors were coded following selected therapist interventions. Results indicated that, while wives responded more positively to therapist reflections, husbands responded more positively to reframing.

Neither of these studies, however, focused on client behaviors that reflect therapeutic change. Only two studies were located that did so. De Chenne (1973) reported that peak emotional experiencing, as measured by the Experiencing Scale (Klein, Mathieu, Kiesler, & Gendlin, 1969), occurred more often after therapist statements than after spousal statements. The nature of those statements was, however, not explored. In an early investigation of group therapy for couples led by Murray Bowen, Winer (1971) observed changes over time in pronoun use that were assumed to reflect changes in differentiation of self, the major construct in Bowen's (1978) theory. Results showing increases in *I* statements and decreases in *we, us,* and *our* statements were said to support the hypothesis of "less intense, symbiotic involvement" (Winer, 1971, p. 245). Conclusions from these studies need to be considered cautiously, however. There was no evidence that the emotional release reported by De Chenne (1973) facilitated a resolution of the couples' problems, nor that the changes in pronoun usage observed by Winer reflected modifications in clients' cognitions or personality.

Client Behavior in Family Therapy

Several studies have provided evidence supporting the widely held belief (e.g., Bowen, 1978; Minuchin, 1974) that exhibition of symptomatic behavior in a therapy session reflects family dysfunction. Zuk, Boszormenyi-Nagy, and Heiman (1963) demonstrated that a client with schizophrenia who laughed inappropriately did so in response to family tension. Crits-Christoph et al. (1991), studying a family with a disturbed adolescent, concluded that the girl's emotional lability was precipitated by pejorative discussions of her problems. Patterson and Chamberlain (1988), studying behavioral therapy for problem youth, reported that within-session parental conflict was associated with greater marital dissatisfaction, parental stress and depression, and the children's antisocial behavior.

In an early process-outcome study of change over time (Postner et al., 1971), family members interacted more with each other and less with the therapist as therapy progressed. More importantly, they increasingly used statements expressing positive ("welfare") and negative ("emergency") emotions. Changes in cognitive variables were studied in three more recent investigations. Munton and Antaki (1988) compared family members' attributions in less versus more successful cases. Although their hypotheses were not supported, the authors observed that only the families with poorer outcomes made stable attributions both early and late in treatment. In explaining their results, Munton and Antaki suggested studying the attributions, or constructions, of individuals rather than of the family as a whole. Doing so, Melidonis and Bry (1995) found that clients' blaming attributions decreased when therapists ignored the negative attributions and repeatedly asked for exceptions to the problem (e.g., "Can you tell me about a time when he did *not* procrastinate?"). In their descriptive study of expert constructionist therapists, Heatherington et al. (1995) found that the majority of clients' causal constructions for specific problems were *internal* (rather than external), *linear* (rather than complex or circular), and *responsible* (rather than blaming). Changes in constructions over time were not assessed, however.

Client resistance or defensiveness was investigated in six studies. Robbins, Alexander, Newell, and Turner (1996) found that the attitude of delinquent adolescents was less negative following therapists' "reframes" than any other kind of intervention. In Shields et al. (1991), families with more disagreements and attempts to structure the therapist were less likely to complete treatment. Similarly, in an early investigation of functional family therapy using the Defensive and Supportive Communication Interaction System, Alexander, Barton, Schiavo, and Parsons (1976) reported an association between premature termination and fewer supportive relative to defensive messages. These results are consistent with those found by researchers of behavioral treatment for troubled youth at the Oregon Social Learning Center, who reported a relationship between treatment dropout and resistance (Chamberlain, Patterson, Reid, Kavanagh, & Forgatch, 1984). Parental noncompliance was likely to follow therapist "teach" or "confront" behaviors as coded by Chamberlain et al.'s (1985) Therapy Process Coding System (Patterson & Forgatch, 1985). On the other hand, in a sequential analysis of the responses of 12 families to one therapist, Barbera and Waldron (1994) reported a contingent relationship between client cooperativeness and therapist "support" and "teach." Likewise, Frankel and Piercy (1990) reported that parents were more cooperative when therapists used support and teach behaviors judged to be of high quality. Notably, the relationship between cooperativeness and these behaviors was nonsignificant when quality of the interventions was not taken into account.

How Do Therapists and Clients Interact?

Despite family theorists' interest in characterizing relationships, communication and interactional patterns, the studies reviewed previously focused on the behaviors of individuals. While it is important to note a recurring pattern of client cooperativeness following therapist support, for example, this pattern is circumscribed by the researcher's choice to observe *therapist* support (not *client* support) and *client* cooperativeness (not *therapist* cooperativeness). In contrast, a relational pattern is one in which sequential behaviors, coded on the same dimension, together define a specific kind of interaction. *Complementarity,* for example, is observed when one person (client or therapist) is dominant and the other submissive; *symmetry* occurs when both parties assume either a dominant or a submissive position.

Two coding systems, the SASB (Benjamin, 1974; Benjamin et al., 1986) and the FRCCCS (Friedlander & Heatherington, 1989; Siegel, Friedlander, & Heatherington, 1992), have most often been used to operationalize complementarity. Complementarity in the FRCCCS is based on sequences of relational control codes ("one-up" or ↑ and "one-down" or ↓) for verbal and nonverbal behaviors like topic change, question, talkover, and head nod. The behaviors observed in this coding system reflect moves toward dominance and submission. Complementarity in the SASB, on the other hand, requires the coder to assess the speaker's friendliness or hostility (e.g., nurturant, sarcastic, or critical behaviors) as well as dominance or submission. The two systems are based in different theoretical traditions (Friedlander, 1993), the SASB in interpersonal theory (Sullivan, 1953), the FRCCCS in communication theory (Bateson, 1936/1958; Ericson & Rogers, 1973).

To date, one descriptive study of family therapy (Laird & Vande Kemp, 1987) has been conducted with the SASB. Early, middle, and late phases were compared in the structural treatment of a family with a daughter with anorexia nervosa. Salvador Minuchin was the treating therapist at the Philadelphia Child Guidance Clinic. As expected, more interpersonal complementarity (e.g., leading/following) was observed in the early and late phases of treatment relative to the middle, restructuring phase.

A similar case study (Raymond, Friedlander, Heatherington, Ellis, & Sargent, 1993), also conducted at the Philadelphia Child Guidance Clinic by a structural therapist with expertise in anorexia, used the FRCCCS to observe relational control dynamics. As in earlier descriptive studies of couples and family therapy with the FRCCCS (Friedlander, Heatherington, & Wildman, 1991; Heatherington & Friedlander, 1990a, 1990c), the predominant therapist/client control pattern was complementarity (Therapist↑/Client↓). Observation of family interactions suggested that important changes may have taken place over time in this family's interpersonal dynamics. Consistent with structural theory, the parent-child interactions became less competitive and the parents communicated in a more competitive symmetrical fashion with one another (Raymond et al., 1993).

What Makes the Relationship Effective?

In an effort to differentiate family treatment from traditional psychoanalytic and humanistic approaches, early theorists focused uniquely on behavior, and relationships within the family were considered to be of far more importance than those with the therapist. Consequently, little attention was paid to the quality of the therapeutic relationship.

Until recently, few published studies had considered the therapist's emotional responsiveness to the family. In an early investigation, Shapiro (1974) found that families whose therapists reported feeling positively toward them after the first session were more likely to stay in treatment. If, and how, this concern was made evident to the family was not, unfortunately, a part of this investigation. In an effort to challenge the notion of neutrality in Milan systemic therapy, Green and Herget (1991) asked team leaders to assess therapist warmth after observing 3-hour consultation sessions with 11 "stuck" families. Although warmth was measured by a single item, results indicated significant, positive correlations between therapist warmth and reports of global improvement and goal attainment at 1- and 3-month follow-ups.

Recent qualitative analyses (e.g., Christensen, Russell, Miller, & Peterson, 1998; Greenberg, James, & Conry, 1988; Sells, Smith, & Moon, 1996) of couples' and family members' perceptions of effective therapy have underscored the importance of therapist warmth. Warmth, along with trust, informality, a sense of safety, and the development of clear goals have been identified as key ingredients of successful therapy from the client's perspective.

Warmth and goal clarity are important aspects of another construct, the *therapeutic alliance*. After the alliance began receiving attention in the individual psychotherapy literature, researchers considered its role in the process and outcome of couples and family therapy. The importance of the alliance was made evident by studies showing that clients' perceived sense of engagement in therapy increases over time (Kuehl, Newfield, & Joanning, 1990; Sigal, Rakoff, & Epstein, 1967) and predicts greater marital satisfaction posttreatment (Holtzworth-Munroe, Jacobson, DeKlyen, & Whisman, 1989), whereas poor collaboration is associated with premature termination (Sigal et al., 1967). Publication of Pinsof and Catherall's (1986) integrative alliance scales for couples and families, which were based on Bordin's (1979) conceptualization of the alliance in individual therapy, allowed research on this important topic to move forward. In these scales, as well as in a recently developed measure for couples (Symonds, 1998), the emotional bond and agreement with the therapist on tasks and goals of treatment are rated with respect to oneself, one's spouse (or other family members), and the system as a whole.

Research has shown associations between alliance ratings and client gender (Quinn, Dotson, & Jordan, 1997; Symonds, 1998; Werner-Wilson, 1997), therapists' conjugal experience (i.e., living with a spouse or partner; Lawson & Sivo, 1998), treatment modality (couples versus family; Werner-Wilson, 1997), session evaluations (Heatherington & Friedlander, 1990b), relational control patterns (Heatherington & Friedlander, 1990c), and marital (Johnson & Talitman, 1997; Pinsof & Catherall, 1986; Quinn et al., 1997) and family (Bourgeois, Sabourin, & Wright, 1990) therapy outcomes. Furthermore, some evidence suggests that a "split" alliance with the therapist occurs fairly frequently in both marital and family therapy (Heatherington & Friedlander, 1990b). In a study of 17 couples, Quinn et al. (1997) found that treatment outcomes were enhanced when wives' alliance scores, obtained after the third session, exceeded those of their husbands. These data were, however, only sampled from those who completed treatment, so that no inferences could be made about the alliance of couples who terminated prematurely (Quinn et al., 1997).

Taken together, these studies clearly indicate that something important happens between therapist and family members and that the creation of a strong bond with each client and with the family as a whole is not to be overlooked, despite its complexity. Recent studies on gender differences (Quinn et al., 1997; Werner-Wilson, 1997) emphasize that family members' roles are a critical ingredient in this regard. Creating an alliance with children can be particularly challenging. An exploratory investigation (Diamond, Liddle, Hogue, & Dakof, 1998) of multidimensional family therapy with urban, substance-abusing teens suggested that a poor alliance can be improved when the therapist attends closely to the adolescent's experience, behaves as an ally, and formulates goals that are meaningful to the client. Unfortunately, only 10 families and 3 therapists were included in Diamond et al.'s sample. Nonetheless, the study sheds light on an important research direction—identifying behaviors that contribute to the development of a strong therapeutic alliance.

What Produces Change?

Although a number of the studies reviewed previously included some index of client change, their purpose was to describe what takes place naturally in successful couples and family therapy, not to identify the specific mechanisms of change. A few experiments have tested the efficacy of various theoretically-based components of couples and family therapy. In an early study of behavioral marital therapy (Jacobson, 1984), a components-analysis design showed that the complete treatment package was not more effective than either component—behavior exchange and communication/problem-solving training—in isolation. Controlled studies have also demonstrated the success of (1) a strategic telephone intervention to engage Hispanic families with drug-abusing adolescents (Santisteban et al., 1996; Szapocznik et al., 1988), (2) team consultation (Green & Herget, 1989a, 1989b) and video feedback (Kemenoff, Worchel, Prevatt, & Willson, 1995) in Milan systemic therapy, and (3) the "formula first session task" intervention in solution-focused therapy (Adams, Piercy, & Jurich, 1991, p. 277).

Apart from these few experimental studies, most process-outcome research has been ex post facto. Caution is needed in interpretation because, as discussed earlier, significant correlations between process and outcome variables do not provide information about the contexts in which important processes take place. Furthermore, *nonsignificant* correlations do not signify that a process variable is *unimportant*. It may be that the frequency of variable X does not predict change, but its timing, quality, uniqueness, or responsiveness to the client's need does make a difference (Stiles et al., 1986).

For this reason, family therapy process researchers have followed the lead of individual therapy researchers (e.g., Greenberg, 1986; Stiles et al., 1986) in attempting to isolate important, recurring moments or episodes in family sessions that seem to account for change. The rationale for this perspective is its clinical relevance. After all, therapists do not make every remark with global goals (like "enhanced marital satisfaction") in mind. Rather, they respond—and revise their responses—as different topics, contexts, problems, and interactions arise in the ongoing stream of therapy. Immediacy is the basis of therapists' evaluations of their work. Therapists ask themselves, for example, "Did a meaningful change take place after that intervention? Did the session end on a high note? Did the family commit itself to a new course of action?"

A variety of qualitative as well as quantitative methods has been applied to identify mechanisms of change in family therapy. [The interested reader is directed to Sprenkle & Moon's (1996) volume on family therapy research methods.] Investigations of effective sessions and therapeutic episodes have highlighted the processes by which change occurs in cognition, emotion, and behavior during couples and family sessions.

With respect to cognition, several intensive analyses of sessions or episodes within sessions have been conducted, reflecting theorists' burgeoning interest in changing family members' constructions, or "narratives," to affect their symptoms and, ultimately, their relationships (e.g., Efran, Lukens, & Lukens, 1990; Sluzki, 1992; White & Epston, 1990). In the earliest study in this group, Holloway, Wampold, and Nelson (1990) analyzed the effects of a successful paradoxical intervention for sleeplessness in a couple's session conducted by Gerald Weeks. Observations showed that the couple's negative symmetry with one another was eliminated after the intervention, and both clients engaged in more deferential complementarity with the therapist.

In a similar study, Gale and Newfield (1992) used a qualitative method, conversation analysis, to identify therapeutic strategies in a single session of solution-focused couple's treatment conducted by Bill O'Hanlon. This couple had recently become reconciled after separating due to the husband's having had an extramarital affair. To move the wife away from blaming and the husband from withdrawing, O'Hanlon used highly structuring interventions along with humor to redirect and prohibit dialogue about problems. Conversation analysis was also used in Buttney's (1990) study of a couple's session conducted by narrative theorist Carlos Sluzki (1992). Sluzki frequently used reframing to modify the couple's constructions of their relationship. As an example, he reframed one client's blame and nagging of the other as "an old discussion." Unfortunately, none of these studies included an assessment of the clients' cognitions.

Using the Cognitive Constructions Coding System (Friedlander & Heatherington, 1998) to operationalize blame, Friedlander, Heatherington, and Marrs (in press) identified blaming episodes in seven family interviews by prominent constructionist theorists (e.g., Harlene Anderson, Bill Lax, Carlos Sluzki, Michael White). A qualitative analysis of the therapists' responses to the blame suggested three core categories—Ignoring/Diverting, Acknowledging/Challenging, and Reframing—subsuming 17 individual codes (e.g., challenging all-or-none thinking, highlighting neutral information, focusing on competence). The most frequent code was focusing on the positive. Although client outcome was not assessed, some evidence suggested that more, and more varied, interventions may have resulted in a quicker and more complete cessation of blame.

Two recent studies have attempted to track the process of cognitive change in an initial family therapy session. Pilot data from an outcome study on family therapy for depressed adolescents (Diamond, Liddle, et al., 1998) suggested that focusing on the teen's need for parental contact, nurturance, and engagement may be one important way to help parents begin to view the child's problem systemically. In this study, changes in parents' constructions were assessed by an interview immediately following the intake session. Along similar lines, Coulehan, Friedlander, and Heatherington (1998) studied intake sessions conducted by therapists trained in Sluzki's (1992) narrative approach. A qualitative comparison was made of successful versus unsuccessful "transformation events." A successful transformation, defined as a shift in the parents' description of the problem from *intra*personal to *inter*personal, was identified by therapists and observers on postsession questionnaires and by the CCCS (Friedlander & Heatherington, 1998). Intensive analysis of eight change events suggested a three-stage process, moving from retelling the "old story," to developing a new, more supportive story, to expressing hope or the possibility of change. Various elements within each stage discriminated the successful from the unsuccessful transformation events.

One important finding in Coulehan et al. (1998) was the occurrence of a shift in the emotional tone of the session as family members began focusing on the child's strengths and the family's values. The creation of an emotional shift in the session has also figured prominently in research on emotionally-focused couples therapy (EFT). In the earliest EFT study, Johnson and Greenberg (1988) compared better and worse outcome cases. In the best sessions (rated by therapists), an emotional "softening" occurred. Softening, an important construct in this approach, occurs when one partner stops blaming and begins to demonstrate vulnerability or ask for closeness or comfort. In subsequent EFT studies, highly rated sessions in successful cases were characterized by "intimate self-disclosure" and deeper emotional experiencing (Greenberg, Ford, Alden, & Johnson, 1993, p. 83). Conflict events, defined as negative interpersonal complementarity on the SASB (Benjamin, 1974), were resolved when the therapist focused the couple on underlying needs and emotions (Greenberg et al., 1993).

In family therapy, conflict events were recently explored in a study of multi-dmensional family therapy, an approach designed specifically for drug-abusing adolescents (Diamond & Liddle, 1996). In this study, parental expressions of hopelessness and helplessness and adolescent expressions of frustration and anger were followed by a "shift intervention" in which the therapist focused on underlying issues (p. 482). Successful shift interventions, those in which the adolescent became more cooperative and less defensive, occurred when the parents began trying to understand rather than control.

A similar process was reported in two qualitative studies of change events in structural family therapy (Friedlander, Heatherington, Johnson, & Skowron, 1994; Heatherington & Friedlander, 1990a). A process of moving family members from "disengagement" to "sustained engagement" began with the acknowledgment of individual contributions to the impasse and communication about underlying thoughts and feelings (p. 438). Successful resolutions of the impasse occurred when family members validated each other's disclosures, made new constructions about one another, and expressed a desire for engagement (Friedlander, Heatherington, et al., 1994).

From this review, it is clear that family therapy process and outcome researchers have been working from very different models. Nonetheless, their efforts have resulted in some important implications for practice. At present, the challenge is to move the empirical literature forward in a coherent fashion. This requires not only a synthesis and integration of existing knowledge but also a consideration of the current state of theory in the field.

IMPLICATIONS AND RECOMMENDATIONS

Building Theory and Informing Practice

Traditionally, theories arose from the practices of successful family therapists who wanted to share their discoveries with others. More recently, theorists have been influenced by the research literature. As one example, studies of clients' phenomenological views of effective therapy (e.g., Greenberg et al., 1988; Sells et al., 1996) have moved theorists away from their almost exclusive focus on technique, to the recognition of nonspecific elements like the therapeutic relationship and the family's emotional experience in therapy. Process research has prompted theorists to look beyond overt behavior to the covert processes that constrain behavior. Discovery-oriented investigations of therapeutic change processes (e.g., Coulehan et al., 1998; Diamond & Liddle, 1996; Friedlander, Heatherington, et al., 1994) have repeatedly shown that family members' unspoken thoughts and feelings play an important role in their relations with one another. By detailing each step in the change process, investigators have modeled how successful therapists can access these latent dynamics. A notable example is the program of research on EFT (Greenberg et al., 1993), which has enabled its authors to delineate in-session processes (e.g., intimate self-disclosure and softening) that bring about important shifts in couples' relationships.

Theory can also be built from unexpected research findings. Diamond, Liddle, et al.'s (1998; Diamond & Siqueland, 1995) pilot work on family treatment of depressed adolescents is a case in point. The investigators found that, contrary to expectation, when the parents sought help for their children, their constructions of the problem were not linear. The parents already knew that their children's depression was systemic in nature, but they were unaware of how to help. Rather than changing the parents' constructions, therapists are helping them see that, despite their children's withdrawal, the children desperately want contact, engagement, and nurturance (Diamond, Liddle, et al., 1998).

As this research program continues to evolve, its authors will likely be able to develop a coherent theoretical model for treating depressed adolescents within a family context. Controlled tests of the approach may suggest not only how to alleviate depression in adolescents but also how to bring parents and children closer. The latter outcome is not trivial. At the outset, we posed the question, "What is a good outcome in family therapy?" Despite the abundant evidence that family therapy "works," too few studies have included changes in relationships as outcome variables. For instance, if a depressed 16-year-old is no longer depressed but decides to leave home, should this outcome be considered successful?

Unfortunately, many outcome researchers tend to focus solely on the symptomatic improvement of individuals who are treated in a conjoint setting. We have clear evidence indicating the value of (1) including spouses in treatments for physical problems (Campbell & Patterson, 1995), agoraphobia, and alcoholism (Edwards & Steinglass, 1995); (2) teaching families how to recognize and avoid relapses of schizophrenic episodes (Goldstein & Miklowitz, 1995); and (3) involving parents in behavior management programs for their troubled children and adolescents (Estrada & Pinsof, 1995). The body of evidence supporting these kinds of treatments is substantial, and the majority of studies are controlled and well executed. By focusing uniquely on symptom reduction, however, many researchers have ignored the family atmosphere (e.g., cohesiveness) and interactional patterns (e.g., competitive symmetry) that maintain the presenting problem. This is unfortunate because treatment success (i.e., problem reduction) is often compromised for highly stressed or disorganized families, and relational difficulties are often the most pressing concerns for therapists who work with couples and families.

The outcome studies reviewed previously need to be considered cautiously. A distinction must be made between *efficacy* research (controlled laboratory studies) and *effectiveness* research (studies conducted in field settings) (Pinsof et al., 1996). To date, the majority of investigations have been manualized efficacy studies that exclude clients with multiple diagnoses and families with multiple problems. There is a paucity of effectiveness research and too few studies on many approaches (e.g., solution-focused therapy, object relations therapy) that are commonly practiced.

There are, nonetheless, some important implications from the outcome literature to guide a clinician's treatment choice. Younger children with conduct problems and eating disorders tend to fare better in family therapy than do adolescents. For couples, behavioral therapy is effective, as are insight- and emotionally focused therapies. For families, behavioral child management approaches as well as functional, structural, and multidimensional therapies have demonstrated success for various problems. On the other hand, family therapy is not recommended for unipolar depression (Prince & Jacobson, 1995) or chronic eating disorders (Campbell & Patterson, 1995).

Although there are few investigations comparing different treatment modalities, with respect to couples, conjoint therapy tends to be superior when the client's primary source of difficulty is the relationship (Prince & Jacobson, 1995). Depression that is not clearly linked with the relationship is better handled with individual treatment (Prince & Jacobson, 1995). On the other hand, involving the spouse in overcoming physical (e.g., hypertension, obesity), sexual, and addictive problems is desirable whenever possible. Likewise, in family therapy, parental involvement is key when the child's problems are externalizing, or directed outward (Estrada & Pinsof, 1995). Children's and adolescents' internalizing problems—anxiety, depression, eating, and addictive disorders—can also be overcome with parental involvement, but there is too little research in this area to substantiate the superiority of conjoint family treatment.

By far, the majority of studies on relationships concern couples' problems. Slowly, a body of evidence is accumulating about the effectiveness of treating other kinds of relationship problems in a family context. One promising new line of research is being conducted on mother-child therapy for children who have witnessed domestic violence (Kahen, Johnson & Lieberman, 1998). Since there are few such studies, the practice implications await further study.

This is not to say that the literature is not informative about treating relationship problems. To the contrary, the process literature is clear about the need for therapists to focus actively on relationship dynamics; to take a central, dominant position with the family; to explore hidden thoughts and feelings about family relations; and to develop clear goals that all family members can agree upon. Gender plays an important role in how therapists behave with family members and how men and women experience what takes place in conjoint sessions. While the therapist's personal qualities have not been the subject of much study, the therapist's warmth and concern are, without a doubt, important factors in treatment success.

Guiding Future Research

Relative to nearly 70 years of research and hundreds of process studies on individual therapy, the 50 or so publications on the process of couples and family therapy are scant. However, because family therapy researchers have kept abreast of the literature and followed the lead of individual therapy researchers, the field is more advanced than one would expect from numbers of studies alone. The most recent process investigations are clinically rich; they focus on therapeutic episodes or change events and take into account important constructs like the therapeutic alliance, cognitive constructions, and emotional experiencing. Increasing numbers of process studies are incorporating outcome data, and the outcome indices are multidimensional and reflect changes in individuals and the family as a whole.

Furthermore, in developing new lines of investigation, researchers are paying close attention to knowledge that has already been generated about crucial processes in family treatment. In the past few years, several areas have gone from being emerging trends in the literature (Friedlander, Wildman et al., 1994) to being recognized as important elements in successful therapy—notably, emotional states (e.g., Coulehan et al., 1998; Greenberg et al., 1993), personal qualities of the therapist (e.g., Lawson & Sivo, 1998; Sells et al., 1996), and the experience of children in therapy (e.g., Alexander et al., 1976; Diamond & Liddle, 1996). A number of recent studies have focused on therapeutic tasks that are unique to conjoint treatment settings: resolving conflict (Diamond & Liddle, 1996; Greenberg et al., 1993), mitigating blame (Gale & Newfield, 1992; Melidonis & Bry, 1995), facilitating engagement (Friedlander, Heatherington, et al., 1994; Santisteban et al., 1996), and reframing presenting problems (Coulehan et al., 1998; Diamond, Siqueland, et al., 1998).

There are, however, many other noteworthy areas of conjoint work that present challenges to therapists, and these areas have only been minimally addressed in the literature. Examples of processes unique to couples and family work that deserve empirical attention include staging enactments (e.g., family members trying something new while the therapist observes), managing secrets in sessions, handling a split alliance, facilitating forgiveness, and redistributing power. Outcome research is needed on (1) when to offer—or not offer—couples therapy in addition to individual therapy, (2) how best to work with low-income, multiproblem families, (3) how to take into account racial/ethnic variables and family structure, (4) how to match treatment strategies to the clients' relational patterns and the developmental task facing the family (e.g., launching grown children, caring for aging parents), and (5) how to work with families with unique needs (e.g., adoptive families, remarried families, gay/lesbian families, three-generation families).

Indeed, there is a large gap between family therapy as practiced and that which is currently being investigated. First, as mentioned, multicultural variables have largely been overlooked. The solutions suggested to a second-generation, Italian American family need to be very different from those offered to a Native American or an Asian immigrant family. Therapeutic interventions that do not respect the family's norms and culture carry risks to both the therapy and the family. Second, some of the newest and most popular approaches to treatment, constructionist/narrative approaches, for example, have received little empirical attention. Third, treatments for the most pressing problems in the lives of families (neglect, trauma, extramarital affairs, chronic illness, violence, divorce, death of a parent) are not being systematically investigated. This is particularly unfortunate since there is a wealth of information available about the needs of families facing these kinds of difficulties.

Future investigative efforts need to move away from the path of individual therapy researchers. Four thrusts are recommended to move the field forward. First, researchers should design process and outcome research that is problem-focused rather than only symptom-focused. Studies should be conducted that focus on relational patterns and concerns (e.g., sexual incompatibility or managing dual family roles). Second, investigations on emerging approaches to therapy are needed, with attention paid to their applicability cross-culturally. Third, researchers need to develop and use instruments that reflect important systemic variables like communication patterns, circular causality, differentiation of self, and intergenerational family dynamics. Fourth, researchers need to incorporate the rich theoretical and empirical base on couple and family interaction into the study of treatment processes and outcomes.

CONCLUSION

Over the past 35 years, the joint contributions of theorists, researchers, and practitioners have moved the field from being an alternative for treating the toughest client problems to a legitimate option for millions of people. No longer a U.S. phenomenon, couples and family therapy is practiced worldwide, and important theoretical contributions have come from Australia, South America, and many countries in Europe.

Undoubtedly, theory has far outpaced research in this field. The empirical literature has, nonetheless, had an important impact in a number of ways. Outcome research, particularly studies comparing individual and conjoint treatments, has induced licensing bodies to credential couples and family therapists, academic programs to develop courses of study in family therapy, and referral sources to recommend family work to their clients. Process research is making important strides in informing therapists, and educators of therapists, about how to provide quality care.

For the future, a stronger partnership of theorists, researchers, and therapists is needed to close the gap between science and practice. After all, the ultimate concern—to help people with family difficulties—is one we all face on a regular basis.

REFERENCES

Abramowitz, I.A., & Coursey, R.D. (1989). Impact of an educational support group on family participants who take care of their schizophrenic relatives. *Journal of Consulting and Clinical Psychology, 57,* 232–236.

Adams, J.F., Piercy, F.P., & Jurich, J.A. (1991). Effects of solution focused therapy's "formula first session task" on compliance and outcome in family therapy. *Journal of Marital and Family Therapy, 17,* 277–290.

Alexander, J.F., Barton, C., Schiavo, R.S., & Parsons, B.V. (1976). Systems-behavioral intervention with families of delinquents: Therapist characteristics, family behavior, and outcome. *Journal of Consulting and Clinical Psychology, 44,* 656–664.

Alexander, J.F., & Parsons, B.V. (1982). *Functional family therapy.* Monterey, CA: Brooks/Cole.

Arnow, B.A., Taylor, C.B., Agras, W.S., & Telch, M.J. (1985). Enhancing agoraphobia treatment outcome by changing couple communication patterns. *Behavior Therapy, 16,* 452–467.

Azrin, N.H., Sisson, R.W., Meyers, R., & Godley, M. (1982). Alcoholism treatment by disulfiram and community reinforcement therapy. *Journal of Behavior Therapy and Experimental Psychiatry, 13,* 105–112.

Bank, L., Marlowe, J.H., Reid, J.B., Patterson, G.R., & Weinrott, M.R. (1991). A comparative evaluation of parent training interventions for families of chronic delinquents. *Journal of Abnormal Child Psychology, 19,* 15–33.

Barbera, T.J., & Waldron, H.B. (1994). Sequential analysis as a method of feedback for family therapy process. *American Journal of Family Therapy, 22,* 156–164.

Barkley, R.A., Guevremont, D.C., Anastopoulos, A.D., & Fletcher, K.F. (1992). A comparison of three family therapy programs for treating family conflicts in adolescents with ADHD. *Journal of Consulting and Clinical Psychology, 60,* 450–462.

Barrett, P.M., Dadds, M.R., & Rapee, R. (1996). Family treatment of childhood anxiety: A controlled trial. *Journal of Consulting and Clinical Psychology, 64,* 333–342.

Bateson, G. (1958). *Naven.* Stanford, CA: Stanford University Press. (Original work published 1936)

Baucom, D.H., Sayers, S.L., & Sher, T.G. (1990). Supplementing behavioral marital therapy with cognitive restructuring and emotional expressiveness training: An outcome investigation. *Journal of Consulting and Clinical Psychology, 58,* 636–645.

Baucom, D.H., Shoham, V., Mueser, K.T., Daiuto, A.D., & Stickle, T.R. (1998). Empirically supported couple and family interventions for marital distress and adult mental health problems. *Journal of Consulting and Clinical Psychology, 66,* 53–88.

Beach, S.R.H., & O'Leary, K.D. (1992). Treating depression in the context of marital discord: Outcome and predictors of response for marital therapy vs. cognitive therapy. *Behavior Therapy, 23,* 507–528.

Benjamin, L.S. (1974). Structural analysis of social behavior. *Psychological Review, 81,* 392–425.

Benjamin, L.S., Foster, S.W., Roberto, L.G., & Estroff, S.E. (1986). Breaking the family code: Analysis of videotapes of family interactions by Structural Analysis of Social Behavior (SASB). In L.S. Greenberg & W.M. Pinsof (Eds.), *The psychotherapeutic process: A research handbook* (pp. 391–438). New York: Guilford Press.

Birchwood, M., Smith, J., & Cochrane, R. (1992). Specific and nonspecific effects of educational intervention for families living with schizophrenia. *British Journal of Psychiatry, 160,* 806–814.

Birnbrauer, J.S., & Leach, D.J. (1993). The Murdoch early intervention program after 2 years. *Behaviour Change, 10,* 63–74.

Bordin, E.S. (1979). The generalizability of the psychoanalytic concept of the working alliance. *Psychotherapy: Theory, Research and Practice, 16,* 252–260.

Bourgeois, L., Sabourin, S., & Wright, J. (1990). Predictive validity of therapeutic alliance in group marital therapy. *Journal of Consulting and Clinical Psychology, 58,* 608–613.

Bowen, M.B. (1978). *Family therapy in clinical practice.* New York: Aronson.

Brown-Standridge, M.D., & Piercy, F.P. (1988). Reality creation versus reality confirmation: A process study in marital therapy. *American Journal of Family Therapy, 16,* 195–215.

Buttney, R. (1990). Blame-accounts sequences in therapy: The negotiation of relational meanings. *Semiotica, 78,* 219–247.

Campbell, T.J., & Patterson, J.M. (1995). The effectiveness of family interventions in the treatment of physical illness. *Journal of Marital and Family Therapy, 21,* 545–584.

Chamberlain, P., Davis, J.P., Forgatch, M.S., Frey, J., Patterson, G.R., Ray, J., Rothschild, A., & Trombley, J. (1985). *The therapy process code: A multidimensional system for observing therapist and client interactions* (OSLC Tech. Rep. No. 1Rx). (Available from OSLC, 207 East 5th, Suite 202, Eugene, OR 97401)

Chamberlain, P., Patterson, G.R., Reid, J., Kavanagh, K., & Forgatch, M.S. (1984). Observation of client resistance. *Behavior Therapy, 15,* 144–155.

Chamberlain, P., & Reid, J.B. (1991). Using a specialized foster care treatment model for children and adolescents leaving the state mental hospital. *Journal of Community Psychology, 19,* 266–276.

Chamberlain, P., & Rosicky, J.G. (1995). The effectiveness of family therapy in the treatment of adolescents with conduct disorders and delinquency. *Journal of Marital and Family Therapy, 21,* 441–460.

Christensen, L.L., Russell, C.S., Miller, R.B., & Peterson, C.M. (1998). The process of change in couples therapy: A qualitative investigation. *Journal of Marital and Family Therapy, 24,* 177–188.

Cline, V.B., Mejia, J., Coles, J., Klein, N., & Cline, R.A. (1984). The relationship between therapist behaviors and outcome for middle- and lower-class couples in marital therapy. *Journal of Clinical Psychology, 40,* 691–704.

Coulehan, R., Friedlander, M.L., & Heatherington, L. (1998). Transforming narratives: A change event in constructivist family therapy. *Family Process, 37,* 465–481.

Craske, M.G., Burton, T., & Barlow, D.H. (1989). Relationships among measures of communication, marital satisfaction, and exposure during couples treatment of agoraphobia. *Behaviour Research and Therapy, 27,* 131–140.

Crits-Christoph, P., Luborsky, L., Gay, E., Todd, T., Barber, J.P., & Luborsky, E. (1991). What makes Susie cry? A symptom-context study of family therapy. *Family Process, 30,* 337–345.

Crowe, M.J., Gillan, P., & Golombok, S. (1981). Form and content in the conjoint treatment of sexual dysfunction: A controlled study. *Behaviour Research and Therapy, 19,* 47–54.

Dadds, M.R., Schwartz, S., & Sanders, M. (1987). Marital discord and treatment outcome in behavioral treatment of child conduct disorders. *Journal of Consulting and Clinical Psychology, 55,* 396–403.

Dadds, M.R., Spence, S.H., Holland, D.E., Barrett, P.M., Laurens, K.R. (1997). Prevention and early intervention for anxiety disorders: A controlled trial. *Journal of Consulting and Clinical Psychology, 65,* 627–635.

Davidson, G.N.S., & Horvath, A.O. (1997). Three Sessions of Brief Couples Therapy: A clinical trial. *Journal of Family Psychology, 11,* 422–435.

De Chenne, T.K. (1973). Experiential facilitation in conjoint marriage counseling. *Psychotherapy, 10,* 212–214.

Diamond, G.M., & Liddle, H.A. (1996). Resolving a therapeutic impasse between parents and adolescents in Multidimensional Family Therapy. *Journal of Consulting and Clinical Psychology, 64,* 481–488.

Diamond, G.M., Liddle, H.A., Hogue, A., & Dakof, G.A. (1998). *Alliance building techniques with adolescents in family therapy.* Manuscript submitted for publication.

Diamond, G.S., & Siqueland, L. (1995). Family therapy for the treatment of depressed adolescents. *Psychotherapy, 32,* 77–90.

Diamond, G.S., Siqueland, L., Diamond, G.M., & Brown, P. (1998, June). Assessing change in the family's understanding of the presenting problem in the first session of family based treatment: The relational reframe. In L. Heatherington (Chair), *Studying the process of change in problem-constructions and solution-constructions in marital and family therapy.* Symposium presented at the annual conference, International Society for Psychotherapy Research, Snowbird, UT.

Dunn, R.L., & Schwebel, A.I. (1995). Meta-analytic review of marital therapy outcome research. *Journal of Family Psychology, 9*(1), 58–68.

Eakes, G., Walsh, S., Markowski, M., & Cain, H. (1997). Family-centered brief solution-focused therapy with chronic schizophrenia: A pilot study. *Journal of Family Therapy, 19,* 145–158.

Edwards, M.E., & Steinglass, P. (1995). Family therapy treatment outcomes for alcoholism. *Journal of Marital and Family Therapy, 21,* 475–509.

Efran, J., Lukens, R.J., & Lukens, M.D. (1990). *Language, structure, and change.* New York: Norton.

Emmelkamp, P.M.G., de Haan, E., & Hoodguin, C.A.L. (1990). Marital adjustment and obsessive-compulsive disorder. *British Journal of Psychiatry, 156,* 55–60.

Emmelkamp, P.M.G., & de Lange, I. (1983). Spouse involvement in the treatment of obsessive-compulsive patients. *Behaviour Research and Therapy, 21,* 341–346.

Ericson, P.M., & Rogers, L.E. (1973). New procedures for analyzing relational communication. *Family Process, 12,* 245–267.

Estrada, A.U., & Pinsof, W.M. (1995). The effectiveness of family therapies for selected behavioral disorders of childhood. *Journal of Marital and Family Therapy, 21,* 403–440.

Everaerd, W., & Dekker, J. (1981). A comparison of sex therapy and communication therapy: Couples complaining of orgasmic dysfunction. *Journal of Sex and Marital Therapy, 7,* 278–289.

Falloon, I.R.H., Boyd, J.L., & McGill, C.W. (1984). *Family care of schizophrenia: A problem-solving approach to the treatment of mental illness.* New York: Guilford Press.

Fals-Stewart, W., Birchler, G.R., & O'Farrell, T.J. (1996). Behavioral couples therapy for male substance-abusing patients: Effects on relationship adjustment and drug-using behavior. *Journal of Consulting and Clinical Psychology, 64,* 959–972.

Forehand, R., & Long, N. (1988). Outpatient treatment of the acting-out child: Procedures, long-term follow-up data, and clinical problems. *Advances in Behavior Research and Therapy, 10,* 129–177.

Frankel, B.R., & Piercy, F.P. (1990). The relationship among selected supervisor, therapist, and client behaviors. *Journal of Marital and Family Therapy, 16,* 407–421.

Friedlander, M.L. (1982). Counseling discourse as a speech event: Revision and extension of the Hill Counselor Verbal Response Category System. *Journal of Counseling Psychology, 29,* 425–429.

Friedlander, M.L. (1993). Does complementarity promote or hinder client change in brief therapy? A review of the evidence from two theoretical perspectives. *Counseling Psychologist, 21,* 457–486.

Friedlander, M.L. (in press). Observational coding of family therapy processes: State of the art. In A.P. Beck & C.M. Lewis (Eds.), *Process in therapeutic groups: A handbook of systems of analysis.* Washington, DC: American Psychological Association.

Friedlander, M.L., Ellis, M.V., Raymond, L., Siegel, S.M., & Milford, D. (1987). Convergence and divergence in the process of interviewing families. *Psychotherapy, 24,* 570–583.

Friedlander, M.L., & Heatherington, L. (1989). Analyzing relational control in family therapy interviews. *Journal of Counseling Psychology, 36,* 139–148.

Friedlander, M.L., & Heatherington, L. (1998). Assessing clients' constructions of their problems in family therapy discourse. *Journal of Marital and Family Therapy, 24,* 289–303.

Friedlander, M.L., Heatherington, L., Johnson, B., & Skowron, E.A. (1994). "Sustaining engagement": A change event in family therapy. *Journal of Counseling Psychology, 41,* 438–448.

Friedlander, M.L., Heatherington, L., & Marrs, A. (in press). Responding to blame in family therapy: A narrative/constructionist perspective. *American Journal of Family Therapy.*

Friedlander, M.L., Heatherington, L., & Wildman, J. (1991). Interpersonal control in structural and Milan systemic family therapy. *Journal of Marital and Family Therapy, 17,* 395–408.

Friedlander, M.L., & Highlen, P.S. (1984). A spatial view of the interpersonal structure of family interviews: Similarities and differences across counselors. *Journal of Counseling Psychology, 31,* 477–487.

Friedlander, M.L., Highlen, P.S., & Lassiter, W.L. (1985). Content analytic comparison of four expert counselors' approaches to family treatment: Ackerman, Bowen, Jackson, and Whitaker. *Journal of Counseling Psychology, 32,* 171–180.

Friedlander, M.L., Wildman, J., Heatherington, L., & Skowron, E.A. (1994). What we do and don't know about the process of family therapy. *Journal of Family Psychology, 8,* 390–416.

Gale, J., & Newfield, N. (1992). A conversation analysis of a solution-focused marital therapy session. *Journal of Marital and Family Therapy, 18,* 153–165.

Glick, I., Clarkin, J., Spencer, J., Haas, G., Lewis, A., Peyser, J., DeMane, N., Good-Ellis, M., Harris, E., & Lestelle, V. (1985). A controlled evaluation of inpatient family intervention: I. Preliminary results of a 6-month follow-up. *Archives of General Psychiatry, 42,* 882–886.

Goldman, A., & Greenberg, L. (1992). Comparison of integrated systemic and emotionally focused approaches to couples therapy. *Journal of Consulting and Clinical Psychology, 60,* 962–969.

Goldstein, M.J., & Miklowitz, D.J. (1995). The effectiveness of psychoeducational family therapy in the treatment of schizophrenic disorders. *Journal of Marital and Family Therapy, 21,* 361–376.

Goldstein, M.J., Rodnick, E.H., Evans, J.R., May, P.R.A., & Steinberg, M.R. (1978). Drug and family therapy in the aftercare of acute schizophrenics. *Archives of General Psychiatry, 35,* 1169–1177.

Green, R-J., & Herget, M. (1989a). Outcomes of systemic/strategic team consultation: I. Overview and one-month results. *Family Process, 28,* 37–58.

Green, R-J., & Herget, M. (1989b). Outcomes of systemic/strategic team consultation: II. Three-year followup and a theory of "emergent design." *Family Process, 28,* 419–437.

Green, R-J., & Herget, M. (1991). Outcomes of systemic/strategic team consultation: III. The importance of therapist warmth and active structuring. *Family Process, 30,* 321–336.

Greenberg, L.S. (1986). Change process research. *Journal of Consulting and Clinical Psychology, 54,* 4–9.

Greenberg, L.S., Ford, C.L., Alden, L., & Johnson, S.M. (1993). In-session change in Emotionally Focused Therapy. *Journal of Consulting and Clinical Psychology, 61,* 78–84.

Greenberg, L.S., James, P.S., & Conry, R.F. (1988). Perceived change processes in emotionally focused couples therapy. *Journal of Family Psychology, 2,* 5–23.

Gurman, A.S., Kniskern, D.P., & Pinsof, W.M. (1986). Research on marital and family therapies. In S.L. Garfield & A.E. Bergin (Eds.), *Handbook of psychotherapy and behavior change* (3rd ed., pp. 565–624). New York: Wiley.

Hahlweg, K., Revenstorf, D., & Schindler, L. (1982). Treatment of marital distress: Comparing formats and modalities. *Advances in Behavior Research and Therapy, 4,* 57–74.

Halford, K.W., Sanders, M.R., & Behrens, B.C. (1993). A comparison of the generalization of behavioral marital therapy and enhanced behavioral marital therapy. *Journal of Consulting and Clinical Psychology, 61,* 51–60.

Hawton, K., & Catalan, J. (1986). Prognostic factors in sex therapy. *Behaviour Research and Therapy, 24,* 377–385.

Heatherington, L., & Friedlander, M.L. (1987). *The Family Communication Control Coding System: Coding Manual.* Unpublished manual. (Available from L. Heatherington, Department of Psychology, Williams College, Williamstown, MA 01267)

Heatherington, L., & Friedlander, M.L. (1990a). Applying task analysis to structural family therapy. *Journal of Family Psychology, 4,* 36–48.

Heatherington, L., & Friedlander, M.L. (1990b). Complementarity and symmetry in family therapy communication. *Journal of Counseling Psychology, 37,* 261–268.

Heatherington, L., & Friedlander, M.L. (1990c). Couple and family therapy alliance scales: Empirical considerations. *Journal of Marital and Family Therapy, 16,* 299–306.

Heatherington, L., Marrs, A., & Friedlander, M.L. (1995, June). *Toward an understanding of how clients' constructions change in family therapy.* Paper presented at the annual conference, Society for Psychotherapy Research, Vancouver, British Columbia, Canada.

Hener, T., Weisenberg, M., & Har-Even, D. (1996). Supportive versus cognitive-behavioral intervention programs in achieving adjustment to home peritoneal kidney dialysis. *Journal of Consulting and Clinical Psychology, 64,* 731–741.

Hogarty, G.E., Anderson, C., Reiss, D., Kornblith, S., Greenwald, D., Ulrich, R., & Carter, M. (1991). Family psychoeducation, social skills training, and maintenance chemotherapy in the aftercare treatment of schizophrenia: II. Two year effects of a controlled study on relapse and adjustment. *Archives of General Psychiatry, 48,* 340–347.

Holloway, E.L., Wampold, B.E., & Nelson, M.L. (1990). Use of a paradoxical intervention with a couple: An interactional analysis. *Journal of Family Psychology, 3,* 385–402.

Holtzworth-Munroe, A., Jacobson, N.S., DeKlyen, M., & Whisman, M.A. (1989). Relationship between behavioral marital therapy outcome and process variables. *Journal of Consulting and Clinical Psychology, 57,* 658–662.

Horn, W.F., Ialongo, N.S., Pascoe, J.J., Greenberg, G., Packard, T., Lopez, M., Wagner, A., & Puttler, L. (1991). Additive effects of psychostimulants, parent training, and self-control therapy with ADHD children. *Journal of the American Academy of Child and Adolescent Psychiatry, 30,* 233–240.

Huber, C.H., & Milstein, B. (1985). Cognitive restructuring and a collaborative set in couples' work. *American Journal of Family Therapy, 13*(2), 17–27.

Hurlbert, D.F. (1993). A comparative study using orgasm consistency training in the treatment of women reporting hypoactive sexual desire. *Journal of Sex and Marital Therapy, 19,* 41–55.

Hurlbert, D.F., White, L.C., Powell, R.D., & Apt, C. (1993). Orgasm consistency training in the treatment of women reporting hypoactive sexual desire: An outcome comparison of women-only groups and couples-only groups. *Journal of Behavior Therapy and Experimental Psychiatry, 24,* 3–13.

Jacobson, N.S. (1977). Problem-solving and contingency contracting in the treatment of marital discord. *Journal of Consulting and Clinical Psychology, 45,* 92–100.

Jacobson, N.S. (1984). A component analysis of behavioral marital therapy: The relative effectiveness of behavioral exchange and communication/problem-solving training. *Journal of Consulting and Clinical Psychology, 52,* 295–305.

Jacobson, N.S., Dobson, K., Fruzzetti, A.E., Schmaling, D.B., & Salusky, S. (1991). Marital therapy as a treatment for depression. *Journal of Consulting and Clinical Psychology, 59,* 547–557.

Jacobson, N.S., Follette, W.C., Revenstorf, D., Baucom, D.H., Hahlweg, K., & Margolin, G. (1984). Variability in outcome and clinical significance of behavioral marital therapy: A reanalysis of outcome data. *Journal of Consulting and Clinical Psychology, 59,* 497–504.

Jacobson, N.S., Schmaling, K.B., & Holtzworth-Munroe, A. (1987). Component analysis of behavioral marital therapy: 2-year follow-up and prediction of relapse. *Journal of Marital and Family Therapy, 13,* 187–195.

James, P.S. (1991). Effects of a communication training component added to an emotionally focused couples therapy. *Journal of Marital and Family Therapy, 17,* 263–275.

Johnson, S.M., & Greenberg, L.S. (1985). Differential effects of experiential and problem-solving interventions in resolving marital conflict. *Journal of Consulting and Clinical Psychology, 53,* 175–184.

Johnson, S.M., & Greenberg, L.S. (1988). Relating process to outcome in marital therapy. *Journal of Marital and Family Therapy, 14,* 175–183.

Johnson, S.M., & Talitman, E. (1997). Predictors of success in Emotionally Focused Marital Therapy. *Journal of Marital and Family Therapy, 23,* 135–152.

Kahen, Johnson, V.J., & Lieberman, A.F. (1998, June). *Child-parent psychotherapy: A relationship based intervention for mothers and children from violent households.* Paper presented at the annual conference, International Society for Psychotherapy Research, Snowbird, UT.

Kazdin, A.E. (1987). *Conduct disorders in childhood and adolescence.* Newbury Park, CA: Sage.

Kazdin, A.E., Esveldt-Dawson, K., French, N.H., & Unis, A.S. (1987). Effects of parent management training and problem-solving skills training combined in the treatment of antisocial child behavior. *Journal of the American Academy of Child and Adolescent Psychiatry, 26,* 416–424.

Kemenoff, S., Worchel, F., Prevatt, B., & Willson, V. (1995). The effects of video feedback in the context of Milan systemic therapy. *Journal of Family Psychology, 9,* 446–450.

Klein, M., Mathieu, P., Kiesler, D., & Gendlin, E.T. (1969). *The Experiencing Scale.* Madison: Wisconsin Psychiatric Institute.

Kuehl, B.P., Newfield, N.A., & Joanning, H. (1990). A client-based description of family therapy. *Journal of Family Psychology, 3,* 310–321.

Laird, H., & Vande Kemp, H. (1987). Complementarity as a function of stage in therapy: An analysis of Minuchin's structural family therapy. *Journal of Marital and Family Therapy, 13,* 127–137.

Lawson, D.M., & Sivo, S. (1998). Trainee conjugal family experience, current intergenerational family relationships, and the therapeutic alliance. *Journal of Marital and Family Therapy, 24,* 225–231.

Leff, J., Kuipers, L., Berkowitz, R., & Sturgeon, D. (1985). A controlled trial of social intervention in the families of schizophrenic patients: Two year follow-up. *British Journal of Psychiatry, 146,* 594–600.

Liberman, R., Levine, J., Wheeler, E., Sanders, N., & Wallace, C.J. (1976). Marital therapy in groups: A comparative evaluation of behavioral and interaction formats. *Acta Psychiatrica Scandinavica, 266,* 1–34.

Liddle, H.A., & Dakof, G.A. (1995). Efficacy of family therapy for drug abuse: Promising but not definitive. *Journal of Marital and Family Therapy, 21,* 511–544.

Lovaas, O.I. (1987). Behavioral treatment and normal educational and intellectual functioning in young autistic children. *Journal of Consulting and Clinical Psychology, 55,* 3–9.

Luepnitz, D.A. (1988). *The family interpreted.* New York: Basic Books.

MacPhee, D.C., Johnson, S.M., & van der Veer, M.M.C. (1995). Low sexual desire in women: The effects of marital therapy. *Journal of Sex and Marital Therapy, 21,* 159–182.

Mas, C.H., Alexander, J.F., & Barton, C. (1985). Modes of express in family therapy: A process study of roles and gender. *Journal of Marital and Family Therapy, 11,* 411–415.

Masters, W.H., & Johnson, V.E. (1970). *Human sexual inadequacy.* Boston: Little, Brown.

Matthews, A., Bancroft, J., Whitehead, A., Hackman, A., Julier, D., Bancroft, J., Gath, D., & Shaw, P. (1976). The behavioral treatment of sexual inadequacy: A comparative study. *Behaviour Research and Therapy, 14,* 427–436.

McFarlane, W.R., Link, B., Dushay, R., Marchal, J., & Crilly, J. (1995). Psychoeducational multiple family groups: Four-year relapse outcome in schizophrenia. *Family Process, 34,* 127–144.

Melidonis, G.G., & Bry, B.H. (1995). Effects of therapist exceptions questions on blaming and positive statements in families with adolescent behavior problems. *Journal of Family Psychology, 9,* 451–457.

Miller, G.E., & Prinz, R.J. (1990). The enhancement of social learning family interventions for childhood conduct disorder. *Psychological Bulletin, 108,* 291–307.

Mills, P.D., & Hansen, J.C. (1991). Short-term group interventions for mentally ill young adults living in a community residence and their families. *Hospital and Community Psychiatry, 42,* 1144–1149.

Minuchin, S. (1974). *Families and family therapy.* Cambridge, MA: Harvard University Press.

Morisky, D.E., Levine, D.M., Green, L.W., Shapiro, S., Russell, R.P., & Smith, C.R. (1983). Five year blood pressure control and mortality following health education for hypertensive patients. *American Journal of Public Health, 73,* 153–162.

Munton, A.G., & Antaki, C. (1988). Causal beliefs amongst families in therapy: Attributions at the group level. *British Journal of Clinical Psychology, 27,* 91–97.

Newberry, A.M., Alexander, J.F., & Turner, C.W. (1991). Gender as a process variable in family therapy. *Journal of Family Psychology, 5,* 158–175.

Odell, M., & Quinn, W.H. (1998). Therapist and client behaviors in the first interview: Effects on session impact and treatment duration. *Journal of Marital and Family Therapy, 24,* 369–388.

O'Farrell, T.J., & Choquette, K.A. (1991). Marital violence in the year before and after spouse-involved alcoholism treatment. *Family Dynamics of Addiction Quarterly, 1,* 32–40.

O'Farrell, T.J., Choquette, K.A., Cutter, H.S.G., Brown, E.D., & McCourt, W. (1993). Behavioral marital therapy with and without additional couples relapse prevention sessions for alcoholics and their wives. *Journal of Studies on Alcohol, 54,* 652–666.

O'Farrell, T.J., Cutter, H.S.G., & Floyd, F.J. (1985). Evaluating behavioral marital therapy for male alcoholics: Effects of marital adjustment and communication from before to after treatment. *Behavior Therapy, 16,* 147–167.

O'Leary, K.D., & Beach, S.R.H. (1990). Marital therapy: A viable treatment for depression marital discord. *American Journal of Psychiatry, 147,* 183–186.

O'Leary, K.D., Riso, L.P., & Beach, S.R.H. (1990). Attributions about the marital discord/depression link and therapy outcome. *Behavior Therapy, 21,* 413–422.

Patterson, G.R. (1982). *Coercive family process.* Eugene, OR: Castalia.

Patterson, G.R., & Chamberlain, P. (1988). Treatment process: A problem at three levels. In L.D. Wynne (Ed.), *The state of the art in family therapy research: Controversies and recommendations* (pp. 189–223). New York: Family Process Press.

Patterson, G.R., & Forgatch, M.S. (1985). Therapist behavior as a determinant for client noncompliance: A paradox for the behavior modifier. *Journal of Consulting and Clinical Psychology, 53,* 846–851.

Pearce, J.W., LeBow, M.D., & Orchard, J. (1981). Role of spouse involvement in the behavioral treatment of overweight women. *Journal of Consulting and Clinical Psychology, 49,* 236–244.

Peed, S., Roberts, M., & Forehand, R. (1977). Evalution of the effectiveness of a standardized parent training program in altering the interaction of mothers and their noncompliant children. *Behavior Modification, 1,* 323–350.

Pinsof, W.M. (1979). The Family Therapist Behavior Scale (FTBS): Development and evaluation of a coding system. *Family Process, 18,* 451–461.

Pinsof, W.M. (1986). The process of family therapy: The development of the Family Therapist Coding System. In L.S. Greenberg & W.M. Pinsof (Eds.), *The psychotherapeutic process: A research handbook* (pp. 201–284). New York: Guilford Press.

Pinsof, W.M., & Catherall, D.R. (1986). The integrative psychotherapy alliance: Family, couple and individual therapy scales. *Journal of Marital and Family Therapy, 12,* 137–151.

Pinsof, W.M., & Wynne, L.C. (1995). The efficacy of marital and family therapy: An empirical overview, conclusions and recommendations. *Journal of Marital and Family Therapy, 21,* 585–614.

Pinsof, W.M., Wynne, L.C., & Hambright, A.B. (1996). The outcomes of couple and family therapy: Findings, conclusions, and recommendations. *Psychotherapy, 33,* 321–331.

Postner, R.S., Guttman, H.A., Sigal, J.J., Epstein, N.B., & Rakoff, V.M. (1971). Process and outcome in conjoint family therapy. *Family Process, 10,* 451–474.

Prince, S.E., & Jacobson, N.S. (1995). A review and evaluation of marital and family therapies for affective disorders. *Journal of Marital and Family Therapy, 21,* 377–401.

Quinn, W.H., Dotson, D., & Jordan, K. (1997). Dimensions of therapeutic alliance and their associations with outcome in family therapy. *Psychotherapy Research, 7,* 429–438.

Raymond, L., Friedlander, M.L., Heatherington, L., Ellis, M.V., & Sargent, J. (1993). Communication processes in structural family therapy: Case study of an anorexic family. *Journal of Family Psychology, 6,* 308–326.

Robbins, M.S., Alexander, J.F., Newell, R.M., & Turner, C.W. (1996). The immediate effect of reframing on client attitude in family therapy. *Journal of Family Psychology, 10,* 28–34.

Russell, G.F.M., Szmukler, G.I., Dare, C., & Eisler, I. (1987). An evaluation of family therapy in anorexia nervosa and bulimia nervosa. *Archives of General Psychiatry, 44,* 1047–1056.

Santisteban, D.A., Szapocznik, J., Perez-Vidal, A., Kurtines, W.M., Murray, E.J., & LaPerriere, A. (1996). Efficacy of intervention for engaging youth and families into treatment and some variables that may contribute to differential effectiveness. *Journal of Family Psychology, 10,* 35–44.

Satin, W., LaGreca, A.M., Zigo, M.A., & Skyler, J.S. (1989). Diabetes in adolescence: Effects of multifamily group intervention and parent simulation of diabetes. *Journal of Pediatric Psychology, 14,* 259–275.

Sayger, T.V., Horne, A.M., & Glaser, B.A. (1993). Marital satisfaction and social learning family therapy for child conduct problems: Generalization of treatment effects. *Journal of Marital and Family Therapy, 19,* 393–402.

Sells, S.P., Smith, T.E., & Moon, S. (1996). An ethnographic study of client and therapist perceptions of therapy effectiveness in a university-based training clinic. *Journal of Marital and Family Therapy, 22,* 321–342.

Selvini Palazzoli, M., Boscolo, L., Cecchin, G., & Prata, G. (1980). Hypothesizing-circularity-neutrality. *Family Process, 19,* 73–85.

Shadish, W.R., Ragsdale, K., Glaser, R.R., & Montgomery, L.M. (1995). The efficacy and effectiveness of marital and family therapy: A perspective from meta-analysis. *Journal of Marital and Family Therapy, 21,* 345–360.

Shapiro, R.J. (1974). Therapist attitudes and premature termination in family and individual therapy. *Journal of Nervous and Mental Disease, 159,* 101–107.

Shields, C.G., & McDaniel, S.H. (1992). Process differences between male and female therapists in a first family interview. *Journal of Marital and Family Therapy, 18,* 143–151.

Shields, C.G., Sprenkle, D.H., & Constantine, J.A. (1991). Anatomy of an initial interview: The importance of joining and structuring skills. *American Journal of Family Therapy, 19,* 3–18.

Siegel, S.M., Friedlander, M.L., & Heatherington, L. (1992). Nonverbal relational control in family communication. *Journal of Nonverbal Behavior, 16,* 117–139.

Sigal, J.J., Rakoff, V., & Epstein, N.B. (1967). Indicators of therapeutic outcome in conjoint family therapy. *Family Process, 6,* 215–226.

Sisson, R.W., & Azrin, N.H. (1986). Family-member involvement to initiate and promote treatment of problem drinkers. *Journal of Behavior Therapy and Experimental Psychiatry, 17,* 15–21.

Sluzki, C. (1992). Transformations: A blueprint for narrative changes in therapy. *Family Process, 31,* 217–230.

Snyder, D.K., & Wills, R.M. (1989). Behavioral versus insight-oriented marital therapy: Effects on individual and interspousal functioning. *Journal of Consulting and Clinical Psychology, 57,* 39–46.

Snyder, D.K., Wills, R.M., & Grady-Fletcher, A. (1991). Long-term effectiveness of behavioral versus insight-oriented marital therapy: A 4-year follow-up study. *Journal of Consulting and Clinical Psychology, 59,* 138–141.

Sprenkle, D., & Moon, S. (Eds.). (1996). *Handbook of family therapy research methods* (pp. 411–428). New York: Guilford Press.

Stiles, W.B., Shapiro, D.A., & Elliott, R. (1986). "Are all psychotherapies equivalent?" *American Psychologist, 41,* 165–180.

Sullivan, H.S. (1953). *The interpersonal theory of psychiatry.* New York: Norton.

Symonds, B.D. (1998, June). *A measure of the alliance in couples therapy.* Paper presented at the annual conference, International Society for Psychotherapy Research, Snowbird, UT.

Szapocznik, J., Kurtines, W.M., Foote, F.H., Perez-Vidal, A., & Hervis, O. (1983). Conjoint versus one-person family therapy: Some evidence for the effectiveness of conducting family therapy through one person. *Journal of Consulting and Clinical Psychology, 51,* 889–899.

Szapocznik, J., Kurtines, W.M., Foote, F.H., Perez-Vidal, A., & Hervis, O. (1986). Conjoint versus one-person family therapy: Further evidence for the effectiveness of conducting family therapy through one person with drug-abusing adolescents. *Journal of Consulting and Clinical Psychology, 54,* 395–397.

Szapocznik, J., Perez-Vidal, A., Brickman, A.L., Foote, F.H., Santisteban, D., Hervis, O., & Kurtines, W. (1988). Engaging adolescent drug abusers and their families in treatment: A strategic structural systems approach. *Journal of Consulting and Clinical Psychology, 56,* 552–557.

Szapocznik, J., Rio, A., Murray, E., Cohen, R., Scopetta, M., Rivas-Vazquez, A., Hervis, O., Posada, V., & Kurtines, W.M. (1989). Structural family versus psychodynamic child therapy for problematic Hispanic boys. *Journal of Consulting and Clinical Psychology, 57,* 571–578.

Turkewitz, H., & O'Leary, K.D. (1981). A comparative outcome study of behavioral marital therapy and communication therapy. *Journal of Marital and Family Therapy, 7,* 159–169.

Waldron, H.B., Turner, C.W., Alexander, J.F., & Barton, C. (1993). Coding defensive and supportive communication: Discriminant validity and subcategory convergence. *Journal of Family Psychology, 7,* 197–203.

Walker, J.G., Johnson, S., Manion, I., & Cloutier, P. (1996). Emotionally focused marital intervention for couples with chronically ill children. *Journal of Consulting and Clinical Psychology, 64,* 1029–1036.

Webster-Stratton, C. (1990). Long-term follow-up with young conduct problem children: From preschool to grade school. *Journal of Clinical Child Psychology, 19,* 144–149.

Werner-Wilson, R.J. (1997). Is therapeutic alliance influenced by gender in marriage and family therapy? *Journal of Feminist Family Therapy, 9,* 3–16.

Werner-Wilson, R.J., Price, S.J., Zimmerman, T.S., & Murphy, M.J. (1997). Client gender as a process variable in marriage and family therapy: Are women clients interrupted more than men clients? *Journal of Family Psychology, 11,* 373–377.

Werner-Wilson, R.J., Zimmerman, T.S., & Price, S.J. (1999). Are therapeutic goals and topics influenced by gender and modality in the initial marriage and family therapy session? *Journal of Marital and Family Therapy, 25,* 253–262.

White, M., & Epston, D. (1990). *Narrative means to therapeutic ends.* New York: Norton.

Winer, L.R. (1971). The qualified pronoun count as a measure of change in family psychotherapy. *Family Process, 10,* 243–248.

Zuk, G.H., Boszormenyi-Nagy, I., & Heiman, E. (1963). Some dynamics of laughter during family therapy. *Family Process, 2,* 302–314.

Author Index

Subject Index